WEIGHT

ROUGH CONVERSION 1 kg. is almost 2¼ lb. 1 lb. is just under 0·5 kg. 1 oz. is about 28 g.

ounces	grams	grams	pounds/ounces	
¼ oz.	7·08 g.	25 g.	– lb.	⅞ oz.
½	14·17	50	–	1¾
¾	21·26	75	–	2½
1	28·35	100	–	3½
2	56·69	125	–	4½
3	85·04	150	–	5¼
4 (¼ lb.)	113·39	175	–	6
5	141·74	200	–	7
6	170·09	300	–	10½
7	198·44	400	–	14
8 (½ lb.)	226·79	500	1	1½
12 (¾ lb.)	340·19	1,000 (1 kg.)	2	3¼
16 (1 lb.)	453·24			
32	907·18			

stones	kilograms	kilograms	stones/pounds	
1 st.	6·35 kg.	10 kg.	1 st.	8 lb.
2	12·70	15	2	5
3	19·05	20	3	2
4	25·40	30	4	10
5	31·75	40	6	4¼
10	63·50	50	7	12¼
15	95·25	100	15	10½
20	127·00	150	23	8¾

pounds	kilograms	kilograms	pounds/ounces	
1 lb.	0·45 kg.	1 kg.	2 lb.	3¼ oz.
2	0·90	2	4	6½
3	1·36	3	6	9¾
4	1·81	4	8	13
5	2·26	5	11	¼
6	2·72	6	13	3
7	3·17	7	15	7
8	3·62	8	17	10
9	4·08	9	19	13
10	4·53	10	22	¾
14 (1 st.)	6·35	25	55	2
56	25·22	50	110	3

cwt.	kilograms	kilograms	cwt./stones	
1 cwt.	50·8 kg.	50 kg.	cwt.	7¾ st.
2	101·6	100	1	7¾
3	152·4	200	3	7½
4	203·2	300	5	7¼
5	254·0	400	7	7
10	508·0	500	9	6¾
20 (1 ton)	1016·0	1,000 (1 tonne)	19	5½

LIQUIDS

ROUGH CONVERSION 1 pint is about 500 ml.
1 litre is just over 1¾ pints.
1 gallon is approximately 4·5 litres.

pints	litres	litres	pints
½	0·28	¼	0·44
1	0·57	½	0·88
2	1·14	1	1·76
3	1·70	2	3·52
4	2·27	3	5·27
5	2·84	4	7·03
6	3·41	5	8·79
7	3·98	10	17·59
8 (1 gal.)	4·55	–	–

gallons	litres	litres	gallons/pints	
½ gal.	2·27	5	1 gal.	¾ pint
1	4·54	6	1	2½
2	9·09	7	1	4¼
3	13·63	8	1	6
4	18·18	9	1	7¾
5	22·73	10	2	1½
10	45·46	50	11	–

fluid ounces	milli-litres	milli-litres	fluid ounces
1 fl. oz.	28·41 ml.	50 ml.	1·75 fl. oz.
2	56·82	100	3·51
3	85·24	150	4·26
4	113·65	200	7·03
5 (¼ pint)	142·66	250	8·78
10 (½ pint)	284·12	500	17·59
20 (1 pint)	568·26	1,000 (1 litre)	35·19

READER'S DIGEST

Household
Manual

PUBLISHED BY THE READER'S DIGEST ASSOCIATION LIMITED
LONDON, NEW YORK, MONTREAL, SYDNEY, CAPE TOWN

HOUSEHOLD MANUAL
was edited and designed by
The Reader's Digest Association Limited, London

First Edition, First Revise 1978
Copyright © 1977 The Reader's Digest Association Limited
25 Berkeley Square, London W1X 6AB
Copyright © 1977 Reader's Digest Association Far East Limited
Philippines Copyright 1977 Reader's Digest Association Far East Ltd

Printed in Great Britain

READER'S DIGEST

Household
Manual

CONSULTANT EDITORS

Elizabeth Gundrey   Barty Phillips

CONTRIBUTORS

Stephanie Blasberg   John McGowan
Shirley Bond MAHE SRD   John Morrell
Anthony Byers   Sheila Morrison
Jarvis Coates   Ann Ord
Sheena Davis   Derek Phillips M.Arch MCD FRIBA F Illum ES
Peter Dewes   John Prizeman, Architect
Kathleen M Dibley MIPR MJI   Nellie Richardson
Dorothy Erskine   Gilian Salter
Alan Field FIHVE AI InfSc MIL Johanna Senior MAHE
Marion Giordan   Jean Sheridan
Jim Haig   Joanna Slaughter
Tamara Hall M.DES RCA   Dr Tony Smith MA BM
Betty Hitchcock   Robert Tattersall
Roger Limbrick   W H Thomas, Solicitor
Dr Stephen Lock MA MB MRCP   John Weiss BA (Arch) Dip TP RIBA FSIAD MSD-C

ARTISTS

Ken Baker MSIAD   Malcolm Kemp
David Baxter (The Garden Studio) Sarah Kensington LSIA
Brian Craker (Saxon Artists Ltd) Sean Milne
Terence Dalley ARCA   Peter Morter MSIA
Michael Davidson   Osborne Marks & Associates
Peter Davies   Stanley Paine ARCA (Saxon Artists Ltd)
Brian Delf   Garry Porter RIBA FFAS
Vana Haggerty   QED
Nicolas H T Hall   Ann Savage
Hayward & Martin Ltd   Ted Williams (Venner Artists Ltd)
William Hill   Roy Wiltshire (The Garden Studio)
Gary Hincks   Ann Winterbotham
Richard Jacobs   Michael Woods

COMMISSIONED PHOTOGRAPHY

John Cook (Whitecross Studios)

Contents of the Household Manual

Home projects

1

IMPROVING YOUR HOME

2

FURNISHING YOUR HOME

3

PLANNING YOUR KITCHEN

Family matters

Improving your home

A coat of paint, a change of curtains, a new lampshade – any of these can alter
a room's appearance. But unplanned change can result in clashing colour,
badly sited lighting and awkwardly placed furniture. The following pages
explain how to set about planning home improvements in a way that
will leave you with a feeling of pride in a job well done.

CONTENTS

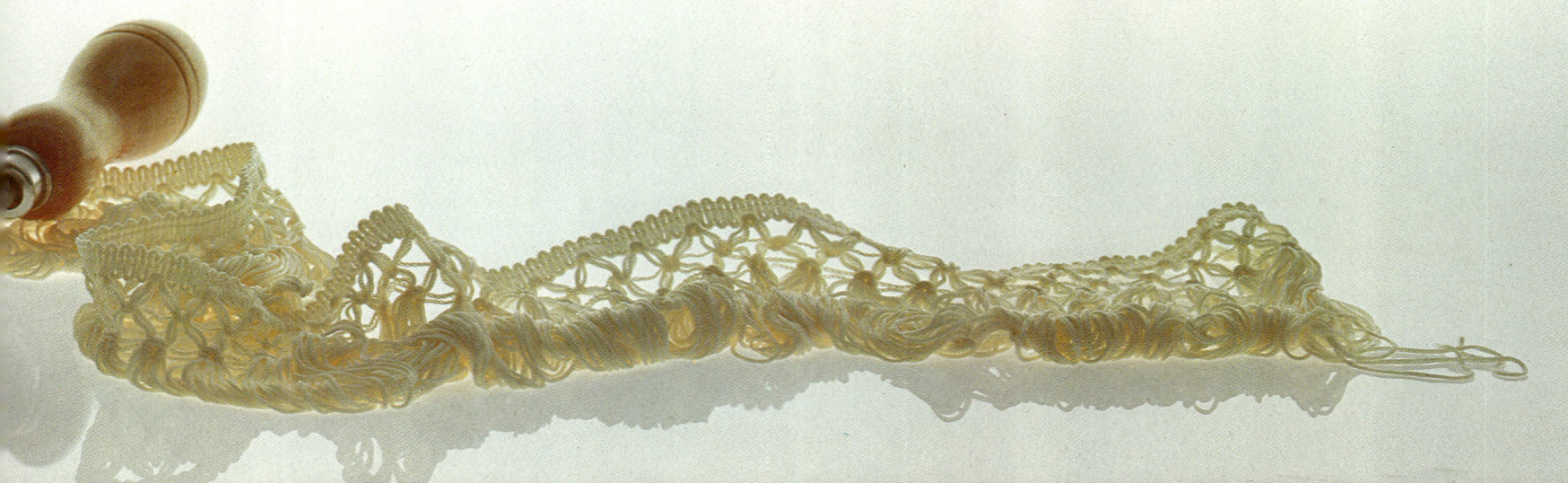

CHOOSING A HOME OF YOUR OWN

House purchase is one of the most important single steps that any individual or couple has to take. It is therefore vital that thorough research and planning should be carried out first. Decide how much you can afford, and what kind of property you need. Spend as much time as you can looking and comparing before offering to buy property. It is generally advisable to engage a solicitor to look after the legal complexities – called conveyancing – and it will be essential to employ a surveyor to examine your chosen property. It may be worth while buying a house or flat that is not in ideal condition. In such a case, find out if you would be eligible for a home-improvement grant, and whether the building society or insurance company from whom you hope to raise the money would be willing to lend the sum you need on a property in a poor state of repair.

A home of your own is likely to be your securest protection against inflation, so it is generally sound economy to buy the best you can afford. In working out your budget, it is reasonable to set off income-tax relief against what might otherwise appear to be insufferably high mortgage repayments. On the other hand, do not fail to take into account all the other continuing, and probably increasing, costs you will have to bear as an owner-occupier, such as rates, insurance, maintenance and repairs.

APPROXIMATE MONTHLY INSTALMENTS FOR REPAYMENT MORTGAGE
If you pay tax at the standard rate, the interest part of each payment attracts tax relief; so for every pound of interest you pay, nearly two-thirds (depending on the standard rate of tax) is allowable when working out your taxable income.

	11%	12%	13%
£6,000 loan			
20 year term	£63	£67	£71
25 year term	£59	£63	£68
£8,000 loan			
20 year term	£84	£90	£95
25 year term	£79	£85	£91
£10,000 loan			
20 year term	£105	£112	£119
25 year term	£100	£106	£114
£12,000 loan			
20 year term	£126	£134	£143
25 year term	£119	£127	£137

- FINDING A HOUSE
- RAISING THE MONEY
- RENTING A HOME
- BUYING A HOUSE IN SCOTLAND
- LOOKING AT HOUSES
- STAMP DUTY AND OTHER COSTS
- BUILDING-SOCIETY INSPECTION
- EXCHANGING CONTRACTS
- INSURING THE PROPERTY
- BUYING IN JOINT NAMES
- MOVING HOME
- IMPROVEMENT GRANTS
- ARCHITECTS' SERVICES
- EMPLOYING PROFESSIONALS
- PLANNING PERMISSION AND BUILDING REGULATIONS

• FINDING A HOUSE

It is probably best to start by approaching estate agents in the area of your choice. They know the neighbourhood and local property prices. But remember that estate agents are employed by the seller.

Go to a qualified agent – he will probably be a member of the Royal Institution of Chartered Surveyors or the Incorporated Society of Valuers and Auctioneers.

Agents will give you addresses and details of houses that are approximately what you want. Check the information carefully before you view anything, and do not waste your time looking at houses outside your price range.

Because of the large fees charged by agents, some sellers advertise their houses themselves in the newspapers. These houses are also worth checking.

Whenever you find a house worth seeing, take the advertised details with you when you go to view it. Take also a notebook and pen and a tape measure, and check the details. Do not accept the description given by an agent or in an advertisement – check the particulars yourself.

• RAISING THE MONEY

Before you start your search for the ideal house, work out how much money you will have available. It is advisable to try for a house that takes up the maximum loan you can raise and afford, if your income is likely to increase with promotion, age and inflation over the years.

The annual cost of paying for the house may also increase, but more slowly.

FINDING A BUILDING SOCIETY

The most obvious source of finance is a building society, and in times of economic difficulty the best way to obtain a building-society loan is to become established as a regular saver with the society of your choice.

Building societies exist to lend their funds for house purchase, but they prefer first-time buyers. So if you already own a house, do not assume that your existing building society will automatically lend you money if you buy another one. Some societies moreover will not normally grant mortgages on houses built before 1920, or on flats or leasehold property.

Most societies limit loans to 80% of their valuation of the property. The amount you can borrow will depend on your circumstances, especially your income. People who have a low basic salary but can depend on earning regular commission should ask their employers to give them a statement confirming this.

Many societies take part of a wife's income into account, but it is sensible to find out whether this applies to the society you intend to use before you start to commit your savings to it. Indeed it is worth shopping around before you decide on a society, because they are not all the same. Interest rates vary, and a high-interest yield on savings will almost always mean a higher-than-average monthly repayment when you eventually obtain a mortgage.

OTHER SOURCES OF MONEY

Insurance companies and the local authorities also finance house purchase. Such loans depend on the economy; when times are hard, funds dry up. Moreover, local councils usually limit their loans to specially needy couples who cannot satisfy building societies' requirements through age or low income. However, they will lend money on pre-1920 houses.

Some employers operate home-purchase schemes for their staff; banks, building societies and insurance companies are examples.

If you have no idea yourself where to try for a loan, a solicitor – when you find one (see pp. 12-13) – may be able to put you in touch with the local manager of a building society. Your bank manager may also be able to help; and estate agents can often recommend sources of finance.

Failing all of these, mortgage brokers exist to find money for clients in difficulty, but the conditions and interest charges imposed are often more onerous than those offered directly by building societies.

While they can be useful if no other source can help, some brokers charge commission in advance, which may be difficult to recover if the loan fails to materialise. The broker is entitled to a fee of only £1 if no agreement is made within six months of his introducing you to a lender.

WHAT KIND OF MORTGAGE

Try to decide at the outset what type of mortgage best suits your finances. The straight repayment mortgage is one where a building society or other lender advances a sum which you pay back by monthly instalments over a period of years. The usual mortgage periods are 20 or 25 years. Instalments vary if interest rates change during the repayment period. You can borrow over a shorter period, but monthly instalments will be higher.

Each instalment is partly interest and partly capital. At the beginning it is mostly interest. Tax relief is available on this interest element and this is very helpful in the early years.

It is wise to insure against death during the period of the mortgage by means of a mortgage-protection policy. If the borrower dies, the insurance company pays off the balance of the mortgage, leaving the house free of debt for the widow or heirs.

An endowment mortgage is one under which you take out a fixed-term endowment insurance policy to cover the amount of the loan. You pay interest on the loan and premiums on the insurance policy, receiving tax relief on both. At the end of the term, the policy matures and pays off the mortgage. If the policy was 'with profits' – which means higher premiums – you will get a cash payment as well. If a borrower dies during the term of such a loan the insurance company pays off the entire mortgage and may make a cash payment to the estate.

It is generally useful to get professional advice on whether this type of mortgage would be advantageous in your particular circumstances.

People who pay little or no tax, and so cannot benefit from tax relief on mortgage repayments, can consider an 'option mortgage'. This allows them a reduced interest rate to compensate for the unclaimed tax relief. A borrower can give up the option mortgage scheme and change to tax relief after a minimum of four years. It is also possible in cases of hardship to change from tax relief to the option scheme.

• RENTING A HOME

There are 20 million homes in Britain. About 11 million are owned by the people who live in them. Public landlords, mostly local councils, control about 6 million, and private landlords own the remaining 3 million.

In many parts of the country it is difficult to find houses or flats to rent. Councils usually have long waiting lists for their accommodation. Private landlords whose activities, and the rents they can charge, are controlled by law, usually try to sell a property if it falls vacant, rather than let it again.

If you want to rent and can find accommodation, the landlord will get you to sign a formal lease or agreement, or simply supply you with a rent book. In addition to paying the rent, you may also be responsible for rates.

In the case of most private tenancies, so long as the tenant complies with the main requirements of the lease and pays the rent on time, the Rent Acts provide that the landlord can hardly ever recover possession. It does not matter whether the property is furnished or not.

The main grounds for possession are as follow:
1. Unpaid rent or breach of the terms of the lease.
2. Nuisance or annoyance to near neighbours, or conviction for illegal or immoral use of the premises.
3. Ill-treatment of the property or furniture (in the case of a furnished letting).
4. Tenant gives notice and landlord arranges to sell.
5. Tenant sublets without permission.
6. Landlord needs the premises for an employee.
7. Landlord needs the place for himself or family, provided he bought it before December 1965.
8. Landlord offers suitable alternative accommodation.
9. Where landlord lets his own residence and tells tenant at the start that he will want to come back and live in it.
10. Farmer wants house back to let to farm worker.

In cases 1 to 8 inclusive, the court has a choice: it may or may not order possession. In cases 9 and 10 it MUST order possession.

Any tenant of private accommodation can apply to a Rent Officer to fix a 'fair rent', which will then be registered. The Rent Officer can increase or decrease an unregistered rent. Once a rent is registered for unfurnished premises it cannot generally be increased for three years unless the landlord has made improvements. In the case of furnished tenancies, the rent cannot be increased unless a Rent Tribunal allows it.

It is illegal to charge a premium or 'key money' as a condition for a tenancy. Sometimes money is demanded for furniture. But the tenant need only pay a fair price for furniture – and can sue to recover any excess.

A weekly tenant must be given a rent book by the landlord. This will contain details of the rent, the day for payment, any notice period, and information about fair rents.

Council tenants, unlike private ones, have no security of tenure, no right to have a rent registered, and no appeal against a rent increase. But in the last resort a council cannot evict a tenant without a court order.

• BUYING A HOUSE IN SCOTLAND

The procedure for buying a house in Scotland differs considerably from that in England and Wales. Although estate agents do exist in Scotland and handle an ever-increasing number of property sales and purchases, the majority of transactions are undertaken from start to finish by solicitors. The house-purchasing service offered by the solicitor can include finding the house, arranging for the mortgage and for any specialist treatment to the house such as woodworm spraying, negotiating the terms of the contract and insuring the property.

The best way to find a house in Scotland is through the advertisement columns of the newspapers, although individual solicitors' offices and estate agents may offer an additional choice. In the cities and several large towns there are also Solicitors' Property Centres, which provide a list of properties being offered for sale by solicitors in that area.

The next stage is radically different from the procedure normal in England and Wales. In the advertisement or in the particulars of the property, a price will be stated above which offers for the property are invited. Once the property has been surveyed and the mortgage arranged, your solicitor will make an offer in writing for the appropriate sum.

If several purchasers are interested in the same house, then the seller's agent will accept the highest offer submitted by a certain day.

Once the written offer has been accepted by the seller's agent, the deal becomes legally binding. A deposit on the purchase price is not necessary. The offer and acceptance – known as the missives – will specify a date on which the purchase price is to be handed over in full, in exchange for a disposition of the property by the seller in favour of the purchaser, or – if a mortgage has been taken out – in favour of the building society. This disposition is drawn up by the purchaser's solicitor after he has received from the seller's agent all the relevant titles to the property. The seller has an absolute obligation to provide a clear and valid title to the property before it is handed over and the purchase money paid.

Scottish solicitors' scale fees for buying a house are:

PROPERTY PRICE	SCALE FEE
£10,000	£120
£11,000	£126
£12,000	£132
£13,000	£138
£14,000	£143
£15,000	£149
£20,000	£178
£25,000	£208
£30,000	£237

These charges are exclusive of VAT and do not include any fee for arranging a mortgage.

A peculiarity of the system of landholding in Scotland is the survival of certain feudal rights. Nearly all property in Scotland derives through a series of feudal grants from the Crown. These grants lay down obligations and conditions applicable to the land, including the payment of duty (now redeemable) by the grantee towards the immediate feudal superior. Provided that the conditions of the grant – and they may be absolutely minimal – are not contravened, the grant is irrevocable.

You may find, for example, that the conditions laid down prohibit the erection of further buildings on the land and you may want to build a garage. If this is the case, you will need not only planning permission from the local authority, but also the permission of the feudal superior.

• LOOKING AT HOUSES

In many legal transactions the law protects the buyer. But when you buy a house you are on your own. Make a full investigation before you exchange contracts, because once the exchange is made you cannot back out of the deal. If the house turns out to have defects, there is no redress unless the sellers have told you lies. Even then, it is not certain that you will have a legal claim for compensation.

When you find a house you like, compare its price with that of a similar property in a similar area. Then haggle. Sellers often ask for more than the house is worth and are almost always prepared to take a drop of 10% on their asking price. If you make an offer in writing be sure to add the words 'subject to contract, and subject to survey'. This ensures that there is no binding legal contract until you want there to be.

Go over the house thoroughly and as often as you need to. Do not worry about upsetting the sellers. They want you to buy. Jot down questions and answers, and take a tape measure. The sizes of rooms given on estate agents' blurbs may not be accurate and it is up to you to check them.

Visit the local planning department and ask to see the plans for the neighbourhood – there may be factories or similar developments in the pipeline which could affect the property.

INSPECTING OUTSIDE

Start with the roof – look for missing or loose tiles. Check for damp stains, mould or cracks in outside walls, gutters, eaves and chimneys. Examine window frames for rotting wood and old putty. Check that ventilation holes are not clogged up. Make sure that the damp course is above the ground level. Look for any large trees whose roots could damage the foundations.

Drains can cause a lot of expense. Lift manhole covers to see how deep they are. If they are less than 2 ft down, or there are large trees near by, suspect possible damage.

If possible, see the house in the rain. Bad weather may show up leaks, overflows and rising damp.

INSIDE CHECKS

Check the timber inside the roof for rot and woodworm, and examine the weather-proofing. Look for signs of leaks. See that the roof is properly insulated with thick glass-fibre. If it is not, ask the seller to cut the price.

Examine the water cistern for corrosion. If it needs replacing, that is another ground for price reduction.

Ceilings and walls may be damp. Newly papered patches are a sign of this. Jump on the downstairs floors to check the state of the floorboards and joists. Look at paintwork and probe into cupboards for rot or damp.

Check the wiring, fusebox, plumbing and lagging. Try all light switches. See if you can look under the floorboards and in the meter cupboard to examine the wiring. Ask the owners what fixtures they are leaving behind.

RUNNING COSTS

Ask about the central heating, its reliability, running expenses and servicing arrangements. Ask to see fuel bills. You will want to know the cost of rates, lighting, cooking and heating, whether there is a woodworm guarantee that can be transferred to you (with the report on any timber treatment); whether there is cavity-wall insulation; if there have been any problems over damp, rot or drains.

Ask the owner why he is selling. There is nearly always a good reason – the seller is retiring, he is moving to a new job in another town, his family is growing, or maybe the children have grown up and are leaving home. There are many more genuine reasons for moving, but once in a while a buyer will be told something that makes him wonder if the seller is desperate to pass on a sorry mistake.

WHAT IT WILL COST

It is easy to underestimate the cost of buying a house. Apart from mortgage repayments and insurance premiums, you will have to pay the building-society surveyor's fee (based on the value of the house); your own surveyor; your solicitor's fees; search fees; stamp duty (for houses costing more than £15,000; Land Registry fees; removal costs; and VAT on professional fees.

Remember that you will have to put down a deposit – probably 10% of the agreed purchase price – when you exchange contracts.

• THE BUILDING SOCIETY'S SURVEY

When you have decided on the house, tell the building society and your solicitor.

The building-society surveyor, whose fee you have to pay, will inspect the property and you will be given a loan based on his valuation. This may be less than the market value of the house, for the building society have to ensure that if they need to call the mortgage in they can get their money back quickly.

YOUR OWN SURVEY

If you are buying an old house, or even a modern house which you feel may be in need of repair, it pays to have a full structural survey done by your own surveyor. You have no claim against the building society surveyor if his report is wrong – you cannot demand to see his report, anyway. But you have a legal claim against your own surveyor if his report is inaccurate or misleading. To save fees, you may be able to employ the same surveyor as the building society.

If you are satisfied with the general state of the house, but concerned about a particular aspect – such as

STAMP DUTY RATES

HOUSE PRICE	RATE	EXAMPLE
£0-£15,000	Nil	
£15,001-£20,000	½%	£18,500 = £92.50
£20,001-£25,000	1%	£21,750 = £217.50
£25,001-£30,000	1½%	£27,450 = £411.75
£30,001-Upwards	2%	£36,000 = £720

THE MONEY YOU NEED TO BUY A HOUSE

To the figures given below, add VAT to professional fees and stamp duty where applicable (see table above).

HOUSE PRICE	£10,000	£12,500	£15,000	£20,000	£30,000
Mortgage	7,000	10,000	12,000	15,000	20,000
Proportion of price to be raised by you	3,000	2,500	3,000	5,000	10,000
Building society survey fee	21	26	31	36	46
Your surveyor's fee	40-80	40-80	40-80	40-80	40-80
SOLICITOR'S FEE FOR PURCHASE Registered title	80	90	100	120	150
Unregistered title	120	140	160	175	200
LAND REGISTRY FEE Registered land	21.60	26.55	31.50	41.40	61.20
First registration	14.40	17.55	20.77	27	39.60
Search fees	6	6	6	6	6
Solicitor's fee for mortgage	65	75	85	90	100
Total (minimum) required by you	3,233.60	2,763.55	3,293.50	5,333.40	10,403.20

chimneys or central heating – you can employ a builder or plumber to make an inspection for less cost than a full structural survey.

WHAT YOUR SOLICITOR DOES

If you have never used a solicitor, ask your bank manager, building-society manager or estate agent to recommend one. Alternatively, consult the local citizens' advice bureau, consumer advice centre or public library.

When you have found a solicitor, ask him to quote his fees and expenses. Scale fees for conveyancing have been abolished, so it is worth asking several firms what they will charge. Fees will be higher if the title is unregistered. Registered land is officially guaranteed to be the property of the person named on the Land Registry.

Your solicitor will receive a draft contract from the seller's solicitor indicating whether there are legal restrictions affecting the property – for example, rights of way or covenants not to erect fences or outbuildings, or to conduct a business on the premises.

'Searches' will be made by the solicitor to see if the road is maintained by the council, if works are planned which will affect the property, if drainage is a public service, and if any planning rules have been broken.

He will also find out from the seller's solicitor about services connected to the property, shared facilities, planning requirements and fixtures, and who owns the boundaries.

If there are any buildings or extensions which look new, tell your solicitor so that he can check up on whether planning permission or other necessary consents were obtained.

Your solicitor will NOT visit the property, measure the garden, or get you a building-society mortgage – though he may make some useful

A STEP-BY-STEP GUIDE TO BUYING A HOUSE

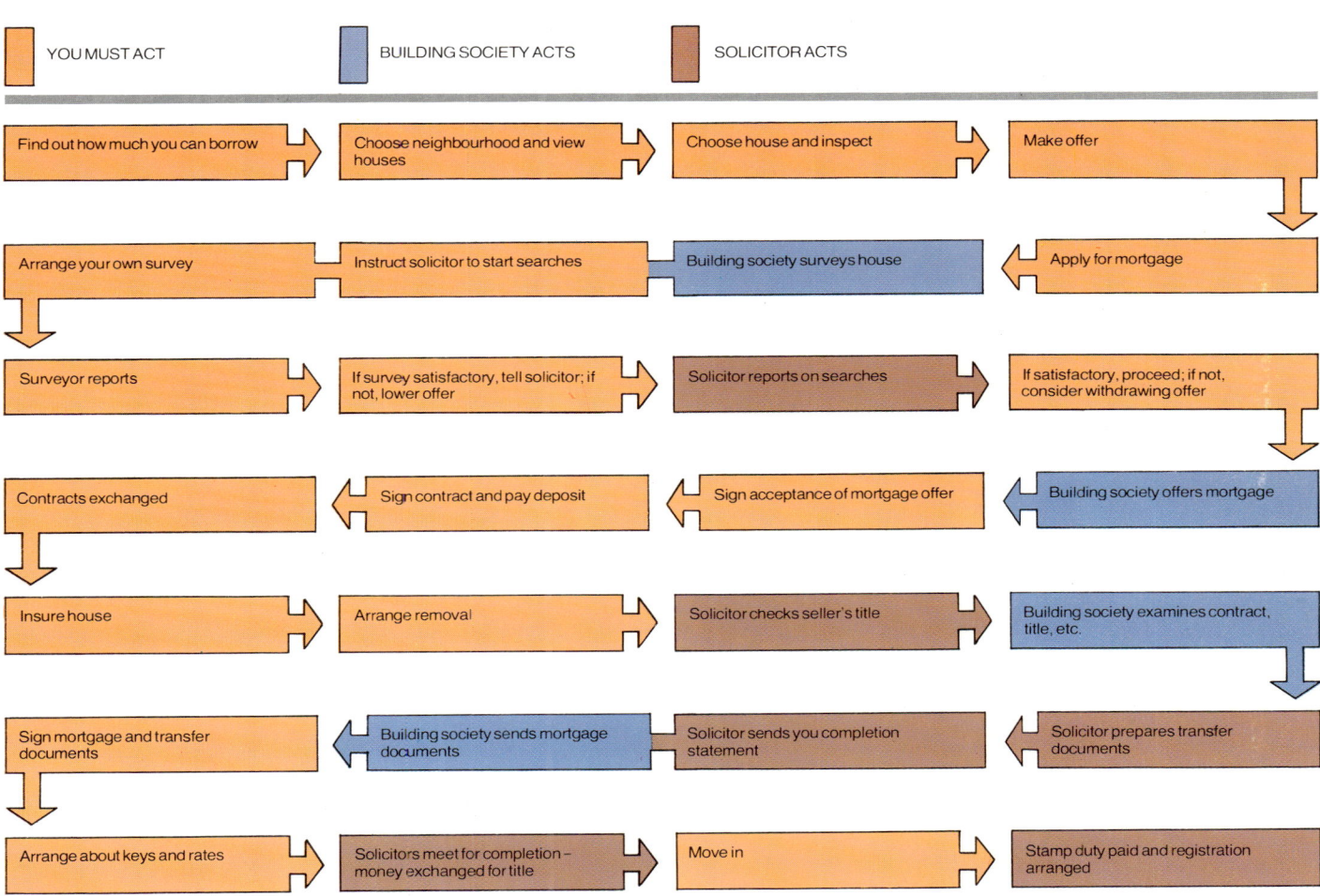

THE HOUSE-BUYING PROCESS It takes weeks of work by many people to complete the purchase of a house. The chart shows who does what at each stage.

suggestions. He is concerned with the title to the land on which the property stands, not with the structure itself, or what condition it is in.

WHEN THE MORTGAGE IS OFFERED

The building society's formal offer of a mortgage may insist on the borrower insuring his life for a sum large enough to pay off the mortgage in the event of his death before repayment is completed.

If their survey reveals defects, the society may withhold part of the money until they have been put right. Alternatively, they may insist that the defects be put right within a set time.

THE CASH YOU WILL NEED

Remember that the mortgage will not cover all your expenditure on the new house (see table on p. 12).

Even without essential items like the removal expenses, the final bill can be considerably higher than it might appear at first glance (see table). For example, a buyer might have to

spend well over £10,200 to buy a registered property for which he is paying the seller £10,000. If he had a 70% mortgage he would get only £7,000, leaving more than £3,200 to raise himself.

On houses that cost more than £15,000 the buyer must pay in addition government stamp duty.

• EXCHANGING CONTRACTS

When the preliminary legal work has been completed, usually after about four weeks, your solicitor will ask you to sign the contract and let him have a cheque for the deposit so that he can exchange contracts.

This is the moment when the deal becomes legally binding. The deposit will be forfeited if you cancel – unless it turns out that the seller cannot prove that he owns the house.

The deposit – to be found from your savings or by borrowing from the bank – is customarily 10% of the agreed purchase price, though some sellers are prepared to accept 5%. The contract and cheque are sent to the seller's solicitor who fills in the date for completion: usually four weeks later, unless agreed otherwise – and sends your solicitor his client's signed part of the contract. (As soon as you know the completion date, start obtaining estimates from removal firms.)

• INSURING THE PROPERTY

It is essential to insure the property as soon as contracts have been exchanged, for you are committed to buying the house, and must pay for it even if it is destroyed. The seller, however, also has a duty to keep the house in good condition until he hands it over on completion.

Check that the building society approves of the insurance company you intend to use, and arrange comprehensive cover against fire and other risks.

The building society will insist that the sum for which you insure the house is adequate to protect their interest in the property. This will normally be a good deal less than the price you have paid, since the land is indestructible.

Remember, however, that costs of building and repairing keep going up with inflation, and unless these are taken into account you run a serious risk of being under-insured. If, for instance, your home were insured for only 80% of its value, the insurance company would be unlikely to pay you more than that percentage of any claim. To minimise this risk, some companies now offer 'index-linked' policies, under which the sum insured – and, of course, the premium paid – is automatically adjusted to keep pace with rising costs.

Do not overlook the contents: the cost of replacing these too will almost certainly go on rising.

It might be worth considering going in for a package-type policy, which will cover everything you need to insure, including a car, caravan, boat, contents of a deep-freezer, and so on. Such a policy is usually cheaper than insuring separately.

MAKING FURTHER INQUIRIES

At the exchange-of-contracts stage, your solicitor receives an 'abstract of title' which shows that the sellers are the actual owners and shows what mortgages have to be paid off. He then sends a draft transfer document to the seller's solicitor for approval.

If the building society is using its own solicitor, it will ask for all the documents, to see that the loan will be legally secure. Both solicitors check at the Land Registry to see that no other claims on the property have been entered on the register.

If the title is unregistered, they find out if there is any significant legal charge registered at the Land Charges Department. There could, for example, be undisclosed mortgages outstanding, or a claim by a creditor; or the seller could be bankrupt and the house not his to sell.

The building society's solicitor will also make inquiries to ensure that you are not bankrupt. People who are bankrupt cannot own property.

COMPLETION AND AFTER

If all inquiries are satisfactory, the seller's solicitor stipulates how he wants the money, and both sides agree on what proportion of the current year's rates they will pay.

Your solicitor sends you a completion statement showing how much money remains to be paid. It is usual for the solicitor to ask for his own costs at this stage. You then sign the transfer document, mortgage deed and any insurance documents.

Notify the Post Office telephone department, gas and electricity boards so that meters can be read. If you are buying fixtures and fittings from the outgoing owner, or if there is coal in the bunker or oil in an oil tank, arrange payment for these items separately.

Collect the keys if possible, or make sure that the seller's solicitor will hand them over at the moment of completion so that you can move in.

Completion takes place when the building-society solicitor and your solicitor meet at the seller's solicitor's office to hand over the money and collect the deeds. You need not be present. The building society retains the deeds until the mortgage is fully paid, but you can obtain copies for a small fee. It is possible to pay mortgage instalments and insurance premiums by a standing order: make the arrangements with your bank.

The building society will tell the Inland Revenue about your new mortgage so that they can adjust your tax code. The Inland Revenue will also examine the transfer document to assess stamp duty (see p. 12). If the title is registered, the transfer mortgage and search certificates will be sent by the building society to the Land Registry so that the ownership change and details of the mortgage can be noted.

Finally, tell the rates department of your local council that you have moved in.

• BUYING IN JOINT NAMES

People who are married or about to be married should consider the advantages of buying the house in their joint names.

If it is in the husband's name only, and he later dies, the house becomes part of his estate, and his widow may not even have a legal right to go on living there. There will certainly be complications and expense if the husband has not made a will.

There are two ways in which a husband and wife can own a house jointly: by *joint tenancy* or by *tenancy-in-common*. Under a joint tenancy, if either partner dies, his or her share of the house automatically goes to the surviving partner, no matter what may be said in the will. Under a tenancy-in-common, the dead partner's share goes according to his or her will. If it is left to somebody other than the husband or wife it will be liable to capital transfer tax.

HOUSE BUYING: TERMS YOU SHOULD UNDERSTAND

Collateral Additional security for the mortgage; usually a life-insurance policy.

Completion The stage when deeds are exchanged by the seller for the money.

Contract A legally binding agreement to sell or buy anything.

Conveyancing The process of transfer of ownership of land.

Covenant Restriction on how land can be used. It is made in the transfer deed and must be observed by the buyer.

Deposit A proportion of the purchase price, paid when contracts are exchanged.

Freehold Absolute right or title to ownership of land.

Joint tenancy Arrangement by which two or more people hold property jointly so that, when one dies, his or her share automatically passes to the survivor. (See also Tenancy-in-common.)

Land charge search Inquiry at national search centre to see if any outstanding charges or claims are registered.

Land Registry Government department which maintains records of all registered titles to land in England and Wales.

Leasehold The right to occupy, for a fixed period, land that belongs to somebody else, to whom rent is paid.

Local land charge search Inquiry to local council to find any planning permissions, and any smoke control and preservation orders affecting a property.

Local searches Inquiries to local council to establish permitted use of a property, if it is connected to main sewer, whether rent restriction applies and if road is adopted and likely to be widened.

Mortgage A signed document detailing property given as security for a loan.

Option mortgage A mortgage scheme for borrowers who pay little or no income tax (and so do not benefit from tax relief). A lower interest rate applies.

Registered title Title to land guaranteed and administered by the Land Registry.

Title The legal right to a piece of land.

Title deeds Documents showing past and present ownership of property. When title is registered, there are no title deeds but a Land Certificate instead.

Tenancy-in-common Arrangement under which two or more people hold property jointly so that, when one dies, his or her share forms part of the estate and is dealt with according to the will (or, if there is no will, according to the rules of intestacy). It does not pass automatically to the survivor. (See also Joint tenancy.)

Transfer Document signed by buyer and seller, agreeing to deal and price.

It is commonly thought that in the event of a divorce a wife has no right to a share of the house if it is in the husband's name only; and similarly that a husband has no right if the house is in his wife's name. This is not so. A court will take into consideration such factors as how long the couple have been married, and divide the ownership of the house accordingly.

• MOVING HOME

Start arranging the move as soon as you know the completion date for the purchase of your new house. This gives you time to find a reliable removal firm and allows you to fix a firm date for the move.

If it is a light move, from a small flat, for example, it may be cheaper to hire a van and driver and do the work with the help of friends. But for anything more substantial use professional removers.

First, seek written estimates. If possible, choose firms recommended by friends. Otherwise, the British Association of Removers (see pp. 410-21) will give you the names of member firms in your area.

Ask the estimator what his firm's arrangements are about packing and insurance. Most firms like to do all the packing and unpacking. In fact, most will not accept liability for damage in transit to goods they have not packed. Most can arrange insurance for the journey, though your own insurance company can do this. Whichever arrangement you choose, proper insurance cover is vital: insist on full details in advance.

Get some idea of the times involved – for packing and loading, for the journey, and for unloading and unpacking.

If you have pets or delicate plants for which special arrangements will need to be made, tell the estimator.

Some contractors will supply cat baskets, for example.

Hi-fi and other delicate equipment should be packed in the containers in which they were supplied.

Arrange to move in the middle of the week, if possible. Weekend moves can be more expensive because of overtime pay to removal men. The weekend can also be inconvenient if you need help with the mains services, or some other emergency arises at the new house.

When the written estimate arrives, check that the date and times are correct and that all the services you require are accounted for, including insurance unless you are arranging this through your own company. Estimates will vary in price, but the cheapest is not necessarily the best, since the service may not be comprehensive.

When you accept the estimate, ask the contractor to confirm the arrangement in writing.

FIXTURES AND FITTINGS

It is important to know which fixtures and fittings you can remove and which stay behind. Buyer and seller can make whatever arrangements they like. The seller, for example, can even remove the chimney pots, provided that he agrees this with the buyer.

Where no agreement is made, some things – such as electric sockets – are legally considered to be sold with the house, while others – such as electric cookers – can be removed by the sellers.

However, there are a number of fixtures and fittings on which the law is vague. These are the most frequent causes of dispute between buyers and sellers.

The most important are fitted curtain rails and tracks; fitted bookshelves and fixed decorative wall mirrors; built-in gas and electric fires; built-in kitchen appliances, including plumbed-in water softeners; garden structures without foundations.

Removable fittings include hanging light fittings, and all electrical fittings which are plugged in; free-standing kitchen appliances, including gas and electric cookers, refrigerators and deep-freezers, washing machines and dish-washers; free-standing kitchen units which are lightly attached to the walls; free-standing gas and electric fires; fitted wardrobes and cupboards which are designed to be easily removed; all floor coverings including fitted carpets; garden furniture and garden ornaments.

If you expect the removers to dismantle fittings or collapsible furniture, discuss this in advance, preferably with the estimator.

Permanent fixtures include plumbing, wiring, including switches and plug sockets; bathroom suite, the central-heating system, except possibly plug-in electric radiators; built-in kitchen units, cupboards and wardrobes which have been 'purpose-made'; outbuildings with foundations, and any plants, trees or shrubs in the garden.

THINGS YOU MUST DO YOURSELF

Removal men will lift and pack fitted carpets, but they will not refit them unless separate arrangements are made. So, if you want carpets refitted, arrange it in advance either with the removal man or with a carpet specialist.

The remover will not accept responsibility for jewellery, cash and other small valuables. So pack these separately, arrange insurance and deal with them yourself. Do not leave them lying around in either house on moving day. It is a good idea to get your bank to look after such things for the period of the move.

Removal men are not allowed to disconnect gas or electric equipment, such as cookers and fires, that are wired to the mains. So remember at least a week in advance to arrange with the gas and electricity boards to disconnect equipment before the removal men arrive. At the same time, arrange to have the meters read on moving day, so that you pay only for what you have used.

You will also need to make separate arrangements for the removal and re-erection of an outside television aerial.

If you have a deep-freezer, use up all the food in it before moving day. The freezer itself should be dried out and aired two days before the move and allowed one or two days to settle afterwards before it is re-stocked.

There are some things you can do to make the move go smoothly.

Visit the new house, locate the water-supply stopcock, the mains gas tap and the electricity mains switch. Check that the plugs on your electrical equipment fit the new sockets.

Write down your new address with a map, if necessary, to give the removal driver. If possible, also give him a spare key in case he arrives before you do: any hold-up in the move can be expensive. Find out if there are any parking restrictions near the new house so that the removers can make advance arrangements with the police.

Put numbered labels on all your furniture. Then draw a plan of the new house and write in the numbers room by room to show where you want the furniture placed.

If you are moving in or out of a block of flats, warn the caretaker so that you can get priority in the use of the lift.

LONG-TERM STORAGE

If you put the contents of your home into storage, clean all fabrics and treat them with a moth repellent. Inflammable and explosive substances will not be accepted for storage.

It is your responsibility to insure the goods and maintain payments to the storage contractor. If payments fall heavily in arrears, the contractor can, after giving you proper notice, sell your goods, take what you owe him from the proceeds and give you the remainder. Seven days' notice is required when you decide to withdraw goods from store.

LAST-MINUTE ARRANGEMENTS

1 Lay out china, glass, cutlery and ornaments, ready for packing – but not on a table that is going.

2 Mark anything that is to be left.

3 Fold bedding.

4 Remove oil from heaters and lamps and petrol from lawn mowers. Remove batteries from gas lighters.

5 Prepare an overnight bag and any food that will be needed quickly.

6 Cancel milk and newspapers.

7 When the removal team arrives, give the foreman the plan of the new house together with the keys, then show him everything that has to go and what has to stay behind.

8 Show him your overnight bag and anything else you want quickly at the new address.

9 If the move takes place in cold weather and the old house is likely to be empty for a while turn the water off at the mains and drain the system to avoid burst pipes.

10 When everything has been loaded, go over the house yourself to check that nothing has been overlooked. Under the standard contract, this is your responsibility.

COLLECTING LOCKS AND KEYS

Man has been preoccupied with the need for security since our ancestors rolled boulders across the openings of their caves. The Greeks had one of the most primitive types of lock – a simple cross-bar with a peg through it. A key lifted the peg out to open the door. But the earliest example of a lock and key as we know them today dates from the reign of the Roman emperor Trajan (AD 90). This was a wooden pin-lock, in which a key lifted several pins to release the lock.

Norman keys of the 11th and 12th centuries were made of bronze with lozenge-shaped tops – as the key shown above (bottom row, right). Between the 15th and 17th centuries, locksmiths were famous for their superb craftsmanship. To qualify as a master locksmith, a French apprentice had to make a lock and key based on a certain architectural style, as with the 17th-century 'Apprentice' key (top right). The iron key (top centre) is an Italian key of the 17th century; the steel key (top row, second right) is English.

During the 17th and 18th centuries treasure chests often had as many as 24 bolts set in a lock. Their security, however, was minimal, as all the bolts could be opened simultaneously with one key. Other locks were fitted with iron spikes, which pierced any hand using a bogus key, or discharged pepper.

Various European courts of the 18th and 19th centuries used ceremonial keys, such as the gilt Chamberlain's key (bottom row, third left) bearing the cipher of George III. These keys originally had a practical use but later became simply a badge of office. This also applied to presentation keys such as the silver-gilt key (bottom row, second right) presented to the Princess of Battenberg when she opened an exhibition in Yorkshire in 1887.

Locks were also exquisitely decorated during this period. The early 18th-century lock (below) has a Tudor rose, leek, daffodil and thistle moulded in brass on a blued-steel background.

From the late 18th century onwards, locksmiths such as Barron, Bramah, Chubb and Yale, concentrated on improving lock mechanisms. The iron key (top row, second left) engraved 'Grosvenor Square Trust' was the key to a famous Bramah lock patented in 1784. Other keys shown above are a 19th-century latch key (top left); a personal key of the Earl of Yarmouth, c. 1800 (bottom row, first left); and a rare Tudor iron key with heart-shaped bow (bottom row, second left).

Interesting old keys and locks may be found today in country ironmongers' stores, where trays of out-of-date stock may be kept. Second-hand shops and market stalls may also yield results.

• GRANTS FOR IMPROVEMENT

Local councils make grants to help owners to bring older houses up to a good standard, or to provide new dwellings by converting large houses. They are not intended for modern or fully equipped houses in good repair, or normally for enlarging a house by adding more bedroom space.

Only the council can tell you what work they will consider subsidising. Normally they must be satisfied that on completion, the house or flat will have the standard amenities, be in good repair and have a useful life of at least 30 years.

Although improvement grants are useful when converting a house, remember that in return for their help the council will expect to keep a close eye on the work. If any changes in the approved plan are proposed in the course of the work, the council should be consulted.

The awarding of grants for owner-occupation is governed by rateable value. If you are to be an owner-occupier of the house which you intend to improve, and its rateable value is greater than £600 in Greater London, or £300 elsewhere, you will not be eligible for an improvement grant. Other types of grant are not affected.

No grant may be awarded for the improvement or conversion of any dwelling built after October 2, 1961.

The upper limit of cost that may be grant-aided, called the eligible expense, is normally £3,200 per dwelling. But where a building of three or more storeys is to be converted to provide flats, the limit is £3,700 for each flat.

You will be entitled to only a percentage of this figure, normally 50%, although more is available if you live in an area designated for improvement.

Repairs and replacements by themselves do not qualify for a grant, except in the limited circumstances in which a repairs grant is available. But up to half your total cost may relate to repair work which is incidental to an improvement, or needed to make improvements fully effective.

The installation of central heating is not eligible for a repair grant unless, like a repair, it is part of a general scheme of improvement.

If you have already had a grant for the provision of standard amenities, or a repairs grant, and now want to make further improvements, you can still apply for an improvement grant. An adjustment will normally be made to take account of the earlier grant.

The council can also give an improvement grant for work to make a dwelling suitable for the accommodation, welfare or employment of a disabled person.

AREAS OF SPECIAL CONCERN

Local authorities can designate Housing Action Areas in districts where bad physical and social conditions interact to create unsatisfactory living conditions. Councils can demand that improvements be made, or even take over properties, compulsorily if need be, from owners unwilling or unable to co-operate.

Councils may also designate General Improvement Areas to cover districts where there is a need to brighten up the environment as well as improve the houses. This kind of work makes a neighbourhood more pleasant to live in, and increases the value of the houses. So it may be worthwhile for a residents' association to approach a council and suggest their area for designation.

Improvements to houses in General Improvement Areas attract grants of up to 60% of the eligible expense.

IF THE BUILDING IS HISTORIC

Additional money may be available for houses that are officially listed as of historic or architectural interest. This is the case if specific works, materials or architectural details are necessary to maintain the character of the building.

APPLYING FOR A GRANT

You will be considered for an improvement grant only if your house is a freehold property or if you have a lease with at least five years to run. The application form, available from the council, explains what information is required about the building, the proposed work, the estimated cost and other related factors.

If you are planning an ambitious scheme, such as the conversion of a house into flats, it is advisable to get professional advice. The council may give you a list of local architects and surveyors who are known to be willing to undertake this kind of work.

Except where a special grant is involved, you must sign a certificate of future occupation. An owner-occupier must certify that he intends to live in the building within 12 months of completing the work, and throughout the following four years. He must also certify that the dwelling will be his only, or main, residence and will be occupied exclusively by himself and members of his household, if any. Grants are not available for second homes.

A landlord must certify that for five years he intends to let the dwelling as a residence – not as a holiday home – to persons other than members of his own family.

WHEN THE GRANT IS PAID

Grants are normally paid when the project has been completed to the council's satisfaction, but they may, in some areas, be paid by instalments during the course of the work. The council may be prepared to pay the grant direct to the builder. Councils usually insist that the work must be carried out within a year of approval – although this can be extended.

They can make loans on mortgage terms to anyone who cannot afford improvements or repairs, with or without the aid of a grant.

OTHER TYPES OF GRANT

Intermediate grants These are given towards the provision of basic amenities, and in addition may cover a proportion of the cost of essential repairs. The grants are available as of right, provided that after improvement the dwelling will have all the standard amenities (bath, wash-basin, sink, lavatory, and hot and cold water supplies); be in a good state of repair and fit for human habitation; and have an expected life of 15 years.

The eligible expense varies, according to the amenities provided, but is subject to an overall maximum of £700. Repairs costing up to an additional £800 may also be approved for grant aid.

An intermediate grant may also be given to provide amenities for a disabled occupant, where the existing amenities are unsuitable because of the disability.

Special grants These are made at the local authority's discretion. Their aim is to improve shared houses where rooms are let out to tenants.

To qualify, a house must be lived in by several people who do not form a single household. Usually, special grants are awarded only for work on old houses that are not worth converting into self-contained flats, or when there is no immediate prospect of conversion.

The standard amenities do not all have to be provided; and more than one amenity of the same kind may be installed. For instance, an extra bathroom may be fitted or a wash-basin put in each bedroom.

The council will fix the eligible expense according to the estimated cost of putting in the amenities that they have approved.

Repairs grants These are available only within Housing Action Areas or General Improvement Areas (see p. 16). Councils make them for essential repairs not associated with improvements or conversion. They are awarded only to people with limited means who cannot afford to pay for the repairs without hardship.

The council will determine the eligible expense, which may not exceed £800, and then fix the grant.

Whatever the type of grant considered, the person applying should check on whether it will have to be paid back, and on any other conditions that may be imposed by the council. In the case of a property that is let, for instance, the council may fix a limit to the amount of rent increase that may be charged because of improvements which they have subsidised with public money.

• ARCHITECTS' SERVICES

An architect can help if you are considering any complicated or expensive alterations or extensions to your present home.

You may need planning permission if anything you do is likely to alter the external appearance of the house or affect its surroundings. And you need building-regulations approval for any major alterations.

The architect will guide you through the maze of by-laws and building regulations, help you to obtain planning permission, and apply for any grant that may be available. His experience in dealing with officials will be valuable, and he will turn your ideas into working drawings. He will help you to select a builder, and will supervise the work.

The money saved by following his professional advice may well outweigh the cost of his fee, and you will have the satisfaction of knowing that the job is properly done.

HOW TO FIND AN ARCHITECT

Personal recommendation, from someone whose judgment you trust, is the best guide when you want the services of any professional.

If you cannot find an architect this way, contact the Royal Institute of British Architects or the Institute of Registered Architects. Tell them exactly what you need, and they will supply the names of qualified members in your area suitable for the job.

If you have the time, interview each of them (first checking whether they will charge a fee for this meeting), and ask them to bring photographs or slides of their work, to see if their style is suitable. It is vital, too, that the architect should be the kind of person with whom you can work well. The better your relationship the better the finished results will be.

If the person you select has a large practice, find out whether he or one of his assistants will be running the job. If it is to be an assistant, ask to meet him.

An architect can take on complete responsibility through every phase of the work, but obviously the more he does the higher his fee will be.

Any partial service should be clearly defined in writing before work begins. If you later want the scope extended, there will be an extra fee which should be negotiated and confirmed in writing.

File dated copies of all correspondence. Do not proceed until all doubts have been clarified.

FEES AND PAYMENT

Scales of fees for architects are given in booklets obtainable from their offices.

Fees are based either on a percentage of the contract price, or by the hour on smaller jobs.

For new building work costing less than £2,500 the architect's minimum fee scale is 10%, reducing to 6% for work up to £25,000; between 6% and 5.75% from £25,000 - £750,000.

On conversions or extensions to existing buildings, minimum fees range from 13% on total costs up to £2,500, to 10% on costs of £25,000.

If you name a sum you are able to budget for – allowing a margin for unforeseen extras – the architect can then see how much he can do for this amount.

Ask for a forecast of how much the fees will come to, plus any extras. If the architect is paid by the hour, ask him to submit weekly or monthly accounts of how many hours he has spent.

Ask him too for a programme of work, stating at what dates fees will be due and what progress will be made by those dates. This ensures that he will keep the job moving along.

THE BRIEFING

Work out with the architect a detailed description of the work – known as the brief – before design work begins.

He will ask about your way of life so that he can design something in harmony with your family's requirements. He may also ask for information on such matters as the rights of neighbouring owners, and for this a solicitor may be needed.

It is important that only one person in the family should give instructions to the professional adviser. He will not be able to work constructively if different people are giving different instructions at different times.

PLAN AND SPECIFICATION

The architect will present his outline ideas as sketch plans, perspectives and possible colour schemes. He should be able to explain the drawings so that the client understands what the finished job will look like.

A specification – a description of materials to be used and work to be carried out – will also be prepared. It will list such things as standards of workmanship and materials to be used.

The client is entitled to have copies of the working drawings and the specification.

As work progresses, the architect will regularly visit the site to make sure the builder is keeping to the drawings and specifications.

An alert client keeping an eye on the site can be a great asset. If he spots anything amiss he should discuss it with the architect – but not instruct the builder directly to make alterations. Unless instructions are always given to the builder by the architect, confusions may be introduced at a later date, affecting the cost of the job.

Each month, or at other regular intervals as agreed, the client will be given a certificate stating what payment is due to the builder. The client then has 14 days in which to pay – otherwise work will cease.

The process of issuing certificates might prove too complex for a small job. A written tender from the builder, with a joint written agreement as to when payments should be made, might be sufficient. The client should be guided by his professional adviser on this.

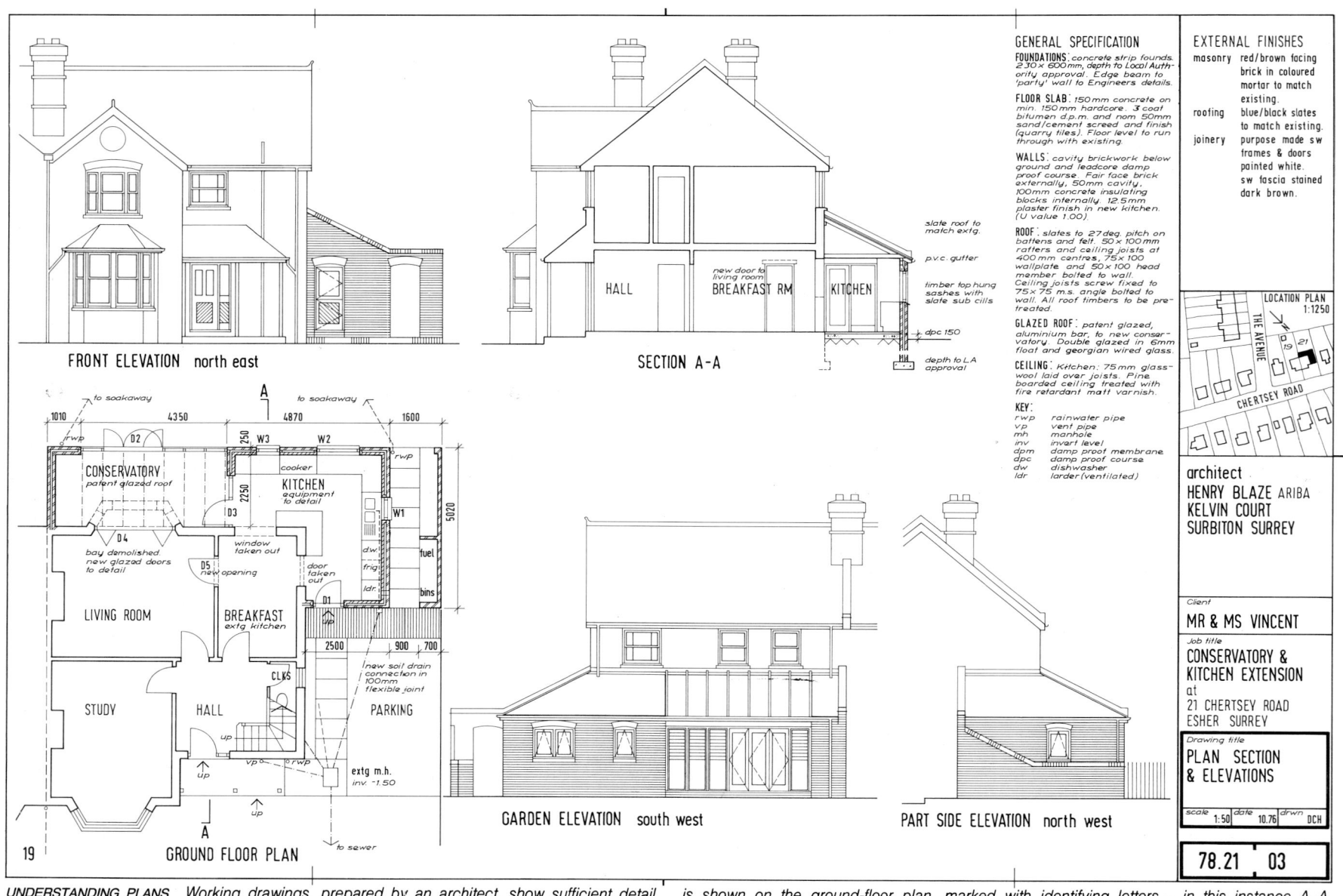

UNDERSTANDING PLANS Working drawings, prepared by an architect, show sufficient detail to obtain planning and building regulation approval, and for a builder to use. There may be one or more drawings, depending upon the size of the job, with elevations and at least one section showing the relationship of new work to old. The imaginary cut line of the section is shown on the ground-floor plan, marked with identifying letters – in this instance A-A. Abbreviations on the plan are explained in the general specification notes column, and new materials, such as brickwork, are usually distinguished from the existing by cross-hatching. A location plan shows the house's relationship to roads and other properties.

• EMPLOYING A BUILDER

If the architect is providing a full service he will advise about a builder. Usually three builders are asked to tender. Following acceptance of the price, it is prudent to get the builder's signature on two copies of the full specification. The builder should be asked to initial each page, adding the price, signature and date and stamp of the firm on the final page. Both parties now have a signed legal contract and know precisely what work is expected for the price (the owner should mentally add 10% to cover unforeseen contingencies).

During the course of the job, extra work or alterations to the original drawings may be needed. Ask the architect to obtain a price. Only when this has been agreed in writing should work proceed.

HIRING A BUILDER YOURSELF

Compile a list of builders from personal recommendations, or ask the local council's building inspector to suggest a few names. Ask those on your list for references of work they have done in the last two years, and then check the work and if possible talk to the people who hired them.

Checking the solvency of small firms is difficult, but the longer they have been in business the better.

A visit to the yard or workshop can help you to assess a firm's efficiency. It is a good sign if materials and tools are tidily stored and there seems to be some organisation.

After these checks, reduce the list to about three. Give each a simple, written specification of the job, setting out exactly what is to be done and what materials should be used, and ask them to quote – in writing. Do not accept a verbal quote. Suspect a tender which is very much lower than the others.

When you accept a tender, get the builder to write saying that he is willing to do the work and at what price.

PAYING THE BUILDER

Builder and client should go through the job in detail on the site to establish what joinery, sanitary ware and other materials are to be used.

It is simplest to allow the builder to appoint sub-contractors unless you have someone you wish to do the work. Ask the builder for a timetable of when the work will start and finish, and when the various stages will be completed.

Ask him, too, about when he wants to be paid. When payment is made, 5% should be kept back for an agreed period against defects. Do not pay in advance – it is not normal practice.

• OTHER EXPERTS

Besides architects and builders, other professionals can help to transform a job from the ordinary to the distinctive.

SURVEYOR

A building surveyor will survey a house, or advise on its condition and any necessary repairs. He is an expert on the various types of grant that may be available, and can ensure that any building work you undertake will not transgress the regulations.

The Royal Institution of Chartered Surveyors provides a free pamphlet, 'The Rehabilitation of Residential Property', which outlines how a surveyor can assist the houseowner. They will also provide a list of chartered surveyors in your area.

INTERIOR DESIGNER

The detailed design and planning of house conversions and extensions is carried out by members of the Society of Industrial Artists and Designers.

An interior designer will redesign complete houses or advise on colour schemes, furnishings, curtains and floor coverings.

INTERICR DECORATOR

A decorator will advise on room design and colour schemes, and carry them out.

Decorators can often provide a complete service, including getting the curtains made up and the carpets laid. Some are experts in antique furniture. They are generally listed in the yellow pages of the local telephone directory.

LANDSCAPE ARCHITECT

The landscape architect will design schemes for a garden and advise on layout and planting. The Institute of Landscape Architects will supply a list of members for each area.

• GETTING PLANNING PERMISSION

Official permission is needed for most major home alterations and improvements, but there are exceptions.

For example, no permission is required for interior alterations, nor for an extension which does not increase the size of the original dwelling by more than 50 cu. m., or one-tenth, whichever is the greater.

But there are limitations. The size of the extension must not exceed 115 cu. m. It must not be higher than the original building, nor project beyond the house frontage. (The 'original' dwelling is taken to be the house as it stood in July 1948 or, if it was built later, as it was originally constructed.) A garage or stable added after the house was built is counted as an extens on to the property.

Other forms of permitted development include small porches, outbuildings and sheds, domestic oil-storage tanks, gates, fences and walls – all subject to restrictions on size, height and position. Also allowed are the construction of hard-standings for private vehicles and certain types of access to the highway.

Other alterations need the local planning authority's permission – usually the local district council (or borough council in Greater London).

Councils in conservation areas, such as those designated as National Parks, have special rules and restrictions of their own.

The authority provides application forms and instructions. It also requires proof that you own the land on which the building is to take place (or that you have notified the landowner of your application).

You must also provide three or four sets of detailed drawings. The drawings must include a location plan showing the surrounding area, a plan of each floor of the proposed building or extension, and elevations showing the sides of the new building or extension. Planning permission is valid for five years. After that it will lapse if work has not been started.

OUTLINE PERMISSION

If you are unsure whether a planning application will succeed, or if you need only an indication 'in principle', you can apply for outline planning permission. Detailed drawings are not normally required, but if the application is granted, full plans will have to be submitted before work can begin. Outline planning permission remains valid for three years, after which it lapses unless a fresh application is made.

LISTED BUILDINGS

If a building is classified as being of special architectural or historic interest, Listed Building consent must be obtained for any alteration that might affect its character. An application is made in exactly the same way as for a planning application.

BUILDING REGULATIONS

Almost all building work must comply with government building regulations. The regulations for England and Wales do not apply to Inner London, which has its own by-laws, nor to Scotland, which also has its own rules. It is an offence to begin work without completing the forms that can be obtained from the Building Control office and the local council. You must give full details of your proposed scheme and provide a set of drawings of the intended work.

You are entitled to a decision within five weeks of application, and approval is valid for three years.

After obtaining approval you will have to notify the building inspector as work proceeds so that he can check that it is up to standard.

If you think that the requirements of any regulations are unreasonable, you can apply to your local authority for them to be relaxed. If permission is not granted, you can appeal to the Department of the Environment within one month.

INNER LONDON

Building work in Inner London (the old L.C.C. area) is controlled by the London Building Acts and by Greater London Council by-laws. Formal approval to begin work is not needed in advance, but a fee – based on the value of the work carried out – has to be paid to the G.L.C. for the services of district surveyors, who supervise all building operations.

Drainage in London is the responsibility of individual borough councils, and they must give formal approval before any work can be carried out.

DESIGNING YOUR ROOMS

Altering an interior to make it more comfortable and attractive to use does not necessarily mean spending a lot of money; but it does require careful thought. The success of the scheme will depend upon the skilful handling of space, colour, texture, pattern, form and light. Note how these elements have been handled in the interiors you admire most – perhaps in other people's homes, in shop displays or in illustrations in magazines and books. These can be not only an invaluable source of ideas for colour schemes but also show in detail how a particular style has been achieved. Watch out for ideas that you can use or adapt to advantage – such as the room schemes illustrated here, and on the following pages. With observation and imagination you can save money while making an attractive home.

• STYLE AND CHARACTER

Try to give every room a character by working to a basic style. This can be based on an historical theme, such as the Regency or Victorian periods; or it can aim at creating a mood with matching colours. Alternatively, a distinctive style can be associated with a particular way of life, such as that suggested by the farmhouse.

Study examples of the particular style you want to achieve, making a careful note of the individual features, fabrics, colours, textures and ornaments that together make a recognisable style.

For instance, a beamed ceiling, a stone or quarry-tiled floor, unpainted woodwork, wrought iron fittings, a Welsh dresser, pewter and copperware are some of the things characteristic of the farmhouse interior.

HISTORICAL THEME   An assortment of old furnishings gives this room an Edwardian style. Net curtains add to the effect and diffuse the natural light.

MODERN SIMPLICITY An elegant interior that derives its interest from a skilful blend of pattern and materials.

• MIXED FURNISHINGS

It is not vital to have furnishings of the same style and period to give a room character. Even if, like most people, you acquire a mixture of furnishings, it is still possible to give a room a distinctive style.

The key to success in mixing furniture of different types is to unify those elements that act as a backcloth; that is, the carpet, walls, ceiling and fabrics. The room below illustrates how, despite mixed furnishings, an interior can be given a striking character.

The unifying elements are: a fitted carpet, neutral in tone and texture; walls and ceiling painted white (or neutral colours); fabric of similar colours on such items as seat covers and cushions; and the repetition of a colour through the use of paint.

OLD AND NEW Complementary colours link modern and period furnishings.

COUNTRY STYLE Plain wood and brick create an air of rustic charm.

• MODERN INTERIOR

To give a room a modern character, aim for simplicity, avoiding the use of too many different materials, colours and conflicting patterns. A strongly defined pattern, if used skilfully, will enhance a modern interior and emphasise its character. This can be achieved by deciding on a basic geometric pattern and repeating it on the furnishing fabrics in the room.

Note how, in the room illustrated above, the pattern of the carpet – which leads the eye towards the natural light – is reflected in the blind and tablecloth. Note, too, how these outcrops of bold patterning are held together by painting the walls and ceiling a neutral colour.

Avoid fussy items of furniture. In this interior the Perspex and polished metal chairs and glass table have

clean, simple lines that go with the aluminium window and picture frame. The single antique – a harpsichord – contrasts with the rest of the furniture in the room without seeming out of character.

Plants provide a softening effect. The pale matt paint on the ceiling and walls eliminates reflections and helps to add to the brightness of the interior.

SCALE AND SHAPE

Dark colours, heavy furniture, ornately framed pictures and mirrors, and overhead lighting all help to make a room seem small.

To make a room seem more spacious use white paint or similar light colours on walls and ceilings; an unpatterned fitted carpet; curtains that cover the whole of a wall when drawn at night; low-level furniture and light-coloured upholstery; plain-framed and modestly sized pictures and mirrors; and low-level lighting. These elements are not all of equal importance in making a room appear large or small. As the illustrations show, a room with light-coloured carpeting and walls will still look spacious, even with dark furniture.

In a large room use strong colours, large pieces of furniture, big pictures, and – to break up the floor area – several patterned rugs or a small carpet that leaves a wide border of the floor showing.

The actual size of doors and windows cannot be altered but their apparent size can. For example, a panelled door, with a heavy moulding around it, will dominate a room more than a flush door that is painted the same colour as the walls and has a simple architrave around it.

A picture rail helps to make a high ceiling look lower, particularly if the ceiling and the area of wall above the rail are painted the same dark colour. Alternatively, removing a picture rail and painting walls and ceiling white, or a light colour, will help to make a room look larger.

Built-in furniture can often improve the proportions of a room, when fitted into awkward spaces, such as a fireplace recess or a bay window, that are difficult to use with conventional furniture. Used like this, it will help to make the floor area seem larger.

MAKING A ROOM SEEM SMALLER   Use dark, tall furniture and patterned carpet.

MAKING A ROOM SEEM LARGER   Use low furnishings and a plain carpet.

LIGHT

When you choose a colour scheme for a room, remember that colours do not look the same in artificial light as they do by day. Under most artificial lighting, reds and yellows appear brighter and blues darker.

A room with a limited amount of colour but a predominance of white, or light tones, can be cool and restful by day and – if lit with subtlety – appear warm and cosy by night. Both natural and artificial light play a significant part in making a room look spacious or smaller, as well as giving emphasis to the style or the mood set by its furnishings.

White and light colours reflect more light than black or dark colours. Therefore the lighter the colours used in a room, the larger it will appear – and vice-versa.

LIVING-ROOM BY DAY Diffused natural lighting highlights form and texture.

LIVING-ROOM BY NIGHT Subtle lighting gives the room a different character.

PRACTICAL APPLICATIONS OF COLOUR

The problems posed when decorating a room that has difficult features can often be solved by the use of colour. It can be used either to disguise or to emphasise such features as an awkward-shaped projection, a low and sloping ceiling, an angled wall or pipework snaking around the walls.

First decide on your basic approach: do you want to camouflage a feature, or to make it more prominent? Both can be extremely effective ways of assimilating awkward features into the general scheme of a room.

DISGUISING PIPES

Pipes can be made to look less prominent if they, and the wall behind them, are painted the same colour – preferably a dark one. With white or a light colour, shadows will show up, giving unwanted emphasis to the pipes.

Alternatively, paint the wall a dark colour to provide a backcloth – and pick out all or some of the pipes in one or more bright lively colours to make a feature of them.

For a more subtle contrast, paint the pipes in a lighter tone of the colour used for the wall. Treated this way, even the untidiest sprawl of pipework can be made less of an eyesore.

AWKWARD SHAPES

Since dark colours tend to make a room look smaller and light colours have the reverse effect, they can be used to advantage in awkwardly shaped rooms. For example, a large high-ceilinged bed-sitter can be made to seem more intimate if it is painted with dark colours, while a small room, painted with light colours, will seem more spacious and be less claustrophobic to live in.

The sloping portion of a ceiling in an attic room can either be painted the same light colour as the walls, in order to disguise its shape and make the room seem larger, or be painted with strong colours to emphasise its form.

ADJACENT WALLS

Painting adjacent walls different colours may also help to change the apparent proportions of a room and create a lively interior. However, if the corner between them is an irregular one – as commonly happens in old houses – use the same colour for both walls or the irregularity will be difficult to disguise effectively.

CENTRAL ARCHES

When two rooms have been turned into one, there is often a square arch left in the centre – either plastered or lined with woodwork. If the shape is an unpleasing one, paint all walls and woodwork the same colour. If the arch is an interesting shape, use a contrasting colour to emphasise it.

The breast of a fireplace and the recesses on either side of it can be similarly treated, to emphasise or to disguise their form.

BAD SURFACES

Avoid using gloss paint on badly plastered walls. Its reflective quality tends to highlight surface irregularities. Use a matt or egg-shell finish.

Paint a recessed plinth or toeboard beneath built-in cupboards matt black or a dark colour. Light colours soon become grubby.

In areas where the atmosphere can be grimy, remember that dark colours will not show the dirt so much and will stay fresh-looking for longer.

As an aid to safety, highlight the handrails and the edge of steps leading down to a basement room or outside area, with a 75 mm. (3 in.) band of white paint.

LIGHT WALLS White or light neutral paint on walls draws emphasis away from the irregularity of the room.

COLOURED WALLS Contrasting colours have the effect of emphasising the different wall shapes.

USING NATURAL COLOUR

In working out a colour scheme for a room that is to be redecorated, exploit where possible the colours of any existing or proposed natural materials, such as wood, cork, brick or quarry tiles, rush matting and canvas, that can be left unpainted.

If you do this, only small amounts of applied colour need to be used, to create an attractive interior. In the illustration below, the use of a bold, heat-resistant, bright red paint has emphasised and made a feature of the water heater and associated pipework.

The red lampshade and matching place-setting mats add to the interest and lively quality of the kitchen. A dark colour helps to make the ceiling seem lower, which in turn gives the kitchen a look of cosiness.

SUNLESS BEDROOM   Warm colours make this north-facing basement room look snug, compensating for a lack of sun.

LIGHT AND COLOUR

Rich dark colours, such as reds and browns, suggest warmth and cosiness, and can make a room look pleasant, even on the greyest of days, compensating for a lack of sunlight. Equally warm, but brighter colours, such as oranges and yellows – used instead of white or pale colours – can create a stimulating interior.

South-facing rooms generally get the most sunshine. In these rooms, provided you have generous windows, you can usually afford to use cooler colours, such as blue and green, which reflect little light. But avoid too many glossy finishes or other highly reflective surfaces.

COLOUR MIX   Natural materials and paint combine to make a cosy kitchen.

SUNNY BEDROOM   Cool colours suit a bedroom that receives plenty of sun.

COLOUR CHANGES

Colour can transform a room in a variety of ways, making it restful, dramatic or intimate.

Schemes based on primary colours (blue, red and yellow), and secondary colours (green, orange and violet), are bright and vigorous; pastel shades and light neutral colours give an impression of delicacy and quiet. The key colour in a room is usually that of the floor covering. Other colours in the room – of walls, curtains, cushions, furniture and so on – should be chosen either to harmonise with the floor-covering colour or to contrast with it.

Avoid colours which you might find tiring after a time and use no more than three or four different colours in a room. Too many will conflict with one another.

USING A SINGLE COLOUR FOR A SPECIAL EFFECT

The use of a single dominant colour can give an interior a striking appearance. It can help to give character to a gloomy and awkward-shaped room, as well as giving a sense of order to a number of unrelated items, such as doors, cupboards, pin-boards, shelves and free-standing pieces of furniture. Remember that colour used over large areas will seem darker and more vivid than when used in small individual areas of paintwork.

Additional emphasis and character can be given to the interior by using the same colour fabrics and fittings, or by using white to create a contrast. The single basic colour will be set off, for example, by having a pale carpet and ceiling contrasting with white blinds, cushions and lampshades.

A fitted wall-storage unit, with plenty of open shelving and display space, will also benefit by being painted in the basic colour or white – giving additional interest and strength to the colour of the items displayed on the unit.

An all-white interior will make the most of a limited amount of daylight, creating a much higher level of reflection.

SUBDUED COLOURS *Warm, matching colours create a quiet and restful room.*

DRAMATIC CONTRAST *Bold colours give the room a more formal character.*

COLOUR AS A FEATURE *The bold use of red, as a background to white furnishings, adds interest to this dining-room.*

MIXED TEXTURES *Soft furnishings provide comfort, and contrast with the shiny surfaces of floor and window.*

HYGIENIC SURFACES *Materials such as mosaic are ideal for bathrooms.*

THE RÔLE OF MATERIALS
The materials you use for furniture and furnishings play just as important a part in evoking an atmosphere as other elements, such as colour, texture, light and pattern.

Natural materials, such as wood, stone, brick and wool, have a charm, colour and texture that automatically evoke a traditional atmosphere. Use them to produce the effect of a room in a farmhouse or country cottage.

Synthetic materials, such as glass, decorative metals, plastics and paint, have all clearly been processed and are therefore ideal when creating a modern and sophisticated interior. An interesting contrast can be made if a small item of one type of natural material – say a panel of hand-made bricks – is incorporated in an otherwise wholly modern interior.

CHARM AND COMFORT *Natural materials suggest a cottage atmosphere.*

TEXTURES SET THE MOOD
The texture of a surface plays a large part in creating atmosphere. Natural materials, such as wood and cork for instance, with their rough finish suggest warmth and have a traditional look. Glass and chrome, by contrast, are smooth and cool and so are suited to a modern décor.

Light and colour also affect texture. The same colour of paint or dye looks different when applied to surfaces of different textures; and light falling on a deeply textured surface can enhance or destroy its effect. A beam of light, falling at an angle, creates shadows, to accentuate texture; an indirect or diffused light will soften it.

EFFICIENCY *Man-made materials create an efficient and easy-to-clean kitchen.*

DELICATE PATTERNS Small-scale patterns add interest to a small room.

BOLD PATTERNS A striking effect gained by giving the contents of a bathroom cabinet a backcloth of bold tiles.

USING PATTERN EFFECTIVELY

There are two kinds of pattern used in decoration – natural and applied.

Natural patterns are those formed by the texture of a material, such as the grain in wood, marble, stone or brick. Applied patterns are those that are engraved or painted on surfaces, or woven into the texture of materials. These applied patterns can be free-flowing or geometric. Free-flowing patterns are generally based on flowers or plant-life and are softer in their decorative effect than geometric or symmetrical designs.

Pattern can direct the eye towards an interesting feature. For instance, a striped rug can lead the way to an alcove, or a frieze can draw attention to an attractive cornice. Often a pleasing effect can be achieved by using the pattern on wall coverings, or furnishing accessories, to echo the shapes of mouldings on furniture.

If a carpet is richly patterned it is generally better to keep the walls plain. Alternatively, counter-balance patterned walls with a plain carpet. A bold pattern in a striking colour can be an effective way of brightening up a hall or passageway.

Pattern can also be used, like colour, to disguise awkward corners or large sloping ceilings. A bold pattern will help to conceal the irregularities in an old or poorly surfaced wall.

• DECORATING TO PLAN

Before decorating a room, consider whether you want to continue using it in the same way as it has always been used.

For instance, is the distance from kitchen to dining-room, or from the parents' bedroom to a child's room convenient? How easy is it for a mother in the kitchen to keep her eye on a child? Can a spare bedroom be converted into a study? Can a room have its use changed in some other way, or can it be adapted so that it will be suitable for more than one purpose?

Perhaps an extension is necessary? If this is the case the work must comply with the current Building Regulations, and it may also be necessary to apply for planning permission (see pp. 18-19).

Often however, a simpler alteration can be almost as effective. Repositioning or re-hanging a door to open the opposite way, for instance, can make it easier to use a room or place an item of furniture.

DRAWING A PLAN

To visualise the alteration or re-decoration of a small room is not too difficult. But planning a large room, containing several large items of furniture, can be tricky.

Draw a plan of the room on squared paper, to as large a scale as possible – the squares representing feet and inches or metres and centimetres, whichever is most convenient.

Show all the major projections, recesses, windows and doors, with arcs representing the space occupied by doors when they are in use.

POSITIONING FURNITURE

Draw on separate pieces of paper or thin card, accurately scaled and shaped templates representing the overall sizes of the principal pieces of furniture you are keeping in the new scheme. Cut these out and position them on the plan. Experiment to find alternative positions where space is used more effectively than it is at present.

First decide on those materials and areas of colour in a room that you are not going to change. For example, you may intend to keep an existing fitted carpet, a polished hardwood floor or a tiled fireplace surround. In this case, colours and textures in your new scheme should take into account those features you intend to keep.

CHECKING SAMPLES

The next stage is to consider and compare the new colours, textures and patterns alongside each other, assembling paint manufacturers'

COLOUR SCHEMES *Experiment with samples to find the best combination.*

PLANNING *Scale cut-outs of furniture help when trying different layouts.*

ARRANGING FURNITURE *Position furniture to match the layout on your plan.*

cards, swatches of furnishing fabrics, samples of wood veneers or laminated plastics and samples of carpet that you like.

When you have decided on the colour or colours that you would like to use, it is a good idea to buy the smallest possible quantity available and paint it on a piece of cardboard. Take the card around the room, holding it up in various places, checking the colour in daylight and in artificial light and against the pieces of furniture and the carpet.

The same applies to wallpapers and fabrics. The small sample from which you made your choice could look very different in a large piece, especially if it has a large pattern.

Ask your supplier for a large sample piece (some shops may require a deposit for this) and check it against the painted cardboard and against any other colours in the room, again seeing how it looks in both daylight and artificial light.

Consider the room from various angles and the relationship of adjoining walls, work tops and furnishings. Do not forget the ceiling. Take into consideration its height and the colour it will need to be to fit the new décor.

EXPLOITING LIGHT
Remember also to exploit windows as much as possible. If they admit plenty of light but overlook uninteresting views, use translucent blinds or put up easily removed shelving across the windows with trailing pot plants. If a room has a small window, use one or more mirrors strategically positioned to help reflect and increase the level of daylight in the room.

Artificial lighting should also be considered carefully. The effect of colours and textures seen in a room by day changes considerably at night when the room is curtained and lit by artificial light. Experiment with your samples beneath the kind of light that will be used in the room, for again, colours will appear different under an ordinary tungsten bulb and under fluorescent lighting.

THE FINAL EFFECT A spacious interior where subtle colours and lighting have been used to complement each other and give emphasis to form, texture and detail.

ROOM-BY-ROOM REMINDERS

Remember these points when planning your home:

HALL
Character: Welcoming and spacious.
Colours: Bright and light.
Floor: Easy to clean.
Storage: Top coats, shoes, umbrellas, possibly pram and telephone.
Telephone will need stand or table for directories and notebook.

LIVING-ROOM
Character: Comfortable for relaxing, reading, or entertaining.
Floor: Warm and sound-absorbent.
Storage: Books, records, stereo, drinks and bric-a-brac.

DINING-ROOM
Character: Warm and stimulating.
Colours: Subtle.
Floor: Easy to clean.
Storage: Tableware, drinks.

KITCHEN
Character: Bright and cheerful.
Colours: Bright, light and lively.
Floor: Easy to clean and not tiring for the feet.
Storage: Kitchenware, food and cleaning equipment.

BATHROOM
Character: Warm and relaxing.
Floor: Warm, waterproof and easy to clean.
Storage: Medicine, toiletries, towels in use and cleaning materials.

BEDROOMS
Character: Personal and comfortable; for children, bright and stimulating.
Colours: Cool if sunny, warm if not.
Floor: Soft, sound-absorbent.
Storage: Clothing cupboards, drawers and possibly shelving.

COMPLETE GUIDE TO FLOORING

There are many factors to be considered when choosing flooring materials, and lack of planning can result in costly mistakes. As floors take a great deal of hard wear, they need coverings with good resistance to the constant movement of people, the weight of furniture, domestic accidents and the effects of dirt and grit brought into the home from outside. Good appearance and comfort are other major requirements. There is a bewilderingly wide range of flooring, including natural materials like cork, stone and ceramic, synthetic materials such as vinyl, and carpets made of wool or man-made fibres. The task of selecting a flooring which is suitable for its location and which will blend with existing furnishings is made easier if you know what you can expect in terms of wear, appearance retention and length of life. But it is not enough to choose the right material. Care must also be taken in laying it correctly and in cleaning it. Laying by a specialist is recommended for most types of flooring, but some materials can be laid successfully by an amateur.

• SUB-FLOORING CONSTRUCTION

When choosing a floor covering, check the type of sub-floor on which it will rest. The two main types are suspended timber and solid concrete.

SUSPENDED TIMBER FLOORS
Tongued-and-grooved or butted boards are supported by timber joists. They are found throughout in pre-war houses, with the possible exception of the kitchen, and from the first floor up in modern houses.

As floorboards move when they are walked on, the choice of floor covering is limited to those types which are not affected by movement. This excludes any form of ceramic floor – quarry tiles, clay tiles or bricks – which may crack or chip if there is any movement in the sub-floor.

A modern development in suspended floor construction is the use of large sheet materials, such as plywood or flooring-grade chipboard, in place of boarding. This provides a very flat floor suitable for thin, flexible flooring materials.

SOLID CONCRETE FLOORS
Concrete is laid directly on to hardcore and earth at ground level in nearly all modern flats and houses.

Precast concrete is used for the intermediate floors of multi-storey blocks of flats. Concrete floors have a cement screed to smooth out the roughness and provide a flat surface on which the flooring can be laid. Concrete provides a very stable floor, suitable for any form of flooring.

DEALING WITH DAMP
Floors of all types at ground level may be affected by damp, which attacks cork, organic materials in carpets and the adhesive of any material stuck to the floor. Modern houses have a damp-proof membrane incorporated in the construction. If there is no damp-proofing, seek specialist advice before new flooring is laid at ground level. In suspended timber floors, the cavity should be ventilated to dry out any damp. If it is not, dry rot may result. It is essential to keep the ventilators free from obstruction.

HEATED FLOORS
Some modern buildings have electric underfloor heating: the cables are laid on a concrete floor and are covered with screed. These floors should not be covered by material with a high insulating capacity such as foam-backed carpet or cork, which prevent the heat from circulating and may affect the thermostat. Other materials which should not be used are those which soften or deform at high temperatures. Thermoplastic and vinyl asbestos tiles are affected by a temperature of more than 27°C (81°F).

Ideal flooring materials for heated floors are those which are inherently stable and have a high thermal capacity – for example, quarry tiles, concrete tiles or bricks. If you want timber flooring, seek specialist advice, as only hardwoods of a low moisture content are suitable.

• CHOOSING FLOOR COVERINGS

Appearance is usually the first consideration when choosing flooring. It is mainly a matter of personal taste, but there are some guidelines which may help in making a choice.

As flooring is often a wide uninterrupted surface, having more visual impact than the furniture set upon it, choose colours to harmonise with the rest of the room.

Closely related to colour is light. A pale or highly polished floor reflects more light than a dark floor, so the amount of daylight and the lighting system in a room may affect your choice. But it is also necessary to consider the use the floor will have. Very light colours may not be suitable for family life unless the material can be easily cleaned.

The effect which flooring has depends also on design. Some people prefer uncomplicated patterns – the natural joints between wood, stone or quarry tiles – to the superimposed patterns on synthetic materials. But a patterned floor is more practical as marks are less noticeable.

Texture is another aspect of appearance and it is also related to the 'feel' of the flooring. Natural materials have their own texture – soft cork, the rippled surface of slate, smooth terrazzo – while synthetic materials may have a texture applied to them.

DURABILITY
Resistance to wear has to be considered in relation to the kind of use the floor has. For example, a living-room will need a more hardwearing

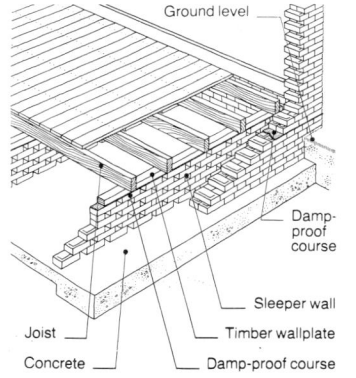

SUSPENDED FLOOR Boards are laid on joists, supported by brickwork and timber wall plates.

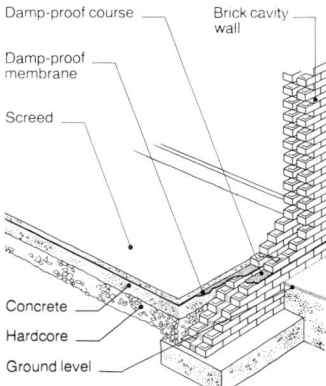

SOLID FLOOR Laid on earth and hard-core, a concrete screed gives a flat surface for flooring.

floor covering than a bedroom, and a kitchen will need a tougher floor than a bathroom.

Most floors come into contact with some of the following hazards and a kitchen floor may be subject to all of them: wear from shoes, particularly high heels, grit and movement of furniture; household chemicals; heat and flame; dropped articles; pressure from furniture; insects; damp.

Hard floors, such as quarry tiles, clay tiles and stone, last longer, but durability must also be related to the length of time a floor retains its good appearance. For example, marble has an indefinite life but is subject to staining. Life and appearance are also dependent on the right sub-floor, good laying and frequent cleaning.

COMFORT

Warmth, quietness and softness of tread are the factors to consider when assessing comfort. People who like to walk about the house in bare feet may regard warmth as the vital factor. To old and disabled people, a non-slippery surface is of primary importance and could be a matter of life or death, since over 50% of accidental deaths at home are caused by falls.

Although hard floors are usually associated with cold, it is the temperature close to the floor that is critical, not the hardness of the surface. A hard floor with underfloor heating at a temperature of 21°C (70°F) gives a sensation of warmth, whereas even a cork floor will appear cold if the air temperature at floor level is cool.

Noise can be softened by absorbent flooring materials such as carpet and cork. There is a greater need for these coverings if the floor is made of modern, lightweight timber joists and boarding with a thin plasterboard ceiling below. Some PVC floor coverings have a noise-absorbing backing.

CORK A feeling of warmth is given by cork tiles with a PVC finish.

CARPET A high-quality fitted carpet in 80% wool and 20% nylon provides warmth, good wear and luxury.

VINYL If the room takes a lot of hard wear, easily cleaned, cushioned vinyl may provide the best surface.

ONE FLOOR: FOUR POSSIBILITIES The drawing-room above has a hardwood strip floor which gives a warm, mellow tone to the room. On the left the same room is shown with three other types of flooring to give an idea of the effect different flooring materials can have on the overall appearance of a room.

• TYPES OF CERAMIC FLOORING

For a long-lasting, hardwearing floor that is easy to clean, ceramics offer an ideal solution provided warmth and quietness are not important factors in choice. Virtually all ceramic flooring needs a solid sub-floor. An exception is mosaic, which can be laid in a small area on a suspended floor, provided the floor is suitably prepared.

CLAY FLOOR TILES

Clay tiles are made from refined natural clays fired at high temperatures and glazed; some are specially made for external use. There is a variety of sizes, shapes, textures, colours and patterns.

Clay tiles require a solid-floor construction and can be laid either directly on to concrete by bedding in cement or they can be fixed to a screed with adhesive.

QUARRY TILES

Hardwearing tiles made from unrefined clays, hard burnt. Only those of first quality can be used outdoors. Colours include heather-brown, red and blue. The standard size of 150 mm. (6 in.) square × 15 mm. ($\frac{5}{8}$ in.) thick is readily available. Larger sizes (which have to be thicker and heavier), such as 200 mm. (8 in.) square, are also made. Random patterns can be formed by using combinations of whole sizes and half tiles. They can be laid directly on concrete by bedding in cement.

MOSAIC

There are three types of mosaic: clay, glass and marble. They are made in small squares and other shapes which are assembled into larger areas, supplied on peel-off sheets for ease of laying. A wide variety of colours, shapes and sizes is available.

Fully vitrified mosaic is made especially for outdoor use.

Ideally, mosaic tiles need a solid floor, but they can be laid on a suspended floor over a small area like a shower compartment if a special construction such as the one shown on p. 41 is used.

BRICK

Special brick paving stones (pavers) are available which, while being of standard brick dimensions, are only 40-55 mm. (1½-2¼ in.) thick, but any hard, well-fired brick can be used, either on edge or flat. Colours include red, brown, blue, purple and yellow, providing a wide choice suitable for inside or outside.

QUALITIES OF CERAMICS

Durability Hardwearing, resistant to chipping and cracking, scratching, indentation, heat and fire, acids, water, oils, fats, alkalis, insects and fungal attack. All types of ceramic flooring retain their appearance; quarry tiles and brick mellow with increasing age.

Comfort Ceramic floors are cold, hard and noisy, and their use has to be considered in relation to the type of heating and noise-absorbing furnishings. Some ceramic floors are slippery when wet, but non-slip finishes are also available.

Cost Ceramic flooring is expensive, but it has good heat-storage capacity, which should be taken into account if underfloor heating is used.

Maintenance Comparatively easy. Sweep and wash regularly. When very dirty, scour with a household cleaner. Quarry tiles may be lightly polished occasionally, but washing with soap and water is usually sufficient. Tiles and bricks rarely break, but if they do, only the damaged area needs to be replaced.

• TYPES OF CONCRETE FLOORING

Most types of concrete are used for outside areas such as garages and patios, but concrete tiles and terrazzo are suitable for indoor use. A solid sub-floor is required for all types of concrete flooring.

GRANOLITHIC CONCRETE

A plain concrete structural floor, used mainly in garages, boiler-rooms and external areas, on which surfacing of granite chippings (aggregate) and cement is cast on site. Final surface is hardwearing but uninspiring. Its appearance is improved if the surface is polished to expose the aggregate in the concrete.

CONCRETE FLAGS

A low-cost flooring, mainly used for terraces and garden paths. A variety of colours, sizes and shapes is available. Concrete paving stones are available with a finish which imitates the texture of natural stone. They should be laid on sand or a bed of weak-mix concrete, using a wooden batten and a spirit level to ensure a level surface.

CONCRETE TILES

Coloured cement and hardwearing aggregate surfaces applied to a concrete backing. They have good wearing properties and are available in sizes from 100 mm. (4 in.) square to 457 mm. (18 in.) square.

TERRAZZO

A material which can be cast on site to form panels up to 1 sq. m. (about 1 sq. yd) or pressed into tiles. The appearance is dependent upon the type of aggregate used; this may be made up of pebbles, marble chippings or other forms of stone chippings. Wide variety of colours and patterns. Terrazzo offers a very hardwearing surface, but some types can be dangerously slippery when wet, unless special non-slip aggregates are used in the construction.

QUALITIES OF CONCRETE

Durability Concrete is good for areas which take hard wear, as it is highly resistant to chipping and cracking, scratching, indentation, heat, insects and rot.

Comfort For indoor use, concrete flooring (tiles and terrazzo) is cold, hard and noisy, but it has good heat retention if used with underfloor heating.

Cost Structural concrete flooring and concrete and granolithic paving stones are relatively cheap, while concrete tiles and terrazzo are in the medium-to-high cost bracket.

Maintenance All types of concrete flooring are easy to clean. Just sweep and wash, or scrub when very dirty. Do not attempt to polish a concrete floor as it can become dangerously slippery.

• TYPES OF CORK FLOORING

A warm, quiet flooring, cork is available as tiles. They can be laid on any sub-floor, but floorboards must

Clay tiles

Quarry tiles

Mosaic

Brick

be covered with hardboard or chipboard. Do not use cork on a heated floor. Tiles with a vinyl backing are available for use on concrete floors.

UNTREATED CORK TILES

Cork tiles are formed by compressing the natural granules of cork and baking them to form tiles bonded by the natural resins. They are made mainly in sizes of 305 mm. (12 in.) square × 3 mm. (⅛ in.) thick, but larger sizes are available up to 457 mm. (18 in.) long. Thicker tiles up to 4.8 mm. (³⁄₁₆ in.) thick provide greater stability and comfort. Tiles may be waxed or sealed with polyurethane or a special cork seal after laying. Ready-waxed tiles are available.

CORK TILES WITH PVC SURFACE

A thin PVC skin is bonded to the cork surface to increase its durability. This also seals in any moisture and makes it even more necessary to ensure that the sub-floor is completely dry before laying the cork.

QUALITIES OF CORK

Durability Good wear, but has low resistance to indentation. Avoid furniture with highly pointed legs. Untreated cork should not be used in rooms where the floor is likely to get wet, but the PVC-faced cork gives protection against splashing. Direct sunlight on cork will bleach out the natural colouring.

Comfort Cork is warm, quiet and resilient, and therefore makes a good flooring for upper corridors, children's rooms and bedrooms. PVC-faced cork is slippery when wet, and can be dangerous for flooring bathrooms and kitchens, especially for elderly and infirm people.

Cost Low to medium cost. PVC-faced cork is the more expensive, but it requires less maintenance than waxed or untreated cork.

Maintenance Clean with a damp mop and polish waxed or untreated tiles occasionally. Sealed tiles and PVC-faced tiles should not be polished.

• TYPES OF STONE FLOORING

For a natural appearance and an almost indefinite life, stone floors are a good choice. All types of stone are very heavy and must be laid on a solid sub-floor.

MARBLE

The variety of marble from the Continent provides a wide range of colours including white, green, grey, pink, brown and black. Marble makes a beautiful surround to recessed carpet and can run through from hall to living-room. It is ideal for bathrooms, where floor construction permits, and for any room which has underfloor heating to counteract coldness.

Marble is available in tiles ranging in size from 305 mm. (12 in.) up to 450 mm. (18 in.) square, but special slabs up to 1.5 m. × 900 mm. (5 × 3 ft) can be obtained.

QUARTZITE

A crystalline rock with a matt finish; the quartz grains give it a slight sparkle. Colours range from silver-grey to olive, yellow and gold. Very hardwearing; non-slip finish suitable for inside or outside.

Italian quartzite tile sizes are 254 mm. (10 in.) square and 304 × 203 mm. (12 × 8 in.), but the quartzite mined in northern Norway can be obtained in sizes up to 600 mm. (2 ft) square, and up to 16 mm. (⅝ in.) thick. The thickness of the quartzite depends on the rock formation.

SLATE

A hard impervious stone obtainable with a polished, sawn or riven surface. Riven slate is split, and the natural undulations give it a rippled surface which is less slippery when wet than a smooth surface. Colours include the blue-grey Welsh and green Lakeland. Interior slate slabs are in standard sizes of 457 × 229 mm. (18 × 9 in.), but larger slabs are available up to 2 m. × 900 mm. (6 ft 6 in. × 3 ft). Slate makes an excellent kitchen floor and is particularly suitable where the same type of flooring is needed to extend from the house to form a patio or terrace.

SANDSTONE, LIMESTONE AND GRANITE

These three stones all make good flooring materials. A popular sandstone is York stone. Colours include various shades of grey, beige and brown. Sizes vary according to quarry and types – up to 2 × 1 m. (6 ft 6 in. × 3 ft 3 in.) although paving stones are usually in smaller random sizes.

QUALITIES OF STONE

Durability Stone floors are resistant to wear, water and indentation and to most household chemicals. But marble stains easily from ferrous metals and oils, and limestone and sandstone are stained by oils and fats and are affected by weak acids and alkalis. Slate and quartzite floors have good resistance to stains; when very dirty from spilt oils or fats, they can be easily scoured clean.

Comfort Cold, hard and noisy, but admirably suited to underfloor heating. Used this way they are warm in winter and cool in summer. Textured surfaces are normally non-slip, but marble with a highly polished surface tends to be slippery, particularly when wet.

Cost Granite is the most costly form of flooring, with other stone floors varying in price from marble down to local stone. Stone flooring is not expensive if a life of 100 years is required, but it is expensive in circumstances where only a short life is needed.

Maintenance Looking after stone floors in the home is comparatively easy. They can be swept, washed and mopped. For highly resistant stains a scouring powder may be needed. Soap should not be used on marble as it tends to make the floor slippery; detergent is preferable. If a marble floor should become badly stained it can be machine ground by specialists to remove the surface and restore the original colour and texture of the natural stone.

Cork

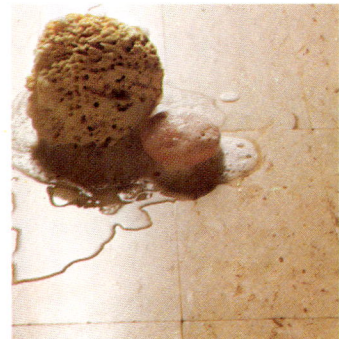
Marble

Quartzite

Slate

Sandstone

THE VERSATILITY OF PLASTIC Cushioned PVC sheeting can be made to look like tiles – but the plastic flooring is quieter, softer and warmer.

• TYPES OF PLASTIC FLOORING

A wide range of colours, designs, textures and prices makes plastic flooring very versatile. Any sub-floor is suitable, except for thermoplastic and vinylised thermoplastic tiles, which need a solid construction. But floorboards should first be covered with hardboard or plywood.

THERMOPLASTIC AND VINYLISED THERMOPLASTIC TILES

The original thermoplastic tiles have, except for dark colours, been replaced by the vinylised version. Vinylised tiles are more pliable, less likely to crack and are available in more colours. Sizes are 250 mm. (10 in.) and 300 mm. (12 in.) square in thicknesses of 2.5 mm. ($\frac{1}{10}$ in.) and 3 mm. ($\frac{1}{8}$ in.). As these tiles are fairly rigid they should be laid on a screeded concrete sub-floor.

VINYL ASBESTOS TILES

A development from thermoplastic tiles. The binder is mainly PVC and the tiles are more flexible and durable. Available with textured or embossed finishes which imitate natural materials. Sizes are 225 mm. (9 in.) and 300 mm. (12 in.) square, and they are in thicknesses of 1.5, 2, 2.5 and 3 mm. ($\frac{1}{16}$ - $\frac{1}{8}$ in.).

FLEXIBLE PVC SHEET AND TILES

PVC flooring is available in tiles or sheet, either plain surfaced or with an embossed or textured finish. Expensive special-quality tiles give the appearance of natural stone such as travertine or brick, ceramic tiles or timber. These tiles have an authentic look, but they do not feel like the genuine product underfoot. A high-grade material is also available, consisting of coloured PVC chips set in a matrix of clear PVC.

The material is available in tiles or sheet, and sheets may be welded by the installer to avoid open joints. Sheets come in widths of 1.2 m. (4 ft), 1.5 m. (5 ft) and 2 m. (6 ft 6 in.). Tiles are squares of 225 mm. (9 in.), 250 mm. (10 in.) and 300 mm. (12 in.) and thicknesses of 2, 2.5 and 3 mm. ($\frac{1}{16}$ - $\frac{1}{8}$ in.). Larger tiles in 500 mm. ($19\frac{1}{2}$ in.) squares are also available in special ranges.

REVERSE-PRINTED PVC

A process in which a pattern is printed on the reverse side of a clear PVC sheet which is in turn bonded to a PVC backing, or it may be printed directly on to the backing. This process allows any type of pattern – imitating cork, timber, ceramic floors or others – but its durability is only that of the clear PVC layer which protects the pattern.

PVC WITH VARIOUS BACKINGS

In order to increase the comfort of PVC sheet floors, which are often relatively thin (1.5 mm./$\frac{1}{16}$ in.) and unresilient, some softer sheet materials have been bonded to the PVC.

QUALITIES OF PLASTICS

Durability The hardest wear is obtained from those floors which contain a high PVC content in the surface; for example, flexible PVC tiles and sheet and PVC with various backings. These are all resistant to wear, water, indentation and to most household chemicals. Minor burns can be removed by rubbing the surface carefully with wire wool.

Thermoplastic and vinyl asbestos tiles last well, but thermoplastic tiles are softened by grease and are not ideal for kitchens. Reverse-printed PVC is not as durable as some other types and there is no easy method of removing burn marks.

Comfort PVC floors with various forms of backing are thicker and therefore more comfortable to walk on. They are also warmer and quieter than the thin reverse-printed PVC and thermoplastic tiles.

Cost Plastic floors range from the cheapest reverse-printed PVC to the expensive ranges of special PVC tiles with embossed finishes. These can cost as much as the tiles or bricks they imitate. The more expensive the floor, the longer its appearance will be maintained.

Maintenance Sweep, mop and polish. Persistent stains can be removed with water and scouring powder.

Vinyl asbestos tiles

Thermoplastic tiles

Flexible PVC

Reverse-printed PVC

• TYPES OF TIMBER FLOORING

Any sub-floor is suitable for timber, except in the case of hardwood block which requires a solid construction. In all cases the sub-floor must be level and damp-proof.

PLYWOOD

Plywood tiles are made to look like wood parquet. Various patterns in herringbone, basket weave or strip are available. Plywood parquet can give a smart appearance initially, but is unsatisfactory in areas of heavy wear. It can be pinned to any timber flooring, but requires plywood under-lay when used over floorboards. It is supplied in various squares from 228 mm. (9 in.) to 914 mm. (3 ft).

WOOD MOSAIC

Hardwood 'fingers' arranged in a basket-weave pattern are stuck to a sheet of backing material to form panels 457 mm. (18 in.) square and 10 mm. ($\frac{3}{8}$ in.) thick. Very good wearing characteristics and a medium-price range have greatly increased the use of wood mosaic.

HARDWOOD STRIP AND BLOCK

A high-quality floor. Woods used include oak, maple, afrormosia, teak and beech. A well-maintained hardwood floor improves with age. Hardwood blocks vary in thickness from 19 mm. ($\frac{3}{4}$ in.) to 31 mm. (1$\frac{1}{4}$ in.), in sizes up to 305×75 mm. (12×3 in.). Strip is used up to 100 mm. (4 in.) wide, and is tongued and grooved to allow concealed nailing. Hardwood block must be laid on a dry solid sub-floor. Blocks are laid with cold bituminous adhesives.

WOOD PARQUET

A high-quality hardwood floor in which special decorative hardwoods are cut into blocks and formed into panels, permitting elaborate geometric designs. The panels vary from 25-32 mm. (1-1$\frac{1}{4}$ in.) thick, in squares from 305 mm. (12 in.) to 610 mm. (2 ft). Parquet may be laid over any rigid wooden sub-floor.

It is rarely used because of its cost, and is not to be confused with plywood parquet.

QUALITIES OF WOOD

Durability The durability of timber floors depends on good maintenance and on the quality of the timber. Hardwoods are resistant to abrasion and indentation, but they should not be used in wet areas, whether the damp is from above or below. Plywood floors are only as good as the thickness of the decorative surface, and will not withstand heavy wear. Cigarette marks can be removed fairly easily from hardwood floors. Softwood timber boarding looks good when it has just been sanded and sealed, but does not wear well under heavy use. It is best used as a surround for other flooring, such as carpet.

Comfort Timber floors are warm to the touch and reasonably resilient. They tend to be noisy, but are not slippery unless too much polish is used. Hardwood block and strip floors can be used with underfloor heating, provided that the timber used has a low moisture content. If in doubt about the wood, specialist advice should be sought.

Cost Plywood parquet is the cheapest of timber floors. Wood mosaic and hardwood block and strip come in the medium-price range, and wood parquet is in the high-cost bracket. A good-quality timber floor will repay itself in excellent wear and appearance over the years.

Maintenance There are three methods of maintaining a timber floor: a spirit-based wax polish (this is hard work but the appearance will improve with age), an oil-resin seal which can be retouched annually; and a hard polyurethane seal which needs to be sanded off and replaced every three or four years. (Instructions for sanding and sealing floors are on p. 44.) Sealed floors are improved by polish and, as timber is susceptible to water, wax emulsion polish (which is water based) can only be used when the floor has been sealed. The floor needs a daily sweeping to remove grit and dirt and an occasional light coat of polish.

TIMBER FLOOR Tongued-and-grooved boarding complements the light natural colours of the furnishings, and a shaggy rug gives a softening effect.

Plywood

Wood mosaic

Hardwood strip

Parquet

• WHAT YOU NEED TO KNOW ABOUT CARPETS

Modern manufacturing processes and the development of man-made fibres have revolutionised the carpet industry, making carpets available in a wide range of materials and textures. The main ways of making carpets are by weaving – the oldest method – and tufting and bonding, which are both modern techniques. Developments in the tufting process have made it possible to produce high-quality tufted carpets which are comparable to the traditional woven carpets. Well-made bonded carpets give good value for money.

The quality of a carpet depends not only on the method of manufacture but also on how well the carpet is made, the fibre used, the quality of that fibre and the density of the pile.

WOVEN CARPETS

Some of the highest-quality carpets are made by the woven method. The pile and backing are woven together so that the pile is locked into position; the backing is woven from jute or polypropylene yarn, and the pile is made with wool, acrylic, nylon, rayon, or blends of two or more of these fibres. The advantage of woven carpets lies in the slight elasticity of the woven back. When correctly laid, the backing fibres hold the pile tufts erect so that they spring back after they have been walked on.

There are two types of woven carpet: Axminster and Wilton. These are not brand names but the names of the looms on which carpets are woven. The main difference is that the Axminster loom allows any number of colours as the threads are cut off and reintroduced according to the pattern. In patterned Wilton carpets the threads are continuous, and each colour is taken into the backing when it is

not part of the design, which makes the carpet thicker. This method often limits the number of colours to five.

The pile of an Axminster carpet is usually cut. Wilton carpets are produced with a variety of piles.

TUFTED CARPETS

The tufts are needled into a backing – usually made of polypropylene in sheet form, but sometimes made of hessian. The tufts are locked into place with a skim of latex along the back. Then, either a foam layer or a secondary back of woven jute sheet or polypropylene is added. If a foam backing is used, an underlay is not needed. The pile is looped or cut, or can be a mixture of both. Tufted carpets are available plain or patterned and can be made with the same fibres as woven carpets. To the untrained eye, a tufted carpet may be indistinguishable from a woven carpet.

BONDED CARPETS

These carpets are neither woven nor tufted. Bonding can produce any appearance from completely flat to a corded or velvet pile. It is also used for flocked carpets which have thousands of small fibres electrostatically bonded to an adhesive-coated backing.

Another method of bonding is needle-punch, or needleloom. A mixture of fibres is punched by needles and entangled through a backing fabric. This fabric is impregnated with an acrylic resin to hold the fibres securely in the backing. The one feature bonded carpets have in common is that the materials used are glued, heat fused or in some way bonded together. They are usually manufactured from man-made fibres. A well-made bonded carpet is hard-wearing and makes an economic floor covering with a good pile.

HOW CARPET FIBRES STAND UP TO WEAR

FIBRE	WEAR For a fibre to give the wear expected of it, the weight and quality must be suitable for the use to which it is put. With a branded fibre this can be assumed to be so.	SOILING Dirt-masking patterns and colours are the best choice with fibres which soil easily.	CLEANING Good results from cleaning are possible only if suitable cleaners are used and instructions are followed closely (see p. 318). For best results, professional cleaning is needed.
Acrylic	Can be expected to wear well in all domestic and many contract locations. The 'A' symbol is a guarantee of quality.	Soils and flattens. A densely woven pile will flatten least.	Cleans easily, releases dirt. But it needs good care to retain its appearance.
Nylon	The hardest-wearing fibre yet created. 100% nylon, or any blend containing more than 15% nylon, gives excellent wear.	Can soil badly and lose its appearance, but manufacturers have produced modifications to mask soiling. Low-density pile or low-loop pile keeps its appearance better than other types of pile.	Cleans easily, but cannot always be returned to its original appearance.
Polyester	Not suitable for heavy wear unless blended with a tougher fibre such as nylon.	Soils fairly quickly.	Cleaning may not return it to its original appearance, especially if it gets very dirty.
Polypropylene	Moderately hard wearing; cord gives the hardest wear.	Soils fairly quickly, but does not absorb water so is resistant to water-borne stains.	Cleans very easily, but may not maintain its original appearance.
Viscose and modified viscose	It is an inexpensive fibre and therefore often used fairly densely, in which case it can wear well.	Can soil badly and flatten.	Releases dirt fairly well.
Wool	Can be very hard wearing, used in the correct qualities. It is often blended with nylon to give extra durability. Woolmark label means all wool, and the woolblend-mark means 80% wool, 20% nylon.	Best resistance to soiling of any fibre. Good appearance, which is well retained.	Cleans easily and well. Too much home cleaning is not good for wool owing to the build-up of detergent residue.

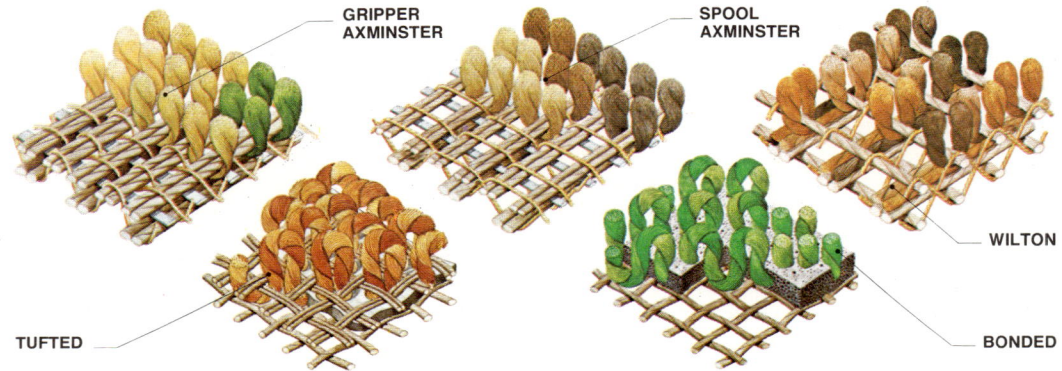

GRIPPER AXMINSTER
SPOOL AXMINSTER
WILTON
TUFTED
BONDED

MANUFACTURING METHODS Axminster and Wilton are woven carpets: tufting and bonding are more recent techniques.

HARD-TWIST PILE
This is a cut pile with a heavy twist built into the yarn, giving a pebbly look. It is used mainly in plain carpets, but it can be combined with other types of pile to give a textured effect. Hard-twist pile does not show shading and tracking as a velvet pile does. Shading is twisting of the pile caused by feet or the moving of furniture, and shows as dark patches. Tracking is the smoothing down of the carpet in heavily used areas.

LOOPED PILE
The pile is uncut and is formed by a continuous series of loops. It can give various textures from a thick and knobbly pile to the closely curled low-loop pile, which is like an irregular cord carpet. Looped pile is used in Wilton and tufted carpets.

SHAG PILE
This is sometimes called Ryatype after the original Rya rug whose surface it imitates. It can be produced on a tufting machine or a Wilton or Axminster loom. The pile is long and shaggy and has a luxurious look. It can, however, look tangled and matted if it has heavy wear.

CUT PILE
Tufted and woven carpets are produced in cut pile, but in Axminster it is the only one used.

WOVEN-CORD PILE
This is produced on a Wilton loom. The pile is left uncut, giving a tight corded effect. It used to be made of haircord, but this is not widely available now. Most cord carpets are made of sisal or man-made fibres. If the fibre is of good quality, cord offers better resistance to wear than velvet pile.

VELVET PILE
Sometimes called velours, this is a close-cut pile which has a smooth, velvety appearance. It is used mainly for plain and two-tone carpets.

SCULPTURED PILE
A combination of cut and looped pile gives a carved or sculptured effect. Different lengths of cut pile, and straight and twisted pile, can also be combined. These combinations are used mainly in Wilton and tufted carpets.

TYPES OF PILE Carpets can be produced with several different kinds of pile. Variations in texture can be used as effectively as colour. The combination of two types of pile, to give a sculptured effect, adds interest to a plain carpet. Long shag pile gives a feeling of luxury, and plain velvet pile makes a good background for decorative rugs.

COCONUT AND COIR
Doormats and hall runners are available in coconut matting, and stair widths can be bought in coir (coconut fibre), which is smoother than coconut matting. It is usually produced in natural colours and can be obtained with a vinyl backing.

EASTERN CARPETS
Hand-woven Oriental carpets and rugs are available in a variety of sizes, patterns and colours from classic designs to simple peasant styles. There is a wide range of sizes; some rugs can be used as bedspreads and others look decorative on the wall. Afghan, Chinese, Indian, Persian and Turkish rugs and carpets are obtainable in this country from large stores or specialist carpet shops.

FELT
Thick carpet felt makes a cheap, warm and colourful floor covering, but it is suitable only for areas where there is light wear as it gets trodden down in use and stains easily.

RUGS
Apart from the Oriental rugs mentioned above, there is a wide range of rugs in all kinds of fibres and with different types of pile. Traditional designs from the East and other parts of the world are also used in modern rugs. Rugs and runners can be used in areas of heavy use to save wear on the carpet. They also look good on stone, cork and wooden floors. For bathrooms, there are cotton rugs which can be machine washed.

RUSH MATTING
Natural rush matting is an inexpensive flooring which can be laid loose on concrete or stone. It is particularly suitable as a covering for a stone floor which is damp, as rush needs to be dampened occasionally to keep it flexible. Dust collects beneath the matting, so it is necessary to lift it to sweep the floor. Rush is woven into squares, circles and lengths, and squares can also be joined to cover larger areas.

SISAL
Sisal is a tough vegetable fibre which is cheap, hard-wearing and easy to scrub. It has a rough texture but can be attractive in a woven floor covering. Dark colours or a blend of two colours are the most practical.

CARPET TILES
Tiles of carpet are available in many qualities, sizes and fibres in a wide range of prices. The smaller ones can be laid by an amateur. Their main advantage is that they can be moved about to give even wear and replaced if they are damaged. Tiles can be laid loose or stuck down. Some have a self-adhesive backing which makes them easy to lay and enables them to be removed if necessary. But it is better to lay tiles loose if they are to be moved about frequently. Some tiles form a pattern; others give the effect of plain carpet.

• CHOOSING A CARPET

Carpets are made in strips, tiles, squares, and broadloom widths of up to 546 cm. (18 ft). If you want a fitted carpet, take into account the types of carpet available. For example, there may be less waste if you carpet an irregularly shaped room with body width rather than broadloom.

BODY OR STRIP

A narrow width of carpet is known as body width, and this is either 69 cm. (27 in.) or 91 cm. (36 in.). For stairs there are widths of 46 cm. (18 in.) and 57 cm. (22½ in.). It may be more economical to use body width for a room that is larger than the maximum broadloom width, or for a room which has a very irregular shape. The carpet can be seamed by the retailer or manufacturer before delivery, or by the carpet fitter when it is being laid.

BROADLOOM

Carpets which are wider than body width are known as broadloom. The most common widths are 275 cm. (9 ft), 366 cm. (12 ft), and 457 cm. (15 ft). Some carpets are also available in a width of 546 cm. (18 ft). Tufted carpets which are being made in metric widths are 3 m. and 4 m. (9 ft 10⅛ in. and 13 ft 1½ in.). Broadloom is a good choice for a fitted carpet if there is a width corresponding closely to one of the measurements of the room, and if the room is regularly shaped.

SQUARES

The advantage of carpet squares is that they can be turned round to even out wear. They also look good on a wooden floor and may be more economical than fitted carpet over a large area. They are usually 366 cm. (12 ft) square or 275 cm. × 366 cm. (9 ft × 12 ft). Squares are also made up from 366 cm. lengths of broadloom with the edges bound.

TILES

Carpet tiles range from 23 cm. (9 in.) square to 50 cm. (20 in.) square. A popular size is 12 in. square; these tiles are sold in packs of nine, so one pack is needed per square yard. As this is a convenient way of estimating and buying, most manufacturers have not changed this size to metric measure.

ESTIMATING QUANTITY NEEDED

Working out how much carpet is needed and whether it is more economical to buy body or broadloom is a job best left to the retailer. But it is useful to have an approximate figure as a guide to cost when shopping around.

First measure the length and width of the room, including bays and recesses. Check these measurements at each side of the room in case the walls are not parallel. A room which appears square may be a little wider at one end. Draw a plan of the room to scale and write in all the measurements. Then compare these measurements with the carpet widths given above and work out which width would be the most suitable. Allow about 100 mm. (4 in.) overlap to allow the carpet to be fitted to the line of the walls. Allow 225 mm. (9 in.) extra for any wall with a door, for fitting under the door.

MEASURING A STAIRCASE

There are two ways of measuring a staircase, and it is advisable to use both to check the results. One method is to measure the riser and multiply this by the number of risers, then measure a tread and multiply this by the number of treads. Then add 450 mm. (18 in.) to the total to allow for moving the carpet occasionally to even out wear (this should be done twice in the first year, then once a year). Check this total by measuring from the top of the staircase to the bottom with a flexible measure, taking care to measure the full width and depth of each tread and riser; add 450 mm. If the carpet is to extend along a corridor, measure the corridor also. For a staircase with a bend, measure each tread and riser on the bend separately at the widest point to be covered by the carpet. Add the total to the amount required for the straight parts of the staircase.

• THE RIGHT CARPET FOR THE PURPOSE

British carpet manufacturers have created a numbered classification scheme which divides their products into five categories, according to the use for which they are recommended. The five categories are:

1. Light domestic use – for bedrooms and other rooms with light use.
2. Medium domestic use/light contract use – for medium use in the home and hotel bedrooms exposed to light use.
3. General domestic use/medium contract use – for general use in the home and hotel bedrooms or public rooms with medium use.
4. Heavy domestic use/general contract use – for living rooms, halls, stairs and other parts of the home where there is heavy use and for public rooms in hotels, restaurants and office buildings.
5. Heavy contract use – for public areas with heavy use such as shops.

A sixth grade is classified as L – for luxury. These carpets are of better quality than category 3, but not necessarily suitable for general use.

Clumsiness, the size and ages of the family, hobbies and pets are

CARPETING A ROOM If a fitted carpet is chosen, it is a good idea to use rugs in areas where there is heavy wear, such as in front of a sofa where scuff marks are likely to appear.

factors which may affect choice of carpet. These things must be considered, as well as the function of each room.

Living-room As most family life takes place in the living-room, a good-quality, hard-wearing carpet is needed if it is to look good and withstand heavy wear for many years. An Axminster made of 80% wool, 20% nylon, in dirt-masking colours and design, would be the best choice. A plain Wilton or tufted carpet would be suitable in a household without children and pets.

Dining-room For a dining-room, an acrylic-pile carpet is practical as stains caused by dropped food can be easily removed. If a liquid is likely to be spilled, choose either a polypropylene carpet, which is easily wiped clean, or an inexpensive carpet with a short life.

Kitchen Carpet is not the most suitable covering for a kitchen floor. For those people who want carpet in the kitchen, a needlepunch or low-loop nylon carpet is recommended as these are the easiest to wipe clean.

Stairs A staircase needs a carpet which is hard-wearing with a surface which is safe, and a good-quality pile carpet fulfils both these requirements. Cord, needlefelt and sisal provide hard wear at low cost, but they could be hazardous for very old people or young children. These dangers arise because these carpets do not grip the feet. An exception is Wilton cord, which is more resilient.

Bedrooms Less-expensive carpets of the light domestic grade can be used in bedrooms, where they get light wear. A room used as a study-bedroom or bed-sitter will need a high-quality carpet, similar to that of the living-room, or a cheap carpet which can be replaced when the room changes its use.

Bathroom The main hazard for a bathroom carpet is water. If the floor is likely to become wet, a polypropylene carpet with a polypropylene back is recommended. In this case it may be unwise to use underlay or have a foam backing, as water may seep down the skirting into the underlay. A low-priced nylon or acrylic carpet would be suitable if the floor does not get too wet.

• BUYING A CARPET

Having decided on the type of carpet and the colour, and whether it should be plain or patterned, the next step is to find out what is available and to compare quality and prices. It is helpful to see carpet on the roll, as it can appear quite different from the small area shown in a sample book, particularly in the case of a patterned carpet. If you have any doubts about the suitability of colour or design, ask for a small sample to take home so that you can look at it in relation to the room to be carpeted. When examining samples, bend them back to see how much of the backing shows through; the less you can see, the denser the pile. Pull at the tufts to see if they are firmly anchored.

Cost Carpet prices vary greatly and there could be a difference of £10 a square metre between top-quality all-wool Wilton and a bonded carpet made of man-made fibre. If you want a hard-wearing carpet at low cost, a printed nylon tufted or a bonded man-made-fibre carpet would probably serve your purpose. On the whole, tufted carpets are medium-priced and woven carpets are in the high-price bracket. When comparing prices you should also take into account the quality and density of the fibre used in manufacture.

Some shops offer 'free' laying, but the cost of this may well be built into the price, so compare prices in different shops, taking into account laying costs where applicable. When you find a carpet you like, ask the retailer to measure the room and give a written estimate. Make sure the estimate includes cost of fitting and underlay.

Underlay All carpets which do not have a foam backing need a suitable underlay. An underlay makes the carpet feel softer and thicker, gives added insulation and prolongs life. There are several kinds of underlay on the market and, provided they are of good quality, there is not much to choose between them. A rubber or latex underlay may be easier to move around than a felt one if the carpet is to be shifted at a later date. Beneath the underlay – or in the case of a foam-backed carpet – place sheets of felt or tar paper. Heavy brown paper can be used, but it is better to have the material designed for the job. The paper stops draughts and dirt from coming up through the floorboards. Where a wooden floor has recently been treated with anti-woodworm fluid, lay sheets of aluminium foil in place of paper to prevent the fluid reaching the carpet.

Care Most new carpets shed fluff for the first few weeks. During this time they should be only lightly cleaned (see p. 318). Cut off any tufts which stand up from the surface – do not pull them out. After the first month, clean with a vacuum cleaner at least once a week, always making the last stroke with the pile so that it lies flat. To even out wear on the carpet, move furniture around occasionally so that indented pile can be brushed up. Avoid dragging heavy furniture over carpets as this damages the fibres. Crêpe and rubber-soled shoes and metal-tipped and stiletto heels also cause wear. For carpet shampooing, see p. 318.

COLLECTING ORIENTAL CARPETS AND RUGS

Hand-knotted Oriental carpets and rugs come from Asia Minor, Persia, the Caucasus, Central Asia, Afghanistan, India and China. The earliest-known hand-knotted carpet dates from the 5th century BC, and was probably made in Central Asia, where the craft began.

Carpets were made of hand-spun sheep's wool, and mixtures of wool, goat and camel hair. Silk rugs were made for royalty and the very wealthy.

Every knot of the pile was laboriously tied by hand across threads stretched on a primitive loom. Dyes were made from plants and minerals.

Each region or town had its particular colours and designs. Carpets from the Caucasus have geometric patterns and positive colours. The best of them, from Dagestan, have diagonal bands or mosaic-like patterns enclosed in boldly decorated borders, such as the rug shown below, left.

In Asia Minor, where religion forbade depicting living creatures, the designs were almost always stylised floral.

Turkoman carpets from Central Asia are frequently made with a blood-red ground and ivory patterns. Similar designs are found on the saddle bags which the nomadic tribes use to carry their possessions. Saddle bags from N. W. Persia are shown above and below right.

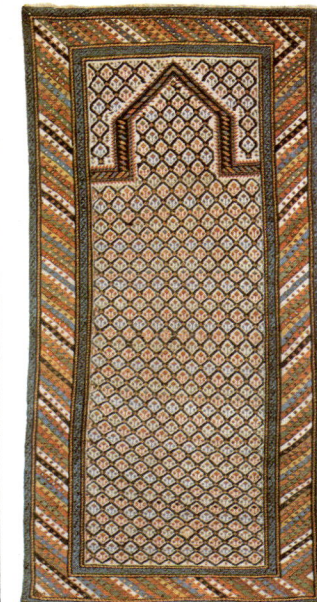

There is a great variety of patterns in Persian carpets. At Tabriz, carpets with central medallions and floral designs are worked. In Kashan, fine wool is used to work paradise motifs of birds and plants.

Chinese carpets show few regional variations. There are instead a range of traditional motifs – dragons representing God, the emperor, or nature; the lotus symbolising immortality; the pomegranate portraying fertility. Indian rug-knotting was learned possibly from the Persians and the designs were basically similar. Indian silk carpets, however, are superior to similar Persian work.

There are many 19th-century Turkish rugs still in good condition, as well as saddle bags from Persia and Turkestan, and scatter rugs from Asia Minor and the Caucasus.

• FLOORING, ROOM BY ROOM

Some parts of the house may need long-lasting flooring, and other rooms may have to be adapted to the changing needs of the family. One room may have to function at different times as a child's bedroom, playroom, study/bedroom or a bedsitter for an elderly relative. If there are small children or old people in the family, non-slip floors are desirable to minimise the risk of falls.

If a house is envisaged as a permanent home, it may be worth investing in the more-expensive hard-wearing flooring. But if there is likely to be a move, it may be better to choose flooring with a relatively short life to keep the cost down.

When all the relevant factors are taken into consideration, some compromise is inevitable. The family house illustrated here shows some of the possibilities. All the rooms have a suspended sub-floor, with the exception of the kitchen and utility room which form an extension built on a solid floor.

PORCH

Granolithic concrete covers the porch area. A recess has been made for a door mat (see below), bringing it level with the floor to prevent people tripping or slipping. Brush mats are available in sizes ranging from 35.5×61 cm. (14×24 in.) to 76×147.5 cm. (30×58 in.) and in varying thicknesses. Hardboard can be placed underneath the mat to bring the mat level with the flooring, if necessary.

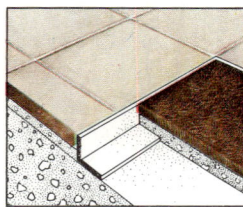
Sunken mat

LIVING/DINING-ROOM

The living-room and dining-room have been combined, so the same flooring was needed throughout to link the two areas. A good quality Axminster in 80% wool/20% nylon was chosen for comfort and hard wear. As children's meals are taken in the kitchen, risk of spills in the dining area is reduced. Where the dining table is used for all family meals, a good compromise would be to have a parquet floor with a carpet square in the living-room section. The carpet could be recessed to prevent tripping. A less-expensive solution would be to sand and seal the floorboards and have a loose-laid carpet square or rugs. On a solid sub-floor, hardwood block could be laid. A room which is used only as a living-room presents less of a problem. If fitted carpet is preferred, choose a high-quality one for long life, or an inexpensive one which can be replaced when a family needs change. Cork, wood or PVC sheet would be suitable in a separate dining-room.

CLOAKROOM

Flexible PVC sheet gives an easy-to-clean floor in the cloakroom. Coving strips, which match the flooring, make a smooth join between the floor and the bottom of the vanity units. Alternatively PVC or thermoplastic tiles could be used.

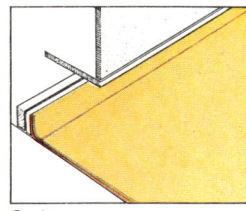
Coving

KITCHEN

The kitchen is a later extension and has a solid sub-floor, so quarry tiles have been used to give a long-lasting, easy-to-clean surface. Coved tiles are fitted round the edges to facilitate cleaning and prevent dirt getting trapped in the angle between floor and wall. A mat could be sunk into the doorway to remove dirt brought in from the garden. A less-expensive flooring, which could also be used on a suspended sub-floor, would be flexible PVC sheet.

TERRACE

The terrace has been laid with quarry tiles of the type used in the kitchen. Only high-quality quarry tiles should be used outside. Brick and slate also make attractive, hard-wearing floors inside and outside.

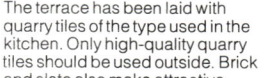

UTILITY ROOM

Quarry tiles have been extended from the kitchen to the utility room. The floor is easily mopped clean and the water runs into a drain. The drain is set into a gully made from standard channel fittings which are part of the range of quarry tiles. This avoids risk of flooding if the washing machine overflows.

HALL AND STAIRS

As the hall, stairs and upper corridor get a lot of wear, they are carpeted with the same quality Axminster as that used in the living/dining-room. A good alternative would be a high-quality tufted carpet. Cord, sisal and needleloom provide cheaper stair coverings, but care should be taken as they can be slightly slippery.

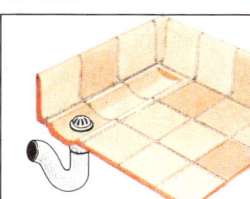
Drain

GROUND FLOOR As dirt from the outside is brought into the hall, kitchen and cloakroom, a hard-wearing floor which is easy to clean is needed. The kitchen has to withstand the additional hazards of burns and spills. A solid sub-floor allows the use of quarry tiles. A cheaper alternative, which can also be used on a suspended sub-floor, is PVC. If carpet is preferred in the hall, it needs to be hard-wearing and in a colour which does not show dirt. The living-room and dining-room need flooring which is durable, warm and comfortable.

THRESHOLDS

Before laying fitted carpet, check to see if the door opens easily over it. If there is a tight fit, and the door rubs the carpet, extra wear will be caused. To prevent this, sandpaper the bottom of the door (see p. 361) or fit rising hinges. Aluminium threshold strips are used where two types of carpet or flooring meet in a doorway. The strip is screwed into the floor and the edge of the carpet is trapped beneath the lip.

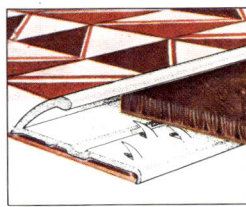

Aluminium strip

NURSERY

A child's room needs a floor which is warm, quiet and easy to clean. Cork tiles fulfil all these requirements – they can be brightened up with colourful, washable rugs. A good alternative is Tretford carpet, made from animal hair. Another possibility is to lay carpet tiles, which can be cleaned or moved out of sight when a small area is stained or damaged. A cheaper solution is to have foam-backed vinyl with washable rugs.

DOORWAYS

When the door is opened the hinge rises so that the door glides over the carpet.

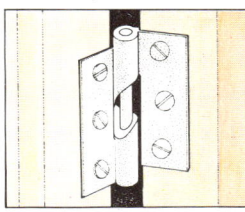

Rising hinge

BATHROOM

On an upper floor which has suspended construction, vinyl tiles or sheet flooring provide a smooth, easily cleaned surface. On a solid floor, ceramic tiles provide practical flooring if the bathroom is adequately heated. As plastic and ceramic can be slippery when wet, it is wise to provide a bath rug. A carpeted bathroom gives a feeling of luxury, but it is not practical if the bathroom is used by children.

SPARE BEDROOM/BEDSITTER

A fitted wool cord gives a hard-wearing floor in the spare room, which may be used as a bedsitter for an au pair or elderly relative, and may later be a teenager's room.

MASTER BEDROOM

As a bedroom gets relatively light wear, a shag carpet can be used to give it a luxurious look, or cheaper-quality tufted carpet can be fitted.

UPPER FLOOR Suspended-floor construction and a need for quiet dictate the use of resilient flooring. Bedroom floors do not take much wear, so less-expensive coverings can be used. But if a bedroom is also used as a study, playroom or bedsitter, a more hard-wearing flooring is needed.

SHOWER-ROOM

The floor of the shower-room, which leads off the spare room, is laid with mosaic, which is also used on the walls. A small area of a suspended sub-floor can be laid with mosaic if the construction shown below is used. The nails in the floorboards are punched down and the floor is sanded if necessary. Marine grade ply, 5 mm. ($\frac{1}{4}$ in.) thick, is laid over the floor, pinned at 150 mm. (6 in.) intervals. Glazed mosaic is bedded in ready-mixed water-proof adhesive and pointed with waterproof grout. A cove is formed by fixing mosaic to a sealed timber fillet or cove.

STAIR TREADS

As the stair treads get most wear, it is advisable to allow an extra 45 cm. (18 in.) of carpet so that it can be shifted occasionally to even out wear. The extra length of carpet is pleated and tacked to the top and bottom risers, so that it is hidden. The carpet should be shifted twice in the first year and once every subsequent year.

Shower floor

41

PREPARING AND LAYING FLOORS

Many modern flooring materials are suitable for laying by the householder. Among these are vinyl tiles, vinyl sheet flooring, cork tiles and carpet tiles. Wooden strips and blocks, slate, quarry tiles and ceramic tiles are best left to the professional floor layer or to the dedicated handyman. Successful laying of the do-it-yourself materials depends largely on careful preparation of the sub-floor and closely following the instructions and recommendations of the manufacturer. Floorboards that are in good condition can be sanded and coated with a clear sealer – this method gives an attractive, natural flooring at low cost. If the floorboards are new, just scrub them with detergent and water, rinse and dry thoroughly and apply a finish.

PREPARING A SOLID SUB-FLOOR

The floor should be level, smooth and free from damp (see p. 30) before any type of flooring is laid on it. If a concrete floor is badly damaged or uneven, have it professionally screeded. Screed is a coat of cement and sand, 25-50 mm. (1-2 in.) thick, which gives a smooth floor surface.

RESURFACING A FLOOR
Slight irregularities can be levelled by using a cement latex smoothing compound sold by builders' merchants and do-it-yourself shops.

This compound can also be used on a stone or brick floor which is to be covered with a flooring material, provided the floor is dry. If the floor has a non-absorbent surface, such as quarry tiles, treat it with a primer so that the compound can stick properly.

If there are any holes or cracks deeper than 3 mm. ($\frac{1}{8}$ in.), fill them with a ready-to-mix cement base (sold in various-sized packs).

Before levelling a floor, first sweep it, then wash it with detergent to remove any grease. Mix the smoothing compound with water according to the manufacturer's instructions. Start at the furthest point of the room from the door and pour about a quarter of the mixture on the floor [A1]. Using a metal trowel at a slight angle, spread the mixture evenly over the floor to a thickness of 3 mm. ($\frac{1}{8}$ in.) [A2]. Cover the whole floor in this way, finishing at the door. As the mixture smooths itself out, the trowel marks will disappear. The surface should be hard enough to walk on after three hours but should not be covered with flooring material until it has completely hardened. This can take 6-12 hours.

PREPARING A WOODEN SUB-FLOOR

If floorboards show signs of rot or woodworm (see p. 378) the boards should be treated by a specialist.

Whatever type of flooring is being laid over floorboards, it needs a firm base – gaps in floorboards cause uneven wear on sheet flooring, and excessive movement in the floor may disturb tiles. Secure loose or creaking boards, remove carpet tacks and punch down protruding nails.

Any faults should be corrected before a new flooring is laid or before the floor is sanded. Hollows in a wooden floor can be levelled with a smoothing compound after gaps have been filled. High spots can be planed off.

SECURING LOOSE BOARDS
First hammer in the existing floorbrads (special nails for floorboards). If the boards are still loose, buy some brads at least 20 mm. ($\frac{3}{4}$ in.) longer than the thickness of the floorboards. Position the new brads about 13 mm. ($\frac{1}{2}$ in.) along the joist from the existing one. Hammer the brads well home, then use a nail punch to knock the heads below the surface of the floorboards. Whenever securing floorboards it is imperative to check that there are no pipes or wires immediately under the boards which could be pierced by a nail.

FIXING CREAKING BOARDS
Creaking can sometimes be cured by sprinkling talcum powder or french chalk between the boards. If this does not work, use a nail punch to knock down the brads just below the surface along all the floorboards in the creaking area. Drill undersize pilot holes for screws, 13 mm. from each nail head. Screw these home tightly into the joist, making sure the heads are below the surface of the floorboards.

FILLING GAPS BETWEEN FLOORBOARDS
Small gaps – less than 6 mm. ($\frac{1}{4}$ in.) wide – between floorboards can be filled with home-made papier mâché.

LEVELLING A SOLID FLOOR

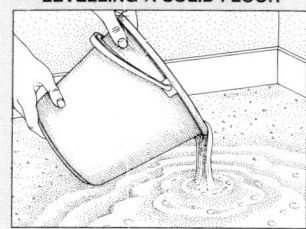

A1. Pour out a quarter of the compound, in the corner opposite the door.

A2. Spread the compound over the floor to a thickness of about 3 mm.

FILLING GAPS WITH PAPIER MÂCHÉ

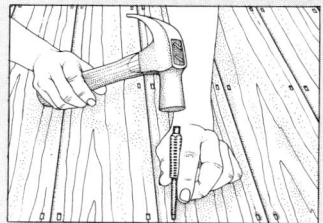

B1. Secure boards by hammering down loose nails. Punch heads below surface.

B2. Pour boiling water over pieces of paper, pounding with a piece of wood.

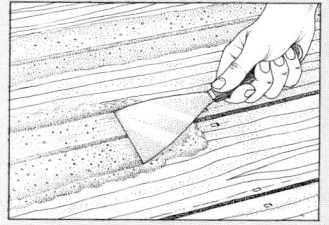

B3. Force papier mâché into gaps between the floorboards, using a scraper.

B4. The filled gaps should be rubbed down with glasspaper when dry.

Any kind of paper is suitable if the floor is to be covered. But if part of the floor is visible round the edges of a carpet, use soft, white and unprinted paper which will give a better finish between the boards – especially if the floor is subsequently stained.

Before starting, make sure all floorboards are secure. Hammer home any loose nails, sinking heads with a nail punch [B1]. Tear the paper into pieces the size of a postage stamp. A bucketful is enough for about 7 sq. m. (80 sq. ft) of floor. Pour boiling water, a little at a time, over the paper and pound it with a piece of wood [B2]. Stir and pound the mixture until it forms a thick paste; if it is too thin add more paper. Leave the mixture to cool for an hour, then pound in wallpaper adhesive until the mixture is very thick. It is better to use too much rather than too little adhesive, to make sure the papier mâché does not contract. It can be dyed to match the floor, using any proprietary liquid dye. When the mixture is cold, force it between the boards with a scraper [B3]. Make sure it is pushed well down. Leave the mixture to dry for two or three days. Then rub along each filled gap with glasspaper and a block

[B4]. Floor sealer can be applied to the papier mâché when it is dry.

LEVELLING A WOODEN FLOOR WITH HARDBOARD
Hardboard gives a level surface for laying sheet flooring and vinyl and cork tiles. Buy the hardboard in squares of 1.2 m. (4 ft). Draw a plan of the room to scale and divide it into squares representing the sheets of hardboard, to find out how many you need. Take into account the offcuts which will be produced as some sheets are cut to fit round the edges of the room.

To prevent the hardboard from buckling, brush the rough side with water and stack the sheets flat, rough side to rough side, for 48 hours to dry. Leave them in the room in which they are to be laid so that they dry out to the moisture content of the room.

Before laying the hardboard, check that the door will open over it, taking into account the thickness of the floor covering to be used.

Prepare the floor by punching down nails and securing any loose boards. Sand any particularly uneven spots and sweep the floor. Lay the hardboard with the smooth side up. Place the first square exactly in the centre of the room (to find the centre point of a room, see p. 46). Working from the centre of the hardboard outwards, hammer in 19 mm. (¾ in.) nails or panel pins spaced 150 mm. (6 in.) apart [C1]. If there are pipes or wires under the boards, use nails shorter than the combined thickness of the hardboard and floorboard. Lay one square directly above the first piece and another below it, but stagger squares each side (see diagram, bottom left) to avoid joins lining up.

Most walls are not absolutely straight and to fill the gaps round the edges of the room will mean marking the line of the wall on the hardboard

as a cutting guide. To do this, place a piece of hardboard squarely on the nailed sections so that a corner of the board touches the skirting [C2]. Take a wooden block about 50 mm. (2 in.) wide, place one edge firmly against the skirting and push it along the skirting, at the same time marking the board with a pencil held against the outer edge of the block [C3]. Cut along the marked line with a saw. Then push the board to fit against the skirting and mark on it the overlap against the edge of the nailed boards [C4]. Cut the board to the size marked and nail it in place [C5]. Fill the remaining gaps in the same way, keeping the joins staggered. Use offcuts where possible.

To mark the shape of the door frame on the board to be placed at the door, position the piece of hardboard over the nailed section so that the edge is touching the skirting.

Measure the distance from the near

edge of the door stop to the face of the skirting, using a ruler and set-square [C6]. Then draw a line on the hardboard to the measured distance, aligning with the inside edge of the door frame. Next cut a wooden block equal to the distance you have just measured. Push the block along the skirting board from the edge of the board towards the door frame, and mark the board with a pencil placed against the outer edge of the block [C7]. Mark all the straight sections of the door frame on the board and join them up, drawing in any curves freehand [C8]. Mark the other side of the door frame in the same way. Cut out the sections with a coping saw.

Lay the board in position and mark on it the edge of the nailed board underneath. Cut the board to size and nail it in position. If a join falls in the middle of the doorway, nail one board in position before marking and placing the other one.

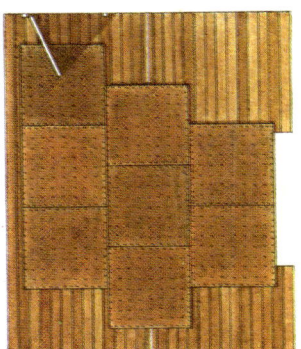

Start from the centre of the room, staggering the joins of sheets at each side.

LEVELLING A FLOOR WITH HARDBOARD

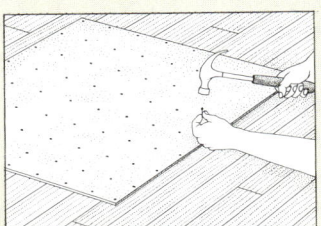
C1. Place hardboard sheet in middle of floor and hammer nails 150 mm. apart.

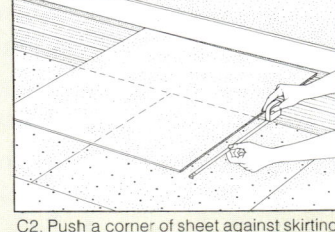
C2. Push a corner of sheet against skirting, keeping it square with fitted piece.

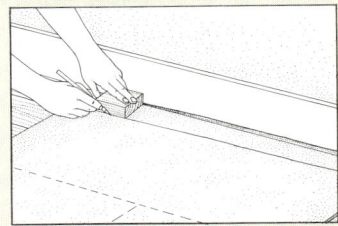
C3. Use a wooden block with a pencil held against it to mark the cutting line.

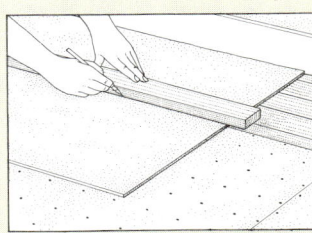
C4. Cut and fit sheet to skirting. Mark line where sheet overlaps on other edge.

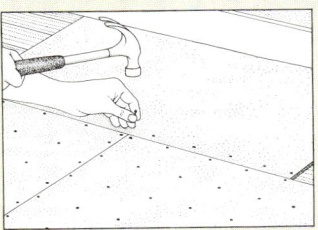
C5. Cut this edge and fit sheet into place. Nail every 150 mm.

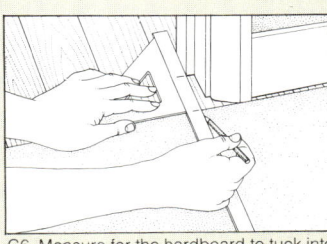
C6. Measure for the hardboard to tuck into the angle of the door frame.

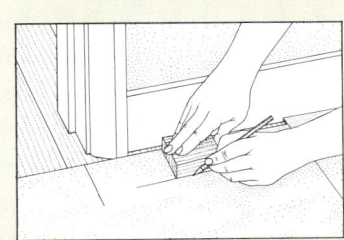
C7. Cut a block of wood to the measured width and use it to mark line of the skirting.

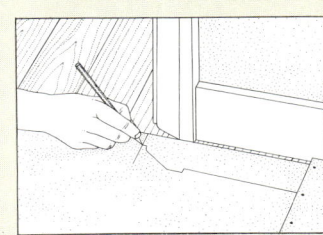
C8. Mark out the other straight sections and join up, drawing curves in freehand.

• SANDING A FLOOR

The purpose of sanding a floor is to level it, to remove grit, dirt, old polish and varnish, and to prepare the surface for a new finish or floor covering. Once it has been levelled, the floor should be resanded only when it has become worn or damaged, or when the finish has to be replaced. A hard plastic finish may need sanding only every ten years as the surface can be re-buffed and given another coat. A polished or varnished floor will need sanding to remove the worn surface; this may be necessary after about four years, depending on the amount of wear the floor gets and how well it is maintained.

HIRING A SANDING MACHINE

Local classified telephone directories usually list firms which hire out sanding machines for domestic use at daily and weekly rates. The hiring firms can sometimes provide an operator if the hirer does not wish to do the sanding himself.

A sanding machine has a revolving rubber-covered drum mounted on a wheeled frame that tilts back to lift the drum from the floor. A sheet of abrasive paper is wrapped tightly round the drum, and a removable linen bag collects the wood dust.

Before hiring a machine, ask the dealer to give a demonstration. Take special note of how the abrasive paper is fitted; if it is not fitted tightly enough it will be ruined as soon as the machine is switched on. Make sure that the machine is in good order and picks up wood dust. Check that the cable is long enough to stretch from the power point to the furthest spot to be sanded; if it is not, ask for an extension lead. Find out if the machine can be serviced straight away if it breaks down.

Sanders for domestic use are usu-ally powered by a 1 hp electric motor. This must not be used with a 5 amp. plug; a 13 amp. circuit is the minimum requirement. Do not hire a more powerful machine, which would be difficult to handle and could damage the floor. Check that the voltage marked on the sanding-machine motor corresponds to the house supply (usually 240 volts).

To sand edges, corners and any area inaccessible to the large machine, hire an edger – a small machine fitted with a sanding disc. If only a small area is to be sanded, it can be done with an edger alone.

Abrasive paper and sanding discs come in several grades, ranging from very coarse to extra fine, which is used when an exceptionally good finish is required. The first sanding is done with the coarsest paper and a progressively finer one is used for each successive sanding. It is sometimes necessary to replace the paper before one sanding is completed as it wears smooth, so obtain a good supply. As sheets of abrasive paper are usually available on a sale-or-return basis, there need be no waste.

PREPARATION FOR SANDING

Clear the room completely, removing all furniture, curtains, paintings and removable fittings such as shelves. If there is a fitting or large piece of furniture which cannot be moved, cover it with a dust sheet.

Remove any floor covering and tacks and make sure that nails in the floorboards are punched below the surface; a protruding nail or tack will rip the abrasive paper and may damage the rubber-covered drum of the machine. After punching down the nails, fill the holes with wood filler.

Secure loose boards and fill any gaps between floorboards (see pp. 42-43). Sweep or vacuum the floor carefully; loose grit will damage the floor if it is rubbed in by the sanding machine. While sanding the floor, keep the windows open and the door closed. It is also a good idea to wear a mask, made from a thin scarf, to avoid breathing in dust. Sanding machines are very noisy, so it is advisable to warn neighbours of your plans.

USING A SANDING MACHINE

Follow the instructions with the machine when fitting the abrasive paper on the drum. Wrap the paper tightly round the drum and secure it well. If the paper breaks during use, make sure there are no particles of paper caught in the fan intake as they will prevent the machine taking up dust. Insert the coarsest abrasive paper for the first sanding.

Most floors will need three or four sandings. If the floor is very uneven, sand diagonally across the floor at first [A1]. Otherwise, sand in the direction of the grain.

Before plugging the machine into the mains, make sure the handle switch is in the 'off' position.

Drape the cable over one shoulder so that it does not come into contact with the drum. Tilt the machine back so that the drum is not in contact with the floor, then switch on. Gently lower the machine until the drum makes contact with the floor. As the sanding paper bites into the floor it makes a screeching sound and the machine moves forward. Resist any temptation to restrain it; keep it moving slowly forward at an even pace until the far end of the room is reached. At this point lift the drum momentarily so that the skirting board is not damaged. Then retrace your steps, moving backwards, and sand over the same line again. Take care not to leave the machine stationary while switched on, as it will make a groove in the floor.

Lift the drum at the beginning and end of each cut.

Continue in this way, overlapping each cut by about 75 mm. (3 in.) [A2], until the whole floor is sanded. This will leave a gap of about 1 m. (3 ft) along the wall where you began. Turn round to sand this area, but remember to switch off before turning the machine.

Sweep or vacuum the floor between each sanding. Change to medium paper and sand again, going in the direction of the wood grain. Repeat the procedure with fine abrasive paper until the floor is level and smooth, with all traces of varnish removed. Empty the dust bag of the machine each time it becomes one-third full and again when the sanding is finished.

Sand the edges and corners with the edger [A3], using the same grades of paper and sanding with the grain. A power drill fitted with a sanding disc can be used as an alternative to the edger [A4]. Again the same grades of sandpaper should be used. Finish off in the corners, where the circular disc cannot reach, with sandpaper on a block.

Vacuum the floor thoroughly to remove wood dust. Then rub over the boards with a damp cloth and leave to dry. Finally, go over the floor with a rag soaked in white spirit. This will ensure that all traces of dust are removed.

APPLYING A FINISH

Have the selected finish (see p. 50) to hand so that it can be applied as soon as possible after sanding, before dirt can get into the wood grain. Even if the floor is to be covered, it is a good idea to seal it with one coat of finish to keep it in good condition. Apply the

SANDING FLOORBOARDS

A1. On uneven boards, the first sanding is made diagonally across the floor.

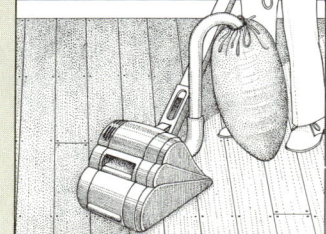

A2. Overlap each run by 75 mm. Subsequent sandings follow the grain.

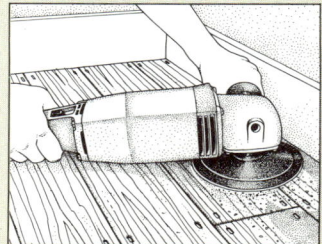

A3. Use an edger to finish off at the skirting and around the corners.

A4. Alternatively, use a power drill with a sanding disc. Follow direction of grain.

first coat of finish with a pad of clean dry cotton, rubbing the varnish well in. Leave to dry; make sure the room is well ventilated and free from dust. This could take from 6 to 24 hours, depending on the type of finish and the weather conditions. When dry, rub the surface with fine steel wool or glasspaper. Apply the next coat and any subsequent ones with a clean, dry paint brush, working with the grain and spreading the finish evenly. Follow the maker's instructions concerning the number of coats. The harder professional finishes usually need only two coats, but others, such as polyurethane, need three or four. Make sure the final coat is thoroughly dry before moving furniture on to it; wait at least 24 hours.

If you want to stain or dye the floor, test the colour on a part of the floor which will be covered by furniture or rugs. Staining must be carried out before the floor is sealed. Use any commercial wood dye or stain and follow the manufacturer's instructions. When dry, apply two or three coats of varnish.

Floorboards before sanding

Floorboards after sanding

THE FINISHED FLOOR   These were once dull and ordinary looking floorboards. At very low cost they were sanded then sealed with two coats of varnish. This has brought out the natural colours of the wood, which give a warm glow to the room.

• LAYING TILES

Any even, dry sub-floor is suitable for laying vinyl, cork and carpet tiles. Thermoplastic tiles need a solid sub-floor. If you are laying tiles on floorboards, cover the floor first with hardboard. If you are using tiles of all the same colour, mix up the contents of the different packets so that any variation in the shade will be unnoticeable.

TOOLS AND MATERIALS

Necessary quantity of tiles, hammer and nails, string, chalk, adhesive and serrated spreader if needed, Stanley knife, scissors, pencil, compasses, felt paper, block of wood. For cork tiles: saw and headless pins. For carpet tiles: double-sided tape and ball-point pen.

MARKING OUT THE ROOM

Tiles are laid from the centre of the room to ensure that they are set out squarely and that there is an even border of cut tiles round the edges.

To find the centre of the room, first mark the centre points of two opposite walls, and tap a nail into the floor at each point. Stretch a chalked string between the nails. Pluck the string sharply [A1] to leave a chalk mark

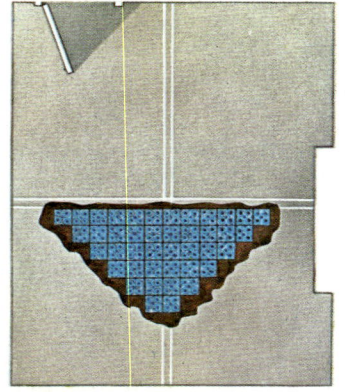

Fit tiles along centre line, then into tile corners. Repeat on the other side.

across the centre of the floor. Repeat from the other two facing walls, so that two chalk lines intersect at right-angles.

The next step is to check the width that will be left around the walls when as many whole tiles as possible have been laid. Starting from an inside angle of the intersecting lines, lay two rows of tiles 'dry' at right-angles towards the nearest walls [A2].

If the space between the last tile and the wall in either row is less than 75 mm. (3 in.), move the whole row half a tile's width away from the wall. If the gap is 75 mm. or more, leave the tiles in position and carry out the same check on the other row.

If either or both rows of tiles are moved in this way, bring them back to form a right-angle at the new point of intersection [A3] without disturbing the adjusted gap between tiles and walls.

Snap fresh chalk lines, parallel to

the first, to mark the new positions of the tiles [A4], and start tiling from the intersection of the second pair of chalk lines.

FIXING VINYL TILES

Warm vinyl tiles before laying them. If forming a pattern from two or more colours, first mark out the pattern on a scaled plan of the room. Tile one half of the room first. Using a serrated spreader, spread adhesive to at least a tile's width along one side of the marker line. Take care not to obscure the chalk mark. When the adhesive is tacky but does not come away on the thumb when lightly pressed, it is ready to receive the tiles. If you are using self-adhesive tiles, follow the manufacturer's instructions.

Place the first tile against the intersection of the chalk lines; working out from this, lay a complete row along the chalk line. To bond the edge of the tile to the dry chalk line, scrape it

lightly across the adhesive so that it picks up enough adhesive to make it stick. Work out from this row, forming a triangle shape (see diagram, left). Butt the tiles against each other, lowering each tile into place rather than sliding it. If any of the adhesive is squeezed up between the tiles, wipe it away immediately with a damp cloth. If the tiles have a grained pattern, place them so that the grain in each tile runs in alternate directions. Continue by fitting tiles into the angles of the corners, up to the border. Tile the rest of the room in the same way.

To cut a border tile, place a tile exactly on top of the last complete tile, making sure the pattern or grain is running the right way. Place another tile on top of the loose one and slide it until the edge touches the wall. Using the outer edge of this tile as a guide, mark a line on the tile below [B1]. Score along the line with a Stanley knife, then bend the tile to complete

---

SETTING OUT THE TILES

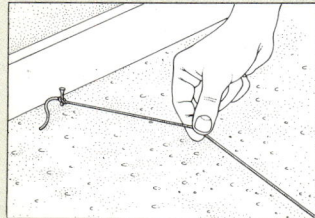

A1. Mark the centre line of a room by plucking string rubbed with chalk.

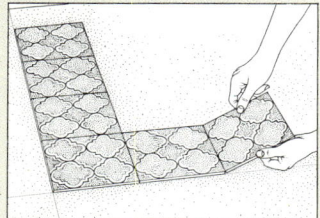

A2. Place tile in angle of corner and set out two rows of tiles towards walls.

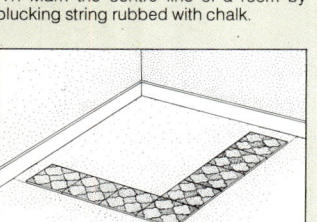

A3. If gaps at ends are 75 mm. or less, move rows half a tile's width from wall.

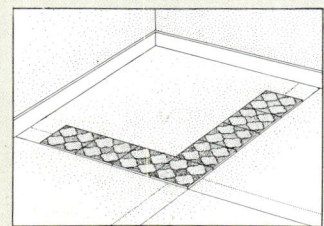

A4. Mark new starting lines and lay tiles against them.

TILING A CORNER

B1. Lay tile over fixed tile. Butt another tile against skirting and mark a line.

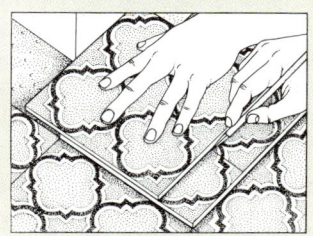

B2. Slide tile to other corner tile and draw a line intersecting the first line.

FITTING A TILE ROUND A PIPE

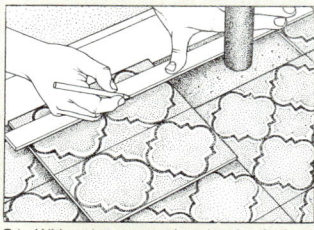

C1. With ruler up against back of pipe, draw horizontal line on the border tile.

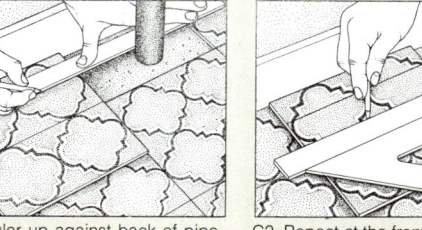

C2. Repeat at the front of the pipe, using set-square to ensure parallel lines.

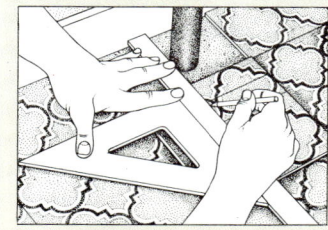

C3. Place the tile on the fixed tile in front of pipe. Mark vertical lines.

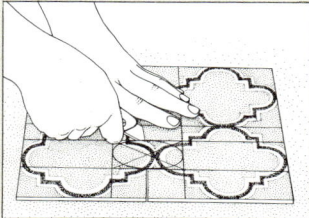

C4. Draw circle inside square formed by lines. Cut down back of tile, cut out circle.

the break. To cut a tile to fit an angle, such as the corner of a chimney breast, first mark it as for a border tile. Then slide the tile, without turning it, or to the fixed tile facing the other side of the corner. Draw a line at right-angles to intersect the first line [B2]. Cut out the oblong section with a Stanley knife or scissors after scoring it. Fit the L-shaped section round the corner. Mark door frames in the same way, drawing in curves freehand.

To mark round a pipe, first cut a border tile to the size of the one adjacent to the pipe. Place it squarely on top of the fixed tile. Place a ruler or strip of wood behind the pipe, with one edge touching it, and use it to mark a horizontal line on the loose border tile [C1]. Then place the ruler or wood strip in front of the pipe and mark another line parallel to the first [C2], using a set-square to ensure accuracy. Slide the tile, without turning it, on to the fixed tile in front of the

pipe; line up the side edges, and mark a vertical line from each side of the pipe [C3].

The four lines will form a square. Find the centre of the square by drawing two diagonal lines from the corners. Place the point of a set of compasses on the centre and draw a circle inside the square so that the circumference just touches the edges. Cut a line from the back edge of the tile to the circle and cut round the circle with a Stanley knife [C4].

To fit tiles round a pedestal basin or lavatory, first stick down as many full tiles as possible round the pedestal. Cut a piece of felt paper to fit roughly round the pedestal. Cut the paper slightly narrower than the space to be tiled, but overlapping about 75 mm. at the front [D1]. Mark on the paper the outline of the pedestal, using a length of wood, pierced with a nail about 50 mm. (2 in.) from one end [D2]. Lay out the tiles that are to be fitted into

the space and transfer the outline on to them. This is done by reversing the piece of wood and using the mark as the guideline, lightly scoring the tiles with the nail [D3]. Cut the tiles along this line [D4].

FIXING CORK TILES
When sticking down cork tiles on a

wooden floor, secure each tile with a headless steel pin at each corner to hold the tile while the adhesive sets.

Cut thin border tiles with a knife; thick tiles with a fine tenon saw.

FIXING CARPET TILES
If using self-adhesive tiles, follow the manufacturer's instructions and

press the tiles down firmly to bond them. If the tiles are to be loose-laid, use double-sided sticky tape to hold the first tile in place. Tiles may be secured with double-sided tape in areas where there is a lot of movement. When marking border tiles, use a ball-point pen on the back of the tiles and cut them from the back.

FITTING TILES ROUND A PEDESTAL

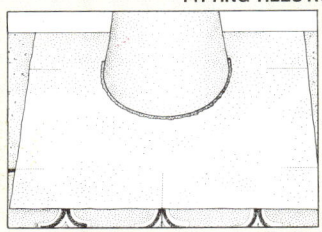

D1. Cut felt paper to fit round pedestal, overlapping the tiles at the front.

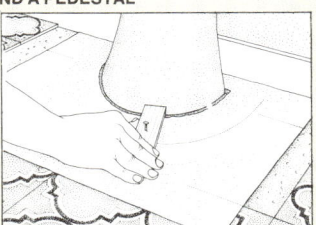

D2. Using nail in length of wood, mark out shape of pedestal on the paper.

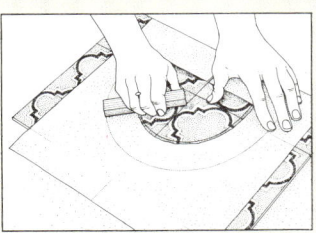

D3. Reverse the piece of wood so that nail marks out pedestal shape on tiles.

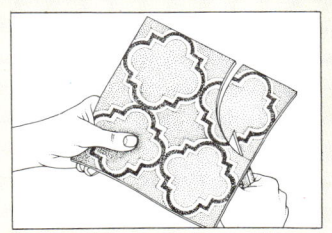

D4. Using Stanley knife, cut tiles along the marked line. Fit into place.

THE ELEGANCE OF TILES   A tiled floor, whether in vinyl, cork, carpet squares or ceramic – as in the room shown here – always looks elegant. Tiled floors are easy to clean and are long lasting.

• LAYING VINYL SHEET FLOORING

Vinyl sheet flooring may be laid on any sub-floor provided the floor is dry, even and free from polish. Fairly rigid sheet flooring can be loose-laid over a small area. But for a larger area, or if the flooring has to be cut round a fitting such as a lavatory pedestal, it should be stuck at the edges and seams. Use double-sided adhesive tape or the adhesive recommended by the manufacturer. When fitting flooring in a doorway, the edge of the sheet should be halfway under the thickness of the door when it is closed.

TOOLS AND MATERIALS

Rolls of vinyl sheet flooring, adhesive and serrated spreader, felt paper, pencil or felt-tip pen, block of wood and saw, Stanley knife, metal straight-edge, hammer, mallet, chisels, decorator's roller, double-sided tape.

ESTIMATING QUANTITY

Vinyl sheet flooring comes in widths of 1.2, 1.5 and 2 m. (4 ft, 5 ft and 6 ft 6 in.). So a room up to 2 m. wide can be covered with a single sheet, which means there is no need for a seam. In this case, measure the length of the room and add about 75 mm. (3 in.) extra for trimming the ends to the shape of the walls.

To cover a large room, allow 75 mm. (3 in.) extra per sheet for trimming and fitting.

If there is a pattern which has to be matched at the seams, allow enough extra vinyl to cover the pattern repeat; measure the pattern and add this measurement to each sheet except the first.

To be sure of ordering the correct amount of vinyl, give the supplier a plan of the room, with dimensions marked, and ask for an estimate.

FITTING SHEET LENGTHS

The method for laying sheet vinyl described here is for cushioned vinyl. Non-cushioned vinyl is less stable and will shrink slightly after being laid. It should therefore be cut to rough lengths, then laid out and left to settle, according to the manufacturer's instructions, before final trimming.

Seams are less noticeable if they are at right-angles to the window. But avoid having seams in the doorway.

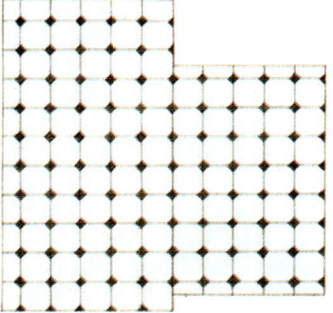

Matching up pattern in vinyl sheets.

Cut a length of vinyl from the roll, 75 mm. (3 in.) longer than the room. Allow an extra length for matching patterns, according to the size of the pattern repeat. Place the first sheet about 50 mm. (2 in.) from a side wall, with the ends lapped up the wall at each end. Use a piece of wood and a pencil to mark the contour of the side wall [A1]. Cut along the line with a Stanley knife or scissors. Fit the sheet flush against the side wall.

To mark the ends of the vinyl, make a pencil mark on the side of the sheet 230 mm. (9 in.) from the skirting [A2]. Pull the sheet away from the wall so that it lies flat. Measure 230 mm. from the pencil mark towards the end of the sheet and make a second mark [A3]. Measure the distance from the second mark to the edge of the vinyl and

cut a wood block to this measurement. This represents the amount to be cut off. Push the vinyl hard against the wall and use the wood block and a pencil to mark the contour of the wall along the vinyl [A4]. Cut along the mark. Mark and cut round door frames in the same way, drawing in curves freehand.

If the vinyl has an overtrim down its edges, lay the next sheet so that it overlaps the first by 25 mm. (1 in.), matching the pattern if there is one. If the vinyl does not need trimming, butt the edges together. If there is an irregular shape such as a chimney breast or bay window, trim the sheet roughly to fit round it. As before, the ends should lap up the end walls.

To trim the seam, use a metal straight edge as a guide and cut through the centre point of the overlap. Peel away offcuts and butt the

sheets together. Then trim the ends as before.

Lay subsequent sheets in the same way. To fit the last sheet to the side wall, place it so that it overlaps the adjacent length with the outside edge butting against the wall. Turn back the end and measure the section that is overlapped [A5]. Cut a piece of wood to this measurement, push the vinyl against the wall and use the wood and a pencil to mark the wall contour on the vinyl [A6]. Cut along this line and fit the vinyl against the wall. Trim the seam, then mark and trim the ends.

Stick the sheets, one at a time, at the ends and seams with double-sided sticky tape or adhesive. Spread the adhesive on the floor with a serrated spreader, making a strip about 50 mm. (2 in.) wide. Press the vinyl firmly on to the adhesive. To make sure it sticks well, go over the seams

with a decorator's roller and tap down the ends with a hammer, using a block of wood to avoid damaging the vinyl. Stick the vinyl at the side walls only if the manufacturers recommend that it should be done.

FITTING ROUND A PEDESTAL

First make a pattern from a large sheet of felt paper. To fit the pattern round the pedestal, measure the distance of the centre of the pedestal from the two nearest walls and mark this point on the pattern. Then cut a line from the edge that will be behind the pedestal to the centre point, and cut out the rough shape of the pedestal [B1]. Fit the pattern to the pedestal and, using a Stanley knife, trim the pattern to leave a gap of about 12 mm. ($\frac{1}{2}$ in.) all round. Fix the felt paper to the floor with pins or weights to prevent it shifting [B2].

LAYING SHEET FLOORING

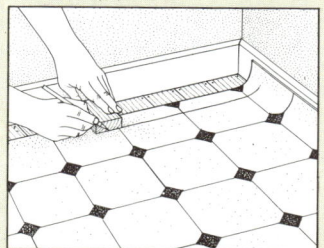

A1. Use a length of wood and pencil to scribe wall contour.

A2. For ends, measure from wall 230 mm. and mark the distance on the vinyl.

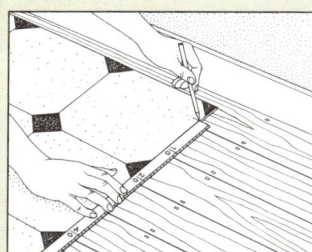

A3. Pull vinyl flat and measure from this mark, 230 mm. back along the sheet.

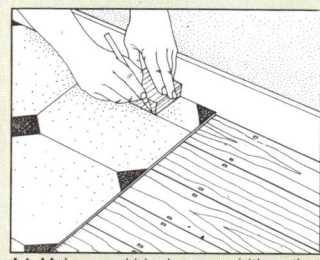

A4. Make wood block same width as that left at end of sheet. Mark the contour.

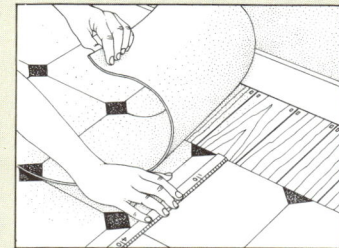

A5. To fit last width, measure the amount by which it overlaps the fitted vinyl.

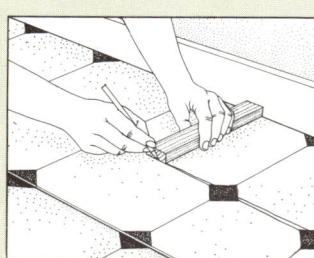

A6. Cut block to this width and scribe edge of skirting as before.

Then take a straight-edged piece of wood, 25 to 38 mm. (1 - 1½ in.) wide. Pierce with a nail about 50 mm. (2 in.) from one end, and use this to trace an outline on the paper. Move the wood round the pedestal so that the nail marks the paper [B3].

Remove the paper and place it on the sheet of flooring material. If the flooring has a tiled pattern, position the pattern so that the pieces on each side of the pedestal will be equal. Fix the pattern to the flooring with pins or weights. Then mark the outline on the flooring by reversing the procedure: place the edge of the wood block on the marked line so that the nail is on the exposed floor covering [B4]. When the outline has been marked on the flooring, cut it with a Stanley knife, at the same time cutting a straight line from the edge of the covering to the outline so that the sheet can be fitted

round the pedestal [B5]. Fit the flooring in place [B6] and stick it down round the pedestal and round the edges. Spread the adhesive on the floor in a strip about 50 mm. (2 in.) wide and press the vinyl on to it. To make sure it sticks firmly, tap it down lightly with a hammer, using a block of wood to prevent marking the vinyl.

• REPLACING DAMAGED TILES

If a tile becomes damaged, remove it and replace it with a new one. If you do not have a spare tile, take a piece of the damaged one to a shop to match it with a replacement. When removing the old tile, take care not to damage surrounding tiles.

VINYL TILES

Chisel out the old tile from the centre, working towards the edges. Scrape

off any remaining bits of tile and adhesive with a paint stripping knife and remove dust. Spread adhesive with a serrated spreader.

Warm the new tile slightly and ease it into the corners. Then press down firmly and rub from the centre outwards to remove air bubbles. Wipe up excess adhesive with a damp cloth.

CORK TILES

Cut along the edges of the damaged tile with a sharp knife, using a metal straight edge as a guide. Use a chisel with the bevelled side down and tap it gently with a mallet to prise the tile from the floor. Scrape old adhesive from the floor with a stripping knife and remove dust.

Apply adhesive with a serrated spreader. Press the new tile into position and, if replacing the tile on a wooden floor, secure with a headless

steel pin at each corner before the adhesive dries. If necessary, wax or seal the tile to match other tiles.

CLAY OR QUARRY TILES

Tap across the damaged tile with a hammer to crack and craze the whole tile. Working from the centre to the edges, chip out fragments with a small cold chisel. When all the tile is removed, use the chisel to smooth the concrete. Scrape the corners clear and brush away dust. Place the new tile in position to check that it is level and just below the surface of the other tiles.

Remove the tile and spread on adhesive or a damp mix of cement and sand – 1 part cement to 3 parts sand mixed with a little water. Press the tile in position. If the tile is not fitted with spacer lugs, place pieces of wood in the gaps to give an even

space all round. Remove surplus adhesive with a trowel.

After 24 hours, remove any wood spacing pieces and grout the joints. Rub a damp mix of 4 parts sand to 1 part cement between the tiles with a rag. Remove surplus grout with a damp sponge, rinsing the sponge frequently in water. Do not walk on the new tile for at least four days.

WOOD MOSAIC

Damaged strips of wood mosaic can be replaced singly or – if they are made of hardwood – in complete panels that are sold by most do-it-yourself shops. First cut out the damaged section using a sharp chisel and a mallet, working from the centre towards the outside edge [C1]. Scrape off any old adhesive from the floor with an old chisel and brush the surface clean. Using a serrated spreader, apply a thin bed of adhesive. When the adhesive is tacky, lay the strip or panel in place. If the last strip, or panel, is tight, tap it down with a mallet [C2]. When dry, smooth the surface with glasspaper. Stain and wax to match the existing floor.

CARPET TILES

A damaged carpet tile can be replaced simply by lifting the old one and putting a new one in its place. But if the rest of the carpet is worn or soiled, a new tile may be conspicuous. In this case, replace the damaged tile with one from under a piece of furniture so that the new tile can be put in a place where it will not show. It is advisable, however, to move the carpet tiles around frequently so that they all get equal wear. If a tile becomes marked or stained, remove it to clean off the stain and replace it when it is dry. If it is treated immediately, water or carpet shampoo may suffice.

FITTING ROUND A PEDESTAL

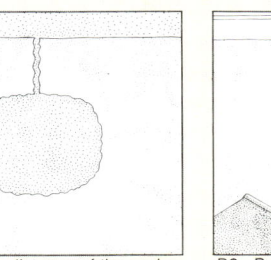

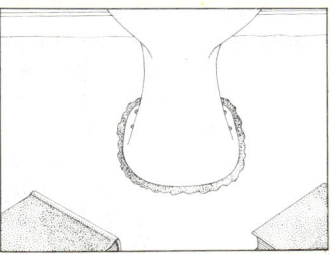

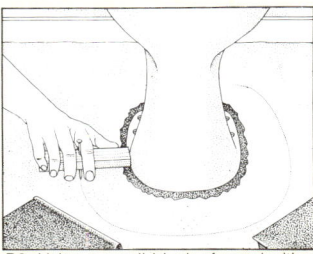

REPLACING WOODEN STRIPS

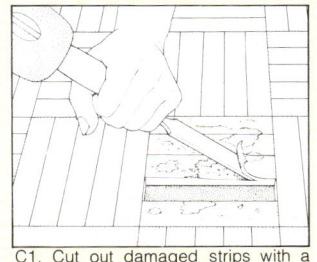

B1. Measure the distance of the pedestal from the walls and cut paper shape.

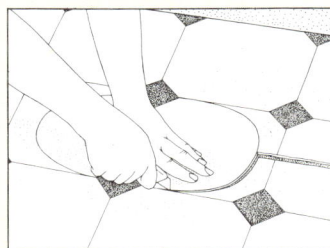

B2. Position paper round pedestal and weight or pin to hold it in place.

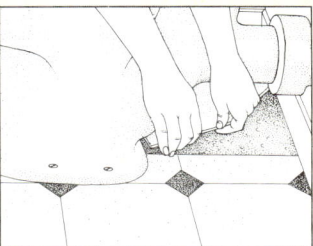

B3. Using a small block of wood with a nail or pencil, mark round the pedestal.

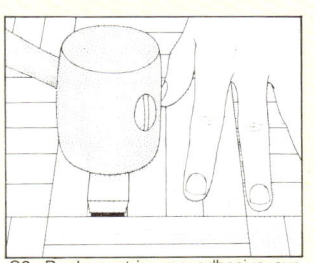

C1. Cut out damaged strips with a chisel, with the bevel side down.

B4. Reverse the block and transfer the outline of the pedestal to the vinyl.

B5. Cut line down vinyl to back of pedestal and cut out pedestal outline.

B6. Fit vinyl into place. Use adhesive round outside edges and round pedestal.

C2. Replace strips on adhesive surface. Tap last one with mallet if tight.

PAINTING AND DECORATING

It costs roughly ten times as much to bring in a professional decorator as it does to buy the materials needed for the job – paint, paste, wallpaper and so on. Clearly it pays to invest in good basic equipment and do your own decorating. In addition to the financial benefits, home decorators have another advantage over the professional – they can take as much time as they like to do a job. This enables them to devote more care to the most vital part of the work – the preparation.

Do not be too ambitious at first. Start on an unimportant room and progress to others later. Choose paint which is easy to apply, and wallpaper which is plain or has a small, simple pattern, to avoid tricky matching.

Do not rush the job and do not overtire yourself. Avoid working under artificial light, if possible. And make sure that all equipment is safe to use before you start work, especially at heights.

Always work to a plan and set yourself a target for each day. Make sure you have all the materials and equipment before you start work.

How long will it take? Much depends, of course, on the size of the room and the amount of preparation needed. But a small room, say 10 ft × 8 ft, to be painted throughout, with two coats, should not take longer than four days even for a beginner. Wallpapering will take a little longer.

If you use quick-drying paints on woodwork, this will speed up the job, especially if the walls are to be papered.

• CHOOSING PAINTS

There are dozens of different paints formulated for different uses, from painting ships to decorating china. The common types used in home decorating are described below.

ALKYD RESIN
See oil-type paints.

EMULSION (VINYL OR ACRYLIC)
A water-based paint which is thinned with water and dries quickly. It is used mainly on interior walls and ceilings. Some types can also be used on interior woodwork, but check the instructions on the label first. Emulsions are available in matt, silk and gloss finishes. All are washable. Acrylic emulsion is also available as a primer/undercoat for use on wood, hardboard and plaster. It is not suitable for use on bare metal.

NON-DRIP OR THIXOTROPIC
This is gelled paint, sometimes called jelly paint. Many gloss, emulsion and most vinyl paints are available in non-drip form. It is easier to smooth out than liquid paint and has better covering capacity.

Non-drip emulsion is particularly useful for painting ceilings, as it virtually eliminates splashes which, when dry, are difficult to remove.

OIL-TYPE PAINTS
Most oil-type paints are now made with alkyd and other resins, blended with oil. Poisonous lead-based pigments have been replaced by non-toxic titanium oxide. These paints, which need an undercoat, are slower drying than emulsion, but they give a tough, hard-wearing finish to most surfaces. Thin with white spirit.

POLYURETHANE
A tough paint which forms a very hard surface that resists moisture, heat and harsh treatment. It is available in gloss and semi-gloss finishes. White is not a good colour for radiators as temperatures above 55°C (131°F) can start to cause yellowing. Thin with white spirit.

VARNISHES AND SEALS
Alkyd and one-pack polyurethane varnish has a hard-wearing surface and a high gloss. It is ideal for woodwork, especially furniture. Polyurethane seals are available in clear and transparent colours. They can be thinned with white spirit. Eggshell-finish varnishes, based on epoxy resin, are also available. These need a special thinning agent.

WASHABLE DISTEMPER
A traditional covering for walls and ceilings, washable distemper is cheaper than emulsion paint but less hard-wearing.

• SPECIAL PAINTS
Flame-retardant paint is available in undercoat, gloss and emulsion. The emulsion is particularly suitable for expanded polystyrene tiles.

Ordinary paint, especially gloss, should not be used on these tiles because the solvents in the paint may soften them.

Anti-condensation paints are available for bathrooms and kitchens where there is heavy condensation. They resist condensation but cannot stop it altogether. Better ventilation and controlled warmth in the room will make them more effective. These paints are simple to apply.

Mould may form on walls because of condensation. Anti-mould paints are available for these situations.

TEXTURED PAINTS
Cracks or irregularities in walls and ceilings can be disguised with textured paint. The paint, a plastic compound, is easy to apply. It is first spread liberally over the surface in an even coat, then treated in various

QUICK CHANGE Light-coloured paint gives a modern look to heavy, old furniture.

ways to create the textured effect. A paint roller run lightly over the surface makes a bark pattern. For a stippled effect, gently bounce a sponge in a polythene bag on the wet paint. Twisting the sponge over the surface gives a pattern of swirls.

• STIRRING, STORING AND THINNING
Stir liquid paints thoroughly with a circular, lifting motion. Do not stand paint containers upside-down to try to distribute pigment that has settled – the solvent may leak from the lid.

Do not stir non-drip paints. Most thixotropic (non-drip) paints should not be thinned, as this will upset the balance of the ingredients. The paint will not gel properly and its covering power will be reduced. The label will indicate whether or not they can be thinned with water.

If water forms on the surface of emulsion paint, pour it off before use.

Skin forms on the surface of some

SUNSHINE LOOK Bright yellow gloss paint adds a warm glow to light entering the window.

PAINTING BRICKS Polyurethane varnish, tinted with wood stain, gives a fine finish to brickwork.

paints after storing. Cut round the skin with a sharp knife and remove it in one piece, if possible. Then stir and strain through an old nylon stocking to remove any remaining skin specks.

Small amounts of paint left over after painting can be stored in a screw-top jar. Label the jar.

Not all paints can be thinned. Read the label for instructions first.

Use water to thin acrylic and emulsion paints. Thin most other types with white spirit. There are some exceptions to this and the label should be your final guide to the correct procedure for thinning.

Non-toxic paints are made for use on toys, cots and other furniture likely to be sucked by children. Not only should the finishing coat be non-toxic, but all the preparation coats as well, including fillers, primers and undercoats.

Stains are used to colour woodwork without concealing its natural texture. They usually consist of solutions of dye in water or spirit and are easy to apply. Oil stains, which are like thin oil paints, are used to colour floors.

Anti-climb paint is a thick compound which forms an apparently firm outer skin but remains plastic underneath. It is for painting on to pipes and walls as a deterrent to burglars.

Metallic paints contain fine particles of aluminium which reflect heat. These paints are especially suitable for radiators and other places subject to heat. They are available in various colours.

• WALL COVERINGS

One of the best aids for amateur decorators is ready-pasted wallpaper. It does away with pasting tables and simplifies the job of wallpapering.

These papers have a paste (usually fungicidal) applied to their backs. A small trough (usually supplied) is filled with water and placed under the strip of wall to be papered. The paper is drawn through the water, allowed to soak briefly, then hung on the wall.

Manufacturers have also simplified the task of stripping paper by introducing easy-to-strip wall coverings. All you do to redecorate is to strip off the top layer of old wallpaper. Wipe the under-surface clean of old paste with a damp sponge and it is ready for the new wallpaper.

The vast range of traditional wall coverings offers an extremely wide choice of textures and patterns.

LINING PAPER

A preliminary covering of plain paper gives a wall an even porosity which helps when painting or hanging the final wall covering. On surfaces such as painted walls, it is essential.

Hang lining paper horizontally so that joins cannot coincide with those of the vertically hung wallpaper.

There are various grades. Avoid thin papers and use a heavy grade to conceal uneven walls.

SURFACE-PRINTED PAPERS

Any one design may contain up to 20 different colours, but 8 to 12 colours are more usual.

The cheaper papers are called pulps. Higher-quality, known as grounded papers, are given a coating of colour before the design is printed.

Papers vary in weight and thickness. Thin papers are cheap, but tear easily when wet. They may stretch if too much paste is applied. Thicker papers help to hide wall defects.

WASHABLE PAPERS

A transparent waterproof film stops moisture, including steam, from damaging the design. These papers are especially suitable for bathrooms and kitchens. Hang washable papers with fungicidal paste. Most are hard to remove. The waterproof film has to be scored, with a wire brush or serrated scraper, to allow water to get through to the backing paper in order to soak it off the wall. A powder wallpaper stripper added to the water helps when removing washable papers.

EMBOSSED PAPERS

The design is pressed into the paper to make it stand out in relief. The process produces wood grain, imitation leather and textile effects.

Duplex embossed papers have deeper designs. Two layers of paper are bonded together before the design is impressed. This material is more resistant to stretch.

CEILING PAPER

Embossed papers are probably the best of the many types available for ceilings. All can be emulsion-painted when they have dried. Papering ceilings is more difficult than papering walls for beginners, but it may be the only way to hide a cracked ceiling.

ANAGLYPTA

Two layers of paper are bonded together and embossed to produce Anaglypta. It can be decorated with matt or silk-finish emulsion paint. Anaglypta can be used to cover a cracked wall. Rolls are 10.05 m. (33 ft) long by 530 mm. (21 in.) wide.

SUPAGLYPTA

This strong, deeply moulded cotton-based paper is good for covering badly cracked walls and ceilings. These surfaces should first be covered with lining paper. Supaglypta looks like plaster and can be emulsion painted. It comes in rolls 10.05 m. (33 ft) long by 530 mm. (21 in.) wide.

INGRAIN PAPERS

These coverings have an oatmeal texture which is useful for concealing a rough wall surface. Small wood chips and sawdust are bonded between two layers of paper during manufacture. Most types can be emulsion painted.

VINYL

Wall coverings of vinyl resist steam and water and can be scrubbed with a soft brush. They are available ready-pasted. For non-pasted types, use a vinyl adhesive containing a fungicide.

VYNAGLYPTA

This is a heavy embossed wall covering made of vinyl. It is tough and easy to handle. Use a vinyl adhesive. Line the underlying surface.

NOVAMURA

With Novamura you paste the wall, not the paper. Work straight from the roll – there is no need to cut lengths first. It is light to handle. Use Polymura wall paste for best results, or a vinyl adhesive. Apply the adhesive by brush or

PRINTED WALLPAPERS These papers are available in a wide choice of traditional and modern designs. Unless treated with a protective finish, a printed paper cannot be wiped clean.

VINYL WALL COVERINGS Resistant to dirt and steam, vinyl can be cleaned with soap and water. It is available in finishes from matt to sheen, and can last up to ten years.

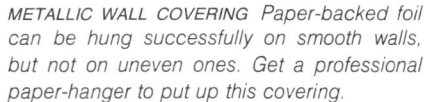

METALLIC WALL COVERING Paper-backed foil can be hung successfully on smooth walls, but not on uneven ones. Get a professional paper-hanger to put up this covering.

INGRAIN WITH ANAGLYPTA These heavy-duty wallpapers have attractive surfaces and, when painted, can provide highly decorative coverings for walls.

roller. Smooth down Novamura with a sponge.

LINCRUSTA

Linseed oil and fillers are bonded to backing paper to make Lincrusta. It is supplied in simulated wood effects or with textured designs, and is sold in rolls 10.05 m. × 530 mm. (33 ft × 21 in.).

CORK

Irregularly shaped cork panels are glued to a background paper to give an attractive textured effect. Walls should be lined before hanging.

FLOCK

Designs stand out in relief and the papers have a velvety pile. This is achieved by gluing nylon, silk or wool cuttings to the surface during manufacture.

HESSIAN

Furnishing hessian is about half the price of backed hessian and comes in two widths – 915 mm. (36 in.) and 1,270 mm. (50 in.). It can be painted with thin oil paint. Spread heavy-duty wallpaper paste evenly on the wall with a roller, then hang the hessian.

METALLIC COVERING

Made from patterned foil glued to paper backing. Its reflective surface accentuates unevenness in walls. Use only on perfectly flat surfaces.

SILK

Woven silk cloth is glued to a background paper for hanging on walls which should first be lined.

HAND-PRINTED PAPERS

Each roll is prepared separately and therefore costs more than machine-printed paper. The designs are outlined more sharply.

• TIPS ON BUYING

Avoid cheap, thin wallpapers. They tear easily when handled, especially when wet with paste.

Buy an extra roll of paper if this is your first wallpapering job. This allows for errors in estimating (see p. 56), and accidents while hanging. Ask your retailer if he will give you a refund on any surplus rolls. Ask him to trim any paper sold with a selvedge.

Beginners are advised to choose plain wallpapers or types with small repeat or random patterns. They are more economical, too.

The colour of wallpaper can vary if the rolls come from different batches.

To check for variations, lay out the rolls so that they overlap. Then look across their surfaces in good light. If colours vary, keep the light lengths together on one wall and the dark together on another wall.

Rolls which vary in colour from one end to the other should be exchanged. Do not stand rolls of paper on their ends when storing; lay the rolls on their sides.

COSTS

Prices of wallpapers vary considerably, but by shopping around you can save money. Price guides are unreliable, as prices change quickly and new collections are being introduced all the time.

Thin wallpaper is the cheapest; prices go higher according to weight, pattern and method of machining.

Washable papers are cheaper than most vinyls. Ready-pasted and easy-strip papers (very useful for beginners) are slightly more expensive.

Prices become progressively higher as you move into the range of flocks, embossed papers, silks, grasscloths and corks, but Anaglypta and Supaglypta are relatively inexpensive.

FELT WALLS A fabric such as felt can be used as a wall covering to create an attractive and warm effect in a living-room. Paper-backed felt can be hung like ordinary wallpaper. When hanging felt with paper backing on brick or plaster, apply a heavy-duty adhesive to the wall. Before pressing the felt to the surface, allow the adhesive on the wall to become sticky. When applying felt to hardboard, use a white adhesive such as Clam.

• TOOLS AND EQUIPMENT

Do not try to do a job with makeshift tools. A suitable kit for preparation work consists of: step-ladders; hop-ups; scaffold board; bucket (plastic); blowlamp; 26 mm. (1 in.) stripping knife – for stripping paint; 51 mm. (2 in.) stripping knife – for stripping paint; 76 mm. (3 in.) stripping knife – for old wallpaper; shavehook – for stripping paint off mouldings; glass-paper and block – a block of wood can be used instead of a glasspaper block; filling knife for filling cracks and holes in plaster (it is more flexible than a stripping knife); sponge.

There are metal hand sanders available with renewable abrasive sheets. These sheets last longer than glasspaper but cost more. They are made in various grades.

Three grades, coarse, medium and fine, should suffice when choosing glasspaper. Wet and dry glasspaper is more expensive, but used wet it cuts out the dust that occurs with ordinary glasspaper.

Step-ladders should be strong. Think ahead when buying and make sure they are suitable for other jobs in the home.

Blowlamps and butane blow-torches can be used for many jobs – from paint stripping to soldering.

Blowtorches are supplied with a selection of burner heads, each of which produces a different jet of flame. The gas cartridges are renewable when exhausted.

PAINT BRUSHES

When buying paint brushes, choose the best you can afford, though a cheaper brush will do for priming and undercoating and for painting unimportant surfaces. Keep a couple for this use only. Brushes with bristles from pigs or boars are best, but nylon is a good substitute.

All new brushes shed hairs at first, so break them in on undercoating jobs before using for top coats.

For walls and ceilings you need a 100 mm. (4 in.) brush. Larger sizes are heavy to handle, especially on ceilings.

Most other jobs can be done with three other sizes: 76, 51 and 26 mm. (3, 2 and 1 in.).

A cutting-in brush has an angled tip useful for painting window frames. A well-worn ½ in. brush will also do the job.

Radiator brushes have long wire handles which can be bent to an angle, enabling you to reach the wall behind.

Any old, but clean paint brush, is suitable as a dusting brush for cleaning the surface just before painting.

PADS AND ROLLERS

Paint pads consist of short mohair bristles, closely packed and glued to a backing pad.

Paint pads are usually sold in sets of various sizes, each size of pad being suitable for a different job – from painting a ceiling to cutting in round a window frame. A set usually includes a paint tray.

Paint rollers cover a surface more quickly than brushes but use more paint. Lamb's wool roller-sleeves are best for gloss and distemper.

Rollers give a slightly textured finish. Foam-sleeved rollers leave a coarser texture than lamb's wool or mohair and splash more easily.

When worn, the sleeves of a roller can be replaced. Keep a couple of spares handy. Rollers are usually sold with paint trays.

Plastic paint kettle This is useful for holding manageable quantities of paint when working with brushes.

S hook Hang this on the step-ladder to hold the paint kettle.

WALLPAPERING TOOLS

Pasting table The ideal size is 1800 × 600 mm. (6 × 2 ft). You can buy or hire one, make one yourself from softwood with a hardboard top, or even make do with the kitchen table, providing it is clean.

Pasting brush A 150 mm. (6 in.) distemper brush is best.

Hanging brush This is used for smoothing the paper on to the wall. A good-quality brush with pure bristles will not scratch the paper.

Scissors Use 253 mm. (10 in.) paper-hanger's scissors.

Plumb-line For marking vertical lines to match edges of paper. A small weight attached to a length of string will do.

Paste bucket Any reasonably sized bucket will do. Make a resting place for the paste brush by tying a piece of string to the handle lugs and stretching it taut across the top.

Angle roller A small boxwood roller used to run along butt joints to ensure adhesion. Do not use on embossed patterns.

Pencil, straight edge, sponge For marking and cleaning.

Folding rule.

Apron with large pocket.

CLEANING TOOLS

After filling in cracks and scraping off paint, clean your tools thoroughly. Wipe off surplus filler from the filling knife as you go. Do not let it dry, or it will have to be scraped off.

Run an oily rag over metal tools when they are clean. Store them wrapped in an oily rag to prevent rusting.

Take care of brushes and they will last longer. Most paint can be removed from a brush with an old kitchen knife or smooth scraper. Clean brushes gently, otherwise you may spoil their shapes.

Lay the brush on thick newspaper and run the blade (or back of the knife) gently along each side of it from the metal case to the ends of the bristles to squeeze out the paint.

Use white spirit, or a brush-cleaning solvent to remove any oil paint, and water to remove emulsion. Then wash the brush in warm water with detergent. Rinse well afterwards.

Brushes on which the paint has hardened can be cleaned with a proprietary brush cleaner or paint stripper. Do not let stripper get on the handle of the brush.

More cleaning may be needed in white spirit, followed by a wash in warm water.

Wrap clean brushes in newspaper. This will help absorb any water left in the bristles and keep off dust.

Rollers and trays should be

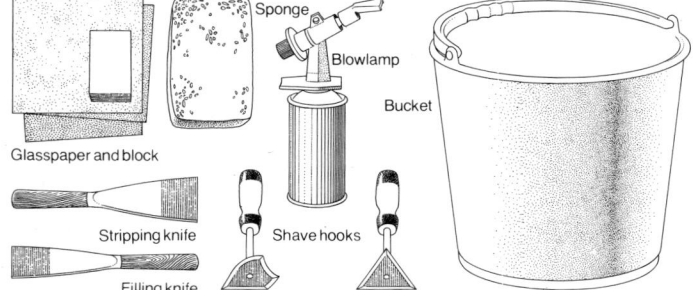

PREPARATION TOOLS *These items are necessary for scraping or burning off old paint, and for cleaning surfaces before starting to decorate.*

Sponge · Blowlamp · Bucket · Glasspaper and block · Stripping knife · Shave hooks · Filling knife

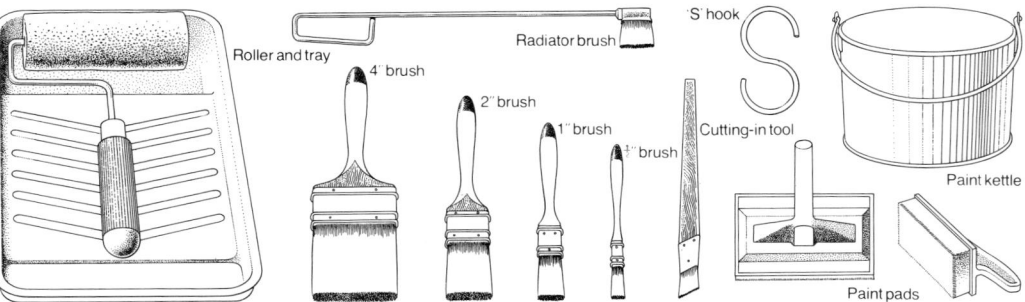

PAINTING TOOLS *The basic equipment for indoor painting jobs includes general-purpose brushes in different sizes, rollers or paint pads. Other useful items are the paint kettle and an S hook to hang the kettle from a high ladder.*

Roller and tray · Radiator brush · S hook · 4" brush · 2" brush · 1" brush · ½" brush · Cutting-in tool · Paint kettle · Paint pads

CLEANING AND CARING FOR BRUSHES

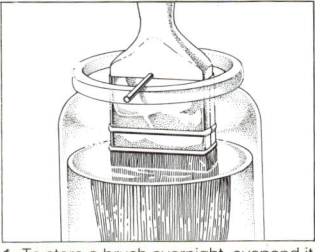

1. To store a brush overnight, suspend it in water from a nail or wire passed through a hole in the handle.

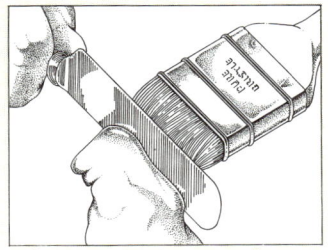

2. To clean a brush, scrape off excess paint with the back of a knife. Scrape towards the tips of the bristles.

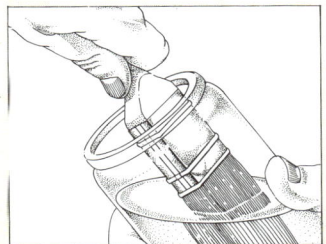

3. Wash the brush – in water to remove emulsion paints; in white spirit to clean off oil-based paint.

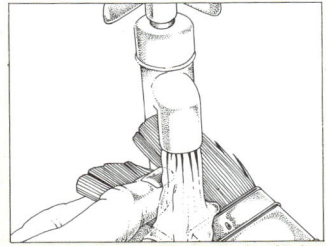

4. Finish removing all types of paint by washing the brush in warm water and soap or detergent. Then rinse under tap.

cleaned with paint solvent if gloss, undercoat or primer is used. Warm, soapy water will clean off emulsion paint. Wrap rollers and trays in paper when dry.

Grease trays to prevent rusting.

Clean off grease before using again.

Paperhanging tools, including brushes, scissors and rollers, can be washed in warm water to remove any paste. Wrap scissors in oily rag after oiling. Wipe clean before the next job.

WALLPAPERING TOOLS Apart from these essential items, wallpapering requires a pasting table, about 1800 × 600 mm. (6 × 2 ft), and two pairs of step-ladders.

• LADDERS AND TABLES

Decorating is tiring, so make sure that your working platform is comfortable – and safe.

For painting ceilings and high walls, two step-ladders or hop-ups are needed, plus a scaffold board to stretch between them. The hop-ups can be used for low ceilings – below 2.5 m. (8 ft 6 in.). Use the step-ladders for higher work.

The scaffold board should be about 3 m. (10 ft) long. This can be bought from a timber merchant or, like most other decorating equipment, hired.

Each step-ladder should be fitted with a tray which clips on the top of it, or have a folding platform. The platform forms the top step on some step-ladders. Many models have a hand-rail rising above this platform.

A scaffold board avoids constant climbing up and down. If you do not feel safe standing on a narrow board, use a step-ladder on its own. The job will take longer, but comfort and safety are more important than speed.

Walls are easier to paint than ceilings, and the same equipment can be used as for ceilings. Often a simple hop-up will be enough, but a step-ladder fitted with a tray is better.

Decorating ceilings above stairwells is a tricky job. Do not try it if you have no head for heights.

Equipment must be strong and firmly secured. An arrangement such as the one shown on the right is suitable. Do not overlook the timber batten which supports the step-ladder on the small landing area.

Use two scaffold boards one on top of the other if the distance they cover is more than 1,500 mm. (5 ft). This will eliminate any sagging when your weight is on it. The boards can be tied together as an extra precaution. Always satisfy yourself that the equipment is secure and cannot slip.

WORKING PLATFORMS To make a safe platform for painting jobs above 2.5 m. (8 ft), use two step-ladders to support a scaffold board about 3 m. (10 ft) long. For jobs below this height, use two hop-ups to support the board.

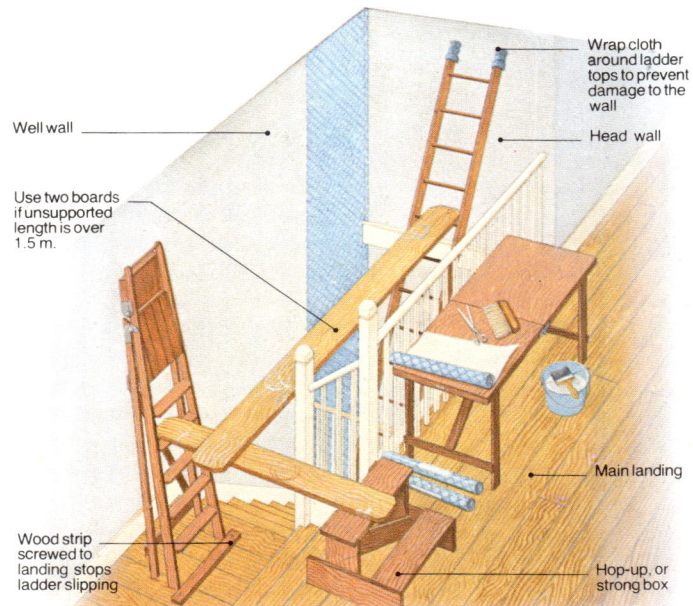

Wrap cloth around ladder tops to prevent damage to the wall

Well wall

Head wall

Use two boards if unsupported length is over 1.5 m.

Main landing

Wood strip screwed to landing stops ladder slipping

Hop-up, or strong box

PREPARING A STAIRWELL Before decorating a stairwell, remove the carpets and arrange ladders and planks so that there is easy access to the walls. For safety, wedge the ladders against wood strips screwed to the landings.

Labels for wallpapering tools: Paste brush, Straight edge, Hanging brush, Wallpaper scissors, Sponge, Angle roller, Plumb-line, Pencil

• ESTIMATING FOR PAINT

Since paint is sold in metric quantities, measure the area to be covered with a metric rule. The usual quantities are: 500 ml., 1 litre, 2.5 litres and 5 litres.

These compare with imperial measures as follows: 500 ml. is 12% less than 1 pint; 1 litre is 12% less than quarter of a gallon (quart); 2.5 litres is 10% more than half a gallon; 5 litres is 10% more than 1 gallon.

When measuring walls, deduct the area of doors and all but the smallest windows.

The spreading power of paint depends on the type, the brand, the temperature of the room and the porosity of the surface. Labels on tins of paint usually state the covering capacity of the paint. An approximate guide is set out in the table immediately below. This will give you a rough idea of your requirements before going to the shop.

Be generous when estimating for paint. Any left over will be useful for touching up later, since it is not always easy to match colours bought at different times.

PAINT COVERAGE
The spreading capacity of paint depends on the type, brand, porosity of surface and on the temperature of the room. Approximate coverage per litre:

TYPE	LIQUID	NON-DRIP
Gloss, lustre, eggshell	16 sq. m. (174 sq. ft)	14 sq. m. (152 sq. ft)
Emulsion	15 sq. m. (163 sq. ft)	11 sq. m. (119 sq. ft)
Acrylic	15 sq. m. (163 sq. ft)	11 sq. m. (119 sq. ft)
Washable distemper	16 sq. m. (174 sq. ft)	
Polyurethane (one-pack)	12 - 18 sq. m. (130 - 196 sq. ft)	

• ESTIMATING FOR WALLPAPER

Measure the height of the room, less skirting and frieze if present, and the distance round the walls, ignoring windows and doors (unless windows are particularly large). Using the chart (foot of page), find the room height on the left. Read across until you reach the distance round walls, shown on the bottom line. The figure at the intersection is the number of rolls required to paper the room.

Wallpaper usually comes in rolls 10.05 m. (11 yds) long by 520 mm. (20½ in.) wide. Most rolls are sold trimmed. The final width of the paper will be 510 to 520 mm. (about 20 to 20½ in.). There are variations, especially in imported and hand-made papers. If using patterned paper, allow 10% for waste when matching.

WALL-COVERING ADHESIVES
Some wall coverings have a label indicating the correct adhesive to use. Where there is no label, follow this chart, or, if in doubt, ask the retailer when buying the covering.

WALL COVERING	ADHESIVE
Anaglypta, ceiling paper, embossed paper, flocks, ingrain, lightweight wallpaper, lining paper, paper-backed fabric, washable paper (but not if used in bathroom or kitchen)	Cellulose, cold-water or starch-ether paste
Cork, Supaglypta	Heavy-duty cellulose or hot-water paste
Vinyl paper, Vynaglypta, washable paper used in bathroom or kitchen	Mould-resistant vinyl adhesive
Unbacked fabrics	Mould-resistant adhesive, such as Clam 143 applied to walls, not fabric

COMMON DECORATING TERMS

Bleeding: this occurs when an old paint or dye dissolves and shows through the new paint. The only effective cure is to remove the affected paint and coat with the appropriate primer (see p. 58) and repaint.

Brushing out: spreading paint, without reloading the brush, to form an even film over the surface.

Butt-joining: hanging lengths of wall-paper or any other wall covering, edge to edge, with no overlap.

Cross-lining: hanging lining paper in the opposite direction to the final wall covering so that the joins do not coincide.

Cutting-in: painting up to an edge to form a straight line. This can be done with an angled brush head.

Efflorescence: white deposit on plaster, brick or concrete. Remove with stiff brush and paint with neutralising fluid. Do not use tap water.

Filler: material for filling cracks and holes; usually a cellulose base which is mixed with water.

Grout: cement-based paste for filling gaps between ceramic tiles.

Key: roughened but level surface to which adhesives and paints can adhere firmly.

Knotting: a solution of shellac and methylated spirit for sealing knots in wood.

Laying on: first application of paint with a loaded brush or roller.

Making good: repairing damage and defects in surfaces before decorating.

Proud: raised above the main surface. A technique used when applying filler to cracks and holes.

Sanding down: using abrasive paper to give a key to painted surfaces.

Selvedge: waste strip down each side of some wall coverings which is trimmed off before hanging.

Size: a glue solution which seals the plaster before hanging wallpaper.

Stripping: removing old paint, distemper and wallpaper.

CALCULATION OF NUMBER OF ROLLS OF WALLPAPER REQUIRED (see Estimating for wallpaper, above)

HEIGHT FROM SKIRTING												
2.13 m. to 2.29 m. (7 - 7½ ft)	4	4	5	5	6	6	7	7	8	9	9	10
2.29 m. to 2.43 m. (7½ - 8 ft)	4	4	5	5	6	6	7	8	8	9	10	11
2.43 m. to 2.59 m. (8 - 8½ ft)	4	5	5	6	6	7	7	8	8	9	10	12
2.59 m. to 2.74 m. (8½ - 9 ft)	4	5	5	6	6	7	8	8	9	10	11	12
2.74 m. to 2.89 m. (9 - 9½ ft)	4	5	6	6	7	7	8	9	9	10	12	13
2.89 m. to 3.04 m. (9½ - 10 ft)	5	5	6	7	7	8	9	9	10	11	12	14
3.04 m. to 3.20 m. (10 - 10½ ft)	5	5	6	7	8	8	9	10	10	12	13	14
3.20 m. to 3.35 m. (10½ - 11 ft)	5	6	7	7	8	9	9	10	11	12	13	15
TOTAL DISTANCE ROUND WALLS	8.53 m. 28 ft	9.75 m. 32 ft	10.97 m. 36 ft	12.19 m. 40 ft	13.40 m. 44 ft	14.62 m. 48 ft	15.86 m. 52 ft	17.07 m. 56 ft	18.29 m. 60 ft	20.72 m. 68 ft	23.16 m. 76 ft	25.59 m. 84 ft

• ESTIMATING FOR TILES

Tile sizes are now measured in millimetres, so all measuring and estimating must also be done in millimetres. First measure the height and width of the area to be covered. If square field tiles (see p. 66) are being used, divide the height and width by the tile size – 100 mm. or 152 mm. – rounding up any remainder. Multiply the two numbers to calculate the total number of tiles. For example, if using 152 mm. tiles and the height of the area being tiled is 1448 mm. (4 ft 9 in.), divide 152 into 1448. This equals 9.526 tiles which, rounded up, means 10 tiles. Say the width is 2337 mm. (7 ft 8 in.), divide this by 152 which equals 15.375, or 16 tiles when rounded up. Multiply the 16 tiles by the 10 tiles, which totals 160 tiles. For 200 × 100 mm. field tiles, divide the height by 100 and the width by 200, then multiply as before to calculate the total number of tiles. In each case, add 5-10 to the total to allow for breakages. If round-edged tiles are being used, count the number needed individually and subtract this figure from the field-tile total.

TILING A BATHROOM When tiling round an outside corner, as seen on the left in this bathroom, always use full tiles at that corner. If tiles have to be cut, use them at the inside corners, where the rough edges will not show.

WALL TILES
General-purpose wall tiles are made in many colours, patterns and textures for use in kitchens, bathrooms and lavatories. Heat-resistant tiles are designed for surfaces where the temperature exceeds 150°C (302°F), such as fireplace surrounds.

USES	SIZES	FINISH	LUGS
General purpose	108×108×4 mm. (4$\frac{1}{4}$×4$\frac{1}{4}$×$\frac{5}{32}$ in.)	Medium glaze	Yes
General purpose	100×100×5 mm. (3$\frac{1}{8}$×3$\frac{1}{8}$×$\frac{3}{16}$ in.) 152×152×6.5 mm. (6×6×$\frac{1}{4}$ in.) 200×100×6.5 mm.(7$\frac{7}{8}$×3$\frac{1}{8}$×$\frac{1}{4}$ in.)	Satin and medium glaze	Yes
Heat resistant	100×100×9 mm. (3$\frac{1}{8}$×3$\frac{1}{8}$×$\frac{3}{8}$ in.) 152×152×6.5 mm. (6×6×$\frac{1}{4}$ in.)	Satin and medium glaze	Some

TILE ADHESIVES
Use this chart to match the adhesive to the surface being tiled.

SURFACE	ADHESIVES
Plaster	Bal-Flex, Bal-Tad, Nic-O-Bond, Cerafix, Polyfix, Bal-Proof, Marley 133
Old glazed tiles	Bal-Flex, Bal-Tad, Nic-O-Bond, Cerafix, Polyfix, Bal-Proof, Marley 133
Building board	Bal-Flex, Bal-Tad, Nic-O-Bond, Cerafix, Polyfix, Bal-Proof, Marley 133
Wood	Bal-Flex, Bal-Tad, Nic-O-Bond, Cerafix, Bal-Proof, Marley 133
Painted surfaces	Bal-Tad, Nic-O-Bond, Cerafix, Polyfix, Marley 133
Cement render	CTF 2, Bal-Flex, Bal-Tad, Nic-O-Bond, Cerafix, Polyfix, Bal-Proof, Marley 133, Nic-O-Bond Waterproof
Shower areas	CTF 2, Bal-Flex, Bal-Proof, Nic-O-Bond Waterproof
Fire-surround repairs	CTF 2, Bal-Flex, Bal-Proof, Marley 133

• PREPARATION

A good decoration job can be done only on a sound surface which has been thoroughly cleaned and cleared of blemishes such as loose paint, cracks and soft plaster.

ORDER OF WORK

Wash the ceiling first, then the walls and woodwork. Wash walls and woodwork from the bottom upwards to avoid dirty streaks running down. Rinse thoroughly. Fill holes and cracks in wood and plaster and rub

down the woodwork with wet and dry.

Paint the ceiling first, then the walls, then the woodwork. If the walls are to be papered, do this *after* painting the woodwork.

Remove as much furniture as possible. Move heavy items to the middle of the room and cover with dust sheets. Take up carpets and take down curtains. Cover tiled or polished floors. Take off all door fittings.

While the carpet is up, attend to any loose floorboards. Use brads about $\frac{3}{4}$ in. longer than before. Drive heads

below the surface with a nail punch.

Fill cracks between boards with papier mâché (see p. 42). Varnish or seal when dry.

New timber Rub the surface down with glasspaper until smooth. Coat any knots with knotting. All new wood needs a coat of primer.

New plaster, brick and concrete Do not apply gloss paint until the surface has dried out. This takes about 12 months. However, emulsion paint can be applied within two or three weeks. At least two coats will be needed.

Hardboard Coat with primer. The surface must be clean and dry before painting. Fill any nail or screw holes.

Primers Priming and undercoating are two separate processes.

The table shows the types of primer for various surfaces. There are 'all-surface' primers available which are claimed to be suitable for wood, metal, plaster and hardboard.

• PAINT STRIPPING

Do not strip paint unless it is flaking or blistering. If this occurs only in small areas, these are the only parts that need to be stripped.

There are three methods: burning; scraping; using chemical stripper.

BURNING OFF

This is the quickest method of removing paint. You need a paraffin blow-lamp or gas blowtorch, a stripping knife or scraper and a shavehook.

Wear an old pair of gloves in case hot paint falls on your hands. Play the flame over the surface, keeping it moving all the time. Avoid burning the wood beneath.

Scrape off the paint as it shrivels.

Use a shavehook for mouldings. Start at the top and work downwards. Use a stripping knife on flat surfaces and scrape upwards. Strip mouldings on doors before the rest of the door.

Do not use a blowtorch on plaster walls or asbestos sheeting, or around panes of glass.

After burning off, rub the surface down with medium-grade glasspaper. Rub away any scorch marks, because paint will not adhere to them. Apply knotting, then primer, and fill holes and cracks with filler.

SCRAPING

Using a scraper without the aid of heat or chemical stripper is a slow process suitable only for small areas.

A Skarsten scraper will speed up the work. This has two blades, one serrated, the other plain.

Score the surface lightly with the serrated edge. Remove the paint with the plain edge.

CHEMICAL STRIPPERS

These do an excellent job, but are expensive. Take care when using chemical strippers, as some types

PATTERNS WITH PAINT An inexpensive way of brightening a bare wall is to cover it with a painted design. In this bathroom, the billowing cloud pattern helps to draw attention from such an ordinary but obtrusive feature as the gas heater.

MATCHING PRIMERS TO SURFACES

SURFACE	TYPE	PRIMER
Timber	Softwood	Wood primer
	Hardwood	Aluminium wood primer
	Highly resinous	Aluminium wood primer
	Oily wood	Teak sealer or aluminium wood primer (wash with white spirit first)
Building boards	Plasterboard	Plaster primer
	Hardboard	Hardboard primer
	Chipboard	Wood primer
	Asbestos	Alkali-resistant primer
Plaster, Brick, Concrete, Stone	—	Alkali-resistant primer Multi-purpose
Metals	Iron and Steel	Calcium plumbate or zinc-chromate primer
	Aluminium	Zinc-chromate primer (rub down first)
	Brass and Copper	Zinc-chromate primer (rub down first)

burn the skin. Wear rubber gloves and dress in old clothes. Move anything likely to be splashed. If any of the stripper gets on your skin or eyes, bathe the affected area in cold water.

Buy the proper stripper for the job; there are various types. Follow the directions implicitly. After applying the stripper, remove the paint with a scraper and shavehook.

Clean the stripped surface thoroughly with white spirit. Rub down with glasspaper. Knot, prime and stop up any holes.

• PREPARING SOUND PAINTWORK

Before any surface can be repainted it must be clean and dry. Paint will not adhere to dirt or moisture.

GLOSS AND SEMI-GLOSS PAINT

Wash with a warm solution of detergent. Rinse thoroughly with clean water. Prepare walls first, then woodwork. Rub down painted walls with wet and dry wrapped around a sanding block or block of wood. Keep dipping it in water and each time rub it on a piece of soap. This lubricates it and prevents it clogging.

For final rubbing down of woodwork, use fine glasspaper or 400 Grade wet and dry paper, using the paper wet.

EMULSION PAINT

Sponge down with warm water and detergent, then rinse with clean water. Scrape off any areas of loose and flaking paint and rub down with fine glasspaper. Prime bare patches before repainting.

WASHABLE DISTEMPER

Treat washable distemper in the same way as emulsion paint, but rub down loose areas lightly.

NON-WASHABLE DISTEMPER

This finish is usually found on ceilings and must be removed before redecorating. Soak with water several times to loosen the distemper, then scrape it off with a broad stripping knife. Wash thoroughly with clean water. Before decorating, seal porous plaster with oil-based primer.

• STRIPPING WALLPAPER

Ordinary wallpapers can be removed by soaking well with water, with a wallpaper stripper added if necessary. Strip with a wallpaper-stripping knife. Hold the knife at an angle to the wall and avoid digging into the plaster. Commercial wallpaper strippers, such as Polypeel, make the job easier.

Washable wallpapers are difficult to remove. Use a serrated scraper, such as a Skarsten, to score the surface. Then soak, and scrape with a wallpaper-stripping knife or the plain blade of a Skarsten scraper.

Vinyl wallcoverings are removed by lifting the top layer from the backing paper which is stuck to the wall. Prise the vinyl from the backing paper at the bottom corners of each strip and peel off upwards. Remove the backing paper in the same way as ordinary wallpaper.

Rub down walls with glasspaper. Fill cracks with cellulose filler and rub down when dry.

Bare walls to be papered should be sealed with size or the adhesive used to hang the paper. This stops the wall absorbing the paste, and helps the paper to slide into position.

• MAKING GOOD

Blistered paint Cut out blisters with a knife and rub down with glasspaper. Knot and prime and fill with stopping. Use cellulose filler on walls and wood filler on wood. Rub down when dry.

Cracks Rake out all loose material from plaster cracks, dampen each crack and fill with cellulose filler. Fill large cracks in stages; let each layer dry before adding the next. Smooth down the final layer with wet and dry glasspaper. Fill cracks in wood with a wood filler such as Brummer stopping, and rub smooth with glasspaper when the filler is dry.

STRIPPING WITH A BLOWLAMP

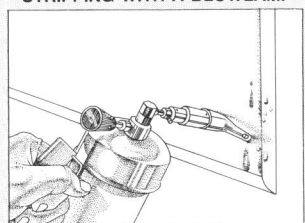

1. Begin stripping the paint from the moulding at the bottom of the door.

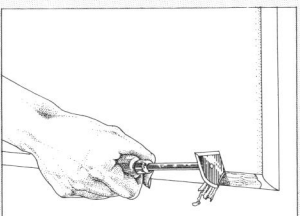

2. Scrape the blistered paint from the moulding with a shavehook.

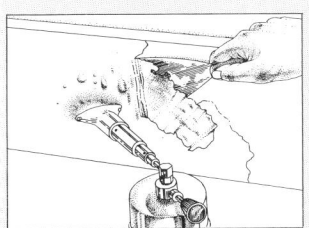

3. Using a scraper, strip the rest of the door. Work from the bottom up.

CHEMICAL STRIPPING

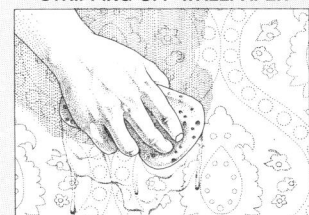

1. Avoid making splashes by applying stripper carefully with a small brush.

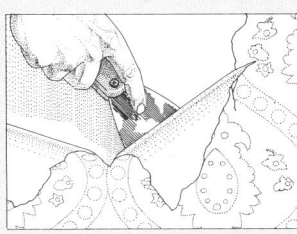

2. Wait until the paint begins to blister before scraping it off with a shavehook.

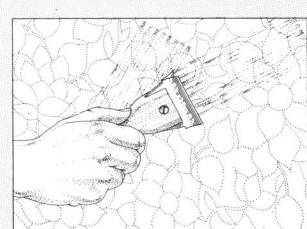

3. Remove all traces of chemical paint remover with white spirit.

STRIPPING OFF WALLPAPER

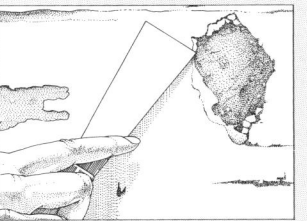

1. Remove the old paper by soaking it well with water or a stripping solution.

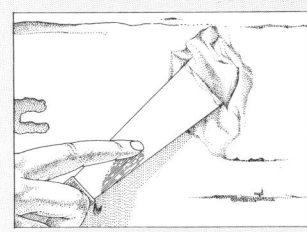

2. Scrape off the paper with a stripping knife, but avoid digging into the wall.

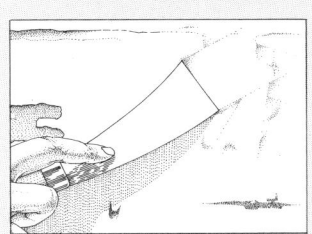

3. To remove a washable paper, score the surface with a serrated scraper first.

FILLING HOLES

1. Scrape off any blistered or flaking paint down to the bare wood.

2. Brush out any loose material and fill. Rub with glasspaper when set.

3. Smooth the final layer down with the filling knife and sand flat when dry.

• PAINTING

Modern tools and materials, such as rollers and paint pads, emulsions and non-drip paints, have helped to make painting one of the easiest jobs – provided a few simple rules are followed.

USING A BRUSH

Unless you are using jelly paint, an overloaded brush will cause drips, sags and runs on the paintwork. To get the correct amount of paint on to your brush, dip it into the paint until about one-third of the bristles are covered. Press the bristles against the inside of the container to force out excess paint. Never draw the bristles across the lip of a container or too much paint will be removed.

When using jelly paint, there is no need to remove excess paint. It will not drip or run.

A piece of string stretched across the mouth of a paint kettle or pot provides a rest for the brush.

Drill a hole through the brush handle so that a piece of wire can be pushed through. If a job using oil paint is halted overnight, the brush can be suspended in a jar of water. The bristles must not rest on the bottom of the jar. Before re-use, shake out the water thoroughly and dry the brush on a dry surface such as a board. The slightest amount of water left in the brush will cause blistering later. Brushes used for emulsion and other water-based paints should be rinsed clean under a running tap for overnight storage.

Never use a brand new brush for top-coat work. Even with a top-quality brush, some bristles will work loose.

USING A ROLLER

Rollers cover large areas such as walls and ceilings quicker than brushes – though they tend to use more paint. They are most suitable for water-based paints, as cleaning them can be tedious if using oil-based paints. Immediately after use the roller must be cleaned.

Lamb's-wool rollers are more expensive than foam rollers, but are the best for all-round use.

Fill the roller tray until the paint comes about one-third of the way up the slope. Load the roller by pushing it backwards and forwards in the paint until covered. To remove excess paint, run it over the 'dry' area.

Follow this order of work:
1. A paint brush is needed to make a neat job of corners; use a 25-50 mm. (1-2 in.) brush.
2. Cover the main part of the surface using the roller in alternate diagonal strokes until the strips of paint are 'interlaced', leaving no bare patches. The roller must not leave the surface suddenly or splashes will result.
3. When laying off, smooth over the paint in straight lines. On ceilings, move the roller in various directions.

USING A PAINT PAD

Walls and ceilings can be quickly and easily painted with pads. A pad consists of a sponge covered with short, mohair bristles held in a plastic cover.

Pads are more economical with paint than brushes or rollers. Various sizes are available.

Though suitable for all types of paint, the largest-size pads are best used only for applying emulsion. Small pads are sold for painting window frames, but these offer no significant advantage over brushes.

To load a pad, immerse the bristles in the paint and remove the excess by pressing against the inside of the container. Use the pad in random directions with overlapping strokes.

PAINTING CEILINGS

Paint a complete room in this order: ceiling, walls, woodwork. Start painting the ceiling by the window. Work continuously; stopping even for short meal breaks will result in a join line showing on the finished surface. Paint in half-metre (2 ft) wide strips, working parallel with the window. Work in sections of about 1 m. (1 yd) along each strip. Do not overlap strips too much.

Start by using the edge of the brush to cut in where the ceiling meets the wall. Turn brush full-face and continue painting the first half-metre strip.

Lay off the paint as you work. That is, smooth over each freshly painted section without reloading the brush, working from a wet edge back into the body of the paint. This technique ensures that all brush marks are obliterated as you go along.

PAINTING WALLS

Allow sufficient time in each work period for one wall to be completed. Leaving a wall half-finished, even for a short break, means that the wet edge will start to dry and a join line will show. Joins in corners will not be noticed.

1. Start by using brush edge-on, where ceiling meets wall near window.

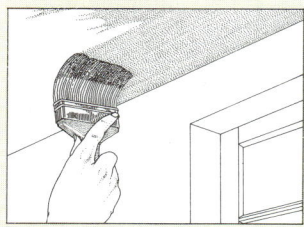

2. Work in 500 mm. wide strips across the ceiling, using the brush full-face.

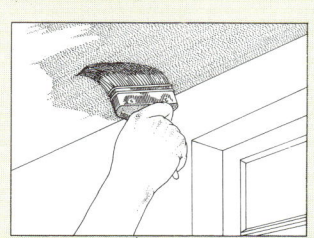

3. Every metre or so, brush back from the wet edge into the body of the paint.

USING GLOSS OR SEMI-GLOSS PAINT

1. Work in sections 600 mm. (2 ft) square. Start at the top right-hand corner of the wall (top left if you are left-handed). Cover the first square with vertical strokes.
2. Cross-brush using horizontal strokes – without reloading.
3. Brush in using vertical strokes; smooth out using horizontal strokes – again without reloading. When the brush glides over the surface, an even paint film will have been applied.
4. Use vertical strokes to lay off the paint – without reloading.

To avoid applying a double thickness of paint at edges of the squares, work towards joins with bristles 'taking off' when the join is reached.

Do not brush undercoat and top coat in opposite directions, otherwise a cross-hatched effect will be produced on the surface.

USING EMULSION

1. Emulsion paint is applied in 200 mm. (8 in.) wide bands of paint,

Order of painting a panelled door

starting the work at the top of the wall.
2. Brush out as for gloss paint; laying off upwards in a criss-cross pattern.

USING JELLY PAINT
Apply a full coat of thixotropic paint and brush it out generously and evenly. Do not overbrush. Follow the gloss or emulsion application method, as appropriate.

PAINTING WOODWORK
When painting woodwork, follow this order of work: windows, picture and chair rails, fireplace, doors and, finally, skirting boards.

On doors, remove all fittings such as handles and finger-plates. Painting round them causes runs.

Paint the panelled doors in the sequence shown. Complete the job in one session; pauses will result in a hard edge that cannot be removed. Do not take too much paint on the brush when working on mouldings – runs will form even with only a slight excess of paint. Glass-panelled doors should be painted in the same

sequence as casement windows.

Paint a flush door in sections, starting at the top and working down. Work continuously – sections must be joined before edges start to dry. Take up fresh paint only when laying on.

There is no need to paint the top edge of an inside door unless it can be overlooked from the stairs.

If only one window of a pair of casements opens, paint the fixed one first, then paint the opening one and finally the frame. Paint the edge of an inward-opening casement the same colour as the inside of the window. Paint the hinged edge to match the outside colour. For an outward-opening casement the reverse applies. Work from the top downwards.

Paint casement windows in this order: (1) the rebates (where the glass joins the wood); (2) the cross-bars; (3) the cross-rails; (4) the hanging stile; (5) the meeting stile; (6) the window-frame. This sequence also applies for metal casements.

If the room is papered with colour-fast paper, brush a 25 mm. (1 in.)

wide strip of glue size on the paper round the frame. Then, if paint gets on the paper it can be wiped off.

When painting sash windows do not paint the cords or they will perish. Thin the paint to cover inside runners – this reduces the risk of sticking. Only the section of the runners visible when the window is open needs to be painted.

To paint a sash window, first pull the bottom sash up and the top sash down – this gives access to the meeting rail. Paint in this order: (1) the

meeting rail, including its bottom edge and rebate; (2) the bars and stiles as far as possible on the top sash; (3) the bottom edge of the bottom sash; (4) the soffit; (5) about 50 mm. (2 in.) down the inside of the outside runners.

Close the window almost completely before painting the top couple of inches of the inside runners (6). Finish off in the same order as for a casement window.

When the outside of the window is painted, you can paint the bottom of

the inside runners (7); and a short way up the inside runners (8).

PAINTING RADIATORS
Allow radiators to cool. If the paintwork is in good condition, wash the surface and apply two coats of gloss if using a matching colour.

Where the colour on the radiator is being changed, wash and rub the metal, touch up with metal primer and apply gloss paint. Do not use an undercoat on a radiator. To avoid runs, load the brush sparingly.

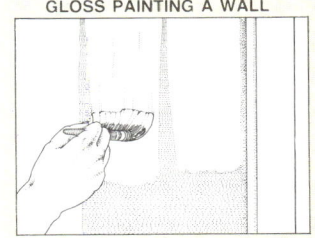

1. Apply gloss paint to the wall, making vertical strokes with the brush.

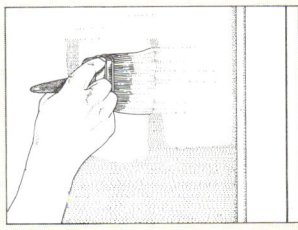

2. Brush over each section of the wall with sideways strokes.

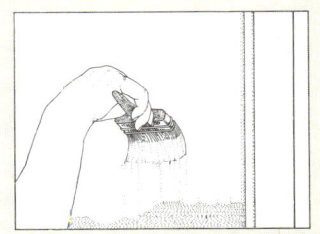

3. After brushing out, work back from the wet edge to the body of the paint.

Order of painting a sash window

Order of painting a casement window

DISGUISING RADIATORS A large radiator can be made relatively unobtrusive if it is painted to tone in with the décor of the room.

• WALLPAPERING

From the first roll of paper cut a length about 100 mm. (4 in.) longer than the height of the wall. The excess allows for trimming. Before cutting a second length, match the pattern with the first [A1]. Continue matching and cutting – allowing .100 mm. excess on each length. Pattern matching at this stage is essential since the sheets will eventually be butt-jointed (laid side by side) on the wall in the order that they are cut from the rolls.

There will be more wastage when matching drop-patterned papers than in matching set patterns. It is often more economical, when you have to match a drop pattern, to work from two rolls of paper at once, taking adjacent lengths alternately from each roll.

Number each length as it is cut, and mark TOP on the back – this will avoid the possibility of a length being hung upside-down or out of sequence.

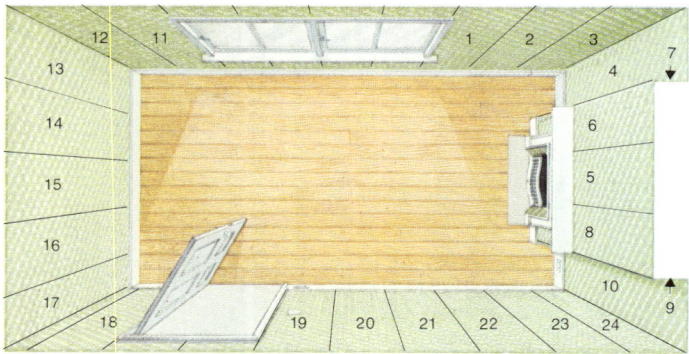

ORDER OF HANGING *Start at the window edge and hang in the order shown.*

Do not throw out odd lengths. Some might fit areas over doors or under windows. Odd pieces can also be stored in case a damaged area needs patching later.

Hang the first length of paper next to the window. Working away from the brightest light source means that should adjoining lengths overlap slightly, a shadow will not be cast, making the overlap more obvious.

Never assume that window or door frames, corners or any other uprights are true verticals against which to align paper – they are almost certain to be out of true.

To establish a true vertical, measure out from the top corner of the window-frame a distance of about 15 mm. ($\frac{1}{2}$ in.) less than the width of the wallpaper you are using.

Suspend a plumb-line from this point and mark the wall at several points exactly behind the line [A2]. Join up the marks with a straight edge.

PASTING

Lay the cut lengths, face down – one piece at a time – on the pasting table, with the ends overhanging the ends of the table. Make sure that they are in numerical order – the first sheet being pasted first. The edge of the top sheet should overlap the side of the table farthest from you by about 5 mm. ($\frac{1}{4}$ in.) to avoid pasting the table.

Dip about one-third of the bristles of the paste brush into the paste; remove excess by pressing against the side of the bucket.

All parts of the back of the paper must be coated with paste – dry patches will not stick to the wall and bubbles will form. Divide the paper into three imaginary strips. First, paste half the central strip [B1].

Then paste strip two – the one farthest from you [B2]. Finish by pulling the paper towards you so that the near edge overhangs the table by about 5 mm.; paste strip three [B3]. Paste the outer strips by brushing towards the edges in herring-bone fashion.

When the first half of the length has been pasted, fold the pasted end into the centre. For easier hanging, make the top fold larger.

Now paste the other half of the length [B4]. When pasted, fold it to centre [B5].

If the paper is a type that requires hanging immediately after pasting, drape the folded length over your arm, with the ends uppermost [B6], and carry it to the wall. If a soaking period is needed, lay the paper to one side on a clean dry surface. Mean-

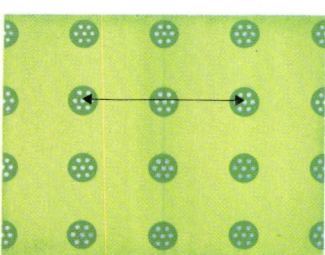

Set pattern

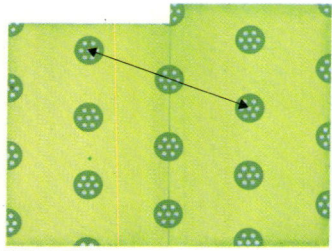

Drop pattern

MATCHING AND MARKING

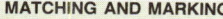
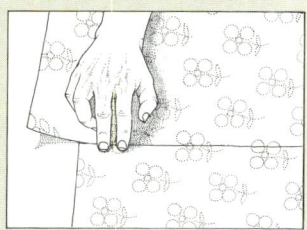

A1. Before cutting a length, match its pattern against the previous piece.

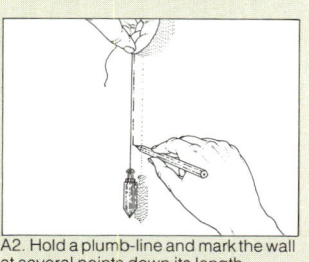

A2. Hold a plumb-line and mark the wall at several points down its length.

PASTING WALLPAPER

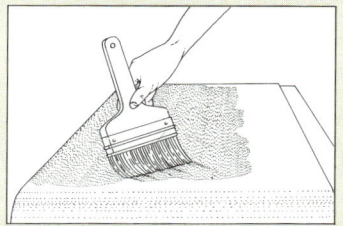

B1. Apply paste halfway down the centre strip of the length of paper.

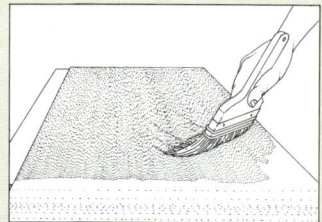

B2. Paste the strip farthest from you. Brush outwards, herringbone fashion.

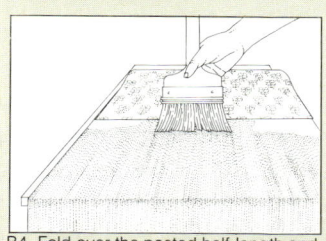

B3. Pull the paper towards you so that it overhangs the table by 5 mm. Paste.

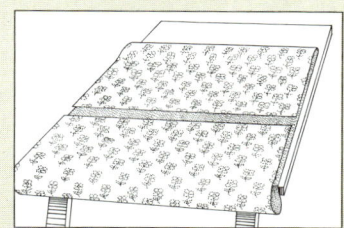

B4. Fold over the pasted half-length and paste the remainder in same way.

B5. Fold the second half, making the top fold larger than the bottom one.

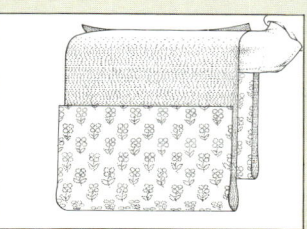

B6. Drape the paper, ends uppermost, over your arm to take it to the wall.

while, paste the next length. While hanging a length, make sure that the next length is soaking for the same time as the previous ones. If paste gets on the patterned side, wipe with a clean, almost dry, sponge.

HANGING

Have a small step stool or hop-up ready to stand on. Unfold the top half of the paper. Position the top edge so that about 25-50 mm. (1-2 in.) overlaps the ceiling for trimming [C1]. Place the right-hand edge against the vertical line marked on the wall. Allow the top fold to drop out gently. Then run the hanging brush down the centre of the sheet first, and brush out towards the edges [C2].

If blisters appear under the paper, this indicates that air bubbles are trapped. Gently peel the paper away from the wall to release the trapped air, then brush the paper back into place.

Run the back of the scissors blade along the paper in the angle of the ceiling and wall. Peel back the paper and carefully cut along the crease. Before brushing back, wipe the ceiling with a damp sponge to remove any paste. Brush the edge back into place to leave a neat finish.

When the top half of the paper is in place, unfurl the lower half [C3] and brush out as before.

Repeat the trimming procedure at the angle of skirting and wall [C4] and along the window frame – should the edge overlap it.

Unfold the top half of the second length and slide it towards the first length so that the adjoining edges of the two lengths butt together. Hang this length in the same way as the first. If the first length was hung vertically, the edge of the bottom half of the second length, when unfurled, will fall neatly into place to form a butt joint.

If the paper curls at the edges, run

an angle roller along the seam. Do not use rollers on embossed patterns.

TURNING A CORNER

No more than 5 mm. of paper should be turned round an internal corner, otherwise it will crease.

Measure the distance from the last length to the corner. Take three measurements, at the top, middle and bottom. Add 5 mm. to the largest measurement and cut this amount from the next pasted length of paper. Keep the matching portion. Hang the first corner piece with its uncut edge adjoining the last complete length [D1]. Hang the other piece of the length on the adjoining wall so that its cut edge overlaps the previous sheet [D2]. Before trimming, drop a plumb-line to make sure that its uncut edge on the adjoining wall is vertical.

The overlapped edges in the corner mean that only about 5 mm. of the pattern will be lost.

HANGING WALLPAPER

C1. Position the paper so that it overlaps the ceiling angle by 25-50 mm.

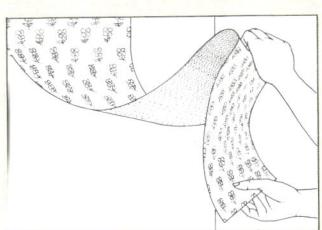

C3. Trim the top edge, then unfurl the bottom half and brush it to the wall.

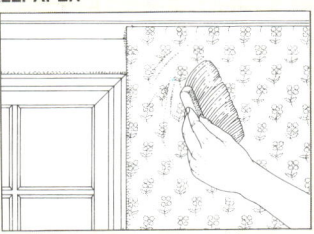

C2. Brush down the centre of the paper, then brush out firmly to each edge.

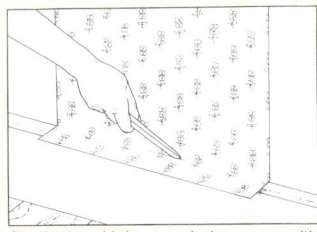

C4. At the skirting, mark the paper with the back of scissors. Peel back and trim.

TURNING A CORNER

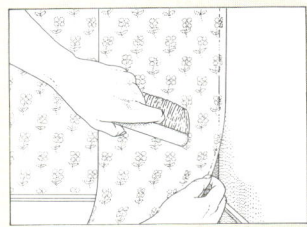

D1. Hang the first strip with its uncut edge next to last full piece of paper.

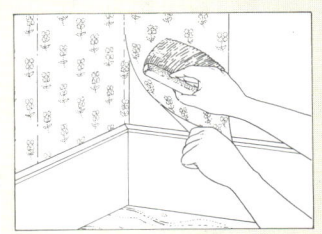

D2. Hang the second piece so its edge overlaps cut edge of first strip.

USING PATTERN A boldly patterned wallpaper adds warmth to a busy hallway where carpets and furniture would be impractical.

• PAPERHANGING PROBLEMS

Places such as chimney breasts and stairwells require extra care when paperhanging because of awkward corners or long drops of paper.

CHIMNEY BREASTS

A chimney breast is usually the focal centre of a room, so a patterned paper – especially one with a large motif – must be hung centrally on this wall. As you work round the room, stop papering when you reach the back corner of the chimney breast. Find the centre of the breast – use a plumb-line to ensure a true vertical – then mark where the edges of the lengths will be to see how the pieces that turn the front corner will fall. Aim to centre the first length on the breast [A1], but if this leaves turns of less than 25 mm. (1 in.) at the corners, matching will be difficult. In this case, butt two lengths to the centre [A2] to give better turns. Hang

the first length, then work back to where papering stopped. Hang the following lengths as shown on p. 62. Those that turn the front corners of the breast are the most difficult to hang.

First, cut a length to allow for a 25 mm. turn round on the external corner down to the skirting board. Retain the matching portion.

Hang the top half of the paper down to the mantelpiece. Do not try to turn the corner with the 25 mm. edge strip – leave it loose.

Press the back of the scissors blade along the back of the mantelpiece to crease a trimming line in the wallpaper. Cut along the line, and also trim off as much waste paper as possible from below the mantelpiece. Aim to leave a surplus edge of about 25 mm. for final trimming.

Take special care when trimming the paper round the fireplace surround; the weight of the paper may cause it to tear. Make scissor snips

and tuck the paper into the moulding at the edge of the mantelpiece [B1]. Work down the surround gradually – creasing and trimming the paper a piece at a time.

Finally, brush out the 25 mm. turn round on to the side of the breast [B2].

SWITCHES

Before papering round a light switch, turn off the electricity at the mains.

There are two types of switches – old-fashioned projecting switches fitted to mountings, and modern flush-mounted switches. The modern switches are simple to tackle. Unscrew the cover plate and trim off the paper 5 mm. ($\frac{1}{4}$ in.) inside the plate area. With projecting switches, press the knob through the paper; make diagonal cross-cuts extending from the knob to about 20 mm. ($\frac{3}{4}$ in.) past each of the four corners of the mounting [C1]. Finally press the scissors blade around the mounting and trim

neatly along the crease lines [C2].

DOORWAYS

Hang the length with the waste area overlapping the door. Press the scissors along the edge of the frame to make a rough trimming line [D1]. Cut out the waste to within about 25 mm. of the frame line. Make a diagonal cut at the top corner to prevent tearing.

Brush the paper into an angle along the top and side of the frame to leave a creased cutting line. Ease the paper off the wall, trim off the waste and brush down the paper [D2].

PAPERING A RECESS

First, paper the inside of the recess, turning a 5 mm. flap on to the outside wall. Overlap the flaps with the paper used on the outside wall [E1].

PAPERING STAIRWELLS

Arrange a working platform as on p. 55. Use a plumb-line to establish a

vertical for the first length on the well wall. Allow for a 5 mm. ($\frac{1}{4}$ in.) edge to turn on to the head wall – the wall facing you as you walk down the main part of the staircase.

The long pieces of paper needed for the well wall may stretch or tear when pasted, so get a helper to support the paper.

• HANGING UNUSUAL MATERIALS

To achieve a special effect, hang one of the more unusual wall coverings instead of paper. Most manufacturers now produce a range of hessians, felts and special, heavy papers in a variety of designs. Hanging techniques for these materials vary.

HESSIAN

There are two types – backed and unbacked – often called prepared hessian and furnishing hessian.

Backed hessian is more expensive. It is specially prepared for use on walls; the paper backing prevents stretching and wrinkling, thus hanging is easier. It is cut, hung and butt-jointed in the same way as wallpaper. Keep the hessian taut during hanging so that the weaving does not distort.

Unbacked hessian has to be hung over a lining paper of the same colour, since it will not obscure sharp differences in colour on the wall.

PAPERING A CHIMNEY BREAST

A1. Centre first length on the chimney breast if this allows corner turns.

A2. Butt two lengths up to the centre line if this gives better turns.

CLEARING THE FIREPLACE

B1. Snip the paper so that it can be brushed neatly up to the moulding.

B2. Brush the turn round the corner. Non-matching patterns will not show.

PAPERING ROUND SWITCHES

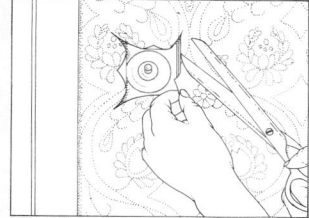

C1. Make diagonal cuts from the centre, past the corners of the switch.

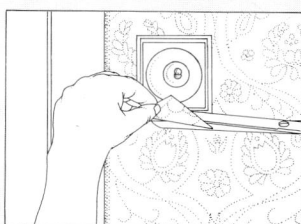

C2. Press the flaps into the edges and trim neatly along the crease lines.

PAPERING ROUND DOORWAYS

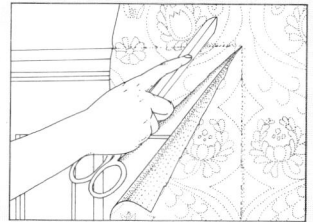

D1. Rub the scissors gently over the overlapping paper to get a crease line.

D2. Ease the paper away from the wall, trim and brush it down into place.

PAPERING A RECESS

E1. Cover the flaps of the interior paper with the short pieces above the recess.

Before either type is hung, the wall must be clean. Strip off any existing wall covering and prepare the wall as for wallpapering.

The manufacturers of backed hessian recommend adhesives and give instructions on how to apply them. Hang unbacked types with heavy-duty wallpaper paste applied to the wall and evened out with a foam roller. Some manufacturers recommend also pasting the back of the hessian.

If any adhesive gets on the face of the hessian, wipe it off with a damp cloth before it dries.

To hang unbacked hessian, position the first strip in a corner. Measure out from the corner a distance 25 mm. (1 in.) less than the width of the hessian. Then, using a plumb-line, chalk a vertical line on the wall at this point.

Cut each length of hessian 50 mm. (2 in.) oversize to allow for a 25 mm. trim at the ceiling and skirting level.

Hang the first length with its edge aligned with the chalk line. Starting from the top of the wall, pat the hessian down gently with your hand, working it into the corner and down.

Finally, smooth the fabric with a clean paint roller, working from the centre. Be careful with unbacked material since it stretches easily and the weave will become distorted.

Hang the second length with a 25 mm. overlap on the first [F1]. Hang and trim succeeding lengths in the same way. However, do not finish the joins until the adhesive on the main surface of the material has dried – there is certain to be some shrinkage.

Next, using a sharp knife against a straight edge, cut through both thicknesses of hessian at the overlap [F2]. Peel off the waste [F3], apply paste to the wall beneath the flaps, then press edges into place [F4].

DECORATIVE FELT

The weight of felt causes the main problem when hanging. This can be overcome by using narrower strips – involving a lot more cutting and joining – or by supporting the roll on a batten between two step-ladders.

With this method, first cut a strip the height of the wall, with an extra 50 mm. (2 in.) for shrinkage and trimming. Roll it on to a batten. Apply the adhesive to the wall.

With the roll supported parallel to the wall and as much as possible of the fabric unfurled, start pressing the material from the bottom upwards, smoothing it with a paint roller. Make joins in the same way as for unbacked hessian. To disguise the joins brush up the nap at the edges.

SUPAGLYPTA

After preparing the surface as for wallpaper, rub down with abrasive paper to form a key.

To make the heavy, embossed lengths of Supaglypta more supple for hanging, dampen them lightly on the back and leave for 15-20 minutes before pasting. Soak each piece for the same length of time to ensure that they stretch evenly. Apply the paste to the paper, not the wall.

LOW-RELIEF ANAGLYPTA

Treat as paper, but if the wall is in poor condition fill any cracks and hang lining paper (using a starch or flour paste). For the Anaglypta use a thick, starch paste. Soak for five minutes, then smooth carefully on to the wall with a brush, not a roller.

VINYL

Prepare the wall as for paper. Do not allow the Vinyl lengths to soak after pasting. Butt-join edges. Where overlaps cannot be avoided – at corners for example – use a latex adhesive to stick down the overlapping edge to the piece underneath.

JOINING HESSIAN

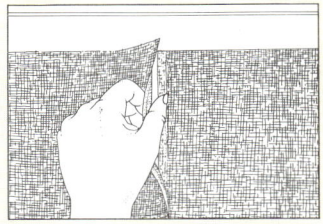

F1. Hang each strip of hessian so that it overlaps the previous one by 25 mm.

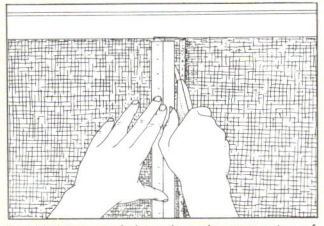

F2. Hold a straight edge down centre of overlap and cut through both pieces.

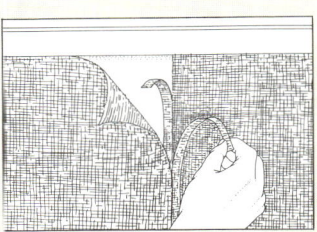

F3. Peel back both strips of hessian and remove the waste that has been cut off.

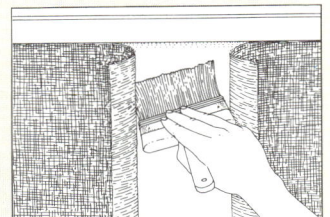

F4. With the hessian folded back, apply paste to the wall. Press hessian down.

A BROWN STUDY Hessian gives a wall an expensive, textured look. The rich and varied colours available will add warmth and depth to a room.

WALL-COVERING SUPPORT To support heavy rolls of felt or hessian, push a batten through the roll and suspend it securely between two step-ladders.

• CERAMIC TILING

Builders' merchants and do-it-yourself shops stock a wide selection of tiles. Most tiles have built-in spacer lugs on their edges to ensure accurate spacing, and modern adhesives make fixing simple.

Plain tiles are available in many colours and tones to match popular colours in sanitary ware.

Textured tiles are produced in a matching range of colours and give different effects. Though these tiles can be used to cover all the walls, they are more often used to give a textured surface to a particular area.

Patterned tiles are available in a wide range of colourful modern and traditional designs.

Heat-resistant tiles are used for areas where surface temperatures are over 150°C (302°F) – fireplace surrounds and areas around solid-fuel cookers.

TILE SHAPES

Three shapes of tile are used in most do-it-yourself jobs. Field tiles are used on the bulk of the area. They have square set edges and most have spacer lugs. Some special-purpose field tiles have no spacer lugs so, to ensure accurate spacing, use matchsticks in the joints to hold the tiles in position until the adhesive dries. This applies to both RE and REX tiles.

RE tiles are used around the perimeter of tiled areas. They have one rounded edge to ensure a neat finish. REX tiles have rounded adjacent edges and are used at external corners in the top row of tiles.

ADHESIVES AND GROUT

Special adhesive is used to fix the tiles; grout is for filling in between tile joints. Most adhesives are ready for use, but some have to be mixed.

Use thin-bed adhesive on smooth,

—Spacer lugs

FIELD TILES
When fixing these, make sure that the spacer lugs on adjoining tiles touch

RE TILES
These have one rounded edge to finish off the borders of tiled areas

REX TILES
These have two rounded edges and are used to finish off corners

level surfaces Spread it on the surface and comb it out in a layer 1.5-3 mm. ($\frac{1}{16}$ - $\frac{1}{8}$ in.) thick.

Use thick-bed adhesive for rough and uneven surfaces.

Water-resistant adhesive is used to fix tiles in shower cubicles and anywhere else that water accumulates. Spread the adhesive in a smooth layer about 3 mm. ($\frac{1}{8}$ in.) thick; do not use a notched trowel. Allow at least 14 days after grouting before the shower is used.

Heat-resistant adhesive is used with heat-resistant tiles.

Grout is a cement-based material. Mix it according to directions on the packet. Use a water-resistant type of grout around sinks, basins and other places where water normally collects on tiled areas.

ACCESSORIES

Most tile manufacturers produce a range of bathroom accessories such as soap dishes and toilet-roll holders. These can be used like tiles since their bases have the same dimensions as tiles. Ceramic edging-cove seals the gap between bath and wall. Produced in colours to match the tiles, cove comes in packs containing sufficient pieces to complete an average-sized bath. Included are two finishing pieces with round ends and four pieces with pre-cut mitres for neat corners. A special rubber-based

adhesive is supplied in the pack; this adhesive is flexible to allow for normal movement of the bath, which would cause ordinary adhesive to crack.

PREPARING THE SURFACE

Always lay tiles on a clean, flat, dry and firm surface.

Plaster Allow one month for new plaster to dry out before tiling. Old, loose plaster must be hacked out and the

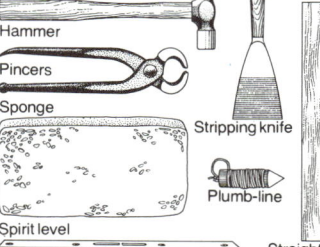

Notched trowel

Metal spreader

Tile cutter

Hammer

Pincers

Sponge

Spirit level

Carborundum stone

Stripping knife

Plumb-line

Straight edge

TOOLS FOR TILING Essential items are the trowel, cutter and pincers.

area dusted to remove loose particles. Treat porous or dusty plaster with a solvent-based primer (such as Bal-Primer) to prevent liquid in the tile adhesive being absorbed too quickly.

Paint A sound coat makes a suitable base for tiles. If in doubt, strip off paint with a sanding disc. Do not use a chemical stripper. Do not use solvent-based adhesives when tiling over paint (see chart on p. 57).

Old ceramic tiles These provide a good base for new tiles, provided they are flat and soundly fixed. Repair chipped or broken tiles with sand and cement or adhesive. Re-fix loose tiles. Wash the surface thoroughly to remove dirt or grease.

Building boards (plywood, blockboard, chipboard) Tiles can be hung on boards that have been braced properly to prevent movement or warping. Seal the back and sides of

the boards with paint undercoat to prevent moisture penetration. If a board has a rough side, make this the working surface – it will provide better adhesion. Screw the boards to a framework of timbers 75 × 50 mm. (3 × 2 in.) spaced at 300 mm. (12 in.) centres, both horizontally and vertically. Brush and wash the surface before tiling.

TOOLS

Plastic or metal spreader This is used for combing out the adhesive on the working surface. On large areas, a notched trowel makes the job easier.

Tile cutter A tile cutter is a scriber with a tungsten-carbide tip. It is used to score a line in the tile which is then broken. An Oporto tile cutter both scores and cuts the tile.

Tile nippers Special tile nippers can be bought, though ordinary pincers

---

COLLECTING TILES

In the mid-19th century, Victorians began to adorn their houses and public buildings with tiles. To meet the demand for these decorative objects, British pottery firms began developing methods for mass-producing tiles. The height of the fashion for tiles was reached in the 1870s, when the transfer-printed kinds (shown below) were manufactured. Popular motifs included plants and flowers and scenes from poems and plays. Some are complete in themselves; others form a pattern over several tiles. Many of the tiles are inexpensive and easy to find in antique shops and markets. But hand-painted tiles of artists such as William De Morgan (1839-1917) command high prices. The strange sailing craft that appears on the De Morgan tile, above, was one of its creator's favourite motifs.

will usually do the job just as well.
Carborundum stone This is used to smooth the rough edges of cut tiles.
Sponge A synthetic sponge is best for working the grout into the joints between the tiles.

In addition you will need a hammer, plumb-line, spirit level, straight-edge and stripping knife.

• PLANNING AND TILING

Plan the layout so that odd spaces are taken up by cut tiles at the ends of the walls, not in the middle. Place cut tiles at the back of window ledges and recesses.

Before starting to tile, find the lowest point on the floor line or skirting. Nail a wooden batten to the wall with its upper edge a tile width above this point. Check that it is horizontal, using a spirit level. Continue the batten around any other walls to be tiled.

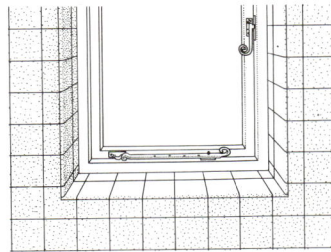

Arranging tiles around a window.

Using a spirit level or plumb-line, draw a vertical guide on the wall at the point where you intend to start tiling. Nail a batten on this vertical guide. Check the junction of the two battens by placing a few tiles loosely in position. The tiles must sit perfectly square in the angle of the battens.

Spread adhesive over about 1 sq. m. (1 sq. yd) of the wall in the angle formed by the two battens. Comb the adhesive with the notched spreader, pressing hard on the wall.

CUTTING L-SHAPED TILES

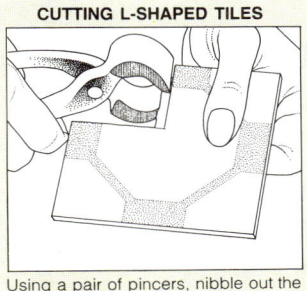

Using a pair of pincers, nibble out the waste in small pieces.

In confined spaces where combing is not possible, spread the adhesive on to the back of the tile. Press each tile in position on the wall with a slight twisting action, ensuring that spacer lugs of adjoining tiles contact each other. Use matchsticks for spacers if tiles do not have spacer lugs. Check the vertical and horizontal

TILING A SURFACE

1. Use a notched trowel to spread the adhesive in ridges across the surface.

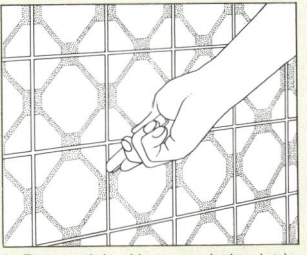

2. Start tiling where the battens meet, and work in horizontal rows.

USING A HORIZONTAL BATTEN

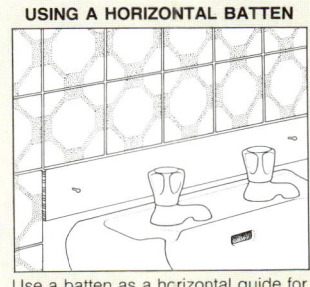

Use a batten as a horizontal guide for positioning tiles above uneven edges.

edges of each square metre of tiles with a spirit level to ensure accuracy before spreading more adhesive. Complete the main area of tiling on the first wall (using whole tiles) before cutting tiles to fit odd spaces.

Allow the adhesive 24 hours to set before filling the joints with grout. Rub it into the joints with a damp sponge,

FILLING THE GAPS WITH GROUT

1. After the adhesive has set, use a sponge to rub grout into the gaps.

2. Run a stick with a rounded point in the joints to give a smooth finish.

FITTING TILES ON LEDGES

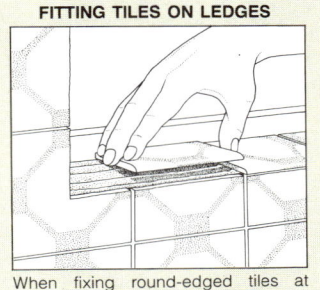

When fixing round-edged tiles at ledges, allow for covering tile edges.

and remove the excess adhesive after it has started to dry.

Work in areas of about 1 sq. m. or the grout may dry before the excess can be cleaned off. Rub a stick with a rounded point along each joint to leave a smooth finish. When the grout is dry, remove the battens and finish tiling in the gaps.

CUTTING TILES TO FIT CORNERS

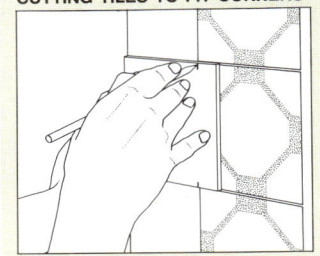

1. Hold the tile to the space, mark the line to be cut, score the glazed side.

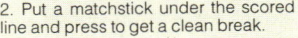

2. Put a matchstick under the scored line and press to get a clean break.

CUTTING TILES

To tile the area outside the battens it may be necessary to cut tiles. Measure each tile for cutting by holding it against the wall, back to front over the space it is to fill. Mark on it the position of the edges of the preceding tile in the row.

Transfer the marks to the face of the tile and score a line across the glazed surface with the cutter. Place a matchstick under the tile, along the line of the cut. Press down gently on the corners of the tile until it snaps along the scored line.

An Oporto tile cutter has a cutting wheel for scoring. It can also be used to break the tile. Smooth the cut edge and fix the tile so that the cut edge sits in the corner of the wall.

CUTTING L-SHAPED TILES

First make a cardboard template of the required shape and transfer this to the glazed surface of the tile. Score the glazed surface, following the marked line closely. Use nippers or pincers to nibble away the waste area. Smooth the cut edges before fixing the tile.

To fit tiles around a pipe projecting from a wall, first cut the tile in half. From each cut edge, mark and cut a semi-circle to fit the pipe. Follow the same techniques as for cutting an L-shaped tile.

POINTS TO BEAR IN MIND

The top edges of sinks, baths and window frames are seldom level. Fix a wooden batten at the height of the nearest line of tiles above the fixture to act as a horizontal guide and support for the tiles above while the adhesive sets. Remove the battens later and cut the tiles to fit the space below.

When measuring RE tiles, allow for the thickness of the tile and the adhesive on the other side of the angle.

WINDOWS, CURTAINS AND BLINDS

Curtains often contribute more to the atmosphere of a room than any other item of furnishing. To create a feeling of formality, use plain, heavy curtains that drape to the floor. By contrast, short curtains made of light, brightly patterned fabric, give a room a relaxed and informal appearance.

A small kitchen, bathroom or dormer window can be made to appear light and colourful by using a blind or a thin, bright curtain fabric. Large windows can make an impact with bold colour or be understated, accenting instead the light they let in or the view they reveal. A window with a poor aspect can be transformed with colourful fabric. One with an unattractive shape can be disguised with curtaining hung beyond the frame – giving an illusion of width.

• FABRICS AND MATERIALS

Most cottons and linen fabrics are ideal for curtains, as they are hard-wearing, easy to clean and economical. It is advisable not to use ticking (a type of linen) for it fades quickly especially in a south-facing room exposed to strong sunlight.

Thin cotton, towelling and plastic-coated materials are ideally suited to bathroom and kitchen windows.

Where as much light as possible is needed as well as privacy, sheers and semi-sheers are a good choice. For heavier curtains, textured fabrics – slubs and bouclés – are effective. Remember that heavier curtains can obscure the window when drawn back. Tie-backs help to overcome this. Alternatively, carry the curtain track across the wall and use the curtains as wall-hangings.

For more formal curtains, velvets, cords, satins and velours are suitable fabrics. Silk makes luxurious curtains, but will eventually rot when exposed to direct sunlight. Most materials are affected by sunlight, so curtains made from expensive or printed fabrics, especially on large windows, should always be lined.

DO-IT-YOURSELF CURTAINS

The essential aids for making your own curtains, available from furnishing shops, are heading tapes and curtain weights. Weights can be individual circular weights, or long strips, inserted into the bottom hem to make the curtain hang properly.

The first stage is to decide which style of heading to use. Next measure the window for the length and width of the curtains. These measurements and the type of heading give the amount of curtain widths required, as shown in the chart on p. 71. If your fabric has a large pattern, extra material will be needed when joining widths (see p. 290).

LINING AND INTERLINING

Cotton sateen lining makes curtains thicker and warmer, and protects the curtains against dirt and fading.

An alternative to sewing lining to the wrong side of the curtain is to make a detachable lining, which can be hooked to the heading tape of the curtain. Such a lining can be taken down and washed independently.

Interlining is a layer of material, usually bump, sewn between the curtain and lining. It creates heavy, thick curtains, ideal for large windows, especially as they prevent some heat loss. As bump can only be dry-cleaned, make sure the curtain fabric can also be dry-cleaned.

A finished full-drape length of interlined curtains will increase by about 2.5 cm. (1 in.) after hanging. Allow for this when measuring.

READY-MADE CURTAINS

Unlined ready-made curtains are inexpensive. They are also quick and easy to put up. Although made in a large range of widths, they come only in three standard lengths, 136, 182 and 228 cm. (54, 72 and 90 in.).

The more expensive ready-made curtains have linings attached. It is possible to buy separate linings to attach to ready-made unlined curtains. The most common headings for ready-made curtains are simple gathers or pencil pleats.

MADE-TO-MEASURE CURTAINS

Have the curtains made by specialists for windows which are an awkward shape, or especially large, or if you want a complicated pleated effect used with expensive curtaining fabric. Most department stores and furnishing shops will send somebody to measure and give an estimate.

Made-to-measure curtains are, of course, more expensive than any other type. They may seem short at first, as the material needs to hang for some weeks before slight creases completely disappear.

• HEADING TAPES

Heading tapes, which carry the curtain hooks, also form the curtains into

Draped curtains, neatly hooked back, soften the lines of a round window.

Beaded curtains for hot weather let the air in and help to keep insects out.

Panel shutters in natural wood can often look attractive when left uncurtained.

Curtains of sheer fabrics give privacy while at the same time letting in light.

the pleats and gathers. Standard tape, which can be bought in various colours, gives a gathered effect and is suitable for all weights of curtains. For nets and sheers there is a lightweight standard tape, which does not show through thin fabric. Standard tapes are reversible, and the pockets for the hooks are formed when the cords which gather the tape are pulled.

Pencil-pleat tapes are made in a mixture of stiffened fabrics for normal curtaining fabrics, and in thin lightweight fabric, stiff enough to hold the pleats in shape, for nets and sheer curtain fabrics.

Most pencil-pleat tapes are not reversible; the pockets for the hooks are on one side only. For tracks fitted less than 7.5 cm. (3 in.) below the ceiling, sew the tape so that the pockets run along the top. If the track is more than 7.5 cm. below the ceiling, fit the tape with the pockets at the bottom.

Fanned pinch pleat tapes come in two depths: 38 mm. (1½ in.) and 89 mm. (3½ in.). If making curtains to hang under a decorative rail or decorative pole, buy underslung, fan-ned pinch pleat tape. If the curtains are to go in front of the track, buy ordinary fanned pinch pleat tape.

A simple gather tape is available for sewing to a separate curtain lining. The lining, gathered to fit the curtaining, can then be hooked to the curtain tape. This makes the lining easy to detach for separate laundering.

All heading tapes are pre-shrunk and can be used with any curtain fabric. When washing, remove the hooks and pull out the pleats and gathers. This ensures that all the curtaining is evenly cleaned. For this reason take care not to cut the cords in the tape, except at the ends where they must be knotted after the tape is cut to length.

The hooks, which connect the curtains to the gliders on the track, are made to match the curtain tape. Plastic hooks are suitable for nets and medium-weight fabrics. For heavy curtains, use rust-proof metal hooks.

If hanging thin fabrics and nets from wires or spring-tension rods, heading tapes are unnecessary. Make the headings by sewing a 5 cm. (2 in.) deep hem along the top.

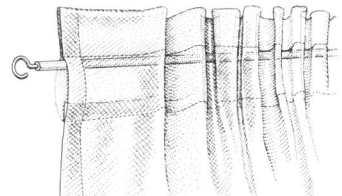

Curtain wires are slotted into open hems.

Machine down one side, closing the hem for 2.5 cm. then sew along the centre of the hem and up the second side. Insert the wire or rod into the open hem space.

SEWING A STANDARD HEADING TAPE ON TO A CURTAIN

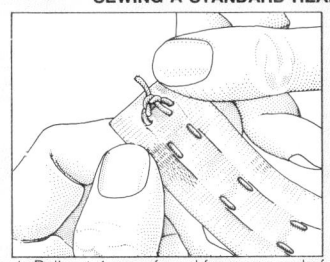

1 Pull out 4 cm. of cord from one end of the tape. Knot the cord. Trim the 4 cm. of tape, without cutting the cord. Turn under this end of tape, enclosing the knot in the turn-under. At the other end of the tape, pull out 4 cm. of cord and turn under the tape, leaving the cord free. Place the top edge of the tape 4 cm. below the top of the curtain.

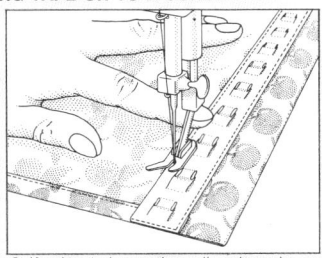

2. If using a decorative rail, pole, valance or pelmet, align the top of the tape with the top of the curtain. To hide the track, fit the tape about 4 cm. below the curtain top. Pin and tack in place. Machine close to the tacks, keeping the stitches outside the cord. Sew each row of stitches in the same direction to prevent the tape distorting the fabric.

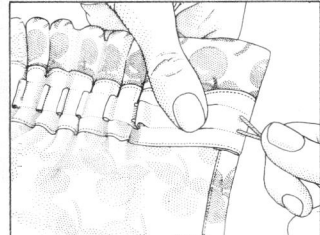

3. Hold the exposed cords in one hand. With the other hand, gather up the curtain, so that it is about 7.5 cm. longer than half the length of the rail. Knot the exposed cords flush to the tape to hold the gathers in place.

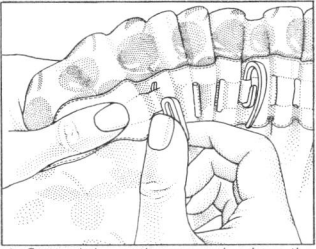

4. Spread the gathers evenly along the width of the curtain. Insert the hooks into the pockets in the tape, formed when the cord was pulled, at 7.5 cm. intervals. Wind surplus cord round a cord tidy. Repeat on the second curtain.

PENCIL-PLEATS

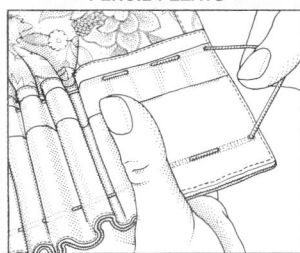

1. Trim the tape and prepare the cords as for a gathered tape. Pin and tack the tape to the reverse side of the curtain, 3 mm. below the top edge, with the tape pockets uppermost. Machine along the top, bottom and sides of the tape, stitching the top and bottom in the same direction to prevent the tape distorting the curtain fabric.

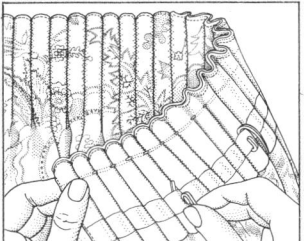

2. Hold the free cords in one hand and gather the curtain to the other end. Pull out the curtain to the required width with gathers even. Tie a knot in the cords to hold the tape in place. Insert hooks each end and 7.5 cm. apart.

DETACHABLE-LINING TAPE

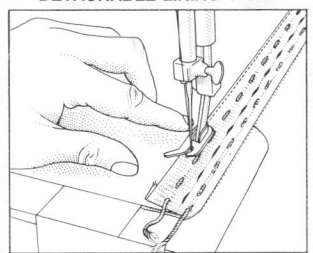

1. Trim the tape and prepare the cords as for a gathered tape. Slot the top of the lining into the fold in the tape. Align the side hems of the lining with the ends of the tape and pin in place. Machine over the knotted end of the tape, then along the bottom edges of the tape. Cut the lining so that the sides are enclosed inside the fold in the tape.

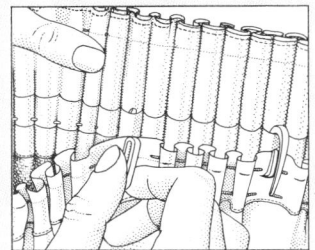

2. Gather the lining to the required width to fit the curtain. Knot the cords to keep the gathers in place. Insert hooks every 7.5 cm. into the holes in the top of the lining tape and through the pockets in the curtain-heading tape.

FANNED PINCH PLEATS

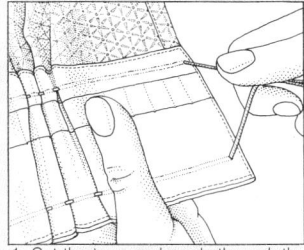

1. Cut the tape and cords through the first group of pleats. Turn the ends, knotting the cords at one end. Lay the tape 3 mm. from the top of the curtain with the ends flush with the sides of the curtain. Tack and machine in place along the top and bottom edges of the tape. A stitching guideline is marked along the bottom of the tape.

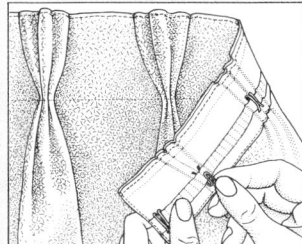

2. Hold the free cords in one hand. Push the curtain into fanned pleats. Tighten the pleats to adjust the width of the curtain in order to fit the track. Insert the hooks at each group of pleats and at the ends of the tape.

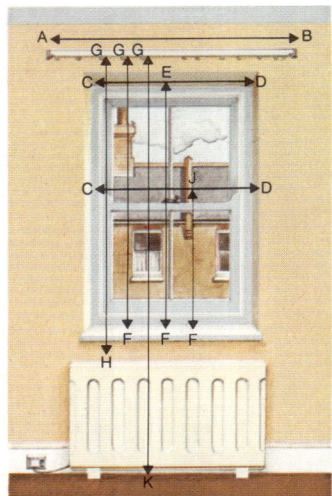

• MEASURING WINDOWS FOR CURTAINS

The first step in calculating the amount of curtain fabric needed is to measure the window. The diagram above shows the basic measurements for different types of curtains.

FOR CURTAINS OUTSIDE THE WINDOW RECESS

Take the following measurements:
Width: A to B, the length of track, whether fitted to wall or ceiling. For a short curtain measure the length from G to H – the hooking point on the track to the top of a radiator. This measurement also applies for sill-length curtains which hang clear of the sill. For a curtain that hangs to the sill measure G to F – a point 5 mm. (¼ in.) above the sill. For a floor-length curtain measure G to K – a point 2.5 cm. (1 in.) above the floor, or 5 mm. above the carpet.

FOR CURTAINS INSIDE THE WINDOW RECESS

Measure the width from C to D. This is the full width of the recess, the length of the wire or rod for nets and café

curtains. The length is measured from E to F, from the curtain hanging point to 5 mm. above the sill; or, for café curtains, from J to F, from the hanging point to 5 mm. above sill.

BUYING THE FABRIC

Using the measuring guide, take the measurements suitable for the type of curtain you wish to fit.

To all length measurements, add a total of 30 cm. (12 in.) to allow for hems, headings and possible shrinkage. In addition, add the length of the pattern repeat if choosing a patterned fabric. Avoid patterns which need matching at the side (see p. 290).

The chart on the next page gives the lengths of material to buy, the number of widths to cut from it, and the length of heading tape required. If your track width falls between two measurements work on the larger.

Nets are made in widths ranging from 120 cm. (48 in.) to 4.3 m. (14 ft 2 in.), so it is possible to make one curtain to fit almost any width of window. Buy whichever width is nearest to one and a half times the length of the track to which they are to be fixed. If using gathered heading tape, buy it the same length as the net width.

• CURTAIN FITTINGS

The support from which the curtains hang should overlap both sides of the window recess. The size of the overlap depends on the width of the window, ranging from 15 cm. (6 in.) on a window 60-100 cm. (24-40 in.) wide, to 45 cm. (18 in.) on a window more than 3.5 m. (12 ft) wide. Thick fabrics need even more overlap, or the window will be partly obscured when the curtains are drawn back.

Decide whether you want a cording control to open and close the curtains. These are useful for tall windows in awkward positions, and also

save the curtains from dirt and wear through constant handling.

Tracks, or rails, are the most widely used supports. The majority are now made of plastic or plastic-covered metal. They are made in a great range of sizes, from 100 cm. (40 in.) to more than 5 m. (16 ft 4 in.). If the exact length you require is not available, buy a longer size and cut to length.

Metal rails are probably best for carrying the heaviest curtains. Plastic rails are pliable enough to bend round the corners of bays, providing the radius of the bend is at least 20 cm. (8 in.) for deep heading rails. Narrower rails can go round tighter bends – down to 12.5 cm. (5 in.) radius. Most rails should have brackets 2.5-5 cm. (1-2 in.) from each end; and at intervals of 30-75 cm. (12-30 in.).

Extension brackets, which extend the rail out from the wall beyond sills and radiators, are available for most tracks. Extension brackets can also be used to carry a second rail. This enables a track carrying nets to run inside a track carrying curtains. Valance brackets are available to hold a valance rail outside a curtain rail.

Where right-angles are unavoidable, a corner joining piece is available for some rails. This makes the fitting look neater, but the gliders which carry the curtains are unable to negotiate the angle.

For thick curtains, it may be necessary to have an overlap at the centre of the window so that there is no gap when the curtains are drawn across.

Net curtains are better fitted to rods, since bare metal curtain wires do not allow nets to move easily and can damage the fabric. However, plastic-coated wires are easy to put up and will not tear the fabric.

Spring-tension rods are easy to use with nets in a recess. These are 19 mm. (¾ in.) in diameter and fit into

the slot headings of net curtains. The rods adjust within four ranges: 40.5-61 cm. (16-24 in.), 56-91.5 cm. (22-36 in.), 91.5-152.5 cm. (36-60 in.) and 120-183 cm. (48-72 in.). The rods are adjusted to slightly more than the width of the recess, then compressed to fit the recess. When the rod expands, it holds firm against the sides.

On most rails, the gliders, into which the curtain hooks fit, run along a track which is either behind or at the bottom of the rail. Some gliders are now designed to hook straight into the heading tape. These gliders have an extra eyelet to which a separate lining can be attached. Use about four gliders to each 30 cm. of rail.

To make gliders run smoothly, wash the track and gliders with soapy

water when curtains are laundered. Rub silicone polish on the track.

Most of the basic rails have a range of decorative versions and there are even rails made to look like brass poles. The pole facing conceals tracks along which run semi-circular gliders. Some models are internally corded. Poles will fit windows from 75 cm. (30 in.) to 6.75 m. (22 ft 6 in.).

Curtain poles in metal or wood are easy to fit. They are available in almost any length and several diameters from 2.5-4.5 cm. (1-1¾ in.). They have matching rings, of which four should be used for every 30 cm. of pole. Poles up to 3-4 m. (10-13 ft) long need only two end brackets. Anything longer needs a third support at the middle.

Curtain poles carried on brackets

DRAMATIC EFFECT Boldly patterned curtains give impact to a plain room.

have decorative finials at the ends. However, poles can be run from wall to wall, or across a recess, with the ends carried in cup fittings.

SECURING CURTAIN TRACKS

Most tracks can be fitted to either walls or ceilings. Check the load-bearing capacity of the wall or ceiling (see p. 109), then mark the bracket positions by pushing a bradawl through the holes in the brackets. Drill holes for the screws, using a masonry bit on reinforced concrete. Plug the holes (see p. 353). Assemble the track, following the manufacturer's instructions. Fit the track into the brackets. Adjust until the same length of track overlaps the window at each side. Tighten the screw in each bracket to secure the track in place.

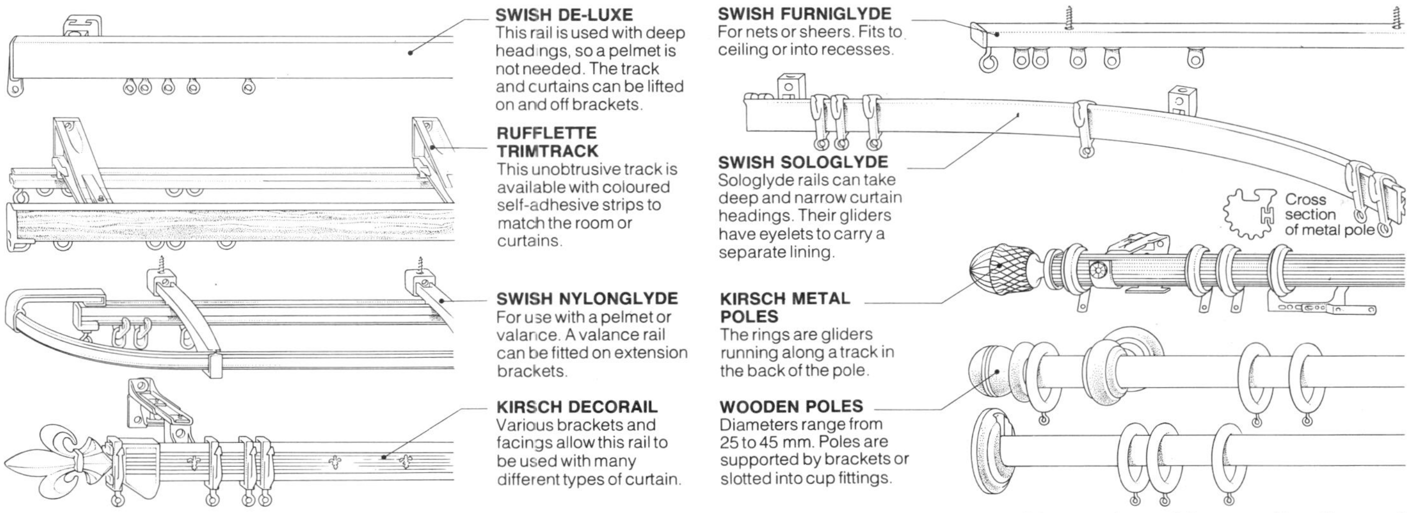
SWISH DE-LUXE
This rail is used with deep headings, so a pelmet is not needed. The track and curtains can be lifted on and off brackets.
RUFFLETTE TRIMTRACK
This unobtrusive track is available with coloured self-adhesive strips to match the room or curtains.
SWISH NYLONGLYDE
For use with a pelmet or valance. A valance rail can be fitted on extension brackets.
KIRSCH DECORAIL
Various brackets and facings allow this rail to be used with many different types of curtain.
SWISH FURNIGLYDE
For nets or sheers. Fits to ceiling or into recesses.
SWISH SOLOGLYDE
Sologlyde rails can take deep and narrow curtain headings. Their gliders have eyelets to carry a separate lining.
Cross section of metal pole
KIRSCH METAL POLES
The rings are gliders running along a track in the back of the pole.
WOODEN POLES
Diameters range from 25 to 45 mm. Poles are supported by brackets or slotted into cup fittings.

CHOOSING CURTAIN TRACKS The choice of track or pole depends on the window and décor of the room, the size of the curtains and the type of heading used.

CURTAIN FABRIC AND HEADING GUIDE

These tables show the amount of plain fabric needed for different sizes of curtain. Read across the curtain-length column and down the track-length column. The indicated figure in metres/yards shows the total amount of fabric for the number of widths shown in the second horizontal column, and includes allowances for hems, headings and shrinkage. If using a patterned fabric, multiply the depth of the pattern by the number of widths, and add to the total.

GATHERED

Track length	m. ft	1.52 (5)	1.83 (6)	2.13 (7)	2.44 (8)	2.74 (9)	3.05 (10)	3.35 (11)	3.66 (12)	3.96 (13)	4.27 (14)
No. of 120 cm. (48 in.) widths	m. yds	2	3	3	3	4	4	4	5	5	6
Curtain 1.22 m. length (48 in.)	m. yds	2.97 (3¼)	4.27 (4⅔)	4.27 (4⅔)	4.27 (4⅔)	5.72 (6¼)	5.72 (6¼)	5.72 (6¼)	7.32 (8)	7.32 (8)	8.53 (9¼)
Curtain 1.37 m. length (54 in.)	m. yds	3.20 (3½)	4.80 (5¼)	4.80 (5¼)	4.80 (5¼)	6.40 (7)	6.40 (7)	6.40 (7)	7.92 (8⅔)	7.92 (8⅔)	9.45 (10⅓)
Curtain 1.52 m. length (60 in.)	m. yds	3.60 (4)	5.18 (5⅔)	5.18 (5⅔)	5.18 (5⅔)	7.01 (7⅔)	7.01 (7⅔)	7.01 (7⅔)	8.69 (9½)	8.69 (9½)	10.36 (11⅓)
Curtain 1.83 m. length (72 in.)	m. yds	4.11 (4½)	6.10 (6⅔)	6.10 (6⅔)	6.10 (6⅔)	8.23 (9)	8.23 (9)	8.23 (9)	10.29 (11¼)	10.29 (11¼)	12.19 (13⅓)
Curtain 2.13 m. length (84 in.)	m. yds	4.80 (5¼)	7.01 (7⅔)	7.01 (7⅔)	7.01 (7⅔)	9.37 (10¼)	9.37 (10¼)	9.37 (10¼)	11.66 (12¾)	11.66 (12¾)	14.02 (15⅓)
Curtain 2.44 m. length (96 in.)	m. yds	5.48 (6)	7.92 (8⅔)	7.92 (8⅔)	7.92 (8⅔)	10.66 (11⅔)	10.66 (11⅔)	10.66 (11⅔)	13.25 (14½)	13.25 (14½)	15.84 (17⅓)
Curtain 2.74 m. length (108 in.)	m. yds	5.94 (6½)	8.83 (9⅔)	8.83 (9⅔)	8.83 (9⅔)	11.89 (13)	11.89 (13)	11.89 (13)	14.85 (16¼)	14.85 (16¼)	17.67 (19⅓)
Amount of heading tape	m. yds	2.74 (3)	3.89 (4¼)	3.89 (4¼)	3.89 (4¼)	5.03 (5½)	5.03 (5½)	5.03 (5½)	6.40 (7)	6.40 (7)	7.54 (8¼)

PENCIL PLEAT

Track length	1.52 (5)	1.83 (6)	2.13 (7)	2.44 (8)	2.74 (9)	3.05 (10)	3.35 (11)	3.66 (12)	3.96 (13)	4.27 (14)
No. of 120 cm. (48 in.) widths	3	4	5	5	6	6	7	8	8	9
Curtain 1.22 m. length (48 in.)	4.27 (4⅔)	5.72 (6¼)	7.32 (8)	7.32 (8)	8.53 (9⅓)	8.53 (9⅓)	10.06 (11)	11.43 (12½)	11.43 (12½)	12.80 (14)
Curtain 1.37 m. length (54 in.)	4.80 (5¼)	6.40 (7)	7.92 (8⅔)	7.92 (8⅔)	9.45 (10⅓)	9.45 (10⅓)	10.97 (12)	12.57 (13¾)	12.57 (13¾)	14.17 (15½)
Curtain 1.52 m. length (60 in.)	5.18 (5⅔)	7.01 (7⅔)	8.69 (9½)	8.69 (9½)	11.36 (11⅓)	11.36 (11⅓)	12.12 (13¼)	13.94 (15¼)	13.94 (15¼)	15.54 (17)
Curtain 1.83 m. length (72 in.)	6.10 (6⅔)	8.23 (9)	10.29 (11¼)	10.29 (11¼)	12.19 (13⅓)	12.19 (13⅓)	14.17 (15½)	16.23 (17¾)	16.23 (17¾)	18.29 (20)
Curtain 2.13 m. length (84 in.)	7.01 (7⅔)	9.37 (10¼)	11.66 (12¾)	11.66 (12¾)	14.02 (15⅓)	14.02 (15⅓)	16.46 (18)	18.75 (20½)	18.75 (20½)	21.03 (23)
Curtain 2.44 m. length (96 in.)	7.92 (8⅔)	10.66 (11⅔)	13.25 (14½)	13.25 (14½)	15.84 (17⅓)	15.84 (17⅓)	18.58 (20⅓)	21.02 (23)	21.02 (23)	23.77 (26)
Curtain 2.74 m. length (108 in.)	8.83 (9⅔)	11.89 (13)	14.93 (16⅓)	14.93 (16⅓)	17.67 (19⅓)	17.67 (19⅓)	20.71 (22⅔)	23.54 (25¾)	23.54 (25¾)	26.51 (29)
Amount of heading tape	3.66 (4)	5.03 (5½)	6.40 (7)	6.40 (7)	7.32 (8)	7.32 (8)	8.69 (9½)	10.06 (11)	10.06 (11)	10.97 (12)

FANNED PINCH PLEAT

Track length	1.52 (5)	1.83 (6)	2.13 (7)	2.44 (8)	2.74 (9)	3.05 (10)	3.35 (11)	3.66 (12)	3.96 (13)	4.27 (14)
No. of 120 cm. (48 in.) widths	3	3	4	4	5	5	6	6	7	7
Curtain 1.22 m. length (48 in.)	4.27 (4⅔)	4.27 (4⅔)	5.72 (6¼)	5.72 (6¼)	7.32 (8)	7.32 (8)	8.53 (9⅓)	8.53 (9⅓)	10.06 (11)	10.06 (11)
Curtain 1.37 m. length (54 in.)	4.80 (5¼)	4.80 (5¼)	6.40 (7)	6.40 (7)	7.92 (8⅔)	7.92 (8⅔)	9.45 (10⅓)	9.45 (10⅓)	10.97 (12)	10.97 (12)
Curtain 1.52 m. length (60 in.)	5.18 (5⅔)	5.18 (5⅔)	7.01 (7⅔)	7.01 (7⅔)	8.69 (9½)	8.69 (9½)	10.36 (11⅓)	10.36 (11⅓)	12.12 (13¼)	12.12 (13¼)
Curtain 1.83 m. length (72 in.)	6.10 (6⅔)	6.10 (6⅔)	8.23 (9)	8.23 (9)	10.29 (11¼)	10.29 (11¼)	12.19 (13⅓)	12.19 (13⅓)	14.17 (15½)	14.17 (15½)
Curtain 2.13 m. length (84 in.)	7.01 (7⅔)	7.01 (7⅔)	9.37 (10¼)	9.37 (10¼)	11.66 (12¾)	11.66 (12¾)	14.02 (15⅓)	14.02 (15⅓)	16.46 (18)	16.46 (18)
Curtain 2.44 m. length (96 in.)	7.92 (8⅔)	7.92 (8⅔)	10.66 (11⅔)	10.66 (11⅔)	13.25 (14½)	13.25 (14½)	15.84 (17⅓)	15.84 (17⅓)	18.58 (20⅓)	18.58 (20⅓)
Curtain 2.74 m. length (108 in.)	8.83 (9⅔)	8.83 (9⅔)	11.89 (13)	11.89 (13)	14.93 (16⅓)	14.93 (16⅓)	17.67 (19⅓)	17.67 (19⅓)	20.71 (22⅔)	20.71 (22⅔)
Amount of heading tape	4.26 (4⅔)	4.26 (4⅔)	5.48 (6)	5.48 (6)	6.70 (7⅓)	6.70 (7⅓)	8.02 (8⅔)	8.02 (8⅔)	9.14 (10)	9.14 (10)

• UNLINED CURTAINS

The seams of unlined curtains, where widths of curtaining fabric join, should always appear tidy from the back. The neatest join is with a self-bound seam. If half widths are used, make sure they lie to the sides of the window frame.

MATERIALS AND EQUIPMENT

Curtain fabric; heading tape; matching thread; fabric shears; steel pins; tape measure; tailor's chalk; sewing machine; curtain weights; iron; Sharps needle; set-square.

CUTTING THE FABRIC

The heading, the depth of the pattern and the length of the curtain track determine the amount of curtaining fabric required. The chart on p. 71 will help you to work out quantities.

Lay the fabric flat, and straighten the ends (p. 291).

Measure the length of the curtain, including hemming and heading allowances, from one of the cut ends. Chalk that length across the fabric from selvedge to selvedge. Cut along the line to give you the first length. Use this as a guide to cut out the rest of the lengths, matching any pattern.

Curtains are often wider than the width of the fabric, so it may be necessary to join two or more widths, or a width and half a width. Make two half widths by folding one full width in half along the length. Press the fold and cut along the crease.

JOINING WIDTHS

Curtain widths are joined with self-bound seams. To make the seam, lay one full width right side uppermost. Place one half width, right side uppermost, next to it, so that the selvedges butt up together. Turn under the selvedge of the half width so that the fold runs along the edge of the design.

Position the half width so that the fold overlaps the selvedge and at least 15 mm. (½ in.) of the design of the full width. Match the pattern by moving the half width, but keep at least 15 mm. of the design of the full width under the fold of the half width. Sew along the edge of the fold with locking stitches [1].

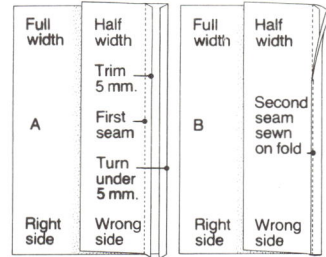

Joining widths with a self-bound seam.

Fold over the half width, so that the right side of the half width lies on the right side of the full width. Machine along the line of stitches.

Open out the fabric, wrong side uppermost. Trim the selvedge of the half width 5 mm. (¼ in.) from the stitches [2]. Fold right sides together.

If the edge of the selvedge on the full width is trimmed, turn under 5 mm. (diagram A). Turn and press again bringing the folded edge to the line of the stitches, so that the trimmed selvedge of the half width is enclosed (diagram B). If the full width selvedge is too wide, trim before folding. Tack and machine as close as possible to the first seam [3]. Press the seam flat from the right side.

BRIGHT AND PRACTICAL Unlined curtains, which are easy to take down and launder, make practical window coverings for bedrooms and bathrooms.

MAKING UNLINED CURTAINS

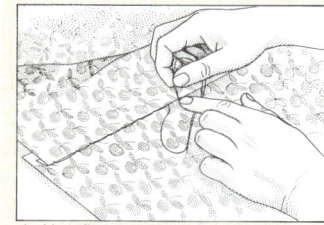

1. Use firm locking stitches to join the width to the half width along the fold.

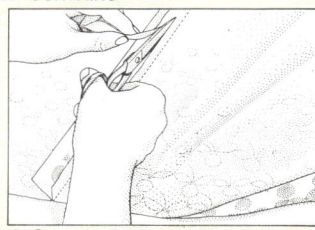

2. Open the fabric, wrong side up, and trim the half-width selvedge.

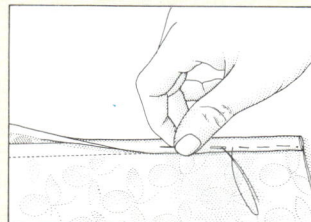

3. Tack the folded seam of the full width to the selvedge of the half width.

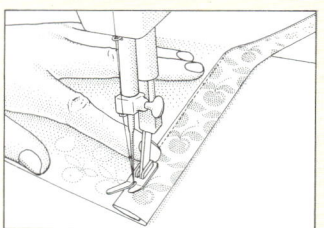

4. Fold a double hem down the side and machine-stitch in place.

5. Turn up and pin the bottom hem 7.5 cm. to allow for shrinkage.

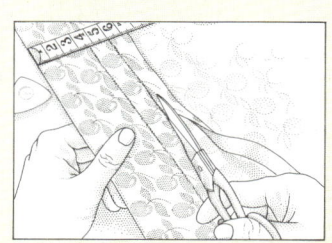

6. Trim the folded piece at the top of the curtain 5 cm. beneath the fold.

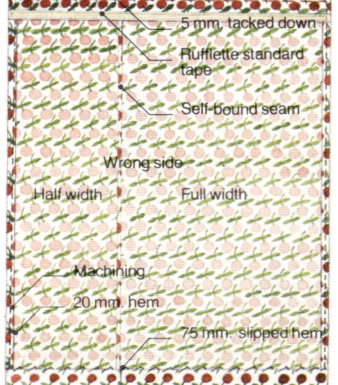

Sewing guide for an unlined curtain.

HEMMING SIDES AND BOTTOM

Turn, press and machine a 2 cm. (¾ in.) deep double hem down the sides of one curtain [4]. Press the seam flat from the right side.

Turn up and press a 5 cm. (2 in.) deep hem along the bottom. Repeat, to make a double hem, and tack in position. Then turn up about 7.5 cm. (3 in.) to allow for shrinkage. Pin in place, keeping the ends open [5]. Slip-stitch along the fold.

Sew thin fabric round each weight with a 5 mm. overlap all round. Insert a weight in the bottom hem, sewing it in place where the self-bound seam meets the hem. Put a weight in each end of the hem under the side hem fold and close the hem with slip-stitches. Repeat for the second curtain.

FORMING THE HEADING

Lay the curtain, right side uppermost, on a flat surface.

From the bottom, measure the finished length, and chalk it across the width of the curtain. Turn the curtain over and fold along the line, wrong sides together. Press the fold. Tack 5 mm. (¼ in.) below the fold to firm it.

Chalk a line across the folded piece 5 cm. below the fold. Cut along this line, going through the folded piece only [6].

Chalk another line across the folded piece, 4 cm. (1½ in.) below the fold. This line is the guide line for the heading tape. The instructions for sewing on different types of heading tape are given on p. 69. To calculate the length of tape needed, see the chart p. 71.

After the curtains have been first laundered, let down the shrinkage allowance and slip-stitch along the fold of the remaining double hem. Close the ends of the hem by slip-stitching.

MATCHING CURTAINS Unlined curtains are cheap and easy to make. It is simple, as here, to use the same fabric elsewhere in the room to give a unified décor.

73

• MAKING LINED CURTAINS

Lining adds weight to the curtain and helps it hang well. It also protects the fabric from direct sunlight, and reduces colour fading. Lined curtains give a house a uniform look outside.

MATERIALS AND EQUIPMENT

The number of fabric widths and the length needed to make the curtains depend on the size of your windows. Use the chart on p. 71 to calculate the total amount of curtaining and lining needed. Equipment: as for unlined curtains (see p. 72).

JOINING THE WIDTHS

If half widths are needed, cut them from full widths in the same way as the unlined curtains.

Join widths for one curtain by laying two widths, right sides facing, and machining 15 mm. (½ in.) from the selvedges, or the depth of the selvedge if that is greater. Add other full and half widths in the same way, always matching any pattern. Press the seams flat.

Join lining widths in the same way, making sure that the seams of curtain and lining will match. If this gives wide lining seams, trim them to about 2.5 cm. (1 in). Lay each curtain with its lining on top, so the seams match. Chalk a line 5 cm. (2 in.) from the bottom of the lining. Turn up a 5 cm. double hem at the bottom of both lining pieces. Machine close to the edge of the hem.

PREPARING THE BORDER

If you decide to have a border going down the sides and across the bottom of each curtain, turn under the ends and the side edges of the border fabric. Press and tack in place.

Lay both curtains flat, face side up. Chalk a line at the position you decide to place the border.

Starting at the top edge of one curtain, pin both edges of the border down the length, as far as the bottom corner. Tack in place. Machine the outer edge of the border in place, ending 20 cm. (8 in.) from the corner. Fold back the border so that its bottom edge lies along the chalk line going across the curtain. Position the border across the curtain to form a mitred corner [1]. Press the fold to form a crease. Chalk a line along the fold, on the face side of the border. Lay the fold and chalk line together and machine along the crease.

Trim the seams 15 mm. from the line of stitches. Snip the material at the two corners [2], so that the seam lies flat. Press the seam flat. Press the turned-over edges in place, turning under the corners where they meet.

Pin and tack the bottom edge of the border along the line going across the curtain. Machine in place, stopping 20 cm. from the next corner. If the border pattern is reversible, repeat at this corner.

If the border pattern goes one way, fold the border at the start of the third chalk line. Cut off 2.5 cm. beyond the line. Reverse the cut-off length of border, so the pattern goes in the same direction as the first vertical length. Pin the end to the end of the horizontal border piece, right sides together. Use a set-square to make a 45 degree angle where the pieces meet [3].

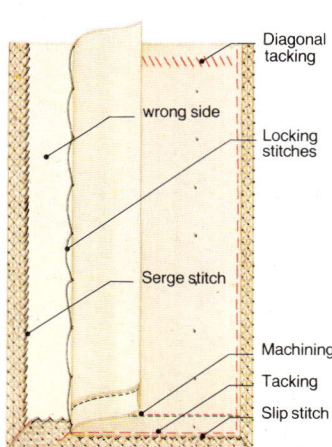

Stitch and seam guide for a lined curtain.

MAKING LINED CURTAINS

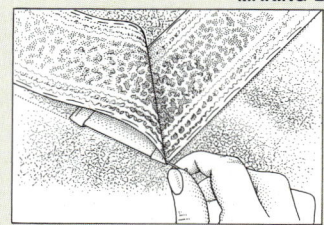

1. Pin the border at the corner. Make a mitred fold and turn along the bottom.

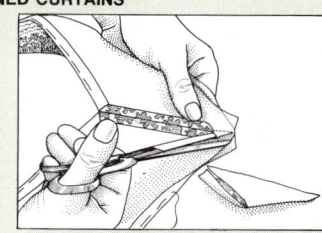

2. Cut into the corner of the seam to allow it to open out and lie flat.

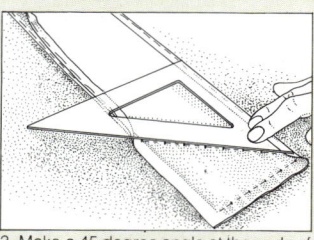

3. Make a 45 degree angle at the ends of the border pieces where they join.

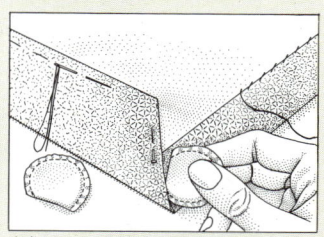

4. Insert a weight at each bottom corner and where the seams meet the bottom.

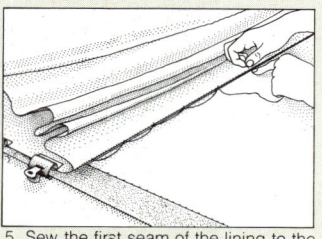

5. Sew the first seam of the lining to the first seam of the curtain.

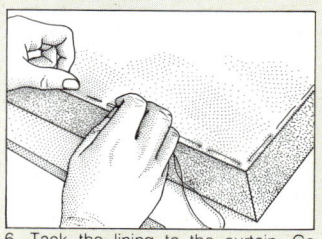

6. Tack the lining to the curtain. Go through the hem, not the front fabric.

LONG CURTAINS Tall windows, to look good, need long curtains, and long curtains need to be heavy. Lining adds weight, helping the curtain to hang well.

Machine together along the line of the angle. Trim to leave a 15 mm. seam allowance. Press the seam open. Lay the border along the chalk line going up the curtain. Machine both edges of the complete border in place. Remove the tacks.

HEMMING THE CURTAINS
Lay the curtain right side uppermost. Measure 5 cm. from the outside edge of the border and down the sides. Fold under and press the fold. Do the same 15 cm. (6 in.) below the border edge along the bottom. Turn under the raw edge along the bottom hem so that a double hem, which is wider than the side hems, is made, then fold a mitre at each corner. Sew the side hems to the curtain with serge stitches (see p. 297). Slip-stitch the bottom hem and corners, sewing in weights [4] at the bottom of each seam and at the corners.

ATTACHING THE LINING
Lay the curtain, wrong side uppermost, on a flat surface, a large table if possible. Clip or weight the hemmed edges, so that the curtain stays flat. Align the hemmed bottom edge with the edge of the table. Lay the lining, wrong side down, on the curtain, 2.5 cm. from the bottom edge. Match the seams.

Fold the lining back on itself at the first seam. Use a long locking stitch (see p. 297) to sew the seam of the lining to the seam of the curtaining along the selvedges [5]. Stop sewing 10 cm. (4 in.) from the top edge. If, when the lining is folded back, a full width of curtaining is exposed, the lining will have to be joined to it by two evenly spaced lines of stitching.

If sewing the lining to a half width of curtaining, sew one row of stitches down the middle. Fold the lining to where the stitches should be and sew

to the curtaining with long, slack locking stitches, catching the back of the curtaining. Finish the rows of stitches 10 cm. from the top. Sew a second row, if necessary, in the same way.

Trim the lining level with the side edge of the curtain. Turn the lining under so the fold matches the mitred side hem of the curtaining. Tack.

Tack the lining to the curtain width along the bottom [6]. Tack to the top, using a diagonal tacking stitch. Stitch to the hems. Do not catch the front fabric.

Continue to join the lining to the rest of the curtain in the same way. Tack along the second side when it is reached.

Slip-stitch the lining to the fabric along the fold of the lining and side hems. Continue for 5 cm. along the bottom at each corner. Make sure the stitches do not penetrate the front fabric. Remove the tacks from the sides. Leave them in the top and bottom.

PREPARING FOR THE HEADING
If you choose a pinch pleat heading tape, prepare the curtain as described here. The instructions for the preparation and sewing of other heading tapes are given on p. 69.

Lay the curtain flat, right side uppermost, on a large table if possible. Clip or weight it flat. From the bottom, measure the finished length of the curtain, plus 15 mm. Chalk a line across the width of the curtain at this measurement. Trim at this line. Turn 15 mm. of the cut edge over to the wrong side and tack, then press.

• INTERLINED CURTAINS
Although large windows make a room bright, they can cause heat loss in winter. Interlined curtains help to overcome this problem. However, they are heavy, so make sure the rail

or other fitting is strong enough to carry them. They look smart, finished with a pencil-pleat heading.

MATERIALS AND EQUIPMENT
As for unlined curtains (see p. 72), plus the same amount of lining and bump interlining as curtain material.

CUTTING AND JOINING FABRIC
Follow the instructions for lined curtains to join widths of curtain fabric and lining. Join bump by butting the edges and oversewing (p. 296).

ATTACHING THE INTERLINING
Lay one curtain flat, wrong side uppermost.

Lay the interlining over it, wrong side down. Smooth the interlining and the curtain flat and clip the edges together.

Release the clips along two sides. Fold the interlining back on itself, so that the fold lies along the first seam where two widths of curtaining have been sewn together. Sew the interlining to the seam allowance nearest the side of the curtain [1]. Leave 7.5 cm. (3 in.) unsewn at the bottom.

If, with the interlining folded back, a

full width of curtaining is showing, sew the interlining and curtain together with two more rows of locking stitches, evenly spaced apart. If half a width is showing, sew one row down the centre. Working across the curtain, join the interlining to the rest of the curtain in the same way. Sew the outer row of locking stitches 4 cm. (1½ in.) from the sides of curtain and lock-stitch across the curtain 7.5 cm. up from the bottom.

Lay the curtain flat, interlining uppermost. Turn up and press a 4 cm. hem along the sides. Turn and press a 7.5 cm. hem along the bottom. Pin in place and mitre the corners (see p. 297). Insert and sew weights in place as for lined curtains.

Sew the side hems with serge stitches (see p. 297), catching the interlining, not the front curtain fabric.

Sew the bottom hem to the interlining with a herringbone stitch [2]. Repeat on the second curtain.

ATTACHING THE LINING
Align the interlined curtain and lining, wrong sides together. Stitch the lining to the interlining with rows of locking stitches, along the lines of the stitches

joining the interlining and curtain.

Trim the sides and bottom of the lining level with the sides and bottom of the curtain. Turn 2.5 cm. (1 in.) of the lining under along the bottom and sides of the curtain. Tack in position, making sure the corners of the lining match the mitred corners of the curtain. Slip-stitch the lining into place across the bottom and down the sides. Sew the lining to the second curtain in the same way.

PREPARING THE HEADING
Turn the curtain right side uppermost. From the bottom edge, chalk-mark the finished length of the curtain and cut 2 cm. (¾ in.) above this line.

Fold the curtain along the chalk line, bringing the lining together. Press the fold. Turn the curtain over and oversew the bottom edge of the folded flap to the lining. Repeat on the second curtain. Attach heading tape (see p. 69).

MAKING INTERLINED CURTAINS

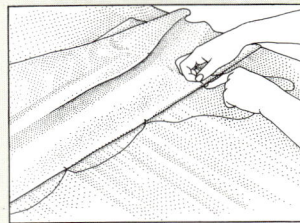

1. Sew the interlining to the curtain seam allowance with locking stitches.

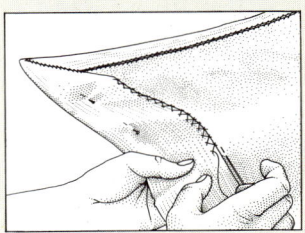

2. Sew the bottom hem to the interlining, using a herringbone stitch.

Attaching interlining to curtain fabric.

Curtain top

Locking stitch

Tacking stitch

Curtain material wrong side

Interlined curtain ready for lining.

Curtain top

Serge stitch

Locking stitch

Interlining

Herringbone stitch

Slip stitch

Curtain material right side

• CAFÉ CURTAINS

Café curtains hide poor views, make awkward windows interesting and let in a lot of light. The curtains made here hang from curtain rings. If you are attaching café curtains to rods or wires, make the scallops deeper so that the points can be looped over.

MATERIALS AND EQUIPMENT

Measure the window, as described on p. 70, to see how wide and long the curtain fabric is needed. (The finished curtain should cover the width of the window, and be long enough to reach the sill); pattern-making paper as long as the width of the curtain; as much Vilene stiffening as is needed to make a strip 15 cm. (6 in.) deep across the full width of the curtain; a pair of compasses; café-curtain hooks (one more than the number of scallops); the rest of the materials and equipment are the same as those needed for unlined curtains as described on p. 72.

CUTTING THE PATTERN PAPER

There should be one more fixing point than there are scallops. Each scallop should be about 11.5 cm. (4½ in.) across at the top and half as deep as it is wide. Allow 15 mm. (½ in.) for the fixing points between scallops. Add the width of a scallop to the width of a point. Divide the total into the width of the curtain to calculate the number of scallops. It should go, with a surplus of 15 mm. for the extra point. If not, vary the width of the scallop by 5-20 mm. (¼-¾ in.) to get as near as possible to an exact division, plus 15 mm., into the fabric width. Any small amount left over can be taken up in the fixing points at each end.

Cut a rectangle 4 cm. wider than the finished curtain and 15 cm. (6 in.) deep from the pattern paper. Mark the positions of the centres of the scallops, centre the compasses at the marks and draw 10 cm. radius semicircles. Cut these out.

PREPARING THE VILENE

Pin together pieces of Vilene to form a strip 15 cm. deep and as long as the width of the curtain.

Pin the paper pattern to the Vilene, aligning the points of the scallops with one long edge. Pencil round the scallops on to the Vilene [1].

HEMMING THE CURTAIN

Straighten the curtain fabric (see p. 291). Press flat. Cut to size.

Lay it wrong side uppermost. Turn up and sew a 2.5 cm. (1 in.) deep double hem along the sides, 5 cm. (2 in.) deep along the bottom. Press.

MAKING THE HEADING

Lay the curtain wrong side uppermost. Turn 16.5 cm. (6½ in.) of the top over to form a flap, with the right sides together. Press the fold. Pin the Vilene to the wrong side of the curtain, with the points of the scallops level with the fold. Tack together along the sides and bottom of the Vilene. Do not tack through the flap.

Machine round each scallop, following the pencil lines marked on the Vilene. Back-stitch at the beginning and end of each scallop. Remove tacks and pins.

Cut out the scallops 5 mm. (¼ in.) above the machining. Cut out small triangles of material every 2.5 cm. (1 in.) round each scallop to ease the curve [2].

Turn the heading right sides out. Push out the scallop corners from inside with the point of a pencil.

Turn under and press a 15 mm. (½ in.) hem along the bottom of the heading. Machine or slip-stitch the hem and the sides to close the heading [3]. Press the completed curtain. Push the pin hooks through one layer of heading and the Vilene fabric at the back of the curtain. The hooks must line up across the curtain, so that they do not show above it [4].

Fit the hooks to the rings on the pole to hang the curtain.

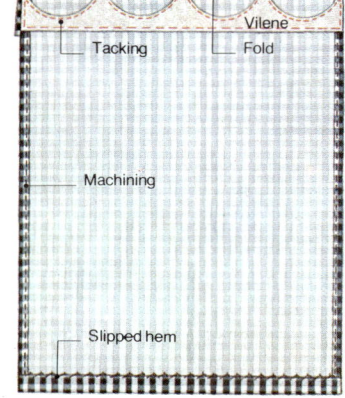

Sewing guide for a café curtain.

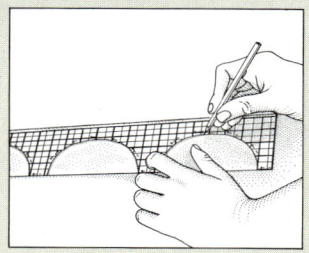
SEWING A CAFÉ CURTAIN
1. Pin the paper scallops to the Vilene and pencil round them.

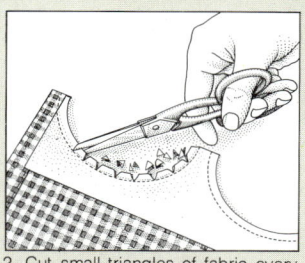
2. Cut small triangles of fabric every 2.5 cm. around the scallop hem.

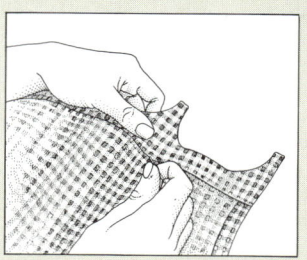
3. Slip-stitch the folded heading down the sides and along the bottom hem.

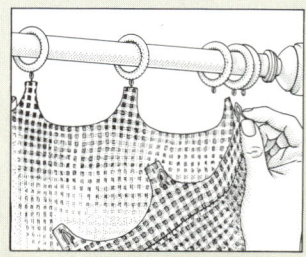
4. Ensure that the hooks are straight and do not show above the curtain.

KITCHEN WINDOW Café curtains give privacy, but at the same time allow in the maximum amount of light for anyone working in the kitchen.

• MAKING A PELMET

A pelmet is a shelf, fitted to the wall above the window recess, which carries a facing of board or fitted fabric to hide the curtain track.

MATERIALS AND EQUIPMENT

Enough upholsterer's buckram to make pelmet deep enough for the curtains; sateen lining; covering fabric (to match the curtain), matching thread and interlining (if necessary) 5 cm. (2 in.) deeper and longer than the buckram; 2.5 cm. (1 in.) curtain tape, 2.5 cm. (1 in.) longer than the buckram; braid or fringe 5 cm. (2 in.) longer than buckram; Sharps needle; latex glue; pins; fabric shears; tailor's chalk; iron; sewing machine; ruler; one packet of tacks (if fitting a pelmet board); one length of 16 mm. ($\frac{5}{8}$ in.) thick softwood, about 15 cm. (6 in.) wide and 10 cm. (4 in.) longer than the curtain rail, and the necessary drills, plugs and screws for putting it up with angle brackets (see p. 108).

FIXING THE PELMET BOARD

Saw a notch at each end of the board, 2.5 cm. (1 in.) wide and deep enough for the pelmet to be tucked in. If no rail is fitted to the window, attach a top-fitting rail to the underside of the board, 7.5 cm. (3 in.) from the front.

Fix the board about 5 cm. (2 in.) above the window recess with angle brackets (see p. 108), with the notches against the wall.

CUTTING THE BUCKRAM

Measure the length of the board and sides. For a pelmet up to 23 cm. (9 in.) deep, buy a little over half this length of 45 cm. (18 in.) wide buckram. Chalk the depth of the pelmet (usually about 4 cm. (1½ in.) of pelmet for every 30 cm. (12 in.) of curtain depth) across the length of the buckram. Cut out this length and repeat on the remaining strip of buckram. Join the two lengths by butting the ends together, and glue a 2.5 cm. (1 in.) strip of buckram over the join. Measure the distance from the notch in the board to the front corner, and mark this distance from each end of the buckram. Fold the buckram at these points to shape it for fixing to the board.

With thin fabrics, put an interlining between the cover and the buckram.

Cut the interlining slightly larger all round than the buckram. Centre the buckram on the interlining, glue together and trim flush.

CUTTING THE COVERING FABRIC

Cut the covering fabric widths 5 cm. deeper than the buckram. For all but the smallest pelmets, the pelmet length will be longer than one width of material. To avoid the seam running down the centre, cut one full width in half and join a half to each end of the other full width. If the pelmet is longer than two widths of material, increase the lengths of the outside widths. Trim the finished length 5 cm. longer than

the buckram. Cut and join the lining in the same way.

JOINING THE COVER TO THE BUCKRAM

Lay the wrong side of the cover on the buckram so 2.5 cm. overlaps all round. Tack-stitch in place 15 mm. from the edge of the buckram. Turn the pelmet over. Use a sponge to damp 2.5 cm. of the edge of the buckram for a distance of 20 cm. (8 in.). Buckram is treated with size which, when wet, forms glue. Fold the front cover over this dampened buckram and press in place with a warm iron. Avoid pressing the buckram.

Stop 5 cm. from the first corner. Dampen the corner. Place the pointed corner of the cover fabric on the dampened corner. Press into place. Damp the buckram on each side of the corner and fold the material to this [1]. Press in place. Slip-stitch together the material that meets at the corner. Continue until the cover fabric is glued round the buckram.

If the buckram fails to hold the fabric, catch-stitch rather than add glue.

FITTING THE TRIMMING

Cut the length of braid or fringe 5 cm. longer than the buckram pelmet. Lay the braid on the right side of the pelmet along one long edge so 2.5 cm. overhangs each end.

Turn one overlapping end of the

braid round to the wrong side of the pelmet. Pin in place and continue round the edge of the pelmet, turning the other end in the same way. Back-stitch (see p. 296) along the top and bottom edges of the braid.

FIXING THE LINING TO THE PELMET

Lay the lining right side uppermost, on the wrong side of the pelmet. Turn under and press 2.5 cm. of the lining all round, so that 4 mm. ($\frac{1}{8}$ in.) of the turned-under front covering is exposed. Pin the lining in position, along the top and bottom edges.

Slip-stitch the lining to the pelmet [2]. Press the edge with a warm iron.

PUTTING UP THE PELMET

Place a strip of curtain tape, 15 mm. longer than the pelmet, along the top edge of the wrong side. Turn under 5 mm. at one end. Sew in place with an open back stitch (see p. 296), continuing along the bottom edge of the tape. Turn under 5 mm. at the other end and sew in place. Catch the top edge of the tape to the cover fabric every 10 cm. (4 in.), with overcast stitches [3]. This forms pockets for securing the pelmet to the board.

Match the pelmet to the board and push a tack through the centre of each pocket. Tuck the 2.5 cm. at each end into the notches next to the wall.

Hammer the tacks into the board, working out from the centre [4].

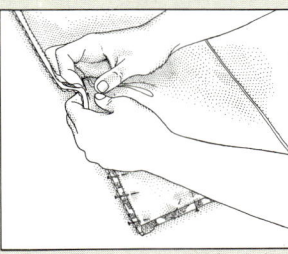

1. Stick down the corner, then fold under excess fabric at the corner.

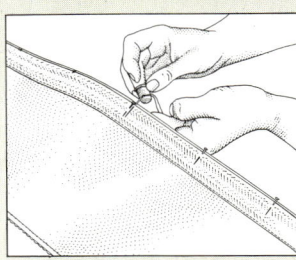

2. Slip-stitch the lining to the pelmet cover all the way round.

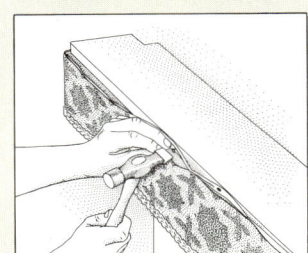

3. Catch-stitch the top edge of the tape to the cover at 10 cm. intervals.

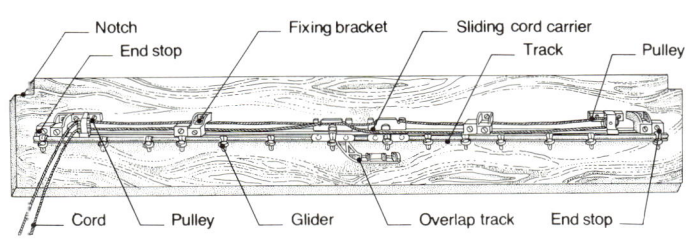

Notch — End stop — Fixing bracket — Sliding cord carrier — Track — Pulley — Cord — Pulley — Glider — Overlap track — End stop

The pelmet will conceal a corded curtain track fixed to the underside of the board.

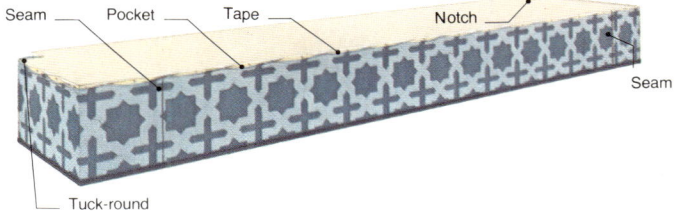

Seam — Pocket — Tape — Notch — Seam — Tuck-round

The finished pelmet, showing how the fabric is centred on the board.

MAKING A PINCH PLEATED VALANCE

There are several ways of attaching a valance to hide a curtain track and enhance the appearance of the window. The method described here uses a board fixed to the wall above the window as for a pelmet (see p. 77), making a valance rail unnecessary.

MATERIALS AND EQUIPMENT

Curtain material; sateen lining; matching thread; heavy-weight dressmaking Vilene; 4 cm. (1½ in.) wide tape; tailor's chalk; steel pins; ruler; fabric shears; iron; sewing machine; Sharps needle; pattern-making paper; 12 mm. (½ in.) tacks.

ESTIMATING THE FABRIC

The length of the curtain and lining fabric is two-and-a-half times the length of the board. The depth is approximately 3 cm. (1⅛ in.) for every foot of curtain drop. Add 6 cm. (2½ in.) for hems. The tape is 5 cm. (2 in.) longer than the valance curtain fabric. Buy enough Vilene to make a 12.5 cm. (5 in.) deep strip, as long as the unpleated valance.

SIZING THE PLEATS

Join pieces of pattern-making paper to make a strip as long as the unpleated valance. From each end, mark with pencil the distance of the returns (the distance out from the wall to the front corner of the valance board). The returns are not pleated. Mark the rest of the paper so that a pleat, which takes up 15 cm. (6 in.), begins at each return line. Mark the centre of another pleat in the centre of the paper. Position remaining pleats with about 12.5 cm. between them.

JOINING WIDTHS OF FABRIC

Follow the instructions for lined curtains (p. 74) to join widths and half widths of curtain and lining.

ATTACHING THE LINING TO THE CURTAIN FABRIC

Measure the finished depth of the valance plus 15 mm. (½ in.) from the bottom of the curtain fabric.

Align the lining over the curtain fabric with right sides together. Pin and tack together along the bottom. Machine-stitch 15 mm. from the bottom edge, beginning and ending about 7.5 cm. (3 in.) from the sides. Press the seam open flat. Turn the fabric right side out, laying the pieces flat together, with the lining side facing. Lift the lining so that 15 mm. of curtain fabric shows along the bottom edge, and press.

Fold in and press flat 2.5 cm. (1 in.) of the curtain fabric along both sides. Mitre the corners (p. 297) where the fold meets the bottom [1].

Cut the sides of the lining flush with the sides of the curtain fabric. Turn in 15 mm. along the sides of the lining. Slip-stitch the lining to the curtain fabric along the fold, starting at the corners and finishing halfway up the

sides. Turn in 2.5 cm. of the curtain fabric along the top edge and press.

ADDING THE VILENE

Fold back the lining to reveal the wrong side of the curtain fabric.

Lay the Vilene under the flap and against the fold at the top of the curtain fabric, with its ends under the folded sides. Tack the Vilene to the top fold, making sure the stitches do not penetrate to the front of the valance. Lay the Vilene and folded curtain fabric flat and machine along the line of tacks. Remove the tacks. Fold the Vilene into the inside of the valance and tack through to the front of the valance to hold in place [2].

FIXING THE TAPE

Lay the lining flat against the Vilene and curtain fabric. Turn under the top of the lining so the fold is 5 mm. (¼ in.) below the top edge of the valance. Align the tape along the top of the valance lining. Turn under 15 mm. at each end of the tape. Machine along the bottom edge of the tape, going only through the tape and lining. Trim the lining 2.5 cm. from the fold [3].

Bring the lining and tape together [4], and pin the top edge of the lining to the curtain fabric. Slip-stitch the lining to the curtain fabric, along the line of the pins, and remove the pins – leave the tape free along the top edge. Continue slip-stitching down the sides, joining the lining to the curtain fabric, until the previous stitching is reached.

FORMING THE PLEATS

Lay the valance right side uppermost. Place the pattern-making paper next to it along the top of the valance.

Insert pins in the valance in positions corresponding to the pleat marks. Chalk 10 cm. (4 in.) lines down from the pin marks. Pinch the pleat lines together to form pinch pleats. Pin in place and tack and machine down the lines (see diagrams at foot of columns 2 and 3).

Pinch each large pleat into three small pleats [5]. Using double thread, sew the pleats at the top and bottom of each group [6]. Repeat at each large pleat. Finish by removing tacking.

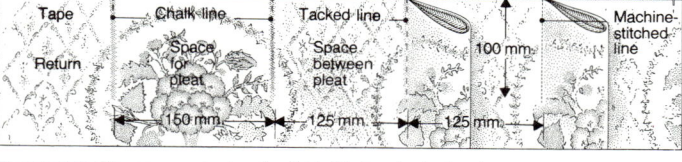

The pleat positions are marked on the right side then tacked and sewn.

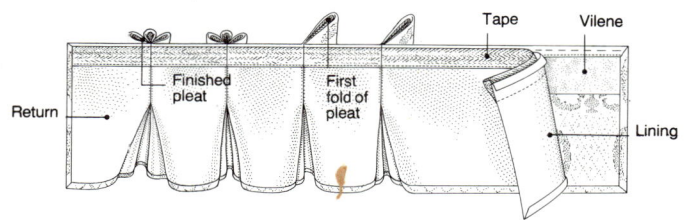

The reverse side, showing finished pleats and assembly of fabric, lining and tape.

MAKING A PINCH PLEATED VALANCE

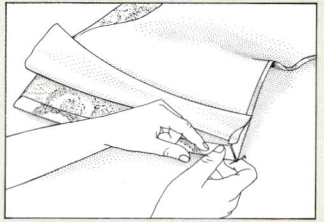

1. Mitre each of the bottom corners of the curtain fabric.

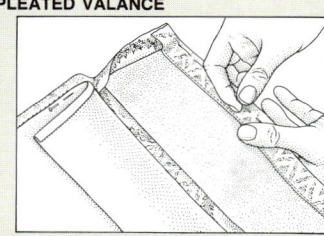

2. Fold the Vilene into the inside of the valance, and tack through to hold it.

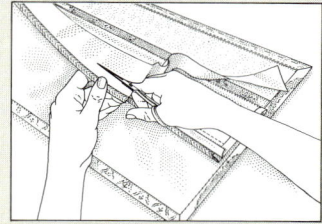

3. Cut off the excess lining to leave 2.5 cm. beyond the fold.

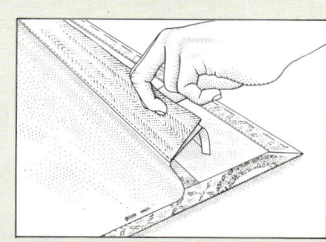

4. Match the tape and lining and lay them against the top of the valance.

5. Divide the large pleat into three equal pleats by nipping it in the centre.

6. Sew the pleats together at the top and 10 cm. down each group.

PUTTING UP THE VALANCE

Push tacks through the centre of the tape between the pleats and along the returns. Attach by knocking the tacks into the edge of the board.

UNLINED VALANCE

A light material, such as cotton, can be used to make a smocked valance to fit on a rail. This is particularly suitable for kitchens and bathrooms since it can be removed for washing.

MATERIALS AND EQUIPMENT

Fabric – twice the length of the rail plus 5 cm. (2 in.); depth as for a pinch pleated valance plus 6 cm. (2½ in.) as backing for the heading tape (length of the rail); smocking thread; matching thread; equipment as for pinch pleated valance, plus large-eyed crewel needle; but omit pattern-making paper.

MAKING UP THE FABRIC

Make a double hem on the bottom and sides, mitring the corners (see p. 297). Turn down the top edge 4 cm. (1½ in.). This gives 2.5 cm. (1 in.) for a stand-up heading, plus 15 mm. (½ in.) to go under the tape. With the crewel needle, put the first line of smocking 2.5 cm. from the top of the valance. Put a second row below this. For smocking stitch see p. 298.

Take a strip of fabric 3 cm. (1⅛ in.) longer than the valance and 3 cm. deeper than the smocking. Press down 15 mm. on each of the long edges, wrong sides facing. Machine the tape to the right side of the strip. Pin the strip to the valance, wrong sides facing, 2.5 cm. from the top.

Slip-stitch the ends of the strip to the valance, turning in the excess. Then slip-stitch along the edges of the strip, catching the backs of the pleats, so that the stitching does not show on the right side.

*HOW A VALANCE HELPS A ROOM   A valance not only conceals the mech-
anics of the curtain track, but can also add character to a room. This pinch*
*pleated valance helps to give a snug look to the bedroom. By reducing
the size of the window, it modifies the cold effect of a large area of glass.*

• BLINDS AND SHUTTERS

Curtains are not the only way to cover windows. Shutters, screens and blinds will also ensure privacy. There are many types of blinds, of which roller blinds and roman blinds can be made at home. Most blinds can be fitted either in the window recess, or on the ceiling or wall outside the recess.

Roller blinds Simple to install and inexpensive to buy in kit form, roller blinds let in plenty of light when drawn up, yet give complete privacy when unrolled. They can be made with

A pinoleum blind allows a soft light to filter through between the slats, which are thin strips of wood held together by cotton.

Venetian blinds permit the amount of light to be controlled by adjusting the slats. Plastic slats are cheaper than the wooden type.

material to blend with any colour scheme.

Roman blinds No special parts are needed to make roman blinds. They are made of fabric attached to cords. When the cords are pulled, the blind rises up in accordion pleats to form a pelmet (see p. 82).

Venetian blinds These blinds are made of parallel slats of plastic or wood. The slats pivot together to any position from horizontal, which lets in most light, to vertical, which cuts out direct light.

Plastic slats are more suitable for

Roller blinds do not have to be vertical: they can be adapted for a roof skylight. They can be bought in kit form, and are easy to install.

A vertical louvre blind, with vertical slats, makes the most of a large window. These blinds are available in several materials.

kitchens, wooden ones, which are more expensive, for living-rooms.

Pinoleum blinds These blinds are an inexpensive covering for large windows. They are made from fine strips of wood, held together by cotton, and let a pleasant, soft light filter through. They may be mounted on a spring-operated roller or moved up and down by cords.

Balastore blinds Another inexpensive blind is the Balastore, which is made of strong paper fibre. It is accordion-pleated to act as a folding blind rather like venetian blinds. Balastores are perforated with small holes to let light through without glare.

Pleatex blinds Made with a stronger paper than Balastores, pleatex blinds have smaller pleats. The paper gives privacy but lets sunlight through, filtered to the colour of the paper. The four main colours are orange, green, blue and parchment.

Vertical louvre blinds Most effective on a large floor-to-ceiling window, these work on the same principle as venetian blinds, except that they close across the window, rather than down. The slats are wider than the venetian type, but less opaque, made from man-made sheer fabric, canvas, silk or thin wood.

Louvre shutters These shutters are like lightweight doors made of overlapping wooden slats, spaced apart to let light through. For large windows they are made in hinged sections, which fold flat against one another to reveal the window.

Screens Hardboard panels with cut-out patterns or fabric stretched on a frame make the best screens. They are attached to the window frame and so cannot be adjusted to let more or less light through. There are now tracks which allow the screen to be moved to one side when an unrestricted view is desired.

• MEASURING A WINDOW FOR A ROLLER BLIND

The measuring guide shows how to calculate the amount of material needed and where to position the roller to make sure the blind covers the window properly.

The position of the brackets must allow the roller to carry sufficient material to overlap the glazed area by 5 cm. (2 in.). Alternatively, attach the brackets outside the recess. In this case the roller should be fitted 7.5 cm. (3 in.) above the window and the fabric should overlap the recess by at least 7.5 cm. each side.

For fitting inside the window recess: measure A to B for the finished length of the blind. Add 16 cm. (6¼ in.) to this for the blind fabric required. Measure C to D for the total length of the roller, including the pins. E to F is the blind width. Add 5 cm. to this for hems, if needed. If the brackets cannot be positioned at least as far apart as the distance from E to F, fit a longer roller outside the window recess.

For fitting outside the window recess: measure G to H for the finished length, which should overlap the recess by at least 5 cm. top and bottom. Add 16 cm. to this for the length of the

blind fabric required. For ceiling-fixed bracket measure from N to H.

Measure J to K for the total roller length, including pin width. J to K should be at least 15 cm. (6 in.) wider than the recess. L to M is the blind width, which should overlap the recess by 5 cm. each side. When buying blind fabric, add 5 cm. to the width for hemming if needed (see below).

• MAKING A ROLLER BLIND

Roller-blind kits, available from large stores and do-it-yourself shops, are cheap. The rollers range in length from 61 cm. to 2.75 m. (2-9 ft) and can be cut to fit any size of window within this range.

MATERIALS AND EQUIPMENT

Roller-blind kit; blind material; hammer; screwdriver; bradawl; iron; tape measure; scissors; needle; thread; set-square; ⅛ in. tacks.

Closely woven fabrics, such as cotton, canvas and linen, are best, as they are firm enough to roll up easily. If the fabric is too heavy it will not wrap smoothly round the roller; if too fragile, it will crease. A thin fabric can be treated with stiffener to prevent fraying and give a spongeable finish. Try to use material that does not need hemming, as hems are bulky on the roller. A spray-can of stiffener covers two blinds, 91.5 × 122 cm. (3 × 4 ft).

If you want to paint designs on plain fabric, the spray will seal the paint or dye. PVC plastic sheeting and vinyl make good blinds, particularly for kitchens and bathrooms. They are thin, easy to fit, easy to clean, require no hems or stiffening and can be sponged clean. Not all PVC is suitable – seek the shopkeeper's advice.

PREPARING THE ROLLER

If you cannot buy a kit with a roller exactly the length needed, buy a longer roller. Measure the required length from the flat-pin end and cut off the surplus at the round-pin end [1]. Smooth the cut with glass-paper.

Place the pin cap on the cut end and push a bradawl through the hole in the cap to indent a mark for the pin. Hammer the pin through the cap, into the hole [2].

PREPARING THE FABRIC

If using a fabric which needs hemming, turn in, tack and sew a 2.5 cm. (1 in.) hem along each side and a 15 mm. (½ in.) hem along the top. Press the hems before machining.

Thin, flimsy fabric, useful if the maximum amount of light is needed in a room, ought to be stiffened. Press, then spray with stiffener, following the manufacturer's instructions, and allow the fabric to dry before continuing. Stiffener will set creases in unpressed fabric.

ATTACHING THE LATH

At the bottom of the blind turn up and sew a 5 cm. hem. Press in place and slip-stitch near the edge and down one end, forming a pocket.

Cut the lath 5 cm. shorter than the width of the blind. Insert it into the pocket and close the open end with slip-stitching.

Thread the pull cord through the holder and knot the end to prevent it slipping through. Thread the other end through the acorn and knot it.

Screw the holder to the lath on the back of the blind, so it is hidden. Prepare the screw holes by pushing a bradawl into the lath through the holes in the holder [3].

FIXING THE BRACKETS

Put the brackets on the ends of the roller. Hold the roller in position at the window, with the spring pin and slotted bracket on your left.

Position the right-hand bracket, which takes the pin end of the roller, at least 5 cm. beyond the point where the glass joins the frame, to give a good overlap at the side. Place the bracket on the recess ceiling if it is a ceiling-fixed bracket. If it is a wall-mounted bracket, place it 4 cm. (1½ in.) below the recess ceiling.

Mark the screw positions of this bracket with a bradawl or a pencil.

Remove the roller and screw the bracket in place [4]. If attaching the bracket to plaster or masonry, use a drill and plugs (see p. 353).

Put the pin end of the roller into the bracket. Position the left-hand slotted bracket so that the spring end of the roller fits into it. Use a set-square and adjust the position of the slotted bracket to ensure that the roller is horizontal and parallel to the window.

Remove the roller, and screw the slotted bracket in place.

ATTACHING THE FABRIC

Lay the fabric on a table, right side up. Lay the roller on the fabric, with the spring end on your left. Bring the top edge of the fabric up over the roller and align it with the fitting line so that the roller is at right-angles to the blind. Glue and tack the material to the roller [5]. Wind the fabric on to the roller and put the blind in the brackets [6].

TENSIONING THE BLIND

Pull the blind down. If it does not cover the whole window, take the roller from the brackets and wind the fabric tighter. Repeat, until the blind locks down in the right position, and rolls up fully when tugged gently.

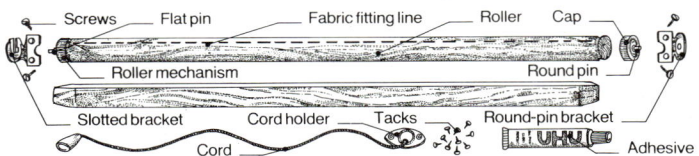
Roller-blind kit. If the roller needs shortening, cut at the round-pin end and shorten lath.

ROLLER BLIND Windows up to 2.75 m. across can be easily fitted with roller blinds. Pulled down they give the occupants complete privacy. Rolled up they expose all the glass and provide maximum light.

MAKING A ROLLER BLIND

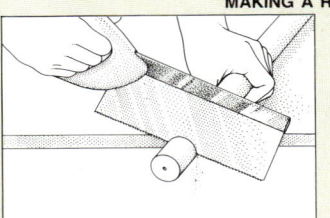
1. Cut the roller to length by measuring in from the flat pin and sawing off the surplus at the round-pin end.

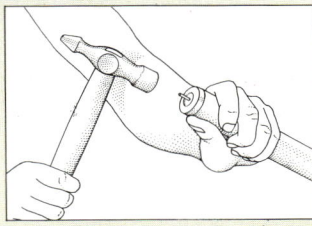
2. Place the cap over the cut end. Push a bradawl through the hole into the roller then hammer round pin through cap.

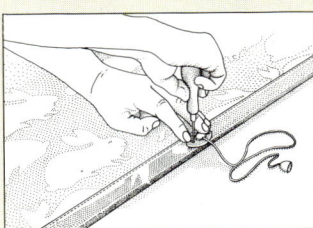
3. Thread the cord through the holder. Screw the holder to the centre of the lath on the wrong side of the blind.

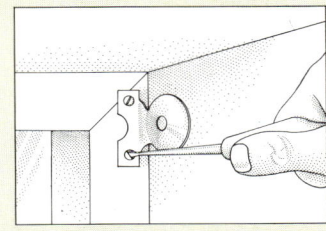
4. Position the round-pin bracket on the frame 5 cm. from the glass and 4 cm. below recess top. Screw in place.

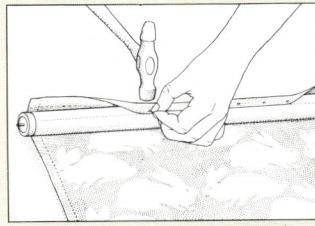
5. Align the end of the fabric with the guideline. Glue and tack the fabric in place, working out from the centre.

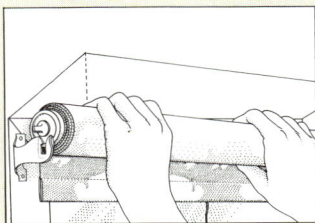
6. Wind the fabric on the roller. Put the round pin in its bracket first, then drop the flat pin into its slot.

• ROMAN BLINDS

Roman blinds are heavier and warmer than roller blinds. They fold up into attractive accordion pleats to hang as a pelmet.

MATERIALS AND EQUIPMENT

Heavy cotton, at least 10 cm. (4 in.) wider and 25 cm. (10 in.) longer than the finished size; same amount of sateen lining; 2.5 cm. (1 in.) heading tape, four times the length of the finished blind plus 10 cm.; one 50 × 25 mm. (2 × 1 in.) wooden batten, as long as the width of the completed blind; tacks; 24 15 mm. (⅝ in.) curtain rings; four medium screw eyes, two 6 × 20 mm. (¼ × ¾ in.) laths, 25 mm. shorter than the width of the blind; one cleat and screws; half a dozen countersunk No. 10 screws and plugs to match; wood and masonry bits; screwdriver; hammer; nylon cord, ten times the length of blind; matching thread; sewing machine; Sharps needle; scissors; ruler; tailor's chalk.

CUTTING THE MATERIAL

Straighten the sides of the blind material (p. 291), and press.

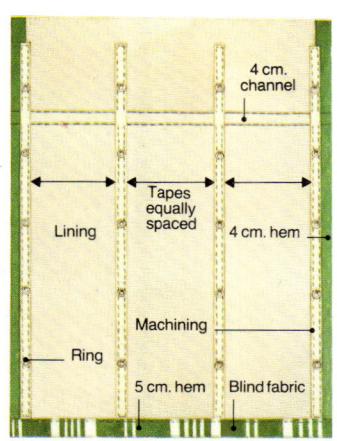

Sewing guide for a roman blind.

Roman blinds can be fitted to the ceiling of the window recess, or the ceiling outside the recess. Measure the window (see p. 80) and cut the material 10 cm. (4 in.) wider than the finished width of the blind and 25 cm. (10 in.) longer than the finished length.

Cut the lining the same length, but 10 cm. narrower than the cut width of the blind material.

LINING AND HEMMING THE BLIND

Align the top and bottom edges of the blind fabric and lining, right sides together, with the blind fabric on top.

Match the sides of the blind and lining [1]. Pin down the sides. Tack the sides of the lining and blind fabric together, 15 mm. (½ in.) from the edges. Machine-stitch along the tacking. Press the seams flat.

Turn right side out and press so that 4 cm. (1½ in.) of the blind fabric shows on each side of the lining.

Spread the blind with the lining uppermost. Turn up the bottom edge 15 mm. and press. Fold over 5 cm. (2 in.) more, tack and machine, leaving the ends open. Turn in the top edges of the blind and lining [2].

Divide the blind length so the rings which guide the cords will be 20 to 30 cm. (8 to 12 in.) apart. Mark the positions near the edge of the lining with chalk.

Chalk a 4 cm. deep channel across the lining, halfway between the positions for the first and second rings. Machine the channel lines. Unpick the lining at one end [3].

SEWING ON THE TAPES

Cut the tape into four lengths, each as long as the finished blind. Place a length over each seam where the lining and the blind fabric are joined.

Turn under 15 mm. at the top of each tape. Machine down both sides of the tapes, stopping at the first line of channel stitches and continuing after the second line. Turn under each tape at the bottom so that they finish at the bottom of the lining.

Sew the other two lengths of tape down the lining in the same way [4], so that all four tapes are equally spaced apart. Press the blind. Lay it flat and sew the curtain rings to the tapes [5]. The rings on all four tapes must line up exactly across the blind.

Push one lath into the bottom, open hem. Sew the hem closed. Push the second lath into the channel [6] and close the opening.

FITTING THE BATTEN

The method of fixing the batten will differ according to whether you are screwing it to the solid lintel inside the window recess, or to the hollow room ceiling outside it.

Drill and deeply countersink screw holes in the batten. For an inside-recess fitting, which will require masonry plugs (see p. 353), allow one screw to every 23 cm. (9 in.) of batten length. For fixing to the room ceiling, locate and position screw holes as described on p. 109.

Place the batten across the recess ceiling, with the countersinks facing down. Push a bradawl through the screw holes to mark the screw positions on the ceiling.

Lay the batten with the countersinks facing down on a work surface. Place the blind, right side uppermost, on the batten. Cover the face of the batten with the top edge of the blind and tack to the batten in this position [7]. Fix screw eyes in the countersunk

CUTTING AND ASSEMBLING A ROMAN BLIND

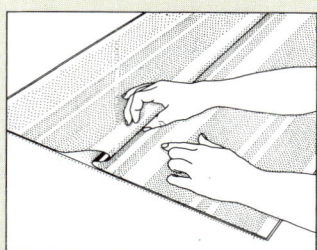
1. Match the edges of blind and lining, taking up blind surplus in an even pleat.

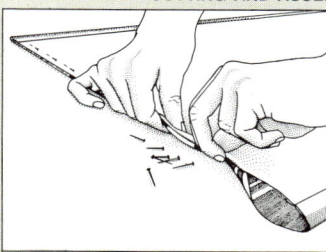
2. Turn the top edge of the blind fabric in under the lining.

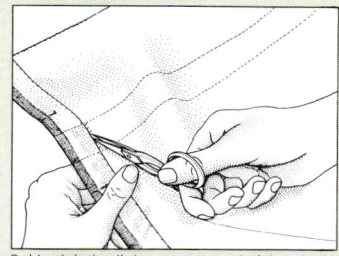
3. Unpick the lining at one end of the channel which is to carry the lath.

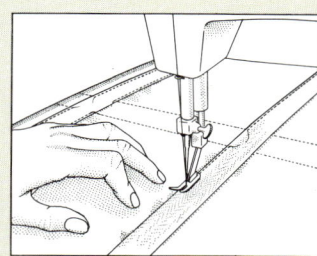
4. Sew the tapes down blind on lining side. Do not sew across channel.

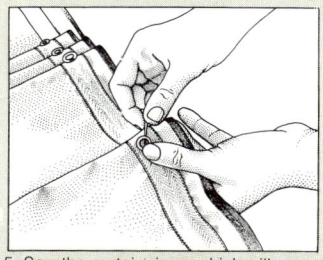
5. Sew the curtain rings, which will carry the cord, to all four tapes.

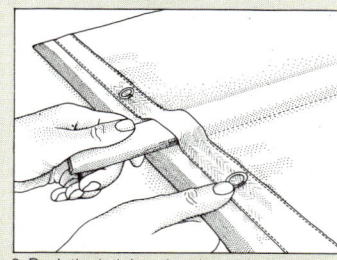
6. Push the lath into the channel at the point where the lining was unpicked.

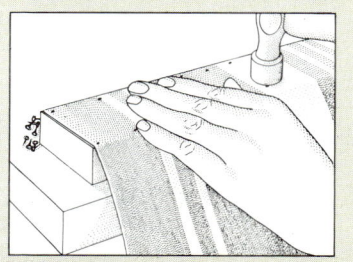
7. Align the top edge of the blind with the back edge of the batten and tack.

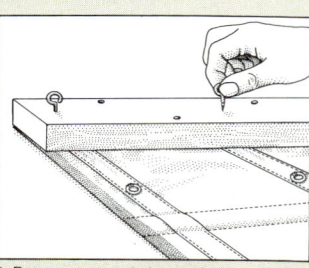
8. Put screw eyes in batten in line with the tapes on the blind.

(uncovered) side of the batten [8].

If fixing the batten inside the recess, use a masonry bit to drill holes at the bradawl marks, and fit plugs

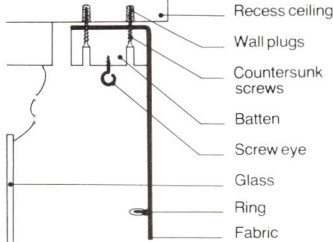

Recess ceiling
Wall plugs
Countersunk screws
Batten
Screw eye
Glass
Ring
Fabric

How the blind fits to the recess ceiling

(see p. 353). If fixing to the room ceiling, drill pilot holes only, with a woodwork bit. Screw the batten firmly in place, with the blind hanging down on the room side.

THREADING THE CORDS

Decide on which side of the window you will fix the cleat round which the cord ends are wound. If on the right-hand side, knot the cord to the bottom right-hand ring, on the lining side of the blind. Thread the cord through all the rings on this tape, and then through the four screw eyes on the batten. Let the cord hang to the bottom of the blind and cut it level.

Thread the remaining cord through the rings on the inside right tape, and then through the inside right, inside left and outside left screw eyes on the batten. Cut the cord at the bottom of the blind. Repeat with the remaining cord for the two lengths of tape on the left. If the cleat is on the left, attach the cords in the reverse order.

Gather the ends of the cords and knot them together, so that when pulled, the pleats of the blind fold up neatly.

FITTING THE CLEAT

Position the cleat on the desired side of the window frame, just above the level of the sill, so that the arms are vertical. Make pilot holes with a bradawl, and screw the cleat in place.

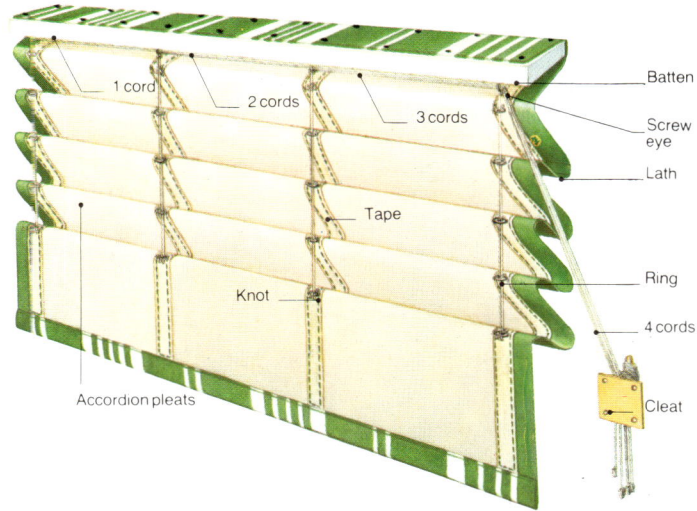

1 cord
2 cords
3 cords
Batten
Screw eye
Lath
Tape
Ring
Knot
4 cords
Accordion pleats
Cleat

A roman blind folds up in accordion pleats, leaving the last pleat to hang as a pelmet.

LIGHT BARRIER *Roman blinds are lined, so they cut out light more effectively than any other type.*

LIGHTS AND LIGHTING

Good lighting can make a house warm and friendly, lively or restful. Bad lighting results in a dreary or glaring interior, and can be dangerous. The difference is often not so much one of cost as of imagination.

Many homes are badly lit only because unsuitable conventional fittings have been accepted without question, or because new fittings have been chosen for their appearance rather than their performance.

In a new house, the lighting can be planned as part of the furnishings and decoration – before the wiring is installed, if possible. In an established house it can be replanned when redecorating.

• UNDERSTANDING LIGHTING

Objects are seen because of the light they reflect back to the eye, and the amount reflected varies according to colour. The lighter the colour, the more light it reflects. Whites reflect about 80% for example, reds and blues 10-20%.

Reflection of light also depends on the quality of a surface – a glossy one reflects more than a matt one, a clean one more than a dirty one.

Under electric light, reflection of colours is not the same as in daylight. The light from a normal household bulb causes red and yellow surfaces to appear brighter than in daylight, and green and blue surfaces to appear darker. Fluorescent lamps have varying effects on colour (see p. 86).

Light and shade give depth to an object; the way the shadows fall depends on the way the light is distributed. Soft shadows, with the light directed from above, are best for general purposes.

Light solely from an overhead central point is, however, likely to make a room flat and uninteresting, and is not generally suitable for a living-room or bedroom. Lighting at different points – such as portable lamps or spotlights – provides highlights and shadows and also direct lighting where it is particularly needed.

For decorative effect, lighting from behind an object throws it into relief in a dramatic way; side-lighting models it in profile; and front-lighting empha-sises its detail. Lighting from below can be used for unusual effects.

HOW MUCH LIGHT IS NEEDED

For general lighting, a good guide is to allow 20 watts per square metre (2 watts per square foot) of floor space for filament lamps and 10 watts per square metre (1 watt per square foot) for fluorescent lamps. So for a room 13.5 sq. m. (150 sq. ft), for example, the total lamp wattage for general lighting should be at least 270 watts for filament lamps or 135 watts for fluorescent lamps.

More light is needed for activities such as reading or sewing, and older people need more light than younger ones. As a guide, a 60 watt bulb is likely to be suitable for a bedside lamp, a 150 watt bulb for a floor standard lamp, and a 100 watt bulb for a table lamp.

But the amount of light that falls on a surface depends not only on the power of the bulb, but also on the degree of reflection from the surface and its distance from the bulb, as well as the way the light is distributed by the fitting (see p. 87).

The best way to find out how much direct light is needed is to experiment with bulbs of various wattages.

THE EFFECT ON THE EYE

Like an automatic camera lens, the eye adjusts to levels of illumination so that it can see clearly. It can adapt to a wide range, from bright to nearly dark, but it cannot see clearly immediately if plunged from one extreme to the other – for example, from daylight into a dark cinema.

It takes longer to adapt from light to dark than from dark to light. As people get older, their eyes take longer to adapt.

To avoid shocks to the eye, such as turning on the main lighting when waking up at night, a low-power night circuit is useful (see p. 89), particularly in stairways and passages. Walking from a brightly lit room into a dark passage can cause accidents.

CONTRAST AND GLARE

Lighting can produce two kinds of glare – discomfort glare and disability glare. The higher the illumination level, the greater the danger of glare from the light source or its reflection.

Discomfort glare may be caused by an over-bright source – such as bright sunlight or an unshielded light bulb – or too much contrast between an object and its background, and can result in eyestrain and headache.

It can be experienced, for example, when reading a book under a lamp in an otherwise dark room. The reflection from the white page in contrast with its surroundings may make reading uncomfortable.

Disability glare can make seeing difficult or even impossible. It often occurs when an object is placed too near a bright light. This happens, for example, when an unshielded bulb is hung low over a work bench. The eye adapts to the brightness of the bulb but cannot see the object on the bench distinctly.

To avoid glare, do not use unshielded lamps, and shade the lamp to screen it from the eye. Do not place lamps and objects to be viewed too close together, and keep the contrasts in brightness in the room within a level comfortable to the eye.

MOOD LIGHTING Fringed shades hanging from wall brackets help to create atmosphere in this bath/dressing-room. Mirror reflections give extra light.

FILAMENT BULBS

PEAR SHAPE
This is the most common type of filament bulb. It is available in a clear or pearl finish (see p. 86); variations include daylight blue and pink pearl. Wattage 25-200. Bulb sizes vary; caps are standard.

SPECIAL SHAPES
Bulbs are made for decorative or particular uses, such as candle shapes (plain or twisted), pilot lamps or pigmy lamps (to fit into a very small space). The finishes available vary. Wattage is usually low, ranging from 6-10 for pilot lamps; 25-60 for candle shapes. Caps may be standard or small.

BLOWN GLASS AND PAR REFLECTORS
Specially shaped bulbs for floodlights or spotlights have internal silvering to concentrate the light beam or disperse it to a wide angle. The PAR 38 bulb, made from pressed glass, is tough and can be used indoors or out. Wattage 40-150.

MUSHROOM SHAPE
Bulbs of this design can be used in shallower fittings than pear-shaped bulbs. They are made with a white finish only, and usually cost slightly more than the pear shape. Wattage 40-150. Bulbs of 100 and 150 watts are bigger, but caps are standard.

PEAR AND MUSHROOM REFLECTORS
Bowl (or crown), silvered pear-shaped bulbs can be used to throw light backwards to a parabolic reflector to give a narrow forward beam. The dark base of the bulb cuts out glare. Silvered mushroom bulbs give more direct light than standard mushroom. Wattage 60, 100.

FILAMENT TUBES

LINEAR FILAMENTS
Tubular filament lamps are used mainly for concealed strip lighting or mirror lighting. Lengths: double cap 222, 285 mm. (8¾, 11¼ in.), wattage 30, 60; single cap 305 mm. (12 in.), wattage 60.

ARCHITECTURAL STRAIGHT AND CURVED
Architectural tubes are used in the same way as other tubular filament lamps, but have peg caps – at each end or in the centre. Lengths 305-1,220 mm. (12-48 in.), wattage 40, 60 curved, 35-150 straight.

FLUORESCENT TUBES

CIRCULAR
Circular tubes are available in three diameters, measured to the outside of the circle. The sizes are: 200 mm. (8 in.) for 22 watts; 300 mm. (12 in.) for 32 watts; 400 mm. (16 in.) for 40 and 60 watts.

MINIATURE STRAIGHT
Straight tubes for use in small spaces are 16 mm. (⅝ in.) in diameter. They vary in length from 150 mm. (6 in.) to 525 mm. (21 in.). The range of colours is limited. Wattage 4, 6, 8, 13.

STANDARD STRAIGHT
Tubes 38 mm. (1½ in.) in diameter are sold in seven lengths from 450-2,400 mm. (18 in.-8 ft) and in a number of colours (see p. 86). Narrower, 26 mm. (1 in.), tubes are also made. Wattage 15-125.

LIGHT SOURCES Bulbs and tubes vary in shape, size and power according to the work they are designed to do.

• LIGHT SOURCES

Domestic electric lamps are either incandescent or fluorescent. Light from incandescent bulbs or tubes is produced by the glow from a tungsten filament heated by electric current, so they are known as filament lamps. With fluorescent lamps, the light is produced by the glow from a phosphor coating on the glass inside the tube, activated by an electric discharge through gases.

Both types are rated according to the electrical power (wattage) they use. This depends on the electrical pressure (voltage). Most household lamps are designed to use the given wattage at 240 volts.

The normal life expectancy of filament lamps is 1,000 hours. Long-life bulbs last for 2,000 hours, but cost more and give less light. They are useful for places where the light socket is difficult to reach. Bulb filaments have either single coil or a more concentrated type of coil, which will give up to 20% more light for the same wattage.

Incandescent lamps get very hot in operation. Do not exceed the maximum wattage recommended for the fitting in which the bulb is to be used.

Domestic fluorescent lamps give about twice as much light as incandescent lamps for the same amount of electricity used. But they need complicated control gear (usually built in), and although cheaper to run are more costly to install. The life expectancy of a fluorescent lamp is 5,000-7,500 hours.

Most bulbs are fitted into the lighting socket by means of two-pin bayonet caps (BC), but Edison Screw caps (ES), widely used on the Continent, are becoming more popular due to the influence of the EEC. In the UK they have been mainly used only for special bulbs, such as reflectors.

COLLECTING OIL LAMPS

Oil lamps have been used for more than 15,000 years. Stone Age men lit their caves by burning animal or vegetable oil in hollow stones or shells. The shell form was imitated in pottery, metal and glass by the Egyptians who probably invented the floating wick. Later, the Greeks and Romans developed a lamp with a closed oil reservoir and a spout for the wick. Large lamps had a dozen or more spouts, each with its own wick.

Spout lamps, burning vegetable and animal oil, remained in use for more than 2,000 years, until the middle of the 19th century, when James Young, a Scot, discovered how to refine paraffin from mineral oil. This made possible the development of the flat-wick oil lamp, with a glass chimney or globe, that was to light even the humblest of Victorian homes.

The cheapest Victorian table lamps had japanned stands and plain-glass chimneys. A little more money bought a cast-iron stand with a decorated glass fount or oil reservoir.

Many better-quality lamps had beautiful shades, such as the etched-glass tulip shape on the table lamp (left), or the cut-glass globe of the lamp on the right.

In country areas, oil lamps were used well into the 20th century, and provincial shops still occasionally provide interesting finds for the collector. Small hand lamps (centre) or harp lamps designed to hang from the ceiling are the most common and are usually the least expensive.

• BULBS AND TUBES

Because of their small, compact shape, bulbs give more adaptable lighting than tubes, which are mainly used for concealed lighting or powerful strip lighting.

Running costs for lighting are as follows: a 100 watt filament bulb is designed to burn for 10 hours on 1 unit of electricity, a 65 watt 1,500 mm. (5 ft) fluorescent tube for 15 hours. At the rate of 2p a unit, a home with ten filament lamps and five fluorescent tubes each burning about 40 hours a week could therefore be lit at a cost of just over £1 a week.

Filament lamps will have a shorter life if they are used in a horizontal position or if they are vibrated or jolted.

Fluorescent lamps will have a shorter life if they are switched on and off frequently. Do not switch off every time you walk out of a room for a short period, as the biggest strain on the tube is in starting.

Sometimes a tube will not start, but constantly flickers and goes off. This may mean that the starter (a small cylinder in the light fitting) needs to be pushed in more firmly or replaced. Switch off before touching the starter.

Keep the tube and diffuser clean, as a coating of dust or grease cuts down the light output considerably. Light output depreciates 15-20% towards the end of a tube's life. Tubes are best changed once they begin to get dull, or start to become black at the ends.

FILAMENT BULBS

Pear-shaped bulbs are also called GLS (General Lighting Service) bulbs. Those with a clear finish give a hard, sharp light and should be used only in opaque fittings or in fittings that have been designed to give a sparkling effect.

A pearl (frosted) finish gives softer shadows without any loss of light output. Pearl bulbs are suitable for most fittings. Pink pearl bulbs give a warm glow without any appreciable light loss.

Daylight-blue GLS bulbs have blue-tinted glass, giving light as close as possible to daylight. These bulbs are good for colour matching, but their light output is reduced by half to two-thirds.

Coloured pear-shaped bulbs are available for lighting effects, but their light output is poor because most of it is absorbed by the colour coating.

Mushroom-shaped bulbs have a white finish from an internal silica coating. This gives a very even light with little shadow, and the glow from the filament cannot be seen.

Because of its slightly smaller size, it is often possible to fit a more powerful mushroom bulb into the space previously occupied by a pear-shaped bulb. But do not exceed the recommended wattage for the fitting, otherwise it could overheat and scorch the shade.

Three-light mushroom bulbs have two filaments that can be used separately or together to give three different light outputs. They are more expensive, have screw caps, and need a special switch to control the use of the filaments.

Reflector bulbs with internal silvering are expensive. A pearl bulb with a clip-on reflector is a cheaper alternative, but the reflector is more likely to get scratched and dirty and therefore to be less efficient.

Low-voltage reflector bulbs are designed to operate at 12 or 24-28 volts, and cannot be connected to the mains supply without a transformer. They give a bright light for a small size, and are mostly used for high-intensity spotlights of narrow-beam reading lamps.

FILAMENT TUBES

Filament tubes can provide strip lighting that is not too powerful. This is an advantage where a fluorescent lamp would be too bright in contrast with other lamps in the room. Double-cap tubes are made with clear and opal (which is similar to white) finishes, single-cap with opal finishes only.

Architectural type linear filaments are often used for strip lighting under glass shelves in display cabinets or for lighting mirrors.

Very powerful tungsten-halogen filament lamps (300 or 500 watts) are available. These are very small and are mostly used for floodlighting.

FLUORESCENT TUBES

There are different 'colours' of white fluorescent tube, varying from cool blue-white to warm pink-white. These different colours produce different effects on the colours in a room. The names of colours are not standard among manufacturers.

Many colours are intended for commercial and industrial use. 'Artificial Daylight', for instance, gives a cool light that allows very accurate colour matching. 'De Luxe Natural', which makes all colours appear brighter and tends to emphasise red, is used in florists' and butchers' shops and for food displays in stores.

'White' and 'Warm White' tubes give the highest light output, and are intended for workrooms where bright light is needed. But they tend to emphasise greens and yellows and give an orange tinge to reds, so have an unkind effect on decorations and complexions. 'Plus White' tubes are designed to combine bright light with good colour effect. They are available only in a limited number of lengths.

The most suitable colours for home use are 'De Luxe Warm White', 'Home-lite', and 'Softone 27'. Although less powerful than White or 'Warm White', and available in fewer lengths, they have a good effect on colour and blend well with tungsten filament lamps.

Many fittings are sold already packaged with 'White' or 'Warm White' tubes. If you do not want this colour, ask the retailer to change it for a 'De Luxe Warm White' or similar colour. This may cost more.

For decorative use, tubes coated with various colours – such as green, gold, pink and blue – are also available, but their light output is reduced. Reflector tubes are made in some lengths.

Three fully recessed downlighters give unobtrusive, direct light for use at bedroom wardrobes and at cupboards.

Direct light for tasks such as reading or sewing is best supplied by a portable, adjustable table lamp.

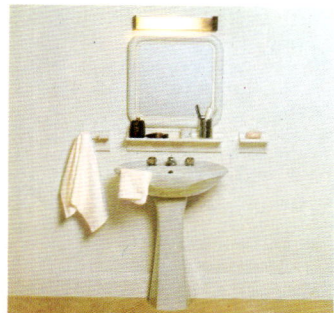
Wall-mounted fluorescent tube with a plastic diffuser gives a good light for use at a mirror over a bathroom wash-basin.

White plastic pendant fitting, suspended on an adjustable rise-and-fall device, throws a direct light on to a dining-room table.

Translucent flat-drum fitting on a hall ceiling gives semi-direct lighting which helps to show the stairs clearly.

• LIGHT FITTINGS

Fittings can be used to direct light, diffuse it, conceal it, release it, or in some other way to control it as needed for a desired effect.

It is a mistake to choose a fitting solely for its appearance; consider whether it will do what you want it to.

The style of fitting chosen can contribute to economy. Ease of cleaning is important, as dirty fittings decrease the efficiency of the lamp. Fittings for bathrooms must be proof against steam and condensation; enclosed ceiling fittings are preferable to pendants, and glass or plastic is more suitable than metal.

There are many fittings for filament lamps, varying from traditional fabric shades to parabolic spotlights. Shades should be light coloured inside to give good reflection.

Fittings may be surface-mounted (on a ceiling or wall); recessed (normally into a ceiling, but sometimes into a wall); pendant (suspended from a ceiling); or portable (to stand on floor or table).

For fluorescent tubes the range of fittings is narrower. They are generally mounted on a batten – on the surface or recessed – and may be bare or covered by a translucent diffuser; there are some pendant types. But tubes can be used in many ways – concealed behind pelmets or baffles, or behind luminous panels to light up a whole ceiling.

LIGHT DISTRIBUTION

Fittings distribute their light directly, indirectly, or by general diffusion. More than half – including most hanging shades and shades for portable lamps – are designed to distribute by general diffusion. This means they send part of the light upwards and part downwards.

The effect of most is to give an even light all round. For a given wattage, the larger the shade the better it will give soft, almost shadowless, glare-free light.

Direct-distribution fittings send more than 90% of their light downwards, and normally give pronounced shadows. They include surface-mounted or recessed ceiling fittings, pendant metal shades, and adaptable fittings such as spotlights and adjustable portable lamps.

The degree of light control varies. A fitting may be designed to give downward light over a fairly wide area, or a narrow beam that can be directed on an object for effect.

Indirect fittings send more than 90% of their light upwards, with very little shadow. They are mostly used in conjunction with direct fittings, to reduce contrast. Light might be directed on a ceiling, for example, so that a bright, direct ceiling fitting that left the ceiling unlit would be seen against a lighter background.

Indirect lighting does not necessarily call for a different type of fitting; it can be a direct fitting used in a different way – a wall-mounted spotlight directed towards the ceiling, for example.

There are intermediate categories – semi-indirect fittings that send 60-90% of light upwards (for example, a suspended glass bowl) and semi-direct that send 60-90% downwards (for example, an opaque cylindrical shade suspended from the ceiling).

When buying a fitting, always ask to see it working so that you can see how the light is directed and how much light the shade absorbs, and thus get an idea if it will be suitable for your purpose.

• LIGHT SWITCHES

Dolly switches – flicked up and down – are most commonly used in the home, but neater, more easily operated, rocker switches are becoming more popular.

Pull-cord switches are the only type of switch that can be used in a bathroom to comply with electrical safety regulations. They are also useful for separate control of wall or ceiling lights in other rooms, and are cheaper to install than wall switches as they do not need wiring down the wall to a switchplate.

Wall-mounted push-button switches need only a very light touch to operate, and are more expensive than dolly or rocker switches. As they can be operated with any part of the body, they are useful for handicapped people.

Dimmer switches vary the amount of light given out by a lamp. They can be used to dim the main room lighting for watching television, for example, or in a child's bedroom to produce a nightlight level of illumination. Or they can be used to alter lighting effects according to mood.

Most dimmers can be fitted in place of a normal switch, but because they are more complex they are more expensive. Since they decrease the power consumed, they can save an appreciable amount on the cost of electricity.

On some types there is only one control for dimming and switching on and off; others have a separate on/off switch so that the dimmer can be left set at a certain level.

Dimmers are rated by the maximum wattage they can carry, which is usually up to 500 watts. They are mainly used with filament lamps – dimming fluorescent lamps is costly because extra equipment is needed. Plug-in dimmer switches can be fitted to portable lamps.

Make sure that the dimmer you buy can be used for two-way switching if required, and that it is well insulated at the back – some are, in fact, completely enclosed. It should also incorporate a suppressor to prevent interference on radio and television.

Door switches that turn on the light when the door is opened and off when it is closed can be used for cupboards. Automatic time switches can be used for outside lighting, night circuits, or as security lighting to deter intruders; they can be set to turn lights on and off at certain hours.

Photo-electric switches can also be used for automatic switching, but they are more expensive. They are sensitive to daylight, and turn lights on at dusk and off at daylight.

Wall-mounted uplighter gives indirect background light to help reduce shadows and contrast in a sitting-room.

Large, pendant Japanese paper shade gives a diffusing, glare-free light, which adds to comfort in a sitting-room.

Spotlights on ceiling-mounted lighting track give easily altered direct lighting for various activities in the nursery.

A parabolic spotlight, with a bowl-silvered bulb, is used to focus attention on paintings on a wall in a sitting-room.

Kitchen work top and sink receive direct light from a small fluorescent tube screened under a cupboard.

• SITING AND WIRING

If the house is being completely re-wired, plan the positions of new out-lets carefully. Take into account maintenance as well as performance, as all lamps will need to be changed and fittings cleaned from time to time, and should be easy to reach.

If the house is not being rewired and there are not enough points for your needs, there are ways of over-coming the shortage.

The simplest way is to fit a two or three-way adaptor to a power socket. Leads can then be run from the lamp and plugged into the socket. But there is a danger of overloading a point if other appliances are used on the adaptor. And trailing flex can cause accidents; if portable lamps are used, they should be placed as near to the plug socket as possible.

A better way is by means of lighting track. This is aluminium track that can be surface-mounted or recessed on a ceiling or wall and wired to a single lighting point. It will then support and supply current to four or five fittings along its length. They are clipped on with special adaptors and can be moved along the track. The electrical conductors are recessed in the track.

Each manufacturer makes light fit-tings for his own track, and the fittings are not interchangeable between makes. Small appliances, such as a hair drier, can also be run from the track, if the loading will allow it.

Up to 1,200 watts can usually be run from a lighting point. The maxi-mum load for a track is normally stated by the manufacturer, but it must not exceed the load that can be carried by the circuit. Always check the loading with an electrician.

Single-circuit track for domestic use is available in lengths of 1,000 mm. (3 ft 3 in.) or 1,200, 2,400 and 3,600 mm. (4, 8 and 12 ft), according to the manufacturer. Straight and right-angled pieces for joining lengths are also available.

Another method is to run a number of flexible pendant lights from one ceiling plate. The pendants can be spread out and screwed into the ceil-ing at different points. Take care not to overload the lighting point.

For a reading light near the centre of the room, ceiling-recessed or ceiling-mounted cylinder downligh-ters or track-mounted spotlights are alternatives to portable lamps.

At least one room switch should be by the door for use on entering. In a room with two doors, there should be a two-way switch at each door so that the circuit can be operated from either position.

• GARDEN LIGHTING

A lighted garden can be arranged for viewing from inside the house, or for effect when viewed from outside. An extra advantage of lighting your house and garden is that it discour-ages burglars.

It is usually most effective visually to have the light sources concealed, with light directed on trees, shrubs, statues or other interesting features.

Lighting from the mains (240 volts) gives the widest choice of equipment, but 24 or 110 volt equipment can be used with a transformer. Equipment must be weatherproof, and is best installed by a qualified electrician.

Surface cable can be used, or for permanent outdoor lighting, a ring-main circuit 455 mm. (18 in.) under-ground, with weatherproof-socket outlets on posts above ground, can be installed. Fittings can be run from the sockets by a length of cable.

Lights outside appear brighter at night than lights of the same wattage indoors, so fairly low-wattage lamps can be used.

BATHROOM/SHOWER
The ceiling is luminous, with 'De Luxe Warm White' fluorescent tubes concealed behind translucent PVC panels. Architectural straight filament 500 mm. (20 in.), 60 watt tubes are each side of the mirror.

Mirror lighting

KITCHEN
Four ceiling-recessed downlighters, 190 mm. (7½ in.) diameter with 100 watt lamps, are supplemented by 900 mm. (3 ft) 30 watt fluorescent tubes fitted under shelves and concealed behind pelmets to avoid glare.

Ceiling-recessed downlighter

LIVING-ROOM
Six eyeball spotlights, adjustable in all directions, are semi-recessed into the ceiling; they have 100 watt lamps and reflectors and are switched in pairs. Over the dining table is a 100 watt rise-and-fall pendant.

Rise-and-fall pendant

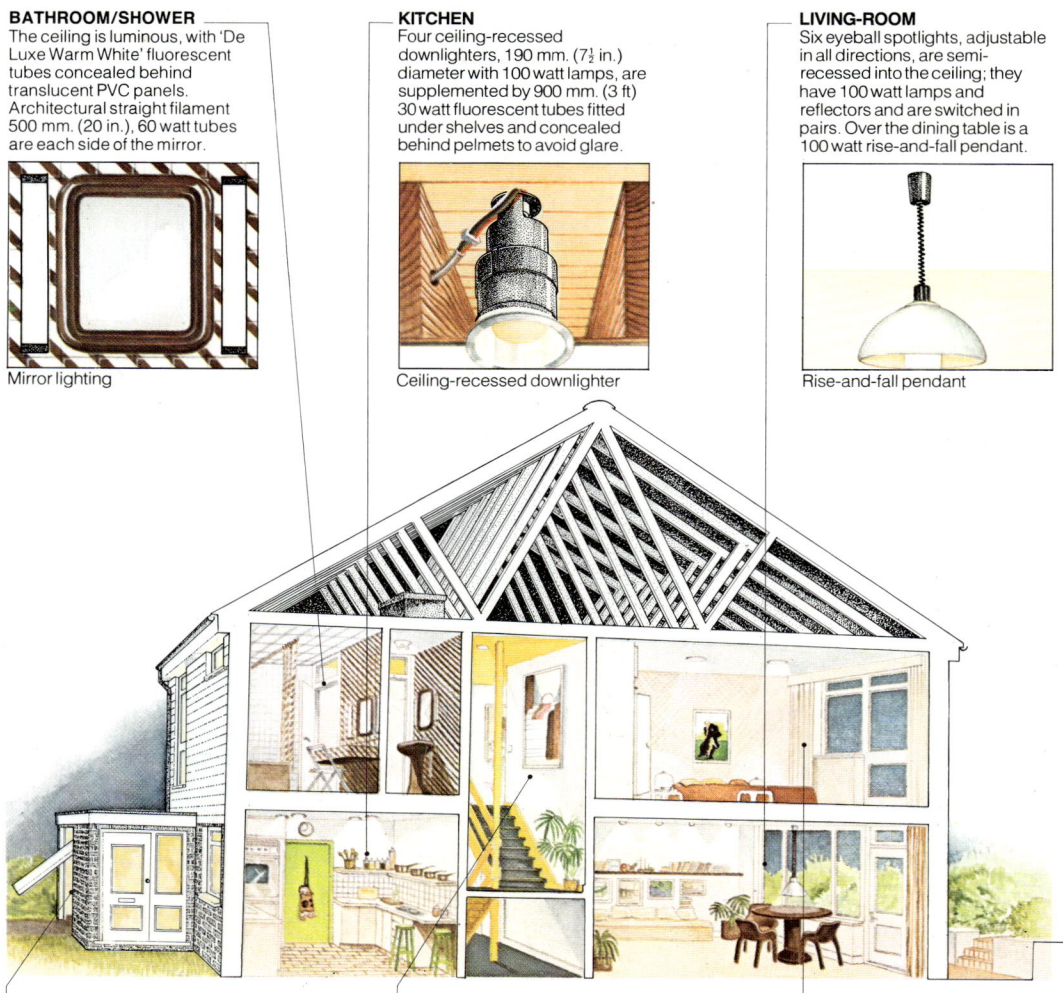

WORKSHOP/GARAGE
Lighting is from a 1,500 mm. (5 ft) 65 watt fluorescent tube; a 900 mm. (3 ft) 30 watt fluorescent tube and wall-mounted adjustable spotlight illuminate the bench. A plug-in distribution board extends the single power socket.

STAIRCASE
Direct lighting from a 150 watt ceiling-recessed cylinder fitting on the landing shows up stairs by throwing light on treads and leaving shadows on risers. There is a similar fitting inside the front door. Both are dimmer-controlled.

BEDROOM
Two 1,200 mm. (4 ft) 40 watt fluorescent tubes are in front of the window behind a pelmet. Two 100 watt recessed ceiling lights are in front of cupboards, a third over the foot of the bed. Table lamps are by the bed.

MODERN SEMI-DETACHED HOUSE Lighting has been used to add character to a house that otherwise resembles all its neighbours. Recessed lights have been built into several rooms, and full use has been made of the many power points to create a flexible system adaptable to the varying needs of the members of the household.

LIVING-ROOM
Diffused general lighting is from a 610 mm. (2 ft) diameter suspended paper shade with a 150 watt clear lamp. Display cabinet striplights are separately switched. Twin-socket power points supply standard, table and reading lamps, record player, TV.

STAIRCASE
A triple spotlight with 60 watt lamps lights the stairs from the first-floor landing. The ground-floor landing has track-mounted spotlights, similar to the hall, trained on pictures down the stairway. Plastic cylinders, 250 mm. (10 in.) across with 100 watt lamps, light the attic and basement landings. All lights can be dimmed for night use.

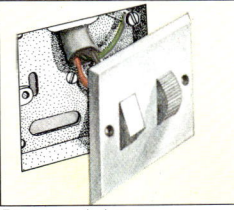

Dimmer switch

NURSERY
Lighting track from the single, central ceiling point carries three adjustable spotlights with 100 watt PAR 38 lamps to reach all parts of the room. A low-wattage nightlight on the wall above the beds can be changed for a study lamp in later years.

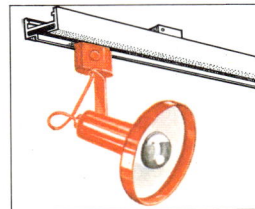

Lighting track

ATTIC BEDROOM/STUDY
The bedhead is lit by a 324 mm. (12¾ in.) 8 watt fluorescent tube, and the 60 watt study light, plugged to a power point, is fixed to adjustable shelving over a work top. A ceiling-mounted pendant lamp has a looped flex that slides on curtain rail.

HALL
Three spherical spotlights with 75 watt reflector lamps are mounted on lighting track from the central ceiling point. They are trained on prints on the wall. The 60 watt porch light, with a switch inside the door, is on a bracket holder.

BATHROOM
Ceiling-mounted plastic cylinders with 100 watt lamps light both the bathroom and the adjoining utility room. Additional lighting in the bathroom is from a wall-mounted heat/light unit and a combined mirror light and shaver point.

LOFT
A 100 watt pearl lamp in a simple batten holder is controlled by a door switch – a push-button switch that turns the light off when it is pressed in by the door edge, and on when released as the door is opened.

BEDROOM
The bed is parallel to the window to avoid too much daylight glare. Twin 60 watt reading lamps, with separate switches, are fitted 765 mm. (2 ft 6 in.) above the bed. The full-length mirror in the recess has a 490 mm. (19¼ in.) 60 watt architectural strip filament lamp just above it. Two recessed ceiling lights, with 100 watt lamps and opal diffusers, are positioned in front of wall cupboards.

Door switch

KITCHEN
There are two ceiling-mounted 1,500 mm. (5 ft) 65 watt fluorescent tubes with prismatic diffusers. In addition, there are slimline tubes, with separate switches, concealed under cupboards. The dining area is lit by a 100 watt rise-and-fall pendant.

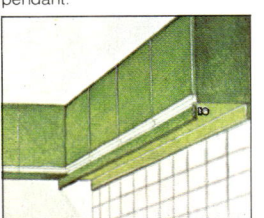

Striplight concealed by batten

• HOW TO GO ABOUT PLANNING

Draw a plan of the hall, landing and each room on squared paper (see pp. 28-29), and mark in doors, windows, fireplaces, radiators, furniture, existing lighting points, sockets and switches. Note special decorative effects – for example, curtains, alcoves, surfaces such as timber or marble – and any danger points.

Beside each plan print a list of practical and decorative requirements and points to note. Then use an overlay on the plan to decide suitable fittings and locations by trial and error. For each one, consider use and future use, comfort, safety, maintenance and effect.

Walk round at dusk noting danger spots such as unexpected changes of level, and make sure they are well lit at night, with switches conveniently sited.

A night circuit for lighting the hall and stairs (or the whole house) during the night can be arranged by dimming the normal lights or by separately controlled low-power lights. Dimmed lights can also be left on while the house is empty to discourage burglars; alternatively, lights can be turned on while the house is empty by means of an automatic switch.

Lighting in the living areas of the house needs to be as flexible as possible, so that it can be adapted according to mood and needs. The total wattage for a room should not be supplied by one fitting only – it is better to use a number of lower-wattage lamps. This reduces the likelihood of glare, allows more light to be directed where it is needed, and gives more scope for lighting effects.

Fluorescent lighting is not generally recommended for a living-room, but is most useful in kitchens, garages and work areas.

MODERNISED VICTORIAN HOUSE This tall, narrow house on several floors shows many of the lighting problems that can occur in an older house. The basement and the attic have little natural light and on three levels the stairwell has no natural light at all. The solutions chosen make use of the existing circuits as far as possible, although some re-wiring had to be carried out to provide adequate lighting in the kitchen and in the main bedroom of the house.

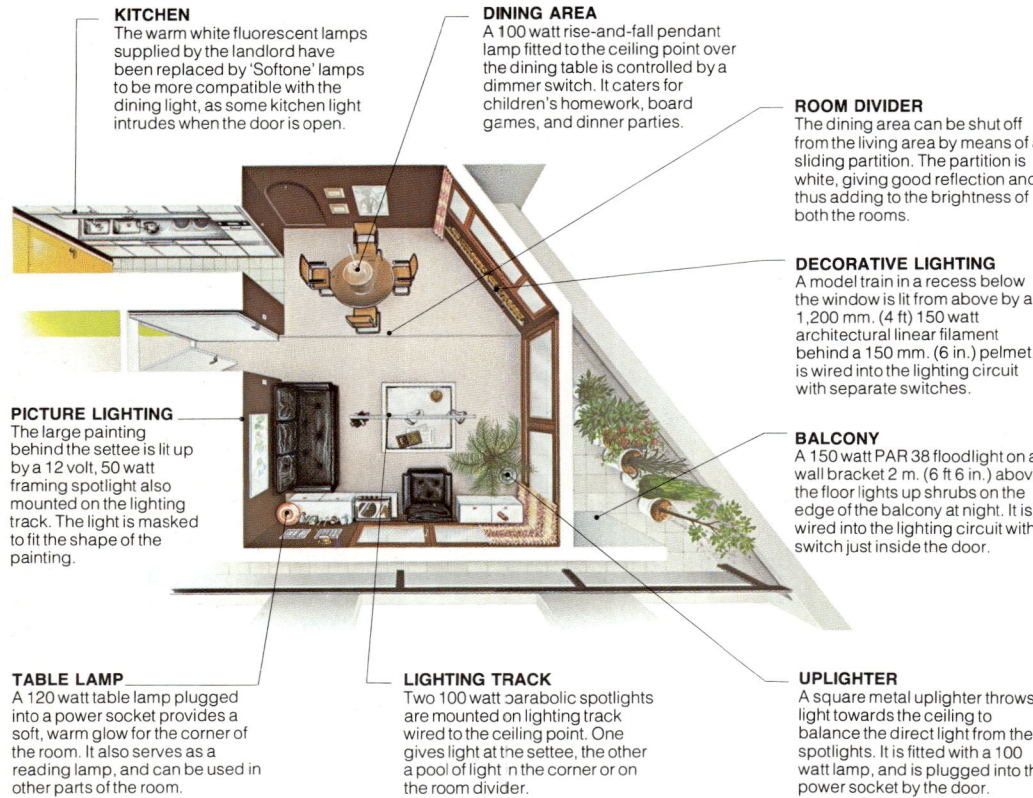

KITCHEN
The warm white fluorescent lamps supplied by the landlord have been replaced by 'Softone' lamps to be more compatible with the dining light, as some kitchen light intrudes when the door is open.

DINING AREA
A 100 watt rise-and-fall pendant lamp fitted to the ceiling point over the dining table is controlled by a dimmer switch. It caters for children's homework, board games, and dinner parties.

ROOM DIVIDER
The dining area can be shut off from the living area by means of a sliding partition. The partition is white, giving good reflection and thus adding to the brightness of both the rooms.

DECORATIVE LIGHTING
A model train in a recess below the window is lit from above by a 1,200 mm. (4 ft) 150 watt architectural linear filament behind a 150 mm. (6 in.) pelmet. It is wired into the lighting circuit with separate switches.

PICTURE LIGHTING
The large painting behind the settee is lit up by a 12 volt, 50 watt framing spotlight also mounted on the lighting track. The light is masked to fit the shape of the painting.

BALCONY
A 150 watt PAR 38 floodlight on a wall bracket 2 m. (6 ft 6 in.) above the floor lights up shrubs on the edge of the balcony at night. It is wired into the lighting circuit with a switch just inside the door.

TABLE LAMP
A 120 watt table lamp plugged into a power socket provides a soft, warm glow for the corner of the room. It also serves as a reading lamp, and can be used in other parts of the room.

LIGHTING TRACK
Two 100 watt parabolic spotlights are mounted on lighting track wired to the ceiling point. One gives light at the settee, the other a pool of light in the corner or on the room divider.

UPLIGHTER
A square metal uplighter throws light towards the ceiling to balance the direct light from the spotlights. It is fitted with a 100 watt lamp, and is plugged into the power socket by the door.

MULTI-PURPOSE ROOMS A room used for a number of activities needs lighting that can easily be adapted.

WINDOWS Dark walls and ceiling absorb very bright sunlight and avoid glare.

• MULTI-PURPOSE ROOMS

A room used for several different purposes, like a living and dining-room, is likely to need several different kinds of lighting. Diffused general lighting will give enough light for moving about. Brighter, more concentrated light will be needed at various points for dining or for reading or sewing. And decorative lighting is required to give the room warmth and character.

The rooms illustrated are the kitchen and combined living and dining-room of a flat. Without any alterations to the wiring, the lighting has been improved to cater for a range of activities and tastes.

No daytime electric lighting is needed. The flat is on the 18th floor and there is plenty of daylight from the large windows. The furnishings have been arranged to make the best use of the daylight and to avoid glare.

Although the living-room has only two conventional ceiling points, seven light fittings have been accommodated – four from the ceiling, one wired into the lighting circuit with a separate switch, and two plugged into power sockets.

The total area of the room is about 30 sq. m. (300 sq. ft), and the total wattage from the seven lamps is 720, giving approximately 24 watts per square metre. For multi-purpose rooms, where there is a variety of needs, the 20 watts per square metre recommended for general lighting (see p. 84) gives a rough guide and starting point only.

Lighting track (see p. 88) has been used for running several different fittings from a single point, and dimmer switches can alter the level of lighting from various fittings.

It is often difficult to avoid fixed light fittings, particularly pendants, being reflected in a television screen, but dimming helps to soften the reflection so that it does not cause annoyance.

GENERAL POINTS TO CONSIDER
Pendant lamps are useful for bringing the light source to a lower level in a room with a high ceiling, but they can be obtrusive in a small room. Wall lights give a subdued light, since the wattage has to be low to avoid glare, and they throw most of their light on the wall. They tend to make a room

DAYLIGHT Consider the natural light available before planning furnishings.

ACCENT LIGHTING   Local lighting giving highlights and shadows is better than dull, even lighting.

LIGHT FOR DINING   Rise-and-fall pendant provides glare-free light at table, and reduces contrast.

look smaller, and are most effective in large rooms.

Unobtrusive general lighting can be supplied by ceiling-recessed fittings, which give fairly bright, glare-free light. The smallest recessed fitting needs at least 125 mm. (5 in.) of space in the ceiling joists. Semi-recessed fittings give a similar lighting effect, but are more obtrusive.

Recessed downlighters also give suitable light for reading directly below them, so are an alternative to the conventional portable table or standard lamp. But as they are nor-

mally on the general lighting circuit, they cannot be used for reading when the lights are dimmed for television.

Another way of providing light for reading or sewing is by means of spotlights. Parabolic reflector spotlamps are useful as they do not cause glare to other people in the room.

Low-voltage spotlamps that give very bright, narrow adjustable beams are suitable for reading or sewing. They cannot be connected to the mains supply (240 volts) without a transformer – some types have one built in.

Spotlights can also be used for lighting up ornaments or pictures, or for throwing light on a curtain or wall, producing the effect known as wall washing. Recessed downlighters are also available with a deflected beam for wall washing.

A dining table needs a pool of direct light, but the lamp should not cause glare to the diners or interfere with their view across the table. If the light is controlled by a dimmer, it can be varied to suit the occasion.

Suitable fittings over a dining table are a recessed downlighter or a rise-

and-fall pendant, which has a counter-weight device so that it can be adjusted to a suitable height for dining, working or playing at the table.

Some subdued background light is needed to reduce contrast, and it is an advantage if the dining-table light is on a separate circuit so that the general lighting can be dimmed – or turned off if there is other background lighting in the room.

A dining-table light needs to be on a separate circuit in a kitchen/diner, where the bright kitchen lights are best turned off during a meal.

DECORATIVE LIGHTING   A display in a recess gives soft background light.

91

MAKING LAMP-SHADES

When it is not possible to buy lampshades which exactly match a particular setting, it is a good idea to buy a frame and cover it with material of your own choice. Three of the most popular shapes – the tiffany, the straight-sided and oval-bowed empire – are described here. The frame of an old, discarded lampshade can also be re-covered. To calculate the covering material required, measure the depth of the shade and add 7.5 cm. (3 in.) for the length. The width should at least equal the shade's widest circumference.

• TIFFANY LAMPSHADES

The tiffany frame can be covered in many ways. A simple fabric cylinder can be stretched over the wires, or more sophisticated covers can be tailored to fit the frame.

MATERIALS AND EQUIPMENT
Frame; lampshade binding tape; between needle; covering material; steel pins; cold-water dye to match the covering material; scissors; paint; PVA adhesive; tape measure; braid.

PREPARING THE TAPE
Work out the amount of lampshade binding tape to buy by adding the lengths of the vertical struts and multiplying by two. Add to this two-and-a-half times the lengths of the rings. Dye the tape to match the covering fabric.

BINDING THE FRAME
File smooth any rough edges on the frame. Paint it to prevent rust.

Cut a piece of binding tape one-and-a-half times the length of a strut.

Begin binding one strut by putting one end of the tape over the top ring, so that 2 cm. (¾ in.) lies against the strut [A1]. Pull the rest of the tape around the ring and wind it round the strut, going over the end of the tape. Keep the tape pulled taut and bind down the strut [A2] until it is covered. At the bottom, take the tape over the ring and sew in place [A3]. Bind all the other struts in the same way.

Begin binding the bottom ring by holding 5 cm. (2 in.) of tape outside the ring, to one side of a strut. Take the rest of the tape over the ring [A4], and

---

BINDING THE FRAME

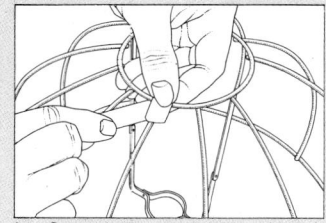

A1. Start binding each strut where it meets the small ring.

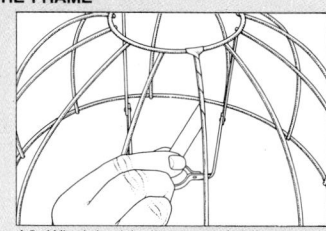

A2. Wind the binding tape tightly around the strut, overlapping each turn.

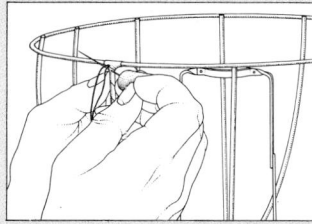

A3. At the bottom of the strut fold the tape over the ring and sew in place.

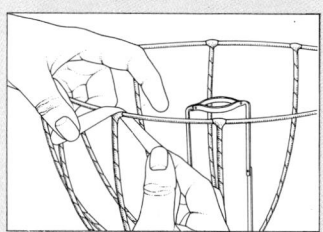

A4. To bind the ring, first pull an end of tape taut across the end of a strut.

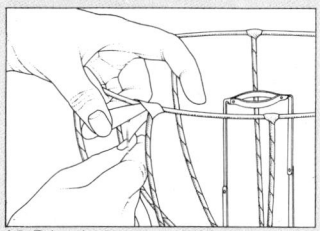

A5. Bring the longer end of the tape under the ring and round the strut.

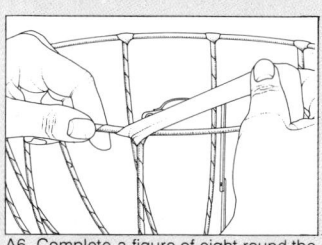

A6. Complete a figure of eight round the strut and start binding the ring.

SEWING ON THE COVERING FABRIC

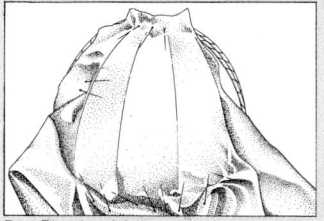

B1. Pin the fabric over three panels, securing it to the outer struts and rings.

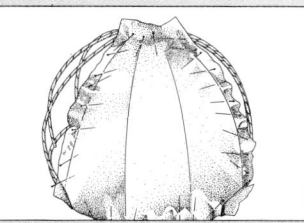

B2. Pull fabric taut and place more pins along rings and struts. Trim excess.

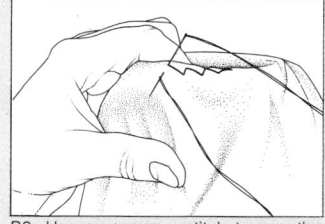

B3. Use an oversew stitch to sew the fabric to the pinned struts and rings.

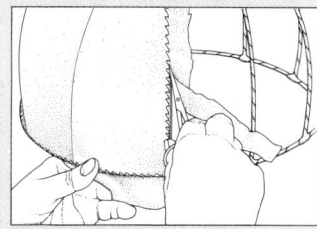

B4. Cut one side of the fabric as close as possible to the strut to which it is sewn.

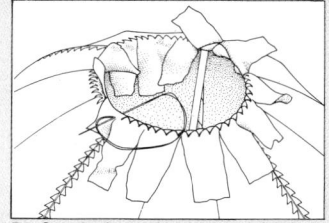

B5. Sew the flaps of folded-back fabric at the top of the shade to the small ring.

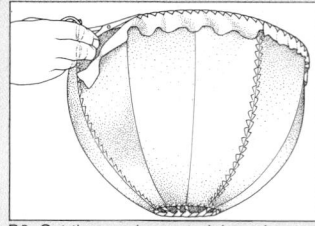

B6. Cut the surplus material as close as possible to the top and bottom rings.

• TIFFANY
• OVAL BOWED
• STRAIGHT-SIDED

pull it through the other side of the strut and over the ring [A5]. Pull the rest of the tape over the uncovered side of the ring to complete a 'figure of eight' round the strut [A6].

Go round the ring, repeating the figure of eight at each strut. At the first strut, bind in the 5 cm. tail and finish with a few stitches. Repeat along the top ring.

SEWING ON THE MATERIAL
Place the material over four struts, i.e. three panels, with the grain going diagonally across the shade. Pin in place halfway along the top and bottom rings, and where they join the outside struts [B1]. Pull the material taut to eliminate all creases. When the material is stretched fully, pin securely down the struts and along the rings.

Trim the material, leaving a 15 mm. ($\frac{1}{2}$ in.) overlap at the struts and 2.5 cm. (1 in.) at the rings [B2].

Using double thread and a between needle (see p. 286), sew the material to the two pinned struts and rings with long diagonal and short straight stitches [B3]. Trim one side flush to one strut [B4].

Repeat the process to sew another panel of fabric across the next four struts, starting at the strut which the first panel is trimmed to. Go on like this until four panels cover the shade. Trim the edges flush with the struts, but leave uncut material at the top and bottom rings. Cut slits in the material at the top, down to the ring, and sew the material to the ring [B5]. Trim the surplus material flush with the ring. Repeat at the bottom ring [B6].

COVERING THE STITCHES
Cut four 3 cm. (1$\frac{1}{8}$ in.) wide strips from the material, each 5 cm. longer than the struts. Fold in each side, to make a 15 mm. wide strip. Press and diagonally-stitch the join [C1].

Sew one end of the strip to the top of a sewn strut. Glue the rest of the strip to the strut, masking the rest of the shade to prevent glue spoiling it [C2]. Trim the strip level with the bottom ring [C3]. Repeat on the other struts.

Cut and sew another strip, 4 cm. (1$\frac{1}{2}$ in.) wide, 5 cm. longer than the circumference of the top ring. Turn under one end of the strip, lay it on the ring, and stab-stitch in place [C4]. Where the strip joins, turn the end under, overlap and sew [C5].

FITTING THE BRAID
Cut the braid the same length as the circumference of the bottom ring plus 2.5 cm. Turn back and sew one end to the ring. Pin, then sew the rest to the ring, securing the top and bottom with a slanting stitch [C6]. Turn the end under and butt to the start.

FITTING THE STRIPS AND BRAID

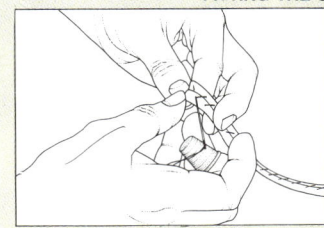

C1. Sew the folded-in edges of the strip together to form a 15 mm. wide strip.

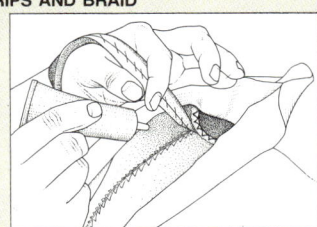

C2. Glue the strip to a sewn strut, sticking it down 5 cm. at a time.

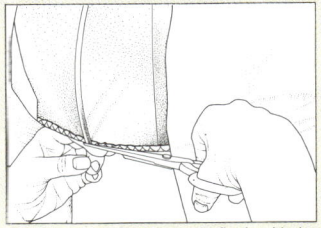

C3. Cut the end of the strip flush with the bottom of the lower ring.

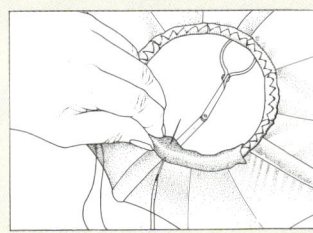

C4. Secure the top strip by stab-stitching under and over the small ring.

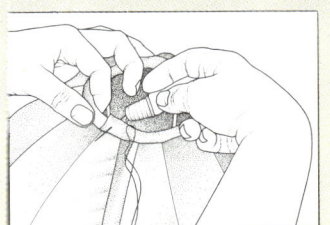

C5. Turn under the ends of the top strip, overlap and sew together.

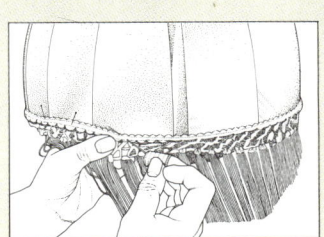

C6. Oversew the braid to the bottom ring. Turn under the end and butt to the start.

TIFFANY LAMPSHADES A dark satin shade directs the light downwards for use as a spotlight. The satin also creates an atmosphere of luxury. Other fabrics create different effects, so that tiffany frames have a wide range of uses.

COVERING AN OVAL-BOWED FRAME

This graceful shape lends itself to a delicate covering material such as broderie Anglaise, crêpe-backed satin or silk. With very thin material, a double lining is needed: an inner balloon lining inside the frame, and a middle lining to fit between the frame and the covering material.

When stretching, fitting and sewing the cover and braid to the frame, the methods and stitches are the same as those used for covering the tiffany lampshade (see p. 92).

COVERING THE FRAME

Paint the frame and bind the oval rings and the two main struts [1].

If you are covering the shade with a soft material such as satin, silk or loosely woven cotton, fold in half across the grain of the fabric (see p. 291). If you are using heavier material, do not fold the fabric.

Lay the material up to the shade with the grain running straight up the centre panel. Pull the material so that it fits tightly round the struts on one of the long sides of the frame. When the material is taut, pin to both rings and the bound struts.

Use contrasting-coloured cotton to put lines of tacking in the material, following the lines of pins. Make sure that the tacking stitches go through the material only, and do not catch the binding on the struts and rings [2].

Unpin the material from the frame. Cut the cover to shape, allowing an extra 5 mm. ($\frac{1}{4}$ in.) outside the strut tacking on each side and 2.5 cm. (1 in.) outside the top and bottom tacking. If the material was doubled, there will now be two halves. If not, because a heavier material has been used, only one half will now be formed.

Mark an edge of this half and a strut or ring of the shade, so that they can be matched. Make the second half of the cover in the same way. Take the pins from the second piece of material to free it from the frame. Lay the halves right sides together and align the tack stitches. Machine-stitch together along the line of tacking, pulling the fabric taut as it is sewn. Remove the tacks.

If you are fitting a middle lining to the shade, repeat the process by folding the lining material and pinning it to the shade. Remove from frame and sew in same way as cover.

MAKING THE INNER LINING

Pin and cut the two halves of the inner lining in the same way as the outer cover. Lay right sides together. Begin machining the two halves together at the tacking on the top of the strut position.

Gradually move the line of stitching in from the tacking until the stitch line is 15 mm. ($\frac{1}{2}$ in.) inside the tacking half way down the side. From this point, move gradually outwards to meet the tacking at the bottom of the strut [3]. This gives a bowed seam which keeps the lining taut. Repeat for the other side.

FITTING THE LININGS AND COVER

Turn the middle lining right side out. Push it over the frame with the seams positioned down the bound struts. Keep the raw edges of the seams together so that the line of stitching runs behind the strut [4]. This conceals the seam and prevents a wide band showing when the light shines through the cover.

Pin the lining to the top and bottom rings and pull taut. Sew to the rings and finish at the top and bottom in the same way as for the tiffany lampshade (see p. 93).

Fit and sew the top cover to the frame in the same way as the middle lining.

Trim the seams of the inner lining 5 mm. ($\frac{1}{4}$ in.) from the stitches.

Position it inside the frame, aligning the seams with the bound struts. Bring the raw edges of the seams together so the stitches lie beside the struts. Pin the bottom of the lining to the bottom ring. Pull the top, so that about 2.5 cm. of material protrudes above the top ring. Unpick about 15 mm. of the seams at the top of the lining so that the open seam fits round the gimbal supports where they join the ring [5]. Pull the lining taut inside the frame, and pin it to the top and bottom rings.

Cut 2 cm. ($\frac{3}{4}$ in.) slits in the lining material where it overlaps the top ring. Stitch the material to the outer surface of the ring binding, hiding the stitches that secure the top cover and middle lining [6]. Trim the material close to the stitches.

Repeat at the bottom ring, although in this case it is not necessary to cut slits in the material before sewing it to the ring.

FINISHING THE FRAME

From the lining material, cut 11.5 cm. ($4\frac{1}{2}$ in.) long strips, 2.5 cm. wide. Fold in and press the edges of each length to form a strip, 15 mm. wide.

Place one strip under one gimbal support [7]. Cross over the ends so that they overlap at the top of the support [8].

Sew the overlapping strip to the ring so that it hides the junction of the gimbal and top ring. Trim close to the stitches. Cover the second gimbal support in the same way.

Finish the top and bottom rings by sewing on a lace ruffle, braid or tape, made from the lining or covering material in the same way as for the tiffany lamp (see p. 93).

FITTING THE COVER AND LINING TO THE FRAME

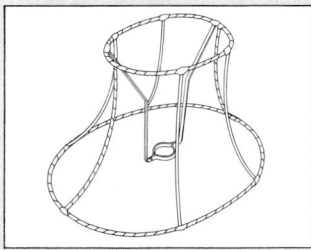
1. Bind the rings and the two struts furthest apart with tape dyed a suitable colour.

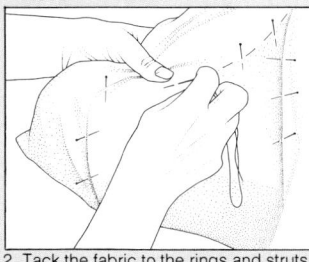
2. Tack the fabric to the rings and struts, taking care not to catch the binding.

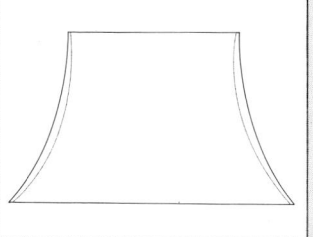
3. Machine the lining, curving out from the tacking at the middle of the seam.

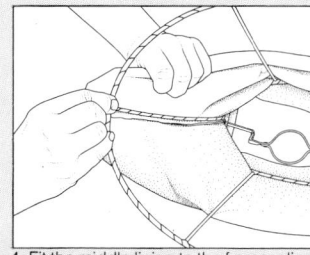
4. Fit the middle lining to the frame, aligning the seams with the bound struts.

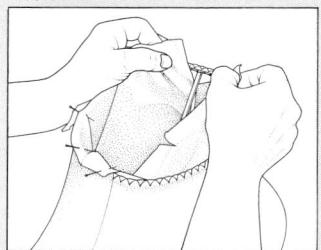
5. Unpick the top of the lining seams to fit the lining round the gimbal supports.

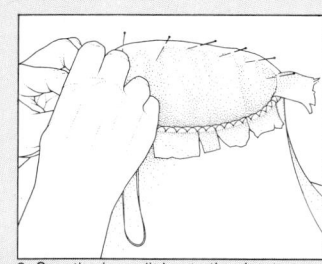
6. Sew the inner lining to the ring to conceal the cover stitching.

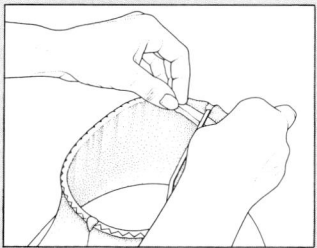
7. Centre one strip under one gimbal support close to the junction with the ring.

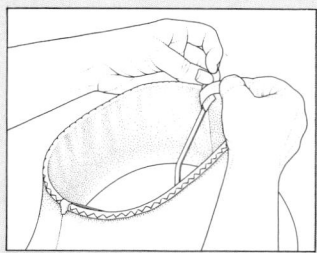
8. Cross the strip over the gimbal support and overlap the ends flat on the top ring.

• STRAIGHT-SIDED LAMPSHADES

The easiest way to make straight-sided shades is to sew ready-bonded lampshade material to two rings, one of which must carry a gimbal. It is also possible to use a thin fabric and iron it to special adhesive-backed lampshade card. Bonded card is ideal for shades in children's rooms as it can be decorated with pictures cut out from books and stuck on.

MAKING THE SHADE

Bind the rings, following the instructions for the tiffany shade (see p. 92).

Cut out the required depth of the shade from a large sheet of paper. Use clothes pegs to clip it to the rings. Overlap the sides of the paper by 15 mm. ($\frac{1}{2}$ in.), cutting off the excess.

Stick the paper to the back of the bonded material with transparent adhesive tape and cut round the paper.

If using adhesive-backed card and separate material, iron the material to the glue side of the card, overlapping the fabric until it is stuck.

Trim the overlapping fabric on one short side to within 5 mm. ($\frac{1}{4}$ in.) of the card. Trim the remaining three sides flush with the card [1]. Stick the overlap to the card with PVA glue [2]. Wipe off any excess glue and allow the joint to dry.

Peg the card to the rings so that it projects 3 mm. ($\frac{1}{8}$ in.) beyond each ring [3]. Sew the cover to the rings with small blanket stitches (see p. 297), as in [4]. Glue the overlapping edges of the cover together.

Cut two lengths of tape, braid or ribbon, 2.5 cm. (1 in.) longer than the circumference of the rings. Turn under 5 mm. ($\frac{1}{4}$ in.) at one end of one piece. Glue round the top. Turn under the raw end and butt to the start. Repeat for bottom ring.

BONDED LAMPSHADES

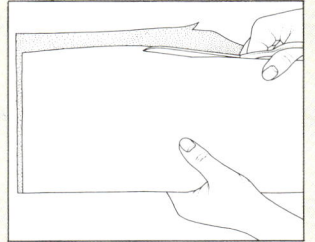

1. Cut the fabric flush with three sides of the card, leaving one short side uncut.

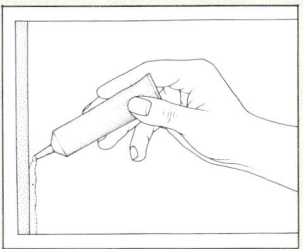

2. Glue the edge of the card which the fabric overlaps.

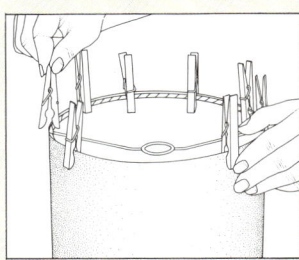

3. Peg the ring so it is about 3 mm. below the top of the card.

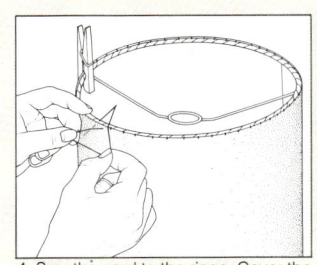

4. Sew the card to the rings. Cover the stitches with braid or ribbon.

STRAIGHT-SIDED LAMPSHADES *Drum or cone shapes are the most common straight-sided shades. They can be fitted to hanging lamps, but are best suited to table or standing lamps since they can be used with any size and type of base.*

Furnishing your home

The secret of success in furnishing a home is not simply
a matter of having money to spend: it is a question of imagination,
and of applying a few simple skills.
This section provides the ideas that will stimulate your imagination,
and teaches the basic skills you need in order to repair and renovate furniture,
and to make cushions, loose covers, bedding
and other soft furnishings.

CONTENTS

CHOOSING FURNITURE

Bentwood and wickerwork, glass and chrome, hardwood and leather; flowing curves or angular shapes – the types and designs of furniture available are broad enough to help you to achieve almost any style you want. Since furniture can be bought from many different sources – furniture shops, department stores, discount warehouses, second-hand and antique shops, auction rooms and private dealers – shopping around beforehand, to compare price and quality, is invaluable. Remember that expensive furniture does not necessarily mean quality furniture; moreover, each piece should be carefully considered to see how well it is likely to satisfy your particular needs and stand up to the wear you will give it.

• GETTING VALUE FOR MONEY

Discount houses advertise widely in the press and, if you are prepared to pay cash and collect yourself, offer the largest reductions on new furniture. Seasonal sales at furniture shops and stores can also be a source for getting new furniture at reasonable prices.

Second-hand furniture that is soundly constructed but otherwise in poor condition can be worth buying. Stripped down to the bare wood and either varnished, painted a bright colour, or re-upholstered, it can be given new life.

Bargains can be picked up in second-hand sale rooms but, since the quality is likely to vary, furniture bought this way needs to be carefully examined beforehand for any signs of damage or woodworm.

Whitewood furniture or prefabricated units that can be assembled at home are also worth considering. The furniture is basic and austere but reasonably priced; and the imaginative use of paint, plastic laminates and self-adhesive plastic coverings can give it a quite different character. Whitewood furniture is particularly suitable for built-in fittings, where its use can save time and effort.

Alternatively, instead of buying relatively inexpensive furniture that you may tire of after a few years, buy a nucleus of good-quality pieces and add to them as you are able.

SYMBOLS OF QUALITY

Furniture that complies with the basic requirements of the British Standards Institution bears the BS kitemark and should stand up to reasonable wear and tear. Good-quality fabrics carry the International Wool Mark or Woolblend-mark (see p. 348).

BEFORE BUYING

Consider first what furniture you already have that you want to keep, and whether you are likely to want further matching pieces later. If so, write to the manufacturer to find out whether the furniture is likely to remain a stock item.

Remember that too much furniture will make a room look small and cluttered. Check not only that you have space for an item of furniture but also that you will be able to get it into a room or perhaps manhandle it up a narrow winding staircase. Take a tape measure with you, if necessary, and measure the piece in the showroom or shop.

Some items of furniture, such as convertible couches or storage units, may be partly dismantled with a pair of pliers and a screwdriver. If you decide to buy such an item, in order to be able to get it in your house make sure there are no particular snags and that you will be able to reassemble it easily; it can be expensive and you may have to wait a long time for a manufacturer to send a craftsman.

WHITEWOOD FURNITURE An example of how the skilful use of paint and colour can give inexpensive whitewood cupboards a distinctive character.

THINGS TO CHECK

Always see and examine furniture before buying it.

Check that the framework is firm and rigid and that the joints are tightly assembled. Veneered or laminated surfaces should not be chipped, cracked, blistered or lifting off at the edges or joins. Look along surfaces at an acute angle to find blemishes, flaws or unevenness due to knots or defects in the base material.

Milky-looking patches in polished wood indicate that dampness was present during the finishing – a fault that cannot be remedied easily. Plastic surfaces should be smooth and even – a texture like orange peel is the result of poor laminating or spraying.

Examine the unfinished surfaces inside and underneath. Splitting at the edges may indicate badly seasoned timber. Look for large knots – any that are loose may soon fall out; any that are sticky have not been sealed and may exude resin for months. Look for protruding nail or screw heads that could cause damage or injury.

Try cupboard doors and drawers to be sure they are not too heavy for the

REVIVED New look for an old chest.

BUDGET FURNITURE Bricks and boards used for temporary shelving.

framework and spoil the balance of a piece of furniture when they are opened. Hinged doors and flaps should be close-fitting – but they should not stick or scrape against the lining when opened. Look underneath shelving to see if it is adequately and securely supported.

Drawers should fit snugly, without sticking or excessive sideways movement. Check that heavy drawers sliding on metal runners do not jump off when fully withdrawn. Check also that drawer joints are sound and that the material used for the bottom is strong

enough for its job. Look underneath to see how it is fixed. Cheap drawer-bottoms are stapled to the drawer frame; good-quality drawer-bottoms are grooved into the sides.

Handles should be securely fixed, conveniently positioned and easy to grasp. Test them carefully to ensure that there are no rough edges to trap fingers or tear finger-nails. Open and close catches to check that they work efficiently and are strong enough to hold the door or flap.

Where possible, look underneath upholstery, to check the condition of the canvas or webbing. It should be taut and secure – not loose or baggy. Cover fabric should be closely woven. It should not be too unyielding to sit on, or so loose that it opens up when used. There should not be any loose or long threads on the surface that might catch or pull.

Always check what an upholstery fabric is made of, whether it is moth-proofed and how it should be removed for cleaning. All upholstered furniture of quality should display a label describing the composition of the covering, or the information should be supplied separately.

Bamboo or cane that is split around the rings may ultimately splinter and be difficult to repair. Examine wickerwork, cane and rush furniture for unravelling or flaking. Some minor defects can be repaired (see p. 122).

Check the screwed joints on bentwood furniture and examine all curved surfaces carefully – splits on the outer edges of a curved frame open up and make it dangerous.

Check that furniture on castors can be moved easily and that the fixings are sound.

CHILDREN'S FURNITURE

This should be strong enough to withstand rough treatment and, if up-

holstered, it should be covered with a material that can be removed and cleaned easily.

Look out for sharp corners or metal fittings with jagged edges; wooden furniture that is badly finished or splintered; and projecting nail or screw heads. Check also that slats or uprights, such as those found on the side of a cot or play-pen, are spaced in accordance with safety standards – not less than 7 cm (2¾ in.) and not more than 8.5 cm. (3⅜ in.) apart.

Some foreign makes of furniture may be finished with a lead-based paint – check with the retailer that only non-toxic paints have been used.

Remember that children's furniture for outdoor use should be sturdily constructed so that it is capable of withstanding the rigours of the weather.

When buying items that have hinged doors or lids, avoid those that close with a scissor-like action, for example, a storage box having a lid that fits within the sides, rather than resting on the top. Furniture hinged this way can trap or sever small fingers.

Similarly, beware of large chests and cupboards, fitted with self-closing catches, in which a child could be trapped.

HOW FURNITURE IS DELIVERED

You can check the general quality of furniture in the shop or warehouse, but make sure that the pieces delivered to you are up to the same standard. It is not always possible to unwrap and check a delivery while the vanman waits, but when you sign the delivery note write 'not examined' beside your signature, and check the furniture as soon as possible. Make sure colours and fabrics are right and that all moving parts work properly. If there are any faults, contact the

BUILT-IN SEATING Painted blockboard and softwood, and cushions, use the awkward space in a bay window to provide seating and display space.

retailer at once (see Consumer problems, p. 344).

BUILT-IN FURNITURE

The chief advantage is that a built-in fitting can save valuable space in a small room, or where recesses and awkward projections make it difficult to position freestanding furniture successfully.

Built-in fittings are cheaper than freestanding furniture and add value to a house. A range of built-in cupboards and work tops, with laminated surfaces, can make a considerable

contribution towards improving both the appearance and the efficiency of an old-fashioned kitchen.

Built-in fittings need less material, thinner sections of wood, and simpler joints than conventional furniture, because they rely upon the walls for a major part of their strength and stability. A built-in cupboard, from floor to ceiling in a deep recess, can be constructed without a top, bottom, back and sides, whereas a conventional cupboard must be strong enough to stand unsupported and be finished on all sides.

• FURNITURE FOR COMFORT

The advantage of good furniture is that in addition to being designed for a specific purpose, it has been carefully related to the user's comfort. For instance, in a well-designed and soundly constructed chair the height and width of the seat and the back, the height of the arm rests and the angle of its various parts will provide the maximum of comfort for the average person to work or relax in.

A well-designed chair should offer more than one comfortable sitting position.

Adjustable easy chairs, which can be moved into a great many alternative angles to suit varied postures, are usually expensive. So it is worth trying various chairs before making a decision to buy.

At one time, most tables and desks were made at the same height; nowadays they are made in different heights, and tables and desks can more easily be bought to suit a specific use, such as for meals, or writing, typing, looking at large books, playing games and so on.

FINISHES AND COVERINGS

Good-quality furniture is often made from solid wood, but a lot of good modern furniture is built mainly from manufactured board, which is less likely to warp or twist. Solid wood is generally used for frames, drawer sides and runners, and – except for cheap furniture – for lipping the edges of manufactured boards.

Surfaces may be veneered – that is, covered with a thin layer of decorative wood. This is used to improve the appearance of some plain woods.

Whether plain wood or veneered, furniture needs a further coating, or finish, to protect it and make it easier to clean. Various clear finishes are used. Wax or oil-based finishes do not give much protection against scratches or stains, but can be repaired in the home (see p. 112). French polish is used only for high-quality or reproduction furniture, and can be damaged by water or other liquids (see p. 114).

More hard-wearing finishes are lacquers or a combination of cellulose and plastics. These have good resistance to denting, scuffing, staining and heat, and are also easy to maintain in good condition.

Plastic laminates can be used as an alternative to veneer. These are made with layers of resin-impregnated paper – the top layer usually decorative – coated with melamine resin.

Upholstered furniture has a wood, metal or plastic frame, with springs, stuffing and an outer covering. Sometimes the stuffing alone provides the springing.

Traditional stuffing materials, such as fibre, horsehair or flock, are often replaced by rubber or plastic foam: materials that are easy to use and hold their shape.

Outer coverings are often woven fabrics – wool or man-made fibre or a blend of both. Blended materials are easier to clean and more hard-wearing than all-wool fabrics.

The weave is as important as the fibre – a close weave generally gives the hardest wear. Wool-pile fabrics, rarely used today, generally give better wear and show dirt less than woven fabrics. Coated fabrics, such as Lurex and Dacron – plastic with a woven or knitted backing – are hard-wearing and easy to clean. Choose a fabric that lets air through, otherwise the surface tends to get sticky after being used for any time.

Leather is hard-wearing and easy to clean (see p. 320), but is expensive. Natural leathers – those with no surface treatment – stain easily..

CARING FOR FURNITURE

In order to extend the life of furniture, as well as preserve its appearance, use only the appropriate cleaning materials and methods recommended for each particular type of wood, fabric and finish.

Of even greater importance are the ways in which you can avoid damaging furniture that is in everyday use.

Never stand furniture directly beside a radiator – excess heat will cause the moisture in the wood to dry out, resulting in shrinkage cracks and joints opening up. Remember that, to a limited extent, this may happen anyway with furniture brought into a centrally heated house, or to furniture in a house when central heating is subsequently installed.

Never put hot dishes or plates on to a finished surface – use a dry table mat. A damp mat will conduct heat. Avoid standing warm or wet cups or glasses on a polished surface. Always wipe up spilt liquids, including water, immediately.

Never use a plastic-laminated surface for cutting bread or vegetables – it will be irreparably damaged; similarly, never place dishes on it that have come straight from a hot oven.

Do not leave upholstered furniture in direct sunlight for too long; otherwise the fabric covering material will tend to fade. In a room that receives a lot of sunlight, use slip-on covers to protect the main fabric.

For the cleaning and care of upholstery, see p. 320.

From time to time and whenever practical, change the position of furniture in a room to avoid the excessive indenting that can occur in soft floor coverings.

Alternatively, use the fittings that can be slipped over the ends of chair and table legs to broaden bearing surfaces (see p. 361).

CHAIRS FOR RELAXATION

Try to achieve an informal arrangement that is suitable for day-to-day use, but flexible enough to rearrange when entertaining on a large scale. Low, comfortable chairs, facing each other across a coffee table, create a natural conversation area. Allow at least 300 mm. (12 in.) space between table and chairs for leg room. Similarly, allow at least 600 mm. (24 in.) between the back of chairs and a wall.

The best height for a low table is about 50 mm. (2 in.) above the seat of an easy chair.

A comfortable wing-back easy chair, that also shields the user from draughts.

A chesterfield sofa, suitable for both traditional or modern interiors.

A relaxing bentwood-and-cane rocker – for reading, writing, knitting or dozing.

Chrome and leather furniture, expensive but characteristic of a modern interior.

Inexpensive foam-rubber seating units that can be arranged as sofas or beds.

DINING AND WORKING CHAIRS

If space is limited and chairs are to be used for dining, as well as working at a table, choose those that provide you with comfortable leg room beneath the table. Remember, too, that chairs having arms, when used at a table, need more space – allow at least 250 mm. (10 in.) between them.

Allow 750 mm. (2 ft 6 in.) between a table and a wall, or similar surface, for a chair to be easily accessible.

Folding or stacking chairs will save space in a small room and make it easier to cope when entertaining.

Bentwood furniture is easy to paint and looks attractive in bright light colours.

Modern and comfortable chairs, with cane seating and resilient tubular framing.

FURNISHING SMALL ROOMS

Where space is limited, a wall-storage unit can be a significant help, particularly if it incorporates a fold-down bed. Unit-storage boxes can be added to as required.

Fold-down tables, often used in the garden, could be a space saver in a small room. Many kinds are made, some painted or stained with bright colours, or with a natural wood finish.

Tubular furniture in a small but modern room creates an illusion of space if the table-tops and seats are of transparent material.

A folding gate-leg table, useful in a bedsitter when it can be stored out of sight.

Folding chrome-and-Perspex chairs that are light enough to hang on a wall.

A lightweight canvas chair, stylish enough to be used in house or garden.

Stackable plastic chairs – space-savers for the small kitchen or dining area.

Chrome-and-glass furniture that can be seen through helps a room to seem larger.

A plastic-and-glass table that serves a dual purpose – also used for storing drinks.

An adjustable office chair, easily adapted to suit most practical heights.

A child's high chair can be used at normal table height or folded to form a rocker.

A pinewood and sea-grass chair – a small and practical chair suitable for the kitchen.

A storage unit with foldaway bed – ideal for a small room used by occasional guests.

Unit storage boxes – adaptable fittings suitable for a variety of storage problems.

STORAGE

No home can be comfortable without sufficient, properly organised storage space. Make sure that the storage space in your home is adaptable enough to cope with changing needs. Always add something extra to your estimated requirements, so there will be space available for new articles as they come along – particularly if there are hoarders in the family. A policy of 'something in, something out' may be necessary if space is very limited, but is usually unpopular and difficult to carry through.

• ASSESSING STORAGE SPACE

Before installing any storage systems, survey the whole house and decide what storage is needed in each room, and where to place it.

As well as noting the obvious places where shelves and cupboards can be fitted, look for places, such as alcoves, where forgotten space can be put to good use. There may be room over doors, for example, or over the staircase. Lofts and cellars are useful storerooms if well organised.

When siting large cupboards, take into account how they will affect the appearance of the room. Built-in cupboards from floor to ceiling, completely filling one wall, may alter the proportions of a room – especially one with high ceilings – and can make it feel narrow and cramped.

• MAKING USE OF AWKWARD SPACES

If there is storage space in out-of-the-way places, use it for long-term storage of things not in everyday use.

LOFTS

Lightweight folding ladders are the best means of access to lofts. They normally fit on the top of a drop-flap trapdoor, folding into the roof when not in use. Several types are available, with instructions for fitting. Some makers will fit them, although this adds considerably to the cost.

Check that the ceiling joists are free of woodworm (see p. 378), and are strong enough for what you plan to store. If in doubt, get professional advice.

If the joists are strong enough, fix flooring-grade chipboard across them. The loft should be well ventilated and free from damp and leaks. If possible, get lighting installed.

Open shelving along at least one side of the loft gives more efficient use of space. Some things can be hung from the rafters – deck chairs, for example, which are best hung away from a wall to avoid mildew.

HIGH-CEILINGED ROOMS

Ceiling racks that are lowered by means of ropes and pulleys are a well-known way of airing clothes. This system can be adapted for storing other light items – baskets, for example, or clothing on coat-hangers.

SPACE ABOVE DOORS

Many doors have sufficient space for an open shelf or small cupboard above them. Make sure the wall is strong enough (see p. 109). If there is an alcove above the doorway, a shelf or cupboard can be supported across bearers on the two side walls.

As such storage space is bound to be about 2 m. (6 ft 8 in.) high, it can be reached comfortably only by using a step-ladder. If the door underneath opens inwards, it should be locked, or warning given when someone is using the shelf or cupboard.

The best type of cupboard door is an up-and-over or shutter door. Alternatively, use a roller blind (see p. 80).

METAL SHELVING Strong and easily fitted, metal shelving provides neat and compact storage in this utility room.

ABOVE AND BELOW STAIRS

The space above the stairs is useful for storage if it can be made accessible. If there is a landing alongside the banisters, a cupboard can be built from the banisters to the far wall of the stair-well, with access from the landing. This is a job for a craftsman.

If you have a walled-in cupboard under the stairs, do not push things to the low end so that they are difficult to get at. Fit shelves the full length of the cupboard wall, and keep the floor clear. This way there is normally just enough room to stand inside.

Under-stair space that is not walled in can be more easily adapted to your needs – by fitting shelves, cupboards or drawer units in descending height, for example.

CELLAR

A cool, dry cellar is useful for storing non-perishable food and wine because of its even temperature.

If the cellar is damp, most items stored there for any length of time will suffer from rust, rot or mildew. Dampness may be caused by condensation, which can be remedied, or by rising damp or seepage, which are costly to treat.

Condensation is usually caused by poor ventilation; check to see if any air vents are blocked. If the cellar is damp, and the cause is not obvious, it is best to get professional advice.

• DIMENSIONS

Throughout this section, the following definitions have been used when the dimensions of shelves and furniture have been given; *width* – the measurement from front to back; *length* – the measurement from side to side.

DECIDING WHAT TO STORE WHERE

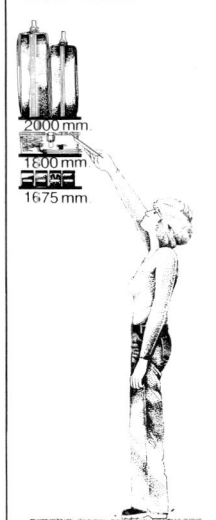 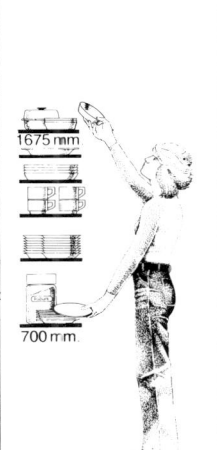 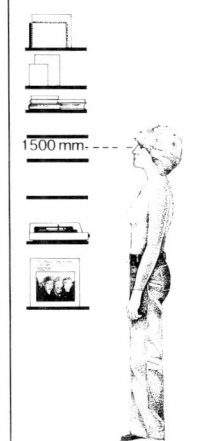 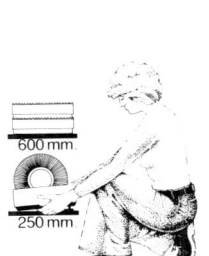  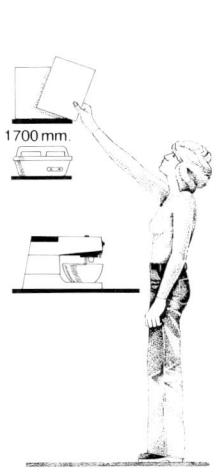 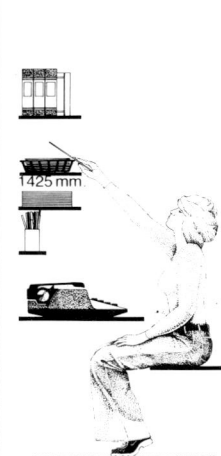

From a standing position, the highest shelf from which a woman of average height (1,625 mm., 5 ft 4 in.) wearing flat shoes can comfortably lift a lightweight article with one hand is about 1,800 mm. (6 ft) – or up to 50 mm. (2 in.) higher if the article is flat. The maximum height she can reach is usually about 2,000 mm. (6 ft 8 in.).

Use shelves higher than 2,000 mm. only for lightweight items not often used.

For a woman of average height, the shelves easiest to get at are those 700 - 1,675 mm. (2 ft 4 in. - 5 ft 6 in.) high. Use the most accessible shelves for storing things used most. Heavy items needing two hands to lift them are best stored at about 700 mm. (2 ft 4 in.).

With a taller woman, her upper reach rises at the same rate as body height, her lower reach at about half the rate. So for a woman 1,780 mm. (5 ft 10 in.) tall, the easiest shelves to reach are those 760 - 1,800 mm. (2 ft 6 in.- 6 ft) high.

To enable the user to see the back of each shelf from a standing position, make the space between shelves greater at high and low levels than near eye level. For a woman of average height, eye level is about 1,500 mm. (5 ft).

Ideal widths for shelves are 100-300 mm. (4-12 in.), depending on the article to be stored. If shelves are too wide from front to back items become difficult to reach.

Items stored below a height of about 600 mm. (24 in.) cannot be lifted out without bending. Use shelves lower than 600 mm. for storing awkward or heavy things that are not often used.

The shape of an article and the way it has to be picked up affect the height at which it is best stored; the lowest shelf height for comfortably picking up something flat is 250 mm. (10 in.).

A person kneeling to take articles from a low cupboard or a pulled-out drawer needs about 700-1,000 mm. (2 ft 4 in. - 3 ft 4 in.) of space in front of the cupboard or chest of drawers to be able to move comfortably.

Plan storage so that it can be used with the least amount of effort and inconvenience by the most frequent user. Take into account any physical handicaps, such as weak wrists or back trouble, which make lifting and bending difficult. Store things as near as possible to the place where they will be used – spare light bulbs and cleaning materials, for example, can be stored both upstairs and downstairs.

For a shelf above a work top, the maximum comfortable height for a woman reaching across from a standing position is about 1,700 mm. (5 ft 7 in.).

If she is sitting at a work top, a shelf at about 1,425 mm. (4 ft 8 in.) is the highest she can reach across to comfortably.

• STORAGE FURNITURE

There are three basic types of storage furniture – individual pieces, unit furniture, and fitted (or built-in) furniture. Storage space is sometimes also provided in furniture designed mainly for another purpose. See p. 98 for points to check when buying furniture.

INDIVIDUAL PIECES

The advantage of individual pieces of furniture – such as a sideboard or chest of drawers – is that they can be moved to another position or room. But normally they take up more floor space than unit or built-in furniture, and can be inconvenient to clean round.

Second-hand furniture is at least as good as modern furniture in materials and construction. It is worth looking for suitable storage pieces in second-hand stores and junk shops, and at furniture auctions.

Pieces that are not suitable for use as they are can often be adapted. A chest of drawers can be made into a desk, for example (see p. 118). Alternatively, they can be dismantled and the timber and fittings used to build something more suitable.

Before buying, make sure that there is no woodworm (furniture beetle). It can be recognised by holes, a little larger than pin holes, from which a fine, white sawdust falls when the wood is tapped. If no dust falls from the holes, then the woodworm has probably been successfully treated and the furniture is safe to take home.

But it should be inspected regularly and re-treated if necessary (see p. 379). Do not store it in an attic or a place where structural timbers could be attacked.

Holes are most likely to be found in rough, unpolished surfaces, so make sure you examine the back, inside and undersides carefully, as well as the bottoms and backs of drawers.

FURNITURE FROM KITS

Many kinds of storage furniture can be bought in kit form for home assembly. Before buying try to see a kit assembled and check the quality and appearance.

Before starting assembly, make sure that the kit is complete and undamaged. Note also how each part is fixed and in what order. If you miss a step in the construction, you may have to dismantle the piece and start again. This can damage the joints.

• UNIT FURNITURE

A manufacturer of unit furniture works to a standard basic measurement, or module, so that different pieces can be joined together in a variety of ways to suit individual requirements.

Because unit furniture is usually built against a wall, it makes the most economical use of space within a room and simplifies floor cleaning. It is not as easy to rearrange as individual pieces of furniture, but it can be dismantled and moved to a new position.

It is made for both living-room and bedroom use, but many pieces can be adapted for use in any part of the house. Kitchen storage units can often be similarly adapted (see p. 192).

LIVING-ROOM UNITS

Most manufacturers make units in matching heights and widths, but in two different lengths so that there is some flexibility in fitting the built-up system to varying lengths of wall.

The units generally available are open shelves, cupboards (closed in or glass fronted), two-drawer or three-drawer chests, drop-leaf writing or cocktail cabinets, record cabinets, and fold-down tables or desks.

Free-standing types normally have a base unit which supports two or three other units. The base unit can usually be levelled so that the alignment of units is not affected by an uneven floor. The top units may be separate pieces that can be stacked on a base, or they may be bought already fixed to a base unit.

There are some systems in which separate units can be supported

STILL USEFUL *A kitchen antique.*

INDIVIDUAL PIECES *Second-hand furniture, such as this Victorian mahogany sideboard, is solid and spacious and can be adapted to modern needs.*

UNIT FURNITURE *Wall storage makes the most economical use of space within a room and can be arranged in various ways to suit individual needs.*

between free-standing side panels or frames.

Free-standing units can be used against a wall or as a room divider. Units used to divide a room should have a polished surface at both front and back, or be used back to back.

Other systems for the living-room are designed for fixing to the wall. They are usually fitted to battens screwed to the wall – several units may be arranged on common, visible battens, or each unit hung on a separate batten that cannot be seen.

Do not plan to use wall-hung furniture until you have checked the construction and load-bearing capacity of the wall (see p. 109).

Whether you plan to use free-standing or wall-hung units, the best way to decide how they can be fitted along the wall is by working it out on a plan (see p. 28). Place a grid ruled out on tracing paper over the plan, then sketch in the units to scale until you find a suitable combination.

BEDROOM UNITS

Bedroom unit furniture is usually free standing, not wall hung, although it may be possible to fix it to a wall if required. There are often link units for combining various pieces.

Unlike fitted furniture, unit furniture has no means of adjusting the height of cupboards, or filling in a gap between a cupboard top and the ceiling. Otherwise many of the systems available, including interior fitments (see p. 106), are similar to fitted furniture.

Units available include wardrobes, cupboards to fit over wardrobes, chests of drawers, single-drawer units, headboards, and bedside units. Wardrobes may include some means of levelling, otherwise wedges can be used to level linked units. Wardrobes with cupboards on top usually reach to a height of about 2.1 m. (7 ft).

Some systems have cupboards that will fit round corners. Some also have low corner units with lift-up lids; they can be butted between cupboards and chests of drawers and used for storing blankets or linen.

Some unit furniture is supplied in pieces for home assembly – these are normally called knock-down units.

CUBE AND STACKING UNITS

The simplest and most adaptable unit furniture is in the form of cubes. These can be separate or interlocking, built up from the floor or fixed to a wall.

Cubes can be used in the basic form – three sides and an open front – or fitted with doors, shelves or drawers. They can serve as bedside tables, bookcases, display cabinets, collection cabinets, chests of drawers and filing cabinets, and are often easy to adapt to other uses.

Cubes are made of plastic, hardboard, wood or plastic-faced board. The most common sizes are 300-400 mm. (12-16 in.) per side. Some makes have units of two-cube or four-cube size, and also special desk or wardrobe units that can be fitted in.

Some types can be bought ready made, others in kits for home assembly. There are some that can be put together without using tools or adhesives – they are made up of hardboard panels that slot into corner joints to form interlocking cube units.

Furniture for stacking need not be cube units. There are rectangular drawer or cupboard units designed for stacking. Some have optional castors or a plinth for free standing.

There are also small cylindrical or square plastic units that can be stacked singly on top of each other. Each unit has a tray top and can be fitted with castors at the base, so that a number can be used to make a small, movable shelved cabinet.

CUBE UNITS The simplest and most adaptable form of unit furniture. Cubes can be used in their basic, open-fronted form or fitted with drawers, shelves or doors. Two stacks of cubes with a flat board laid across form this desk.

• SPACE-SAVING STORAGE

Storage compartments in furniture designed mainly for another purpose can be great space savers.

Beds, for example, may have drawers underneath, useful for storing blankets, linen, or other articles. One of the simplest pieces is an ottoman – a seat about 1,200 mm. (4 ft) long without back or arms. Under the seat is a trunk suitable for blanket storage.

When buying a bed with drawers, remember that it must stand in a position where the drawers can be opened. A standard-size double bed needs about 900 mm. (3 ft) of space on each side for the drawers to be opened fully.

Convertible bed settees often have space in the base for bedding to be stored. Armchairs and matching stools are available with storage space below both seats.

Occasional tables often include space for magazine and book storage, and there are designs with lift-up tops and interiors that can be used for drinks, toys, needlework or papers.

• FITTED CUPBOARDS

Fitted cupboards are made from pre-fabricated parts designed so that they can be built into a room from floor to ceiling and, if required, from wall to wall. Some are designed for do-it-yourself assembly, others are fitted by the retailer or a builder.

Although they are intended mainly for bedroom storage, cupboards can be used in any part of the house where there is a convenient space.

Many systems have a matching range of other bedroom furniture and fitments, such as free-standing dressing-tables and headboards.

Some fitted cupboard systems are simply floor-to-ceiling sliding doors enclosing an alcove, or sliding doors and an end panel against a wall.

The doors are hung on metal track fixed to the ceiling, and a guide track for the door bottoms can be laid over carpeting. The bottom door guides include springs to compensate for the unevenness of floors.

Other systems are made up of separate units that can be linked together. They are usually about 450-600 mm. (1½-2 ft) in length and width.

Manufacturers usually make fitted cupboards in several different heights. If you cannot get a cupboard of the exact height required, a small gap between the top of the cupboard and the ceiling can be panelled in. Vertical panels can be used to fill gaps between cupboards and walls.

Make sure the type of door you choose is suitable for the space available round a cupboard. Doors side-hung on hinges give maximum access to the cupboard, but there must be enough space in front for the door to be opened.

Folding doors are pivoted on running gear so that they fold and slide concertina fashion. They are usually narrow for their height and do not take up as much space when open as a side-hung door. Access to the cupboard is limited at each end by the combined thickness of the doors when folded back.

Although sliding doors save space in front of a cupboard, only half the cupboard is accessible at a time.

Cupboard doors can be papered to match the room if desired, and some are made so that the panels can be removed and covered to match curtains or wallpaper.

INTERIOR FITTINGS

Shelves are usually adjustable. They may be fitted on block joints, or rest on studs clipped into holes in the side walls of a unit. Short hanging rails may be suspended below shelves.

Drawers are often lightweight trays or baskets on plastic runners. Drawer runners may be clipped into holes in the same way as shelf studs, so that the positions can be changed easily.

FREE-STANDING UNITS

For cupboards that are areas enclosed by floor-to-ceiling doors, the shelves and drawers are fitted into free-standing units inside.

A top shelf for the cupboard can be supported by two tall units, and small units can be used below short hanging clothes. A hanging rail is normally fixed below the top shelf, supported by brackets fixed to the tall units at each end and to the shelf above. Hanging clothes can be heavy – long runs of rail need to be supported about every 750 mm. (2 ft 6 in.).

Before buying a system, check the shelf lengths available and work out how you can arrange units so that a top shelf and hanging rail will be well supported, otherwise both will sag. A long top shelf should rest on the tall units, not be suspended between them. A shelf longer than about 600 mm. on block joints at the corners will hold lightweight articles only.

SPACE-SAVING FURNITURE Storage capacity in furniture, such as in this convertible sofa/bed, is particularly useful where space is limited.

CONVENIENT STORAGE SPACE Bedding kept in the cavity below the mattress base is neatly out of the way during the day but easy to get at when needed.

OPEN SHELVES
Household linen, folded clothing, hats, handbags and various other articles stored on open shelves are easy to get at but neatly out of the way. Do not have shelves too deep – things piled too high are difficult to get out and soon become untidy.

UNDERCLOTHES
Light clothing such as underclothes, ties and socks can be stored in shallow drawers below eye level for easy selection. Alternatively, ties and belts can be hung on a pivoted rail fixed to a wall or door. Wire baskets can be used for laundry.

BACKLESS UNITS
If the units are backless, make sure the back of the cupboard is wallpapered or covered with gloss or emulsion paint that will not rub off on clothes.

HANGING RAILS
The usual height of a hanging rail is 1,650-1,800 mm. (5 ft 6 in.- 6 ft). The hanging depth needed for a jacket or skirt is about 1,000 mm. (3 ft 3 in.), for an overcoat about 1,350 mm. (4 ft 6 in.), and for a long dress about 1,500 mm. (5 ft).

SPACE FOR CLOTHES
Hanging rails that run parallel to the wall need to be about 300 mm. (12 in.) from the wall for coathangers to be hung at right-angles to the wall. If the cupboard is not wide enough to hang clothes sideways, they can be hung from front to back on an extending rail, but they are then not so easy to select.

GROUPING CLOTHES
Group long and short clothes separately on hanging rails so that the space below short clothes can be used for shelves or drawers, or another rail. A low rail is useful for a child's clothes at a height that the child can reach.

AWKWARD THINGS
Things normally awkward to store tidily, such as knee-length boots, can be placed in a compartment. A knee-length boot is generally about 500 mm. (20 in.) high. Heavy bags and suitcases can be stored at the bottom of a storage system where they are easy to lift out. Their weight puts no strain on the shelving.

SHOES
Shoes are best stored on racks for good ventilation. Racks can be made up of two parallel rods 100 mm. (4 in.) apart and about 75 mm. (3 in.) off the floor. Some storage systems have drawers fitted with shoe racks.

STORING CLOTHES A man generally needs about 1,050 mm. (3 ft 6 in.) of hanging rail for his clothes, and a woman probably about 1,650 mm. (5 ft 6 in.). A child is likely to need about 750-900 mm. (2½-3 ft) of rail. Hang outdoor coats in everyday use near the entrance to the house; allow one or two extra hooks for visitors. A free-standing coat rack gives better ventilation for coats than wall hooks.

OPEN SHELVES *One of the simplest and cheapest forms of storage, open shelves are useful in kitchens particularly for dry goods and cooking utensils.*

• TYPES OF SHELVING

The two basic methods of supporting shelves are on brackets or battens fixed to a wall, or on free-standing frames. Free-standing shelves take up more space than wall-fixed ones.

Wall shelves can be either fixed or adjustable. Some of the types available are illustrated below. The shelving is normally bought separately from the supports.

With free-standing shelves the shelves and supports are usually bought together, either ready assembled or in do-it-yourself kits. Many types have adjustable shelves.

Making existing shelves in cupboards or bookcases in your home adjustable can be difficult, but the dowels, wires or strip (see below, next page) needed can be bought in do-it-yourself shops. Strip is generally the simplest way.

One of the strongest and cheapest types of free-standing shelving is metal industrial shelving, which is generally used for workshops or garages. It can sometimes be fitted into a decoration scheme for use in the living areas of a home.

When planning shelves, think beyond your immediate needs. Try to assess how your use of them will develop. Most shelves have to carry more as time goes on.

MATERIALS AND LOADS

Chipboard is a commonly used shelving material because it is comparatively lightweight and cheap. Veneered or melamine-faced chipboard is stronger than unfaced chipboard, which will sag under fairly light loads. It varies in its ability to hold screws or nails according to its density.

Blockboard is stronger but more expensive than chipboard. Use it with its wooden core lengthways.

Plywood varies in strength and cost according to the number of plies and the quality of timber used. It can be stronger than solid wood.

Solid wood shelves are strong but likely to be heavy and expensive, and the choice of widths available is limited. Plywood, blockboard and chipboard are available in wider sections than solid wood. See p. 354 for the choice and use of wood.

Glass shelves can be bought from a glazier ready-cut with all edges, or just the front and side edges, polished. These are mainly suitable for bathrooms and are generally 6 mm. ($\frac{1}{4}$ in.) thick, 100, 125 and 150 mm. (4, 5 and 6 in.) wide, and in lengths of 450-600 mm. (18-24 in.). Louvre window blades, 100 and 150 mm. (4 and 6 in.) wide with edges smoothed, make ideal shelves.

Glass shelves for displays are usually about 10 mm. ($\frac{3}{8}$ in.) thick, and can be cut to the size you require.

The load a shelf can carry depends on the strength of the supports, the distance between them, and the shelving material. A long span of glass, particularly, bends and finally breaks under a heavy load.

For a shelf carrying a heavy load, such as large books, the distance between supports should not be greater than given in the chart below.

Before buying a support system, find out how strong it is – either from the retailer or from the manufacturer's leaflet. Some adjustable wall brackets are designed for light loads only.

If you want to increase the strength of a bridging shelf in an alcove, fix a hardwood batten measuring about 50 × 25 mm. (2 × 1 in.) all the way along its length at the rear, between the side supports. If the shelf is wider than 250 mm. (10 in.), use a second batten at the front.

DISTANCES BETWEEN SHELF SUPPORTS

SHELF MATERIAL	THICKNESS	MAXIMUM SPAN
Wood	16 mm. ($\frac{5}{8}$ in.) 22 mm. ($\frac{7}{8}$ in.) 28 mm. (1$\frac{1}{8}$ in.)	500 mm. (20 in.) 900 mm. (3 ft) 1050 mm. (3 ft 6 in.)
Plywood	18 mm. ($\frac{3}{4}$ in.) 25 mm. (1 in.)	800 mm. (2 ft 8 in.) 1000 mm. (3 ft 3 in.)
Blockboard	12 mm. ($\frac{1}{2}$ in.)	450 mm. (18 in.)
Veneered chipboard	12 mm. ($\frac{1}{2}$ in.) 18 mm. ($\frac{3}{4}$ in.) 25 mm. (1 in.)	400 mm. (16 in.) 600 mm. (2 ft) 750 mm. (2 ft 6 in.)
Glass	6 mm. ($\frac{1}{4}$ in.) 10 mm. ($\frac{3}{8}$ in.)	300 mm. (12 in.) 450 mm. (18 in.)

METAL BRACKET
Metal L-shaped angle brackets are fairly cheap. If the sides are of unequal length, the long side is screwed to the wall, either directly or on a wooden mounting, the short side to the underside of the shelf.

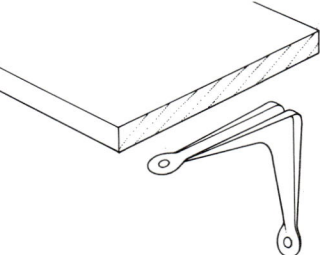

WOODEN BATTEN
A shelf spanning an alcove can be supported by wooden battens about 25 mm. (1 in.) thick screwed to the side walls. Battens can be hidden by a wooden strip along the shelf front.

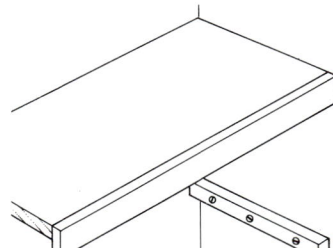

ANGLED METAL SUPPORT
Bearers for side walls can be right-angled pieces of aluminium or mild steel. The shelf can rest on them or be grooved to slide on to them, so they are barely visible once the shelf is in place.

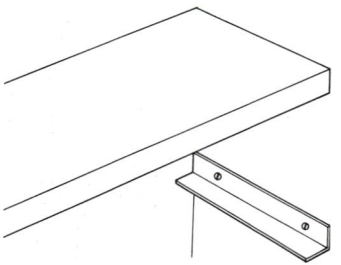

Alternative methods of supporting fixed shelving on a wall, or between alcoves, using proprietary metal brackets or softwood.

SHELF UNITS Simple whitewood shelves are cheap and can be adapted for many uses. The wood can be left bare or stained or painted.

CHECKING THE STRENGTH OF A WALL

Do not plan to fix shelves against a wall until you have found out if the wall is strong enough to take the load. Test it in the way described below. For methods of plugging walls, see p. 353.

If your walls do not appear to be made of any of the materials listed in the chart below, get professional advice before fixing shelves. Some walls, especially in high-rise blocks, need particular care. A wall may be strong enough to carry a shelf – until it is loaded.

Walls erected in the course of home improvements or extensions, such as partitions put up to convert a large bedroom into two, are often hollow, consisting of plasterboard or similar manufactured board nailed over a timber frame. Screw shelf supports into this solid timber, using screws long enough to give a good penetration into the wood, or special fixing bolts (see p. 353) in the plasterboard.

CONSTRUCTION	HOW TO TEST	SUITABLE FIXINGS AND SUPPORTS
Stud wall – timber uprights (studs) usually 400-450 mm. (16-18 in.) from centre to centre, covered with plasterboard or similar material	Tap along wall lightly with a hammer and listen for change in sound between hollow board and solid stud. Or locate timber by probing with bradawl – make several holes to mark stud centre and edges. Studs are load-bearing	Screws must be long enough to go through plasterboard into stud to a depth of 15-20 mm. ($\frac{1}{2}$-$\frac{3}{4}$ in.). If necessary, studs can be spanned by crosspieces so that brackets can be positioned between studs
Lath and plaster – wooden laths about 25 mm. (1 in.) wide nailed horizontally to timber studs and the whole covered with plaster. Often used in old buildings. Studs are usually about 50 mm. (2 in.) thick, placed 450-600 mm. (18-24 in.) from centre to centre	Locate studs by probing with a bradawl or 3 mm. ($\frac{1}{8}$ in.) masonry drill at an inconspicuous spot near bottom of wall. Some studs may be horizontal – make sure you locate an upright one. Check that plaster is sound and there is no woodworm in timber (see p. 379). Studs are load-bearing	As for stud walls
Brick and plaster	Bore a hole with a bradawl or 3 mm. ($\frac{1}{8}$ in.) masonry drill in wall at an inconspicuous spot near skirting. There should be white dust from plaster and orange dust from brick, which will be harder to penetrate. Make sure plaster is not damp or crumbling. Load-bearing good	Use fibre or nylon wall plugs. Make sure screw goes into brick to a depth of 15-20 mm. ($\frac{1}{2}$-$\frac{3}{4}$ in.). Depending on shelf material (see Distances between supports opposite), supports every 600 mm. (2 ft) should allow shelf to carry fairly heavy articles
Breeze blocks and plaster – breeze blocks are made from lightweight aggregate (graded stone chippings)	Test as for brick and plaster. Dust from breeze blocks will be bluish grey. Modern breeze blocks are load-bearing; some older types are not. Judge by resistance to drill – if it goes in easily, the wall is not load-bearing	Use fixings as for brick walls. For load-bearing breeze blocks, support as for brick walls. Non-load-bearing breeze blocks will support shelving for light articles but not for heavy loads such as a lot of books

TEBRAX
Metal brackets, suitable for shelves up to 600 mm. (2 ft) wide, fit into slots in aluminium uprights screwed to the wall. Lipped brackets are made for glass shelves.

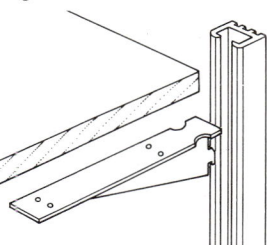

CLICK
Brackets click into channelled uprights. A flexible reading light and an adjustable spot-light can also be fitted into uprights; a cover strip hides the cables.

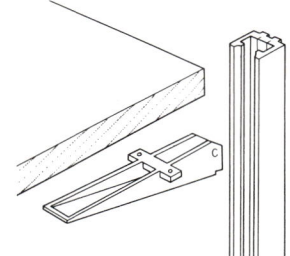

REMPLOY/LUNDIA
Adjustable wooden shelves, 250-750 mm. (10-30 in.) wide, supported on a wooden frame. The extendible frames may be up to 3 m. (9 ft 9 in.) high.

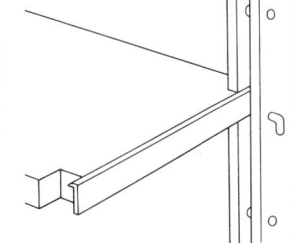

INVISIBLE WIRE
No support is visible when a wire is used at each side. The shelf is grooved to slide over the wires, which clip into pairs of holes in the sides of the bookcase.

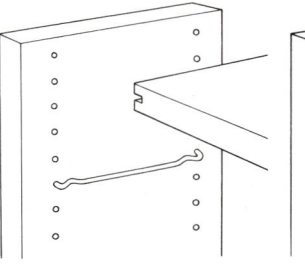

DOWEL OR STUD
Shelves can be supported on dowels or studs plugged into holes in the bookcase sides. Plastic studs or rubber buffers can be used to cushion glass shelves.

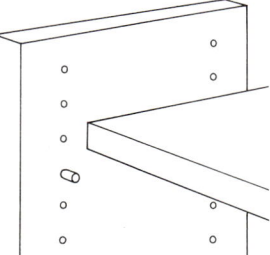

METAL STRIP AND STUDS
Metal clips or studs fit into slots on vertical metal strips screwed in pairs to both of the side walls of the cupboard or bookcase. Height of the shelves is adjustable.

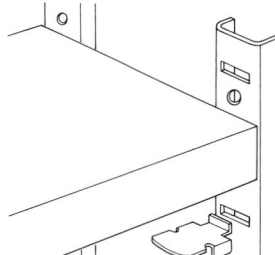

Alternative methods of supporting adjustable shelving for cupboards, books or display-ware, using either a cantilevered system, from the face of a wall, or a dowel or stud system between alcove walls.

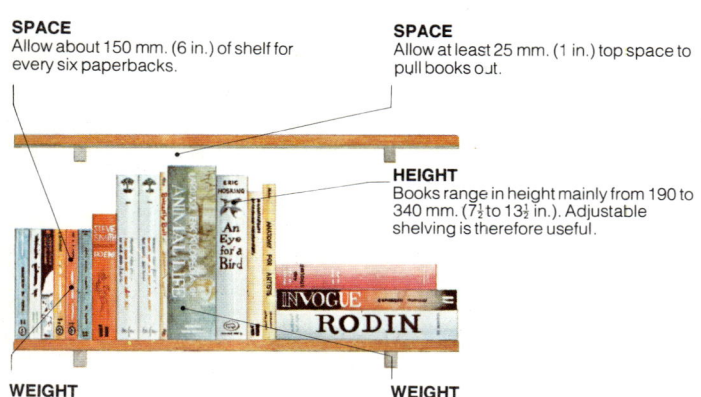

SPACE
Allow about 150 mm. (6 in.) of shelf for every six paperbacks.

SPACE
Allow at least 25 mm. (1 in.) top space to pull books out.

HEIGHT
Books range in height mainly from 190 to 340 mm. (7½ to 13½ in.). Adjustable shelving is therefore useful.

WEIGHT
Six average-size paperbacks weigh about 1 kg. (2¼ lb.).

WEIGHT
Six average-size hardbacks weigh about 2 kg. (4½ lb.).

STORING BOOKS Keep books away from direct heat and damp. Heat can cause bindings to crack, while damp allows mould to develop.

• FIXING SHELVES TO A WALL

Before fitting shelves draw a scale plan of your proposals, then mark the positions lightly on the wall. Note the location of lighting switches and points, and do not fix uprights or brackets in places where you are likely to drill into an electric cable. Check the position of water pipes also.

Do not rely entirely on measurements for positioning screw holes, as walls may not be true. Level shelves by the method illustrated below.

Supporting brackets fitted a little way in from each end of a shelf reduce the central span and increase the load-bearing capacity. If the span between the two end brackets is greater than that recommended (see p. 108), add extra brackets.

MAKING GOOD USE OF SPACE Roomy storage units built into an alcove allow this living-room to be used as a work-room as well.

FIXING ADJUSTABLE SHELVES TO A WALL

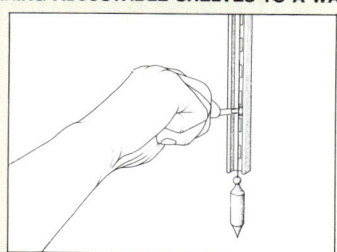

1. Plug the wall for the top screw of the first upright in the position required. Loosely screw the upright to the wall.

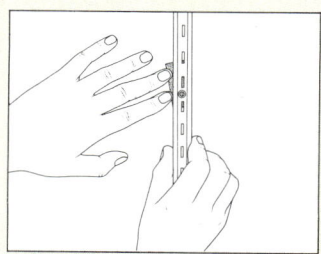

2. Align the upright vertically with a plumb-line. Mark the bottom screw hole, plug, and fix screw loosely.

3. If the wall surface is uneven, pack small pieces of wood or cardboard behind the upright where needed. Tighten screws.

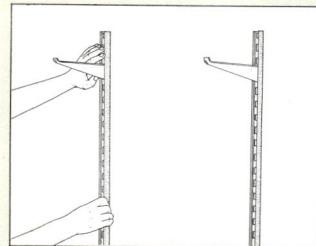

4. Fix a bracket into the fitted upright and another in a matching position in the second, unfitted upright. Fix end uprights before intermediate ones.

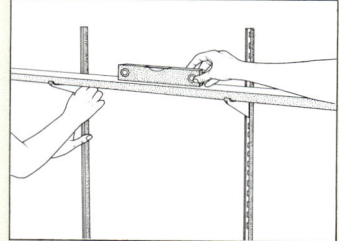

5. Get a helper to hold the second upright and bracket in position while you lay a shelf board across the brackets and place a spirit level on it.

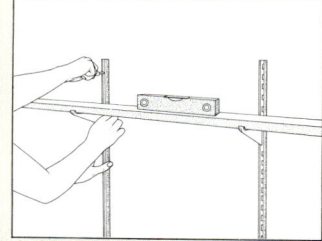

6. Adjust the position of the second upright until the shelf is level. Then mark the position for the top screw and complete fixing the upright as before.

BUILT-IN CUPBOARDS Designed to house records, record player and control panel, these cupboards disguise a disused fireplace and chimney corner.

ONE-ROOM LIVING *Where space is limited, well-planned and adaptable storage is essential for comfort and convenience. In this bed-sitter, compact wall units provide book shelves, display shelves, space for a record player, a record cabinet, a drinks cabinet, a work cupboard, a writing desk, a telephone table and a room divider, leaving the centre of the living area uncluttered.*

RESTORING FURNITURE

Understandably, most homeowners become extremely fond of their various pieces of furniture, whether bought or inherited, and are loath to part with their own particular treasures however dilapidated they may become. Rather than bury these pieces away in some corner of the attic they can be given a new lease of life using basic skills that are simple to acquire. The work need not involve a lot of expense, and furniture restored in this way will give its owner that personal sense of satisfaction that comes with having actually carried out the work. Remember, however, that the repair or restoration of valuable furniture should be left to experts. The following pages take you through the basic techniques of cutting and joining wood, and cleaning and renewing the various finishes used on furniture. Then there are step-by-step examples on restoring a Welsh dresser and converting a chest of drawers into a desk.

• BASIC TECHNIQUES

Before starting to repair or renovate a piece of furniture, you need to know a few basic woodworking techniques. If you have not worked on wood before, practise by sawing on a spare piece of timber. (See also the section on tools, p. 352.)

CUTTING TIMBER

To cut narrow pieces of wood, mark the length to be cut with a sharp knife. Keep the knife on this mark and line up the blade of a try square against the knife. Draw the knife across the wood, using the try square blade as a guide. Mark each side of the wood in this way. If a wide piece of timber is to be cut, make two or three marks across the wood and join them with a straight edge, marking cutting line.

Use a tenon saw for cutting small timber and a panel saw for large pieces. Hold a small piece of timber steady on a bench hook (see p. 353), hold the saw handle firmly and extend your forefinger along the side of the blade to give control over the direction of the saw. Place the handle end of the blade on the far edge of the timber, against the waste side of the marked line. Draw the saw slowly towards you, with the thumb of the other hand placed lightly against the side of the blade to guide it. Make four or five back strokes, then saw forwards and

backwards without forcing the blade, holding the saw horizontally.

When cutting large sheets of wood, use a saw-horse or box, placing one knee on the wood to steady it. Hold the saw at an angle of 60 degrees to the wood and keep your wrist straight. The force should come from the shoulder, not the arm. When you near the end of the cut, saw lightly and hold the waste end to stop it falling and splintering the work.

USING NEW WOOD

The wood should be as free as possible from saw marks, rough edges, discoloration and knots.

Smooth with glasspaper those cut edges which will show in the finished article. Treat knots with knot-sealer to prevent resin leaking, which would eventually result in the knot working loose.

PUNCHING IN NAILS

When using nails on parts of the furniture which will be seen, punch the nail heads below the surface with a nail punch. Then fill the nail hole with a coloured wood filler (see Surface repairs, p. 115).

USING ADHESIVE

First scrape off old adhesive and smooth with glasspaper. PVA woodworking adhesive is suitable for most

jobs. Smooth it on to the wood with a finger to get an even surface. When the wood is glued in place, clamp it if necessary and leave to dry for ten minutes. Wipe off excess glue with a damp cloth. Spots of glue which dry hard should be rubbed with glasspaper. When using a clamp, place spare pieces of wood within the clamp to protect the work.

MAKING A SPANISH WINDLASS

To hold four sides of wood together while glue is drying – for instance, the sides of a drawer, or the base of a dining-room chair to which legs are being re-fitted – use a Spanish windlass instead of a clamp.

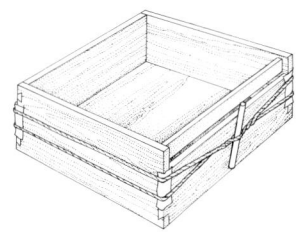

How a Spanish windlass is used.

To make a Spanish windlass, take a piece of string, wind it loosely round the four pieces of wood twice and tie the ends, allowing a little give in the string. Slot a piece of protective card between the string and the finished work at the corners. Then place a sturdy stick of wood between the two pieces of string on one side and twist it round until the string tightens, like a tourniquet. Make it just tight enough to hold the pieces of wood in position while the glue dries, but not so tight that it bends the wood or distorts the joints that are being glued (see illustration above).

If you are using a Spanish windlass on a drawer which has a back that is lower than the sides, cut a piece of

timber to fill the gap exactly. Fit the piece of wood in place so that it is flush with the sides, then use the Spanish windlass. This stops the sides of the drawer bending inwards at the back.

STRIPPING

The stripping process removes wax, dirt, varnish, paint, polish and tar. Use a commercial stripper, unless you are stripping french-polished furniture, in which case you may wish to use the method described under french polishing on p. 114. Wear rubber gloves to work, as the stripper can burn the skin.

If it gets in your eyes, bathe them with cold water but if the burning sensation persists, call a doctor. If possible, do the job outdoors or make sure the room is well ventilated, because the fumes may be toxic. Do not smoke while working as the stripper is inflammable.

Pour some stripper into a can. Using an old paint brush, cover the surface of the furniture fairly thickly with stripper. Leave for at least five minutes, then rub the surface with a pad of grade 3 wire-wool to remove the stripper. Any paint or varnish on the surface will have bubbled up. Remove this with a stripping knife. Do not let stripped paint lie on the floor. The stripper contained in the paint is still corrosive.

Apply a second coat of stripper and again clean the surface with wire wool, rubbing with the grain until the surface is dry. Wash down with cold water or methylated spirit, making the wood really wet. This must be done thoroughly to remove all traces of stripper. If any stripper is left on it will act against the new paint or varnish. If you use water, leave the furniture to dry overnight before carrying out the next stage. Methylated spirit will evaporate straight away, so use this if you want to continue with the job the same day.

BLEACHING

Bleach the wood after stripping, to remove stains and marks and to make the wood look lighter. If the wood is not too badly stained, undiluted domestic bleach may be sufficient. Rub it all over the wood with a clean rag, then wash it off with two lots of cold water, using a fresh rag the second time. Leave to dry.

Otherwise use ultra-bleach A and B. It is in 5 l. (1 gallon) containers and can be bought from french-polish makers. Pour a small quantity of both liquid A and liquid B into separate containers made of china, glass or earthenware – do not use metal as it causes a reaction. Always replace corks on the bottles after use.

Apply liquid A with a cotton rag, rubbing it all over the timber. Then apply the B solution in the same way, but wear rubber gloves and make sure that the liquid does not get on your skin. The reaction of B on A turns the wood a whitish colour. Leave the bleach on for at least 24 hours. Any liquid A left over may be poured back into the container, but left-over B bleach should be thrown away as it is likely to have become contaminated with liquid A when the cloth was dipped into it.

Wash off the bleach with two lots of cold water, using a fresh rag the second time. The cold water neutralises the action of the bleach. Let the wood dry thoroughly.

MAKING REPAIRS AND FILLING HOLES

Before putting a finish on the wood, carry out any repairs needed (see pp. 114-15). Surface stains or burn marks which have not been removed with bleach and are likely to show through one finish, can be treated as also described on p. 115. Fill nail holes and any other small holes. Use wood filler if the furniture is to be varnished, polished or lacquered. If the piece is to be painted, use alabastine or Polyfilla. Press the filler into the holes with a knife or finger so that the filling comes above the surface. Old wood absorbs wood filling, so you need to be quite generous with it.

After about 30 minutes, when the filler will be dry, rub over the fillings with fine glasspaper to level them off. Then glasspaper the whole piece.

APPLYING POLYURETHANE FINISH

Next apply a coat of semi-matt polyurethane. Lay the polyurethane on with the flat of a brush, going with the grain. If it runs, pick up the drips with the brush. Give the furniture a good coating without making it too wet. Leave overnight to dry. Apply another coat of polyurethane. Rub with fine glasspaper before each coat. For a glossy finish, use a gloss polyurethane. Finally, apply furniture wax with a pad of fine wire-wool (grade 0), working with the grain, until there is an eggshell finish. Then rub it down with a soft rag. The waxing gives a good sheen and smooths down the polyurethane. If applying polyurethane to new wood, use shellac sealer or cellulose sealer before putting on the polyurethane.

Other finishes For a waxed finish, apply wax with wire wool as described above but use more wax. Lacquer is applied in the same way as polyurethane. (French polishing, see p. 114; Painting, see p. 119.)

NAILING

Always nail through thin wood into thick wood. Choose nails that are two and a half to three times the thickness of the thin timber. Drive nails in at an angle to get a stronger fixing. When you are using a lot of nails in one length of wood, try to stagger them, instead of putting them in a straight line, to avoid splitting the wood. When nailing into hardwood, and when nailing into end grain, drill pilot holes for the nails so that there is no risk of the wood splitting. Use a Warrington hammer for driving home small nails. To start off the nail use the flat pein (the part of the head opposite the hitting end) to avoid hitting your fingers.

When the nail can stand upright on its own, turn the hammer round and hammer the nail with the hitting end of the head. To drive in very small nails – such as panel pins – without hitting your fingers, put the nail through a piece of card and hold this. Remove the card when the nail is firmly held in the wood. For nails which are large enough to hold without hitting your fingers with the hammer, use a claw hammer (the claw part of the head is for withdrawing nails).

To conceal the nail, drive its head below the surface with a nail punch, then cover with wood filler.

SCREWS

When screwing pieces of wood together, fix the thinner piece to the thicker piece. Before screwing into hardwood, drill a clearance hole for the shank and a countersunk hole for flat-headed screws. It is advisable also to drill a pilot hole half the diameter of the screw thread. (Drilling, see p. 352.)

When screwing into softwood, use a bradawl to start the hole. If you do not want the screw head to show, make a deep countersunk hole, drive the screw head below the surface and cover it with wood filler. Glasspaper smooth when the filler is hard.

COLLECTING BAMBOO FURNITURE

Japanese furniture, first shown at the International Exhibition in London in 1862, sparked off an interest in the Oriental style that was to become a craze by the 1870s. The most popular Japanese furniture was made of bamboo – stems of a giant tropical grass.

At the height of its popularity, desks were found in the study, aspidistra stands in the hall, cabinets in the drawing room – all made of bamboo. Originally the bamboo was left in its original honey-brown state, but a tortoiseshell effect, achieved by painting brown flecks on the bamboo, was popular in late Victorian times.

Bamboo furniture often incorporated lacquered panels. The lacquer work, usually a black background decorated with birds and foliage in scarlet and gilt, was a delicately ornate touch. Fine examples, like the hall stand (above, left) are rare and expensive.

By the 1890s English manufacturers were beginning to imitate the Japanese, using natural and simulated cane. Shelves and panels of desks and tables were usually made of strips of woven rattan, a pliable type of cane. Whole stems of rattan were plaited to make cane furniture like the chair (above, right).

Because so much bamboo furniture was turned out at the end of the 19th century, there are still quantities of it about in antique shops. The tortoiseshell type is the most common and cheapest. The plant stand (above, centre) is an example. Ornate pieces of pale bamboo with lacquered panels like the cake stand (right) are sure to be Japanese imports, and so more expensive than home-made examples.

Avoid damaged pieces, unless you feel they can be repaired at home. Bamboo furniture is apt to splinter rather than break. Chair and table legs are particularly vulnerable. If the damage is not too great, insert dowelling in the hollow bamboo and stick the splinters to it.

Because it is lightweight, bamboo furniture harmonises with most contemporary furniture. A canterbury, for instance, originally designed to hold sheet music, would make a magazine rack. A whatnot – a shelved stand, sometimes with drawers in the base or top – can stand alone as a decorative piece.

• RESTORING FRENCH-POLISHED FURNITURE

French polish is a mixture of shellac and spirit applied in several thin layers to give a high gloss. As the polish is soft and marks easily it is used for decorative, lightly used, pieces of furniture. If you have a badly worn piece of french-polished furniture which is in constant use, it may be better to strip it and give it a polyurethane finish (see p. 113) rather than re-polish.

If you are not sure whether a piece of furniture is french-polished, make the following test. On a part of the furniture which is hidden from view, remove any wax polish with turpentine substitute. Then rub the cleaned area gently with a cloth dipped in methylated spirit. A french-polished surface will immediately soften and the cloth will be stained. Any other finish will leave the cloth unmarked.

MATERIALS

Commercial stripper; methylated spirit; pure turpentine; oxalic-acid crystals; soda crystals; commercial wood dye or colouring powders; wood filler; coloured beeswax; french polish; linseed oil; antique wax; coarse wire wool; fine wire wool; clean, soft cloths; cottonwool or unbleached wadding; very fine glass-paper called flour-paper (No. 7/0); fine brushes.

PREPARING THE SURFACE

A surface which is simply dull can be re-polished without stripping provided it is not too scratched. But a surface which is grazed or badly marked needs to be stripped first. If there is no need to strip the furniture, wash it with turpentine or a very weak solution of soda crystals in warm water. Leave it to dry and apply french polish as described next. There is no

need, however, to give it as many applications as are required for french polishing bare wood.

To strip off the old polish, use a commercial stripper as described on p. 112 or, if the furniture is of good quality, use methylated spirit. Pour a liberal amount on to the furniture and rub with a pad of coarse wire wool. But be careful. As methylated spirit attacks glue, try not to let it run down over the furniture joints. Keep wiping the surface with wire wool and methylated spirit until all the polish has been removed. Then wipe with fresh methylated spirit on a soft cloth. Finally, wipe the surface with a clean, dry cloth.

If you want to lighten the wood, bleach it by wiping with a solution of oxalic acid made by dissolving 50 g. (2 oz.) oxalic-acid crystals in 600 ml. (1 pint) warm water. After bleaching, wipe the wood with methylated spirit to remove bleach. Leave to dry.

Treat any stains, burns or scratches, and fill any tiny cavities or chip marks (see next page). Tinting can be done now or during polishing (see Tinting and colouring), but if you wish to stain the wood, do so at this stage (see Staining).

FRENCH-POLISHING

Ready-mixed french polish can be bought from a good ironmonger or french-polish manufacturer. Use a colour matched to the wood you are working on, or transparent polish if you want to retain the natural colour of the wood.

To apply the polish, sprinkle it on a wad of cotton wool [A1], which is then wrapped in a piece of clean cotton cloth. Always sprinkle the polish on the wadding – not on the outside cloth where a sticky build-up of polish would develop. Make sure, too, that the outside cloth is not wrinkled [A2],

otherwise ridges may occur in the polish being applied. Before starting to polish, squeeze out any excess polish from the pad [A3].

Work on one area of the furniture at a time. Stroke the polish on evenly, going with the grain. Keep the pad moving over the furniture at all times to avoid it sticking. When the pad feels dry, unwrap the cloth and pour a little polish on the wadding, squeezing out as before. Leave the surface to harden slightly, then go over it again. When the second layer has hardened, go over it lightly with a very worn piece of flour-paper (No. 7/0).

Tiny cracks or chips which you missed before may now become noticeable and can be filled (see Filling scratches and gouges). After filling, dust the surface with a soft cloth. If you are tinting with powders and did not carry out the work earlier, do so at this stage.

Apply more polish to the wadding and squeeze out the pad as before. Then put a few drops of linseed oil on the cloth. This stops the polish sticking and helps the cloth to glide over the surface. Go over the furniture in a figure-of-eight movement [A4] without removing the pad from the surface until you get to the edge of the furniture. Then slide the pad off. Do not lift it. The oil will show as a slight smear on the surface. Go over the surface two or three times in this way, applying more polish if necessary. If the pad sticks to the surface, apply a drop more oil to the cloth.

Then work with polish only to remove all traces of the oil. If any oil is left it will leave smears on the surface and will go rancid. Keep polishing until all smears have disappeared. A good shine indicates that the oil has been removed. Leave the polish to dry, then continue polishing with french polish only, building up thin

layers of polish until you have the degree of shine you want. It should be possible to see your reflection in the finished piece.

During polishing, you may notice that some parts of the wood come up a different colour. Match them up by colouring the wood (see Tinting and colouring) and continue polishing. When the polishing is finished, leave it to harden for three or four days. The surface will not need any maintenance.

If you want a matt finish, follow the same french-polishing procedure but with fewer applications. After the final application, leave the piece overnight, then wax it. Use a good antique wax matched to the colour of the furniture, and apply it with a pad of fine wire wool. Go over the surface, following the grain of the wood, until the shine has been taken off. Then wipe it

with a soft cloth. This finish needs to be polished once every six months.

• SURFACE REPAIRS

Most surface damage can be treated without having to strip the furniture. Deal with marks as described next, then resurface the damaged area with french polish. Over a very small damaged patch, apply the polish with a fine brush, building it up in layers until it is level with the surrounding surface. A coat of french polish over the entire surface will blend the new polish with the old.

WATER MARKS

Damp vases and glasses and water splashes may leave white rings and spots on furniture. To remove them without stripping the surface, wipe the marks with a little methylated spirit on a soft cloth. If this does not remove

FRENCH-POLISHING

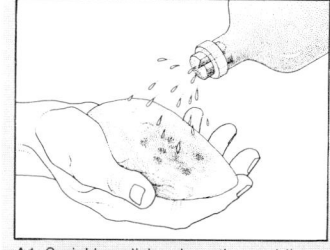
A1. Sprinkle polish only on the wadding – not the outside cloth.

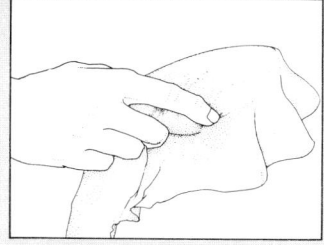
A2. To ensure an even finish, always keep the pad free from wrinkles.

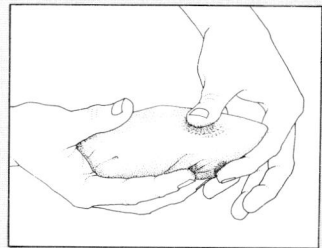
A3. When topping up with polish, squeeze the pad to remove any surplus.

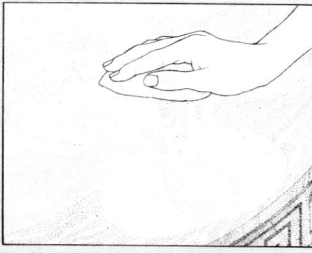
A4. The figure-of-eight movement to follow in the final stages of polishing.

them, mix equal quantities of methylated spirit, pure turpentine and linseed oil. Shake the mixture and rub it over the stains very gently with a piece of fine wire wool.

If you have removed the french-polished surface, treat any remaining water marks with a solution of oxalic-acid crystals and warm water, using the same proportions as for bleaching (see Preparing the surface). Apply the solution with fine wire wool, rubbing in the direction of the grain. Wash down with methylated spirit to remove all traces of the acid and leave it to dry.

BLACK SPOTS

A black mark may be a spot of varnish or old polish. Remove these with coarse glasspaper, then flour-paper and wipe with a cloth. Black spots which are caused by water getting under the finish can be coloured to blend with the wood. If the furniture is stripped, try rubbing the spot with flour-paper (No. 7/0). If that does not remove it, rub with fine wire wool and oxalic-acid solution as for water marks.

INK STAINS

You may be able to remove ink stains from stripped and polished furniture with domestic bleach applied with fine wire wool. If that fails, use oxalic-acid solution as for water marks. If the stain remains, tint it.

CIGARETTE BURNS

On stripped furniture, a slight burn may be removed by sanding with fine glasspaper. If that does not remove the mark completely, tint it. If the burn is deep, rub it with glasspaper to remove the charred wood, then fill with wood filler or wax, and tint. If the furniture is not being stripped, lightly rub the charred surface with glasspaper,

then tint it. This time if the burn is deep, treat it as for stripped furniture and re-polish.

HEAT MARKS

To remove marks left by hot dishes on a polished surface, rub with equal quantities of raw linseed oil and pure turpentine, or rub with a vinegar-and-water solution. You may need to make several applications to remove the marks.

SPIRIT MARKS

Spilled spirit such as whisky or gin softens or completely removes french polish. If possible, wipe up the spilled spirit immediately and leave the surface to harden. Then rub over it with french polish. If the polish has been removed, build up layers of french polish with a brush, going with the grain, until it is level with the surrounding polish. Then go over the whole surface with a pad of french polish to blend in the treated patch.

FILLING SCRATCHES AND GOUGES

Surface scratches can be removed without stripping. Mix equal quantities of methylated spirit, pure turpentine and linseed oil in a jar and shake it. Apply the mixture to the scratched surface with a soft cloth. Scratches and small chips on stripped furniture can be filled by rubbing in a piece of coloured beeswax, matched to the wood. If you need to push the filling into a crack, do so with a piece of soft wood. After filling, smooth down with very worn flour-paper (No. 7/0). If necessary, tint the piece that has been filled (see below).

TINTING AND COLOURING

Stains and fillings can be tinted before polishing. Use a commercial wood dye to match the furniture.

Apply the dye with a fine brush and allow it to dry before polishing. Alternatively, you can tint the spots between applications of polish, using various colouring powders mixed to the required shade. Correct mixing takes practice and it is a good idea to try the colour first on a part of the furniture which will be hidden. To mix colours, first pour a small amount of the french polish into a small pot, then mix in the colouring powders, adding a little at a time, until you have the right shade.

To paint out cigarette burns, use red lead mixed with yellow ochre. For matching with mahogany, use red lead with yellow ochre and bismark brown. Mix orange chrome, yellow ochre and brown umber to match light walnut. Black and red powders for darker-coloured woods are also available. Paint the colour on with the tip of a fine paint brush and leave to dry before applying polish.

To colour a large area of furniture, mix the colour to a watery consistency with french polish. Put the colour on a pad and wrap a cloth round it. Add a drop of linseed oil and apply as for french-polishing.

STAINING

Use a commercial wood stain and try it out first on a spare piece of wood to make sure it is the colour you want. When staining a large area, start at one edge and work methodically across the piece of furniture. Apply the stain evenly with a brush or pad of soft cloth.

Try not to put the stain on too liberally as it may become streaky and will take a long time to dry. Use a clean, soft rag to wipe off any surplus and to even out the colour. Leave to dry in a place where all surfaces are exposed to light and air in a calm atmosphere free from dust.

• REPAIRING CHAIRS

When joints between the seat legs and chair frame become loose and need to be re-glued, it will be necessary to remove corner blocks strengthening the framework. Remove any screws, then tap blocks free by hitting them with a hammer [B1]. To release the joint itself, place a block of wood firmly against the leg upright or rail, hitting this with a hammer to save damaging the chair. To release a back rail that is narrower than the others, place a block of wood between the side rails. Force joints apart by hitting the wood into the narrower part of the chair [B2].

Scrape off old glue from the joints. Smear strong glue on the joints and put the rail back in position. Use a cramp to hold the joints while the glue is drying or make a Spanish windlass (see p. 112). Leave 24 hours to dry.

If the old corner blocks are no longer serviceable, or get damaged in removal, they should be replaced by making new ones from hardwood.

Hold a length of wood diagonally under the joint of the chair where the new block is to be placed [B3] and draw two pencil lines where the cuts will need to be made. Cut the wood along the pencilled lines and, using a vice to hold the wood, drill two holes for screws, each about 25 mm. (1 in.) from one end. Finish off with a countersunk bit to allow for countersunk screws.

Smear PVA adhesive on the inner edges of the block and press it into place. Hold the block firmly in place and push a bradawl down through the screw holes to help to start the screws. Fit two countersunk screws [B4], screw them in tight and wipe off any excess adhesive.

REPLACING A CORNER BLOCK

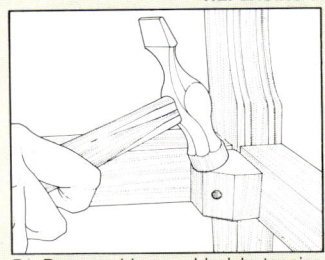

B1. Remove old corner block by tapping firmly with a hammer.

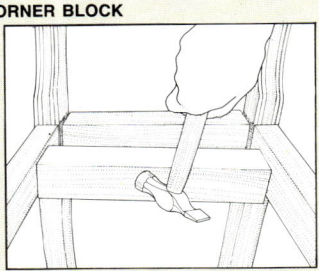

B2. Where a chair-back narrows, force in a wood block to open up joints.

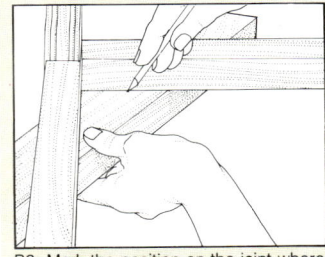

B3. Mark the position on the joint where the new corner block is to be placed.

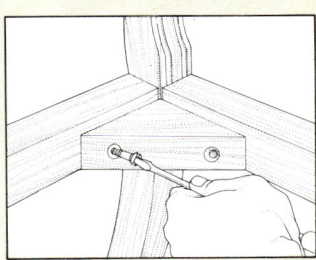

B4. Note the angle of the hole drilled at each end of a new block.

• RESTORING A WELSH DRESSER

For simple restoration work, such as stripping off varnish, bleaching the wood and making small surface repairs, see pp. 112-15.

More extensive repairs – such as reinforcing the shelf unit, putting in new shelves and replacing the drawer handles – are detailed here. The basic techniques you will need for these jobs are given on pp. 352-7.

TOOLS

Nail punch; two hammers (a Warrington No. 2 is a very useful hammer and will do most jobs); knife or small scraper; pumice stone; trimming knife; small hand drill and bits; small tenon saw; ruler; pencil; bradawl; screwdriver; large dusting brush; 2 small paint brushes; soft cloth; medium wire wool; try-square.

MATERIALS

Wood filler; glasspaper: coarse (S2), medium (M2 and M5), fine (0 and 00); polyurethane clear gloss varnish; white wax polish; high-gloss wood stain; small tin green lacquer; 100 g. (4 oz.) green flocking; new handles; brass cup hooks; softwood battens: for the back – 12 mm. ($\frac{1}{2}$ in.) thick, 50 mm. (2 in.) wide, twice times length of back of shelf unit; for the top – 19 mm. ($\frac{3}{4}$ in.) thick, 50 mm. (2 in.) wide, four times depth of shelf unit top; wood for new shelves; plate stops (softwood/hardwood): 6 mm. ($\frac{1}{4}$ in.) thick, 12 mm. ($\frac{1}{2}$ in.) wide, for all new shelves; 6 mm. ($\frac{1}{4}$ in.) dowelling; oval nails: 25 mm. (1 in.) and 50 mm. (2 in.); panel pins: 15 mm. ($\frac{1}{2}$ in.) and 19 mm. ($\frac{3}{4}$ in.); countersunk brass screws and brass cups; 2 dome-headed brass screws.

STRENGTHENING THE SHELF UNIT

The shelf unit can be strengthened by fixing battens to the back and top. Fix the back battens with the shelf unit in position on the base.

Measure across the back of the unit. Cut two pieces of softwood 12 mm. ($\frac{1}{2}$ in.) thick by 50 mm. (2 in.) wide to this measured length. At each end of the battens, cut a 45 degree

FIXING A BACK BATTEN

Bending the nails. Note the bevelled end of the batten, and its flush fit.

bevel, using the tenon saw.

Mark the position of the first batten parallel with and about 100 mm. (4 in.) down from the top of the dresser. Mark the same distance plus 25 mm. (1 in.) on the front to give a guide for the nails. Place the top edge of the batten along the pencilled marks on the back, with the bevelled side facing outwards so that the batten will not show from the front of the dresser.

Get someone to hold the batten in position while you nail it from the front. The person holding the batten should place a heavy hammer head near the point where each nail comes through. This will prevent the old wood of the dresser from vibrating and possibly splintering or cracking.

Use 25 mm. oval nails. Hammer one in at each end of the batten and one in the centre. Then hammer a nail in the centre of every remaining plank. Finally, put a nail in each end of the batten from the back so that it goes through the side piece of the shelf unit. Punch nail heads below the surface.

When all the nails are in, hammer the ends over, along the grain of the wood. Position the second batten about 75 mm. (3 in.) up from the base. Cut a piece of wood 75 mm. long, using a try-square to get both ends straight. Use this as a guide to mark a line where the lower edge of the batten is to go. When putting in the first nail at each end, keep the measuring gauge between the base and bottom of the batten to ensure it is positioned correctly. Nail the batten in place as before.

To fix battens to the top of the unit, first remove the unit from the base. Measure the top from back to front and cut four pieces of 19 × 50 mm. ($\frac{3}{4}$ × 2 in.) softwood to this measurement. Position them at equal intervals along the top with the outer pair about 300 mm. (12 in.) in from each side. Measure and mark the nail positions on the underside, so that the nails are centred on the battens.

Secure each batten with a 50 mm. oval nail at each end. Then hammer in a 25 mm. oval nail at each end from the underside.

There is no need to sink these nail heads as the nails will not be seen. Fill other nail holes with wood filler and smooth down with glasspaper. After carrying out this work, attention can be given to the pelmet, the curved edges of which may be rough. First rub behind the curves with a coarse glasspaper (grade S2). Then wrap the paper round a short rod, and smooth the curved edges with an in-out sawing motion. Do this again with a medium paper (grade M2), then a fine paper.

FILLING HOLES IN THE BASE

Remove the shelf unit from the base. Use a nail punch to hammer all nails below the surface of the wood so that they can be hidden by wood filler. To avoid damage, get someone to hold a heavy hammer head behind the piece of wood at the point where the nail is being driven in.

Fill all holes with wood filler in a shade matching the wood. Push the filler into the holes with a small scraper, chisel or knife. Overfill the holes slightly. Do not try to smooth the filler at this stage as it may shrink during hardening.

Allow two hours for the filler to dry, then smooth down the filler with medium glasspaper (grade M5), followed by fine glasspaper (grade 0). Do not use a sanding block as old wood is uneven and the block will ride over dents and hollows. Wipe away any dust.

DRAWER STOPS

A block of wood, nailed to the bottom front strut of the drawer housing, stops the drawer being pushed in too far. If a drawer stop is missing, make a new one. Measure an existing stop and cut a piece of wood to match it. Place the new stop the same distance from the front edge of the strut as the existing stops [A1]. Hammer a 12 mm. panel pin through the stop

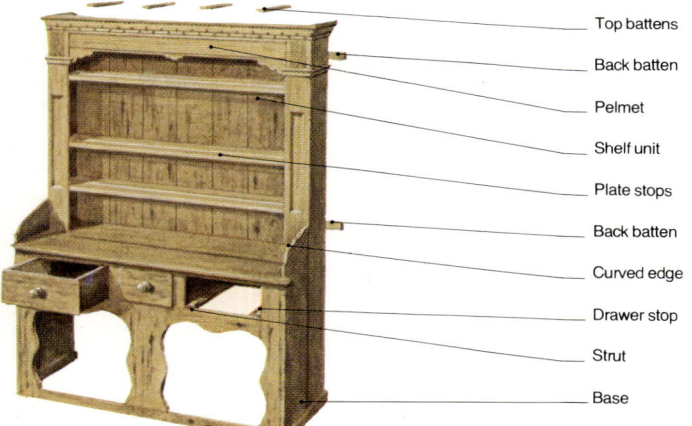

THE PARTS TO NOTE The back battens of the Welsh dresser have been extended sideways to show the fixing position. These battens must fit flush.

	Top battens
	Back batten
	Pelmet
	Shelf unit
	Plate stops
	Back batten
	Curved edge
	Drawer stop
	Strut
	Base

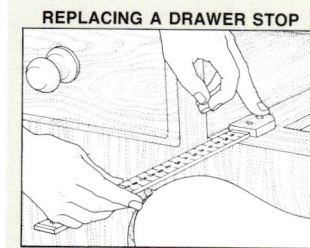

REPLACING A DRAWER STOP

A1. Check the new stop's position by comparing with existing stops.

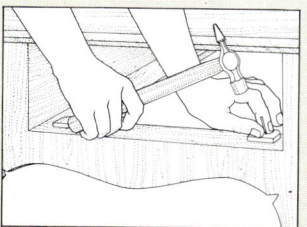

A2. Secure stop with panel pin. A second pin is put at the back of the stop.

[A2]. Push in the drawer to check that the stop is in the correct position, adjust if necessary, then hammer a second panel pin at the back of the stop to make it firm.

REPLACING HANDLES

If odd handles are missing, it is unlikely that you will be able to buy new ones to match the existing handles. Buy a complete new set. If the new handles do not fit the existing holes, plug the holes and make new ones. To fill the old holes, cut a piece of 6 mm. (¼ in.) dowelling slightly longer than each screw hole.

Whittle it with a trimming knife or chisel until it fits the hole, then put some PVA adhesive in the hole and tap the dowelling in with a hammer. When the glue has dried, saw off the protruding end and rub it down flush, using a medium glasspaper (grade M2).

To position new handles, pencil in the diagonals on the front of the drawer to locate the centre. Using a try-square, draw a vertical line through the centre. Mark the position of the new handle on the line.

Place the handle so that it conceals the filled hole. If it is positioned slightly nearer the bottom of the drawer than the top, it will more easily take the weight of the contents when the drawer is being opened. Drill a 6 mm. hole through the front of the drawer at the point marked, but do not fit the handle.

REPLACING SHELVES

Always use old timber to replace missing or damaged shelves, as new wood will not tone in with the original timber.

Old boards can be purchased from secondhand timber yards. If the boards have been stored in the open, do not put them in a warm place immediately as they may warp. Rub them with a pumice stone to remove the worst of weathering. Cut the boards to length, then smooth them with medium glasspaper (grade M2). Fill any holes with wood filler, then smooth with a fine glasspaper.

To make a plate stop for a shelf, take a strip of wood 6 mm. thick and 12 mm. wide and cut it to the same length as the shelf. Mark a line on the shelf about 30 mm. (1¼ in.) from the back edge [B1]. Place the back edge of the strip, broad side down, along this line, and secure with 19 mm. (¾ in.) panel pins, 38 mm. (1½ in.) from each end [B2]. Place three more at equal spaces between. Punch pins below the surface and smooth with glasspaper.

FLOCKING THE DRAWER

Buy about 100 g. (4 oz.) green flocking from a handicraft shop, and some green lacquer paint. Remove the cutlery drawer's old flocking with paint stripper. Clean off the stripper thoroughly. Cover the upper edges of the drawer sides with masking tape. Paint the inside of the drawer with lacquer paint. Work swiftly because the paint dries quickly. While the paint is still wet, sprinkle flocking thickly over the inside of the drawer surfaces [C1]. Quickly cover the drawer with paper, stuck down with tape. Pick up the drawer and shake it in all directions to distribute the flocking evenly [C2]. Remove the paper, tip out excess flocking and leave to dry.

FINISHING OFF

When wood filler dries, it may show up lighter than the timber. Touch it up with a high-gloss wood stain matched as closely as possible to the colour of the dresser. Paint it on with a fine brush and leave for two hours to dry. Remove all the drawers, and take the shelf unit off the base. Start on the base and coat with polyurethane or clear lacquer, to give a hard surface. Coat the front of the drawers and round the front edges. Then give the shelf unit one coat. Leave to dry for 16 hours or for the length of time recommended on the can. Smooth the painted surface lightly with fine glasspaper (grade 0), and wipe off dust. Apply a second coat of polyurethane and allow to dry.

WAXING

To give an egg-shell finish to the polyurethane, apply white wax on a pad of medium wire wool. As the pad dries out, add more wax to the wire wool. Rub along the grain on all surfaces until you have the finish you require. The surface is easier to wax if the handles are removed from the drawers. Remove the cup hooks to wax along the edge of the shelves.

Wipe down with a soft cloth, then go over any shiny patches again with wax. Cover your fingernail with cloth and scrape the wax from joints. To maintain the finish of the dresser, polish with white wax or a good household wax about every six months.

If cup hooks are wanted, they can be screwed in along the front edges of the shelves at about 100 mm. intervals. Start a hole for each with a bradawl. Fit and secure the shelf unit. Finally, fit the new handles and replace the drawers.

FIXING THE SHELF UNIT
Use brass countersunk screws at rear, brass dome heads on curved front.

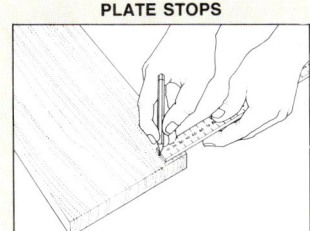
PLATE STOPS
B1. Marking the position of the plate stop – 30 mm. from the back.

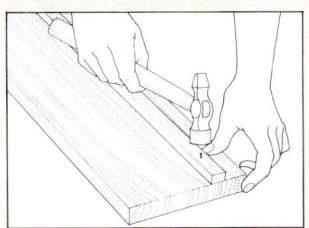
B2. Secure with panel pins: one at each end, three spaced in between.

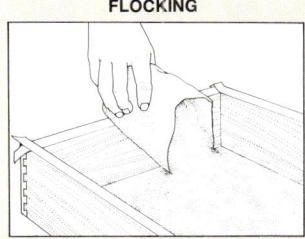
FLOCKING
C1. Pour loose flocking into the freshly lacquered cutlery drawer.

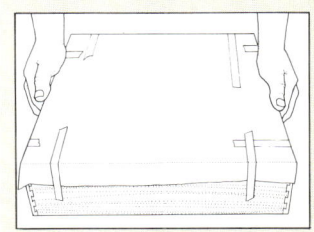
C2. Seal with paper and shake the drawer to spread the flocking evenly.

THE WAY IT WILL LOOK The restored Welsh dresser, with its display of china and crockery, can be given an eggshell finish, as here, or a shiny, lacquered finish.

• CONVERTING A CHEST OF DRAWERS INTO A DESK

A chest of drawers can be converted into a desk by fitting a plywood top. One end of the plywood is fixed to the top of the chest and the other end to a support piece of blockboard or laminboard.

TOOLS

Screwdriver; hammer; bradawl; nail punch; pincers; scraper (or old kitchen knife); small tenon saw and a junior hacksaw; coarse glasspaper; medium glasspaper (M5 & M2); fine glasspaper (F2 and 0); cork sanding block; pencil; rule; 150 mm. (6 in.) cramp, Jointmaster or a quick-clamp; chisel; Surform; hand drill and bit.

MATERIALS

Stripper; alabastine or Polyfilla; PVA adhesive; 40 mm. (1½ in.) and 25 mm. (1 in.) oval nails; 20 mm. (¾ in.) panel pins; No. 8 screws and brass screw cups in sizes 25 mm. (1 in.), 34 mm. (1⅜ in.), and 50 mm. (2 in.); 19 mm. (¾ in.) thick blockboard for support piece; 25 mm. (1 in.) thick plywood for desk top; 19 × 12 mm. (¾ × ½ in.) hardwood; 75 × 25 mm. (3 × 1 in.) hardwood for back lipping and rail; 50 × 25 mm. (2 × 1 in.) softwood; 25 mm. (1 in.) square hardwood; odd piece of hardwood for new drawer runners; primer; undercoat; paint; handles.

PREPARING THE CHEST

First renovate the chest by stripping off its varnish or paint (see p. 114). Remove the old handles if you intend to fit new ones. If a handle is held by staples, nails or glue, gently push a screwdriver under the handle's top edge and prise it off. To remove staples that remain, place the flat edge of the screwdriver blade on the staple points outside the drawer, and hammer the blade to drive the staple back through the wood [A1], where it can be pulled out with pincers [A2]. Punch any nail heads below the surface and fill all holes with alabastine or Polyfilla. Sand when dry with a fine glasspaper (grade F2). To fill a larger area, scrape the filler on, then smooth it across. Rub down with F2 glass-paper. Use a sanding block and work with a circular movement to ensure that the whole area is rubbed down evenly.

REPAIRING DRAWERS

Before removing drawers, number each one and its opening so that you can fit them back the same way.

If a drawer has loose dovetail joints, prise them apart, squeeze PVA adhesive into the dovetails, then push them back in place. If the wood is split, gently separate the parts, put adhesive into the crack [B1] and push the wood back in place. If the cracks are large, hold them in place with a spanish windlass (see p. 112) until the adhesive is dry. Drive a 20 mm. (¾ in.) panel pin into each joint and punch down the head [B2].

REPAIRING A RUNNER

If a bottom runner is beginning to split, put PVA adhesive in the split, then hammer a panel pin up through the runner, punching down the head of the pin below the surface of the wood, or the drawer will not run smoothly.

To fit a new bottom runner first pin the bottom of the drawer firmly to the sides with panel pins. Pare off the split edge with a chisel or Surform [C1] so that the side of the drawer is flush with the bottom. Smooth with medium glasspaper.

Measure the length, width and thickness of the runner on the opposite side of the drawer. Cut a new runner to these dimensions from a piece of hardwood [C2]. Use PVA adhesive to stick the new runner in position. Hammer a 20 mm. panel pin into each end of the runner to hold it in place and punch in the pins. Smooth the join using a medium grade of glasspaper.

MAKING THE UPRIGHT SUPPORT

Cut a piece of 19 mm. (¾ in.) block-board (or laminboard) to exactly the same height as the chest. Cut it to 25 mm. (1 in.) less than the width of the chest to allow for lippings – which fix to the two long edges of the block-board to give it a finish – at each side. Cut two lippings from hardwood 12 mm. (½ in.) thick and 19 mm. wide. Make sure each lipping is about 50 mm. (2 in.) longer than the supporting board.

Put PVA adhesive along an edge of the board and along one 19 mm. edge of the lipping. Place the two glued edges together, keeping the lipping flush with the bottom of the board. The overlap at the other end will be cut off later. At each end, hammer a 25 mm. oval nail through the lipping into the board. Drive a 25 mm. nail in at the centre and two more nails between the centre and each end. Attach lipping to the other edge in exactly the same way and leave it to dry. Saw off the surplus lipping, and

Back lipping
Plywood
Batten
Blockboard
Lipping
Back rail
Upright support
Dovetail joint
Bottom runner
Chest of drawers

MAKING A DESK This is how the desk top is fitted, using the chest of drawers at one end and an upright support of blockboard at the other.

REMOVING STAPLES

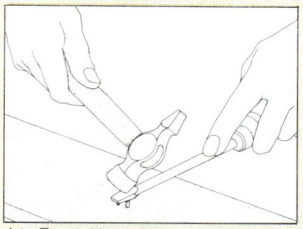

A1. Tap with a screwdriver blade to force down the points of the staples.

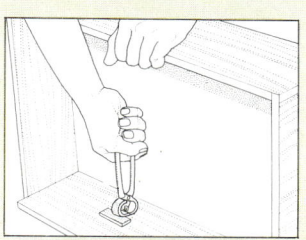

A2. Pull staples free with pincers, using a block to protect surface.

REPAIRING A DRAWER

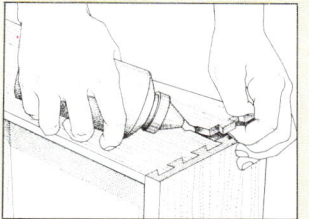

B1. Hold open the damaged joint and squeeze in adhesive.

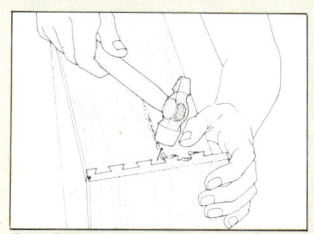

B2. Panel pins are fixed through dovetails for added strength.

ADDING A NEW RUNNER

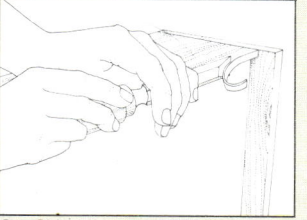

C1. Chisel the old runner down flush with the drawer base.

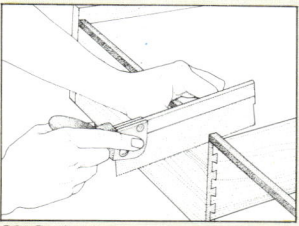

C2. Cutting the new runner to the correct size.

glasspaper joins between lipping and board.

MAKING THE DESK TOP

For the desk top, use a piece of plywood 25 mm. thick, and at least the width of the chest. It should be long enough to allow for a knee-hole about 750 mm. (2 ft 6 in.) across for the desk to be comfortable.

Lipping is fixed on all four edges of the desk top. The back lipping extends above the top, forming a ledge. This is screwed on, not nailed.

For the front lipping, cut a piece of softwood 25 mm. thick and 50 mm. wide, so that it measures 100 mm. (4 in.) longer than the desk top. Hold the lipping with its 50 mm. side facing the front edge of the plywood. Make sure that it is flush with the top surface and that it overhangs 50 mm. at each end. Fix with PVA adhesive and 40 mm. (1½ in.) oval nails in the same way as the lipping on the support.

Lay the desk top upside-down to fit the side lippings on. Use the same size softwood as for the front lipping and cut two pieces 50 mm. longer than the desk sides. Glue each lipping in place so that it fits against the overlap of the front lipping and overhangs at the back by 50 mm. Nail.

When the glue has dried, saw off overhangs on both desk top and support board.

For the back lipping cut hardwood 75 mm. (3 in.) thick by 25 mm. wide so that it is 50 mm. longer than the length of the desk top (including the side lippings). Place the desk top on a bench so that the back juts out slightly. Line up the lipping against the back of the desk top so that it extends above and below the top by 25 mm., and so that there is an overhang of 25 mm. at each end. Get someone to hold the lipping in position while you pencil a line along the lipping where it meets the top of the desk [D1]. Then mark three points 9 mm. (⅜ in.) below the line [D2]: one at the centre and one about 75 mm. from each end. Drill through the lipping at the three points with a No. 8 bit. Smooth with glasspaper.

Line the lipping against the desk top again and push a bradawl through the drilled holes to make holes for the screws on the desk top edge. Place screw cups over the holes on the outside edge of lipping, and drive screws through into the desk top. Saw off the overhangs and smooth the cuts with glasspaper.

FIXING THE UPRIGHT SUPPORT TO THE TOP

The upright support is secured to the top with a batten. Cut a piece of 25 mm. square hardwood to the width of the desk top (excluding the front and back lippings).

On one side of this batten make marks 38 mm. (1½ in.) from each end, slightly above the centre. Then mark three more points equidistant between the first two. Drill through the batten at these points with a No. 8 bit. Smooth with medium glasspaper.

On the adjacent edge of the batten, make four marks halfway between the five points on the other edge. Drill through the batten at these points with a No. 8 bit. Smooth with glasspaper.

Lay the desk top upside-down. Hold the support piece at right-angles to the top, so that it is flush against the inner edges of the lipping. Place the batten against the support piece with the four holes facing up. Hold in place with a cramp while you push a bradawl through the holes to mark the screw positions on the support.

Remove the support piece and drill holes where marked with a bit 2 mm. (1/16 in.) smaller than the screw.

Smear PVA adhesive along the in-side of the end lipping and along the inside of the end of the desk top (where the support will be fixed), and position the support. Clamp the batten firmly in position and put five 50 mm. screws through the batten into the support piece, and four 34 mm. (1⅜ in.) screws through the batten into the desk top. Start with the two middle screws in the top of the batten, then put in the middle screw in the side of the batten. Continue working from the middle of the batten to the ends. Smooth with glasspaper.

FIXING THE DESK TOP

Remove all the drawers and turn the chest upside-down. Draw diagonal lines across the inside of the chest top. Make a pencil mark on each line 75 mm. in from each corner. Then drill a hole with a No. 8 bit at each marked point. The No. 8 screws should be about 3 mm. (⅛ in.) shorter than the combined thicknesses of the chest and the desk top. (Do not screw the two pieces together yet, as it will be easier to paint them separately.)

MAKING THE BACK RAIL

For the back rail cut a piece of 75 × 25 mm. (3 × 1 in.) hardwood as long as the plywood top. Smooth the cut ends with glasspaper. Position the rail high enough to clear the skirting board in the room where the desk will be used. Mark this height on each of the back uprights of the chest frame and on the back of the upright support.

Find the centre line of the two frame uprights. Then, with someone holding the rail in place, mark these positions on the rail. Mark the centre line of the upright support at the other end of the rail. At each mark, drill and countersink two holes, 19 mm. in from each edge of the rail. Hold the rail in place again and push a bradawl through the drill holes to mark the screw positions on the uprights. Drill the uprights at these marks.

FITTING DRAWER HANDLES

Draw a horizontal line through the middle of the drawer fronts. Drill pilot holes for screws on handles, 100 mm. (4 in.) in from the sides.

PAINTING AND FINISHING

Smooth the wood with glasspaper and prime and undercoat the chest, the fronts of the drawers and the new wood.

When it is dry, rub down lightly with fine glasspaper (grade 0). Wipe with a cloth dampened with white spirit to remove dust. Apply top coat.

When the first top coat is dry, rub down and wipe and apply second coat. When that has dried, screw the desk top to the chest. Fit the new drawer handles and replace the drawers. Glue and screw the back rail in place.

FIXING THE LIPPING

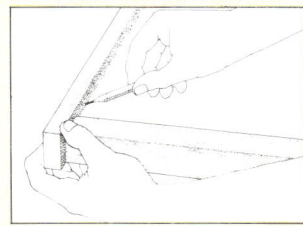

D1. Mark a line along the lipping where it meets the top of the desk.

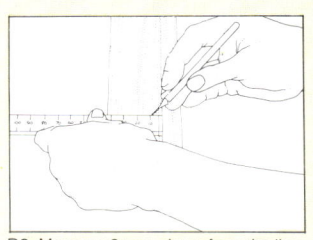

D2. Measure 9 mm. down from the line on the lipping to position the screws.

BEDROOM DESK   The converted chest of drawers makes an ideal desk for a teenager's bedroom, allowing the room to double as a study.

• RE-CANING A CHAIR

Re-caning a chair is not a difficult job – it merely requires patience and care. Follow the instructions carefully and keep in mind the following points.

1. Do any repairs to the frame first. A weak frame will pull apart under the strain of caning.

2. Soak each length of cane in water for a couple of minutes before use, and wind it round the hand to make it more flexible.

3. When changing to a new length of cane, secure the loose ends with pegs.

4. Keep the glossy side of the cane facing upwards.

5. To avoid twisting the cane, pass it through the fingers.

6. Keep the tension even.

MATERIALS AND EQUIPMENT

Chair-seating cane: No. 2 – approx. 1 oz., No. 4 – approx. 1 oz., No. 6 – 4 strands; pegs to hold cane – tapered willow or thicker cane or dowel; awl or long nail; trimming knife, or sharp kitchen knife; scissors; tweezers; pincers; hammer.

REMOVING OLD CANE

Push the knife blade under the beading cane and cut away from the seat frame, lifting it as it is freed. When the beading is removed, cut away the seating cane [A1].

Push the awl through the holes to clear out dirt, cane and plugging [A2]. If any cane or plugging sticks in the holes, pull it out with pincers.

When the holes are thoroughly clear, brush away the debris and wipe the seat frame with a damp cloth.

MAKING A NEW CANE SEAT

The strongest style of caning for chairs is known as the seven-step pattern, because it involves seven steps, or stages. The first four stages

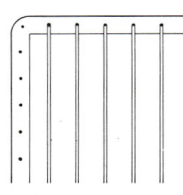 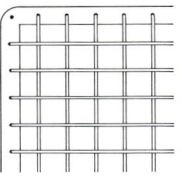 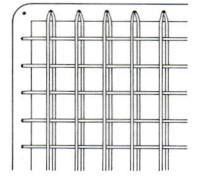 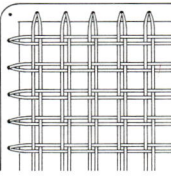 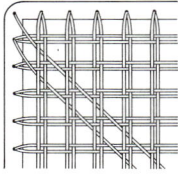 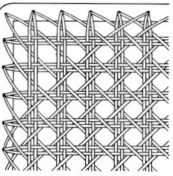 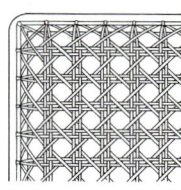

| STAGE ONE | STAGE TWO | STAGE THREE | STAGE FOUR | STAGE FIVE | STAGE SIX | STAGE SEVEN |

are known as crossing, the fifth and sixth as setting and the seventh is the beading. Beading hides the holes in the rails and gives a neat finish. But it is not essential, and some people prefer the appearance of unbeaded cane.

STAGE ONE

Place a peg in the centre hole of the back rail of the seat frame (or, if there is an even number, in the left one of the two centre holes). Then do the same on the front rail so that the two pegs are opposite each other. Take a strand of wetted No. 2 cane. Remove the back peg and push one end of the cane through the hole, glossy side up. Leave about 100 mm. (4 in.) of cane hanging and peg it [A3].

Remove the front peg, pull the other end of the cane through the hole and replace the peg. Keep the cane taut, but make sure it gives slightly when touched. If it is too tight, it may snap during weaving.

Push the cane up through the next hole on your right [A4]. Peg this hole and pass cane across to the opposite hole. Repeat this procedure until the side rail is reached. But leave the corner holes free. Repeat the whole procedure on the left side. The pegs may be moved about as you work, but leave a peg in any hole where there is a loose end of cane. When one strand of cane comes to an end, secure it with a peg. Start a new strand of cane in the next hole and peg it.

If the front rail is longer than the back rail, there will be more holes at the front than the back. Connect the extra ones to the holes immediately above on the side rail, keeping the strands parallel to those already threaded [B1].

To secure ends of cane, thread them through the loops of cane on the underside of the frame [B2]. Use the awl to stretch the loop to make way for the cane. Thread the end through two or three times, pull tight and cut off.

STAGE TWO

Leaving the corner hole empty, thread a strand of No. 2 cane through

---

REMOVING OLD CANE AND STARTING NEW CANE

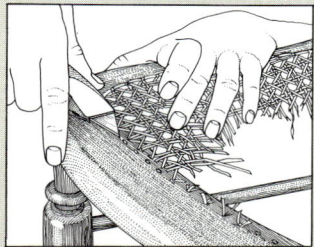
A1. Cut the old beading with a trimming knife, then cut the cane from the seat.

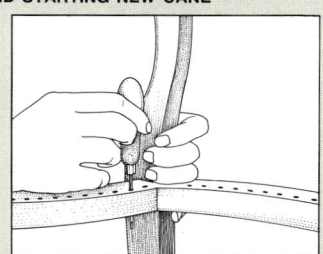
A2. Clear the holes of dirt, cane and plugging by pushing through with an awl.

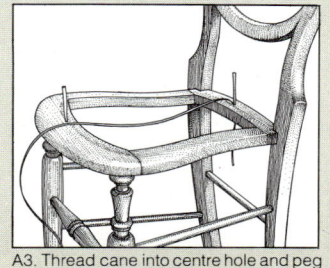
A3. Thread cane into centre hole and peg it, leaving 100 mm. below the hole.

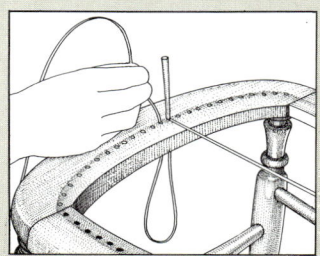
A4. Bring the cane up through the next hole on the right, keeping glossy side up.

PATTERN GUIDE A cane chair with a broken seat can be renovated at little cost. If the old seat is not too badly damaged, use it as a pattern.

the next hole at the back of the left rail. Peg the hole and thread the cane in the same way as for the first crossing, taking it over the first strands to form a criss-cross pattern [B3]. Continue until all the side holes have been threaded, except the corner holes. If the front of the chair is curved, however, it may be necessary to use the front corner holes at this stage. This will ensure that there is not a large gap between the last strand and the middle of the front rail.

STAGE THREE

Thread No. 2 cane exactly as in the first stage, starting from the middle hole on the back rail. This layer goes over the first and second.

STAGE FOUR

Leaving the corner hole empty, thread No. 2 cane through the next hole on the left of the back rail. (If the seat frame is straight rather than curved, start from the first hole at the top of the left rail.)

To make weaving easier, cut the end of the cane to a point. Weave over the first strand and under the next. Continue over and under to the end, then pass the cane through the last hole before the corner. Bring the cane up through the first side hole. Weave under the first strand, then over the next one [B4]. Continue in this way until the other side is reached. Keeping to the pattern formed by these two rows, continue weaving until the whole frame is completed.

When weaving close to the frame, lift the strands with tweezers so that the cane can be passed through easily. On the corners, where the cane is stretched fairly tightly over the wood, it may be easier to weave two strands together (over two, under two), using the tweezers to lift them.

STAGE FIVE

Change to No. 4 cane and start at the back left-hand corner, in the empty hole. Weave diagonally across, going over the side-to-side strands and under the front-to-back strands until the opposite corner is reached [B5]. Bring the cane up through the hole on the left and weave diagonally to the left, still going over and under and keeping the strand parallel to the first. Continue in this way until the left side is completed [B6].

If the front rail contains more holes than the side rail, it will sometimes be necessary to thread one hole twice on the shorter rail.

Weave in the same way on the right side, starting in the back left corner hole as before and weaving the first strand to the bottom right corner hole. Continue working to the right until the whole frame is woven. If the back rail has fewer holes than the side rail, leave a few holes empty where convenient on the side rails (these holes can be used in the next stage).

STAGE SIX

Still using No. 4 cane, start in the empty hole in the back right corner. Take the cane under the side-to-side strands and over the front-to-back strands (reverse of the previous weaving). Weave the left side first, then the right side.

When the weaving is completed, turn the chair upside-down, secure loose ends and hammer them flat.

STAGE SEVEN

Cut 4 mm. ($\frac{3}{16}$ in.) plugging cane into 20 mm. ($\frac{3}{4}$ in.) lengths. Insert a plug in every alternate hole along the front rail, starting in the third hole from the corner [C1]. This holds the cane firmly in the holes.

Take a length of No. 6 beading cane, and cut the end to a point. Push the other end of the cane through the front right corner hole and peg it. Take the cane across the front rail and down through the left corner hole [C2]. Take a length of No. 2 cane, pass it up the first unplugged hole, over the beading and down the same hole, making a loop over the beading cane [C3]. Then bring it up the next unplugged hole and repeat the procedure until the corner is reached. Repeat on the other three sides, using fresh beading cane each time.

Hammer a plug into each corner hole and cut off the ends of beading cane. Secure the ends of the No. 2 cane [C4], and flatten with a hammer.

CANING THE CHAIR

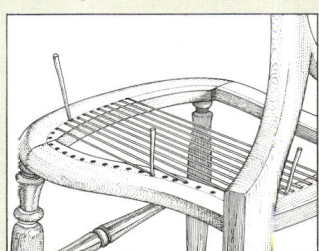

B1. If the front has more holes than the back, use the sides when back is full.

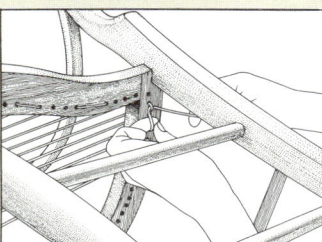

B2. Secure loose ends of cane by threading them through loops under seat frame.

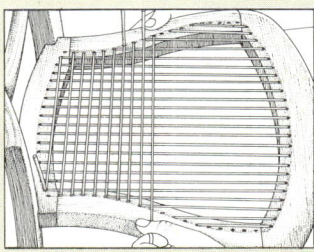

B3. Keeping cane taut, take it across the first layer to form a criss-cross pattern.

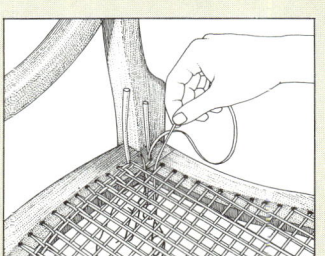

B4. Use both hands to weave the cane; run it through fingers to prevent twisting.

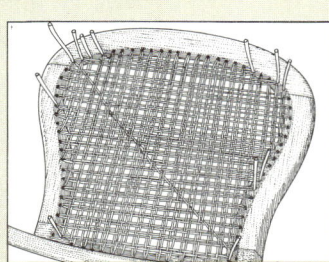

B5. From a back corner hole, weave across the strands to the opposite corner.

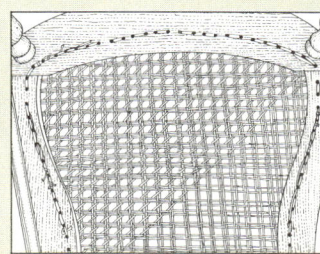

B6. Underside of chair, showing how ends have been tied round the loops.

PLUGGING AND BEADING

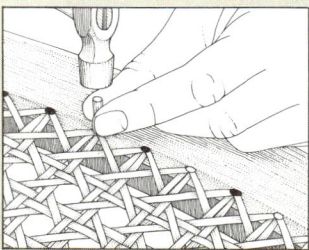

C1. Hammer plugging cane into alternate holes to hold the cane in place.

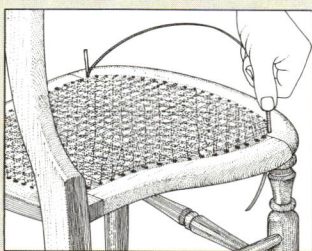

C2. Take beading cane across the front seat rail and peg it in corner holes.

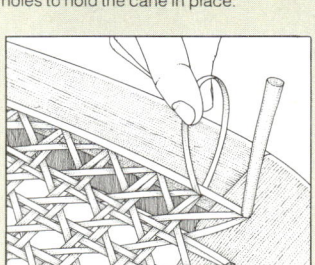

C3. Pass cane up through hole, over the beading and down through the hole.

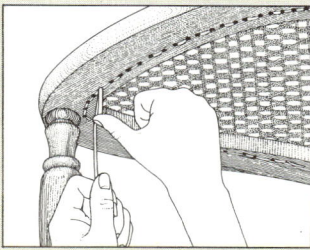

C4. When the beading is finished, secure loose ends of cane under the loops.

TRADITIONAL UPHOLSTERY

Upholstering a traditional chair from the frame outwards requires skill in handling a hammer, tacks, twine and a variety of shaped needles. The first job is to tack and strain webbing between the seat rails to form a base for the seat padding. Coil springs are stitched to the webbing, then a hessian cover is tacked over the springs. The hessian cover is also stitched to the springs and forms a base for the first filling, usually a fibre, which is covered with scrim or hessian and stitched into shape. The second filling of flock or horsehair rounds out the shape, bringing the seat to its full size, and is covered by calico. Cotton wadding, which is used to provide an extra-smooth surface as a base for the top cover, is placed over the calico before the cover is fitted and trimmed. The underside is covered with black calico.

The basic techniques are applied to all shapes and sizes of chairs. They are best learned on the loose frame of a drop-in seat (see p. 124). Modern chairs often have simpler springing systems based on rubber webbing, which are easier to replace than traditional metal springs. The methods shown here for replacing covers can be used for most types of upholstered chairs.

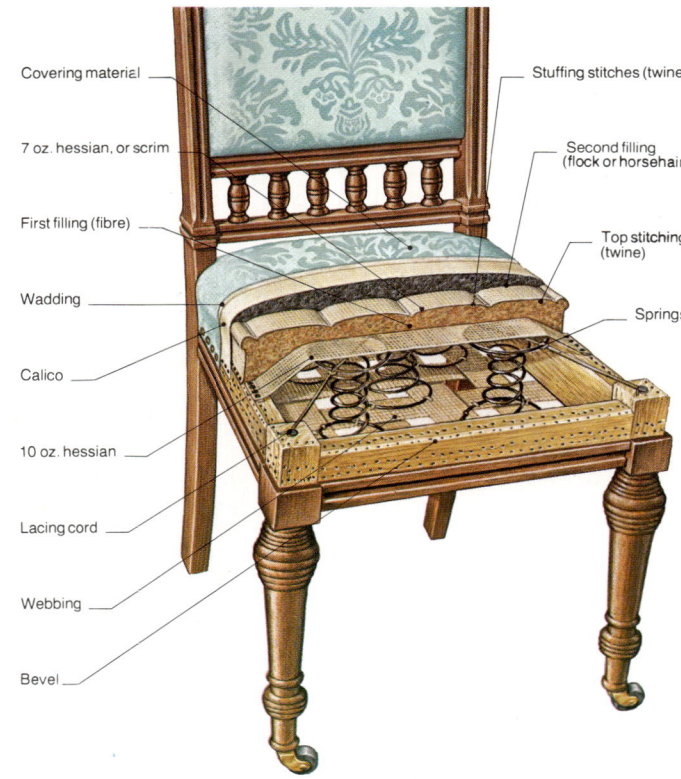

Covering material
7 oz. hessian, or scrim
First filling (fibre)
Wadding
Calico
10 oz. hessian
Lacing cord
Webbing
Bevel

Stuffing stitches (twine)
Second filling (flock or horsehair)
Top stitching (twine)
Springs

ANATOMY OF A CHAIR Up to seven layers of fabric and fibre are built up on springs to form the seat of a traditional sprung chair.

• BUYING SECOND-HAND CHAIRS

There are three factors to consider when buying a second-hand chair: the shape, the comfort and the extent of the repairs needed to put it in order.

To test the comfort, sit well back in the chair for a few minutes, then sit forward as if at a table or in conversation. If your feet rest easily on the floor in both positions, the seat is the right height. The thighs should be supported comfortably, otherwise the seat is the wrong depth from back to front. It is possible to adjust the height and softness of the seat when re-upholstering, by varying the thickness and texture of the padding materials and fitting or removing castors. The depth, too, can be altered by adding or taking away back fillings.

To find out what repairs are needed, turn the chair over to check the webbing, springs and fillings. Pull away a corner of the underside covering and look into the seat. Sagging or broken webbing can be replaced without too much difficulty. If the hessian which covers the springs is torn and filling is spilling out, all the seat upholstery will have to be removed to make repairs.

Test the strength of the chair frame by pushing the back outwards while holding down the seat. There should not be much movement. Check the frame for signs of woodworm (see p. 378) and of previous repairs.

When buying a set of dining chairs, examine the condition of each one. Completely remaking the seat of one chair is a reasonable task, but upholstering six is a major project for an amateur with limited equipment.

• EQUIPMENT AND MATERIALS

Professional upholsterers use a wide range of specialist tools, but the amateur tackling limited repairs can find adequate substitutes for most of them in the house. The main exceptions to this are the specially shaped needles used for the various upholstery stitches.

MATERIALS

When buying fabric for final covers, make sure the manufacturer recommends the fabric for upholstery. If a fabric is intended only for loose covers or curtains, it will not stand up to constant wear if used for upholstery. Check any cleaning instructions with the retailer and follow these exactly.

Very large pattern repeats are wasteful of material when used on small seats in a set of chairs. It is difficult to keep the lines on a striped fabric straight without practice, and these are best avoided by beginners.

Calico Unbleached calico is a tightly woven cotton fabric often used to shape the second filling. Lightweight hessian or scrim are commonly used under leather covers, but they are too bulky under lightweight fabrics. Black calico is used to cover the underside of the seat.

Scrim A lightweight, coarsely woven fabric, scrim is made of flax and is used for shaping the first filling where hessian would be too bulky. It is softer and easier to handle than hessian.

Hessian This coarsely woven fabric is made from jute and is usually sold in 7 or 10 oz. weights. The heavier hessian is used as the base on which the first filling rests. The lighter version is interchangeable with scrim as a cover for the first filling and is less expensive than scrim.

Webbing Webbing stretched across the seat frame is the basis of all traditional upholstery. The best-quality webbing, called English or black-and-white, is a twill weave of pure flax. There is also another version, slightly less strong, made of jute and cotton.

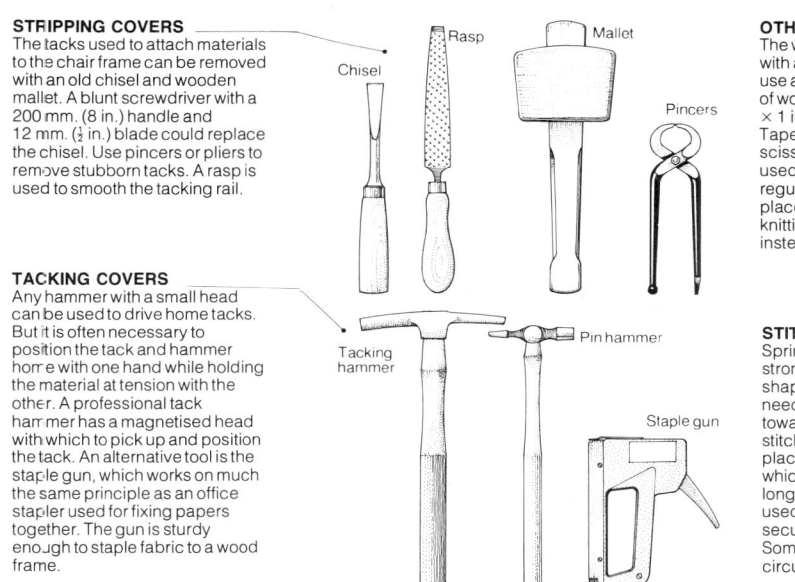

STRIPPING COVERS

The tacks used to attach materials to the chair frame can be removed with an old chisel and wooden mallet. A blunt screwdriver with a 200 mm. (8 in.) handle and 12 mm. (½ in.) blade could replace the chisel. Use pincers or pliers to remove stubborn tacks. A rasp is used to smooth the tacking rail.

Chisel
Rasp
Mallet
Pincers

TACKING COVERS

Any hammer with a small head can be used to drive home tacks. But it is often necessary to position the tack and hammer home with one hand while holding the material at tension with the other. A professional tack hammer has a magnetised head with which to pick up and position the tack. An alternative tool is the staple gun, which works on much the same principle as an office stapler used for fixing papers together. The gun is sturdy enough to staple fabric to a wood frame.

Tacking hammer
Pin hammer
Staple gun

OTHER EQUIPMENT

The webbing is stretched tight with a web strainer. Professionals use a bat and dowel, but a block of wood 150 × 75 × 25 mm. (6 × 3 × 1 in.), can be used instead. Tape measure, tailor's chalk, scissors and a trimming knife are used when cutting the covers. A regulator is used to pull fillings into place through the inner covers. A knitting needle can be used instead.

Bat and dowel
Wood block
Scissors
Trimming knife
Tailor's chalk
Tape measure
Regulator
Knitting needle

STITCHING

Springs are sewn in place with strong twine, using a specially shaped needle. The spring needle is curved and flattened towards the tip. It is essential for stitching springs and fillings in place. The stitching needle, which is about 250 mm. (10 in.) long and pointed at both ends, is used with a lighter-weight twine to secure and shape the fillings. Some twine work is done with half-circular needles.

Stitching needle
Skewer
Spring needle
Half circular needles

STRIPPING AND REPLACING COVERS Professional upholsterers use specialist tools which enable them to work efficiently and quickly. Some of these tools – particularly the needles – are essential for the amateur. Others, such as the bat and dowel and the hammers, can be replaced by tools or materials available in most homes where a basic kit is kept for do-it-yourself jobs.

The cheapest webbing, quite suitable for most purposes, is brown and made of jute. Webbing comes in 50, 65 and 75 mm. (2, 2½ and 3 in.) widths and 7 lb., 9 lb. or 11 lb. weights. Weight indicates strength – 9 lb. × 2 in. is the most widely used grade.

Wadding Soft cotton wadding, sold as skin wadding, is laid over the calico cover to give softness and conceal small lumps in the second filling. When calico is not being used and the cover is laid directly on to the second filling, Lintafelt, made of cotton waste, is used to cover any lumps.

Fillings The fibres most commonly used as fillings or padding are coir or coconut fibre, Algerian fibre, made from palm leaves, and horsehair. Horsehair is the most resilient, but it is expensive. It is sometimes mixed with other animal hairs. The other fibres are cheaper. Use a fibre for the first filling and horsehair or flock for the second. The fillings from existing pads can often be used again.

Twine and threads Spring twine is used to stitch springs to webbing and hessian. A lighter-weight twine is used for other stitching. The springs are laced down with laid cord, which is not twisted but has the fibres laid side by side to prevent stretching.

Gimp and braiding Tacks and the raw edges of fabric on chairs are concealed under banding or gimp. Bands of the cover fabric may be laid over the tack heads and fixed with decorative nails. Gimp is a narrow braid used for the same purpose. Another traditional finish is leather boarding fixed with decorative nails.

Tacks, nails and pins Always use steel tacks for upholstery. These have cut ends with fine sharp points and may be fine or improved. Fine tacks have smaller heads. The most common sizes are: improved, ⅜, ½ or ⅝ in.; and fine ⅜ or ½ in. Gimp pins, used to attach gimp or braid, have very small heads. Decorative nails, used to conceal raw edges, are made in several finishes.

Coil springs These springs have a vertical double cone and are made of copper-covered steel wire or galvanised steel wire. They are graded by height and gauge (thickness of the wire). Sizes range from 100 mm. to 355 mm. (4-14 in.). The smallest are used for chair arms and the largest for seats. An 8-10 gauge is used in seats while 12-13 gauge is used for backs and arms. Springs break only when put under pressure while distorted. However, they do bend and then must be replaced. When buying new ones, take a spring from the damaged chair and ask the shop to match it.

WHERE TO BUY

Tools, including needles, can be bought from craft suppliers. Tacks, decorative nails, gimp and other braids, and webbing are available from many department stores stocking upholstery fabrics. Many small upholsterers will supply fillings and wadding in small quantities.

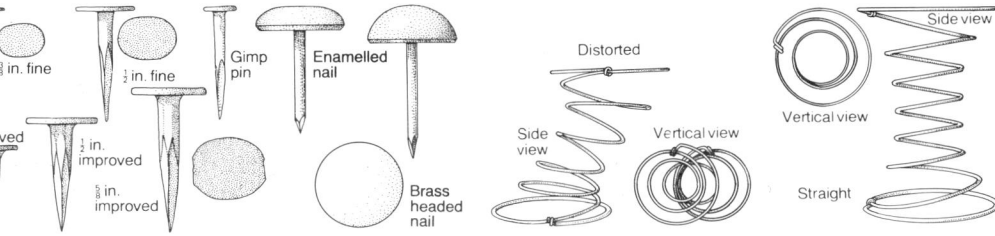

TACKS, NAILS AND PINS *Use steel tacks for all fabrics. Fix gimp with gimp pins. Finish with decorative nails.*

SPRING CHECK *Look down into the spring, and examine it from the side, to see that the coils are not distorted.*

• UPHOLSTERING A DROP-IN SEAT

All old covers and fillings have to be removed so that the seat can be re-built from the frame upwards. If the pad is not too bumpy, it can be used again; but discard everything else.

MATERIALS AND EQUIPMENT

5 cm. (2 in.) wide brown webbing; 10 oz. hessian; stitching twine; black and unbleached calico; fibre or hair filling; cotton wadding; cover fabric; ½ in. fine and ⅜ in. improved tacks; old screwdriver; wood mallet; tack hammer; scissors; tape measure; tailor's chalk; spring needle; upholstery skewers; web strainer.

CALCULATING QUANTITIES

Take the seat out and measure it both ways, measuring from the underside of the frame over the cover. Add about 5 cm. (2 in.) all round for fitting. Find the length and number of the existing webs and allow 15 cm. (6 in.) excess on each length. Keep the full length of webbing intact.

STRIPPING THE OLD COVERS

Work on a table covered with an old blanket. Spread an old sheet on the floor to catch materials and tacks.

First, lay the seat upside-down. To lever out old tacks, put the screw-driver beside a tack head and strike the handle with the mallet. Work the blade under the tack head and strike again. Work in the direction of the wood grain [A1]. Turn the seat over, lift off the covers, and cut the twine holding the filling to the hessian. Set the pad of filling aside if it can be used again [A2]. Mark the position of the webs, then remove the hessian and webbing. Mark the centre of the front and back rails on both sides.

FITTING THE WEBBING

Follow the pattern of the old webbing, allowing about 5 cm. between webs. The webbing is attached to the top of the frame. Take the full length of webbing and turn up 2.5 cm. (1 in.) at one end. Place the fold halfway across the frame's front or back rail.

Secure with five staggered ⅜ in. improved tacks [A3].

Place the strainer on the outer edge of the opposite rail. Wrap the webbing round the strainer. Hold the frame down. Replace the strainer on the edge, then press down to stretch the webbing [A4]. Pull it as taut as you can. Secure with three tacks on the centre line of the rail. Then trim the webbing to within 2.5 cm. of the tacks. Turn up the excess and tack twice, between the previous tacks.

Complete the back-to-front webbing. Attach the cross webs in the same way, after weaving between the back-to-front webs [A5].

FITTING HESSIAN

Cut a piece of hessian large enough to overlap the frame by 5 cm. all round. Lay it over the webbing with the grain straight from front to back.

A1. Hammer the screwdriver blade under the tack head and knock or prise it out.

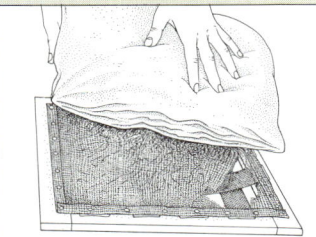

A2. Remove the pad of filling and check if it can be re-used.

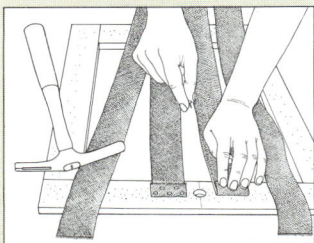

A3. Make a 2.5 cm. fold in one end of the webbing and secure with five tacks.

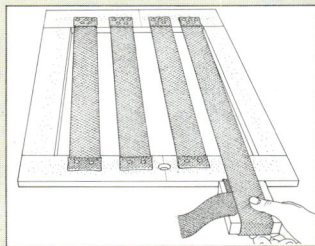

A4. Wrap the webbing once round the strainer and press down.

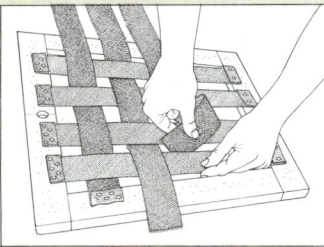

A5. Weave the cross webbing between the back-to-front strips before tacking.

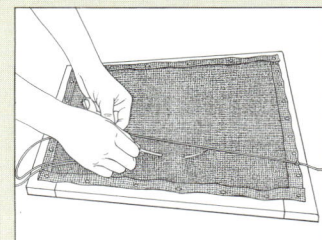

A6. Secure the twine in the front hem, then make a back stitch halfway across.

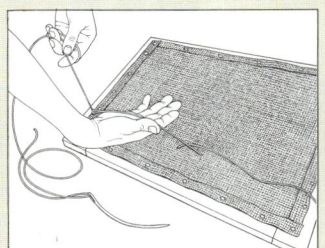

A7. Use a hand to allow about 5 cm. of play under each loop before knotting.

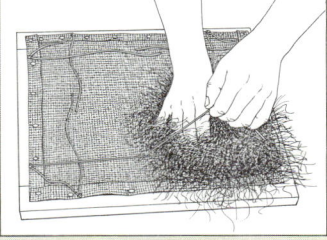

A8. Push filling under the loops until the seat is covered to a depth of 7.5 cm.

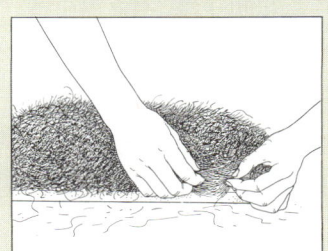

A9. Tease out humps and excess fibre until the density is even throughout.

DROP-IN SEAT All the basic upholstery skills can be learned on a drop-in seat, which is simpler to repair than a conventional sprung dining chair.

Starting from the front edge of the seat, turn up about 10 mm. (⅜ in.) of the edge of the hessian. Make the fold line up with the ends of the webbing.

Using ½ in. fine tacks spaced about 2.5 cm. apart, tack the hessian to the front of the frame with a straight row of tacks just inside the fold line.

Strain the hessian to the back of the seat and tack it down in line with the folded ends of the webbing, spacing the tacks 5 cm. apart. Do not turn up the edge of the hessian at this stage. Repeat on both sides.

Cut away surplus hessian at the back and sides about 2.5 cm. from the lines of tacks. Turn up the hems and tack them down, spacing the tacks between those underneath.

BRIDLE TIES AND FIRST FILLING

If the old seat pad can be re-used, position it on the new hessian and cover with a layer of cotton wadding.

To make a new pad, first thread the spring needle with twine. Make a knot in the end to secure and make the first stitch in the front hem of the hessian, 5 cm. in from the side. Put the needle in again halfway down the side towards the back of the seat and make a small back stitch [A6]. Pull the twine loosely through, then make a small back stitch in the back hem. Wrap the twine twice round the needle. Adjust each loop of twine to hold about 5 cm. of compressed filling [A7]. Pull the end knot tight.

Take the twine across the corner and make a stitch in the side hem to start the next bridle stitch, which runs parallel to the back. Repeat with the other side and the front, so that there is a set of bridle stitches, along each side of the seat. On a large seat, put a tie down the centre from front to back.

Push the filling under the twine, a handful at a time [A8]. Continue until all the loops are filled. Pull or tease the fibre over the centre and out to the sides. The loose filling should be about 7.5 cm. (3 in.) deep. Shape the filling to a dome at the centre, and taper it towards the back. Make the filling rise straight from the frame all round. Tease and press the fibre until the density is even over the entire seat [A9]. Smooth the edges.

CUTTING AND FITTING CALICO

From this point, all the covers are tacked to the underside of the frame. Cut the unbleached calico to cover the filling and overlap the underside of the frame by about 5 cm. Fold in half lengthways and nick each end of the fold to mark the centre.

Lay the calico over the filling, grip it firmly to the filling and frame at the sides, then turn the seat frame over [B1]. Match one notch in the calico with the centre mark on the underside of the frame at the back. Using ⅜ in. improved tacks, fix at the centre and work out towards the corners. Leave the corners free. Hold the calico over the front frame and stand the seat upright on the back edge. Smooth the calico over the filling and down on to the underside of the front frame. Match the centre marks and tack at the centre [B2]. Pulling the fabric down and sideways, tack out along the front, leaving the corners free [B3].

Tack the sides in a similar manner, starting in the centre and keeping the grain of the fabric straight.

Pull each corner of the calico over the filling and down on the underside of the frame. Pull on a line from the centre of the seat to the corner. Tack at the centre of the corner. Gather the fullness at either side of the corner into two pleats. Pull back each pleat, away from the frame, then fold forward on to the frame so that the fold lies parallel with the adjacent side. Tack, then trim off the excess. The second pleat lies over the first at right-angles [B4]. Trim the calico up to the tacks all round.

Remove any lumps in the filling with a skewer or needle. Push it through the calico, catching up some filling, and lever the filling into place [B5].

FINAL COVER

Measure the finished seat, from front to back and side to side, from the underside over the calico. Mark the centre of front and back frames.

Mark the size and the shape of the seat on the cover fabric, keeping the pattern central. Cut the cover fabric, allowing 5 cm. excess all round. Fold the fabric in half from back to front and nick each end of the fold to mark the centre.

Cover the seat with cotton wadding and trim to fit the seat. If the cover fabric is bulky, fray the wadding at the sides to reduce the bulk. Lay the cover over the wadding, matching the notches with the centre marks on the frame [B6]. Skewer the centre of the fabric to the centre of the seat.

Hold the fabric in place and turn the frame over. Tack the cover in the same way as the calico. If using a bulky fabric, cut a narrow V out of the fullness at each side of each corner [B7]. Then fold down and tack off. Trim the fabric close to the tacks.

Cut the black calico to cover the tacks on the underside, allowing 2.5 cm. excess all round. Fold under the excess and tack the calico to the back rail [B8]. Next tack the front, then both sides. Fold the hems over each other at each corner and tack.

CUTTING AND FITTING THE CALICO AND COVER

B1. Put the calico over the filling. Hold it tightly in place and turn the seat over.

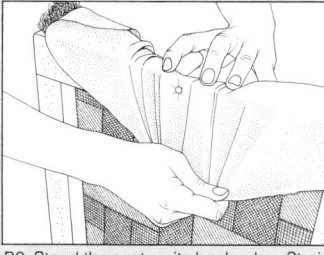

B2. Stand the seat on its back edge. Strain calico over the front edge, and tack.

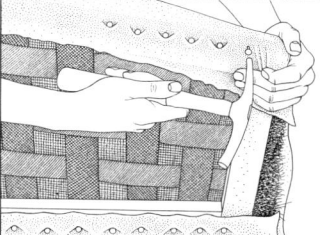

B3. Tack along the front, outward from the centre, leaving the corners free.

B4. Fold a second pleat over the first, at right-angles, to finish the corner.

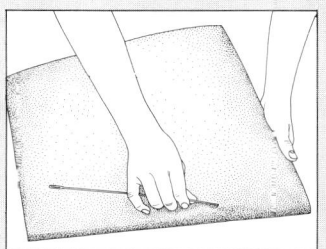

B5. Push needle or skewer through calico and tease the filling to an even density.

B6. Position the cover from back to front over the frame, making sure it is centred.

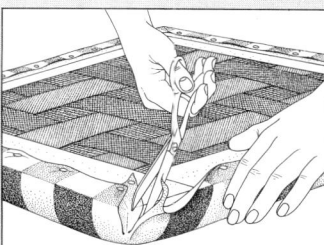

B7. Cut a narrow V into the fabric on either side of the corner to reduce bulk.

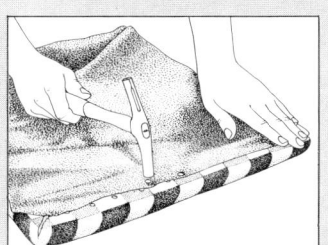

B8. Tack black calico to the underside of the seat to conceal tacks and raw edges.

• UPHOLSTERING A SPRUNG DINING CHAIR

If the webbing and hessian base of the seat are broken and the springs are distorted, the seat can be re-made. This involves fixing new webbing, positioning and securing the springs, forming the first and second fillings and putting on the final cover.

To estimate quantities for fabrics, measure the existing cover and add 5 cm. (2 in.) all round Measure the length and number of existing webs and add 15 cm. (6 in.) for each length to estimate quantity of webbing.

MATERIALS AND EQUIPMENT

5 m. (16 ft 6 in.) of 5 cm. (2 in.) webbing; 1 m. (3 ft) of 10 oz. hessian; laid cord; spring and stitching twine; ⅝ in. and ½ in. improved and fine tacks; gimp pins; 1 m. (3 ft) each of 5 oz. scrim, black and unbleached calico; 2.5 m. (8 ft 3 in.) gimp or braid; fibre and horsehair or flock fillings; contact adhesive and cardboard; old chisel or screwdriver; mallet; tack hammer; rasp; regulator; webbing strainer; spring needle; 25 cm. (10 in.) stitching needle; half-circular needle; scissors; trimming knife; tape measure; tailor's chalk.

• FITTING NEW WEBBING AND SPRINGS

Turn the chair upside-down on a table, protecting the surface with a blanket. Spread paper or an old sheet on the floor round the table. Clear away old tacks and materials regularly while working. Before freeing the webbing and springs, note the number and pattern of both. Follow this when replacing these items.

STRIPPING OFF OLD MATERIALS

Loosen and knock out the old tacks as described on p. 124, working in the direction of the wood grain.

When all the tacks have been removed, turn the chair right side up. Lift away the covers and snip the twine which holds the fillings and springs to the hessian and webbing and remove all tacks and upholstery from the frame [A1].

Rasp the top outer edges of the seat rails above the polished wood to create a clean bevelled edge [A2].

WEBBING

Turn the chair over and position the first web on the back seat rail. Turn up 2.5 cm. (1 in.) on the end of the webbing and tack to the middle of the back rail, using five ⅝ in. improved tacks. Rest the webbing strainer on the outer edge of the front rail opposite. Pull the webbing over the strainer. Wrap it once round the block. Replace the strainer on the edge, press down and hold [A3]. Secure the stretched webbing with three tacks. Trim to within 2.5 cm. of the tacks, turn up the excess and secure with two tacks between the first three.

Place the remaining webs not more than 5 cm. (2 in.) apart. Fit the cross webs in the same way but weave between the first webs before straining and tacking in place [A4].

FITTING COIL SPRINGS

Use the existing springs, replacing only those that are broken or distorted. The springs will be of 9 or 10 gauge and between 12.5 and 15 cm. (5-6 in.) high, depending on the height of the finished seat. The springs, all the same size, are compressed about 5 cm. during fitting. Dining chairs may have four to nine springs. Arrange according to the previous pattern.

Place the chair upright on the floor and position the springs. The base coil of each spring should be evenly supported by the webbing [A5]. Space the springs evenly and check

---

STRIPPING THE SEAT AND FITTING NEW WEBBING AND SPRINGS

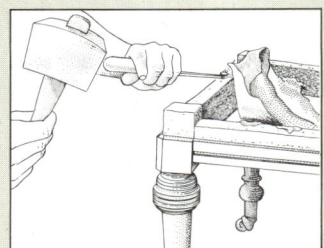

A1. Use a mallet and screwdriver to loosen and prise out the old tacks.

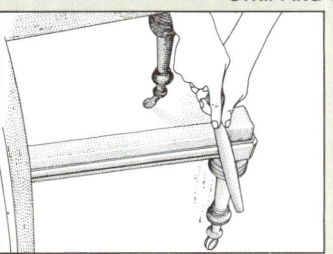

A2. Rasp a clean bevelled edge to the raw wood of the frame. Avoid polished wood.

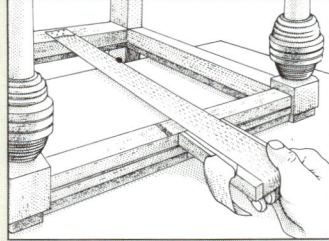

A3. Pull the webbing, wrap it once round the strainer and press down.

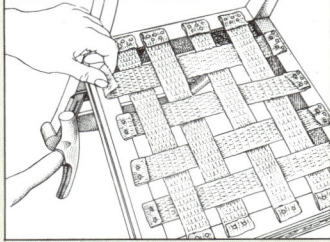

A4. Weave the cross webs between those running back to front and tack down.

A5. Position each spring so that it is evenly supported by the webbing.

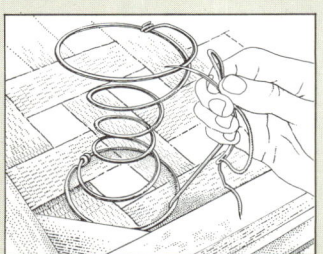

A6. Push the needle up through the webbing inside the base of the first spring.

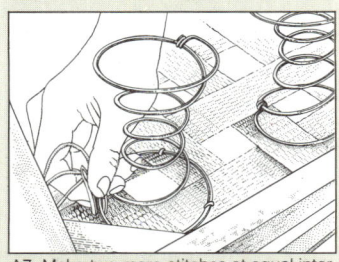

A7. Make two more stitches at equal intervals round the base coil.

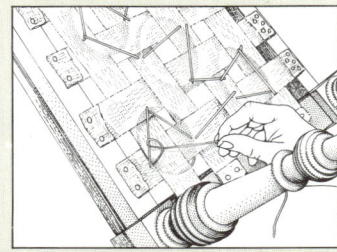

A8. Turn the chair over, pull all the stitches tight and knot the twine.

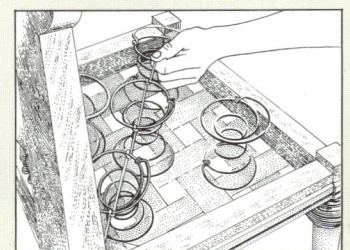

A9. Put a slip knot in the cord on both sides of the top coil of each spring.

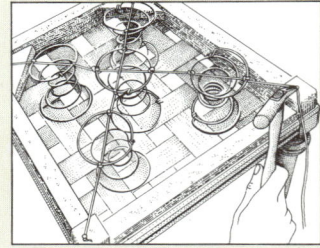

A10. Check that all laced springs are upright and evenly compressed.

that each one is standing straight.

Thread the spring needle with about 2 m. (6 ft) of spring twine. Starting from below, push the needle through the webbing to come out just inside the base coil of the first spring in the back left-hand corner [A6]. Put the needle in again just outside the coil Pull most of the twine through anc knot with the tail under the seat.

Make two more stitches at equal intervals round the base coil [A7]. Pull the stitches tight, then pass to the next spring. Stitch this down in the same way. Move on from spring to spring, until all are stitched to the webbing. Turn the chair over and on the final stitch make a slip knot with the twine. Before pulling the knot tight, pull tight each stitch in turn, starting from the beginning [A8]. Pull the final knot tight, tie firmly, and cut the twine.

LACING THE SPRINGS

The springs must remain upright or they will distort and break. To keep them in place, lace them tightly to each other and to the chair frame. Laid cord is used for this because it is stronger than twine. If the springs are arranged in two diagonals, lace across the diagonals. Springs arranged in a square or in parallel lines are laced from front to back along each row, then from side to side.

Drive a ⅝ in. improved tack half home on each corner block and on top of each front post. Cut two pieces of cord, each one-and-a-half times the length of the diagonal over the springs. Wrap and knot one end of each length round a back corner tack and hammer home to secure.

Press the springs down about 5 cm., with the arm across one of the diagonals to gauge the height to which the springs should be compressed. Take the cord over this diagonal. With finger and thumb hold

Slip knots used in lacing a spring.

the cord to the top coil of the first spring in the back corner. Wrap the cord under and over in a slip knot. Keeping the cord taut, stretch to the opposite side of the top coil and make a second slip knot.

Keeping the springs compressed to the same level, attach the cord to each side of the top coil of each spring, working across the diagonal to the front corner [A9]. Check that the

springs are upright and are still under even tension, then wrap the cord tightly round the front tack and hammer home. Cut off the excess cord. Lace down the other row of springs in the same way as the first [A10].

FITTING THE HESSIAN BASE

Lay the hessian over the springs and cut it roughly to size, allowing 5 cm. outside the frame all round [B1].

Replace the hessian on the springs with the selvedge to the back. Fold up the excess fabric at either side of the seat and tuck the back of the hessian through between the back posts. Use ½ in. improved tacks to attach the hessian to the top of the back seat rail. Keep the grain of the fabric straight at all times. Leaving about 2.5 cm. excess hessian, tack half home at the centre of the back rail. Pull the fabric towards the corner post and tack half

home again, leaving the corner free. Tack towards the other corner. Check that the fabric is straight, then tack home. Turn up the excess hessian along the back and tack in place.

Pull the hessian to the front, making it tight over the springs, and tack to the front rail in the same way as the back [B2]. Pull down and outwards when tacking towards the front posts. Leave the corners free. Tack the sides in the same way. Check that the grain of the fabric is straight, then tack home. At the back posts, cut into the corner of the hessian up to the inner corner of the post [B3]. Pull the hessian tight over the frame and tack down all round [B4]. Trim the hessian to within 2.5 cm. of the tacks all round [B5]. Then turn up the excess and tack home [B6]. At the front, fold the hem of the front hessian over the hem at either side and tack to the top of the

front post through the two hems.

STITCHING THE HESSIAN TO THE SPRINGS

Stitch the hessian to the springs using the same pattern as for stitching the springs to the webbing. Thread the spring needle with twine. Put the needle into the hessian inside the top coil of the first spring. Go under the coil and bring the needle out just outside the top coil. Pull the twine through but leave a tail [B7]. Make a running knot with the tail and pull the knot tight.

Make two further ties, evenly spaced round the top coil. Each tie is made by wrapping the twine twice round the needle before pulling the rest of the twine through. Move from spring to spring, making three ties on each. Make a double knot [B8] on the last tie and cut the twine.

CUTTING AND FITTING THE HESSIAN BASE

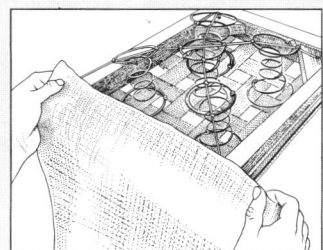

B1. Lay the hessian on the springs and cut it 5 cm. outside the frame all round.

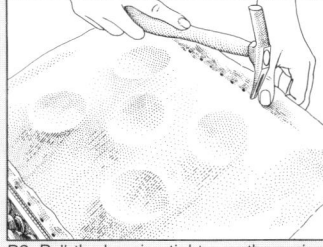

B2. Pull the hessian tight over the springs and tack to the front rail.

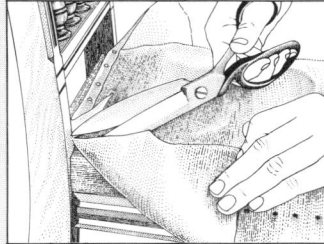

B3. Cut into the corner of the hessian up to the inside corner of the back post.

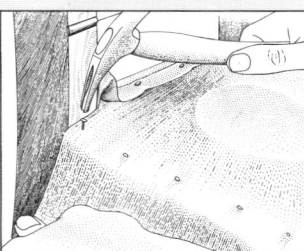

B4. Pull the hessian tight over each of the side rails and tack down.

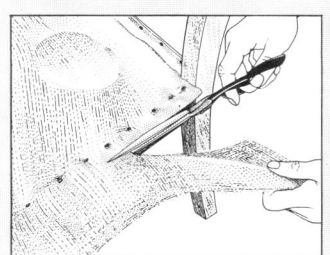

B5. Trim the hessian to within 2.5 cm. of the tacks all round the frame.

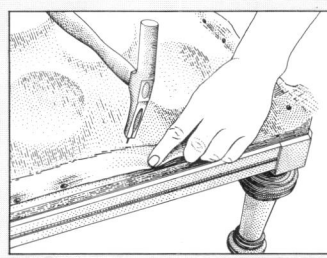

B6. Turn up the 2.5 cm. excess all round and tack down.

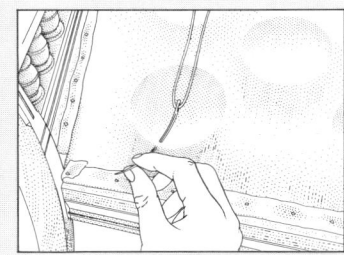

B7. Loop the needle through the hessian under the top coil of the first spring.

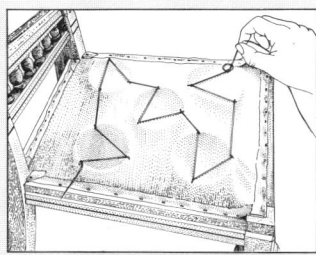

B8. Put three ties round each spring. Make a double knot on the last tie.

• DINING CHAIR - MAKING THE FIRST FILLING

Loosely stitched loops, called bridle ties, are sewn to the hessian base to hold the fibre which is the first of two layers of filling which pad the seat of the chair. The fibre is teased and patted into shape, then covered with scrim. The scrim is tacked temporarily into place while further stitches are put in to hold the filling to the centre of the seat. The scrim is then tacked down and trimmed. Then another series of stitches are put in to pull the filling into a roll along the edge of the seat, ready for the next stage in shaping the seat.

BRIDLE TIES

Each bridle tie is made up of two long stitches with a smaller back stitch at the centre, and is knotted to the hessian at each end. The ties run parallel to all four sides and lie 7.5 cm. (3 in.) in from the frame. Each loop must be large enough to hold 5 cm. (2 in.) depth of compressed filling.

Thread a spring needle with stitching twine. Take a small back stitch in the hem of the hessian at the front and knot with the tail of the twine. Put the needle in again just over halfway to the back of the seat and make a 5 cm. back stitch through the hessian [A1].

Pull the twine through loosely and make a small back stitch in the back hem of the hessian. Wrap the twine twice round the needle near the eye and pull through, but not tight. Lift each loop to check that there is about 5 cm. clearance above the hessian [A2]. Pull the knot tight.

Take the twine across the corner to the adjacent side, put a back stitch in the hem and make two ties across the back. Continue making ties round the other two sides [A3]. Knot and cut the twine after the last stitch.

BUILDING UP THE FILLING

Lift up the first loop of the tie on one side of the seat and push a handful of fibre underneath [A4]. Press the next handful against the first and continue until the loop is filled. Fill the ties so

---

BUILDING UP AND SHAPING THE FIRST FIBRE FILLING

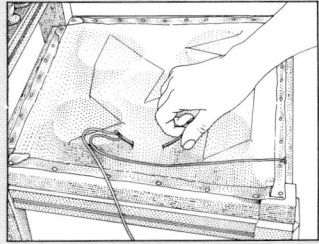
A1. Secure the twine and take a back stitch just over halfway across the seat.

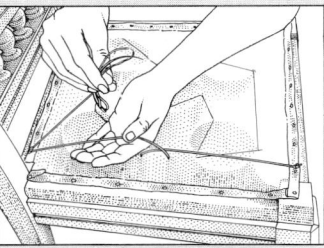
A2. Lift each loop to check that there is 5 cm. clearance above the hessian.

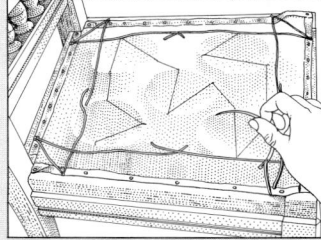
A3. Make bridle ties along all sides. Put the last stitch in the hem and knot.

A4. Lift the loops to push fibre underneath. Pack all eight loops tight.

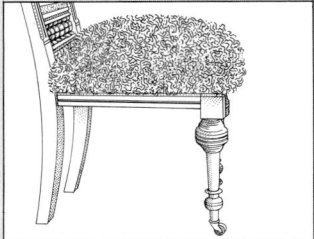
A5. Shape the fibre so that it is evenly distributed over all the seat.

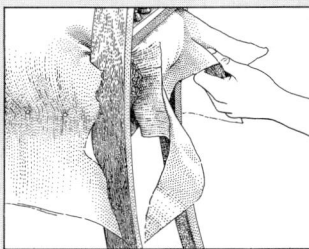
A6. Tuck the inner edge of each flap between the filling and the back post.

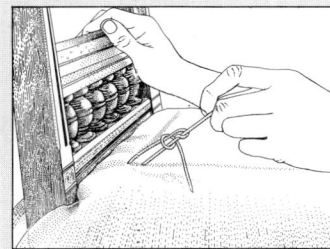
A7. Make a slip knot with the tail of the twine as the needle comes clear.

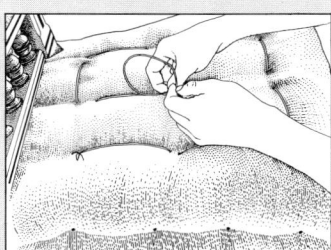
A8. Pull all the stitches tight and make a double knot on the last stitch.

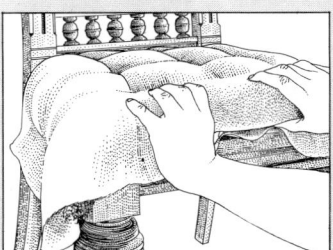
A9. Straighten the scrim and tuck it under the filling at the front.

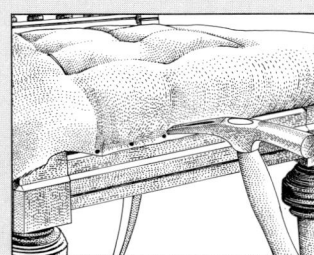
A10. Tack the scrim to the bevelled edge of the front rail, starting at the centre.

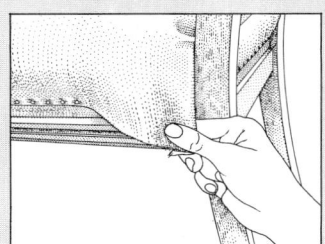
A11. Fold in the flap beside the back post. Pull the fold parallel to the post.

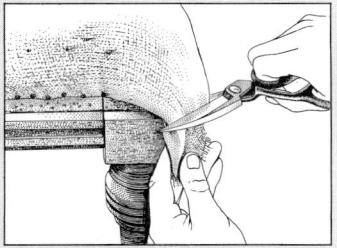
A12. Pull the scrim down over the front corners and cut off the triangle formed.

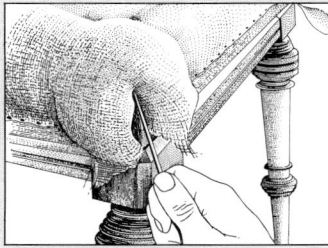
A13. Use the regulator to push a dent in the filling at the front corner.

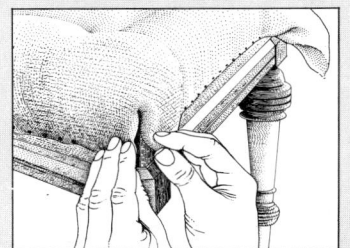
A14. Pinch together the folds formed on each side of the dent at the corner.

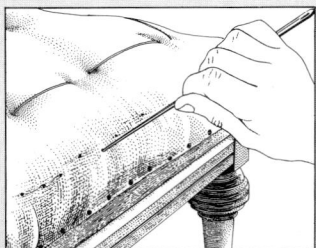
A15. Use the regulator to even out the filling and pull it out to the edge.

that each loop holds the fibre tightly.

Pull or tease the fibre with your fingers to spread the filling to the centre of the seat and outwards, so that it is evenly distributed over the seat and slightly overhangs the frame [A5]. Press down to check that the density is even. The fibre should be about 10 cm. (4 in.) deep, except under the ties.

PUTTING ON THE SCRIM COVER

Cut the scrim to cover the filling, and overlap the underside of the seat frame by about 5 cm. Lay the scrim over the filling, selvedge to the back. Fold up the excess at each side and push the scrim under the lower back rail. Using $\frac{1}{2}$ in. improved tacks, tack half home to the bevelled edge on all four sides of the frame. Use about five tacks on each edge and leave the corners free. Keep all the filling under the scrim and keep the grain of the fabric straight from front to back.

At the back posts, pull back the triangular flap of scrim and cut from the corner of the flap to the inner corner of the post. Push the inner edges of each flap down between the filling and the post on either side [A6].

STUFFING STITCH

Chalk a rectangle on the seat top, 7.5 cm. in from the edge all round. This is the guideline for the stuffing stitches which hold the stuffing in place. Thread the stitching needle with twine. Start at a back corner of the guideline and work towards the front. Stab the needle through scrim, filling, hessian and webbing. Pull the eye of the needle free of the hessian, but not through the webbing. Move the eye about 2.5 cm. (1 in.) along the underside of the hessian, before stabbing it up to come out about 2.5 cm. along the guideline towards the front. Pull the needle clear of the scrim and

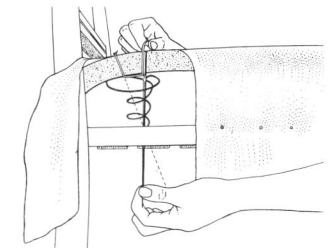

Detail of stuffing stitch.

make a slip knot with the tail of the twine [A7]. Pull the twine through and tighten the knot, pushing it down into the seat.

Move 15 cm. (6 in.) along the guideline and repeat the stitch through scrim, filling and hessian, without the eye going through the webbing, as before. Move the eye about 2.5 cm. along the guideline and stab upwards and out. Repeat round the guideline to the middle of the back, and there make a final stuffing stitch to the centre of the seat. Before finishing the last stitch, pull all the stitches tight, starting from the beginning. Make a double knot on the last stitch and cut the twine [A8].

TACKING THE SCRIM

Remove the temporary tacks on the front seat rail, and straighten the scrim. Tuck the scrim under the filling [A9], then pinch between finger and thumb and tack to the bevelled edge of the front, moving from the centre to the sides [A10]. Keep the tension on the scrim even and the grain straight. Place tacks 15 mm. ($\frac{1}{2}$ in.) apart. Tack the back, then the sides in the same way, leaving the corners free.

At the back posts, pull down the folded flaps on either side of the post, with the fold parallel with the edge of the post [A11]. Tack to the seat rails in line with previous tacks. Trim the scrim up to the tacks along the back.

To finish the front corners, use the regulator to push the fibre so that the corners will finish at the same height as the front of the seat. Pull the scrim down firmly over the corner and trim off the excess triangle of fabric [A12]. Use the regulator to dent in the centre of the corner [A13]. Pinch the folds on either side of the dent together [A14], and push the scrim under the filling. Tack the folds to the top of the front post on the bevelled edge.

When both corners are complete, check that the tacks at sides and front are straight. Then tack home at 15 mm. intervals all round.

Smooth away lumps in the filling, using a regulator. At the same time, pull the filling firmly into the scrim round the edge of the seat top [A15]. Push the regulator in at the side and out on top, outside the stuffing stitches. Lever the filling to the edge. Repeat right round the seat.

BLIND STITCH

This stitch pulls the filling to the edge and holds it in place round the outside edge of the seat top. Thread the stitching needle with twine. Start alongside the back post on one side of the chair. Right-handed people should work from left to right. Put the needle through the scrim on the side of the filling immediately above the tack line. Push the needle through the filling to come out on top outside the line of the stuffing stitches [B1]. Pull the eye of the needle free of the scrim, angle the eye slightly towards the back of the seat, then push the eye back in the same hole. Bring the needle out alongside the tail of the twine [B2]. Before pulling all the twine through, make a slip knot with the tail, then pull the knot tight.

Take a stitch about 4 cm. (1½ in.) along the side, bring the eye out at the top, and angle the needle towards the

back of the seat. Then put the eye into the same hole. Bring the needle out to the side, at the centre of the long loop of twine made by the stitch [B3]. Wrap the left-hand part of the loop twice round the needle [B4], then pull the twine tight [B5]. Stitch along the side to within 2.5 cm. of the corner. Finish the last stitch, then take the twine round the corner. Leaving the twine in a loose loop, put the needle in 2.5 cm.

along the front of the seat to come out on top in the centre of the corner. Angle the needle to the front of the corner, put it back through the same hole and bring it out on the corner. Wrap the left and then right-hand parts of the loop round the needle [B6] before pulling the twine tight.

Blind-stitch round the remaining three edges. Make a double knot on the last stitch and cut the twine.

BLIND STITCHING

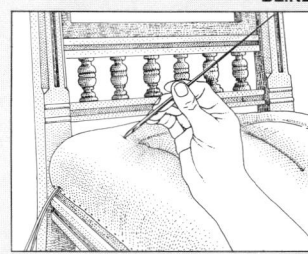

B1. Push the needle up through the side to emerge outside the stuffing stitches.

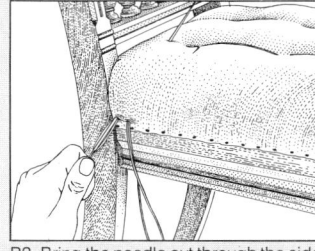

B2. Bring the needle out through the side beside the tail of the twine.

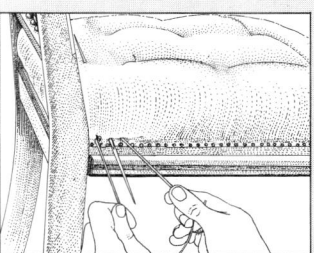

B3. Push the needle eye through centre of loop formed with the previous stitch.

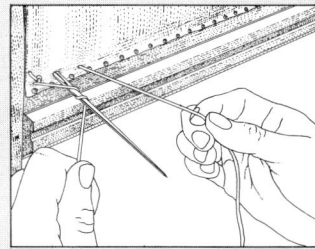

B4. Wrap the left-hand part of the loop twice round the needle.

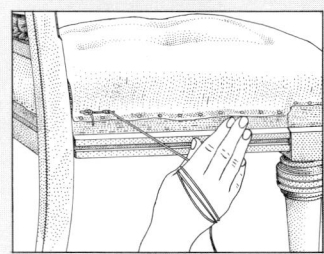

B5. Pull the needle through and pull the twine tight in direction of stitching.

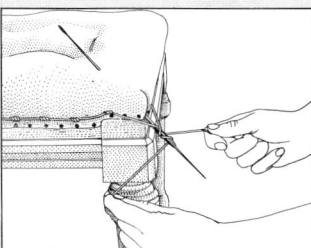

B6. Bring the needle out at the corner and wrap both sides of the loop round it.

• DINING CHAIR – SHAPING THE SECOND FILLING

Top stitching forms a roll which gives a firm shape to the seat. A second filling of horsehair or flock is built up under bridle ties. This filling is tightly covered with calico to shape the seat. A layer of cotton wadding over the calico provides a smooth, even surface. Raw edges and tacks are covered with gimp, or braid.

Chalk lines on the top and sides of the seat, 4 cm. (1½ in.) from the edge, at the front and on both sides. The back is not top-stitched on this chair because there is no room.

TOP-STITCHING THE EDGE ROLL

Thread a stitching needle with twine. Starting near the back post on one side, push the needle through the side chalk line. Bring the eye of the needle out on the top chalk line. Take a stitch about 2.5 cm. (1 in.) along the line towards the back post; put the needle in eye first and bring out beside the tail of the twine [A1]. Make a slip knot with the tail. Pull the twine through and tighten the knot.

Take a 3 cm. (1¼ in.) stitch along the side, bring needle out on top, leaving the stitch at the side as a large loop of twine. Move the needle back and

needle out on the top chalk line. Take a stitch about 2.5 cm. (1 in.) along the line towards the back post; put the needle in eye first and bring out beside the tail of the twine [A1]. Make a slip knot with the tail. Pull the twine through and tighten the knot.

Take a 3 cm. (1¼ in.) stitch along the side, bring needle out on top, leaving the stitch at the side as a large loop of twine. Move the needle back and

push it, eye first, into the last hole made by the twine. Wrap the left-hand twine clockwise twice round the needle [A2]. Pull the needle and twine through and tighten the knot.

Stitch and knot to within 2.5 cm. of the corner. Take the twine round the corner and put the needle into the side at the front, 2.5 cm. from the corner. Bring the needle out on top and move the needle back. Midway

TOP-STITCHING THE EDGE OF THE FIRST FILLING

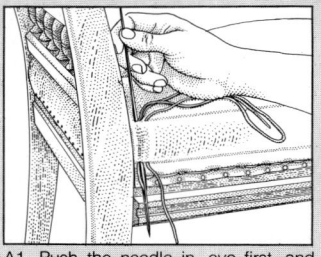

A1. Push the needle in, eye first, and bring it out at the side beside the twine.

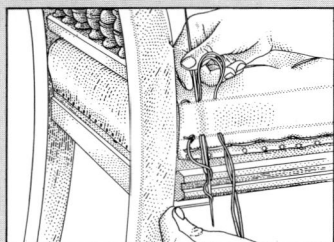

A2. Wrap the left-hand twine twice round the eye end of the needle.

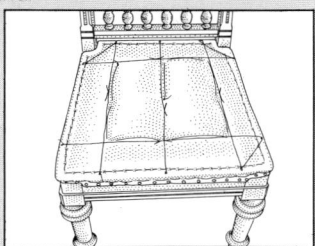

A3. Make the last tie down the centre of the seat from back to front.

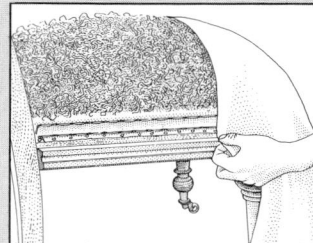

A4. Measure the calico over the filling and add 5 cm. all round.

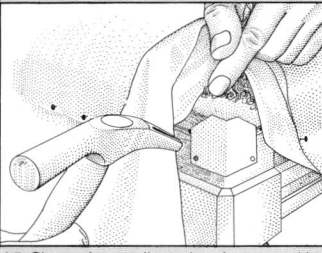

A5. Shape the cardboard and secure with a tack on each side of the corner.

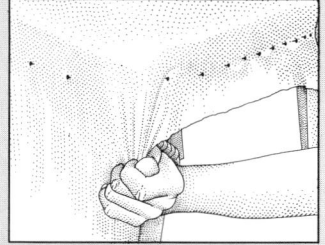

A6. Pull the corner of the calico firmly down over the corner post.

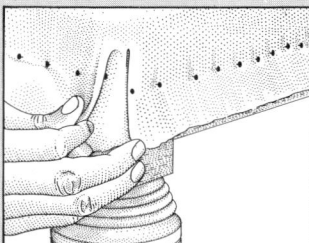

A7. Form a pleat in the calico and pull it forward to conceal the tack.

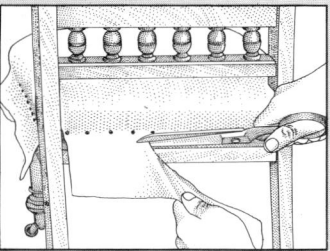

A8. Trim the calico as close to the tacks as possible all round.

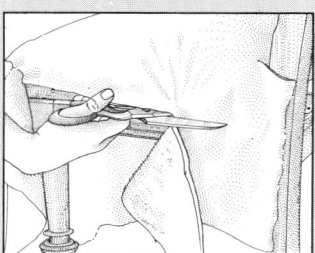

A9. Cut the cotton wadding to fit just above the polished wood all round.

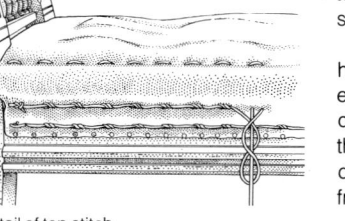

Detail of top stitch.

between the two twines, push the needle through, coming out on the corner. Twist the left and right twines round the needle – left, right, left – and pull tight. Sew the front and the other side in the same way. At the end of the second side, finish with a double knot and cut the twine. Smooth out any lumps in the roll by rubbing hard with a handful of filling material.

With a spring needle and twine, make bridle ties in the same way as for the first filling. Put an extra tie down the centre of the seat from back to front [A3]. Before knotting the twine at the end of each tie, test to see that each loop will hold 4 cm. of compressed filling.

Build up a second filling of flock or horsehair. Push it under the ties a handful at a time, working in bands across the seat. Tease and shape the filling so that it is slightly domed at the centre and tapers to the back. It should be about 5 cm. (2 in.) deep above the hessian when not com-

pressed, and stand straight up from the front and sides of the frame.

FITTING THE CALICO COVER

Cut the calico to fit the seat, allowing 5 cm. excess all round. Lay the fabric over the filling with the selvedge to the back [A4].

Fold up the excess along either side of the seat and push the back of the calico under the lower back rail. Use ⅜ in. fine tacks to tack the calico temporarily to the outside of the back seat tacking rail.

Start at the centre and tack half home; then tack to within 5 cm. of each post. Ease the fabric forward over the filling, pull it taut and tack it to the centre front rail. Strain the fabric down and to the side, and tack the front to within 5 cm. of each corner.

Tack the sides half home in the same way as the front, starting near the highest point of filling. Check that the grain of the fabric is straight from front to back.

Pull the corner of the fabric away from one back post. Cut into this triangle, following a diagonal line from the outer to the inner corner of the post. Cut right up to the wood. Pull down a flap of calico on either side of the post. Use a regulator to push the inner edge of each flap between the post and the filling. Pull each flap out at right-angles to the frame, and cut off the flap to within 2.5 cm. of the frame. Fold the cut edge under. Pull the fold down parallel to the back post and tack to the rail close to the post. Complete the other back post in the same way.

FRONT CORNERS

Cut a piece of stiff cardboard to measure 5 × 5 cm. (2 × 2 in.). Fold the card in half across the width. Push the card, with the fold on the corner of the frame, under the edge roll, and fit above the polished wood. Cut the top outside corners to fit. Secure with a tack on either side of the corner [A5]. The card supports the corner of the edge roll while the calico is fitted.

Take the corner of the calico and pull it down firmly over the centre of the corner [A6]. Hold the fabric taut round the front post with the fingers. Tack halfway down the unpolished wood on either side of the post.

Take the fullness at the side of the corner into a pleat. Pull the fold back, then forward and down to the corner, covering the first tack [A7]. Secure with two tacks placed in line with the side tacks. Trim off the calico up to the tacks. To deal with the fullness at the front, first remove the corner tack. Pull the pleat back from the corner to tighten the calico, then tack the single layer. Next, fold the fullness forward and tack. Trim the excess.

Check that the tacks are straight, then hammer home at 2.5 cm. intervals right round the seat. Trim the calico up to the tack line all round [A8]. The calico should be tight, but the strain of the tacks should not produce creases on the top of the seat.

Cover the calico with cotton wadding cut to fit above the polished wood all round the seat frame [A9].

FINAL COVER

Fit and tack the cover in the same way as the calico, except for the corners.

Lay the cover fabric face up on the work surface. Measure the seat from front to back and side to side, from the underside of the frame over the cover. Use these measurements to mark the shape of the seat on the fabric with the pattern in the centre. Allow 5 cm. excess all round, then cut. Fold it in half lengthways across the centre of the

pattern. Nick the corner of the fold at either end. Chalk mark the centre front and back of the seat frame.

Lay the cover on the seat. If using velvet, make sure the pile runs forward. Fold up the excess at each side and push the back of the cover under the back rail. Match the nicks in the fabric with the centre marks on the frame. Then put a skewer through the fabric to hold the pattern in the centre. Tack the cover half home, leaving the corners free. Make sure the tacks are above the polished wood [B1].

Pull the corner of the fabric away from one of the back posts. Cut into the point of the triangle of fabric up to the inside corner of the back post [B2]. Pull the back flap down over the back of the seat, and fold the excess on each side inwards, so that the folds are parallel to the back posts. Trim each flap to within 2.5 cm. of its post,

fold the raw edge under and tuck between the post and the seat [B3]. Tack to the back rail.

Pull out the side flap, trim to within 2.5 cm. of the post. Turn under the cut edge. Fit the fold up to the back post and tack. Finish the second post in the same way.

At the front corner, pull the fabric down over the corner, keeping an equal amount of fullness on either side. Tack to the edge of the corner just above the polished wood [B4]. Stretch the fabric round the corner and tack about 4 cm. up from the centre tack on both sides of the post.

Pull back the fullness on one side and cut a narrow V from the fabric pointing to the side tack [B5]. This reduces the bulk of fabric at the corner. Fold in the cut edge and pull the fold down and forward. Tack the fold close to the corner. Repeat for the

fullness on the other side. Remove the centre tack, trim off the excess and tack home. Finish the second corner.

Check that the pattern is still centred and the grain of the fabric straight. Then tack home at 2.5 cm. intervals all round. Keep the tacks in a straight line just above the polished wood. Trim the excess fabric right up to the tack line.

COVERING THE UNDERSIDE

Cut the black calico large enough to cover all the tacks on the underside of the seat frame with 2.5 cm. excess all round. Fold under 2.5 cm. at the back of the seat and tack the calico to the frame, using ⅜ in. fine tacks.

Leave the corners free. Turn under the excess and tack the calico to the front, then to either side. At each post, cut into the point of the loose triangle of fabric up to the inner corner of the post [B6]. Fold under the excess on either side of the post and tack home.

FITTING THE GIMP

Start at the left-hand back post on the side of the seat. Turn under 2.5 cm. of the gimp and fit the fold up to the back post. Use gimp pins to tack the gimp to the side as near the post as possible, covering tacks and raw edges.

Spread fabric adhesive on the wrong side of the gimp, on the turn-up and about 25 cm. (10 in.) along the gimp [B7]. Press the gimp over the raw edge of the cover. Tack half home at 10 cm. (4 in.) intervals.

Glue and tack the gimp in this way round the seat to the right back post. Trim off, leaving 2.5 cm. excess.

Turn under the excess and secure with a gimp pin as close to the post as possible [B8]. Attach the gimp between the posts at the back in the same way. Allow the adhesive to dry, then remove the tacks. Flatten the gimp by tapping with a tack hammer.

FITTING THE COVER AND FINISHING OFF

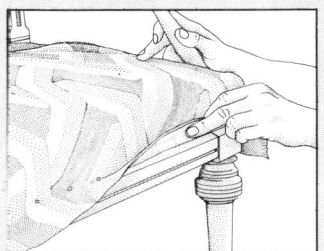
B1. Tack the cover half home above the polished wood, leaving the corners free.

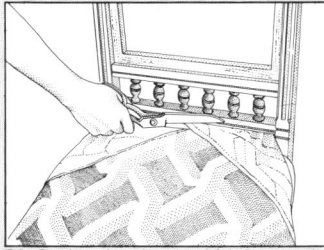
B2. Cut into the triangle of fabric up to the inside corner of the back post.

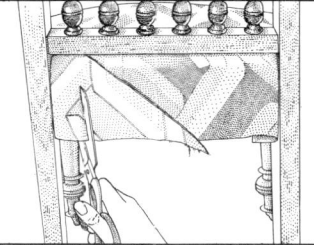
B3. Trim the excess on each flap to within 2.5 cm. of the back post.

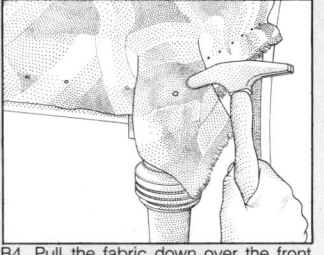
B4. Pull the fabric down over the front corner and tack above polished wood.

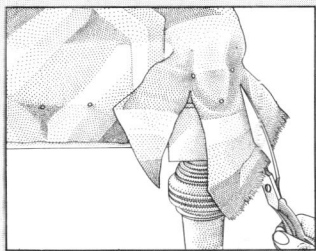
B5. Cut a narrow V into the fabric on each side of the post to reduce bulk.

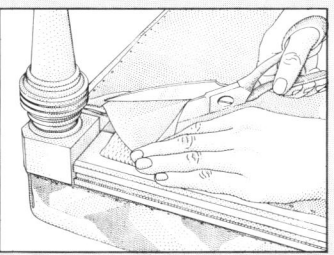
B6. Pull back the calico and cut into the triangle up to the inner corner of the post.

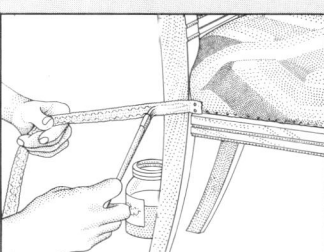
B7. Spread contact adhesive on the first 25 cm. of gimp and press down.

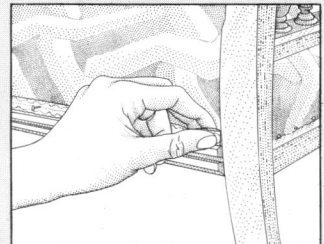
B8. Turn under the excess gimp and tack close to the post with a gimp pin.

• DINING CHAIR — PADDED BACK

The final stage of re-upholstering a dining chair is to renew the padded back. All the covers are tacked to the tacking frame, set into the front of the chair back. All fitting is done with the chair on its back.

STRIPPING DOWN TO THE FRAME

Protect the table with a blanket, and lay the chair on its back on the table. Take off the old covers and filling, layer by layer, using mallet and chisel to remove tacks. If the filling is not too dusty and brittle, tease out any lumps and it can be used again.

Measure the inside of the frame, from side to side and top to bottom. Mark the centre of the outer frame at the top and bottom with chalk.

Lay the fabric face up and mark out the shape of the back, centring the pattern. For the back cover, allow 2.5 cm. (1 in.) excess all round. Allow 5 cm. (2 in.) excess all round for the front cover to accommodate the filling. Fold each piece in half, along the length, down the centre of the pattern. Nick each end of the fold to mark the centre line of the fabric.

TACKING ON THE BACK COVER

Lay the outside back cover face down on the frame. If using velvet, arrange the pile to run from top to bottom. Match the centre marks on the frame with the notches in the cover. Fix to the tacking frame with ⅜ in. fine tacks placed as close as possible to the polished frame. Start at the bottom centre, and move out towards the corners, tacking half home at 2.5 cm. intervals. Leave corners until last.

Pull the fabric to the top of the frame and tack in the same way. Repeat along the sides. Check that the pattern is centred and the grain of the fabric straight, then tack the corners before tacking home all round. Trim the fabric close to the tack line [1].

Cut the hessian 5 cm. larger than the frame all round. Tack in the same way as for the outside cover, but at a greater tension and just inside the previous line of tacks. Trim the hessian to within 2.5 cm. of the tacks. Turn up the excess and tack home.

PUTTING IN THE FILLING

Use a half-circular needle and stitching twine to make a bridle tie (see p. 128) about 2.5 cm. from the frame on each side of the hessian. Avoid catching the back cover. Make the loops loose enough to hold about 2.5 cm. of compressed fibre. Shape the filling, a handful at a time, forming a slight dome at the centre.

Cut the calico cover 5 cm. larger than the frame all round. Fold in half and mark the centre with a nick at each end. Lay the calico over the filling and tack to the bottom of the frame, starting at the centre as for the back cover. Pull the calico to the top and tack. Tack both sides and finally the corners. Tack home and trim the calico close to the tack line.

FINAL COVER AND GIMP

Match the centre marks on the cover to those on the frame. Using gimp pins, tack to the bottom, then pull the cover back. Lay wadding over the calico and cut to fit [2].

Pull the cover to the top of the frame and tack half home, working from the centre to the corners [3]. Leave corners until last. Tack half home at each side, then check that the pattern is centred. Tack home at 2.5 cm. intervals, then use the trimming knife to cut the fabric close to the pins.

Protect the cover with a piece of calico while attaching the gimp. Turn under 2.5 cm. of gimp, fit the fold into the bottom left-hand corner of the frame and secure with a gimp pin. Spread adhesive on the back of the gimp a few inches at a time and press and tack to the frame.

Turn each corner with a mitred fold. To make this, first run the gimp right into the corner and temporarily tack with a gimp pin. Then fold the gimp back along itself. Next make a diagonal fold across the corner, and

THE VELVET TOUCH Old dining chairs are given new life and a look of luxury when they are re-upholstered and covered with velvet.

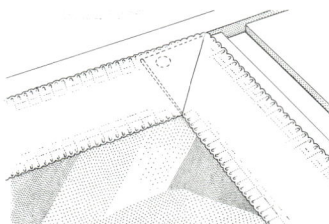

Detail of mitred corner

bring the outside edge of the gimp along the next side of the frame. Hide the pin with the fold, moving the pin if necessary. Glue under the fold. At the last corner, fold the gimp and butt the fold to the start [4].

PADDING A CHAIR BACK

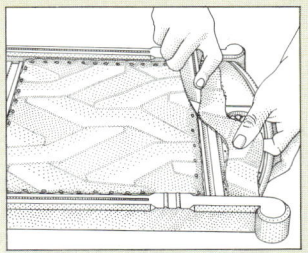

1. Trim the back-cover fabric close to the line of tacking.

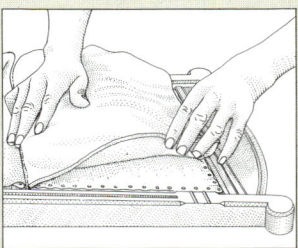

2. Lay wadding over the calico and cut it to fit the frame.

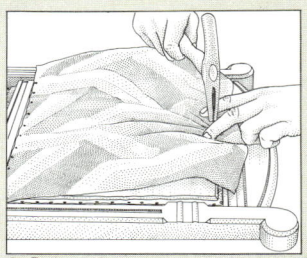

3. Pull up the cover and tack it half home to the top of the frame.

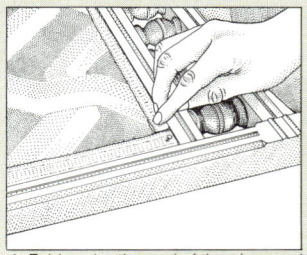

4. Fold under the end of the gimp and butt the fold to the start.

• PADDING AND COVERING A SOLID SEAT

Hide is expensive unless bought as offcuts, but choose offcuts carefully, as they often have blemishes. Other materials required: horsehair or fibre filling; stitching twine; 3/8 in. fine tacks; gimp pins; medium-density foam, 2.5 cm. (1 in.) thick; unbleached calico; decorative nails; strong paper. Cotton wadding can be used instead of foam.

PREPARING THE SEAT AND TEMPLATE

Remove tacks and nails with chisel and mallet, working in the direction of the wood grain. Lift off the covers, snip the twine holding the filling, and remove all old materials.

With the chisel, score a line round the seat, about 4 cm. (1½ in.) from the edge, as a guide for the final shape of the covers and pad. Fix the paper to the seat with two tacks hammered half home. Trace the seat shape with a pencil, following the scored line [1]. Lift off the paper and cut round the pencil line with scissors.

BRIDLE TIES AND FILLING

Ties for a solid seat are made by stretching twine across the seat between tacks in the frame. Place a tack centre front and back, inside the scored line, and hammer half home. Wrap the twine loosely round both tacks, making sure there is about 4 cm. clearance between the twine and the seat, then hammer the tacks home. Make similar ties on either side, about 2.5 cm. inside the scored line.

Push the filling under the bridle ties a handful at a time, to make a pad about 4 cm. deep [2]. Dome the centre and taper to the sides, keeping within the scored lines.

FITTING THE FOAM

Use the paper template to mark out the seat shape on the foam. Cut 15 mm. (½ in.) outside this line, using fabric shears or scissors.

Lay the foam over the filling. Using 3/8 in. improved tacks and starting at centre back, tack through the centre of the foam edge, angling the tacks inward on the seat [3]. Tack the centre of the front and sides first, then complete the tacking all the way round, through the edge, at 2.5 cm. intervals. This will make the edge fold and taper within the scored line.

TACKING AND FITTING CALICO

Cut the calico roughly to the shape of the seat, allowing 10 cm. (4 in.) excess all round. Lay the calico over the pad with the grain straight from front to back and side to side. Hammer a 3/8 in. fine tack into the calico at centre back. Hold temporarily with five tacks. Stretch the calico to the front and tack in the same way [4]. Keep all tacks 10 mm. (3/8 in.) within the guideline.

Place three tacks temporarily at either side. Check that the fabric is straight, then pull it down firmly over each corner and tack.

Check that the tension is even, then tack home. Finish tacking at 2.5 cm. intervals all round. Trim the calico close to the tack line. Cover the pad with a thin layer of cotton wadding, cut to fit inside the guideline.

FINAL COVER

Lay the paper template over the best part of the leather. Using a trimming knife, cut the leather 5 cm. (2 in.) wider than the template. Lay the leather over the seat pad. Tack and stretch into place in the same way as for the calico. Use gimp pins if there is not enough room for fine tacks. Keep within the guideline. Trim the leather close to the tack line [5].

Chalk a guideline for the nails, joining up the tacks on the edge of the leather. To avoid marking the nails, hammer them in with care. Start at the back of the seat and place the nails head to head so that they cover the raw edge and all tacks [6]. Remove any tack that cannot be hidden as you go along, and replace in a more convenient position.

A TOUCH OF COMFORT Desk chairs often have a solid seat. This can be made softer with a hide-covered pad, which is quick and easy to fit.

COVERING A SOLID SEAT

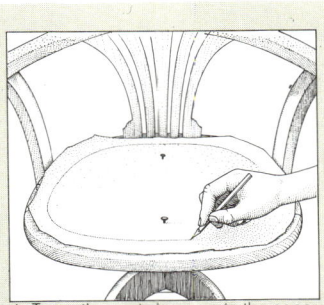

1. Trace the seat shape on to the paper, following the scored line.

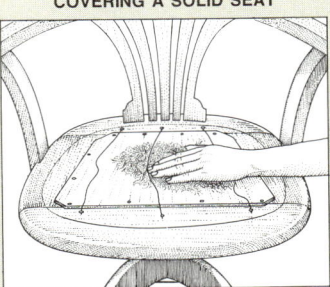

2. Push the filling under the ties to make a pad about 4 cm. thick.

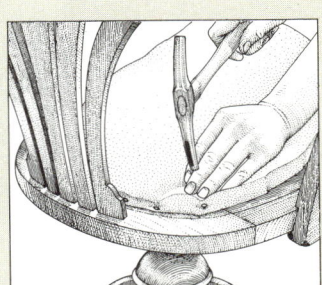

3. Tack through the foam edge, angling the tacks inward on the seat.

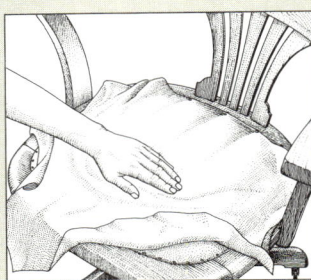

4. Pull the calico forward over the pad and temporarily hold with five tacks.

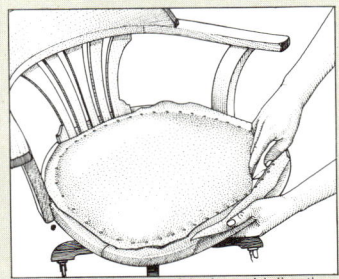

5. Tack the leather inside the guideline then trim close to the tacks.

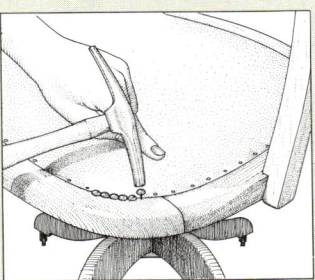

6. Place the decorative nails head to head, covering the raw edge and tacks.

MAKING LOOSE COVERS

There are many reasons for fitting loose covers – to protect new furniture, to enhance the appearance of a worn chair or sofa, or to harmonise a piece of furniture with a new colour scheme. The best fabrics are hard-wearing cotton and linen mixtures. Plain material is easier to make up, but may show creases. If fabric with a large pattern is used, the motif must be centred on the inside back and seat and matched on the arms.

There is no need to wash the cover fabric before fitting; remove and wash it when it gets grubby. Any shrinkage will be overcome by putting the washed cover on when still slightly damp. Piping cord should be washed before use.

Measure each part of the chesterfield at its widest and deepest. Cut rectangles to these measurements from the covering fabric, then pin them together on the chesterfield. They are then cut to shape, taken from the sofa and sewn together, adding piping and the skirt. Where other types of chair or sofa differ in shape from the chesterfield, the variations in methods are described.

• MEASURING FOR LOOSE COVERS

When measuring any chair or sofa, add 5 cm. (2 in.) to all dimensions to allow for seams. If the cover has a tie-under finish (see p. 140), add 15 cm. (6 in.) to the depth of the outside back and arm, and the front border pieces. Follow the illustrations below and right when measuring.

MATERIALS AND EQUIPMENT

Covering fabric; matching thread; sateen lining for the skirt; piping cord (No. 2); Velcro to length of opening plus 10 mm. (⅜ in.); an equal length of 2.5 cm. (1 in.) wide cotton tape; sewing machine; fabric shears; steel pins; iron; 1 sheet (approx. 1 sq. m.) of pattern-making paper; tailor's chalk; crayon; 30 cm. ruler; wrist pincushion; tape measure.

CHESTERFIELD

1. Outside back (A to B × C to F) Measure between points where the arms join the back [1]. Then from where back padding is fullest to bottom of upholstery, taking in bulge.

2. Inside back (A to B × C to D) For C to D measure from a point on the padding fullness to where the top of the seat meets the back, plus 15 cm. (6 in.) for tuck-in [2].

3. Outside arms (B to H × E to P) B to H is the line from the point where the back joins the arm to the edge of the front facing. For E to P, measure from the arm to the bottom of the sofa, taking in the bulge [3].

4. Inside arms (B to H × E to G) E to G is from the fullness of the arm padding to where the arm meets the seat, plus 15 cm. for tuck-in.

5. Seat (D to L × G to G) D to L is the width of the seat plus 15 cm. for tuck-in. G to G is the length of the seat from arm to arm, plus 30 cm. (12 in.) for tuck-ins on each side.

6. Front border (J to K × L to Q) J to K is the line along the front edge of the seat [4]. L to Q is from the top of the front edge of the seat to the bottom of the upholstery.

7. Front facings (H to M × N to R) H to M is the widest part of the arm scrolls. N to R is measured from the top of the arm scrolls to the bottom of the upholstery.

8. Skirt The depth of the skirt is measured from the carpet or floor to the bottom of the sofa, plus 4 cm. (1½ in.) for seams and hems. Cut six widths this depth from the width of the covering fabric. Measure and cut the lining for the skirt in the same way.

When measuring furniture for loose covers, every part must be measured across its widest and deepest span.

USING THE TAPE

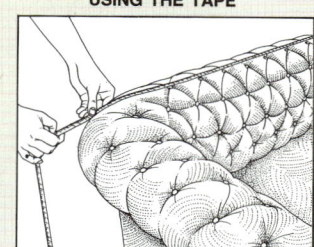

1. Measure the outside back from where the arms join the back.

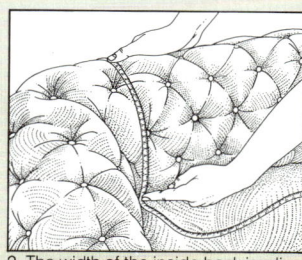

2. The width of the inside back is a line from the back bulge to the seat.

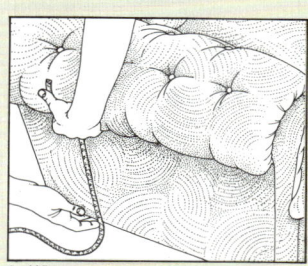

3. When measuring the outside arm, take the tape under the arm bulge.

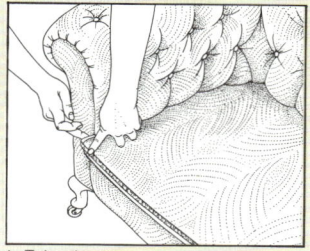

4. Take the tape measure round any angles at the front of the sofa seat.

MEASURING SOFAS AND CHAIRS

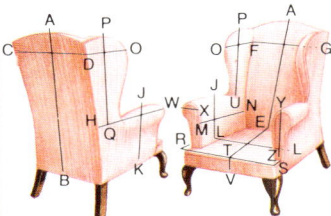

STRAIGHT-SIDED SOFA

Remove the fitted seat cushions and cover them separately as described on p. 146.

Measure all the dimensions of the sofa in the same way as those of the chesterfield, remembering to measure each part where it is at its widest and deepest span.

However, as there is no padded bulge on the back and arms, measure from the back edge of the back and arm borders. If the back and arm borders are wider than 12.5 cm. (5 in.) measure and make them as separate pieces, A to B × C to D for the arm borders; B to B × E to F for the back border.

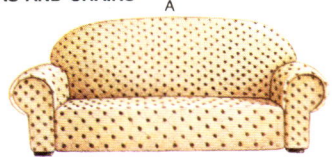

ROUND-BACKED SOFA

If the sofa has individual fitted cushions, these should be removed and covered separately as described in detail on p. 146.

Measure the sofa's dimensions in the same way as measurements were taken for the chesterfield.

Remember to measure the depth of the back pieces from the highest point, A, and all other pieces across their widest and deepest spans.

Add the allowances for seams, tuck-ins and tie-unders wherever these are necessary.

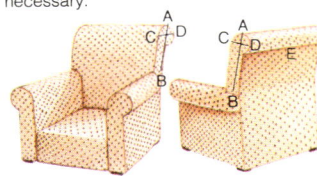

CONVENTIONAL ARMCHAIR

Remove any fitted cushions from the armchair and cover them separately (see p. 146).

Measure the chair in the same way as the chesterfield. For the side facings of the back measure A to B × C to D. Measure the length of the outside back piece from the point under the scroll at the back, marked E. The width should be measured across the widest span.

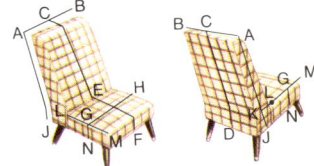

TV CHAIR

Measure the outside back, A to B × C to D plus 15 cm. (6 in.) for tie-under. The inside back measurement is A to B × C to E, plus 15 cm. for tuck-in between back and seat. The seat is measured from G to H × E to F, plus 30 cm. (12 in.) for tuck-in and tie-under. The side facings are A to J × K to L, and the side borders measure from L to M × G to N plus 15 cm. for tie-under.

WING CHAIR

If there is a fitted seat cushion, remove and cover it separately as described on p. 146.

Measure the rest of the chair beginning with the outside back, A to B × C to D, adding 15 cm. (6 in.) to the A–B measurement for the tie-unders. A is the highest point on the back and C to D is the widest part of the back. Next measure the inside back A to E × F to G. Add 10 cm. (4 in.) to A to E for a tuck-in. The outside arm dimensions are H to W × J to K plus 15 cm. for the tie-unders. Measure the inside arms J to L × M to N plus 10 cm. The outside wings are D to O × P to Q. D to O is the widest part of the wing. The inside wing measurements O to F × P to U must take in the bulge. The front border is R to S × T to V, plus 15 cm. The facings are measured from W to X × Y to Z and the seat from T to E × L to L, plus 10 cm. to each dimension for tuck-ins.

• CALCULATING THE FABRIC

Once the measurements have been taken, the next stage is to calculate the amount of fabric needed.

Join the pieces of pattern-making paper to make a long strip. Mark the width of the cover fabric across the width of the pattern-making paper, counting each small square as 1 sq. cm. if you are using metric measurements. If you are working in feet and inches, count each small square as 1 sq. in. Draw two lines down the length of the paper so that the distance between them represents the width of the material.

Mark the rectangles of the cover pieces between these lines. If you are working with patterned fabric, remember that the pattern on adjoining pieces will have to run the same way.

When a piece is wider than the fabric, joins will have to be made. Divide the surplus width of the piece in half and draw these on to the paper, allowing 5 cm. (2 in.) for seams. When you come to join the actual pieces of fabric, one of the halves will be joined to each end of the main piece.

To avoid confusion, pencil the name of the pieces (outside back, seat, and so on) on each rectangle.

Use spare areas to represent fabric needed for piping covering.

Add together the lengths of the pieces to see how much fabric is required, and add 1 m. (39 in.) for piping covering. To allow for pattern matching, add to this three times the depth of any pattern there may be.

CUTTING THE FABRIC

Trim the ends of the fabric square, as shown on p. 291.

Using tailor's chalk, draw the pieces full-scale on the wrong side of the fabric. Write the name of each piece on the back with crayon. Mark the top and bottom of each piece. Cut them out with fabric shears. Cut out the lining for the skirt from sateen, the same size as the skirt widths.

JOINING FULL WIDTHS

Match the pattern when pinning the side widths to main piece. Pin, tack and sew together, using a straight machine stitch 15 mm. ($\frac{1}{2}$ in.) from the edges. Press open seams.

Sew two skirt widths together, then sew another three together forming two lengths for the skirt. The sixth width remains separate, so that it can be added if necessary.

SHAPING THE SOFA An old chair or sofa loses its regular shape with use so measure matching parts, such as arms and facings, separately. Some parts may be so distorted they will need to be built up with padding.

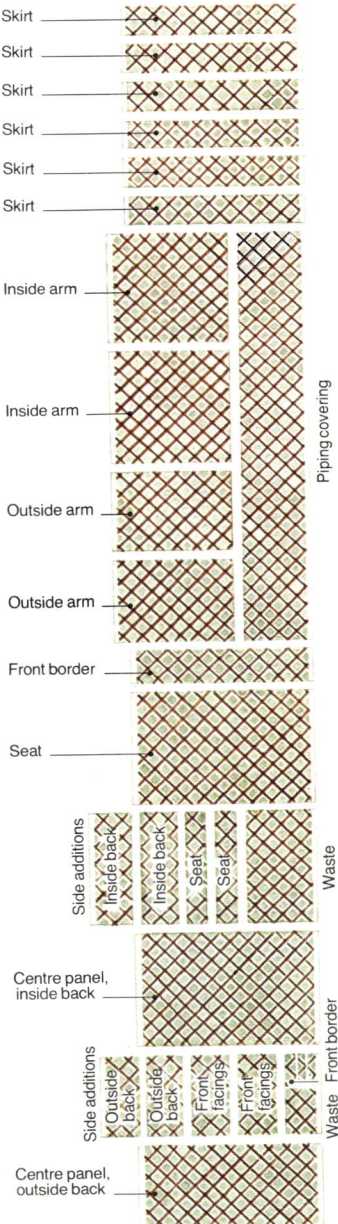

Skirt
Skirt
Skirt
Skirt
Skirt
Skirt

Inside arm

Inside arm

Outside arm

Outside arm

Front border

Seat

Side additions — Inside back, Inside back, Seat, Seat — Waste

Piping covering

Centre panel, inside back

Side additions — Outside back, Outside back, Front facings, Front facings — Waste — Front border

Centre panel, outside back

Cutting guide for a chesterfield

• PINNING THE PIECES

The next stage is to pin the cut-out pieces together on the sofa or chair so that they fit the shape. When they are pinned together, they are cut to match the shape of the sofa or chair.

Tip the sofa on to its front so that the back faces up. Measure the width of the back and mark a centre line from the top to the bottom of the back.

Fold the outside back piece along the width to find the centre. Pin the top centre of this piece to the back of the sofa, at the centre line right side out [A1]. Align the top edge of the outside back piece along the imaginary line A to B where the padded curve on the back of the chesterfield is at its fullest (see p. 134). As a guide, it is advisable to chalk these lines along the back and arms of the sofa.

Stand the sofa on its feet. Fold the inside back piece in half along its width to find the centre. Pin it to the outside back piece, top centre to top centre, then pin the two pieces together along the edge, wrong sides together, matching the seams [A2].

If necessary, pin darts in the in-

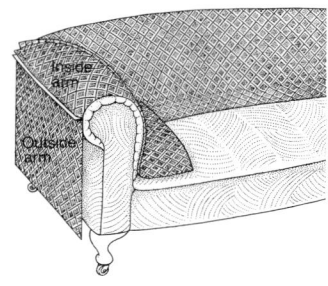
Arm and inside back piece pinned in place.

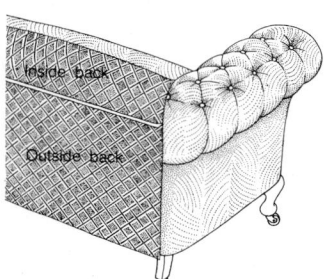
Outside back piece pinned in place.

side back piece, where the arms join the back, to allow the fabric to hang properly.

Take one outside arm piece and pin it about 15 mm. (½ in.) above the padded bulge line B to H (see p. 134),

running along the padding of the arm. Ensure that the front edge of the outside arm piece protrudes about 15 mm. in front of the arm of the sofa.

Fit one inside arm piece over the arm. Pin to the outside arm piece, leaving a seam allowance. Remove the pins holding the outside arm piece to the sofa to adjust the arm pieces. When both arm pieces have been adjusted, pin together with the seams wrong sides together.

Pin the outside arm piece to the outside back piece, about 15 mm. from the edges.

Fold the inside arm piece so that the fold follows the curve at the shoulder of the sofa. Fold the inside back piece in the same way, and pin this to the inside arm piece along the fold, wrong sides together.

Repeat the process to fit and pin the other arm pieces together and to pin them to the two back pieces.

Adjust the outside back and the inside back pieces to fit neatly the curve of the sofa at the back corner [A3]. If necessary, pin darts in the back pieces, using as few darts as possible.

Fold back the inside arm and inside back pieces at one shoulder of the sofa. Chalk both pieces along the fold on the wrong sides, removing the pins joining them together.

Cut the inside arm and back pieces 2.5 cm. (1 in.) outside these lines, cutting about 15 cm. (6 in.) at a time, stopping 10 cm. (4 in.) from the seat. Pin the inside arm and back pieces together close to the chalk line [A4]. Repeat at the second arm.

Turn the chesterfield on to its front. Remove the pins holding the outside back piece to the sofa. Re-pin the outside arm pieces to the outside back piece, following the shape of the sofa's corner, from the join of the arms and the back to the bottom of the upholstery.

Use this pinning to pull the pieces tight, without pulling the seams apart, or making them crooked.

Trim the surplus material from the back and arm pieces, along the pinned seams. Leave the seams about 10 cm. wide for slight tuck-in. Remove the pins holding the back pieces to the sofa to allow the outside back piece to hang free. Stand the sofa back on its legs.

TUCK-INS

Push the inside back and one inside arm piece together into the tuck-in where the back and one arm of the sofa meet in a gully.

Chalk a line at this position on both pieces. Push a pin into the pieces, tucked into the gully, at a position level with the seat [A5].

Withdraw the material from the tuck-in gully. Hold the pieces together, so that the inside back piece is uppermost. Chalk two lines on this piece, one 15 cm. from the pin, and running parallel to the front edge of the seat, the other 15 cm. from the pin, parallel to the arm. These two lines

---

PINNING THE PIECES TOGETHER

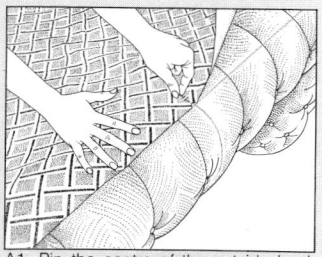
A1. Pin the centre of the outside back piece to the centre of the back bulge.

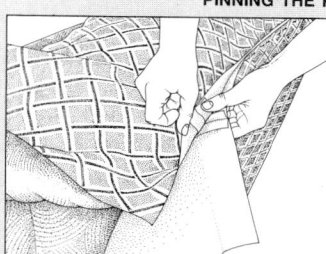
A2. Match the seams of the inside and outside back pieces when pinning.

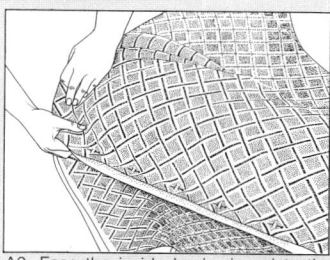
A3. Ease the inside back piece into the shape of the curve at the back corner.

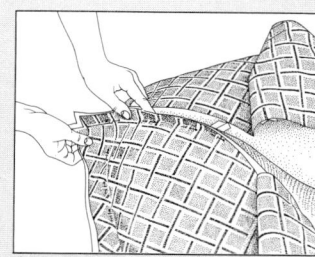
A4. Join the inside arm and back pieces at an angle from the back to the seat.

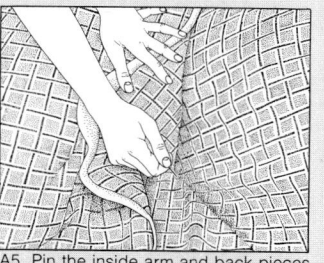
A5. Pin the inside arm and back pieces together where they meet the seat.

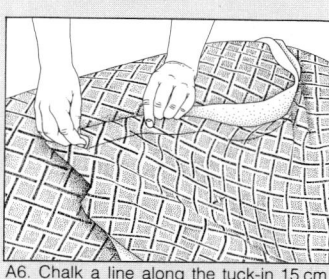
A6. Chalk a line along the tuck-in 15 cm. outside the corner pin.

A7. Pin the centre of the seat piece to the centre of the front edge of the seat.

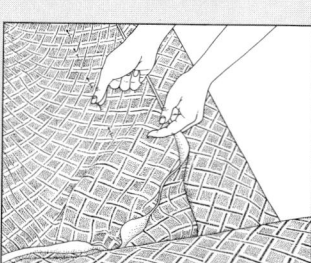
A8. Temporarily pin where back and seat meet. Measure from pins for tuck-in.

shculd meet at a right-angle, about 16 cm. (6½ in.) from the pin [A6].

Cut the fabric exactly along these lines, continuing to the edges of the pieces. Pin the edges together, the surplus material being the tuck-in allowance.

Repeat this at the second arm, forming a tuck-in allowance for this gully, where the arm joins the back.

THE SEAT TUCK-IN

Lay the seat piece, right side up, flat on the sofa seat. Find the centre of the front edge and pin it to the centre of the front edge of the seat [A7].

Put in a temporary row of pins where back and seat meet [A8]. Measure from this line for the tuck-in. Remove pins and pin along the tuck-in edge, allowing for a seam.

Smooth the seat piece flat, and push the sides down the gully be-

tween the arm and the seat of the sofa.

With the material pushed down as far as the frame of the sofa, pin or chalk the front edge of the seat tuck-in at its deepest point [B1].

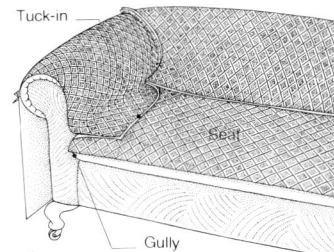

Seat and back tuck-ins pinned in place.

Cut this tuck-in material in a straight line, 15 mm. outside the pin or chalk mark. Fold back the seat cover and push the inside arm piece into the

gully. Pin or mark this at the deepest point, and cut in a straight line, 15 mm. outside the mark. Pin the seat piece to the arm piece [B2] and the back piece, leaving generous tuck-ins. Repeat at the other arm.

THE FRONT BORDER

Position the border piece against the border of the sofa. Pin the centre of the top edge to the centre of the seat piece, at the front edge. Pin together, working out from the centre, about 15 mm. from the edges [B3]. Tuck the arm and seat pieces into the tuck-in gully between the seat and arms. Turn the sofa on its back.

Cut small slits along the edges of the seat and border pieces when pinning them together round the curve at the ends of the border [B4].

Pin the front border piece and seat piece together along the edges that

lie in the gully between the seat and arm [B5]. Repeat at the other arm.

FRONT FACINGS

Place one front facing to the front of one arm. Chalk the shape of the scroll on the fabric [B6]. Cut off surplus material 2.5 cm. outside the line.

Pin the facing from the top of the inside arm piece [B7]. Avoid large pleats forming at the top of the scroll. Continue pinning the facing to the inside arm piece down the gully where the seat piece and border meet. Carry on to pin the facing to the border piece below the tuck-in [B8]. Repeat with the second facing.

• PREPARING FOR SEWING

Follow these instructions for all types of covers fitted on to any shape of chair or sofa. The equipment essential for sewing is listed on p. 134.

When sewing loose covers you will need a large work surface.

With the cover pieces pinned together on the chair or sofa, open the seams and chalk a line on both seams where they meet.

At one of the seams, where the outside back piece meets the outside arm piece, draw horizontal chalk lines [C1]. This seam will not be sewn, as it is the one which remains open so the cover can be fitted. Remove the pins joining this seam, but leave all other seams pinned.

Lift off the cover. Lay it flat and trim the seam allowances 15 mm. from the chalk lines.

Cut facing pairs of 5 mm. (¼ in.) notches along all seams, as a position guide [C2]. Space out the notches irregularly to avoid confusing their positions when the seams are brought together.

PINNING THE PIECES TOGETHER

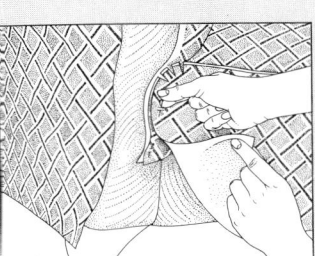

B1. Mark the front of the seat piece at the deepest part of the tuck-in.

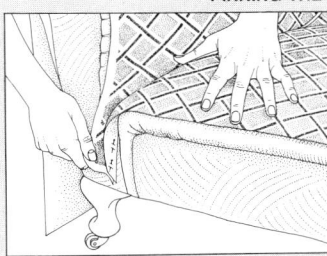

B2. Position the inside arm piece in the tuck-in and pull taut.

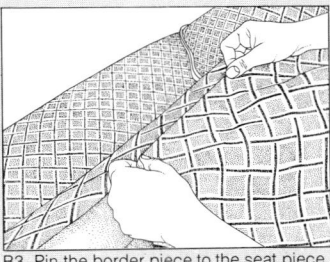

B3. Pin the border piece to the seat piece, starting at the centre and working outwards.

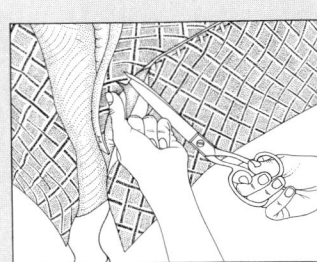

B4. Cut small slits in the pieces where the border curves to prevent creases.

CHALKING AND NOTCHING

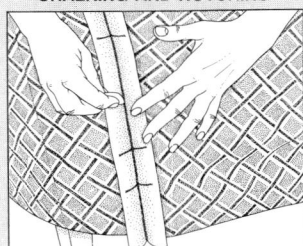

C1. Chalk across the opened seam so that both parts of the seam are marked.

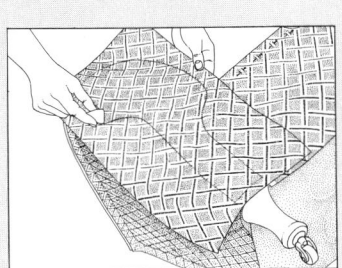

B5. Pin the seat piece and the border piece together at the front tuck-in.

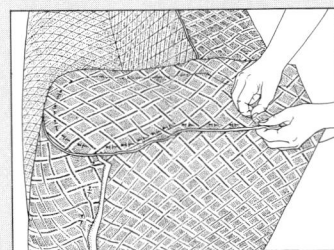

B6. Lay the front facing on the front of the arm and chalk the shape of the scroll.

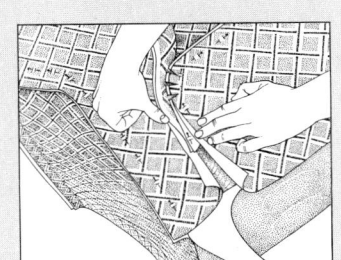

B7. Pin the facings carefully to prevent folds forming at the top of the scroll.

B8. Pin the facing to the border below the tuck-in of the seat and arm pieces.

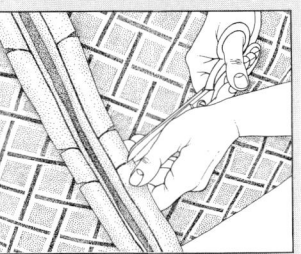

C2. Cut notches so that seams can be matched when sewing together.

PINNING THE PIECES ON OTHER TYPES OF CHAIRS AND SOFAS

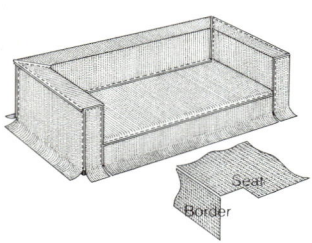

STRAIGHT-SIDED SOFAS

The straight-sided sofa is pinned in the same order as the chesterfield, adding the arm and back borders to the inside and outside arm and back pieces.

If the sofa has separate cushions, pin the inside arm pieces to the seat piece. At the front edge, allow 15 mm. ($\frac{1}{2}$ in.) seams for 10 cm. (4 in.), then allow normal tuck-in along the side of the seat and the bottom of the arm.

WING CHAIRS

Pin the inside and outside back pieces together along the top of the chair. Cut the wing pieces roughly to shape. Pin to the back pieces. Then pin the wing pieces together around the wing, cutting darts to get round the tip of the wing. Cut as few darts as possible. Pin the inside and outside arm pieces together along the outside of the arms.

Pin the outside arm to the outside back and outside wing. Readjust the pins to fit the inside arm to the inside back and wings. Pin the seat, front border and front facings in the same way as the chesterfield, reducing the tuck-ins to 2.5 cm. (1 in.) if the chair seat has tension springs.

ROUND-BACKED SOFAS

Pin a round-back sofa in the same order as the chesterfield, allowing for normal tuck-in.

To achieve the rounded shape on the back, pin darts in the back pieces. Limit

the number used by careful pinning and adjustment. Allow plenty of surplus material when shaping the front facings.

CONVENTIONAL ARMCHAIRS

A quick way of fitting covers to armchairs is to fold the pieces lengthways and pin to one side of the chair. Chalk a line down the centre of the chair and fold the pieces in half lengthways, with the wrong sides together.

Pin the folded edge of the inside back piece to the chalk line, with the top extending 7.5 cm. (3 in.) over the back of the chair. Pin the outside back to the inside back at the top of the chair. Pin the seat to the inside back and to the front border.

Place both inside arm pieces, wrong sides facing, and pin to seat and inside back pieces. Extend the inside arm piece across the bottom of the side facings, level with the top of the arm. Put the outside arm pieces wrong sides together and pin to the inside arm pieces at the top edge and to the outside back piece.

Cut the front facings, folded with the wrong sides together, and pin to the outside and inside arm pieces, the seat piece and the front border. Cut the side facings in the same way and pin to the inside and outside back and inside arm pieces.

Finally, trim all the seams to give an allowance of 15 mm. ($\frac{1}{2}$ in.).

TV CHAIRS

Pin together as for a conventional armchair without arms and a front border.

• SEWING THE PIECES TOGETHER

The next stage in making a cover is to sew the cover pieces together, adding the piping at the same time.

SEWING THE PIPING COVERING

Work out how much piping is needed. The position of piping on a chesterfield is usually round the joins of the back and arm pieces, round the front facings, across the top of the front border, and round the top of the skirt.

Cut and join 4 cm. (1½ in.) wide strips of piping covering until the required length is made. Sew to the piping cord (see p. 299).

SEWING THE COVER TOGETHER

Turn the cover wrong side out. Set the tension of the sewing machine at ten stitches to the inch. Use a straight machine stitch for all seams, and begin and end each line of stitching with 2.5 cm. (1 in.) of back stitching.

Match the notches when sewing the pieces together. Remove the pins on the seam which is being sewn, keeping to the chalk lines on both pieces. The other pieces remain pinned together. Sew in this order.

1. **Inside back to the seat** Begin 15 mm. (½ in.) from the edges.

2. **Bottom of an inside arm piece to the seat** Start 15 mm. from where the arm joins the back. Repeat with the second arm.

3. **The side of the inside arm to the inside back piece** Begin where the back joins the seat. Repeat with the second arm.

4. **One outside arm piece to the out-**side back piece Sew this seam to the bottom of the material. Join the other

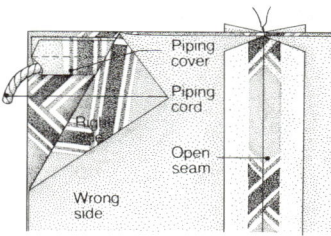

Open the seams when sewing on piping.

end of the outside back piece to the other arm by sewing only 4 cm. (1½ in.) together at the top. Leave the rest open. Sew together any darts on the inside back.

5. **Piping along the back and arms** Unpin the outside arms and back from

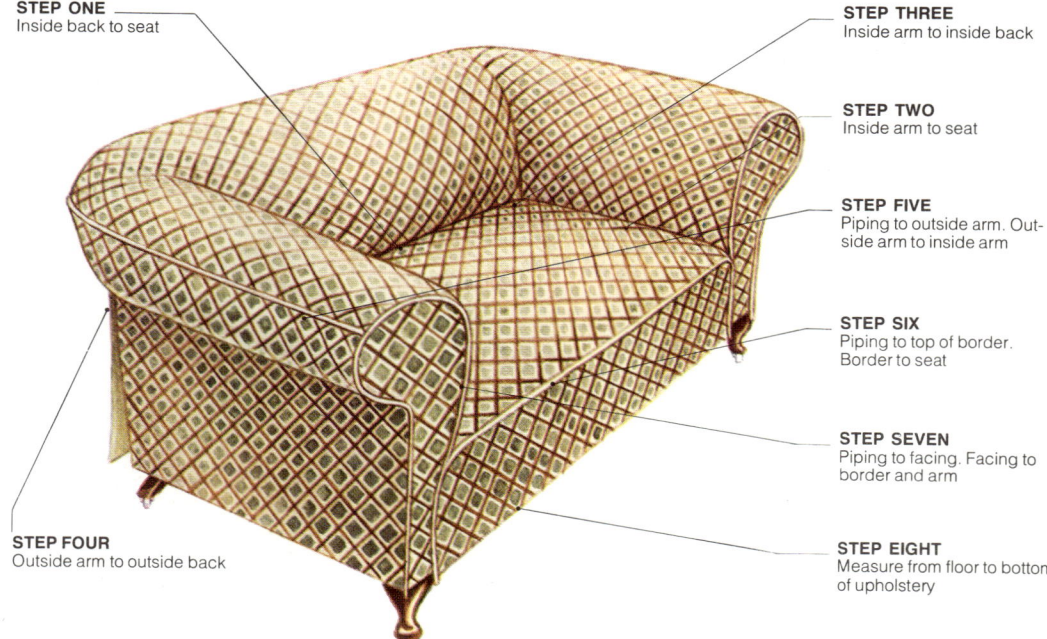

STEP ONE Inside back to seat

STEP TWO Inside arm to seat

STEP THREE Inside arm to inside back

STEP FOUR Outside arm to outside back

STEP FIVE Piping to outside arm. Outside arm to inside arm

STEP SIX Piping to top of border. Border to seat

STEP SEVEN Piping to facing. Facing to border and arm

STEP EIGHT Measure from floor to bottom of upholstery

ORDER OF SEWING A step-by-step guide to joining the pieces of a loose cover.

the rest of the cover. Fit a piping foot or zipper foot to the machine. Lay the raw edges of the piping covering on the raw edge of the top of the outside arm, right sides together. Sew a long length of piping along the top of the outside arm and back pieces, opening any seams that are in the path of the stitching. Pin the outside back and arms to the inside back and arms, matching notches, right sides together with the piping enclosed. Sew the inside arms and back to the outside arms and back, placing the piping at the top, for the piping foot to use as a guide. Stitch on or inside the previous stitches.

6. **Piping round the border** Where the tuck-in seams join the front border, mark with a pin pushed into the border at both tuck-ins. Unpin the border from the facings and seat. Sew piping

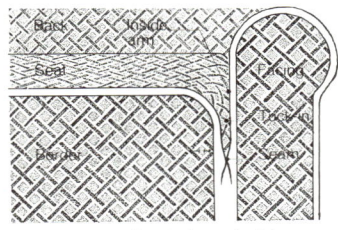
How the arm and seat pieces tuck in.

around the top of the border. Start and finish sewing at the pins but leave 4 cm. of piping and covering unstitched beyond the pins. The remaining piping around the border is added when the arm facings (stage seven) are sewn to the border piece. Make three or four cuts in the covering down to the cord, to allow the piping to go round the bends in the border. Pin the

border to the seat and sew together from the bottom of the tuck-in where it meets the seam of the seat and inside arm, laying the raw edges of the piping covering along the top edge of the border.

7. **Piping round the facing** Unpin the facings from the cover. Leaving the

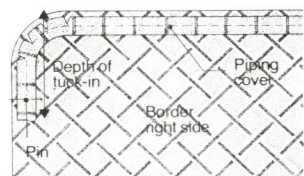
Sewing piping round the corner.

bottom of the facings free of piping, sew piping round the facings. When attaching piping to curves on the fac-

ings, cut the piping covering down almost as far as the cord.

Pin one front facing to the outside and inside arm pieces and front border. Where the facing meets the piping on the arm, pin the piping raw edges flat. Sew these pieces together, if necessary by hand if there is too much material to pass through the sewing machine. Where the piping on the front border joins the facing, cut notches in the piping cover so that it lies neatly along the corner. Pin the raw edges so that they are turned away from the facing pieces. Sew the pieces together. Repeat with the second facing.

8. **Piping round the bottom edge** Turn the cover right side out. Fit it over the sofa by placing the back and arms in position, leaving the seat and tuck-in

material loose on the seat. Kneel on the seat to push the tuck-in securely down.

Be prepared for a lot of adjusting and pulling of the material before the fit is satisfactory. Pin the opening together so that it gives an accurate hang.

Measure the distance from the floor to the bottom of the upholstery. Draw a line along the bottom of the cover, flush with the upholstery, so that the cover is the same distance from the ground all round. Take the cover off and trim on the line.

Sew piping round the bottom edge, holding open seams crossed by the stitching. However, when crossing the piping at the facings, keep the seam closed and fold the raw edges towards the centre of the facings.

MARKING THE OUTLINE Piping emphasises the lines of a chesterfield.

SEWING THE PIECES ON OTHER TYPES OF CHAIRS AND SOFAS

STRAIGHT-SIDED SOFAS
Sew the loose cover pieces together in the same order as those for the chesterfield. Use piping to emphasise the lines of the sofa along both edges of the arms and back and down facings. If there are no piped cushions, pipe along the front of the seat cover.

WING CHAIRS
Sew the inside back and inside arms to the seat. Join the inside wings to the inside back and inside arms. Sew the outside back to the outside wings, leaving all but the first 5 cm. (2 in.) unsewn at one seam to form the opening. Sew piping round the outside arms, and across the top of the outside back. Pipe the top of the outside arms and join them to the wings and back on the side where the inside arms and back are joined.

Work out how much piping you will need. Attach the outside back, wings and arms to the inside back wing pieces and arms. Pipe the border and join to the seat if there is no piped cushion. Pipe round the front facings, and join to the front border, and to the inside and outside arm pieces.

ROUND-BACKED SOFAS
Follow the sewing and piping instructions for the chesterfield. If the sofa has piped seat cushions, there is no need to pipe the front edge of the seat.

CONVENTIONAL ARMCHAIRS
Join and pipe the pieces as for the chesterfield, except that side facings for the back are added. Sew piping round the side facings, leaving enough unattached piping to reach the bottom of the chair.

Sew the side facings to the inside back, outside back and inside arm pieces. Continue sewing the piping down the outside arm to within 5 cm. (2 in.) of the bottom of the covers if finishing with tie-unders. If attaching a skirt, sew on the piping as far as the bottom of the cover. Cut the piping cord level with the bottom of the material, leaving about 2.5 cm. (1 in.) of piping covering loose beyond the bottom.

TV CHAIRS
Join the back of the seat to the bottom of the inside back along the tuck-in. Sew piping across the top of the outside back and join to the inside back.

Sew piping to the side borders, finishing 5 cm. (2 in.) short of the ends which join the side facings. Sew the side borders to the seat. Add piping to the side facings and sew them to the inside and outside back, and to the side borders.

TIE-UNDER FINISHES

Loose covers can be finished with tie-unders or a skirt. Use tie-unders to achieve a tailored look, or on chairs with legs you do not want to hide.

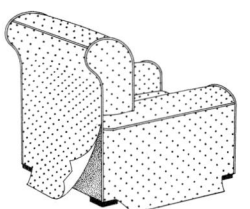

After the cover is fitted, pin it to the upholstery immediately above the outside middle of each leg. From a point 15 mm. (½ in.) below the pin, cut a line, parallel to the upholstery, in each side of the cover to within 15 mm. of the inside edges of the cover. At the end of each line, cut downwards at 45 degrees to the bottom of the cover.

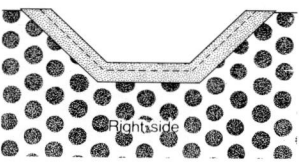

Cut a 5 cm. (2 in.) wide facing to the shape of each corner. Machine to the cover, right sides together, 15 mm. from the edge. Turn the facing in, and press. Oversew the edge to the cover.

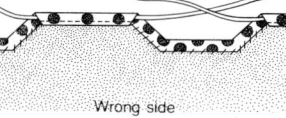

Hem the four straight bottom edges of the cover. Thread a tape through each hem, with plenty of excess at each end. Sew a tape at right-angles to the middle of each hem. Pull all tapes tight, and tie under the chair as shown below.

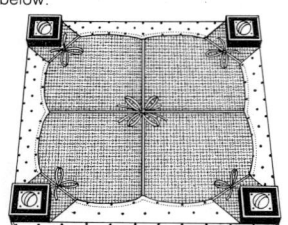

• FORMING THE SKIRT

Lay the border piece of the cover on a flat surface. Pin the centre of the top edge of the long skirt length to the centre of the bottom edge of the border. Pin out from the centre to each corner. Insert a pin in the skirt at the point below the outer line of piping on each front facing [A1]. At the corner diagonally opposite the opening in the cover, insert four pins beyond the first at 10 cm. (4 in.) intervals [A2]. Form a box pleat by bringing the outer pins to the centre pin [A3]. Secure the pleat with pins. (See also p. 160.)

Pin the outside arm piece to the skirt up to the second corner. If 35.5 cm. (14 in.) of skirt overlaps the corner, form another box pleat and pin to the cover. If the overlap is less than 35.5 cm., join the shorter skirt piece to the first, pinning them together with a 15 mm. (½ in.) seam allowance. Form the pleat as before.

On some sizes of chair and sofa, a join may be on or near the pleat, which will look conspicuous. To avoid this, form the second pleat as before. Unfold the half pleat nearest the free end of the skirt, and cut anywhere between the first and third pin [A4].

Pin the short skirt length to the long one at this cut with a 15 mm. seam allowance on each piece. Re-form the pleat and continue pinning.

Continue pinning the skirt length along the back, as far as the opening. Insert a pin in the skirt 15 mm. before the opening. Place another pin 20 cm. (8 in.) further along the skirt length. Form half a box pleat by bringing this pin to the first, so that the second pin lies behind the first. Trim the end of the skirt level with the opening [A5].

Arrange the material so that the front of the skirt and cover are upper-

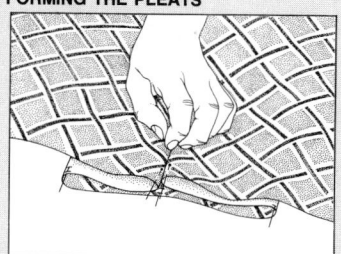

Third (open) corner / Second corner / Opening / Back / Second side / First side / Front / Centre marker pin / Fourth corner / First corner / Long skirt length / Front seams centred

Fitting the skirt.

most. Make a box pleat at the second front corner. Continue pinning the skirt to the cover along the second side. Join the single skirt width to the end of this length. Pin to the cover until the opening. Form half a box pleat as before, so that the two halves make one box pleat at the opening [A6].

SEWING THE SKIRT PIECES

Unpin the skirt from the cover. Cut small notches at the pleat folds at the top of the skirt. Chalk the position of seams. Machine-sew the seams to make one long strip. Sew the same amount of lining together to form another strip. Press open the seams of lining and skirt, right side uppermost, on a flat surface. Place the lining on it, seams uppermost. Pin together closely along the bottom edge [A7]. Trim the ends of the lining level with the skirt. Sew together, leaving a 15 mm. seam allowance along the bottom edge. Press open the seams. Turn 15 mm. of the skirt over as a hem.

Hold in place with pins and iron flat. Tack-stitch 2.5 cm. (1 in.) from the top and bottom. Trim the top edge of the lining level with the top edge of the skirt.

Pin the pleats in position and stitch along the top edge of the skirt, 5 mm. (¼ in.) from the top [A8].

FITTING THE SKIRT AND FORMING THE PLEATS

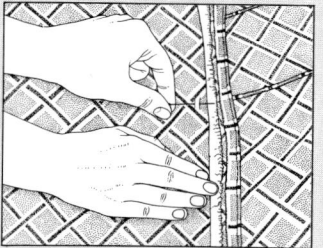

A1. Pin skirt at a point matching the corner piping on the front facing.

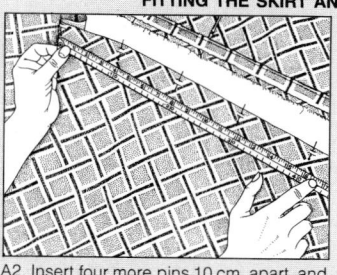

A2. Insert four more pins 10 cm. apart, and align the centre pin with the corner.

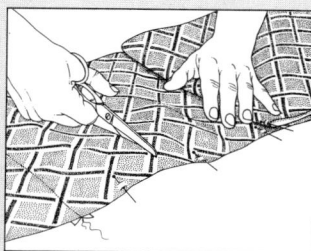

A3. Bring the outer pins to meet the centre pin, forming a box pleat.

A4. Unfold one half of the box pleat and cut through the unfolded skirt.

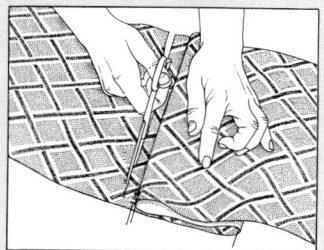

A5. Cut the skirt 15 mm. beyond the fold of the half box pleat.

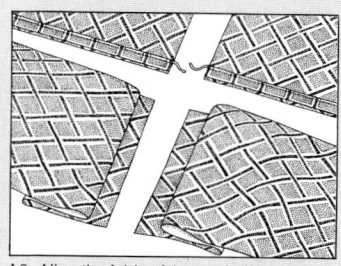

A6. Align the folds of the two half box pleats with the edges of the opening.

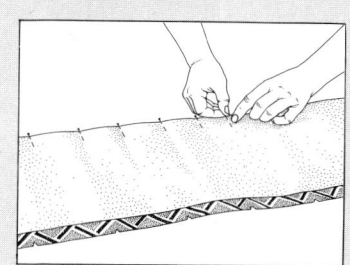

A7. With the lining and skirt pinned at the top, pin closely along the bottom.

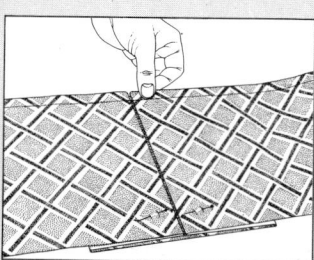

A8. Pin and tack the pleats before machining 5 mm. from the top.

SEWING ON THE SKIRT

Lay the cover and skirt right sides together with a length of piping cord and piping covering between them. Align all the raw edges, making sure the opening of the cover is level with the opening on the skirt. Pin and tack-stitch together 5 mm. from the edge. Machine along the line of tacks.

• ATTACHING THE VELCRO

Lay one of the Velcro strips on a 2.5 cm. (1 in.) wide length of cotton tape. The strips of Velcro and tape should be long enough to reach from the top of the sofa to the floor. Sew the Velcro and tape together, right sides outside, along one long edge.

Insert the raw edge of the outside back cover between the tape and Velcro, so that the right side of the fabric faces the same way as the nylon nap on the Velcro. Pin in place.

Tack the Velcro, cover and tape together [B1], then machine.

Cut the other side of the Velcro the length of the first. Lay the second strip, smooth side next to the right side of the outside arm piece. Pin together, with 15 mm. of cover under the Velcro [B2]. Machine together.

Lay the Velcro strips face to face, with the cover pieces right sides together. Pin the tops of the strips together and machine across them [B3]. Fold at the Velcro seam, bringing the outside arm piece over the outside back piece, so that both pieces are right side up. Fold the Velcro on the arm piece under to the wrong side, bringing 3 mm. ($\frac{1}{8}$ in.) of the right side of the cover to the wrong side. Hem-stitch the free edge of the Velcro to the cover [B4].

Trim the seam edges straight and oversew them with a zigzag stitch.

SEWING ON THE VELCRO TAPES

B1. Slot the tape-backed Velcro over the edge of the outside back piece and tack.

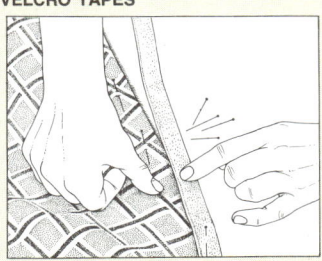

B2. Pin the Velcro to the outside arm piece, covering the raw edge by 15 mm.

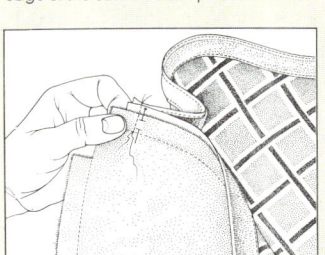

E3. Match and pin the Velcro strips, then machine across the ends to secure.

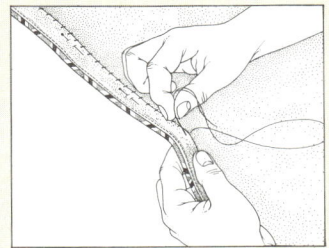

B4. Fold the Velcro to the wrong side of the cover and hem-stitch in place.

COVER PATTERNS   Fabrics with small patterns make economical loose covers. Large patterns are wasteful to match. Moreover, to look good, large patterns need to be centred on the back and seat – involving more waste.

MAKING CUSHIONS AND FOAM SEATING

Chosen with care, cushions of various shapes and sizes can give even a sparsely furnished room a look and feel of comfort. They soften the stark lines of modern furniture and transform stools, window seats and box tops into comfortable seating. Colourful covers can be used to brighten plainly furnished rooms. Large cushions, scattered around the floor, can be used as sofas and chairs, and even replace more conventional seating.

There are two ways of making cushions. A basic cushion shape can be bought and then covered, or the filling can be bought and shaped in inner covers of your own design. When choosing a covering fabric, select a hardwearing easy-care fabric, with a design and colour which will harmonise with the decor of the room. Other materials can be used – a small oriental bedspread would make an unusual cover – but avoid loosely woven fabrics which soon become misshapen on anything other than decorative cushions.

Foam, which is widely used as a filling for cushions, can also be cut and shaped into simple items of furniture.

• CUSHION FILLINGS

The choice of filling depends on price and the use to be made of the cushion. Cheap fillings are adequate for decorative cushions, such as small scatter cushions, which will not get much wear.

Box cushions for stool and chest tops, or window seats and squab cushions for kitchen chairs, all need to be precisely shaped and able to withstand hard wear. They are best filled with firm foam.

Fillings for cushions used in children's bedrooms or play areas should be as washable as their covers. Fibre, such as Terylene, or foam chips are the best fillings for these.

All fillings give off poisonous fumes if they catch fire. If there are careless smokers in the family, or if you have some other cause for concern about fire, make covers of fire-resistant material. Wool moquette is one of the safest.

FEATHER MIXTURES

The best-quality ready-made cushions are filled with feather or feather and down mixtures. Feathers retain

SEAT AND BED Half-a-dozen large box cushions can be arranged to make a single bed and a low seat. They can also be arranged to make a double bed.

SOFA The same six cushions make a large sofa. They can also be made up into individual seats. Colourful scatter cushions brighten the plain covers.

their resilience almost indefinitely and 'fall' or 'drape' gracefully as scatter cushions. It is not worth making the cushion base from scratch, since the cost of the raw materials is more than most shops charge for the ready-made cushion. But it is worth remaking old cushions or pillows that have begun to leak feathers. The new inner cover must be made of feather-proof cambric.

 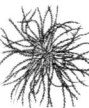

Goose and duck down This is the most expensive cushion filling. It is also the softest and most resilient and, as it bulks large for its weight, it makes the lightest cushion.

Feathers and down A feather-down mixture is less expensive, but heavier, than pure down. The cushion will also be harder.

Goose and duck feathers Because feathers do not bulk as large as down, more are needed to fill a cushion and it will be heavier than one filled with feathers and down.

Chicken feathers These make the cheapest feather filling. They are usually curled to increase their bulk and resilience, but even so they pack more densely than duck or goose feathers and so make heavier cushions. However, they are still lighter than most other fillings.

KAPOK

This vegetable down, imported from Indonesia, is cheap, soft and resilient, but it tends to become lumpy after it has been in use for some time. Kapok cannot be washed, and deteriorates if dry-cleaned. It is best used for decorative cushions, not for hard wear.

FIBRE FILLING

Terylene (a polyester fibre) can be used for pillows, cushions, soft toys, quilts and duvets. It is a light, resilient filling which is non-allergic, non-absorbent and completely washable. If bought in bulk, cover the amount required for a cushion in thin gauze for easy handling. Use drip-dry fabric for the inner cover, then cover and filling can be washed together.

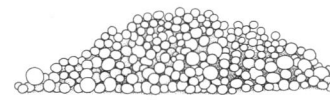

POLYSTYRENE BEADS

Available in bags of 6 and 12 cu. ft, polystyrene beads are mainly used for large floor cushions. They are packed fairly loosely in the inner cover, but compress under weight and so make a filling firm enough to sit on, and comfortable enough to lie on. Because the beads give a bumpy outline to the cushion they should be covered with a sateen cotton lining before the final cover is put on.

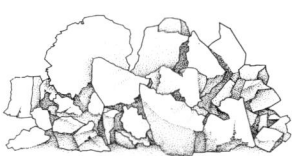

FOAM CRUMBS AND CHIPS

Plastic foam crumbs are the cheapest commercial filling. They are sold in 450 g. (1 lb.) bags, one of which is enough for a 40 × 40 cm. (16 × 16 in.) cushion. Foam crumbs and chips are rather lumpy, and the lumps tend to show through even a double covering. They are not affected by washing and do not produce dust. Foam crumbs are best used for small scatter cushions. If used to fill large cushions, mix in larger pieces of foam. This will prevent the crumbs moving around when sat or laid upon. As with fibre, make the inner cover of drip-dry fabric, so that cover and filling can be washed together.

TIGHTS

Discarded tights, cut into 15 cm. (6 in.) strips are the cheapest cushion filling. Packed firmly together, until the cushion is as hard as you require. Tights are soft and resilient. Throw away the feet and machine wash the rest inside a pillowcase before using. If the inner cover is drip-dry, filling and cover can be washed together.

● FOAM

Foam is widely used for cushions and furniture because it is comfortable, easy to use, inexpensive, non-allergic and long-lasting. It weighs little in relation to its bulk and can be shaped into strong, but lightweight, furniture that stands up to constant use without distortion.

There are two types of foam, latex foam, made from natural and synthetic rubber, and polyether, or plastic, foam. Latex foam is the more expen-

sive of the two. But it is more resilient. Both types of foam deteriorate and eventually break down if exposed to sunlight, so they should always be covered. Normal upholstery fabrics give adequate protection.

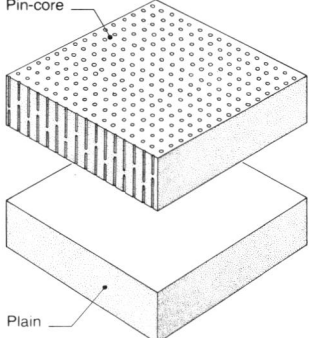

LATEX FOAM

Latex foam is graded according to firmness. All grades, except that made specially for pillows, are suitable for seating. Latex is made in sheets and in moulded units.

The sheets are approximately 183 × 137 cm. (72 × 54 in.), and in three thicknesses, 12, 25 and 30 mm. ($\frac{1}{2}$, 1 and 1$\frac{1}{4}$ in.). Plain latex is suitable for arm pads, bar stools, kitchen and dining chairs.

Pincore latex is also made in sheets up to 100 mm. (4 in.) thick. This foam has small holes on both sides of the sheet.

POLYETHER FOAM

Polyether foam is made in various degrees of density and hardness. The hardness depends on the chemical make-up of the foam, not the density. The density varies according to the amount of air in the foam.

High-density foam costs more, but lasts longer than low-density foam. Avoid hard, low-density foam for cushions or seats in constant use,

because it will eventually collapse.

The density of polyether foam ranges from 1 to 3 lb. per cubic foot. Densities of less than 1$\frac{1}{2}$ lb. are suitable for back cushions, headrests and arm supports. For seating, it is always better to use higher-density foams. Once the density is chosen, select the hardness which you find the most comfortable to sit or lie upon. Always explain your requirements to the supplier, who will advise which is the most suitable foam.

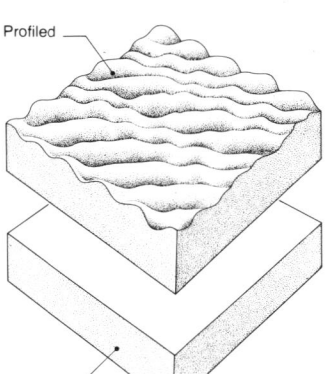

Basic types of polyether foam.

Firm grades should be at least 90 mm. (3$\frac{1}{2}$ in.) thick if attached to a hard base. Softer grades should be at least 110 mm. (4$\frac{1}{2}$ in.) thick, on a hard base. Thickness can be reduced by 12 mm. on softer supports, such as webbing.

To reduce the thickness, it is possible to laminate different hardnesses of foam. This technique can also be used to make seats and floor cushions harder in the centre to compensate for the extra weight applied there. This is achieved by sandwiching a piece of hard foam between two layers of softer foam. Alternatively, 25 mm. thick medium foam can be stuck to 25 mm. hard foam.

• USES OF FOAM

Using the techniques shown here, pieces of foam can be shaped and glued together to make simple items of furniture.

For example, circles of foam can be built up into a pouffe. The circles are glued one on top of the other. The lower circles should be of high-density foam, to support the weight and provide stability. Use contact adhesive to glue a thin piece of hardboard to the bottom layer. Cover the pouffe by the method used for a circular cushion (see p. 147).

It is possible even to make a foam sofa which converts into a bed. Two 150 mm. (6 in.) thick sheets of medium-density foam are cut to the desired size, and reinforced with harder foam glued round the edges. Hinge the sheets together with 5 cm. (2 in.) wide linen tape. When the two sheets are folded together they make a sofa, which can be covered with a simple tailored cover. Opened out, they become a standby bed.

CUTTING FOAM

Cut foam sheeting with a fine-toothed hacksaw blade or an electric carving knife. Foam should be cut 5 mm. ($\frac{1}{4}$ in.) larger all round than the desired size of the finished item. This minimises the risk of wrinkles.

BASES

If you put foam on to a solid base, rather than on jute or rubber webbing, the base must be ventilated. Wood and hardboard are the most suitable bases for seating units, pouffes and mattresses. Perforate the mattress base by drilling 2 cm. ($\frac{3}{4}$ in.) diameter holes through the board, 18 cm. (7 in.) apart across the width and 25 cm. (10 in.) apart along the length. Drill 2 cm. holes, about 20 cm. (8 in.) apart on other solid bases. A foam mattress needs a 50 mm. (2 in.) layer of profiled foam glued to the base, profiled side down, to allow air to circulate. Polyether foam with an egg-box profile is best.

To fit foam to the webbing base of a chair, or if replacing springs, measure the area of foam required and cut to shape. Position the foam on the webbing and hold in place by nailing or tacking the cover to the frame.

COVERS

Feather or down-filled cushions should be lined with down-proof cambric or feather-proof ticking before covering, as shown on p. 150.

When covering cushions, or any item made with polyether or latex foam, make sure that the fabric is air-permeable, which will allow the air to escape when the cushion or foam is compressed.

When covering latex foam, choose a tightly woven fabric, to protect the foam which perishes in direct sunlight. A further precaution is to cover the latex foam with calico or sateen lining before making the outer cover.

Always use white or light colours for inner covers, since strong colours

CURVING FOAM TO A BASE	CUTTING CIRCLES OF FOAM	ROUNDING THE SIDES	DOMING	MAKING CONVERTIBLE SEATS

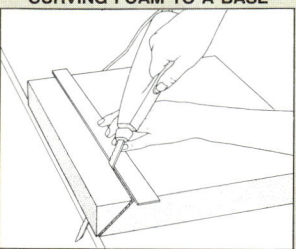

1. Cut an angled edge, using a metal ruler and the edge of an old table as guides. The wider the edge cut, the more gradual the curve becomes. An electric carving knife is the best tool. Alternatively, use short strokes with a fine-toothed hacksaw blade.

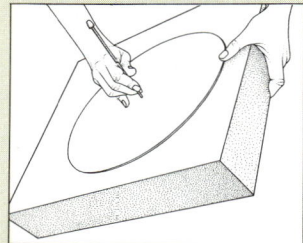

1. Cut two matching circles of hardboard or stiff card the required diameter of the foam. Pierce a hole in the centre of each circle. Sandwich the foam between the circles and secure by pushing thick wire or a steel knitting needle through the holes.

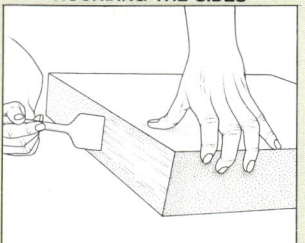

1. Apply contact adhesive to the side to be rounded. Ensure that the glue covers all the surface of the side. Allow the glue to become tacky; the time depends on room temperature. Starting at one end of the side, press in the centre with the forefinger or side of the hand.

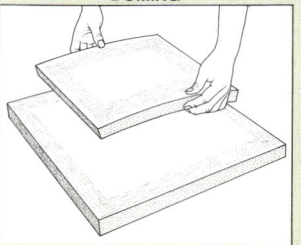

1. Cut two matching pieces of soft foam to the size you have chosen for the cushion, and one piece of hard foam the same shape, but 7.5 cm. (3 in.) smaller all round. Carefully glue the piece of hard foam to the centre of one of the soft pieces. Leave glue to set.

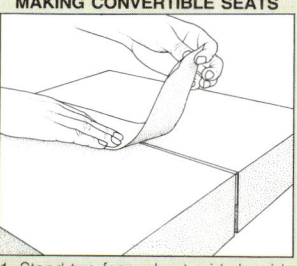

1. Stand two foam sheets side by side together along their long edges. Glue a strip of 5 cm. (2 in.) wide tape along the join where the top edges meet. When the glue is dry, fold the sheets together with the fold in the tape inside. Glue a second length of tape along the join.

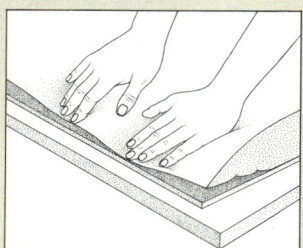

2. Glue the smaller surface of the foam to the board, aligning the edges of the larger surface with the edges of the board. When stuck, glue the angled sides of the foam. Push them downwards and outwards, flush with the board edges, to form a curved border.

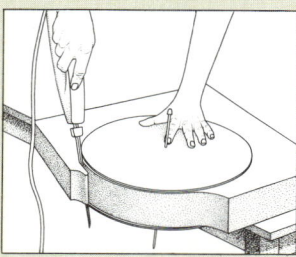

2. Cut round the sandwich to form a circle of foam, taking care not to cut the hardboard or card. Repeat, if necessary, until you have enough circles to achieve the required depth of the cushion, seat or pouffe. If more than one circle is used, glue them together.

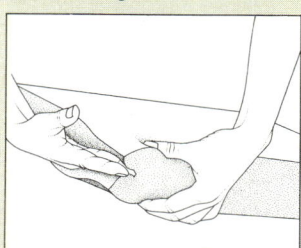

2. Bring the top and bottom edges together, ensuring that they align to form an even curve. Continue folding the glued sides together until the whole length is curved. Repeat with the other sides if desired. Curved sides can be used for cushions and seat edges.

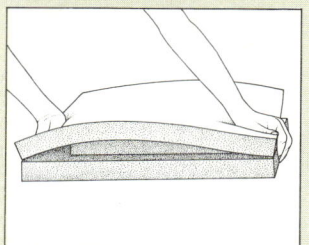

2. When the two pieces are stuck, spread glue over their combined surface and one side of the other piece of soft foam. Place them together, to make a sandwich of the hard foam. The hard centre makes a cushion better able to withstand weight.

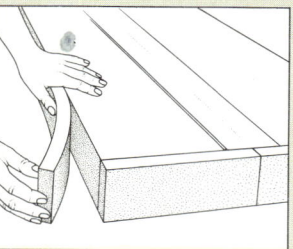

2. Reinforce the edges of the foam sheets with 25 mm. (1 in.) thick strips of hard foam. Cut the strips to the depth of the sheet and glue them to the sides and ends of each sheet. Make sure the side strips match the folding edge or the sheets will not open properly.

could show through the outer cover.

Outer covers can be made from all types of fabric, though loosely woven and fluffy fabrics create problems with pulled threads and pilling. Washable, easy-care, man-made fibres make the most practical cover from the point of view of wear and cleaning.

REMOVABLE COVERS

Covers for cushions and foam furniture should be easily removable for cleaning.

For soft cushions, use popper tape, which has press studs attached, or a zip. On tighter-fitting covers, Velcro tape and zips are more suitable.

MOULDED MANUFACTURED SHAPES OF FOAM

Foam sheets, bought from do-it-yourself suppliers, cannot be made into very complicated furniture, because of the limited depth of cutting achieved with domestic tools and blades. However, foam suppliers will cut foam to any shape you require. This can then be covered at home.

It is often more economical to buy foam furniture already made than to make it yourself. Many furniture makers work in conjunction with foam manufacturers to produce hard-wearing chairs. The designs usually exploit the lightness of foam, so that different parts and units can be moved apart or joined together to make adaptable, versatile furniture. Some of the shapes that are generally available, and the ways in which they are used, are shown on this page.

Many suppliers sell their designs in kit form, with instructions, so the foam can be joined and covered at home (see p. 134). They will also make up the furniture, covered with the customer's own choice of fabric. Covers are usually closed with zips, so they can be removed and washed.

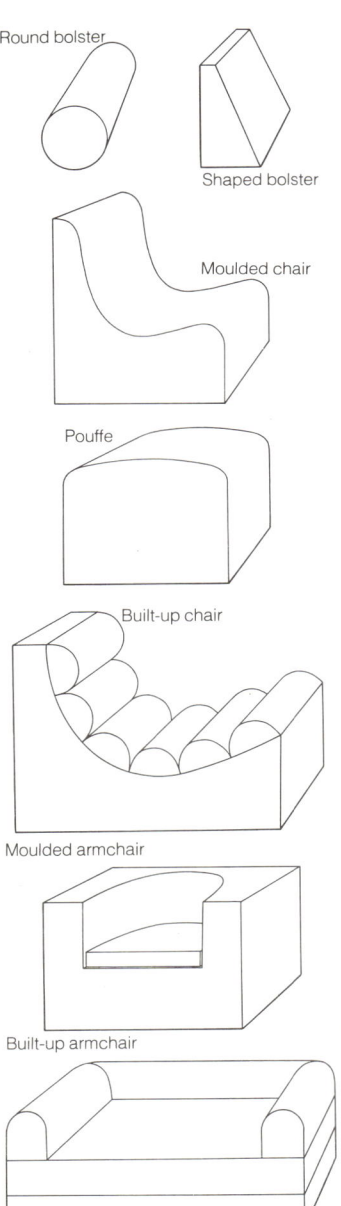

Round bolster

Shaped bolster

Moulded chair

Pouffe

Built-up chair

Moulded armchair

Built-up armchair

FOAM FURNITURE *Moulded foam makes a wide range of seating.*

VERSATILE FOAM *A unit made of hinged pieces of foam can be folded to make three different items of furniture: a bed, a reclining chair or an easy chair. Units can also be grouped together with corner pieces to make a large sofa.*

• TAILORED BOX CUSHION

A block of foam, covered with soft furnishing fabric and piped along the main seams, turns a plain wooden chest into a useful occasional seat. The method can be used for any size of square or rectangular cushion.

Use high-density foam 10 cm. (4 in.) deep. Cut the foam (see p. 144) or order it 5 mm. (¼ in.) longer and wider than the required size of the finished cushion. The chest illustrated is 67.5 × 49.5 cm. (26½ × 19½ in.), and the foam block is 68 × 50 cm. (26¾ × 20 in.).

The top and bottom covers are cut to the same size as the foam. But the side pieces are 3 cm. (1 in.) deeper than the foam to allow for seams. This compresses the foam round the sides without distorting the edges and corners.

MATERIALS AND EQUIPMENT

68 × 50 × 10 cm. (26¾ × 20 × 4 in.) high-density foam block; 140 × 120 cm. (55 × 48 in.) cover fabric;

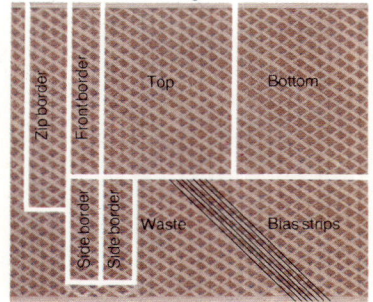

Cover cutting guide for a box cushion.

5 m. (5½ yds) No. 2 piping cord; 100 × 120 cm. (40 × 48 in.) cotton sateen lining; 1 reel mercerised cotton to match lining; 1 reel thread to match cover; two 40 cm. (16 in.) zips; fabric shears; tape measure; rule and set-square; tailor's chalk; pins; zipper and/or piping foot for the machine; iron; sewing needle.

The lining is made from four pieces of fabric. The top and bottom panels are two rectangles, 68 × 50 cm. (26¾ × 20 in.). The border is two equal rectangles, 115 × 12.5 cm. (45¾ × 5 in.).

The main panels are also 68 × 50 cm. but the border of the cover is in four pieces. The front is 68 × 12.5 cm. (26¾ × 5 in.); the sides are 45.5 × 12.5 cm. (18 × 5 in.), and the back is 83 × 15 cm. (33 × 6 in.), to allow for the two zips, which are placed head to head and go round both back corners.

MAKING THE LINING

Press the lining fabric. Straighten one end (see p. 291). Using tailor's chalk and tape, measure and mark out the main panels and border pieces on the matt, or wrong, side, following the cutting guide.

Cut top and bottom panels 68 × 50 cm., side by side across the width

Lining cutting guide for a box cushion.

of the lining fabric. Cut two border pieces 115 × 12.5 cm. (45¾ × 5 in.).

Place the two border pieces right sides together. Match the ends, and machine 15 mm. (½ in.) from the raw edge. Join the other ends in the same way. Press the seams flat.

Pin one panel all the way round one edge of the border, right sides together [1]. Machine 15 mm. from the edge. Pin the other cover halfway round the other edge of the border and machine. Press a 15 mm. seam allowance on the unsewn edges of the border and cover.

Oversew (see p. 296) the raw edges. Turn the cover right side out. Fit the foam block inside the cover, then slip-stitch (see p. 297) to close the opening.

MAKING THE COVER

Press the cover fabric. Measure, mark and cut the pieces, following the cutting guide.

On the remaining fabric find the bias (see p. 291). Mark and cut 4 cm. (1½ in.) wide bias strips, and make up the piping (see p. 299). Cut the completed length of piping in half.

Cut the back border in half along its length. Place the lower half right side up. Lay both zips face down and head to head on this half. Overlap the zip tapes where the heads meet. Match the top edges of the tapes with the top edge of the border. Pin as close to the edge as possible.

Use a zipper foot, with thread to match the cover, and machine as close as possible to the metal teeth of the zip. Start and finish where the teeth end. To avoid making a curve in the seam, machine to within 5 cm. (2 in.) of the head then open the first zip before stitching on [2]. Open the second zip 5 cm. before stitching. Repeat to attach the other edge of the zips to the other half of the

border. Machine both sides in the same direction.

Pin a pleat along each half-border piece so that the folds meet over the centre of the zip and conceal the teeth [3]. Press the pleats and machine along them as close to the teeth as possible. Machine across the width of the zip tapes at each end.

Place the back border and one side border right sides together. Match up the ends and pin. Machine 15 mm. from the pinned edge. Top-stitch (see p. 296) 2 mm. from the seam on the

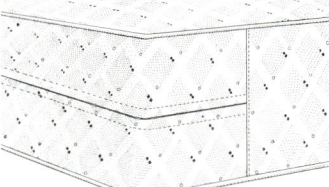

Finished corner, showing zip and seams.

side panel to strengthen the end of the zip opening [4]. Repeat for the other side border. Join the front border to the side pieces in the

---

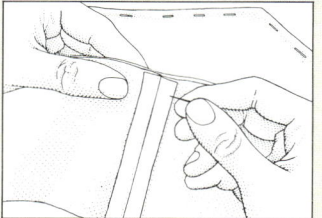

1. Pin and sew lining border all round one panel edge, half round the other.

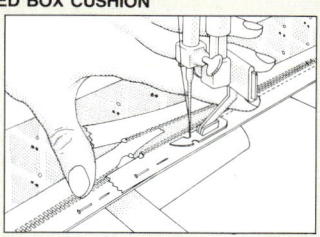

2. For zip seam, machine to within 5 cm. of zip end. Open zip, continue machining.

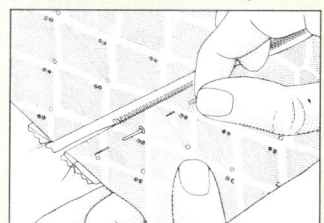

3. Pin a narrow pleat along each length, so that folds meet over zip to conceal it.

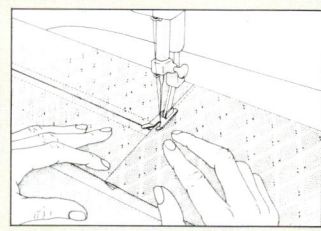

4. To strengthen the zip opening, top-stitch down the depth of the border.

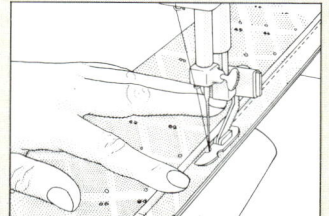

5. Machine piping to one edge of border, right sides together. Sew close to piping.

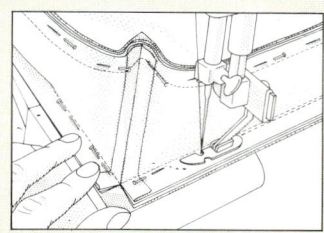

6. Sew panels to border. Notch piping tail and border seam to ease corners.

same way, except that top-stitching is not needed. Pin one strip of piping to one edge of the border, right sides facing, and leaving the two ends loose. Use a piping or zipper foot to machine as close to the cord as possible [5]. Join the two ends of the piping (see p. 299). Pipe the other edge of the border in the same way. Open the zip.

Place the border, right side down, on the right side of the top panel. Match the front corner seams on the borders to the corners of the panel.

Pin the border to the panel. Arrange the bottom panel on the other edge of the border in the same way. To ease machining at corners, notch the piping fabric and border seam allowance. Cut in towards the point of the corner, stopping short of the piping cord. Use the zipper foot, and machine as close as possible to the piping [6].

Oversew all the raw edges. Trim the zip tails if necessary. Press both seams down on to the border, then turn the cover right side out.

• MAKING A CIRCULAR CUSHION AND COVER

If possible, have the foam circle cut by the supplier. Otherwise, use the method described on p. 144.

MATERIALS AND EQUIPMENT

Pin-core latex, 7.5 cm. (3 in.) thick and 37.5 cm. (15 in.) square; 50 cm. (20 in.) of 120 cm. (48 in.) cotton sateen lining fabric; 70 cm. (27½ in.) of 120 cm. (48 in.) cover fabric; strip of calico 117 × 7.5 cm. (46 × 3 in.); 240 cm. (95 in.) of No. 2 piping cord; 45.5 cm. (18 in.) zip; 1 reel white cotton; 1 reel matching thread; contact adhesive suitable for use with foam; adhesive tape; stiff paper; large compass; soft pencil; tape measure; tailor's chalk; scissors; hacksaw blade; fabric shears; pins; iron; zipper and/or piping foot for the machine.

MAKING THE PAD

To shape the foam, draw, then cut a circle, radius 17.5 cm. (7 in.), from stiff paper. Pin the circle to the smooth side of the foam and pencil round it. Cut the foam (see p. 144).

Spread contact adhesive on the

calico strip, 7.5 cm. (3 in.) wide and 117 cm. (46 in.) long. Wrap it tightly round the side of the foam pad, overlapping the ends. Keep the join closed with adhesive tape until the contact adhesive has dried. Make two more paper circles, radius 19 cm. (7½ in.), as patterns for the top and bottom lining and cover fabric.

MAKING THE LINING

Press the lining fabric and straighten one end (see p. 291). Place the paper patterns side by side across the width of the fabric and pin. Mark circles on the fabric with tailor's chalk and cut.

Mark and cut out a rectangle 113 × 10 cm. (45 × 4 in.) for the lining border. Match the two ends, shiny sides facing. Machine 15 mm. (½ in.) from the edge at each end.

Pin the top panel to one edge of the border, right sides facing. Machine 15 mm. from the edges all round. Pin the bottom to the other side of the border, leaving about half the circumference unpinned. Machine 15 mm. from the edges up to the opening. Oversew (see p. 296) the seams and press them down on to the border. Press a 15 mm. seam allowance along the edges of the opening. Turn the cover right side out and fit to the foam pad. Slip-stitch (see p. 297) the opening.

MAKING THE COVER

Press the cover fabric and straighten one end (see p. 291). Use the paper circles to mark and cut the top and bottom covers. Mark two border

pieces across the width: 66 × 10 cm. (26 × 4 in.) for the front; 50 × 12.5 cm. (20 × 5 in.) for the back (allowing for the zip). Find the bias (p. 299) on the remaining fabric and mark and cut 4 cm. (1½ in.) bias strips. Cut and make the piping (see p. 299). Cut the piping in half. Cut the back border strip in half lengthways.

Place one half face up and lay the zip face down on it. Centre the zip on the length of the fabric. Match the raw edge of the fabric with the edge of the tape. Pin, then tack, close to the edge. Pin and tack the zip to the other half of the back border in the same way. Use a zipper foot and machine as close to the zip teeth as possible on both sides, up to the end of the teeth. Leave the zip tails free.

Turn the border right side up and take a small pleat in the fabric along one side of the zip, so that the fold lines up with the centre of the teeth. Press the pleat and stitch as close as possible to the teeth along the length of the zip. Repeat on the other side of the zip. Oversew the seams (see p. 296).

Machine the back and front border pieces together, end to end, allowing 15 mm. seams. Top-stitch 2 mm. (1/16 in.) from each seam on the front border (see p. 299). Press the seams, oversew the edges and open the zip.

Tack the top and bottom cover pieces to paper-pattern circles and pipe round both circles. Cut the piping fabric almost to the cord to ease round the circle where necessary. Join the piping (see p. 299).

Tear the paper off the top circle and pin it to the border, right sides facing. Machine as close to the piping stitches as possible. Repeat for the bottom circle. Oversew the raw edges of the seams. Press the piping tail down on to the border on either side. Turn the cover right side out.

EXTRA SEAT   A plain wooden chest is transformed into a useful occasional seat when fitted with a tailored box cushion.

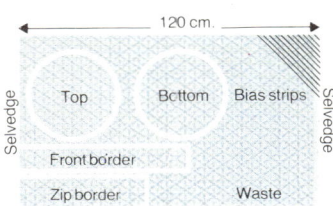

Cover cutting guide for a circular cushion.

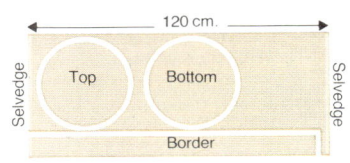

Lining cutting guide for a circular cushion.

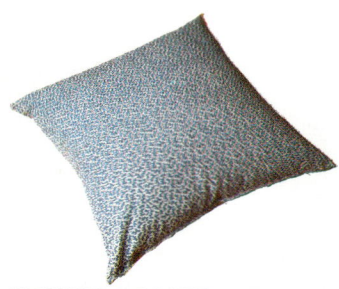

• MAKING A COVER FOR A PLAIN FLOOR CUSHION

A rectangular floor cushion is the simplest to cover, and this method can be used to cover any other rectangular cushion. Make the cover a tight fit for a polyester-filled pad, and 2.5 cm. (1 in.) smaller if the pad is filled with feathers or foam chips. This gives a firm outline to the finished cushion.

MATERIALS AND EQUIPMENT

Use the pattern guide below. For a finished cushion of say 87 × 87 cm. (34 × 34 in.) you need: 190 cm. (75 in.) of 120 cm. (48 in.) fabric; 1 reel matching thread; 80 cm. (32 in.) of 12.5 mm. (½ in.) Velcro; sewing

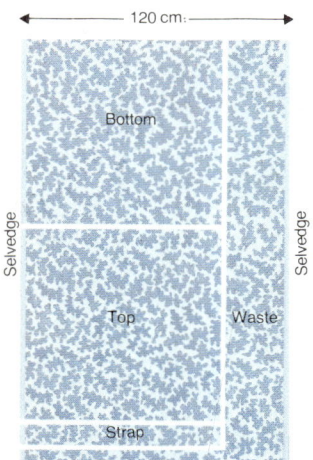

Cutting guide for a rectangular cushion.

machine; tape measure; tailor's chalk; fabric shears; set square; rule; iron.

METHOD

Press the fabric and straighten one end (see p. 291). Mark and cut two pieces 90 cm. (35 in.) square. From the remaining fabric, cut a piece 90 × 5 cm. (35 × 2 in.) for the strap.

Pin the strap, wrong side up, on the wrong side of the bottom cover, with one edge 5 mm. (¼ in.) from one edge of the cover. Machine together

15 mm. (½ in.) in from the edge of the cover [1] and press.

Turn up a 10 mm. (⅜ in.) hem on the other side of the strap and press [2]. Fold the hem edge of the strap up and over the edge of the cover so that the strap just covers the first line of stitches on the right side of the cover [3]. Pin and machine close to the hem edge of the strap, then press.

Pin one side of the Velcro, fuzzy side up, to the centre of the strap on the right side of the cover [4]. Machine round all sides of the Velcro.

MAKING A FLOOR CUSHION COVER

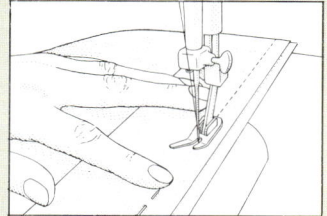

1. Sew the strap, wrong side up, to the wrong side of the bottom cover.

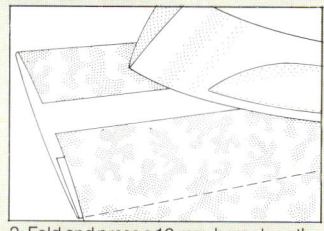

2. Fold and press a 10 mm. hem along the unsewn edge of the strap.

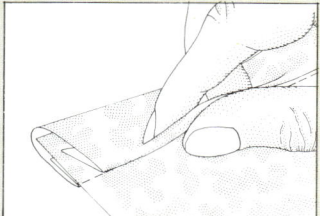

3. Bring the hemmed edge of the strap over the edge of the cover.

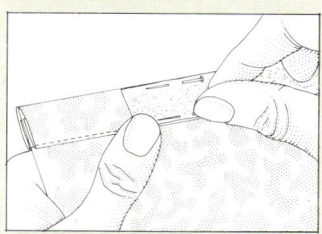

4. Pin one strip of Velcro, fuzzy side up, to the strap on right side of cover.

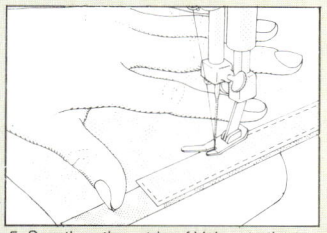

5. Sew the other strip of Velcro to the top cover hem, covering the edge of the hem.

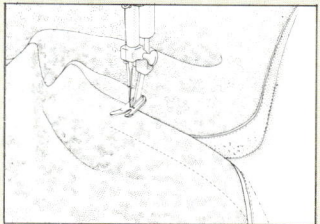

6. Machine across the ends of the Velcro strips to secure them.

Turn down a 15 mm. hem on the top cover. Pin the second piece of Velcro to the hem, covering the raw edge and machine as before [5].

Pin the covers, right sides facing, close to the edges on the three plain sides, then machine 15 mm. (½ in.) in from the edges. On the fourth side, pin the two edges together from each corner only to the Velcro and machine 15 mm. from the edge. Turn cover right side out, close the ends of the Velcro and machine across each end [6]. Oversew seams (see p. 296).

• MAKING A BOLSTER CUSHION AND COVER

The cushion pad is made from 25 mm. (1 in.) thick foam wrapped round foam chips and covered with cotton sateen. The method can be used for any size of bolster.

MATERIALS AND EQUIPMENT

50 × 95 cm. (20 × 37½ in.) of 25 mm. (1 in.) foam; 1 lb. foam chips; contact adhesive; 90 cm. (36 in.) of 120 cm. (48 in.) cotton sateen; 1 reel mercerised cotton; sheet of stiff paper; 90 cm. of 120 cm. cover fabric; 1 reel

matching thread; 1.8 m. (63 in.) of No. 2 piping cord; 43 cm. (17 in.) popper tape; two 2.5 cm. (1 in.) curtain rings; cottonwool; compasses; tape measure; soft pencil; tailor's chalk; pins; scissors; fabric shears; sharp knife; set-square and rule; piping or zipper foot for the machine; Bulldog clips; iron; adhesive tape; needle.

MAKING THE FOAM PAD

Measure, mark and cut (p. 144) a rectangle 50 × 74 cm. (20 × 29 in.) from the foam. Cut a paper circle, diameter 20 cm. (8 in.), and use as a guide to cut two discs from the remaining foam [A1].

Spread adhesive on the edge of each short end of the foam rectangle and press together to form a tube. Hold the ends in place with Bulldog clips until the adhesive dries [A2]. Spread adhesive around the rim of one disc and inside one end of the tube to a depth of 2.5 cm. (1 in.). Fit the disc into the tube, flush with the end. Press together and leave to dry.

Fill the tube with foam chips, leaving 2.5 cm. at the top for the other disc. Glue and fit it [A3]. The finished tube should be 50 cm. long with a 25 cm. (10 in.) diameter and a 78.5 cm. (31 in.) circumference.

Press the lining fabric and straighten one end (see p. 291). Mark a rectangle with one side 3 cm. (1 in.) longer than the tube – 53 cm. (21 in.) – and the other 3 cm. longer than the

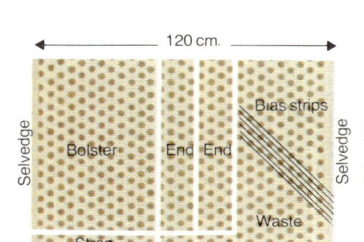

Cutting guide for bolster cover.

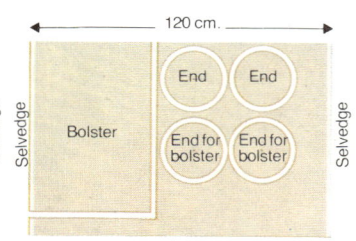

Cutting guide for bolster lining.

circumference – 81.5 cm. (32 in.). Cut a paper circle, diameter 28 cm. (11 in.). Use this to mark four pieces of lining fabric.

Fold the rectangle, short edges together, right side in. Machine 15 mm. from the edge [B1]. Press the seam.

Pin one circle, right side inwards to one end of the fabric tube. Machine 15 mm. from the edge all round [B2]. Turn the lining right side out and insert the foam pad. Slip-stitch (p. 297) the second circle, right side outwards, to the open end [B3].

MAKING THE COVER

Mark a rectangle 53 × 81.5 cm. (21 × 32 in.) on the wrong side of the cover fabric. This allows 15 mm. seams.

For the ends of the cushion, cut two rectangles 81.5 × 14 cm. (32 × 5½ in.). These will be gathered to form the circles.

Cut a smaller rectangle 53 × 7.5 cm. (21 × 3 in.) to make a strap for one side of the popper tape.

Find the bias (p. 299) on the remaining fabric. Mark and cut 4 cm. (1½ in.) wide piping strips. Make up

the piping (see p. 299) and cut into two equal lengths. From the remaining fabric, cut two circles about 15 mm. larger than the curtain rings.

Use a running stitch to machine along one long side of each cushion end piece, 5 mm. (¼ in.) from the strip edge. Place the ends of the strip together, right sides facing, and machine 15 mm. from the edge [B4]. Press the seam flat. Draw up the gathers tightly to make a gathered circle. Secure with small hand stitches. Cover each circle, wrong

side up, with a lining circle and pin round the edge. Tack about 10 mm. (⅜ in.) in from the edge all round. Lay the large rectangle of fabric wrong side up. Attach the strap, right side up, along one of the 53 cm. sides, following the method used on the floor cushion cover.

Centre the stud side of the popper tape on the right side of the strap. Turn under the raw ends and pin. Stitch close to tape edge [B5].

Turn the cover right side up, fold down a 15 mm. hem on the raw edge

opposite the strap. Pin the presser side of the popper tape to the hem, matching it carefully with the stud side and covering the raw edge of the hem [B6]. Stitch round all four edges of the tape.

Position the cover, right sides facing, and match the taped ends. Pin the two edges together up to the start of the tape from both sides. Machine 15 mm. in from the edge, up to the tape. Machine across the two ends of tape – through all layers – to secure tape ends [B7].

Pin one piece of piping to each of the gathered end pieces, on the right side, matching the raw edges. Clip up to the stitch line at 4 cm. (1½ in.) intervals on the raw edge of the piping to ease round the circle [B8]. Using the piping foot, stitch as close to the cord as possible [B9]. Join the ends of the piping (see p. 299).

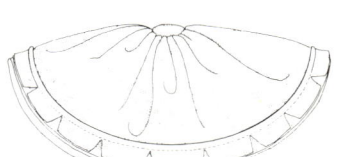

Finished bolster end.

With right sides inwards, pin the circles to the ends of the main cover piece. Machine as close as possible to the piping stitch line. Oversew all the seams. Press the piped seams down on to the circles, then turn the cover right side out.

To make the buttons, sew running stitches (see p. 296) round the edge of each small circle, by hand. Wrap a curtain ring in cottonwool and place in the centre of the circle. Pull the gathers tight to cover the ring and the cotton. Secure with small hand stitches. Slip-stitch a button to the centre of each end of the bolster, gathered side down.

MAKING A FOAM BOLSTER

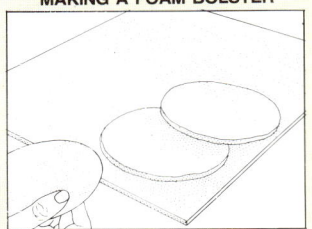

A1. Use a paper pattern, 20 cm. diameter, to cut two discs from the foam.

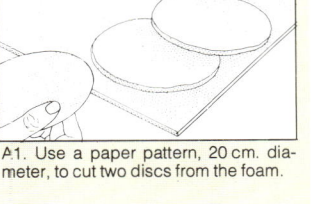

A2. Butt and glue the edges of the short sides of the foam to form a tube.

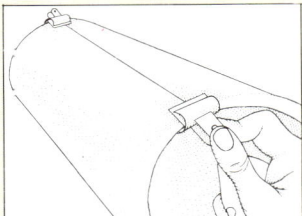

A3. Fill the tube with foam chips to within 2.5 cm. of the top. Seal with disc.

MAKING A BOLSTER LINING AND COVER

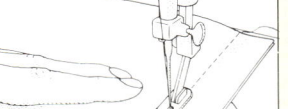

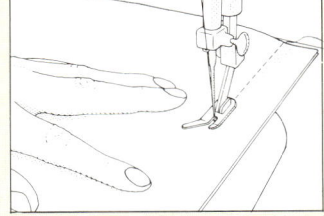

B1. Machine together the short sides of the lining rectangle, right side inside.

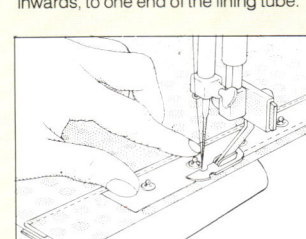

B4. Machine the short ends of the strip fabric together, right side inside.

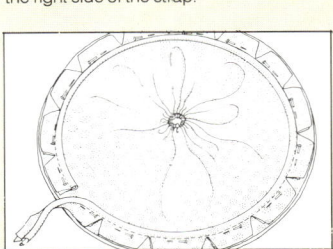

B7. Secure the tapes by machining across the ends, going through all layers.

B2. Machine one lining circle, right side inwards, to one end of the lining tube.

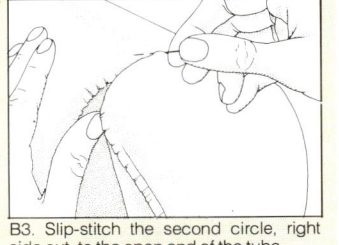

B5. Sew the stud side of the popper tape to the right side of the strap.

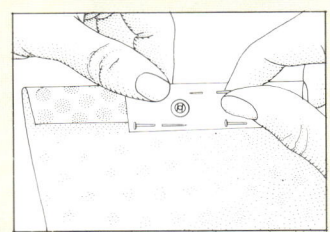

B8. Clip the raw edge of the piping every 4 cm. to ease it round the circle.

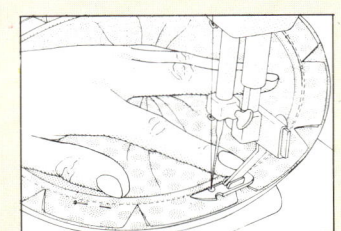

B3. Slip-stitch the second circle, right side out, to the open end of the tube.

B6. Match the presser side of the popper tape to the stud side and pin to hem.

B9. Sew the piping to the circle, keeping close to the piping stitches.

• FEATHER-FILLED SCATTER CUSHION

The made up feather cushion is 50 × 50 cm. (20 × 20 in.), but the cushion pad is made slightly larger to give a firm outline. Piped seams and a zip closure make a neat, tailored finish. Scatter cushions can of course be made with other fillings, such as foam chips or kapok.

MATERIALS AND EQUIPMENT

Allow 1 lb. pure down; 1½ lb. of a 50/50 down-and-feather mixture, or 2 lb. of pure feathers; 60 cm. (23½ in.) of 120 cm. (48 in.) feather-proof cambric; 1 reel mercerised cotton; 80 cm. (32 in.) of 120 cm. (48 in.) cover fabric; 210 cm. (84 in.) of No. 2 piping cord; a 45.5 cm. (18 in.) zip; tailor's chalk; tape measure; pins; set-square; rule; fabric shears; Bulldog clips; iron; zipper and/or piping foot for the machine.

CUSHION PAD

Press the cambric and straighten one end (see p. 291). Measure and mark 55 cm. (22 in.) down each selvedge,

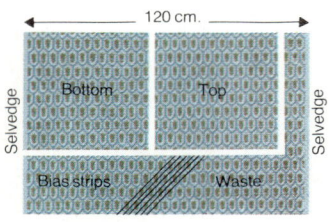

Cutting guide for scatter-cushion cover.

join the marks and cut. Measure and mark 107 cm. (43 in.) from the left-hand selvedge along the top and bottom edges. Join the marks and cut. Fold the fabric in half down the centre shiny side out.

Keep the fabric folded and raw edges matched. Using a large stitch, start from one end of the fold and machine round the three open sides 15 mm. (½ in.) from the edge. Stop 30 cm. (12 in.) from the other end of the fold [1]. Oversew (see p. 296) the seams. Turn the bag right side out and press in the seam allowance on either side of the opening.

Push the feathers into the bag, a handful at a time until full [2]. For this job, work with the feathers and bag in a dry bath with the bathroom door closed, so that the feathers do not blow about and any that fall are easy to pick up. Fasten the opening with Bulldog clips, then machine to close.

CUSHION COVER

Press and straighten one end of the fabric. From the left-hand selvedge, measure and mark two points – at 53.5 cm. (21½ in.) and 107 cm. along the straightened edge. Measure and mark three points 53.5 cm. down from the straightened edge: one on the left-hand selvedge, the others below the two previously marked points. Join the three horizontal marks and the two pairs of vertical marks. Cut along all three lines.

Find the true bias on the remaining

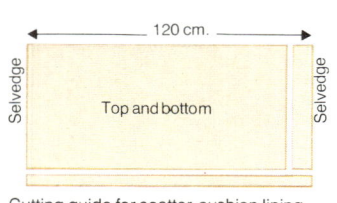

Cutting guide for scatter-cushion lining.

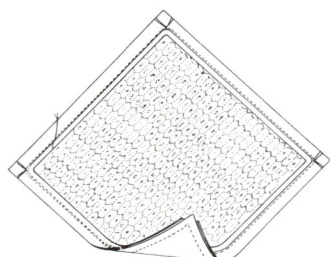

Detail of piped side of cover

fabric (see p. 291). Mark up and cut 4 cm. (1½ in.) wide bias strips and make up the piping (see p. 299).

Pin the piping on the right side of the top cover, raw edge matching the edge of the cover. Start pinning about 10 cm. (4 in.) in from a corner. Cut into the piping up to the stitch line to ease it round corners. Allow a 2.5 cm. (1 in.) overlap where the two ends of the piping meet, and trim off excess.

Use a piping or zipper foot, and machine close to the piping cord. Join the ends (see p. 299).

Place the bottom cover face up on the work surface. Lay the zip, face down, on the cover and match the edge of the zip tape and one raw edge of the cover. Pin close to the zip edge. Pin the other side of the zip tape to the right side of the piped cover, with the zip teeth as close as possible to the edge of the piping [3]. Using a zipper foot, machine close to the zip teeth on both sides. To avoid a curve in the seam, machine halfway down with the zip closed, then open the zip and continue. Leave the tails of the zip unstitched.

Fold a small pleat on the unpiped side of the cover and pin it alongside the zip so that the fold of the pleat meets the piping and therefore completely hides the teeth of the zip [4].

With the zip flat, start on the right side of the unpiped border at one end and stitch across the end of the zip tape.

Lift the foot, leave the needle down and pivot the fabric (see p. 289). Then sew along the pleat as close to the teeth as possible [5]. Pivot again and stitch over the other end of the tape.

Open the zip for 5 cm. (2 in.) and place the covers right sides facing, with the piped side uppermost. Match the sides all the way round and pin. Using the piping foot, start at one end of the zip and machine all the way round as close as possible to the piping stitches. Hold the piped side taut as you work to compensate for the tightening of the first stitches [6].

Trim off the zip tails to line up with the seams, then oversew the seams to prevent fraying. Turn the cover right side out and press.

MAKING THE CUSHION AND COVER

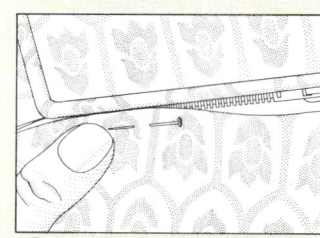

1. Using a large stitch, machine from one end of the fold round the open sides to within 30 cm. of the other end of the fold.

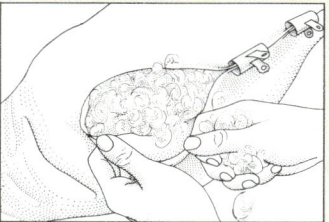

2. Push the feathers into the bag a handful at a time, then close the opening with Bulldog clips and machine.

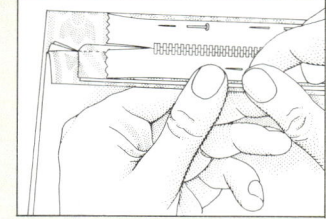

3. Pin the zip to the right side of the piped cover with the teeth as close as possible to the edge of the piping.

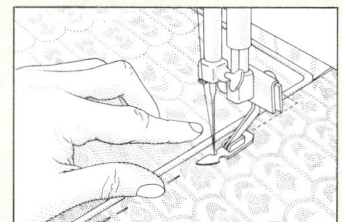

4. Pin a small pleat on the unpiped side of the cover, so that the fold meets the piping and hides the zip teeth.

5. Machine across the ends of the zip and along the unpiped side, keeping as close as possible to the teeth.

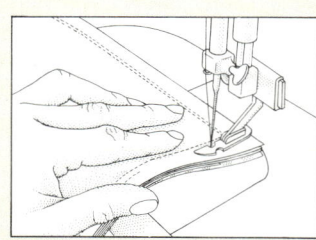

6. Machine the top and bottom covers together, keeping as close as possible to the piping stitches.

COLOURFUL, COMFORTABLE CUSHIONS *Home-made cushions add comfort to furniture and colour to a room. The seat and back of this cane sofa are padded with large deep cushions. Scatter cushions in a variety of sizes and patterns help give the setting its dramatic effect. The large floor cushion, besides creating a new focus of attention in the room, makes a more than ordinarily comfortable seat. Floor cushions, like these, are not only easy to make; they are also versatile and inexpensive substitutes for conventional armchairs and sofas.*

BEDS AND BEDDING

A good bed is an investment in comfort and health – we spend one-third of our lives there. It should hold the body in any sleeping position, taking over as the muscles relax. A very soft bed turns natural body movements into hard work for the muscles. A very hard one leaves the body unsupported between shoulder and hip, causing aches and pains. Heavily built people, however, need a firm bed, as do back sufferers and invalids. Elderly people also do better with a firm bed, while children must have a firm, level mattress to support their growing spines. A bed may last from 10 to 15 years.

• BUYING A BED

The first sign that a bed needs replacing is a tired and aching body in the morning. Examine the mattress for lumps and hollows caused by broken or sagging springs. One which has moulded itself to the body may be comfortable for going to sleep, but will not give proper support during the night. Check the base for worn-out springs, tears in the covering, and damaged legs or castors.

Buy a complete bed, as base and mattress are designed to go together: a foam mattress should not be used on a base intended for a spring mat-tress, nor the other way round, as the base will not provide the correct support for the body.

There are four basic bed sizes: small single; standard single; small double; and standard double. Beds and bedding are now made in metric measurements (see p. 155). Beds are available outside these basic sizes and shapes, but they are more expensive.

For comfort, choose a bed that is at least 6 in. longer than your height. The bed should be wide enough to ac-commodate the many dozens of com-plete changes of body position during the night. To make sure that the width of a single bed is right, lie down on the mattress and link your hands behind your head. If your elbows protrude over the side, the bed is too narrow. A narrow bed is suitable for only occa-sional use.

TYPES OF MATTRESS

The two most popular kinds of mat-tress are interior sprung and foam. A third kind, the hair mattress, is now rare and costly.

Spring mattresses come in three types. Open springs have hourglass-shaped wire coils sandwiched be-tween wire frames. Pocketed springs are cylindrical, and each is enclosed in a fabric or foam pocket. Continuous springing is made from wire which is linked and intertwined in a mesh-like pattern.

Open-coil mattresses and continuous-spring mattresses are ideal for double beds, because they compress to the shape of the body. Pocketed mattresses are also excel-lent because each spring works inde-pendently and body pressures do not affect adjacent springs.

The BSI Kitemark label guarantees that a mattress has passed a stringent test for durability.

A well-made foam mattress has layers of latex or polyether foam – the firmest at the bottom and the softest at the top. Cheaper versions have a single-density foam slab. There is no BSI Kitemark for foam mattresses.

The rarer hair mattresses are made of horsehair and white fleece, and last a lifetime.

BED BASES

The most expensive type of base is a rigid platform with springing taken to the edge (sprung edge). Firm-edge bases have springs set within a solid frame, allowing storage or easy cleaning beneath. The so-called orthopaedic base is a foam-covered platform without springs for those who prefer a firm bed – or must have one because of back trouble.

TESTING BEDS

Choose and test your bed at a shop or store which has a wide range. See that the base gives a firm, level sur-face for the mattress. Ask for a pillow and lie on the bed in various sleeping positions, noting whether the mat-tress supports the body at pressure points.

A double bed should be tested by both people concerned – at the same time – to see that the mattress gives individual support. For couples whose weights differ considerably there are zip-together mattresses, each of which gives a different degree of support. These can be joined together to make a double bed. Alternatively, use a double-size pock-

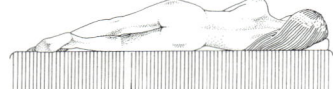

OVER-FIRM BED   On a hard bed the sleeper cannot relax because the body is not satisfactorily cushioned.

OVER-SOFT BED   A sagging sleeping surface may be deceptively comfort-able but fails to support the body.

CORRECT SUPPORT   A good bed cra-dles the body, while its underlying firmness maintains correct posture.

FOUR BASIC TYPES OF MATTRESS

Linked coils of continuous springs are held between two metal frames.

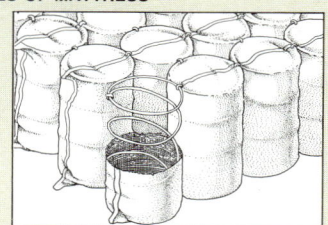

Pocketed springs, each tucked into a separate calico pocket.

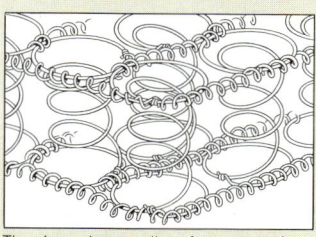

The hourglass coils of open springs are held together by a wire frame.

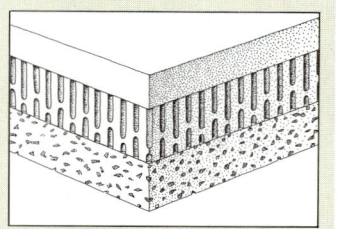

Foam mattresses, made of rubber or plastic, offer varying degrees of firmness.

eted mattress with its independent springing.

Examine the covering: a closely woven material is best for durability. If it is an interior-sprung mattress look at the BSI Kitemark to find the type and quantity of the springs.

If it is a foam mattress, ask whether it is the more durable latex, or the cheaper and firmer polyether foam, and whether it is single or multi-layer.

• TYPES OF BED

Next to comfort and durability, the main consideration in choosing a bed is the space it will occupy. Divans, bed-settees, fold-up beds, stacked beds and bunks are all practical where space is limited.

Divans Single or double divans consist of a base and mattress. There are also twin divans – single units that can be put together to form a double.

Some divans have storage drawers built into the base; others have a hinged top to give access to storage space in the bed frame.

Bed-settees These convert from a settee and are useful for putting up the occasional guest. They can also be used as a regular bed, but as the requirements for sitting and sleeping are quite different this is not generally advisable.

Some bed-settees incorporate a mattress as they unfold; or use the back and seat as a sleeping surface. Others convert by removing the back cushions, or by re-arranging the unit seating.

If a bed-settee must be used regularly – for example, in a bed-sitting room – it is best to buy the type that disguises its dual function but converts quickly. Choose one, for example, that folds away with bedclothes in

position. A bed-settee that is wide enough to sleep on – 90 cm. (3 ft) – will need a movable back-rest for comfortable sitting.

Fold-up beds The cheapest folding bed has a light steel frame and can be folded and pushed away on castors – on some types the head forms a table top when folded.

Dearer versions fold or pivot into a wall recess and can be hidden behind curtains or cupboard doors.

Stacked beds Most of these can be stacked with the bedding in place, ready for sleeping. One type has folding legs and slides under the main bed; others are designed to stack one on top of the other.

Bunk beds Bunks are useful where children have to sleep in small rooms. Bunk beds usually split into two separate single beds.

Children under three should not sleep in bunk beds, and the top bunk should not be used by under-fives who might fall off by accident. Many bunks are only 75 cm. (2 ft 6 in.) wide, but it is better to buy the 90 cm. (3 ft) size – this will still be wide enough when the children grow bigger.

Bunks for young children should have a safety rail running the length of the bed; the space between the top of the mattress and the rail should not be sufficient to allow a child's head to slip through. A strong ladder, firmly attached, is needed to reach the top bunk.

For older children there should be enough headroom above the bottom bunk to allow them to sit up.

• CARING FOR THE BED

The polythene wrapper must be removed, or the new mattress will not be able to 'breathe'. Covers of plain or quilted cotton can be bought. They are held in place by elastic, are easy to remove and wash, and will help to

preserve the mattress. Lay down a rubber sheet for bed-wetting children or incontinent adults.

Turn spring mattresses over weekly for the first six weeks, and every three months after that time. Reverse the mattress from head to foot.

Never roll or bend a spring mattress. The springs will 'set' and the mattress will not lie flat afterwards. Foam mattresses do not need turning, though a single-layer one can be turned if desired.

Sit on the edge of the bed as little as possible, as the concentrated weight can damage the springs. For the same reason, do not allow children to bounce on the bed.

Clean mattress and base with a soft brush every month; do not use a vacuum cleaner as this may pull the upholstery out of shape. At the same time, check for loose or missing buttons; tears, distorted springs and any other damage. Periodically check screws and nuts on legs or castors and tighten if necessary.

Throw back the covers each morning and allow at least 20 minutes for the bed to dry out the moisture absorbed from the body during the night. The body loses about 900 ml. (1½ pints) of fluid every night.

BEDMAKING

Bedmaking is easier if the bed has smooth-running castors, so that it can be pulled away from a wall or corner. If space allows, the bed can be moved to the centre of the room, giving all-round access.

If the bed cannot be moved easily, try to position it so that there is at least 70 cm. (2 ft 4 in.) of space on each side.

A mattress height of about 50 cm. (20 in.) from the floor is the most comfortable for bedmaking, and the task can be further eased by using a con-

tinental quilt – or duvet. A fitted bottom sheet, which can be bought separately, also reduces the work involved in bedmaking, and will stay in place during the night.

DEALING WITH STAINS

Act quickly to prevent stains from soaking into the mattress. Mop up the stain and stand the mattress on edge.

If the stain is non-greasy, sponge with cold water. In the case of a grease stain, use an absorbent, such as talcum powder. Remove the stain by following the correct treatment (see p. 326).

• SHEETS

These are sold in both metric and imperial measurements (see chart, p. 155). It is possible to buy sheets to fit all basic bed sizes. Always buy the size of sheets shown in the chart to give sufficient allowance for tucking-in and shrinkage.

If you are making your own sheets, fitted or otherwise, follow the diagram and instructions on p. 155 for taking the necessary measurements.

Materials vary from a cheap coarse weave to the finer and dearer Egyptian cotton percale. Look for a regular weave and watch for dressing – a powder that is added to improve the appearance, and which quickly washes out. Test by rubbing the material between your fingers to see if a powder comes away.

Flannelette has a raised surface, and is soft and warm. However, it shows the dirt and needs to be washed often.

Nylon and Terylene are hardwearing, easy to wash and dry rapidly. But they do not absorb body moisture and need frequent washing. A mixture of cotton and polyester feels like cotton, but wears well and needs no ironing.

STORAGE UNDER BEDS A drawer under a built-in base for a mattress can be used for storing sheets, blankets or duvets.

• BLANKETS

These are available for all standard beds (see chart, p. 155).

Wool blankets are soft, warm and wear well, but check on the label that they are mothproof and shrink-resistant. It is best to dry-clean wool blankets. Acrylic blankets are not as warm as wool and shrink less; they dry more quickly and are mothproof. Rayon is cheaper but not as warm as wool or acrylic. A wool-and-rayon mix gives warmth and good wear.

Lightweight cellular blankets are made up of a series of pockets or cells which hold warm air. They provide good insulation if used under an ordinary blanket. They should be dry-cleaned, rather than washed.

Cotton blankets give less warmth, but are easy to wash and are ideal for children's cots.

ELECTRIC BLANKETS

There are three types of electric blanket: the overblanket; the pre-heat underblanket; and the low-voltage underblanket.

The all-night overblanket is used above the top sheet and should have a light covering above it to prevent loss of warmth. A special device prevents it from overheating, and it can safely be left on all night.

A thermostat adjusts to keep the warmth constant, whatever the temperature of the room.

A pre-heat underblanket is laid between the mattress and the bottom sheet. It should be tied to the bed with tapes or tucked in with flaps attached to the border. An underblanket is used to pre-heat the bed and must be switched off before going to bed.

An all-night low-voltage underblanket works from the mains, but has a transformer which reduces the risk of a shock even if the blanket becomes wet. This makes it suitable for elderly or infirm people and invalids.

Always follow the manufacturer's instructions on use, cleaning and servicing. Blankets made before 1971 should be inspected and overhauled. Do not use an underblanket as an overblanket, or the other way round. Air a damp electric blanket over a clothes-horse. But if a blanket gets soaked, send it back to the maker to be cleaned and dried. Do not attempt to dry it by switching it on.

Electric blankets can be bought for single or double beds. Many doubles have separate controls, so that one side can be switched on or off independently of the other.

Underblankets need not cover the whole mattress. Suitable sizes range from about 150 × 75 cm. (60 × 30 in.) for a single bed, to 150 × 120 cm. (60 × 48 in.) for a small double. Overblankets need to be about 50 cm. (20 in.) longer, and wide enough to overhang the bed.

• DUVETS AND EIDERDOWNS

Continental quilts, or duvets, give warmth without weight, or the restricting 'tucked-in' feeling of ordinary bedclothes. An undersheet, a duvet with its cover, and a pillow, are all that are needed on the bed.

Ordinary bedclothes weigh about 15 lb. A duvet weighs about $3\frac{1}{2}$ lb. and is just as warm.

Duvets are made for all sizes and types of bed, but allow an overhang of 23 cm. (9 in.) on either side. Look for the BSI Kitemark when buying.

A duvet is made of light but bulky material sewn between two layers of cloth. Feather or down fillings are the warmest. Synthetic fibres may be less warm, but are ideal for people allergic to natural fillings. They are also the only type of filling suitable for children aged less than 18 months.

When cleaning and refilling duvets, follow the manufacturer's instructions. Duvet covers can be bought or made from cotton/polyester sheeting. Make the cover 5-10 cm. (2-4 in.) bigger than the duvet to give the duvet room to expand.

If the feathers of an old eiderdown are still in good condition, remake the eiderdown (see p. 156). Or use the feathers as part of the filling to make a duvet (p. 158).

• PILLOWS

When buying a pillow, always look for the BSI Kitemark and test several pillows before you make your choice. A good way to test a pillow is to press down on it. It should spring back. If it is wrapped in polythene, ask the shopkeeper to remove it – you cannot judge the feel through the plastic.

The best and most expensive pillows are filled with down. Others have a mixture of down and feathers, and some are filled with man-made fibres. Foam pillows – latex or polyether – are suitable for people allergic to dust and feathers. They have a different feel – soft and spongy – from down and feather pillows, and are available with various degrees of firmness.

The life of a pillow varies according to the filling. A good-quality down pillow used constantly will last up to ten years, a feather pillow less. Foam pillows last up to ten years.

• SLEEPING BAGS

These can be used as bedding on bed-settees and fold-up beds. The standard size for a single sleeping bag is 185 × 68 cm. (6 ft × 2 ft 4 in.). Some can be zipped together to form a double bag or quilt. If a child's size is unavailable, buy an adult bag and tuck in the extra length.

Most sleeping bags are made of cotton or nylon, with a filling of man-made fibre, such as Terylene. To keep a sleeping bag clean, a sheet bag can be fitted inside it.

MATCHING BED LINEN Boldly patterned sheets and pillowcases are attractive enough to be left uncovered in daytime.

• MAKING YOUR OWN BEDDING

Many items of bedding can be made easily and economically at home. The range of materials available is wide, and many manufacturers supply do-it-yourself kits.

Before buying materials, always measure the bed. It is not enough to know whether it is a single or a double bed, as sizes vary within these categories (see table below). Take into account the thickness of the mattress, as this affects any allowance needed for tucking in.

For bedspreads, valances and divan covers, measure also the height of the bed from the floor.

Sizes of bedding given in the table are generally what the shopkeepers would recommend, but your particular preferences may differ. Some people, for instance, like a more generous overhang of sheets and blankets. Never underestimate: few mistakes are more likely to guarantee restless nights than bedding that is too small.

Shrinkage can be an important factor with sheets. It is advisable to buy shrink-proof or pre-shrunk material: and even with these materials, the British Standards Institution recommends making an allowance of 5% to 7%.

Pounds can be saved by making your own duvet, either by following the instructions on p. 158, or by buying a kit, or by using an old eiderdown for the filling. The down from a set of bedding that has been in the family for a generation or more could be worth £50.

Down will last for many years, but it is very expensive. Terylene P3 is one of the best synthetic substitutes, and can be bought in varying weights in the form of a fibre pad cut to the size you require. A ready-made single-bed duvet usually weighs about 3½ lb., but if you are making one to use in a centrally heated bedroom, you can reduce the weight of the filling.

A duvet can never be too big, but it *can* be too small. Make it at least 45 cm. (18 in.) wider than the bed. A good duvet should last a lifetime, so if you make one for a child's bed, look ahead and measure with an adult bed in mind.

MEASURING YOUR BED

When measuring up for materials for home-made bedding, use the diagram at the foot of column 5 for the basic bed measurements. Add 5 cm. (2 in.) for any seam allowances, and 12.5 cm. (5 in.) to the length and width for hemming. Add an extra allowance for shrinkage of washable materials. Add a further allowance for matching patterned materials. Use the table on this page as a guide to the finished article only, not the fabric required to make it.

SHEETS

Length: Length of the mattress (A to J), plus twice the depth (F to G), plus 70-80 cm. (28-32 in.) for fold-over and tuck-in. Width: Width of mattress (E to F), plus twice the depth (F to G), plus 70-80 cm. (28-32 in.) for tuck-in.

FITTED SHEETS

Length: Length of the mattress (A to J), plus twice the depth (F to G). Width: Width of the mattress (E to F) plus twice the depth (F to G).

BEDSPREAD

With the bed made, measure from the floor at the foot of the bed, over the pillows to the head of the bed (D to C), plus 30 cm. (12 in.) tuck-under, if wanted. The width of the centre panel is the width of the fabric. The width of the side panels is the height of the bed from the floor to the centre panel plus seam and hem allowances. See also pp. 162-3.

FITTED DIVAN COVER

If the divan is left made up during the day, measure over the bedding. Size of the top panel equals the size of the mattress (A to J and E to F). Depth of the border equals depth of the mattress (F to G). Depth of the valance is from the bottom of the mattress to the floor (G to H, plus feet or castors), plus 4 cm. (1½ in.). See also p. 160.

EIDERDOWN

Length: Front edge of the pillows to the foot of the bed (A to B), plus 8 cm. (3 in.). Width: same as the mattress (E to F) plus 8-16 cm. (3-6 in.). For re-making an eiderdown, see p. 156.

DUVET

Size equals size of the mattress (A to J and E to F) plus 23 cm. (9 in.) in width at each side. Make a cover about 5-10 cm. (2-4 in.) longer and wider. See instructions, p. 158.

BEDDING SIZES

This table gives the approximate minimum sizes of ready-made bedding for standard-size mattresses. Following the convention in the trade, width is given first. Exact sizes vary according to the manufacturers, materials and brand names. Metric and imperial equivalents are approximate: any apparent inconsistencies are due to different standards of conversion followed in the trade. Sizes of sheets and blankets are based on a mattress thickness of about 18-20 cm. (7-8 in.). Allowance is made for tuck-in and shrinkage. Sizes of bedspreads and fitted divan covers should be adjusted to height from the floor of the made-up bed.

MATTRESS SIZES	SMALL SINGLE 90 × 190 cm. 3 ft × 6 ft 3 in.	STANDARD SINGLE 100 × 200 cm. 3 ft 3 in. × 6 ft 6 in.	SMALL DOUBLE 135 × 190 cm. 4 ft 6 in. × 6 ft 3 in.	STANDARD DOUBLE 150 × 200 cm. 5 ft × 6 ft 6 in.	QUEEN SIZE 165 × 200 cm. 5 ft 6 in. × 6 ft 6 in.	KING SIZE 180 × 200 cm. 6 ft × 6 ft 6 in.	COT 70 × 140 cm. 2 ft 4 in. × 4 ft 8 in.
Sheet sizes	175 × 250 cm. 70 × 100 in.	203 × 295 cm. 80 × 117 in.	225 × 270 cm. 90 × 108 in.	270 × 295 cm. 108 × 117 in.	270 × 295 cm. 108 × 117 in.	295 × 315 cm. 117 × 126 in.	
Fitted sheet sizes	Supplied in sizes corresponding to the mattress sizes, with drop allowed for						
Pillowcase size	Supplied to fit standard-size pillows, suitable for all sizes of bed						
Blanket sizes	180 × 250 cm. 70 × 100 in.	203 × 250 cm. 80 × 100 in.	230 × 250 cm. 90 × 100 in.	250 × 295 cm. 100 × 118 in.	250 × 295 cm. 100 × 118 in.	270 × 295 cm. 108 × 118 in.	75 × 100 cm. 30 × 40 in.
Eiderdown sizes	100 × 170 cm. 39 × 68 in.	115 × 170 cm. 45 × 68 in.	144 × 170 cm. 57 × 68 in.	158 × 180 cm. 63 × 70 in.	180 × 180 cm. 70 × 72 in.	190 × 180 cm. 75 × 72 in.	
Bedspread sizes	198 × 260 cm. 78 × 104 in.	213 × 260 cm. 84 × 104 in.	245 × 260 cm. 98 × 104 in.	260 × 260 cm. 104 × 104 in.	275 × 260 cm. 110 × 104 in.	290 × 260 cm. 116 × 104 in.	
Duvet sizes	135 × 190 cm. 53 × 75 in.	144 × 203 cm. 57 × 80 in.	180 × 190 cm. 70 × 75 in.	198 × 203 cm. 78 × 80 in.	213 × 203 cm. 84 × 80 in.	230 × 203 cm. 90 × 80 in.	80 × 100 cm. 31 × 39 in.
Duvet cover sizes	Supplied in sizes corresponding to standard sizes of duvet						
Fitted divan cover sizes	Supplied in sizes corresponding to mattress sizes, usually with drop of about 50 cm. (20 in.) allowed for the border						

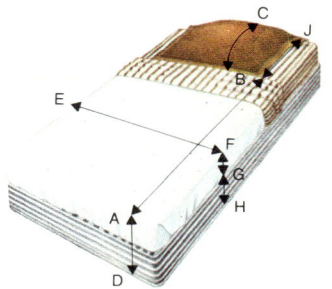

Key dimensions of a bed

• MAKING SHEETS AND PILLOWCASES

These instructions are for all sizes of sheets, but the amount of sheeting required depends on the size and depth of the mattress. For how to take the measurements, see p. 155.

MATERIALS AND EQUIPMENT

Sheeting; fabric shears; ruler; tailor's chalk; sewing machine; zigzag foot; matching thread; Sharps needle; one 61 cm. (20 in.) length of 6 mm. (¼ in.) wide elastic; steel pins; set-square.

MAKING SHEETS

To make a plain top sheet, lay the sheeting flat. Square the top and bottom (see p. 291). Sew a 2.5 cm. (1 in.) double hem at the top and a 5 cm. (2 in.) single hem at the bottom.

To make a fitted sheet, lay the sheeting on the floor. Square the top and bottom. Chalk-mark the length and width of the mattress, leaving an equal margin all round. At each corner, cut cut a square of fabric about 3 cm. (1 in.) less each way than the square formed by the intersection of the length and width marks. Snip from the inside corner of the square to the intersection of the chalk lines.

At each corner, pin together the wrong sides of edges A to B (see cutting guide). Sew together 15 mm. (½ in.) from the edges. Trim 5 mm. (¼ in.) from the seam and turn the fabric right sides together. Sew together 15 mm. in from the seam.

Fold and sew a 15 mm. double hem round the sheet, leaving 7.5 cm. (3 in.) unsewn on each side of each seam at the corners of the sheet.

Cut four 13 cm. (5 in.) lengths of elastic. Stitch one end of a length to the beginning of a corner opening. Lay the elastic inside the unsewn hem and stitch the other end where the open hem ends. Sew the hem closed. Repeat at each corner.

TWO PLAIN PILLOWCASES

Lay the sheeting flat. Square the ends (see p. 291). To make two pillowcases, cut out two pieces 76 × 51 cm. (30 × 20 in.) and two 91.5 × 51 cm. (36 × 20 in.).

Sew a 15 mm. (½ in.) double hem along one 51 cm. (20 in.) width of each piece. Lay one small piece on top of a large piece, right sides together, aligning the raw ends. Tack together round the aligned edges.

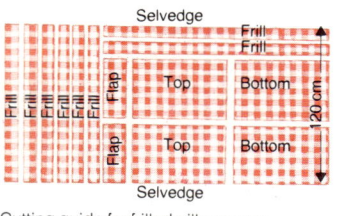

Sewing guide for plain pillowcases.

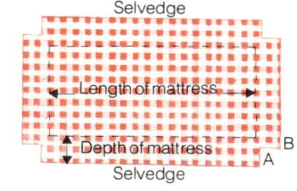

Cutting guide for a fitted sheet.

Fold the overlap of the long piece over the short piece and pin in place.

Machine the pieces together 15 mm. from the edges, leaving the folded end unsewn. Neaten the raw edges with zigzag stitches. Turn right sides out. Repeat to make a second pillowcase.

TWO FRILLED PILLOWCASES

Buy 2.5 m. (8 ft 4 in.) of 120 cm. (48 in.) wide sheeting material. Cut four pieces 76 × 51 cm. (30 × 20 in.) and two 51 × 15 cm. (20 × 6 in.). Cut the frill pieces 9 cm. (3½ in.) wide.

Sew one long and three short frill pieces together (see cutting guide) to form a circle. Press the seams flat.

Sew a 15 mm. (½ in.) double hem along one edge of the circle. Machine short sections of gathering stitches along the raw edge. Pull the gathers until the frill measures 2.5 m.

Lay the frill round one of the large pieces, right sides together, so that the outside edge of the frill is facing inwards. Align the gather-stitched edge of the frill with the edge of the fabric. Pin and tack in place, then remove pins and machine together 15 mm. from the edge. Remove the tacks.

Sew a 2.5 cm. (1 in.) hem along one width of a second large piece. Pin this piece over the first large piece, right sides together, with the frill flat between them, so that the hem of the second piece lies about 2.5 cm. below the edge of the frill.

Sew a 15 mm. hem along one of the long sides of one of the flap pieces.

Align the raw edge of the flap with the raw edge of the frill, so that the right side of the flap lies on the wrong side of the second large piece. Machine 15 mm. from the edges.

Turn the pillowcase right side out and press. Repeat with the remaining pieces to make a second pillowcase.

• REMAKING AN EIDERDOWN

The filling from an old eiderdown is suitable for making a new one. To add body, dry-clean the old eiderdown and add new feathers as required.

Cotton or cotton mixture is the most suitable covering material.

When buying the fabric, allow 45 cm. (18 in.) extra for piping cover. If using a patterned fabric, add twice the depth of the pattern to match the top and bottom covers. If the material has to be joined to make up the width of the eiderdown, add three times the depth of the pattern. The cutting guide below is for a single-bed eiderdown, using 90 cm. (36 in.) wide covering fabric to match the bedroom curtains, 120 cm. (48 in.) wide cambric lining, and 450 g. (1 lb.) of new feathers.

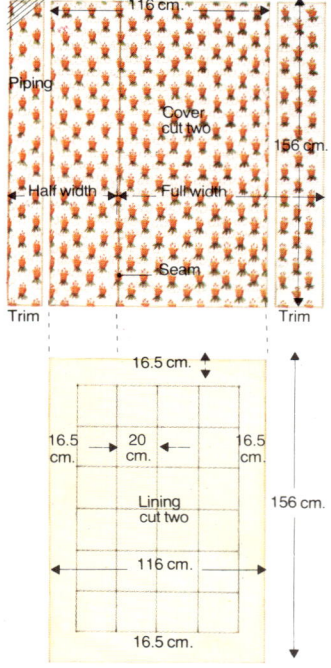

Cutting guide for a single-bed eiderdown.

CHILD'S BED Patterned fabrics make gay and practical sheets and pillowcases.

MATERIALS AND EQUIPMENT

Cover fabric; down-proof cambric; dry-cleaned feathers from an old eiderdown; 450 g. (1 lb.) of new feathers; sewing machine; piping foot; iron; steel pins; piping cord (No. 1); ruler; tailor's chalk; pencil; scissors; set-square; four large Bulldog clips.

CUTTING THE MATERIAL

Iron the covering material, square the ends (see p. 291), and cut three 156 cm. (61 in.) lengths. Fold and cut one piece in half lengthways, and lay one half alongside one full piece.

Turn back 15 mm. (½ in.) of the half width and move until the patterns on the two widths match. If this leaves less than 15 mm. of material turned back, fold back to the next pattern repeat. Press the fold. Open the fold and sew the pieces together along the crease with a locking stitch (see p. 297). Machine on the reverse side along the stitches. Press open the seams. Join the other full and half widths.

Cut and join 6.25 m. (20 ft) of piping cover and fit the cord (see p. 299).

Cut two pieces from the cambric, each 156 × 116 cm. (61 × 46 in.). Allow 15 mm. all round for seams, then pencil squares and a border on the shiny side (see cutting guide).

MATCHING COVER TO LINING

Lay one piece of cambric shiny side down and place one cover right side up on top of it. Align the seam of the cover with the second lengthways pencil line. Tack along the seam. Trim the cover to match the lining. Pin and tack together along the edges.

Turn the material over and pin, then tack along the pencilled lines [1]. Repeat with the other cover and lining.

SEWING ON THE PIPING

Leave about 5 cm. (2 in.) of piping free and pin the piping to the right side of the top cover, aligning the raw edges.

Fit a piping foot to the machine and begin sewing 7.5 cm. (3 in.) from one corner keeping close to the cord. About 15 mm. (½ in.) from the first corner, clip the piping cover almost down to the cord. Machine as far as the cut, then stop with the needle in the fabric. Lift the piping foot and turn the fabric at right-angles to the previous line of stitches. Turn each corner in the same way. Sew open any seams in the path of the stitching. Stop sewing 10 cm. (4 in.) from the start. Take the cover out and join the piping (see p. 299).

JOINING THE COVERS

Align the top and bottom covers, right sides facing. Pin together at the corners. Clip two corners to the table. Pin round the seam allowance. Tack close to the pins, leaving a 30 cm. (12 in.) opening on one short side [2].

Machine along the piping stitches, except for the opening. Pull out the tacks round the seam allowance, except those joining the unpiped cover to the cambric at the opening.

Turn the cover right side out. Pull the piping square at the corners.

STITCHING THE PANELS

Pin through both covers at the junction of every square. Pin, then tack round the border and down the channels. Remove the pins. Machine along the tacks from one corner of the border, down one length, across the closed width and up the other border length. Do not sew the border facing the opening. Sew the lengthways channels only up to the tacked border at the open side. Back-stitch to finish each line.

Remove the tacks on the lengthways channels and side borders. Leave all other tacks. Press the cover.

FILLING THE QUILT

Unpick the pockets of the old eiderdown. Cut a 30 cm. opening across a corner and add any new feathers. Oversew this opening to the opening of the new cover [3].

Distribute the feathers evenly into the new cover.

Starting at the bottom of the channels, pin along the tacked lines dividing the channels into squares [4], making sure that each square has the same amount of filling. Pump excess feathers into the border and release the old eiderdown. Oversew the cambric and unpiped cover at the opening. Lay this seam to the piped edge and slip-stitch (see p. 297) to close the opening.

If available, fit a wide foot to the machine, then with the feed teeth down, position the quilt to sew the cross channel next to the bottom border. Raise the feed teeth, then lower the foot on the fabric. If there is no way to lower the feed, remove your foot every time the quilt is repositioned.

Begin by back-stitching. Sew only a little at a time, with the seam held taut. Check that no folds form in the seam on the underside. Sew along the tacked lines. Back-stitch where the channels cross to form squares.

RE-COVERING AN EIDERDOWN

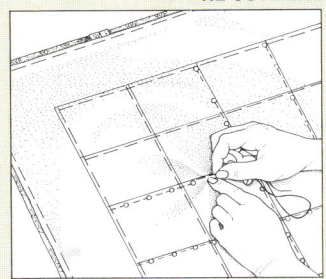
1. Pin and tack the lining to the cover along the pencilled lines of the squares.

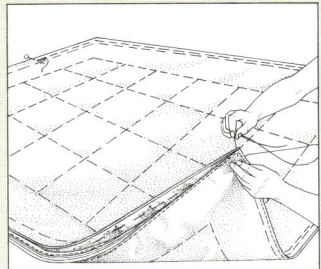
2. Tack the covers together, leaving a 30 cm. gap at one end.

3. Sew the opening in the old eiderdown to the opening in the new cover.

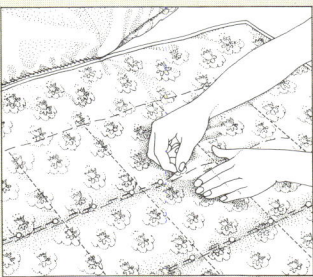
4. Close the filled squares by pinning the covers together along the tacks.

AS GOOD AS NEW An old eiderdown can be completely remade, giving not only added warmth to the bed but also a new look to the room.

• MAKING DUVETS

The weights of filling needed for various sizes of duvet are given in the chart on p. 159. Do not use feathers or down for children under 18 months.

Polyester/cotton sheeting can be used for making both duvets and covers. Use featherproof cambric for feather-and-down duvets. The cover is best made from cotton, linen or a cotton mixture fabric. For measurements, see instructions on p. 155.

FIBRE-FILLED DUVET

For a bed 100 × 200 cm. (3 ft 3 in. × 6 ft 6 in.), the finished size of the duvet is 144 × 203 cm. (57 × 80 in.).

MATERIALS AND EQUIPMENT

145 × 200 cm. Terylene P3 fibre pad; 3.2 m. (3½ yds) of 205 cm. (80 in.) polyester/cotton sheeting; 2 reels polyester thread; 7½ m. (8 yds) insertion piping tape; 1 reel coloured tacking thread; long tacking and sewing needles; fabric shears; piping foot for machine; ruler; set-square; tape measure; Bulldog clips; glass-headed pins and tailor's chalk.

Method Unroll the fibre on the work surface, keeping on the gauze with which it is covered. Hold the pad to the table with Bulldog clips and oversew the gauze covers together round all four sides of the pad [A1].

Press the sheeting and straighten one end (see p. 291). Cut off two 153 cm. (61 in.) pieces. The longer side of each rectangular piece is for the length of the duvet.

MAKING THE CHANNELS

Spread one rectangle on the table. Leaving a 15 mm. (½ in.) margin all round, mark six equal divisions across the width at both ends, and two or three times in between. Use a ruler to join up the marks into parallel lines along the length of the fabric.

Tack along these lines. Repeat with the second rectangle.

Keep the second rectangle in place. To make the piped edge allow 5 cm. (2 in.) of insertion tape to overlap the first corner. Match the edge of the tape to the raw edge of the fabric and pin near the edge. Make right-angled turns at each corner. Back at the first corner, where the ends of the piping meet, pull both ends out with the corded sides touching. Pin together [A2]. Use the piping foot to machine the piping to the fabric, stitching close to the cord. Pin the second rectangle to the first with the piping between them. Turn the cover over and machine as close as possible to the piping stitches. Leave a gap of about 1 m. (1 yd) at the centre of one end.

Arrange the fibre pad on top of the cover. Slip-stitch the gauze to the

seam of the cover all round [A3]. Turn the cover right side out. Make sure the fibre goes right into each corner. Slip-stitch the opening in the cover.

Use glass-headed pins to pin the top cover to the bottom, through the fibre. Follow the tacked lines. Make sure the top and bottom lines match. Use coloured tacking thread and a long needle to tack the cover together following the pins [A4]. Remove the pins as you go along. Keep the fibre evenly spread between the channels.

Using a long needle and polyester thread, back-stitch (see p. 296) along the channels. Check that each stitch catches both covers. Start and finish each length of thread with a treble stitch. Remove the tacking.

FEATHER-AND-DOWN DUVET

When making a feather duvet, avoid pinning and tacking wherever possible and use a large stitch when machining. This reduces the number of holes in the cambric through which the feathers can work their way out.

MATERIALS

For a duvet to fit a double bed 150 × 200 cm. (5 ft × 6 ft 6 in.): 8.2 m.

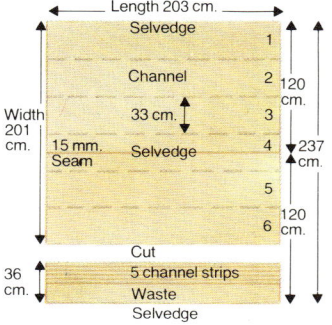
Cutting guide for a feather-filled duvet

(9 yds) of 120 cm. (48 in.) cambric; 1950 g. (4 lb. 4 oz.) feather-and-down mixture; 2 reels mercerised cotton thread.

Method Press the cambric and straighten one end. Measure, mark and cut four pieces each 203 cm. (80 in.) long from the length.

Match two lengths, matt sides facing, and sew together along one selvedge with a 15 mm. (½ in.) seam. Repeat with the other two pieces. Using the cutting guide, mark and cut each joined piece parallel to the seam to a width of 201 cm. (79 in.). From the remaining fabric, cut five strips, each 5 cm. (2 in.) wide and 198 cm. (78 in.) long, for the channel pieces. Press a 10 mm. (⅜ in.) fold on either side of each strip [B1].

MARKING UP THE CHANNELS

Mark the channels on the shiny side of

MAKING A FIBRE-FILLED DUVET

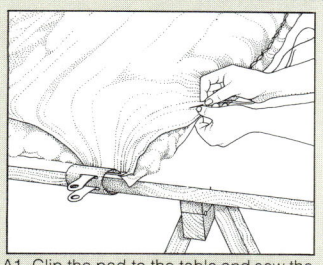
A1. Clip the pad to the table and sew the fibre pad into its gauze cover.

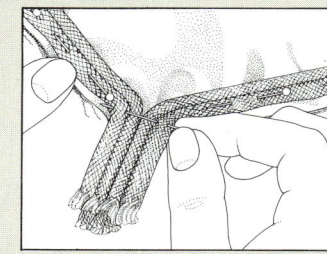
A2. Pin the two ends of the piping together, corded sides touching.

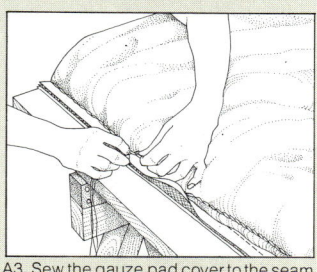
A3. Sew the gauze pad cover to the seam of the duvet cover all round.

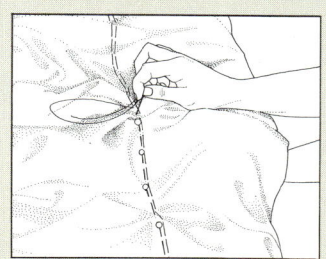
A4. Tack the top and bottom covers together, through the fibre.

THE FINISHED DUVET A duvet keeps a bed as warm as several blankets for a fraction of the weight. The bed is also easier to make and does not create fluff.

each rectangle of fabric in the same way as for the fibre duvet. Allow 15 mm. either side for the seams. Make five lines 33 cm. (13 in.) apart with a soft pencil, making six channels in all.

Lay the first channel strip on the first channel line on the left of the top cover. Keep the top of the strip 15 mm. below the top edge of the cover with the right-hand fold of the strip on the line. Machine to the cover [B2]. Repeat with the other strips.

When all the strips are attached, turn the top cover over and place it on top of the bottom cover, shiny sides together. Turn back the top cover to the first strip on the left-hand side. Machine the free fold of the strip to the bottom cover, following the first pencil line [B3]. Attach the remaining strips.

The duvet is now divided into six feather-proof pockets [B4].

Turn inwards a 15 mm. hem round all sides of both top and bottom covers and press in place. At one end, turn the hem on the bottom cover over the ends of the channel strips [B5]. Join top and bottom covers on both sides and one end with a double row of machine stitches.

FILLING THE DUVET

To fill the duvet, put it, if possible, in a dry bath and close the door of the bathroom – this will trap any feathers that escape. Close the ends of the channels with Bulldog clips. Open one channel at a time and push in a handful of feathers [B6]. Work from right to left in sequence until all the feathers have been used up.

Machine the end of the duvet closed, close to the edge, taking out the Bulldog clips as you go along. Put in a second row of stitching.

QUANTITIES OF FILLINGS FOR DUVETS

The quantities of fillings given in this table are calculated to give equal warmth, whatever the filling used. Temperatures in Britain are never likely to be so low that a duvet made to these specifications would prove inadequate, even on cold winter nights. In summer, a duvet would be too warm only on the hottest nights. Feathers and down should not be used for very young children. Use fibre filling only, for children under 18 months old. Check the size of duvet required from the chart and instructions on p. 155.

DUVET SIZE	TERYLENE P3	85% FEATHER 15% DOWN	PURE DUCK DOWN	PURE GOOSE DOWN
135 × 190 cm. 4 ft 5 in. × 6 ft 3 in.	1280 g. 2 lb. 13 oz.	1190 g. 2 lb. 10 oz.	860 g. 1 lb. 14 oz.	680 g. 1 lb. 8 oz.
144 × 203 cm. 4 ft 9 in. × 6 ft 8 in.	1830 g. 4 lb.	1420 g. 3 lb. 2 oz.	960 g. 2 lb. 2 oz.	800 g. 1 lb. 12 oz.
180 × 190 cm. 5 ft 10 in. × 6 ft 3 in.	2060 g. 4 lb. 10 oz.	1600 g. 3 lb. 8 oz.	1130 g. 2 lb. 8 oz.	900 g. 2 lb.
198 × 203 cm. 6 ft 6 in. × 6 ft 8 in.	2350 g. 5 lb.	1950 g. 4 lb. 4 oz.	1330 g. 2 lb. 15 oz.	1080 g. 2 lb. 6 oz.
213 × 203 cm 7 ft × 6 ft 8 in.	2500 g. 5 lb. 8 oz.	2070 g. 4 lb. 8 oz.	1410 g. 3 lb. 2 oz.	1170 g. 2 lb. 9 oz.
230 × 203 cm. 7 ft 6 in. × 6 ft 8 in.	2680 g. 6 lb.	2160 g. 4 lb. 11 oz.	1500 g. 3 lb. 5 oz.	1260 g. 2 lb. 13 oz.

• DUVET COVER

This cover is for a double duvet 198 × 203 cm. (78 × 80 in.) for a standard double bed. The length of the cover is cut from the width of the fabric for all sizes of duvet. The cover is made slightly larger than the duvet, to allow for easy fitting.

MATERIALS AND EQUIPMENT

4.25 m. (4¾ yds) of 225 cm. (90 in.) polyester cotton sheeting; 2 reels of matching thread; 1 m. (1 yd) × 2.5 cm. (1 in.) Velcro; tape measure; rule; set-square; tailor's chalk; fabric shears; pins; sewing machine.

Method Press out any creases in the sheeting and straighten one end (see p. 291). Cut two rectangles each 211 × 213 cm. (83 × 84 in.). Place them together, right sides facing, match the edges and pin together, near the edge. Leave a central gap of about 1 m. (1 yd) at one end for fitting and removing the cover.

Starting from one side of the opening, working all round and finishing at the other side of the gap, machine the two sides of the cover together, 15 mm. (½ in.) from the edge [C1]. Do not make right-angled turns at the corners, but put a stitch across each corner (see p. 289). Clip off the corner diagonally almost up to the stitch line.

Press down the seam allowance on either side of the opening. Turn the cover right side out. Press down the seams.

Pull the Velcro fastening apart and pin one strip to each side of the opening, covering the raw edge [C2]. Machine round each Velcro strip, close to the edge.

Machine from one side of the opening round the cover to the other side of the opening, in line with the stitches on the inside edge of the Velcro. This makes a firm finish to the cover, which can easily be removed for washing.

MAKING A FEATHER-FILLED DUVET

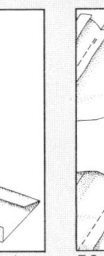

B1. Fold in and press a 10 mm. hem along each side of the channel strip.

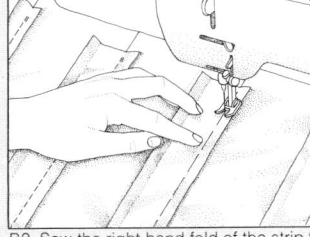

B2. Sew the right-hand fold of the strip to a channel line on the top cover.

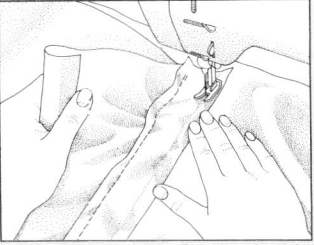

B3. Sew the free fold of each strip to its channel line on the bottom cover.

MAKING A DUVET COVER

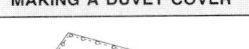

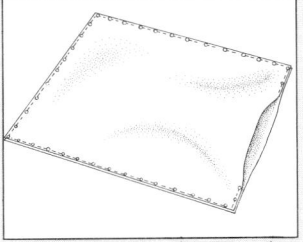

C1. Sew the cover pieces together, face to face, leaving a 1 m. gap.

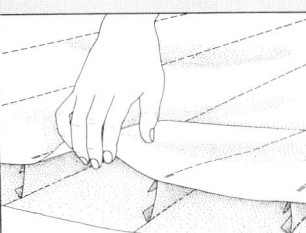

B4. Channel strips sewn are between top and bottom corners to form pockets.

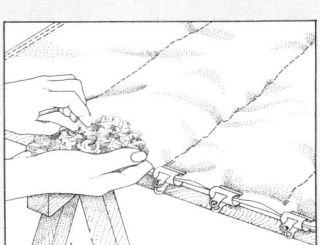

B5. Fold the top cover hem over the bottom cover to close the channels.

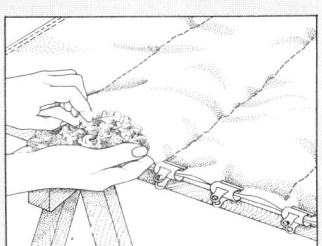

B6. Open one channel at a time and put a handful of feathers into each in turn.

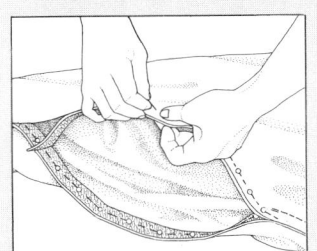

C2. Pin Velcro along each side of the gap, covering the edges of the hems.

• FITTED DIVAN COVER

A well-made divan cover not only protects the bed, but also transforms it into an attractive sofa for day-time use. Blankets and sheets can be made up and concealed beneath the cover instead of being stored separately. It is best to use plain material. If a patterned material is used, there is likely to be waste because of the need for matching.

MATERIALS AND EQUIPMENT

Cover material, such as furnishing cord or other hard-wearing fabric; sateen lining for the valance; matching thread; No. 1 piping cord; tape measure; ruler; tailor's chalk; crayon; fabric shears; steel pins; Sharps needle; sewing machine; piping or zipper foot; set-square; iron.

CUTTING THE MATERIAL

To make a cover to fit a single divan, calculate the amount of material from the instructions on p. 155. Add two valance widths to the length of material for box pleats.

Roll the cover material open, wrong side uppermost. Straighten the ends (see p. 291), then iron.

Chalk the outlines of the pieces to be cut on to the material, following the appropriate cutting guide (see below), according to whether you are making a cover for a large or a small divan. To allow for seams, the top piece should be 3 cm. (1¼ in.) wider and longer than the top of the mattress and the border pieces should be 3 cm. deeper and longer than the sides of the mattress. Cut the valance pieces 4 cm. (1½ in.) wider than the distance between the mattress and the floor. This allows for a 15 mm. (½ in.) seam with the border and a 2.5 cm. (1 in.) hem at the bottom. Chalk the piping section in 5 cm. (2 in.) strips on the bias (see p. 299) for the piping cover.

Draw a curve at each corner on the wrong side of the top cover, using a plate as a guide. Cut out the pieces of cover material.

From the lining material, cut strips to the number and length of the valance pieces, but 15 mm. narrower.

JOINING THE BORDER PIECES

Cover one side border with one end border, right sides together. Machine sew, 15 mm. from the raw edges of the ends. Repeat with the second end and a side border piece.

Lay the two strips of border pieces, right sides together, so that one end border is against one side border. Sew together as before at both ends to form a large loop. Press all the seams flat.

PIPING ROUND THE BORDER

Join the piping covering and sew round the piping cord (see p. 299).

Lay the raw edges of the piping covering against one of the raw edges of the border, right sides together, and pin, leaving 5 cm. of piping free at the start and finish.

Fit a piping foot to the machine and sew the piping to the border, stitching close to the cord. Leave the unpinned ends free. Remove all pins.

Join the piping (see p. 299). Repeat, to sew piping to the other raw edge of the border. Press the border, keeping the vertical seams open [A1].

SEWING THE BORDER ON

Lay the border against the top, right sides together, with the piping on the border lying between them. Position the border so that the end-piece

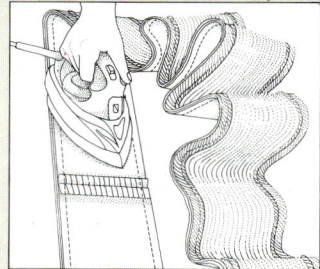

Divan cover border, wrong side out.

seams correspond to the centre of the curved corners on the top and pin in place [A2].

Machine sew border and top together, close up to the piping cord.

Oversew the raw edges of the border and the top.

MAKING THE VALANCE

Sew the valance strips together, end to end, to form a complete loop. Sew the lining strips together in the same way.

Lay the valance and lining right sides together, with the raw edges aligning along one side, and pin [A3]. Sew the raw edges together, 15 mm. from the edge. Press open the seam.

Turn the valance and lining right sides out and match the unsewn top edges of the valance and lining. This forms a hem of cover material at the bottom. Pin the top edges together

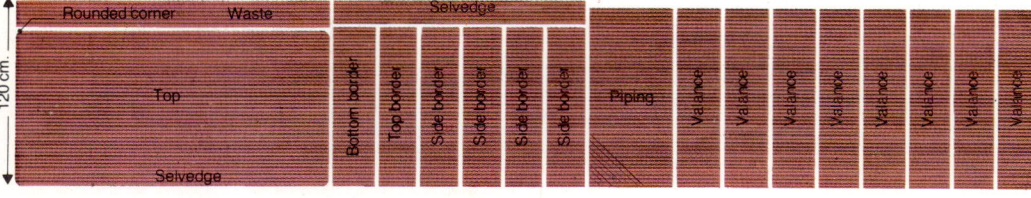

Cutting guide for a cover to fit a single divan, using 120 cm. fabric.

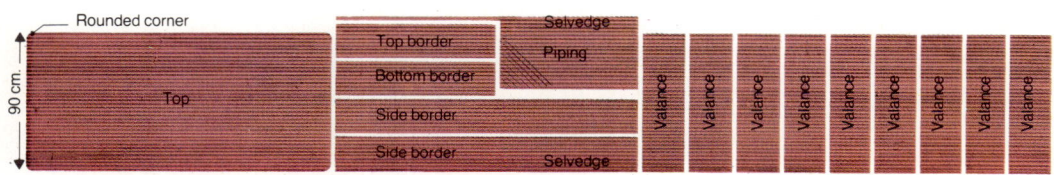

Cutting guide for a cover to fit a small single divan, using 90 cm. fabric.

SEWING THE BORDER AND VALANCE

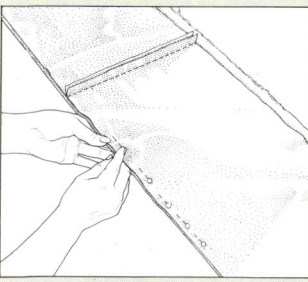

A1. Press the border with the piping in place along each edge. Press all the vertical joining seams open.

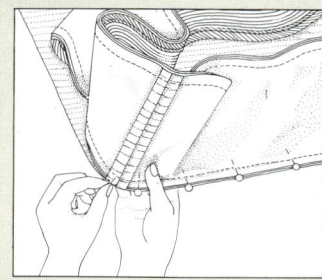

A2. Pin the border and top pieces together. Centre the seams joining the side and borders on the corner curves.

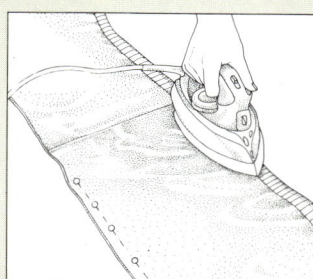

A3. Lay the lining and valance, right sides together. Align one side and pin, leaving a 15 mm. overlap on the other side.

A4. Align the unsewn raw edges of the valance and the lining to leave the hem on the other side. Press the hem.

ard press the hem [A4]. Tack the lining to the valance 15 mm. below the raw edges.

FORMING THE PLEATS

Lay the valance on the floor and chalk the lengths of the bed sides and ends on it. Mark one bed corner on the top edge of the valance with a pin then put four pins beyond it at 10 cm. (4 in.) intervals. Place five pins in matching positions on the bottom edge of the valance.

Fold a line between one of the outer pairs of pins and align this fold with the centre pins [B1]. Repeat with the other pair of outer pins to form a box pleat [B2]. Pin to secure, then tack-stitch the pleats in place [B3]. Repeat at each of the other three corners.

JOINING VALANCE AND COVER

Match the centre of the pleat with the seams of the border (which correspond to the corners of the top), so that the right sides of the material are together. Pin together with the piping flat between them.

Tack-stitch in place before machining with a piping foot, keeping close to the cord. Back-stitch when crossing pleats and when ending.

Oversew the raw edges. Remove the tacks and pins except for the tacks holding the pleats together. Leave these in place for a few days and the pleats will hang better. Press the cover and fit to divan [B4].

MAKING A BOX PLEAT

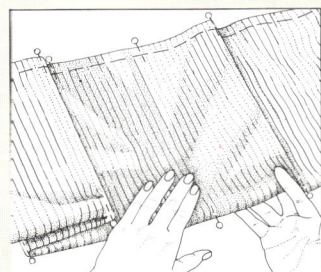

B1. Fold a line between one pair of outer pins, and align the fold with the centre pins. Repeat on the other side.

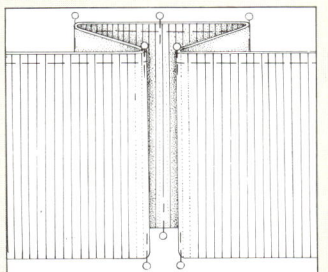

B2. The fully formed pleat in the valance, showing the inner and outer folds before the pleat is pinned in place.

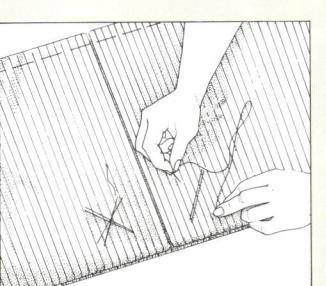

B3. After pinning the two folds of the pleat in place down the centre line, tack through all three layers to hold in place.

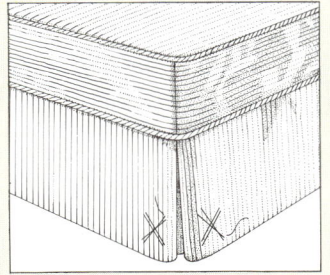

B4. The valance is fitted to the border with the centre fold of the pleat matching the corner seams in the border.

DUAL-PURPOSE DIVAN *A divan makes the most of the space available in a bed-sitting room. A fitted cover allows it to be used as a bed by night and a sofa by day. The bedclothes can be made up and left under the cover, or they can be stored under the bed when not in use. Some divans are made with drawers for this purpose.*

• LINED BEDSPREAD

This bedspread is made to fit a double bed, size 150 × 200 cm. (5 ft × 6 ft 6 in.). The technique is the same for any size of bedspread, but the amount of fabric differs. Consult the measuring instructions on p. 155.

MATERIALS AND EQUIPMENT

Cover material (furnishing-weight fabrics, such as cotton rep or linen union); sateen cotton lining; No. 2 piping cord; matching thread; Sharps needle; steel pins; scissors; tape measure; ruler; tailor's chalk; sewing machine; piping foot; iron; set-square.

CUTTING THE MATERIAL

If you use material with a printed border, as in the photograph, buy a matching piece of plain material for the side panels. Press the material and square the ends (see p. 291). Cut each piece 295 cm. (115 in.) long. Centre the patterned fabric lengthways on the bed.

The width of the side panels is the height from the floor to the selvedge of the centre panel, when in position on the bed, plus 5 cm. (2 in.) for seam allowances. Trim any excess from the cut edge of the side panels.

JOINING WIDTHS

Sew the piping covering together and insert the piping cord (see p. 299), to make two strips of piping, each about 3 m. (9 ft 10 in.) long.

Lay a piping length on each long edge of the centre panel, right sides together, aligning the raw edges. Fit a piping foot to the machine and stitch the piping to the cover, keeping close to the cord.

Lay one of the side panels on the centre panel, right sides together, with the piping flat between them. Align the selvedge of the border piece with the raw edge of the piping and pin along the side. Machine sew along the wrong side of the centre-panel material, keeping to the stitches of the piping. Remove any pins in the path of the stitching. Zigzag-stitch the raw edges of the piping and cover together. Repeat on the other side.

Cut the lining fabric in the same way as the cover. Lay one side panel of lining on the centre panel, wrong sides together. Align the selvedge of the side panel with the edge of the centre panel. Machine together, 15 mm. ($\frac{1}{2}$ in.) from the edge. Repeat with the other panel. Press the seams open.

Spread the cover out on the floor, seams uppermost. Arrange the lining over this, so the seams of the lining and cover exactly match. Sew the seam allowances of the lining to those of the cover with locking stitches (see p. 297). Tack lining and cover together well inside all outer edges.

CURVING THE CORNERS

Fold the cover in half lengthways. On each of the bottom corners chalk a square, the sides of which are equal to the height of the bed including the mattress. Pivot a ruler, or a piece of string the same length as the sides of the square, from the inside corner of the square to form an arc (see illustration). Draw the arc with tailor's chalk and cut along the line through both thicknesses.

Turn in to the wrong side a 15 mm. single hem on both the cover and lining edges. Press the hems. Slip-stitch the hems together to secure the lining to the cover.

LINED BEDSPREAD Not only does this bedspread add warmth to the bed; it is also a vital part of the room's décor.

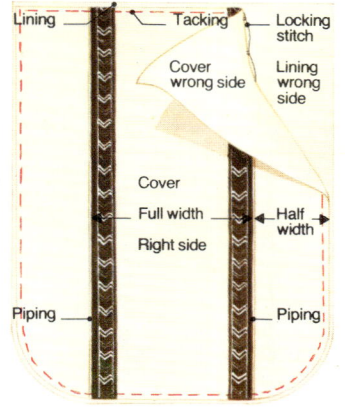

Assembling the cover.

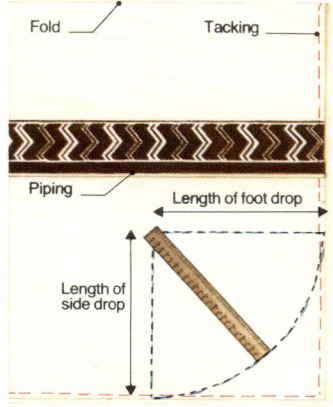

Making the curved corner.

• A PATCHWORK BEDCOVER

The technique used for making a bedcover with hexagonal patches can be applied to any patchwork article, with any shape of patch. To determine the size of bedspread, see measuring instructions on p. 155.

MATERIALS AND EQUIPMENT

Scissors; trimming knife; stiff paper or thin card; steel pins; Between needle; fine thread; pre-shrunk lining; bump or thin blanketing for interlining; patches (cotton is best – if using scraps do not mix heavy and light fabrics or different fibres, and avoid fragile materials); iron; sewing machine; templates; pencil; tailor's chalk; tacking cotton.

USING THE TEMPLATES

Templates can be bought at crafts shops (see diagrams on right). To make a hexagonal patterned bedcover you need one solid hexagonal template, for paper shapes; and one larger template with a 'window' cutout of the same size. The frame of the window template is about 10 mm. (⅜ in.) wide, to allow for a uniform turning of the material round the paper shapes.

Cut out all the paper shapes you will need before going any further, or work in batches of seven at a time.

For the paper shapes, pencil all round the solid template and cut several thicknesses of paper together with a pair of scissors. Alternatively, lay the paper on a sheet of tough cardboard and cut round the template with a trimming knife.

For the fabric patches, position the window template on the material so that the desired pattern or design is seen inside. Align two opposite sides of the hexagon to the grain of the fabric. Chalk round the outside of the template [1] and cut out. Do not attempt to cut out more than one patch at a time, as this could waste material.

FORMING THE PATCHES

Pin a paper shape to the centre of the wrong side of a patch, leaving the fabric overlapping equally all round. Turn this material over the paper and tack the fold all round. Remove the pin. Make six more patches.

JOINING THE PATCHES

Place two patches, right sides together, with the grain of the fabric running in the same direction. Oversew closely along one edge [2]. Join the other patches to these in the same way [3].

Cut out another seven paper shapes and make and join another seven patches.

Join groups of patches by placing them right sides together and oversewing adjacent edges. Continue like this, making and joining groups of seven until there are enough joined patches to form the body of the cover.

Straighten the sides of the patchwork by sewing half hexagons in the spaces. Lay the patchwork right side up and iron with a damp cloth. Remove the tacks and the paper shapes. Oversew the outer edges of the patchwork all round.

LINING THE PATCHWORK

Lay the interlining flat. Place the patchwork over the interlining, right side uppermost. Match the edges, trimming the interlining if necessary.

Lay the lining on the patchwork, right sides together. Pin and tack 15 mm. (½ in.) from the edges, leaving open 45 cm. (18 in.) on one of the short sides. Machine close to the tacks, removing the pins. Leave the 45 cm. opening unsewn.

Trim the edges of the interlining 5 mm. (¼ in.) from the stitches.

Turn the patchwork cover right sides out through the 45 cm. gap, so that the interlining is sandwiched between the lining and the patchwork. Oversew the edges to close the gap.

Press the patchwork. Lay it flat, lining uppermost. Sew firm stitches through the three layers about 15 cm. (6 in.) apart, inserting the thread through the seams of the patches to hide the stitches.

JOINING THE PATCHES

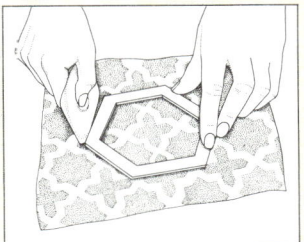

1 Adjust the open hexagon on the fabric until the pattern fits.

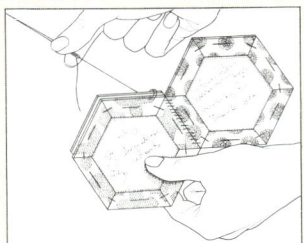

2. Place two hexagons right sides together and oversew along one edge.

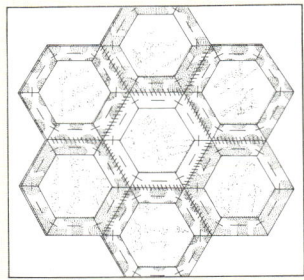

3. Join a patch to each side of the first hexagon, making seven in all.

AMERICAN PATCHWORK Hexagonal patches make a colourful bedcover.

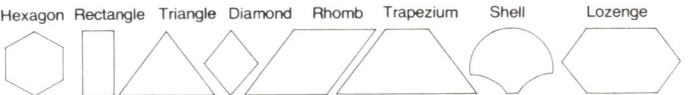

Hexagon Rectangle Triangle Diamond Rhomb Trapezium Shell Lozenge

QUILTED ELEGANCE The patchwork effect on this quilted bedcover was created by an appliquéd design of squares and triangles.

PICTURE FRAMING

Framing a picture can enhance its appearance, and putting it under glass protects it from the effects of sunlight, dust and changes in the atmosphere. Humidity, for example, can cause an unframed print to wrinkle, and damage a delicate water-colour or pastel drawing.

Three ways of do-it-yourself picture framing are: using a new or secondhand frame; buying a framing kit; or buying the basic materials and equipment needed to make your own frame. Framing your own pictures needs care and a degree of skill. A beginner should avoid starting with valuable or delicate pictures and practise on old prints first.

• PROFESSIONAL FRAMING

The professionally made frame is generally more expensive than any other, but worthwhile with a valuable picture. It is also advisable if the picture to be framed has sides longer than 1 m. (3 ft) – a frame this size is difficult for a beginner to handle.

SECONDHAND FRAMES

To avoid the expense of new frames, it is often profitable to look for secondhand ones. Provided the mouldings are in reasonably good condition, an old frame can be worth restoring, even though the corner joints may be loose, the glass broken and the back-ing board missing. To fit new glass and a backing board, see p. 167.

Prise the corner joints apart carefully, working from the back of the frame. Scrape off the old adhesive from the mitred faces and clean them with glasspaper. Apply a film of PVA adhesive to each. Clamp the sides together and secure them with panel pins. A frame clamp, ideal for this purpose, is available from most tool shops. To ensure that the corners are at right-angles, adjust the frame before the adhesive has set, until both diagonals are the same length. Remove clamp when adhesive is dry.

To reinforce the corners of large frames, cut out triangular pieces of

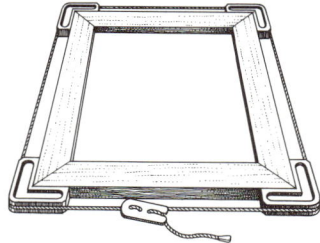

A simple but effective frame clamp.

3 mm. ($\frac{1}{8}$ in.) thick plywood, and glue and panel-pin them to the back of the corners. Alternatively, screw a metal plate to each corner.

Remove grease and grime with soapy water, except on glued corners and on frames that have plaster mouldings. Expensive frames may have carved woodwork mouldings, but cheaper secondhand frames are more likely to be plasterwork cast on a timber base. Provided the plaster is not flaking or crumbling, repair chipped areas with filler paste or gilder's compo, obtainable from art shops.

To repair larger areas, buy some dental-impression compound from a dental suppliers and use it to make a mould from a sound part of the frame.

Badly chipped plaster mouldings can sometimes be chiselled off to expose a simple but serviceable frame underneath. To soften the plaster, lay damp rags over it for several days. Clean the exposed wood with glasspaper.

A gilded frame may have a gold, bronze or silvered appearance. A golden-coloured frame may be surfaced with gold leaf or gold paint. Identifying which it is and restoring it are jobs best left to an expert.

Small chipped areas can be touched up with wax gilt, obtainable from art shops. Remove old varnish with a proprietary paint stripper and glasspaper.

ASSORTED FRAMES An attractive arrangement of new, secondhand, professionally made and do-it-yourself frames.

• FRAMING KITS

Kits simplify the most difficult aspects of framing – making the mitred joints.

One of the cheapest and simplest kits consists of a shallow Perspex box, with a close-fitting piece of polystyrene or cardboard to hold the picture in place. Mount the picture on card (see p. 168). Lay it face down in the Perspex box and fit the polystyrene or cardboard in place. The box is hooked over nails in the wall.

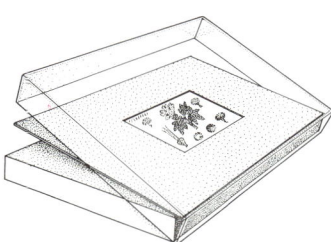

Perspex and cardboard framing kit.

More sophisticated kits contain four pieces of aluminium or plastic moulding, supplied with clips and fastenings to hold and hang the frame together – the corners are mitred and ready for assembly. With most kits you buy the board and the glass separately.

A similar type of kit has grooved metal edges. Three sides are assembled to form a V-shape, with the picture – sandwiched between glass and backing board – pushed into place. The fourth side, sealing the open ends and stabilising the frame, is fastened to them.

Although most framing kits are manufactured with variations of assembly, finish and colour – metal frames are sold in matt black, polished aluminium, gold, silver and pewter colours – their limited size range can be a drawback.

Some kits are available to frame pictures up to 1 m. (3 ft) long, but most are no longer than 455 mm. (18 in.). To fit an intermediate-sized frame, it may be necessary to trim a picture or use a mount (see p. 168).

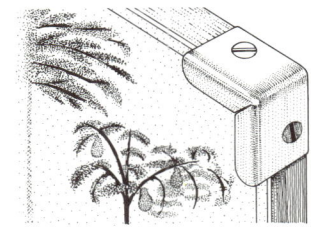

Corner framing with mirror clips.

An alternative to the conventional frame is to sandwich a picture between a sheet of board and glass, clipped together at the edges. This is a simple method for an amateur,

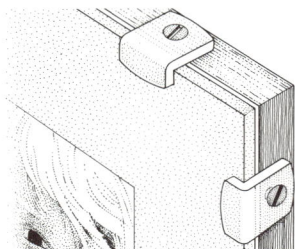

Using Perspex framing clips.

since it eliminates cutting and assembling joints.

Spring-loaded clips are inexpensive and can be bought from picture framers or art shops. Clip sizes vary and they should be bought to suit the combined thickness of backing board, glass and mount. Metal or plastic mirror clips, sold at ironmongers or by glass merchants, can be used for frameless pictures.

COLLECTING PICTURE FRAMES

With the development of photography during the mid-19th century, framed pictures became commonplace in homes throughout the country. Frames were produced in their thousands – initially in plain or painted wood and metal; subsequently in more elaborate materials, such as shell, brass or ormolu.

Frames varied in size and shape, from small square ones of linked brass rings or oval shapes, set with garnets, to large rectangular shell frames, and brass frames engraved with flowers and scrolls. Hinged frames with velvet linings, and painted metal frames, were at the cheaper end of the market, with the silver frame at the other. The more costly ormolu frames were also produced – often in combination with other materials, such as pottery.

Although English pottery frames are rare, 20th-century transfer-printed ones – rather than hand-painted versions – can be found in antique shops.

Victorian silver frames in good condition should be treasured – many have lasted better than, say, shell or velvet, and still retain their value. Sometimes the backing board may be loose or missing, in which case it can be repaired or replaced. But, generally speaking, expensive frames do not lend themselves easily to restoration.

Much easier to come by are brass, wood and metal frames dating from the turn of the century. Look for art nouveau frames in copper or cast iron – silver too, though this tends to be expensive – with decorative patterns of garlands and trailing leaves.

REPAIRING A DAMAGED MOULDING

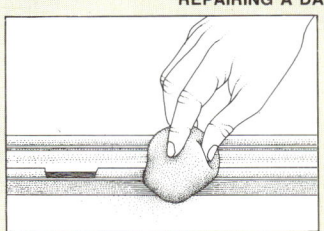

1. Heat dental compound in hot water, to soften it, and press it on a section of moulding matching the damaged area.

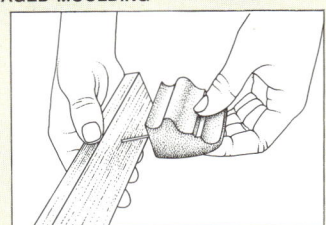

2. Press a strip of wood, with a nail through it, on to the bottom inner edge of the compound to hold them together.

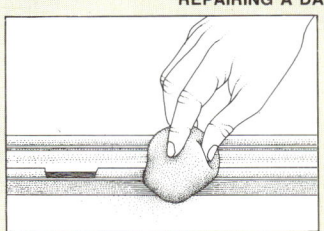

3. Mix cellulose filler and fill the cavity formed by the compound and wooden strip, flush with the top of the strip.

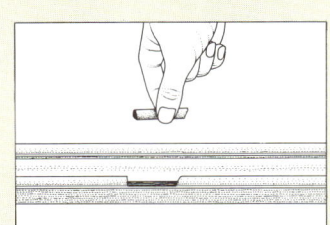

4. Glasspaper the cast to fit the gap in the moulding. Coat surfaces with epoxy resin and stick moulding in place.

FITTING SPRING CLIPS

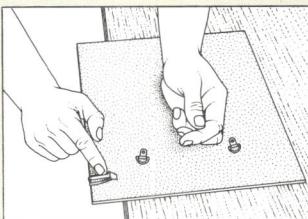

1. Push a spring-clip over the backing board and make a pencil mark where the inner edge of the clip meets the board.

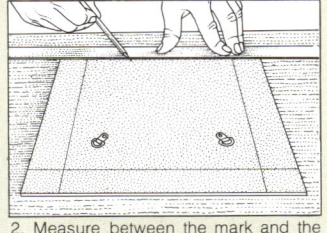

2. Measure between the mark and the edge of the board and draw lines this distance away and parallel to all edges.

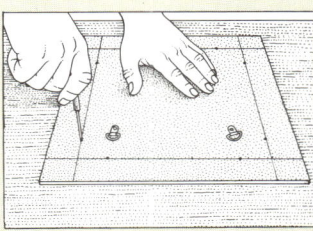

3. Make holes with a bradawl on the lines through the smooth side of the board, a quarter of its width in from each corner.

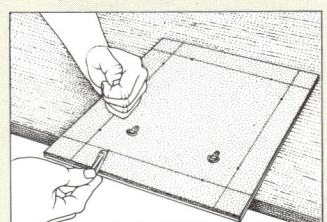

4. With glass, mount and board face down on cloth, fit the spring-clips so that the inner ends notch in the holes.

• MAKING A PICTURE FRAME

Mouldings suitable for picture frames can be bought at most do-it-yourself stores and handicraft shops, and from some professional framers and timber yards.

Mouldings which are the simplest in shape are the easiest for the beginner to use. But with practice it is possible to make attractive frames using the more complicated traditional mouldings. Metal mouldings – usually aluminium – are simpler in section than those made of wood, but are more difficult to join at the corners. Aluminium frames are manufactured in natural, pewter, black, gold and silver colours, with a brushed or polished finish.

Wooden mouldings may be natural, stained or wax-polished hardwood. They can also be bought with the front and side surfaces covered with a factory-bonded finish such as plastic, fabric, lacquer, gilt or gesso – a thin coating of plaster with a gilded surface. Silver and gilt mouldings are also sold with a distressed finish – one which simulates the appearance of an antique.

If you are uncertain what kind of moulding to use, try the picture or print against a sample. Shops often have short lengths of corner sections made up and will usually advise on the most suitable type and size.

As a rough guide, slim, waxed-wood mouldings and Hogarth frames – those with a black, white or brown finish and gilt edging – look well with small prints in a room furnished in traditional style.

Pictures or prints in a room decorated in the modern style tend to look better in thin metal frames or deep, angular wooden surrounds. The finish can be natural, painted or fabric.

A wooden mitre-box or metal mitre-cutter to guide the saw is essential. Without one of these tools it is impossible to cut mitred joints accurately. The mitre-cutter is more expensive but can be used for metal as well as wooden mouldings. It is easier to use, since it has corner clamps to hold the mouldings rigidly in place during cutting, gluing and nailing.

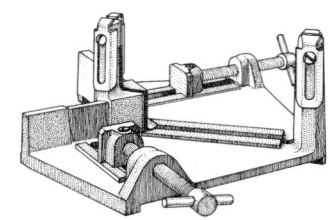

A metal clamp and mitre-cutter.

MATERIALS AND EQUIPMENT

Mitre-box or cutter; moulding; tenon saw; rule; small hammer; tapered bradawl; nail punch; fine-grade glasspaper; 20 mm. ($\frac{3}{4}$ in.) panel pins; PVA adhesive; 50 mm. (2 in.) brown, gummed paper tape; scissors; picture glass; backing board; D-rings.

MEASURING THE PICTURE

There are two ways of measuring a picture for a frame, depending on whether or not you use a mount (see p. 168).

For a frame without a mount, measure the length and width of the picture and add an extra 3 mm. ($\frac{1}{8}$ in.) to each measurement. If the picture is out of square, add this fitting allowance to the longest and widest dimensions. This will give the rebate size – the area of the recessed opening at the back of the frame, in which glass, picture and backing board are fixed.

For a frame with a mount, measure the glazed area that will be seen within the frame.

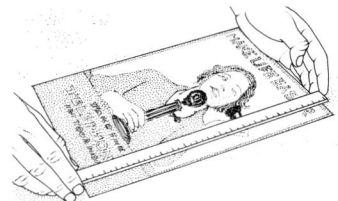

Measure the picture or print carefully.

The length of moulding required is the combined length of the mount's four sides, plus eight times the width of the moulding, and an extra 50 mm. (2 in.) to allow for cutting.

MEASURING AND CUTTING THE FRAME

Clamp the moulding squarely in the mitre-cutter [A1]. If necessary, pack out complex-shaped mouldings with small off-cuts of wood so that the moulding is held firmly. On mouldings

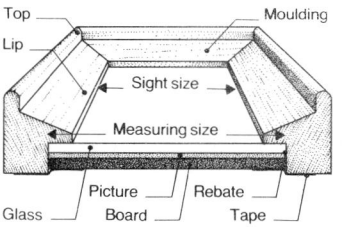

The parts of a picture frame.

with delicate carvings, use small pieces of cardboard to avoid damaging them with the clamps. Saw off an angle as close as possible to the end.

Remove the moulding and measure for the first length [A2] allowing for the mitre – angled the opposite way – at the other end. Repeat this procedure with each of the other three lengths. Always keep the mitre saw level and use a smooth action [A3].

When all four joints are sawn, lightly clean the cut edges with glasspaper to remove any whiskers of wood.

Arrange the four cut sides on a flat surface, in the way they will ultimately be assembled. Apply adhesive to each cut face. Clamp two adjoining pieces of moulding together, in the mitre-cutter, to form a tight and correctly aligned joint [A4]. Use the bradawl to make starter holes for the panel pins, driving two pins through the shorter of the two mouldings [A5]. Lightly punch the heads of the pins below the surface.

Joint the diagonally opposed corner with the remaining two pieces of moulding, to make the second L-shaped frame [A6]. Join the two L-shaped frames in the same way. Fill all nail holes with cellulose filler. Adjust the frame, if necessary, to ensure the diagonals are the same length.

With all four joints glued and nailed, lay the frame flat and leave it for several hours to dry. If it does not lie flat, twist the frame slightly, and press it under a piece of hardboard with weights on top.

FINISHES

Paint, stain or wax-polish the frame. Use a plastic paint – which can be thinned with water – and apply two or three thin coats, working it well into the grain of the wood. When dry, rub the second and third coats down with fine steel wool to get a smooth surface.

Liquid stains can be bought in many different shades of timber and a few colours. Smooth the wood beforehand with glasspaper, and apply the stain with a soft pad of cloth, working the stain well into the grain with a gentle rubbing action.

When dry, polish the stain with a dry cloth for a subtle sheen. For a brighter finish, rub with fine steel wool before polishing with the cloth.

A wax finish, like stain, can give emphasis to an attractive grain. Apply

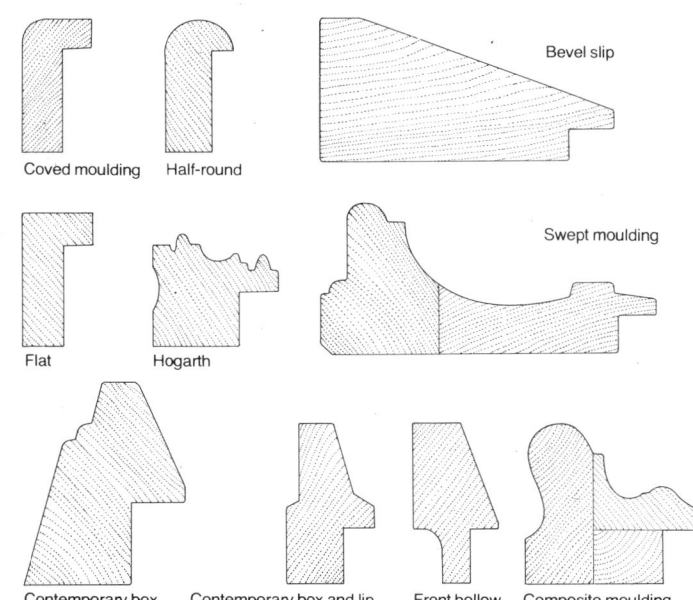

Bevel slip

Coved moulding   Half-round

Swept moulding

Flat   Hogarth

Contemporary box   Contemporary box and lip   Front hollow   Composite moulding

WOODEN MOULDINGS Some of the many shapes – shown in cross section.

the wax thinly and work it well into the wood with a dry cloth and vigorous rubbing.

GLASS

Get a glazier to cut the glass for you so that it fits the rebate size of the frame. The glass should be about 1.5 mm. ($\frac{1}{16}$ in.) smaller all round. If the glass is too tight, it could easily crack when being fitted into the frame.

Ask for picture glass. This used to be called 18 oz. glass (its weight per square foot) but is now known by its thickness, which is 2 mm. Picture glass is thinner than ordinary window glass and, correspondingly, slightly cheaper.

Non-reflective glass is a lot dearer, but useful in places where glare is unavoidable, for example on a south-facing wall. The drawback of this glass is its tendency to dull the colours of a picture seen through it.

When buying glass for a frameless picture (see p. 165), ask for the edges to be smoothed.

MAKING THE BACKING BOARD

Cut hardboard the same size as the glass. For small pictures – those up to about 600 × 300 mm. (24 × 12 in.) – with frame mouldings less than 20 mm. ($\frac{3}{4}$ in.) wide, use single D-ring fixings in the back board; double D-rings for larger pictures. Alternatively, use screw eyes in the inside back edge of the frame mouldings.

Measure and make a pencil mark one-third down from the top of the frame and 50 mm. (2 in.) in from each side. Use a bradawl to make holes through the smooth side of the hardboard for the D-rings [B1]. Push the split tails of the rings through the holes and hammer them flat [B2].

Clean one side of the glass and lay the glass clean side up in the frame, followed by the picture and backing board.

Press the backing down gently but firmly and secure it with panel pins [B3], tapped into the inside edge – and half the thickness – of the frame mouldings. Position the pins about 100 mm. (4 in.) apart.

Secure a length of picture wire to the D-rings, allowing sufficient for the hook, when the frame is suspended on the wall, to be about 25 mm. (1 in.) down from the top of the picture and concealed from view [B4].

To seal the picture in as a protection against dust, use the gummed paper over the backing board and the back of the mouldings. Trim the edge of the paper, if necessary, with a razor blade.

Clean the face of the glass.

GROUP FRAMING *Gilded frames and cut mounts used to link assorted prints.*

MAKING THE PICTURE FRAME

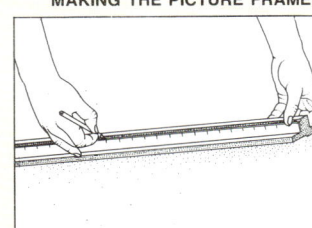

A1. Clamp moulding – face up, and inside edge facing away. Cut off angle as close as possible to end of length.

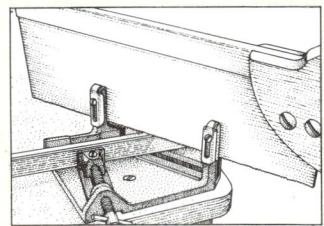

A2. From this angle, measure the first length of moulding. Allow for angle, sloping opposite way, at other end.

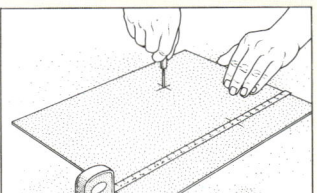

A3. Repeat this procedure with other three lengths. Always carefully check angles before sawing them off.

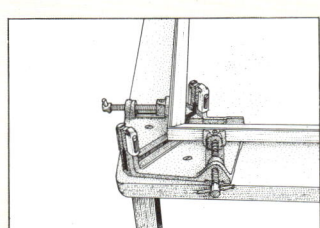

A4. Glue and clamp mitred faces together in the mitre-cutter. Adjust them carefully to get perfect alignment.

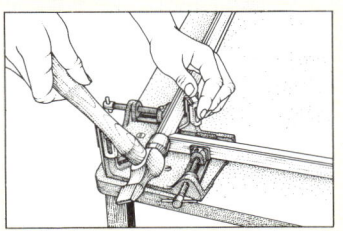

A5. Tap in panel pins to secure each corner joint and lightly punch the heads below the surface.

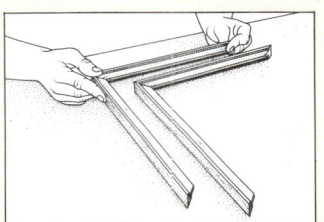

A6. Assemble the opposite corner next, so that you have two L-shaped frames, before gluing and nailing together.

MAKING AND FITTING THE BACKING BOARD

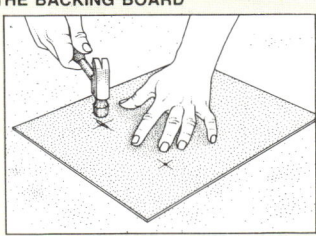

B1. Make holes with a bradawl through the board, one-third down from the top and 50 mm. in from the sides.

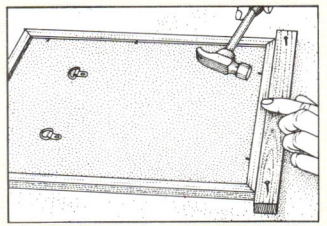

B2. Smooth the edges of the holes and fit a D-ring in each. Hammer split ends of each ring flat on a hard surface.

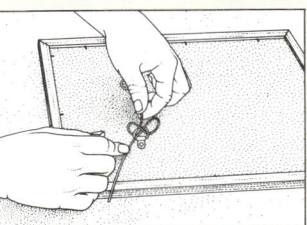

B3. Fit glass, picture and board in the frame, press down gently and hammer panel pins into edges of mouldings.

B4. Secure cord or wire to the D-rings. Adjust the length so that it will be concealed behind the picture.

MAKING A PICTURE MOUNT

A mount is a white or tinted card which provides a border for a picture. A cut mount has a window in it through which a picture can be seen. In a bevelled mount, the window has bevelled edges.

Prints, pastels and water-colours – particularly small pictures which would otherwise look insignificant – look better with a mount. The mount is effective because it gives a border to a picture and separates it from the frame. A cut mount has the added protective value of separating a picture from the glass – essential when mounting pastels and delicate water-colours.

The size, colour, texture and proportion of a mount are matters of personal taste. An optical illusion causes the margin around a picture, when mounted centrally, to look narrower at the bottom. To compensate for this it is usual to increase the bottom margin by about 15 mm. (½ in.).

Mount boards can be bought at art-supply stores in varying thicknesses, textures and colours. A 4-6 sheet – about 1.5 mm. ($\frac{1}{16}$ in.) thick – is adequate for most purposes, but get professional advice when mounting a valuable picture. Some materials are less suitable than others and, over a period of time, could cause a picture to deteriorate.

MATERIALS AND EQUIPMENT

Mount board; straight edge; trimming knife (with heavy-duty blades); set-square; rule; glasspaper; spare card for use as cutting surface; 25 mm. (1 in.) thick board that is longer and wider than the straight edge.

MEASURING THE MOUNT

Position the straight edge along the centre line of the board and drive two small screws part of the way in, near each end, for the straight edge to butt against [A1]. Move the card under the mount when making a fresh cut, otherwise the cut edges of the mount will be fluffy.

Measure and mark on the face of the mount the rebate size of the frame (see p. 166) and, if the mount is to have a window cut in it, the size of the picture. Allow for the edges of the window to overlap the print or picture by at least 5 mm. (¼ in.).

Use the set-square to mark and check that the corners of the mount and the window are at right-angles, and that the sides of both are parallel to each other [A2].

CUTTING A BEVELLED MOUNT

Lay the mount on the spare card and cutting board. With the straight edge resting against the screws, start cutting out the window. Hold the knife at about 45° to the vertical [A3] and try to maintain gentle but firm pressure.

Keep the blade at the same angle and cut to the marked corners [A4]. When the centre panel has been cut out, use the blade of the knife to snick out any fluffiness in the mitred corners, and clean them with fine-grade glasspaper.

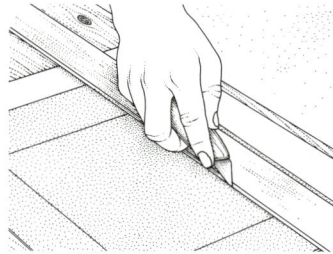

Hold knife at an angle. Use firm pressure.

MAKING A CARD MOUNT

A1. Place the straight edge on the board, resting against partly driven-in screws. Slide card under the straight edge.

A2. Mark on the mount the position of the window. Make the bottom margin 15 mm. wider than the rest.

A3. Align the straight edge against the edge of the window and start cutting the card. Use firm cutting pressure.

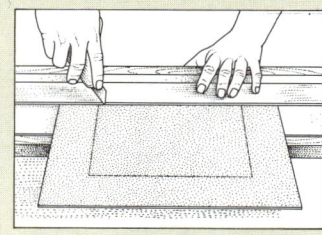

A4. Keep the blade at the same angle and cut to the marked corners. Remove the centre panel. Clean any fraying edges.

A5. Position picture and mount so that they project beyond a table edge and apply strips of clear tape underneath.

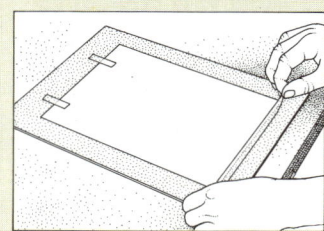

A6. Turn the mount over and fix a strip of tape along the top of the picture. Remove the tape from the other end.

MAKING A FABRIC MOUNT

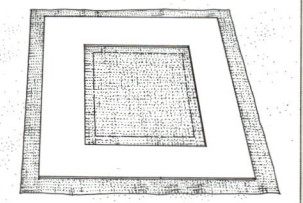

B1. Cut the fabric about 50 mm. larger than the mount, and mark the position of the window on the fabric in pencil.

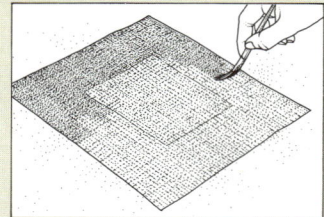

B2. Apply a thin coat of adhesive to the fabric, up to the edges of the inner window, and to the face side of the mount.

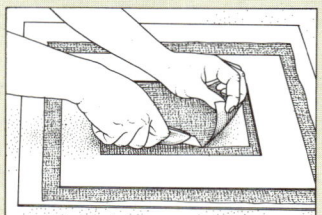

B3. When touch-dry, press the mount and fabric together. Cut out the centre window with the knife or razor blade.

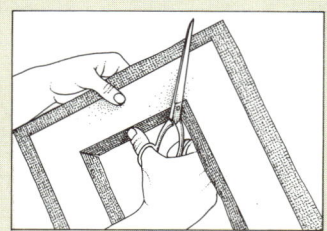

B4. Use scissors to cut from the inner corners of the fabric window to the inner corners of the mount's window.

B5. Turn the inner edges of the fabric over the edges of the window and press them flat with the fingertips.

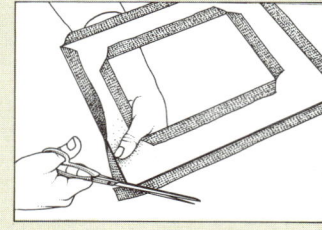

B6. Cut the outer corners of the fabric off at 45°, and turn the remaining edges over. Leave under pressure for two hours.

MOUNTING THE PICTURE

Lay the mount over the picture, adjusting it for its correct position. Lay both on a table so that the picture projects beyond the table.

With one hand keeping mount and picture together, use the other to apply two small strips of clear adhesive tape to the underside of picture and mount [A5]. Reverse the mount and picture and tape the top edge of the picture to the mount [A6]. Carefully remove the two pieces of tape at the bottom of the picture.

• MAKING A FABRIC-COVERED MOUNT

Linen and silk make good fabric mounts but linen, being thicker, is easier for the beginner to handle.

MATERIALS AND EQUIPMENT

Fabric; trimming knife or razor blade; scissors; small paste brush; natural latex; rolling pin.

PREPARATION WORK

Cut the fabric about 50 mm. (2 in.) larger than the mount and lay it face down on a flat surface.

Mark the position of the window in the centre of the fabric and a second window, about 25 mm. (1 in.) smaller, within it [B1]. Apply a thin coat of adhesive to the reverse side of the fabric, around the edges of the smaller window [B2], and to the face side of the mount.

When the two are touch-dry, press them together with hand pressure. Use the knife or razor blade and cut out the centre of the smaller window [B3]. Cut mitres from the hole to each corner of the mount [B4].

Gently knead the inner edges of the fabric over the edges of the window, pinching the fabric tightly to the mount [B5].

Cut the corners of the fabric off at

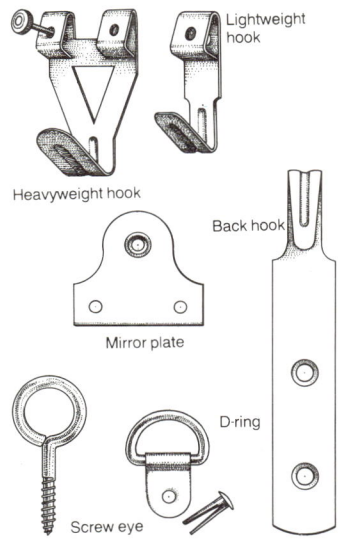

HANGING PICTURES Frame and wall fittings are made for all sizes of picture, and to suit all weights.

45° – at a tangent to the outer corners of the mount [B6].

Turn the mount over, fold the outer edges of the fabric over the mount and roll the fabric down flat, to remove any bubbles of air. Leave it flat under pressure for two hours to dry.

• HANGING PICTURES

Use nylon cord or three-ply picture-wire – never string – knotted to D-rings, screw-eyes or back hooks. Screw-eyes are suitable where the moulding is thick enough to take the screw without splitting, and not less than 15 mm. (½ in.) wide. For lighter mouldings, use D-rings in the backing board. For heavy pictures use back hooks, screwed to the back of the frame mouldings.

Hang pictures on hook-eyes, sold as single or double hooks, complete with needle-like masonry nails that can be hammered into a wall.

ASSORTED PICTURES A cluster of pictures, having different styles, shapes and framing materials, can be grouped together informally, if those at the top or bottom line through with the ceiling or a dominant piece of furniture.

PICTURES AND FURNITURE A skilful arrangement, making a set piece of pictures, furniture and antiques.

SINGLE LINE A formal arrangement can be achieved by hanging pictures with their top edges aligned.

BALANCED ARRANGEMENT Hang large, or heavy-framed pictures at the centre or top of a group.

169

FLOWERS AND PLANTS IN THE HOME

The best time to cut garden flowers is either early in the morning, before the sun gets to them, or in the evening when they can be left in water to regain moisture overnight. Avoid cutting flowers in the heat of the day, because the sun draws the moisture from the petals.

When buying flowers, avoid any that have been standing in the sun. Check that the flowers do not have slimy or dark-coloured ends to their stems. Never buy flowers if the pollen is falling off, or spring flowers, such as daffodils or tulips, with slightly transparent petals. To ensure freshness, flowers are sent to market while still in tight bud. This helps them to last. Try to get the shop to wrap flowers so that their heads are out of the air and are protected from the weather, particularly on extremely hot or windy days.

Immediately after cutting and treating the stems, place all flowers in deep water for some hours, or overnight, using a bucket, a deep jug or a large bowl. Do not crowd the flowers together, because this causes damage.

• PREPARING FLOWERS

Flowers must be taking up water well before they are arranged in any display. To ensure the quick uptake of water, there are methods of treating different kinds of stems.

In all cases, remove the bottom leaves on the stem first. Cut 15 mm. ($\frac{1}{2}$ in.) off the end (except with soft-stemmed flowers) to remove a seal that may have formed while the stem was out of water. Make the cut on the slant, using florist's stub scissors, or a sharp knife. Split all stems, except soft or hollow stalks, from the base upwards for 15 mm. or more, depending on the length.

Cutting and splitting exposes the inner tissues of the stems to water, and speeds the flow of water to the leaves and petals before they wilt.

Soft-stemmed flowers, such as daffodils and irises, need only have the ends of the stems snipped off.

Hollow-stemmed flowers, such as delphiniums, are not easy to arrange if the stems are split. Cut the stems on a slant while the ends are under the water. Another method is to hold the flowers upside-down, fill the stems with water, and then plug the opening with cottonwool.

WOODY STEMS

The bottom 50 mm. (2 in.) of the stem of a woody plant may be crushed with a mallet. Alternatively, cut the stem on a slant and peel off the outer leathery skin with a knife, leaving the white under-stem showing for at least 50-75 mm. (2-3 in.). The stem may also be cut upwards for 25 mm. (1 in.) or 50 mm. to expose the inner tissue to water. When arranging the flowers, make sure that the peeled section of the woody stem has been well covered by the water.

Woody plants can also be treated by standing the stems in hot water. This treatment is also good for roses, poppies, bluebells and clematis; for

COLLECTING JARDINIÈRES AND CACHE-POTS

Ornamental two-piece porcelain jardinières, such as the large dark blue art nouveau pot and stand shown above, were used to display flowers in well-to-do Victorian homes. Introduced into Britain from France early in the 19th century, the jardinière remained popular until the First World War. In the last half of the century, porcelain manufacturers such as Wedgwood and Minton produced jardinières and the smaller cache-pots. The hand-decorated cache-pot on the right below was made about 1860, and the Bretby pot in the middle reflects the elaborate style of the 1880's. The cache-pot on the left commemorates the coronation of George V in 1911. Jardinières and cache-pots can still be found in antique shops. When displaying plants and flowers in jardinières, choose those that complement the rich colours and the ornate mouldings of the containers.

SPLITTING STEM ENDS

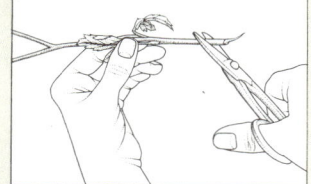

1. Cut the stem on the slant with florist's scissors to expose the stem core.

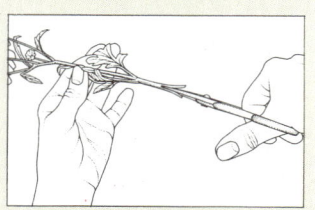

2. Split all stems from the base upwards to a length of 15 mm.

PREPARING WOODY STEMS

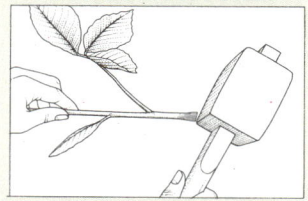

1. Crush the bottom 50 mm. of a tough woody stem, using a wooden mallet.

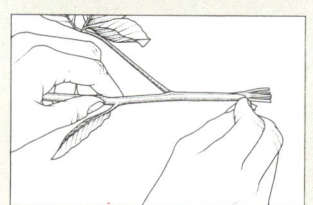

2. A woody stem can be cut on the slant. Peel off bottom 50 mm. of bark.

PRICKING THE STEM

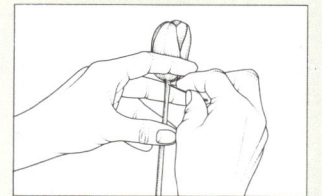

1. Prick the stem of the flower below the head, using a needle.

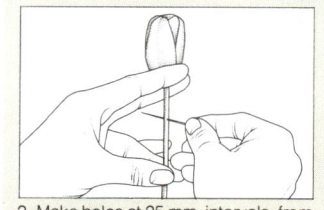

2. Make holes at 25 mm. intervals, from the head down to the stem end.

hothouse plants such as *Begonia rex* and caladium; and for hollyhocks, euphorbias, viburnums and young hydrangeas, which are slow to take up water.

Place the ends in a bucket containing 50 mm. of very hot water and leave for one minute. Then fill the bucket with tepid water and allow the stems to stand in it for several hours.

Cover the heads of delicate flowers, such as clematis, with newspaper or tissue paper to protect the petals from steam. Punch holes in the tissue paper, insert the stems through the punched holes, and then fold over the paper to cover the heads of the flowers.

MILKY STEMS

A white substance, known as latex, oozes out of euphorbias such as poinsettias when the stems are cut. The plants cannot take water until this flowing juice coagulates. The easiest way to prevent this bleeding is to singe the stem end with a gas flame or a match immediately after cutting.

HELLEBORES AND TULIPS

Pierce the stalks of hellebores (plants of the Christmas rose family) and tulips right through at intervals of about 25 mm., using a needle, from the head down to the stem end. This treatment allows the flower to drink freely. An alternative method is to score the whole length of the stem with the point of a pin or needle.

REMOVING LEAVES

Some flowers, such as lilacs and philadelphus, wilt quickly because their leaves give off most of the moisture absorbed through the stems. If the leaf stems are long enough, cut off the foliage and arrange it separately. Treat flowers with tough-fibred stems, such as wallflowers, in a similar way.

STIFFENING LEAVES

All leaves can be stiffened by complete immersion for up to 12 hours in a bath or sink filled with tepid or cold water. After removing the leaves from the water, leave them to drain on a piece of dry newspaper. Never submerge any grey foliage because immersion of this material spoils its silvery-grey effect.

• USING WILD FLOWERS AND PLANTS

Take wild flowers only from sites where they are plentiful, and choose those, such as buttercups, daisies and hedge parsley, which are abundant in the countryside. Never take wild flowers on private property or farm land without first asking the owner's permission.

Cut wild flowers about 50 mm. above the ground, using scissors. The root or bulb of the plant should never be uprooted or loosened. Never tear flowers or foliage from wild plants.

If it is not possible to place wild flowers in tepid water after picking, place them head first into a polythene bag. Blow into the bag and fasten the end with an elastic band. The trapped air cushions the plants, and the protective polythene prevents any loss of moisture.

If a polythene bag is not available, wrap the flowers in newspaper, covering their heads. Always shake wet plants before storing them in bags or wrapping them up.

Rushes, grasses and leaves can be used in fresh or dried arrangements. Pick rushes and grasses just after the flowering section grows from its outer protective sheath. Do not cut riverside plants or those with very flimsy petals, because they die quickly without water. If a wild flower droops when lightly touched, do not take it.

PLASTIC CONTAINER *For displaying flowers, a plastic trough can be as attractive as a traditional vase.*

GLASS JUG *An arrangement of dried or artificial flowers can be shown to advantage in a glass jug or vase.*

EARTHENWARE CASSEROLE *For massing flowers, such as daisies, a casserole is suitable: there is no danger of its overbalancing because of the weight.*

METALLIC CACHE-POT *A potted house plant can be placed in a more decorative container which has been filled with damp peat to create a humid atmosphere.*

• FLOWER-ARRANGING EQUIPMENT

Flower stems can be held in position by using wire-netting, plastic foam or pin-holders, which are available in a variety of sizes. For cutting wire-netting use pliers if you do not have a special wire-cutting tool.

WIRE-NETTING

A 50 mm. (2 in.) mesh wire-netting is the most pliable stem-holder. It can be crumpled to fit any container. Cut a piece of netting about twice the size of the mouth of the container. Use more wire for thin stems, and less wire for thick ones. Bend the wire into a U-shape and then crumple it into an irregular ball to fit the shape of the container. Wind the cut ends around some of the stems to hold them in position.

After use, wash the wire-netting in water, containing a little disinfectant, to remove scum and bacteria. Once the container has been emptied, cleaned and dried, the dry netting can be placed back inside it.

Always fix the wire firmly in the container. This can be done by hooking the wire over the lip of the container. Then run a fine string or length of wire round the container, tying it to a strand of the wire-netting on each side. A strong rubber band may also be used to hold the wire-netting firmly.

Galvanised wire-netting does not slip, but it may scratch a container. Plastic-covered wire causes no damage, but it may slip, even if the ends are hooked over the rims of the con-tainer, and it is also bulky and less pliable. It is best held in position with a few strips of transparent sticky tape. If the tape shows it can be cut away when the arrangement is finished.

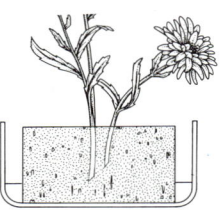

PLASTIC FOAM

Water-retaining plastic foam, such as Oasis, is sold by florists. It holds most stems easily in any position, but it is not suitable for very soft stems. It is particularly useful for holding flowers in shallow saucers and vases.

Cut the plastic foam with a knife to the required shape. Before putting the foam into the flower container, soak it in a bowl of cold water. The level of the water must be deeper than the block of foam. Leave a small block of plastic foam to soak for five minutes. A large block should be left for 15 minutes or until the foam sinks down and is level with the surface of the water. No more water is absorbed by longer soaking. Insert the bottom 25 mm. (1 in.) of the stem ends into the wet foam at any angle.

If the plastic foam is used in a shallow container without water, make sure it is kept moist by pouring in a little water every day or two. Foam does not easily absorb water a second time. Eventually it becomes full of holes and disintegrates. Keep the foam in a plastic bag between uses, to prevent it from drying out.

If necessary, foam can be secured to a container with a special green or white adhesive tape stocked by florists. It may also be impaled on a pin-holder made for this purpose.

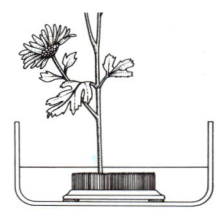

PIN-HOLDERS

These consist of a series of metal points, placed closely together, which project upwards from a heavy metal base. The shapes and sizes of the bases vary. The most useful base is round, and about 75 mm. (3 in.) in diameter. The stems are gently pressed on to the points. Slender stems are not suitable for pin-holders.

To secure the pin-holders, stick a small ball of Plasticine or floral clay on the base. Press the pin-holder on to the bottom of the container, twisting slightly as you press down. The pin-holder, the Plasticine and the container must all be dry.

• METHODS OF ARRANGING

When making up an arrangement, work on a polythene sheet where the flowers and other materials to be ar-ranged can be clearly set out. This method of working also prevents mess and damage to furniture.

MASSED ARRANGEMENTS

The simplest arrangement is a bunch of cow parsley or marigolds, massed together tightly in a container. The emphasis in this type of arrangement is on the colour rather than the design.

The stems can be cut to a length slightly taller than the height of the container. The only support needed for a bunch in a deep container is the rim of the vessel. However, in a shal-

---

ALL-ROUND DESIGN

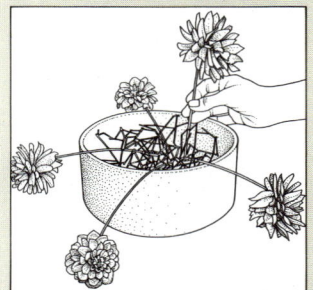

1. Crumple the wire-netting to form a mound and place in the middle of a wide-necked container. Insert the tallest stem in the centre of the netting.

2. In this display of dahlias, the side stems radiate out from the centre at different angles and distances to form the outline of the arrangement.

CONE-SHAPED DISPLAY

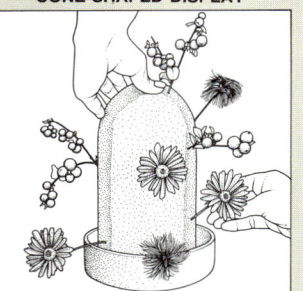

1. Cut a rounded cylinder from a block of foam. Soak the foam before fixing the straight end in the container. Insert the foliage and then the flowers.

2. This display consists of clematis seedheads, snowberries and American spray chrysanthemums. A cone is suitable for a vase or a shallow dish.

FRONT-FACING ARRANGEMENT

1. Mound the wire-netting higher at the back of the container. Set the centre stem towards the back rim. Place the side stems at angles to the centre.

2. A front-facing arrangement of flowers and other materials can be set on a side table against a wall. This design consists of daffodils, catkins and ivy.

low container the stems must have some extra support inside.

ALL-ROUND DESIGN

With equipment to hold stems in position, flowers can also be arranged in a definite outline. A basic shape is the all-round design, with the stems radiating out in all directions. The design must be arranged so that the flowers look attractive when viewed from any angle.

A wide-necked container is best for the all-round design because it gives more room for the radiating stems. Lift the wire-netting in the centre to form a mound above the rim of the container. This mound gives additional support for the central stems.

The main feature of the all-round design is the tall central stem, which defines the height of the arrangement. This stem must be vertical. Next arrange stems of roughly the same length all round the sides of the container and at right-angles to the central stem.

Place the intermediate stems between the central and the side stems. All these stems should lean away from the central stem. Allow some of the flowers at the lower levels to lean over the side to conceal the hard line of the container rim.

Never complete one side of an all-round design first. To create a well-balanced display, keep turning the container until a three-dimensional shape is achieved. Then fill in the gaps of the arrangement with shorter stems or leaves.

CONE-SHAPED DISPLAY

Other arrangements can be made from the basic all-round design by varying the lengths and the proportions of the centre and the side stems. For example, a cone-shaped arrangement can be created by elongating the centre. The side stems become shorter and shorter as they reach the rim. A cone shape can also be achieved by inserting a mass of short-stemmed flowers in a cone of plastic foam.

LONG, LOW ARRANGEMENTS

This type of arrangement is suitable for the centre of a dining table because it does not obstruct the view. The method of creating the long, low arrangement is the same as for the all-round design. However, the centre stem is cut short, while the long side stems are left longer so that they flow over the rim of the container.

FRONT-FACING ARRANGEMENTS

This type of arrangement has an outline similar to the all-round design, but it faces only one way. It is suitable for decorating a container on a side table that stands close to a wall.

In making the front-facing arrangement, set the centre stem about three-quarters of the way back in the container. Create the semi-circular outline shape with the other long-stemmed flowers. Arrange the front-facing flowers down from the top centre to below the rim level. To fill out the arrangement and give added depth to the display, alternate foliage with the flowers. Use extra flowers at the sides.

MODERN ARRANGEMENTS

Conventional rules of flower arrangements are not followed in many modern floral designs. Rather than trying to create a balanced or rounded design, the arranger may use materials to express an idea, a mood or an emotion. A modern design usually consists of only a few flowers and other plant materials. Elements from outside the plant world, such as scrap metal, rope and plastic, and unusual containers are sometimes part of modern arrangements. In its present form modern floral design is a purely Western development, although it was originally influenced by Japanese floral art.

CARING FOR FLOWERS

Fill the vase or container three-quarters full of water before arranging the flowers. This adds to the weight, and the vase is not likely to overbalance. When the flowers are arranged the vase can be filled to the top. Do not place the arrangement in full sun, by a fire or radiator, on the television set or near strong lamps, because the heat will cause the flowers to wilt or die. Never place the arrangement in a draught because it causes loss of water.

It is not necessary to change the water daily if a little mild disinfectant is used. But fresh water must be added daily to keep up the water level.

Flowers displayed in a dry, centrally heated room benefit from being sprayed with water. If this is difficult to do in a living-room, remove the vase to the kitchen or bathroom where it can be sprayed from above. Wilted flowers can be revived by re-cutting the stem under water, boiling the end, submerging the flower or by floating it in water.

Foul water shortens the life of flowers. Always strip off any leaves from the portion of the stem which is under water. Glass vases are not ideal containers for flowers because they admit sunlight. The light causes bacterial activity, which makes the water foul. There are preservatives, such as Bio-flower or Chrysal, that help to maintain freshness.

MASSED ARRANGEMENT

1 Use a container that holds the bunch together tightly. Cut the flower stems so that they are slightly taller than the height of the container.

2. Choose full-faced flowers, such as marigolds, for massed arrangements. If the container is deep enough, the wire support should not be necessary.

MODERN ARRANGEMENT

1. A low container is ideal for a modern arrangement. Cut the stems on the slant so that they lean at specific angles when impaled on the pin-holder.

2. Modern arrangements need only a few flowers and natural materials. This display consists of twigs, rayonnate chrysanthemums and bergenia.

LONG, LOW ARRANGEMENT

1. A long, low arrangement is basically the same as an all-round one, but the centre stem is kept short. The side stems are long and flow over the rim.

2. This long, low arrangement consists of ranunculus, eucalyptus and laurel leaves. This type of display is ideal as a centre-piece for a dinner table.

**COLLECTING
POT-POURRI VASES**

Pot-pourri is a mixture of dried flower petals, herbs and spices kept in a vase or other container to make a room smell sweet. The scent of the flowers escapes through holes pierced in either the vase itself or its lid. During the 18th century, such aromatic mixtures were essential to indoor comfort, because most aristocratic and well-to-do people believed that washing was unnecessary and even injurious to their health.

French manufacturers began making pot-pourri vases, known as *bouquetiers*, after the process for producing objects in artificial soft porcelain was discovered in St Cloud in the late 17th century. The Germans discovered hard porcelain at the beginning of the 18th century. With this material, they created fine pot-pourris, such as the porcelain ball shown above at the famous Meissen works near Dresden.

In Britain the manufacture of pot-pourris started in the mid-18th century. Large ornamental vases, gilded and painted with sprays of flowers, were produced at Worcester late in the century. During the Victorian period pot-pourris came from the Coalport and Minton china works. In Britain these containers remained popular as decorative household objects until the end of the 19th century.

Exquisite examples of 18th-century pot-pourri vases are exhibited at the Victoria and Albert Museum, London. They are expensive and difficult to obtain, but anyone wishing to collect these objects can still find 19th-century pot-pourri baskets and balls. These can be filled with aromatic floral mixtures, which you can make up yourself from such familiar garden plants as lavender or scented rose petals, or buy from herbalists, some department stores and chemists.

• LONG-LASTING ARRANGEMENTS

Preserved flowers and foliage make attractive long-lasting arrangements on their own, or they can be used as part of a fresh display. There are two methods of preserving plants, either by drying or by treating leaves and seed heads with glycerine solution.

DRYING PLANTS

Plants can be hung up to dry, pressed, or dehydrated by the use of drying agents. Gather the plants on a dry day, because this prevents mildew and speeds up dehydration, so helping to retain the colour. Select flowers just before they are fully developed, and avoid badly formed or poor and damaged specimens.

The flowers that are easy to preserve because they dry easily are the everlastings or 'immortelles'. These include helichrysum, statice, rhodanthe, ceranthemum and ammobium. They can be grown specifically for drying, and thrive in sunny places. Apart from everlastings, there are other flowers – for example, hydrangeas – which can also be successfully preserved by drying.

Many kinds of grasses can also be dried. They should be picked early in the summer, before they are fully mature and begin to shed their seeds. Other materials to use in dried arrangements include cones, nuts, driftwood and grains.

DRYING PLANTS BY HANGING

The simplest way of preserving plants is to hang them head down in a warm, dry, well-ventilated place, or near a boiler, until they feel dry and crisp. Keep them out of direct sunlight, which bleaches the colours.

Before hanging up flowers for drying, remove the leaves on the stems, because these shrivel and slow down dehydration. Tie the stems in small bunches, and hang them upside-down. Place hydrangeas, heather and bells-of-Ireland in 15 mm. ($\frac{1}{2}$ in.) of water, and leave until the water has evaporated. Pick hydrangeas for hanging up when the petals begin to have a papery texture.

WIRING FOR DRIED FLOWERS

Before drying immortelles, strip away the leaves on the stems. Because the stems of some immortelles shrivel during drying, they cannot support the weight of the blossom. Therefore, a wire stem must be inserted while the flower is soft and fresh.

Snip off most of the stem of the flower, leaving about 25 mm. (1 in.). Push a piece of wire into the face of the flower, and gently pull it through the cup-like calyx that holds the blossom. Hook the end of the wire and embed it in the face of the flower. The flower tightens on the wire as it dries.

After attaching the wire, twine it round a twig or cover it with a corn stalk. The wire can be hidden by binding it with florist's tape.

PRESSING PLANTS

Bracken, ferns, flat flowers and single petals can be preserved by pressing. This method flattens the plant and is not suitable for very thick or succulent plants, but it prevents curling and shrivelling.

Delicate flowers, leaves and petals can be placed between sheets of clean blotting-paper and pressed in a flower press or under a book. The longer the material is left, the better it will retain its colour when it is exposed to the light. Heavier leaves need to be placed between sheets of newspaper under a carpet or under heavy books. Large flat leaves may be placed between sheets of newspaper and pressed with a warm iron. Place these leaves under a carpet for a week to complete the drying process.

PRESERVING WITH DRYING AGENTS

Alum and borax powders, silica-gel crystals and sand can be used to dry flowers. These drying agents remove moisture from flowers, but preserve the colour and the shape of petals.

Spring flowers, such as daffodils, hellebores, mimosa, narcissi, primroses and tulips, can be treated with drying agents. In summer, pick carnations, clematis, peonies, pinks, marigolds, roses, dahlias and zinnias for preservation with drying agents.

Because some flowers are fragile, choose a drying agent that will support rather than crush them. Alum and borax are ideal for delicate flowers, but too fine for heavier blossoms. These drying agents take about six to ten days to dry out the flowers.

Silica gel is the fastest-acting drying agent. Flowers need only two or three days to dry out, but if left in silica gel too long they become brittle and the colour changes greatly.

DRYING WITH SAND

Heavier flowers can also be dried in sand. This process may take as long as three weeks. Before use, the sand must be cleaned. Place the sand in a bucket, fill with water, stir well and pour off the excess. Repeat the process several times. Spread the sand on trays and dry in the sun, or in an oven at a very low temperature for three or four hours.

DRYING WITH CHEMICAL AGENTS

Pick flowers and plant material on a dry day. Avoid plants and flowers that are badly formed, damaged or past their prime. Remove the stems and leaves. Before placing the flowers in the drying agent, wire the blossoms.

Place the flowers on a 15 mm. ($\frac{1}{2}$ in.)

WIRING FLOWERS

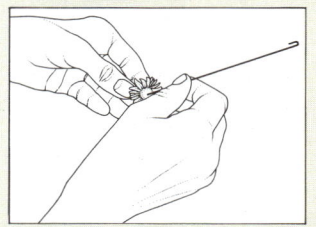

1. Hook one end of the wire and push the other end through the flower face.

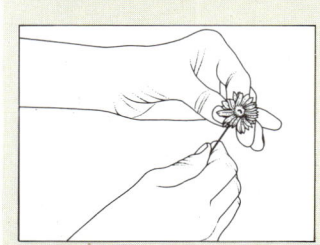

2. Pull the wire through the flower and embed the hook in the flower face.

DRYING WITH SILICA GEL

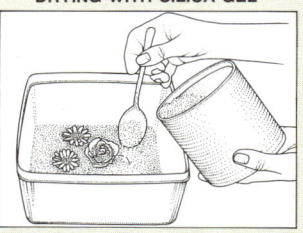

1. Rest the wired flower on the silica gel and add the crystals to cover the flower.

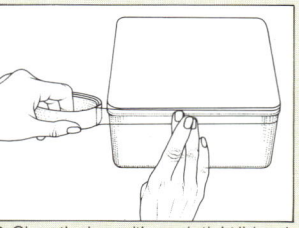

2. Close the box with an air-tight lid and seal it by running a tape around the join.

layer of drying agent which has been spread over the bottom of an air-tight tin. Gently spoon more of the drying agent over the petals. Continue until the flower is covered by at least 15 mm. of the drying agent. Place the lid on the tin and seal it by running a tape around the join. Label the tin with the contents and the date.

When opening the tin to check whether the flowers have dried sufficiently, brush away the top layer of crystals or powder. If the flowers are not dry and papery, re-cover them with the agent and reseal the box.

All drying agents need to be dried out after use. Spread them on baking trays, and place in an oven at a temperature of no more than 130°C (250°F; mark ½) for an hour or two. Store the drying agents in a sealed container.

PRESERVING WITH GLYCERINE

Many leaves and some seed heads can be preserved with glycerine solution. The suitable plants include aspidistra, beech, fatsia, ferns, ivy, hellebore, laurel, magnolia, oak and rhododendron. As the solution is absorbed by these plants, the leaves change in colour from green to shades of brown, creamy-beige or almost black.

Pick mature foliage for preserving with glycerine, but avoid damaged leaves and sprays. Young leaves do not take up glycerine easily. The best time to collect most foliage is in July. Remove the lower or damaged leaves, and prune out the crowded ones. Cut the stem end on a slant. Split thick stems and scrape the bark off the woody stems with a knife for about 50 mm. (2 in.).

Prepare a mixture of 1 part glycerine to 2 parts hot water. Stir the mixture well, and place about 50 mm. of the stem in the solution. Do not allow the stems to dry out during the preserving process. Top up the solution as it is drawn up into the stem.

Keep the stems in the solution until the leaves change colour. This may take from a few days to several weeks.

Submerge small, tough leaves, such as ivy, because they absorb moisture slowly. Aspidistra and large fatsia leaves which are too large to submerge can be wiped on both sides, using cottonwool or a tissue, before standing the stems in a glycerine solution.

STORING AND HANDLING

When not in use, preserved plant material can be placed in cardboard boxes or tins with lids. Store the boxes in a dry place to prevent the plant material from reabsorbing moisture. Preserved plant material can also be stored standing up in jars or left hanging up if the atmosphere is dry.

Wrap preserved material individually in tissue paper. Do not store plant material preserved by different methods in the same box.

When used with fresh flowers, plant material, preserved with glycerine, may develop mildew on the stems. To prevent this, lacquer the stems with varnish or nail polish or dip them in wax. Dried material should be arranged with other fresh or preserved material without water.

Damp air makes dried flowers go limp. Coat them with an aerosol plastic spray, or a fixative from an art shop.

Arrange dried or preserved materials in the same way as fresh flowers and foliage. As water is not used, arrangements placed in lightweight containers should be weighted with sand or gravel for additional stability. Although a dried-flower display is long-lasting, it can be rearranged every few weeks to give more interest.

HANGING FLOWERS   Bunches of flowers hanging upside-down from a rafter dry quickly in a well-ventilated place.

• PLANTING IN BOXES AND TUBS

Containers such as window-boxes and tubs are normally used for growing flowering plants and shrubs. They can also be planted with herbs, vegetables and fruit, such as miniature tomatoes and strawberries.

Window-boxes made from heavy materials, such as stone or concrete, are too heavy and dangerous to be placed on window sills. Fibreglass and plastic containers have the advantage of being light but are still strong enough to support the weight of soil and water.

Untreated wooden window-boxes warp and rot quickly unless they are made of hardwoods, such as teak, elm or oak. Before planting in a wooden box, paint the outside and treat the inside with a non-poisonous preservative, such as Cuprinol.

Tubs may also be made of oak, teak or stone, and some are made from large casks sawn in half. They can be used on terraces and balconies.

PREPARING BOXES AND TUBS

All containers intended for outdoor use must have drainage holes in the base. Bore 20 mm. ($\frac{3}{4}$ in.) holes at 150 mm. (6 in.) intervals in the bottom of the container. Use large terracotta tubs without drainage holes only for containing plants in their own pots.

When filling the container with soil, first cover the bottom with a 25-50 mm. (1-2 in.) layer of broken crockery, clinker or small stones. Do

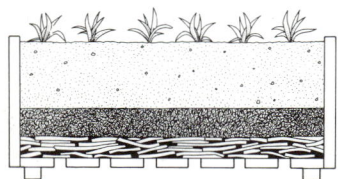

Fill a box with potting mixture and peat.

not pack these so tightly that the water cannot seep through. On top of this layer, add another layer of partly decomposed leaves or moss.

Fill the box, up to 25 mm. (1 in.) from the rim, with potting mixture, such as John Innes No. 2, or an all-peat compost. Plant lime-hating plants, such as rhododendrons, azaleas, camellias and some heathers, in lime-free soil, such as John Innes acid compost, or limeless peat compost. Water it well and allow it to settle. Top up the container annually with fresh potting mixture.

FIXING BOXES AND TUBS

When placing a window-box on a sill, make sure that it fits the space snugly. Secure the box by means of wedges driven between the ends of the box and the side walls, or with hooks fastened to eyelets in the window-frame. Use two wooden blocks to raise the box above the sill. Place a metal drip tray beneath the holes.

Sink pot plants in a box filled with peat.

If there is no window-sill, the box can be fixed to the outside wall on strong brackets. Because the boxes are heavy when filled with soil, place them in position before filling them up, watering and planting.

Prepare a wooden tub in the same way as a wooden box. Castors can be fixed underneath the tub for easy movement. If castors are not used, stand the tubs on bricks or wooden blocks to allow drainage and a good circulation of air.

PLANTING IN CONTAINERS

When planting a window-box or tub, put the plants straight into the soil. Alternatively, put the plants in pots and then put the pots in the box. Surround the pots with soil and damp peat.

This method of planting makes it easy to remove a plant if it dies. During the winter the plants in pots can be brought indoors and put outside when the weather grows warmer.

The best bushy plants for tubs include camellias, fatsias, hydrangeas, marguerites and roses. The following climbing plants are recommended for growing in tubs: jasmine, morning glory, passion flowers and roses.

WHEN TO PLANT IN BOXES

Plant bulbs and other spring-flowering plants in boxes in September or October. When they have finished flowering they can be immediately replaced by summer-flowering plants. During winter, the window-box can be filled with dwarf evergreen shrubs. However, if these remain in the boxes some of the spring or summer-flower display may have to be sacrificed.

MAINTAINING PLANTS

Because the soil in window-boxes dries out in the sun and the wind, it must be watered regularly. In the hottest periods of the summer, plants may need watering once or twice a day. But at other times, several times a week will be sufficient. Prick the soil in the window-box with a pointed stick or hand fork from time to time to keep it aerated. Add plant food occasionally, following the maker's instructions.

When plants are removed at the end of the spring or summer season, turn the potting mixture lightly and add a fertiliser. If possible, change the soil during the winter.

BOXES FOR WINDOW-SILLS *The traditional containers for flowering plants and shrubs are window-boxes which can be used to brighten the exterior of a house.*

SUGGESTIONS FOR OUTDOOR PLANTINGS

ASPECT	SUMMER	WINTER
South and west:	Geranium (zonal pelargonium) Pelargonium Petunia Trailing *Lobelia erinus* *Alyssum maritimum* *Tagetes* (marigold) Nicotiana (tobacco plant) Tuberous begonia *Ageratum houstonianum* Marguerite Nasturtium *Cineraria maritima*	Hebe (veronica) Hedera (ivy) Christmas cherry Dwarf cupressus Daffodil Tulip
North and east	Ever-flowering begonia Fuchsia Impatiens (busy lizzie) Italian bell flower Hedera (ivy) Hebe (veronica) Hydrangea	Aucuba (Japanese laurel) Fatsia Polyanthus Myosotis (forget-me-not) Crocus Snowdrops

URNS FOR GARDENS *An exotic urn, set on a pedestal and filled with plants and shrubs, provides a simple but striking feature in a small paved garden.*

BALCONY CONTAINERS *During the summer a balcony is a delightful sitting-out area which can be enhanced by plants in a variety of different containers.*

POTS AT THE WINDOW *Most herbs like plenty of light – so they are easy to grow in pots on a kitchen window-sill. At the same time they are instantly available when cooking.*

177

CARE AND TREATMENT OF HOUSE PLANTS

Most house plants are easy to care for. But they can be harmed by strong draughts, sudden changes in room temperature, too much or too little water, or long periods in direct sunlight or darkness. Although fresh air is not essential to indoor plants, a gentle movement of air is beneficial.

Do not buy house plants with damaged leaves or spindly stems. Indoor plants are usually sold with labels which give information about growing conditions and maintenance. If there is no label, ask for information about the plant's requirements.

Never place indoor plants in garden soil. They must be grown in an appropriate potting mixture.

WATERING

Ideally, the soil surrounding a house plant should be moist but not soggy. Over-watering will rot the roots of the plant and cause the leaves to turn yellow and drop off.

Submerge a dry plant up to the pot rim.

The most effective way of watering is to submerge the pot in a bucket of tepid water, and leave it until the water stops bubbling. Then allow it to drain and replace it in its saucer.

Do not leave the pot standing in water. Only semi-aquatic plants, such as cyperus, can survive with permanently waterlogged roots.

Most flowering plants may require a lot of water, whereas cacti need very little. Plants in hot rooms need more than those in cool rooms, because the rate of evaporation is greater in a warm atmosphere. Plants in plastic pots lose less water than those in porous clay ones, which need frequent watering.

If you use a can, pour tepid water on the soil, rather than on the plant. A long-spouted watering-can makes this easy. Fill the pot to the rim. Any surplus should drain through the hole in the bottom of the pot and collect in a saucer or outer pot.

Water a very dry plant thoroughly and leave it until the soil appears dry. Do not give it small amounts daily.

Give plants more water during their period of growth, when new foliage and flowers are forming. With most, this is in the warm months. But winter-flowering plants should be watered and fed in winter, and can be safely left unwatered and unfed in the spring and summer.

Some plants, including cyclamens, gloxinias (sinningia), miniature orange and lemon trees and African violets, can also be watered from below. To do this, stand the pot in water to the level of the potting mixture and leave it to soak until the water starts to moisten the surface of the soil. Allow the water to drain before replacing the pot.

PROVIDING HUMIDITY

Most central-heating systems absorb moisture from the air, and this is harmful to plants. Humidifiers, radiator troughs and saucers of water left about the room help to provide humidity.

Spraying plants with tepid water also provides moisture. Stand about a foot away from the plant and direct the spray at the leaves. Do not spray plants in direct sunlight, because the moisture will scorch the leaves.

Stand a pot on pebbles or place in peat.

An effective way of supplying house plants with sufficient moisture is to place the pot in a larger container lined with moist peat or sand.

Another method is to put a 25 mm. (1 in.) layer of pebbles in a container. Add water to just below the top of the pebbles and stand the pot on them. Top up the water as it evaporates.

The steamy atmosphere of bathrooms and kitchens is a good source of moisture. Plants in other rooms will benefit by a move to such conditions.

FEEDING

Give house plants a liquid feed at fortnightly intervals during the growing and flowering seasons. Liquid compound fertilisers, which contain all essential plant food, are sold by chemists, florists and garden centres. The instructions for use are given on the labels. It is better to give too little rather than too much food.

LIGHT

Many plants need full sun during the late autumn to early spring and then light shade for the rest of the year. Generally, plants with dark green foliage tolerate deep shade best, whereas plants with variegated or coloured leaves need good light. The only indoor plants which should be left in full summer sun are desert cacti, succulents, and some flowering plants such as geraniums.

The leaves of plants tend always to grow towards the light, making them spindly and unbalanced. Turn them occasionally, particularly if they are sitting on a sunny window-sill, so that they grow evenly all round and do not turn away from the room.

If necessary, natural light can be supplemented or replaced by fluorescent lighting. For best results, it is advisable always to use 'warm white' tubes for flowering plants, and 'daylight' tubes for foliage plants.

Stand the plants about 400-800 mm. (16-32 in.) beneath the fluorescent tube. For maximum benefit the plant needs about 12 hours of artificial light each day.

PTERIS TREMULA. This easy-to-grow fern is a popular house plant.

TEMPERATURE

Most house plants can tolerate temperatures which are too low for human comfort. But they prefer constant temperatures, ideally 10-18°C (50-64°F), and not above 24°C (75°F).

LEAF CARE

Because plants breathe and absorb light through their leaves, any dust that settles on them could be harmful.

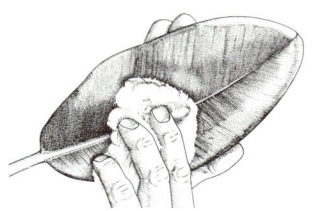

Wipe leaves with damp cottonwool.

Remove it with a dry cloth. To give leaves a glossy finish, wipe them carefully with cottonwool or a cloth dipped in water.

FUMES

Only sturdy plants with thick leathery leaves will survive in rooms with fumes from gas, coke, oil and anthracite-coal heating. Fresh paint and ripe apples also give off fumes that harm house plants.

HOLIDAY CARE

Before going on holiday, remove the plants from positions beside windows or radiators. Water them thoroughly. If it is not possible to get a neighbour or friend to take care of the plants, there are several ways of making sure that they do not dry out while you are away. Place the plants on trays of gravel and water and let them draw what moisture they need. Or, stand the pots closely together in buckets, or a sink, in a bed of damp peat.

Placing large bowls of water near the plants helps to create a humid atmosphere. Another way to maintain humidity is to water the plant generously then cover it with a plastic bag with as much air as possible trapped inside.

RE-POTTING

House plants need regular re-potting. In the case of young plants re-potting should be done once a year, in the spring before the growing season starts. The most useful pot sizes for growing plants are 2½ in., 3½ in. and 5 in. As the plants grow, they need to be placed in correspondingly larger pots. Established plants need re-potting in the same size pot with fresh compost every two or three years.

A plant is pot-bound when the root ball is too big for the container. The plant is slow to grow even in good light and warmth, or with frequent watering and feeding. The soil surrounding a pot-bound plant also dries out quickly when watered. The roots of the plant may grow through the drainage holes. However, several plants – for example, clivia – grow well and flower more freely when pot-bound, but they must be fed and watered regularly.

POTTING MIXTURE

Pot-grown plants need soil or compost that contains the right proportion of potash, nitrogen and phosphate. The compost should be free of pests and diseases, and sterilised before being used. There are ready-made sterilised composts available for pot-grown plants. For example, there are three grades of John Innes compost mixtures which consist of the same proportions of loam, peat and sand, but these differ according to the amount of fertiliser they contain. John Innes No. 1 potting compost can be used primarily for young or slow-growing plants. No. 2 potting compost has twice as much fertiliser as No. 1 and is suitable for fast-growing plants. Use No. 3 for vigorous growths such as chrysanthemums. There is also a John Innes seed compost for seed sowing. All-peat or loamless composts are also suitable for house plants.

REMOVING THE PLANT

To make sure that potting on is necessary, carefully remove the plant from its pot. Cover the soil with your fingers and turn the pot upside-down. Make sure that the compost in the pot is dry before removing the plant. Hold the plant with the stems projecting between your first and second fingers. Give the pot a sharp tap to release the plant. Allow the root ball to fall out of the pot into your hand.

If there appears to be plenty of space and soil for the roots, slip the root ball into the pot again. However, if the roots are matted on the outside and there is very little soil, transfer the plant to a slightly larger pot. If an old pot is used, it must be cleaned first. Soak a new clay pot in water overnight. Remove any old crocks and put new ones in the new pot. Plastic pots do not need crocks because there are more drainage holes.

When re-potting, scatter 15 mm. (½ in.) or so of John Innes No. 2 potting compost on the base of the pot. Use the same type of compost if you want to keep the plant small. However, to ensure that plants, such as annuals, reach the flowering stage, re-potting in the stronger, No. 3 – type of compost is necessary.

Place the plant on top of the new layer of potting mixture in the larger pot. Fill the space around the root ball until the surface of the soil is about 15 mm. from the rim.

CUTTING BACK

Some indoor plants can be cut back to keep them neat, and to encourage them to grow in a particular shape. Prune plants which have a vigorous growth, such as geraniums and fuchsias, by cutting back just as growth begins. Cut straggly shoots cleanly just above a leaf joint.

Indoor plants can be 'stopped' to encourage bushy growth, which gives more flowers. Stopping means pinching out the growing tip of the stem or the young shoot just above a leaf joint. The best time for stopping is in the spring.

SUPPORTING PLANTS

Indoor climbing plants – for example, ivies – need support to grow strongly. Triangular, square or circular trellis frames made of plastic or bamboo can be used. Alternatively, insert bamboo canes in the pot and tie the climber loosely with soft raffia or wire.

Train a plant with aerial roots on a pole.

Philodendrons and other plants with aerial roots can be trained on poles covered with moss obtained from garden centres. Secure the moss with green plastic-covered wire, and spray regularly with water.

HOW TO RE-POT A PLANT

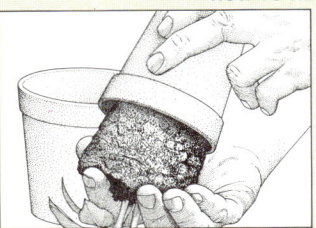
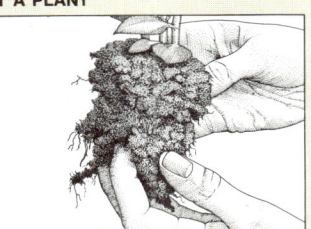

1. Turn a pot-bound plant upside-down with your hand over the soil and shake out the root ball into your hand.

2. Before re-potting the plant in a larger pot, ease away some of the old soil from around the roots.

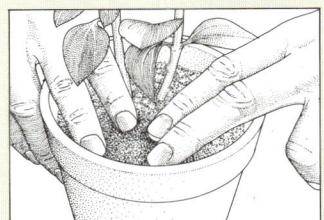

3. Set the plant on compost in a new pot and fill in the space around the root. Fill the pot to within 15 mm. of the rim.

4. Water the plant before lightly firming down the fresh compost with your fingers or a stick.

• PROPAGATING PLANTS

If a house plant is multi-stemmed at or below ground level, new plants can be grown by dividing the plant into two or more pieces. Do this during the growing period, from late spring to early autumn.

Turn the plant upside-down and gently knock it out of its pot. Expose the points at which the plant can be divided by tapping away the soil round the crown and root ball. Using a small stick or your fingers, pull the base of the plant apart. If the crown or rootstock is thick or tough, cut the roots or stems with a knife. Pot the separated pieces at once. Water sparingly at first. Keep the pots in a shaded, warm position for a few weeks.

PLANTS FROM CUTTINGS

New plants can be propagated by taking cuttings. This can be done by snipping off a young shoot, a piece of stem or root, or even a piece of leaf.

Put the cuttings in a mixture of equal quantities of peat and washed sand, or in John Innes No. 1 potting compost. Some plants, such as African violets, develop roots simply by being placed in water for a time. Because their roots are tender, they must be potted very gently.

Cuttings can be rooted in pots and trays. Insert several cuttings round the edge of the pot.

A cutting needs warmth and moisture to grow. Initially, the water uptake is slow, because the cutting has no roots. Therefore, a moist atmosphere is essential to prevent wilting. An ideal method of creating such an atmosphere is to cover the pot with a clear plastic dome, jam jar, tumbler or plastic bag.

Spray uncovered cuttings with a fine mist of water from time to time. Once the roots of the cuttings are growing, transplant them into separate pots of John Innes No. 1 potting compost.

Tip cuttings These offer one of the easiest methods of propagation. Cuttings from hollow-stemmed plants, such as tradescantias, and from ivies root quickly. Take 75-100 mm. (3-4 in.) cuttings from the tips of young, non-flowering stems or side-shoots. Strip the lower leaves from each cutting, and trim the stem cleanly below a leaf node. Stand the cuttings in a glass of water. After 10-14 days, roots appear and the plants can be potted.

Cuttings from other house plants can be inserted in the potting mixture immediately. With a sharp knife, cut about 100 mm. (4 in.) from a stem or side-shoot. Pull off the lower leaves

---

DIVIDING PLANTS

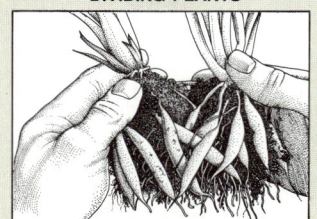

1. After tapping away the old compost, carefully pull the plant roots apart.

2. Sever any tangled roots using a sharp knife or a razor blade.

3. Pot the separated pieces in John Innes compost or an all-peat mixture.

HOW TO ROOT TIP CUTTINGS

1. Take cuttings from the stems of young, non-flowering stems during the summer.

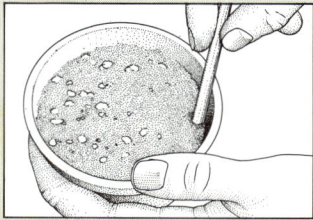

2. With a small stick, make four to six planting holes round the edge of the pot.

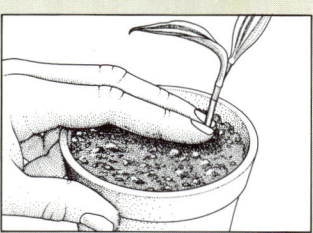

3. Insert the cuttings in the planting holes so that the stems rest against the pot.

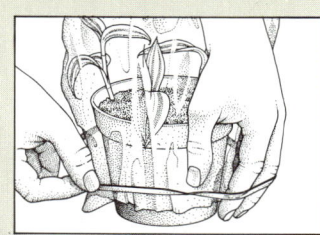

4. Cover the pot loosely with plastic and keep it in a shaded place.

5. When the cuttings are rooted, remove them carefully from the soil.

6. Pot the new plants in John Innes No. 1 compost and water them in.

ROOTING LEAF CUTTINGS OF AFRICAN VIOLETS

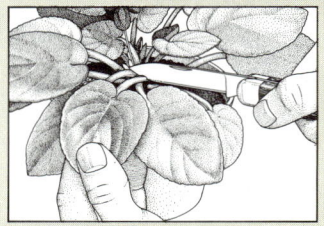

1. Cut young healthy leaves from the plant, with the stalks attached.

2. With a small stick, make a few planting holes in a pot of compost.

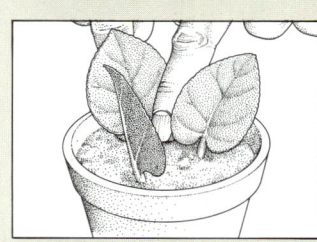

3. Insert each cutting so that the leaf blade is clear of the compost.

4. Fill the pot with water to the top and then let it drain completely.

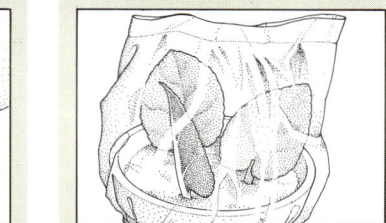

5. Enclose the top of the pot with a plastic bag, secured by an elastic band.

6. When the leaf cuttings are rooted, remove the cuttings and pot separately.

and make a clean cut across the stem just below a leaf node – the point where a leaf joins the stem.

Plant four to six cuttings round the edge of a 90 mm. (3½ in.) pot. Cover the pot with a clear plastic dome or plastic bag. Leave the pot in a shaded position where a temperature of 18°C (64°F) can be maintained. The cuttings should take root within three or four weeks.

Remove the cuttings by carefully inverting the pot, supporting the soil with the hands. Pot each cutting singly in John Innes No. 1 compost.

Leaf cuttings Plants with thick, hairy leaves, such as African violets or begonias, are easily propagated by leaf cuttings. The best time for taking cuttings is from June to September.

Cut two or three healthy young leaves, with about 25 mm. (1 in.) of the stalk attached. Trim the end of each leaf stalk cleanly with a sharp knife. Almost fill a 90 mm. (3½ in.) pot with a mixture of equal quantities of peat and coarse sand. Most leaf cuttings can be either laid flat on the compost or inserted in it. But insert only the stalk of the African violet in the compost because the leaf may otherwise rot.

Fill the pot with water to the top and let it drain completely. Cover the pot with a plastic bag and secure it with an elastic band to ensure that the atmosphere is kept moist.

Roots will form within three to five weeks, and new leaves will appear at the base of the leaf stem. When this happens, invert the pot and remove the cuttings carefully. Place them singly in 65 mm. (2½ in.) pots of John Innes No. 1 compost. Keep the plants in a warm shaded place for two or three weeks.

PLANTS FROM FRUIT

The stones of many fruits, such as avocado pears, and the seeds of lemons, oranges and grapefruit, can be grown to form attractive household plants.

To grow a house plant from an avocado, first wash the stone to remove any loose skin. Pierce the stone with a skewer at three points and insert three matchsticks to half their length in the holes. Suspend the stone over the mouth of a jar of water. The water should reach about 20 mm. (¾ in.) up the stone. Put the stone and the jar in a warm, dimly lit place and keep the water level topped up.

In three to eight weeks, the stone will split, and a root and shoot will emerge. Put the stone about 75 mm. (3 in.) deep in a large pot of John Innes No. 1 compost. It will grow rapidly in a warm sunny spot, developing lush, green-pointed leaves and a woody trunk. Pinch the growing shoot to make the avocado plant bush out. Keep the plant out of draughts, and water whenever the potting mixture gets dry. Spray the foliage occasionally. The plant grows rapidly and needs frequent re-potting (see p.179).

A handsome house plant can be grown from a pineapple top. Slice off the fresh leaf top, together with 25 mm. (1 in.) of flesh, retaining the top row of 'pips' on the flesh. Leave the cutting to dry for two or three days – this prevents rotting.

Fill a 90-100 mm. (3½-4 in.) pot to within 20 mm. (¾ in.) of its rim with moist potting compost. On top of this, sprinkle a thin layer of coarse sand.

Plant the pineapple top in the shallow layer of sand sprinkled with compost. Cover the fleshy part with fresh compost. Keep the plant in a warm place at a temperature of 20-23°C (68-73°F). Cover the pot with a plastic bag. Remove the bag to spray the plant regularly. Rooting takes place in about eight weeks. Once fresh leaves appear, remove the plastic bag, and re-pot several months after rooting.

The plant may grow to about 450 mm. (18 in.) high. Water and feed it regularly. If the plant is kept in considerable humidity and warmth it may eventually produce fruit of its own.

GROWING AN AVOCADO

1. Suspend the stone from matchsticks then almost fill the jar with water.

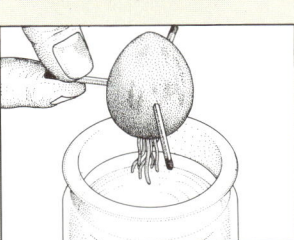

2. In three to eight weeks, roots emerge from the base of the stone.

3. Half bury the stone, roots down, in a pot containing John Innes compost.

GROWING A PINEAPPLE

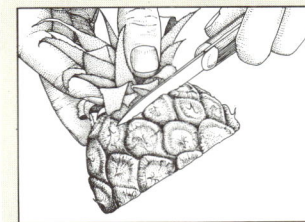

1. Slice off the leafy crown and the top row of 'pips' from a fresh pineapple.

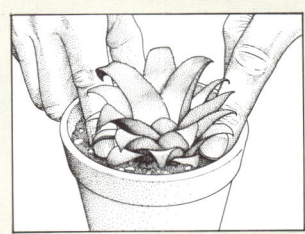

2. Set the pineapple top in a shallow layer of sand sprinkled over compost.

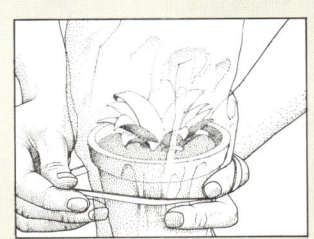

3. Cover the pot with a plastic bag secured with an elastic band.

PLANTS FOR GROUPING *Flowering house plants such as calceolaria can be grouped together in a large container to create a massed floral display.*

EASY PLANTS FOR THE HOUSE

All house plants need light, but few will tolerate scorching sunshine. As a general guide, flowering plants do best in good light; those with thick, dark-green foliage prefer some shade. All the plants listed below are easy to grow, and with reasonable care most will last for years.

NAME	DESCRIPTION	LIGHT	REMARKS
Asparagus fern	Feathery foliage	Not fussy	Water well in summer
Aspidistra	Foliage	Not full sun	Sponge leaves
Busy lizzie	Long-flowering	Sun	Keep moist
Calceolaria	Flowering	Light shade	Discard after flowering
Campanula	Trailing	Light shade	Water well during flowering
Chrysanthemum	Flowering	Sun	Avoid waterlogging
Ivies	Climbing or trailing	Light shade	Tolerant to central heating
Mother-in-law's tongue	Tall, narrow leaves	Not fussy	Water moderately
Palm	Grows up to 6 ft	Sun	Keep in humid place
Pelargonium (geranium)	Bushy or trailing	Sun	Avoid over-watering, especially in winter
Philodendron	Vine, up to 4 ft tall	Light shade	Tolerates gas
Rubber plant	Grows up to 6 ft	Light shade	Avoid draughts
Wandering jew	Trailing	No direct sun	Water well in summer

PLANTS FOR WINDOWS During the winter, plants may be left on a south or west-facing window, but they must be moved elsewhere in the summer.

• PESTS AND DISEASES

Incorrect watering, insufficient lighting and a dry atmosphere can stunt plant growth. Improving growing conditions (see chart) may restore the plant to health. Avoid over-watering because this can cause root rot.

PLANT PESTS

Greenfly, red spider mite, thrips and scale insects are the most common insect pests that attack house plants.

Greenfly The first sign of greenfly is a twisting or warping of the tender shoots of the plant. Because these pests multiply quickly, fast action is required to prevent damage to the plant. Spray with an insecticide, such as malathion, outside on a still day. Soapy water will also get rid of greenfly.

Red spider mite The sign of an attack is a fine pale or reddish mottling on the leaves, followed by browning or premature leaf-fall. This pest also attacks when humidity is low. Raise the humidity and spray with malathion.

Scale insects A wilting plant with clusters of scab-like scales on its shoots will be under attack by scale insects. They are immobile, and live by sucking the plant's sap. Wipe off with a cloth dampened with soapy water or methylated spirit.

Thrips Silvery-white patches on leaves are caused by thrips – minute insects which puncture the leaves. Spray the plant outside on a still day with malathion, BHC or derris.

PLANT DISEASES

Fungus diseases are not easy to cure. A cause of fungus disease is standing a plant in a position that is too cool, damp and dark. Improving growing conditions and applying a fungicide may help. But it is best to throw out a sick plant, because the disease may spread to nearby plants.

PESTS, DISEASES AND AILMENTS OF HOUSE PLANTS

PLANT TROUBLE	CAUSE	TREATMENT
Brown patches on the leaf and around the edges	Hot dry air, paraffin, coal-gas fumes, over-watering, sun-scorch, water splashes, over-feeding, pot-bound	Remove badly affected leaves, improve growing conditions
Dropping leaves, buds or flowers	Sudden change in temperature or light, over-watering, over-feeding, dryness of roots, red spider mite	Improve growing conditions. Spray pests with malathion
Failure to flower	Over-feeding may be the cause, if there is excessive foliage; too much or too little heat; dryness at roots	Check the fertiliser balance. Correct pruning may make the plant flower. Make sure the plant never lacks water
Frost damage	This may occur when the plant is left too near to a window during cold weather, and is perhaps cut off from room heat by a heavy curtain	To thaw the plants, put them in a cool place and spray with cold water. To prevent future frost damage, move the plants from the window to the centre of the room
Holes in leaves	Leaf-eating insects, such as caterpillars and earwigs	Spray leaves with malathion
Leaf spots	Thrips, sun-scorch, spraying with incorrect or over-concentrated pesticides	Spray with malathion. Remove from sunlight. Check manufacturer's instructions for spray
Lopsided growth, with stems and leaves bending to one side	Light deficiency	Give the pot a quarter turn every day to provide even light
Mottled leaves	Red spider mite, thrips and other pests	Spray leaves with malathion
Poor or slow growth, plants with spindly stems and pale leaves	Problems may be caused by under-feeding, over-watering or insufficient light during the growing season; pot-bound	Feed regularly, reduce watering. If plant is pot-bound, re-pot in a larger vessel
Stunted plants with poor roots	Over-watering	Let plants dry out completely between waterings
Wilting	Soil or atmosphere too dry, too much sun or heat, over-watering, pot-bound	Spray leaves frequently, reduce watering and check on drainage. If plant is pot-bound, re-pot
Yellowing leaves	Lime in compost or tap water used for lime-hating plants; over-watering	Re-pot in John Innes acid compost or a loamless compost. Water with rain water, but avoid making compost waterlogged

PLANTS FOR BIG ROOMS *A wide range of house plants can be used to harmonise with the colour scheme and the furnishings of a room. Before buying a plant, consider the space that is available and choose one that seems to be in proportion to its surroundings. Big, bold plants can be effective in large rooms, and can be used against an empty wall or to fill a bare corner.*

Planning your kitchen

No single factor has a greater impact on reducing the burden of housework than a well-planned kitchen. The following section shows how ergonomics – the study of human efficiency in a working environment – can be applied in the kitchen to create labour-saving working areas. Whether you are fitting out a brand new kitchen or seeking ways to improve your existing one, you will find dozens of ideas in these pages.

CONTENTS

IMPROVING YOUR KITCHEN

Anybody with a house to run is likely to spend more of the working day in the kitchen than in any other room – cooking, washing up, and possibly washing and ironing too. All of these jobs can be done easily and efficiently even in a small kitchen, provided that the kitchen is planned in a logical way, to ensure a smooth work-flow.

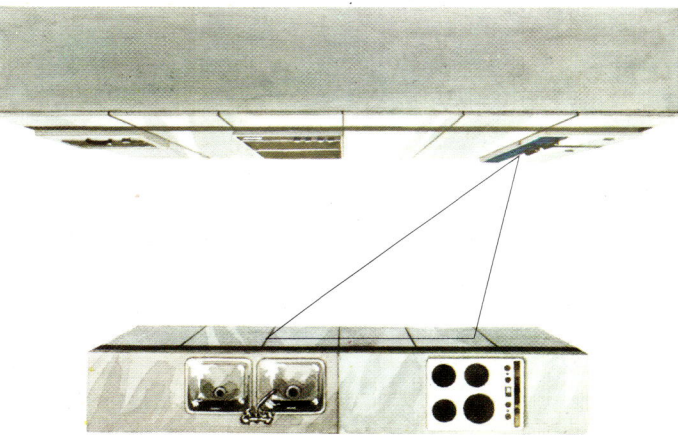

THE WORK TRIANGLE   The total distance from refrigerator to cooker to sink and back to refrigerator should never exceed 6 m. (20 ft).

• WORK TRIANGLE

Producing a meal involves a natural work sequence: food storage, preparation, cooking, serving, washing up and clearing away. These jobs are linked to refrigerator, cooker and sink, which should form a work triangle. For maximum efficiency, the total distance between these three points should not be more than 6 m. (20 ft). The cooker and sink should be fairly close to each other, divided by a work surface for food preparation.

If possible, have a work surface on each side of the cooker and sink, giving an uninterrupted sequence of: work top, sink, work top, cooker, work top. Keep tall cupboards out of this working area.

POSITION OF MAIN APPLIANCES

Unless you are replanning your kitchen, the siting of large pieces of equipment is probably determined by the position of the sink. This is usually near a window, which gives a good light for washing up and possibly a view. The disadvantage is that there may be no convenient wall for fixing a plate rack or cupboard. If you have a choice of sink position, you will have to decide which is preferable. Avoid having a sink jammed up against a corner, as this reduces access and makes it difficult to have someone helping with the washing up. This does not apply, of course, if a dishwasher is used.

Avoid placing a cooker *squarely* in a corner – if a corner is the only place for it, fit it *across* the corner. Access is otherwise difficult and only one side is left free for a work top.

Nor should a cooker be in front of a window as there is a risk of curtains catching fire and of accidents being caused by leaning across the cooker to open or clean the window. Another danger is that a draught from the window may blow out a gas flame on the hob. For the same reason, do not place the cooker near a door; there is an extra risk of pan handles being knocked by people going in and out.

Avoid having a wall cupboard above the cooker as there is risk that it may catch fire. There is also a danger of burning or scalding yourself when reaching over the hob to a cupboard.

The refrigerator, which is the third point of the triangle, should be placed within easy reach of the cooker and a work top. It is preferable not to have the cooker and refrigerator next to each other, but if there is no alternative, place an asbestos sheet between them for added insulation, or have a wide gap which can be used for tray storage.

The work triangle should be free from obstructions and arranged so that other people do not pass through it when you are working there. Accidents can be caused by a child rushing across your path while you are carrying something hot or heavy. There are more accidents in kitchens in a year than on the roads.

ERGONOMICS: HOW TO MINIMISE THE STRAIN WHILE YOU WORK

CALCULATING THE IDEAL HEIGHTS FOR YOUR KITCHEN WORK TOPS

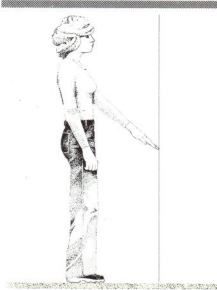 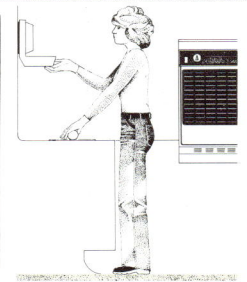 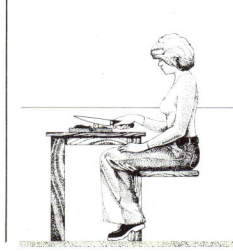 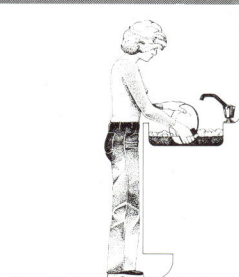

Stand upright, 450 mm. (18 in.) from a wall, and raise one arm until your fingers touch the wall. The point of contact is the ideal height for your work top.

Grills, wall-mounted equipment and oven controls should be at eye level. Position a high-level oven so that its bottom shelf aligns with a work top.

The comfortable height of a work top used when seated is 700 mm. (28 in.), with the seat height at 400 mm. (16 in.). When using a bowl, place it on your lap, not on the table.

If a sink unit is separate from a continuous work-top surface, the bottom of the sink should correspond to your work-top height (see first illustration).

• FOOD STORAGE

The work area should also incorporate storage for food and cooking equipment. Make the most of the space available by using internal cupboard fittings. A great deal of lifting, stretching and carrying can be avoided if items are stored near the area where they are used and if cupboards and shelves are within easy reach. (See the section on relating storage to the user, pp. 102-3.)

Have a cupboard or shelf near the cooker and work top to store items which are used frequently during the day, such as flour, salt, sugar, stock cubes, herbs and spices. Keep tea, coffee and other beverages near the kettle.

If you do a great deal of baking, keep a supply of baking ingredients and utensils together in a cupboard near the work top where you do the mixing. You can get them out, and later put them away in one movement, if kept in a removable wire basket fitted on runners in a cupboard.

Foods which are rarely used and stocks of preserves, canned and dried foods can be kept in less-accessible cupboards. Fresh fruit and vegetables are most conveniently stored near the sink where they are washed and prepared. Keep them in wire racks in a ventilated cupboard.

If you have a larder near the work area, most food can be stored in it. Reserve high and low shelves for rarely used items and long-term food supplies. A larder which is some distance from the work area is best kept for long-term storage items.

If the larder is used for perishable foods, it should have fly-proofed ventilation and preferably a cold slab for foods such as cheese and butter, unless these are kept in the refrigerator. (For detailed information on food storage, see pp. 222-5.)

EFFICIENT GALLEY KITCHEN *The narrow, but meticulously planned galley-style kitchen is one of the best examples of the efficient work triangle in practice.* *Because all the units are so close together, across the narrow passageway, the time and effort needed to move from one to another are minimised.*

COLLECTING BISCUIT TINS

Biscuit tins can be collected for their curious shapes, or as a pictorial record of events such as royal marriages, coronations and jubilees. Children's novelty biscuit tins – made in the shapes of boats, vans, buildings, furniture and animals – could also be the basis of a collection.

Biscuit tins were decorated with paper labels until the late 1860s when a process of transfer-printing onto tin plate was developed. By the mid-1870s manufacturers were printing and moulding boxes into many complicated shapes. Lifelike objects such as the 'Library' book tin of 1900 (third from right, above) continued to be made until the late 1930s.

Other novelty tins were made, such as the 1923 'Castle' tin (above, right). But by the outbreak of the Second World War, production costs had so risen that most manufacturers had reverted to plain shapes.

Look around your own home for tins. There may be some hidden away in the attic or in use as a pencil-box or button-tin. If you are lucky, you may well find a 1929 'Grandfather Clock' tin (above).

Rare discoveries would be the first three from left to right – 'Juvenile' (1895), 'Tea Caddy' (1928), Rocking tin (c. 1900) and, second from right, the 'Motor Van' of 1912. Another rare biscuit tin is 'Anvil', 1910 (below). But even quite common tins, such as Art Deco examples from the 1930s, can make an attractive collection.

Old biscuit tins can still be picked up at jumble sales or on junk stalls, but they are also sold in expensive antique shops, since they are now sought by serious collectors.

When starting a biscuit-tin collection, remember that the condition of a tin will affect its value. Avoid badly scratched or dented tins and tins that have damaged or missing parts, such as hinges or catches. If you want your tins to increase in value, treat them with care. Never use them, since scratches will reduce their market value.

• STORING EQUIPMENT

Frying pans, roasting tins and casseroles are most conveniently stored near the work top and cooker, where they are used. You may prefer to have saucepans near the sink where vegetables are prepared. They can be kept on a shelf or hung on hooks from a butcher's rail, or stacked in a pyramid-shaped rack. Alternatively, keep them in a deep drawer divided into sections like a filing cabinet. Saucepan lids can be kept in a special rack fitted to a wall.

Keep heavy utensils in low or waist-high cupboards, and light, rarely used items in high cupboards.

Mixing bowls need to be near the work surface where you mix and prepare food. Kitchen scales, mixers, and other frequently used pieces of equipment should be easily accessible. Mixers can be kept in a unit which has a pull-out shelf for easy access. Alternatively, build them into a work top. If you have scales which can be fixed to the wall, put them at a convenient height over the work top. Otherwise, keep these items on a shelf above the work top.

Spatulas, whisks, sieves, knives and other tools should be near the cooker and work surface. Hang those which can be hung on a rack or peg board; keep other items in compartmented drawers below the work surface. Kitchen knives should be out of reach of children. A pull-out rack in a kitchen unit is a safe place.

STORING CLEANING ITEMS

Keep small cleaning materials and those used for wet cleaning near the sink. Harmful substances should be

USING WALLS AND UNDER-SHELF SPACE Providing adequate storage space need not involve a lot of expense. Intelligent use of wall space and the underside of kitchen shelving not only creates extra storage areas; it is also an efficient means of ensuring that often-used equipment is readily to hand.

kept out of reach of children, or in a locked, ventilated cupboard.

STORING MISCELLANEOUS ITEMS

Articles which are not in frequent use can be stored in odd corners in less-accessible cupboards. Picnic equipment and empty bottling jars, for example, can be stored in a high cupboard when not in use. They need not even be in the kitchen – a shelf in the garage, for instance, could be just as suitable.

Rolls of kitchen and greaseproof papers and aluminium foil can go on a special rack fitted inside a cupboard door or on a wall. Such things as plastic bags, clothes pegs, towels and dish cloths can be stored in compartmented drawers or removable wire baskets on runners. Towels in use can be hung on hooks, on telescopic rails in a work top gap, or on a concertina rail attached to a wall. Keep them close to the sink. Trays can be kept in a gap between kitchen units or on a slotted shelf.

WHERE TO STORE TABLEWARE

Store cutlery, china and glass and other table items near where they will be used or cleaned. A room divider which has a cupboard with doors on the kitchen and dining sides is a good storage place for tableware. Failing that, store tableware in a cupboard near the kitchen sink. Serving dishes may be more conveniently stored near the cooker where they can be warmed before being filled.

LAUNDRY

If you do your laundry in the kitchen, keep everything you need in as compact an area as possible so as not to take up too much cooking space. If you wash by hand, laundry equipment will be needed in the sink area. Keep bleaches, rinses and detergents together, out of the reach of children, or in a locked cupboard. If you have a spin drier, it can be stored under a work surface and wheeled out when needed. A large sink, 500 × 400 × 200 mm. (19½ × 15¾ × 7¾ in.) deep, is needed if you wash large items by hand, and the operation is less messy if the drainer has a good slope.

In a small kitchen, it is probably more convenient to have the washing machine next to the sink. But if you have a larder which is not needed for food, it may be possible to install a washing machine in there. Make sure there will be no plumbing problems if you want a plumbed-in machine. If you have a machine which does not need to be plumbed in, make sure it can be moved out easily when needed. If you do laundry only once a week, it may be worth the inconvenience of moving the machine to save working and storage space.

In a large kitchen, it may be possible to segregate the laundry area with a line of fittings or a room divider (see Kitchen planning, p. 205).

The kitchen is not a good place to dry off washing; wet clothes pick up cooking smells, and they also get in the way and create additional moisture. But if you have no alternative, use an extended line stored in a box which fits on the wall. The line can be pulled out above the sink when needed. Alternatively, use a rack which can be hoisted up to the ceiling, out of the way. Do not dry clothes above the cooker as there is a risk of fire.

Drip-dry clothing is best dried on a rack which fits over the bath. An extended line can also be fitted in the bathroom, so that it stretches over the bath when needed. Work top or table space of about 1,200 mm. (48 in.) is needed for sorting and folding the laundry. If there is not a convenient space in the kitchen for the ironing board, keep it in a broom cupboard or under the stairs. Or consider buying a kitchen unit which houses a fold-away ironing board. An adjustable typist's chair takes the backache out of ironing and other kitchen jobs.

• MAKING THE MOST OF A SMALL SPACE

Even a very small or awkwardly shaped kitchen may be transformed into an efficient working unit by repositioning equipment and making the most of the space available (see Kitchen layouts, p. 202). In a narrow or awkwardly shaped room, space can be saved by removing doors completely or by substituting sliding doors or louvred shutters or blinds. It may be possible to split a door down the middle and hinge it at both sides. Windows which are difficult to reach over kitchen units can be rehinged; or new, easy-opening ones may be installed. Try to remove any equipment which is not essential to the main kitchen tasks. A freezer, for example, could be housed in a garage, hall or spare bedroom; the bathroom could take a plumbed-in washing machine; and an old kitchen range could be removed to make use of the chimney space.

If you are buying new equipment, a split-level cooker – with hob set into the work top and oven built in at chest level – may fit into the scheme better than a combined cooker. A refrigerator can also be mounted at chest height.

Most kitchen appliances are now made in metric sizes, so they may not be the same height as your existing appliances. Adjust differences in height by fitting a continuous work top over all units (except the cooker). Many manufacturers make narrow units for gaps of over 100 mm. (4 in.) and filler pieces for smaller gaps. If the kitchen is an awkward shape, make use of odd spaces by building shelves or cupboards into them. Use the wall space between work top and wall cupboards for hanging cooking utensils, or fit narrow shelves for storing jars of dried herbs.

To save space, store pots and pans inside one another in one drawer or cupboard. Stack the lids in a separate place.

Two cupboards in one have been made by hinging one in front of the other in place of a conventional door.

Cupboards with up-and-over doors can be fitted in places where there is no room to open side-hung doors.

Semi-circular shelves fitted to the door of a corner unit swing round to provide storage in the corner space.

Foil and paper stay tidy and easy to reach if hung on rollers fitted to the inside of a cupboard door.

To maximise use of shelf space, vary heights of shelves according to articles being stored.

• PLANNING REGULATIONS

If your kitchen is too small for your needs, consider converting another room into a kitchen, or extending the kitchen into the dining-room by having all or part of the connecting wall removed. Or it may be possible to build an extension into the garden. Another possibility is to build an extension for a utility-room to house laundry equipment, a freezer, a boiler and cleaning utensils.

There are regulations about the siting of kitchens, so consult the local council before making plans to re-site the kitchen. Planning permission is not always required for an extension, but check with the planning department of the local council before going ahead. Simple extensions can be worked out with a builder or with the advice of the local council.

The local council's building inspector will give advice on official requirements for all structural alterations and on building regulations if you plan to knock down walls, put in hatches or enlarge doors and windows. If you are improving a property and there is no sink in the kitchen, you can apply to the local authority for a grant. Banks are usually willing to lend money for home improvements and building societies will also consider applications for loans. It is cheaper to borrow from building societies than from banks or finance companies.

• POWER

Planning is made easier if there are enough electric sockets in strategic places to serve all the existing appliances and those you may acquire later. Allocate at least two sockets for each work surface, at work-top height. Six sockets should be enough for a small kitchen which is used just for cooking and washing up. A larger kitchen which is used for other pur-

poses may need up to ten points. If you do not have enough sockets you can get an electrician to add more to an existing circuit; double sockets are preferable to single ones as they allow two appliances to be used in the area and avoid the need for adaptors.

An electric cooker does not plug into a socket. It is wired in to a separate circuit (see p. 371).

All new wiring connected to the main supply should be inspected and approved by the local electricity board, who charge a small fee.

Position all electrical equipment so that there are no trailing flexes, which can cause accidents. New kitchen units may have space at the back for wires, flexes and piping.

• HEATING

The temperature in a kitchen fluctuates more than in any other room, as the cooker and other appliances generate heat when in use. The heating system in a kitchen therefore needs to be flexible; a radiator which is part of the central heating needs a sensitive thermostat to avoid overheating. If possible, avoid having the central-heating boiler in the kitchen as it will take up valuable space and may impair ventilation.

If the kitchen is not included in the central-heating system, choose a form of heating which will warm the room rapidly and will cool down quickly when it is not needed. Wall-mounted radiant heaters, which are switched on by a cord, heat almost instantaneously and do not use much electricity. A wall-mounted electric fan heater is also a good way of heating the room quickly, and it can be used as a cool-air fan during hot weather.

Electric storage heaters are not economical unless used for at least 12 hours a day, and they are bulky.

WATER HEATING

If your main water heater does not give enough hot water for your needs, consider installing a water heater for the kitchen sink. There are gas and electric heaters which heat a small amount of water quickly. They are sited on a wall as close to the sink as possible. If the wall is some distance from the sink, an extended spout can be fitted. They should be plumbed in, not fitted on the end of a tap. A gas heater may need a flue to the outside; it should be serviced every six months.

There is another type of electric water heater which needs no plumbing. It can be filled with up to 4 l. (7 pints) of water from the tap by a flexible hose and it boils a pint in under two minutes, ending with a musical warning when boiling. The water can be used for washing up and for making drinks.

• VENTILATION

Cooking smells, fumes and steam make the atmosphere in the kitchen unpleasant and can spread to the rest of the house if there is not adequate ventilation.

Moisture can also cause condensation; when the moisture in the air touches a cold surface it turns to drops of water. This can spoil decoration and rot window frames and, if it is very bad, can cause dry or wet rot. The solution is to get rid of as much moisture as possible with good ventilation, to have efficient background heating and insulating materials on walls and ceilings.

The area most in need of ventilation is around the hob, particularly a gas hob which creates a lot of vapour.

There are two main methods of kitchen ventilation – an extractor fan or a cooker hood.

An extractor fan draws fresh air across the head of the cooker and extracts the stale air. For maximum effect, it should be placed high in the wall or window as near to the cooker as possible and opposite the door. Some of the more expensive fans incorporate a grease filter. To make sure you get the right size for your kitchen, give your supplier a plan of the kitchen, showing dimensions of walls and position of cooker, doors and windows. Cooker hoods are designed to go on an external wall, an internal wall, or for suspending over an island unit. Most models incorporate lighting. A hood fitted to an external wall is vented directly to the out-

side air. This type of hood can incorporate a fan or can operate without one, but a fan is preferable. Or a wall-mounted extractor fan can be used in addition. The hood should preferably contain a grease filter, which should be easily removable for washing. A hood with a fan and filter removes grease, moisture and fumes efficiently, but it has the disadvantage that it can make the kitchen cold.

A ductless hood for an internal wall does not extract the air but purifies it. A motor-driven fan extracts grease and fumes and recirculates clean air. The advantage is that the air retains its heat. But this kind of hood does not remove all moisture, and you may need a louvred ventilator or louvred glass windows, which provide ventilation without creating draughts.

A hood designed for an island unit has an extractor pipe which can be inserted between the ceiling joists and taken to the outside air.

Whatever method of ventilation you have, it helps to cut down on moisture in the first place. Set the hot-water cylinder thermostat to 60°C (140°F). Turn cold taps on before running hot water and do not let the kettle boil longer than necessary. If possible, use one that switches itself off. Where possible, cook in tightly closed casseroles instead of boiling, and have a window open when cooking.

• WASTE DISPOSAL

Waste can be divided into three categories: paper; plastic wrappings, cans, bottles and cartons; food waste. These can all be disposed of separately. Paper can be collected in some areas for recycling; wrappings and containers can be put in a dustbin or sack for collection; and food waste, except bones, can be put on a compost heap or in a waste-disposal unit (see p. 193). Do not put cooked

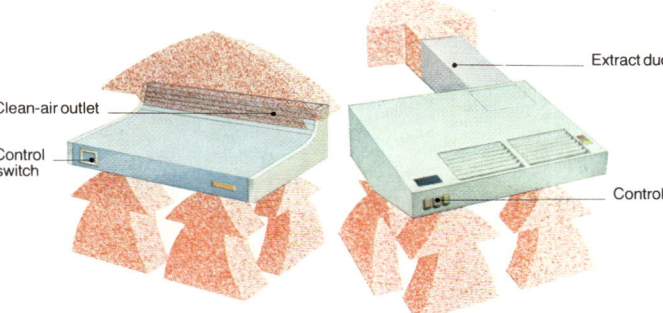

DUCTLESS HOOD This type does not remove moisture. It is an air purifier.

HOOD WITH FAN Stale air is drawn up and extracted through a duct.

Clean-air outlet

Control switch

Extract duct

Controls

or greasy scraps on a compost heap.

In country areas where there are no collections, or infrequent ones, most rubbish can be disposed of on a bonfire, but plastic, tin and glass have to be buried or taken to a public rubbish tip. Another solution is to install an electric or gas incinerator, which burns kitchen waste and other rubbish (including packaging and plastic bottles) to a fine ash. These incinerators are, however, expensive.

Kitchen-waste containers are best kept near or under the sink. Choose a container that is easy to clean and has a tight-fitting lid to keep smells in and flies out. Suitable containers include pecal bins and bins that fit inside a cupboard, some of which open when the cupboard door is opened, and swing-lid bins. Line bins with plastic bags, tie them when full and put in the dustbin. Strong paper or plastic bags, sometimes with a built-in heat sealer, can be fitted on a bracket inside a cupboard door – the bag is clipped to the bracket which carries a lid. When the bag is full it is put in the dustbin.

It is possible to have a waste chute installed. The waste is put through a hatch in the kitchen and drops into a container below, which is emptied from outside by the refuse collector.

Dustbins should have tight-fitting lids. Plastic bins with plastic or rubber lids are light and quiet to use, but they cannot be used for hot ash. A metal bin with a rubber lid is a good compromise. If bins have to be moved to a collection point, this is made easier if they are mounted on wheels or a trolley. The local council may be able to make special arrangements for elderly or disabled people. Officially, dustbin men collect only domestic waste, but most councils will collect larger items on request. All councils are obliged to dispose of domestic rubbish delivered to their refuse depots.

MAKING THE BEST USE OF STEEL *Although it is costly, stainless steel makes an attractive durable, kitchen work surface. In this design, cooking rings have been incorporated into the work-top surface, with an extractor fan positioned in the external wall above the cooking area.*

KITCHEN UNITS AND MAJOR FITTINGS

The smooth functioning of a modern kitchen is almost entirely dependent on appliances and machinery. The following pages show what is available, what features to look for, and how to get the best out of kitchen equipment. This section deals with kitchen units, sinks, waste-disposal units, refrigerators, freezers and dishwashers. Washing machines are covered in the laundry section on p. 328. Most equipment is now made in standard metric sizes, which makes planning much easier. If you have to combine existing appliances with new ones in metric sizes, you will need to realign them and adjust the heights, possibly covering them with a new work surface.

• KITCHEN UNITS

It is possible to create an efficient kitchen with self-assembly units which you put together at home, or with ready-made whitewood units which you can paint or varnish yourself. More expensive, but less trouble, are the ready-made units which can be installed by the supplier. If you want to build a new kitchen on a low budget look for second-hand units which you can renovate yourself (see p.112). You can fit a continuous work top over them to give a neat, uniform appearance, and fill any gaps with whitewood or self-assembly units.

All types of manufactured units are made in standard sizes, but the range of sizes is so great that units can be fitted even into an awkwardly shaped kitchen. There is a wide selection of wall cupboards, corner cupboards, base units, full-length cupboards, work tops, housing units for ovens and other appliances, and island units which can also include hobs and sinks.

CHOOSING UNITS

Kitchen centres are the best places to start looking. If there is not one in your area, look at displays in department stores and builders' merchants.

Before buying units, try to see them assembled in a showroom. Check that drawers slide out easily and that cupboard doors close properly. Make sure that door handles are big enough to grasp but do not stick out too far. Look for base units with a recessed plinth (the strip covering the gap between cupboard base and floor). This allows space for your toes when you are standing at the unit.

If you are buying self-assembly units, check that they are easy to put together and that the instructions are clear. Check if screw holes are already drilled and if screws are supplied. You should need only a screwdriver to assemble the units.

Some suppliers provide a planning kit with squared paper, cut-out scale models of units and appliances, and instructions for measuring and planning. If no planning service is available, make a scale plan of your kitchen and take this to the showroom when selecting units.

MATERIALS

Most units are made of solid wood, such as pine, or manufactured board, such as plywood or chipboard. They are finished on the outside with varnish, lacquer, paint or melamine – a plastic veneer that will withstand knocks. The more coats of finish there are, the tougher it is. This also applies to whitewood units which you paint or varnish yourself.

Cupboards may be melamine inside, or painted with washable paint or an impact-resistant paint, which is much stronger. Melamine interiors are easier to clean, but are more expensive than painted ones. One company makes moulded interiors – like the inside of a refrigerator – which are smooth, rounded, very tough and easy to clean, but not heat resistant.

Most work tops which are sold with standard units have a melamine laminate finish. This is smooth, shiny, easy to clean and fairly tough, but it is not completely heat and stain resistant, and it shows knife marks.

The work tops are available in a wide range of colours and patterns and some have a ledge at the back and a drip stop at the front. Stainless-steel work tops are also available, and boiling rings can be set into them. A good-quality stainless-steel work top wears well and cleans easily, but a cheaper one may scratch and stain.

Work tops in other materials can be made to order or by a skilled handyman. As no one surface is suitable for all jobs, a combination of materials is best. Oiled teak is good for general food preparation, and end-grain sycamore is the best surface for cutting and chopping. Marble is excellent for pastry making, and stainless steel, ceramic, mosaic or quarry tiles withstand great heat. Different materials can be used where there is a change in level, or a chopping board or marble slab could be set into a continuous work top. (For information on cleaning different surfaces, see pp. 318-27.)

DIMENSIONS

All units are now built to standard metric measurements. Heights of units (including work top) are 850 mm. (33½ in.) or 900 mm. (35½ in.). If

A FITTED KITCHEN The fitted units make the most of space and incorporate many of the appliances essential to a kitchen's smooth functioning.

neither of these heights is suitable, it may be possible to adjust the plinth to give the desired height. The ideal height for working is 75 mm. (3 in.) below elbow level when you stand with your arms bent. If you have a special work top for rolling pastry, it is better to have it a little lower than other work tops, about 750 mm. (29½ in.), to allow you to apply pressure.

The width (front to back) is either 500 mm. (19½ in.) or 600 mm. (23½ in.). Lengths (left to right) range from 300 mm. (11¾ in.) to 1,200 mm. (3 ft 10 in.) in multiples of 100 mm. (4 in.). Gaps can be filled with special filler pieces. Work tops are in the same widths as units and are available in lengths from 300 mm. (11¾ in.) to 2.2 m. (6 ft 9 in.). Longer or wider work tops usually have to be made to order; delivery may therefore take longer. L-shaped work tops can also be cut to order.

Housing units for built-in appliances are 2 m. (6 ft 6 in.) or 2.25 m. (7 ft 4 in.) high. The length and width vary according to the dimensions of appliances for which they are designed.

● SINKS

If you are thinking of buying a new sink, first consider whether the single type will meet all your requirements or whether a double sink would be preferable.

A double sink gives greater scope for organising kitchen tasks efficiently, as two jobs can be done at the same time. It also leaves working tops free of the clutter of dirty dishes. It is possible to have two equal-sized sinks or one large one, for washing clothes and large items like oven trays, and one small one, for rinsing dishes and washing vegetables. Make sure that the large one is big enough to wash oven and refrigerator shelves – at least 500 × 350 mm. (20

× 14 in.) and 175-200 mm. (7-8 in.) deep. For washing clothes – a minimum depth of 250 mm. (10 in.) is needed. The small sink can be set into the work top lengthways to make better use of the available space.

If the small sink is fitted with a waste-disposal unit, you can dispose of waste while washing up – which is not possible if you have a single sink unit. Some sink units have a small third bowl fitted with a disposal unit. If you cannot afford a waste-disposal unit straight away, but plan to fit one later, get a sink with a waste outlet large enough to take a unit – about 90 mm. (3½ in.) in diameter. In the meantime, you can fit a waste-strainer the same diameter as the outlet.

If a double sink seems a luxury, or will not fit in the kitchen, consider installing a very large sink with mixer taps, and use two plastic bowls.

CHOICE OF SINKS

The most popular material for a sink is satin-finished stainless steel. It is hygienic, easy to clean, and has a durable surface.

Vitreous enamel is available in a wide range of pastel colours, but it can chip. Glazed fireclay is an attractive, but old-fashioned, material which is liable to chip, crack and lose its glaze, and is not easy to clean.

Most sinks already have holes for pillar or mixer taps, but it is possible to order one which can be used with wall-mounted taps.

DRAINING BOARDS

The sink and draining board are available as one unit. The draining board may be on the left or right of the sink, or there may be one on each side. Choose the arrangement which suits your way of working and/or the site of the sink in your kitchen.

Sinks can also be fitted into a work

top. The disadvantage of this arrangement is that a flat work top does not allow the water from draining dishes to flow back into the sink. A solution to this problem is to have a draining rack with a drip tray fitted. The joint between the sink and work top must be completely watertight.

If your sink is adequate, but the surroundings are old or damaged, you can get a replacement sink top to fit round your existing sink. Sink tops and combined sink and draining boards are also available as complete built-in cupboard units.

TAPS

Swivel mixer taps have a combined outlet for hot and cold water, so that the two can be mixed to the temperature required. When fitted to double sinks the tap can be swivelled to serve either sink. They make it easier to fill buckets and kettles. They are not suitable, however, if a washing machine or dishwasher has to be connected directly to the taps.

Separate taps of the old pillar type are the least expensive and the easiest to grip and turn. The modern acrylic type is much more expensive and can be difficult to grip. Spray taps have the advantage of using about half as much water as the ordinary kind, but the holes can clog. A long-handled surgeon's tap can be turned on with your elbow.

SINK CLEANING

Always rinse the sink with hot water after use. Brush out corners regularly with a stiff pot brush, and clean once a week with hot water and detergent. Put washing soda down the outlet occasionally and pour boiling water down it. Use a soft cloth and liquid detergent to clean a stainless-steel sink. Do not use salt and vinegar or undissolved detergent powder, and

do not scrub with steel wool. For glazed fireclay, use bleach and scourers.

Never pour fat down the sink, as it will congeal and block the drain. Ideally, the grille of the plug-hole should be small enough to stop carrot scrapings and tea-leaves from being washed down. If it is not, use a sink strainer. For information on unblocking sinks, see p. 376.

● WASTE-DISPOSAL UNITS

The advantage of a waste-disposal unit is that food waste can be disposed of immediately. It takes small bones, fruit stones and small wrappings, but not metal, plastic, rags, string, cottonwool, large cartons, china or glass. The waste is ground into pulp and flushed into the drainage system with cold water. Do not use hot water which melts grease, making it stick to the pipes.

Modern waste disposers do not need any special wiring or plumbing. They can be connected to a standard drain, but the sink outlet should be 90 mm. (3½ in.) in diameter. It is usually not possible to connect them to a cess-pool drainage system.

Units are operated from a 13 amp. socket. There are two types: continuous feed, which lets you add waste while the machine is running, and batch feed, which cannot operate until a safety lid is fitted. Batch-fed machines are more expensive and slower in use, but they are safer, particularly if there are children, and there is less risk of items such as teaspoons being lost.

THREE WAYS TO SAVE EFFORT A surgeon's tap with swivel nozzle, a waste-disposal unit in a double sink, and a waste bin fixed to the cupboard door.

• COOKERS

When choosing a cooker, the first thing to consider is the kind of fuel the cooker is to run on – gas, electricity, solid fuel or oil. Your choice may be narrowed by the availability in your area, although bottled gas can be used in place of mains gas. If both mains gas and electricity are available, it is worth comparing the cost of each fuel. Take into account the fuel used for central heating or other appliances, as you may get a cheaper tariff for gas if you use more than a certain amount. If you have a white meter for electricity, an electric cooker may be more economical if you use it much during the cheaper period. You also need to take connection costs into account if you introduce a second fuel.

If hot water and central heating are not already provided for, and if you do a lot of cooking, it may be more economical to have a heat-storage cooker (fired by solid fuel, gas or oil) which supplies hot water or a certain number of radiators. If you are considering buying a heat-storage cooker, remember that you may need storage space for oil or solid fuel. The local distributor will be able to supply addresses of fuel suppliers.

All types of cooker are safe as long as they are properly installed and well maintained. Electrical equipment should carry the BEAB sign – mark of the British Electrotechnical Approvals Board – or foreign equivalent. British gas equipment is given the 'Seal of Service' which guarantees that the appliance conforms to safety standards. Good domestic solid-fuel cookers are approved by the Domestic Fuel Appliances Approvals Scheme of the National Coal Board.

Apart from considerations of availability and cost, there is personal preference to be taken into account. A person who has been cooking happily with one particular fuel for many years may see no reason to change. Some people find gas easier to adjust, and some people think an electric oven and grill have more even heat. Electricity is cleaner. New developments in both gas and electric cookers have evened out most differences in operation, but electric cookers offer more extra features. People who prefer a gas hob, but would rather have an electric oven, may find that the ideal solution is to have a split-level cooker with a gas hob and a separate electric oven. There is now such a wide range of cookers that every cook should be able to find one that suits her.

ASSESSING YOUR NEEDS

Before choosing a cooker, sum up your requirements and decide which features are essential. If, for example, you do a lot of grilling, look for a large grill. If you like baking, or if you entertain frequently, a cooker with two ovens may suit you best. People who go out to work, or like to prepare meals in advance, will find an automatic timer useful. The size of the family and whether it is likely to change must also be considered. It is also important to measure carefully the space available in the kitchen, and to decide whether a combined cooker or a split-level one will fit into the scheme better. Someone who finds it difficult to stoop will be more comfortable with a waist-high oven.

POSITION OF THE COOKER

The cooker should be placed in relation to the refrigerator and sink (see Work triangle, p. 186). Avoid putting it against the wall opposite the window as you will be standing in your own light. Do not position it under a window to avoid fire risk with curtains. If you want a gas cooker with automatic electric control clocks, make sure there is a power point near by.

Check that there is room for the oven door to open fully and which way the door should swing – you can choose between a left or right hung door. If you want a drop-down door, make sure there will be enough space in front for the door and the cook.

Heat-storage cookers are larger than the standard gas and electric cookers and are usually permanently installed with flues (see p. 195).

ALLOWING FOR COST

You need not limit your choice to the amount of cash you have available at the time of buying. Instalment payments can be arranged by the gas or electricity showroom or supplier. Sometimes a discount is allowed if you trade in your old cooker for a new one. It is worth looking at reconditioned second-hand cookers in the showroom and at advertisements in local papers. But if you do buy a second-hand cooker, have it checked and installed by a trained man.

If you wish to buy a heat-storage cooker, remember that you may have to leave it behind if you move. Although it may add to the value of the house, it may not appeal to prospective purchasers.

Read the small print on any service agreement attached to your new cooker. British cookers are guaranteed for one year provided the customer has complied with certain terms which should be noted. Repair work should be carried out by a trained man from a service centre recommended by the manufacturer.

GAS COOKERS

All gas burners give direct heat and can be instantly controlled. Some gas cookers have burners of varying size and power on one hob to suit different types of cooking. Some gas hobs have one burner which is thermostatically controlled – once it is set, the contents of the pan keep at a constant temperature without further adjustment. This is useful for deep-frying or for heating milk.

Gas ovens have burners along the back of the bottom of the oven and heat by convection. The heat rises and flows round the oven, creating zones of heat. The top of the oven is the hottest part and the bottom is the coolest zone. The temperature of the oven is thermostatically controlled. Many ovens have an easy-clean lining which only needs wiping over.

There are two types of gas grill. The conventional type has two frets which glow and radiate heat. The surface combustion grill has a plate or gauze instead of a grill fret and the gas burns over the whole surface, giving even heat all over. Some large grills can be heated on one half only. See also the general information on grills, p. 196.

ELECTRIC COOKERS

Solid hot plates or discs have mostly been replaced by the faster radiant rings. They heat up and cool down at the turn of a switch, so there is not as much wasted heat as with solid plates which can take longer to heat and cool. On most cookers one ring has a dual control so that the centre coil only can be heated for use with a small saucepan.

Element
coil

Dual-setting electric ring

The elements of an electric oven are at the sides, and the top of the oven is the hottest zone. Continental ovens have the elements at the top and bottom; some ovens have exposed elements which give direct radiant heat, and this may alter cooking times. A fan oven has the element at the back and the heat is distributed by a fan. This gives even heat in every part of the oven and wider shelves as there are no side elements. A fan oven is more economical as it heats up more quickly than the traditional type, and slightly lower settings are adequate. Cooking times may also be slightly shorter than a recipe states. Read the instruction book carefully and adjust your recipes accordingly. A fan oven is often incorporated in a double-oven cooker. It is particularly useful for people who do a lot of

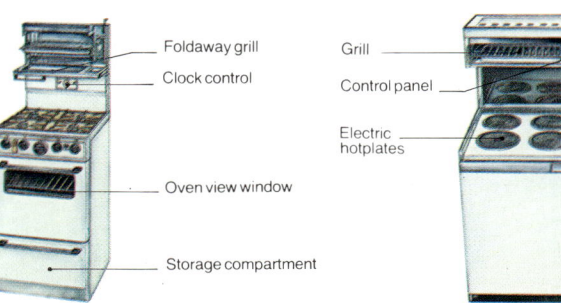

Foldaway grill
Clock control
Oven view window
Storage compartment
Grill
Control panel
Electric hotplates

GAS AND ELECTRIC COOKERS Many features, such as internal lighting and eye-level grills, are now common to both types of cooker.

baking and cook large quantities at a time for freezing.

Many electric ovens have a specially coated lining which cleans as it cooks by the reaction of oven heat on the coating. The coating is not suitable for the oven floor which is cleaned in the ordinary way. Some ovens have an automatic self-cleaning device. The oven is set to a very high temperature and any grease or dirt is burned off. The process takes about two hours, but since the oven switches itself off, the job can be done at any time.

Electric cookers may have a hob light set in the control panel and an automatic oven light which comes on when the oven door is opened. The control panel may include indicators to show which parts of the cooker are switched on. There may also be an automatic timer and buzzer timer.

Electric elements in a grill are positioned so that heating is uniform, and browning is even over the whole area. Some electric grills have a dual control which allows you to use only half of the grill.

HEAT-STORAGE COOKERS

The traditional heat-storage cooker, which runs on solid fuel, is now available for use with mains gas, bottled gas, wood or oil. There is even a model that works off electricity stored at the cheaper night rate.

The cooker is continuously refuelled and provides instant heat for all types of cooking. Some models also heat water and can be used to supply a few radiators. They are much more expensive than standard gas or electric cookers, but they can be economical to run if they are used regularly for large quantities of cooking and to supply hot water. A heat-storage cooker may be ideal for a large family or for someone who entertains on a

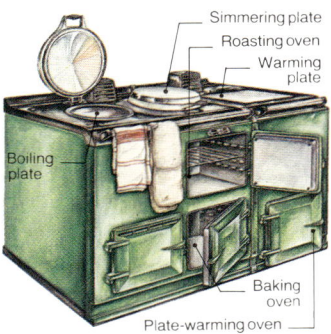

HEAT-STORAGE COOKER Fuel can be gas, oil, solid fuel, wood or electricity.

big scale, but it would not be economical for a small family which has only breakfast and an evening meal at home.

A cooker which does not heat water uses about $2\frac{1}{2}$ tons of solid fuel a year, or 54-63 litres (12-14 gallons) of oil a week, or $14\frac{1}{2}$ therms of gas a week. A model which heats water, about 405 litres (90 gallons) a day, uses approximately $3\frac{1}{2}$ tons of solid fuel a year, or 65-75 litres (14-17 gallons) of oil a week, or 19-20 therms of gas a week.

A heat-storage cooker can be placed in a recess or against a wall. It needs a flue, and if it is heated by solid fuel it must have a plinth. A representative of the supplier will inspect your kitchen to make sure there are no installation problems. You will also need storage space for fuel if the cooker is run on oil or solid fuel.

Heat-storage cookers are generally larger than gas or electric cookers, and take up more space. One two-oven model, for example, is 851 mm. high, 984 mm. long and 679 mm. wide ($33\frac{1}{2}$ in. × $38\frac{3}{4}$ in. × $26\frac{3}{4}$ in.); a four-oven model is 1,480 mm. ($58\frac{1}{4}$ in.) long. They are available in different colours.

On standard models there are two hot plates. The one directly above the

fire is used for boiling and the other is used for simmering. Insulating lids cover the hot plates to conserve the heat when it is not required.

There are two ovens, one which gives high temperatures for roasting and baking and one which can be used for simmering, slow cooking and meringues. The heat is thermostatically controlled, and is available instantly for all types of cooking.

Grilling is done on the top runner of the hottest oven, under the solid shelf, or by means of a special pan which can be bought as an extra. There is also a toaster available. It is a racket-shaped gadget which is used on the boiling hot plate. You must use pans with a machine-ground base.

The advantages of cooking on a heat-storage cooker are that the food does not shrink and it retains its moisture. The floor of the oven can be used and is particularly good for cooking pastry, as the bottoms of pies and flans get crisp. You can cook whenever and for as long as you like without wasting heat.

As the oven is always hot, grease and spills get burnt to a very fine carbon dust, so the oven just needs to be wiped with a damp cloth.

INSULATED COOKER

A smaller version of the heat-storage cooker costs about half the price of the original type, but it does not have such effective insulation and may need more fuel if used a lot. The main difference is that the air flow is controlled manually and high temperatures are not available instantly. There is a warming oven in place of a simmering oven and this is intended mainly for keeping things hot, although it can be used for slow, overnight cooking. When at maximum heat, an insulated cooker is as efficient as a heat-storage cooker.

GAS COOKER FOR A LARGE FAMILY This second-hand gas cooker – bought from an hotel – satisfies the needs of a large family, as well as helping to evoke the atmosphere of a country kitchen.

195

• GRILLS

Whichever fuel is used, the grill heat is fully variable and all heat at approximately the same speed. Grills require little cleaning as the high temperature reached during grilling burns off the grease. If necessary, the frets or elements may be brushed with a soft dry brush. Some grill pans have an anti-splash grid in the base to prevent spitting and improve safety and cleanliness. Some grills have a rôtisserie/kebab attachment, or it may be an optional extra.

To make it easier to turn food over, some grill pans can be pulled part of the way out without tilting. To remove them completely it is necessary to tilt them upwards.

WAIST-HEIGHT GRILLS

These are often wider than eye-level grills, as the whole width of the cooker can be used. They usually have a drop-down door which can serve as a shelf. There are two or three grill-pan runners so that the distance from the heat can be adjusted.

EYE-LEVEL GRILLS

These work in the same way as lower grills but are usually narrower. They may not be a good choice for a short person, as it is not desirable to have to remove the grill pan to look at the food. Fewer electric models than gas models have eye-level grills. Heat-storage cookers do not have eye-level grills.

WALL-MOUNTED AND TABLE-TOP GRILLS

A grill can be bought as a separate item if you have a split-level hob and oven and can be fitted where convenient, on the wall or on a work top. They usually have a rôtisserie/kebab attachment.

GRILLS IN THE OVEN

Grills in the oven have the same features as eye-level grills. A disadvantage can be that the oven cannot be used at the same time. Even when the grill is turned off, the elements or burners will have heated to such a high temperature that the oven cannot be used immediately for food which requires a lower temperature.

• SPLIT-LEVEL COOKERS

The advantages of having a split-level cooker are that the oven can be built in at eye level, it is possible to have a gas hob and an electric oven (or vice versa), it allows storage space beneath hob and oven, and it gives more scope for planning a flexible layout.

But a split-level cooker costs more than a combined cooker and there are two installation charges if you have a combination of gas and electricity. If you have a built-in oven, you will also have the extra cost of an oven housing (see Ovens, below).

An oven at work-top height may take up valuable space in a small kitchen, or it may interrupt the work sequence.

Many ovens incorporate the grill, which means that the two cannot be used at the same time. So if you do a lot of grilling, you may need to have two ovens or a separate grill, or a combined hob and grill.

Before deciding on a split-level cooker, measure the space available and make sure the oven will fit in at the end of a work sequence or on another wall. A hob can be fitted in the middle of a work top. Make sure that power connections are suitably placed.

OVENS

Split-level ovens generally have the same features as the ovens in standard cookers. They can be supplied singly or doubly and some of them are

CONVERTED KITCHEN *The cooker has been set into space originally occupied by the kitchen range. The table, with its storage for pots and pans, forms part of a compact work triangle with the sink and refrigerator.*

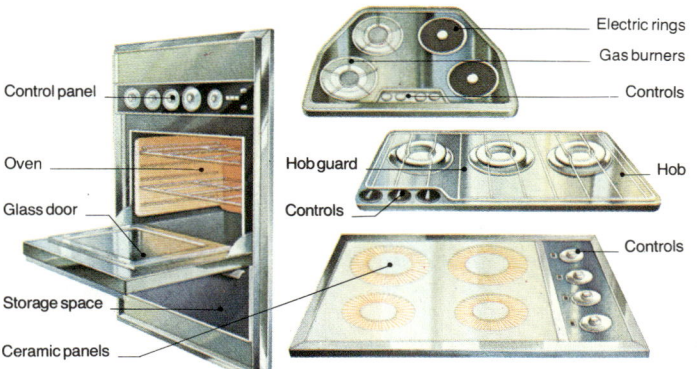

WALL-MOUNTED OVEN *One advantage is that it cuts down on stooping.*

HOBS *Some have gas and electric rings. Ceramic hobs (electric) are flat.*

operated by a heat distributing fan.

Some ovens are supplied in their own cabinet. If you buy a housing separately, check that the measurements correspond to the measurements of the oven. Some manufacturers make their own housings or have an arrangement with kitchen-unit manufacturers who make housings for their appliances (see Kitchen units, p. 192).

• HOBS

Hobs are available with their boiling rings set in a semi-circle, one long line or a square. The first two arrangements leave more space to draw off pans and make it easier to see and reach them. Boiling rings can be set individually into a work surface.

Controls are supplied to the left or right, whichever is preferred, or in front of the hob.

A hob which combines both gas and electric boiling rings is useful if one source of power should fail. They may be close to each other within the same stainless-steel surround, or separated by a work-top space.

A few models are available with an eye-level grill combined.

A hob with controls arranged in a line – from front to back – is a safe layout where there are children.

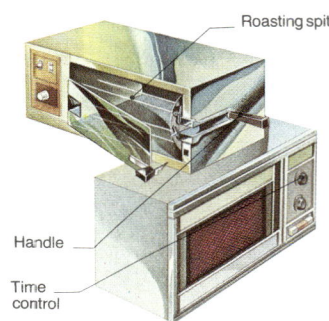

SEPARATE OVEN AND SPIT A wall-mounted spit and a microwave oven.

CERAMIC HOBS

A ceramic hob can be bought as part of a cooker or as a separate unit. The hob is made of very tough, heat-resisting, opaque glass. It is completely flat and has four circular electric heating elements concealed on the underside. The heated areas are marked on the ceramic in the form of a circular pattern which glows yellow when in use. Although the heating elements get very hot, the ceramic surround remains cool. Each element has a variable switch with a neon light to show when it is on. The heat control is very sensitive and is quick and economical. Pans with a machine-ground base are recommended for use with ceramic hobs.

The outside edges of the hob are sealed to prevent liquids getting underneath. The plate is easily wiped clean with a damp cloth. For cleaning off marks, a special cleaning agent is available – abrasives should not be used. When not being used for cooking the ceramic top can be used as a work surface, but it should not be used for cutting or chopping.

This type of hob is about two-and-a-half times the price of a conventional gas or electric hob.

• RÔTISSERIES

If the cooker does not incorporate a rôtisserie, it is possible to buy a separate one to put on a work top or for mounting on a wall.

The roasting spit is fitted with holding forks and these are pushed into the joint of meat so that it balances. If a bird is being cooked, a shaft is passed through it and the forks hold the shaft. The spit is automatically turned by an electric motor.

Kebab attachments are supplied with some units. They consist of long revolving skewers on which the small pieces of meat are threaded.

The food bastes itself as it revolves and is more moist than ordinary roasts. There is no splashing, so only the drip pan collects grease.

If the spit or skewers are greased lightly before loading, the cooked food is easier to remove.

• MICROWAVE OVENS

Although used mainly by the catering trade at the moment, there is no reason why microwave ovens should not be used in the home. They can be expensive to buy but, for certain foods, they save a great deal of time and fuel. No special installation is needed, as the oven plugs into a 13 amp socket. The microwaves penetrate the food and are converted into heat. This means that the food cooks inside as quickly as it does outside. Only the time the food is in the oven needs to be controlled, not the temperature. The oven can cook raw foods in minutes and can heat liquids. Frozen foods can be cooked straight from the freezer.

One disadvantage is that the food does not brown as there is no direct heat. If a brown, crispy finish is required, the food must be finished off under a grill. Because they cannot cope with all the different kinds of cooking required, microwave ovens should not be used as a substitute for conventional cookers.

FREE-STANDING FOR MAXIMUM ACCESS This island unit has an inset marble slab for making pastry, a chopping board for cutting meat, bread and vegetables, a stainless-steel hob with four boiling rings, and cupboards below.

Roasting spit

Handle

Time control

• REFRIGERATORS AND FREEZERS

A refrigerator stores fresh food at temperatures between 2°C and 8°C (35°F and 46°F). The temperature and storage times for frozen food depend on the star rating (see below).

For people who have a large quantity of fresh fruit and vegetables available, and for those who live in remote areas, a freezer might also be extremely useful. It is a convenience in any home, reducing greatly the number of shopping trips required in a week or month.

When buying a refrigerator or freezer, look for the mark with the initials BEAB, which shows that it meets the safety requirements of the British Electrotechnical Approvals Board.

CHOOSING A REFRIGERATOR

Before buying a refrigerator, you need to take into account the number of people in the family, what sort of food you eat, how often you shop and whether you already have a freezer. If you have, you will not need a frozen-food compartment. If you only wish to store a small quantity of frozen food, an ordinary refrigerator with a frozen-food compartment will be enough. Consider also how long you may need to store frozen food and look for the appropriate star rating.

If you wish to store larger quantities of frozen food and to freeze a small quantity of fresh food occasionally, consider buying a two-door refrigerator with a freezing compartment, or a freezer and refrigerator combined in one cabinet. The disadvantage of some two-door refrigerators is that when food is being frozen the whole refrigerator gets very cold, as both compartments are operated by the same compressor. The combined refrigerator/freezer usually

has separate compressors, so they operate independently.

The space inside a refrigerator is measured in litres or cubic feet. Allow 28 litres (1 cu. ft) for each person in the family, and then add 28 litres extra. If in doubt, buy a larger refrigerator. As the motor is the most expensive part of the refrigerator, it does not cost much more to have an extra cubic foot.

STAR RATING OF REFRIGERATORS

The temperature of the frozen-food compartment and the length of time frozen food can be stored, depend on the star rating, usually shown on the flap of the frozen-food compartment.
* Approx. −6°C (21°F). Stores frozen food up to one week.
** Approx. −12°C (10°F). Stores frozen food up to one month.
*** Approx. −18°C (0°F). Stores frozen food up to three months.
**** This is the freezer symbol shown on freezers and on refrigerators which have a frozen-food compartment which can freeze small quantities of fresh food.

POSITION OF REFRIGERATOR

The refrigerator should be in a cool part of the kitchen and should be conveniently placed in relation to the cooker and sink (see Work triangle, p. 186). A gas refrigerator needs to be near the gas supply; an electric refrigerator needs a 13 amp socket.

Measure the space available and allow about 50 mm. (2 in.) at the back for the heat from the refrigerator to escape. If the refrigerator is to fit under a work top, allow a small gap at each side also, or between the top of the refrigerator and the work surface. If the refrigerator is to form part of the work surface, choose one with a suitable top.

A small refrigerator can be fitted on a wall or put on a work top. Wherever you put the refrigerator, make sure there is room for the door to be opened wide enough to get the freezing-compartment drip tray out.

FROZEN-FOOD COMPARTMENT

Most refrigerators contain a compartment where frozen food can be stored and where ice cubes can be made. This compartment can also be used for making ice cream. The length of time frozen food can be stored is indicated by the star rating (see left) which is marked on the flap of the frozen-food compartment.

DOOR SEAL

Most door seals consist of a plastic gasket with a magnetic strip. The purpose of the seal is to stop cold air leaking out of the refrigerator. When buying a refrigerator, test the seal by shutting the door on pieces of paper placed at different points. If you have to give a slight tug to pull the paper out, the seal is effective.

It is useful to have a seal that is removable, so that it can be replaced if it perishes or deteriorates.

Make sure that the door swing suits your kitchen plan, or buy a model with doors that can be hung on either side.

ADJUSTABLE FEET

A refrigerator needs to be level if it is to work efficiently and with minimum noise. If the floor is uneven, choose a model with adjustable feet.

DOOR STORAGE

Some refrigerators have fixed door fittings and some have flexible fittings. Check on the number of milk bottles the door will hold and whether there is space for extra tall bottles (a tip-up shelf may allow for these). Door fittings may include an egg rack,

cheese and butter compartments and a shelf.

SHELVES

To store items of varying heights you will need flexible shelving, with several shelf runners, half shelves and lift-up shelves for storing tall items. For safety and convenience, it is also useful if the shelves have stops or anti-tip devices.

DEFROSTING SYSTEM

The defrosting system can be manual, push-button, or automatic. If it is manual, you have to empty the freezing compartment and switch the refrigerator off. This can be done by turning the dial in the refrigerator to zero. (The numbers on this dial do not indicate the temperature; they simply enable you to regulate it – usually the higher the number, the lower the temperature.) When the ice has melted, remove and empty the drip tray.

In the case of a push-button refrigerator, pushing the button inside the refrigerator switches off the power supply. When the defrosting is completed, the button is automatically thrown back, and the supply is reconnected. But you have to remove the frozen food and empty the drip tray.

If defrosting is automatic, ice is prevented from forming in the cabinet and the moisture is channelled out of the cabinet, where it evaporates. About three times a year it is necessary to defrost manually to clear any build-up of frost.

CARE OF A REFRIGERATOR

Defrost when the ice in the frozen-food compartment is about 6 mm. ($\frac{1}{4}$ in.) thick. If something is spilt, clean it up straight away. Wash with a cloth wrung out in warm water – the door compartments and the salad compartment are the parts which get dirtiest. It helps to wipe jars, bottles and yoghourt containers before putting them in the refrigerator. From time to time, unplug a free-standing refrigerator and dust the radiator at the rear of the cabinet.

The door of the refrigerator is potentially the weakest part, so do not force bottles and jars into the storage compartment and do not slam the door. Do not put hot food into the refrigerator as it creates steam which causes frost to build up on the cooling unit.

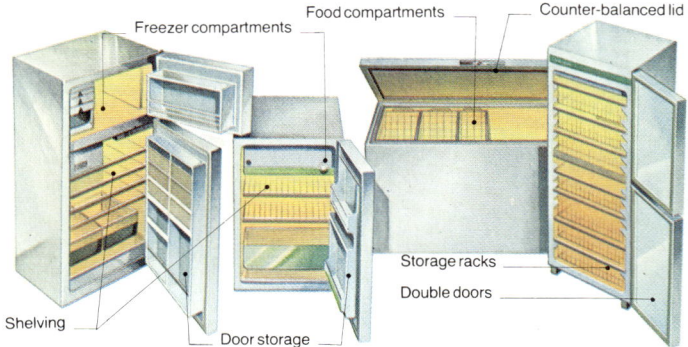

TYPICAL MODELS From left to right, a refrigerator with 4-star freezing compartment; work-top model; chest freezer; and combined freezer/refrigerator.

CHOOSING A FREEZER

The first thing to consider when selecting a freezer is whether you want it mainly for storing bought frozen food or for freezing and storing fresh food or food you prepare yourself. Then decide how much storage space you are going to need. If you want only to store bought frozen food, a double-door refrigerator or refrigerator/freezer may suit you. If you already have a refrigerator but need more frozen-food space, or if you wish to freeze small quantities of food, choose between a small upright freezer and a table-top freezer.

If you plan to do a moderate amount of freezing, but are short of space and would like to keep the food in the kitchen, choose between a refrigerator/freezer and a small upright freezer. One of these would also suit someone who wanted a freezer to cut down on shopping trips, and also to freeze occasional home-made dishes for family use and entertaining.

If, however, you want to do large-scale freezing, and are likely to have large quantities of fresh produce in the summer, or if you want to store bulk packs of food from discount suppliers, then you will need a large upright or chest-type freezer.

CHEST FREEZER

The chest freezer has a top-opening lid which is counter-balanced to remain open. The advantage of this is that there is minimum loss of cold air when the freezer is opened (as cold air does not rise), and this reduces running costs. It is also cheaper size for size than the upright type, and has more flexible storage space. It is usually available with an interior light, and it is possible to have a lock fitted to the lid. These last two features are particularly useful if you keep the freezer in an outhouse or garage.

The disadvantages are that the chest takes up more floor space than the upright type, and you cannot use the top. And it may be difficult for you to reach to the bottom of the cabinet if you are small.

UPRIGHT FREEZER

An upright freezer looks like a refrigerator and requires little floor space. This makes it easier to fit into a kitchen. It can be free-standing, matched in size with a refrigerator or it can be built into a unit. It is easier to load and unload than the chest type and is easier to clean. The door may have storage space in the form of racks.

The disadvantages of many upright freezers are that some cold air is lost when the door is opened, and they are thus slightly more expensive to run than a chest freezer. As frost builds up more quickly in the cabinet, due to loss of cold air and reactivation of the motor, they need more frequent defrosting. They are also more expensive to manufacture and, therefore, to buy. Storage space in the door may not be as cold as in the cabinet and, therefore, the door should not be used for long-term storage.

FREEZER CAPACITY

Manufacturers often quote the gross capacity, or the gross and net capacity. The net capacity does not include the space occupied by the baskets, partitions and shelves, so this is the better figure for assessing the usable space inside the freezer. For each cubic foot of net volume, calculate an average possible storage space of 9 kg. (20 lb.) of frozen food. This depends, however, on the type of food and the way it is packaged. For example, a sponge cake with a cream topping, which needs to be packed in a box with space between the cake and

the lid, may take up more space than a heavier, closely packed item.

The freezing capacity varies from one make to another, so check the manufacturers' leaflets. But, as a rough guide, 1 kg. (2lb.) of fresh food per cubic foot of freezer capacity can be frozen in any 24 hour period.

WHERE TO KEEP A FREEZER

A freezer must never be connected to the domestic lighting circuit. Always make sure that it has a fused 13 or 15 amp power supply. Ideally it should be connected to its own fuse box at the electricity board's consumer unit, so that it can be left on when all other power is switched off for holidays.

Leave space round the condenser (usually at the back of the cabinet) to allow the warm air to escape. Upright freezers are supplied with spacers which fit at the back of the cabinet to keep it the required distance of 20-100 mm. ($\frac{3}{4}$-4 in.) from the wall. The door on most upright models is hung on the right of the cabinet. On some models, however this can be changed to the left, and some manufacturers provide for either.

If a small freezer is kept under a work top, make sure there is space all round to allow the warm air to escape, and that the controls are not hidden under the work surface.

A freezer needs a well-ventilated, dry position with a cool temperature. The floor should be firm. If the freezer is stored in an upper room, make sure the floor can take the weight (a loaded freezer can weigh up to 250 kg. ($\frac{1}{4}$ ton). If you are buying a large freezer, make sure it will go through the door of the room where it is to be kept.

LOOKING AFTER A FREEZER

When a new freezer is delivered, wipe the inside with a damp cloth. Do not use a detergent solution, as most

detergents have a perfume which could be transferred to the food.

To make sure the freezer is not switched off accidentally and that the plug is not removed, cover the plug and switch with adhesive tape, or have the electrician fit a fused connector unit where the cable is to be taken directly to the consumer unit.

DEFROSTING AND CLEANING

Defrost the freezer when food stocks are low. Disconnect the freezer from the power supply. Remove any food, wrap in thick layers of newspaper and store it in a cool place.

Place some newspaper on the floor of the cabinet and scrape the excess frost from the sides, using a freezer scraper or plastic spatula. Do not use anything sharp, as you may damage the freezer linings, which will be expensive to repair.

If there is a defrost drain-hole in the freezer, just leave the frost to melt and put a container under the outlet hole. Make sure the container is large enough to collect all the water.

Leave the freezer lid or door open and when all the frost has melted, mop up the water with a clean cloth. Wipe out the inside of the cabinet with water. If there are food stains, clean with some bicarbonate of soda dissolved in warm water. Do not use abrasive cleaners, which could damage the cabinet lining.

When the cabinet is dry, reconnect the freezer, switch to the lowest temperature and leave closed for one hour before replacing the food.

POWER FAILURE AND BREAKDOWN

Most power cuts do not last long enough to affect the frozen food, which should keep in good condition for at least eight hours. (It takes 12-24 hours for food in an unopened

freezer to thaw.) If you do have a power failure, do not open the lid of the freezer as this will introduce warm air into the cabinet. Leave it closed for at least two hours after power has been restored.

You can insure the contents of your freezer against loss due to a power failure, but not if it is caused by a strike. An insurance broker can give advice on this type of insurance.

Make sure there are reliable service facilities in your area, because if anything goes wrong with your freezer it will need servicing quickly.

Keep the telephone number of the service engineer where you can find it quickly – for instance, on a label stuck to the cabinet.

MOVING HOUSE

If you are planning to move, it is advisable to use up your freezer stocks. If there is food left in the freezer, make sure the removal men are prepared to handle the loaded cabinet. In this case, turn on the fast-freeze control the day before you move.

Make sure that the freezer is the last item on the van and the first off, and check that the power supply in the new house is connected and that you have a suitable plug.

HOLIDAYS

It is quite safe to leave the freezer running while you are away, but check that the electricity supply is left on. It is advisable to leave a key with a neighbour so that some quick action can be taken if the power supply is cut off for any extended period while you are away. If, at any time, the freezer is not being used, it should be disconnected, then cleaned and dried and left with the lid open. If there is a risk of children climbing into the cabinet, however, either remove the lid or lock it and remove the key.

• DISHWASHERS

Apart from saving you the chore of washing dishes by hand, a dishwasher can save up to ten hours a week of your time. It also keeps the kitchen tidier, as the dirty dishes can be stored in the machine until there is a full load to wash. Machine washing is more hygienic than hand washing, because the water used in a machine is much hotter, 55-65°C (131-149°F), and so kills more bacteria.

CHOOSING A DISHWASHER

The size of dishwasher needed does not necessarily depend on the size of the family. Because it is more economical to use a machine with a full load, a small machine which can be fully loaded after each meal may be more suitable for a large family. On the other hand, if you do not use much crockery at each meal, you may prefer to leave the dirty dishes in the machine from one meal to the next, and have one wash when the machine is full. In this case, a large machine may be preferable. A large-capacity machine takes large pans and mixing bowls and may have an intensive programme to deal with heavily soiled casserole dishes, so someone who entertains a great deal may need this type of dishwasher.

When buying a dishwasher, consider the number of wash programmes available (and which of these you need), the amount of crockery and cutlery the machine will take, the overall size of the machine, and installation requirements.

The capacity of a machine is measured in standard place settings. A standard place setting consists of a soup plate, dinner plate, side plate, cup and saucer, glass and a set of cutlery, and allowance is made for a set of serving dishes. Although you may not always use complete settings, and will want to wash other items as well, the description of capacity will enable you to make comparisons. To make sure your tableware fits the machine you select, take to the shop some of the items you will want to wash and try them in the racks. Such items might include one of your largest dinner plates, any particularly large item in frequent use, glasses, and soup bowls with curved rims (which may not slot into racks).

TYPES AVAILABLE

A small dishwasher can stand on a work top or draining board. It must be close to the water supply if it cannot be permanently plumbed in. This saves installation costs but means that the tap cannot be used while the machine is operating. Some models can be built in.

Most dishwashers are free-standing, and take 8-14 place settings. As they are front-opening, they can be used as work tops or be fitted under an existing work top. Some models can be built into a unit.

Some dishwashers can be filled from the hot-water supply (up to a given temperature only), but most are designed for a cold fill.

DISHWASHER/SINK UNIT

A single unit combining sink and dishwasher saves space, but is more expensive than other models. It takes 11-12 place settings.

HOW A DISHWASHER OPERATES

The machine rinses, washes, re-rinses and dries the dishes. The water drains away between each stage. The various stages, or combination of stages, of the washing process are called programmes. Machines vary in the number of programmes they offer, but they all provide the basic stages which make up a complete wash.

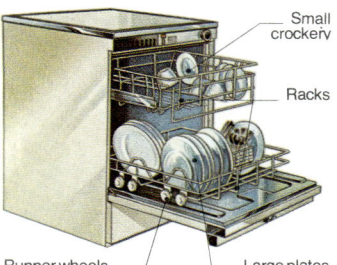

Small crockery

Racks

Runner wheels — Large plates

CHOOSING A MACHINE The size should be determined by space and washing needs.

The whole sequence takes from 65-100 minutes, depending on the number of stages used. The average time for a normal wash from a cold fill is 85-90 minutes. An intensive wash adds 20 minutes to the time.

PRE-RINSE

Clean water is flushed through the base of the cabinet and is pumped out. This process removes liquids (such as tea or coffee) spilt in the machine during loading, and pumps away any water left in the machine from the previous wash. At the same time, or immediately afterwards, cold water is sprayed over the dishes to remove loose food particles and liquids and is drained away. This pre-rinse stage can also be used on its own to rinse surface dirt from dishes which are being stored in the machine until there is a full load; this prevents staleness and stops stains from drying firmly on to the dishes.

Some machines also have a heated pre-wash with detergent, usually as part of an 'intensive' programme for washing very dirty dishes and pans.

MAIN WASH

For glasses, dishes that are virtually clean (such as side plates) and for china and glasses which have been stored and not used for some time, it is possible to have a series of heated rinse cycles without detergent.

For normally soiled dishes and cutlery used for a meal, a pre-set volume of water is taken in and is gradually heated while agitation takes place. Detergent is added, usually automatically, at the beginning of agitation. The washing therefore takes place with cold, warm and hot water, 55-65°C (131-149°F), which cleans a range of food stains. Egg remains, for example, can be removed in the warm pre-wash before they can be 'cooked on' in the hot wash. To wash very dirty items, an intensive programme combines the main wash with the pre-wash using detergent.

RINSING AND DRYING

Two or three cold rinses remove any remaining detergent and food stains. There is then a final heated rinse during which a rinsing agent is automatically added, leaving the dishes almost dry and streak-free. Drying is completed by heat left in the machine or by a built-in electric heater.

ADDITIONAL PROGRAMMES AND VARIATIONS

There may be a special wash for fragile items, a short programme for lightly soiled dishes, and a bio-intensive programme which washes heavily marked or burnt items.

A plate-warming programme allows the final hot rinse to be dialled on its own, so that the dishes can be taken from the machine warm.

LOADING THE MACHINE

Remove large food scraps before putting dishes in the machine. Always stack bowls, cups and glasses with the rim downwards to allow the water to drain away at the end of the wash programme. If you are buying new crockery look for items with a flat base – if a cup, bowl or glass has a depression in the base, water collects there.

When loading, take care not to block the outlet of the detergent dispenser. Look carefully at the inside of the dishwasher and note how the water is dispersed throughout the cabinet. When you have worked out the spray pattern, keep it in mind when loading the machine and make sure that one item does not shield another from the spray. Check also that there is no cutlery projecting through the basket as this may hinder the spray arms.

Some plastics become soft at high temperatures. If in doubt, wash thin or light plastic items by hand.

Hand-painted china or antique pieces should always be washed by hand. If the pattern has been coated with a glaze, it will be safe to wash it in a dishwasher as the glaze protects the pattern. Lead or fine crystal glassware should be washed at the low-temperature glass programme. If the pieces of glass are valuable or irreplaceable, it is safer to wash by hand. Crystal can become opaque after many machine washings and this effect is irreversible. When in doubt, wash the glass by hand or try one piece first at the low-temperature programme.

Knives with bone, wood or plastic handles need special care as the glue used to fix the handle to older types may melt at high temperatures. Knives are made from a harder steel than forks or spoons to give them a harder cutting edge. As this hard steel has less corrosion resistance, more care is needed. The condition most likely to cause pitting in knives is contact with water over a long period. In the dishwasher this could happen if the load is pre-rinsed and left until the machine is full before being washed.

It could also happen if the machine is programmed last thing at night and the cutlery is left damp until morning.

When unloading the machine, unload the bottom basket first – otherwise items on the top basket which did not dry properly will drip on those underneath as they are removed.

WASHING AIDS

Special detergents made for use with washing machines are much stronger than ordinary detergents. To avoid possible damage to your china, use a detergent recommended by the British Ceramic Research Association. Ordinary washing-up liquid will not give good results.

A rinse aid is used in a dishwasher to help the dishes to dry efficiently. It causes the water to run off in a sheet so that drops of water do not dry on the dishes and leave marks.

Hard water can cause a build-up of white deposits on the crockery. If this happens, either have the water softened before it enters the machine or buy a dishwasher with a built-in water softener – this is a reservoir in the cabinet which holds cooking salt or rock salt to neutralise the calcium in the water. If you have a dishwasher without a water softener, experiment with different brands and quantities of detergent or try a different rinse aid. Otherwise put some powder water softener on the door before you close it. This will soften the water for the first wash only.

It is best to use a rinse aid and detergent made by the same manufacturer as they complement each other. There is not one detergent which suits all machines, so follow the manufacturer's recommendations. (In some cases, using a detergent other than that recommended can invalidate the guarantee.) If you get bad results, check that you are using the correct quantity of detergent, that the rinse aid dispenser is filled and the water has been softened if necessary. If you are still not satisfied, experiment with different brands until you find one that is satisfactory. Try each one for at least a week before deciding.

LOOKING AFTER THE MACHINE

When the machine is not in use, leave the door ajar so that the air can circulate. Clean the machine regularly, paying particular attention to the area round the door seal where food particles tend to get caught. Clean the filter after each wash. If the filter is not cleaned, the food particles caught on it will be recirculated in the next wash and may be deposited on the dishes. If the machine is not going to be used for a long period, rinse it and make sure it is clean. Dry the inside with a soft cloth and leave the door ajar.

Dishwashers need to be serviced regularly. Most manufacturers offer a service-maintenance contract once the guarantee is ended. This involves a yearly payment, in return for which servicing and repairs are carried out. Before entering into such a contract, make sure you know exactly what you are entitled to and find out if there are any extra charges. Without a contract, you will have to pay for servicing and repairs as they are needed.

SITING A DISHWASHER

It is more convenient to have a dishwasher permanently plumbed in (see p. 375), but it can be connected temporarily to the sink tap by a hose each time it is used, and emptied through a hose into the sink. In either case it is advisable to have the machine close to the drainage, electricity and water supplies.

Measure the space available and compare this with the sizes of machines. Allow for a space of 5 mm. ($\frac{1}{4}$ in.) at each side of the machine to enable the servicing engineer to pull it out for servicing, and a space at the back for the fill and drain hoses. Free-standing and built-in machines made to a metric standard are 600 mm. ($23\frac{1}{2}$ in.) square and 850 mm. ($33\frac{1}{2}$ in.) high. Those made in imperial measures vary in size, so make sure you get the exact measurements if size is important. Some machines which are designed to be built in have removable side panels so that the machine will fit easily into a standard housing unit. Work-top models also vary in size, but the following measurements give a general indication of the range: 635-660 mm. (25-26 in.) high, 533-584 mm. (21-23 in.) from side to side, and 482-533 mm. (19-21 in.) from back to front.

POSITIONING THE DISHWASHER In many kitchens, the position of water pipes will determine where the dishwasher can be sited. Try, where possible, to fit it unobtrusively under an existing work top and – for ideal convenience – beside the sink.

INSTALLING A NEW KITCHEN

The ideal kitchen is very much a personal problem. What will suit one family will not necessarily suit another. Kitchen units that fit neatly into place in one house need not fit the same floor area in another. Windows will be in the wrong place; doors will open inwards when outwards would be preferable; fuse boxes and pipes tend to protrude in all the wrong places. Creating a new kitchen therefore needs careful thought and a lot of planning with pencil and paper to overcome these problems. The kitchen installations opposite and overleaf show how the accommodation in three different types of house was adapted by their owners to provide up-to-date and easily run kitchens.

• THE PLANNING STAGE

Most people have rigid ideas of how they want their new kitchen to look and what appliances they want installed. With this basic knowledge, take a sheet of graph paper and first draw out a scale plan of the size and shape of the area (see Planning your rooms, p. 28), marking the position of doors and windows, including how much space doors take up if opening into the kitchen. All measurements should be in metric because kitchen units and appliances are sold in metric sizes, and it will therefore be easier when plotting the various units on to the plan.

Double check these measurements. For instance, if measurements are taken at floor level, re-check by measuring 1 m. (1 yd) up from the floor where the walls could be out of square. If there is a variation, always mark down the smallest measurement. This will mean that when the units come to be fitted, the only problem will be having to extend a unit top back to the wall, rather than having to chop away parts of the wall.

Next mark the following items on the plan: electric-cooker point and its height from the floor; other electric points and their heights; light switches and light points; gas and water pipes; waste outlet; height of window sill from floor; ceiling height; any obstructions such as pipes, airbricks and flues; and boiler.

The shape of the room you have drawn and the position of doors and windows will probably decide what the basic layout of the kitchen will be. When fitting the units to your drawing, always remember the importance of the work-triangle (see p. 186), and that the total length of the triangle sides should be between 3.6 m. (12 ft) and 6.6 m. (20 ft). Decide on your needs for can-storage space, pan and equipment storage, and fresh-food storage, and allow for these in your choice of cupboards. Do not forget, either, that appliances, such as a dishwasher, that are not fixed and have to be moved for servicing, will need extra space.

FINAL CHECK

Finally, re-check all the measurements by making cardboard cut-out miniatures of the various units and appliances, scaled down to fit your scale-plan drawing. The cut-outs can be moved around on the plan to find the best arrangement that fits the room.

You can, of course, call in an expert to help with the design. This can be an architect, an interior designer, the man from the kitchen centre at your local store, or even the local builder. The one rule to follow when employing outside assistance is to ensure that you have actually seen work carried out by the particular designer, so that you will know that the type of plan being prepared is going to suit your own requirements.

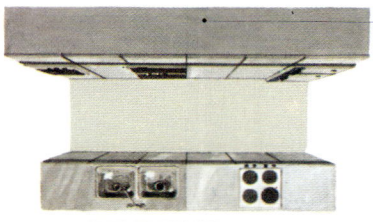

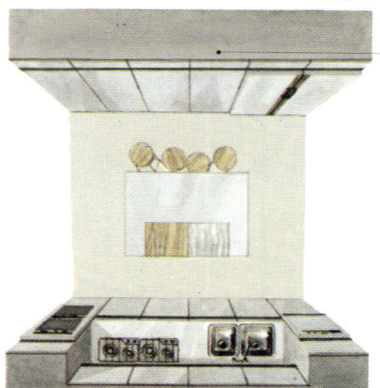

SINGLE-LINE KITCHEN
The simplest kitchen design, suitable for rooms where space is limited. All the fittings are along one wall.

L-SHAPED KITCHEN
Sink and washing machine are on one wall, with hob, cooker, refrigerator, and more work-top space along the return. If one arm of the 'L' is made up of storage units, it can be used as a room divider creating a dining or working space within the area of the kitchen.

GALLEY KITCHEN
The compact layout of this kitchen is ideal for a small house or flat. The units are set against two facing walls. A good galley arrangement is to have sink, hob and work top against one wall with food-storage cupboard, refrigerator, ovens and dishwasher housed in full-height units against the other.

U-SHAPED KITCHEN
This is probably the most efficient kitchen design, providing the maximum work-top area for the minimum amount of walking to and fro. The sink (the centre of the work-triangle) is in the middle of the 'U' shape and four boiling rings are recessed into the work top to the right of the sink. The layout also allows for three working heights – standing, sitting and comfortable sink-working.

ISLAND KITCHEN
This kitchen is basically a 'galley', widened sufficiently to accommodate an 'island'. Full-height units on one wall provide all food and china storage. Ovens, hobs, sinks, dishwasher (incorporated into the tall unit next to the sinks) and utensils are along the opposite wall. A wooden chopping board (on the left) and a marble pastry slab are recessed into the work top of the central preparation area, which also provides room for bar-top snacks.

FIVE BASIC PLANS At least one of these layouts will suit any kitchen.

• A NEW KITCHEN FOR A SEMI-DETACHED HOUSE

Typical of thousands of homes, this semi-detached house had a long, narrow section at the back that was originally split into four small rooms – scullery, larder, built-in store cupboard and coal store. The scullery on its own was not large enough to create a modern family kitchen. But, by removing the internal partition walls of the section and making one room out of the four, an area was created large enough to accommodate a family-size kitchen.

ADDITIONAL LIGHT

Careful thought and planning kept expensive structural alterations to a minimum. A window in the coal store (it had been put in when the store was converted to an outside w.c.) was extended sideways to give additional light over a work top. The existing w.c. door and the larder window were removed and the openings bricked up.

Before completely sealing the window opening, an air-vent brick was incorporated into the space at the point where the new food-storage cupboard was to back on to the wall.

A quarry-tiled floor was laid over the existing floor surface, and to give more light to the kitchen's eating and laundry areas, the wooden half-glazed scullery door giving access to the garden was replaced with a fully glazed door.

IN TWO PARTS

The completed design (below right) shows how the kitchen has been split into two distinct parts. At the far end the facilities for food preparation, cooking, occasional eating and washing-up are all grouped together. The other end accommodates the laundry and has storage cupboards for cleaning materials and equipment.

These two parts are separated by the door to the garden, and through-traffic to and from the garden does not intrude into the kitchen work area.

The original scullery was dark and cramped, a depressing place in which to work. The conversion has transformed it into a well-planned kitchen, which is not only easy to work in, but is also a cheerful place for an occasional meal. In addition, the conversion has added to the value of the house.

MONEY-SAVING IDEAS Costs were kept down by buying whitewood units and painting them. The use of quarry tiles, built in as a table top around the cooker, means that splashes from cooking are simple to wipe up.

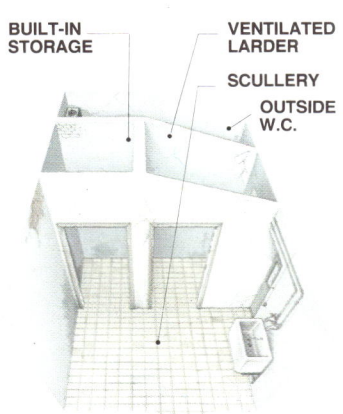

BUILT-IN STORAGE

VENTILATED LARDER

SCULLERY

OUTSIDE W.C.

THE OLD KITCHEN These were the original four rooms. The scullery's only light came from a half-glazed door.

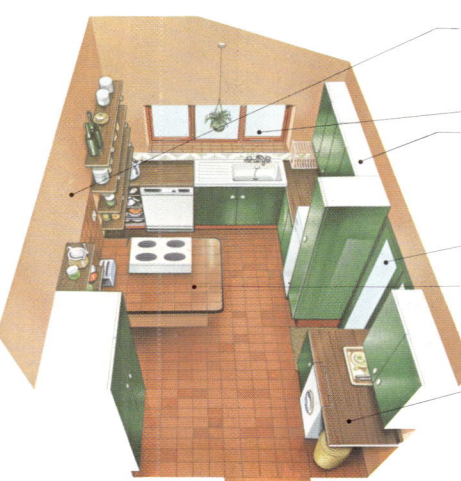

EXTRACTOR FAN
A fan will be fitted later to help clear the room of cooking smells.

WINDOW EXTENDED
This increases light to the kitchen and the work-top area.

W.C. AND LARDER WINDOWS BRICKED UP
During the work, an air-brick was fitted for the new larder cupboard.

EXTERIOR DOOR FULLY GLAZED
By fitting a modern fully glazed door, the central area of the new kitchen became brightly lit.

TILED WORK TOP
The area around the cooker can be used for informal meals.

LAUNDRY AREA
The laundry work top doubles as a serving annexe to the dining area, in the main part of the house.

THE NEW KITCHEN The scullery and three cubicles have been knocked into one, making space for floor and wall units, cupboards, shelves, washing machine, cooker and refrigerator.

203

• RESTYLING A VICTORIAN TOWN HOUSE KITCHEN

The previous owners of this Victorian town house used a room at the back of the house as the kitchen. Restyling the kitchen gave the new owners the opportunity of moving the kitchen to a completely new room – identical in shape and size – at the front of the house at the same time installing modern units and equipment.

THE ADVANTAGES

The switch round had the advantage that the new kitchen would be out of the way of people passing to and from the back garden. The sink unit, larder and dishwasher were positioned so that outlets for air vents and waste pipes could be fitted through the house's front wall.

The old kitchen could now be used as a living-cum-dining-room. It was away from the traffic noise at the front of the house, and it overlooked the garden.

In restyling the new kitchen, no alterations were made to the room, apart from removing the fireplace surround so that units could be fitted. While re-decorating the room, the windows overlooking the road were double-glazed to cut down the noise from passing traffic.

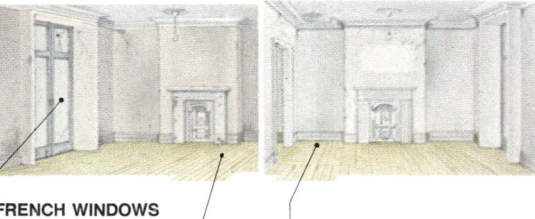

FRENCH WINDOWS

ORIGINAL KITCHEN
This room at the back of the house is the only way out to the garden.

ORIGINAL LIVING-ROOM
A noisy room, facing a busy main road, and with an unprepossessing outlook.

CHANGING THE ROOMS The kitchen is to go on the right, the living-room on the left. The new kitchen is more conveniently sited for attending to the front door; at the same time, people using the garden are not constantly passing through.

RISE-AND-FALL UNIT
The light can be set at various heights by a pull of the shade. Useful when working or dining.

VICTORIAN DETAILS
Ceilings of Victorian houses are high. Units can be fitted without disturbing attractive cornices.

SINGLE-RUN UNITS
A variety of units can be linked in different ways to make runs. This run includes refrigerator, wall and floor units, cooker, hob, sink.

WORK TRIANGLE
Cooker, sink and work top are handily placed to save labour. The work top is also a table for informal meals.

SERVICES
The food cupboard was positioned so that its vent could be fitted through the outside wall. Waste pipes also run through this wall.

THE NEW KITCHEN The units stand proud of the wall each side of the fireplace. This helps to increase ventilation behind equipment such as refrigerators.

A FEELING OF SPACE The choice of white units accentuates the spacious feeling that comes with high ceilings. Double-glazing has been fitted to the large window overlooking a busy road, which will help to keep out traffic noise, reduce condensation and cut down heat loss.

• CONVERTING A COUNTRY KITCHEN

Old-fashioned farmhouse kitchens are often large, recalling those days when farm wives stored, prepared and cooked virtually all the food eaten by their large families. Such kitchens would be too big for most families today, but in making the kitchens smaller and labour-saving, the same set of problems still have to be considered. With so much home-grown food being produced, cooking and preserving will almost certainly be on a large scale; without shops near at hand, other foods will need to be stored in large quantities.

DIVIDED BY WALLS

The problems were solved when re-styling this particular country kitchen by erecting partition walls, dividing the kitchen so that roughly two-thirds became an area for food preparation and cooking; the remaining one-third being split into a walk-in larder with a deep-freeze, and a laundry room.

Light to the kitchen was increased by enlarging two windows and by painting the brick walls white. The central-heating boiler for the house was fitted by the side of the original fireplace so that it could be vented up the existing chimney. The crude door at the side was replaced by one more in keeping with the restyled room without spoiling its character.

The walk-in larder gives ample food-storage space, and the laundry room – which is the main rear entrance to the house – is particularly useful in the winter as a store for muddy boots and working clothes.

LOOK OF WELCOME The low, wood-slatted ceiling adds a feeling of warmth to what is traditionally a place of welcome – the country kitchen. The units for the new kitchen were purpose-built to fit the out-of-square walls, and painted to match the Aga cooker. An unusual feature is the bench-type seating arrangement at the table.

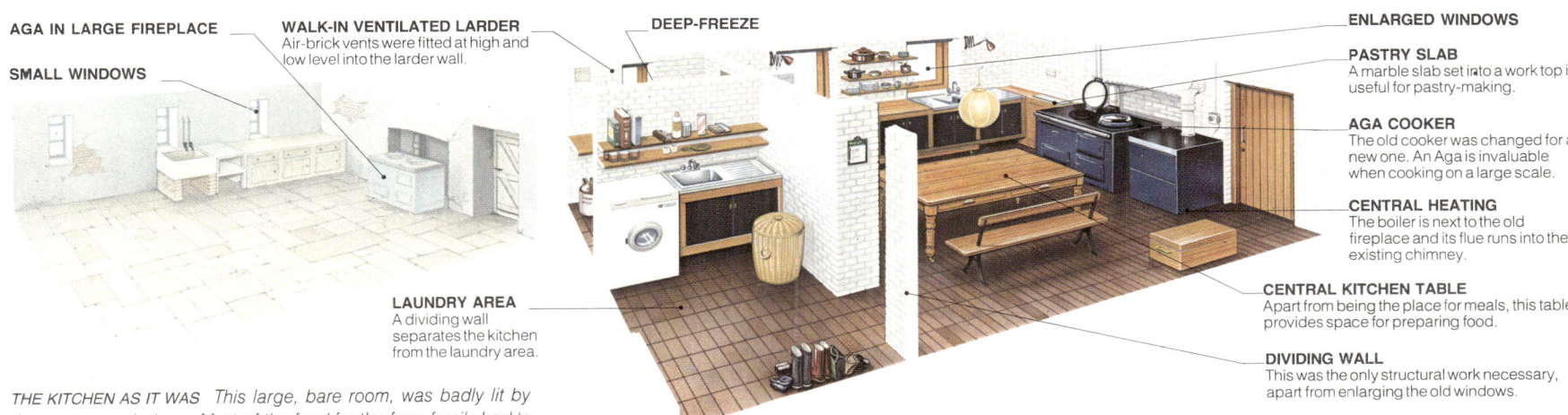

AGA IN LARGE FIREPLACE

SMALL WINDOWS

WALK-IN VENTILATED LARDER
Air-brick vents were fitted at high and low level into the larder wall.

LAUNDRY AREA
A dividing wall separates the kitchen from the laundry area.

DEEP-FREEZE

ENLARGED WINDOWS

PASTRY SLAB
A marble slab set into a work top is useful for pastry-making.

AGA COOKER
The old cooker was changed for a new one. An Aga is invaluable when cooking on a large scale.

CENTRAL HEATING
The boiler is next to the old fireplace and its flue runs into the existing chimney.

CENTRAL KITCHEN TABLE
Apart from being the place for meals, this table provides space for preparing food.

DIVIDING WALL
This was the only structural work necessary, apart from enlarging the old windows.

THE KITCHEN AS IT WAS This large, bare room, was badly lit by three narrow windows. Most of the food for the farm family had to be prepared on the small work top in the far corner of the kitchen.

THE KITCHEN NOW The large space has been divided into separate working and storage areas, with plenty of room for meals.

• USING THE KITCHEN FOR OTHER ACTIVITIES

If your kitchen is habitually used as a workroom, playroom, dining-room or office, allow for this in the planning. This also makes it easier to supervise children while they are playing or doing their homework.

KITCHEN/DINING-ROOM

It is convenient to be able to have meals in the kitchen, even if there is space only for breakfast and snacks. A pull-out table, lift-up flap, island unit, or a counter with a width of at least 460 mm. (18 in.) will be sufficient for casual meals and snacks. All these surfaces can be used as work tops when not needed for meals. Folding chairs or stackable stools can be stored under a work top or in a cupboard when not in use.

A kitchen large enough to take a dining table comfortably can be used for family meals and entertaining. The dining area can be separated from the working area by a unit which can serve as a sideboard, by a ladder-type room divider which can be used for storage, by a curtain or a blind.

If there is not space for a divider, you can make the dining area appear separate with carpet, differently coloured walls and the clever use of lighting and decorating. Have a lamp suspended over the dining table and use dimmer switches (see lighting section, p. 87) in the work area so that it is not obtrusive when you are eating. Use plants and pictures to give a relaxed atmosphere and to distract attention from the work area. Alternatively, the whole room can be decorated in a softer, less kitchen-like manner, using wooden units rather than plastic.

If the dining table is likely to be used for kitchen jobs, make sure it has an easily cleaned and stain-resistant surface. To save space when the room is not being used for meals, have an extendable table. But make sure that there is room for people to sit comfortably around the table when it is fully extended.

KITCHEN/PLAYROOM

As small children need constant supervision and as a mother has to spend much of her time in the kitchen, it seems sensible to create a safe area in the kitchen where a child can play.

Once a child can crawl or walk, he needs space to move around and toys to play with. He must be kept away from electric points, gas jets, hot pans, poisonous substances and trailing flexes. If there is enough space, consider dividing the working part of the kitchen from the play area with a peninsular unit, and close the gap with a child's safety gate. If the kitchen is not large enough to divide in this way, there are other solutions. If you have a hatch which enables you to see into the dining-room or living-room, create a safe play area in that room.

Failing that, sit the child near the end of a work top or kitchen table. Keep a nearby cupboard or drawer just for his toys and paint a square of wall or cupboard with blackboard paint. If possible, give up some time to playing with him. Many children like to copy their mother, so give a child some pastry to play with and a few plastic dishes to 'wash up' in a bowl of water.

Make a few safety rules and stick to them. Never leave a child alone in the kitchen, even in his own separate play area. Always turn pan handles inwards, or keep pans screened by safety guards. Always keep out of a child's reach all harmful substances, including bleaches, detergents, disinfectants, polishes and any kind of spray, knives and sharp instruments. Fit childproof electric sockets (see p. 372). Never let a small child open a refrigerator, climb on work surfaces or climb to look out of a window.

KITCHEN/SEWING-ROOM

Unless you have a very large kitchen and a long table suitable for cutting out, full-scale dressmaking is best done elsewhere. But mending, embroidery and small sewing jobs can be done quite comfortably in the kitchen if you have a suitable work top, and storage space for the equipment you will be using.

SAFE PLAY AREA UNDER MOTHER'S EYE   The kitchen is the natural place for a young child to play, but the problem of ensuring his safety is all the greater because of the equipment near by. The ideal solution is to use a safety gate.

There is a kitchen storage unit which has a pull-out shelf designed to hold a sewing machine. When not in use, the machine is stored out of sight under a work surface. If you have to use a table or work surface, try to set aside a special corner for sewing. As a sewing machine is quite heavy to lift, keep it close to where you are going to use it, or store it on a shelf at the same level. In the same area, keep a shallow drawer for threads, scissors, needles and other sewing materials, and a deep drawer, box or basket to store items to be mended. An adjustable typist's chair is ideal for sewing-machine work, and a comfortable armchair or folding garden chair – if there is space for one – makes hand-sewing a relaxing task. A wall-mounted angled lamp, which can be directed where needed, is probably the best source of light (see p. 84).

KITCHEN/WORKROOM

A good-sized kitchen with a large, solid table can be adapted for a certain amount of woodwork, modelling, drawing, painting, flower arranging and other crafts. Store equipment in one part of the room away from the kitchen work area. A pegboard is useful for hanging light things, and a wall-storage unit for heavier things such as tools. A set of adjustable shelves can hold larger items and a rack can be used for storing short lengths of timber. For model making, painting and craft work, shallow drawers are needed for small tools, adhesives, paints and brushes The drawers can be kept tidy by dividing them into compartments, or using cutlery holders. Clay modelling can be done in the kitchen if the clay used is the type that does not need firing. Access to a sink and a good sized work top or table is needed. Adjustable shelves can be used for storing the models while they are drying. Plastic-coated steel shelving is both practical and cheap.

Flower arranging is most conveniently done at the sink, so store vases, wire and other necessary items in a cupboard or on a shelf near the sink. If plant potting is done in the kitchen, make sure earth does not get into the sink, and keep hormone rooting powders and other potting aids away from food.

KITCHEN/OFFICE

As the kitchen is the place where you are likely to deal with accounts, write letters and school notes, make shopping lists and telephone calls, it makes sense to have an organised space where all these things can be done. A small desk or kitchen table in a corner of the room, with plenty of wall space for shelves, is ideal. A wide shelf at a comfortable sitting height serves the same purpose. The shelves can be used for cookery books, stationery, files of leaflets, recipes, guarantee cards and pens. A pegboard is useful for pinning up reminders, shopping lists, a message pad and calendar. If you use a typewriter, have an adjustable typist's chair. Good lighting is needed here – a light that fits on the wall or a shelf will save desk space.

CARING FOR PETS

Pets are almost bound to find their way into the kitchen: it is impossible to keep a cat or dog away from the smell of food, the warmth and companionship, and almost impossible to prevent a child from bringing his hamster or guinea-pig cage in from time to time. Rather than trying to keep them out provide a space where they will neither harm themselves nor the family.

Make sure that any pet is healthy. Get a book about the care and treatment of the animal and if in doubt always go to a vet, RSPCA, People's Dispensary for Sick Animals or Blue Cross branch (see pp. 410-18).

Some ailments, such as worms, can be caught by humans. Fleas from cats and dogs, on the other hand, cannot live on humans but they can bite and they do carry disease. Make sure that the animal is wormed and clear of fleas. Wash or destroy its bedding regularly.

Cats and dogs should have a basket lined with hessian, old blanket or cushion. Always keep it away from food and do not let children play in it.

Feeding and drinking dishes should be of glazed earthenware or enamel and should be washed after every meal, separately from any dishes used by the family. Keep pet powders, tonics, grooming equipment and so on, out of the kitchen.

DINING IN THE KITCHEN Built-in seating and the imaginative use of colours and materials can create a compact dining area in the kitchen.

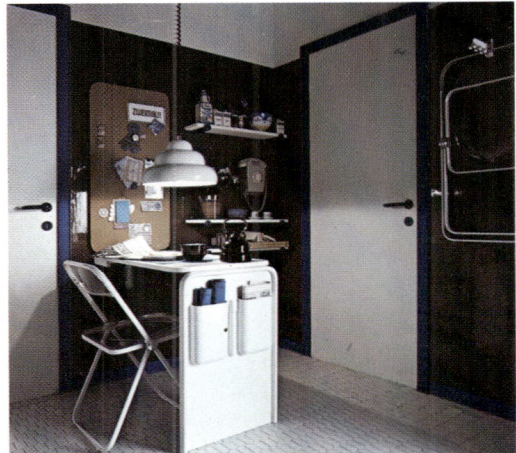

HOME OFFICE The kitchen is often the most convenient, if not the only, place to provide a desk or study area.

WHEN WORK IS OVER Specially designed foldaway units ensure that floor space can be reclaimed when needed.

USEFUL KITCHEN EQUIPMENT

Given the opportunity to re-equip her kitchen with all the various utensils and tableware she needs, a housewife today would be faced with a bewildering choice. New materials, coupled with modern manufacturing methods, have produced various types of pots and pans in a host of shapes and sizes. Cutlery, glassware and table linens are made in a multitude of designs, while electrical gadgets can be loaded with attachments. This section is a guide to what is available, and what you should consider when buying kitchen equipment.

• POTS AND PANS

The five main materials used to make saucepans and other cooking utensils are aluminium, iron, steel, copper and heat-resistant glass. Consider the advantages, and disadvantages, of each before making your choice.

ALUMINIUM

Saucepans made from aluminium are inexpensive, light and durable. They do not rust, are easy to clean and conduct heat evenly. The best aluminium pans have a thick heat-retaining base, and are suitable for use on the hot plates of electric and solid-fuel cookers. Very lightweight aluminium pans should be avoided. They can become distorted if dropped. This may affect the pan's balance, making it dangerous to use.

Care and cleaning Use hot, soapy water and a soap scouring pad. To remove stubborn stains, make up a weak solution of vinegar and water and boil it in the pan. Never clean aluminium pans with soda. This will corrode the metal, causing food to stick to the pan and burn.

COPPER

The great advantages of copper kitchenware are that it is an excellent conductor of heat, is extremely hard-wearing and, when cleaned properly, looks most attractive in a kitchen. Its drawbacks are that it is expensive and needs frequent cleaning. Modern copper saucepans are lined with non-toxic metals – tin or silver. A lining needs replacing about every three years if the pan is in constant use.

Care and cleaning Treat the pan as carefully as you would a non-stick pan. Wash the inside with soapy water and dry immediately. Never scour the pan. Stubborn food deposits are best removed by soaking. The outside surface can be cleaned with a proprietary copper polish.

STAINLESS STEEL

Because stainless steel is not a good conductor of heat, the bases of pans are clad in aluminium or copper to distribute heat evenly. The most expensive pans are made in three layers – a mild-steel centre layer with the outside layers in stainless steel. This saves costs when cooking. It retains heat well, so that only a low flame is needed once the food begins to cook.

Care and cleaning Avoid scouring. Use hot, soapy water. A stainless-

LIDS
The lid should fit reasonably tightly to avoid wasting heat. The knob on the lid should be made of wood or thermo-setting plastic which will not conduct heat. Ensure, too, that the knob is large enough to grip without burning your fingers on the lid.

HANDLES
The ideal length of handle on an average-sized pan is 150 mm. (6 in.). Longer handles can upset the pan's balance. Avoid metal and ceramic handles, which conduct heat, and make sure the handle is secure.

CORNERS
Choose pans where the base and sides are joined inside with a slight curve. Square, right-angled corners are difficult to clean and are less efficient when stirring liquids.

RIMS
Curved rims are best for draining liquids from pans. Milk pans can have a pouring lip.

BASES
The base of aluminium pans should be thick to distribute heat evenly. Stainless-steel pans should have a copper or aluminium base, or be made throughout of an inside core of mild steel, sandwiched between two layers of steel.

SAUCEPAN CHECK-LIST Apart from size, there are five main parts of a saucepan to check when deciding on the right type to buy. Make sure that the saucepan you are buying matches up to these requirements and it will give you good results – and long service.

steel cleaner will restore the original mirror finish to the *outside* of the pan.

HEAT-RESISTANT GLASS

The three main types of heat-resistant glass that can be used in the oven are Pyrex, Cordalite and Pyroflam. Only Pyroflam can withstand the direct heat of a hot plate.

Care and cleaning Avoid using harsh abrasives or wire scourers. Clean with hot, soapy water. Deposits that are baked on are best removed by soaking the dish in warm, soapy water.

CAST IRON

Utensils made of cast iron are among the most economical to use. Cast iron not only conducts heat evenly, but it also retains heat, allowing dishes to keep boiling or simmering at low temperatures. Their big disadvantage is their weight.

Care and cleaning Wash in hot, soapy water. Dry immediately, then rub with cooking oil to prevent rust.

ENAMEL-COATED PANS

Enamel can be fused on cast-iron, steel and aluminium utensils. Apart from the visual appeal of the colours and patterns produced by this process, enamel-coated pans are easy to keep clean. Considerable publicity has been given recently to the health hazards that could be created if cadmium or lead are used in the enamelling process. Check either with the manufacturer's literature, or with the store, that the particular utensil you are buying meets safety standards.

Care and cleaning Use only wooden or plastic spoons or spatulas. Metal may chip the edges. Do not use harsh abrasives for cleaning. To remove stubborn stains, soak the pans in warm soapy water.

NON-STICK COOKWARE

Pans with non-stick linings, such as Teflon or Fluon, are popular because they are far easier to clean. Take care not to over-heat a pan of this type or the non-stick surface will gradually break down and food will burn.

Care and cleaning To preserve the non-stick surface for as long as possible, always wash the pan in clean soapy water, rinse it out and dry thoroughly. A wipe with a damp cloth may appear to have cleaned the surface, but tiny food particles left

The parts of a pressure cooker.

behind will burn, destroying the non-stick surface. Never use metal tools, which will scratch the surface.

• PRESSURE COOKERS

When boiling water is trapped, the build-up of steam creates extremely high temperatures. This is the principle on which a pressure cooker works. Cooking by this method has a number of advantages. Food is cooked faster, saving fuel. Because the juices are trapped within the cooker, food is tastier, and with the pressure forcing heat into the food, tough pieces of meat become tender. Fewer vitamins are destroyed and various foods can be cooked at the same time.

Because different pressures are needed to cook different foods, two main types of cooker are sold. The first has a pressure fixed at 15 lb. to the square inch, and is suitable for all meat and vegetables. The second has a range of pressure controls that can be altered. Bottling fruit in a pressure cooker, for instance, needs 5 lb. of pressure; bottling vegetables, 10 lb. of pressure.

Care and cleaning Keep the valve free from dirt. Wash the cooker with hot, soapy water and store carefully with the lid off so that air circulates inside the pan. The sealing gasket will need replacing after a time, but its life can be prolonged by occasionally lubricating with cooking fat. Stains inside the pan can be removed with a weak solution of cream of tartar and water, boiled up in the sealed cooker. Leave the cooker sealed for three hours. Empty out, wash and dry.

• BAKING EQUIPMENT

Most trays and moulds used in baking are made from tinned steel, which is not affected by normal oven temperatures or by the mild acids used in baking. Large baking tins used for cakes have a loose bottom so that the cake, when cooked, is easier to remove from the tin.

Tin melts at a temperature of 232°C (450°F), so never leave an empty tray on a hot plate. With constant use tin will wear off. It is cheaper to buy a new tray than have the tray re-tinned.

When following recipes, it is essential to use the correct size of baking tin. As a temporary measure, a simple shallow tray can be made to the correct size by folding double-thickness foil to the required shape.

Care and cleaning The idea that bakeware left dirty will 'mature' and therefore produce better cakes and pastries is not correct. Tins should be washed in hot, soapy water to remove all burned food deposits. Dry thoroughly afterwards. Do not scour harshly. Soak the tin in hot, soapy water to remove stubborn food particles, if necessary rubbing them with a nylon pad.

Stainless steel

Copper

Aluminium

Cast iron

Non-stick finish

Heat-resistant glass

Enamelled cast-iron

Stoneware

• TABLEWARE

Crockery is manufactured in two distinct forms – as traditional plates and dishes on which meals are served, and as oven-to-tableware in which food can be cooked and which can then be used for serving at the table. This cuts down on the number of pieces of crockery required.

When buying tableware, therefore, always consider whether pieces could be used as ovenware to save doubling up on unnecessary items.

OVEN-TO-TABLEWARE

Some oven-to-tableware is flameproof, which means that it can be used on the direct heat of either gas or electric rings. But always check this point with the manufacturer's instructions and, unless it is clearly stated that it is flameproof, use the piece only in the oven.

Ovenware items should not be subjected to sudden changes of temperature such as being taken from a hotplate and put into cold water. The only dishes able to withstand this are known by the trade names 'Pyrosil'or 'Pyroflam'; these can be used direct from freezer to cooker.

Before buying oven-to-tableware, check that handles are large enough to grip with an ovencloth, but not so large that they take up too much oven space; some flameproof ware can be fitted with long, lock-on, detachable handles for use on the cooker top. Check that casseroles are large enough to hold a stew for your family or guests; that they have easy-to-lift lids which can be safely held with an ovencloth; and, finally, that they harmonise with the pieces from which you eat at the table. The different types of oven-to-tableware available are as follows:

Borosilicate glass This is the most

ALPHABETICAL GUIDE TO KITCHEN UTENSILS

A bewildering number of utensils equip a modern kitchen, and many items will be unnecessary for your needs. Use this list to check that you have allowed for your own particular requirements.

B

BAKING AND ROASTING EQUIPMENT
baking tin (large and small)
baking trays
bulb baster
bun tins (1 set)
cake tins (3 sizes)
casseroles with lids (oven and/or flameproof)
cream-horn tins
flan rings (plain and fluted)
gratin dishes (oven and/or flameproof)
loaf tins (450 g. and 900 g. – 1 lb. and 2 lb.)
pie dishes (deep and shallow)
pie funnel
pie plates (2 sizes)
ramekins (1 set)
sandwich tins
soufflé dishes
Swiss roll tins and tartlet tins
terrine

BOWLS AND JUGS
coffee pot
milk jugs
mixing bowls (large and small)
pudding basins (3 sizes)

C

CLEANING UTENSILS
bottle brushes
dish mops and brushes
glass and tea cloths
scourers

CONTAINERS
bread bin
flour bins
plastic storage containers
storage jars and tins

CUTTING TOOLS
apple corer
ball scoop
cheese slicer
cherry stoner
egg slicer
kitchen scissors
knife sharpener
knives (2 sizes of chef's knives, serrated knife, vegetable knife)
mandolin slicer
meat cleaver
meat saw
pastry cutters (plain and fluted)
pastry wheel
potato chipper (fluted)
vegetable peeler

G

GENERAL EQUIPMENT
balloon whisk
biscuit cutters (assorted)

cake racks
cake-decorating equipment
chopping board
flour sifter
forcing bag and nozzles
funnel
jelly bag
meat lifters
muslin
needles (larding and trussing)
nutcrackers
palette knives (2 sizes)
pastry board and brush
rolling pin
rotary whisk
skewers
spatula
squeezer
sugar sifter
tongs (for grilling and frying)
trivet
waffle irons
wooden cocktail sticks

GRINDERS AND GRATERS
coffee mill
food blender
garlic press
grater (stainless steel)
mincer
nutmeg grater
pepper and salt mills
pestle and mortar

H

HOLLOW WARE (POTS, PANS)
deep fryer

double saucepan
egg poacher
fish kettle
frying pans
kettle
milk pan
preserving pan
pressure cooker
saucepans (3 sizes minimum)
steamer

K

KITCHEN STATIONERY
aluminium foil
cutlet frills
greaseproof paper
kitchen paper (absorbent)
non-stick and waxed paper
paper cases (for cakes and sweets)
plastic food bags
rice paper
self-clinging plastic foil
string

M

MEASURING EQUIPMENT
cooking thermometer
kitchen timer
measuring cup
measuring jugs
measuring spoons

MOULDS
charlotte mould

jelly moulds
pie moulds
ring mould
savarin mould

O

OPENERS
bottle openers
corkscrew
screw-top openers
tin openers

S

SPOONS AND FORKS
draining spoon (perforated)
fish slice
kitchen cutlery (stainless steel)
skimming ladle
soup ladle
wooden kitchen fork
wooden spoons (3 sizes)

STRAINERS
colander
salad shaker
sieve (hair)
sieve (nylon)
strainers

W

WEIGHING EQUIPMENT
scales

Earthenware

heat-resistant material for oven-to-tableware. There is no glaze to crack and collect dirt, which makes it also the cleanest and the most hygienic to use. It is usually known by the trade names of 'Pyrex' and 'Pyroflam'.

Cast-iron (non-enamelled) Very hardwearing, and both ovenproof and flameproof. Heat distribution is even, but dishes are heavy. They need seasoning before first being used to prevent rusting. Dishes not pre-seasoned by the manufacturer need seasoning by the buyer. Normally, the dish has to be washed in mild soap and water then thoroughly dried before seasoning, which is done by rubbing the inside surface (including the lid) with cooking oil, and heating in a slow oven for about two hours (or as long as instructed).

After each use, excess oil is wiped off with paper and the dish washed if necessary. If it is washed in strong detergent or scoured, it needs re-seasoning.

Enamelled cast-iron This has all the advantages of non-enamelled cast-iron oven-to-tableware. In addition, enamelling makes the surface easier to clean. However, enamel chips easily if knocked, and will flake off if put under cold water immediately after use. Allow slow cooling. Do not bang on the rim of the dish with a spoon or similar utensil.

Earthenware Ovenproof earthenware is inexpensive, is available in a large variety of designs, and retains and spreads heat efficiently. Its disadvantage is that the glazing 'crazes' (forms hairline cracks) under extreme temperatures. Once such crazing occurs, the porous nature of earthenware makes it unhygienic to use.

A new type of casserole has an earthenware crockpot, inside an electrically heated container made of plastic and lined with aluminium.

Enamelled steel This does not hold or distribute heat as well as cast-iron, but is cheaper and lighter. Because its base is thin it is not suitable for slow stewing. It is ideal for quick cooking, such as boiling vegetables. Some types have stainless-steel rims to protect the enamel.

Royal Worcester porcelain Although expensive, it is hardwearing, well designed and withstands quick changes in temperature.

Stainless steel Strong and durable, with a hard, smooth surface that is hygienic and easy to clean, but it develops heat marks in hot ovens.

Stoneware Strong and difficult to chip, but check the manufacturer's instructions – some stoneware oven-to-tableware is not flameproof.

• CROCKERY

There are three main categories of crockery for the table – the classical, such as the heavily embossed Wedgwood; the traditional, such as the elegant Minton or Royal Crown Derby; and the modern, with its streamlined shapes, geometric patterns and bold colours.

Whatever sort of crockery you choose, it is very important to consider it from a practical point of view. Make sure that plates and saucers sit flatly; that cups are well balanced in the saucers (when the cups are full as well as empty); that jugs and pots have openings large enough to make cleaning easy; that lids of tea and coffee pots do not fall off when the liquid is poured; and that spouts pour liquids properly. A cup should feel comfortable to hold and the handle should be so designed that it can be held without fingers being pressed against the cup's side. If you have a dishwasher, do not choose cups with a concave base. These bases trap water when the cups are placed upside-down in the dishwasher for cleaning. Also bear in mind that if cups are too shallow, the contents will cool rapidly.

When you have finally decided on a design, it is best to buy one piece first and use it for at least a month to test its durability. Wash it regularly in very hot water, then take it back to the shop and compare it with the stock. If the pattern has not faded and there is no crazing in the glaze, the design is sturdy enough for practical use.

It is not necessary to buy complete sets of crockery. Instead you can build up a set by buying a few items at a time. But do make sure from the shop assistant that the design you choose is likely to stay in stock for some time.

If you use a dishwasher, ask the retailer if the decoration on the crockery will stand up to being washed in the high temperatures of these appliances. Decorations beneath the glaze are usually safe, being protected by the glaze. Decorations that have been fired on over the glaze may need to be test-washed in the machine first.

Some of the most attractive types of crockery you can buy are as follows:

Earthenware Very porous. Once the glaze is chipped, it should not be used – it could be unhygienic. Also available in oven-to-tableware.

Bone china One of the most expensive makes of crockery. It is white and translucent, and although it looks delicate is extremely hardwearing.

Porcelain True porcelain – vitreous and translucent – is available in both oven and tableware.

Faience A tin-glazed Italian pottery also known as 'majolica'. The tin-oxide used comes from Faenza, a city in northern Italy famous for pottery since the 15th century.

Jasper The blue or green unglazed stoneware with white embossing which most people call simply by its designer's name – Wedgwood.

Black basalt An unglazed stoneware stained with manganese dioxide and cobalt. It is expensive but hardwearing, and is made only by Wedgwood.

Bone china

Porcelain

Faience (or majolica)

Blue Jasper

Black basalt

• PLASTIC AND WOODEN KITCHENWARE

Traditionally, many of the utensils found in the kitchen were made of wood. Plastic has replaced wood in many instances, because it is cheap, hygienic, colourful and easy to clean. But wood still has an important role to play in today's kitchen.

PLASTIC KITCHENWARE

There are two kinds of plastic used in the kitchen – *thermosetting plastics*, which cannot be softened by heat, and *thermoplastics*, which melt when heated.

Thermosetting plastics are used for the handles of saucepans, kettles and irons, for heatproof kitchen boards and kitchen surfaces, for cups, saucers and beakers, and for salt and pepper pots.

Most plastic kitchen utensils are made from the more flexible and much lighter thermoplastics. The most common types are poly-propylene, nylon and polystyrene. They are used to make mixing bowls, measuring jugs, sieves, colanders and containers.

Care and cleaning All types of plastics are easy to clean by washing in hot soapy water, but care is needed when using plastics as they scratch easily. Avoid using scouring pads, and remember that it is not wise to wash plastics in an automatic dishwasher (see pp. 200-1).

WOODEN KITCHENWARE

Salad bowls, salt boxes and chopping boards are usually made from wood, although there are excellent alternatives available in synthetic materials.

A salad stays fresher in a wooden bowl which should be made of teak to absorb some of the oil from the salad dressing. If using garlic in a salad, rub a peeled garlic clove around the inside of the bowl. The wood will retain the garlic flavour so the bowl should be used only for salads.

Salt and pepper stay drier in wooden containers, the wood itself absorbing any dampness in the atmosphere. Because of this, always choose wood for a salt-store container and use wooden salt and pepper pots.

Chopping blocks are usually made from lengths of beech wood, pinned and glued together. To add strength to the board, metal rods are inserted through the length and width. Cutting boards are normally made from two or more pieces of sycamore glued together, and may also have strengthening rods inserted through them.

Meat tenderisers are usually made from wood, although the teeth may be metal. When using a tenderiser, dampen the teeth with cold water. This will help prevent meat tissue sticking to the teeth.

Because wooden spatulas do not damage the surfaces of saucepans, they are ideal to use with non-stick kitchenware. The handles of wooden utensils will not get hot, but if left in a hot pan for some time may scorch.

Use wooden utensils when making jam. Plastic utensils could melt, and metal utensils could affect the taste.

Care and cleaning A salad bowl should be cleaned by wiping thoroughly with paper towels after use. Do, not wash it unless oil absorbed by the wood becomes rancid. Then soak in hot water with a little detergent. Give it two or three rinsings with clean hot water and dry thoroughly. Chopping blocks and cutting boards should be wiped with a damp cloth after use. Never soak them in water. This can loosen the

---

ALPHABETICAL GUIDE TO SMALL ELECTRICAL APPLIANCES

When buying any electrical appliance, always check that it has been approved as electrically safe (see p. 370).

BLENDER/LIQUIDISER
A blender consists of a motor that turns cutting blades inside a lidded goblet. It will pulp fruit and vegetables (cooked or raw) and blend such things as soups, batters and milk shakes. Some will also chop dry foods, and make breadcrumbs.
Advantage Food preparation can be done quickly and effortlessly.
Points to consider It is noisy. Some low-powered models run for only 45 seconds at a time, yet foods can take a lot longer than this to blend.

COFFEE GRINDER/MILL
A coffee grinder crushes beans between discs; a mill chops them with rotating blades. Either type can be an attachment to a food mixer or a separate appliance.
Advantage Both produce freshly ground coffee quickly and easily.

Points to consider The consistency of coarse and fine grinds varies with the make of machine, so does the amount that can be ground at a time.

COFFEE MAKER
There are three types of electric coffee maker – percolator, drip filter and vacuum machine. Each has a different method of forcing boiling water through a container of ground coffee.
Advantage All make coffee automatically (in about ten minutes).
Points to consider Percolators are the simplest method and keep coffee hotter, but some will not make less than 500 ml. (1 pint) at a time. Filters and vacuum machines use finely ground coffee, which is more economical.

FOOD MIXER
The range of food mixers varies from large, powerful table models to small, hand-held models. All types have beaters that fit into the mixer head and can be used for rubbing in fat and flour, beating cake and pudding mixtures, whisking egg whites, and mixing batters and sauces. Table models

include a bowl and stand, and some hand-held models have them as extras. Optional attachments available include can openers, potato peelers, mincers and blenders.
Advantages Mixers save time and hard work. Those with stands can be left to work unattended.
Points to consider Table models are large and heavy to move, but they have more attachments and can cope with heavy mixtures and large quantities. Hand-held types can be used at the cooker; but are not strong enough for heavy mixtures – large quantities have to be mixed in batches.

JUICE EXTRACTOR
There are two types – a citrus-fruit press, which is a rotating corrugated cone on which the halved fruit is pressed, and an enclosed unit with rotating blades that will pulp fruit and vegetables, the juice running out through a spout. Both can be separate appliances or mixer attachments.
Advantages Juice is cheaper to make than buy. A citrus-fruit press is quicker and more efficient than hand squeezing.

Points to consider Juicers are expensive, and dismantling and cleaning them is irksome. Juice can be made (not as efficiently) in a blender/liquidiser, but separate straining is needed.

KETTLE
Capacities of kettles vary from about 1-3.5 litres (2-6 pints). Automatic types switch off when the water boils; others have to be switched off.
Advantage All types are fast boiling – under four minutes for 1.7 litres (3 pints).
Points to consider Automatic kettles are more expensive but more economical to use. If you want to boil small amounts some kettles will not work with less than 850 ml. (1½ pints) of water. Spout-filled kettles should have a water-level indicator. Stainless-steel kettles last longest, especially in hard-water areas.

PLUG-IN COOKERS
These include a contact grill, which cooks steaks and small

joints between two closed-in plates; a multi-cooker, which has a deep lid and cooks like an oven; a deep-fat fryer; a casserole.
Advantages They can be plugged in for use in any room. Contact grills and deep-fat fryers cook fast and economically. Multi-cookers and casseroles can be unplugged and used at the table.
Points to consider The average-sized contact grill usually cooks only enough for two people. Cooking by casserole is slow, so meat must be sealed, vegetables fried and stock boiled first. Some multi-cookers and deep-fat fryers can be immersed in water for cleaning; others cannot.

SLICER
There are two kinds: one consists of a cutting table and rotary blade for slicing meat, bread, cheese and vegetables; the other is a slicer/shredder (usually a mixer attachment), an enclosed unit into which food is fed to a cutter and passed out through a chute.
Advantages Food slicing is quicker, smoother and more economical than by hand.
Points to consider A rotary-type slicer should have a guard, and no niches where food can accumulate. The slicer/shredder is irksome to clean.

TOASTER
Most types toast two slices of bread at a time; these pop up when ready and the heating element switches off.
Advantage It uses less electricity than a cooker grill.
Point to consider Some types toast one side at a time and slices have to be turned by hand.

YOGHOURT MAKER
A container with a heating element at the bottom. Warm milk (boiled, then cooled) and live yoghourt or yoghourt ferment is placed in the inner container and kept at an even temperature to produce fresh yoghourt.
Advantage It makes live yoghourt more cheaply than it can be bought.
Point to consider Yoghourt can be made anywhere without a maker if the temperature is correct.

glued joints and may rust the ends of any strengthening rods.

• CUTLERY

In Victorian times it was a sign of affluence for the table to be laid with elaborate silverware and for a kitchen to be stocked with every type of knife. Few household budgets today can stretch so far, but modern cutlery designs and materials are such that a table can be set out attractively without a lot of expense – and food can be prepared using a basic kitchen knife set of eight pieces.

TABLE CUTLERY

Strictly speaking, the word 'cutlery' refers only to knives. The correct name for forks and spoons is 'flatware', but it has now become acceptable to call all eating utensils cutlery.

Most cutlery today is made of stainless steel. Good stainless steel is referred to as 18/8 (indicating that it contains 18% chromium and 8% nickel). It does not rust, but can become discoloured if left in contact with mild acids such as vinegar and lemon juice. Chromium-plated and nickel-plated cutlery were once widely used, but now only cheaper-quality items are plated with these metals.

Cutlery that has been electroplated with nickel silver (known as EPNS cutlery) is more expensive, but very hard-wearing. If stamped A1 it has been given a top-quality plating which should last at least 20 years before replating becomes necessary.

Silver cutlery is extremely expensive, but in times of inflation it can turn out to be a good investment. It contains 92.5% silver and will have a hallmark that guarantees its purity.

When buying cutlery, check that it feels comfortable to hold and that the blades of knives stay rigid under pressure as well as cut properly. Fork prongs should be smooth and evenly spaced to ease cleaning. The bowl of the spoon should be deep enough to scoop up liquids without spilling. If you are building up a canteen of cutlery over a period of time, check with the shop or store that the design you choose will not be discontinued.

Care and cleaning Thorough drying after washing helps to prolong the life of cutlery. While acids from foods can lead to corrosion, long contact with water – especially hard water – is the cause of most pitting of stainless-steel surfaces. A stainless-steel polish should remove these marks. Do not wash knives in very hot water or leave them immersed in water for any length of time, as this could melt the adhesive holding the handles to the blades. Silver-plated and silver cutlery will be scratched if jumbled up together; wash pieces individually.

Certain foods, such as eggs and brussels sprouts, will tarnish EPNS cutlery. Remove stains with silver polish before washing.

KITCHEN CUTLERY

Stainless-steel knives will be adequate in most family kitchens, although their blades do not stay as sharp as those of knives made from carbon steel. When choosing kitchen knives, check that the handle is firmly riveted to the blade and not just fixed with adhesive. Choose knives that fit the palm of your hand comfortably.

Never store knives loose in a drawer. Apart from the damage it can do to the blades, fingers may be cut badly when sorting out knives. Store knives in a rack or in a case with individual compartments. (For sharpening knives, see pp. 364-5.)

Care and cleaning Wash in hot, soapy water after use, and dry thoroughly. Carbon-steel knives will rust if not dried immediately.

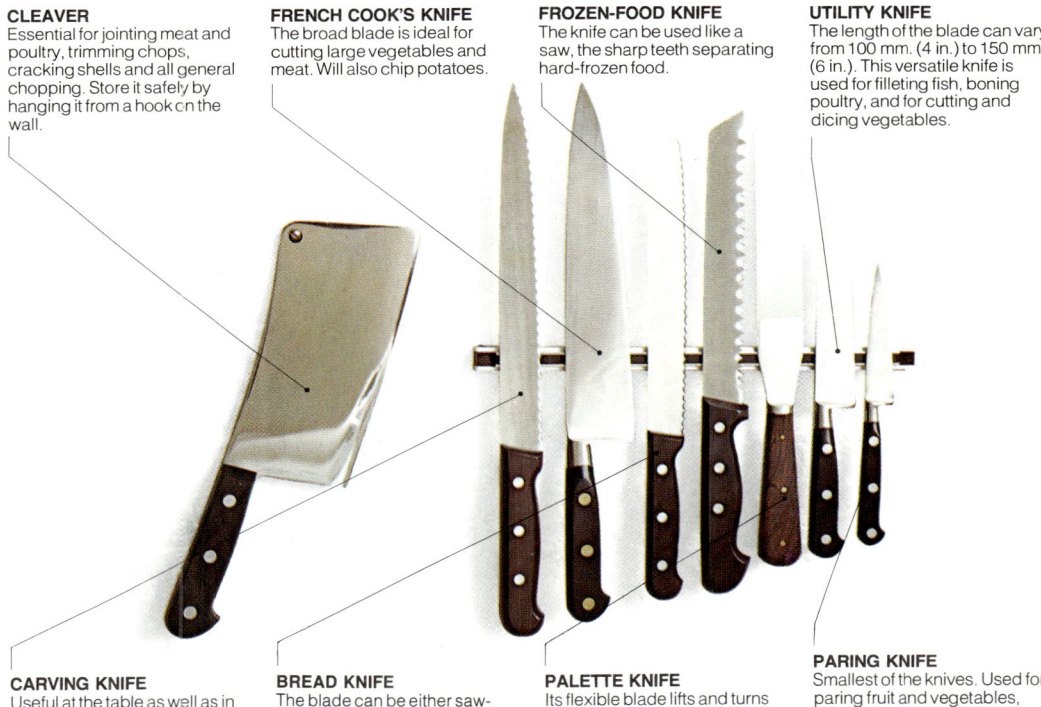

CLEAVER Essential for jointing meat and poultry, trimming chops, cracking shells and all general chopping. Store it safely by hanging it from a hook on the wall.

FRENCH COOK'S KNIFE The broad blade is ideal for cutting large vegetables and meat. Will also chip potatoes.

FROZEN-FOOD KNIFE The knife can be used like a saw, the sharp teeth separating hard-frozen food.

UTILITY KNIFE The length of the blade can vary from 100 mm. (4 in.) to 150 mm. (6 in.). This versatile knife is used for filleting fish, boning poultry, and for cutting and dicing vegetables.

CARVING KNIFE Useful at the table as well as in the kitchen for carving.

BREAD KNIFE The blade can be either saw-toothed or scalloped.

PALETTE KNIFE Its flexible blade lifts and turns food. Also spreads cream.

PARING KNIFE Smallest of the knives. Used for paring fruit and vegetables, chopping herbs and for coring.

KNIVES FOR THE KITCHEN These seven knives, and the cleaver, make up the basic knife set suitable for the average family kitchen. Note the firmly riveted handles, and how the knives are safely racked on a magnetic holder.

TEASPOON This can 'double' as a coffee spoon and also be used for grapefruit, melon and ice-cream dishes.

DESSERT SPOON

SOUP SPOON Can also be used in the kitchen as a serving spoon.

LARGE KNIFE Unless it is silver, or silver-plated, this can be used with the large fork for both meat and fish dishes. Silver retains the taste of fish so a separate knife and fork should be used for fish if cutlery is silver.

DESSERT KNIFE Can 'double' as a butter knife and fruit knife.

LARGE FORK

DESSERT FORK Used with the dessert knife, this is also suitable for hors-d'oeuvre dishes.

CUTLERY FOR THE TABLE There is no need to buy a whole range of table cutlery. Many pieces today can serve a dual purpose, and the seven pieces above would be ample for the needs of each member of the family.

• GLASSWARE

Drinking glasses, decanters and vases can be bought in four different qualities: in heavy and lustrous full-lead crystal; in the slightly less expensive but equally elegant lead crystal; in plain crystal; and in the all-purpose soda-lime glass, which is hand-made in its best quality and machine-moulded for the cheaper, mass-production market. Full-lead crystal contains a minimum of 30% lead oxide, and lead crystal contains 25%. It is this addition of lead oxide that gives glassware its brightness, clarity, weight and strength.

GLASSES

You can always tell a glass that is made of lead crystal by the ringing tone produced when you tap the rim lightly with your fingernail. Glass described as 'crystal' quality has a small lead oxide content, but the amount of oxide is not specified.

Glasses take on added elegance when decorated. The most popular type of decoration is the hand-cutting carried out on lead crystal, where the lead content makes it easier to cut, and on crystal glass. The cutting is done by holding the glass against the edge of an abrasive wheel. The incisions made are polished with concentrated acid. Hand-cut incisions are usually made deep into the glass and have sharply defined edges. Imitation cut-glass, produced in a mould, has a shallow cut, and the edges of the incisions tend to be rounded.

Other forms of decoration are copper-wheel engraving, which is similar to abrasive-wheel cutting, but with a shallower incision; frosting, carried out by dipping the glass when it is still hot into cold water, leaving uneven marks on the surface; acid engraving, in which the glass surface is etched away by an acid solution; sandblasting, in which a jet of abrasive cuts away the surface; and colouring, achieved by adding metallic oxides to the glass when it is molten.

A full glass set comprises eight main types as shown above (from the left): champagne flute, port glass, wine goblet, hock glass, whisky tumbler, tulip-shaped wine glass, brandy thistle and sherry copita. If you are starting to collect a full set of glasses, begin with three basic types: the

A complete eight-piece set of glasses.

sherry glass, which will also be suitable for port and for liqueurs; one of the wine glasses (medium size, 175-225 ml., 6-8 fl. oz.); and the whisky tumbler (about 225 ml., 8 fl. oz.) which can also be used for beer and for long drinks.

Choose clear glasses for wines and spirits, so that the colour of the drink can be seen and appreciated.

When buying glasses, examine each one carefully, making sure there are no chips around the rim and base, and no cracks or tiny bubbles in the glass. Also check that they stand level on their bases. If buying glasses individually to make up a set, check with the shop assistant that the design is likely to be available for some time, so that you can build up a complete set, or replace breakages.

DECANTERS, JUGS AND VASES

The popularity of decanters – now used to hold port, whisky and brandy – resulted from the discovery in the 18th century that the taste of port improved when it was decanted from its large cask into a smaller container.

Decanters are produced in the same quality-range as glasses, and in many shapes and sizes: tall and elegant; with large bases and tapered necks; with drum-shaped bases and short necks; and in square, squat cubes. The choice of shape is a personal one, but when buying a decanter make sure that the liquid pours properly and also that the stopper fits securely.

When choosing a jug, make sure that the handle is large enough to hold the jug properly and that the spout pours the liquid without gushing or dripping. The neck should be wide enough to allow the inside of the jug to be cleaned easily, and the base should be wide enough for the jug to stand squarely. A jug from which iced drinks will be poured needs a curled, narrowed lip to hold back the ice cubes.

Vases and bowls need to be balanced so that they remain stable when filled with flowers or fruit.

Care and cleaning Glasses should always be washed separately, in warm soapy water, to ensure that they do not chip against each other. Rinse in warm water and dry with a soft cloth. Always store upright to avoid damaging the rim, which is the most delicate part of a glass. Use a soft brush to clean marks within the engraving. A stopper that is stuck in a decanter can be removed by rubbing a little cooking oil around the joint. Leave the decanter for an hour or two in a warm place, then gently ease the stopper out (see also Care and Cleaning, pp. 322-3).

COLLECTING GLASS

The most popular collections are those of Georgian glasses, manufactured in the 18th century when the art of glass-making reached its peak in Britain. The full range is immense. Below are six examples, varying from 165-216 mm. ($6\frac{1}{2}$-$8\frac{1}{2}$ in.) high. From left to right:
1. An ogee bowl on a colour-twisted stem (c. 1765); 2. A round-funnel bowl on an eight-sided Silesian stem (c. 1740); 3. A wide-funnel bowl on a medium baluster stem (c. 1730); 4. A rare toasting-glass, its bell bowl engraved with a portrait of William, Duke of Cumberland (c. 1745); 5. A trumpet bowl, on an opaque white spiral-twist stem (c. 1765); 6. A round-funnel bowl on a double corkscrew air-twist stem (c. 1750).

The goblet, above (c. 1850), is 180 mm. (7 in.) high, has a capstan stem, and is engraved with a sailing ship, a rose and a thistle.

Georgian glasses can be expensive, but plain-stemmed glasses of the period can often be found at reasonable prices at antique shops and auction rooms. To recognise the surface sheen of Georgian glass, study the best examples. Harvey's Wine Museum, in Bristol, and the Victoria and Albert Museum, London, have excellent collections of glass, illustrating centuries of fine craftsmanship.

Soda-lime glass.

Lead crystal glass.

Full-lead crystal.

• TABLE ARRANGEMENTS

Well-cooked food and carefully chosen wines need the background of an attractive table-setting if you are to reap the full rewards of your work in the kitchen.

TABLE LINEN AND TABLE MATS

When buying tablecloths it is worth considering the non-iron range, made from seersucker or linen and cotton mixes. Also, check whether the cloth has been chemically treated to prevent stains penetrating through the material. A tablecloth should overhang all sides of the table by at least 23 cm. (9 in.). Tablecloths are usually sold 135 cm. (54 in.) wide and from 1.75-3 m. (2-3¼ yds) in length.

Napkins are made in a number of traditional sizes, according to use. Tea napkins are 28 cm. (11 in.) square; dinner napkins range from 38 cm. (15 in.) to 45 cm. (18 in.) square. Banquet cloths up to 60 cm. (24 in.) square are also available.

When using table mats – with or without a tablecloth – remember that fabric mats will not protect a polished table surface from the heat of dishes. The best protective mats are those made of cork, woven rush, wood or Melamine. Cork or Melamine are the most heat-resistant.

FLOWERS AND LIGHTING

Any flower arrangements on the table should be kept simple and not built up too high. Tall flowers will restrict the view of guests and inhibit conversation. If using candles, set them either above or below eye level so that guests are not looking directly at the flickering flames.

PLACE-SETTING

Whether a meal is a formal one or a family affair, the layout of a place-setting has the same objective – to tell a person exactly which piece of cutlery to use with each course.

Forks go on the left in the order in which they will be used, working from the outside in, and knives on the right, in the order of use. The soup spoon goes on the outside of the knives.

The dessert spoon and fork should be laid across the top of the setting – the spoon above the fork with the handle ready to be picked up in the right hand. The fork is placed for picking up in the left hand. A small knife, or butter spreader, may be placed horizontally above these, or across the top of the side plate – which is to the left of the setting – with its blade facing left.

Any dish requiring special cutlery – for example, oysters, lobster, melon and grapefruit – should be served with the correct piece. If an individual sweet is to be served, a spoon is brought with the sweet. If fruit is being served, a dessert plate, with a dessert knife and fork, and a finger bowl should be brought to the table.

Glasses can be arranged in various ways. The French tend to set them out to the right of the place-setting in a direct line facing the guest, the nearest glass being the one to use first. Another way is to place them diagonally on the right, the nearest glass again being used first. Glasses can be placed in a triangle just above the tip of the knives, with the two largest glasses at the back and the smallest at the front. Glasses for port are generally brought to the table at the beginning of the dessert course. Table napkins can be put either on the side plate, in the centre of the place-setting, or in one of the wine glasses. There are many ingenious ways of folding napkins, but the modern trend is towards simplicity – folding them into squares or rolling and inserting them into napkin rings.

DINNER FOR TWO Shining cutlery, gleaming glasses and attractive flowers – all add pleasure to a meal. Always strive for harmony in choice of colours. Flower arrangements and china should fit in with the decor of the room.

Cooking for the family

A good cook starts work long before setting foot in the kitchen. This section
will help you to plan meals ahead, and to get value for money when shopping.
There are basic cooking guides for meat, fish, poultry, vegetables –
every type of food from apples to venison, with advice on the
appropriate wine for each dish.

CONTENTS

BUYING AND STORING FOOD AND WINE

Advance planning, wise shopping and efficient food storage are the three essentials to keeping food costs down. Time spent planning meals is time saved on shopping and cooking, and good shopping depends on knowing what to look for in terms of freshness as well as cost – the most expensive food is not necessarily highest in food value. Wise shopping is wasted, however, if the food is not properly stored. Keeping food at the correct temperature and knowing how long it remains fresh will prevent wastage.

• BUDGETING

Most housewives know by experience how to balance their housekeeping budget. However, even the most experienced can make their money go further by careful planning.

To create a budget, divide the weekly food allowance into amounts to be spent on separate items: meat, fish, fruit and vegetables, dairy produce, groceries, bread and cakes and extras. If it is necessary to spend more on one item, cut that amount off another purchase. If there is some budget money left at the end of the week, use it for store-cupboard goods and to take advantage of special offers, gluts or seasonal foods.

Before shopping, draw up a plan of the week's menus. This can include ingredients for the main meals each day rather than specific recipes, and can be varied to take advantage of cheaper offers which may be available in the shops.

Make a detailed shopping list based on the menu plan and including canned, bottled and packaged foods for the store-cupboard. A list of standard foods such as cereals, coffee, sugar and tea, which need to be replaced regularly, can be pinned up in the kitchen and checked when making up the list.

It is time-consuming to shop more than twice a week and daily shopping inevitably means spending more money. The best days for twice-weekly shopping are Tuesday and Friday when food is fresh and shelves well stocked. Monday is not a good day to buy perishable foods, because most shops will not have had a delivery since Friday.

Shopping at a supermarket saves time because most food can be bought under one roof. Many goods are sold at cut prices, and supermarkets often have their own brands which are cheaper than other equivalent proprietary goods. But meat and fresh vegetables are often more expensive than at a separate butcher's or greengrocer's because they are prepacked. The disadvantage of shopping in a supermarket is the temptation to buy extra foods on impulse.

Many shoppers enjoy the personal contact with the salesman at a small food store and he can often give sound advice. However, in a small shop the choice of foodstuffs may be restricted, goods tend to be more expensive than in a supermarket and there may be fewer special offers.

Prices of perishable foods vary from one area to another, but shopping some distance from home is worthwhile only if the price of the fare or petrol is saved in the lower cost of the food.

Street markets have fresh fruit and vegetables at lower prices than the shops because stall-holders do not have to pay overheads and need a quick turnover. In country districts local produce, such as free-range eggs, vegetables and, possibly, meat, may be more reasonably priced at farm shops. Prices are low because the food is brought straight from the farm to the shop. It is also cheaper to buy potatoes and onions in bulk, and other vegetables in season, direct from a farm. In the summer it is often possible to go to a farm and pick your own soft fruit and vegetables at reasonable prices.

BUYING FRESH FOODS

Fresh foods can be bought two or three days in advance, if meat and fish are stored in a refrigerator, and fruit and vegetables in a cool larder. Some dairy products, such as eggs, fats and cheese, can be purchased weekly or fortnightly.

Most fresh foods are cheaper than canned, frozen or dried food, but there are exceptions. For example, fresh peas may be more expensive than canned or frozen ones, and canned milk, which can be diluted and used for cooking, is sometimes cheaper than fresh milk.

Buy only small portions of perishable food, to avoid wastage and possible tainting of other food in the refrigerator. Perishable food that cannot be used immediately can be cooked and then stored in the refrigerator (see chart, pp. 222-3).

DATE-STAMPING

Date-stamping is often found on packed meats, sausages, cream, vacuum-packed bacon, butter and other fats and some bread and cakes. It may indicate the date by which the product must be sold or the date by which it should be used. However, there are no legal requirements for manufacturers to stamp any date or other indication of freshness. Never buy outdated goods.

STORE-CUPBOARD BUYING

Dry goods, such as flour, sugar and dried fruit, as well as canned and bottled food have a long shelf life and

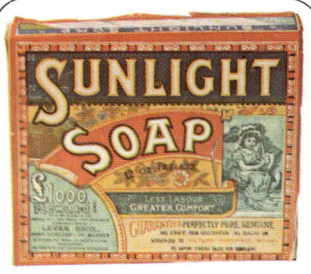

COLLECTING PACKETS AND WRAPPERS

The consumer packages of today – the yoghourt cartons, the cornflake boxes, the butter wrappers and the flour packets – could be highly prized tomorrow.

This thought is borne out by the way that product-packaging of the early 1900s is now collected for its fascinating insight into Britain's social history. Early Oxo and Bovril jars, Sunlight soap packets, Bryant and May matchboxes, Camp coffee labels, Bisto Kids pictures . . . all are sought by collectors.

Modern packaging has roots stretching back more than 100 years when a shopkeeper, buying his goods loose and in bulk, had labels and paper bags printed with his name and address. Then, as the volume of trade increased in the 19th century, shopkeepers found it more convenient to handle prepackaged goods. Manufacturers took over their own labelling, and the era of the brand-name had begun.

Collecting such packaging from the past is difficult because, understandably, few householders kept empty packages. Saving today's interesting packages, however, would provide a valuable social commentary for your great grandchildren. Except for the Sunlight soap packet (c. 1890) above, and the cocoa tin (c. 1910) second from right below, all the items shown here span no more than half a century.

can be bought once monthly or even every three months, if the housekeeping budget can be planned over a long period.

Canned foods, with the exception of prunes (9 months) and rhubarb (a year) keep indefinitely if left unopened, provided that the cans are sound. Before buying, make sure cans are clean, have no leaking seams and are not misshapen.

Dried and packaged goods include pulses, cereals, dried fruit, nuts, coffee, tea, sugar, flour, dehydrated vegetables, vacuum-packed fruit and vegetables and convenience foods. Their weight is marked in imperial and metric units, and an increasing number of foods are now being sold solely in metric packs.

When buying packaged food, check that the container is sound, particularly vacuum-sealed packs, which keep food in good condition only when it is held in a vacuum.

Some dried fruits, pulses, and sugar are sold loose and may be cheaper than the ready-packed.

By law, canned, bottled and other pre-packed foodstuffs, with certain exceptions, which include chocolate, confectionery and biscuits, must have the following information on the label: name of food; a description of the food if the name is not self-explanatory or more than 30 years old; a list of ingredients in descending order of weight; the name and address of the seller, packer or manufacturer; the net weight of the entire contents; and the country of origin, if imported.

The use of any food additives, colourings and artificial sweeteners must also be declared on the label. The only permitted artificial sweeteners are saccharin, saccharin calcium and saccharin sodium, which must also be listed on the label.

THE IDEAL LARDER A large, cool larder is a good place to store a wide variety of foods. In modern homes, kitchen cupboards often must be used instead. But dried shallots and herbs can be hung up to give a country feeling, and dried goods attractively displayed in storage jars on open shelves.

COOKING FOR THE FAMILY

SEASONAL FOODS

Even though most foods are available throughout the year, either fresh, frozen, canned or dried, many are still seasonal, in the sense that they are more plentiful, cheaper and tastier at particular times.

Most people, for example, eat strawberries only in June and July when the home-grown crop is available. Fresh strawberries imported in winter are expensive and the flavour is not comparable with home-grown fruit.

Similarly, a wide range of canned and frozen fruit is available all year round. But the flavour and texture is quite different from that of fresh fruit.

The foods illustrated on the right all have seasons lasting several months. In general, the flavour of fruit and vegetables is best when they are young. However, towards the middle of the season is usually the best time to buy because quality is still good but prices are lower than early in the season.

Some foods, such as soft fruit, can be well worth buying at the end of the season. Strawberries, for example, are past their best as dessert fruit by late July, but they are then cheap and still good for jam-making.

Game birds, such as pheasants, may be rather tough by January but they are less expensive at the beginning of the season and the flavour is good. Buy them to casserole.

Scallops and mussels are cheaper in March, near the end of the season.

Imported fruit and vegetables, although available for most of the year, are in better condition at certain times. Celery from America and Israel, for example, is youngest and best in February. Aubergines are best in July and August, and peppers from August to November.

Oranges, imported from the Mediterranean countries and Israel, are sweeter after Christmas, when they are more mature. They are now being supplemented by increasing supplies from the United States.

April is a bad month for fruit because even imported varieties are of poorer quality, and little home-grown fruit is available.

THE BEST TIME TO BUY

WINTER, WHEN GAME IS CHEAPEST

VEGETABLES

KALE
Available: All year
Cheapest: Nov.-May

SWEDES
Available: Sept.-May
Cheapest: Nov.-Jan.

TURNIPS
Available: All year
Cheapest: Nov.-Feb.

CABBAGES
Available: All year
Cheapest: Autumn and winter, Dec.-Jan.
Summer varieties: Aug.; red cabbage, Nov.-Dec.

CELERIAC
Available: Sept.-Mar.
Cheapest: Dec.-Jan.

BAKING POTATOES
Available: All year
Cheapest: Nov.-Jan.

FRUIT

CRANBERRIES
Available: Oct.-Feb.
Cheapest: Jan.

BRAMLEY COOKING APPLES
Available: All year
Cheapest: Nov.-Jan.

NUTS (Chestnuts, almonds, brazils, cobnuts, walnuts)
Available: Oct.-Jan.
Cheapest: Little variation

FISH

SPRATS
Available: Nov.-Mar.
Cheapest: Jan.-Feb.

MACKEREL
Available: All year
Cheapest: Dec.-Mar.

SCALLOPS
Available: Sept.-Mar.
Cheapest: Feb.-Mar.

HALIBUT
Available: Aug.-April
Cheapest: Dec.

MEAT

HARE
Available: Aug.-Mar.
Cheapest: Oct.-Mar.

PHEASANT
Available: Oct.-Jan.
Cheapest: Dec.-Jan.

PARTRIDGE
Available: Sept.-Feb.
Cheapest: Nov.-Feb.

GROUSE
Available: Aug.-Dec.
Cheapest: Oct.-Dec.

THE BEST TIME TO BUY

SPRING, FOR GREENS AND RHUBARB

VEGETABLES

CAULIFLOWER
Available: All year
Cheapest: April

SPRING CABBAGE
Available: Jan.-May
Cheapest: April-May

WATERCRESS
Available: All year
Cheapest: Little variation

SPROUTING BROCCOLI
Available: Sept.-April
Cheapest: Mar.-April

NEW POTATOES
Available: Mar.-Aug.
Cheapest: June

FRUIT

RHUBARB
Available: Jan.-July
Cheapest: May-June

SEVILLE ORANGES
Available: Feb.-Mar.
Cheapest: Mar.

FISH

WHITEBAIT
Available: All year
Cheapest: April

THE BEST TIME TO BUY

SUMMER – FRESH SALADS AND STRAWBERRIES

VEGETABLES

SWEET CORN
Available: July - Oct.
Cheapest: Home:
Sept. Imported: Aug.

RUNNER BEANS
Available: July - Oct.
Cheapest: July - Aug.

LETTUCES
Available: All year
Cheapest: June - Aug.

MARROWS
Available: July - Oct.
Cheapest: Aug. - Sept.

PEAS
Available: May - Oct.
Cheapest: June - July

CARROTS
Available: All year
Cheapest: Oct. - Dec.

CUCUMBERS
Available: All year
Cheapest: Home and
Dutch: June - July
Canaries: Jan. - Feb.

BROAD BEANS
Available: June - July
Cheapest: Mid-June

TOMATOES
Available: All year
Cheapest: Home and
Dutch: June - July
Canary: Dec. - Jan.
Spanish: Dec.

RADISHES
Available: All year
Cheapest: June

BEETROOT
Available: All year
Cheapest: July

COURGETTES
Available: May - Sept.
Cheapest: Aug. - Sept.

FRENCH BEANS
Available: All year
Cheapest: June –
but never really cheap

FRUIT

PEACHES
Available: Most of
year
Cheapest: July - Aug.

STRAWBERRIES
Available: All year
Home-grown:
June - July
Cheapest: End June

**RED, WHITE AND
BLACKCURRANTS**
Available: June - Aug.
Cheapest: July - Aug.

PLUMS
Available: Aug. - Oct.
(home-grown)
Cheapest: Aug.

CHERRIES
Available: May - Aug.
Cheapest: June - July

GOOSEBERRIES
Available: May - Sept.
Cheapest: June

RASPBERRIES
Available: June - Sept.
Cheapest: July - Aug.

LOGANBERRIES
Available: July - Aug.
Cheapest: End July

FISH

PLAICE
Available: All year
Cheapest: Aug.

DOVER SOLE
Available: All year
Cheapest: June

SCOTCH SALMON
Available: May - Aug.
Cheapest: July

HERRINGS
Available: All year
Cheapest: May - Sept.

TROUT
Available: All year
Cheapest: Mid-June

CRABS
Available: All year
Cheapest: July - Sept.

TURBOT
Available: All year
Cheapest: June - Aug.

MEAT

ENGLISH BEEF
Available: Aug. - Mar.
Cheapest: Aug. - Oct.

ENGLISH LAMB
Available: April - Nov.
Cheapest: Sept. - Nov.

THE BEST TIME TO BUY

AUTUMN, THE HIGH SEASON FOR FRUIT

VEGETABLES

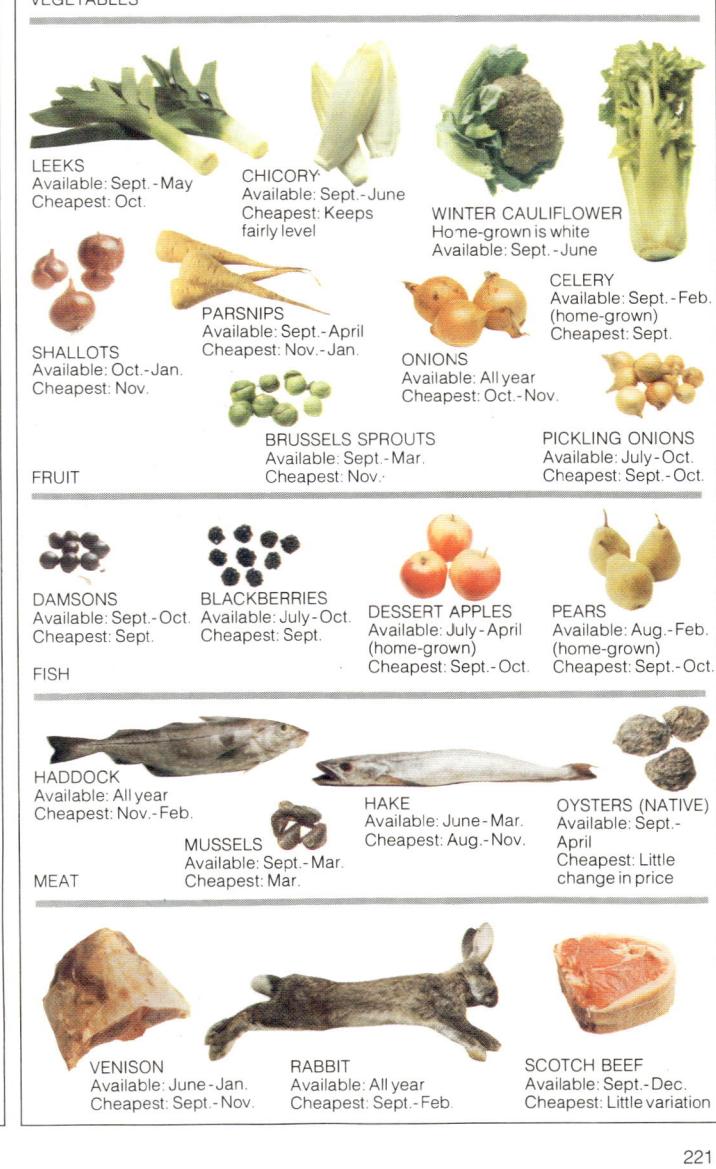

LEEKS
Available: Sept. - May
Cheapest: Oct.

CHICORY
Available: Sept. - June
Cheapest: Keeps
fairly level

WINTER CAULIFLOWER
Home-grown is white
Available: Sept. - June

SHALLOTS
Available: Oct. - Jan.
Cheapest: Nov.

PARSNIPS
Available: Sept. - April
Cheapest: Nov. - Jan.

CELERY
Available: Sept. - Feb.
(home-grown)
Cheapest: Sept.

ONIONS
Available: All year
Cheapest: Oct. - Nov.

BRUSSELS SPROUTS
Available: Sept. - Mar.
Cheapest: Nov.

PICKLING ONIONS
Available: July - Oct.
Cheapest: Sept. - Oct.

FRUIT

DAMSONS
Available: Sept. - Oct.
Cheapest: Sept.

BLACKBERRIES
Available: July - Oct.
Cheapest: Sept.

DESSERT APPLES
Available: July - April
(home-grown)
Cheapest: Sept. - Oct.

PEARS
Available: Aug. - Feb.
(home-grown)
Cheapest: Sept. - Oct.

FISH

HADDOCK
Available: All year
Cheapest: Nov. - Feb.

HAKE
Available: June - Mar.
Cheapest: Aug. - Nov.

OYSTERS (NATIVE)
Available: Sept. -
April
Cheapest: Little
change in price

MUSSELS
Available: Sept. - Mar.
Cheapest: Mar.

MEAT

VENISON
Available: June - Jan.
Cheapest: Sept. - Nov.

RABBIT
Available: All year
Cheapest: Sept. - Feb.

SCOTCH BEEF
Available: Sept. - Dec.
Cheapest: Little variation

• FOOD STORAGE

Food can be stored in three ways: dry, in a cupboard, drawers or storage jars; cool (12°C, 54°F) in a larder or well-ventilated cupboard; and cold, in a refrigerator (2-8°C, 36-46°F) or a freezer (−18°C, 0°F).

DRY STORAGE

Canned and ready-packed food will last a long time on cupboard or larder shelves (see chart), but it will not stay palatable for ever. Write the date of purchase on the labels, and check from time to time to see if foods are nearing the end of their shelf life.

After packets of sugar, flour and other dry goods have been opened, transfer the contents to storage jars.

Steam and condensation in the kitchen may cause food in dry storage to deteriorate. Heating and an extractor fan can prevent this problem.

COOL STORAGE

A small, ventilated walk-in cupboard or larder, built on a north-facing outside wall, provides the best cool storage. It should have a window covered with mesh, or one that will open.

Fresh vegetables, bread, cheese, eggs and preserves can all be kept in a larder. Leave cooked foods there to cool before putting them into the refrigerator. Conversely, food from the refrigerator can be left in the larder before serving or cooking.

Most food needing cool storage can also be put into the refrigerator. The larder is seldom cool enough all the year round to be an adequate substitute for a refrigerator.

COLD STORAGE

A refrigerator with a normal running temperature of 5°C (41°F) can be used for short-term storage of all perishable foods. The coldest part of the refrigerator, just under the frozen-food compartment, is best for meat or fish. The door and bottom of the refrigerator keep food chilled and can be used for butter, other fats and salads. Before food goes into the refrigerator, it should be put in covered containers or wrapped or covered in foil or plastic film to prevent evaporation and smells. Cover meat and fish lightly to allow for air circulation.

Most refrigerators have a frozen-food compartment, star-marked to indicate the length of time that food can be safely stored. One star means that food will keep for one week; two stars, for one month; and three stars, for three months. Only ready-frozen food can be stored in this compartment. The chart on these pages gives the minimum safe storage periods for a number of foods. Many can be kept for longer if correctly stored.

FOOD STORAGE IN A LARDER OR REFRIGERATOR

TYPE OF FOOD		METHOD	COMMENTS	LARDER	FRIDGE
Beverages	Cocoa and drinking chocolate	Leave in packet or tin	Keep dry	1 year	
	Coffee, beans (roasted)	Keep in airtight container		3 months	
	Coffee, ground	Keep in airtight container	Unopened vacuum packs will keep indefinitely	1 month	
	Coffee, instant	Keep in airtight container	Keep very dry	1 year	
	Fruit juice, bottled	Keep sealed, away from the light	Once opened, use within a week	3 months	3 months
	Fruit juice, canned	Keep sealed, away from the light	Once opened, use within a week	1 year	
	Fruit squash	Leave in bottle with tightly sealed lid		6-8 months	6-8 months
	Tea	Leave in packet or store in airtight tin		1 year	
Bread	Uncooked dough	Put into sealed plastic bag	There is no advantage in keeping bread in a refrigerator. It prevents mould but may hasten staling	overnight	one day
	White and brown loaves	Lightly wrap and put in bread bin		1 week	
	Wholemeal bread	Lightly wrap and put in bread bin		3-4 days	
Cakes and biscuits	Biscuits	Keep in airtight tin or jar		2-4 weeks	
	Sponge cake	Keep in airtight tin		3 days	
	Rich fruit cake	Wrap in plastic film then foil and put into an airtight tin	Do not put a fruit cake directly into foil because the acid in the fruit will pit the foil and let in air	6 months	
Canned food	Fish in oil	Write date of purchase on labels and keep cans in a larder or storecupboard. Inspect occasionally to see that they are still in good condition	It is not necessary to keep unopened cans in a refrigerator, but once opened refrigerate and store as fresh food. Cans are now sterile and it is not necessary to remove the food for storage. Tinned ham should keep for 2 years, and prunes for 9 months	5 years	
	Fish in tomato sauce			1 year	
	Fruit (except prunes)			2 years	
	Meat (except large tins of ham)			5 years	
	Milk (condensed)			1 year	
	Vegetables			2 years	
Cereal products	Cornflour	Leave in sealed packet. Once opened, put into an airtight jar	All cereal products are liable to attack by weevils	1 year	
	Plain flour	Leave in bag or put into container with lid	Once opened, use within 3 months	6 months	
	Self-raising flour	Leave in bag or put into container with lid	Once opened, use within 2 months	2-3 months	
	Wholemeal and wheatmeal flour	Leave in bag or put into container with lid	Once opened use within 1 month	2 months	
	Oatmeal and porridge oats	Store in airtight jar	Becomes bitter. Use within 3 months, once opened	6 months	
	Rice, semolina, tapioca	Store in airtight container		2 years	
Dairy products and fats	Butter, unsalted	Keep in wrapper or in covered container		1 week	10 days
	Butter, salted	Keep in wrapper or in covered container		10-14 days	2-3 weeks
	Cheese, hard	Wrap in foil or keep in container with lid	Remove cheese from the refrigerator half an hour before it is needed	5-7 days	1-2 weeks
	Cheese, grated	Keep in container with lid or plastic bag			3-4 weeks
	Cheese, cream or curd	Wrap in foil or keep in container with lid		2-3 days	5-7 days
	Cooking fat	Leave in wrapper or container		1 year	1 year
	Eggs, whole	Leave in box or put in egg compartment of refrigerator		1-2 weeks	3 weeks
	Eggs, yolks	Cover with water		1 day	4-5 days
	Eggs, whites	Keep in covered plastic container		1 day	1 week

FOOD STORAGE IN A LARDER OR REFRIGERATOR

TYPE OF FOOD		METHOD	COMMENTS	LARDER	FRIDGE
Dairy products and fats continued	Margarine	Leave in wrapper or tub		6 weeks	2-3 months
	Milk, pasteurised	Leave in bottle		2-3 days	3-4 days
	Milk, sterilised	Leave in bottle		1 week	1 week
	Milk, dried	Leave in sealed packet or tin		3 months	
	Yoghourt	Leave in carton		2 days	3-4 days
	Suet, fresh	Grate and mix with a little flour. Put in covered container		3 days	1 week
	Suet, packet	Leave in packet	Once opened, use within 4 months. Do not put in refrigerator	6 months	
Dried fruit	Currants, prunes, apricots, dates	Leave in packet		1 year	
Fish (fresh)	Oily and white fish	Remove head, gut and wipe	Keep lightly covered	1 day	1-2 days
	Smoked fish	Wipe with a damp cloth	Keep lightly covered	2 days	3-4 days
	Shellfish	Keep in coldest part of refrigerator	Keep lightly covered	a few hours	1 day
Meat	Uncooked joints	All raw meat should be unwrapped, wiped with a damp cloth and stood on a rack, over a clean plate, and lightly covered		1 day	2-3 days
	Minced meat, offal and giblets		Use on day of purchase if not stored in refrigerator		1 day
	Bacon rashers, green	Lightly wrap in foil or put into container with a lid	Vacuum-packed bacon is usually date-stamped	2 days	5 days
	Bacon rashers, smoked	Lightly wrap in foil or put into container with a lid		3 days	1 week
	Sausages	Lightly wrap in foil or put into container with a lid		1 day	4 days
	Cooked meat	Keep covered	Stale left-overs can cause food poisoning	a few hours	1 day
	Sliced meat and pâté	Keep covered	Some of these are in date-stamped packs	1-2 days	2-3 days
	Poultry and hung game, plucked and drawn	Wipe bird, stand on a rack over a clean plate and cover lightly	Put frozen birds, covered, on a rack in a larder to thaw before cooking	1-2 days	2-4 days
Pasta (dried)	Macaroni, noodles and spaghetti	Leave in packet or store in airtight container	All subject to weevils and mites	2 years	
Prepared food	Shortcrust pastry, dry mix	Put into plastic bag		2-3 weeks	3 months
	Shortcrust pastry, dough	Wrap in foil or plastic		1-2 days	2-3 days
	Shortcrust pastry, cooked blind	Put into airtight tin		7-10 days	
	Pancake batter	Keep in covered bowl		1 day	2-3 days
	Pancakes, cooked	Keep in plastic bag, interleaved with greaseproof paper		1 week	1 week
Pulses	Dried beans, peas and lentils	Store in airtight container	All subject to weevils and mites	1 year	
Preserves	Honey and jam	Store in jar with tightly fitting lid	Once opened, use jam within 2 months	6 months	
	Pickles, sauces and chutney	Store in jar with tightly fitting lid	Sauces and ketchups may thicken with keeping	2 years	
Sugar	Caster and granulated sugar	Bags are fragile, so store sugar in airtight container	Keep all sugar very dry	Indefinitely	
	Demerara and soft brown sugar	Store in airtight container	Tends to go lumpy if kept too long	1-2 years	
	Icing sugar	Leave in cardboard packet	Tends to go lumpy once it is opened	6 months	
Sundries and packet foods	Baking powder	Store in airtight container	Keep very dry	3-4 months	
	Custard powder, cake mixes, etc.	Leave in sealed packet		at least 1 year	
	Dehydrated soups and sauce	Leave in sealed packet		at least 1 year	
	Dried herbs	Keep in airtight container	Flavour diminishes the longer they are kept	6 months	
	Instant potato	Leave in sealed packet		1 year	
	Mayonnaise and salad cream	Leave in bottle with tightly fitting lid	Home-made mayonnaise keeps 1-2 weeks in a refrigerator	4 months	
	Nuts, ground	Leave in sealed packet		6 months	
	Nuts, whole and desiccated coconut	Keep in airtight container		1 year	
	Oil	Leave in bottle with tightly sealed lid	Keep away from the light	3 months	
	Spices and essences	Keep in airtight containers	Lose flavour if kept too long	1 year	
	Tomato paste	Leave in tube with tightly sealed lid		3 years	
	Yeast, fresh	Keep in loosely tied polythene bag		4-5 days	Up to 1 month
	Yeast, dried	Leave in sealed packet in airtight container		6 months	
	Stock cubes	Leave in carton		3 months	
Vegetables and fruit	Green and salad vegetables	Wash and put into plastic bags	All vegetables can be stored in a cool airy place, or in a plastic box in the refrigerator	1-2 days	2-3 days
	Root vegetables	Do not wash. Store in vegetable rack		2 weeks	
	Soft fruit	Remove bad and damaged fruit, sprinkle with sugar, cover	Citrus fruit, if undamaged, will keep for weeks, and apples for months	1 day	1 day
	Stone d and hard fruit	Remove damaged fruit and put the rest in a dish		3-7 days	

• FREEZER STORAGE

Food stored in a freezer will keep its flavour from one month to a year, depending on the type (see chart). But once frozen food has been thawed, it must be treated as fresh food.

Many firms supply commercially frozen food in bulk at less than normal retail prices, and some provide a delivery service. Study price lists from several frozen-food stores before deciding where and what to buy.

RULES FOR HOME FREEZING
All food for the freezer must be prepared and packed correctly. Always follow the freezer manufacturer's instructions. The following rules apply to freezing food, fresh or cooked:

1. All utensils and packaging must be clean.
2. Food must be in perfect condition.
3. Package food in quantities to suit family size.
4. Seal containers to exclude air.

5. Cool food rapidly when it has been cooked or blanched. But never put warm or hot food into a freezer.
6. Label packages with contents, date to be used by, and number of servings. Keep a check list of the

FOOD STORAGE IN A FREEZER

TYPE OF FOOD		METHOD	COMMENTS	MAX. STORAGE TIME
Dairy Produce	Butter	In wrapper, overwrapped in foil		12 months
	Hard cheese	Double wrap in foil or plastic		6 months
	Soft cheese		Does not freeze well	
	Cream, single and double	Leave in carton	Only freeze pasteurised cream	
	Ice cream, home-made	In plastic box		4 months
	Ice cream, commercial	In plastic box		1 month
	Egg yolks	In plastic box or ice-cube tray with teaspoon salt or sugar		3 months
	Egg whites	In rigid sealed container or ice-cube tray	Do not freeze eggs in shell	10 months
	Milk, pasteurised and sterilised			10 months
	Milk, homogenised	In waxed carton, leaving 2 in. head space	Do not freeze	
	Yoghourt		Do not freeze	1 month
Fish	Oily and smoked	Wrap in plastic		3 months
	White	Wrap in plastic		6 months
	Shellfish	Put in sealed plastic bag	Do not freeze mussels or clams	1 month
	Cooked fish	Wrap in plastic in foil box		2 months
Fruit	Soft	Whole or as purée in plastic box		8 months
	Stone and hard fruit	In plastic box, whole, sliced or puréed with sugar/syrup		12 months
Vegetables	Green	Wrap in foil or plastic	Blanch before freezing	12 months
	Fresh herbs	In plastic bags		6 months
Cooked meat	Casseroles, curries, pâtés	Wrap in plastic		2 months
	Sliced	Wrap in plastic		1 month
Uncooked meat	Bacon	Wrap in plastic		1 month
	Beef and lamb	Wrap in plastic		12 months
	Pork	Wrap in plastic		9 months
	Offal, mince and sausages	Wrap in plastic		6 weeks
Poultry and game	Chicken, turkey	Wrap in plastic, whole or in pieces	Remove giblets, do not stuff	9 months
	Pheasant, partridge	Wrap in plastic, whole or in pieces		9 months
	Giblets	Separately in covered container		6 weeks
Bread and buns	Bread	Wrap in foil or plastic	All kinds of bread can be frozen	1 month
	Scones and buns	In plastic bags		6 months
	Uncooked dough	In greased plastic bags	Each bag should contain enough for one baking	5 weeks
Cakes	Sponge	In plastic or foil box with waxed paper between slices	Do not fill or ice sponges	6 months
	Rich fruit cake	Wrap in foil and put in plastic bag or box		12 months
	Uncooked mixes	In sealed containers	Do not freeze whisked sponge	2 months
Pastry	Shortcrust, or rich raw	In plastic bag		5 months
	Cooked, unfilled	In foil container		6 months
	Cooked, fruit-filled	In foil container		6 months
	Cooked, meat-filled	In foil container		4 months
Puddings	Steamed sponge mix	In rigid or foil container	Pre-cook for two-thirds of cooking time	4 months
	Cooked sponge	Cover and overwrap with foil		3 months
	Suet pudding mix	Cover and overwrap with foil		2 months
	Cooked pancakes	Interleave with foil in plastic bag		2 months

freezer contents, to be ticked off as they are used.

7. Use frozen food within the recommended storage period (see chart).

8. Fresh food from the freezer should not be refrozen after it has thawed unless it is cooked first. Bread and cakes can be thawed and refrozen.

WHAT NOT TO FREEZE

Food with a high moisture content, such as lettuce and watercress, does not freeze well.

Soft fruits, including bananas, should be frozen slightly under-ripe or they become mushy.

Single cream and mayonnaise tend to separate and curdle, and eggs must be frozen out of their shells.

PREPARING THE FOOD

Bread, pastry, hard cheese and cooked dishes need no special preparation before freezing, apart from the correct packaging. Freeze fish only if it is absolutely fresh – almost straight from the sea or river. Scale fresh fish if necessary and remove the fins. Flat fish and herrings are best gutted. Oily fish, such as herring, should be washed in fresh water, and dried. Wash other fish in salt water.

Meat needs little preparation, but remove excess fat, as it tends to go rancid before the flesh. Whenever possible remove meat bones, which take up freezer space.

Do not stuff raw poultry before freezing it, because this slows up freezing and thawing times. Remove giblets and freeze them separately.

Buy soft fruits firm, not over-ripe, if they are to be frozen whole. Ripe fruit can be used for frozen purée.

Strawberries and raspberries can be sprinkled with sugar before freezing, which preserves the colour and helps to prevent mushiness. A free-flow pack is also a good way to freeze whole soft fruit; place each berry separately on a tray and freeze until firm, then pack in a rigid container.

Tough-skinned fruit, such as blackcurrants and gooseberries, can be frozen without special preparation. Firm-textured fruit, such as peaches and apricots, are best frozen in syrup made by dissolving 450 g. (1 lb.) of sugar in 600 ml. (1 pint) of water. Chill the syrup in the refrigerator. Pour it over the halved and stoned fruit, using about 300 ml. (½ pint) to each 450 g. of fruit, and cover. Keep the fruit under the liquid with crumpled waxed or greaseproof paper.

Apples should be peeled, cored, sliced and dropped into cold water, then blanched in boiling water for 2-3 minutes. Cool in ice-cold water before packing in layers with sugar.

Most vegetables need to be blanched before freezing to kill enzymes which cause loss of colour and flavour. Prepare the vegetables and put them into boiling water, using the biggest saucepan that is available. Return the water to the boil after the vegetables have been added. Check boiling times for specific vegetables in a freezer handbook.

PACKAGING AND LABELLING

Packaging for the freezer should be moisture and vapour-proof, grease-proof, durable and resistant to low temperatures. It is best to buy special freezer packaging.

Polythene bags are the cheapest packaging. Fasten them with plastic or paper-coated ties, which are easily loosened. These bags can be used for all foods, although they are less suitable for liquids and foods which might be crushed, such as soft fruits.

Rolls of plastic sheeting sealed with special adhesive tape are used to wrap meat, poultry and pies.

Foil may be fitted round the food, but it can be easily punctured and may need to be put into a plastic bag. Cover protruding sharp corners with an extra layer of foil. Foil containers with lids are useful for cooked dishes – they can go straight into the oven.

Plastic boxes or wax cartons, with tightly fitting lids, which do not need extra sealing, stack easily in the freezer, can be washed and re-used, and are suitable for storing most foods. Wax cartons are cheaper than plastic boxes but are not so durable.

Waxed paper is used to separate sliced meat, which makes separation easier after thawing.

Package solid foods tightly so that as much air as possible is expelled. This is difficult with a polythene bag but can be simplified by lowering the full bag into a bowl of water; the water pressure forces the air up and out of the bag. Dry the bag thoroughly before freezing.

Liquids need space at the top of the container. For every pint of liquid, there should be 2.5 cm. (1 in.) head-space to allow for expansion. Do not leave too much space because ice crystals form, and they affect the storage time and flavour of the food.

Polythene bags can be used to store liquids which have been frozen into solid shapes. Put a polythene bag into a clean, empty box and fill with the liquid, leaving a head-space. Freeze until solid, then remove the carton and seal the polythene pack.

Freezer adhesive and tie-on labels are sold in inexpensive packs. Write on labels and plastic containers with a wax crayon or pencil.

WHAT CAN GO WRONG

Storage beyond the specified time and poor wrapping causes food to deteriorate.

Greyish-brown areas known as freezer burn are caused by poor wrapping. Oxidation and rancidity happen when oxygen penetrates the packaging and reacts with the contents to give a bad taste and smell.

Bad packaging also causes cross-flavouring of strongly flavoured foods.

THAWING AND REHEATING

For the best results, food should be thawed gently before it is cooked or reheated. The best place to do this is in a refrigerator where 450 g. of food can take up to six hours to thaw out. Once thawed, the food should be used immediately.

Poultry must be completely thawed before use and should be left in a refrigerator overnight.

Vegetables, stews, pre-cooked dishes, some fish and meat can be cooked from the freezer.

In general, frozen food should be cooked as rapidly as possible to preserve the flavour and texture. However, frozen joints of meat should not be cooked at a high temperature as the outside will be overdone before the inside is cooked. A meat thermometer will help avoid this problem.

BLANCHING VEGETABLES

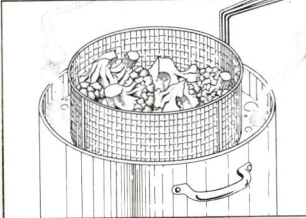

1. Lower the vegetables into boiling water in a wire basket or colander. Blanch only 450-900 g. at a time.

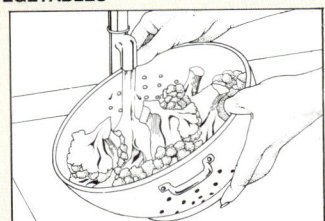

2. After blanching for the required time, wash the vegetables in ice-cold water. Drain thoroughly, then pack immediately.

FREE-FLOW PACKS

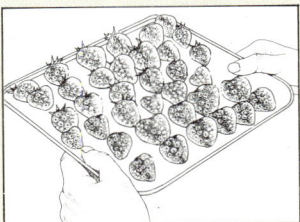

To freeze soft fruit, space them out on a baking tray and freeze until firm before packing in a container and storing.

PREFORMING LIQUIDS

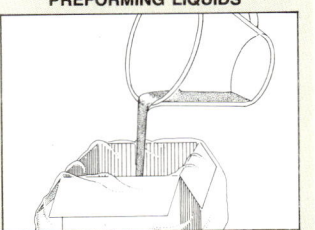

To freeze liquid in a plastic bag, put the bag into an empty box and pour in the liquid. Freeze solid and remove box.

SEPARATING PORTIONS

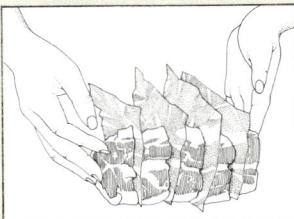

Put waxed paper between chops, slices of meat and fish fillets before freezing, for easy separation.

• CHOOSING WINE

Wine is produced by fermentation – the chemical reaction between the natural sugar in the grape and the yeast enzymes in the film that develops on the skins as they mature.

All wine is red, rosé or white. The first two gain their colours from the time the blue-black grape skins are left with the fermenting juice. White wines are from green-gold grapes and the skins are usually separated from the fermenting juice.

TYPES OF WINE

Wine falls into three classes. Table wines are intended for drinking with food: they are still (non-sparkling), and normally contain not more than 14% alcohol. However, this alcoholic content usually ranges from 8½% to 11% for white wine and 10% to 13% for red. By comparison, spirits have an alcohol content ranging between 40% and 50%.

The second type is sparkling wine, which can be served at any time – with or without food. All wine gives off carbon dioxide during fermentation, but with sparkling wine carbon dioxide is sealed in by secondary fermentation in bottles (the champagne method) or in large closed vats, as in Germany, Italy and parts of France.

The alcoholic content of French champagne is limited by law to 14%. Only wine made by the champagne method in the region round Rheims can legally be called by this name.

The third type is fortified wine, such as port and sherry, to which brandy has been added. They contain between 18% and 21% alcohol. Because of their higher alcoholic strength these wines are normally drunk before or after meals.

BUYING WINE

A bottle of wine selling for 90p bears duty of about 41p and Value Added Tax of about 7p. Bottling charges are 14p, while profits, promotion and distribution costs amount to 18p, leaving 10p as the cash value of the wine. Costs and duties are roughly the same, whatever the retail price, so that a £1 bottle will contain a wine that is twice the value of a 90p one.

The cheapest wines are the branded and blended ones. They are imported in bulk and usually sold in litre bottles. Next in price come table wines from named localities, shipped in bottles from France, Germany or Italy. At one time they came in barrels and were bottled in Britain, but today the trend is towards shipping in bottle, to ensure stricter supervision. Good value among reds are the Côtes du Rhône wines of France, and Chianti and Valpolicella from Italy.

Among the whites, the best are those German wines with the sub-region title of Bereich, such as Bereich Bernkastel from the Mosel, and Bereich Nierstein from the Rhine.

GRADING WINE

Most countries ensure standards by laying down the types of grape to be used, the minimum alcoholic strength, and the maximum yield per acre to prevent weakening the vines by over-production.

The top 15% of French wines are grouped as Appellation Contrôlée (controlled name); these words are shown on the label. Then come VDQS – Vins Délimités de Qualité Supérieure (wines of good quality for the region in which they are produced) – followed by the Vins du Pays, or run-of-the-mill local wines.

In Germany the top grade is Qualitätswein mit Prädikat (quality wine with special attributes). The word Prädikat refers to qualities such as Spätlese, meaning that the wine is made from riper and sweeter grapes. Below this comes Qualitätswein bestimmter Anbaugebiete (QbA) – quality wine of designated regions.

The third grade is Tafelwein. This does not carry the vineyard names permitted to the first two. It comes from five large vine-growing regions and is made from approved grapes. It may be blended with wines from other Common Market countries, although Deutscher Tafelwein must be solely German wine.

In Italy the top grade is Denominazione di Origine Controllata e Garantita (DOCG) – Controlled and Guaranteed Denomination of Origin – a highly restricted class. The second grade, Denominazione di Origine Controllata (DOC), is the one most commonly found in Britain.

The third is Denominazione di Origine Semplice (DOS), and refers to local wines not usually seen in Britain.

Wines from the Mediterranean countries and Southern Europe – as well as Hungary and Yugoslavia – have become popular since the Second World War. The reds are light; but the whites do not match the best of Northern Europe, where the colder climate has caused greater acidity and hence a more positive taste.

Bordeaux, red Beaujolais pot Côte de Provence Loire Moselle Bordeaux, white Vintage port

Burgundy Chianti Franconian flagon Hock Alsace Champagne Port

WINE BOTTLES *A wine can often be identified by the shape of its bottle.*

Spain produces huge quantities of red, white, rosé and sparkling wine – plus, of course, sherry.

The white wines of Portugal tend to be superior to those of Spain, but the reds are surpassed by the best Spanish reds.

Wines of all types, including sherries and ports, are produced in South Africa; the main vineyards being in the Paarl Valley in the Cape. Australia has an important wine industry. Its best-known wine-producing area is the Barossa Valley in South Australia. Because of their consistent climate, vintage is not an important consideration in either of these countries.

TASTING WINE

Wine gives of its best when handled with care. The best shape for a wine glass is one which curves inwards at the rim, trapping the fragrance of the wine for you to savour. Never fill it more than half full. Swirl the wine round to release its bouquet, put the rim to your nose and sniff.

Next, half-fill your mouth and let the wine wash round your teeth – even bite it. This will release the extra flavour. Swallow and wait to feel the aftertaste left in your mouth.

If you prefer sweet wine, that is what you should drink, no matter what the experts say. But sweet wine is sweet all through and almost inevitably this begins to cloy and prevents you from noticing the flavour of the food. So most people drink dry wine with food.

Sweet whites have their place with fruit or pâté de foie gras. France's Sainte Croix du Mont and Monbazillac are lower-priced examples, but the superb – and expensive – Chateau d'Yquem is the best. Germany, too, produces splendid sweet wines from

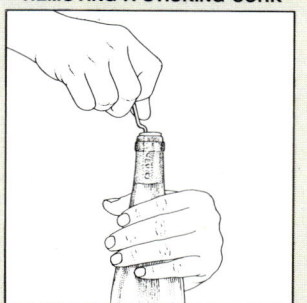

REMOVING A STICKING CORK

More leverage can be achieved by inserting the corkscrew at an angle.

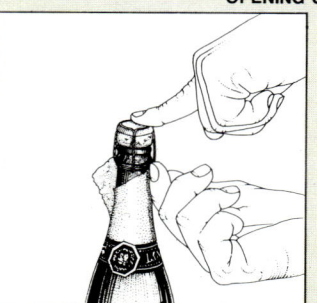

OPENING CHAMPAGNE

1. Remove the foil, press down on top of the cork and undo the wire muzzle.

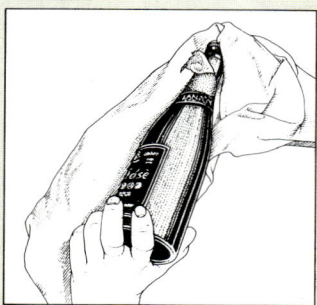

2. Hold the cork in a towel and twist the bottle, holding it away from yourself.

Auslese (selected) grapes.

WINE AND FOOD

Pleasing as wines can be on their own, they reach their best when carefully matched with food.

Traditionally lighter wines are served before big-bodied ones and dry before sweet. A dry white is served before a red and a red before a sweet wine. This is the normal order of the dishes that accompany them at a meal which includes fish, meat and sweet or fruit courses.

Aperitifs such as dry champagne or dry sherry stimulate the gastric juices. Offer an amontillado sherry to those who do not drink the dry, but nothing sweeter which will cloy the palate.

Hors-d'oeuvres, or salads with French dressing, do not go with wine, though the Italians drink a rosato (dry rosé) with them. Serve dry sherry or dry Madeira with most soups.

With oysters and shellfish, including lobster, usually choose a Chablis, although a cheaper Muscadet de Sèvre et Maine is satisfactory, being light and dry. Sancerre, Pouilly-Fumé, dry Graves and dry Rhine and Mosel wines are also suitable.

With plain grilled fish, select a dry white such as Bandol, or a rosé from the Côtes de Provence or from Italy.

Fish with a rich sauce needs a wine capable of standing up to the rich flavour. A good choice would be Meursault, a full-bodied white burgundy. Less expensively, choose demi-sec (semi-dry) wine, such as Vouvray, or a semi-sweet Rhine wine.

Smoked salmon or smoked trout call for Chablis, or Pouilly-Fuissé.

Chill all these white wines for an hour in the refrigerator to achieve crispness without killing the bouquet.

It is generally agreed that red wine goes best with beef and lamb. A Beaujolais, a Chateauneuf-du-Pape or a simple Côtes du Rhône would be suitable. If price is no barrier a good burgundy such as Chambertin would partner roast beef, but Nuits-Saint-Georges and Beaune are cheaper.

For lamb, buy a Bordeaux, ideally one of the fine wines from the region, such as Chateau Cos d'Estournel, Chateau Giscours or Chateau Lascombes. Chateau Gloria is a good Bordeaux which is less expensive. Or you could choose a Volnay from Burgundy for the lamb, a Barolo from Italy for the beef, a Chianti for either.

Open all red wines at least an hour before use, so that they can 'breathe' in the dining-room.

VINTAGE YEARS

The very best vintages are often very expensive. The next grades may be almost as good as the best and much better value for money.
KEY: 1 – Best 2 – Very good 3 – Good

YEAR		61	62	63	64	65	66	67	68	69	70	71	72	73
Red	Burgundy	2	3		2		2	3		1	3	1	2	3
	Claret	1	2		2		2	2		3	1	2		3
	Rhône	1	2		2		2	2		3	2	2	2	2
White Bordeaux		2	3		3		2	3		3	3	2	3	3
	Burgundy	3	3		2		1	2		1	1	1		2
	German wines	3			2		2	3		2	3	1	3	3
Champagne		1	2		1		2	3		2				
Port				1			1	2			1	3		

TYPES OF WINE

COUNTRY OF ORIGIN	WHITE DRY 1	MEDIUM DRY 2	SWEET 3	SPARKLING 4	RED LIGHT BODIED 5	MEDIUM BODIED 6	FULL BODIED 7	FORTIFIED 8
France	Alsace Chablis Muscadet Vouvray Pouilly-Fuissé Edelzwicker	Pouilly-Fuissé White Burgundy Entre Deux Mers Macon Blanc White Beaujolais Graves Sancerre Mersault	Barsac Montbazillac St Croix du Mont Sauternes Côteaux du Layon	Vouvray Champagne	Provençal wines Entre Deux Mers Bandol Macon Côte du Rhone Villages Beaujolais Premiers Côtes de Bordeaux	Côte Rôtie Beaujolais (named) Medoc (non-vintage)	Côte de Nuits Côte de Beaune Châteauneuf du Pape Paulliac Hermitage Gigondas Bordeaux (vintage)	Vermouth
Germany		Niersteiner Steinwein Mosel	Beeren-auslese Auslese Eiswein	Sekt	Any German red wine			Vermouth
Italy	Soave Trebbiano	Frascati Valpol-icella Soave Orvieto		Asti-Spumante	Chianti Valpol-icella Bardolino Merlot	Bardolino Valpol-icella Barbera Chianti	Chianti Riserva	Marsala Vermouth
Spain and Portugal	Minho Douro Rioja		Grandjo		Rioja Valdepeñas	Valdepeñas (named)		Port Sherry
Others	Turkish Trakya Hungarian and Yugoslav Riesling	Yugoslav Traminer Bulgarian Chardonnay	Yugoslav Tiger Milk Samos and Commandaria from Cyprus		Greek Demestica Romanian red wines	Hungarian Bull's Blood		Madeira

DISHES AND APPROPRIATE WINES

Check numbers with the table above X = no wine

DISH	PREPARATION	WINE	DISH	PREPARATION	WINE	DISH	PREPARATION	WINE
Hors-d'oeuvres	Vinegar dressing	X	Fish	Shellfish	1	Offal	Liver, kidneys, hearts	6 7
				Pâté, mousse	1		Sweetbreads	1
				Smoked	1			
Soup	Thin	X		Grilled, fried	1 2 5	Ham and bacon		1 6
	Thick	8		With bland sauce	1 2 5			
	Cream	X		With strong sauce	1 6 5	Game		6 7
	Cold	8						
			White meat	Grilled, fried, poached	1 2	Cheese	Cream cheese	1 2 5
Pâté	Fatty	1		With bland sauce	1 2		Blue and hard cheese	6 7
	Meaty	2 6		With strong sauce	1 6			
	Foie gras	1 4 3		Roast stuffing	1 6	Puddings	Ices, puddings, cakes	X
Eggs	Mayonnaise	X					Pastries	4
	With tomato sauce	2 6	Red meat	Roasts, grills	7		Cooked fruit	3
	Other methods	1		Casseroles, pies	6			

ALL ABOUT MEAT AND POULTRY

The food value of different types of meat varies, but cheap and expensive cuts are equally nutritious, providing protein, mineral salts and B vitamins. The fat gives the meat added flavour and contains vitamin D.

During the life of the animal, the harder its muscles work the tougher its flesh will become. Cheaper, tougher cuts are good buys, provided they are properly prepared and cooked. Less active, protected parts of the animal are the most tender; they need less preparation and cooking but, being in greater demand, are also more expensive.

Those who dislike fatty or bony meat may prefer the more expensive cuts, even for stews and casseroles, because there is less wastage. It is no economy to buy a cheaper cut of meat if much of it is discarded. Where meat is bought on the bone, the ratio of meat to bone should be taken into account.

Throughout Britain and the Common Market countries, there are variations in the way meat carcases are jointed. The London and Home Counties method – the joints and cuts described in this book – is most widely used in Britain. By law, all pre-packed meat must be labelled with the country of origin, weight and cost per pound. Uses and descriptions of the joints and cuts are not compulsory.

Economies can be made with meat by serving plenty of vegetables and accompaniments, such as sauces or stuffings, or by putting it into pies and puddings. A boned, stuffed joint is easier to carve and is more economical. Pulses, such as lentils and haricot beans, can be added to stews and casseroles to make the meat go further. Textured vegetable protein, usually made from soya beans, increases the quantity of minced-meat dishes.

Leftovers from joints of meat, if not eaten cold, can be used for a variety of dishes: stuffed vegetables and pancakes, meat pies, fritters or croquettes and risotto and pasta sauces.

All cooked meat should be used quickly because it is liable to contamination. Keep leftovers in cool, clean conditions and re-heat thoroughly and quickly before serving.

• VEAL

Veal is the meat from calves between four and five months old. There are two kinds of veal – one from milk-fed calves and the other from those fed on grass. Milk-fed veal is the most tender, but grass-fed veal has a better flavour. Most British calves are fattened to be sold as beef, so home-produced veal is expensive. It is also hard to find except in London and southern towns where demand makes it more easily available. Butchers will not stock veal unless there is a regular demand, because it does not keep well and must be sold within about four days of being slaughtered. 'Bobby' calves, slaughtered before they are three weeks old,

provide some cheaper home-produced veal. Milk-fed veal is imported, refrigerated, from Denmark, Holland and France, where calves are reared for this purpose.

WHAT TO LOOK FOR

Good-quality grass-fed British veal is pale pink. Imported milk-fed veal is off-white and should be soft and moist, but not flabby. It has a fine texture and puffy connective tissue around the flesh. There is little fat, but the bones are large in proportion to the amount of meat.

Veal from 'Bobby' calves is moister and flabbier than that of older calves, with a puffy appearance and more connective tissue. Apart from the leg,

veal from 'Bobby' calves is best for braising and stewing, when extra flavour can be added. Some butchers sell 'pie veal' which consists of trimmings from the breast, shoulder, knuckle or neck cut into small pieces ready to stew or casserole.

HOW TO COOK VEAL

All veal tends to be dry and bland because it comes from a young animal and there is very little fat. Its flavour is improved by adding sauces, seasonings and stuffings.

Grilling or frying Best-end-of-neck cutlets can be cooked by these methods. But escalopes, from the fillet end of the leg or from the loin, beaten into thin slices, are the most popular way of serving fried veal. Dip the cutlets first in beaten egg and then in breadcrumbs, and fry in butter for 5 minutes. They are served with a variety of sauces and accompaniments.

Roasting Leg, loin and shoulder of veal can be roasted at a moderate temperature, and should be well done. The meat needs frequent basting to keep it moist. The breast, stuffed and roasted, makes an economical meal.

Stewing Neck, breast, shoulder, knuckle and hock are all cooked in this way. If veal is overcooked, it becomes dry and unpalatable. A stew or casserole needs cooking for about an hour. Lemon juice and thyme are flavours that combine well with veal.

The knuckle bone, cut from the foot end of the hind leg of the calf, is quite meaty. The meat can be cut off for stews and casseroles and the bone stewed for soups and stock. The bone contains a lot of marrow and when stewed it produces a rich, gelatinous stock.

Boiling Boned, stuffed and rolled breast of veal can be boiled to serve hot or cold. Breast and knuckle are

boiled to make jellied veal and veal moulds, as is the neck. In general, it is better to boil larger pieces of meat as small ones tend to lose their flavour.

Braising Most cuts can be cooked by this method, but boned shoulder, chops and cutlets are most usual. Boned, stuffed and rolled breast is also good for braising. For a small family, half the breast could be roasted and the other half braised, making it an economical buy.

TRADITIONAL ACCOMPANIMENTS

Veal can be served with bacon rolls, slices of fat ham or bacon, baked streaky pork, lemon and thyme stuffing, and thickened gravy.

Alternative stuffings are bacon or ham and rice, raisin and walnut, and sage and onion. Accompaniments can also include cranberry, mint or apple jelly.

Escalopes of veal are often served with spaghetti or risotto.

Vegetables: boiled, roast or creamed potatoes, green vegetables, roast parsnips and buttered courgettes. Stuffed mushrooms go well with veal.

BUDGET RECIPE – VEAL RAGOUT

Ingredients 15 g. ($\frac{1}{2}$ oz.) butter; 15 g. lard; 2 level tablespoons flour; 700 g. (1$\frac{1}{2}$ lb.) neck, breast or pie veal; 10 small onions or shallots; $\frac{1}{2}$ litre (1 pint) stock; bouquet garni; 1 level teaspoon salt; $\frac{1}{4}$ teaspoon pepper; 225 g. (8 oz.) frozen peas.

Method Melt butter and lard and, away from the heat, add the flour. Return to the heat and cook until the mixture is yellow and frothy. Add veal and onions and cook, stirring occasionally, for about 10 minutes. Add stock, bouquet garni and seasoning, bring to the boil and simmer, covered, for 1 hour, stirring occasionally. Add the peas and simmer for a further 30 minutes. Serves four.

CARVING LOIN OF VEAL

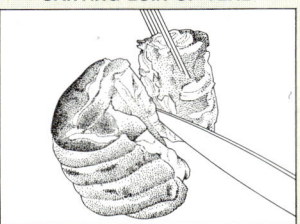

1. Remove the chined bone by putting the point of the knife under the bone and cutting down the back.

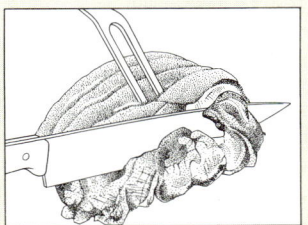

2. Turn joint on to cut side and carve down in slices, starting furthest away and working towards you.

CARVING BEST END OF VEAL

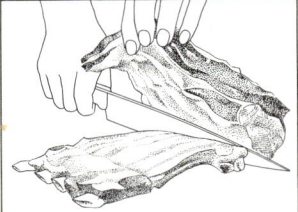

1. After removing chined bone, cut off the meat by putting blade under rib.

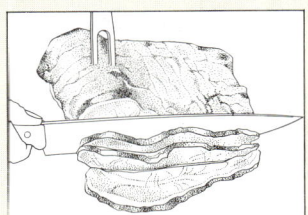

2. With thick end of joint towards you, cut slices through thick and thin end.

LOIN
Large joint from the back, usually sold boned. Loin is one side of the saddle – the back section. Cooking method: stuff and roast.

LEG
Large joint from the back legs, usually divided into two – knuckle end and cushion. Cooking methods: stew or boil knuckle to make jellied veal or moulds; roast the cushion.

ESCALOPES
Slices about 15 mm. thick cut from the cushion end of leg or from the loin. Beat the slices until they are very thin. Cooking method: dip in seasoned flour or egg and crumbs, and fry.

VEAL CUSHION (Fillet)
Cushion or fillet is the section cut from the top of the leg and is the most expensive joint. Sold whole, boned and rolled, or cut into thin slices for escalopes. Cooking methods: roast whole joint, fry escalopes.

VEAL CUTLETS
Cut from the best end of neck, cutlets are about 25 mm. thick and have a good eye of lean meat. They have more bone than chops. Cooking methods: fry, grill or braise.

VEAL CHOPS
Very meaty chops, 25-40 mm. thick cut from the loin and with little bone. Veal chops contain a portion of the kidney. Cooking methods: fry, grill or braise.

PRIME CUTS Even the best cuts of veal tend to be dry and bland because they come from very young animals and have little fat. Larding a joint, with strips of fat, or serving accompaniments such as fat bacon, make roast veal more succulent and give it extra flavour.

SHOULDER
Large joint, including forehock. Shoulder contains a large bone, making carving difficult. The butcher may remove the hock meat and sell it as 'oyster'. Cooking methods: roast the shoulder and use oyster in stews, particularly blanquette of veal.

BEST END OF NECK
Sold in cutlets or one piece, best end consists of seven rib bones and the shoulder blade. A fairly inexpensive joint. Cooking methods: roast or braise, on the bone or boned and rolled.

BREAST
Sold on the bone or boned and rolled. It may also be cut into thick strips. Cooking methods: roast, stew, braise or make into pies.

SCRAG
Bony cut sold in one piece or already chopped. Cooking methods: boil, stew or use chopped up in casseroles.

MIDDLE NECK
Cut containing a high proportion of bone and sold as cutlets or boned and diced. Cooking methods: stew, braise, use in pies and pâtés.

KNUCKLE AND HOCK
Lower part of the hind or foreleg. Hind knuckle is more tender and meaty. Cooking methods: hind knuckle can be slow roasted on the bone or cut into pieces for stews such as Osso Bucco. Forehock or shin can be boiled, or diced and stewed or put into fricassees and pies. Use the marrow bones to make stock.

MEDIUM CUTS Veal has no poor cuts but these medium joints are more economical to buy, although they have a high proportion of bone. Many butchers sell the boned meat, cut into pieces ready to use, as 'pie veal' for braised and casseroled dishes as well as pies.

• BEEF

Young, well-fattened heifers and bullocks provide the best beef. The grazing animals are not slaughtered until they are at least 18 months old. However, many butchers consider this is too young for the meat to have a good flavour. Intensively fed animals, known as 'barley beef', are killed at 11 or 12 months when they are tender but lack flavour.

Some beef from cows (animals that have calved) is also available. Beef from a one-calf cow is of a good quality and has a full, rather strong flavour. It is sold by some butchers, particularly in the north of England, and makes good stews and pot roasts.

The meat is dark red and tends to be dry, but long slow cooking with a little liquid makes it succulent.

The bulk of beef sold in Britain comes from cross-breeds of cattle, such as Friesian, Hereford, Aberdeen Angus and Charolais. Chilled and frozen beef is imported from Argentina, Australia and New Zealand, and when sold raw is marked with the country of origin. It must be boned before entry, and most is used for manufacturing.

The many cuts of beef and their names vary in different parts of Britain. The following are some variations. Scottish names are also used in northern England.

ENGLISH	SCOTTISH
shin	fore hough
shin and cow-heel	fore-knap bone
buttock and	
silverside	hind hough
sirloin	pope's eye
back rib	rib roast
roll of silverside	rump
neck	sticking piece

FORE RIB
Large joint from the back, between the wing and back ribs. The long rib bones may be cut off for a joint called Jacob's ladder. Fore rib can be boned and rolled. Cooking methods: slow roast, pot roast or braise.

WING RIB
Excellent roasting joint, similar to sirloin but without fillet. It is less expensive and not so tender or tasty. Cooking methods: quick or medium roast.

SIRLOIN
Large joint cut from the back of the animal, containing the fillet. Best cooked on the bone, sirloin can be cooked off the bone and with or without the fillet. The best joints weigh not less than 2.5 kg. and contain two or three bones. Cooking methods: quick or medium roast.

FILLET
The undercut from the sirloin, removed in one piece for roasting. Lean, tender and boneless, fillet weighs about 1 kg. Extra fat is needed. Cooking methods: quick or medium roast.

FILLET STEAK
The undercut from the sirloin, sliced into steaks. Names vary according to thickness: fillet mignon, 15 - 20 mm.; tournedos, 25 - 40 mm. Cooking methods: grill or fry.

T-BONE STEAK
A cut of sirloin between 25 and 60 mm. thick, containing a T-shaped bone. Cooking methods: fry or grill.

PORTERHOUSE STEAK
Similar to entrecôte steak, cut from wing rib and 25 - 40 mm. thick. Cooking method: excellent grilled, especially over charcoal.

RUMP STEAK
A slice up to 30 mm. thick cut from the rump of the animal. Excellent flavour but tougher than fillet steak. Cooking methods: grill or fry.

ENTRECÔTE STEAK
A slice 15 - 25 mm. thick, cut from the top of the sirloin and also called sirloin steak. Cooking methods: fry or grill.

TOP RIB
A cut from between the shoulder and the fore ribs, top rib is half the section known as middle rib. Sold boned and rolled. Cooking methods: braise or slow roast.

TOPSIDE
A lean, boneless joint from the hindquarters of the animal. Fine grained and tough unless cooked slowly. Extra fat is needed during cooking to prevent dryness. Buttock steaks are cut from topside for casseroles. Cooking methods: slow roast, pot roast or braise.

TOP RUMP or THICK FLANK
Cut from the hindquarters. This is a fairly lean joint with a close grain. Cooking methods: pot roast or braise.

LEG-OF-MUTTON CUT or THICK TOP RIB
Cut from the neck, this cut is a compact, lean joint, usually sold boned. Cooking method: braise.

CHUCK AND BLADE BONE STEAK
Also known as shoulder steak. The hard gristle and excess fat should be removed before cooking. Excellent for long, slow cooking. Cooking methods: braise, stew or use for pies and puddings.

BACK RIB
The other half of the middle rib. A medium cut with less bone than fore rib. Sold on the bone or boned and rolled. Cooking methods: slow roast, or braise.

SILVERSIDE
A close-grained, boneless joint adjoining the top rump. Cooking methods: if salted, soak to remove salt, and boil with root vegetables such as carrots. Boil or slow roast a fresh joint.

PRIME CUTS Although the quality of beef is more variable than other meats, all these cuts and joints should be tender and have a good flavour when they are cooked.

MEDIUM CUTS Some of these joints can be slow roasted with added fat to prevent dryness. All medium cuts are excellent for braising and pot roasting.

The continental method of cutting up a carcase and the names of the joints are different from the English and Scottish ones. However, they are rarely seen in British shops at present. If in doubt, ask the butcher's advice.

WHAT TO LOOK FOR

When good-quality beef is first cut the flesh should be bright red, smooth, firm and just moist. When the meat is exposed to the air, it takes on a brownish tinge. If the meat is very red, it can mean that the carcase has not been hung for a sufficient length of time and the meat is tough. The lean should be flecked with fat, or marbled, and surrounded by a layer of creamy-white fat, although the colour varies according to the breed and feeding of the animal.

A joint of beef from an old animal has a layer of gristle under the outer layer of fat and needs long, slow cooking. If there is a great deal of gristle, the meat will be tough unless it is stewed for at least 3-4 hours.

HOW TO COOK BEEF

Beef contains more iron than any other meat, apart from offal. It also provides B vitamins. The nutritive value is equally good whichever cut of meat or cooking method is used.

Grilling and frying Steaks cooked by these methods need little additional fat. For maximum tenderness they can be marinated in oil seasoned with salt and freshly milled pepper for an hour before cooking.

Stewing Leg and shin, chuck and blade bone steak, skirt, clod or sticking are all stewing cuts. Meat labelled 'stewing steak' by butchers can be a mixture of any of these and is sometimes cheaper than a specific cut such as chuck steak. Red wine, beer or cider can be used instead of stock for beef stews and casseroles to turn an economical meal into a dinner-party dish.

Roasting Sirloin and rib joints should be roasted at a medium temperature (190°C, 375°F; mark 5) to avoid drying, hardening and shrinkage. Joints such as topside, silverside and brisket are best roasted slowly (160°C, 325°F; mark 3) in a covered tin or foil to keep them moist.

Braising or pot roasting Rolled and boned joints are best cooked by this method. The joint is cooked in a covered pan with vegetables and a little stock. This is a good way to prepare topside, top rump, rib and leg of mutton cuts of beef.

Boiling Silverside, if salted, must be soaked well before boiling. Brisket, fresh or salted, makes delicious cold meat when cooked on top of the stove. When the meat is cooked, the bone is removed and the joint is pressed and served cold. Flank of beef, boned and rolled, is cooked in the same way.

TRADITIONAL ACCOMPANIMENTS

Roast beef can be served with Yorkshire pudding; horseradish cream or grated, pickled horseradish; mustard; Cumberland sauce; and gravy. Vegetables: roast potatoes, cut up and cooked round the joint, green beans, marrow, cauliflower, cabbage, sprouts or mashed swede. Chipped potatoes, grilled tomatoes and mushrooms are usually served with grilled or fried steak.

OTHER BEEF PRODUCTS

Corned beef Imported from Argentina and some African countries, corned beef is the meat left after meat extracts have been made. It is lower in vitamin B than fresh beef but is a more concentrated source of iron. The meat is pickled, pressed into cans and processed. By law, corned beef must be 100% beef. If bought loose, it should be used the same day.

Salt beef Jewish salt beef is brisket, with the fat, cured and freshly cooked to sell hot or cold. The salt beef sold in many supermarkets and delicatessens is brisket, without the fat, or silverside which is cured and cooked to sell cold. It is widely available in plastic packs but is also cut off and sold loose in some shops. These are pure-beef products, but beef is also used with cereals and other meat, to make sausages (see p. 240).

BUDGET RECIPE – GOULASH

Ingredients 450 g. (1 lb.) thin flank or stewing steak; 25 g. (1 oz.) dripping; 2 onions; 2 level teaspoons paprika pepper; 1 level teaspoon salt; 75 ml. (3 fl. oz.) tomato juice or 2 tomatoes; pinch of caraway seeds; 150 ml. (5 fl. oz.) stock; 450-700 g. (1-1½ lb.) potatoes.

Method Peel and slice the onions and cut the meat into 25 mm. (1 in.) cubes, removing gristle and fat. Heat the dripping in a saucepan and fry the meat until brown. Add the onions and cook for a few minutes. Add all the other ingredients except the potatoes. Cover the saucepan and simmer over a low heat for 2-3 hours. The goulash can also be cooked in the oven for 2-3 hours at 150°C (300°F; mark 2). While the goulash is cooking, peel and boil the potatoes. Cut them into quarters and add to the goulash 10 minutes before the end of the cooking time. Serves four.

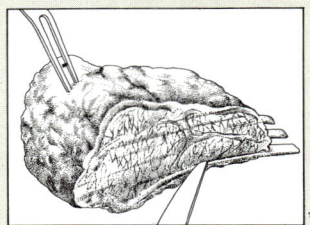

LEG AND SHIN
Lean cuts containing gristle and connective tissue, which disappear with long cooking. Leg comes from the hind leg; shin from the fore leg. Cooking methods: stew, and use for pies.

BRISKET
Cut from the forequarters and sold fresh or salted, brisket may be boned and rolled for easy carving. Cooking methods: braise or slow roast. Boil a salted joint.

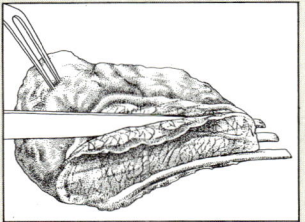

FLANK
Layers of fat and lean meat from the belly of the animal. It is sold boned and rolled, with the inner skin and gristle removed. Cooking method: pot roast.

CLOD AND STICKING
A steak from the neck of the animal. It is inexpensive, but has a fair proportion of gristle which must be cut away. Cooking methods: stew or casserole.

SKIRT
Cut from the diaphragm of the animal. There are several kinds of skirt, the best being rump skirt. Cooking methods: stew, use for soup.

COARSE CUTS Slow cooking is necessary to make these cuts of beef tender. They are not economical if there is too much gristle and fat.

CARVING WING RIB

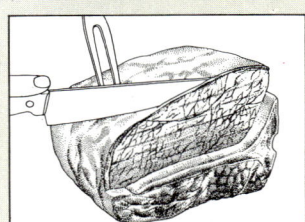

1. After removing the chine bone, loosen the meat by sliding the point of the knife along between the meat and the rib bones.

2. Carve downwards through the meat in thin slices which should come away easily from the loosened rib bones at the base.

CARVING SIRLOIN

1. Stand the joint on the uppercut. Carving is easier if the meat is first loosened by inserting the knife blade between the meat and the bone.

2. Carve down towards the bone to remove the meat on this side, then turn the joint and remove the bone. Carve the rest of the meat downwards.

• LAMB

Five times more lamb is eaten per person in Britain than in any other European country, and there is a good supply all the year round. About 40% of lamb is home-produced, and the rest is imported from Australia and New Zealand. Mutton is cheaper but not easy to find in the shops.

The following are the English names of joints of lamb, and their nearest Scottish equivalents:

ENGLISH	SCOTTISH
leg	gigot
scrag	neck
breast	flank
saddle	double loin
loin chops	cutlet end
best end of neck	back rib cut
shoulder	runner cut

WHAT TO LOOK FOR

The flesh of the lamb varies in colour from light pink to dark red, depending on the age of the animal and the variety. Dark meat usually comes from an older animal and is less tender, but some breeds – hill lambs for example – are a deeper colour regardless of age. Home-produced lamb is available in the shops from spring onwards and is slightly paler than imported. It is cheapest from September-November.

The surrounding fat should be firm and white, not yellow and oily, and the legs plump and small-boned. The bones should be translucent, with a bluish tinge around the knuckle. Brittle, white fat indicates that the carcase has been refrigerated for a long time and the meat will be tough.

HOW TO COOK LAMB

Lamb should be served slightly underdone, it must not be overcooked, or the flesh will dry out. When grilling lamb chops, preheat the grill. Turn the chops once during cooking.

Grilling and frying Lamb chops and cutlets can be grilled, or trimmed and coated with egg and white breadcrumbs for deep-frying, or shallow-fried at a moderate heat.

Stewing Breast, scrag and neck, the usual stewing cuts of lamb, should be well trimmed. A lamb stew can be made in 1½-2 hours.

Roasting Leg and loin of lamb are the prime joints for roasting. All joints are best cooked at a moderate temperature. Allow the meat to rest in a warm place for 15 minutes before carving, as it shrinks if cut at once.

ACCOMPANIMENTS

Young roast lamb is served with mint sauce, new potatoes and thin gravy. Lamb can be served with thyme-and-parsley stuffing or onion sauce, redcurrant jelly and thick gravy.

Vegetables: any green vegetables, marrow, courgettes, celery, braised onions, green or bean salad.

BUDGET RECIPE – FRICASSEE OF LAMB

Ingredients 1 breast of lamb (boned); 1 onion; 50 g. (2 oz.) fat; 2 bay leaves; 2 cloves; pinch of dried mace; 6 peppercorns; salt, pepper; 600 ml. (1 pint) boiling stock or water; 25 g. (1 oz.) flour; 1 dessertspoon capers (optional).

Method Cut the meat into 50 mm. (2 in.) pieces. Melt the fat. Cook the onion and meat with bay leaves, cloves, mace and seasoning, over a gentle heat for 30 minutes, stirring frequently. Add stock or water and simmer for 1½ hours. Mix flour with a little water until smooth, then gradually add 300 ml. (½ pint) liquid from the pan. Add the meat to this sauce and bring to the boil in another pan. Sprinkle with capers and serve with mashed potatoes and greens. Serves four to six.

CARVING LEG

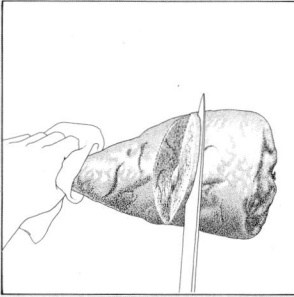

Have the fleshiest side uppermost and hold the shank bone with a cloth. Slice down through the centre of the joint, to the bone, and take out two slices, 5-15 mm. thick. Continue to take slices from either side of this centre cut, angling the knife to cut longer slices. Turn the joint over and remove excess fat. Carve the meat in horizontal slices.

CARVING BEST END

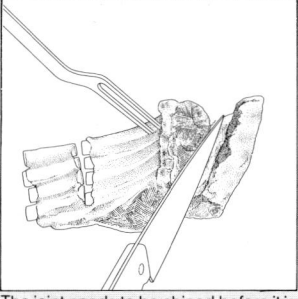

The joint needs to be chined before it is cooked. The butcher will do this and he will also strip off the thin, outer layer of skin. To carve the joint, have the fat side uppermost, and find the fleshy parts between the rib bones with the point of a knife. Divide the best end into cutlets by cutting down between the bones. Serve two cutlets per person.

CARVING LOIN

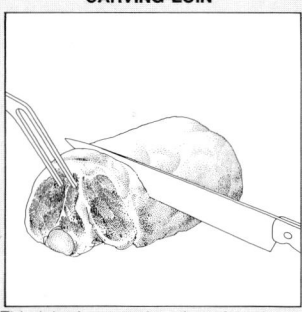

This joint is a continuation of the best end. Ask the butcher to cut through the sections of the backbone. When the joint is cooked, remove this chined bone – which should come away quite easily. This will loosen the meat. Find the natural divisions between the bones with the point of the knife and carve the joint downwards into chops.

CARVING SADDLE

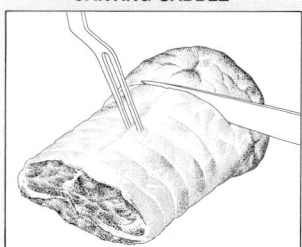

1. Make two cuts in a T-shape – one across the chump end and the other at a right-angle to this down the centre of the joint.

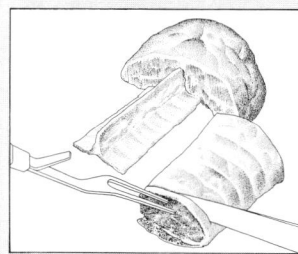

2. Remove the meat from the bone. Carve the chump end from each side in turn, the knife angled to the centre. Slice the fillet lengthways.

CARVING SHOULDER

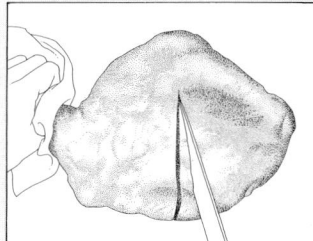

1. Use a cloth to hold the shank end. With the fat side uppermost, cut a long slice, 15 mm. thick, from the centre of the joint right down to the bone.

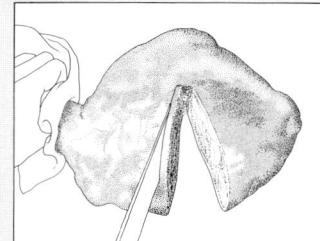

2. Carve slices from both sides of the first cut, making smaller slices over the hump of the blade bone. Make the slices thick at the outside, tapering inwards.

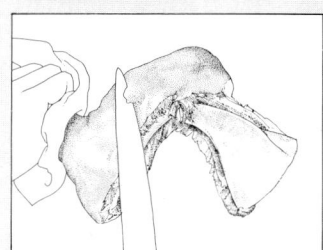

3. Still holding the shank end with a cloth, carve horizontal slices from the shank bone until all the meat has been removed from this side of the joint.

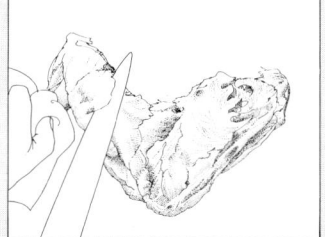

4. Turn the joint over and trim off any excess pieces of fat from the undercut. Carve the meat in thin horizontal slices, parallel to the bone.

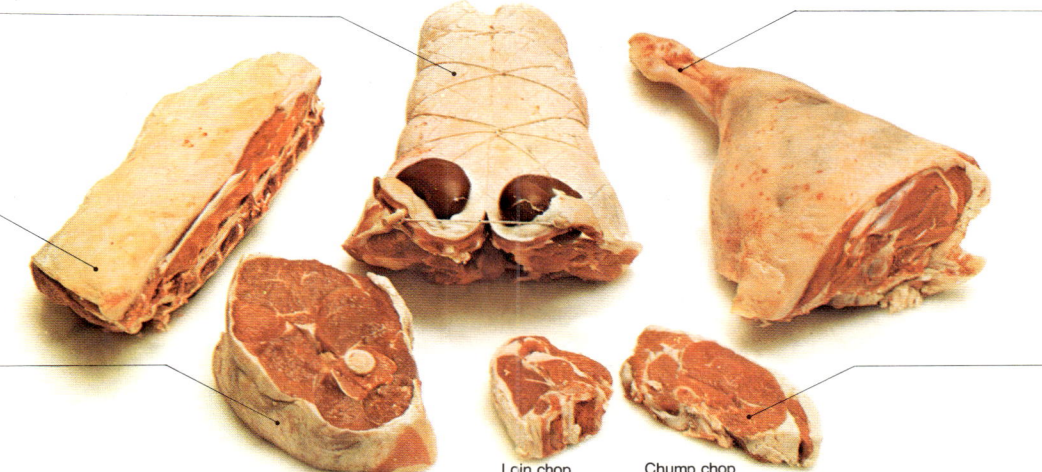

SADDLE
For saddle of lamb, the carcase is not cut in half in the usual way, but the whole loin section is cut out in one saddle-shaped piece. The butcher needs notice to prepare this joint. Cooking method: roast at a moderate temperature

LOIN
Cut from the centre back, this joint has a good eye of lean meat and a thin layer of fat. Cooking methods: roast on the bone, or boned and stuffed

LEG FILLET
Slices are cut from the fillet end of the leg. These should be 20-25 mm. thick for grilling whole and 40 mm. thick when cubed for kebabs. Cooking methods: fry or grill

Loin chop   Chump chop

LEG
Cut from the hindquarters of the animal, this is an expensive joint, but there is little waste apart from the centre bone. The usual weight is 2-3 kg. The leg can be divided into shank and fillet of lamb. Cooking method: medium roast

LOIN AND CHUMP CHOPS
Cut from the neck end, loin chops contain small T-shaped bones. Chump chops, from the thick end of the loin, are meatier with a small, round bone. Cooking methods: grill or braise

PRIME CUTS A large part of a lamb can be cut into joints which are suitable for roasting. However, the prime joints – and the most expensive ones – are the leg, loin and saddle of lamb. The saddle is a very large joint which is suitable for dinner parties and banquets rather than family meals. The loin, half the saddle, is more manageable and can be cut into chops.

BEST END OF NECK
An excellent small joint from the end of neck, which joins on to the loin. It usually contains six or seven bones. The butcher will chine the joint and saw through the cutlet bones. Two best ends of lamb make a crown of lamb. Cooking methods: medium roast, braise or pot roast

SHOULDER
Cut from the fore-quarters, the shoulder usually weighs 1.5-2 kg. It is fatty, but the meat is sweet. Large shoulders are often cut in half, but the blade bone makes carving difficult. Cooking methods: roast, on the bone or boned and rolled

NECK FILLET
This is the middle neck after it has been boned. There is quite a lot of fat but the meat is tender and inexpensive. Cooking methods: slice and fry, grill or stew

BEST-END CUTLET
Six to seven cutlets are cut from each best end of neck. They have a long bone and less lean meat than chops. Excess fat should be trimmed off. Cooking methods: fry, grill or braise

MIDDLE NECK
Small, bony section between best end and scrag. Sold in one piece with the scrag, middle neck is also cut into individual joints. It is cheap and has a good flavour, but a great deal of bone and fat. Cooking methods: stew, or use for soup and broth

SCRAG
Cut from the neck end where it joins the head, scrag is sold in a long piece or divided into round portions, with a large proportion of bone to meat. Cooking methods: stew or braise

BREAST
Breast of lamb is best boned, rolled and stuffed because of its awkward shape. A cheap, small joint, it has layers of fat between the lean strips. Cooking methods: roast slowly, braise or stew

MEDIUM CUTS These have more fat than the prime joints, but the meat is tender and quite suitable to roast or grill. Shoulder and best end of neck make reasonably priced family joints.

COARSE CUTS These are the parts of the animal where there is a lot of fat and bone in proportion to meat. However, they are inexpensive and have a good flavour when stewed or braised.

• PORK

About 96% of pork sold in Britain is home-produced. Demands for lean meat have brought about the breeding of longer, leaner pigs, usually Large White, Landrace or Saddlebacks. Most pork pigs are slaughtered when they weigh about 45-50 kg. (100-120 lb.). Some larger pigs are bred for food-manufacturing trades.

At one time, pork was sold only during the winter because it did not keep in hot weather. Because of refrigeration and more hygienic, scientific breeding conditions, pork is now available all the year round. However, the meat still keeps less well than beef and lamb, and needs careful handling and cooking. Pork is a better source of B vitamins than other meat, but contains less protein, weight for weight, than beef.

Pork joints are tender and almost all can be roasted. However, the meat is rich and some people find it indigestible. There is no waste and every part of the pig is used either for eating or manufacturing purposes.

The following are the English names for joints of pork, with their nearest Scottish equivalents:

ENGLISH	SCOTTISH
fillet-end of leg	gigot
tenderloin	loin
belly	flank
hand and spring	fore hough

WHAT TO LOOK FOR

Pork is a red meat but, after slaughter, it is 'bled', leaving the flesh a pale pink. Prime pork should be firm, a delicate pink and finely grained. Coarse, darker-coloured meat with a brownish tinge comes from an older animal and may be tough.

There should be a good surround of firm, white fat with a milky tinge. Very lean pork lacks flavour. The bones should be small, and pink and white in colour. The skin should be pink, smooth and supple on a young pig. It thickens and toughens with age.

HOW TO COOK PORK

Pork should always be thoroughly cooked, to make it more digestible.

Grilling or frying Trim excess fat from pork chops before cooking. This surplus fat can be melted down and used to fry the chops.

Stewing Hand, spare rib and belly of pork make economical stews, but are rather fatty. Apples added to pork dishes help to offset the richness of the meat.

Roasting Leg, loin, hand and blade of pork are the best roasting joints. The joint should be placed on a rack with the fat side uppermost and cooked at a high or moderate temperature. It will be more tender cooked at a moderate heat, but higher temperatures ensure that the skin, or 'crackling', is crisp and brown. Before cooking make 15-20 mm. ($\frac{1}{2}$-$\frac{3}{4}$ in.) wide cuts in the skin, brush with oil or rub in salt for added crispness.

Braising and pot roasting Pork is a rather fatty meat and can be greasy when cooked in these ways. Spare-rib chops are most suitable for braising.

TRADITIONAL ACCOMPANIMENTS

The usual accompaniments for roast pork are sage-and-onion stuffing, apple sauce, cranberries or cranberry jelly and thickened gravy. Fruit flavours combine well with pork, and it can be served with gooseberry, apricot or prune sauce, or baked and sliced apples, pineapples and apricots. Dried fruit and nuts such as prunes and walnuts, almonds and raisins can also be used in stuffings for pork.

Vegetables: roast or creamed potatoes, roast parsnips, boiled onions, braised celery, courgettes, runner or french beans.

PIG'S HEAD

A pig is the only carcase usually delivered to butchers with the head attached. The head is an economical buy and has a high proportion of meat to bone. The cheek is sometimes removed to salt and boil. This is sold as Bath chap, which can be eaten cold and is also very good sliced and fried.

The rest of the head can be soaked for 2 hours, and boiled for 2-3 hours so that the bones are easily removed. Use the meat to make brawn.

BUDGET RECIPE – BARBECUED SPARE RIBS OF PORK

Ingredients 15 g. ($\frac{1}{2}$ oz.) butter or oil; 1 small onion; 1 stalk celery; 1 level tablespoon brown sugar; 2 level teaspoons dry mustard; 1 level teaspoon salt; $\frac{1}{2}$ level teaspoon paprika pepper; 2 teaspoons tomato paste; 1 tablespoon Worcester sauce; 150 ml. ($\frac{1}{4}$ pint) water; 1 tablespoon vinegar; 2 tablespoons lemon juice; 4 thick, spare-rib chops.

Method Peel and finely chop the onion and celery. Bake the chops, uncovered, in a shallow dish for 30 minutes at 200°C (400°F; mark 6) until brown. Pour off excess fat. While chops are cooking, fry the onion in the butter or oil until brown. Mix and add remaining ingredients to the onion and pour over the chops. Cover and cook for 45 minutes. Serves four.

CARVING LEG OF PORK

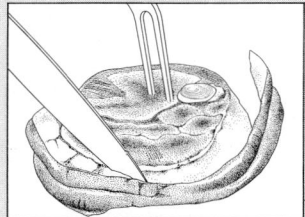

1. The leg has a circular bone at an angle through the middle. It is easier to carve if the crackling is removed first, with a sharp knife.

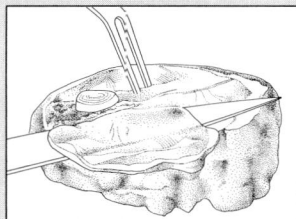

2. Cut small slices from each side of the bone until the surface of the joint is level. Cut slices across the top, easing the knife round the bone.

CARVING BLADE OF PORK

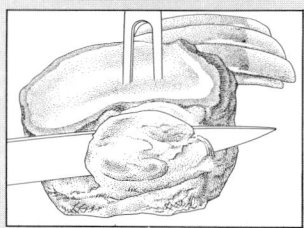

1. Remove the crackling by sliding the knife along between it and the meat. Carve slices downwards, round the hump-shaped bone.

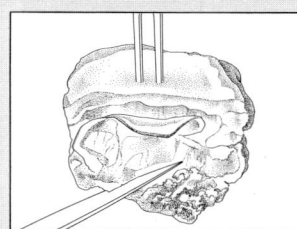

2. Cut two or three slices down to the bone, leaving them attached at the base. Cut across the base of the slices and round the bone to free the meat.

CARVING HAND OF PORK

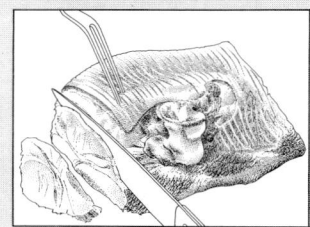

1. Remove the crackling from the top, and the rib bones from the underside of the joint. Carve slices downwards, alternately, from each side of the bone.

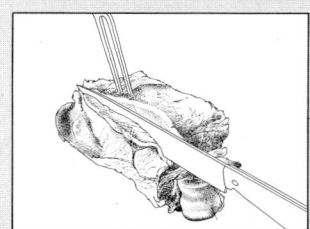

2. Continue carving slices from each side of the joint, up to the bone. Turn the joint over and carve the remaining meat horizontally, across the grain.

CARVING LOIN OF PORK

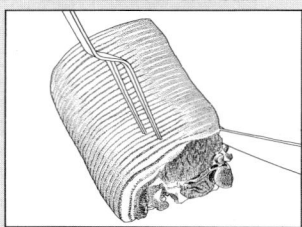

1. Remove the chine bone from the base of the joint. It should come away quite easily. This allows the carver to cut straight through the joint.

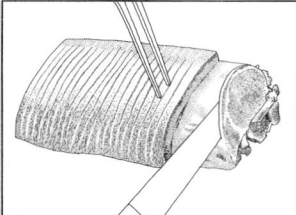

2. To simplify carving, remove part of the crackling. Carve downwards at a slight angle to get good-sized slices of meat, fairly thick and not too small.

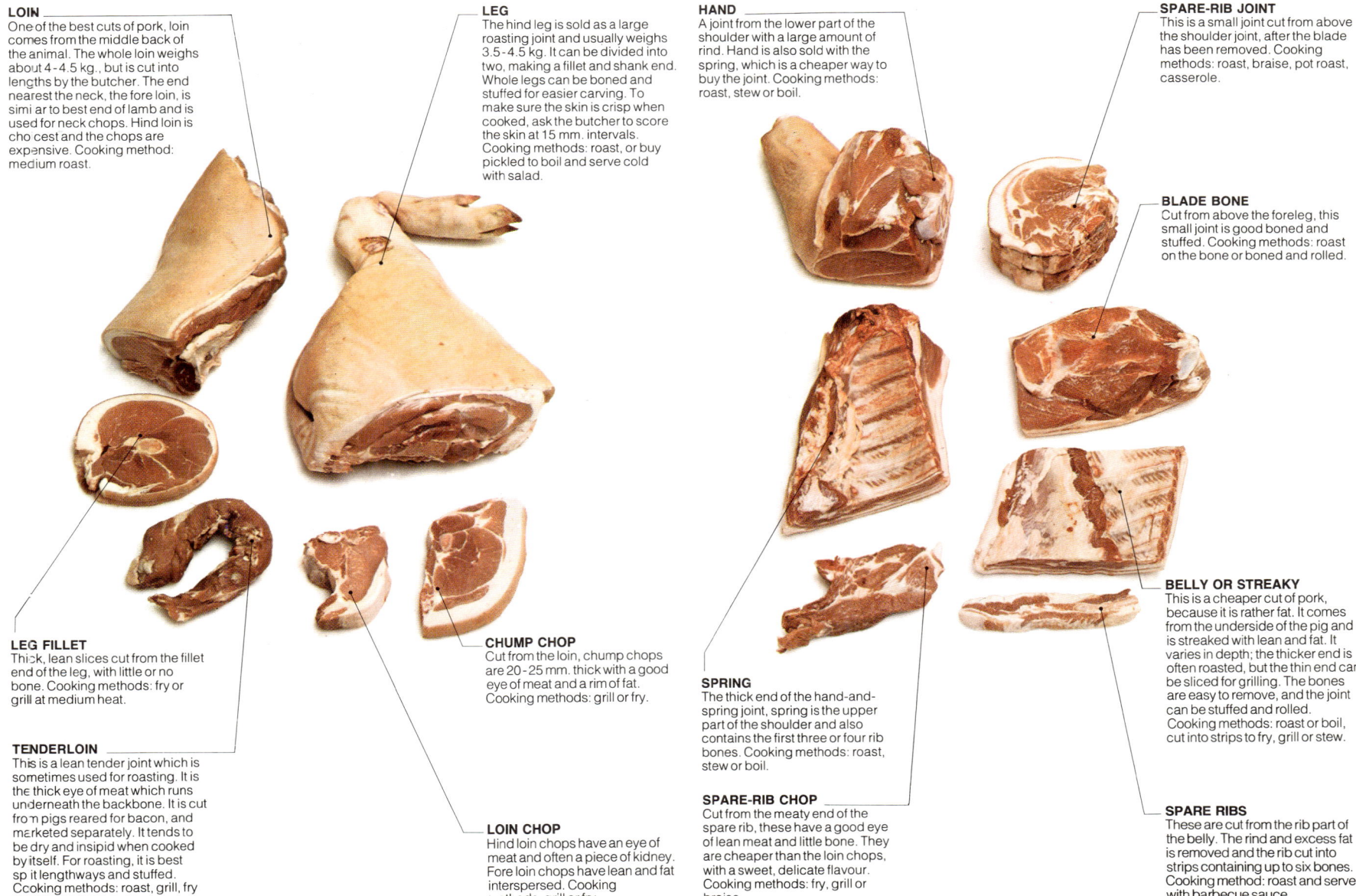

LOIN
One of the best cuts of pork, loin comes from the middle back of the animal. The whole loin weighs about 4-4.5 kg., but is cut into lengths by the butcher. The end nearest the neck, the fore loin, is similar to best end of lamb and is used for neck chops. Hind loin is choicest and the chops are expensive. Cooking method: medium roast.

LEG
The hind leg is sold as a large roasting joint and usually weighs 3.5-4.5 kg. It can be divided into two, making a fillet and shank end. Whole legs can be boned and stuffed for easier carving. To make sure the skin is crisp when cooked, ask the butcher to score the skin at 15 mm. intervals. Cooking methods: roast, or buy pickled to boil and serve cold with salad.

HAND
A joint from the lower part of the shoulder with a large amount of rind. Hand is also sold with the spring, which is a cheaper way to buy the joint. Cooking methods: roast, stew or boil.

SPARE-RIB JOINT
This is a small joint cut from above the shoulder joint, after the blade has been removed. Cooking methods: roast, braise, pot roast, casserole.

BLADE BONE
Cut from above the foreleg, this small joint is good boned and stuffed. Cooking methods: roast on the bone or boned and rolled.

LEG FILLET
Thick, lean slices cut from the fillet end of the leg, with little or no bone. Cooking methods: fry or grill at medium heat.

TENDERLOIN
This is a lean tender joint which is sometimes used for roasting. It is the thick eye of meat which runs underneath the backbone. It is cut from pigs reared for bacon, and marketed separately. It tends to be dry and insipid when cooked by itself. For roasting, it is best split lengthways and stuffed. Cooking methods: roast, grill, fry or casserole.

CHUMP CHOP
Cut from the loin, chump chops are 20-25 mm. thick with a good eye of meat and a rim of fat. Cooking methods: grill or fry.

LOIN CHOP
Hind loin chops have an eye of meat and often a piece of kidney. Fore loin chops have lean and fat interspersed. Cooking methods: grill or fry.

SPRING
The thick end of the hand-and-spring joint, spring is the upper part of the shoulder and also contains the first three or four rib bones. Cooking methods: roast, stew or boil.

SPARE-RIB CHOP
Cut from the meaty end of the spare rib, these have a good eye of lean meat and little bone. They are cheaper than the loin chops, with a sweet, delicate flavour. Cooking methods: fry, grill or braise.

BELLY OR STREAKY
This is a cheaper cut of pork, because it is rather fat. It comes from the underside of the pig and is streaked with lean and fat. It varies in depth; the thicker end is often roasted, but the thin end can be sliced for grilling. The bones are easy to remove, and the joint can be stuffed and rolled. Cooking methods: roast or boil, cut into strips to fry, grill or stew.

SPARE RIBS
These are cut from the rib part of the belly. The rind and excess fat is removed and the rib cut into strips containing up to six bones. Cooking method: roast and serve with barbecue sauce.

PRIME CUTS Loin is the best and most expensive pork roasting joint. It is often easier to remove the crackling and cut it into portions before carving. The leg can be boiled fresh to serve cold.

MEDIUM CUTS Although quite suitable for roasting, these cuts contain more bone than the prime cuts and some are fatty. Trim off the fat and dice the meat to use in stews and braises.

• BACON, GAMMON AND HAM

Bacon and ham come from pigs, specially reared for the purpose, which give a certain proportion of lean meat to fat. They are larger than pork pigs, and can weigh up to 180 kg. (400 lb.). In addition to home-produced varieties, bacon is also imported from Eire, Poland and Denmark.

Green bacon is produced by pickling the carcase in a salt solution, or injecting it under pressure with a salt solution, and curing it for four days. The green bacon is sold after maturing for a further seven to ten days. It is less expensive than smoked bacon, but does not keep so well. Green bacon is popular in Scotland, the north of England and the Midlands.

Smoked bacon is produced by further drying and smoking over wood shavings, producing a stronger-flavoured bacon which is popular in the south of England.

After curing, the bacon sides are cut into joints, steaks and rashers. The hind leg is cut off and sold as gammon; the rest of the carcase is used as bacon.

Ham is the hind leg of the pig, corresponding to gammon, but is usually cured or pickled separately from the rest of the carcase. York ham is cured with dry salt, lightly smoked and matured for several months. Wiltshire ham is cured before it is removed from the side of pig and, strictly speaking, is green ham. Bradenham and Suffolk hams are both soaked in molasses, which turns the skin black and gives red rather than pink meat. They are then hung for several months. Wiltshire ham is the least expensive English ham, whereas Bradenham and Suffolk hams are expensive and not readily available.

Other cures sold in most supermarkets and delicatessens are the mild-flavoured ones such as Virginia,

MIDDLE GAMMON
A succulent joint from the centre portion of gammon, weighing 1.5-2 kg. Cooking methods: boil or bake. Slices 15-20 mm. thick are cut from the joint for gammon rashers to fry or grill.

CORNER GAMMON
Thick, triangular end of the gammon, cut off to make a joint of 1.5-2 kg. Plenty of lean meat, little bone and an even surround of fat. Cooking methods: boil or bake to serve hot or cold.

GAMMON HOCK
Cheapest gammon joint, cut from the shank end. It has more bone than other gammon joints but gives plenty of lean slices. Cooking method: boil on the bone. Meat removed from knuckle end is good for minced dishes.

GAMMON SLIPPER
A small, triangular joint cut from the inside hind leg. Lean with a small, round bone. Sufficient for two or three people. Cooking methods: boil or bake.

PRIME COLLAR
End of the collar, weighing about 3 kg. Sold as smaller cuts. Prime collar has a large proportion of lean meat flecked with fat and a good rim of fat, which adds flavour. Cooking methods: boil or use as rashers to fry or grill.

LONG-BACK
Lean rashers cut from the end of the back, where it joins the gammon. Also cut into thick bacon steaks. Cooking methods: grill or fry.

TOP BACK
Cut adjoining the collar, top back is sold sliced into lean rashers. Cooking methods: best grilled or fried.

SHORT-BACK
Prime rashers with an equal amount of fat and lean. They may be cut into chops. Cooking methods: grill or fry.

PRIME CUTS The corner, middle and hock are all part of the whole gammon and these are the prime baking or boiling joints which can be served hot or cold.

Slices from the middle gammon are sold as rashers to grill. Prime collar can be baked or boiled and bacon rashers to fry are cut from this.

Maryland and Honey-roast hams. The hams are boned and cured in moulds for easy slicing. Virginia ham is wet-cured in brine and is slightly moist and succulent. Honey-roast ham and Maryland are cured in a similar way, but the honey-roast is coated with honey and brown sugar to give a slightly sweeter taste and a dryer texture.

Ham sold loose in square or rectangular slices has been previously tinned. It tends to have a softer texture than freshly cooked ham.

Home-produced smoked ham is also sold ready-sliced. This is closer in flavour and texture to the traditional, dry-cured hams such as York and Bradenham.

The best-known imported hams are Parma, Prosciutto and Westphalian which are smoked and dry-cured but not cooked. They are thinly sliced and eaten raw as hors-d'oeuvres.

Shoulder and collar joints of bacon can be cured in the same way as ham.

The cured shoulder is often described as picnic ham or picnic shoulder. These cured bacon joints are less expensive, but lack the delicate flavour and texture of ham.

WHAT TO LOOK FOR

Green bacon is pale pink with a pale, supple rind.

Smoked bacon has a dark, firm but elastic golden-brown rind and darker red flesh. All bacon should have white or cream fat, with no green or yellow tinges, and should be firm, not soft and oily. The flesh should be firm and moist. The rind should be thin, covering a layer of fat about 15 mm. ($\frac{1}{2}$ in.) thick between it and the meat.

Stale bacon is easily recognised by its brown, dry appearance and unpleasant smell.

Rashers of back and streaky bacon are available in date-stamped vacuum packs and should be used by that date to be in prime condition. Store them in a refrigerator, and once

the packs are opened the bacon must be treated as fresh and used within three or four days.

Bacon and gammon joints should be short and thick, not too fat and with a thin rind.

Gammon slices are sold for grilling. These are expensive, and shoulder bacon slices (sometimes called 'picnic steaks') are a good substitute. Bacon chops, which are the short back cut into chops 5-15 mm. ($\frac{1}{4}$-$\frac{1}{2}$ in.) thick, can also be grilled.

Freshly cooked ham, usually sold sliced, should look moist and fresh with white fat and pale pink flesh. Ham on the bone is expensive but has a better flavour than boned ham.

COOKING BACON AND GAMMON

Bacon and gammon joints should be soaked for at least an hour and preferably longer, to remove excess salt.
Grilling and frying Thin rashers of bacon are best fried; thicker ones grill well. Prepare the rashers by cutting

off the rind and removing any small bones with scissors. Snip the fat to make the rashers cook flat. For frying very lean bacon, heat a little oil or lard first and put the bacon into a hot pan, then cook gently. Bacon and gammon rashers and steaks for grilling should be brushed with fat if they are very lean, and turned often under a hot grill.

Boiling Soak bacon joints for boiling in cold water for at least three hours. Some joints require as much as 12 hours. After soaking, put the bacon into a saucepan and just cover with cold water. Bring it to the boil, remove the scum and simmer gently until tender, allowing 25 minutes to the pound and 25 minutes over. After cooking, the rind can easily be removed with a knife. The joint can then be served hot with a sauce, or left to cool in the cooking water for eating cold. When it is cold, drain off the water and finish by sprinkling the fat with a mixture of browned crumbs and brown sugar.

COLLAR
Thick, fleshy joint from the neck end of a side of bacon. A whole collar weighs 3.5-4 kg., but it is usually cut into smaller joints. Cooking methods: boil or bake.

OYSTER CUT
Fatty end of the long-back sold sliced, or as a small joint with the bone in. Cooking method: boil to serve hot or cold.

BUTT
Leanest and best end of forehock, weighing up to 2 kg. Cooking methods: boil or bake.

OYSTER RASHERS
The oyster cut is often sliced and sold as small rashers. Cooking methods: grill or fry.

SMALL HOCK
Knuckle end of forehock. A cheap cut, weighing 500 g. - 1 kg., small hock needs to be soaked well because it may be salty. Cooking method: best boiled and the flesh removed for minced dishes or casseroles.

FLANK
A very fatty cut from the end of the streaky joint. It is best used for larding lean meat.

FORE SLIPPER
Fatty end of the forehock. Cooking method: boil to serve cold. Use with chicken, veal or game, or for minced dishes.

END COLLAR
Good small joint, weighing about 1 kg., useful for serving with leaner meats. Cooking methods: boil or use as a base for soups and stews.

STREAKY RASHERS
Rashers with a good flavour but containing some gristle. Cooking methods: grill or fry.

STREAKY JOINT
Cut from the underside of bacon, streaky has layers of fat and lean. Cooking methods: bake or boil.

MEDIUM CUTS Good baking and boiling joints, these cuts are less expensive than the prime cuts because they are less tender or have more fat.

COARSE CUTS Because they have a high proportion of fat these are the least expensive of the cuts of bacon. They can all be boiled to serve hot or cold, but are best served with lean meat such as chicken or used in minced ham dishes.

Baking Bacon and gammon joints can all be cooked by this method. They should first be boiled for half the cooking time, then drained and wrapped in foil. Bake in a moderate oven (180°C, 350°F; mark 4) until 30 minutes before cooking is completed. Then raise the oven temperature to hot (220°C, 425°F; mark 7). To give the joint a crisp, golden skin, remove the foil before raising the oven temperature. Remove the rind from the joint, and coat with a sugar glaze made from 2-3 tablespoons brown sugar, 25 g. (1 oz.) butter and 1 tablespoon water, brought to the boil in a small saucepan. The exposed fat can be scored with a knife, and cloves inserted before the glaze is applied. Replace the glazed joint in the oven, without the foil, until crisp.

TRADITIONAL ACCOMPANIMENTS
Bacon and gammon joints tend to be rich and fatty. Accompaniments similar to those for pork are best served

with these joints. Boiled bacon served hot is usually accompanied by parsley sauce. Apple, gooseberry, cider and raisin, Cumberland, tomato or barbecue sauces can also be served, and cranberry or redcurrant jelly. Fruit, such as pineapple, cherries, peaches or apricots, lightly grilled, or cooked, sliced apples can also be served as accompaniments.
Vegetables: serve with broad or french beans, boiled potatoes, pease pudding, ratatouille, courgettes or vegetable marrow.

BUDGET RECIPE – BACON AND PASTRY ROLY-POLY
Ingredients 225 g. (8 oz.) suet pastry (see p. 274); salt if required; 325-350 g. (12 oz.) finely chopped, cooked bacon; 1 finely chopped onion; 1 level teaspoon sage or mixed herbs; 1 tablespoon chutney; 1 beaten egg.
Method Roll out the pastry to a rectangle about 300 × 150 mm. (12 × 6 in.). Mix together the rest of the in-

gredients and bind them together with a beaten egg. Spread this mixture over the pastry to within 15 mm. (½ in.) of the edges. Damp the edges and roll up the pastry to make a Swiss roll. Wrap the roll in grease-proof paper or foil and fold over the edges to seal it. Cook in boiling water, on top of the stove, for 2-2½ hours, topping up with boiling water, if necessary. Sufficient for four people.

CARVING MIDDLE CUT OF GAMMON

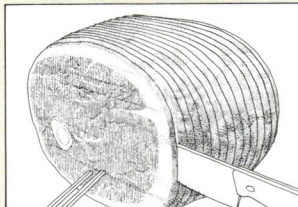

The joint narrows towards the bone end. Carve downwards in slices that are about 15 mm. thick at the outside but taper towards the bone.

CARVING GAMMON HOCK

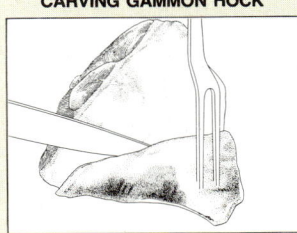

1. Slide the knife round the edges then under the centre section to remove the skin. Fold back the skin and scrape it away from the fat.

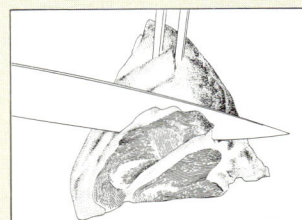

2. Carve in straight, downward slices, starting at the far side and working towards you. Buy this joint boned and rolled for economy and easy carving.

CARVING CORNER OF GAMMON

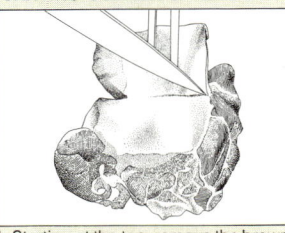

1. Starting at the top, remove the brown skin by sliding the point of the knife down one side and then the other. Sever the skin from the fat.

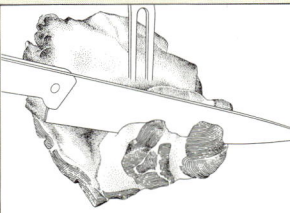

2. Carve downwards in thin slices, slightly wider at the outside and tapering towards the centre, similar to the method for middle cut of gammon.

• OFFAL

The edible insides of beef cattle, lambs, pigs and calves (such as the liver, the kidneys and the heart) are known as offal. The head, tail and feet of the animal are often included in this category, although strictly speaking they are not offal.

Most types of offal contain protein, mineral salts and vitamins, and can be cooked in a variety of ways to provide nutritious meals. Offal is usually cheaper than other meat. The exception is calf's offal, which is expensive and scarce, because Britain produces few home-killed calves.

Lamb offal has a better flavour and texture than pig. Equally nutritious, ox offal is coarse-textured and has a strong flavour.

Liver, kidney and sweetbreads have little gristle or fat, and are economical and easy to prepare.

Offal does not keep well and should be used on the day of purchase.

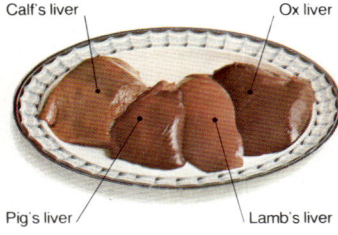

Calf's liver Ox liver
Pig's liver Lamb's liver

LIVER

Liver is richer in vitamins than any other kind of meat. It has little gristle or fat and, with the exception of calf's liver, is inexpensive. Overcooking makes it tough.

Calf's liver Light brown, with a delicate flavour, calf's liver is a delicacy. Imported calf's liver is less expensive than home-produced, but the flavour is not as good.

To prepare calf's liver, remove the outer skin and cut the liver into slices

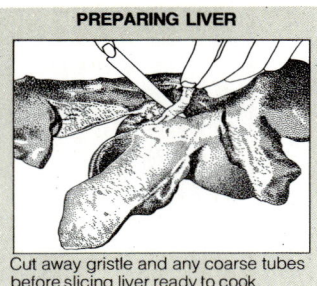

PREPARING LIVER

Cut away gristle and any coarse tubes before slicing liver ready to cook.

5-15 mm. (¼-½ in.) thick. Season and brush with melted butter before grilling. If the liver is to be fried, dredge it with seasoned flour first to prevent the outside hardening.

Lamb's liver Home-produced lamb's liver is pinky-red, tender and soft. It comes from young animals up to six months old and is delicately flavoured. Darker-red liver from an older animal has a strong flavour and is less tender. New Zealand lamb's liver is imported frozen. Make sure it is completely thawed before cooking.

Before cooking lamb's liver, remove the skin, cut out any gristle and cut the liver in slices 5-15 mm. (¼-½ in.) thick. Fry or grill gently, turning it over as soon as the blood runs out. Lamb's liver can also be braised or used in pâté.

Pig's liver Cheaper than lamb's, pig's liver is dark red and shiny. It is soft and tender, but has a strong flavour.

Prepare pig's liver, like lamb's, by removing any gristle and skin, and slicing it. Pig's liver can be grilled or fried, but the strong flavour makes it more suitable for pâtés, meat loaves and stews.

Bullock or ox liver Cheapest and coarsest of the livers, ox liver is not suitable for grilling or frying.

Make sure the butcher has cut out the coarse tubes. Chop and use the liver for stews and braised dishes.

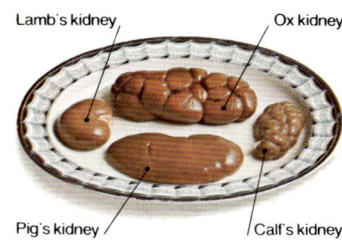

Lamb's kidney Ox kidney
Pig's kidney Calf's kidney

KIDNEYS

Strongly flavoured, ox kidneys are best cut into small pieces and braised or stewed, but pig's, calf's and lamb's kidneys can be grilled or fried. Allow two of these kidneys for each person.

Calf's kidneys These are the same shape as ox kidneys, but are small and lighter brown in colour. They are tender with a delicate flavour, but are not readily available.

Remove the outer skin and cut the kidney into 15 mm. (½ in.) thick slices, removing any white core. Sauté or fry lightly.

Lamb's kidneys These are smooth and dark red. They should be firm, with the outer skin slippery but not dry. The kidneys are usually sold in a thick layer of white suet. If this fat is left on when the kidneys are baked or grilled, it provides a natural baste, but it does mean that the core cannot be removed before cooking.

Remove the outer skin and halve the kidney to remove the central core.

Fry, bake or grill on their own, as kebabs or in a mixed grill.

Pig's kidneys Larger than lamb's kidneys, pig's kidneys vary in size – the older the animal the larger the kidneys. They are flat, light brown, with a strong flavour.

Slit the kidney along the outer edge and remove the skin, pulling it towards the central core. Cut the kidney in half and remove the core. Slice for frying or grilling, or dice the meat to stew or braise.

Bullock or ox kidneys These are large, weighing about 700 g. (1½ lb.), lumpy and dark red. They are rather coarse and tough, unless cooked slowly.

Remove the outer skin and cut the red, fleshy part away from the central core before cooking the kidneys. Cut into pieces and use for stews, or with steak for pies and puddings.

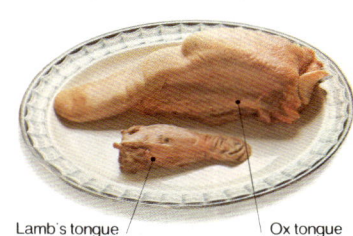

Lamb's tongue Ox tongue

TONGUE

Ox and lamb's tongue are most widely available, fresh, cooked and sliced or tinned. Calf's tongue is difficult to

obtain and pig's tongue is usually sold only with the whole head.

Lamb's tongue A lamb's tongue is small, weighing 100-150 g. (4-5 oz.), and does not have such a good flavour as the more popular ox tongue. It is usually served fresh.

Soak for 2-3 hours, then boil or braise. Cook the tongues until the skin can be removed easily – about an hour. Serve hot with parsley sauce or cold with salads, allowing one-and-a-half tongues for each person.

Bullock or ox tongue Available either cooked and sliced or raw. A whole ox tongue weighs 2-2.5 kg. (4½-5½ lb.) and can be bought fresh, but is usually salted. It has a good flavour and a velvety texture.

To cook a fresh tongue, blanch (see p. 282) then simmer until tender (it will take 2½-3 hours). Pickled tongue should be soaked in cold water for 24 hours before cooking for 2-3 hours. Remove the skin and bones. To press the tongue for serving cold, fit it tightly into a saucepan or other suitable container after it has been cooked. Put a plate over it with weights on the top and leave to set for about 12 hours. The tongue can be sliced for salads and sandwiches.

To serve hot, sprinkle browned breadcrumbs over the skinned tongue and accompany with parsley or tomato sauce.

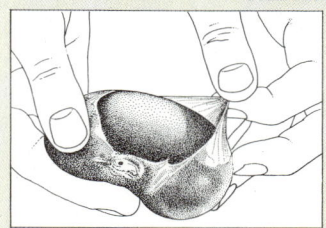
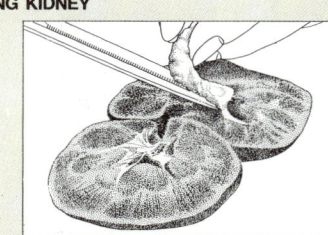

PREPARING KIDNEY

Remove the transparent, outer skin, which peels off easily, and any fat.

Slice the kidney in half, lengthways, and cut out the white, central core.

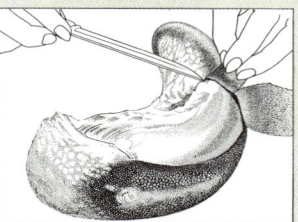

SKINNING TONGUE

When the tongue is cooked, peel off the thick skin, starting at the tip.

Lamb's sweetbreads | Calf's sweetbreads

SWEETBREADS

These glands of lamb or calf, which are considered a delicacy, are pink and lumpy, and covered with a fine skin. They are usually sold by the pound, which is sufficient for three or four people.

Calf's sweetbreads These are slightly larger and a deeper pink than lamb's sweetbreads.

Soak for 2-3 hours. Blanch (see p. 282) and skin the sweetbreads. Fry in butter, or dip first in beaten egg then in breadcrumbs, and fry.

Lamb's sweetbreads Small and pale pink, lamb's sweetbreads are tender and have a good flavour.

Soak for 2-3 hours. Blanch and skin the sweetbreads, and remove the black veins and any gristle. Fry, serve in a cream sauce, or use for fricassées or for filling pastry cases.

Calf's heart | Lamb's heart | Pig's heart

HEARTS

Hearts are tough and muscular, but make cheap, nourishing meals if cooked slowly for several hours.

Calf's heart This weighs approximately 700 g. (1½ lb.) and is bright red.

Calf's heart is sliced for braising and stewing. It is too large and tough for stuffing and baking.

Lamb's heart The smallest and most tender of the hearts, a lamb's heart is dark red and weighs about 225 g. (8 oz.).

Wash the heart thoroughly, and cut out any tubes and skin from the inside. It can be stuffed whole and roasted in foil or braised for 1½-2 hours.

Pig's heart Inexpensive and light red, it is slightly larger than a lamb's heart.

Pig's heart can be cooked whole or in slices. Wash and remove tubes and skin. Slice and use for stewing or braising. The whole heart can be stuffed and roasted slowly.

Bullock and ox heart Although less popular than other hearts, bullock and ox heart is cheap and nourishing. Dark red in colour, the hearts are large and tough but very lean and muscular, with little fat. The usual weight is about 2 kg. (4½ lb.).

Slice the heart into 15-20 mm. (½-¾ in.) pieces and remove any large tubes. Stew or braise, cooking the meat very slowly for a long time, with gravy and vegetables to offset the dryness of the heart. It is not suitable for roasting.

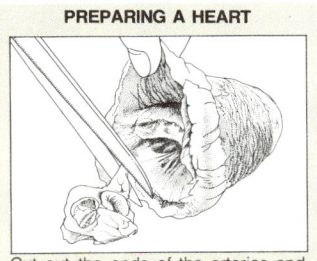

PREPARING A HEART

Cut out the ends of the arteries and tendons before putting in the stuffing.

FEET

Pig's feet, or trotters, are readily available. When cooked in a stew they make it rich and gelatinous. Cow heel and calf's feet have almost disappeared from the shops due to lack of demand.

Pig's trotters These are pink and they are sometimes sold lightly pickled.

Wash the trotters and split in half. Simmer gently for about 3 hours, and serve hot, using the stock for a sauce or soup. After boiling, the bones can be removed and the trotters can be dipped first in beaten egg, then breadcrumbs, and fried.

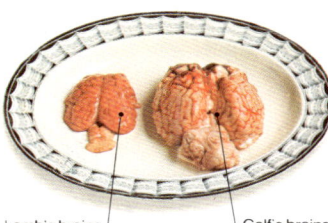

Lamb's brains | Calf's brains

BRAINS

Lamb's brains are more plentiful, but the rarer calf's brains have a better flavour. Both types must be soaked in cold water for about 2 hours before cooking to remove all the blood. Buy brains fresh and use them quickly.

Lamb's and calf's brains These look alike, being very pale pink in colour and forming a bumpy, oval mass. The lamb's brain is slightly smaller.

Prepare both types in the same way. After soaking, blanch the brains and simmer them gently in a good stock for about 20 minutes. Serve hot with lemon sauce, or drain and press them. Cold brains can then be cut in 15 mm. (½ in.) slices and fried. They are often served with black butter (see p. 282). Two calves' brains will serve three people. Allow one lamb's brain per person.

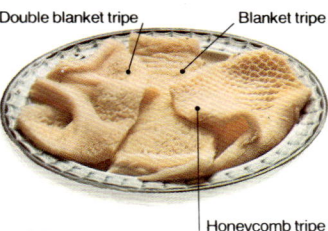

Double blanket tripe | Blanket tripe | Honeycomb tripe

comes away easily from the central bone. Add a little more stock during cooking if the oxtail is drying out.

TRIPE

Tripe, the inner lining of the stomach of the ox, is sold blanched and partly cooked. The main kinds are blanket tripe, which is the smoothest and comes from the first stomach of the animal, double blanket, a fold of the stomach lining, and honeycomb tripe, which has a rough surface and comes from the second stomach. All types should be firm and white. Stale tripe is flabby and has a slimy look.

Before being sold, the tripe will have been partly cooked, which will affect subsequent cooking time. Ask the butcher how much more cooking it needs. Wash and blanch the tripe. Cut into pieces or slice and use with onions in stews or braised dishes.

OXTAIL

The tail of the bullock or ox is sold whole or in pieces. Its meat should be bright red, the fat creamy-white and there should be an even ratio of meat to bone. Oxtail used to be cheap, but is now quite expensive.

Wipe the meat and cut off excess fat. The meat makes a rich soup, stew or braised dish, but needs to be cooked slowly for 2-3 hours, until it

MARROW BONES

The fore and hind legs of beef cattle are available from most butchers already cut into pieces. They contain marrow which should be pinky-white in colour. The bones can be used for stock, and when cooked the marrow can be pushed out with a skewer. It is considered a delicacy, served on toast as a savoury or hors-d'oeuvre.

To cook the bones, seal the ends with a paste made from flour and water and wrap each bone in a cloth. Simmer gently in a *court bouillon* (see p. 282) for 1½-2 hours.

BUDGET RECIPE – LIVER SHASHLIK

Ingredients 450 g. (1 lb.) of calf's, lamb's or pig's liver; 2 medium-sized onions; 8 medium-sized tomatoes; 225 g. (½ lb.) mushrooms; fresh bay leaves; oil, vinegar, salt and pepper; juice of 1 lemon; chopped parsley.

Method Wash the liver and remove any coarse tubes. Dry it on kitchen paper and cut into 40 mm. (1½ in.) slices. Peel and slice the onions, quarter the tomatoes and wipe mushrooms with a damp cloth. Thread the ingredients on to eight long kebab skewers in order: bay leaf, liver, mushroom, tomato, onion, bay leaf, liver and so on. Brush with oil and place in grill pan. Sprinkle with a little vinegar, salt and pepper and marinate (see p. 282) for about 30 minutes. Cook under a medium grill for about 10 minutes, then remove and put on to a warm dish. Add a little water to the grill pan and boil on top of the stove, either in the pan or a small saucepan. Add lemon juice and parsley and pour over the meat. Serve with rice and salad or mashed potatoes and vegetables. Sufficient for four.

• MINCED MEAT AND SAUSAGES

Minced meat can be coarse or fine, depending on the size of the mincer blades used. Coarse mince is suitable for making shepherd's pie, pasties and hamburgers. Fine mince is best for bolognese sauce, pâtés and stuffing.

The cheapest kind is minced beef made from the trimmings of joints and other cuts. This contains about 20% fat. Lean minced beef, which is more expensive, is made from chuck steak and other lean cuts. It contains about 10% fat.

Some butchers and large supermarkets have minced veal and pork, made from the leg and shoulder, and some will mince lamb on request. These kinds of mince are all good quality, containing about 10% fat. If you have any doubts about the quality of mince on display, buy an appropriate cut and ask the butcher to mince it. Alternatively, mince it yourself at home.

Home-made mince may be cheaper, and has the advantages that all excess fat and gristle can be trimmed off if very lean mince is preferred, and the meat can be minced just before cooking so that it is really fresh. Inexpensive, tougher cuts of meat cook more quickly if they are minced, because the mincing breaks down the connective tissues.

Mince does not keep well, and should be used on the day of purchase and kept in a refrigerator until it is needed.

WHAT TO LOOK FOR

Minced beef is bright red, and veal, pork and lamb are a lighter pink. Any tinge of brown or dryness means that the mince is stale. A large number of white flecks in the mince indicates a high proportion of fat.

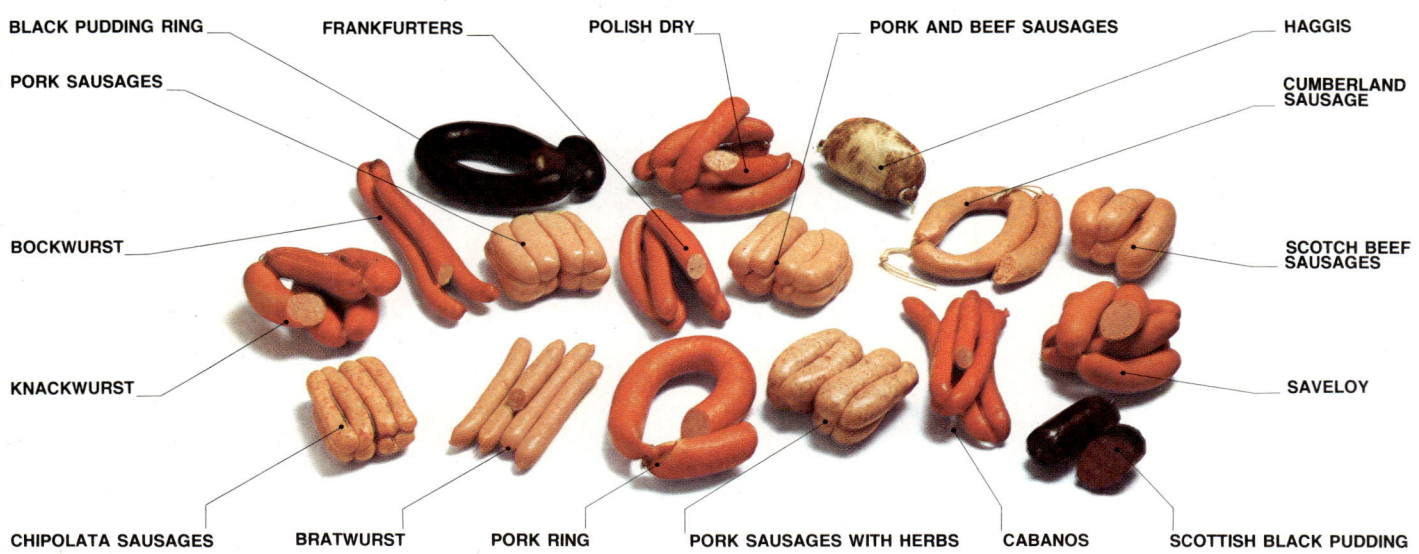

BLACK PUDDING RING — FRANKFURTERS — POLISH DRY — PORK AND BEEF SAUSAGES — HAGGIS — CUMBERLAND SAUSAGE — PORK SAUSAGES — BOCKWURST — KNACKWURST — SCOTCH BEEF SAUSAGES — SAVELOY — CHIPOLATA SAUSAGES — BRATWURST — PORK RING — PORK SAUSAGES WITH HERBS — CABANOS — SCOTTISH BLACK PUDDING

SERVED HOT Fresh sausages, which are usually fried, grilled or baked in the oven, are sold in edible, synthetic casings. Skinless sausages, which tend to be dry, are less popular than those with skins. Some pre-cooked sausages, such as frankfurters, black pudding and saveloys, are heated before serving.

HOW TO COOK MINCE

Mince should be browned quickly in the frying pan and the excess fat drained off. The meat is then cooked slowly in a stock or sauce for about 45 minutes or added to pies, sauces or pasta dishes. Lean mince can be mixed with onions, herbs and other flavourings, bound with a beaten egg, milk or wine and made into hamburgers or rissoles for grilling or frying. Commercially made hamburgers can be bought fresh or frozen from butchers and supermarkets. These are made from a mixture of minced beef, onion and flavourings. By law, they must contain 80% raw meat, but added cereal is permitted.

Minced beef can also be mixed with minced liver and herbs to make an economical meat loaf which can be eaten hot or cold.

In general, minced meat tends to lack flavour, and benefits from being cooked with herbs and spices and strongly flavoured vegetables such as onions and tomatoes.

FRESH SAUSAGES

Factory-produced sausages are available ready-packed, and many butchers make their own.

Sausages are made from minced meat mixed with cereal, herbs and flavourings. The mixture is put into casings made from cleaned pigs' intestines or synthetic material.

By law, sausages must contain 50% meat; those named as pork or beef must contain at least 65% of that meat. Cumberland sausages have a meat content of 85-90%.

If sausages contain preservatives, sulphur dioxide, for example, this must be stated on the label or pack. The salt content also inhibits the growth of bacteria. Sausages will keep four or five days in a refrigerator.

In 450 g. (1 lb.) of sausages there are about eight large or 12-16 small, or chipolata, sausages.

HOW TO COOK SAUSAGES

Fresh sausages should be cooked over a gentle heat to avoid shrinkage. Pricking the skins before cooking prevents the sausages from bursting, but this should not be necessary if they are cooked slowly. Sausages can be fried or grilled for 15-20 minutes, cooked in a moderate oven (180°C, 350°F; mark 4) for 30 minutes, or put into pies, casseroles and pasta dishes. Sausage meat is used in sausage rolls, forcemeat and pâtés.

READY-COOKED SAUSAGES

Delicatessen shops and cold-meat counters of large supermarkets stock a wide range of cooked sausages which may be home-produced or imported, mainly from France, Italy, Germany, Spain and Poland. The following are usually heated before serving.

Black pudding Popular in the north of England and Scotland, this sausage is made from pigs' blood, barley and pork fat. Scottish black pudding is slightly different from the English version, being leaner and finer and containing oatmeal. The ingredients are stuffed into cleaned pigs' intestines and then boiled. Black pudding is usually cut into 5 mm. (¼ in.) slices and fried or grilled.

Frankfurter A highly seasoned, smoked sausage which originated in Germany but is now produced in Britain as well. A variety of meats, but mainly lean pork, beef and a little bacon fat, are ground to a fine paste and put into long, thin, synthetic casings. The sausages are hung up to dry for a day and a half, then smoked. Although they can be served cold, or

ARDENNES PÂTÉ   HAM SAUSAGE   TURKEY PÂTÉ   PORK PÂTÉ   MORTADELLA   CERVELAT   DANISH SALAMI

STRASBOURG
LIVER SAUSAGE

SALAMI

CONTINENTAL
LIVER SAUSAGE

FRENCH
GARLIC SAUSAGE

TONGUE SAUSAGE

GERMAN
GARLIC SAUSAGE

BRUSSELS PÂTÉ

COARSE
LIVER SAUSAGE

BREAKFAST
SAUSAGE

ENGLISH LIVER SAUSAGE   FAGGOTS   METTWURST   CHORIZO   POLONY   LIVER AND HAM PÂTÉ   BEER SAUSAGE

consistency. The Italian and German sausages are the true salami, the Danish variety is an imitation of these. It does not usually contain garlic and is a lighter red. There is now also a French version of salami. Although whole salami can be kept for several months, and then may need to be soaked, they are often sold earlier when they are firm and moist.

Other slicing sausages are cervelat and beer sausage, ham sausage and tongue sausage.

Faggots Popular in East Anglia and the north of England, faggots are made from minced pigs' liver, fresh or salted pork, rusk, spices and flavourings. The mixture is divided into individual rissoles and wrapped in pigs' intestines before being baked. Faggots are usually fried.

PÂTÉS AND TERRINES

These are made from minced and pounded meats and offal with a variety of flavourings, which often include garlic. Most pâtés contain a high proportion of pork or pork fat mixed with duck, goose, goose liver, veal and other meats, depending on the region where the recipe originated. The most expensive is pâté de foie gras, made from goose liver.

Pâtés are sold in tins, foil packs or sausage-shaped plastic casings. The consistency of pâté can vary from very fine, like Brussels pâté, to coarse, like Ardennes pâté. Fine pâté can be spread on bread and is useful for making sandwiches. It can also be used for savoury piping. Coarse pâté is usually served in slices with toast and salad or pickles.

Pâtés are served cold as hors-d'oeuvres or with salad.

The word terrine means an earthenware dish and originally was used to describe pâtés made in these dishes, which often had a layer of aspic jelly.

SERVED COLD Pre-cooked sausages such as polony, liver sausage, mortadella and cervelat, and smoked dry salamis, are eaten cold as hors-d'oeuvres or with salad. Ham and garlic sausages are eaten cold, but can also be added to stews and flans. All these sausages are usually sold thinly sliced.

---

in a salad, frankfurters may also be heated. The traditional German way to serve frankfurters is to simmer them for about five minutes in hot water and serve them with sauerkraut – pickled white cabbage. 'Hot dogs' are made by grilling the frankfurters before putting them into split, long bread rolls.

Saveloy Although the saveloy originated in France, it has become a traditional British sausage. It is made from salt pork, lights, cheek, brains and other pickled pork meat. Saveloys keep well because they are well cooked and dried. They do not need to be stored in a refrigerator.

Saveloys, before heating, have a soft consistency and can be used as a spread for sandwiches. To serve hot, simmer for ten minutes and then eat with pease pudding or mashed potatoes. Cold saveloys can be sliced and served as hors-d'oeuvres.

Other boiling sausages include Bockwurst, Cabanos, Knackwurst, Polish Dry and Pork Ring. Haggis, a pudding of chopped offal, suet, onions and oatmeal, is boiled in a sheep's stomach lining. Grill or fry Bratwurst, Mettwurst and Chorizo.

Uncooked sausages and those with a moist texture should be kept in a refrigerator. Dried sausages, such as salami, should also be refrigerated if sliced and will last for four to six days. Left whole, or in the piece, dried sausage is best kept in a cool larder where it will last for up to two months.

Although sliced sausages are usually eaten cold, in sandwiches, with salads, and as hors-d'oeuvres, they can be added to stews and flans.

Breakfast sausage This sausage is home-produced and is particularly popular in Scotland. It is made from pork, beef, bread and flavouring, finely minced and pressed into a pig's windpipe or synthetic casing. It is

smoked, well cooked and is a deep pink colour, about 75 mm. (3 in.) in diameter and with a close texture.

Garlic sausage Imported or home-produced garlic sausage is made from finely minced pork, diced fat, garlic and other seasoning. The well-mixed ingredients are pressed into the casings, hung in a warm, airy place for four days, then stored at a cool temperature for about five months before being sold. Garlic sausage is 50-125 mm. (2-5 in.) in diameter and is sold whole or sliced.

Liver sausage Produced in Britain from a mixture of cooked livers, rusk and flavourings, the minced ingredients are filled into natural casings, made from pigs' intestines, and then boiled. Liver sausage is light brown in colour, about 75 mm. (3 in.) in diameter and has a soft consistency. It can be used as a spread.

Luncheon sausage A bland, pale

pink English sausage with flecks of fat, luncheon sausage is made from a mixture of finely minced salt pork, lean beef and fat. Small pieces of fat are added just before the mixture is put into the casing. The whole sausage, which is about 100 mm. (4 in.) in diameter, is boiled and then smoked.

Mortadella The best comes from Bologna, in Italy. It is made from finely minced pork with large pieces of fat, peppercorns and other seasonings. The largest of the cooked sausages – 230 mm. (9 in.) in diameter – mortadella is pale pink with white flecks.

Salami Imported from Denmark, Germany and Italy, this dried, smoked sausage is made from finely chopped pork, beef and fat, and is dark red marbled with white. The ingredients are put into natural or synthetic casings and hung and dried before being smoked. The flavourings may include garlic, and the sausage has a firm

• POULTRY

Poultry, such as chickens, turkeys, ducks, geese and guinea fowl, are sold fresh or frozen. Chickens and turkeys are readily available because they can be produced by battery methods. Ducks, geese and guinea fowl cannot be successfully reared in this way. Battery-raised birds usually have less flavour than free-range ones but are cheaper. Giblets are usually sold with the bird, but can also be bought separately to make pies, pâtés and stock. Chicken livers are also sold for pâtés and other dishes such as risotto.

WHAT TO LOOK FOR

In general, young birds are more tender, but older birds have a better flavour.

Make sure a frozen bird has no discoloured patches of skin, caused by freezer burn. All frozen poultry should be thoroughly thawed before cooking.

Chicken Usually sold plucked, drawn and trussed ready to cook, a fresh chicken should have a plump, white breast, pliable breastbone and smooth, pliable legs. A rigid breastbone and large scales on the legs indicate an old bird, more than 12 months old and suitable for boiling rather than roasting.

Chickens are sold whole as poussins, capons, spring chickens or roasting birds, depending on the age and size. They are also sold in pieces.

Turkey The hen has a better flavour than the cock bird. Fresh and defrosted birds should have plump, firm breasts, whitish with a slightly blue tinge, black legs that are not too scaly and supple feet.

Frozen turkeys may need to be thawed for two or three days, depending on the size of the bird. Turkeys are also sold cut into pieces.

TURKEY
Weight ranges from 2.5-15 kg. but a bird weighing between 6 kg. and 7 kg. is most convenient. Cooking method: rub with fat and roast on a rack or in foil.

GOOSE
The average weight of a goose is 2.5-5.5 kg. The proportion of bone to meat is high. Cooking method: roast as for duck.

CHICKEN
Size varies, but a 1.5-2 kg. bird is sufficient for four people. Cooking methods: best roasted, but can be braised or stewed.

SPRING CHICKEN
A bird about three months old, weighing 1-1.5 kg. Spring chickens are usually produced by broiler methods for freezing. Cooking methods: can be roasted, but best casseroled with added flavourings such as herbs and vegetables.

DUCK
A duckling weighs about 1.5 kg. and is sufficient for two people. A fully grown duck weighs 2-3 kg. Cooking method: prick through the skin all over the bird and roast on a rack. Duck is a fatty bird and best not wrapped in foil as the fat cannot escape and the skin and meat will be greasy.

CAPON
Weighing 3.5-4.5 kg., a capon is a castrated cock bird reared to give a high proportion of flesh to bone. One bird is sufficient for 8-12 people. Cooking method: rub with bacon fat or butter and roast on a rack or in foil.

POUSSIN
A baby chicken weighing 450-700 g. Tender and juicy but not very fleshy, one poussin serves only one person. Cooking methods: spit roast or grill whole.

POULTRY Chickens are classified in many different ways, but these are the roasting birds most frequently seen in the shops. Most poultry is sold ready to cook, either fresh or frozen and, with the exception of geese, there is a good supply in shops and supermarkets for most of the year.

Duck Fresh duckling are available only in the summer, although frozen ones can be bought all the year round. A fully grown duck, fresh or frozen, is expensive and not economical, as there is a high proportion of bone to meat, but it has a very good flavour. Fresh, fully grown birds are best from August to December.

The flesh should be white, the breast plump and the feet pliable.
Goose Not as readily available as other poultry, a goose can be bought frozen all the year round, although it may have to be ordered. Fresh birds are available between October and February. The flesh is darker and richer than other poultry, and rather fatty. Like ducks, geese do not have much flesh in proportion to the bone.
Guinea fowl Usually sold fresh, guinea fowl were originally game birds but are now bred for the table. They have grey feathers mottled with white, but are usually sold plucked, drawn and trussed. The meat is firm, creamy-white and the flavour a cross between chicken and pheasant. They

are available all the year round but are most plentiful and at their best from February to April.

HOW TO COOK POULTRY

Whole birds are usually roasted (see chart, p. 247), but chickens and chicken and turkey pieces can be cooked in a variety of other ways. For example, a whole chicken can be braised or stewed. Hens, after they have stopped laying, are sold for boiling. Chicken and turkey joints can be fried, grilled, casseroled or curried.

TRADITIONAL ACCOMPANIMENTS
Roast poultry is usually served with stuffing and other accompaniments depending on the type of bird.
Chicken: bread sauce, thyme and parsley stuffing, sausages, gravy.
Turkey: bread sauce, chestnut stuffing, sausages, bacon rolls or ham, cranberry sauce, thin gravy.
Duck: apple sauce, sage-and-onion stuffing, thin gravy, orange salad.
Goose: apple sauce, sage-and-onion stuffing, slightly thickened gravy.
Guinea fowl: bacon, cranberries.

PIGEON
Very young birds have pink legs and downy feathers. Older birds tend to be tough. The meat is dark red. Cooking methods: roast or grill a young bird, casserole older ones, allowing one per person.

GROUSE
Sufficient for one person, grouse has dark meat which tends to be dry and has a gamey flavour. Cooking methods: roast. Older birds, with rounded wings, are best casseroled.

PHEASANT
A hen bird is sufficient for three or four people; a cock for four or five. Check before buying that a feathered bird has not been badly shot. Pheasants are often sold unplucked but are also available ready dressed for the oven. Cooking methods: roast a young bird, casserole or stew an older one.

Hen pheasant

Cock pheasant

VENISON
The best meat, which is dark red with firm, white fat, comes from the young male deer. It is sold cut into joints. Cooking methods: roast leg and saddle of venison. Shoulder, chops and cutlets are best braised or casseroled.

RABBIT
Wild rabbit has a gamey flavour, quite different from the blander tame ones. A young rabbit will serve four people. Cooking methods: roast whole or joint and casserole.

HARE
There are two types: the brown English hare and the blue Scottish one. A young hare weighs 2.5-3 kg. and is sufficient for four to six people. Hare is sometimes sold as joints. Cooking methods: young hare is roasted whole, older ones casseroled or jugged.

GAME Unlike poultry, most game is seasonal and is available unplucked or with the fur on as well as ready for the oven. Butchers will pluck or skin and draw game for a charge. Game birds are expensive and young birds are best simply roasted. Braise or casserole an older bird to make the most of the flavour.

• GAME

Wild animals and birds that are hunted and eaten are called game. These include pheasant, partridge and grouse, hare and venison, all of which are protected by law so that they can only be hunted outside their breeding season. Pigeons and rabbits are available fresh throughout the year.

It is best to buy game from a licensed poulterer and game dealer, who will pluck or skin the bird or animal and prepare it for the table.

Unprepared game should be hung in a cool airy cupboard for 10-14 days after shooting, depending on the weather and the type. Hares should be hung by the feet, birds by the neck.

WHAT TO LOOK FOR

Young birds, best for roasting, have pliable beaks and feet, soft feathers and plump breasts. Prepared game is sometimes labelled as 'young' or 'casserole' birds. Most types of game are available frozen throughout the year, but the flavour does not compare with that of well-hung, fresh game.

Pheasant The birds are reared for shooting, and the season is from the beginning of October to the end of January. Hen and cock birds are sold singly or as a brace, or pair. The hen bird is considered to have the better flavour.

Grouse The most common is red grouse, and the young birds have downy breast feathers and pointed flight wings. Grouse are in season from August 12 to December 16.

Pigeon Wood pigeons are the least expensive of the game birds. They are available all the year round, but are best from August to October. The flesh is firm and dark red.

Hare Young hares have soft ears, small teeth, and claws that are usually covered with fur. The older animals have projecting claws and white hairs on the muzzle. Hares are in season from the beginning of August to the end of March, but are at their best from October onwards.

Rabbit Young wild rabbits are most tender, and have soft, smooth fur, small teeth, and claws covered with fur. Paunching, or removing the entrails, must be done as soon as they are shot. If the weather is warm, skin them immediately.

Most rabbit meat in the shops comes from tame animals and is sold whole or jointed. Tame rabbit can be used in the same way as wild rabbit, but it does not have the same gamey flavour.

Venison The meat from the red or roe deer is known as venison, and should be dark red and fine grained. It is available fresh from June to January. Young venison up to 18 months old is very tender and has a good flavour. Venison is sold cut into joints. Haunch, loin and saddle of venison are large roasting joints.

HOW TO COOK GAME

Game is usually sold already hung (check this when buying) and is then roasted. Because there is little fat on game, all types should be larded (see p. 282) or covered with bacon or pork fat before roasting, and basted frequently. Small, tender birds can be grilled. Older animals and birds will be more succulent if they are braised. Venison, unless it is from a young animal, should be marinated in wine, oil and herbs for at least 12 hours before being roasted or stewed.

TRADITIONAL ACCOMPANIMENTS

Game birds are not usually stuffed but served with bread sauce, fried breadcrumbs and game chips or potato crisps and thin gravy. Bacon rolls are served with pheasant and partridge, and cranberry jelly with grouse. Hare, rabbit and venison can be accompanied by forcemeat balls, redcurrant jelly and thickened gravy flavoured with port.

• PREPARATION OF POULTRY AND GAME

Birds are usually sold already hung, plucked and drawn. Poultry should be plucked as soon as possible after killing, because the feathers come out more easily. After plucking, hang a chicken for 24 hours, a turkey for three to five days, and a goose or duck for one or two days. Reduce the hanging time if the weather is very warm. An older bird needs to be hung for slightly longer than a young one. Game birds are hung for several days before plucking.

After hanging, draw game and poultry by cutting off the head and pulling out the entrails and fat. Keep the giblets to make stock for gravy.

Hare should be hung by the feet for about a week before skinning. After that time, skin it and remove the entrails – called 'paunching'. It is not necessary to hang rabbit.

Frozen chicken, duck and turkey are best thawed at room temperature, the length of time depending on the size of the bird. Chicken and duck will thaw completely in a cool larder in one or two days, but turkeys take up to three days.

If poultry and game are to be stuffed, do so before trussing. Various stuffings can be used, and these make the bird a better shape for carving, and improve the flavour.

Stuffing made with a base of about 125 g. (4 oz.) slightly stale, white breadcrumbs is sufficient to stuff a bird weighing 1.6 kg. (3½ lb.). It should be loosely packed, as it expands during cooking.

TRUSSING A BIRD

After stuffing a poultry or game bird, truss it – that is, tie it into a neat shape ready for the oven. The following method is suitable for most birds.

Fold the loose neck skin up and over the back of the bird to close the neck opening. Fold the wing tips over the body to hold the neck skin in place. Turn the bird so that the breast is uppermost and make a slit above the back opening. Pull the parson's nose through this slit. Lay the bird on its back and push the legs towards the neck. Insert a skewer through the body, just below the thigh bone, to come out below the thigh bone on the opposite side. Turn the bird over and pass a piece of string over the wings, then underneath the bird and back over the ends of the skewer. Cross the string over the back. Turn the bird on its back, loop the string round the thighs and parson's nose and tie.

JOINTING A HARE OR RABBIT

Young hares and rabbits can be roasted whole, older ones cut up to casserole. After they have been paunched and skinned, the animals are divided into eight pieces.

Use a sharp knife and cut off and discard the flaps of skin below the rib cage. Cut the carcase in half, lengthways, along the backbone then remove the hind legs. Do this by breaking the bone and cutting off the top of the thigh, close to the body. Cut round each shoulder to remove the front legs. Divide each of the two remaining halves of the carcase into two pieces, making eight portions in all.

The back section, or saddle, of hare is sometimes roasted whole. In this case, remove the flaps of skin and the back and front legs as described but do not cut along the backbone.

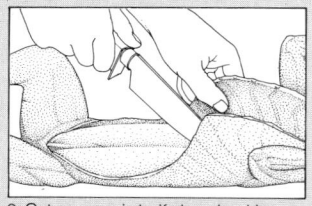
JOINTING A HARE
1. Remove skin flaps below rib cage.

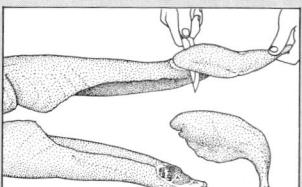
2. Cut carcase in half along backbone.

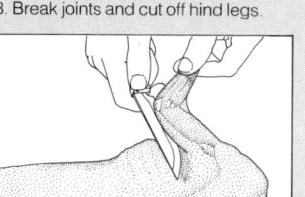
3. Break joints and cut off hind legs.

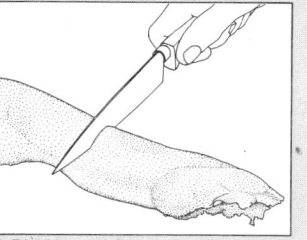
4. Cut off forelegs round shoulders.

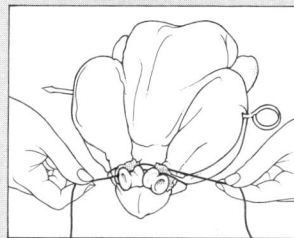
5. Divide remaining carcase in half.

TRUSSING A CHICKEN

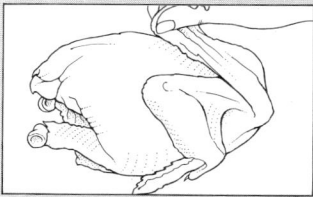
1. Fold neck skin up over the back.

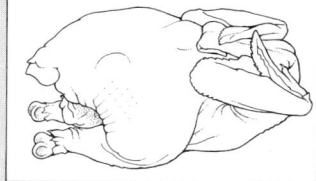
2. Fold wing tips to secure neck skin.

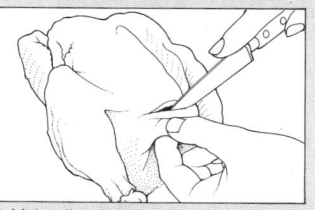
3. Make slit to hold parson's nose.

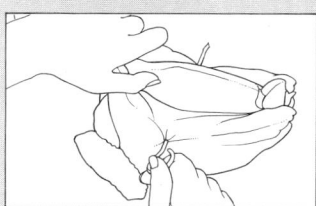
4. Insert skewer through the body.

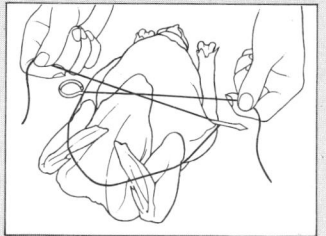
5. Cross the string over back of bird.

6. Turn bird and tie string round thighs.

JOINTING A CHICKEN OR DUCK

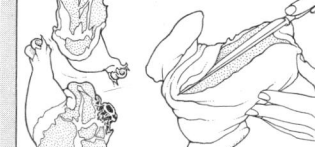
1. Cut through skin joining legs to body.

2. Break joints. Cut off legs close to body.

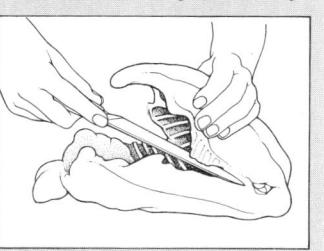
3. Remove wings, cutting towards joints.

4. Remove breast and cut it in half.

• CARVING POULTRY AND GAME

Poultry and game, like other meat, should be left in a warm place for 10-15 minutes after cooking and before carving so that the meat does not crumble. The basic method is the one shown here for duck. Carving is easier if the wishbone is removed from the bird before it is cooked.

To carve most birds, first remove the wings and the legs, which are divided into thighs and drumsticks. If the bird is stuffed, cut thick slices across the stuffed end. Carve the breast meat downwards, in slices.

Large birds, such as turkeys and capons, are carved in this way, but because the drumsticks are very meaty, slices are also carved off these. Give each person some brown meat from the leg and some white meat from the breast.

Chickens can be carved in the same way, but a small bird can be divided equally between four so that each person is given a portion of breast meat and a piece from the leg.

Small birds, for example duckling, grouse and partridge, can be cut in half to make two portions.

In addition to the method shown, a large saddle of hare can be carved as follows. Cut straight through the meat at the base, or chump end, about two-thirds of the way along the back. Make a cut at right-angles to the first one, along the centre back, so that the cuts form a T-shape. Cut off the chump end so that it is separate from the back section and carve it in alternate slices, first from one side and then the other. Carve the remaining back section as shown. Saddle of venison is carved in the same way.

DIVIDING DUCKLING IN HALF

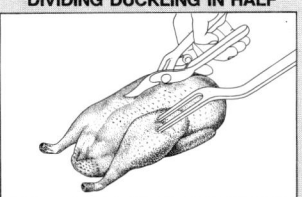

Remove the trussing string or skewers. Use poultry shears, a carving knife or strong kitchen scissors. Split the bird in half by inserting the shears or knife in the neck and cutting along the centre of the breastbone to the back opening. Cut through the backbone to separate the two halves. Small game birds such as grouse can be divided in the same way or served whole, one per person.

CARVING SADDLE OF HARE

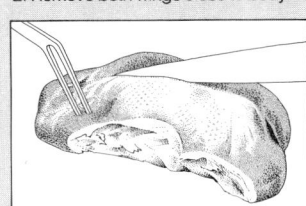
1. With larding fat in, carve far side first.

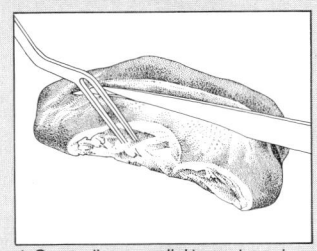
2. Cut along rib bones to release slices.

CARVING DUCK

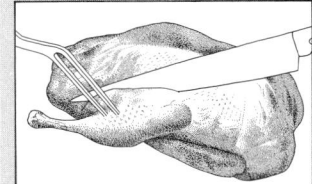
1. Cut off thighs where they join body.

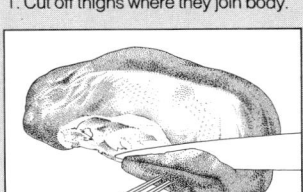
2. Remove both wings close to body.

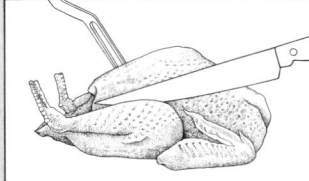
3. Cut down through centre of breast.

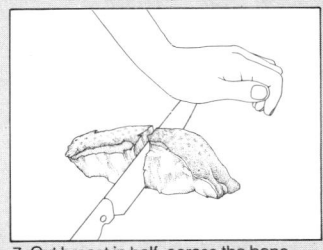
4. Carve slices parallel to centre cut.

DIVIDING A CHICKEN INTO FOUR PORTIONS

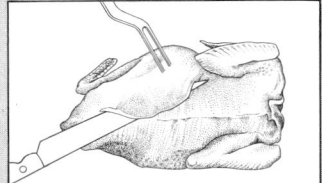
1. Insert knife into top of thigh.

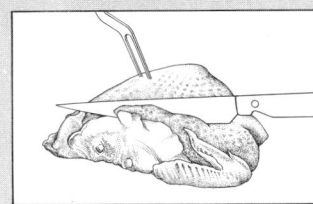
2. Turn bird and cut round thigh.

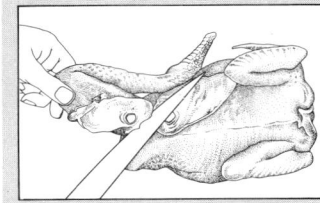
3. Hold thigh firmly and remove legs.

4. Cut off wing with a portion of breast.

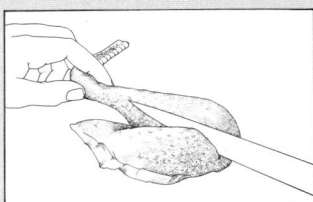
5. Divide thigh into two equal portions.

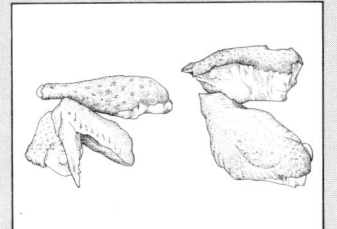
6. With bird on end, cut off breast.

7. Cut breast in half, across the bone.

8. Serve leg/breast, wing/drumstick.

CARVING TURKEY OR CAPON

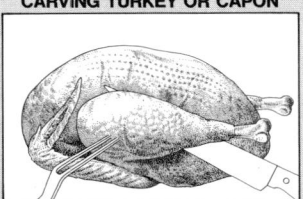
1. Remove drumsticks, close to body.

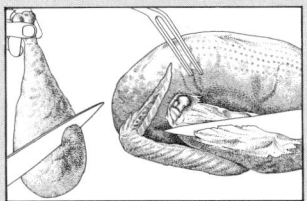
2. Carve from drumsticks and thighs.

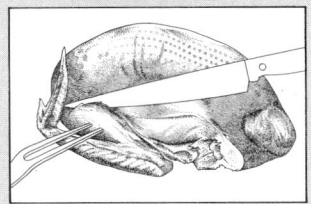
3. Cut off wings, where they join body.

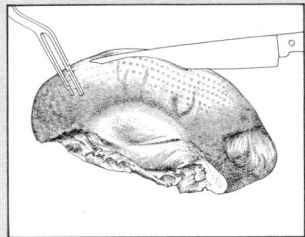
4. Carve breast in downward slices.

• HOW TO COOK MEAT

Cooking makes meat tender, digestible and more palatable by breaking down the connective tissue. It also destroys bacteria. Overcooking – either for too long or at too high a temperature – spoils the flavour and dries the meat.

ROASTING

Prime and medium joints of meat, either on the bone, or boned and rolled, are cooked by this method.

All meat to be roasted should be taken from the refrigerator an hour before cooking. Frozen meat should be fully thawed for the best results but small joints can be cooked straight from the freezer, allowing slightly longer cooking time.

Wipe the joint with a damp cloth or kitchen paper, and bone, stuff, roll and tie as required. Weigh the joint and calculate the cooking time (see chart below).

Heat the oven to the required temperature before putting in the meat. Put a few knobs of fat, preferably of the same kind as the meat, on to a very lean joint. Other joints do not need additional fat. Stand the joint on a rack in a shallow tin, fat uppermost.

OVEN TEMPERATURE

Medium roasting is best for most joints. Put the meat into a fairly hot oven (200°C, 400°F; mark 6) for the first 15 minutes. Reduce the oven temperature to 180°C (350°F; mark 4) for the remaining cooking time. Cooked by this method, the outer surface of the meat is brown and crisp and the rest of the joint is succulent and juicy. To prevent dryness, the joint should be basted from time to time, or it can be covered with foil after the first 15 minutes' cooking.

QUICK ROASTING

By this method the joint is put into a hot oven (220°C, 425°F; mark 7), and cooked at this temperature for the full cooking time, allowing about 20 minutes per lb. and 20 minutes extra. The outer surface of the meat is quickly seared and the meat juices are contained in the meat. The joint needs frequent basting. Although quick roasting gives delicious results, it is wasteful as the joint shrinks when cooked in this way.

SLOW ROASTING

There is less shrinkage by this method, which is particularly suitable for medium cuts of meat. The oven temperature should be 180°C (350°F; mark 4). Most joints will need 35-40 minutes per lb. and 35-40 minutes extra. The meat remains moist and succulent when roasted slowly, but does not brown.

MEAT THERMOMETER

Tastes vary as to how rare or well done the meat should be, and a meat thermometer enables an accurate judgment to be made of when a joint is ready. Insert the thermometer into the thickest part of the meat (avoiding fat and bone). This registers the internal temperature, which should be 60°C (140°F) for rare meat, 70°C (158°F) for medium, 75°C (167°F) for well done.

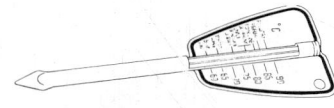

Meat thermometer

FOIL ROASTING

This method not only makes basting the meat unnecessary, but it also prevents fat from splashing inside the oven. Before putting the joint on the rack in the roasting tin, wrap it loosely in foil and pinch the edges together. Because foil deflects heat, add an extra 30 minutes to the cooking time to allow for this. Open up the foil 20 minutes before the end of the cooking time and replace the joint in the oven to allow the meat to brown.

Special transparent roasting bags and film are available for cooking joints without making the oven dirty. These do not have to be removed until the meat is done.

SPIT ROASTING

Many cookers have an electrically operated rotisserie to attach to the grill. The horizontal shaft goes through the meat and turns at an even speed in front of the radiant heat. Fairly large joints and poultry can be cooked on a rotisserie, but a regularly shaped joint is essential so that the spit turns evenly and the meat is properly cooked. The joint is basted with its own juices and is cooked evenly on all sides.

Heat the grill or rotisserie until it glows (5-10 minutes) before fitting the shaft into place. Cook the meat at an intense heat for about 15 minutes to seal it, then reduce the heat. Baste lean joints.

POT ROASTING

This is a useful cooking method for less tender joints of meat, such as brisket and flank of beef.

Prepare the meat as for roasting and melt a little dripping in a heavy, fire-proof casserole with a well-fitting lid. Dredge the meat with seasoned flour and fry in the hot dripping until it is well browned. Drain off the fat, put the lid on the casserole and cook in a slow oven (150°C, 300°F; mark 2), allowing 45 minutes per lb. and 45 minutes over.

BRAISING

Cheaper cuts of meat, large and small, are excellent when cooked by this method. Prepare the meat as for roasting, and then fry it in a little melted fat until browned all over. Remove the meat from the pan and fry a mixture of diced root vegetables, such as onions, carrots, turnips, leeks or swedes. Season, add a bouquet garni (see p. 278) and stand the meat on top of the vegetables in an oven-proof casserole. Add enough stock or water to reach to the top of the vegetables. Put on the lid and cook in a slow oven (170°C, 325°F; mark 3) allowing 40 minutes per lb. of meat.

COOKING TIMES FOR MEAT

TYPE OF MEAT	MEDIUM ROASTING (At 200°C, 400°F; mark 6, for 15 min., then 180°C, 350°F; mark 4 unless otherwise stated)	STUFFED JOINTS	SPIT ROASTING	BOILING	GRILLING OR FRYING
Beef	Rare, on the bone: 20 min. a lb., 20 min. over Off the bone: 25 min. a lb., 25 min. over Medium, on the bone: 25 min. a lb., 25 min. over Off the bone: 30 min. a lb., 30 min. over	+ 5-10 min. a lb.	20 min. a lb.	Pickled beef: 25 min. a lb., 25 min. over	Steak: Rare, 6 min. Medium, 8 min. Well done, 10 min.
Veal	On the bone: 25 min. a lb., 25 min. over Off the bone: 30 min. a lb., 30 min. over	+ 5-10 min. a lb.	30 min. a lb.	20 min. a lb., 20 min. over	Chops: 12-15 min. Escalopes: 4 min.
Lamb	On the bone: 20 min. a lb., 20 min. over Off the bone: 25 min. a lb., 25 min. over	+ 5-10 min. a lb.	35 min. a lb.	20 min. a lb., 20 min. over	Chops: Medium rare: 8 min. Well done: 10 min.
Pork	On the bone: 30 min. a lb., 30 min. over Off the bone: 35 min. a lb., 35 min. over	+ 5-10 min. a lb.	40 min. a lb.	20 min. a lb., 20 min. over	Chops: 12-15 min.
Bacon and Gammon	Can be cooked in the oven, but must be par-boiled first (see p. 236)			Cured bacon and gammon (ham): 25 min. a lb., 25 min. over	Bacon rashers: 5-10 min. Gammon steaks and bacon chops: 10-15 min.

Remove the meat from the casserole and finish cooking in a roasting tin with a little fat for 30 minutes. Use the left-over vegetables and stock to make soup.

STEWING

Similar to braising, this method is used for tougher cuts of meat which are diced first and have their fat and gristle removed. The meat and vegetables are cooked, covered in stock, on top of the cooker or in the oven.

To make a basic stew for four, dice 450 g. (1 lb.) of meat into 25-40 mm. (1-1½ in.) pieces and roughly chop 225 g. (½ lb.) of mixed root vegetables. Toss meat in 35 g. (1½ oz.) of seasoned flour, shaking off the excess. Brown the meat in hot dripping, remove it and fry the vegetables. Put the fried vegetables with the meat and add the remainder of the seasoned flour to the pan. When it is well browned, gradually add 600 ml. (1 pint) of stock and bring to the boil, stirring until thickened. Return the meat and vegetables to the pan, with a bouquet garni, bring to the boil and simmer for 2-3½ hours, or cook in the oven at 160°C (325°F; mark 3) for the same length of time.

BOILING

By this method, meat or poultry is immersed in simmering stock or water and cooked until tender (see chart). Whole hams, gammons, large bacon joints, pickled meat, tongue and boiling fowl are cooked in this way.

The meat is prepared as for roasting, but never stuffed as this would boil out during cooking. Before boiling, soak pickled or cured meat in cold water for not less than 12 hours. If this is not possible, the meat can be soaked for 1 hour, then put into fresh water and brought to the boil, before being cooked in more clean water.

PRESSURE COOKING

Stews, braised dishes and boiled meat can all be prepared in a pressure cooker, which cuts down on the cooking time by about three-quarters.

For the best results, follow recipes from the manufacturer's instruction book. Less stock is needed than for other cooking methods because there is no evaporation. The liquid should be only halfway up the pan.

GRILLING

This is the best method for cooking small prime cuts of meat, such as steaks, chops and cutlets. Kidneys, sausages and bacon and chicken legs can also be grilled.

The grill should be red-hot before cooking. Brush the meat with melted butter or oil. Put the meat on to the grid, in the low position, if it is adjustable, and cook under the grill until it starts to brown. Turn the meat over, using tongs or two spoons to avoid puncturing it, and brown the other side. Lower the heat so that the meat cooks through. Then return to the first side to complete cooking.

FRYING

This is a fast method of cooking meat. It is best for thin steaks and chops, some offal and bacon rashers and sausages. Very thick pieces of meat or chops tend to burn on the outside unless the heat is very low.

Use a thick frying pan or cast-iron griddle to give an even spread of heat. Melt a little fat (butter or dripping is best) and put the meat to cook over a gentle heat until brown. Turn over and brown the other side.

Bacon and sausages should not need extra fat for cooking. Liver and kidneys are best fried in bacon fat over a very gentle heat.

MEAT PUDDINGS

The tougher, coarse cuts of meat, often stewed, can also be used to make meat puddings. Line a basin with suet pastry, made in the same way as suet pudding (see p. 274), leaving enough over to make a pastry lid. Dice the raw meat and toss it in seasoned flour. Put the meat into the lined basin with 4-6 tablespoons of stock or water. Cover with the pastry lid and foil or a pudding cloth. Boil or steam for 4 hours. Serve the pudding with extra gravy.

Steak and kidney, bacon and onion, and steak and pigeon breasts are all suitable for meat puddings.

MEAT PIES

Put the meat into a pie dish with stock, and cover with shortcrust or flaky pastry. The meat is diced and can be used raw or cooked. If raw filling is used cook the pie in the oven for 15 minutes at 230°C (450°F; mark 8) then reduce to 190°C (375°F; mark 5) for a further 1¾ hours. A pie containing cooked meat needs only 30 minutes at 230°C (450°F; mark 8).

BRAISING A JOINT

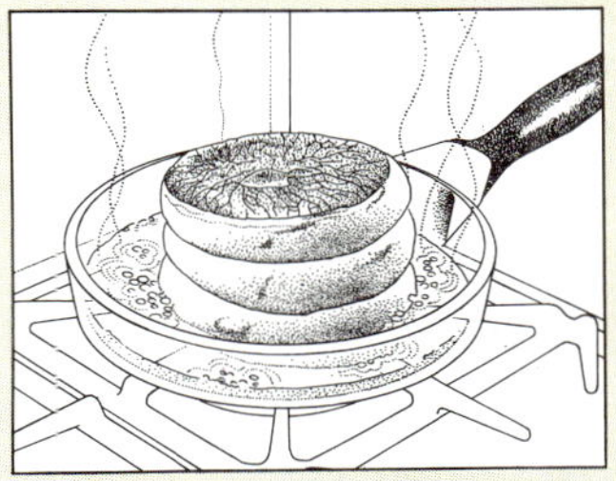

1. A combination of stewing, steaming and roasting, this method gives flavour and succulence to cheaper cuts of meat. First brown the joint all over in a little fat to seal in the juices.

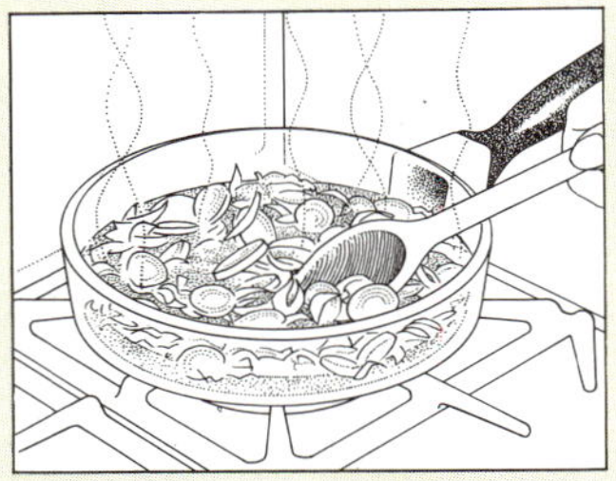

2. Remove the meat from the pan. Lightly fry a mixture of prepared and diced root vegetables in the remaining fat for about 5 minutes. Season them with salt and pepper and add a bouquet garni.

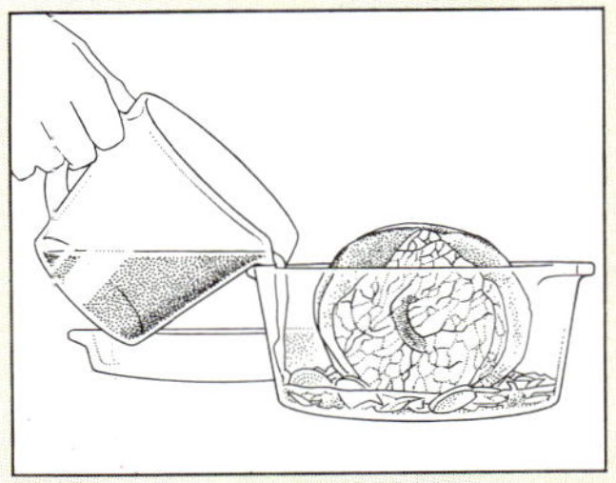

3. Remove the vegetables from the pan and put them into an oven-proof casserole. Place the meat on to the bed of vegetables and pour in enough stock to cover them. Put a lid on the casserole.

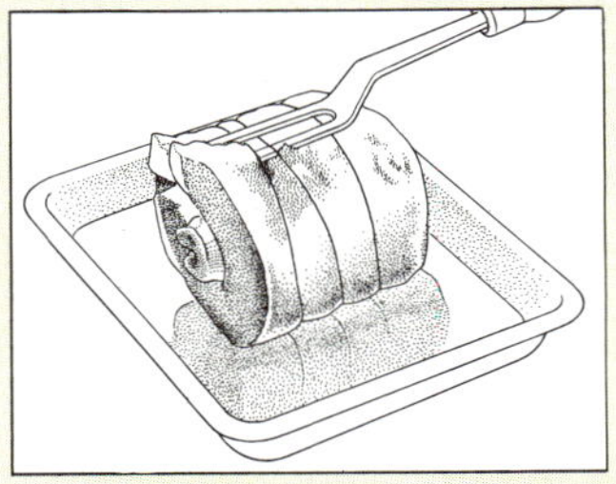

4. After cooking the meat and vegetables in the oven, remove the casserole and put the meat into a roasting tin with a little melted fat. Roast the joint for 30 minutes to brown and crisp the outside.

COOKING TIMES FOR POULTRY AND GAME

TYPE OF MEAT	WEIGHT	MEDIUM ROASTING	REGULO C	F	GAS
Turkey	6-14 lb. (3-6 kg.)	20 min. a lb., 20 min. over	190°	375°	5
	14-20 lb. (6-9 kg.)	30 min. a lb., 15 min. over	190°	375°	5
Chicken	1-1½ lb. (450-700 g.)	30 min.	190°	375°	5
	2-3 lb. (1-1.5 kg.)	1 hour	190°	375°	5
	4-12 lb. (2-5 kg.)	20 min. a lb., 20 min. over	190°	375°	5
Goose	8-18 lb. (4-8 kg.)	15 min. a lb., 15 min. over	190°	375°	5
Duck	3-6 lb. (1.5-3 kg.)	15 min. a lb., 15 min. over	200°	400°	6
Hen pheasant		¾-1 hour	190°	375°	5
Cock pheasant		1-1½ hours	190°	375°	5
Grouse		30-40 min.	190°	375°	5
Pigeon		15-20 min.	230°	450°	8
Hare	6-8 lb. (3-4 kg.)	1½-2 hours	190°	375°	5
Rabbit	2-2½ lb. (900-1 kg.)	1-1¼ hours	190°	375°	5
Venison		20 min. a lb., 20 min. over	190°	375°	5

ALL ABOUT FISH

The wide variety of fish available in Britain can be divided into four broad categories: white fish, which have the oil concentrated in the liver; oily fish, with the oil distributed throughout the flesh; freshwater fish; and shellfish. These types are all available fresh, and many can be bought frozen, canned, dried or smoked from the fishmonger or supermarket.

For an island people, the British consume comparatively little fish – a yearly average of 7 kg. (15 lb.) per person. This is surprising considering that most fish is no more expensive than meat and is very nutritious, providing more protein, weight for weight, than meat. Fish also contains vitamins and mineral salts. Oily fish and the livers of white fish, such as cod and halibut, are particularly rich in vitamin D, which aids growth and bone formation. White fish, such as cod, is good for anyone on a low-fat or slimming diet, as white flesh contains hardly any fat at all. It is not necessarily the most expensive fish which is most nutritious – herrings, for example, are cheaper than many others but are one of the best for food value. Freezing and canning does not make fish any less nutritious. Canned sardines are the richest-known source of fluorine, which is particularly good for children and pregnant women, as it strengthens bones and teeth.

• BUYING FISH

Many people prefer to buy fresh fish, when it is available, as it has a better flavour and texture than most frozen and canned varieties.

Fishmongers, supermarkets and delicatessens also sell a wide range of smoked fish, from kippers to cod roe and eels.

But rising costs and increased supplies of frozen fish have led to the closing of many small fishmongers' shops which previously supplied fresh fish.

FRESH FISH
Fish does not keep well and, ideally, should be eaten on the day it is bought. In fishing towns it is often possible to buy from the fishermen or at a quayside market. Apart from local catches, the widest variety of fresh fish is found in inland towns with large markets, such as Manchester.

The signs of good-quality, freshly caught fish are bright, full eyes, firm flesh, red gills, and a clean, sea-water smell. Fish sold whole should have slightly slimy skins, and if they have scales these should be plentiful. Dull, dry skin, sunken eyes, flesh that dents when it is touched and any smell of ammonia are signs of staleness.

Fresh fish will keep one day in a refrigerator, and white fish keeps slightly better than oily fish. Prices fluctuate because the catch varies from season to season, and bad weather can create shortages and high prices. Most fresh fish, such as cod, plaice and herrings, are available all the year round.

FROZEN FISH
Fish caught as far north as Greenland and Newfoundland is cleaned, gutted and deep-frozen on the trawler. Some is packeted at sea ready for the frozen-food market. Nearer catches are brought into port fresh, and are frozen and packeted in factories.

White fish, shellfish and smoked fish are sold frozen, but oily fish has not so far been successfully marketed in frozen packs.

It is difficult to judge the quality of frozen fish but, as much of it is frozen as soon as it is caught, it is often better quality than so-called fresh fish which may have been in transit for at least one day before it reaches the shops. Fillets of frozen white and smoked fish, like haddock and kippers, are sold in date-stamped vacuum packs.

Avoid damaged or mis-shapen

TURBOT
Firm with good flavour. Whole, fillets or steaks. Best Apr.-July

DOVER SOLE
Firm, with scaly skin. Delicate flavour. Sold whole. Best May-Feb.

LEMON SOLE
Less flavour than Dover sole. Sold whole. Best Dec.-Mar.

WITCH SOLE
Similar in flavour to lemon sole. Sold whole. Best Aug.-Apr.

SKATE
Only the bony, pink-fleshed 'wing' of skate is sold. Best Oct.-Apr.

BRILL
Similar to turbot. Sold whole or in steaks. Best Nov.-Mar.

PLAICE
Soft, and creamy flavoured, sold whole or filleted. Best Feb.-Apr.

HALIBUT
Firm, dry white flesh. A large fish, sold in steaks. Best Aug.-Apr.

FLAT WHITE FISH These are all sea fish with a low fat content and very white flesh. They can be bought whole or in fillets. Large flat fish such as turbot is usually cut into steaks and cutlets. When buying flat fish do not choose a large one because it will probably be old and have coarse flesh.

packets of frozen fish, since the texture will be impaired and it will be dry and stringy when cooked.

Frozen fish has the advantage of being ready to cook, having been cleaned, gutted and often coated with breadcrumbs, batter or a sauce before it is packed. It can also be stored for about a week to three months in the frozen-food compartment of a refrigerator, depending on the star-marking (see p. 222). Once thawed, fish should not be refrozen because of the danger from bacteria. Frozen fish can be cheaper than fresh fish because it is not subject to the same fluctuations in supply, and there is no storage problem.

CANNED FISH

Though the flavour of canned fish differs from that of fresh fish, it is an excellent product, equally nutritious, and a good store-cupboard standby. Oily fish, such as herrings, mackerel, and sardines, are used for canning, rather than white fish, and are usually preserved in oil or tomato sauce. Shellfish, roes of cod and herrings are usually canned in brine. Tuna and pink or red salmon are canned and processed in their own juices.

PRESERVED FISH

Kippers, smoked cod and smoked haddock are the commonest preserved types of fish and are available from most fishmongers and supermarkets. Smoked trout, mackerel, eels, salted herrings, smoked salmon and smoked cod roe, are also all widely available (see p. 250).

Salt has been used for preserving fish for many years because it inhibits the growth of harmful bacteria. But too much salt makes the fish unpalatable, so fish today is only lightly salted.

Salting can be combined with drying and this is the method used for cod and other white fish such as haddock which are first split open. Salted herrings are usually pickle-cured, which means they are plunged into barrels of brine and made airtight. This is how matjes herrings are prepared. Pickled herring pieces and roll-mops are marinated in liquor containing vinegar, sugar, salt and spices.

• WHITE FISH

In these fish the oil is concentrated in the liver, and the flesh is very white and lean. Most white fish eaten in Britain can be divided into flat fish, such as plaice and sole, and round fish, such as cod and haddock.

White fish is sold whole, filleted or cut into steaks and cutlets. Steaks from round fish are cut from between the middle of the body and the tail. Cutlets come from between the head and the middle of the body. Steaks and cutlets contain a small, circular bone – a section of the backbone – easily removed after cooking.

Most fishmongers will clean, gut, bone and cut up fish as the customer requires. However, it is quite possible to do this at home (see p. 252) when any dark, tough skin is also removed.

White fish usually has less flavour than oily fish, but it is easily digested.

Small, young fish usually have a better flavour and texture than large ones, and it is better to buy a thick slice from a small fish than a thin slice from a large one.

In addition to those illustrated, the following white fish can also be bought fresh from a fishmonger. They are less common varieties, but are generally cheaper.

Coley Also called saithe, coley is an inexpensive fish of the cod family. Its greyish, coarse flesh looks unattractive raw, but when it is cooked, coley turns white and can be used in the same way as cod or haddock. It is available all the year round.

Dab Rather like small plaice, but with paler spots and rougher scales, dab is usually cooked whole. It can be fried, grilled or steamed. Dab is at its best from April to September.

Flounder This is also a member of the plaice family and has a light, brown-mottled top skin, and a creamy-white underside. Flounder is best fried and served with tartare sauce (see p. 269). It is available in September.

Red fish Despite its name, red fish is a round white fish, sometimes called ocean perch or soldier. It usually weighs about $2\frac{1}{2}$ kg. ($5\frac{1}{2}$ lb.) and is sold whole or in fillets. The flesh is firm and pinky-red with a good flavour. Serve it poached or baked. Look for red fish in the shops in late summer and autumn.

Rock salmon This is one of the names fishmongers use for several kinds of white fish such as cat fish, rock eel or dog fish. It is usually sold skinned and has firm, pink flesh. Use rock salmon in fish stews and pies.

GREY MULLET
Scaly, grey estuary fish with firm, coarse flesh. Best July - Feb.

COD
The flesh forms large flakes, has little flavour. Best July - Feb.

ROE
Hard cod roe is sold fresh, or boiled and cut into portions to fry

CONGER EEL
Sea eel with slightly tough, pinkish flesh. In season Mar. - Oct.

WHITING
Similar to cod. Sold whole. Best Nov. - Mar.

BASS
Also called dace or perch. Pink flesh. In season May - Aug.

SEA BREAM
Bony fish with coarse, pink-tinged flesh. Filleted. Best June - Dec.

HADDOCK
White, flaky flesh, similar to cod but firmer. Best Nov. - Feb.

HAKE
Almost boneless fish with tender, flaky flesh. Best July - Mar.

ROUND WHITE FISH *These are also salt-water fish, although grey mullet is found in estuaries rather than in the sea, like cod and haddock. Small, round fish such as whiting are sold whole, but large ones like cod and haddock are usually sold in cutlets, steaks or fillets. Small cod, called codling, are sometimes sold whole.*

FLAT-FISH FILLET

STEAK   **ROUND-FISH FILLET**

CUTS OF FISH *Flat fillets can be cut in half, round ones into portions.*

• OILY FISH

Most of the oily fish caught at sea belong to the herring family. This includes herrings, sprats, anchovies, sardines and pilchards. In addition, there are mackerel, smelt and red mullet. The oil content of all these fish is spread throughout the flesh, but varies with the seasons. Oily fish are rich and less digestible than white fish, but very nutritious. The fish are usually sold whole, and the fishmonger will remove the heads and gut them if required. Oily fish are often very bony, but can be filleted at home before cooking (see p. 252).

Some fish, such as anchovies, sardines, pilchards and brisling, are more easily available canned than fresh. They are all similar to herrings, but smaller. Anchovies are mostly caught in the Mediterranean and are filleted, salted and canned in Italy or Spain. They are 7-10 cm. (3-4 in.) long, with a very strong, salty flavour.

Pilchards are 15-23 cm. (6-9 in.) long and, although most of them are caught off the coasts of Devon and Cornwall, they are not usually available fresh, because they deteriorate quickly. They are canned in brine or tomato sauce.

Sardines are 10-15 cm. (4-6 in.) long and are the young of pilchards. Most of them come into Britain, already canned in oil or tomato sauce, from France and Portugal. However, fresh sardines are becoming more popular, and are imported from France from March to September.

Brislings are young sprats, about the same size as sardines, sold canned in oil or tomato sauce.

• SMOKED FISH

Some white fish, such as haddock and cod, are sold smoked as well as fresh, but it is mainly oily fish which are prepared in this way. Sometimes the fish, which may be whole or boned, are lightly salted or soaked in brine first and smoked, either cold or hot.

Cold-smoked fish are hung some distance from smoking wood chips, ensuring that they never reach more than 30°C (86°F).

If fish are properly cold-smoked, they take on a brown colour naturally.

A quicker and cheaper method used by some curers is to dye fish beforehand, to give them the appearance of long smoking. This applies particularly to kippers and white-fish fillets. Genuine Arbroath 'smokies' (haddock) and Manx kippers (herring) are not dyed but smoked over oak chips. Other fish which are cold-smoked include salmon, mackerel, whiting and coley.

If they are to be hot-smoked, the fish are hung over smouldering wood chips or sawdust at a temperature of 66-93°C (150-200°F). By this method the fish are wholly or partly cooked, and have a smokier flavour than cold-smoked fish. Fish that are usually hot-smoked include bloaters, sprats, mackerel, trout, eel and oysters, mussels and cod roe. Buckling are hot-smoked herrings cured for a longer period than kippers or bloaters.

BUYING SMOKED FISH

In general, cold-smoked fish are sold by fishmongers, and hot-smoked varieties in delicatessens. Supermarkets often sell both kinds whole, as well as vacuum packs of smoked and filleted haddock and kippers, and smoked shellfish and roes in jars and cans.

Hot-smoked fish do not keep well, and are best eaten on the day they are bought. Fish that have been cold-smoked will keep for up to a week in a refrigerator. Vacuum packs may be stamped with the date by which they should be eaten, but once opened treat as smoked fish bought loose.

Look carefully at smoked fish before buying, because they can go mouldy. The flesh should be firm and dry, the skin glossy and the smell wholesome. Most of the cold-smoked fish can be fried, grilled or poached. Smoked haddock have several forms. They can be golden cutlets (double fillets of haddock or whiting); Finnan haddock (whole fish named after a village near Aberdeen); Glasgow pales (small, split haddocks); or Arbroath 'smokies'.

Smoked salmon and mackerel and some of the hot-smoked varieties are served cold, without further cooking.

• SHELLFISH

There are two groups of shellfish: softer-shelled crustaceans, such as crabs, lobsters and prawns; and hard-shelled molluscs, such as oysters, mussels, winkles and whelks.

BUYING SHELLFISH

Depending on type, shellfish can be bought raw or cooked, in or out of the

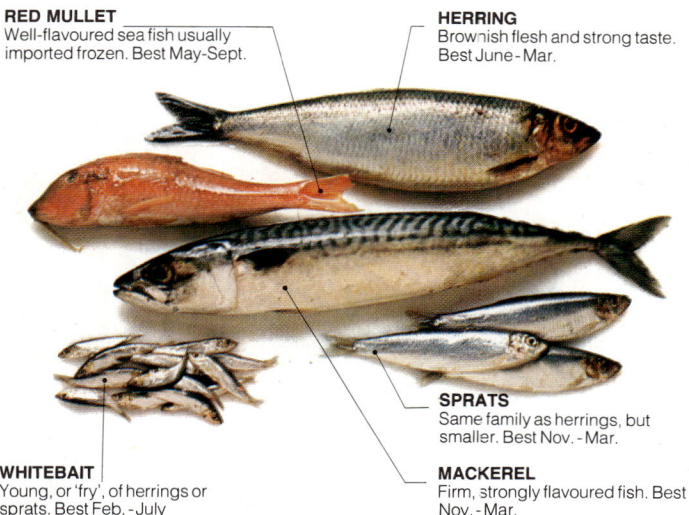

RED MULLET
Well-flavoured sea fish usually imported frozen. Best May-Sept.

HERRING
Brownish flesh and strong taste. Best June-Mar.

SPRATS
Same family as herrings, but smaller. Best Nov.-Mar.

WHITEBAIT
Young, or 'fry', of herrings or sprats. Best Feb.-July

MACKEREL
Firm, strongly flavoured fish. Best Nov.-Mar.

OILY FISH Most of the oily fish live in the sea, although some freshwater fish are also oily. The skin should look bright and the eyes prominent.

BUCKLING
Whole smoked herrings which need no further cooking

SMOKED MACKEREL
Smoked in winter or spring and sold whole, in fillets or canned

HADDOCK
Finnan haddock smoked on the bone are best

SMOKED SALMON
Salted and marinated in rum and other flavourings before smoking

SMOKED COD ROE
Hard cod roes are brined and smoked a pinkish brown

KIPPER
Herring that has been split open, gutted, and salted before smoking

SMOKED EEL
Common, freshwater eels are sold smoked, skinned and filleted

SMOKED TROUT
Gutted rainbow trout are smoked and sold whole or in fillets

BLOATER
Whole herrings only lightly smoked. They do not keep well

COD
Similar to smoked haddock, fillets are dyed yellow

SMOKED FISH The main reason for smoking fish today is to give it additional flavour rather than to preserve it. Smoked herrings and white fish, such as cod and haddock, are fairly cheap, but salmon, eel and trout are expensive.

shell, frozen, and in cans and jars. Shellfish sold loose, either in or out of the shells, should be available from good fishmongers. Preserved shellfish, either frozen or canned, are sold in most supermarkets.

Shellfish decompose quickly, and molluscs can harbour harmful bacteria: buy them fresh and use them quickly. Thorough cooking eliminates the bacteria. All shellfish should look clean and fresh, and the mollusc shells should be tightly closed when uncooked. Discard open ones.

Lobsters are often considered the finest-flavoured shellfish. They are dark blue when alive, but turn deep red when boiled. Freshly cooked lobsters should have springy tails and deep coral-red shells, with no trace of white which is a sign of age. They vary from 325 g. - 1.5 kg. (¾ - 3 lb.) in weight, and a 450 - 900 g. (1 - 2 lb.) lobster is best. The male is a brighter colour with larger claws. The female,

known as the hen, has a broader tail and more tender flesh.

Crayfish weigh 1.8 - 2.7 kg. (4 - 6 lb.) and do not have large claws like a lobster. Most of the meat, which is fairly coarse, comes from the tail. Crayfish are sold whole, live or cooked, and the tails are sold frozen.

True scampi are caught only in the Bay of Naples, and shellfish sold under this name in Britain are usually Dublin Bay prawns. Most of them come from Scotland, rather than Ireland. They are the largest British prawns – about 100 mm. (4 in.) long – and are sold cooked, either shelled or unshelled, and frozen.

Oysters, usually eaten raw, are the most expensive of the molluscs. They are usually graded according to size and sold by the dozen. Native British oysters come from Colchester, Whitstable and Helford and these are in season from September to April. Imported ones, known as Portuguese

oysters (although they come from various countries), are available all the year round.

• FRESHWATER FISH

Although most freshwater fish have some of the fat distributed throughout the body they are usually classified as white fish. These fish are usually only available in season, and are sometimes called game fish. Some freshwater fish, such as the carp family and trout, live permanently in lakes and rivers. Rainbow trout are the most easily available freshwater fish, and are reared on fish farms.

Other game fish live in fresh water for only part of their lives. Salmon, for instance, hatch in rivers, then migrate to the sea. They return to fresh water to spawn. Their young are called grilse.

Some freshwater fish – trout and salmon, in particular – are readily available fresh from fishmongers.

Carp, pike and perch are caught mainly by amateur anglers.

In addition to rainbow trout, there are brown river trout, and sea or salmon trout. River trout have a spotted skin and are darker than rainbow trout. Superior in flavour and texture to rainbow trout, they are available from March to September and, although in short supply, are worth buying when they are in the shops. Salmon trout, as the name implies, are similar to salmon but the flesh is less rich and firm, and not such a deep colour as that of true salmon. They weigh 450 g. - 1.5 kg. (1 - 4 lb.) and are in season from March to August.

Salmon have oily, red flesh with a strong flavour. Fresh salmon, of which Scottish are considered the finest, are at their best in June and July. Chilled salmon are imported from Canada, Japan and Norway. Salmon are cheaper if bought whole. They can also be bought canned.

Carp are round, greenish-brown fish which usually weigh from 1 - 4 kg. (2 - 9 lb.), although some can be as large as 14 kg. (30 lb.). Carp have a rather coarse texture and those caught in lakes and rivers tend to have a muddy taste. Soak the fish in salted water for about three hours to remove this.

Pike are long fish with white, well-flavoured flesh, at their best when they weigh about 2 kg. (4 lb.). Large fish tend to be coarse and dry. Perch are round fish, about 300 mm. (12 in.) long, with bright mottled skin and hard scales. Carp, pike and perch are all in season from mid-June to mid-March.

Smelt are an almost transparent, delicately coloured and flavoured fish 125 - 250 mm. (5 - 10 in.) long. Like salmon, they are salt-water fish that spawn and are caught in rivers. The season is January to March. Smelt are sold prepared and packed in boxes.

SCALLOP
Sold in the open shell, or shelled and frozen. Best Sept. - Mar.

LOBSTER
Sold fresh in the shell, live or cooked. Best Apr. - Aug.

DUBLIN BAY PRAWNS
Also called scampi. Sold cooked or frozen. Best May - Nov.

PRAWNS
Boiled before being sold, shelled or unshelled. Best June - Aug.

SHRIMPS
Like small, pinkish-brown prawns. Sold fresh in their shells

COCKLES
Tiny molluscs, usually cooked and shelled. Best Sept. - Apr.

CRAB
Boiled and sold fresh in the shell. Best May - Oct.

OYSTER
When sold live, the shell should be closed. In season Sept. - Apr.

CRAYFISH
Rather like lobster but flesh is coarser. In season Apr. - Sept.

WHELKS
Tough, greyish molluscs, cooked and shelled. Best Sept. - Feb.

WINKLES
Sold cooked in the shells. Best Oct. - May

MUSSELS
Like oysters, mussels are sold live in the shell. In season Sept. - Mar.

CLAM
Sold live in the shell. Can be eaten raw or cooked. Best Sept. - Nov.

SALMON
Sold whole, in pieces or cutlets. In season Feb. - Sept.

SALMON TROUT
Pink-fleshed trout, like young salmon. Season Mar. - Aug.

RAINBOW TROUT
White-fleshed trout available, fresh or frozen, all year round

SHELLFISH They are not so plentiful now as a few years ago and most are expensive. When fresh, all shellfish should look clean and shiny and mollusc shells should be closed, or close rapidly if the shell is tapped.

FRESHWATER FISH These are the best-known ones. Carp and perch are more popular on the Continent where they are bred for the table. A few are imported.

• HOW TO PREPARE FISH

Large, round fish are sold in fillets and steaks. Other fish may need to be cleaned, skinned and boned at home, though the fishmonger will gut them and remove the heads if required.

CLEANING

To clean round fish, such as herrings, first remove the loose scales. Hold the fish by the tail and scrape a knife along the back from tail to head. Rinse the fish continually.

To remove the entrails from round fish, slit the belly, with a sharp knife or kitchen scissors, from just below the head to halfway along the body. Discard fish entrails. Herring roes can be left in the fish or removed to cook separately. Wash out the inside of the fish and rub with salt to remove any black skin. The head can be left on, or cut off just below the gills. Trim away the fins and gills and cut off the tail.

Heads and tails can be boiled up to make stock for fish soup or the basis for a sauce to serve with the fish.

Red mullet is cleaned by cutting a slit under the gills and squeezing out the entrails. Wash and dry.

Small, round fish, such as sprats and smelt, need little preparation. Wipe the fish with a damp cloth and cut off the head. Gently squeeze out the entrails and wash and dry. The tail can be left on.

With flat fish, such as sole and plaice, first cut off the fins on both sides and remove the gills. Cut open on the dark-skinned side, just below the head, and scrape out the entrails.

Wash the fish in cold water. If pre-ferred, remove the head and tail also.

To clean fish steaks, fillets and cutlets, simply wash them in cold water and dry with kitchen paper.

SKINNING

Round fish are usually cooked with the skin on, but can be skinned.

To skin haddock, whiting or other whole, small, round fish, loosen the skin on one side of the head with a sharp knife. Dip fingers in salt and grip the skin firmly, drawing it down to the tail. Repeat on the other side.

The rough, dark skin of whole flat fish, such as sole, is usually removed before cooking. But the white skin can be left on. To remove the skin, lay the fish with the dark side uppermost and make a cut across the tail. Press a thumb between the skin and flesh and run it round the sides of the fish to loosen the skin. Dip fingers in salt, hold the head with one hand, pressing the thumb down on the backbone to prevent the flesh from coming away with the skin. Strip off the skin, from tail to head, with the other hand.

The dark skin can be removed from fillets of round or flat fish by putting the fish dark-side down on a board and inserting a sharp knife between the skin and the flesh, starting at the tail. Carefully saw off the flesh.

FILLETING

Although fillets of flat fish and large, round fish are prepared by fishmongers, it can be cheaper to buy the fish whole and fillet them at home.

To fillet a large, round fish, such as haddock, after cleaning, remove the head then cut along the centre of the back, down to the bone, with a sharp knife. Remove the first fillet from the bones, working from head to tail and cut it off at the tail. Gently ease out the backbone and cut the tail from the other fillet.

Plaice and sole are the flat fish most often bought whole, and can be filleted to make four pieces. Put the fish on a board and run a sharp knife down the backbone. Make a semi-circular cut just below the head and with short, sharp strokes remove the first fillet from the side nearest to you, cutting it off at the tail. Turn the fish round to cut off the second fillet from tail to head. Turn the fish over and remove the remaining two fillets.

BONING

Herrings and mackerel are often boned before cooking. Before boning, remove the head, tail and entrails. Slit the fish on the underside and spread it flat on a board, cut side down. Press lightly down the entire length of the backbone to loosen it.

Turn the fish over and ease away the backbone with the tip of a knife, removing as many small bones as possible at the same time. The fish can be folded back into shape or cut into two.

SHELLFISH

Most shellfish are bought boiled and sometimes shelled, ready to eat. The exceptions are oysters and mussels, which must be alive if in the shell.

Discard any mussels or oysters with broken or opened shells, and scrub the remainder with a stiff brush to remove grit. Mussels are cooked unopened, oysters usually eaten raw.

Boiled lobsters and crabs can be bought with the flesh removed from the shells – 'dressed' – but it is quite easy to 'dress' a crab at home. Use the handle of a heavy knife to crack

---

CLEANING A ROUND FISH

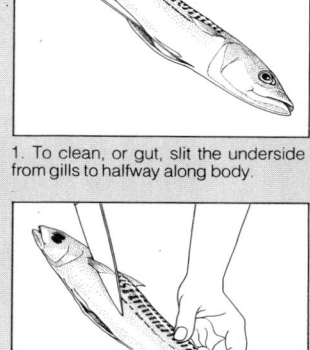

1. To clean, or gut, slit the underside from gills to halfway along body.

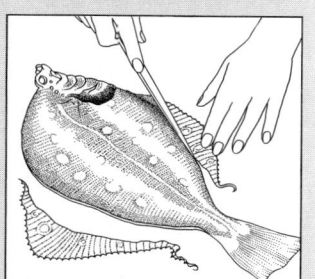

2. After scraping out the entrails, cut off the gills and fins on either side.

CLEANING A FLAT FISH

1. Make a slit on the dark side, behind the head, and scrape out the entrails.

2. Wash the fish before cutting off the fins close to the body on each side.

FILLETING A ROUND FISH

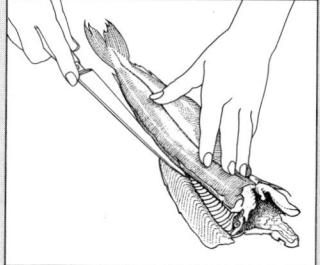

1. First cut off the head, then cut along the backbone, from head to tail.

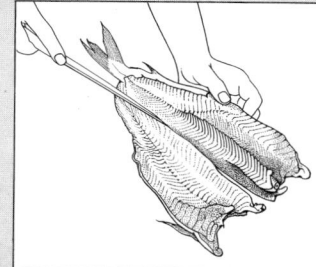

2. With the blade at an angle to the backbone, cut the first fillet off the bone.

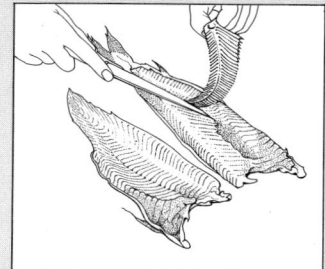

3. Insert the knife point under the bone and gently ease it away from the flesh.

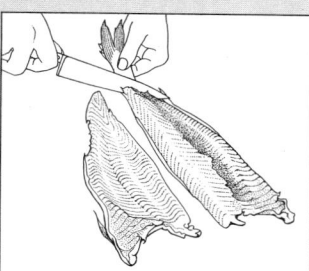

4. Cut off the tail from the remaining fillet. Divide large ones into portions.

the crab's shell. Discard the stomach sac behind the head, and the grey, feathery gills. Remove the legs and pull the round body part away from the rest of the shell. Crack and scoop out the white meat from the large claws and the body, and remove the brown meat from the outer shell.

Shrimps and prawns can be bought ready-shelled, but are less expensive unshelled.

• HOW TO COOK FISH

Whether fish are whole, filleted or in steaks or cutlets, they can be fried, grilled, poached or baked. Do not overcook fish or it will be tough and tasteless. Fish is cooked when the flesh separates easily from the bones. Test for this by gently pressing the thickest part of the fish. The appearance of a white, curd-like substance indicates that white fish is cooked.

BAKING

Bake small, whole fish and fillets, steaks or cutlets, including cod, turbot, halibut and salmon. The prepared fish can be stuffed first, put into a buttered, fireproof dish, and then seasoned with lemon juice, salt and pepper, and brushed with melted butter. Cover with foil or greaseproof paper and bake in the centre of the oven, pre-heated to 180°C (350°F; mark 4). Allow 10-20 minutes for fillets, 20 minutes for steaks and 25-30 minutes for small, whole fish.

SHALLOW-FRYING

Particularly suitable for fillets, steaks and small, whole fish, including sole, plaice, dabs, bass, bream, cod, haddock, mackerel, herrings and trout.

Coat the fish with seasoned flour, or in beaten egg and then in dry breadcrumbs. Heat enough fat to cover the base of a frying pan. The fat can be cooking oil, or butter with oil added to prevent the fat from discolouring. Put the fish into the hot fat and cook over a moderate heat until brown on the underside. Turn it carefully with a fish slice and cook on the other side. Allow approximately 5 minutes each side.

DEEP-FAT FRYING

This method is most suitable for fillets coated with egg and breadcrumbs, or batter (see pp. 268-9), which will protect the fish from the intense heat, and for small, whole fish such as sprats, fresh sardines and whitebait.

A pan 10-10.5 cm. (4-4½ in.) deep with a wire frying basket fitted inside is best. Half fill the pan with dripping, lard or oil, and heat. Test that the fat is hot enough by dropping in a 25 mm. (1 in.) cube of bread, which should turn brown in 60 seconds. Lower the fish into the fat – egg and crumbed pieces should be put into the wire basket, but battered fish goes straight into the pan. The fish is cooked when the outside is golden-brown, which should take 5-10 minutes.

GRILLING

Most fish, whole, filleted, or in steaks or cutlets, can be cooked by this quick method. Put whole fish, such as herrings, on to the greased grid of the grill pan but remove the grid for fillets, steaks and cutlets. Put them into the greased pan so that they do not break when turned over or taken out of the pan.

Oily fish need no additional fat, but white fish should be brushed with melted butter and basted.

To keep kippers moist, stand them in a pan of boiling water for 2 minutes, then drain and grill for 5 minutes.

Score plump, whole herrings or mackerel with three or four diagonal cuts on each side so that the heat can penetrate. Cook thin fillets and steaks on one side only, but turn thicker pieces and whole fish once. Grill the fish under a moderate heat. Thin fillets take 4-5 minutes, thick pieces and whole fish 10-15 minutes.

POACHING

This method is good for white fish (whole or in pieces), salmon, trout, smoked haddock and kippers.

The fish can be poached either on top of the cooker or in a covered casserole at 180°C (350°F; mark 4).

Heat salted water, fish stock or milk, to which parsley, onion, mushroom stalks or lemon juice have been added, until it is simmering. Put in the fish and simmer for 8-10 minutes. Use the liquid to make a sauce.

STEAMING

Fillets of white fish such as turbot, halibut, plaice and sole are best for cooking by this method.

Dot the fish with small pieces of butter and put it in the perforated compartment of a steamer. Put the steamer over a pan of boiling water and cook for 10-15 minutes.

Thin fillets can be steamed between two buttered plates, or wrapped in foil and put on a plate over boiling water. The sealed foil contains the fish juices which can be used for sauce.

ACCOMPANIMENTS TO FISH

Poached, steamed, baked and sometimes fried fish are often served with a hot sauce (see p. 269).

Fried or grilled white fish, shellfish and cold fish such as salmon, can be served with a cold sauce based on mayonnaise (see p. 279). Chives, parsley, gherkins and capers are added to mayonnaise to make tartare sauce, which is often served with grilled or fried white fish.

Some sauces are particularly associated with one type of fish, such as mustard sauce with herrings and gooseberry sauce with mackerel.

Stuffing is used inside whole fish, such as herrings; between two fillets, rolled inside thin fillets, or in the centre of a fish steak.

The fish is grilled or baked, and the stuffing can be a mixture of breadcrumbs, melted butter, lemon juice, parsley and seasonings bound with milk or a beaten egg. Flavourings such as chopped onions, herbs, mushrooms or chopped shellfish can be added.

FILLETING A FLAT FISH

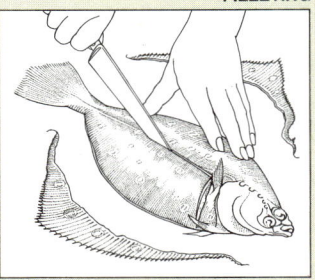

1. Lay fish, with the fins off, dark side up and cut down the backbone.

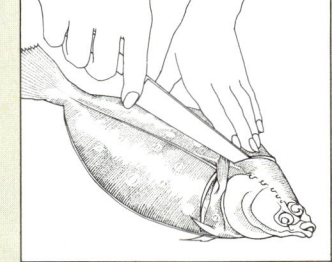

2. Make a semi-circular cut behind the head, through half thickness of fish.

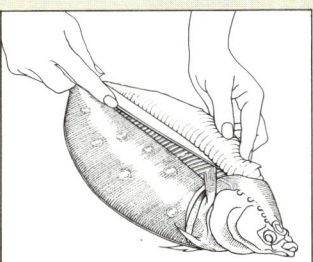

3. With the knife at an angle, cut off the first fillet with short, sharp strokes.

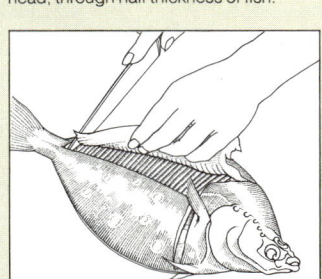

4. Cut off fillet at tail. Remove second fillet. Repeat on the other side.

BONING A HERRING

1. Cut off the head, tail and fins and slit the fish open along the belly.

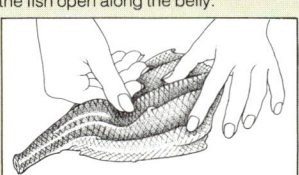

2. Flatten out the fish and firmly press along the length of the backbone.

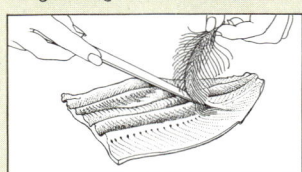

3. Start at the head end and, with the knife point, ease out the backbone.

ALL ABOUT FRUIT AND VEGETABLES

Most of the fresh vegetables and much of the fruit sold in Britain are home-produced. These are supplemented by imported produce and the numerous frozen, canned and dried varieties, which means there is a wide choice all the year round.

Vegetables and fruit are an essential part of a balanced diet, providing vitamins, minerals, some carbohydrate and protein, as well as roughage. Preserved vegetables and fruit lose no more of their valuable nutrients than cooked fresh produce. However, overcooking and keeping vegetables warm after they have been cooked does result in loss of food value. Many fresh vegetables and fruit must now conform to EEC grading regulations. They are given a grade from 1 to 3, depending on quality, and this must be clearly marked – on the plastic bag if they are prepacked and on a display ticket if sold loose.

• BUYING VEGETABLES

The flavour of really fresh vegetables is much better than frozen or canned. But preserved vegetables are always better than stale and limp produce from the greengrocer.

Choose medium-sized vegetables as a rule, since small ones can be flavourless and very large ones tend to be coarse.

Although they look attractive and are cleaner to handle, pre-packed fresh vegetables cost more and do not keep so well as those sold loose. Some dirt on root vegetables and potatoes helps to keep them fresh.

Use green vegetables as soon as possible, to retain the maximum flavour and vitamin C. Most root vegetables will keep for at least two to three weeks, and onions and potatoes for much longer, so they are worth buying in bulk.

FROZEN VEGETABLES

Supermarkets stock a wide variety of frozen vegetables in small packs containing from one to four servings. Shops specialising in frozen foods stock large packs of the more popular vegetables, such as peas, beans and broccoli, for storing in a home freezer.

When buying frozen vegetables, as with all frozen food, make sure the pack is in good condition.

Fresh vegetables can be frozen at home to store in a freezer (see p. 224).

CANNED AND BOTTLED VEGETABLES

Special varieties of a number of vegetables, including peas, broad and green beans, potatoes, carrots, tomatoes and celery, are grown for canning and freezing. The vegetables are gathered while in prime condition, blanched (see p. 225) and canned in salted water, sometimes with added colouring or other preservatives.

Canned vegetables should keep up to two years in a larder or store cupboard, provided the tins are clean and free from dents.

DEHYDRATED VEGETABLES

Some vegetables, such as carrots, potatoes, turnips, onions, mushrooms, celery and peppers, are sold dried and sometimes flaked in packets and are useful for the store cupboard as they keep indefinitely. Dried peas and beans are also popular.

Dried vegetables usually have to be soaked to increase their volume before being used. Instructions for reconstituting them should be on the packet.

HOW TO COOK VEGETABLES

Fresh, young vegetables are best simply boiled or lightly fried to retain and enhance their natural flavour.

It is best to undercook vegetables slightly rather than overcook them.

Whichever cooking method is used, fresh vegetables should be washed thoroughly.

Scrape young root vegetables with a sharp knife and peel older ones. The most nutritious part of these vegetables, and also of potatoes and onions, is just below the skin; so only a thin layer should be removed.

The following cooking methods are most frequently used for vegetables.

Baking Potatoes are cooked in their skins but onions and parsnips are peeled. Wash them first and brush with melted butter (although this is not essential for potatoes). Put into a moderate oven (180°C, 350°F; mark 4) and cook until they are tender.

Boiling There should be sufficient water just to cover the vegetables. Add about ½ teaspoon of salt to each 300 ml. (½ pint) of water.

Put root vegetables and potatoes into cold water and bring them to the boil. Add green vegetables to boiling water and then return to the boil.

For all types of vegetables, after they have reached boiling point, reduce the heat and simmer until they are tender but still firm.

Braising Fry the vegetables in butter for 2-3 minutes, before adding 150-300 ml. (¼-½ pint) of stock for each 450 g. (1 lb.) of vegetables. Season, cover the pan and simmer gently until the vegetables are cooked. Root vegetables, whole onions and celery hearts are cooked by this method.

Frying Tender vegetables, such as courgettes, mushrooms and aubergines, and also sliced onions, can be shallow-fried in butter until lightly browned. Par-boiled (see p. 283) potatoes, carrots, green beans and most other vegetables can also be cooked in this way.

Deep-frying A suitable method for cooking raw vegetables such as potatoes. Par-boiled cauliflower florets, onion rings and diced marrow, can be dipped in batter (see p. 269) and deep-fried.

Roasting Roots and tubers, such as carrots, parsnips and potatoes, are often cooked in the fat round a joint of meat. Put the prepared whole or halved vegetables in hot fat and cook them at 220°C (425°F; mark 7) for about 1 hour. A dusting of flour gives them a crisp finish.

Roasting time can be reduced if the vegetables are par-boiled for 10 minutes first.

Steaming Most vegetables can be steamed. Cut large root vegetables into small pieces.

Put the prepared vegetables into a steamer or a colander over a pan of boiling water. Sprinkle them with salt, cover with a tightly fitting lid and steam until tender.

• BUYING FRUIT

Most fresh fruit is expensive because it has a short season, or is imported. Fruit will not keep long and it is more economical to buy good-quality, slightly under-ripe fruit.

One exception is soft fruit in season. This may be inexpensive because it is fully ripe and must be sold quickly.

Appearance is not always a certain guide to the quality of fruit. But, in general, the skins should be smooth and unblemished and the fruit firm.

FROZEN FRUIT

Soft fruits – strawberries and raspberries in particular – are grown for the frozen-food market. The fruit is picked when it is in prime condition, and is frozen in sugar or sugar-syrup. Apples, pineapples and many other fruits are also frozen.

Frozen fruit is more expensive than canned, but the flavour and texture are nearer to that of fresh fruit. It should be thawed slowly, in a refrigerator, to avoid mushiness.

CANNED AND BOTTLED FRUIT

Foreign-grown fruits, such as peaches and pineapples, are cheaper canned than fresh, although the flavour is not usually so good. Home-produced plums, apples, pears and cherries are also sold canned. Fruit is usually canned in heavy syrup and is best used within two years of purchase. The same legal requirements apply to fruit as to other canned foods (see p. 219).

Commercially bottled fruit, such as peaches, apricots and cherries, look attractive but they are expensive, especially when brandy or liqueurs have been added.

Canned and bottled fruit are equal in food value and both are a good source of vitamins.

VACUUM-PACKS

Home-grown fruit, such as rhubarb and gooseberries, as well as some vegetables, are sold ready to use, sealed in vacuum packs. These keep well out of a refrigerator – up to three months if the seal is unbroken. The texture and flavour is like that of frozen produce.

DRIED FRUIT

Dried fruit, such as currants, raisins, sultanas, prunes, apricots and apples. is sold ready for use in cakes and puddings. It can be bought ready-washed in packets or loose, in which case it needs to be washed thoroughly in cold water. Spread the washed fruit on kitchen paper to dry.

Dried fruits are a good source of minerals and vitamins (especially vitamin B) and provide roughage.

Raisins are available either small and seedless, large with the seeds removed, or large with seeds. Removing the seeds is tedious, but these large raisins often have the best flavour. Dried fruit to be cooked in cakes and puddings does not need to be soaked. But when larger fruit, such as prunes, peaches, apricots and apples, are to be stewed, soak them overnight in cold water. Stew the fruit in this water with sugar and a piece of lemon peel.

Dessert dates are sold loose and in boxes. They are available only from October to February. Other dates are sold stoned in solid packs for cooking, and are in the shops all the year round. Dried figs are sold in similar packs.

COOKING AND PRESERVING FRUIT

Fruit is most nutritious eaten raw, but very little goodness is lost if it is stewed and the cooking liquid eaten with it. Use puréed, stewed or canned fruit to make cold soufflés, mousses and ice cream.

Raw or tinned fruit can be combined with sponge mixtures or pastry to make a variety of baked or steamed puddings, pies and tarts.

• MAKING JAM

Fruit for jam should be firm though not under-ripe. Setting depends on pectin, which is not present in over-ripe fruit. Pectin also improves the colour and flavour of the jam, and prevents the sugar from crystallising. Apples, gooseberries, damsons and blackcurrants are rich in pectin and acid; plums, greengages, apricots and raspberries contain less, and strawberries, blackberries and cherries lack pectin and acid. To improve the setting quality of fruit lacking pectin and acid, add the juice of 1-3 lemons,

or 1-2 teaspoons citric or tartaric acid (see chart), to each 4-6 lb. of fruit, or use a commercially bottled pectin, following the manufacturer's instructions.

Use a thick-based aluminium or stainless-steel pan for making jam. Wash the prepared fruit (see chart for quantities), put it into the pan with water and simmer gently until soft – 15-30 minutes. Remove from the heat and stir in the sugar. Boil the fruit and sugar rapidly until it reaches setting point, which can take 3-20 minutes, depending on the type of fruit.

A cooking thermometer is the most accurate means of testing the setting temperature – 105°C (221°F). Alternatively, put a teaspoon of jam on a cold saucer and allow to cool. If setting point has been reached, the surface of the jam should wrinkle when a spoon is pushed across it.

Pot the jam in clean, warmed jars, cover with a waxed disc and then with cellophane. Jam should keep at least six months.

• BOTTLING FRUIT

All types of fruit can be preserved if sterilised and sealed in airtight jars. It will then keep for up to a year. The fruit should be of good quality, fully ripe but not mushy.

Oven baking and pressure cooking are the simplest of the many bottling methods. Special jars are sold for bottling fruit. Prepare the fruit according to type, slicing apples, pears and peaches, for example, but leaving plums and cherries whole. Pack the fruit closely in the jars, which should be perfectly clean. Soak the rubber sealing rings in warm water and dip them into boiling water just before using them.

To oven-bake the fruit, make a syrup with water and sugar – 125-225 g. (4-8 oz.) to 600 ml. (1 pint) of

water, depending on taste – boiled for 2-3 minutes. Pack the fruit into the jars, and stand them on a baking tray lined with four thicknesses of newspaper. Fill the jars with boiling syrup to within 2.5 cm. (1 in.) of the tops. Put on the rings and lids and stand the jars on the shelf below the centre of the oven, set at 150°C (300°F; mark 2), for 30-50 minutes (60-80 minutes for pears and tomatoes). These times are for jars holding 450 g. -1.8 kg. (1-4 lb.) of fruit. Remove the jars from the oven, put on the screw bands at once and tighten them. Leave the jars for 24 hours, test the seals and store.

To cook bottled fruit in a pressure cooker, pack it into warm jars and pour boiling syrup over the fruit to within 2.5 cm. of the top. Put on the

tops, loosening screw bands a quarter turn. Put 2.5 cm. depth of water into the pressure cooker, with 1 tablespoon of vinegar to prevent the pan from staining. Bring the water to the boil before putting in the jars. Stand them on the trivet in the bottom of the pressure cooker so that they are not touching each other, or the sides of the pan. Put on the lid and raise to 5 lb. pressure in 5-10 minutes. Close the vent immediately steam begins to escape. Most fruit needs only 1 minute cooking at pressure, but peaches and pineapples take 3-4 minutes and tomatoes 5 minutes. Remove the cooker from the heat and cool for at least 10 minutes before opening. Remove the jars, tighten screw bands and leave to get cold.

QUANTITIES FOR MAKING JAM
Commercial pectin can be used, following the manufacturer's instructions.

FRUIT	SUGAR	SETTING AGENT	WATER	APPROXIMATE YIELD
Blackberries, 2.7 k. (6 lb.)	2.7 k. (6 lb.)	Juice 2 lemons or 2 level teaspoons tartaric acid	150 ml. (¼ pint)	4.5 k. (10 lb.)
Blackberries, 1.8 k. (4 lb.) and prepared sour apples, 700 g. (1½ lb.)	2.7 k. (6 lb.)	None	275-300 ml. (½ pint)	4.5 k. (10 lb.)
Blackcurrants, 1.8 k. (4 lb.)	2.7 k. (6 lb.)	None	1.5 l. (3 pints)	4.5 k. (10 lb.)
Dark cherries, stoned, 1.8 k. (4 lb.)	1.6 k. (3½ lb.)	Juice 3 lemons or 3 level teaspoons citric or tartaric acid	None	2.3 k. (5 lb.)
Gooseberries, 2.7 k. (6 lb.)	2.7 k. (6 lb.)	None	1 l. (2 pints)	4.5 k. (10 lb.)
Plums, 2.7 k. (6 lb.)	2.7 k. (6 lb.)	None	900 ml. (1½ pints)	4.5 k. (10 lb.)
Raspberries, 1.8 k. (4 lb.)	1.8 k. (4 lb.)	None	None	2.7-3.2 k. (6-7 lb.)
Strawberries, 1.8 k. (4 lb.)	1.6 k. (3½ lb.)	15 g. (½ oz.) citric or tartaric acid	None	2.3 k. (5 lb.)

A-Z OF FRUIT AND VEGETABLES

This list includes the best-known home-grown and imported fruit, vegetables and also nuts, as well as some more exotic varieties.

A

APPLES
Dessert apples vary in size and the colour can be green, yellow or red, depending on the variety. They are often cheaper than cooking apples and can be used instead in most recipes.

The best-known cooking apples are Bramleys, which are larger than dessert apples, with firm flesh and a sharp taste.

Home-grown apples are in season from July to April. Some varieties mature during storage. Popular dessert varieties are: Worcester Pearmain, which is pale green and crimson with juicy, white flesh; Egremont Russet, reddish-brown skin and crisp flesh; and Cox's Orange Pippin, with orange-yellow skin and crisp, juicy flesh.

Imported eating apples, available all the year round, include Golden Delicious and Granny Smith.
Cooking methods Stew, use in pies and puddings; core and bake whole, and use for bottling and jam.

APRICOTS
Apricots are in season from May to August, when they are cheapest, and from December to February.
Cooking methods Stew, use in cold desserts and for jam and bottling.

ARTICHOKES, GLOBE
Mostly imported from the Continent, although they are grown in this country, artichokes should have fresh green, tightly closed leaves with no brown streaks on them. The flavour is sweet and slightly nutty. They are available from April to November.
Preparation Cut off the stalk near the base of the leaves and remove the outside layer of leaves. Part the leaves and scrape out the hairy choke in the centre with a teaspoon. Soak the artichokes for about 10 minutes in cold water and drain upside-down in a colander.
Cooking method Boil in salted water until the leaves can be removed easily – 20-40 minutes, depending on size. Serve hot with melted butter or hollandaise sauce, or serve cold with salad dressing, allowing one per person as an hors-d'oeuvre. The leaves are pulled off and dipped into the sauce, the base only being eaten. The heart, considered the best part, is eaten with a knife and fork.

ARTICHOKES, JERUSALEM
Brown-skinned vegetables rather like small, knobbly potatoes, Jerusalem artichokes have white flesh which has a sweet, aromatic flavour when cooked. They are home-grown and measure up to 10 cm. (4 in.) long and 5 cm. (2 in.) across. Small, dirty or misshapen artichokes will be of poor quality. They are available November-March.
Preparation Peel them and put into cold water with a squeeze of lemon juice.
Cooking method Boil in salted water with a little lemon juice or vinegar until soft – about 20 minutes. Serve with melted butter.

ASPARAGUS
Sold in bunches, asparagus stems should be clean, even-sized and fresh, with the top firm and pinkish-green. Stems not more than 15 cm. (6 in.) long and of medium thickness are best. The home-grown crop is in season only in May and June, imported from February to June.
Preparation Cut off the end of the stalk and lightly scrape the white part, towards the bud. Wash the stalks and tie in bundles with the heads together.
Cooking method Stand bundles upright in boiling, salted water reaching to just below the heads. Boil for 10 minutes. Do not overcook.

Serve hot as a first course with melted butter or hollandaise sauce, or serve cold with vinaigrette (p. 279), allowing eight to ten stems per person.

AUBERGINES (Egg plants)
A fresh aubergine should have a shiny, purple skin which is a uniform colour all over. Generally, the larger they are the better. Aubergines are imported and available all the year, but are at their best from July to October.
Preparation Wipe with a damp cloth and cut off the stalk. Do not peel aubergines unless a recipe specifies it. Cut into slices, sprinkle with salt and leave about 30 minutes. Drain well. This removes the slight bitterness. The flavour is delicate and the texture, when cooked, rather like marrow, but not so watery.
Cooking methods Dip slices in flour and fry in oil or butter until brown and tender. Stuff with minced ham, tomato, onion and breadcrumbs and bake as a supper dish. When cooked, sprinkle with grated cheese.

AVOCADO PEARS
The colour of avocados varies from bright green to a purplish-brown, and the skins can be smooth and shiny or rough. They are ripe when the bulbous end yields under gentle pressure. The creamy-yellow flesh should be soft. It is rich, with a mild, rather fragrant taste. Avocados are available all the year round, but scarce from June to August.
Preparation Slice lengthways, remove the stone and fill the centre with cream cheese or prawns and mayonnaise, or serve with vinaigrette dressing.

B

BANANAS
There are two main types of banana – those from the West Indies, which are quite large with white flesh and do not have a very strong flavour; and Canary bananas, which are smaller and have creamy, slightly pink-tinged flesh and a stronger flavour.

Under-ripe, slightly green, bananas are usually cheaper than fully ripe fruit and will mature in a warm room. They should keep for a week, but do not put them in a refrigerator. Bananas are available all the year round.
Cooking methods Fry in batter, use in fruit salads and cold desserts, and sliced, raw with lemon juice, as an accompaniment to curry.

BEANS, BROAD
These beans are at their best when the pods are 20-25 cm. (8-10 in.) long, and the beans small and tender. Home-grown broad beans are in season from mid-June to late July.
Preparation Shell the beans or, if they are very young, cook and eat them in the pods.
Cooking method Put the beans into boiling water and simmer for 10-15 minutes.

BEANS, FRENCH
Smooth-skinned and stringless, French beans should be firm-looking. The flatter the pod the better, as long as it is not undersized. French beans are at their best when young and tender, and not more than 10-12 cm. (4-5 in.) long. Home-grown beans are in season from June to August.
Preparation Wash, top and tail the beans, then either leave whole or slice into 5 cm. (2 in.) lengths.
Cooking method Boil in salted water until tender – about 10 minutes. Toss in butter and serve hot or dress with vinaigrette sauce and eat cold as a salad dish.

BEANS, KIDNEY
A type of French bean, but larger, kidney beans are usually purple, but turn green when they are cooked. When they are fresh, the beans have a distinct bloom. They are in season from June to November.
Preparation Top and tail the beans and string them, as they are not so tender as French beans. Cut into lengths.
Cooking method Boil the beans in salted water for 5-10 minutes.

BEANS, PEA
The short, green pods are about the same size as pea pods and the beans are round. They are in season in early summer.
Preparation Wash, top and tail the beans. Leave the pods whole.
Cooking method Cook in the same way as French or kidney beans. They can also be served cold with French dressing.

BEANS, RUNNER
The pods of fresh runner beans should be crisp and firm. They are larger than French beans and have a stronger flavour. They are in season July-October.
Preparation String the beans, remove the tops and tails and slice thickly.
Cooking method Boil for 5-10 minutes in salted water.

BEAN SHOOTS (Mung beans)
The crisp, white shoots of the mung bean, used extensively in Chinese cookery, are now grown commercially in Britain. They are sold in some supermarkets and delicatessens.
Preparation Wash and use raw in salads.
Cooking method Blanch for 15 seconds in boiling salted water, so that the shoots are still crisp, and serve as a hot vegetable.

BEETROOTS
Globe-shaped beetroots are sold raw. The smaller they are the more tender they will be. They should have some foliage attached and the roots intact. They are in season from June to September. Cooked beetroots should be fresh and moist. Stale ones are slimy to the touch.
Preparation Trim foliage but leave the root. Wash carefully and avoid damaging the skin, as this causes the beetroot to 'bleed'. Ready-cooked beetroots simply need skinning, and are usually served cold, often in spiced or sweetened vinegar.
Cooking method Boil whole in

A-Z OF FRUIT AND VEGETABLES

salted water until tender. This can take up to 2 hours, depending on size. When the beetroot is cooked the skin slides off easily. Serve hot with white sauce or cold in salads.

BILBERRIES (Whortle berries)
These dark blue berries, slightly smaller than blackcurrants, grow wild on moors and hills in England and Wales, and some are sold fresh from June to August. Bilberries can sometimes also be bought dried.
Cooking method Bilberries are tart and are best cooked with sugar in pies and puddings.

BLACKBERRIES
Those sold in the shops are usually cultivated blackberries, which are larger and juicier than wild ones and are in season from July to October. Blackberries are often cooked with apples, because pies or jam made just of blackberries have rather a lot of pips.
Cooking methods Stew, use in mousses, jam or jelly.

BROCCOLI
Sprouting broccoli should have firm compact florets, fresh green leaves and no thick, coarse stalks.
The florets can be white, purple or green. The purple and white varieties are generally in season December to April, the green from September to April.
Preparation Wash and remove any coarse, outer leaves and the tough stalks.
Cooking method Boil in salted water until tender, about 5-10 minutes. Serve with butter or Bearnaise sauce.

BRUSSELS SPROUTS
Small, tight sprouts are best. If the outside leaves are yellowing the sprouts are stale. Brussels sprouts are available from September to March.

Preparation Wash, remove loose outer leaves and trim stalks. Slice raw sprouts and toss them in French dressing, with a little French mustard added, to make a winter salad.
Cooking method Put into boiling, salted water, then simmer for 10 minutes.

CABBAGES
Spring cabbages, in season in April and May, are small, with bright green leaves and cone-shaped hearts. Use as soon as possible after buying, as the leaves wilt.
Summer cabbages, in season from June to October, are firm and green with large hearts. Winter cabbages, such as Savoys, are similar to the summer ones in shape, but the leaves are more curly. These cabbages will keep for two or three days in a cool place.
White cabbages are usually in season throughout the winter from October to February.
Red cabbages, in season from November to March, have a purplish bloom when fresh. They lose some of their colour usually when they are cooked.
Both red and white cabbages are round and solid with very tight leaves and no loose outer ones.
All cabbages should feel firm, with crisp leaves and clean stalks. Stale cabbages have wilting, yellow outer leaves and slimy stalks.
Preparation With all cabbages, remove coarse or damaged leaves. Wash thoroughly before shredding greens finely and cutting solid cabbages into wedges. White and red cabbages can be finely sliced and served raw in salads.
Cooking method Put greens and green and white cabbages into boiling, salted water for 5-8 minutes if they are shredded, 10-15 minutes for wedges, except red cabbage which takes up to 30 minutes.
Red cabbage is often pickled, but can be braised in vinegar and cider with a little brown sugar. Serve with pork, duck or goose.

CALABRESE
A type of sprouting broccoli which has firm compact heads of green florets and matures in late summer and autumn.
Preparation Cut off woody stalks and divide into florets.
Cooking methods Like cauliflower, calabrese can be boiled for 15-20 minutes and served with white or cheese sauce. The florets can also be deep fried with breadcrumbs.

CAPE GOOSEBERRIES
Golden berries from the Chinese lantern plant, Cape gooseberries are sold in some luxury fruiterers in February and March. They have an aromatic flavour and are eaten raw.

CARROTS
Young carrots, with the leaves attached, are sold in bunches from May to August. Choose those that are a uniform pale orange, as carrots that are green at the top have been pulled too early. Large, coarser, mature carrots are available from September throughout the winter.
Home-grown varieties are supplemented, particularly during the summer and autumn, by imported carrots. These are more like early carrots, but larger and less tapering.
Preparation Remove tops and tails, including the leaves, if any. Lightly scrape young and imported carrots, thinly peel mature ones.
Cooking methods Cook small carrots whole, and slice large ones into quarters, rings or sticks. Cook carrots in not more than

150 ml. (¼ pint) boiling water for 10-30 minutes, depending on size and age. Slice old carrots and add them to stews and soups.

CAULIFLOWERS
A good-quality cauliflower has fresh green leaves and a firm, compact, creamy-white head with no brown patches. Cauliflowers are in the shops all year.
Preparation Cut off yellow or damaged outer leaves and, if the cauliflower is to be cooked whole, cut a cross in the stalk so that it cooks through. Alternatively, the cauliflower can be separated into florets.
Cooking method Boil or steam for 9-12 minutes in salted water in a covered saucepan. Serve with white sauce to accompany a main course or with cheese sauce as a supper dish.

CELERIAC
Celeriac is the root of one variety of celery, which it resembles in flavour. Celeriac varies from the size of an apple to the size of a coconut and has a brown, fibrous skin and creamy-white flesh. The root should be firm and hard. It is in season September to March.
Preparation Wash, peel, and slice. Grate to use raw in salads.
Cooking methods Boil in salted water, with the lid on, for 25-30 minutes, or sauté in butter for 30 minutes.

CELERY
Home-produced celery, with white stalks and pale green leaves, is in season September to February. If the small leaves are at all yellow or turning brown the celery is stale. The stalks should be firm. Green-stalked, imported celery is in the shops from January to April.
Preparation Remove the outer stalks and trim the root. Cut the heart into sections, lengthwise. Scrub in cold water and remove

coarse fibres. Serve raw on its own, with cheese, or in salads.
Cooking methods Cut into 5-6 cm. (2-2½ in.) lengths and boil, covered in salted water, for 15-20 minutes, or blanch (see p. 225) for 10 minutes, then cover with stock and braise for 40-50 minutes.

CHERRIES
Dessert cherries – usually bright red or black – are imported from Italy and France from May to August.
Home-grown cherries are in season only in June and July. The most popular varieties are White Heart, which are yellow and red and firm and sweet, and Black Heart which are purple-black, slightly softer and juicier.
A few black Morello cooking cherries are sold fresh in August.
Cooking methods Dessert cherries as well as Morello cherries, which are too sharp to eat raw, can be stewed, put into pies and puddings and used for jam and bottling.

CHICORY
A cone-shaped white vegetable, chicory has a head of tightly-packed white leaves 10-12 cm. (4-5 in.) long, with pale yellow tips. Green or brown tips show that the chicory is stale. Chicory is at its best from November to March. It has a bitter taste, which is more pronounced when the chicory is cooked.
Preparation Wash, trim root ends and remove any discoloured outer leaves. For salads, break off the leaves.
Cooking methods Boil in salted

COLLECTING JELLY MOULDS

Moulds to shape food came into general use in the 18th century. Wooden moulds were used for gingerbread, iron for wafers, and ceramic and copper moulds for cheese and jellies.
Moulds holding more than one portion were introduced by Josiah Wedgwood in the 1780s. They were in two parts. The jelly was poured into an outer case and a decorated inner section was fitted into it. When the jelly was set, the outer case was removed.
One-piece china moulds in a variety of shapes gained popularity in the early 19th century. Moulds with animal patterns were probably used for savoury jellies. Pressed moulds (hand-shaped) and cast ceramic moulds were mostly made in Staffordshire, although a type of smooth-glazed, stone mould came from Bristol. A few moulds were also made in London. However, most 19th-century manufacturers did not mark their moulds.
Two-part 18th-century jelly moulds are rare, but Victorian moulds can still be found quite frequently. Look in antique and china shops and markets. Prices vary from a matter of pence to several pounds.
Pictured in the back row (left to right) are: hand-made Staffordshire pottery mould (1830-40); star-shaped, cast china mould (1930s); pottery mould, probably made in London (c. 1850). At the front are a mosque-shaped cast mould (1840-60); and a rare, pressed mould made for Queen Victoria's coronation (1837).

A-Z OF FRUIT AND VEGETABLES

water for 15-20 minutes. The bitter flavour disappears if the chicory is blanched (see p. 225) for 5 minutes before being cooked.

CHINESE CABBAGE
Chinese cabbage is similar to a large cos lettuce. The texture is between that of an English cabbage and a lettuce. It is best in autumn and winter.
Preparation Wash thoroughly, remove coarse stalks and chop for salads.
Cooking method As for cabbage.

COURGETTES
A variety of marrow grown for early harvesting when about 4-6 in. long, home-produced courgettes are in season from May to September. Imported ones are available the rest of the year. Look for firm straight courgettes, not more than 15-18 cm. (6-7 in.) long with glossy skins.
Preparation Wash, trim both ends but do not peel.
Cooking methods Slice and fry in butter or boil whole for 10-15 minutes.

CRANBERRIES
These berries, which mostly come from America, are usually dark red. They are slightly smaller than cherries, and have hard, creamy-yellow, seed-filled flesh. The berries are sour with a slightly bitter taste. Some are home-produced, and are in season in July and August. Fresh, imported cranberries are available from October to February.
Cooking methods Stew with apples for tarts and pies, and use to make cranberry sauce or jelly.

CUCUMBERS
Greenhouse cucumbers – long, thin with smooth, dark green skin – are available all the year round, but are at their best in spring and summer. Ridge cucumbers, which are grown outside and are shorter and fatter with a ridged lighter skin, are in season from July to September. All cucumbers should be crisp and firm. If they feel soft and flexible, they are past their best.
Preparation Usually sliced raw for salads. Thinly sliced cucumber mixed with a carton of natural yoghourt is a good accompaniment to curry and other spicy, savoury dishes.
Cooking method Cook gently in butter in a covered pan for 10-15 minutes.

CURRANTS
Black, red and white currants are home-grown, and a few are sold fresh from June to August.

Blackcurrants are most plentiful, but they are grown commercially for freezing and making soft drinks.

Redcurrants have bright red, glossy skins. White currants have almost transparent skins and are sweeter.
Cooking methods Remove the stalks and top and tail the currants. Use blackcurrants in pies, cold sweets and for jam. Red and white currants can be eaten raw and redcurrants are used to make jam and jelly.

D

DAMSONS
Oval, purple-skinned, small plums, the flesh is yellow and sour, unless the fruit is fully ripe. They should be firm, but not hard.

Damsons are in season in September and October.
Cooking methods Stew, use for fools, pies, puddings and jam.

DATES
Fresh dates are sold in luxury fruiterers and some large supermarkets from October to February. They look very much like dried dessert dates, but are darker brown with smooth, shiny skins and are sold by the pound, unlike dried dates which are usually in packets or boxes.

E

ENDIVES
Endives have curly, light green leaves that should look crisp. They are in season from September - November.

A hardier type, with wavy leaves, called Batavian endive, is grown during the winter.
Preparation Separate the leaves and wash thoroughly, discarding damaged ones. Use raw.
Cooking method Blanch (see p. 225) for 5-6 minutes. Wash in cold water and drain thoroughly, then braise in a covered casserole in 275-300 ml. (½ pint) stock with a knob of butter for 40-45 minutes at 160°C (325°F; mark 3). Leave whole, and serve with Béchamel sauce.

F

FENNEL
The variety used as a vegetable is Florence fennel and has solid,

pale green or white stems that look like celery, but have a bulbous base. If the stems are dark green the fennel is old. It has a distinctive, aniseed flavour and is cheapest June-November.
Preparation Remove discoloured or damaged outer stems and wash. Thinly slice to eat raw.
Cooking method The trimmed head can be braised as for celery.

FIGS
It is possible to grow figs in the open in the south of England, but most are grown in hot-houses, and fresh figs are usually imported from the Mediterranean countries. They can be green or purple skinned with yellow flesh, or purple with red flesh. Both should feel firm, but not hard. Fresh figs are juicy and full of seeds. They are in season from August to December. Eat figs as a dessert fruit or serve them with ham, as an hors-d'oeuvre.

G

GOOSEBERRIES
Early gooseberries, in season in May and June, are home-produced. These are small, green and hard, and are best for cooking. Popular varieties are May Duke, which is round with a hairy skin, and Keepsake, which is oval and slightly hairy.

Most dessert gooseberries are imported and are available from July to September. They are larger than cooking gooseberries, often hairy, and have soft, sweet flesh and large seeds.
Cooking methods Use early, green gooseberries stewed, in pies and puddings, to make fools, as sauce for mackerel, and in jam.

GRAPEFRUIT
Imported grapefruit are available all the year round and can vary

from the size of a large orange up to a giant fruit weighing several pounds. Smooth skins usually indicate juicy fruit. Rough, slightly spongy fruit can be dry.

Most grapefruit have pale yellow skins and flesh, but pink-tinged ones are imported from America and are slightly sweeter.

Eat grapefruit for breakfast or sprinkled with brown sugar and grilled, as an appetiser, mixed with seafood or vegetable salad to start a meal, and in fruit salads. Grapefruit can also be used in marmalade.

GRAPES
Home-grown hot-house grapes are in season in the late autumn and are considered best for appearance and flavour.

Small, seedless green grapes from Cyprus are available in July and August, and larger green or black grapes with a few seeds for the rest of the year.

Fresh grapes should have a bloom on the skin and feel firm, not squashy.

GREENGAGES
These belong to the plum family and are fairly small – about 2-4 cm. (1-1½ in.) in diameter – and round with a very good flavour. Few home-produced greengages reach the shops, but some are imported. These lack the flavour and juiciness of English fruit. Greengages should be firm with a white bloom which, as with damsons and plums, is a sign of freshness.
Cooking methods Eat large, ripe greengages raw. Small, firmer fruit is best stewed, cooked in pies, or used for jam and bottling.

GREENS
Spring greens are spring cabbages pulled before they are mature. But cabbages can be grown throughout the year, and any picked before developing hearts may be sold as greens.

This term also covers the top leaves from broccoli and brussels sprouts.
Preparation Discard woody stems and shred green leaves.
Cooking method As for cabbage.

K

KALE
A member of the cabbage family, kale has curly leaves and a strong flavour. It is home-grown and is in season from November to March.
Preparation Separate leaves, remove the central ribs and wash thoroughly.
Cooking method As for cabbage.

KIWI FRUIT
These luxury fruits are imported from New Zealand. They are about 5 cm. (2 in.) long and oval, with hairy brown skin and juicy green flesh pitted with seeds. The flavour is aromatic and not very strong. They are in season from July to February. Peel off the skin and eat the fruit raw. Also known as Chinese gooseberry.

KOHL RABI
The globe-shaped white or purple stems grow above ground, topped with curly green leaves. Buy kohl rabi when they are small and young – not larger than an

A-Z OF FRUIT AND VEGETABLES

orange – or they will be coarse.
Preparation Remove the top leaves, if any, and peel thickly.
Cooking method Boil or braise for 30 minutes to 1 hour, depending on size. Serve whole with white sauce, or glazed with butter, or mashed.

KUMQUATS
These small citrus fruits are about the same size as plums, but are otherwise very like oranges. They have orange, slightly pitted skin and juicy, bitter flesh. Kumquats originated in Japan and China, but are now imported from Morocco.
Cooking method Can be used for marmalade.

L

LEEKS
In season from September to May. Look for chunky, thick-stemmed leeks with 15-20 cm. (6-8 in.) of white stem and 4-5 cm. (1½-2 in.) diameter. If the leaves are yellowing, the leeks are old.
Preparation Remove coarse outer leaves and trim tops and roots. Wash thoroughly, splitting down the centre, to remove grit.
Cooking method Boil whole until soft – 20-25 minutes. Serve leeks hot with white sauce or cold with French dressing. They also add flavour to soups and stews.

LEMONS
Varieties include small, juicy, smooth-skinned lemons and large, knobbly ones with thicker skins and less juice. Thin-skinned lemons are a better buy than thick-skinned, even if the skin is wanted for flavouring. They are imported all the year round and the most common variety is the Genoa lemon.
Cooking methods Both rind and juice are used as a flavouring in sweet and savoury dishes and to make drinks. Slices of lemon are used as a garnish to some fish and meat dishes. Lemons can also be included in marmalade, with oranges, limes or grapefruits.

LETTUCES
Round, cabbage-shaped lettuces can be soft-leaved or crisp and curly-leaved. Cos lettuces have long, closely packed, crisp leaves which taste sweeter than round lettuces. Cheapest and best are the home-grown outdoor lettuces, available from May to October. Look for those with crisp, bright green leaves and with no traces of brown or slimy patches.
Preparation Trim base and damaged leaves, separate and wash. Drain well and use in salads. Leave the lettuce whole if it is to be cooked.
Cooking method Blanch for 5-6 minutes, then hold under cold running water to refresh the lettuce. Put in the oven in a casserole with a little fried bacon, onion and carrot, and enough stock to cover the contents. Cook for 40 minutes at 180°C (350°F; mark 4).

LIMES
Small, pale green to yellow fruits similar to lemons, limes have a slightly more aromatic flavour. Scarcer and more expensive than lemons, limes are in season from February to July.
Cooking methods Use in the same way as lemons for flavouring and garnishing food, making drinks and marmalade.

LOGANBERRIES
A cross between blackberries and raspberries, loganberries are elongated, reddish-black and juicy. They can be up to 5 cm. (2 in.) long and are seedless with a hard, white core. They are home-produced and in season from June to August.
Cooking methods Core the fruit and cook them in puddings, pies and jam.

LOQUATS
Imported from Israel, loquats, also called Japanese medlars, are similar in shape and size to plums.

The smooth skin can be yellow, orange or reddish-brown. Loquats are available in only a few fruiterers, but they are in season all year. Eat them raw, like plums.

LYCHEES
Originally from China, lychees are now grown in South Africa. Fresh ones are in season in January and February. They are about the size of very large cherries and have a hard, scaly, red-brown skin. Do not buy lychees if the skin is brown, dry or slightly shrivelled. The flesh is white, juicy and slightly tough, and the distinctive flavour is sweet and aromatic, with a hint of sharpness.

Peel the fruit and serve on their own as a dessert. Lychees also make an interesting addition to fruit and vegetable salads.

M

MANGOES
Mangoes in the shops are usually 12-25 cm. (5-10 in.) long and roughly kidney or pear-shaped. The skin is tough. The yellow flesh is juicy with a delicate, slightly spicy taste. They are available most of the year.

Peel and slice mangoes to eat raw, chilled.

MARROWS
Marrows are best bought young, when they are not more than 30 cm. (12 in.) long and the flesh is watery with a delicate flavour. They are in season from July to October.
Preparation Peel off the skin with a sharp knife and remove the seeds. Cut the flesh into even-sized pieces.
Cooking methods Boil for about 10-15 minutes in 2.5 cm. (1 in.) of salted water, and serve with white sauce or melted butter. Marrow can also be roasted round a joint of meat, or stuffed with a mixture of minced meat, breadcrumbs and herbs, and baked, wrapped in greaseproof paper, for 1 hour at 180°C (350°F; mark 4).

MELONS
Melons are available all year round, although they are less plentiful in the winter. Most melons are imported, but a few are grown commercially in this country.

Cantaloup has dark green, ridged skin, is about the size of a football and has pinkish-yellow scented flesh.

Charentais melons are small and round with green, striped skin and yellow flesh. They are the most expensive variety.

Honeydew are the least expensive and most plentiful melons and they are cheapest in the early autumn. They are shaped like rugby footballs, with yellow, ridged skins and pale green to pink flesh.

Watermelons are largest of all, with a glossy dark green skin and watery pink flesh with black seeds. They are large and are usually sold cut in slices.

Fully ripe melons feel soft when the ends are pressed and should be used at once. Firm ones can be ripened at room temperature.

Eat melons raw (halved or sliced, with the seeds removed) as an appetiser, cubed, in fruit or vegetable salads, and in jam, usually mixed with ginger.

MUSHROOMS
Most of the mushrooms sold in greengrocers and supermarkets are cultivated. Field mushrooms, which may have a better flavour, are sometimes found in markets and country areas. Very young, round mushrooms are sold as 'button' mushrooms; slightly larger, more open ones as 'cups'; and the largest and most mature as 'flats'. Mushrooms are available all the year round and field ones are in season from late August to October.

Preparation Cut or break off the stalks, which can be used in soups and stews. Wipe the cap of cultivated mushrooms and peel the field ones. Slice button mushrooms and add them to salads.
Cooking method Season the mushrooms with salt and pepper and fry in butter for 4-6 minutes, turning once. They can be served on toast, in a cream or wine sauce or stuffed as an appetiser.

MUSTARD AND CRESS
Although known as mustard and cress, this salad vegetable is really vegetable rape. It is sold in punnets and is easy to grow at home on damp cottonwool or blotting paper. The leaves should be bright green.
Preparation Snip off the cress with scissors and wash it under running water.

N

NAARTJE
Similar to tangerines, naartje have a loose, bright orange skin. They are seedless and are imported from South Africa. The season is from November to January and a few are sold fresh, although they are more often sold as crystallised whole fruit. They are expensive to buy fresh and are best peeled to eat raw.

NECTARINES
Similar to peaches, but with a smooth shiny skin, nectarines have slightly firmer, less-juicy flesh. Do not buy nectarines when they are hard and under-ripe. Most nectarines are imported, and are in season from December to May and in August and September. A few home-grown ones are available in July and August.

Use nectarines in the same way as peaches.

Brazil
Cob
Walnut
Almond

NUTS
Almonds The sweet kernel is sold whole or chopped and ground for cake-making. Almonds are served with chicken and fish, such as trout, and also used to make almond paste for cakes.
Brazil nuts Firm, oily nuts with hard, dark brown shells. Used in cakes and sweets.
Cashew nuts Kidney-shaped, aromatic kernels, used as a cocktail savoury and in sweet-making.
Chestnuts Sold in the shells, peeled in tins, either plain or in syrup, and as a sweetmeat, called *marrons glacés.* Fresh nuts can be boiled for cold desserts and to make stuffing for turkey.
Cob nuts Also called hazel nuts or filberts, they are used ground in cakes and desserts.
Coconuts Some are sold whole but they are most widely used dried and flaked or grated for

Pecan
Cashew
Chestnut

cakes, puddings and sweets, such as coconut ice.
Peanuts Available fresh, roasted and salted. Ground peanuts are made into peanut butter.
Pecan nuts The shell is oval, smooth and red, and the kernel is like an elongated walnut. They are used in cakes, biscuits and sweets.
Walnuts The kernels should be fresh and damp-looking with a brown skin over the creamy-white

A-Z OF FRUIT AND VEGETABLES

nut. Buy them ready-shelled for cakes and sweet-making.

OKRAS (Ladies' fingers)
Aromatic, green beans native to the West Indies, where they are called Gumbo. The whole pod, which can be up to 23 cm. (9 in.) long, is eaten. Okras are in season from June to December, and those in the shops are usually 8-15 cm. (3-6 in.) long.
Preparation Wash the pods.
Cooking method Par-boil (see p. 283) for 5 minutes, then cook in butter for 10 minutes until tender.

ONIONS
All onions should be firm with feathery brown skins. If onions are shrivelled or feel at all soft round the top they are likely to be bad. Large onions with a mild flavour include Spanish onions, which originated in Spain but are now also home-produced. These varieties are available all the year.

Shallots are smaller than true onions and have a stronger flavour. They are in season from July to January and can be used for pickling.

The third main type is the spring or salad onion, which may be thinnings from large onions before they reach maturity, or varieties which only grow to this size. They are available most of the year but are best from May to October. Some of these salad onions are used for pickling when they are mature.
Preparation Peel away the thin skin and trim the roots. Spring onions, which are usually left whole or chopped and used in salads, may have their green leaves trimmed.
Cooking methods Boil large onions and shallots in salted water for 20-30 minutes or slice and fry gently in hot fat.

ORANGES
Sweet oranges are imported from many countries all the year round,

and bitter or Seville oranges from Spain are in season in January and February. They have coarse skins with green patches, numerous pips and are very acid.

Sweet oranges include Jaffa oranges from Israel, which are large and oval with thick skins and are very sweet and juicy.

Navel or Brazil oranges are seedless. They have a growth like an embryo orange at one end and are thin-skinned and juicy.
Cooking methods Sweet oranges although mostly eaten raw on their own or in fruit salads, can be included in cooked sweets and the rind and juice are used for flavouring cakes and sauces. Bitter Seville oranges are used to make marmalade and sauces to serve with rich meat, such as duck.

ORTANIQUES
A cross between an orange and a tangerine, an ortanique looks like a large, yellowish navel orange. It has a thin skin, sweet, juicy flesh and is imported from Spain from October to March.
Cooking methods Use ortaniques in marmalade, mixed with other citrus fruit.

PARSNIPS
Small to medium parsnips – 20-23 cm. (8-9 in.) long and about 5 cm. (2 in.) in diameter – are sweeter than large ones. They are in season September-April.
Preparation Peel off the skin with a knife or potato peeler and cut the parsnip into quarters. Remove the hard core.
Cooking methods Boil in salted water for 30-40 minutes, or par-boil (see p. 283) and roast round meat. Use in soups and stews. Very large, coarse parsnips are not very palatable but can be grated for soups.

PASSION FRUIT
Juicy, tropical fruit, with a sharp, tangy flavour, there are several varieties. They are not widely available fresh but the best known is probably the American passion fruit which has a hard, purplish-brown skin and soft, orange pulp with black seeds in it. There is no need to remove the pips. The flesh is eaten raw, with a little sugar, or used to flavour cocktails and fruit drinks.
Cooking methods The peeled fruit can be stewed and used hot in pies or cold in fruit creams, mousses and fruit salads.

PAWPAWS
Large, smooth-skinned tropical fruit, pawpaws look rather like pear-shaped melons. The skin is green, yellow or orange, depending on ripeness. The pulp is orange and juicy and similar in texture to melon. There are dark brown seeds in the centre. Use like melons.

PEACHES
A few home-grown peaches are available from July to October. Most are imported from South Africa and Italy during the same period. Test peaches for ripeness by lightly pressing the stalk end, which should be soft. If peaches are difficult to peel, put into hot water for a few seconds and then into cold.
Cooking methods Stew in syrup or wine for flans. Peaches are also used in salads and with gammon, and for bottling and jam-making.

PEARS
Home-grown pears are available from August to February and imported ones all the year round. Dessert pears include Conference, which are elongated with green, russet-speckled skin, and William pears, which are yellow-skinned and fatter. Cooking pears are smaller than dessert ones, and green-skinned.
Cooking methods Dessert and cooking pears can be stewed, cooked in red wine, and used in cold desserts.

PEAS
Fresh peas are in the shops from about May to October. The pods should be bright green, smooth and not too fat, or the peas will be old. Peas with wrinkled pods are likely to be hard.
Preparation Shell fresh peas.
Cooking method Boil gently in salted water, containing a sprig of mint and 1 teaspoon sugar, for 5-15 minutes.

PEAS, MANGETOUT
The earliest peas, they are picked when the pods are flat and are eaten whole.
Preparation Wash the pods.
Cooking method Boil the pods until tender, about 5-10 minutes, and toss in butter.

PEPPERS (Capsicums, pimentoes)
Semi-tropical vegetables, peppers can be red, green or yellow, depending on ripeness. They are usually 8-13 cm. (3-5 in.) in diameter and have a mild, piquant flavour.
Preparation Wash and either cut in half lengthways or cut round the stalk end. Remove the stalk, seeds and white membrane. Slice and use raw in salads.
Cooking method Boil in salted water for 10 minutes, drain, then stuff with meat or vegetables mixed with cooked rice and herbs. Bake for 25-30 minutes at 180°C (350°F; mark 4). Chop and add to stews, and risotto.

PERSIMMONS
Orange-red, smooth-skinned tropical fruits about the size of a large tomato. The skin is thick and rather tough, and the pulpy flesh juicy and slightly acid. Some types are seedless. They are in season from March to November, but are not plentiful.
Cooking methods Persimmons can be used to make jelly and jam.

PINEAPPLES
Fresh pineapples are imported from many tropical countries and are available most of the year, but are usually expensive. Small Cape pineapples, in the shops from February to May, are more reasonably priced. Large pineapples are plentiful from October to December. Pineapples are ripe when the leaves, which should be stiff and not drooping, come away easily when lightly pulled.

Remove the hard, rough outside skin and slice to eat raw.
Cooking method Stew in syrup, made by boiling sugar and water, and use for cold desserts or with gammon.

PLANTAIN
A variety of large banana which can be more than 30 cm. (12 in.) long, plantain are popular in India and the West Indies.
Preparation Peel and slice.
Cooking methods Green, under-ripe plantain can be fried in oil, then just covered with water and cooked for about 15 minutes, until tender. Serve as a vegetable.

PLUMS
Most plums sold in the shops are home-produced. They are in season from August to October, but a few large dessert plums are imported from Italy and South Africa in June and July.

Home-grown plums can be divided into those for cooking, and those suitable for dessert as well as cooking.

Cooking plums: Santa Rosa, a small purple plum, and the greenish-yellow Golden King, both juicy but rather acid, are the most usual cooking plums.

Dessert plums: Czar is dark blue with golden-yellow flesh; Early Rivers, a small, purple plum and the first of the home-grown varieties to come into the shops; and Victoria, a large, oval fruit with yellow and red skin and juicy flesh.
Cooking methods Stew, cook in pies and puddings and use for jam and bottling.

POMEGRANATES
This hard-skinned fruit, about the size of an orange, is imported September-January.

The thin, tough skin is removed with a knife and the pink, juicy flesh sucked from the seeds.

POTATOES
There are two main types of potato – early, or 'new', and maincrop, or 'old'. Most are home-grown, but some early potatoes are imported and are in the shops in February or March. The home-grown varieties are in season from June to August.

Maincrop potatoes are available for the rest of the year and will keep at home for several weeks in a dark, dry place.

Of the early potatoes, Maris Peer and Red Craigs Royal are recommended by the Potato Marketing Board, and can be boiled, used in salads, chipped or sauté. If these varieties are not available, Arran Pilot and Home Guard are good.

During the winter, maincrop varieties available include King Edward, which are good boiled, mashed or jacket-baked; and Majestic, recommended for chips and sauté potatoes.
Preparation Wash and lightly scrape new potatoes, or cook with

A-Z OF FRUIT AND VEGETABLES

the skins on. Scrub old potatoes and leave the skins on for baking, or thinly peel and cut into even-sized pieces to boil.

Cooking methods Boil for 15-20 minutes, or fry in deep fat for 5-8 minutes. Boiled potatoes can be served in pieces or mashed with a little milk and butter. Old potatoes can be roasted round a joint for the last hour or roasted on their own for 40 minutes. To jacket-bake old potatoes, prick the skin all over, and bake at 180°C (350°F; mark 4) for 45 minutes to 1 hour, until tender.

PUMPKIN
The orange, pulpy flesh is similar to marrow, and should be close-textured and not stringy.

Preparation Peel, remove the pith and seeds, and cut the pumpkin into small cubes.

Cooking methods Boil for 20-30 minutes and serve in a cheese sauce, or roast round a joint.

QUINCES
Uncommon fruit which is available in a few shops from September to November. The pear-shaped fruit is very hard and solid with tough, yellow or russet skin and acid, aromatic flesh.

Cooking methods Quinces add flavour to cooked apples or pears and can be made into jam and jelly.

RADISHES
Radishes can be round, oval or pointed, and they should be crisp and sweet with a mild flavour. Buy small radishes – 1-2 cm. (½-¾ in.) in diameter – as large ones may be dry and pithy. Test for this by gently pressing the radish between finger and thumb. It should be hard and not give at all. Home-produced radishes are best from May to September.

Some winter radishes are available, from November. They can be round or long and are larger than salad radishes.

Preparation Trim off the leaves and root ends and wash in cold

water. Radishes are eaten raw in salads and with cheese. Winter radishes can be boiled.

RASPBERRIES
Home-grown raspberries are available June-September. Do not buy soft or mildewy ones, or fruit in a stained punnet. Raspberries keep very well in a freezer.

How to use Serve raw with cream, purée for cold sweets and sauces or make into jam.

RHUBARB
The stalks of rhubarb are treated as fruit, although they are really vegetables. The leaves are poisonous and the stalks are sour. 'Forced' rhubarb, which has pale pink stalks and yellowish leaves, is sold from January to March. The main crop is on sale March-July.

How to use Stew, or cook in pies and puddings and use in chutney and jam.

SALSIFY
Long, thin root vegetable with a brown skin, salsify has soft white flesh and, when fresh, grey-green leaves. They are in season from October to May.

Preparation Scrub well, scrape off the skin and trim the roots. Cut into 3-5 cm. (1-2 in.) lengths.

Cooking method Boil for 45 minutes in salted water and serve with butter. Use the leaves in salads.

SCORZONERA
This is similar to salsify, but with black skin. The season is from October to March.

Preparation Peel off the black skin and prepare as salsify.

Cooking method As for salsify.

SEA KALE
A vegetable with dark green, crinkly leaves and white stalks. The leaves and the stalks are eaten. Sea kale is in season from August to March.

Preparation Wash thoroughly, remove the leaves, trim the roots

and tie the stalks in bundles.

Cooking methods Boil the stalks for 25 minutes. Cook the leaves in the same way as spinach.

SPINACH
Summer spinach has smooth, rounded mid-green leaves, but the winter variety has larger, prickly leaves which are tougher and take longer to cook. Summer spinach should be used on the day of purchase. It is at its best in March and April.

Preparation Spinach needs several washes in cold water to remove all the dirt and grit. Cut off thick stalks and any discoloured, slimy leaves. Use raw in salads.

Cooking method Put the wet spinach into a saucepan with no extra water, sprinkle with salt and cook gently for 5-8 minutes, shaking the pan occasionally. Drain and add a good-sized knob of butter. Spinach diminishes during cooking and 1-1.5 kg. (2-3 lb.) is needed for four helpings.

SPINACH BEET
Better known as perpetual spinach, this all-the-year-round vegetable is very similar to winter and summer varieties, but has smaller leaves and longer stalks.

Preparation Wash thoroughly in running water to remove grit.

Cooking method As for spinach.

STRAWBERRIES
Home-grown strawberries are in season in June and July, and some late crops and Scottish ones are in the shops in September. A few imported strawberries are available throughout the year, but the flavour is not comparable. Strawberries should be bright red.

Cooking methods Use strawberry purée in cold sweets, and ripe fruit to make jam and on cakes.

SWEDES
The orange flesh of swedes has a milder flavour than turnips. Swedes are in season from September to May.

Preparation Peel thickly to remove the tough skin and trim roots and stalks. Cut into even-sized pieces.

Cooking methods Boil in salted water for 30-40 minutes and serve mashed with butter, or roast round a joint, allowing 1-1¾ hours, depending on the size of the pieces.

SWEET CORN (Corn-on-the-cob)
Choose cobs that are pale gold and shiny, with stiff, bright green leaves. When punctured, fresh corn exudes a milky liquid. Home-grown corn is in season from July to October, but imported varieties extend the season.

Preparation Trim away the leaves and silky fibres.

Cooking method Put whole cobs into boiling, unsalted water. Cook for 12-20 minutes, depending on size. Cobs fresh from the garden can take as little as 3 minutes. Drain well and serve with butter.

SWEET POTATOES
Sweet potatoes, widely used in parts of the United States, can be white, pink, purple or red skinned with creamy-yellow flesh which

has a sweet, slightly perfumed taste. They are available from September to June.

Preparation Scrub well and peel if preferred.

Cooking methods Boil whole in salted water for about 25 minutes, or cut into pieces and boil for 15 minutes. Serve as ordinary potatoes.

T

TANGERINES
This small, delicately flavoured fruit is related to the orange. Varieties include: clementines, which have a closer skin, and are not as sweet as tangerines; mandarin oranges which are sweeter and have thin skin and a rather flattened shape; and satsumas, seedless, with a paler skin.

All these fruits are in season from October to March.

Cooking method Tangerines make very good marmalade.

TOMATOES
Home-grown tomatoes, available from March to October, have a good flavour and are best for salads. Imported tomatoes are available throughout the year. Use soft, fully ripe tomatoes for cooking.

Preparation Remove the stalk, wash and peel if necessary. To remove the skins, plunge tomatoes into boiling water for 1 minute, then into cold, and the skins can be peeled off.

Cooking methods Cut in half and grill under a moderate heat for 5-10 minutes, or bake in a shallow greased dish for 15 minutes at 180°C (350°F; mark 4), or fry in shallow fat.

TURNIPS
Small, early turnips, which have tender, yellow flesh, and a pale skin, tinged with light green near

the foliage, are sold in bunches from April to July.

Stronger-flavoured, maincrop turnips, which are larger and coarser, keep well during the winter and are available from August to April. They are sold individually or by weight.

Preparation Wash, trim stalks and roots and peel thickly. Early turnips can be grated for salads or cooked whole. Wash and peel maincrop turnips in the same way, then cut into quarters.

Cooking methods Boil in salted water for 20-30 minutes. Serve early turnips whole, tossed in butter, and mash maincrop ones with butter and seasoning. Add chopped, maincrop turnips to soups and stews. Tender leaves can be used as greens.

U

UGLI FRUITS
This irregularly shaped citrus fruit is a cross between a grapefruit and a tangerine, and is the size of a small grapefruit. Ugli fruits have thick, loose, green-yellow skins. The yellow flesh is sweeter than grapefruit and there are few pips. Uglis imported from Jamaica are in season from October to February, but supplies can sometimes be limited.

Use ugli fruit in the same way as grapefruit, as an appetiser for breakfast, and also as a dessert fruit.

W

WATERCRESS
Home-grown watercress, sold in bunches, is available all the year round. It should be fresh, crisp and dark green with no yellowing leaves.

Preparation Separate the watercress, trim the stalks, wash and drain well and use in salads, in soups and for garnishes.

MILK, FATS, CHEESE AND EGGS

Milk contains almost all the nutrients required for a balanced diet, but is low in iron and vitamin C. Cheese is the natural way to preserve the food value of milk. The curd, which is the most nutritious part of the milk, is separated from the whey – usually by using rennet – then ripened to make cheese. Butter is the conglomeration of fat from the cream of the milk, and is rich in vitamins A and D. Margarine and other vegetable oil spreads usually contain about 10% butter or other added nutrients to make their food value equivalent to that of butter, although this does not apply to lard and cooking fats. Eggs are the original convenience food – quick and easy to cook, versatile and nutritious, rich in protein, fat, iron, mineral salts and vitamins.

All these foods are high in cholesterol which can harm the circulation and, in some people, even be a cause of heart attacks. It is a good idea, where possible, to substitute corn oil (see p. 279) or other vegetable fats for cooking.

• MILK

Milk is a food, as well as a drink, containing about 13% solids – more than some fruit and vegetables. Processing, such as pasteurising, drying, evaporating and condensing, results in only a small loss of vitamins.

FRESH MILK

The grading, description and price of fresh milk sold in Britain are state controlled. All dairy cattle in the country are now free from bovine tuberculosis, which used to infect milk and was a common cause of T.B. in people. The standard of milk is maintained by regular government inspection of herds and dairies.

Most milk is heat-treated – pasteurised or sterilised – to kill bacteria and delay souring. It has a minimum butterfat content of 3%. Pasteurising, evaporating or drying milk all reduce the vitamin B1 content by 20% and the vitamin C content by 20%. However, this loss of food value is outweighed by the benefits of having 'safe' milk. Small quantities of untreated milk are sold, mostly in rural, milk-producing areas such as Devon and the Channel Islands. Although this milk is not pasteurised, the herds and dairies are regularly inspected and the producer must have a government licence to sell untreated milk.

There is a slight risk of infection.

At present, dairies use their own form of date coding, usually a number on the cap. There are plans for a standardised code that everyone can understand.

Fresh milk should be kept in a dark, cool place and never left standing outside, because sunlight quickly destroys the vitamins and impairs the flavour. Milk is best kept in the bottle. All containers should be kept covered to keep out dirt and germs and to prevent the milk from picking up the flavour of other foods.

Once milk has been poured into a jug or glass it should not be put back into the bottle, and one day's milk should not be mixed with that from the day before because there is a risk of contamination.

Homogenised milk can be frozen in a container, such as a plastic bag or waxed carton, but it should not be kept in a freezer longer than one month.

BUTTERMILK

This is the liquid that is left after the cream has been removed from milk to make butter. It contains between 0.1 and 1.5% fat and is pasteurised and sold in cartons.

Buttermilk can be drunk on its own, chilled, or used to make scones.

CONDENSED MILK

To make condensed milk, whole milk is heat-treated to reduce the volume by about 40% and sweetened so that the final product contains about 42% sugar. It will keep for up to two years. Use it for milk puddings and sweets.

DRIED MILK

Between 90 and 98% of the moisture is removed from whole milk so that it becomes a powder. Dried milk can easily be reconstituted by the addition of water. It is sold in tins and will keep for about three months. Skimmed dried milk is economical to use –

STERILISED
The milk is homogenised, then sterilised in the bottle by being held at a temperature of 104 - 110°C for 30 minutes. Caps are changing to blue. Keeps a week, unrefrigerated

PASTEURISED
The milk is heated to at least 72°C (160°F) for 15 seconds, then rapidly cooled, which slightly reduces the vitamin content but kills all harmful bacteria. It will keep two or three days

UNTREATED SOUTH DEVON AND CHANNEL ISLANDS
This raw milk is available only in the Channel Islands and West Country. It is creamier than other untreated milk

PASTEURISED SOUTH DEVON AND CHANNEL ISLANDS
This is milk treated in the same way as pasteurised, but which contains not less than 4% butterfat

HOMOGENISED
After pasteurisation, the milk is treated to distribute the cream evenly throughout so there is no separate layer of cream on top. The flavour is creamy. Homogenised milk will keep for up to five days

UNTREATED
Milk produced under government licence, but not heat-treated. Not all the herds are tested for brucellosis so there is a slight risk of infection, unless the milk is boiled. Only available in some country areas

ULTRA-HEAT TREATED
The milk is homogenised then heated to 132°C (290°F) for one second. The carton is labelled UHT; the new plastic bottles will have a pink cap, and the milk will keep for three months, unopened

FRESH MILK All milk, except untreated, is heat-treated in some way so that it stays fresh longer. These are the types of milk available and how they are processed. The grade and type of milk are identified by the colour of the cap.

50 g. (2 oz.) of powder makes 600 ml. (1 pint) of milk. It can be used dry in tea, coffee and for cooking. Dried milk-type powders sold for adding to coffee usually contain casein, the main milk protein, but no butterfat.

EVAPORATED MILK

The water content is evaporated from full cream fresh milk so that it is reduced to about 60% of its original volume. Vitamins B1 and C, lost during evaporation, are often added to the milk after it has been processed. After evaporation it is canned and sterilised. Evaporated milk can be substituted for cream in tea or coffee, in cooking and on fruit. It can also be diluted and used as fresh milk.

SKIMMED MILK

Similar to buttermilk, with a fat content of only about 0.1%, skimmed milk is whole milk with the cream removed. It is sometimes sold as a liquid, but is most frequently dried.

Use skimmed milk in the same way as fresh milk for low-fat diets.

YOGHOURT

This consists of whole milk to which beneficial bacteria, such as *Lactobacillus bulgaricus*, have been added. It ferments the sugar in the milk turns to lactic acid and the milk becomes soft and clotted, rather like soured milk. Yoghourt continues to mature, becoming thicker and sharper the longer it is kept. It can be bought ready-frozen for freezer storage. Natural yoghourt has a tart flavour, but more is sold sweetened, with fruit. The unflavoured kind is added to sauces, and casseroles.

HOME-MADE YOGHOURT

All you need is 600 ml. (1 pint) of fresh milk and a 150 ml. (¼ pint) carton of natural, unflavoured yoghourt. Check when you buy the yoghourt that it is 'live' and contains the organisms that will induce fermentation. Some yoghourts sold in supermarkets are not 'live', but those from health shops usually are.

Heat the milk to 37°C (98°F), which is lukewarm, then remove from the heat and whisk in the yoghourt. Cover and leave in a warm place (an airing cupboard is ideal) for up to 12 hours, until it is set. The best temperature is 85-90°C (185-194°F). Chopped fruit can be mixed with the yoghourt.

• CREAM

The butterfat is separated from whole fresh milk and sold as cream. It can be bought in various grades according to the butterfat content, but no product can be sold as cream unless it has a minimum of 18% fat.

Most cream from dairies and supermarkets is pasteurised and packed in cartons or small bottles. This will keep for about three days in a refrigerator. A small amount of Channel Island and South Devon cream is sold untreated. The flavour is rich, but it does not keep fresh for more than one day. The types of cream are:

CLOTTED CREAM

This comes from Devon and Cornwall and is produced by heating milk to 82°C (180°F), cooling it, then skimming off the thick, creamy crust. Clotted cream contains 55% butterfat and is very thick. In summer, clotted cream will keep for two or three days and in cooler weather for three or four.

Clotted cream is most often used to spread on scones or to decorate cold desserts.

DOUBLE CREAM

Thick and rich, double cream must contain 48% butterfat. It is pasteurised and some, usually described on the carton or bottle as 'extended life', is homogenised, vacuum-sealed and then reheated so that it will keep, unopened, for two or three weeks.

Double cream is poured on to fruit, whipped to decorate cakes and cold desserts, used in mousses and cold soufflés and added to soups and sauces. It should not be boiled.

STERILISED CREAM

Most frequently sold in cans, sterilised cream contains 23% butterfat. It is homogenised, and will keep for up to two years if not opened. Pour it on to hot or cold puddings, and add to soup. If the can is not shaken before being opened the colourless liquid, 'whey', can be poured off and the cream used to decorate desserts.

WHIPPING CREAM

Pasteurised, but not homogenised, whipping cream is a grade between single and double cream and must contain 35% butterfat.

As the name implies, this cream whips easily and is the best kind for decorating cakes and cold desserts.

SINGLE CREAM

There must be at least 18% of butterfat in single cream which is pasteurised and homogenised. Long-lasting single cream, in cartons marked UHT, has been ultra-heat treated. It is produced in a similar way to UHT milk and keeps for up to three months if not opened.

Pour single cream on fruit and add to coffee. It is also used in cooking, and can be boiled.

SOURED CREAM

Cultured or soured cream is produced in a similar way to yoghourt and has a slightly acid taste. It contains 18% butterfat.

It can be substituted for fresh cream in most savoury sauces and soups, and put on jacket-baked potatoes.

• BUTTER

It takes the cream from 18 pints of milk to make 450 g. (1 lb.) of butter, which is rich in fat and vitamins A and D.

BUYING BUTTER

About 11% of the butter sold in Britain is home-produced. The rest is imported from Eire, the Continent, New Zealand and Australia.

British butter and that imported from New Zealand and Australia is usually 'sweet' butter, which means it has been made from fresh cream and has a firm texture and bright yellow colour. Continental butter is often of the type known as 'ripe' butter. It is made from soured cream, and is paler and softer than sweet butter.

Salted butter can be sweet or ripe and is cheaper than unsalted.

Keep butter in its wrapper and store it in a dark cool place, preferably a refrigerator.

COOKING WITH BUTTER

Butter can be used for most cooking purposes where fat is required, but many people prefer to use margarine and other fats as they are cheaper.

A firm, sweet butter is best for cooking, except for cake making when softer, ripe butter is easier to cream. Unsalted butter is most suitable for making butter cream.

BUTTER CREAM

The following recipe makes sufficient to cover the top and sides of a cake 18 cm. (7 in.) in diameter. Ingredients: 100 g. (4 oz.) butter, 175-225 g. (6-8 oz.) icing sugar, vanilla essence (optional), 1-2 tablespoons milk. Method: beat the butter until it is creamy then beat in the sifted icing sugar, a little at a time. Add the vanilla essence. Various flavourings can be added to the basic butter cream.

• OTHER FATS

Margarine, lard, dripping and cooking fats can be substituted for butter for many cooking purposes, and soft margarine can be used for spreading.

COOKING FATS

Usually sold under various brand names, cooking fats can be similar to cooking margarine – yellow and hard – or white and firm like lard. They are made from vegetable oils, without added nutrients. Cooking fats can replace butter or margarine in most recipes, but not in rich cakes.

DRIPPING

The rendered-down fat from beef and mutton, dripping is more expensive than lard, but can be made at home from fat trimmings. It has a good flavour and is best for roasting meat and frying.

LARD

Pure pork fat rendered down is called lard. It is white and firm, but fairly soft textured, and keeps well. Use lard for shallow or deep frying and, mixed with butter or margarine, for cooking.

MARGARINE

Vegetable oils with added milk solids and vitamins are used to make margarine, which has a similar nutritional value to butter. Some margarine contains about 10% butter and this is marked on the wrapper.

The cheapest margarine is bright yellow, hard and suitable for cooking. Soft margarine, usually sold in plastic tubs, is pale yellow. It is more expensive and a good substitute for butter.

Special low-calorie margarine is available to use in slimming diets.

● CHEESE

All cheese is made from milk solids – the curds – after they have been separated from the liquid whey, processed, moulded and pressed to remove more whey. The finished cheese is then stored to allow it to mature. Variations in this basic process, the different quality and type of milk used, local climatic conditions and vegetation give rise to the enormous variety of cheeses available.

In spite of price increases, cheese is still one of the cheapest sources of protein. It is also rich in calcium, riboflavin and vitamin A. The only variation in the nutritive value of different types of cheese is in the fat content. This depends on whether the milk used is skimmed or whole, and whether it is all cream or has added cream.

There are five main types of cheese: hard-pressed, such as Cheddar, which has a firm texture; lightly pressed like Caerphilly, which is slightly softer, more moist and crumbly; blue vein, such as Stilton, which is treated with moulds to give a distinctive flavour and blue markings; soft cheese, including cream and cottage, containing more whey than pressed cheeses; and processed cheeses, made by heating a mixture of hard cheeses and adding flavourings, salts and preservatives.

BUYING CHEESE

Few shops now stock whole cheeses and sell pieces cut from them. Supermarkets in particular sell hard and medium cheeses already cut into pieces and packed in plastic. Look for those without too much rind, for minimum wastage.

Cottage, curd and cream cheeses may be sold loose, but are often packed in cartons. Imported soft cheeses are sold wrapped in foil in boxes, or as individual portions.

COTTAGE CHEESE (English)
Made from soured, skimmed milk, it has acid taste

BRIE (French)
Delicately flavoured farm-produced cheese

DOLCE LATTE (Italian)
Strong-flavoured cheese, creamy when ripe. Similar to Gorgonzola

DANISH BLUE
Crumbly with sharp, salty flavour. Very white cheese is under-ripe

GORGONZOLA (Italian)
Rich, strong, blue cheese matured for up to a year

BOURSIN
Triple cream cheese flavoured with garlic, herbs or pepper

MOZARELLA (Italian)
Firm, soft, unpressed cheese. Sharp taste. Use in pizza

STILTON (English)
Blue double-cream cheese matured for six months

CABOC (Scottish)
Rich, mild cheese rolled in toasted oatmeal

BEL PAESE (Italian)
Mild and rich, foil packs are softer than loose cheese. Use on pizzas

MYCELLA (Danish)
Very soft with rich flavour. Should be spreading consistency

ROQUEFORT (French)
Rich, blue cheese with sharp, peppery taste and strong smell

CREAM CHEESE (English)
Double-cream cheese is 45-50% fat, single, 25-30%

PETIT SUISSE (French)
Cream cheese made from whole milk and cream. Serve with sugar

CAMEMBERT (French)
Originally from Normandy, now widely imitated. Best when soft

DEMI-SEL (French)
Bland taste, like fresh cream. Use with fruit and in cold desserts

BLEU DE BRESSE (French)
Soft, creamy blue cheese with a buttery flavour. Can be salty

BLUE-VEINED CHEESE AND CREAM CHEESE The various blue-veined cheeses are strongly flavoured and are best used on the cheeseboard. Soft cheeses include soft curd cheese, such as cottage and Boursin, cream cheeses, such as Petit Suisse and Demi-sel, and soft-ripening ones like Brie.

Hard cheese should look smooth and fresh. Dryness, cracks or darkening of colour, indicate staleness. Sweatiness means that the cheese has been kept at too warm a temperature and the quality will be impaired. Blue cheese should not be too moist. Imported soft cheese, such as Brie and Camembert, should feel soft and not rubbery when the foil is pressed gently.

Most people store cheese in a refrigerator, although hard cheese keeps well in a cool cupboard. Soft imported cheese to be eaten ripe, like Brie, should not be put into a refrigerator but kept in a cool place and used as soon as it is ripe. Buy cheese in small quantities and use it quickly because, like most dairy produce, it does not keep well.

Wrap cheese loosely in polythene or foil, or keep it in a polythene box. Grated cheese for cooking can be stored, loosely covered, in a jar in a cool cupboard.

Always remove cheese from the refrigerator at least an hour before it is to be used so that it reaches room temperature and regains its full flavour.

Cheese may be frozen, but hard varieties tend to crumble when thawed. Freeze soft cheeses when they are ripe. Unripe cheese will not ripen after freezing. Grated cheese freezes well.

SERVING CHEESE

Cheese is nutritious and convenient to serve uncooked in snacks, salads and on the cheeseboard. The cheeseboard should offer a choice of at least one hard or medium, one blue and one soft cheese. In addition to

CHESHIRE (English)
Mellow, slightly salty flavour. Can be white or red. Grills well

ORKNEY
Type of Cheddar cheese with a fairly strong flavour

DANBO (Danish)
Mild, nutty flavour. Caraway seeds sometimes added. Grills well

SAMSOE (Danish)
Similar to Cheddar in flavour but with waxy texture. Cooks well

EMMENTHAL (Swiss)
Hard cheese with sweet, nutty taste. Expensive

GLOUCESTER (English)
Rich-flavoured, crumbly cheese, useful for most cheese recipes

PORT-SALUT (French)
Bland cheese with a rich, creamy texture. Eat when slightly soft

WENSLEYDALE (English)
Mild, sweet, crumbly cheese from Yorkshire. Good for cooking

CAERPHILLY (Welsh)
Moist, white cheese matured for two weeks. Mild, salty, acid taste

TÔME AU RAISIN (French)
Rich, firm, chewy cheese coated with grape pips

LEICESTER (English)
Flaky, mild cheese. Eat fresh as it soon dries out. Good for cooking

JARLSBURG (Norwegian)
Mild flavour, similar to Gruyère, but cheaper. Use in fondues

LANCASHIRE (English)
Crumbly, firm cheese, it hardens if kept long. Good for grilling

CHEDDAR (English)
Can be mild, medium or strongly flavoured

EDAM (Dutch)
Slightly rubbery, mild cheese made from skimmed milk

DERBY (English)
Mild, distinctive flavour. Sometimes with layers of sage

GOUDA (Dutch)
Firm and mild. Made from whole milk. High butterfat content

HAVARTI (Danish)
Mild, semi-soft. Mix with stronger-flavoured cheese for cooking

SMOKED CHEESE (Austrian)
Firm cheese with mild, smoky flavour. Made in sausage shapes

PARMESAN (Italian)
Group of expensive hard cheeses ripened for two years. Use grated

GRUYÈRE (Swiss)
Expensive hard cheese with fairly sweet taste. Use in fondues

DUNLOP (Scottish)
Similar to Cheddar, but milder. Use for most cheese recipes

HARD AND MEDIUM CHEESES The majority of English cheeses are in this category as well as Italian Parmesan and Swiss Emmenthal and Gruyère. While most cheeses can be used for cooking, hard and medium ones, which grate easily and have a distinct flavour, are best. Irish Cheddar has a stronger flavour than New Zealand and is less expensive than English or Canadian Cheddars.

bread or biscuits and butter, salad vegetables such as radishes, watercress, spring onions and celery are good accompaniments to cheese.

COOKING WITH CHEESE

Almost any cheese can be used for cooking, but those that are firm and grate easily such as Cheshire, Cheddar and Lancashire, are best.

Italian Parmesan cheese, which is hard and dry with a strong flavour, is finely grated to sprinkle on soups and pasta dishes. Buy Parmesan in the piece if possible as packs of ready-grated cheese are more expensive and may go stale. Use a rotary grater, as Parmesan is very hard.

Some recipes specify Swiss Gruyère, Italian Mozarella or Bel Paese cheeses (these are used for pizzas), but they are all expensive, and cheaper cheese such as Cheddar can usually be substituted without spoiling the dish.

Use grated cheese as a filling for omelettes or pancakes, or mixed with other ingredients to stuff tomatoes or hard-boiled eggs. Sprinkle it on cooked egg, fish and vegetable dishes, then brown under a hot grill.

Slices of Cheddar cheese make a tasty addition to hamburgers and fish fillets. Lay the cheese over the cooked hamburger or fish and melt under a medium-hot grill.

BUDGET RECIPE – CHEESE PUDDING

Ingredients 300 ml. ($\frac{1}{2}$ pint) milk, 25 g. (1 oz.) butter or margarine, 1 egg, 50 g. (2 oz.) white breadcrumbs, 50 g. (2 oz.) grated Cheddar cheese, salt and pepper.

Method Grease a 600 ml. (1 pint) pie dish. Heat the milk, add the butter and when it has melted remove from the heat. Add crumbs, cheese and seasoning and cool slightly. Mix in the beaten egg yolk thoroughly. Stiffly whip the egg white and fold it into the mixture. Pour into pie dish and bake for 20 minutes at 220°C (425°F; mark 7), when the pudding should be firm and light brown on top.

• EGGS

Eggs are the cheapest available source of high-quality protein and the yolk is a rich source of iron, vitamins and minerals. The British eat an average of 256 per person every year. It takes 72 million hens in this country, producing 14,500 million eggs annually, to meet the demand.

However, since one egg contains 300 mg. of cholesterol, which is two-thirds of the acceptable daily amount, the number of eggs eaten should be balanced with the intake of other high-cholesterol foods such as butter.

EGG PRODUCTION

Most eggs come from battery farms – 91% of all hens are kept by this method. The birds live in cages, are fed on a balanced diet and the light and temperature conditions are controlled. The battery hens are usually kept for about a year and then they are sold as boiling fowl.

Only 4% of birds in this country are kept free-range and allowed to run about in the open. The other 5% are in deep-litter systems where the birds move freely in groups of several hundred on deep layers of straw or wood shavings. Hens are put into deep-litter houses at five months old and are usually sold at about 16 months when they have passed their peak laying time.

Some poultry farmers have their own packing stations, but eggs from others are collected once or twice a week and taken to one of over 500 packing stations in different parts of the country. At the packing stations the eggs are 'candled' – held before a bright light to check for quality – graded and packed, then distributed.

BUYING EGGS

Check the date stamp on the carton before you buy to make sure the eggs are as fresh as possible (see illustration). They should not be more than two weeks old and, ideally, less than a week. Do not buy dirty eggs as the shells are porous and can absorb bacteria.

Eggs are priced according to size. It is worth comparing the prices of the different sizes because it is possible to economise by buying small eggs when, for example, four small eggs cost less than three standard ones and give about the same quantity.

Brown eggs can cost more than white, but there is no difference in food value.

Eggs labelled 'Farm fresh' are sold in some shops. These come direct from farms and do not go through the packing stations. There is no guarantee that these eggs are particularly fresh or that they are free-range, unless this is specifically stated.

Eggs bought direct from the farm in country districts are often free-range eggs. Free-range eggs are also sold in some small shops and usually cost about 20% more per dozen than battery-produced ones.

There is no evidence that free-range eggs are more nutritious than battery-produced ones, or that those with deep yellow yolks are better than eggs with pale yolks. Some people, though, prefer their flavour.

There is no way to tell the freshness of an egg before buying if it is not dated, but fresh eggs sink when put in water and stale ones tend to float.

Another test of freshness is to break an egg on to a plate. A fresh egg has a rounded yolk and a firm raised white with two distinct layers. A stale egg has a flat yolk and the white is runny, but can still be used for cooking.

Eggs not more than a week old are best for boiling and for recipes where the eggs must be separated and the whites whisked.

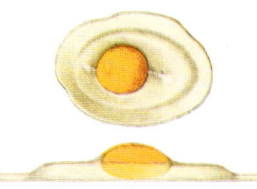

CLASS A Top-quality egg, which has a firm white, and thin outer layer.

CLASS B Fair-quality egg which has a flattened yolk and a soft white.

Eggs that are not quite so fresh can be used for cakes and puddings.

Fresh eggs will keep for three weeks at room temperature. Since shop eggs are usually one week old, they will keep for two weeks. They can be stored for up to six weeks in a refrigerator. Take them out of the refrigerator and keep them at room temperature for about half an hour before use. Very cold eggs tend to crack when boiled and the whites do not whisk easily.

Eggs are plentiful all year round and the price is fairly stable, but the peak laying time is still the spring and this is when eggs are cheapest. It is worth bulk buying at this time if you have a freezer. Eggs break if frozen in their shells. To freeze eggs they should first be shelled. Yolks and whites can then be separated and frozen separately, or lightly mixed together before freezing.

EGGS FROM OTHER BIRDS

Ducks often lay eggs in muddy places where harmful bacteria may penetrate the porous shell. It is therefore advisable to hard-boil the eggs

WEIGHT GRADING OF EGGS			
BRITISH GRADES	WEIGHT	EEC GRADES	WEIGHT
Large	2⅜ oz. or over	Grade 1	70 g. or over
		Grade 2	65 - 70 g.
		Grade 3	60 - 65 g.
Standard	1⅞ - 2⅜ oz.	Grade 4	55 - 60 g.
		Grade 5	50 - 55 g.
Medium	1⅝ - 1⅞ oz.	Grade 6	45 - 50 g.
Small	1½ - 1⅝ oz.	Grade 7	45 g. or under

REGISTERED NUMBER
This is the packing-station number. If the eggs are British it will begin with a 9

NAME AND ADDRESS
The name and address of the enterprise which graded the eggs or its trademark

'EXTRA' LABEL
This means that the eggs are not more than a week old. The label must be removed not later than the 7th day after packing

QUANTITY
The number of eggs the carton contains – usually six

DATE CODE
The week number (or date) on which the eggs were packed. The weeks of the year are numbered 1 - 52, week 1 being the first complete week in January

QUALITY
Eggs in the shops are Class A (excellent internal quality) or B (fair internal quality). Class C eggs are not sold to the public. They go direct to food manufacturers

WEIGHT GRADE
At present UK weight grades – Large, Standard, Medium and Small – are used, but EEC grades (see chart) are scheduled to be introduced in this country in 1978

BUYING FRESH EGGS   Common Market (EEC) regulations cover all eggs sold in the shops, which must have the quantity, weight, quality, packing-station number, grader's name and the date of packing clearly marked on the carton.

for at least 10 minutes. Duck eggs are larger and more strongly flavoured than hen eggs. The whites have a slightly blue tinge when cooked and the yolks are deep orange. Use them for cakes and puddings. They should not be frozen. Eggs from pheasants, gulls, plovers and guinea fowl are all edible and usually hard-boiled for 10-15 minutes to serve as hors-d'oeuvres.

• COOKING EGGS

It is surprising how often simple egg dishes turn out badly.

One reason is that eggs should be cooked slowly, except when they are used in omelettes. Fast cooking toughens the white of a boiled or fried egg and makes scrambled eggs rubbery. Cook omelettes over a medium-to-high heat for not more than 2 minutes, or they become leathery.

BAKED EGGS

Break the eggs into individual, buttered, fire-proof dishes. Heat the oven to 180°C (350°F; mark 4), then stand the dishes in a pan containing hot water to half the depth of the dishes. Bake for 8-10 minutes. Cream, pâté, sauces, such as cheese or tomato, or puréed vegetables can be put into the dish before the egg.

BOILED EGGS

Pierce the rounded end of the shell with a pin to prevent boiled eggs from cracking while they are being cooked. Gadgets are available for this but a pin is just as effective. Put the eggs in a saucepan and cover with cold water. Bring the water to the boil and immediately lower the heat to a simmer. Timing after the water boils should be: soft boiled – large size 3 minutes, standard 2¾ minutes, medium 2½ minutes; medium boiled – large size 4½ minutes, standard 4 minutes, medium 3½ minutes; hard boiled – large 8 minutes, standard 7 minutes, medium 6 minutes.

Tap the pointed end with a spoon as soon as it is cooked to crack it and to prevent further cooking.

If the shell does crack when the egg is in the water, quickly put in a teaspoon of vinegar to prevent the white running out. If the white is already escaping, put in a tablespoon of salt.

CODDLED EGGS

Easily digestible, coddled eggs are ideal for babies and invalids. Lower the egg, in its shell, into a pan of boiling water. Remove the pan from the heat at once, cover and leave to stand: 9 minutes for a large egg; 8 minutes for a standard; and 7 minutes for a medium; then serve.

FRIED EGGS

Cook the eggs gently in butter, lard or dripping, hot but not sizzling. Break each egg into a cup before sliding it gently into the hot fat to prevent the yolk from breaking, and check that the eggs are of good quality. Baste the eggs with a spoon.

POACHED EGGS

Special poaching pans steam the eggs rather than poach them because the eggs are cooked over the water put into the lower pan.

True poaching can be done in a shallow pan half-filled with simmering water, to which a teaspoon of vinegar has been added. Break each egg into a cup and slide it into the pan. Cook gently until set.

SCRAMBLED EGGS

Use a heavy pan so that the eggs cook evenly. Allow two eggs per person. Mix the eggs with 2 tablespoons of milk or water to lighten the mixture and make it go further, and season with salt and pepper. Melt 15 g. (½ oz.) butter in a saucepan and add the eggs, reserving 1 tablespoon. Stir them to prevent sticking and to ensure they cook evenly. Remove the pan from the heat just before the eggs have set and add the reserved egg. The pan heat will finish the cooking.

OMELETTES

There are two main types of omelette – plain, with the yolks and whites mixed together, and soufflé, with the whites whisked separately and folded into the yolks. Plain omelettes are usually served on their own or with a savoury filling, soufflé omelettes often contain fruit or jam. Do not use more than four eggs – large omelettes are difficult to cook properly.

Any heavy frying pan can be used. A pan kept for making omelettes and wiped out with kitchen paper rather than washed prevents sticking.

How to make a plain omelette Beat the eggs lightly in a basin using a fork and adding a tablespoon of water to lighten the mixture. Season with salt and pepper. Meanwhile, melt 15 g. (½ oz.) of butter in the pan and, when the butter is sizzling, pour in the eggs. Draw the mixture from the sides to the centre of the pan with a fork as it sets, and let the liquid egg from the centre run to the sides. Cook for a further minute once the egg has set then fold in half, or fold either side to the middle, and slide the omelette out of the pan. Suitable fillings: herbs, chopped ham, cooked meat or grated cheese, can be stirred into the egg mixture before it is cooked. Add hot fillings, such as fried bacon mushrooms or fish in a little cheese sauce, when the omelette has set, just before folding it.

How to make a soufflé omelette Separate yolks of the eggs from the whites. Whisk the yolks until they are creamy and, for a two-egg omelette, stir in a level tablespoon of caster sugar. Stiffly beat the whites and fold them into the yolks. Melt 15 g. (½ oz.) of butter in a heavy-bottomed pan, without browning it, then pour in the eggs. Cook over a moderate heat until the underside of the omelette is golden brown. Remove from top of the cooker and put the pan under a medium grill to brown the top of the omelette. Fold it in half and slide on to a warm plate. Suitable fillings: rum, vanilla and other liquid flavourings are stirred into the egg yolks with the sugar. Spread jam or puréed fruit on the cooked omelette before folding it.

• USING EGGS

Apart from the use of eggs as dishes in their own right, they are indispensable for cooking.

BINDING WITH EGG

Whole whisked eggs, or just the yolks, will bind the dry ingredients for breadcrumb-based stuffings, rissoles and meat loaves. Rich pastry and creamed potatoes to be moulded or piped can be mixed with beaten egg.

COATING WITH EGG

Food – usually fish or meat, such as veal escalopes – brushed with beaten egg and dipped in breadcrumbs is protected from very hot fat and comes out with a crisp coating.

GLAZING

Whisked whole egg, or the yolk mixed with a little water or milk, is used to glaze pastry, bread and scones. Brush the top with egg before baking, to give a rich brown gloss.

RAISING

Eggs act as raising agents because they retain the air beaten into them. They are used for this purpose in batters (see p. 269) and many cakes, particularly sponges. A whole egg can be beaten to a pale yellow foam with added sugar (about 2 tablespoons to each egg). Whisked egg whites are used for extra light mixtures (see below).

SEPARATED EGGS

The usual way to separate an egg is to break the shell in half over a basin, then tip the yolk from one half to the other, allowing the white to drain off. Another method is to break the egg on to a saucer, turn a cup upside-down over the yolk and drain off the white.

SEPARATED YOLKS

In addition to being used for binding and glazing (see above), egg yolks combine with oil or melted butter to make an emulsion. This emulsifying property is used in making mayonnaise (see p. 279) and hollandaise sauces.

SEPARATED WHITES

The volume of separated egg whites increases as much as six times when they are whisked at room temperature. If whisked whites are not used at once, the air disperses and they collapse. Whisked whites are used in meringues, sponge cakes, soufflés and soufflé omelettes.

THICKENING

Whole whisked eggs, or just the yolks, act as a thickening agent when heated gently with liquid to make custard, soups and sauces. One egg will thicken about 275-300 ml. (½ pint) of liquid. Do not add the egg directly to hot liquid but mix it with a tablespoon of cold water or milk. Stir in some of the hot liquid then return the mixture to the pan and stir over a gentle heat until it is thick. Do not boil. If there is any sign of curdling put the liquid in a cold bowl and beat vigorously.

COOKING WITH FLOUR

In Britain, over 3½ million tons of wheat flour is produced annually, an average yearly consumption per person of about 65 kg. (140 lb.). Flour contains protein, carbohydrate, mineral salts and vitamins, as well as roughage in the wholemeal varieties. In cooking, flour is important because the protein in it forms gluten. This gives an elastic dough which, with raising agents such as eggs, yeast or baking powder, makes light, spongy mixtures for cakes, bread and puddings. Flours from other cereals, such as oats and rice, contain little gluten and are usually mixed with wheat flour for baking.

• TYPES OF FLOUR

Most flour sold in this country is made from milled wheat.

A grain of wheat consists of the embryo, or wheatgerm, the white, starchy endosperm covering it, and the tough, brown outer skin, also called the husk or the bran.

The aim of milling is to reduce the wheat grain to a fine flour. To make white flour the endosperm is separated from the wheatgerm and the husk. Break rollers in the mills crack open the wheat grains, scrape and partly crush them. The wheat then passes through a series of increasingly fine nylon or silk meshes which separate the flakes of husk and wheatgerm, leaving the endosperm. This is finely ground into flour.

Vitamins, iron and calcium are lost during milling and so are replaced in white and wheatmeal flour. Bleaches and improvers are also added to facilitate bread manufacture. All these additives are strictly controlled by the Food Standards Committee.

Wheat is classified according to its hardness, or strength, and hard wheat contains most protein. Hard wheat makes strong flour, because it contains a high proportion of gluten and absorbs more liquid than soft flour. Strong flour is the kind used for making bread.

Most wheat grown in Britain is soft, because our summers are not usually hot enough to fully ripen hard wheat. **White flour,** which is the most widely used, consists of home-grown wheat, blended with hard wheat imported mainly from Canada and France. The wheatgerm and the outer skin are removed, leaving the pure endosperm.
Wheatmeal, which is also called brown flour to avoid confusion with wholemeal, has only the coarsest particles of bran, or outer skin, removed. It does contain the wheatgerm.
Wholemeal flour, sometimes known as wholewheat, includes the whole wheat grain with nothing added and nothing taken away, and is slightly more nutritious than other flours. The bran also provides roughage.
Self-raising flour can be white or brown and contains raising agents. When heated, these give off carbon dioxide which makes cakes and puddings rise.
Super-sifted flours, also called superfine or super-graded flours, are prepared from specially blended wheat by modified sifting techniques which give a free-running white flour with no lumps. It is easy to use and does not need sieving, but is more expensive than ordinary white flour.

Most wheat is ground between metal rollers, but stone-ground flour is still made by the centuries-old method of milling between two stones. There is no proof that stone-ground flour has higher food value than flour milled on rollers.

Compost-grown flour, sold mostly in health-food shops, is made from wheat grown on naturally fertilised land, free from artificial chemicals. Only small quantities are available and the flour is soft. Bread sold as being made from compost-grown flour will almost certainly contain some flour made from hard wheat.

OTHER FLOURS

With the exception of rye flour, which may contain a little, the following flours do not contain gluten to make dough rise, and are not suitable for making bread. They are used to thicken soups, sauces and custard, or mixed with wheat flour to give a lighter texture to cakes and puddings.

ARROWROOT

The root of the maranta plant is ground to make arrowroot, a fine powdery starch. When heated with water it makes a clear, thick liquid for coating fruit flans and making cold desserts.

CORNFLOUR

The outer husk and oil are removed from maize, or sweet corn, and the starchy grain is ground to make cornflour. It is finer than wheat flour and is easier to blend into a smooth sauce. The cornflour swells and thickens when it is heated, and can be used in sauces, soups and stews. It forms the basis of custard powder and packet blancmange mixtures.

POTATO FLOUR

Sometimes called farina or fecule, the refined starch from potatoes is used for thickening soups and sauces. It thickens at a lower temperature than other starches.

RICE FLOUR

Rice is milled to a fine, cream-coloured powder which can be mixed with wheat flour to give a lighter texture to cakes and puddings.

RYE FLOUR

This dark brown, coarse flour, made from whole grains of rye, is not widely available. It is used on its own to make dark, moist Pumpernickel bread. It is also mixed with wheat flour to make brown rye loaves.

TAPIOCA FLOUR

The finest siftings produced during the manufacture of tapioca, which is made from the root of the cassava plant, are sold as tapioca flour. It is used mainly to thicken soups.

STORING FLOUR

Flour deteriorates if it is stored in a damp, warm place or if it is kept too long. It is best left in the bag and put on a dry, airy shelf. In a damp, steamy kitchen, put the bag in a tin with a

USES OF WHEAT FLOURS

TYPE OF FLOUR	PERCENTAGE OF WHOLE WHEAT	USES, FOR BEST RESULTS
Plain strong white	70-72%	White bread, puff pastry and flaky pastry
Plain soft white	70-72%	Short pastry, biscuits, shortbread
Self-raising white	70-72%	Sponges, cakes and puddings
Wheatmeal (Brown)	80-90%	Bread and heavier-textured cakes and pastry
Wholemeal	100%	Bread, cakes and pastry with a grainy, wholemeal texture

tight-fitting lid, or in a stoppered jar.

If stored under good conditions, plain flour will keep up to six months, self-raising for two to three months, after which it loses its raising power, and wholemeal and wheatmeal flours for two months. Buy wholemeal flour in small quantities and use it quickly as it goes rancid if kept too long.

• USES OF FLOUR

Flour is the basis of batters and sauces, which are easy to make and can be used for a wide variety of sweet and savoury dishes.

BATTERS

Basically a mixture of flour, eggs and milk, batter can be made thick or thin, according to the amount of liquid, the thoroughness of the beating (to add air to the mixture) and the cooking method.

The two types of batter – pouring and coating – are made in the same way, but pouring batter is thinner and contains more liquid.

BASIC RECIPE FOR BATTER

Ingredients 100 g. (4 oz.) plain flour; 1 standard egg; a good pinch of salt; 300 ml. (½ pint) milk for pouring batter or 150 ml. (¼ pint) milk for coating batter.

Method Sift the flour and salt into a bowl, make a well in the centre and break the egg into it. Gradually stir in half the milk, mixing the egg well in. Beat the mixture thoroughly, then stir in the remaining milk. To make a lighter mixture use half milk and half water. A balloon whisk is more effective than a rotary one, or use a liquidiser.

POURING BATTER

To make a pancake, pour two or three tablespoons of the mixture into a little sizzling lard or oil. Only sufficient fat is needed to coat the pan, so pour off the excess before putting in the batter. Tilt the pan so that the mixture thinly covers it. Fry until golden brown underneath and set on top, then turn with a fish slice and fry until brown on the other side.

Pancakes can be served plain, with sugar and lemon juice, traditionally eaten on Shrove Tuesday, or stuffed with savoury or sweet fillings, like omelettes (see p. 267).

Do not use more than 10 g. (¼ oz.) of fat, and put in only enough batter to thinly cover the pan or the pancake will be stodgy. Cook over a medium heat because if the heat is too low the pancake will be flabby, not crisp.

Pouring batter is also used to make Yorkshire pudding. Heat the oven to 230°C (450°F; mark 8). Put 25 g. (1 oz.) fat into a baking tin and heat in the oven for two to three minutes. Pour all the batter mixture into the tin, return to the oven and cook for 30-35 minutes, until well risen and crisp. This is traditionally served with roast beef.

Alternatively, put tablespoons of the mixture into individual, greased bun tins and cook for 20 minutes. These can be served with syrup.

COATING BATTER

This is used to give a crisp covering to fish, chicken or rissoles. Fruit or vegetables are coated with the batter and deep fried to make fritters. Cut the food into evenly sized pieces, dip into coating batter and cook in deep fat for four to ten minutes, depending on whether the food is cooked or raw.

French coating batter is made with the same ingredients but the egg is separated, the white whisked stiffly and folded into the batter just before it is cooked. This gives a crisper coating.

Yeast coating batter also makes a very crisp covering. Sift 100 g. (4 oz.) plain flour and a pinch of salt into a basin. Stir in 1 teaspoon of dried yeast or 10 g. (¼ oz) fresh yeast, mixed with 150 ml. (¼ pint) of warm water and 1 tablespoon of oil, and leave for 20 minutes before using.

• SAUCES

The starch in flour, mixed with liquid, swells when heated, and acts as the thickening agent for many savoury and sweet sauces.

Most flour-based sauces are made by the roux method, which means that the flour is cooked in butter or other fat first. The liquid is added to this roux, which can be white or brown depending on how long it is cooked.

Sauces can be of pouring or coating consistency, like batters. A very thick sauce is called a panada.

Savoury pouring sauces are served with fish, meat and vegetable dishes, and sweet sauces with hot stewed fruit and puddings.

Coating sauces are used as a basis for mousses and creams or chaud-froid sauces to coat meat and fish.

QUANTITIES FOR BASIC WHITE SAUCES			
INGREDIENTS	POURING SAUCE	COATING SAUCE	PANADA
Fat (butter or margarine)	15 g. (½ oz.)	25 g. (1 oz.)	50 g. (2 oz.)
Plain flour	15 g. (½ oz.)	25 g. (1 oz.)	50 g. (2 oz.)
Milk, stock or wine	300 ml. (½ pint)	300 ml. (½ pint)	300 ml. (½ pint)

MAKING A BASIC WHITE SAUCE

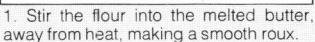
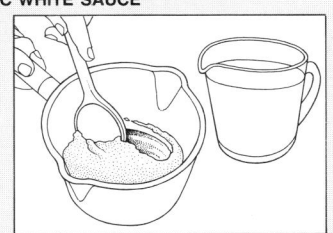

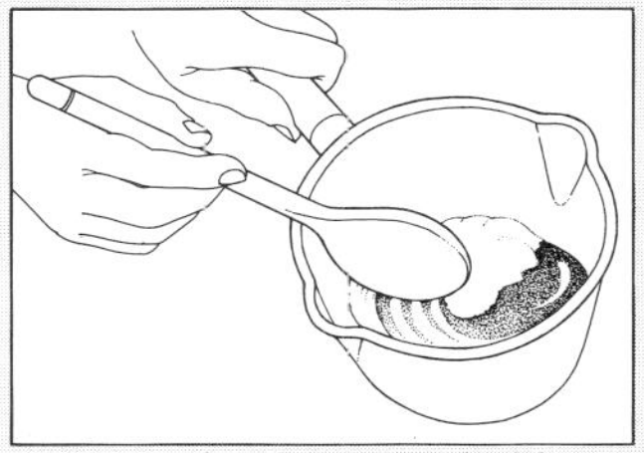

1. Stir the flour into the melted butter, away from heat, making a smooth roux.

2. Stir a little liquid into the roux, and cook over a gentle heat.

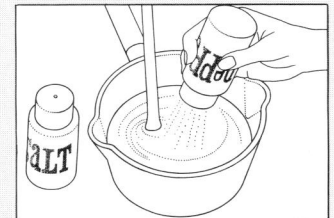

3. Mix in the remaining liquid away from heat. Cook and stir until sauce boils.

4. Allow the thickened sauce to simmer for five minutes and add seasonings.

A panada is used to bind cooked or raw meat for croquettes and other savoury rissoles, for vol-au-vent and patty fillings and to make sweet or savoury soufflés.

BROWN SAUCE

The basic method and ingredients are the same as for white sauce, but the fat used can be dripping, bacon fat or olive oil and the liquid is usually meat or vegetable stock rather than milk or wine.

Cook the flour over a gentle heat, stirring frequently until it turns a rich brown, before adding the liquid.

Brown sauce is used only for savoury dishes. Pouring brown sauce can be served as gravy or put into soups and stews. Coating sauce is used for meat dishes in a thick sauce, and for reheating left-over meat.

Flavourings for brown sauce include: herbs, tomato paste, curry powder, onion and mushrooms.

DRIED SAUCES

Packets of savoury dried sauces are sold in most shops. They are quick and easy to use. Water or other liquid is added to the sauce powder then brought to the boil. It is worth experimenting with different brands because they vary considerably.

FRUIT SAUCE

Fruit juice or purée is made into sauce by the blending method. For 300 ml. (½ pint) of juice or purée, sweetened with 25 g. (1 oz.) of sugar, blend 15 g. (½ oz.) cornflour, arrowroot or potato flour, with two tablespoons of cold water. Heat the juice or purée to boiling point and add 2-3 tablespoons of the boiling liquid to the cornflour and water. Re-boil, stirring.

Serve fruit sauce with steamed, baked or boiled puddings and as a filling for cakes and pancakes.

• BUYING AND MAKING BREAD

Less bread is eaten in the home than at any time in the past. Britain's average consumption per head is just over a loaf a week. Yet for most people, bread and flour still supply more energy and the B vitamin thiamine than any other food. Only milk supplies more calcium and only meat more protein, iron and niacin, another B vitamin. This is because of the quantity eaten rather than comparable food value, ounce for ounce.

Government regulations control the ingredients and nutritional value of bread and flour (see p. 268). In addition to the basic ingredients, the regulations allow oils and fats, milk, sugar, enzyme active preparations such as malt extract, wheat gluten and germ, poppy and caraway seeds, oats, yeast-stimulating agents to improve texture, anti-mould agents such as acetic acid, emulsifiers (lecithin, for example), permitted bleach, improving agents and preservatives.

These regulations apply to brown and wheatmeal bread as well as to white bread, but the flour used must also contain at least 0.6% fibre, and wholemeal bread must be made from the wholewheat grain (see Wholemeal flour, p. 268).

Wheatgerm bread, such as Hovis, must contain at least 10% processed wheatgerm. Loaves described as granary are made from flour containing a small amount of rye flour and malted wheat.

Starch-reduced breads must contain at least 22% protein. This means that, slice for slice, there is less carbohydrate than in other bread.

BUYING BREAD

The large, wrapped, sliced white loaf accounts for 50% of total bread sales in Britain, although most bakers stock at least a dozen different sizes and shapes of bread. Traditional shapes – made from the same basic dough – are pictured right. They include bloomer, cob, cottage, farmhouse and sandwich loaves as well as plain, finger and crescent rolls. The cholla is a Jewish loaf made of plaited dough covered with poppy seeds. Matzo is Jewish bread made with flour, salt and water, but no yeast. Crispbreads are also made without yeast.

Sliced bread comes in thin, medium or thick slices and is convenient to use, particularly for toast and sandwiches.

Wrapped loaves keep better than others, but they are not crusty. Partly cooked brown and white loaves and rolls are sold in many shops and need only a short final baking to make them crisp and brown.

Milk breads, such as French sticks and Vienna loaves, and those enriched with fat or eggs, also keep well because the crumb content is softer. Baps and French rolls – croissants and brioches – are made with this type of mix.

To freshen stale bread, wrap it in foil and put it into a hot oven, 230°C (450°F; mark 8) for five to ten minutes. Allow the bread to cool slightly in the foil and when it is unwrapped it will taste freshly baked. Crusty bread tends to lose its crispness after a day, and this can be restored by putting the loaf, unwrapped, into a hot oven for five to ten minutes.

STORING BREAD

Leave wrapped bread in the paper and put other loaves or rolls into a clean polythene bag, wrapped loosely so that the air can circulate. Put the wrapped bread into a dry, clean, well-ventilated bread crock or bin and keep it at room temperature. To keep the crust crisp and the bread soft, moist and free from mould, the container should not be airtight. Wash it out in hot soapy water once a week, and add a little vinegar to the rinsing water to prevent mould from forming.

Most bread will keep for about one week stored in this way and a wrapped sliced loaf will keep for a few days longer. Bread can be wrapped in a sealed polythene bag and put into a freezer for at least a month, though crusty bread does not freeze well.

• HOME-MADE BREAD

White and wholemeal strong flour and dry or fresh yeast, needed to make bread, are available at supermarkets and health shops.

Home-made bread is not necessarily cheaper than bought loaves or rolls, but the taste and texture are much better.

INGREDIENTS

Fresh yeast Unlike other raising agents, such as baking powder, yeast is a living plant. Mixed with flour and water, in a warm temperature, yeast grows and carbon dioxide is formed. The bubbles in the gas make the bread dough spongy, and the alcohol produced by the growing yeast gives freshly baked bread its characteristic taste and smell.

Fresh yeast looks like putty and should be creamy grey, cool to touch and easy to break. It is not as easily available as dried yeast, but gives better results. It will keep for four or five days, loosely wrapped in polythene, in a cool cupboard, a month in a refrigerator and six months in a freezer. Before freezing, wrap the yeast in convenient 15 g. (½ oz.) packs. Before using, either grate the yeast or leave it to thaw for 30 minutes at room temperature.

Dried yeast Stored in an airtight tin in a cool cupboard, dried yeast will keep for up to six months. It is sold in 100-125 g. (4 oz.) packets or tins or 25 g. (1 oz.) packets in chemists, grocers

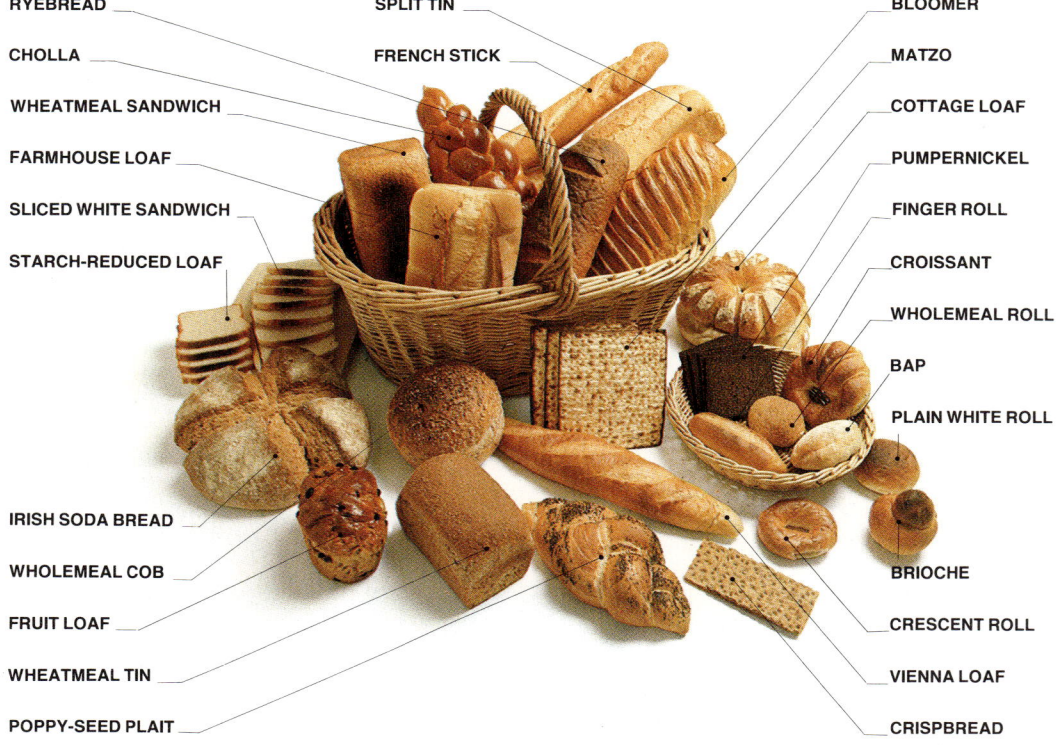

RYEBREAD
CHOLLA
WHEATMEAL SANDWICH
FARMHOUSE LOAF
SLICED WHITE SANDWICH
STARCH-REDUCED LOAF
IRISH SODA BREAD
WHOLEMEAL COB
FRUIT LOAF
WHEATMEAL TIN
POPPY-SEED PLAIT

SPLIT TIN
FRENCH STICK

BLOOMER
MATZO
COTTAGE LOAF
PUMPERNICKEL
FINGER ROLL
CROISSANT
WHOLEMEAL ROLL
BAP
PLAIN WHITE ROLL
BRIOCHE
CRESCENT ROLL
VIENNA LOAF
CRISPBREAD

BREAD LINES Bakers sell bread in dozens of shapes, from the age-old cottage loaf to the latest sliced sandwich.

and health food shops. Dried yeast is more concentrated than fresh yeast and only half as much is needed in most recipes.

Flour Flour labelled 'strong' or 'bread flour' gives the best results in home baking, producing a spongy loaf.

Wholemeal, wheatmeal and stone-ground flour can also be used to make bread with a dense, coarser texture and nutty flavour.

Rye flour is mixed with wheat flour to make rye bread, and with bran and wheat to make pumpernickel.

Salt Some salt is needed in home-made bread to prevent the yeast from fermenting too quickly. Be careful not to add more than the recipe specifies.

Sugar Although sugar is a food which helps yeast to grow, ensuring well-risen bread, too much kills some of the yeast cells and gives the bread a very yeasty flavour.

Fat Oil or lard can be added to dough to enrich it, although it is not essential for plain mixtures. A small amount of fat makes the crumbs soft.

Other ingredients Milk adds food value, strengthens the dough, improves the keeping quality and gives a crustier loaf. The dough can also be mixed with milk and water, or water only. Other ingredients, such as eggs, dried fruit and malt, can be added to doughs to enrich them and give variety.

PLAIN WHITE BREAD

The following recipe is for two 450 g. (1 lb.) loaves or 18 bread rolls.

Ingredients 700 g. (1½ lb.) strong, plain flour; 2 level teaspoons salt; 15 g (½ oz.) fresh yeast or 2 level teaspoons dried yeast and 1 teaspoon sugar; 450 ml. (¾ pint) warm water; 15 g (½ oz.) lard.

Method This basic method is used for all types of bread.

1. Blend fresh yeast with the warm water. If dried yeast is being used, dissolve a teaspoon of sugar in the warm water, sprinkle on the dried yeast and leave it in a warm place until it is frothy (about ten minutes).

2. Mix together the flour and salt and rub in the fat.

3. Mix the yeast and water with the dry ingredients to make a soft dough. Put this on to a board and knead it thoroughly for about ten minutes. Always flour your hands rather than the board, as too much flour will spoil the elasticity of the dough. Knead by pushing, pulling and slapping the dough repeatedly.

An electric mixer with a dough-hook attachment can be used to knead the dough. Start the mixer on the minimum speed and after one minute switch to speed 1 for two minutes, or follow the mixer manufacturer's instructions. The dough should leave the sides of the bowl cleanly.

4. Put the dough into a greased, plastic bag or back into the bowl, covered with a damp cloth. Leave it to rise for 30-40 minutes in a warm place, until it has doubled in size.

5. When the dough has risen, knead it again by hand, or in the mixer for two minutes at minimum speed.

6. For two small loaves, divide the dough into two equal pieces. Roll up each piece, fold under the ends and put into a greased and floured 450 g. (1 lb.) loaf tin or on a baking sheet with the folded side underneath.

7. To make rolls, divide the dough into 18 pieces and roll each one into a ball. For soft-sided, pull-apart rolls, put the pieces of dough 20 mm. (¾ in.) apart on a baking sheet and lightly dust with flour. For crusty rolls put the pieces of dough 25 mm. (1 in.) apart.

8. The dough is now left to rise a second time, which is called proving it, until it again doubles in size. This will take 20-30 minutes at room temperature. The dough should spring back into shape when it is pressed.

9. Bake the loaves in a very hot oven (230°C, 450°F; mark 8) for 15 minutes, then reduce the heat to 190°C (375°F; mark 5) for 30 minutes. Test that they are cooked by tapping the bottom of the tins, which should sound hollow.

Put rolls near the top of the oven and bake for 20-25 minutes at 230°C (450°F; mark 8).

10. Cool on a rack.

ENRICHED DOUGH

This recipe makes a softer, shorter textured dough which can be used for loaves or buns. The amounts given

MAKING BREAD DOUGH

1. Add the yeast and water to mixed dry ingredients, and stir to a soft dough.

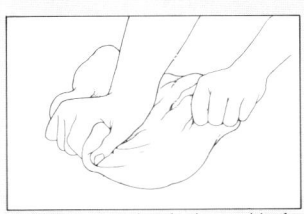

2. Knead the dough thoroughly for about 10 minutes to make it elastic.

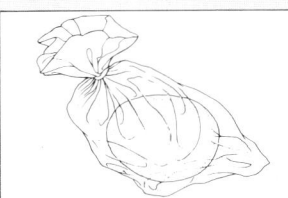

3. Leave the dough to rise in a greased plastic bag until it doubles in size.

will make two small loaves or 12 buns.

Ingredients 450 g. (1 lb.) strong, plain flour; 1 teaspoon sugar; 15 g. (½ oz.) fresh yeast or two teaspoons dried yeast; 300 ml. (½ pint) warm milk; 1 teaspoon salt; 50 g. (2 oz.) butter or margarine; 1 egg.

Method For buns or loaves, the method is basically the same.

1. Weigh out a quarter of the flour into a bowl with the sugar and fresh or dried yeast. Add the warm milk and beat. Leave the mixture to stand for 30 minutes, until frothy.

2. Mix together the remaining dry ingredients and rub in the butter. If the dough is to be used to make buns add an extra 50 g. (2 oz.) sugar.

3. Whisk the egg and stir it into the yeast batter. Add the rubbed-in flour and fat and mix to a soft dough.

4. Knead thoroughly for about ten minutes and leave to rise for 20-40 minutes in a warm room until doubled in size.

5. Re-knead the dough then shape it into loaves or buns. Extra flavourings, such as grated cheese, herbs, spices or dried fruit, can be added at this stage. Put loaves into tins or, for buns, place rounds of dough 20 mm. (¾ in.) apart on a baking sheet.

6. Put the bread or buns into a polythene bag to prove for 20-30 minutes, then remove and brush with beaten egg.

7. Bake loaves for 45 minutes at 190°C (375°F; mark 5), and buns 15-20 minutes at 220°C (425°F; mark 7).

TIME-SAVING DOUGHS

Bread making can be speeded up by adding an ascorbic-acid tablet (available from chemists) to the yeast liquid. It is essential to use only fresh yeast. Continue as for making plain, white bread and mix the ingredients to a soft dough. After kneading, leave the dough to prove in a greased polythene bag or covered bowl for five minutes at room temperature.

Re-knead the dough for about two minutes and then shape, prove and bake as for white bread.

SODA BREAD

Raising agents other than yeast, such as baking powder or bicarbonate of soda and cream of tartar, can be used to make bread. They are quick and easy to use although the bread tends to have a more cake-like texture. It does not keep so well as bread made with yeast.

Ingredients 450 g. (1 lb.) plain flour; 1 level teaspoon salt; 1 level teaspoon bicarbonate of soda; 1 heaped teaspoon cream of tartar; 25 g. (1 oz.) butter or lard; 300 ml. (½ pint) fresh milk. Buttermilk can be used instead of fresh milk and the cream of tartar omitted.

Method Sift the flour, salt, bicarbonate of soda and cream of tartar into a bowl and rub in the butter or lard. Make a well in the centre and add the milk. Mix it in with a knife to form a non-sticky ball of dough.

Turn on to a floured board and knead until smooth, then shape into a round. Flatten until it is about 5 cm. (2 in.) thick, then put on a tray and bake in the centre of a hot oven (200°C, 400°F; mark 6) for 35-40 minutes.

GLAZES

Various finishes can be added to home-made bread and rolls to give them an attractive appearance.

Glaze rolls before putting them in the oven, but bread 20 minutes before it has finished cooking, otherwise it will be too brown.

For a shiny, yellow glaze use cream, top of the milk or beaten egg. To make the crust crisp use salted water. Glaze buns with sugar and water.

• HOME-MADE CAKES AND PUDDINGS

Cakes and puddings have a high carbohydrate and calorie content because of the amount of flour, fat and sugar they contain. If the fat used is butter or margarine this will provide some vitamins A and D, and the flour contains small quantities of B vitamins, protein, calcium and iron.

BASIC INGREDIENTS

Flour Plain, white flour and baking powder can be used but self-raising flour gives a more open texture. It is particularly suitable for sponge cakes and puddings.

Butter For the best flavour use butter to make plain cakes and baked or steamed sponge puddings.

Margarine Usually more economical than butter, margarine can be substituted in most cakes and puddings.

Suet Available shredded, in packets, or in a piece from the butcher.

Oil Corn or vegetable oils are particularly useful for cakes, made by the 'melted-in' method.

Eggs Recipes refer to standard-sized eggs weighing approximately 50 g. (2 oz.), unless otherwise stated. Eggs act as a raising agent.

Caster sugar Use fine caster sugar in sponge cakes and rich steamed puddings to give a fine texture.

Granulated sugar Coarser and cheaper than caster sugar, granulated sugar can be used for cakes and puddings made by the rubbed-in method.

Brown sugar Use moist, dark brown sugar to improve the flavour of fruit cake or gingerbread. Demerara sugar gives a grainy texture and is best used as a topping.

Syrup and treacle Used with sugar to give colour and flavour to rich fruit cakes and gingerbread.

Milk Used in most cakes and sponge puddings. In general, the richer the cake, the less liquid is needed. Cakes and scones that include bicarbonate of soda are mixed with sour milk, which increases the raising action.

CAKE TINS

Use shallow tins, in which cakes cook fairly quickly, to make plain cakes and sponges to be eaten within a few days of baking. Deep tins are best for rich cakes to be kept for some time.

A square tin holds the same amount as a round one which is 25 mm. (1 in.) more in diameter than one side of the square. For example, a 180 mm. (7 in.) square tin holds the same amount as a round tin 205 mm. (8 in.) in diameter.

Grease all tins before use and dust sponge tins with a dessertspoon of flour mixed with a dessertspoon of caster sugar, to give a crisp coating. Line sandwich tins and large cake tins with greaseproof paper to protect the cake during cooking. Two thicknesses of greaseproof are best for rich, large cakes. Christmas cakes usually have two thicknesses of brown paper tied round the outside of the tin as well.

• BASIC RECIPES

Cakes can be divided into a few basic types depending on the method and the proportion of fat, sugar and eggs. Plain cakes contain only half as much fat as flour, rich cakes have more fat, and sponges do not contain fat. Gingerbreads, made by the melted method, are plain cakes, and those made by the all-in-one method are rich cakes.

Although these recipes are for specific cakes, the mixtures can be used for a wide variety of cakes and puddings.

RUBBED-IN METHOD: PLAIN CAKE

This recipe is sufficient for a cake in a round tin 150 mm. (6 in.) in diameter.
Ingredients 225 g. (8 oz.) self-raising flour; pinch of salt; 100-125 g. (4 oz.) butter or margarine; 100-125 g. (4 oz.) caster sugar; 2 eggs; 4 tablespoons milk.

Method Put the flour and salt into a bowl and add the fat, cut into small pieces. Rub the fat into the flour with the fingers, or use an electric mixer, until it resembles fine breadcrumbs. Stir in sugar. Whisk the egg lightly with the milk and stir it into the dry ingredients. Mix thoroughly until the mixture drops softly from the spoon. Put into the prepared cake tin. Bake for 1-1¼ hours in the centre of the oven pre-heated to 180°C (350°F; mark 4).

CREAMED METHOD: VICTORIA SANDWICH

This recipe is sufficient for two sandwich tins 180 mm. (7 in.) in diameter.
Ingredients 100-125 g. (4 oz.) butter or margarine; 100-125 g. (4 oz.) caster sugar; 2 eggs; 100-125 g. (4 oz.) self-raising flour; 2 tablespoons jam.

Method Cut the fat, softened at room temperature, into pieces and put into a bowl. Beat with a wooden spoon or in an electric mixer until creamy. Beat in the sugar until the mixture is pale, light and fluffy. Beat in the eggs, with 1 tablespoon of the flour to prevent curdling. Gradually fold in the rest of the flour, adding a tablespoon of milk if the mixture is too stiff. It should be soft enough to drop easily from the spoon. Divide the mixture evenly between the two prepared sandwich tins and bake just above the centre of the oven for 20 minutes at 190°C (375°F; mark 5). The cake should be well risen, firm and golden.

When the cake is cool, spread the jam on one half and put the other half on top. Sprinkle a tablespoon of caster sugar over the top.

ALL-IN-ONE METHOD: FRUIT CAKE

Prepare a 180 mm. (7 in.) diameter round, or 150 mm. (6 in.) square tin.
Ingredients 50 g. (2 oz.) glacé cherries; 225 g. (8 oz.) self-raising flour; pinch of salt; 3 eggs; 175 g. (6 oz.) soft margarine; 175 g. (6 oz.) sugar; 325-350 g. (12 oz.) mixed, dried fruit; 2 level teaspoons mixed spice; 1 teaspoon grated lemon rind.

Method Quarter the glacé cherries, then put them, with all the other ingredients, into a bowl. Beat all the ingredients together for one minute, either with a wooden spoon or in an electric mixer. Put into the tin and bake in the centre of the oven for 1½ hours at 160°C (325°F; mark 3).

WHISKED SPONGE: SWISS ROLL

Although many sandwich cakes are described as sponges, a true sponge does not contain fat. Prepare a Swiss roll tin 280 × 180 mm. (11 × 7 in.).
Ingredients 3 eggs; 75 g. (3 oz.) caster sugar; 75 g. (3 oz.) plain flour;

CREAMED-CAKE METHOD

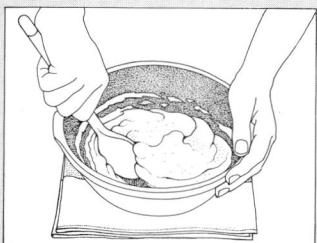

1. Beat the fat and sugar with a wooden spoon until light and fluffy.

2. The eggs can be broken straight into the bowl, or beaten first and added.

3. Fold in sifted flour, adding a little milk if mixture is too stiff.

MAKING A SWISS ROLL

1. Turn on to sugared paper, trim, and spread jam to within 15 mm. of edges.

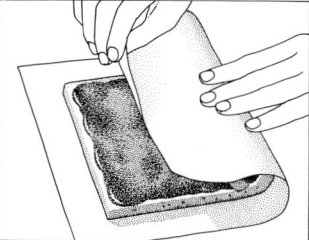

2. Protect sponge with the paper for first turn. Remove paper and roll up.

CREAMED METHOD
Used for Victoria sandwich and plain cakes, the sponge-type mixture has a light, close texture.

RUBBED-IN METHOD
Easy way to make cakes, rock buns and scones. It produces crumbly and loose-textured cakes.

MELTED METHOD
Slightly sticky, dense-textured cakes like chocolate cake and gingerbread are made in this way.

WHISKED METHOD
Usually without fat, whisked cakes, including Swiss roll, sponges and buns, have a soft, light texture.

ALL-IN-ONE METHOD
A time-saving alternative to the creamed method, all-in-one cakes are made with soft margarine.

BASIC METHODS Most cakes are a variation on these five basic types, but many variations can be made with flavourings, fillings and decorations. In general, plain cakes, with half as much fat as flour, need a high temperature and rich cakes, with a high proportion of fat, low to moderate. Small cakes are risen and golden-brown when cooked, and shrink from the sides of the tin.

pinch of salt; 100-125 g. (4 oz.) jam.
Method Whisk the eggs and sugar together in a bowl over a pan of warm water, or in an electric mixer, until creamy. Fold in the flour and salt with a metal spoon. Spread the mixture evenly over the tin. Bake near the top of the oven for 10 minutes at 200°C (400°F; mark 6) until firm, risen and golden brown. Turn the cake out quickly, on to sugared paper, trim the edges and spread with warmed jam. Roll up the cake evenly, and cool on a wire rack.

GINGERBREAD

Traditionally, gingerbread is baked in a square tin, and this recipe makes sufficient for a tin 180 mm. (7 in.) square by 25 mm. (1 in.) deep.
Ingredients 100-125 g. (4 oz.) butter; 100-125 g. (4 oz.) black treacle; 100-125 g. (4 oz.) soft, brown sugar; ½ teaspoon bicarbonate of soda; 4 tablespoons milk; 225 g. (8 oz.) plain flour; pinch of salt; 1 teaspoon ground ginger; 1 egg.
Method Melt together the butter; black treacle and sugar, stirring it frequently. Dissolve the bicarbonate in 1 tablespoon of milk. Mix the dry ingredients. Beat in the treacle, egg and

remaining milk, using a wooden spoon, then mix in the bicarbonate of soda. Put the mixture into the tin, and bake in the centre of the oven for 1 hour at 160°C (325°F; mark 3).

COOKING TEST

Test a cake by pressing with a finger. If it leaves a mark, the cake is not cooked. To make sure, insert a skewer into the centre of the cake. If it comes out clean, the cake is cooked.

Sponges and small cakes can be taken out of the tin while they are hot. Cool them on a cloth-covered, wire rack. Leave large, rich cakes and cakes made by the melted-in method in the tin until cool.

STORING CAKES

Sponges and small cakes are best eaten within three days of baking. Gingerbread will keep for at least a week, and large, rich fruit cakes can be kept for at least six months.

Store cakes in an airtight tin and wrap those to be kept for some time in greaseproof paper and foil.

PUDDINGS

Baked puddings Use the basic plain cake or Victoria sponge mixture, in a

greased pie dish, as a topping for jam, syrup or fruit purée. Alternatively, add 100-125 g. (4 oz.) dried fruit to the mixture. Bake for 45 minutes at 180°C (350°F; mark 4).
Steamed and boiled puddings Sponge puddings, which can be flavoured with jam, syrup, spices or dried fruit, are made with a creamed Victoria sandwich mixture.

Grease a basin thoroughly. The mixture should only three-quarters fill the basin to allow the pudding to rise.

Cover the basin with a double layer of greaseproof paper or foil. Cook sponge puddings, in a steamer or in a saucepan, with enough boiling water to reach halfway up the basin. Put a lid on the saucepan and simmer gently, adding boiling water, as necessary, during cooking.

A pudding made with 100-125 g. (4 oz.) fat, 100-125 g. (4 oz.) flour, 175 g. (6 oz.) sugar and 2 eggs should be steamed or boiled gently for 2 hours.
Suet puddings Plain suet puddings, to which dried fruit can be added, are boiled, either in a basin or a cloth, baked or steamed. Plain flour can be used, but self-raising gives a lighter textured pudding.

Ingredients 175 g. (6 oz.) plain or self-raising flour; pinch of salt; 75 g. (3 oz.) shredded or finely chopped suet; 50 g. (2 oz.) caster sugar; 150 ml. (¼ pint) milk or water.
Method Mix together the flour, salt, suet and sugar. Stir in the milk or water to make a soft dough.

Grease a pudding basin and three-quarters fill it with mixture, as for steamed pudding. Cover with a double layer of greaseproof paper or foil and tie on a floured cloth.

Round or roly-poly suet puddings can be loosely wrapped and tied in a floured cloth and put straight into boiling water.

Put the pudding into a steamer, or a saucepan of rapidly boiling water so that the basin is covered. Lower the heat and simmer the pudding for 1½-2 hours, topping up with boiling water when necessary. To bake a suet pudding, put the mixture into a greased dish and cook for about 1 hour at 200°C (400°F; mark 6).

WHAT CAN GO WRONG WITH CAKES
If a cake turns out badly, check with the chart, to avoid mistakes next time.

PROBLEM	REASON
Coarse texture	Too much raising agent
Uneven texture	Too little rubbing in or too much liquid
Close texture	Too much fat
Fruit sinks to the bottom	Too soft a mixture, or oven too cool
Sunk in the middle	Too much liquid, opening the oven door while cake is cooking, or using self-raising flour when recipe specifies plain
Dry	Oven too hot, tin not lined properly, or insufficient liquid
Too moist and 'heavy'	Oven too cool, or the cake stored before it is cool
Surface is cracked	Oven too hot or mixture too dry

• MAKING PASTRY

Pastry can be divided into shortcrust, flaked pastry, choux, hot-water pastry and suet pastry. These are all made basically from fat and flour mixed with water, but the methods differ. Pastry has a high calorific value because of the flour and fat, and also contains protein, iron, calcium and vitamins.

BASIC INGREDIENTS

Flour Plain white household flour is best for making pastry. Self-raising flour can be used to make shortcrust and suet pastry, giving it a rather soft, spongy texture. Shortcrust pastry made with wholemeal flour has a heavy, more cake-like texture and a brown, speckled appearance.

Fat Butter and margarine give pastry a good flavour and crisp texture, lard and white cooking fat make it short and crumbly. Most people prefer to use half butter or margarine and half cooking fat for shortcrust pastry. Vegetable oil, whipped fats and soft margarine give good results using the fork-mix method.

Eggs Rich and choux pastry contain eggs and an egg or its yolk can be used to mix shortcrust pastry.

Salt A small amount of salt is included because it acts with the gluten in the flour to make the mixture elastic.

Flavourings Sugar is added to rich, shortcrust pastry for flans and tartlets and spices, grated strong cheese, such as cheddar, and herbs can be added to shortcrust and suet pastry before it is cooked. As a rule, add 1 teaspoon of dried herbs or 100-125 g. (4 oz.) cheese to 100-125 g. (4 oz.) flour. With spice, add one teaspoon to 225 g. (8 oz.) flour.

POINTS TO REMEMBER

All pastry should have a light texture, and this depends on the amount of cold air incorporated. Hands, ingre-

dients (except for choux and hot-water pastry) and all utensils should be cool.

Handle the pastry as little as possible and roll it out lightly, moving the rolling pin away from your body. Do not roll the pin off the edge of the pastry as this presses out the air. To prevent the cough from sticking, flour the surface and the rolling pin lightly.

Leave pastry to rest in a covered bowl for at least five minutes before cooking it, particularly in hot weather.

BAKING 'BLIND'

Flan cases and tarts are often baked 'blind', which means without a filling. To do this, put the pastry into a tin and cut out a piece of greaseproof paper slightly larger than the base of the tin. Butter the paper, put it, butter side down, on the pastry and weight it with uncooked rice, haricot beans or stale crusts. Bake the case for 10-15 minutes (see individual recipes for oven temperature), then remove the paper and cook the pastry, uncovered, for a further five minutes.

GLAZING PASTRY

Brush pies, patties and sausage rolls with a beaten egg or a little milk before baking to give a glossy, brown finish. Egg yolk alone gives a deeper brown glaze. Fruit pies and tarts can be brushed with cold water and dredged with caster sugar.

• BASIC RECIPES FOR PASTRY

Shortcrust is the quickest and easiest pastry to make, used in sweet and savoury flans, tarts, pies, patties, sausage rolls and baked dumplings.

RUBBED-IN SHORTCRUST PASTRY

Ingredients 225 g. (8 oz.) plain or self-raising flour; $\frac{1}{4}$ teaspoon of salt; 50 g. (2 oz.) lard; 50 g. (2 oz.) margarine; 2 tablespoons water.

Method Sift the flour and salt into a bowl, cut the lard and margarine into pieces and rub it into the flour with the fingertips until the mixture resembles fine breadcrumbs. Sprinkle the water on to the mixture and stir it in with a broad-bladed knife to form a firm dough. Lightly knead the dough and roll it out.

FORK-MIX SHORTCRUST PASTRY

Use the same ingredients as for rubbed-in shortcrust pastry, but substitute 100-125 g. (4 oz.) soft margarine or whipped fat or 5 tablespoons of vegetable oil for the margarine and lard.

Method Put the soft margarine, whipped fat or oil, 3 tablespoons of flour, salt and water into a bowl and mix together with a fork. Add the remaining flour and mix to a dough.

FLAKED PASTRY

These types of pastry include flaky, rough puff and puff pastry. The air is incorporated between layers of pastry instead of being distributed throughout the dough so that the result is thin layers of rich, crisp pastry used for savoury pies, sausage rolls, vol-au-vents, patty cases and pastry cakes such as mille feuilles and cream horns.

FLAKY PASTRY

Ingredients 225 g. (8 oz.) plain flour; $\frac{1}{4}$ teaspoon of salt; 175 g. (6 oz.) butter, margarine or half butter and half lard; 150 ml. ($\frac{1}{4}$ pint) of very cold water.

Method Slightly soften the fat (this can be done by working it on a plate with a broad-bladed palette knife) and divide it into four equal parts. Rub a quarter of the fat into the flour until it resembles fine breadcrumbs, then mix to a soft dough with the water, using a palette knife. Knead the dough on a floured surface and roll it

into a rectangle about 30 × 15 cm. (12 × 6 in.). Cut another quarter of fat into flakes and dot these over two-thirds of the pastry rectangle. Fold the pastry so that half the fat is covered and fold the remaining piece over the top. Seal the edges and put the pastry into a floured plastic bag or covered bowl to rest in a refrigerator for 15 minutes.

Remove the pastry from the bag or bowl and put it with the folded edge on the right. Roll out to a rectangle, flake the third quarter of fat on to two-thirds of the pastry and fold and seal as before. Turn the pastry at right-angles, and roll, fold and seal again, and leave to rest and chill for 15 minutes. Repeat with the remaining quarter of fat then leave the pastry to rest and chill for 15 minutes.

ROUGH PUFF PASTRY

A variation of flaky pastry, rough puff pastry is crisp but has larger flakes and not such a light texture. The basic recipe is the same as for flaky pastry, but the method is different.

Method Cut the fat into 20 mm. ($\frac{3}{4}$ in.) dice – it should be just firm but not hard. Put the flour and salt into a bowl, add the fat and mix well with a knife. Stir in the water lightly to form a firm, elastic dough. Knead the dough and roll it out as for flaky pastry. Fold, seal, rest and cool the pastry for 15 minutes, as for flaky pastry. Repeat the folding and resting three times.

PUFF PASTRY

Puff pastry is made with equal quantities of fat and flour mixed with water and a little lemon juice. The best results are obtained with strong flour.

Ingredients 225 g. (8 oz.) strong, white flour; $\frac{1}{4}$ teaspoon of salt; 225 g. (8 oz.) unsalted butter; 1 teaspoon lemon juice; 150 ml. ($\frac{1}{4}$ pint) iced water.

Method Sift the flour and salt into a bowl. Shape the softened butter into a

MAKING SHORTCRUST PASTRY

1. Rub the fat into the flour until the mixture resembles fine breadcrumbs.

2. Sprinkle a little cold water on to the mixture and stir to a firm dough.

3. Knead the pastry lightly on a floured surface until it is smooth.

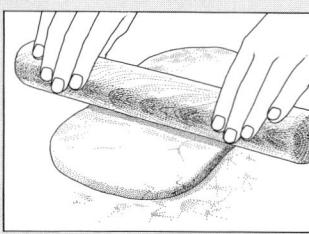

4. Roll out the pastry lightly but firmly, moving the rolling pin away from you.

pat about 100 mm. (4 in.) square and leave it in a cool place. Add the lemon juice and water to the flour to form a soft dough. Put the dough on to a floured board and knead and pummel it well. Roll out to form a rectangle about 25 × 12.5 cm. (10 × 5 in.). Put the butter on to one end of the pastry rectangle, fold over the other piece of dough and seal the edges. Roll out the pastry again and fold the lower one-third half-way over the other two-thirds. Fold down the remaining one-third of pastry, seal the edges and put the pastry to rest, covered, in the refrigerator for at least 15 minutes. Remove the pastry and roll it out again, this time with the folded edge on the right. Repeat the resting and rolling out four times more.

BAKING FLAKED PASTRY

Cook flaky and rough puff pastry for 10 minutes at 220°C (425°F; mark 7). Then reduce the heat to 180°C (350°F;

mark 4) for a further 10-20 minutes.

Start puff pastry at 230°C (450°F; mark 8) for ten minutes, then reduce the heat to 180°C (350°F; mark 4) for the rest of the cooking time.

CHOUX PASTRY

This is a light, airy pastry, hollow in the centre, used for éclairs, cream buns, and gateaux.

Ingredients 50 g. (2 oz.) butter; 150 ml. (¼ pint) water; pinch of salt; 65 g. (2½ oz.) strong white flour; 2 eggs.

Method Melt the butter in a saucepan, add the water and bring to the boil. Tip in the flour and salt quickly, away from the heat, then beat over a gentle heat until the mixture leaves the sides of the saucepan. Cool the mixture a little, then beat in the eggs, one at a time, until they have been absorbed, making a glossy mixture. Put the pastry into a forcing bag with a 15 mm. (½ in.) nozzle and pipe 5-7.5 cm. (2-3 in.) lengths on to a baking

tray to make éclairs. For profiteroles or cream buns put dessertspoons of the mixture on to the tray.

BAKING CHOUX PASTRY

Cook at 220°C (425°F; mark 7) for 20 minutes, then reduce the heat to 180°C (350°F; mark 4) for a further 10 minutes. Split open éclairs and buns when they come out of the oven to allow the pastry to dry inside.

HOT-WATER PASTRY

Used as a crusty casing for savoury pies, hot-water pastry is moulded into shape while it is warm. The water for mixing it should be boiling, to make the dough pliable enough to mould. It is necessary to work quickly before the dough cools and stiffens. Keep a quarter of the dough for the lid.

An easy way to make these pies – sometimes called 'raised pies' – is to roll out the pastry and line a greased cake tin, preferably a loose-bottomed one. Put in the filling and roll out and put on the lid, then bake the pie in the tin. The pastry is strong, and with care the pie can be removed from the tin when it is cooked.

Ingredients 225 g. (8 oz.) plain flour; ¼ teaspoon of salt; 1 egg yolk; 6 tablespoons water; 75 g. (3 oz.) lard.

Method Put the flour and salt into a warmed bowl, make a well in the centre and drop in the egg yolk. Put the water and fat into a small pan and heat to boiling point. Pour this liquid on to the flour and stir it in quickly with a wooden spoon. Put the dough on to a flat surface and knead it until it is smooth.

BAKING HOT-WATER PASTRY

Pies made from hot-water pastry are usually filled with raw meat such as chicken, pork, veal and ham, or game. The meat should be boned and cut into 15 mm. (½ in.) dice. Sea-

son it and moisten with a little stock. Cook these pies for 20 minutes at 200°C (400°F; mark 6). Reduce the heat to 160°C (325°F; mark 3) and cook individual pies for a further hour, and family-sized pies for a further 2-2½ hours.

SUET PASTRY

Suet pastry is the same as suet pudding (see p. 273), but the dough is rolled out and used to line basins which are filled with raw meat or fruit and covered with a lid of suet dough. Boil a fruit pudding in a 1½ pint basin for 2½ hours, at a steady simmer, and puddings containing raw meat for 5 hours.

Suet pastry is also used to make dumplings, which are added to a stew 20 minutes before the end of the cooking time. The pastry can also be put into a greased pie dish and baked for 20 minutes at 200°C (400°F; mark 6), to be served with meat dishes.

COLLECTING ROLLING PINS

Nailsea rolling pins, made of glass decorated with coloured enamel, were first made at Nailsea glassworks, near Bristol, in the 18th century. They became very popular between 1830 and 1860 and were widely copied. Among the rarest, and most valuable, are those flecked with dark maroon or yellow.

In the collection illustrated, the oldest (bottom) probably dates from the late 18th century; the most recent (second from top) was made 100 years later. It is of clear glass with pictures stuck on the inside. The inside was then painted with an opaque varnish.

MAKING FLAKY PASTRY

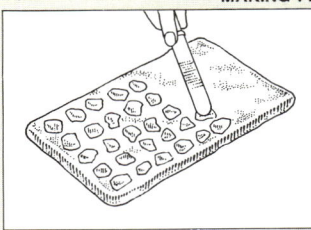

1. Dot two-thirds of the pastry with a quarter of the fat, cut into small pieces.

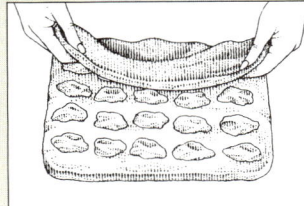

2. Fold over one end of the pastry so that half the fat is covered.

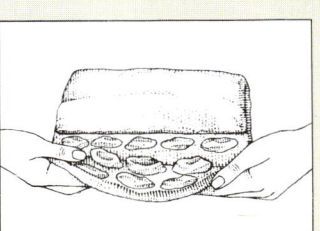

3. Fold over the other end so that all the fat is enclosed in the pastry.

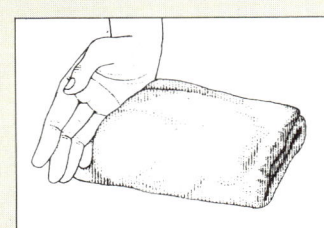

4. Seal the edges of the pastry with the side of one hand, or the rolling pin.

Hot-water pastry

Choux pastry

Flaky pastry

Shortcrust pastry

STORE-CUPBOARD COOKERY

Dried foods such as pasta, pulses and cereals are useful in the storecupboard because they keep well and can be used for quick, filling, economical meals. They can be bland and tasteless, but combine well with herbs, spices and other strong flavourings and are often used to supplement or accompany meat and fish dishes and as the basis of sweet puddings. The food value of pulses and cereals varies, but all contain carbohydrates, protein and vitamins.

• PASTA

Basically pasta is dried dough made into various shapes and sizes, such as spaghetti, noodles or cannelloni. Sometimes eggs are added to the pasta, or spinach purée, which tints it green – called pasta verde.

Fresh pasta, sold in some delicatessens, should be used within two or three days, but dried pasta will keep indefinitely in a cool cupboard.

HOW TO COOK PASTA
Dried pasta swells in cooking, 50 g. (2 oz.) raw yields 175 g. (6 oz.) cooked. Allow 75-100 g. (3-4 oz.) of cooked pasta per person for a main course or 50 g. for a starter.

Cook dried pasta for the following times: vermicelli, stars and other shapes, 6 min.; spaghetti, noodles, tagliatelle, 10-12 min.; macaroni, mafalde and lasagne, 12-15 min.; cannelloni, ravioli, 15-20 min.

Fresh pasta needs only about five minutes and does not increase in bulk. Quick-cooking pasta has instructions on the packet.

Cook all pasta in boiling water, allowing 600 ml. (1 pint) of water and half a teaspoon of salt to every 50 g. of pasta. When cooked, drain in a colander, add 25 g. (1 oz.) butter or 1 tablespoon olive oil and toss pasta in this until coated.

Serve pasta with grated Parmesan cheese or freshly chopped herbs as a starter or with a main dish.

With the addition of cheese, meat or tomato sauce, pasta makes a filling supper dish such as spaghetti bolognese, cannelloni or lasagne.

Vermicelli, noodles and small pasta shapes, such as conchiglie are used in soups and broths.

Spaghetti, ravioli and pasta shapes are also sold canned in tomato sauce.

• RICE

Most rice consists of polished, white grains with the husks and brown cuticles removed. The two main types are long-grain, used for savoury dishes, and short-grain, or 'pudding', rice.

Brown, unpolished rice, which is rich in protein, is sold in health shops.

Ground rice consists of finely milled, broken white grains and is used for milk puddings and some cakes.

'Instant' rice has been pre-cooked then dehydrated. Soak it for five minutes in boiling water and use without further cooking.

HOW TO COOK RICE
Long-grain rice is usually boiled. It trebles in bulk when it is cooked and 50 g. (2 oz.) of uncooked rice is sufficient for one person. An average-size cup holds 225 g. (8 oz.) rice – enough for four people.

To boil rice, put into a saucepan, and add two cups of water for each cup of rice; then add a teaspoon of

SPAGHETTI CANNELLONI MAFALDE TAGLIATELLE VERDE FRESH RAVIOLI VERMICELLI SOUP GARNISH CONCHIGLIE NOODLES LASAGNE VERDE MACARONI

PASTA, IN ALL SHAPES AND SIZES Pasta can be divided into four main types: solid strings, which include vermicelli, noodles, spaghetti; hollow pasta tubes, such as macaroni, cannelloni; ribbon pasta, from tagliatelle to lasagne; and stuffed pasta, of which the best known is ravioli.

salt and bring to boil. Stir rice, put lid on saucepan, lower heat, and simmer until all water has been absorbed – usually about 15 minutes.

• OTHER CEREALS

Barley Pearl barley, which is the polished grain, is used to thicken soups and in pilaff, mixed with meat or fish and spices.

Oatmeal The whole grain is dried, husked and ground to make coarse, medium or fine oatmeal, all used for porridge, oatcakes and oatmeal biscuits.

Rolled oats This is the crushed, partly cooked grain, sold under various brand names. It is cooked to make quick porridge; mixed with fruit and nuts to make muesli, and used as the basis of cakes such as flapjacks.

Semolina, sago and tapioca All these are used to make milk puddings. Semolina, coarsely milled, hard wheat, is also made into gnocchi – savoury dumplings, deep-fried and served as a starter. Sago is made from the pith in the trunk of the sago palm. Tapioca comes from the root of the West Indian cassava plant.

MILK PUDDINGS

Make rice and flaked tapioca puddings as follows:

Ingredients 40 g. (1½ oz.) short-grain rice or flaked tapioca; 25 g. (1 oz.) sugar; 600 ml. (1 pint) milk; spice, such as grated nutmeg, or other flavouring.

Method Put cereal into oven-proof dish and add sugar and milk. Cover and cook at 150-160°C (300-325°F; mark 2 or 3) for two hours. Remove from oven, stir, add spice or flavour-ing and cook for a further half-hour.

Fine tapioca, sago and semolina puddings are made as follows:

Ingredients 600 ml. (1 pint) milk; 25 g. (1 oz.) tapioca, sago or semolina; 25 g. (1 oz.) sugar; vanilla or other flavouring.

Method Bring milk to boil, remove from heat and sprinkle with tapioca, semolina or sago. Stir well, return to a gentle heat and bring to boil, stirring until mixture thickens. Add sugar and flavouring, put pudding into pie dish and brown in oven (180°C, 350°F; mark 4) for 30 minutes.

• PULSES

Dried peas and beans of various types are known as pulses. They are rich in protein, inexpensive and keep well. The best known are butter, haricot and kidney beans. Haricot beans are used for baked beans in tomato sauce.

Dried peas are a specially grown variety of garden pea, sometimes called blue peas. Lentils, one of the most nutritious pulses, are a type of pea widely grown in the south of Europe.

Textured vegetable protein Dried soya beans are sold in health food shops. They are also processed to make textured vegetable protein, which is sold under various brand names. Vegetable protein can be used on its own or mixed with fresh meat for hamburgers, minced-meat dishes and stews.

HOW TO COOK PULSES

Soak dried peas and beans (except for lentils which need only two hours soaking) overnight before cooking; alternatively, bring them slowly to the boil, simmer for two minutes, then leave for an hour before cooking.

To cook, put the pulses into a saucepan and cover with fresh cold water. Add salt to taste, bring to boil and cook gently until soft.

Average cooking times are: butter beans, chick peas and black beans, 60 min.; haricot and soya beans, 45 min.; split peas 30 min.; lentils and dried peas 25 min. Stored beans may need more time.

Pulses, particularly butter beans and dried peas, are served as an accompanying vegetable. Haricot, chilli, black and black-eye beans, as well as dried whole or split peas, can be added to soups and stews. Red kidney beans are used in chilli con carne, mixed with minced beef, onion and chilli powder. Lentils are cooked in soups and also in croquettes.

LENTILS • PEARL BARLEY • DRIED PEAS • SEMOLINA • BLACK-EYE BEANS • SAGO • LONG-GRAIN RICE • BLACK BEANS

OATMEAL • BROWN RICE

SHORT-GRAIN RICE • HARICOT BEANS

CHICK PEAS • RED KIDNEY BEANS • TAPIOCA • SOYA BEANS • BUTTER BEANS • WILD RICE • ROLLED OATS • SPLIT PEAS

A SELECTION OF CEREALS AND PULSES These foods tend to be bland on their own, but can easily be varied in flavour with the addition of spices and other ingredients. Wild rice, which is expensive, is the seed of an American grass and is served as an accompaniment to game. Chick peas are grown in the tropics and are used in soups and stews or cold in salads.

• HERBS

Many herbs are best used fresh, but only a limited number are easily available unless they are grown at home (see p. 176). Bay leaves, chervil, fennel, parsley, rosemary, sage and thyme are sometimes sold fresh in shops, and are in season all the year round.

These herbs, as well as many less well-known ones, are also sold dried. They should be kept well sealed and used within six months as they lose their flavour after a period.

DRYING HERBS

Most herbs can be dried during the summer for use in winter. Pick the herbs just before flowering time when the flavour is best. Wash them thoroughly then shake off the excess moisture. Tie the herbs into small bunches and hang them in a cool, airy place or spread them out on a clean cloth and put them to dry in a warm place such as an airing cupboard. Dry different types of herbs separately or the flavours will mingle. When they are dry and brittle, strip off the leaves and store them in air-tight, labelled jars.

FREEZING FRESH HERBS

Soft-leaved herbs, such as basil, chives, fennel, mint and parsley, freeze well. Wash the herbs, shake off the excess water and dry them. Put the herbs into sealed plastic bags, label them and put into a freezer.

A convenient way to freeze parsley for flavouring sauces and stews is to finely chop the fresh parsley and pack it into a refrigerator ice-cube tray. Fill the tray with water and put it into the freezing compartment of the refrigerator until solid. Remove the cubes from the tray, put them into a sealed polythene bag and store in the freezer, where they will keep for up to

six months. To use the cubes, remove from the bag and drop into the sauce or stew to dissolve two or three minutes before it is cooked.

• SPICES

Most spices are seeds from plants grown in hot climates. They are sold whole or ground. Ground spice loses flavour more quickly than whole spice, but is easier to use because it is added to sweet and savoury dishes straight from the pack. Most spices keep well for up to a year, but after this they will taste musty. Usually, only a

small pinch of spice is needed to flavour a dish.

Allspice The popular name for Jamaica pepper, or pimento, allspice looks like peppercorns and tastes like a combination of cinnamon, cloves and nutmeg. Use allspice whole in pickles, soups and stews or ground in cakes, puddings and pies.

Caraway Small, brown, striped seeds with a pungent flavour. Use to flavour lamb and veal stews and in cakes and bread.

Cayenne A very hot, powdered spice used in cheese and fish dishes and

sprinkled on smoked salmon, oysters and prawn cocktails.

Chillies The fruit of a species of capsicum, fresh chillies have small, shiny red pods and are very hot. Whole chilli peppers are ground to make chilli powder. Use fresh chillies in pickles, and chilli powder, sparingly, in curries, tomato and spaghetti dishes.

Cinnamon The sweet, aromatic bark of a tree which grows in Sri Lanka and India, sold ground or in sticks about 50 mm. (2 in.) long. Use ground cinnamon to flavour cakes and biscuits. Add the sticks, which can be used

more than once, to syrup for preserved fruit, and in stews.

Cloves Dried, unopened flower buds from a tree native to the Moluccas Islands, cloves have a strong flavour and are sold whole or ground. Use them with cooked apples, in bread sauce and veal stews.

Coriander Fawn to yellow ribbed seeds with a mild, aromatic flavour. Use them in curries and lamb stews.

Cumin A greenish-brown seed with an aniseed flavour. Use in pork and cheese dishes, curry and bread.

Ginger Ginger root is available in

BASIL
Spicy herb that can be grown in pots or boxes. Does not lose pungency when it is dried.

SAGE
One of the best-known herbs, sage grows well in this country and can be used fresh or dried.

TARRAGON
Usually used dry, but the fresh leaves are particularly good for flavouring egg and tomato salads.

MARJORAM
Spicy, bitter herb which can be used instead of basil, sprinkled on meat. More pungent dried.

FENNEL
The leaves and seeds of the herb are used to counteract the richness of oily fish and in sauces.

CHIVES
Not easily available in the shops, chives are simple to grow and are best when freshly cut.

BAY
The leaves can be used fresh or dried to flavour savoury dishes, particularly sauces and stews.

DILL
The leaves have a delicate, aniseed flavour, which enhances the flavour of grilled fish.

GARLIC
The very pungent cloves should be used sparingly. Garlic keeps for several months in a dry place.

ROSEMARY
The shrub grows well in Britain and the sweet, aromatic leaves are more pungent fresh.

PARSLEY
Mild-flavoured parsley leaves are rich in iron and vitamins. Use them in sauces and as a garnish.

BOUQUET GARNI
Ready-made bouquets garnis are available, in muslin, and include bay leaf, thyme and parsley.

THYME
Widely used herb; fresh or dried. The strongly flavoured leaves go well with most meat dishes.

CAPERS
Flower buds, usually sold pickled, capers are most often used to make sauce for mutton or fish.

OREGANO
Wild marjoram, used in Greek and Italian dishes. Usually sold as a dried powder in this country.

MINT
Widely grown, popular herb used in fruit tarts and cocktails as well as with meat and vegetables.

HERBS AND THEIR USES These fresh herbs are widely used in cooking. Many of them, not just the more usual ones, such as mint, parsley and thyme, can *be grown in the garden or in pots. This allows you to use them fresh, or to freeze or dry them at home. Most of these herbs can be bought dried.*

irregularly shaped grey-brown pieces or ground to a brown powder. The hot, pungent spice is used ground in cakes and puddings. Root ginger is added to curries and pickles and needs about 30 minutes' cooking.

Mace The outer skin of the nutmeg seed, mace is sold ground to an orange powder or in blade-shaped pieces. Use ground mace in fruit cakes, sauces for fish, and the blades for home-made pickles.

Mustard Sold in powder form, to mix with water, or ready-mixed. Ready-made English mustard does not have the same strength or flavour as mustard powder. Ready-mixed French and German mustards are milder than English mustard and are mixed with vinegar instead of water. French Dijon mustard is made from specially grown mustard seeds mixed with white wine and spices. It is mild with an acid flavour.

Nutmeg A slightly sweet, brown kernel, sold whole or ground. If the nutmeg is bought whole, a mill or special grater is useful as the kernel is very hard. Use nutmeg to flavour cakes, milk puddings and sauces.

Paprika A mild, red powder made from the ground pods of a plant of the capsicum family. Use, more generously than other spices, to flavour goulash, chicken and veal stews and to garnish fish, meat and egg dishes.

Pepper Black and white pepper are both made from the dried seeds of the same plant, the white being the riper seeds which are further processed after drying. Black pepper is stronger than white and both are sold whole or ground. A pepper mill is needed to grind the whole peppercorns.

Saffron A bright yellow powder made from the powdered stigmas of a type of crocus, saffron is expensive and has a bitter taste. Use it to flavour and colour cakes and savoury rice.

Turmeric A root which is dried and ground to a bright orange powder, turmeric is a member of the ginger family and has a mild, earthy flavour. Use it in curries and pickles.

Curry Different spices such as cayenne, coriander, cumin, turmeric, ginger, mace, cloves and pepper are blended to make curry. It is sold either ground to a rich yellow powder or mixed to a brown paste with oil or vinegar, and is labelled according to its strength. Use curry as a sauce to serve with meat, fish or egg dishes and in soups.

Mixed spices A blend of spices which includes cinnamon, nutmeg, cloves, mace and ginger, sold ground to use in cakes and puddings.

Pickling spice A mixture of dried spices such as mustard seed, peppercorns, chilli pods, cloves, ginger, mace and coriander, used for pickles and chutney.

OTHER FLAVOURINGS

The best and most expensive essences, such as vanilla, are made from small quantities of oils of spices, flowers and plants, but most bottled essences are synthetic. In addition to vanilla, these flavourings include peppermint, rum, chocolate, coffee and many fruit flavours.

Vanilla pods give a better flavour than essence and are not so strong. Put the pods in milk which is being heated to make custard, milk puddings and cold desserts. Remove the pod for re-use once the milk is hot. Keep one or two pods in a screw-top jar of caster sugar, to improve the flavour of the sugar in cakes and puddings.

• OILS

The fats from a number of vegetables, nuts, cereals and seeds are manufactured into edible oils and used in cooking. Like butter and other animal fats, oils are a source of energy and vitamins. However, vegetable oils are low in cholesterol (see p. 262) and for a healthy diet should be substituted where possible for animal fats. Pure oils such as olive, sunflower and corn oil have the best flavour for baking and salad dressings.

Buy oil in 4 litre or 1 gallon cans rather than smaller bottles, if possible, because it is cheaper. Sometimes, too, it is cheaper to buy oil from a chemist rather than a supermarket or grocer's shop. Oil will keep for up to three months in a cool place.

OLIVE OIL

Virgin olive oil is the finest and most expensive. It is either the oil from the first pressing of the olives, or that which is drawn from the top of the settling tank.

French olive oil has a delicate flavour whereas that from Italy, Spain and Greece has a stronger olive taste and is deeper in colour.

OTHER OILS

Other edible oils are maize (corn oil), palm kernel, coconut, groundnut, rape, sunflower and soya. These are sometimes blended together with the addition of preservatives and anti-foaming agents.

DEEP-FRYING

Oil is the best fat to use for deep-frying because it can be heated to a high temperature without burning. Use a heavy-based, deep saucepan or a deep-fryer with a wire basket. Any oil can be used, but corn and groundnut oils have a good flavour.

The oil should be 50-75 mm. (2-3 in.) deep, and not more than halfway up the pan. Most food can be deep-fried at 190°C (375°F), which can be checked with a food thermometer. A cube of bread will brown in 60 seconds at the correct temperature.

Frying times vary, but food containing cooked ingredients, such as croquettes, should take 2-3 minutes; fritters 3-5; potato chips 4-5; and chicken joints 15 minutes.

• VINEGARS

All vinegar is a weak solution of acetic acid, obtained from the fermentation of cider, wine or beer, and can be used for cooking, preserving and pickling. Wine or cider vinegar give the best flavour in cooking.

MARINADING WITH VINEGAR

One of the properties of vinegar is its ability to break down tough fibres of meat and the cellulose of green vegetables. In marinading, vinegar is used with oil, spices, herbs and vegetables to make a liquor in which raw meat is steeped for up to 24 hours.

Malt vinegar The cheapest vinegar, which is made from malt after it has been used in beer-making. Use malt vinegar spiced for pickles and chutney. Boil the vinegar with spices such as mace, allspice, cloves, cinnamon and peppercorns, then leave it to cool before use.

Cider vinegar Slightly paler than malt vinegar, and with an aroma of apples, cider vinegar is used to marinade pork or rabbit for casseroles.

Wine vinegar Most wine vinegar is produced in France from grape juice and sour wine. It can be pale gold or rose-coloured, and is excellent for salad dressing, aspic and mayonnaise.

Flavoured vinegars When strongly flavoured herbs are added to vinegar, it takes on their flavour. The best known is tarragon vinegar. Other flavourings include chilli, dill, garlic and shallots. Use flavoured vinegar for marinades and salad dressing.

SALAD DRESSING

Oil or vinegar are combined to make a basic dressing. Flavours such as crushed garlic or chopped yolk of hard-boiled egg can be added.

French dressing Put 1 teaspoon made English or French mustard, $\frac{1}{4}$ teaspoon of salt, $\frac{1}{4}$ teaspoon of sugar and a pinch of freshly milled black pepper into a bowl. Stir in 4 tablespoons of olive or other pure oil, then gradually whisk in 2 tablespoons of vinegar (preferably wine vinegar).

Vinaigrette dressing Add 1 tablespoon of chopped, mixed, fresh herbs, such as parsley, chives, thyme or marjoram, and 1 teaspoon of chopped capers to the French dressing.

MAYONNAISE

Ingredients 1 egg yolk; $\frac{1}{4}$ teaspoon salt; $\frac{1}{2}$ teaspoon dry mustard; $\frac{1}{4}$ teaspoon caster sugar; pinch of white pepper; 150 ml. ($\frac{1}{4}$ pint) olive, corn or sunflower oil; 1 tablespoon wine or flavoured vinegar.

Method Put the egg yolk into a basin and stir in the dry ingredients. Add the oil, drop by drop, until about one-third of the oil has been used, beating all the time so that the mixture thickens to a smooth, shiny consistency. Add the remaining oil in a slow, steady stream. Beat in the vinegar.

Alternatively, put the egg yolk and all the dry ingredients into an electric blender, switch on and pour in the oil in a steady stream. Add the vinegar.

The mayonnaise will curdle unless the oil is added very slowly at first, and the ingredients are at room temperature. If it does curdle before all the oil has been added, quickly whisk in 1 teaspoon of boiling water, or start again with another egg yolk, in a clean bowl, and beat the curdled mixture into this.

• SUGAR

Sugar is manufactured from sugar cane and sugar beet. The beet or cane is heated to produce molasses and crystals which are then refined to produce white sugar.

Sugar is a carbohydrate – an energy-giver. It has no other food value, and any excess over the body's energy needs is bad for health. Refined sugar should not be confused with the natural sugar which is contained in honey, fruit and vegetables. These also contain B vitamins, particularly thiamin, which help to digest carbohydrates.

Too much refined sugar, as well as creating weight problems, can clog the digestive system and cause tooth decay. There is little to choose between brown and white sugar except flavour: for sweetness alone, use white.

The following is a list of the sugars and other sweeteners in general use.

Granulated sugar The cheapest sugar, it consists of coarse, white crystals and is used for most sweetening purposes.

Caster sugar Fine, white sugar which dissolves quickly, caster is used in cake-making and sprinkled on fruit.

Cube sugar The sugar is formed into large slabs and then mechanically cut into small cubes, packeted and sold for use in hot drinks. Cube sugar can be white or brown. It dissolves more quickly than granulated sugar.

Demerara Sold in Britain as 'London Demerara', this is usually fully refined sugar mixed with molasses to give it a distinctive flavour. It is used on breakfast cereals and in cake-making. Other sugar sold as Demerara is made from beet sugar, flavoured and coloured.

Preserving sugar This is white sugar made in large crystals. It produces less scum than granulated sugar when making jam and preserves.

Soft brown sugar Usually less refined than white sugar, soft brown is made in several shades. Store it in an airtight tin to stop it going lumpy, and use it for cakes and sweets.

Barbados sugar Similar to Demerara but darker and finer, Barbados sugar is not generally on sale in British shops. It has a rich flavour but less sweetening power than white sugar. Use it for rich fruit cakes.

Icing sugar This is white sugar, ground finely and used for cakes and sweets. It contains corn starch to prevent lumps forming.

Golden syrup A by-product of the early stages of sugar refining, golden syrup is used for sweets, puddings, sauces and cakes.

Treacle A thick syrup with a rich, slightly bitter taste, obtained from molasses. Spread it on bread or use in cakes and puddings.

OTHER SWEETENERS

In addition to sugar, several other products can be used as sweeteners in cooking or as spreads and flavourings.

Glucose Sold as a powder, glucose can be used to sweeten drinks. It is made from maize starch.

Maple sugar and syrup The sap of the North American maple tree is evaporated to produce a very rich, sweet sugar or syrup. The syrup is more easily available than the sugar, which is used sparingly in cooking as it is twice as sweet as granulated sugar. The syrup is obtained by evaporating the maple sap but stopping the process before it solidifies into sugar. The syrup, which is expensive, is most often used on pancakes and waffles.

Honey More expensive than other sweeteners, honey has a distinctive flavour which varies with the source of the nectar collected by the bees. There is no generally accepted evidence that honey is particularly beneficial, although it is a natural source of sugar. It is usually spread on bread, but it can also be used on cereals and in cakes and puddings.

Sugar substitutes Several types of artificial sweeteners, in tablet, liquid or powder form, are sold for use by slimmers and diabetics. They consist of saccharin, saccharin calcium or saccharin sodium.

COOKING WITH SUGAR

Apart from its use in cakes and puddings, sugar is dissolved in water to make sugar syrup, used for sweet-making and for sweetening fruit or cold drinks. It is also used for preserving fruit and for making jam.

Sugar syrup A simple sugar syrup is made with 2 parts of granulated sugar to 1 part water. Boil the sugar and water together until slightly thickened and then use as required.

Caramel Sugar changes flavour and colour when it reaches a high temperature, going from white to light brown to black.

When the melted sugar or syrup turns amber it is known as caramel and is used in sweets, flavourings and desserts, such as caramel custard.

Dry sugar can be dissolved to make caramel, but the results are better if water is added.

Put 450 g. (1 lb.) of granulated sugar into a heavy saucepan and stir in 150 ml. (¼ pint) of water. Leave to stand to dissolve some of the sugar, then heat very gently until all the sugar is dissolved. Do not let the syrup boil at this stage, but when it is clear, boil rapidly, with a lid on the saucepan, for 2-3 minutes. Do not stir the syrup or the sugar will crystallise. Remove the lid and continue to boil the syrup until it turns amber. Remove it from the heat immediately and carefully add 2 tablespoons of water before using it.

ICING

The two basic types of icing are glacé icing, which is soft and used for small cakes, Victoria sandwiches and sponges, and Royal icing which is harder and more suitable for decorating fruit cakes.

A quick and easy way to turn an ordinary cake into a party one, icing also helps to keep the cake moist.

Glacé icing The following recipe makes sufficient icing to coat the top of a cake 15-20 cm. (6-8 in.) in diameter, or 12-18 buns.

Ingredients 100-125 g. (4 oz.) icing sugar; 1-2 tablespoons warm water; food colouring and flavouring (if desired).

Method Sift the icing sugar into a deep bowl and gradually add the water, stirring with a wooden spoon until the mixture is thick enough to coat the back of the spoon. Add more water or sugar, if necessary, for the required consistency, and add a few drops of food colouring, if desired.

Flavours can be added to the basic icing by substituting liquid flavouring for an equal amount of water. Cocoa and coffee powder should first be dissolved in a little hot water.

Royal icing This recipe makes enough Royal icing to cover the top and sides of a cake 25 cm. (10 in.) across and 5 cm. (2 in.) deep.

Ingredients 4 egg whites; 800-900 g. (1¾-2 lb.) icing sugar; 1 tablespoon lemon juice; 2 teaspoons glycerine (optional).

Method Put the egg whites into a large bowl and beat them lightly with a wooden spoon. Gradually stir in the sifted icing sugar, then beat until the icing is smooth. When half the sugar has been added, beat in the lemon juice. Add more sugar, beating the mixture well until it forms soft peaks. Add a little more sugar to make a firmer icing for piping decorations on to cakes. If glycerine is used, stir it into the finished icing. This helps to keep

DECORATING WITH ICING SUGAR

Allow the cake to cool a little, then sift icing sugar over the top.

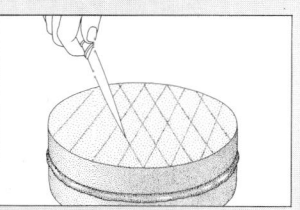

Use the point of a sharp knife to draw a lattice pattern in the icing sugar.

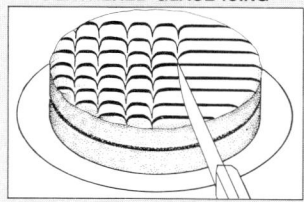

FEATHERED GLACÉ ICING

Use a knife to score lines across icing at right-angles to the piping.

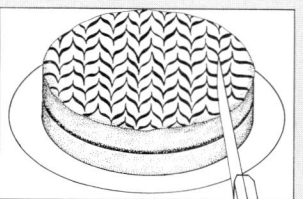

Turn the cake right round and score again across the first set of lines.

the icing soft and makes it easier to cut on the cake without crumbling.

If possible, leave the icing, covered with plastic or a damp cloth to prevent a crust forming, for 24 hours before using it.

To make Royal icing in an electric mixer, set the control to medium and whisk the egg whites before adding the sifted sugar. Do not overbeat or the icing will not spread smoothly.

• TEA

About four-fifths of the tea drunk in this country is black tea, most of which comes from India and Sri Lanka (Ceylon). The rest is made up of oolong tea, green tea, usually called China tea in Britain, and tea made from herbs.

The quality of tea depends on where it is grown and the part of the plant from which the leaves are picked. The finest tea is produced from the small, growing tips of the plant.

Black tea The leaves are dried with hot air, rolled to bruise them and bring out the flavour, then allowed to ferment in the air so that they turn brownish-black. When fermentation is complete the leaves are dried, or 'fired', with hot air.

Oolong tea The leaves are allowed to ferment slightly but the process is stopped and the leaves dried in an intense heat. The tea is greenish-brown and produces a lighter-coloured brew than black tea.

Almost all the black and oolong tea we buy is a blend of different leaf grades and regional teas sold in branded packets or tea-bags.

Unblended teas are more expensive. They are graded by leaf quality and place of origin. Pekoe tip or flowery Pekoe is high-quality tea made from the leaf tips. Pekoe is made from medium-sized leaves and Orange Pekoe from large ones. Pekoe tip

makes the strongest tea and is more economical to use than the weaker Pekoe and Orange Pekoe. Souchong tea is made from large leaves picked early in the season, and also makes fairly weak tea.

Unblended Indian teas include Assam, a dark, pungent tea from the north-east of the country, and Darjeeling, with a delicate flavour, considered by connoisseurs to be India's finest tea.

Pure Ceylon tea has a strong flavour produced by drying the leaves at a very high temperature to seal in the flavour, so that it stays fresh longer.

How to make black tea Warm the tea-pot with hot water, empty it, then put in the tea. One level teaspoon for each person and one for the pot makes medium-strength tea. Pour boiling water on to the tea, stir, and leave 3-4 minutes before pouring. Oolong tea is made in the same way.

Green or China tea Made from unfermented leaves, green tea is milder flavoured than black or oolong tea. It is sold in different leaf sizes. Gunpowder tea consists of the smallest leaves rolled into tiny pellets. Imperial tea is made from slightly larger leaves, rolled into larger pellets, and hyson tea is made from leaves of the early crop. Regional varieties of green tea include Hoo-chow, a very fine tea which makes a light, fragrant brew; Ping-suey, which is a slightly inferior grade; and teas from Kwangtung, which all have a good flavour.

China tea is made in the same way as black tea, but without an extra spoonful for the pot. It infuses more quickly and can be poured after 2-3 minutes. It is served without milk.

Herb tea Almost any herb, usually dried, can be used to make tea. Simply pour boiling water on to the herbs, using sufficient for the strength re-

quired. Many herbs are also now sold in tea-bags, among the most common being mint, rosehip and camomile.

Instant tea The tea is first brewed and then dehydrated to form a powder. It is used, like instant coffee, by putting 1 level teaspoon into a cup and pouring on boiling water.

• COFFEE

Bought as beans, ground or instant, coffee is usually a blend of beans from different varieties of the coffee plant. The flavour varies, depending on the country or region where the coffee is grown. The best flavour comes from freshly roasted and freshly ground beans. Ready-ground coffee cannot be quite so fresh and the flavour is not quite so good. Instant coffee has a much blander and less-distinct flavour than ground coffee.

Beans or ground coffee described as blended are usually a mixture of coffees from different parts of one country. For example, Kenya blend, which has a rich, slightly acid flavour, is made from several African coffees. Similarly, a Brazil blend is Brazilian beans blended with other mild coffees. These blends are cheaper than unblended beans from one particular area. Examples of the pure types are Costa Rica, a mild coffee from central America; Mysore coffee, full-flavoured, rich and smooth from southern India; and Mocha from Ethiopia, which has a strong flavour and is used to make Turkish coffee.

Coffee beans and ground coffee can be in three different strengths and colours: light, medium and dark, depending on the length of time the beans have been roasted.

Coffee beans Sold loose, in packets and in vacuum packs, the beans can be prepared using a hand grinder, but electric grinders (see p. 212) make the job easier.

Ground coffee Once the packet is opened, ground coffee quickly loses its flavour. The coffee can be ground fine, medium or coarse. Fine coffee is the most economical, but medium and coarse grinds are best used in a percolator. Ready-packed ground coffee is usually medium roast and medium grind, which is suitable for most methods of coffee-making.

The main ways to make ground coffee are in a percolator, with a drip-filter or a vacuum machine, and these are all available as electrical appliances (see p. 212).

The simplest method, requiring no special machine, is to put ground coffee into a warm earthenware jug, pour on boiling water and leave for 5 minutes. Use 50 g. (2 oz.) coffee to 600 ml. (1 pint) of water. Pour the coffee through a strainer.

Chicory The dried root of this herb is ground and roasted and added to ground coffee to give it body and a distinctive aroma. Coffee with chicory is slightly cheaper than pure coffee.

Turkish coffee Very strong, very sweet coffee made by boiling finely ground beans with sugar. It is served black in small cups.

Instant coffee Available as a liquid, powder, or in granules, instant coffee is made from blended ground coffee beans which have been percolated. The liquid is then bottled to sell as an essence; or first spray-dried (powder) or freeze-dried (granules) before being packed in tins and jars. Instant coffee soon loses its aroma once it is opened.

De-caffeinated coffee Coffee contains 1.5% caffeine which stimulates the nervous system. Pure caffeine is a white powder extracted during de-caffeination. De-caffeinated coffee is sold ground or as instant coffee powder and is made in the same way as ordinary coffee.

STORECUPBOARD CHECK LIST

The following products all keep well (see p. 222) and can be used to make a variety of meals at short notice.

Baked beans
Baking powder
Beef or yeast extract
Bicarbonate of soda
Biscuits (dry and sweet)
Bouquet garni
Breadcrumbs
Breakfast cereals
Cake mix
Cocoa and chocolate
Cook-in sauce
Cornflour
Cream (canned)
Cream of tartar
Curry powder or sauce
Dried fruit
Dried mushrooms
Dried pulses (peas, beans, lentils)
Dried sausage (salami)
Fish (canned)
Flavouring essences
Flour (plain and self-raising)
Fruit (canned or bottled)
Fruit juice (canned)
Gelatine
Golden syrup
Gravy browning
Herbs (dried) and spices
Honey
Horseradish (grated)
Instant milk pudding (dried or canned)
Jam, jelly and marmalade
Lemon juice
Mango chutney
Meat (canned)
Milk (dried, evaporated, condensed)
Mustard
Nuts (shelled)
Oatmeal or rolled oats
Oil
Olives
Packet meals (dried curry, risotto, etc.)
Pasta (macaroni, spaghetti)
Pâté (canned)
Pickles
Rice (long and short grain)
Salad cream
Salt and pepper
Sauces (bottled)
Semolina
Soup (canned or packet)
Stock cubes
Suet (packet)
Sugar (white, brown and icing)
Tea and coffee
Tomato purée
Vanilla pods
Vegetables (canned and dried)
Vinegar (malt and wine)
Yeast (dried)

GLOSSARY OF COOKERY

A

ASPIC
Clear jelly made from cooked juices of meat, chicken or fish.
AU GRATIN
A crusty topping made by sprinkling food with breadcrumbs and cheese and browning it.

B

BAIN MARIE
A large, open dish, half-filled with hot water in which a smaller pan, containing soups, sauces, etc., is stood to cook or warm.
BAKING BLIND
Pastry cooked without a filling.
BARDING
Covering poultry, game or lean meat with pork or bacon fat.
BASTING
Moistening meat, poultry and game during roasting by spooning the pan juices over it.
BATTER
Mixture of flour, eggs and liquid used for Yorkshire puddings, pancakes and coating food.
BÉCHAMEL
A rich white sauce.
BEIGNETS
Fritters or deep-fried pancakes.
BEURRE MANIÉ
Equal quantities of flour and butter, mixed together to make a paste for thickening liquids.
BEURRE NOIR
Butter heated until it turns nut brown. Usually served with fish or meat.
BINDING
Adding eggs, liquid or melted fat to hold together dry ingredients.
BISQUE
Thick soup made from shellfish.
BLANCHING
Plunging food into boiling water to loosen the skin; or bringing food to the boil to whiten it, to reduce saltiness or, with vegetables, to prepare for freezing.
BOUCHÉES
Small puff pastry patties.
BOUQUET GARNI
Small bunch of herbs tied together in muslin and used to flavour stews and soups.
BRAISING
Browning meat in hot fat then cooking slowly, covered, with vegetables and a little stock.
BRIOCHE
Soft, rich yeast roll.
BROCHETTE
Skewer used to grill pieces of meat, fish and vegetables.
BROWNING
1. Searing the outer surface of meat to seal in the juices.
2. Placing a cooked dish under the grill or in a hot oven to brown.

C

CANAPÉS
Small pieces of fried bread, toast, pastry or biscuits with savoury topping.
CARAMEL
Sugar heated very slowly in a thick pan until it turns a rich brown.
CASSEROLE
1. Ovenproof dish with a lid.
2. Slow, oven-cooked stew.
CHAMPIGNON
Small, button mushroom.
CHAUD-FROID
Cold, cooked savoury dish coated with sauce and aspic.
CHINE
A pair of pork loins, undivided.
CHINING
Separating the rib bones of a joint from the backbone.
CHOWDER
Thick soup made from fish and vegetables.
CLARIFIED BUTTER
Butter heated gently and sieved so that it does not discolour when used for frying.
CLARIFYING
Clearing fats (as above) and clearing jellies and consommés with beaten egg white.
COCOTTE
Individual, oven-proof dishes for cooking and serving eggs.
CODDLING
Cooking eggs by putting them into boiling water, away from the heat.
COMPÔTE
Fresh or dried fruit, cooked in syrup and served cold.
CONSERVE
Whole fruit preserved with sugar.
CORN STARCH
Maize flour, finely ground and used for thickening.
CORN SYRUP
Maize syrup used in cakes and confectionery.

COURT BOUILLON
Liquid, containing wine and herbs, in which fish is cooked.
CRÈME BRULÉE
Cream custard with a caramelised topping.
CRÈME CARAMEL
Cold egg custard with caramel topping.
CRÊPE
Thin pancake.
CRIMPING
Decorating pie crust by pinching it with the fingers.
CROQUETTES
Cooked meat, fish or potatoes moulded into small shapes, egg and crumbed and deep-fried.
CROÛTES
1. Pastry covering for meat, fish or vegetables.
2. Slices of baked or toasted bread on which savouries are served.
CROUTONS
Small cubes of bread, fried or toasted and used as garnish.
CURD
Semi-solid part of soured milk.
CURDLE
Separation of fresh milk into liquids and solids, or of sugar and fat in a creamed mixture.
CURE
Preserve fish or meat by drying, salting or smoking.

D

DARIOLE
Individual, cup-shaped mould.
DEVIL
To cook meat, poultry or fish with highly seasoned ingredients.
DICE
To cut food into small cubes.
DREDGING
Sprinkling with flour or sugar.
DRESS
1. To pluck, draw and truss game and poultry.
2. To prepare cooked crab and lobster meat in the shell.
DROPPING CONSISTENCY
Cake or pudding mixture soft enough to drop from a spoon.

E

ÉCLAIR
Choux pastry filled with cream.
EGG-AND-CRUMBING
Coating fish, rissoles, croquettes, etc., first with beaten egg and then breadcrumbs.
EN CROÛTE
Meat or fish in pastry.
ESCALOPE
Thin slice of meat (usually veal), beaten flat and shallow fried.

F

FAGGOT
Savoury rissole made from pork offal, onion and bread.
FARINA
Fine flour made from wheat, nuts or potatoes.
FILLET
1. The undercut from a loin of beef, veal, pork and game.
2. Boned breasts of poultry.
3. Slices of boned fish.
FINES HERBES
Finely chopped herbs, usually parsley, chervil, tarragon and chives.
FLAKING
1. Breaking up cooked fish.
2. Grating chocolate into slivers.
FOIE GRAS
Pâté made from the livers of specially fattened geese.
FOLDING IN
Adding dry ingredients to a whisked or creamed mixture.
FONDUE
Melted cheese mixed with white wine.
FOOL
Cold dessert of fruit purée cream and custard.

G

GALANTINE
Boned poultry, game or veal, served cold, usually glazed with aspic.
GARNISHING
Improving the appearance of a savoury dish with edible decorations such as parsley.
GELATINE
Protein from animal bones and tissue, which melts in hot liquid and forms a jelly when cold.
GLAZE
To give food a glossy finish by brushing it with beaten egg, milk, sugar syrup or jelly.
GNOCCHI
Small dumplings of semolina, potatoes, or choux pastry.

GOULASH
Hungarian beef and onion stew with tomatoes and paprika.
GRAVY
Sauce made from juices of roast meat or poultry boiled with stock or wine; sometimes thickened with flour.

H

HAGGIS
Scottish pudding made from chopped offal, suet, onions and oatmeal, encased in the lining from a sheep's stomach.
HAMBURGER
Minced beef rissole often served in a bread bun.
HANGING
Suspending meat or game in a cool, dry place to improve the flavour and make it tender.
HARICOT VERT
Green bean.
HERBS
Aromatic plants whose leaves or seeds are used in cooking.
HORS-D'OEUVRE
Originally, small, cold dishes served before the soup. Now used to mean any 'starter'.
HULLING
Preparing soft fruit such as strawberries and raspberries by removing the calyx.

I

ICING
Coating for cakes, consisting basically of sugar mixed with water, butter or egg whites.
INFUSING
Extracting the flavour from herbs, spices, tea or coffee by pouring on boiling liquid, covering, and leaving to stand.

J

JARDINIÈRE
A garnish of cooked, diced vegetables.
JOINT
1. A large cut of meat.
2. To divide meat, poultry and game into pieces.
JUGGED
Meat, usually hare, stewed in a covered pot.

K

KEBAB
Cubes of meat marinaded and grilled on a skewer.
KEDGEREE
Breakfast dish of fish (usually smoked haddock), rice and hard-boiled egg.
KNEADING
Working dough with the hands in bread and pastry-making.
KOSHER
Food prepared according to the Orthodox Jewish law.

L

LARD
Pork fat, natural or refined.
LARDING
Threading small strips of pork or bacon fat through lean meat.
LEAVEN
Fermenting agent, such as yeast, which makes dough rise.

M

MACEDOINE
Cooked, diced fruit or vegetables used as a garnish and sometimes set in jelly.
MARINADE
A mixture of oil, vinegar, wine or lemon juice with herbs and spices in which meat or fish is steeped.
MASKING
Coating cooked meat or fish with a savoury sauce or jelly.
MERINGUE
Stiffly whisked egg whites mixed with sugar and baked at a low temperature until crisp.
MEUNIÈRE
Cooking fish in butter, and garnishing with lemon juice and parsley.
MILANESE
Veal escalopes coated with egg and breadcrumbs, seasoned with grated Parmesan cheese and fried.
MIREPOIX
Diced mixed vegetables and ham, fried and used as the base for brown sauces and stews.
MIXED HERBS
A blend of dried herbs which usually includes chervil, chives, parsley, tarragon and thyme.

GLOSSARY OF COOKERY

MOUSSAKA
Greek dish of minced lamb, aubergines and tomatoes topped with a savoury custard.
MOUSSE
Cold dish made with cream, gelatine and whisked egg whites.
MUESLI
Breakfast dish of rolled oats with fruit and nuts.

NAVARIN
Mutton or lamb stew with vegetables and often haricot beans
NEAPOLITAN
Cakes and ice cream in layers of different colours and flavours.
NIÇOISE
Salads and cooked dishes with tomatoes, onions, garlic and black olives.
NOISETTES
Small round or oval pieces of trimmed lamb or beef.

OFFAL
Edible organs such as liver, heart and kidneys.
OSSO BUCO
Veal marrow bones braised with wine and tomatoes.

P

PAELLA
Spanish dish which includes chicken, shellfish, onion and saffron rice.
PANADA
A thick flour or bread sauce used for binding.
PAR-BOILING
Boiling for part of the cooking time and then completing cooking by roasting or frying.
PARING
Peeling fruit or vegetables thinly.
PASTY
Individual pastry case with a filling, usually savoury.
PÂTÉ
Savoury meat or fish paste, usually baked, and served cold.
PATTY
Small, flat savoury cake, such as fish cakes or potato cakes.

PECTIN
A thickening material present in fruit and vegetables.
PETITS FOURS
Small iced sponge cakes.
PETITS POIS
Small, young green peas.
PICKLE
To preserve food in a salt or vinegar solution.
PIZZA
Yeast pastry topped with cheese, tomatoes, anchovies and olives.
PLUCK
1. Offal.
2. To remove the feathers from game and poultry.
PROSCIUTTO
Thin slices of smoked ham.
PULP
Soften food by crushing or boiling.
PURÉE
Food, usually fruit or vegetables, cooked, and sieved.

QUENELLES
Savoury dumplings made with meat or fish.
QUICHE
Pastry tart with a savoury filling.

RASPINGS
Grated crumbs of stale bread.
RATATOUILLE
Stew of onions, aubergines, tomatoes and peppers.
REDUCING
Concentrating a liquid by boiling.
RELISH
Sharp or spicy sauce.
RENDERING
1. Melting down the fat from meat trimmings.
2. Clearing frying fat by heating it.
RENNET
Extract from inner membrane of a calf's stomach, used to curdle milk for cheese and junket.
RISOTTO
Savoury fried rice cooked in stock and served with grated cheese.
RISSOLE
A round cake of minced meat.
ROE
Fish eggs.
ROUX
Paste of fat and flour used to thicken soups and stews.

SALAMI
Spiced, pork sausage which can be fresh or dried.
SAUTÉ
To fry quickly, in shallow fat.
SCALD
To pour boiling water over food to clean it or to loosen the skin.
SCORING
Shallow, parallel cuts in the surface of food to help it cook more quickly.
SEARING
Browning meat at a high temperature to seal in the juices.
SIFTING
Shaking dry ingredients through a sieve.
SKIMMING
Removing the fat from the surface of stews, the cream from milk or scum from jam.
SMOKING
Curing food over wood chippings.
SORBET
A fruit-flavoured water ice.
SOUFFLÉ
Light pudding, sweet or savoury, thickened with egg yolks and with stiffly whisked whites folded in.
SOUSING
Pickling food, usually fish, in brine or vinegar.
SPIT
Metal rod on which meat and poultry is cooked by revolving over a fire or under a grill.
STEEPING
Leaving food to stand (usually overnight) in hot or cold water to soften it or to remove salt.
STERILISING
Heating food, particularly milk, to destroy harmful bacteria.
STOCK
Liquid used as the base for stews and soups. Made by simmering meat or fish bones and trimmings, vegetables and herbs, in water.
STRUDEL
An Austrian pastry consisting of leaves of dough with fruit or savoury filling.
STUFFING
Bread or rice mixed with meat, vegetables, fruit or herbs and used as a filling.
SWEATING
Cooking vegetables gently in fat to extract the juices.

SYLLABUB
Rich, cold dessert made from double cream and wine.
SYRUP
Sugar boiled with water or fruit juice, until it is thick.

TERRINE
Originally the earthenware pot used to cook pâté, now used to describe the contents as well.
TRUFFLES
Rare, expensive, edible fungi.
TRUSSING
Using skewers and string to tie a bird into a compact shape.

V

VELOUTÉ
Smooth, white sauce made with veal, chicken or fish stock.
VINAIGRETTE
Salad dressing made from oil, vinegar, salt and pepper.
VOL-AU-VENT
Puff-pastry case.

WHEY
The liquid part of the milk, left when the curd solidifies.
WHIPPING
To beat air into a mixture.
WIENER SCHNITZEL
Escalope of veal, egg and bread-crumbed, fried and garnished with anchovies and capers.

Y

YEAST
Fungus plant used as a fermenting or raising agent.
YOGHOURT
Sour milk treated with a fermenting agent.

ZABAGLIONE
Italian dessert of egg yolks, sugar and Marsala or white wine.
ZEST
The oily outer skin of citrus fruit, peeled thinly or grated.

WEIGHTS AND MEASURES

Many recipes are now given in metric as well as imperial measures. Exact conversions between the two systems are not practical.

In this book, 1 oz. is taken as the equivalent of 25 g. and 1 pint as the equivalent of 600 ml.

When large quantities are being used, as in party catering, jam-making and bread-making, 1 lb. is taken as the equivalent of 450 g. The full conversion tables are on the inside cover.

Where both metric and imperial measures are given in a recipe, use one or the other – never a mixture of the two.

The metric measures make about 10% less in quantity than the imperial equivalents and cooking times for cakes and puddings will need to be reduced by about four minutes in each half-hour. Existing kitchen equipment can still be used.

However, scales, spoons and jugs are now available marked in metric measures so choose these when buying new ones.

The amount of food bought in a shop may yield a much smaller quantity by the time it has been prepared. (See chart below.) It is worth bearing this in mind when comparing prices. Prawns, unshelled, may seem cheap in comparison with ready-shelled ones, but will produce only half as much food for the table.

Where recipes specify one egg, this refers to a standard egg, weighing about 50 g. (2 oz.). One medium onion should weigh 75-100 g. (3-4 oz.).

Catering for large numbers of people can be simplified and wastage avoided if quantities are bought and cooked according to the number of servings they will provide. Some guidance is given in the chart below.

HANDY QUANTITIES

FOOD BOUGHT	YIELD
1 lemon	50 ml. (2 fl. oz.) juice
225 g. (½ lb.) peas in pods	75-100 g. (3-4 oz.) peas
10 fl. oz. (½ pint) prawns in shells	150 g. (5 oz.) shelled
1.8 kg. (4 lb.) crab in shell	575 g. (1¼ lb.)

PARTY QUANTITIES

FOOD AND DRINK	NUMBER OF SERVINGS
1 large loaf of bread	approximately 20 slices
100 g. (4 oz.) butter	spreads 20 slices of bread, 24 rolls
cooked meat, fish and cheese	25 g. (1 oz.) per sandwich
hard-boiled eggs	2 eggs will fill 3 rounds of sandwiches
7 in. sponge cake	8 portions
7 in. fruit cake	12 portions
1 lb. shortcrust or flaky pastry	makes 36 tarts, patties or 24 small pies
1 bottle champagne	6-8 glasses
1 bottle squash	15-20 glasses
1 bottle of wine	6 glasses
1 bottle spirits	20 tots
1 bottle sherry	12 glasses

Sewing for the family

Many of the things to make which are described elsewhere in this
book depend on a knowledge of sewing. The equipment, materials, basic
stitches and skills needed to make your own bedding, curtains, loose
covers, cushions and other projects are described in this section.
Here too is information on repairs and alterations to clothing,
from making the simplest darn to shortening a fur coat,
and on how to alter a shop-bought pattern to suit a particular figure.

CONTENTS

TOOLS AND MATERIALS

Sewing is one of the basic skills of the homemaker. Many of the projects outlined in this book – from making curtains to repairing upholstery – involve sewing either by hand or with a machine. This chapter brings together all the techniques needed in these various projects as part of a basic guide to sewing. At the same time, the chapter sets out the principles of dressmaking and explains how to repair and alter clothes.

The first essential for successful sewing is a good working area. Ideally, it should be a small room set apart for the purpose, or a well-lit corner kept solely for sewing. Your basic equipment should include a work-table, an ironing board, a sewing machine and sufficient storage space for fabrics, patterns and smaller equipment. A peg-board screen is useful for hanging tools, clothes and storage bags. Your work surface should be large enough – about 2 × 1 m. (6 × 3 ft) – for cutting and pinning, and firm enough to carry the sewing machine. If you use a polished table, fit it with a hardboard cover, since pins, scissors and other tools will soon mark it. Alternatively, a folding wallpaper pasting table can be used – also with a hardboard top to give the width needed for cutting. Store small items such as thread, zips and trimmings, in a basket or workbox, or in a set of shallow office file drawers.

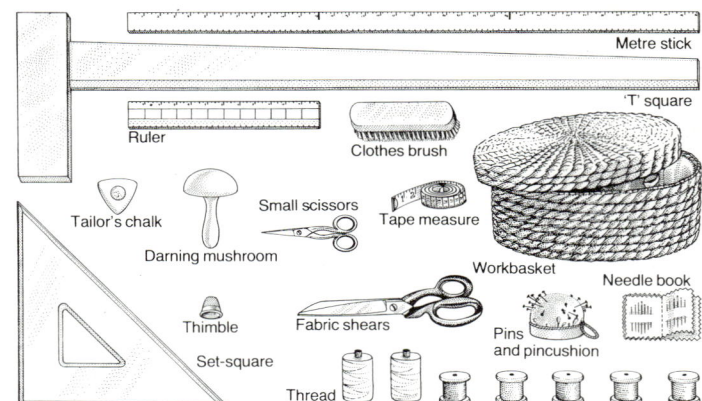

BASIC SEWING EQUIPMENT This includes basket, rulers, T-square, pincushion, scissors, mixed threads, tailor's chalk, needle holder and thimble.

SEWING AREA A spare bedroom can be adapted as a sewing room. The bed is kept under the work top. Make sure a power point is available for machine.

• BASIC WORKBASKET

Choose even the simplest items with care. Good quality tools will make sewing easier and the results will look more professional.

CUTTING TOOLS

The best size for dressmaking shears is 25-30 cm. (10-12 in.). Pinking shears give a zigzag fray-resistant finish to raw edges. Use fabric shears only for cutting fabric, as paper will blunt them. Electric scissors, battery or mains-operated, make light work of cutting out. Use small scissors with sharp, pointed ends for buttonholes, embroidery and cutting the ends of cotton. A seam ripper, which has a tiny protected blade, cuts stitching without harming the fabric.

MEASURING TOOLS

Choose a fibre-glass tape measure – which will not stretch – marked in metric and imperial measurements. A metrestick is essential for soft furnishing work. It is also useful for marking long lines on patterns or checking hem levels.

A set-square is needed when cut-ting curtain or upholstery fabric to ensure a true right-angle at the corners. Perspex rulers and set-squares allow you to see the grain of the fabric.

PINS AND PINCUSHION

Use fine, sharp dressmaker's pins, preferably 18 mm. ($\frac{3}{4}$ in.) long. Shorter pins can be used for lightweight fabrics and paper. Glass-headed pins can be used for sheer or lacy fabrics, and 30 mm. ($1\frac{1}{4}$ in.) pins are needed when cutting out loose covers.

A pincushion held on the wrist on a band of elastic keeps pins and needles instantly available when working. It can also be hung on the dress stand or the sewing machine.

NEEDLES AND THIMBLE

Needles are sized by number, ranging from No. 1, the longest and thickest, to No. 24, the smallest and finest. For general sewing, use 7 or 8 in the Sharps range. For fine work use Betweens or long, small-eyed milliner's needles. These are also useful for tacking. For suede and leather you will need a strong sharp needle, preferably a three-sided glover's needle.

Use ballpoint needles for sewing stretch or knit fabrics. Keep needles in a dry place, such as a felt-paged needle book, to protect them.

Silver or steel thimbles are best. They should fit your second finger. Keep a darning needle and mushroom in your workbasket. A needle threader is also useful.

BULLDOG CLIPS AND WEIGHTS
When cutting a long piece of fabric fix it to the edge of the table with Bulldog clips. Weights are also useful for preventing the material from slipping or twisting off grain.

PATTERN PAPER
Special pattern paper is marked with squares to make pattern drawing easy. But large sheets of lining paper or brown paper can also be used for soft-furnishing patterns. Tissue-

paper patterns that are being used a lot should be transferred to heavier paper.

MARKING EQUIPMENT
Tailor's chalk is used for marking alterations. Test fabrics first to make sure the chalk will not permanently mark them.

Coloured carbon paper can be used with a tracing wheel to transfer pattern markings on to fabric. For delicate fabrics use a smooth-edged wheel. For everything else use a spiked wheel.

CARE OF FABRICS WHILE SEWING
Brush off dust, fluff and loose threads as they collect on the fabric.

Remove spots immediately with dry-cleaning fluid. Sewing-machine oil can mark the fabric permanently. Plastic or wooden (not wire) hangers

are best to hold garments while working on them.

TRIMMINGS AND THREADS
Buy bias and hem tape in black, white and beige, and narrow tape and elastic, both woven and shirring, in black and white. Buy white and coloured tacking cotton, buttonhole twist, the large-size reels of mercerised sewing thread and darning wool. Buy the appropriate threads when buying the fabric (see chart, below).

ELECTRIC IRON
An iron, preferably with thermostatic control and steam setting, is needed for pressing seams and darts.

FASTENINGS
For zips and other fastenings, see p. 302. Buy press studs, hooks, eyes and bars in black and plain metal.

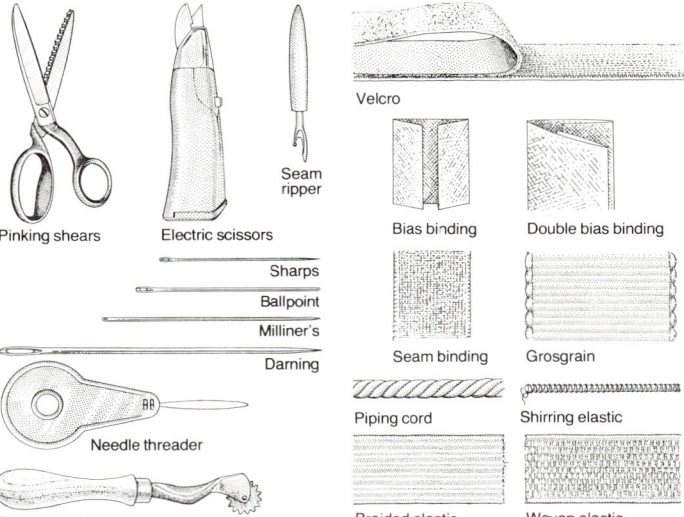

USEFUL ADDITIONS If you intend to do a lot of sewing, add the tools (left) to your equipment. Also stock up with braids, bindings and elastic (right).

CHOOSING YOUR NEEDLE AND THREAD

FABRIC (EXAMPLES)	FIBRE	THREAD	NEEDLE SIZES HAND/MACHINE	
FINE: Lawn, georgette, voile, chiffon, organdie, net, lace	synthetic/mixtures	synthetic 60	9	9-11
	cotton/linen	mercerised 50	9	9-11
	wool	mercerised 50	9	9-11
	silk	silk	9	9-11
LIGHTWEIGHT: Pop in, gingham	synthetic/mixtures	synthetic 60	8-9	11-14
	cotton/linen	mercerised 50	8-9	11-14
	wool	mercerised 50	8-9	11-14
	silk	silk	8-9	11-14
MEDIUM WEIGHT: Gaberdine, brocade, tweed, waterproofed	synthetic/mixtures	synthetic 60	8-9	11-14
	cotton	mercerised 50	7-8	11-14
	linen	mercerised 40	7-8	11-14
	wool	mercerised 50	7-8	11-14
	silk	silk	7-8	11-14
HEAVYWEIGHT: Coatings, canvas, heavy furnishing fabrics	synthetic/mixtures	synthetic 40	6	16-18
	cotton	mercerised 40	7-8	14-16
	linen	mercerised 40	6-7	14-16
	wool	mercerised 40	7-8	14-16
	silk	silk	7-8	14-16
VELVET	synthetic/mixtures	synthetic 60	8-9	11-14
	cotton	mercerised 50	7-8	11-14
	silk	silk	7-8	11-14
LEATHER AND PVC		synthetic 40	3-8	14-18

COLLECTING THIMBLES AND TAPE MEASURES

Until 1851, when the sewing machine first appeared in Britain, every article of clothing and every piece of household linen was stitched by hand. This in turn resulted in a bewildering array of sewing aids – particularly thimbles and tape measures which would today be ideal subjects for the amateur collector.
Thimbles The Anglo-Saxons used the word 'thymel' to describe the bell-shaped protective leather cover worn on the thumb when sewing. This word became thimble, and over the centuries thimbles were made in materials as diverse as wood and ivory, pewter and glass and – as shown in the selection on the right – gold, silver and porcelain. Silver thimbles, which first appeared in the 16th century, were often decorated. The one in the centre has shamrock leaves, its top inset with Connemara marble. The very small thimble immediately in front of it is a child's, or doll's, thimble made in 1906. Some Victorian thimbles were sold in souvenir cases. The case, top left, which holds the gold thimble standing in front of it, is inscribed 'Hastings from the Sea'. It was made in 1895. Silver and gold thimbles are not recommended for someone starting a collection. They are very expensive and rarely found outside a museum. Brass and bronze thimbles are cheaper, and many interesting examples can often be picked up at market stalls.
Tape measures Ribbon tapes wound into cases by hand have been in use since the 17th century, but these would be hard to find today. Ingenious tape measures however were made during the Victorian era – as the selection on the left shows. Tapes are re-wound into the measures by twisting the tail of the donkey, turning the steering wheel of the car, winding the handle on the mandolin and turning the three-pronged base of the owl. Even more intricate is the tape-measure model of Nuremberg Cathedral. As the tape is pulled out, the figures set around the outside of the model revolve.

• THE SEWING MACHINE

Before buying a sewing machine see as many as possible demonstrated in order to decide which machine best suits your needs.

A machine with a swing needle for zigzag stitching is adequate for most basic sewing and mending.

Free-arm machines have a small arm raised above the base of the machine: this is useful for setting sleeves into armholes and making children's clothes.

Semi-automatic machines have a limited range of special stitches such as stretch, blind hemming and buttonhole stitches.

Fully automatic machines are the most expensive type and should be bought only if you are sure you will make use of their wide range of embroidery and other special stitches.

Do not dismiss an old treadle or hand machine if you have one. These old machines were beautifully made, and usually need only cleaning and oiling and perhaps a new driving belt to make them run smoothly. Beginners may find old machines useful to learn on, as their pace is controlled by the person using them. It is also possible for a sewing machine repairman to fit an electric motor to a hand-powered model.

Another possibility in place of an expensive new machine is a second-hand, reconditioned model. Sewing-machine shops usually sell them with at least a six months' guarantee.

BASIC CARE AND USE OF THE MACHINE

New machines will have a comprehensive manual giving full instructions for their care and maintenance with details of extra accessories you can buy later. Manuals for older models can usually be obtained from the manufacturers.

Brush Use a small, firm-bristled paintbrush to remove dust from around the bobbin area. Dust the machine every time it is used.

Screwdriver Needle screws, sewing plates and other machine fittings occasionally need tightening with a small screwdriver.

Oiling The sewing machine must be oiled regularly according to the plan given in the manufacturer's working manual. Keep the machine clean. Brush out fluff from under the needle plate and lightly oil the working parts before use. Take care not to use too much oil. Stitch through a scrap of fabric to remove any excess oil from the needle plate.

Machine needles Most needle sizes are matched to the type and thickness of fabric. The low numbers indicate the finest needles and the high numbers the thicker needles for thicker fabrics. (See Needle and Thread chart on p. 287.) Needle sizes sometimes vary according to the make of the machine. There are needles with special points for sewing knitted fabrics and leather.

Bobbins Keep a number of bobbins wound in various colours ready for use. Do not put too much thread on a bobbin or it will not fit its case.

Bobbin case The bobbin case fits underneath the sewing plate. It holds the bobbin which feeds the lower thread to the needle.

THREADING UP

Check that the correct size of needle is inserted the right way – normally with the fine groove facing you – and the needle pushed up as far as possible before being screwed into place [A1]. The bobbin must also be in-

---

THREAD GUIDE
The guide directs thread from the spool to the take-up lever.

THREAD TAKE-UP LEVER
Thread is carried up and down by the lever in time with the needle.

PRESSURE REGULATOR
This adjusts the spring which pushes the foot on to the fabric.

FOOT LIFT LEVER
The lever lifts the foot to allow the fabric under the needle.

NEEDLE CLAMP SCREW
This holds the needle in place. Make sure it is tight.

NEEDLE
The shank must be the right way round in the clamp, or the machine will not sew correctly.

FOOT CLAMP SCREW
This holds the presser foot in place. Unscrew to exchange feet.

PRESSER FOOT
The foot presses the fabric on to the feed dogs which move it under the needle.

FEED DOGS
The teeth shuttle to and fro to draw the fabric under the needle.

UPPER THREAD TENSION REGULATOR
High numbers indicate high tension. Adjust with the foot down.

SLIDE PLATE
The plate covers the bobbin which feeds the lower thread to the needle.

SPOOL PIN
The spool which supplies thread to the needle unwinds on this pin.

BOBBIN WINDER PIN
Wind thread evenly on to the bobbin as it turns on this pin.

BOBBIN WINDER SWITCH
Controls the bobbin winder pin.

HAND WHEEL
Turn wheel by hand for first few stitches to ease the load on motor.

NEEDLE-POSITION SELECTOR
This offsets stitches to one side. It is useful for sewing buttons.

REVERSE-STITCH SELECTOR
Reverse-stitch to anchor the start and finish of each seam.

STITCH-LENGTH REGULATOR
Stitch length has to be varied to suit the type of fabric.

STITCH-WIDTH REGULATOR
This controls the side-to-side needle movement in zigzag sewing.

LAMP
A lamp under the machine arm illuminates the sewing area.

KNOWING YOUR MACHINE These are the important working parts of a sewing machine – their names, and what they do.

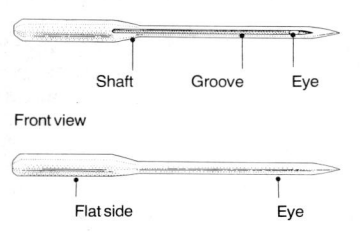

Shaft   Groove   Eye

Front view

Flat side   Eye

Side view

The machine needle.

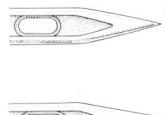

REGULAR
These needles (size 9-18) can be used on all woven fabrics.

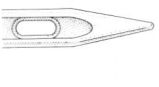

BALLPOINT
Rounded points (size 9-16) are used for knitted fabrics.

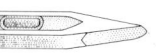

WEDGE-POINT
Wedge needles (size 11-18) are designed for sewing leather.

Needles for different purposes.

THREADING UP

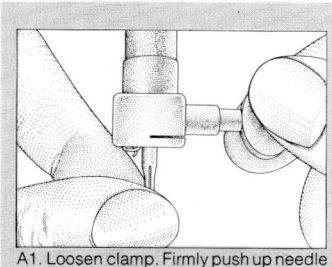

A1. Loosen clamp. Firmly push up needle (with groove facing user). Re-clamp.

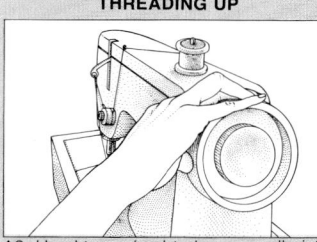

A2. Hand-turn wheel to lower needle into needle hole. Keep turning to raise needle.

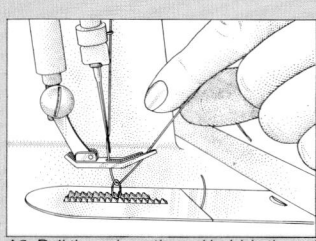

A3. Pull thread gently and bobbin thread will come up through the needle plate.

serted correctly. The top and bobbin threads must be identical and the needle should be threaded with the presser foot raised. Once the needle is threaded, lower it into the needle-hole in the plate, then bring the needle up by turning the machine wheel by hand [A2]. Pull the thread gently and the bobbin thread will come up through the needle plate [A3].

TENSION

Do not alter the tension once it is set correctly, except when gathering or applying decorative top stitching. Uneven stitches, or 'looping' and puckering, are caused by incorrect tension. If the loops are underneath the fabric, the top tension is wrong. Conversely, if the loops are on the top, the bottom tension is wrong. Try to make all adjustments, both up and down, with the upper tension-adjusting screw, which is above the needle on most machines. Adjust the lower tension only as a last resort. Most tension problems are caused by:

1 incorrect thread for the fabric
2 wrongly inserted or damaged (bent or blunt) needle
3 tension mark wrongly set
4 bobbin tension wrong

If adjustment is unavoidable, consult the machine handbook since different machines have different methods of adjusting thread tension.

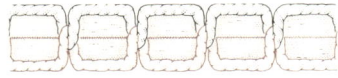

Correct tension.

Tension too tight.

Tension too loose.

BREAKING THREAD

This common problem may be caused by:

1 thread tension too tight
2 incorrect size of needle
3 damaged or incorrectly inserted needle
4 faulty thread
5 tiny ends of thread or fluff around bobbin area and plate

MACHINE STITCHING

Place fabric under the raised presser foot, lining up the needle on the seam line. Take long ends of bobbin and needle threads to the back of the needle plate. Lower the presser foot and turn the wheel by hand to insert needle in fabric. This takes the load off the motor for the first stitch and reduces the risk of breaking the

thread. Stitch for 15 mm. (½ in.) then reverse-stitch to lock ends. Go forward again to follow the seam line. Guide the fabric evenly, without pulling or pushing. Hold it lightly at the side and towards the back with the fingers of the other hand. Do not watch the needle, but look at the presser foot for the guide to stitching along the marked line. Leave at least 5 cm. (2 in.) of thread on the machine before cutting off, so that the thread is available for the next line of stitching.

Beginners should practise several rows of stitching, including turning right-angled corners. Do not do this in one continuous movement, but stop machine at corner, leaving needle in fabric [B1]. Raise presser foot, turn the fabric to the new sewing line, lower presser foot and start stitching [B2]. Practise with different types of fabric and different stitch lengths and tensions. Draw curves, squares and circles on fabric and practise sewing along the outlines.

Practise turning sharp corners. This is done in two moves instead of the one needed at a right-angled corner. Stop at the corner as before [C1], but only half turn the fabric [C2]. On thin material put one stitch across the corner (two or three stitches on thicker material), then turn again to the new seam line [C3]. Turn through to right side, pushing the corner out carefully

Trimming off excess at corners.

with the point of a knitting needle.

Points and curves are always stitched before the actual shape is cut out. If cut out first, the shape can distort during machining. Scallops are also stitched before being cut, with one stitch across the points between scallops. Move the fabric gently while stitching so that the curved line is followed exactly. Notch the outward curve by cutting a tiny V-shape a fraction from the stitching line, to leave less bulk in the seam and let the curve lie smoothly. Similarly, if the curve is to lie inwards when finished, the allowance is snipped, not notched, so that it can spread out without puckering the seam (remember that notches close up, and snips open out).

Snip inside curves, notch outside curves.

ATTACHMENTS

A wide range of attachments is available for modern machines. When buying attachments, make sure they fit your machine.

Zipper foot For stitching a seam which has more bulk on one side than the other. Its design allows the needle to sew very close to the zip teeth on one side. Essential for seams where the stitching needle must be as close as possible to the raised surface.

Piping foot Similar in function to a zipper foot, but more efficient for attaching piping and cording. Not available for all makes of machine.

Zigzag foot This foot allows the needle to make zigzag stitching in a variety of widths for finishing seam edges, and to do decorative stitching such as satin stitch. If the needle is set to the centre of the foot, it can be used for normal straight stitching.

Seam guide This keeps the outer edge of the fabric on course when sewing seams.

HELP AND ADVICE

Some sewing-machine manufacturers give free lessons to customers. Sewing-accessory shops and department-store pattern departments are usually staffed by dressmaking experts who will help with advice. Evening classes in dressmaking are available in most areas.

A RIGHT-ANGLED CORNER

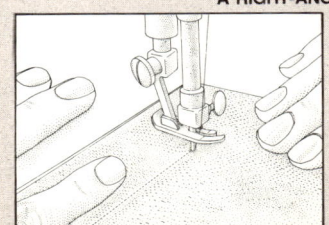

B1. Stop at the corner point. Keep needle in the fabric and raise the presser foot.

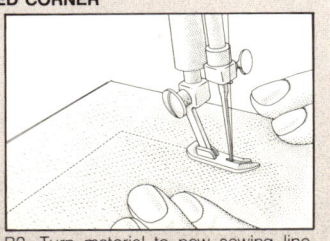

B2. Turn material to new sewing line. Lower presser foot and continue sewing.

A SHARP CORNER

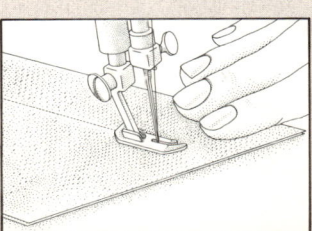

C1. Stitch to the corner point. Keeping needle in the fabric, raise presser foot.

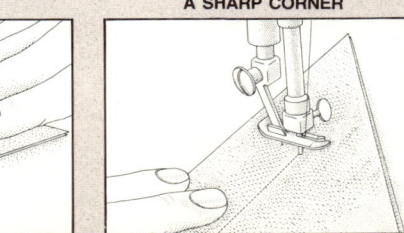

C2. Turn fabric halfway. Lower presser foot and make two or three stitches.

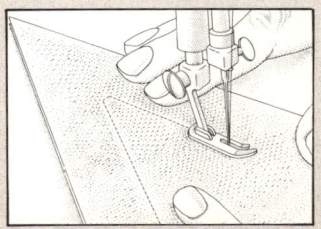

C3. Raise foot. Again leave needle in, turn fabric. Lower foot, continue sewing.

• GUIDE TO FABRICS

There are five main categories of fibre: man-made fibres, such as nylon, and the four natural fibres – cotton, linen, wool and silk. Natural fibres are easier to use and more comfortable to wear, but man-made fibres often have special features, like drip-dry or crease-resistant qualities.

For dressmaking or soft furnishing, the ideal fabric may be a combination of natural and man-made fibres. For instance, a cotton/polyester blend has the crease-resistance of polyester plus the coolness of cotton.

Woven, non-stretch fabrics like flannel, fine tweed, gingham, etc., are easiest to cut and sew. When buying fabric, ask the shop assistant to say what it is made from, whether it should be washed or dry-cleaned, and if it has any special qualities.

Ask to see the fabric unrolled, preferably in daylight. Stand back from it

 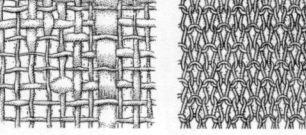

Woven fabric   Knitted fabric

to see the total effect of pattern and texture. This helps to decide whether, for instance, curtains will need lining or whether chair covers would be improved by a contrast piping trim.

Examine the fabric closely and rub a piece between the fingers to make sure its 'body' is not a glue-based dressing which will powder when rubbed and will wash out.

USING DIFFICULT FABRICS

The following hints will help you avoid costly mistakes when using fabrics such as velvets, crêpes, checks and lace. These 'difficult' fabrics are not recommended for the beginner.

Velvets Fabrics with a pile – such as velvet or corduroy – or with a one-way nap – such as broadcloth – change colour according to the way the nap or pile lies. Lay all pattern pieces on the fabric so that the nap or pile will face the same way on each. When making up velvet curtains be careful to indicate the top of each curtain as you cut it out, with a marker of coloured thread. To cut velvet, have the pile side down, but mark the direction of the pile with chalk arrows on the wrong side. Pin inside the seam allowance, as pins can damage velvet, and sew in the direction of the pile.

Sheers Chiffon, voile, organdie and other sheers should be made up in a design requiring as few seams as possible. Clip the tight selvedge of chiffon to let it lie evenly. Mark sheers where necessary with tacking rather than chalk. The softest of these fabrics, such as sheer curtains, should be machine-sewn with tissue paper below, to prevent slipping on the needle plate. Cut strips of tissue, lay them underneath the tacked seam and stitch through. Gently tear the paper away afterwards.

Lace Back lace with net to accentuate the design, or sew it to a lining. Seams can be disguised by cutting round the individual motifs and oversewing them across the seams. A narrow seam can be machined twice and finished with a zigzag.

Crêpe Because it stretches in handling, crêpe is a difficult fabric to cut and sew. Pin carefully and tack all slanted seams and curves while the fabric is still flat on the table. Stay-stitch neckline curves by making a line of machine stitching just inside the seam line. Garments with bias seams should hang for a few days to drop before being hemmed.

Knitted fabrics The firm doubleknits are relatively easy to make up, but the finer, softer knits tend to sag and stretch. Avoid circular shapes and curved seams and treat the rib of the knitting as the grain. Avoid stretching it when cutting. Use a small zigzag machine-stitch with a ball point needle, to avoid splitting the fibres. Reinforce shoulders and waistlines with cotton tape sewn in with the seams.

Satins Their colour effects vary according to the way light hits the surface, so cut them the same way.

Lining fabrics Garments that are lined will keep their shape and resist creasing. The lining should be able to accept the same cleaning treatment as the outer fabric. Rayon taffeta is one of the cheapest and best linings for fabrics which will need dry-cleaning. Washable linings are expensive.

Interlinings While linings are treated almost as a separate part of a garment, interlinings are cut exactly as the main fabric and handled with it as one. Interlinings add weight and body to a limp fabric, or back a loose weave. Lawn, organza or lightweight taffeta are the usual interlining fabrics.

Interfacings These are firm fabrics used to add crispness, body and shape to necklines, facings, collars and pockets. Interfacings can be ironed on or sewn to the garment. Iron-on interfacings are easy to use though too stiff for light fabrics. There

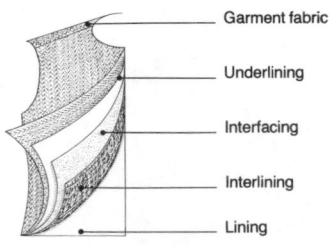

Order of interlinings and linings

is an iron-on canvas for heavy woollen cloths. Woven canvas is the best interfacing as it is more flexible than the iron-on varieties.

Underlinings Lightweight fabric is used to give added strength and durability, to maintain the shape of a garment and hide inner stitching.

HOW THE DESIGN AFFECTS SEWING

Additional material will usually be required when using patterned material so that the design can be matched up exactly. These extra amounts of material may be specified on the pattern envelope. If not, calculate them as follows:

One-way prints When using these, lay out pattern pieces so that material is cut with a minimum of waste. If width of garment at top and bottom is roughly the same, no extra fabric should be needed. If the width differs a lot – as in a widely flared skirt – allow

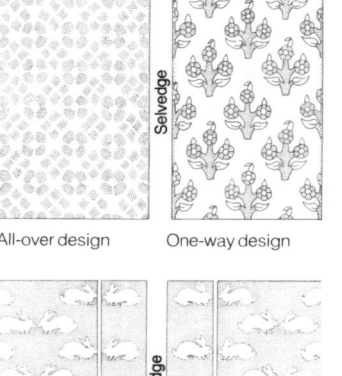

All-over design   One-way design

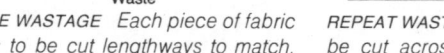

SIDE WASTAGE Each piece of fabric has to be cut lengthways to match.

an extra 30 cm. (12 in.) to each metre or yard of material specified.

Large prints Matching up can mean a lot of wastage. To calculate additional fabric for dressmaking, add one 're-peat' – the depth covered by one motif of the design – to each metre or yard of material. For curtains, add one repeat for each curtain length.

Checks, plaids and stripes These need careful laying out to make sure that the right parts of the paper pattern match when sewn together. Unless the pattern is specially designed for checks and stripes, allow extra material for matching – 25 cm. (10 in.) more for small checks, about 50 cm. (20 in.) for stripes and up to 90 cm. (36 in.) for large plaids, depending on the depth of the pattern repeat. If possible, avoid uneven plaids, which are difficult to match. With plaids, the thickest or most dominant colour bar will be the most obvious in the made-up material. Mark with a pencil on the

First curtain

Waste

Second curtain

REPEAT WASTAGE One piece has to be cut across the width to match.

pattern where dominant parts of the pattern appear near any notches at the seam line, so that they can be matched to the joining pieces. Checks and stripes must have all pieces laid out and cut one way, otherwise they will not match. If the checks cannot match all along the seam, make sure that they match in the most obvious places. Tack together all pieces before sewing them, as a final check on matching.

• PREPARING FABRICS FOR SEWING

Unless the fabric is guaranteed as being pre-shrunk, test for shrinkage. Cut two identical squares of the material and soak one in water. Press it when it is almost dry and compare the two. If there is a difference, pre-shrink the whole length of fabric by pressing on the wrong side with a damp cloth or with a steam iron. Press down only – do not slide the iron.

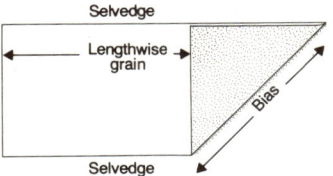
Folding the fabric to find the bias.

Grain Lengthwise grain is the un-stretchable warp thread in a fabric (see above). Patterns must be placed carefully with the grain-line arrows following the lengthwise grain. Garments or curtains cut off the grain will not hang properly.

Bias The crosswise line running at a 45 degrees angle to the straight grain is called the bias (see above). Flared and circular skirts and piping are cut on the bias to give them stretch and movement. To find the true bias, sometimes called 'cutting on the cross', fold the material so that the straight cut edge aligns with the

Drawing a thread to find a straight line.

selvedge. This forms a triangle, the folded edge of which is the bias.

STRAIGHTENING FABRIC ENDS

It is important to start with a straight edge when cutting. One way to ensure this, with a suitable woven fabric, is to pull out one of the crosswise threads (see above) and cut along the line it leaves. If the fabric does not permit this method, use a T-square or set-square to draw a line with tailor's chalk at right-angles to the selvedge.

LAYING OUT THE PATTERN

Buy the right amount of fabric for the width given, and follow the cutting layout given with the pattern. Check the grain of the fabric, especially for curtains and loose covers, as some pieces must be cut on the straight grain while others, like the arm sections of chair covers, should be cut on the bias.

Lay the material flat. Fold in half lengthways with the selvedges pinned together at intervals. Place the pattern sections carefully, noting which must be butted against the fold line so that they open out in one piece, and which butt against the selvedge.

Pin the pattern through the two thicknesses of fabric. Use tacking, chalk or dressmaker's carbon paper to mark any special points.

Cut around the pattern with long, even strokes and without stretching or twisting the fabric. Cut balance-mark notches outwards into the seam allowances.

EVEN PLAIDS

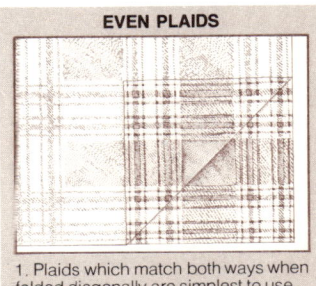
1. Plaids which match both ways when folded diagonally are simplest to use.

2. These even plaids also match when folded vertically through a repeat.

UNEVEN PLAIDS

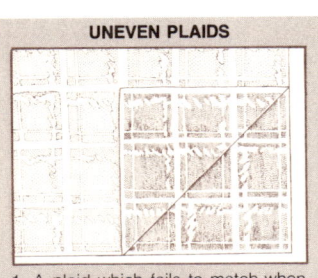
1. A plaid which fails to match when folded diagonally is uneven.

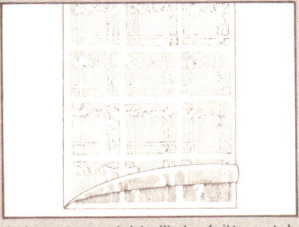
2. An uneven plaid will also fail to match when folded vertically.

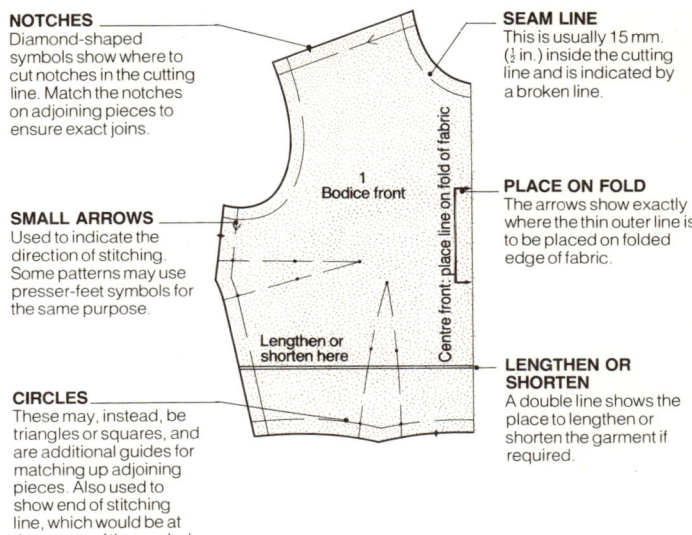

NOTCHES Diamond-shaped symbols show where to cut notches in the cutting line. Match the notches on adjoining pieces to ensure exact joins.

SMALL ARROWS Used to indicate the direction of stitching. Some patterns may use presser-feet symbols for the same purpose.

CIRCLES These may, instead, be triangles or squares, and are additional guides for matching up adjoining pieces. Also used to show end of stitching line, which would be at the centre of the symbol.

SEAM LINE This is usually 15 mm. (⅝ in.) inside the cutting line and is indicated by a broken line.

PLACE ON FOLD The arrows show exactly where the thin outer line is to be placed on folded edge of fabric.

LENGTHEN OR SHORTEN A double line shows the place to lengthen or shorten the garment if required.

1 Bodice front

Centre front: place line on fold of fabric

Lengthen or shorten here

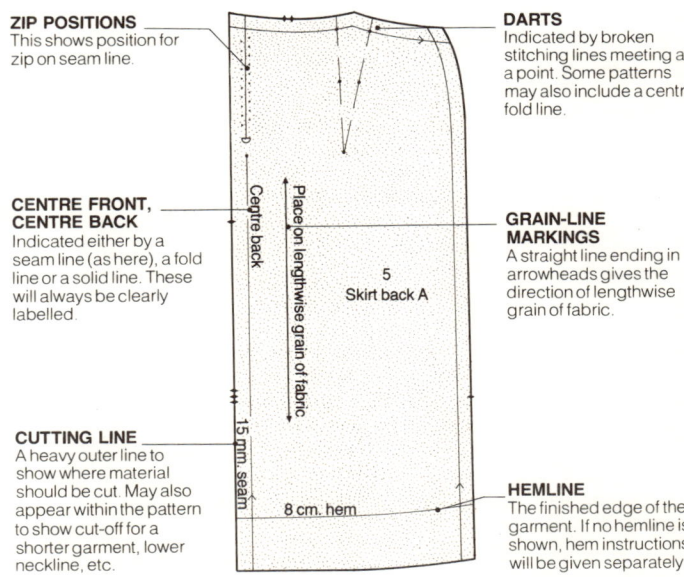

ZIP POSITIONS This shows position for zip on seam line.

CENTRE FRONT, CENTRE BACK Indicated either by a seam line (as here), a fold line or a solid line. These will always be clearly labelled.

CUTTING LINE A heavy outer line to show where material should be cut. May also appear within the pattern to show cut-off for a shorter garment, lower neckline, etc.

DARTS Indicated by broken stitching lines meeting at a point. Some patterns may also include a centre fold line.

GRAIN-LINE MARKINGS A straight line ending in arrowheads gives the direction of lengthwise grain of fabric.

HEMLINE The finished edge of the garment. If no hemline is shown, hem instructions will be given separately.

Centre back

Place on lengthwise grain of fabric

5 Skirt back A

15 mm seam

8 cm. hem

PATTERN MARKINGS An understanding of the various symbols on patterns is essential to good dressmaking. These are the markings – and what they mean.

• HOW FABRICS ARE MADE

All fabrics are made from a basic fibre. Most fibres are formed into yarns and knitted or woven together.

Fibres may be natural – from animal, vegetable or mineral sources – or man-made. They may be available in short lengths (staple) or continuous lengths (filament).

Cotton, wool, flax and silk are the natural fibres normally used for clothing fabrics. The cheapest is cotton. Wool, more difficult to process, is more expensive. Animal hairs or fleeces classified as wool (alpaca, angora, camel, cashmere, llama, mohair, vicuña) are all expensive.

Flax, used to make linen, is not widely available and is difficult to process, so is fairly expensive. Silk is the only natural fibre available as filament, but is scarce and expensive.

Chemically produced man-made fibres are in two groups – those derived from natural materials such as cellulose, and those produced from by-products of coal and oil.

Commonly used man-made fibres are acetate, triacetate and viscose rayon (regenerated from natural materials); acrylic, elastomeric, modacrylic, nylon, polyester (coal or oil-based).

All man-made fibres are produced in filament form, but many are cut into staple form and spun into yarn to vary the texture and appearance. Although man-made fibres vary in their particular qualities, they are mostly resistant to moths and mildew, and all tend to develop static electricity.

Man-made fibres are generally less expensive than natural fibres, with the exception of cotton. Viscose rayon is one of the cheapest.

Yarns are strands made up from single fibres. Staple fibres are spun (drawn and twisted) into strands. The tighter the strand is twisted, the stronger the yarn. Filaments need only be twisted to make yarn.

Yarns may be single (one strand) or ply (several strands twisted together). Combining strands adds strength and improves texture.

STRUCTURE AND FINISHING

Fabrics vary in weight from light to heavy, depending on the fineness of the yarn. A fabric may be made from more than one fibre. Different fibres can be blended together to form a yarn, or different yarns can be mixed in a fabric structure.

This may be done to produce a cheaper fabric (cashmere with wool, for example), to take advantage of the particular qualities of each fibre (such as the washability of cotton and the warmth of wool), or to obtain a decorative effect.

Woven fabrics Weaving is a process of interlacing yarns. Those lengthways in a fabric are known as the warp, those across its width as the weft (or filling).

The weave can be varied by the spacing of the yarns, by different patterns of interlacing, and by mixing yarns of different weight and character. The three basic weaves are plain, twill and satin (see Glossary).

Knitted fabrics Machine-knitted fabrics are formed by interlocking loops of yarn, and may be weft knitted – with loops linked across the width – or more complex run-resistant warp knits – with loops linked along the length of the fabric.

Finishing Once the fabric has been formed, it may be treated in some way to give it a particular quality – such as a polished, embossed or napped surface or resistance to creasing or shrinking. There are many different treatments, some of them patented processes. The main ones are described in the glossary.

FABRIC GLOSSARY

Cleaning instructions for fabrics should be given on the care label (see p. 330). Advice is given here for a few difficult fabrics.
* Indicates trade name.

ACETATE
Silk-like man-made fibre derived from cellulose, but not very strong. Often blended with other fibres. Drapes well and does not crease or shrink. Some types are flame resistant. Used to make dresses, blouses, lingerie, linings. Trade names include Celafibre, Dicel, Lancola, Lansil, Lo-Flam.

*ACRILAN See Acrylic.

ACRYLIC
Wool-like man-made fibre derived from acrylonitrile, a by-product of oil and coal. Lightweight, fairly strong, crease resistant. Used for knitwear, dresses, suits, sports clothes. Trade names include Acrilan, Courtelle, Dralon, Novacryl, Orlon.

ALPACA See Llama.

ANGORA
Silky hair of angora rabbit. Used for knitwear. Usually blended with wool or nylon.

*ANTRON See Nylon.

APPLIQUÉ
Design or motif fixed to a completed fabric or garment.

*ARNEL See Triacetate.

ASTRAKHAN
Heavy fabric made with a pile of deep loops or curls to look like Persian astrakhan lamb. Used for coats and hats.

*BAN-LON See Nylon.

BARATHEA
Closely woven fabric with a fine, pebble-like surface resulting from a special twill weave. High-quality barathea is made from worsted, but blends with wool and viscose rayon are also made. Used for suits, coats, dresses, trousers. Dry-clean.

BATIK
Fabric with a multi-coloured design formed by coating parts with wax and dyeing the uncoated parts. Used for soft furnishings, blouses, scarves. Hand wash.

BATISTE
Fine, soft semi-sheer fabric made from cotton or man-made fibre. Used for handkerchiefs, lingerie, blouses, linings. Wool-woven batiste is used for dresses.

BEDFORD CORD
Hardwearing cloth with heavy, regular cords. Made from wool, cotton, man-made fibre, or mixtures. Used for suits, trousers, sportswear, dresses, children's wear.

BENGALINE
Heavy, finely woven ribbed fabric, a heavier version of faille. Made from cotton, silk or worsted. Used for coats, suits, dresses, trimmings.

BIAS
Diagonal direction across fabric. True bias is an angle of 45 degrees to the grain.

BIRDSEYE See Piqué.

*BLUE C See Nylon.

BONDED FABRICS
Fabrics joined back to back by an adhesive to give extra thickness or stability. May be two fabrics bonded together, or one with a foam backing.

BONDED FIBRES
See Felt; Non-woven fabrics.

BOUCLÉ
Woven or knitted fabric made from yarn with tight loops, giving it a curly appearance and springy feel. Made from wool or man-made fibres. Used for coats, suits, dresses. Dry-clean.

*BRI-NOVA See Nylon.

*BRI-NYLON See Nylon.

BROADCLOTH
Hardwearing fabric with a glossy, napped finish. Usually made from wool or cotton. Wool is used for coats, cotton for shirts. Dry-clean.

BROCADE
Rich fabric with raised, intricate, woven design. Made from various fibres; raised pattern may be of metallic threads. Used for heavy drapes and evening gowns. Brocatelle is similar, but with more pronounced design. Dry-clean.

BROCATELLE See Brocade.

BRODERIE ANGLAISE
Cotton fabric with cut-out and embroidered designs. Used for blouses, dresses, lingerie, children's wear.

BRUSHED FABRICS See Nap.

BUCKRAM
Coarse fabric of cotton, linen or jute that has been stiffened with size. Used for stiffening belts, pelmets. Dry-clean.

BULKED YARN
See Textured yarn.

BUMP
Non-woven fabric made from cotton waste. Used for interlining heavy curtains. Dry-clean.

CALENDERING
Finishing treatment in which fabric is pressed through heavy rollers. Effects include embossing, glazing, moiré, polishing.

CALICO
Firm, plain-woven cotton fabric with a matt finish. Used for dresses, sportswear, interlinings, soft furnishings.

CAMBRIC
Soft, lightweight cotton or linen fabric with a glossy finish. Used for lingerie, dresses, children's clothes, soft furnishings.

CAMEL HAIR
Lightweight fabric made from camel hair. May be mixed with wool. Soft underhair used for dresses, coarser outer hair for coats.

CANDLEWICK
Woven cotton fabric with pattern formed by pile made from inserted tufts of yarn. Used for bedspreads.

CANVAS
Strong, tightly woven fabric in plain or rib weave made from cotton, linen or man-made yarn. Duck is similar but slightly heavier. Used for sportswear, upholstery.

CASHMERE
Very soft, lustrous fabric made from underhair of the Asian cashmere goat. May be mixed with wool. Used for suits, coats, sweaters.

CAVALRY TWILL
Strong, firm fabric with pronounced, steep diagonal double ribs. Made from worsted, wool or man-made fibre. Used for suits, coats.

*CELAFIBRE See Acetate.

*CELON See Nylon.

CHALLIS
Soft, lightweight fabric, usually wool, often printed with delicate floral pattern. Used for dresses and dressing-gowns. Hand wash.

CHANTILLY See Lace.

CHEESECLOTH
Cool, gauze-like fabric made from cotton or cotton and polyester. Used for blouses and dresses. Hand wash in warm, soapy water.

FABRIC GLOSSARY

CHECK
Fabric patterns in blocks and stripes, usually twill woven with two or more colours. Common patterns include houndstooth, tattersall, shepherd.

CHIFFON
Soft, sheer, very lightweight fabric made from silk or viscose rayon. Used for scarves, lingerie, blouses, dresses. Hand wash.

CHINTZ
Cotton fabric with a glazed finish, usually brightly printed. Used for soft furnishings and drapes.

CIRÉ
Shiny, wet-look fabric finish. Now produced with PVC coating or by heating material such as nylon. Hand wash nylon types. Sponge down PVC types with damp cloth.

CLOQUÉ
Fabric woven with several different types of yarn to give it an irregular, blistered surface. Used for formal dresses. Dry-clean.

*CLYDELLA
Warm, lightweight fabric made from 80% cotton and 20% wool. Used for children's clothing.

COMBED COTTON
Cotton yarn that is combed to make it finer and smoother.

CORDS
Raised lines along length of fabric, produced by plain-weave variation in which weft threads pass over and under two or three warp threads at a time.

CORDUROY
Tough, hardwearing fabric woven with extra weft threads to produce cut-pile cords of varying widths. Narrow-ribbed corduroy is known as needlecord. Made from cotton or man-made fibre. Used for skirts, dresses, trousers, suits.

COTTON
Natural fibre spun from the downy covering of the ripe seed pod of the cotton plant. Fabrics woven from cotton are strong, cool and comfortable. The finest cottons are Egyptian and Sea Island (West Indies); American types are the most widely used; Asiatic cottons are the coarsest. Cotton is very versatile, and can be woven into fabrics of many different weights and colours and given a variety of finishes. It creases easily unless treated.

*COURTELLE See Acrylic.

COVERT
Twill-woven fabric with a speckled appearance achieved by using yarns of different shades. Made from wool, cotton or man-made fibre. Used for suits, coats.

CRASH
Rough-surfaced cotton or linen fabric woven from thick, uneven yarns. Used for towels, curtains, upholstery linings.

CREASE RESISTANT
Resin treatment given to cotton, linen and viscose rayon fibres so they do not crease easily.

CRÊPE
Fabric with a crinkly surface, made by using highly twisted yarns, by a special weave, by embossing, or by chemical treatment. Made from silk, cotton or man-made fibre. Used for blouses and dresses. Dry-clean.

CRÊPE DE CHINE
Glossy, lightweight crêpe made from silk or man-made fibre. Used for lingerie, dresses, blouses. Dry-clean or hand wash.

CRÊPON
Crêpe-like fabric with crinkles resembling the texture of tree bark. Made from cotton. Used for shirting, dresses, blouses.

CRETONNE
Unglazed cotton or linen fabric printed with floral design. Used for soft furnishings. Dry-clean.

*CRIMPLENE See Polyester.

*DACRON See Polyester.

DAMASK
Glossy fabric with intricate, jacquard-woven designs, similar to brocade but with flatter surface. Made from silk, cotton, viscose rayon, or mixtures. Used for table linen, soft furnishings, dresses.

*DARELLE See Viscose rayon.

DENIER
Measurement indicating fineness of silk or man-made yarns. Lower deniers are finest.

DENIM
Strong fabric, twill woven with coloured warp and white weft. Made from cotton or man-made fibre. It can have a brushed finish. Used for shirts, trousers, skirts.

*DELUSTRA See Viscose Rayon.

*DICEL See Acetate.

*DIOLEN See Polyester.

DOBBY WEAVE
Weave that includes small dots, geometrical designs or motifs.

DOE-SKIN
Napped wool or cotton fabric that resembles doe-skin leather. Used for suits, trousers, coats. Dry-clean wool, hand wash cotton.

DONEGAL TWEED
Irish tweed with bright flecks of colour and an uneven surface, due to the use of slubbed yarns.

DOUBLE KNIT See Interlock.

*DRALON See Acrylic.

DRILL
Hardwearing, smooth, cotton fabric, twill or satin woven. Used for shirts, trousers, uniforms.

DRIP-DRY See Easy care.

DUCK See Canvas.

DURABLE PRESS See Easy care.

DUPION
Silk woven from an uneven, double-thread produced when two cocoons nest together. Used for furnishings, dresses. Dry-clean.

*DURAFIL See Viscose rayon.

*DYNEL See Modacrylic.

EASY CARE
Fabrics that can be washed and worn with little or no ironing; termed minimum care, drip dry, durable press, crease-resistant, non-iron, etc. Some man-made fibres, such as acrylic, have inherent easy-care properties. On cotton, linen and viscose rayon it is usually achieved by a resin finish applied to the completed garment. Wool can be chemically treated to give permanent pleats.

ELASTOMERIC FIBRE
Man-made polyurethane fibre that resembles rubber. Although not as elastic as rubber, it is lighter and more durable. Used for belts, brassieres, girdles, sock tops, swimsuits, tights. Do not iron. Trade names include Lycra, Spanzelle.

*ENKALON See Nylon.

*EVLAN See Viscose rayon.

FAILLE
Soft fabric with flattened ribs, between poplin and poult in weight. Made from silk or man-made fibre. Used for formal dresses, lightweight coats, scarves. Dry-clean.

FAKE FUR See Fur fabric.

FANCY YARNS
Yarns made deliberately uneven, looped, etc., to produce special effects in the weave (see also Slub).

FELT
Non-woven fabric made from fibres bonded together by moisture, heat and pressure. Made mainly from wool fibres, which interlock naturally. Has no grain, does not fray, but will not spring back to original shape. Used for hats, craftwork, soft toys, wall coverings. Dry-clean.

*FIBREGLASS See Glass fibre.

*FIBRO See Viscose rayon.

FLAME RESISTANCE
Fabrics that burn easily, such as cotton and viscose rayon, can be chemically treated to make them flame resistant (they smoulder rather than burn). Treatment may not be durable, and re-treatment may be needed after cleaning. Man-made Modacrylic fibres are inherently flame resistant (see also Modacrylic). Flame-resistant fabrics do not give protection against heat.

FLANNEL
Soft fabric with a slight, non-directional nap. May be plain or twill woven from wool. Used for dresses, nightwear, slacks, suits.

FLANNELETTE
Flannel woven from cotton or viscose rayon with other fibres. Used for children's clothes. Cannot be sold as children's nightwear unless given a flame-resistant finish (see Winceyette).

FLOCKING
Fabric with design formed by loose fibres dusted on adhesive. Used for wall coverings, trimmings. Dry-clean.

FOULARD
Twill-woven fabric, usually silk or man-made fibre; often patterned. Used for ties and scarves.

FUR FABRIC
Deep-pile fabric simulating animal fur. Made from cotton or man-made fibre. Used for coats, hats, jackets, trimmings.

GABERDINE
Strong fabric in tight twill weave. Made from worsted, cotton, man-made fibre, or blends. Used for suits, dresses or sportswear. Can be given a showerproof finish.

GEORGETTE
Crisp, sheer, crêpe-like fabric. Made from wool, silk or man-made fibre. Used for lingerie, scarves, dresses. Dry-clean.

GINGHAM
Crisp fabric with coloured stripes or checks. Made from cotton or man-made fibre. Used for lingerie, dresses, children's clothes, aprons, soft furnishings.

GLASS FIBRE
Very fine fibres spun from molten glass. Fabrics are crease resistant, flame resistant, non-absorbent, but will not stretch, and wear easily on folds. Used for curtains and upholstery. Trade names are Fibreglass, Marglass.

GLAZING
Fabric resin-treated, then calendered and polished to give a smooth, shiny appearance.

GRAIN
Term used in tailoring for the fabric threads. Lengthwise grain is the warp, crosswise the weft.

GROSGRAIN
Fabric with narrow, pronounced ribs. Once made from silk, now usually from man-made fibre. Used for coats, formal dresses, soft furnishings. Dry-clean.

GUIPURE See Lace.

HARRIS TWEED
Tweed handwoven in the Hebridean island of Harris.

HERRINGBONE See Twill weave.

HESSIAN
Coarse fabric with plain, loose weave. Made from hemp or hemp and jute (both coarse, natural fibres from India). Used for upholstery, curtains, craftwork, wall coverings. Dry-clean. Sold with paper backing for walls.

HOPSACK
Rough-surfaced fabric, plain-woven with double threads. Made from cotton, linen, man-made fibre. Used for suits, coats.

I / J

INTERFACING
Non-woven fabric, felt or calico used to shape garments or soft furnishings. Dry-clean; some (such as Vilene) are washable.

FABRIC GLOSSARY

INTERLOCK
Fabric weft-knitted with two yarns knitting across each other, giving a smooth face on both sides. Made from wool, cotton. Used for underwear, double jersey knits.

JACQUARD WEAVE
Intricate and elaborate designs produced on a Jacquard loom, which is controlled by a punch-card system. Used for brocades, damasks, tapestries.

JERSEY
Smooth, weft-knitted fabric made from wool, cotton, silk or man-made fibre. Can be single or double knitted. Jacquard jersey is patterned double jersey using up to four colours. Used for dresses, suits, coats, lingerie.

JUTE See Hessian.

L

LACE
Openwork fabric, hand or machine made by looping, interlacing, plaiting or twisting threads to form a pattern. Made from cotton or man-made fibre. There are various types with distinctive patterns, such as Chantilly, Guipure. Ribbon lace has the pattern motifs outlined in ribbon. Leavers is a delicate machine-made lace first produced in Nottingham. Used mainly as trimming for lingerie, dresses, blouses; sometimes for bedspreads, curtains.

*LAMÉ See Metallic yarn.

*LANCOLA See Acetate.

*LANSIL See Acetate.

LAWN
Fine, closely woven fabric made from cotton, linen, or man-made fibre. Used for lingerie, dresses, shirts, children's clothes.

LEAVERS See Lace.

LENO WEAVE
Openwork weave in which warp yarns are twisted round each other as weft yarns pass through. Used for gauze, net.

LINEN
Strong, cool, absorbent fabric with natural lustre and slightly uneven appearance due to irregularity of yarn made from flax. Pure linen tends to shrink unless treated, does not dye well, and frays badly. Often blended with man-made fibre. Used for skirts, dresses, sportswear, bed and table linen, soft furnishings.

*LIRELLE See Polyester.

LLAMA
Long hair of the South American llama; hair from the alpaca, a smaller relative, is similar. May be white, brown or black. Often blended with wool. Used for knitwear, coats, suits.

LOCKNIT
Warp-knitted fabric with vertical rows of double loops on face and cross-lapped threads on back. Usually made from polyester, nylon. Used for lingerie, shirts.

*LO-FLAM See Acetate.

*LUREX See Metallic yarn.

*LYCRA See Elastomeric fibre.

M

MADRAS
Fine cotton fabric woven in stripes or checks. Used for blouses, shirts, dresses.

MALIMO
Fabric construction in which weft threads are laid across the warp without interlacing, and secured by a warp-knitted third thread.

*MARGLASS See Glass fibre.

MAROCAIN
Heavy, ribbed crêpe made from wool, silk or man-made fibre. Used for dresses.

MARQUISETTE
Lightweight mesh fabric, leno woven or warp knitted. Made from cotton, silk or man-made fibre. Used for veils, dresses, curtains.

MATELASSÉ
Fabric with a quilted appearance, produced by different shrinkage of yarns or dobby or jacquard weave. Made from cotton, silk, wool, man-made fibre. Used for evening wear. Dry-clean.

MELTON
Thick, hardwearing felt-like woven fabric with a short, dense, non-directional nap. Made from wool or cotton warp, wool weft. Used for coats. Dry-clean.

MERCERISE
Finishing treatment by which cotton and linen is stretched and swelled. This increases strength, affinity for dyes, and adds permanent lustre.

METALLIC YARN
Decorative yarn made from aluminium coated with plastic. The plastic coating is laminated to sheets of aluminium foil, then slit into filaments. Without colouring the yarn is silver; colouring is applied to the adhesive used for lamination. Trade names include Lamé, Lurex, Metlon.

*METLON See Metallic yarn.

MILANESE
Strong, warp-knitted fabric with plain-knit face and diagonally crossing threads on the back. Used for suits, stockings.

*MILIUM
Fabric finished with a metal insulating treatment. Used for linings, ironing-board covers.

MODACRYLIC
Flame-resistant man-made fibre, similar to acrylic but not quite as strong. Brand names include Teklan – used for night wear, particularly children's – and Dynel, used for fur fabrics.

MOHAIR
Hard-wearing fabric woven or knitted from the long silky hair of the angora goat, which is white and slightly waved. Often mixed with wool or man-made fibre. Used for knitwear, suits, coats, rugs, upholstery.

MOIRÉ
Wavy, watermarked finish applied by pressure (see Calendering).

MOQUETTE
Pile fabric, cut or uncut, made from wool pile on a backing of cotton or man-made fibre. Once popular for upholstery.

MOUSSELINE
Fine, crisp muslin made from silk or man-made fibre. Used for evening wear.

MUSLIN
Cotton fabric with plain, loose weave made in various grades. Cheap muslin may be finished with starch. Used for linings, shirts, underclothes. Hand wash in warm, soapy water.

N/O

NAP
Downy fabric finish produced by brushing short fibres to surface. This makes the fabric warmer and more durable. Fibres are usually raised from the weft; fabric is specially woven to give weft extra strength. Fibres may be brushed in one direction (dress face), have no direction, or be flattened to hide weave. Some warp-knitted fabrics can be given a nap finish.

NEEDLECORD See Corduroy.

NET
Mesh fabric of knotted or twisted thread. Can be woven or knitted. Made from cotton, silk, man-made fibre in various weights: tulle, for example, is fine silk or nylon net used for veils, dresses, trimmings; fishnet is coarse, open-weave net used for tights and veiling.

NON-WOVEN FABRICS
Fabrics made from a web of fibres bonded together, usually with chemical solution (but see Felt) or by heat treatment.

*NOVACRYL See Acrylic.

NYLON
Strong, hardwearing man-made fibre. Almost non-absorbent but with good elasticity. Dries quickly, is crease resistant, and can be set into permanent pleats. Blends well with other fibres. Used for lingerie, tights, shirts, overalls, curtains. Brand names include Antron, Ban-Lon, Blue C, Bri-Nova, Bri-Nylon, Celon, Enkalon, Tendrelle, Ultron.

OILSKIN
Fabric treated with oil to make it waterproof. Made from cotton, linen, silk, man-made fibre. Used for heavy-duty rainwear. Clean by sponging with a damp cloth.

ORGANDIE
Fine, crisp, sheer fabric made from cotton or man-made fibre. Used for trimmings, children's clothes, dresses. Hand wash and lightly stiffen with starch.

ORGANZA
Light, sheer fabric similar to organdie but made from silk or man-made fibre. Used for dresses.

*ORLON See Acrylic.

P/Q

PEAU DE SOIE
Soft, lustrous, satin-woven fabric. Once made from silk, now usually man-made fibre. Used for dresses.

PICOT
Decorative edge on selvedges of lace, ribbon. Made from cotton or man-made fibre.

PILE
Soft, raised surface on fabric formed by short tufts from yarns specially introduced into weave and cut or left as loops. Backing fabric is known as ground, and may be made from different fibre. Pile fabrics can also be knitted.

PIQUÉ
Firm fabric embossed or dobby woven with various patterns, such as cords (wale or waffle piqué), diamond shapes (honeycomb) or diamond shapes each with a centre dot (bird's eye). Made from cotton or man-made fibre. Used for trimmings, dresses.

PLAIN WEAVE
Simplest form of weave, with warp and weft interlaced alternately. Closely woven it is one of the strongest weaves. Woven with double threads it is known as basket or hopsack weave.

PLISSÉ
Cotton fabric with chemically produced puckered stripes, or man-made fibre with puckering produced by heat treatment. Used for lingerie, children's clothes, furnishings. Dry-clean.

POLISHED COTTON
Shiny cotton fabric produced by satin weave or calendering.

POLYESTER
Strong man-made fibre similar to nylon but less elastic and with greater resistance to colour fade. Can be heat-set into textured yarns or permanent pleats and knitted or woven into easy-care, crease-resistant fabrics. Often blended with cotton and wool. Used for lingerie, dresses, children's clothes, bed linen. Brand names include Crimplene, Dacron, Diolen, Lirelle, Tergal, Terlenka, Terylene, Trevira.

POLYVINYL CHLORIDE (PVC)
Fabric treated with a fine plastic waterproof film. Used for aprons, rainwear, upholstery.

POPLIN
Firm fabric with fine ribs. Made from mercerised cotton or man-made fibre. Used for dresses, sportswear, children's clothes, soft furnishings. Hand wash.

POULT
Stiff fabric with pronounced ribs. Made from silk, man-made fibre. Used for dresses and linings.

PRE-SHRUNK
Finishing treatment to reduce shrinkage to a small percentage.

QUILTING
Layers of fabric stitched together, with padding between. Stitching is in rows forming all-over pattern. Used for bed covers, dressing-gowns, anoraks. Dry-clean.

R

RASCHEL
Warp-knitting process producing openwork fabrics such as lace, net and pile fabrics. Vertical looped chains anchor the interlaced, openwork yarns.

FABRIC GLOSSARY

RATINÉ
Rough wool fabric with knobbly surface. Woven from fancy yarn. Used for coats and suits.

RAYON See Viscose rayon.

REPP
Fabric with prominent ribs. Made from wool, cotton or man-made fibre. Used for suits, furnishings.

RIBS
Raised lines crossways on fabric. Produced by variation of plain weave, with pairs of weft yarns and single warp, or a thicker weft. On weft knits by alternate knitting to back and face.

RIBBON LACE See Lace.

*RIBBONFIL See Viscose rayon.

SAILCLOTH
Strong, stiff, ribbed fabric made from cotton, man-made fibre. Used for casual wear, upholstery.

*SARILLE See Viscose rayon.

SATEEN
Shiny cotton fabric, woven with a variation of satin weave. Used for linings and soft furnishings.

SATIN WEAVE
Weaving method with closely set warp yarns passing over several weft yarns and under one to form a smooth, lustrous surface. Reverse side is dull and coarser.

SATIN
Smooth, shiny fabric satin-woven from silk or man-made fibres or mixtures. There are various types such as duchess and slipper (fairly stiff), panne (very shiny finish), double (shiny both sides). Used for lingerie, evening and wedding dresses, furnishings.

SCANDAIR See Viscose rayon.

SEERSUCKER
Lightweight cotton fabric with crinkled stripes or checks formed by chemical treatment, or by varying tension of warp threads. Used for lingerie, children's wear.

SELVEDGE
Narrow, tightly woven edge of fabric, which prevents fraying.

SERGE
Heavy, hardwearing twill-woven fabric. Made from wool, worsted or wool mixed with cotton or man-made fibre. Used for skirts, suits, school uniforms. Dry-clean.

SHANTUNG
Silky fabric, plain woven with slubbed yarn to give an uneven surface like wild silk from Shantung, China. Made mostly from acetate. Used for blouses, lightweight suits, coats, dresses.

SHEER
Term describing translucent, flimsy fabrics, such as chiffon.

SHOT
Any lustrous fabric woven with warp a different colour from weft, giving effect of changing colour from different angles.

SHOWERPROOF
Chemical finishing process to prevent fabric absorbing water. Not 100% waterproof. Used for rainwear. Dry-clean and re-proof.

SHRINK RESISTANT
See Pre-shrunk; Superwash wool.

SILK
Long thread spun by the silkworm when making its cocoon. Silk yarn is fine, strong and elastic, and can be woven into soft, warm fabrics. Various types include lightweight Jap, rough Pongee, uneven Shantung. Spun silk is made from short lengths of silk waste. Wild (or Tussore) silk, taken from wild silkworms, is darker and coarser than that from domesticated worms fed on mulberry leaves. Pure silk is silk that has not been weighted – a process giving it extra body and weight. All silks are suitable for dresses, suits, blouses, scarves, lingerie, soft furnishings.

SLUB
Single-ply fancy yarn of varying thickness, giving an uneven fabric surface, known as linen look.

*SPANZELLE See Elastomeric.

STRETCH FABRICS
Fabrics made from yarns with an elastomeric core; they return to their original shape after stretching. Used for foundation garments, tights, stockings, dresses, trouser suits, swimwear, upholstery.

SUEDE CLOTH
Woven or knitted napped fabric simulating suede leather. Made from cotton, wool, man-made fibre, or blends. Used for coats, handbags, upholstery, wall coverings. Dry-clean.

SUPERWASH WOOL
Wool made from fibres chemically treated and given a fine plastic coating to prevent shrinkage caused by felting of the fibres.

SURAH
Soft, lustrous twill-woven fabric made from silk or man-made fibre. Used for scarves, blouses, lightweight coats, dresses, suits.

TAFFETA
Crisp, plain-woven fabric, usually lustrous. Once made from silk, now mainly from man-made fibres. Types include faille taffeta (with fine rib), moiré taffeta (watermarked). Used for evening dresses, soft furnishings, linings.

*TEKLAN See Modacrylic.

*TENASCO See Viscose rayon.

*TENDRELLE See Nylon.

*TERGAL See Polyester.

*TERLENKA See Polyester.

TERRY TOWELLING
Absorbent fabric with looped pile on one or both sides. Usually made from cotton. Used for towelling, bathrobes, beachwear.

*TERYLENE See Polyester.

TEXTURED YARN
Man-made filament yarns given permanent loops, crimps, twists – usually by heat treatment – to increase stretch and bulk

TICKING
Strong, striped cotton fabric. Used for mattress covers.

*TREVIRA See Polyester.

TRIACETATE
Man-made fibre similar to acetate, but with higher heat resistance and better easy-care qualities. It is crease resistant and can be set in permanent pleats. Often blended with wool or other man-made fibres. Used for dresses, knitwear, linings. Brand names include Arnel, Tricel, Tricelon.

*TRICEL See Triacetate.

*TRICELON See Triacetate.

TRICOT
Strong, warp-knitted fabric with crossways rib on back. Made from cotton or man-made fibre. Used for lingerie, T-shirts, and as a backing for bonded fabrics.

*TRIPLE A See Viscose rayon.

TUSSORE See Silk.

TWEED
Rough-surfaced woollen fabric, often woven with two or more colours to form a pattern of checks or chevrons. There are various types, named for their pattern (see also Check) or place of origin (see also Donegal, Harris). Used for coats, suits, curtains, upholstery.

TWILL WEAVE
Weave in which interlacings are progressively stepped to form a diagonal rib across the fabric. There can be many variations, warp threads passing over and under two or three weft threads, or passing over two or three and under one. Variations include reversal of the rib direction to produce a chevron pattern known as herringbone. Twill weaves produce a more supple fabric than a plain weave.

*TYREX See Viscose rayon.

*ULTRON See Nylon.

VELOUR
Thick, velvet-like fabric with a short, dense pile. Made from wool or cotton. Used for coats, hats, dresses, furnishings. Dry-clean.

VELVET
Fabric with a soft, lustrous pile. Can be made with an extra warp thread which is looped then cut, or woven in two layers with shared warp yarns which are slit apart. Made from silk, cotton, nylon or other man-made fibres in a variety of weights and types, such as panne velvet (with pile crushed in different directions), stiff Lyons velvet, Utrecht velvet (with long pile, often mohair), uncut velvet (with looped pile), or figured velvet (with pile in patterns on a flat background). Used for dresses, coats, evening wear, ribbons, trimmings, soft furnishings. Dry-clean.

VELVETEEN
Cotton fabric with a short, all-over pile, resembling velvet. Pile formed by extra weft threads which float over several warp threads and are then cut. Used for children's wear, dresses, trimmings, soft furnishings.

VICUÑA
Fine, soft fabric made from underhairs of vicuña (wild relative of the llama). Used for dresses and suits. Vicuña hunting has now been banned.

*VILENE
Non-woven fabric used for shaping and interfacings.

*VINCEL See Viscose rayon.

VISCOSE RAYON
Widely used man-made fibre derived from cellulose. Drapes well but creases easily unless treated. Recent polynosic types are similar to cotton. Often blended with other fibres. Used for clothing, household textiles, soft furnishings, carpets. Trade names include Darelle, Delustra, Durafil, Evlan, Fibro, Ribbonfil, Sarille, Scandair, Tenasco, Triple A, Tyrex, Vincel (polynosic).

*VIYELLA
Lightweight, twill-woven fabric

made from a blend of wool (55%) and cotton (45%). Used for lingerie, blouses, dresses.

VOILE
Crisp, sheer, plain-woven fabric. Made from cotton, silk, viscose rayon. Used for lingerie, blouses, dresses, evening wear, curtains.

W

WATERPROOF
Fabrics that will not let water through, achieved by coating with rubber or oil compounds or PVC coating (see also Oilskin, PVC, Showerproof). Most should be cleaned by sponging with clean, warm water.

WET-LOOK See Ciré; Polyvinyl Chloride.

WHIPCORD
Sturdy fabric, twill woven with pronounced, steep diagonal ribs. Usually made from cotton or worsted. Used for children's clothes, suits, coats, slacks, riding clothes. Dry-clean; cotton types can be washed.

WINCEYETTE
Warm, lightweight, twill-woven napped fabric. Made from cotton, wool or blends; fabric made with flame-resistant acetate fibre is used for children's nightwear.

WOOL
Fine, soft fibre from the fleece of the sheep. Wool-woven fabrics are warm, soft and resilient, but need care in washing to avoid shrinking and matting of fibres. The finest, warmest wools are merino and botany, but these are not as strong as lower-quality wool. Virgin wool or pure new wool is wool prepared direct from the fleece. Re-manufactured wool from old woollen fabric may be blended with new wool to provide reasonably priced fabric. See also Superwash wool.

WORSTED YARN
High-quality wool yarn produced by combing the fibres before spinning to make them fine and smooth. Used for suits, coats, dresses, children's wear.

BASIC SEWING

The more expensive a sewing machine, the more it can do. Gathering, shirring, darning, blind-hemming and buttonholing are among the many extra stitches that can be sewn by modern machines. However, there are still many sewing tasks at the beginning as well as the finishing of dressmaking and soft-furnishing projects which require hand stitching. If this is carried out carefully it can only add to the appearance of the finished article.

• HAND STITCHES

Use a short thread in hand sewing – 45-60 cm. (18-24 in.) for permanent stitches, longer for temporary ones.

TAILOR'S TACKS

These are used to transfer pattern symbols to two or more layers of fabric. Using a double length of unknotted thread – fairly long in this instance – make a 5 mm. (¼ in.) stitch through the pattern and all layers of fabric [A1]. Leave a 20 mm. (¾ in.) end. Repeat stitch to make a 25 mm. (1 in.) loop. Cut off thread to leave a 20 mm. tail [A2]. When all symbols have been marked in this way, cut the top off each loop [A3] and lift off paper pattern. Gently pull apart the layers of fabric, cutting the threads that join them [A4].

TACKING AND TRACE TACKING

The stitch used for both tacking (sometimes called basting) and trace tacking is a temporary one. Tacking is used to hold fabrics together during fitting, or before permanent sewing.

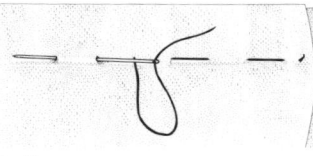

Tacking

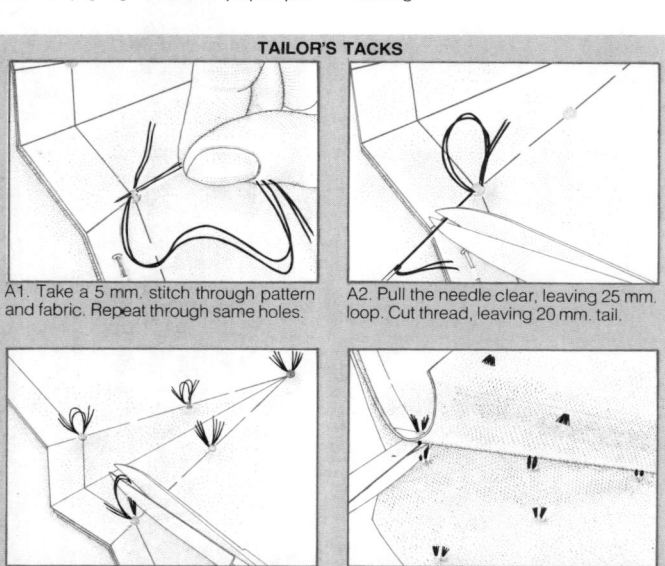

TAILOR'S TACKS

A1. Take a 5 mm. stitch through pattern and fabric. Repeat through same holes.

A2. Pull the needle clear, leaving 25 mm. loop. Cut thread, leaving 20 mm. tail.

A3. When all tacks are made, cut the top of each loop and lift off pattern.

A4. Ease the two layers of fabric apart, cutting the threads that join them.

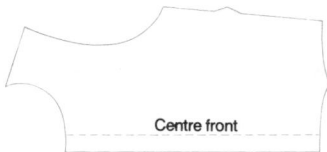

Centre front

Trace tacking

Stitches should be about 10 mm. (⅜ in.) long. Fasten with two or three back stitches. Trace tacking is a line of tacks used to mark design details.

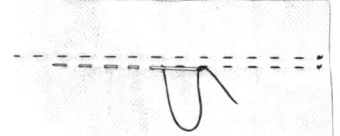

RUNNING STITCH

A small, even stitch used mostly for hand gathering (in two parallel rows) or as a decorative top stitch. For gathering, knot one end and make even stitches about 2 mm. (⅛ in.) long. Leave loose end for pulling up, and wind this excess thread around a pin (see below) in the fabric at the end of each row until gathers are adjusted.

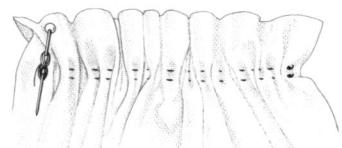

Using a pin to hold gathers

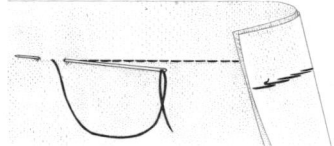

BACK STITCH

Another small hand stitch which is very strong, and is used for zips set in by hand or areas where machine stitching is not possible. Make a

2 mm. stitch, take the needle back to the point where the stitch ends and make another. A variation of back stitch is stab stitch (see below). The needle is taken back only fractionally so that the stitch hardly shows. This is useful for strengthening.

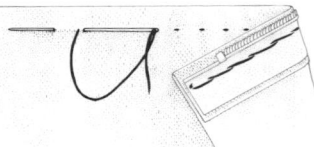

Stab stitch

OVERSEWING

Used to finish raw edges, to join knitting, and to apply appliqué pieces. Pass the needle from back to front of the material, making slanting stitches. Do not pull thread tight.

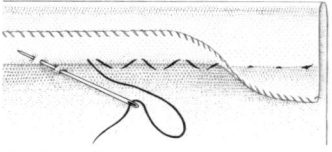

BLIND STITCH

Because this stitch is almost invisible on the right side, it is the best all-purpose stitch for hems. It lies quite flat because of its single turning. It is suitable for almost all but very fine, sheer fabrics. The raw edge is finished with a zigzag machine stitch or by hand oversewing. The hem is turned up and tacked a little way from the finished edge. With this edge folded back slightly, take a very small stitch on the garment side under the fold, then another on the inside hem turning. Do not pull thread tightly.

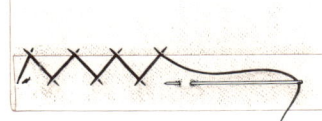

HERRINGBONE

Unlike most other stitches, the herringbone is worked from left to right. It is used for hemming, with a single fold turning which can be made on the raw edge without a finishing stitch. Tack the hem in place, make a knot in the thread and take one stitch in the hem turning with the needle facing backwards. Make the next stitch above the turning, 10 mm. (⅜ in.) along, but made small so that it does not show on the right side.

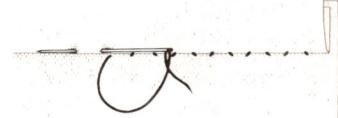

SLIP STITCH

This stitch is taken through a fold in the hem turning and is used on thin fabrics and, for example, on double-fold sheers and curtains. Stitch through the edge of the hem turning fold for 10-20 mm. (⅜-¾ in.). Bring the needle out and make another tiny stitch on the garment or main side of the hem. Slip stitching is also used on very narrow folded or rolled hems.

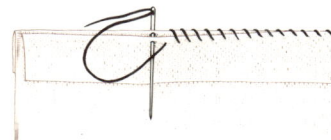

WHIP STITCH

A small overhand stitch for joining edges, lace, patchwork or appliqué. The small, slanting stitches are made very close together.

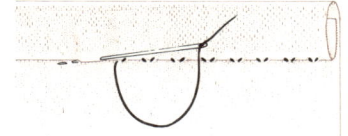

FELLING

A very tiny hemming stitch, felling is mainly used in tailoring for attaching linings to coats and jackets or for sewing hems of handkerchiefs and scarves. The small stitches should take in only a thread or two of the lining hem edge and a thread or two just below. They should be made firmly, but should not pull the fabric.

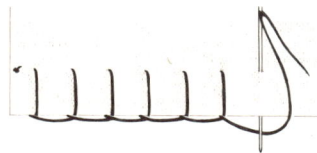

BLANKET STITCH

This can be used to finish raw edges, or as a decorative way of attaching appliqué. A variation of blanket stitch, in which the lower fabric is 'caught' in, can be used for hemming. The needle is taken through the fabric about 5 mm. (¼ in.) from the edge and brought through the loop of its thread to form a chain edge.

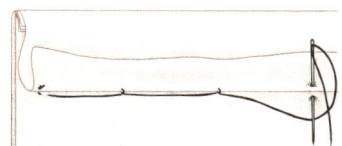

LOCK STITCH

This stitch keeps a curtain and its lining hanging together and prevents the lining dropping below the curtain hem. Locking stitches catch in one or two threads of the curtain fabric and the lining. The stitches are made in rows spaced about 10 cm. (4 in.) apart. To make a row, fold the lining in half lengthways and place the fold line down the centre of the wrong side of the curtain. Lock-stitch along the fold line. For a very wide curtain it may be necessary to make two or more rows of lock stitches.

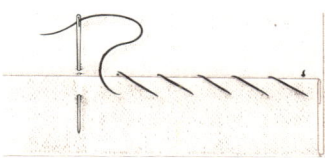

SERGE STITCH

Another invisible stitch, serge stitch is used to hem curtains before attaching linings. Sew from the right. Bring the needle forward through the hem, then pick up a thread in the main fabric about 15 mm. (½ in.) to the left, close to the hem. Bring the needle back through the hem and repeat.

• HEMS

Level off hems with a metrestick or ruler held at right-angles to the floor. Make a straight hem at least 5-7 cm. (2-3 in.) in depth as the weight of the fabric helps it to hang well. Circular hems should have a narrow turning. Pin at right-angles to the edge to distribute the turning fabric evenly.

Blind-stitched hem The hem is turned once and the raw edge finished with oversewing, zigzag or blanket stitch. After tacking the hem 10 mm. (⅜ in.) from the finished edge, blind-stitch in place.

Herringbone-stitched hem Unless the fabric is very frayable, the hem can be turned up and herringbone stitched without the raw edge being finished first.

Slip-stitched hem Turn in the edge of the hem to make a fold through which the slip stitch is made. On sheer fabrics make the turn to the same depth as the hem itself, to prevent layers of fabric showing on the right side.

• CORNER MITRES

Mitres are used to turn corners in braid or on a straight run of fabric, without creating bulky corners.

The key to making successful mitres is accurate pressing of the folds at the corners [B1, B2], and trimming the seam allowances at exactly the right place [B3]. The mitre joins can be secured by a slip stitch to keep them in place [B4]. A stitched mitre should never be used on plaited braid as the open weave of the braid would spread the seam. For this and other similar fancy braids, make a folded mitre, snip off the corner outside the mitre fold [C1] and pin down [C2]. A simple stitched mitre on a 90 degree corner can be formed by folding and then stitching the line of the angle. This can be used, for example, on a tablecloth.

MITRING HEM CORNERS

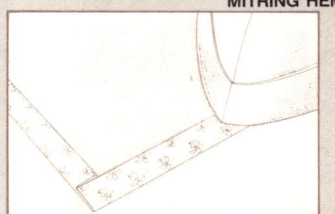

B1. Fold in seam allowance, wrong sides facing, and press.

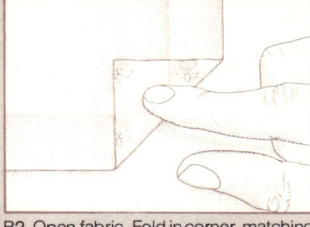

B2. Open fabric. Fold in corner, matching fold to pressed seam allowance corner.

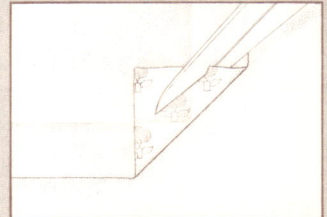

B3. Press diagonal fold, then trim off corner triangle 10 mm. outside line of fold.

B4. Fold in again along seam allowances. Slip-stitch hems together at the corner.

MITRING BRAID

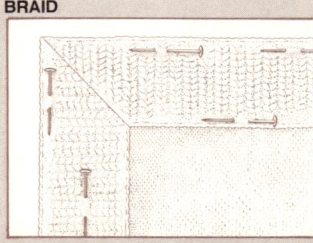

C1. Fold braid and match fold to corner. Sew braid to fabric diagonally in from corner. Trim bottom corner of braid.

C2. Fold and pin braid down from stitched diagonal to run along next side. Repeat at the remaining corners.

• BASIC SEAMS

Seams are the basic joins used in the making of any garment. The main types are explained here.

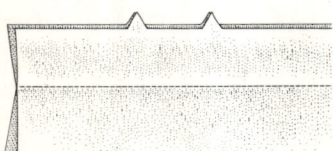

FLAT OPEN SEAM

The most simple type of seam, made with the right sides of the fabric facing, is the flat open seam. Match up the notch-mark guides in the two pieces of fabric (above), pin then tack the pieces together.

On fabric that is likely to fray, finish the raw edges with hand-oversewing or zigzag machine-stitching. Finish seams on very fine materials with a narrow machine-edged turning.

If it suits the style of the garment, finish an open seam by top-stitching an even line on each side of the seam. Stitch on the right side of the fabric.

FRENCH SEAM

Tack mark seam line on each piece of fabric. Place fabric wrong sides together, match tack lines, then machine half-way between the tacks and the edge of the fabric [A1]. Press this seam open, fold fabric right sides together and press again with sewn line on edge of fold. Sew along tack line to enclose first seam [A2].

FLAT FELL SEAM

A strong seam which is used for denims and sportswear. First make a flat open seam with wrong sides together, then trim one seam edge to 3 mm. (⅛ in.) from the stitching [B1]. Press a 3 mm. fold on the wider edge, then turn this seam over the narrower one so that it lies flat [B2]. Tack and machine-stitch to the garment along the turned-in edge.

WELTED OR RAISED SEAM

The welted seam is similar to the flat fell seam, but is sewn with the right sides of the fabric facing [C1]. Trim one side about 5 mm. (¼ in.) from the stitching. Fold untrimmed side to enclose trimmed edge [C2] and machine close to the edge. The enclosed seam allowance gives a raised, or welted, seam. This is a particularly useful seam for thick woollen fabrics.

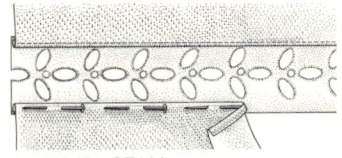

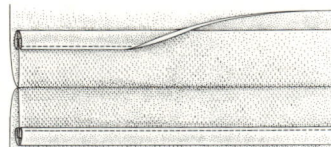

BOUND SEAM

On heavy, unlined garments or curtains, machine-stitch a binding – such as a narrow commercial bias binding – over the raw seam edges (see above).

CHANNEL SEAM

Fabric in a contrasting colour, or lace, leather or ribbon, can be laid between two main sections of fabric for decorative effect. This is a useful way to lengthen a child's dress, for instance. Press in the seam allowance on the two main sections and lay them on the channel strip (see above) which, to help you position the fabric correctly, should have its centre line marked with tacking. Stitch close to edges.

TUCKED SEAM

This is used for invisible joins. Fold one seam allowance to the wrong side and tack along the edge [D1]. Press the fold and lay this on the seam line of the other piece of fabric. Stitch together through all three thicknesses close to fold. Stitch along the tacking line [D2] and remove tacks.

• DECORATIVE SEWING

Attractive and colourful finishes can be given to garments and soft furnishings by using decorative stitches.

SMOCKING

Fabric folds, stitched together at regular intervals, create a patterned effect known as smocking.

The most popular parts of garments for smocking are yokes, bodices, sleeves, pockets and waistlines. Almost any fabric can be smocked, but you will need two-and-a-half to three times the finished width of material.

Smocking is based on a pattern of evenly sewn dots (see below). Bring the thread through at dot 1, make a small stitch behind dot 2, then dot 1, pull the thread taut and return it through dot 2. Repeat at 3 and 4, and

---

FRENCH SEAM	FLAT FELL SEAM	WELTED SEAM	TUCKED SEAM	SMOCKING
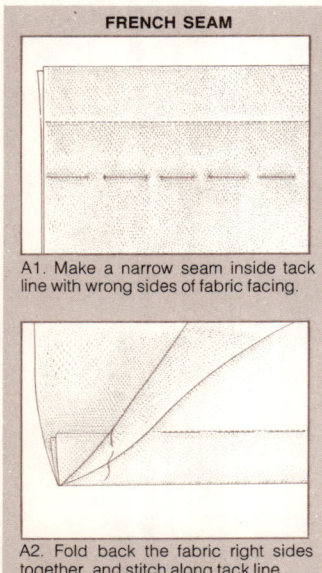	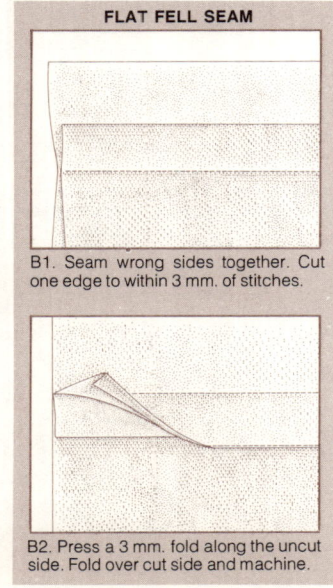	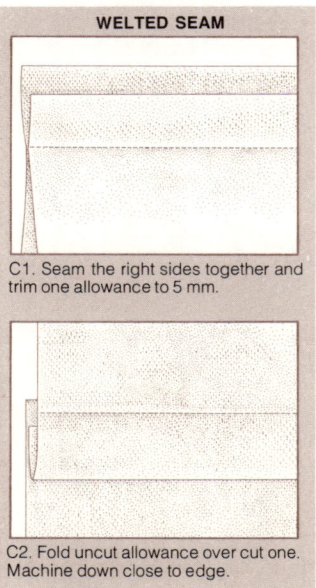	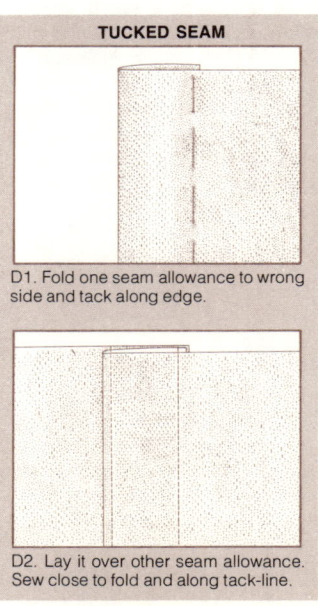	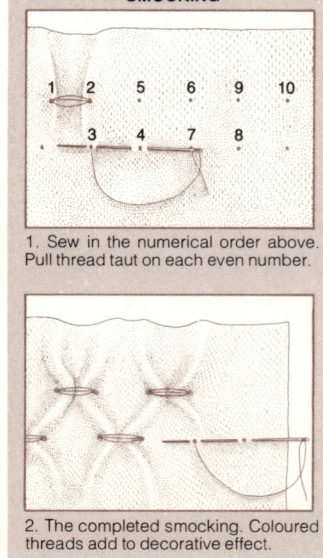
A1. Make a narrow seam inside tack line with wrong sides of fabric facing.	B1. Seam wrong sides together. Cut one edge to within 3 mm. of stitches.	C1. Seam the right sides together and trim one allowance to 5 mm.	D1. Fold one seam allowance to wrong side and tack along edge.	1. Sew in the numerical order above. Pull thread taut on each even number.
A2. Fold back the fabric right sides together, and stitch along tack line.	B2. Press a 3 mm. fold along the uncut side. Fold over cut side and machine.	C2. Fold uncut allowance over cut one. Machine down close to edge.	D2. Lay it over other seam allowance. Sew close to fold and along tack-line.	2. The completed smocking. Coloured threads add to decorative effect.

so on. Gingham is an easy material to use as its pattern serves as a grid for the sewing points. To add colour to smocking, use a decorative thread.

FRILLING

Complete the hem edge of the frill first. Gather the other edge by hand or by using the longest stitch on the machine. Draw in the gathered edge evenly until it is the same length as the edge to which it is to be sewn. The frill can be attached in various ways:

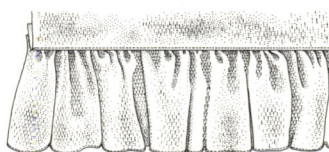

Method A Turn and press seam allowance on edge of fabric to which frill is being attached. Tack and top stitch gathered edge of frill to the fold. Trim seam allowance and oversew.

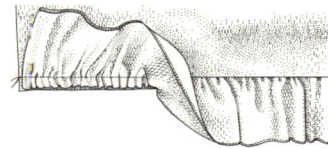

Method B Lay the frill's gathered edge on the fabric, right sides together. Pin, tack and stitch. Oversew seam and lightly press to finish.

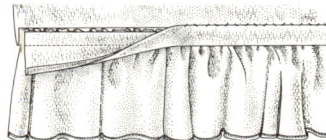

Method C When using facing or binding to attach the frill, follow Method B, then add the facing or binding to the stitching line on top of the frill. Sew the other binding edge to the inside, after the seam is pressed.

To pipe frilling Stitch piping on the seam line of the fabric. Lay gathered edge of the frill right side down on top of the piping and stitch through all layers using a zipper or piping foot.

APPLIQUÉ

When cutting motifs from fabrics that fray easily, allow extra for a small hem all round. Tack or press under this hem before attaching the motif. Tack the motif in place then slip-stitch, blanket-stitch or oversew by hand. If machining the motif in place, use a small zigzag stitch. Motifs cut from felt do not require hems.

QUILTING

Although used mainly on bed and cot covers, quilting added to collars, pockets and sleeve trimmings can give a rich, textured look to garments.

Quilting fabric is either backed with wadding or has a thick interlining.

The quilting pattern is made simply by stitching down the fabric, following straight lines for the traditional squares or diamonds, or following shapes for matching the design of a patterned fabric. Some sewing machines have a quilting guide, which clips on to the presser foot, to keep stitching lines straight.

On large areas of quilting, work outwards from the middle of the fabric. Working inwards from the edges may ruck the material in the middle.

TOP STITCHING

A plain, straight stitch, which can be machine or hand-sewn. It is used to emphasise the lines of yokes, pockets, collars and belts. If used alongside a flat open seam, top-stitching will give a garment added strength as well as decoration.

Ordinary sewing thread is normally suitable, but on thick fabrics and for prominent stitching, use a thicker thread. This requires a large needle and a big-stitch setting on the machine. Use ordinary thread on the bobbin.

PIPING

A cord is enclosed within a fabric strip to make piping This in turn is sewn into the seams of a garment or article of soft furnishing to make a piped seam.

Piping cord, usually made of twisted white cotton, comes in various diameters – from very fine for dressmaking to 10 mm. (⅜ in.) for soft furnishings.

To make piping, the fabric enclosing the cord is cut on the bias (see illustration, p. 291). Find the bias by folding over a corner of the fabric until the cut edge aligns with the selvedge. Press along this fold, open up and cut along this crease. Cut into parallel strips about 5 cm. (2 in.) wide until you have enough strips to cover the complete length of cord.

Sew these pieces together [1] and trim off the angle corners [2]. Fold the strip in half along its length and enclose the cord, then pin [3] and stitch as close to the cord as possible [4].

To fit the piping, leave about 5 cm. free and lay it on to the seam of the upper piece of fabric, matching raw edges. Make sure that the piping seam lines up with the fabric seam.

Tack, then machine-stitch with a zipper or piping foot. Pin and tack the lower fabric piece over it and machine-stitch again as close as possible to the cord.

To join the piping, leave the last 5 cm. of piping free and overlap this with the 5 cm. at the start. Cut the cord to a butt joint. Trim the ends of the piping cover [5] and overlap. Sew a seam down the join [6] and press open. Fold cover over cord ends [7]. Machine cover over cord [8].

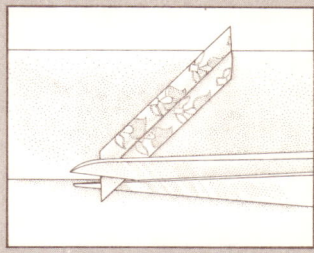
1. Sew strips of bias-cut fabric together with right sides facing.

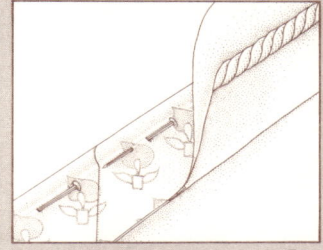
2. Press open seams and cut off the 'ears' which overlap the strip.

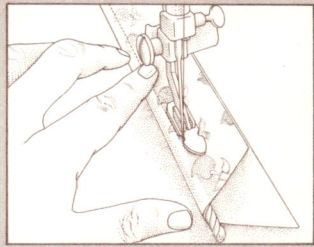
3. Lay cord along wrong side of strip. Fold strip, enclosing cord, and pin.

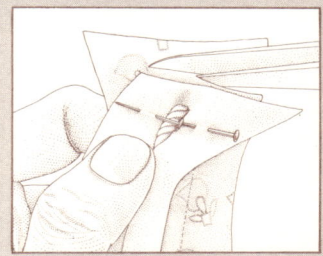
4. Machine down the length of the strip, keeping as close as possible to cord.

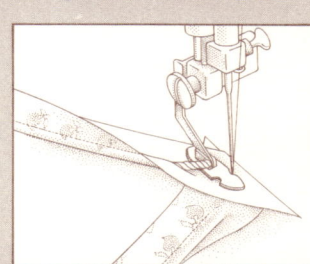
5. To join piping, open cover at each end and pin together. Trim excess.

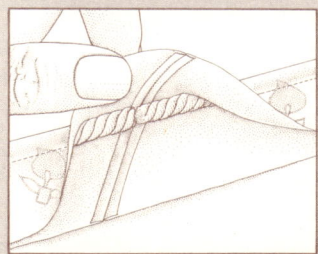
6. Cut cord so that ends butt together. Sew pinned seam, press open and trim.

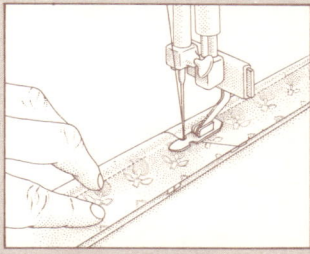
7. Fold joined cover over butted ends of cord.

8. Machine the cover strip closed, keeping as close as possible to cord.

299

• BUTTONHOLES

There are two basic types of button-hole – worked and bound. A worked buttonhole is stitched all round, and a bound buttonhole uses fabric to bind the edges.

It is important to make buttonholes exactly the right length. For bound buttonholes, this size is calculated by adding together the width and thickness of the button. For example, a button 2.5 cm. (1 in.) wide and 3 mm. (⅛ in.) thick, would need a hole 2.8 cm. (1⅛ in.) long. For worked buttonholes, however, add a further 3 mm. to allow for the finishing work required at each end of the hole.

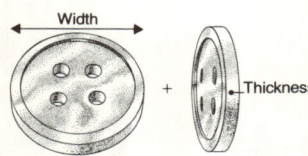

Add these two for buttonhole size.

HAND-WORKED BUTTONHOLE

Tack three parallel lines down the fabric. The outer lines mark the length of the buttonholes; the inner line marks the button positions. Mark the length of a buttonhole. Make a running stitch all round about 3 mm. from the mark to indicate the depth of the buttonhole stitch. Put a pin at each end of the mark and cut between them. Oversew the raw edges. For the buttonhole stitches, knot the thread and bring the needle through the opening, taking it out just below, on the line of running stitches [A1]. Bring the cotton around the back of the needle and underneath its point. Draw the needle out, pulling the thread gently until it forms a small twist or ridge on the cut edge [A2]. Sew closely, about one stitch per millimetre (25 per inch). Fan the stitches into a curve at the outer end of the cut. Put bar stitches at the inner end [A3]. Finish with buttonhole stitches over the bar stitches [A4].

BOUND BUTTONHOLE

Use this method for small buttonholes on fine fabrics. Cut a patch of fabric about 2.5 cm. longer than the buttonhole, and centre it, right sides together, over a tack-line marking the hole. Pin and tack in place [B1]. Turn to wrong side of garment and machine about 3 mm. from each side of the line and across the ends [B2]. Working from the wrong side, cut along the line, through both patch and fabric, and snip into the corners [B3]. Pull the patch through to the wrong side and flatten [B4]. Fold the patch flaps so that the folds meet along the centre of the opening and tack in place [B5]. Finish each end of the opening with bar stitches. Trim excess fabric of patch [B6].

COLLECTING BUTTONS

Over the centuries, buttons have been made from almost every conceivable material. The selection on the right and below includes buttons made of glass, gold, silver, pottery, mother-of-pearl and metal, hand-painted and enamelled.

The best way to become familiar with all types of buttons is to study collections, or buttons on period-costume displays. Some of the best are in the Somerset County Museum at Taunton, the Birmingham Museum, the Museum of Costume at Bath, and the Victoria and Albert Museum in London.

Buttons are not easy to date, and their age does not necessarily make them valuable. Of more importance is the material from which the button is made, the condition of the button and whether it is part of a set. Victorian buttons can often be bought cheaply in street markets and at jumble sales, and a button-box 30 or more years old could yield an interesting hoard.

Display buttons by mounting them on cards, which can first be covered with fabric. Glass and silver buttons look best on richly coloured velvet, black glass or enamelled buttons on creamy satin, and wooden buttons on wool.

MAKING A HAND-WORKED BUTTONHOLE

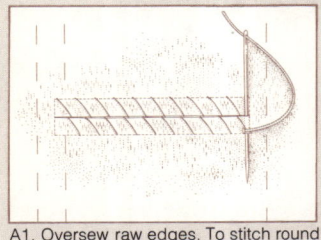

A1. Oversew raw edges. To stitch round hole, bring needle out on line of stitches.

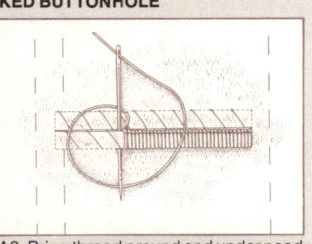

A2. Bring thread around and under needle point to form ridge on buttonhole edge.

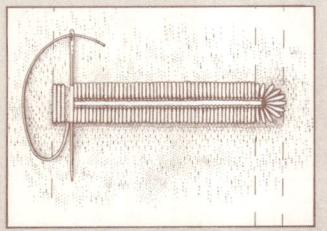

A3. To turn corner, turn fabric and fan stitches. Finish with bar stitches.

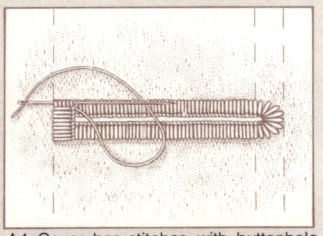

A4. Cover bar stitches with buttonhole stitches, fastening thread on underside.

MAKING A BOUND BUTTONHOLE

B1. Pin and tack patch over the buttonhole line, with right sides facing.

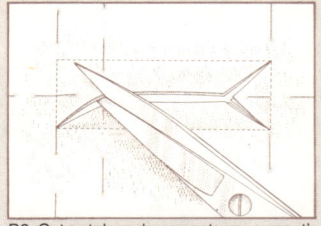

B2. Turn garment to wrong side and machine round the line to within 3 mm.

B3. Cut patch and garment, on garment's wrong side, along line and into corners.

B4. Remove tacks and pull patch through hole to wrong side.

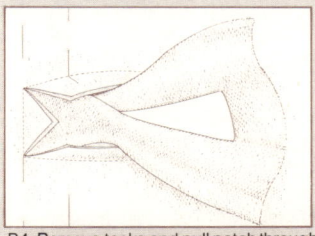

B5. Fold over patch edges, butting them centrally. Tack into place.

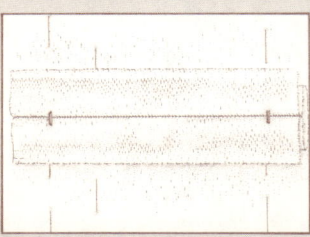

B6. Bar-stitch ends of opening and trim off excess pieces of fabric.

BUTTON LOOPS

Loops in fabric, ribbon, cord or thread make easy, decorative buttonholes. To make fabric loops, cut long bias strips about 2.5 cm. wide. Fold in half lengthways, right sides together, and stitch about 5 mm. (¼ in.) from the fold to make a tube. At one end, make a few stitches with double thread. Tie the end of the thread to a bodkin and push the bodkin through the tube to pull it right side out. To make button loops on a faced edge – between two layers of fabric – lay loops facing away from the opening and with their ends on the edge of the fabric. First test that the buttons will pass through the loops easily, then tack them securely to the seam line. Sew the facing on top [C1]. When the fabric is turned back, the loops are in position along the edge [C2]. Instead of each loop being made separately, some dressmakers prefer to set them in the seam as a continuous strip.

THREAD LOOPS

Useful for fine fabrics and for babies' and toddlers' clothes, thread loops are made with a double thread or a single, buttonhole twist. Sew a few loose threads, the width of the button, near the edge [D1]. Work a blanket stitch around them [D2].

SLOT BUTTONHOLES

A band of fabric, ribbon or braid can be added to the opening edge of a garment, leaving vertical slots in the seam for buttons. It is particularly useful when altering clothes or when making a new opening. The band should be at least twice as wide as the button, plus the seam allowance. Tack, then stitch, the band to the fabric, leaving unsewn spaces in the seam for buttons [E1]. Secure the ends of the button openings with bar stitches [E2]. Press flat the seam. Turn back the band and hem it to its seam allowance [E3].

• POCKETS

The two main types of pocket used in dressmaking are patch pockets and side seam pockets. A patch pocket is fitted to the outside of a garment; a side seam pocket fits inside.

LINED PATCH POCKET

Cut the fabric to double the depth of the proposed finished pocket, plus seam allowances. Mark the halfway point by trace-tacking. Cut interfacing to exactly the size of the finished pocket and iron on, or tack it in place, on the wrong side of the fabric with one edge to the halfway line [F1].

Fold the fabric in half, right sides together, and stitch round the seam line, leaving a gap opposite the fold [F2]. Cut off excess fabric on seam allowance (if pocket is to be curved, notch this seam allowance). Pull pocket through the gap and hand-sew the opening. Press and top-stitch the pocket to the garment.

SIDE SEAM POCKET

A seam allowance of 10 mm. (⅜ in.) is needed to fit an inside pocket. Cut the two sides of the pocket (see pattern, above right). Make sure the seam is firmly stitched above and below the pocket opening. Through the opening, place the straight edge of each pocket piece along the right side of each seam allowance, raw edges together. Pin, stitch [G1] and push pieces through opening. Turn the garment and, on the seam allowance op-

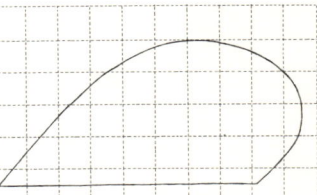

Pattern for side seam pocket.

posite the side the pocket will lie, snip above and below the pocket stitching [G2]. Tack and stitch the pocket pieces together [G3].

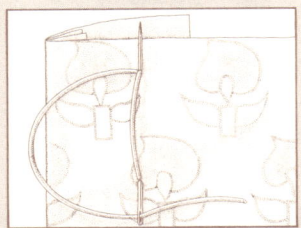
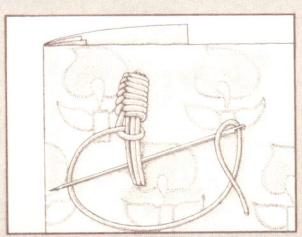

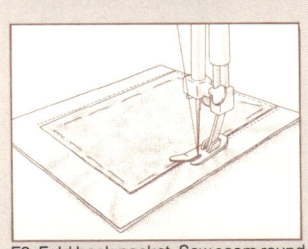

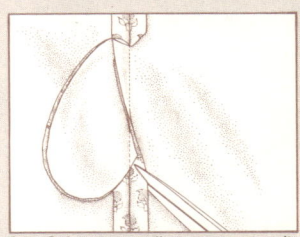
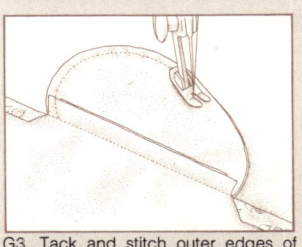

• FASTENINGS

The way that openings could be secured in garments was revolutionised in 1893 with the invention of the zip fastener. There are many types of zip today – strong metal chain zips for overalls and other working clothes;

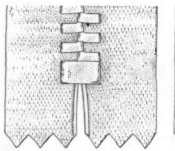 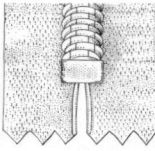

Chain teeth   Coil teeth

light nylon coil zips that are easy to insert but which can be damaged by a hot iron; open-ended zips for cardigans and anoraks; curved zips for trousers.

HOW TO SHORTEN A ZIP

To reduce the length of an existing zip, first pull the zip closed. Make several bar stitches over the zip teeth at the bottom of the zip (see below), approximately 2.5 cm. (1 in.) below

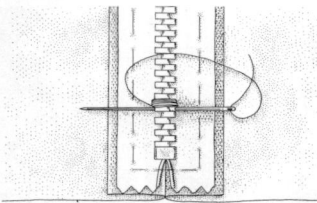

Bar stitching to shorten a zip

the desired new length of opening. Tie off thread on wrong side of zip and cut off the excess length of zip and tape 6 mm. (¼ in.) below the stitches.

CONCEALED ZIP OPENING

One side of the opening overlaps the zip completely to conceal it. Leave an opening in the seam long enough to take the zip. On the overlap side, fold

the seam allowance on the seam line and tack. On the underlap side, make the fold 3 mm. (⅛ in.) out from the original seam line and tack [A1]. Tack the right side of the zip tape to the wrong side of the underlap and stitch close to teeth [A2]. Tack, then stitch tape in place through overlap [A3]. Bar-tack across end of tape.

SEMI-CONCEALED ZIP OPENING

The semi-concealed opening is used on dresses with collars, medium to thick woollen skirts, trousers and for

---

CONCEALED ZIP

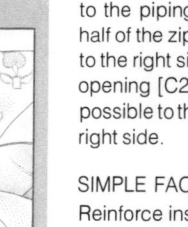

A1. Fold one seam 3 mm. out from original line for underlap. Tack both seams.

A2. First tack, then stitch right side of the zip to wrong side of the underlap.

A3. Turn the overlap seam over the zip. Tack, then stitch zip into place.

---

open-ended zips. Press the seam allowance along each side of the opening and tack together with diagonal basting stitches [B1]. Place the top of the zip tapes level with the top of the opening. Lay the right side of the zip on to the seam allowance so that the zip teeth are centred exactly on the butting seam lines. Pin, then tack along the tapes [B2]. Using the zipper foot of the sewing machine stitch close to the teeth [B3]. Start at the top on one side, go past the bottom stop of the zip, across the end, then up the

---

SEMI-CONCEALED ZIP

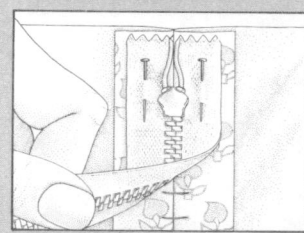

B1. Press, then tack seams together with a diagonal basting stitch.

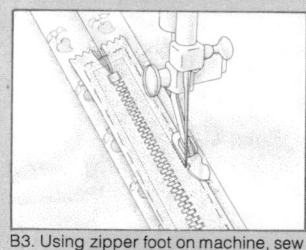

B2. Lay zip, right side down, on seam allowance. Pin in place, then tack.

B3. Using zipper foot on machine, sew zip in position, keeping close to teeth.

---

other side. Remove the tacking and press under a damp cloth. For silk and sheer fabrics, hand-sew zip with a strong, small, back stitch (see p. 296).

ZIPS IN PIPED OPENINGS

Because of extra bulk in the seam, fitting zips next to piping requires extra care. First tack piping to the seam line on the right side of fabric. Pin and tack one half of the zip, wrong side uppermost, to the piping side of the opening [C1]. Machine with piping or zipper foot as close as possible to the piping. Pin and tack the other half of the zip, wrong side uppermost, to the right side of the other side of the opening [C2], and stitch as close as possible to the teeth. Press and turn to right side.

SIMPLE FACED OPENING

Reinforce inside of opening with iron-on interfacing, or lawn or organza for

---

ZIP IN A PIPED OPENING

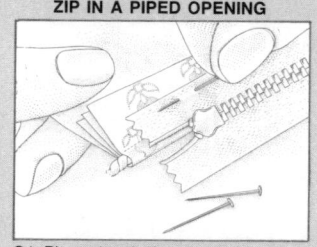

C1. Pin and tack zip, wrong side up, to piped edge. Sew close to piping.

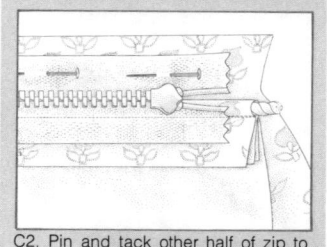

C2. Pin and tack other half of zip to other side of seam. Machine sew.

---

very fine fabrics, then mark the opening with trace tacks [D1]. Lay facing section over opening mark, placing the right side of facing to right side of fabric. Tack into position and turn the fabric over. Use the trace tacking as a guide and machine-stitch around the opening mark, starting 5 mm. (¼ in.) from the edge of the opening at the top. Taper the stitches in towards the point and put two stitches across the point. Sew a matching line of stitching up the other side.

Cut the opening [D2]. Turn facing to

SIMPLE-FACED OPENING

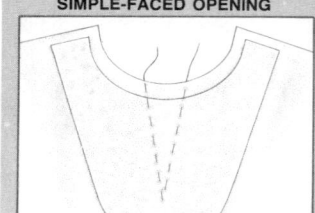

D1. Reinforce inside with interfacing or fabric, and trace-tack the opening.

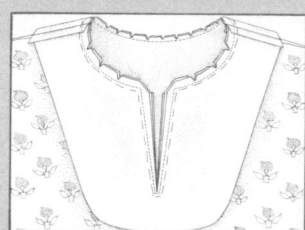

D2. Tack facing to right side of garment. Stitch round opening, then cut.

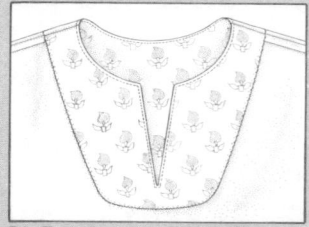

D3. Turn garment to inside. Tidy raw edges of facing. Top-stitch top edge.

---

inside. Neaten the raw edge of the facing, and hold it in place with blind stitches. Top-stitch the edge of the opening [D3]. If loop buttonholes are to be used, stitch them on before the facing (see p. 301).

CONTINUOUS OPENING

This strong, neat opening is useful for women's shirts, casual skirts and children's clothes. Mark and cut the opening along the straight grain of the fabric [E1]. Cut a bias strip about 6 cm. (2½ in.) wide and twice the

E1. Trace-tack, then cut out opening along straight grain of fabric.

E2. Pull opening edges out as straight as possible. Stitch to bias strip.

E3. Press over 5 mm. of strip's other edge. Fold to enclose stitched edge.

length of the opening plus 2.5 cm. (1 in.). Hold the opening straight and place its cut edge to one edge of the bias strip, right sides facing. Machine the two together, with the stitching as close as possible to the edge at the centre point [E2]. Press the strip over the cut edge and turn in a 5 mm. (¼ in.) seam along the other edge of the strip. Fold the strip lengthways so that the seam line is level with the back of the stitched line. Slip-stitch along this line and press [E3]. The opening can be fastened with buttons, press studs, or hooks and eyes.

BUTTONS AND FASTENINGS

Mark the positions of buttons on garments with pins through the buttonholes. For buttons with two or four holes, sew fairly loosely through the holes and back through the fabric. On thick material ensure an even shank by placing a matchstick across the top of the button [F1]. After sewing,

SEWING ON A BUTTON

F1. Insert matchstick across top of button and sew stitches over it.

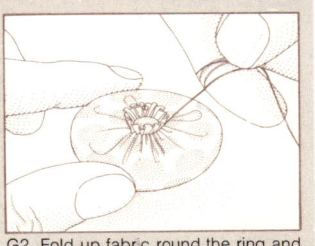
F2. Remove matchstick. Pull button taut and wind cotton round shank.

remove the matchstick and wind the cotton several times round the shank of thread between the button and fabric [F2]. Secure by back-stitching into this shank. If the button already has a shank or metal loop, simply sew it firmly to the fabric. Buttons which are likely to be under strain, such as the top and bottom buttons on a coat, should be strengthened by a keeper button – a shirt button will do – sewn at the back of the main button.

In most cases, sew four-holed buttons with two bars of stitches. The crossover method is generally used only on those buttons with recessed centres, where the build-up of thread at the centre crossover point does not protrude above the button and subsequently become worn.

Covered buttons A fabric-covered button should be used only with a bound buttonhole as the friction of a stitched buttonhole would wear away the fabric cover. Use a soft, loosely

COVERING A BUTTON

G1. Make running stitch round fabric. Place ring in centre with cottonwool.

G2. Fold up fabric round the ring and pull in running stitches.

woven fabric – lined if it is delicate fabric – to cover the button. There are special button mounts with press-in backs which are easy to cover, but curtain rings can also be used. Cut a circle of fabric half as large again as the ring and make running stitches round the edge. Place the ring in the centre on the wrong side of the fabric and a pad of cottonwool under the ring [G1]. Draw in the running stitches to take up the fullness on the reverse [G2]. Knot the thread to fasten.

Press studs Whether you buy them separately or on strips of tape, make sure the ball-and-socket parts are exactly matched on both sides of the opening before sewing into place. Sew the ball part on first, then press it against the facing fabric so that the ball makes an impression on which the socket can be placed correctly.

Hooks and eyes (or bars) On overlapping facings, use a bar instead of an eye. On edge-to-edge openings, use an eye because it protrudes slightly so that when the hooks fit into it, the edges of the opening meet. Instead of a metal bar or eye, a hand-stitched loop can be made as for thread buttonholes. Sew the hook just inside the wrong side of the fabric edge. Take a few stitches under the hook and through the loops to hold the hook in position, then sew it down firmly with buttonhole stitches. Work the loops of the eye or bar in the same way.

Hook tape Chair and cushion covers are often closed with hook tape, a strong fastening fixed in much the same way as a zip fastener. Fold in the seam allowance on one side of the opening. Place the eye tape under the seam, matching the fold to the open sides of the eyes. Machine as close to the eyes as possible and down the other edge of the tape, enclosing the raw edge of the seam.

Fold in the seam allowance on the

other side of the opening. Place the outer edge of the hook tape to the fold, making sure that the hooks and eyes align. Machine down the tape as close to the fold as possible, then down the other edge of the tape, enclosing the seam allowance.

Velcro fastening This consists of two tapes – one with nylon loop nap, the other with nylon hook nap. The two adhere firmly when pressed together. It is particularly useful for soft furnishings. Machine round all sides of each tape, close to the edges.

Press stud

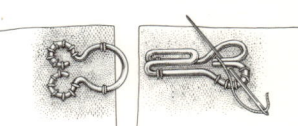
Hook and eye

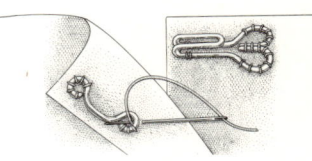
Hook and bar

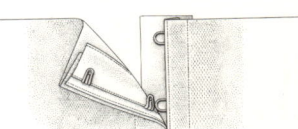
Hook-and-eye tape

Velcro fastening

ALTERING AND REPAIRING

Commercial patterns for women are made not only according to size, but also to figure type as well. So, before buying a pattern, measure the person for whom the garment is intended and decide the figure type to which she approximates by checking against the chart on a pattern envelope. Generally, choose a dress or shirt pattern by bust or chest size, as the waist and hip measurements are easier to adjust. Patterns are sold in size groups, but the names of these groups are not always a sufficient guide. Junior Petite size, for instance, could fit a small adult. Choose simple patterns to start with. Some pattern catalogues include special patterns for beginners, giving fuller instructions than usual.

• ALTERING PATTERNS

Patterns often need adjusting in order to fit the individual figure. The simplest pattern changes for the beginner are those involving length and width. First compare the individual's exact measurements with those on the pattern to find which need changing. Then press the pattern with a warm iron so that the paper is flat and smooth before marking the alterations.

The easiest alteration to make is that to length, since patterns always include thick printed lines labelled 'lengthen or shorten here'. Making the alterations at these lines ensures that the proportions of the garment do not change.

Start with alterations to length above the waist, then below the waist to adjust the overall length of the garment. Then make any necessary adjustments at the sleeves. Finally, make sure that all darts are the right length and pointing the right way.

To alter the width of a garment remove or insert the excess at seams. A total of 5 cm. (2 in.) can be taken from or added to the seams.

Use tissue paper, pinned in place,

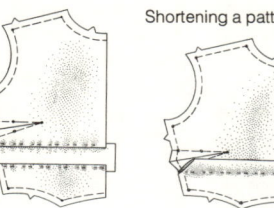

Shortening a pattern

Lengthening a pattern

to add to the pattern width or length.

In all alterations keep the grainline marked on the pattern straight. Where more than one alteration is needed, always change the length first, otherwise changes in width will not fall at the correct place.

SHOULDER LENGTH
Take measurement from base of neck to edge of shoulder.

BACK WAIST LENGTH
Taken centrally down back from prominent vertebra at base of neck to natural waist.

CROTCH DEPTH
Sit on a firm chair and keep feet flat on the floor. Measure from natural waist to the chair seat.

APEX OF BUST
Measured from base of neck to point of bust.

BUST
Measured across widest part of back, under arms and across full bustline. Note distance across front, side seam to side seam.

WAIST
Mark waist by wincing tape measure snugly round your middle. It will adapt to the natural waist. Measure round waist at this mark.

SLEEVE LENGTH
With hand on hip, measure from shoulder joint to wrist bone. Note length from shoulder to elbow for positioning of elbow darts.

CROTCH LENGTH
Measure from waist at the back, through legs to waist at the front. Divide this into front and back crotch lengths at the midpoint between the legs. It will not necessarily be an even division.

FINISHED LENGTH
For dresses, measure from base of neck to hem. For skirts, subtract back waist length from this measurement. For blouses, use back waist length, plus tuck-in allowance.

HIPS
Measure round the fullest part, keeping tape parallel to the floor.

FINISHED TROUSER LENGTH
Measure down side of leg from waist to hem. May vary from pattern size, depending on curve of hips.

WHERE TO MEASURE YOURSELF Accurate measurements are essential to good dressmaking. When taking measurements use a tape that does not stretch.

Stand naturally and wear normal underwear. If recording measurements for future reference, check every six months to see if any have changed.

Often, a change in one pattern piece will affect others. This applies particularly to changes in width. For example, a change in the waistline of a dress skirt will affect the bodice. Match the pattern pieces to check, and alter the bodice as necessary.

DRESS STANDS

Because good dress stands are expensive, they are worth buying only if you intend making most of your own and your family's clothes. When buying a dress stand, choose a slightly smaller size so that you can pad it out to your own proportions. Tailor's wadding or cottonwool can be used for padding. Cover the dress stand with an old nylon jersey slip, or adapt a standard bodice-and-skirt pattern to make a close-fitting cover in a stretch fabric as a working surface.

• FITTING GARMENTS

Almost everyone has a figure that differs from a standard size in at least one respect. Once corrected on the garment, a particular adjustment can be marked on all future patterns.

FITTING SEQUENCE

After cutting out the pieces of fabric for a garment, place them on a flat surface right sides up. Pin and tack darts. Pin and tack bodice fronts to backs along side and shoulder seams with right sides facing.

Leave centre front or centre back seam open. If there is no centre front seam, mark the centre front line with coloured tacking to help to check the hang of the garment while fitting.

Pin and tack skirt seams, gathering skirt to correct size with running stitch if necessary. Pin and tack bodice and skirt together.

Try on the garment or place it on a dress stand. Close openings with pins. If sides need letting out or taking in, make the alterations equal on both sides and do not cut away any of the surplus fabric until the fit is exact. If neck or armholes are strained, carefully snip seam allowances at intervals until they lie flat. Mark the new seam lines with tacking or tailor's chalk. If alterations are made to the shoulder line, use the pattern to re-mark the neck and armhole positions.

Once all alterations are marked, begin stitching the garment. Tack sleeve seams and set in the sleeves, checking the balance marks to make sure they are inserted the right way round. Try on the garment again. Check the armhole position and adjust if necessary. Check sleeve and hem lengths and make sure vertical seams hang straight. Adjust pocket and trim positions if necessary.

Machine-stitch according to new adjustments. Press. Have the last fitting of an unlined garment just before the final inside finishing, and of a lined one just before inserting the lining. Always fit garments over the clothes you will wear beneath them, and with the shoe height you will be using.

NOTE: The garments illustrated below are right side out, but seams have been drawn on the outside to show where alterations are made. All fitting is done with the garment right side out. Alterations are marked on right side with tailor's chalk or tacks.

BODICE-FITTING PROBLEMS

Tight armholes and neck Snip into the bodice's seam allowance round the armholes and neck, and mark a new seamline with tacking or tailor's chalk. Snip to this line so that the bodice fits without straining at any point.

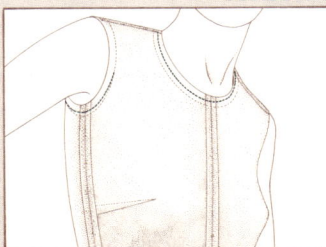

Thin arms and neck This will result in the armhole and necklines being too big. To reduce them in size, raise the underarm-seam curve into the seam allowance, then raise the neckline-seam curve into the seam allowance.

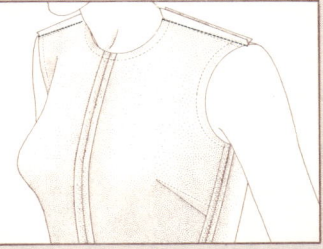

Straight shoulders The fabric will strain at the outer seam edges. Let out the shoulder seam. Starting from the neck edge, re-stitch a tapered seam, progressively narrowing out the seam while working towards the edge of the shoulder seam.

Sloping shoulders The seam will rise above the shoulder and drag at the underarm seam. Take the surplus fabric on top of the shoulder into the shoulder seam. Correct armholes at front and back in the same way as for tight armholes.

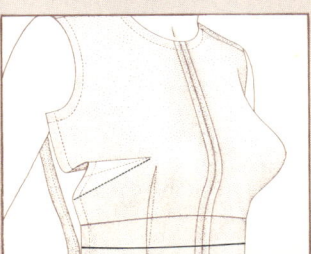

Too full a bust This will make the fabric drag towards the side seams. Undo the seams and lift fabric into side bust dart on lower stitching line. Since this shortens the side seams there will be less seam allowance at the waist.

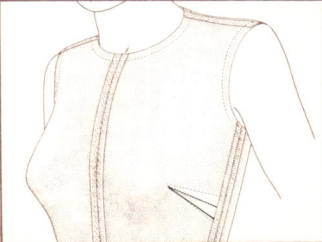

Side bust darts in wrong position The dart should always run from the side seam towards the point of the bust. If wrongly placed, unpick the dart stitching, and raise or lower the dart to the correct position. Re-stitch in new position.

Flat bust There will be too much fullness in the bodice front. Undo side seams and let out side bust dart on lower stitching line. Re-pin the side seams, taking in surplus width from front. Re-shape front of armhole if necessary.

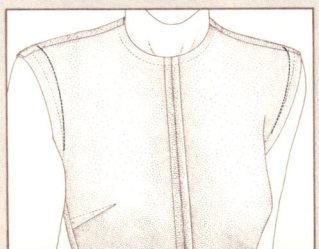

Shoulders too wide, or too narrow Mark the correct armhole-seam position by following line of underarm crease round the front to the top of the outer shoulder points. Continue marking line down towards back. Allow for ease of movement.

SKIRT-FITTING PROBLEMS

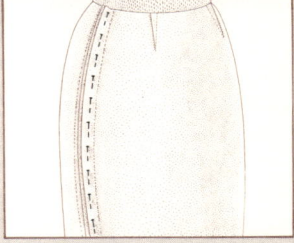

Tight skirt width If the fabric is pulling across waist and hips, this will cause the skirt to ride up. Unpick the side seams and re-pin them to fuller width. Check that new width fits correctly before re-stitching the seams.

Tight skirt seat This will cause the fabric to pull in just below the seat. Undo side seams and pin new seams to allow more fabric to seat. Take any extra width at the waist into the back darts.

• RENEWING COLLARS AND CUFFS

Replace worn cuffs and collars by taking a pattern from the old one and making the new one in a contrasting or, if the garment is plain, a patterned fabric. On women's shirts, an old cuff can be removed and elastic slotted through a hem, or the sleeves can be cut to elbow length and turned up to form a new cuff.

Collars To make a new collar and stand (the upright base), cut two collar sections and two stand sections. Cut 15 mm. ($\frac{1}{2}$ in.) outside the old stitching line to allow for seams. Cut interfacings for collar and stand.

Tack the interfacing to the wrong side of the underpiece of the collar, and lay both collar sections together, right sides facing. Tack and stitch the three outside edges, taking one stitch across at each point. Trim the seam allowance [A1], turn the collar right side out and press. Top-stitch (see p. 299) if desired. Attach interfacing to the wrong side of one stand piece. Sandwich the collar between the stand pieces, right sides facing with the interfacing at the bottom. Align the top edge of the stand with the bottom edge of the collar. Tack and stitch together [A2]. Trim seam, notch the curves and turn stand down. Press in the seam allowance of the inside edge of the stand. Pin the unpressed edge to the outside of the neck of the shirt, right sides together, matching raw edges [A3]. Tack and stitch. Fold over the pressed edge of the stand to the inside neck edge to enclose the neck edge within the stand. Tack and fell-stitch (see p. 297) to shirt [A4].

Cuffs The method for attaching a cuff depends on whether the cuff is cut in two pieces or folded in half; whether it overlaps or meets edge to edge (see illustration).

If it is cut in one piece, attach interfacing to the under cuff, or the lower half of it. Tack and stitch. Trim seam allowance [B1], turn to right side and press. Press in the seam along one edge, and lay the unpressed edge to the gathered or main part of the sleeve, right sides together. Adjust the sleeve fullness to the correct length, pin in place [B2]. Stitch seam allowances then trim this seam [B3]. Notch the edge of the sleeve fabric. Turn in the pressed edge of the cuff to inside of the sleeve and fell-stitch to the seam line [B4]. Make buttonhole(s) as necessary (see p. 300).

• RELINING A COAT

Remove the old lining carefully and press each section. Cut a new pattern from this, adding seam allowances of 15 mm. ($\frac{1}{2}$ in.) all round. Mark any darts. Stitch all darts and seams. Press. With coat inside out, either on a dress stand or flat on a table, pin the shoulder-seam allowance of the lining to the coat's shoulder-seam allowance (see illustration, below). Back-stitch through both these seam allowances without pulling thread too tightly. Do the same with the side seams. This holds lining in place. Turn back lining to let it fall naturally, and pin all the way round to the previous lining

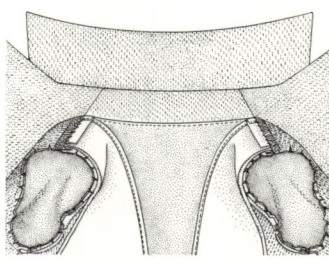

Attaching lining to a garment.

position. Do this on a stand or a coat-hanger to stop the lining distorting. Turn to the right side and adjust the lining if it is pulling at the coat fabric. Fell-stitch all the edges, leaving a small tuck at the hems to allow ease in wearing.

• WAISTBANDS

To take in a waistband, remove the old band then take in all darts and seams on the garment evenly. Replace the waistband. It will now have more overlap, which can be taken up by moving the fastenings. When letting out a waistband, there is seldom enough material in the band to allow for the extra length. In this case, replace the waistband with a new one of petersham. First let out all darts and seams in the garment evenly to fit the new waist measurement. Lay the petersham on the garment with one edge to the seamline of the old band, overlapping each end. Pin and stitch

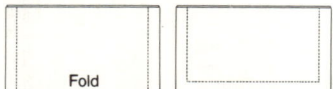

The two ways of making a cuff.

ATTACHING A NEW SHIRT COLLAR

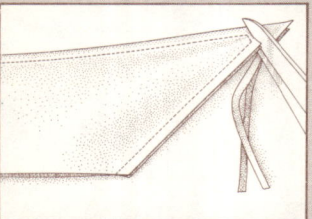

A1. Sew the collar pieces together, right sides facing. Trim off excess material.

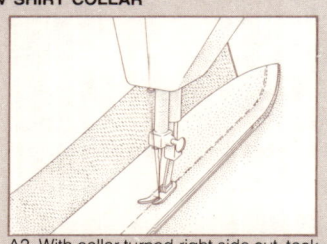

A2. With collar turned right side out, tack and stitch edge of stand to collar.

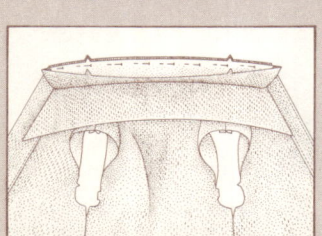

A3. Pin the stand to the shirt neck edge, matching raw edges. Tack and stitch.

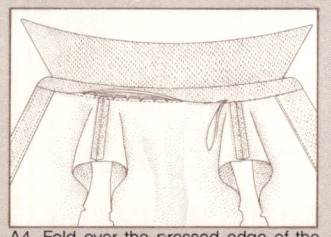

A4. Fold over the pressed edge of the stand to inside neck edge. Fell-stitch.

ATTACHING A NEW CUFF

B1. Stitch interfacing to the under cuff and trim seam allowances.

B2. Lay unpressed edge to sleeve, right sides together, and pin in place.

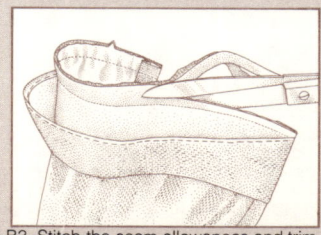

B3. Stitch the seam allowances and trim the unpressed seam.

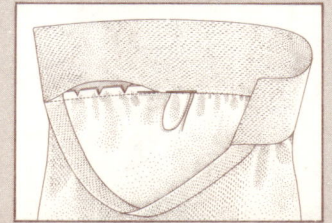

B4. Turn in the pressed edge of cuff to the inside of the sleeve, then fell-stitch.

ATTACHING A PETERSHAM BAND

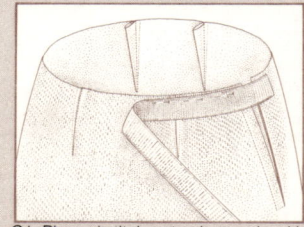

C1. Pin and stitch petersham strip with one edge to seamline of old band.

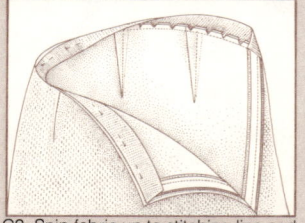

C2. Snip fabric up to stitching line and turn the petersham to the inside.

the petersham along this line [C1]. Snip the skirt fabric seam allowance up to the stitching line and turn petersham to the inside [C2]. Press, and press in opening ends. Top-stitch the outside edge for firmness. Sew on fastenings.

• HEMS

When taking up a hem, especially if the skirt is flared, avoid creating too deep a turning which will cause puckers in the skirt fabric. Trim the hem, levelling it if necessary. To let down a hem, first remove all the old threads and press under a damp cloth to remove creases. Check the hem level. If there is not enough turning to let down, make a false hem in a matching, lining-weight fabric or with ready-made hem binding. To make the binding, cut strips on the bias and join them together (see p. 299). Press a narrow turning along one edge. Trim the hem edge, and lay the binding

MAKING A FALSE HEM

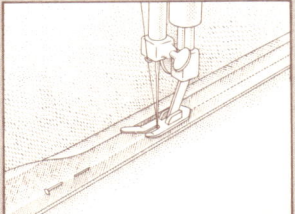

D1. Lay binding against hem edge, right sides together. Machine-stitch.

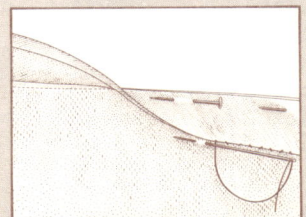

D2. Turn up false hem to inside. Press, then slip-stitch it to inside of garment.

against it, right sides together. Machine-stitch about 3 mm. (⅛ in.) from edge [D1]. Turn up false hem to inside. Press, then slip-stitch false hem to inside skirt [D2]. Frequently, when letting down old hems there are irremovable hem creases or fade marks. Even rows of machine stitching in the same or a contrasting colour will cover the hem and marks. For children's clothes, there are many decorative ways of covering a hem mark; braid, ribbon or lace, for instance, or a channel seam (see p. 298) can lengthen the skirt and decorate it at the same time.

• RENEWING A FLY-FRONT ZIP

To fit a curved trouser zip, cut a shaped facing to fit the right-hand side of the opening. Sew it to the opening, right sides together.

Snip and press the seam. Lay the zip right side down on the faced side of the opening with the left tape edge along the seamline. Place the bottom stop 20 mm. (¾ in.) above bottom edge of facing. Stitch right edge of tape with the zip foot, as close as possible to the teeth. Make a second row of stitching just outside the first. Turn the facing to the inside. Tack and stitch it down. Remove tacking from left side of zip tape, leaving it free.

Fold and tack left side seam allowance. Undo zip, and pin the seam to the free edge of the zip next to the teeth. Make a fly shield to cover the inside from two pieces of fabric shaped like the previous facing strip. Tack the fly shield behind the zip, matching all the seam edges inside, stitch through all layers. Snip lower end of seam and strengthen with a few stitches. The same method applies when resetting a zip, except that the fly shield will have to be removed, pressed and then resewn. For fixing and shortening a zip, see p. 302.

RENEWING A FLY-FRONT ZIP

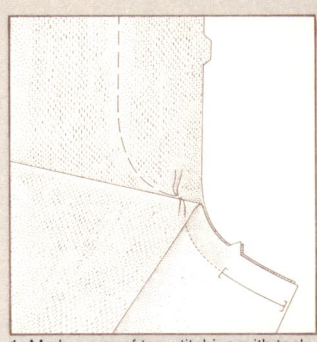

1. Mark curve of top-stitching with tacking on right front. Also mark the bottom of the opening with knotted thread.

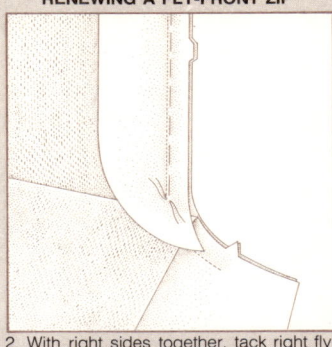

2. With right sides together, tack right fly facing to right front edge. Stitch up from opening mark to the waist.

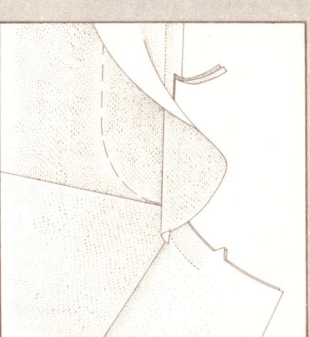

3. Trim the seam allowances. Open out the facing, then press the facing and the seam allowances away from the garment.

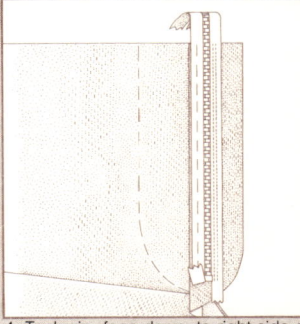

4. Tack zip, face down, to right side of facing, turning up zip tape at bottom left. Sew two rows on right edge, near teeth.

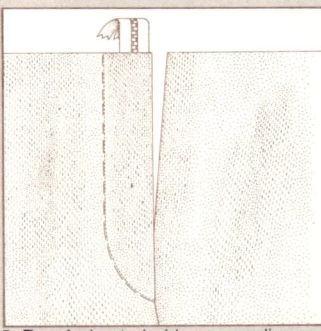

5. Turn facing to inside on seamline and press. On outside, tack fly facing to front. Top-stitch, working from bottom to top.

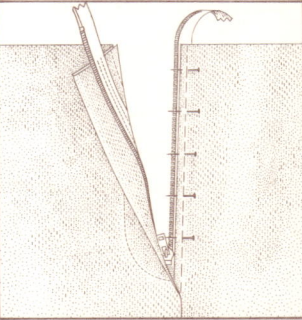

6. Open zip and pin zip tape to wrong side of left front. Tack in place and close zip to check it is positioned correctly.

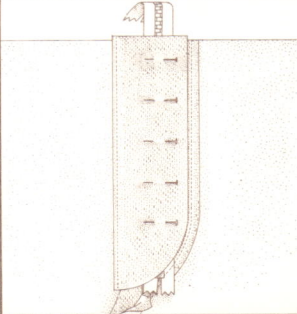

7. Position fly shield, working from the wrong side. Match curve of shield to curve of top-stitching. Pin temporarily.

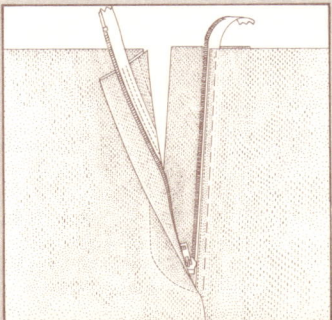

8. Turn back to right side and tack through all layers of garment, zip and shield. Open zip and stitch through all layers.

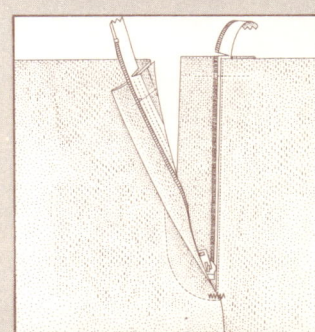

9. With zip open, stitch across tapes at waist seamline. Cut off excess zip, level with top of garment. Bar-tack at bottom.

• RE-SETTING SLEEVES

The top, sometimes called the cap, of a sleeve is larger than the armhole so that the sleeve will fit over the top of the arm. This extra fabric must be eased in to fit the armhole curve. With stretchable fabrics it is relatively easy to stretch the armhole slightly, as the sleeve is pinned in, or to shrink the top of the sleeve first by pressing under a damp cloth.

More care must be taken with closely woven fabrics to avoid puckers and creases in the sleeve. When pinning, tacking and stitching sleeves into armholes, work from the sleeve, not the bodice. Mark to the top of the sleeve to align with the shoulder seam. To help distribute the fullness, make two rows of running stitches around the top of the sleeve [A1]. Then draw the stitches until the cap is the same size as the armhole [A2]. Wind the excess thread around a pin pushed through the fabric across the seam. Pin the sleeve in place, matching the balance marks and placing pins at right-angles to the seam line.

Tack, then machine sleeves in place, sewing between the two gathering rows [A3]. Trim the seam allowance and oversew raw edges.

RE-SETTING SLEEVES

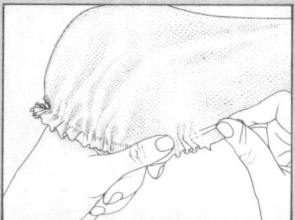

A1. Sew two rows of running stitches round top, or cap, of the sleeve.

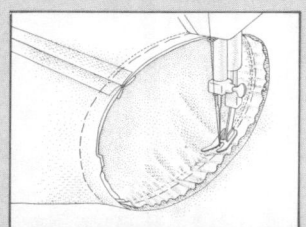

A2. Draw threads in until the cap is the same size as the sleeve armhole.

A3. Tack, then machine into place. Stitch in between the running stitches.

• PATCHING

Patches are used for holes too large to be darned, and on garments, household linen and loose covers where the strength and durability of the repair is more important than the appearance. Trim away the ragged edges of the hole to make a square or rectangle [B1]. Cut the patch at least 5 cm. (2 in.) bigger than the hole all round. The best patch is a piece of fabric from a hidden part of the same garment – on a shirt, from the tail for instance – as it will have faded with the main fabric. If it is necessary to use a new piece of fabric, first age it slightly by leaving it to soak in a solution of soapy water and baking soda. Tack the patch in position over the hole on the wrong side. Turn in the edges of the patch and machine or slip-stitch over the hole [B2]. Turn in the edges of the hole and slip-stitch to the patch [B3].

Patches need not always be inconspicuous. Multi-coloured patches sewn on the right side of the garment can be used on children's clothes. Appliqué motif patches can cover worn spots on pillowslips and blankets. Ordinary white tape is useful for patching small holes in the corners of towels, face cloths and tea towels.

• DARNING

Repairs to small holes in most fabrics and to all holes in stretch and knit fabrics are best made by darning – a reweaving process which should follow as closely as possible the way the original fabric was made. Use a wooden darning mushroom or darning egg to hold the fabric evenly. Any loosely knitted fabrics can be darned over a clothes brush, the bristles holding the edges of the hole in place. Match the thread as closely as possible to the original in colour, texture and weight. Too thin a darn will wear through very quickly, while too coarse a thread will make the darn clumsy and its weight will strain the surrounding fabric. Make a circle of running stitches around the hole about 2.5 cm. (1 in.) from the edge [C1]. This will help to hold and strengthen the worn and frayed edges around the hole. Take darning thread back and forth across the hole [C2], then weave cross-wise rows in and out [C3]. Leave a small loop at the end of each row to allow for any shrinkage of the new thread. If the hole is very big, darn it on a net base made by cutting out and tacking down a net patch first. Most woven upholstery should be darned (preferably with threads pulled from an inside seam). Some sewing machines have a special darning foot which produces an almost invisible darn of closely woven stitches.

PATCHING

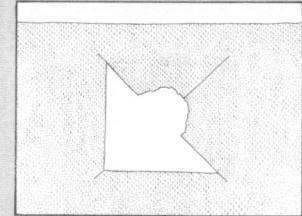

B1. Trim off ragged edges of the hole. Cut mitres in each of the corners.

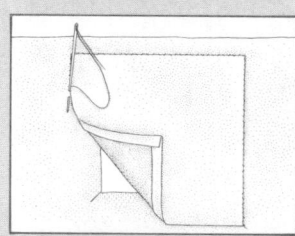

B2. Fit patch over the hole, turning in the edges. Stitch into place.

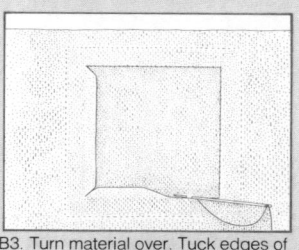

B3. Turn material over. Tuck edges of hole under and slip-stitch into place.

DARNING

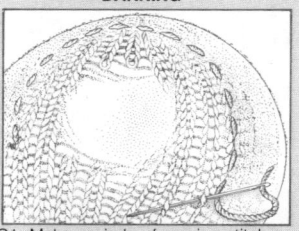

C1. Make a circle of running stitches round the hole to strengthen edges.

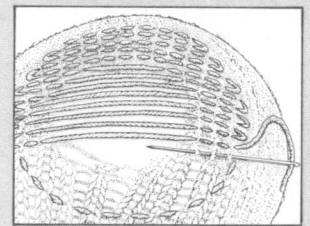

C2. Take thread back and forth across the hole, keeping threads close.

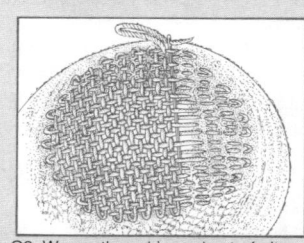

C3. Weave thread in and out of alternate rows. Again, keep threads close.

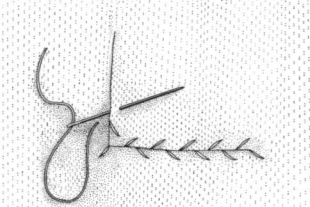

DARNING A TEAR

Tack the tear, right side out, over a piece of paper to hold the slit together while darning across it. An alternative is to apply a patch of iron-on interlining to the back of the tear first. Make small, slanting stitches by bringing the needle up on one side of the tear, down through the tear and up through the other side (see above). Triangular tears can also be mended this way.

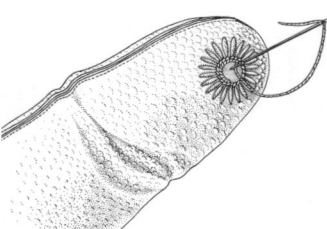

DARNING A LEATHER GLOVE

Darn gloves on the hand. A three-sided glover's needle, made for leather work, must be used for mending skin gloves. With silk thread, make a buttonhole-stitch edging around the hole, then work around it in narrowing circles filling in the hole with closely worked buttonhole stitches (see p. 300). Splits between the fingers are repaired in the same way, but work lengthways instead of in a circle.

• SMALL REPAIRS

Small repairs can be expensive when carried out professionally. Most simple repairs, such as those examples given here, can be undertaken by anyone with a basic knowledge of sewing, saving both time and money.

REPLACING WORN FUR

A worn patch on a fur garment can be replaced, provided it is not too large, by using a piece of fur from the inside of either the facings or sleeves. After making sure the piece will match, undo the stitching on the section from which the replacement patch is to be taken, and open the fur out flat. Using a razor blade, cut the patch out, slightly larger than the piece it will replace. When cutting fur, always cut from the skin side and hold the pelt up to avoid cutting hairs on the fur side.

On the skin side of the worn part, mark out in chalk the area to be cut out. Cut along the chalk lines with the blade. Shape the replacement patch to the same size, making sure that the hairs on the patch run in the same direction as those on the garment. Use a heavy-duty needle and stitch the edges together with small oversewing stitches. Smooth the hairs round the patch with a fine brush.

If the worn part is near the hem edge, the garment can be shortened, to three-quarter or jacket length. First undo and turn back the lining at the hem and, on the skin side of the fur, chalk in the new length. Cut along this line very carefully with the blade.

Hand-stitch tape, or a wide binding, to the edge with very small oversewing stitches. The tape should be placed against the fur side, but sewn from the skin side. Tack a narrow strip of soft fabric, such as flannel, around the skin side of the fur. Turn the tape to the inside, and herringbone-stitch it down. Cut lining to length and slip-stitch it into place.

REPLACING ELASTIC

Elastic is run through seams to gather material at the waist or wrist on garments such as underclothes and pyjamas. It may be necessary to unpick part of the seam to pull out the old elastic. Cut the new elastic the desired length less 3 cm. (1¼ in.). Attach a plastic threader or a small safety pin to one end of the elastic, and push through the channel. Fix a large safety pin to the other end of the elastic so that it cannot pull through. Overlap the ends of the elastic and slip-stitch together, then slip-stitch the seam opening. Special wide elastic is available for replacing the tops of underpants (machine-stitch along one edge, stretching the elastic as you stitch). And there are soft elastic straps and brassière backs complete with hooks and eyes for lingerie repairs.

SHIRRING

Shirring is formed by rows of gathering, often with elastic thread. To tighten old knitted ribbing on sweaters and sock tops, machine a few rows of thread and shirring elastic round the ribbing, or hand sew rows of running stitch with double elastic.

TURNING SHEETS

When sheets show signs of wear in the centre, cut them in half lengthways and rejoin the selvedges with a flat fell seam to make a new centre.

Make new hems at the sides, first trimming off any frayed edges.

TABLECLOTHS

Wear in tablecloths tends to take place along the fold lines. Trim 5 cm. (2 in.) off one end or one side of a tablecloth and hem. When it is folded, the new folds will fall in unworn places. Holes and stains on tablecloths can be hidden with appliquéd flower patterns or circles – patterned on plain cloths and vice versa. Make matching table napkins in the appliqué fabric.

BATH TOWELS

These usually wear first at the edges. Trim the worn edges and bind or face them with matching or contrasting cotton tape. Wash and dry the tape first to pre-shrink it. A very worn bath towel can be cut up and the pieces hemmed to make hand towels and face cloths.

REPLACING BUTTONS

Use strong button or crochet thread when replacing buttons on children's and work clothes. Buttons which take extra strain, such as the lowest one on a shirt or dress, can be reinforced by being stitched through a square of tape or a keeper button at the back. (See Sewing on a button, p. 303.)

DECORATIVE MENDING

This is the only method possible if a stain or a hole appears in a place where any patch or darn would look obvious. The possibilities of decorative mending depend on the type of garment and the extent of the damage. They can range from a small embroidered appliqué motif to a new skirt or bodice in a contrasting fabric. New patch pockets or, on cushions, contrast panels can help to hide a stain or tear (see illustration, right).

Embroidery, braiding, frills and rucking will also conceal damage.

• EMERGENCY REPAIRS

Department store haberdashery counters have a wide range of materials for making emergency repairs – ready-made pockets, iron-on patches, braids and bindings, belt-making kits, button-covering kits and eyelet kits. Build up a stock of these items so that dressmaking repairs can be made as quickly and as simply as possible.

TORN HEM

One of the most common forms of damage to a garment is a torn hem. The easiest repair is simply to raise the hem so that the tear is hidden. But do not use safety pins to secure a hem that has become unsewn, unless no better makeshift is possible.

Sellotape strips are preferable; and on dark fabrics, staples can be used

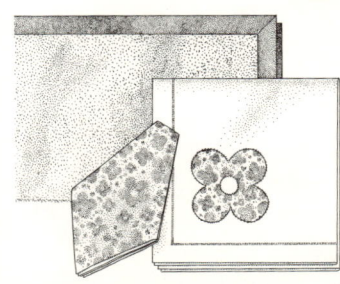

Examples of decorative mending

as a temporary measure. Press the staples into the fabric on the wrong side. Iron-on hem tape makes a more lasting repair, although it will eventually come off with washing unless it is slip-stitched in place.

LADDERS IN TIGHTS

Prevent ladders from spreading with a dab of nail polish or, until they are washed, a rub with dampened soap at the top of the run.

BROKEN ZIP

A zip-fastener runner that has come free of the teeth on one side can be temporarily repaired. Pull the runner to the bottom of the zip. Then, about 5 mm. (¼ in.) above the runner on the unattached side, cut into the zip tape between two teeth [D1]. The teeth above the cut can then be worked into the runner. Pull up the runner and just above the cut, oversew across the zip [D2] to create a new bottom stop.

MENDING A ZIP

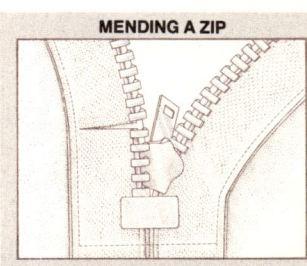

D1. Pull runner to bottom of zip and cut zip tape about 5 mm. above it.

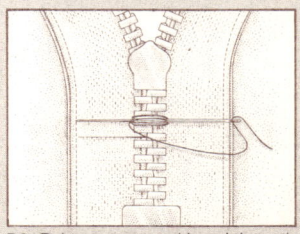

D2. Raise runner, working zip's teeth into it. Oversew just above cut.

Home management

Like any other skills, those that go into running a home
can be learned the hard way – by trial and error – or the easy way,
by following sound advice. The following pages set out the short cuts
through housework, and give advice on balancing the family budget.
Successful home management has always demanded practical
knowledge of the outside world, and with the help of this section
you will be able to plot a course through the jungle of laws, rules and
regulations covering taxation, savings and shoppers' rights.

CONTENTS

PLANNED HOUSEWORK

Some people spend no more than an hour a day on housework. Others find that household chores last from breakfast to bedtime. At whichever end of the scale you come, it saves time and effort to work according to a set plan – provided that the plan is flexible enough to allow for unscheduled demands on your time: a crying baby, the arrival of an unexpected visitor, children wanting a knee bandaged, the breakdown of a vacuum cleaner and so on. A plan assists flexibility, since it helps you to decide what jobs can be put off to a later date.

• WORKING OUT A PLAN

Planning does not necessarily require elaborate timetables. At its simplest, all that is needed is a rough outline of the week's programme on a calendar (keep one in the kitchen with room for making notes). Set aside a short time each day to assess the needs of the next 24 hours.

It helps to make check lists, especially if the tasks are divided between members of the family (see p. 314).

There are three main types of work in a house: essential jobs that need to be done frequently; regular tidying and cleaning for freshness and comfort; and occasional major cleaning and checks for repairs and overhaul.

How frequently essential jobs need to be done – two or three times a day, once a day, or every few days – depends on the job, the size of the family, and such things as the weather or the time of year. Regular tidying and cleaning may be a weekly or fortnightly job, or it may be done at whatever intervals are convenient. Occasional jobs are likely to be necessary only once or twice a year.

FREQUENT JOBS

Essential jobs include shopping, preparing meals, clearing up after them, washing clothes, and whatever cleaning is absolutely necessary for health and comfort. In cold weather, organising the heating system must be added to the list, whether it is laying and lighting fires and keeping a supply of fuel handy, or merely filling a coin meter.

A good approach to essential tasks is first to cut down the amount of work involved wherever possible – by means of equipment such as a dishwashing machine and an automatic washing machine. (See also Ways of cutting down cleaning, p. 316.)

Secondly, brush aside any preconceived ideas of what ought to be done when – such as washing on a Monday. Washing by machine can be done at home whenever a load is available, or at whatever time the local laundrette is least crowded.

Washing up after each meal has traditionally been considered good practice, but it is not the best way to use a dishwasher (see p. 200). Many people complete the day's cleaning before going shopping, but it is best to shop at the start of the day. Shops are usually less crowded with customers, and assistants are fresher. Whatever time you do your shopping, it helps to make a shopping list. Keep a pad in the kitchen and write items you need on it as you go along, then take it when you go shopping.

Give cookers, sinks and the bathroom a frequent, quick wipe round. If they are left too long they become difficult to clean. Similarly, if milk boils over on the cooker, or some other mishap occurs, clean up at once.

REGULAR TIDYING AND CLEANING

Regular tidying – emptying ash trays, straightening cushions, books and magazines – helps to keep a room pleasant and comfortable. It is usually convenient to empty wastepaper baskets once a week, just before the dustmen call.

Old newspapers and magazines can be bundled up and left out for the dustmen every other week or so. Hold a few in stock for such uses as putting on the floor when cleaning shoes.

Cut down the amount of tidying up needed by providing as much storage space as possible (see p. 102).

A lost-property drawer for depositing things not tidied away by their owners can be useful, but in the long run may only create another task – that of clearing it out when it fills up.

Provided that crumbs and tramped-in dirt are cleaned up fairly soon after they appear, regular thorough cleaning – vacuuming, dusting, polishing – need only be tackled at convenient intervals.

The order in which you clean rooms is not important, but it saves effort to clean adjoining rooms, or rooms on the same floor, at the same time. The order in which you clean out a particular room makes a difference to time and efficiency. A suggested order is given in the check lists (see p. 314).

First, do the dust-creating jobs – such as hearth cleaning and sweeping. It is usual to vacuum a carpet before dusting, but most cleaners have attachments that can be used for dusting ceilings, picture rails, curtains, upholstery, ledges over doors, and so on. If you dust these places with a dusting mop, it is best to do so before vacuuming the floor.

Use a vacuum cleaner systematically across the floor with a slow, deliberate movement. The head of a cylinder model should make a good seal with the surface for efficient suction. Generally, two or three backward and forward strokes are needed – more for a very dusty surface. The last stroke of an upright cleaner should follow the pile of the carpet. Work from top to bottom when cleaning stairs.

If you sweep a room with a broom, use short, forward strokes, brushing the dirt towards a central collection point for sweeping into a dustpan.

Dust metal surfaces like those on gas or electric fires with a damp cloth, and dry with a paper towel. Disconnect any plugs first. For thorough room cleaning, place ornaments and small objects on a tray and move them out of the way before dusting.

Dust shelves and furniture with a dry duster folded into a pad, then polish them or wipe them with a damp cloth, according to the surface. (See Cleaning furniture, p. 320.)

OCCASIONAL CLEANING

Before the days of smokeless fuel and washing machines, the ritual of spring cleaning used to be necessary to clean the grime of winter smoke and fogs from curtains and coverings.

Occasional jobs, such as washing down paintwork, and cleaning carpets, curtains and chair covers, still need to be done, but whenever convenient – not especially in spring. Some jobs, such as washing blankets, getting boilers serviced or chimneys swept, are obviously best done in spring or summer.

The amount of occasional major cleaning needed depends to some extent on the system of regular cleaning. If this is fairly extensive, major cleaning will not be such a large-scale operation.

• SAVING TIME AND ENERGY

Much of the time and energy spent on housework goes in sheer mileage. Find ways to reduce the effort spent in going to and fro, and up and down stairs.

Keep some cleaning equipment upstairs as well as down, or carry

HOW TO CARRY, PUSH, LIFT AND BEND

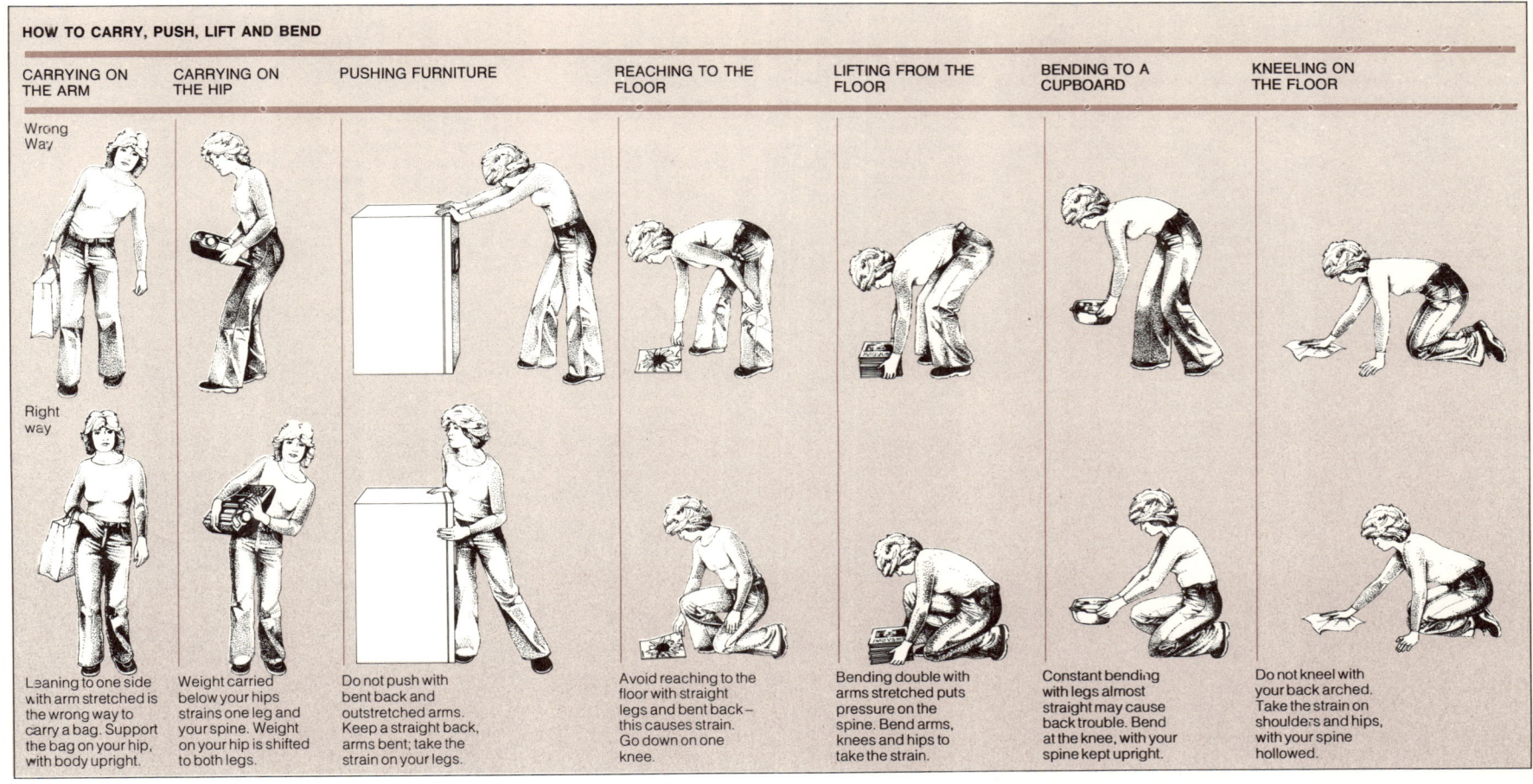

CARRYING ON THE ARM	CARRYING ON THE HIP	PUSHING FURNITURE	REACHING TO THE FLOOR	LIFTING FROM THE FLOOR	BENDING TO A CUPBOARD	KNEELING ON THE FLOOR

Wrong Way

Right way

Leaning to one side with arm stretched is the wrong way to carry a bag. Support the bag on your hip, with body upright.

Weight carried below your hips strains one leg and your spine. Weight on your hip is shifted to both legs.

Do not push with bent back and outstretched arms. Keep a straight back, arms bent; take the strain on your legs.

Avoid reaching to the floor with straight legs and bent back – this causes strain. Go down on one knee.

Bending double with arms stretched puts pressure on the spine. Bend arms, knees and hips to take the strain.

Constant bending with legs almost straight may cause back trouble. Bend at the knee, with your spine kept upright.

Do not kneel with your back arched. Take the strain on shoulders and hips, with your spine hollowed.

equipment in a basket. When emptying ashtrays and waste bins, take round a plastic bag to save trips to the dustbin. Load up the tea trolley with what is necessary for laying the table, to save several journeys. Arrange cupboards and shelves so that you can reach things easily.

Save energy by avoiding the strain and fatigue that results from using the body muscles incorrectly. Develop a relaxed working tempo. Hurrying causes tiredness and tension and

can lead to accidents. Work with natural, rhythmic movements, not sharp jerky ones that are likely to cause stiff, tense muscles. It is easiest to clean windows and large surfaces with a circular motion.

When you lift, use the muscles that are strongest for the task. The legs, for example, are stronger than the back, so bend at the knees and hips rather than at the waist. Avoid stooping, as it causes pressure on the spine. Keep your spine as upright as you can.

When pushing or pulling, get close to the object and use the weight of your body rather than just the strength of your arm muscles. When carrying, take the strain of a weight on your hip.

Hold whatever you are lifting or carrying with the palm of your hand and the base of your fingers whenever possible; strain on the fingertips causes tension in the upper arms and chest. Avoid gripping objects tightly, unless they are very heavy – hold them lightly but

firmly. Keep your elbow into your side when pouring, to reduce the strain on your arms and shoulders.

When standing, keep your feet slightly apart with one foot in front of the other for ease and balance. Standing takes more energy than sitting, so sit down for whatever jobs you can – ironing or vegetable peeling, for example. Try to alternate working positions by doing a sitting job after you have been standing for some time.

GETTING PROFESSIONAL HELP

Professional cleaning services, such as carpet and upholstery cleaners, are available on a long-term or short-term basis. Ask friends for recommendations, or look up firms in the yellow pages of the telephone directory, or in local directories or newspapers. Wherever possible, get written estimates from more than one firm, making it clear to them that the work is domestic, not commercial.

HOUSEWORK PROGRAMME CHECK LIST

A check list helps to sort out priorities and to plan and share out tasks.

FREQUENT JOBS

1 Check contents of food store, refrigerator and freezer
2 Check household store
3 Work out menus for meals
4 Check pet food supplies
5 Make out shopping list
6 Clean pet dishes and feed pets; ensure water bowl is full
7 Clear hearth and lay fire
8 Fill coal scuttles, coke hods
9 Vacuum up crumbs, etc.; empty ash trays if necessary
10 Tidy away books, magazines, papers, toys
11 Water house plants, window boxes, if necessary
12 Top up flower vases if needed
13 Make beds; put clothes away
14 Sort dirty linen for washing
15 Put out clean towels, tea cloths, glass cloths
16 Wash dishes or load dishwasher (empty its filter)
17 Empty kitchen waste
18 Put out milk bottles
19 Wind clocks if necessary

REGULAR JOBS

Jobs marked with an asterisk do not need to be done every time the room is cleaned, but are included to show order of work.

1 Clean living/dining-room

*1 Remove ornaments and small objects to kitchen for cleaning
2 Empty waste bins, ash trays
3 Clean fireplace
*4 Dust high places, such as ceiling, picture rail, light fittings and ledges over doors with mop or vacuum-cleaner attachment
*5 Vacuum cushions and upholstery. Shake or beat out dust
6 Clean floor
7 Dust paintwork, skirting board, ledges, picture frames, door handles
8 Dust furniture, and polish it
9 Clean mirrors, picture glass, etc.
*10 Clean ornaments according to their material
11 Refill humidifier
12 Clean table-mats; top up salt and pepper pots

2 Clean bedrooms

1 Tidy away clothing, etc.
2 Strip bed and vacuum mattress
3 Turn mattress over from head to foot to equalise wear (but do not turn a foam mattress)
4 Make bed and fold up edges of bedspread away from floor
*5 Cover bed with old sheet or newspaper, and place on it small furniture to clear floor
*6 Clear small objects, such as alarm clocks, from shelves and dressing-tables on to a tray and place on bed
*7 Dust high places, as for living-room
8 Clean floor
9 Dust paintwork, skirting board, ledges, door handles and so on
10 Dust furniture and polish if necessary, replacing small furniture; straighten bedspread
11 Clean mirrors and other glass
*12 Clean and replace small objects from tray

3 Clean bathroom/lavatory

1 Tidy away objects such as toothpaste, shaving kit
2 Remove mats, laundry basket, towels, scales, and any small furniture
*3 Dust high places as for living-room
4 Sweep or vacuum floor
5 Wipe down tiles and dry
6 Clean cabinet exteriors, mirrors, towel rails. Ensure that heated towel rail is switched off before wiping with damp cloth and drying
7 Clean bath/shower, hand-basin (particularly the overflows), drain holes and taps
8 Clean lavatory cistern and seat. Wipe seat dry
9 Clean lavatory pan and brush
10 Renew flush block, if needed
11 Wash or polish floor according to surface material. When floor is dry, clean and return any rubber mats and small furniture; provide clean towels and put down clean bath and lavatory mats
12 Remove, clean, and replace shower head, tooth-cleaning mugs or any similar equipment
13 Check supplies of soap, toothpaste, etc., and renew where necessary

4 Clean hall, stairs and landings

*1 Remove ornaments and small objects for cleaning, and dust high places as for living-room
2 Vacuum carpets. While doing stairs check that stair rods or fittings are secure
3 Dust, mop or polish any uncarpeted floor
4 Dust or polish banisters, paintwork, furniture
5 Clean mirrors and telephone

5 Clean kitchen/utility-room

1 Tidy away stray articles to cupboards or shelves
2 Clear work tops of any articles that may be kept there, such as scales or mixers
3 Remove waste bins, and any mats or small furniture
*4 Dust high places as for living-room
5 Sweep or vacuum floor
6 Dust paintwork, ledges, skirting board, door handles
7 Wipe surfaces such as cooker, refrigerator
8 De-frost and clean refrigerator
9 Clean work tops according to surface material – usually plastic
10 Wash and replace items such as scales, food-mixer stand
11 Wash articles such as washing-up rack, soap dish, waste bin; disinfect waste bin
12 Clean sink, taps and draining board
13 Clean sink drainpipe by putting washing soda in and around plughole and pouring boiling water over it
14 Wash or clean floor according to surface material
15 When floor is dry, clean and replace mats and small furniture

6 General cleaning/maintenance

1 Wash, dry, and iron clothing and other linen
2 Refill steam iron with water
3 Mend any clothing in mending basket
4 Wash hair brushes and combs. After removing hair from brush, wash bristles by beating them up and down in warm soapy water. Clean backs of brushes according to material. Hang to dry
5 Remove and clean doormats and sweep and wash doorsteps

6 Empty vacuum cleaner
7 Empty carpet sweeper
8 Tie up old newspapers and magazines; put out for dustmen
9 Polish any silverware, brass
10 Check solid-fuel supplies and re-order if necessary
11 Check oil level, central heating
12 Clean bird cage, goldfish tank, animal beds/mats
13 Brush and comb dog/cat
14 Clean windows inside and out
15 Clean outside drains
16 Clean and disinfect dustbin
17 Sweep backyard or entry; damp down dust

OCCASIONAL JOBS

1 De-frost and clean freezer
2 De-scale kettle, steam iron
3 Put salt in dishwasher water softener. Check rinse-aid level
4 Clean filters in washing machines and spin driers
5 Get gas water heater serviced
6 Get washing machine serviced
7 Thoroughly clean cooker/oven
8 Clean filter on cooker hood
9 Clean contact grill
10 Check pots and pans for loose handles, worn non-stick or tin linings, etc.
11 Clean inside toaster
12 Sharpen cutlery as necessary
13 Get scissors, shears, etc. re-sharpened
14 Clear and clean bookshelves. Dust and replace books
15 Clear and wash insides of cupboards and drawers. Do not wet wood too much; wipe out with vinegar-and-water solution to remove grease and dirt marks – 1 tablespoon vinegar to 600 ml. (1 pint) lukewarm water
16 Tidy sewing box, drawers
17 Remove and dust pictures and check metal wires, chains, or fittings for security and rust
18 Turn carpets to equalise wear; move stair carpet 150 mm. (6 in.)
19 Shampoo carpets
20 Send floor mats for cleaning
21 Wash or clean ironing board cover
22 Check shoes for repair
23 Turn out and clean linen store; check contents and note any replacements or repairs needed
24 Turn out and clean wardrobes; hang clothes to air while cleaning

25 Turn out old clothes for ragbag or charity
26 Clear out old medicines and return to a chemist's shop
27 Wash dustpan and household brushes, mops and cloths Re-impregnate mop heads with fresh polish if necessary
28 Check vacuum cleaner. Renew filter on cylinder model. On upright model check drive belt and brush and adjust or renew if necessary. Lightly oil wheels
29 Brush dust from intake grilles of fan heaters
30 Remove and clean light fittings; clean bulbs and tubes in position with dust mop; use foam spray for chandeliers (see p. 316)
31 Check electrical flexes and plugs for safety and security
32 Check action of door or flap stays, catches, hinges, locks or stays. Oil if necessary
33 Oil metal curtain rails
34 Check action of furniture castors; oil or renew as necessary
35 Clean sliding-door tracks
36 Check furniture, floors, wooden articles (stepladders, etc.) for damage or woodworm
37 Cream polish insides and undersides of wooden furniture to prevent warping and cracking and guard against woodworm
38 Check action of drawers and rub furniture cream on runners
39 Check taps for drips; renew washers (and funnels if any) as necessary
40 Get watches/clocks cleaned and overhauled
41 Check that burglar alarms, fire alarms are in working order
42 Check stylus of record player
43 Oil sewing machine
44 Check dates of pets' booster inoculations

OCCASIONAL JOBS FOR SPRING AND SUMMER

1 Get chimneys swept (fix date for day before rooms are cleaned)
2 Clean wall coverings
3 Wash paintwork inside and out
4 Clean cushions, loose covers, upholstery, curtains, roller and venetian blinds. Check for repairs
5 Wash or dry-clean bedspreads, quilts, blankets
6 Send any feather pillows and quilts for cleaning and to have filling renewed

7 Send electric blankets for cleaning and servicing
8 Put furs and blankets in mothproofed storage. Expensive furs should be stored by a furrier at a controlled temperature of about 4°C (40°F); alternatively, cover the fur in an old cotton sheet (not a plastic bag), to allow to breathe, and hang it in a well-used cupboard where moths are less likely to breed. Store small fur articles in a pillow case
9 Order oil or solid fuel, taking advantage of summer rates
10 Empty oil stoves; send them for servicing if necessary
11 Send rainwear for reproofing
12 Get winter coats cleaned
13 Clean and store winter sports equipment. Check for repairs

OCCASIONAL JOBS FOR AUTUMN AND WINTER

1 Check that gutters are not blocked or in need of repair
2 Oil and store garden tools
3 Get lawnmower serviced
4 Clean, store summer sports equipment. Check for repairs
5 Inspect food stores and preserves (such as apples, roots, chutney)

CHECK LIST FOR RENEWALS AND PAYMENTS

1 Building society
2 Charity covenants
3 Club and society subscriptions
4 Dog licence
5 Electricity account
6 Gas account
7 Ground rent
8 Hire-purchase payments
9 House insurance
10 Life insurance
11 Magazine subscriptions
12 MOT (now DoE) vehicle test
13 Motor insurance
14 Motoring organisation subscription
15 Mortgage account
16 Professional organisation fees
17 Rates
18 Rent
19 Season ticket
20 Telephone account
21 Television licence
22 Television rental
23 Union fees
24 Vehicle excise licence
25 Water rates

• CLEANING EQUIPMENT

Cleaning is easier if you have the right equipment. Avoid wasting money on elaborate equipment you will rarely use, but do not make do with inferior or worn out tools that increase the time and energy needed for the job.

VACUUM CLEANERS

Electrically powered vacuum cleaners are the easiest and most efficient way of getting up dirt and dust. There are three main types: upright, cylinder or globe-shaped.

Some globe-shaped models float on a cushion of air, making them easier to pull about. Small, hand-held cylinder types are also available, for jobs such as dusting.

Upright cleaners are the quickest and easiest to use on large areas of carpet, and they include a revolving brush that helps to raise the pile. Some also have built-in beaters. Most upright models have a hose attachment that can be bought as an extra.

Some models have extras such as a light for dark corners, a brush that adjusts to the carpet pile, or a filter to catch objects such as pins.

Cylinder models are easier to carry about, and are generally simpler to use on stairs and to adapt to surfaces such as hard floors or curtains. Some have extras, such as a swivel for the hose. Both cylinder and upright models may have retractable flexes and suction regulators for different thicknesses of carpet and hard surfaces.

Disposable dust bags add to expense but are cleaner to empty than permanent bags. Some disposable bags can be used more than once. Clean permanent bags by brushing them lightly; do not wash them, as this may open the weave of the fabric. If the bag on a cylinder model becomes porous, dust can damage the motor.

When buying a vacuum cleaner, check that the flex is long enough, how much noise the cleaner makes, whether it is approved by the British Electrotechnical Approvals Board (BEAB, see p. 370), and how easy it is to remove the dust bag. Make sure an upright will go under low furniture and clean right up against a wall. Check how well the attachments of a cylinder fit together, and whether they are easy to disconnect and assemble. Test the weight, especially if you will have to carry the cleaner about. Find out about servicing and repairs.

If your cleaner is not working properly, there are a few checks you can make before arranging for servicing. First, examine the plug and fuse (see p. 370). Make sure that the bag is not too full (cleaners work best with the bag less than half full). Check the brush bristles on an upright for wear. They should touch a ruler placed across the brush opening, otherwise they need adjusting, if possible, or replacing (see p. 368); check also that the drive band is all right and that nothing has jammed the fan blades.

On cylinder cleaners renew the filter regularly. A blocked hose can be cleared by fitting it to the exhaust hole (sometimes hidden by the filter and grille) and switching on. Direct the hose outdoors when you do this.

CARPET SWEEPERS

A carpet sweeper has a revolving brush that throws dirt into built-in dust pans, which are hinged at the bottom for emptying after use.

Choose a sweeper with a wide base that is low enough to be pushed under furniture, and that will clean close to a wall. On some the brush can be lowered to sweep hard floors.

CARPET SHAMPOOERS

A carpet shampooer has foam rollers (and/or brushes) that work shampoo into a carpet as the cleaner is pushed back and forth. The shampoo solution is fed to the rollers from a tank on the handle, with the flow controlled by a push button. When the carpet is dry, the residue and dirt are taken up with a vacuum cleaner.

Empty and rinse the tank after use, otherwise the distribution holes will get clogged. Clean fluff from brushes and rollers. Store by hanging.

Electric shampooers (often combined with electric polishers) can be hired on a daily basis if needed for occasional thorough cleaning.

ELECTRIC FLOOR POLISHERS

An electric floor polisher is worth buying only if there are large areas of smooth floor to be polished. The polish is applied by hand before use, although some models can be fitted with a liquid-polish dispenser.

The polisher head has two or three motor-driven brushes. Different sets are fitted on as needed. The better types have mild suction to prevent dust being ground into the surface.

BRUSHES AND MOPS

Brushes with fine, soft bristles are best for smooth, hard surfaces, and brushes with hard bristles for carpets and rough surfaces such as concrete. Bristles should be closely set in tufts, and the head well covered with tufts.

If you have a vacuum cleaner with the necessary attachments, you can probably do without a soft broom for uncarpeted floors and a soft, long-handled wall or cornice brush for ceilings and picture rails. A stiff yard broom may still be necessary, as well as a dustpan and hand-held brushes, a scrubbing brush, and a lavatory brush. Houses with open fires also need a soft hearth brush and a flue brush. In the kitchen, pan, bottle and spout brushes are useful.

Shake sweeping brushes well after use to remove clinging dust. Store all brushes by hanging. Do not leave them resting on their bristles. Occasionally, wash brushes in warm, mildly soapy water; add disinfectant for lavatory brushes. If brushes with natural bristles (not man-made, such as nylon) have been used for wax polishing, add washing soda to remove grease – 1 tablespoon to 2 litres ($\frac{1}{2}$ gallon) of water.

Wash brushes by beating the head up and down on the water surface, so that water reaches well into the bristle tufts. Rinse in the same way in cold water. Shake well and dry with bristles downwards to prevent water collecting at their bases.

Dusting mops with heads of twisted yarn, feather, or man-made fibre are useful for light dusting and awkward surfaces; long-handled ones can be used for out-of-reach places such as picture rails. For floor dusting there are long-handled mops with hinged heads fitted with removable, washable pads. Both floor and dusting mops are available with heads impregnated with siliconised oil to pick up dust easily and polish and preserve surfaces. Heads can be re-impregnated after washing.

Shake mops well outdoors after use and wash them occasionally in warm, soapy water. Rinse well and dry.

The easiest way to wash a hard floor is with a long-handled cellulose-sponge mop with a replaceable, lever-controlled head, hinged for wringing. Short-handled sponge mops are available for cleaning windows (although not as effective as a rubber mop or a chamois leather) and washing up; dish mops may also have cotton heads. Make sure the head of a dish mop is securely fixed and that the handle is not poking through. Never use disinfectant or bleach with a cellulose-sponge head. Wash and rinse sponge heads after use, and wring and dry well. Store by hanging.

CLOTHS AND LEATHERS

Dusters should have a plain, unraised surface, so are usually made from cotton, or cotton and rayon mixture. Polishing cloths need to have a fleecy, napped surface.

Floor cloths need to be tough and absorbent, dish cloths soft and absorbent. Both are available as disposable cloths (such as J-Cloths), which can be used more than once; some can be machine-washed. There are also sponge cloths that can be used for dishes.

Always rinse and wring washing cloths well after each use. Wash all cloths and dusters regularly; boil or bleach cotton cloths occasionally.

Chamois leathers for cleaning windows and flat glass surfaces are expensive but hardwearing. Cheaper but less hardwearing man-made leathers are also available. Chamois leathers are flexible when wet, leave no lint on a glass surface, and are more absorbent than sponges or cloths. (See also pp. 320, 325.)

A good supply of cotton drying cloths for china, cutlery and kitchenware is essential. To give glasses a good shine use a linen glass cloth.

BUCKETS, BOWLS AND LADDERS

At least one 8 litre (2 gallon) bucket in which to carry water for cleaning is needed in the home. Plastic buckets and washing-up bowls are light to use and less likely to damage surfaces than metal ones.

A step-ladder with five steps is generally suitable for most jobs in the home. Make sure it is sturdy and stable, and easy to store. It should have a platform on which to place a bucket, and non-skid steps and feet.

• WAYS OF CUTTING DOWN CLEANING

The way a room is planned and furnished can help to minimise the cleaning needed. Choose colours and textures that do not show the dirt.

Choose furniture that is easy to move or clean under, and has a surface that needs no polishing. Above all, choose simply shaped furnishings that do not contain dust traps. Some of the worst dust traps are in light fittings and ornaments, and ledges and struts in furniture.

Wooden floors are easier to clean if they are sealed with clear polyurethane lacquer (see p. 50). But keep uncarpeted floors to a minimum; it is quicker to vacuum a carpet than brush and mop a smooth floor, even if it is plastic-coated.

Where possible, choose soft furnishing fabrics and blankets that can be put in the washing machine. Loose covers made from fabric such as Dralon can be replaced while still slightly damp so that they dry smooth and need no ironing.

To simplify dusting, avoid having too many ornaments. They are awkward to clean round, and moving them out of the way takes time. Large, self-closing ashtrays are tidy and do not need frequent emptying. Simplify bed making by using duvets (see p. 154) and fitted under-sheets. Cut out drying-up with a tea towel by rinsing dishes after washing and leaving them to drain in a rack. Choose a cooker with an easily cleaned hob. Gas or electric fires, or an overnight-burning stove, make less work than open fires.

If you have pets, cut down cleaning by taking protective measures where possible. Guard against animal hairs, for example, by keeping a washable cover, such as an old towel, over a pet's favourite chair.

CLEANING AND PROTECTIVE AGENTS

AGENT	DESCRIPTION AND USE	SOME BRANDS
Before using a cleaning agent, always read the manufacturer's instructions; even for an apparently familiar brand, changes in the formula may require a new technique. Note whether the product is inflammable, dangerous to the skin or eyes, or poisonous, and take the precautions necessary. Examples of some common brands are given, but for most products there are many others, including supermarket 'own brands'.		
Abrasive cleaner	For removing stubborn grease and dirt from hard surfaces if detergent will not do so; can be used diluted for some floors. All types clean by rubbing away a surface – powders are harshest abrasives, liquids mildest. See p. 324 for vitreous enamel	Ajax, Vim (powders); Gumption, Chemico (pastes); Jif, Liquid Gumption, Ajax Cream (liquids).
Air freshener	For keeping sick rooms, lavatories, etc., sweet smelling.	Airwick, Racalet, Astral, Haze, Glade
Bath cleaner	Mild abrasive cleaners mostly designed for vitreous enamel baths, and not suitable for plastic baths unless stated on packet. *For plastic baths:* Shimmer, Plasheen	Jif, Cleen-o-Pine, Bathbrite, Sprinkle.
Bath-stain remover	For removing stains caused by drips, hard water; or rust from baths, sinks, lavatory pans.	Jenolite Bath Stain Remover, Polyclens Plus, Renubath RB 70
Bleach	Liquid household bleach is chlorine bleach. Use undiluted or diluted, as instructed on the container, for cleaning and disinfecting drains, lavatories, etc., and for bleaching fabrics during laundering (see p. 333).	Brobat, Domestos, Parozone
Blacklead	Polish for cast-iron grates/stoves.	Zebrite
Carpet cleaner	Liquid or spray shampoos. Liquids have to be diluted and can be used in shampooers.	Bissell, Sabco, Betterwear, Glory, Fab Clean, 1001
China/glassware stain remover	For removing stains from china, glass and melamine ware.	Chempro T, Stainfree
Detergent	A detergent is any surface cleaner, such as soap, but the term is now usually applied to synthetic detergents.	Flash (floors, etc.), Daz, Tide, Persil, Fairy Liquid (washing-up)
Dishwasher powder	Low-foaming powders for use in electric dishwashers.	Sun, Freedom, Focus, Hygleam, Colston
Disinfectant	For killing or checking the growth of bacteria. Some are poisonous and should not be allowed to contact the skin.	Jeyes Fluid, Parador, Pynol, Scentol, Mistral, 3-Hands, Ibcol, Jeypine, Sanpic, Dettol, Lifeguard
Drain cleaner	For putting down drains to clear blockages. Harmful if used carelessly; caustic soda can burn.	Caustic Soda (Boots, Kleenoff, Mangers), Clearway, Drainfree
Dustbin powder	A disinfectant and insecticide powder for sprinkling in dustbins.	Bingard, Keating's, Jeyes, Zal Pinefresh

CLEANING AND PROTECTIVE AGENTS (CONTINUED)

AGENT	DESCRIPTION AND USE	SOME BRANDS
Fabric cleaner	For cleaning fabrics, shoes, handbags, etc. See also Suede cleaner, Upholstery cleaner.	Meltonian Denim Cleaner; Radium Suede/Fabric Shampoo
Fabric protector	A silicone coating for spraying on clean, colourfast fabrics to repel water and grease stains.	Miss Dylon Rain and Stain Repellent, Scotchgard
Fabric retexturiser	Spray containing ingredients to add body and feel to fabrics (not very dark colours) when ironing.	Fabulon
Fabric softener/ conditioner	For making laundered fabrics soft and easier to iron. It reduces the static electricity that causes synthetic fabrics to cling and crackle. Added to final rinse.	Lenor, Comfort, Softlan
Floor polish	Polishes are either spirit based or water based. Spirit-based polishes need to be rubbed in, water-based ones leave a shiny film as they dry. Cleaner/polishers are self-shine polishes with detergent added. Self-shine polishes need applying about every six weeks (floors can be wiped in between); occasionally old polish has to be stripped off and a fresh start made; see Polish stripper.	*Spirit based:* Mansion Wax, Mansion Guard Shine, Goddard's Silicone Wax, Johnson Beautiflor, Ronuk, Lavendo, Cardinal (for unglazed quarry tiles, brick, cement). *Self-shine:* Seel, Goddard's, Novashield, Marley Clearseal, Cardinal (tiles, etc.); Dual (cleaner/polisher)
Furniture blemish remover	For removing scratches or heat and water stains from furniture.	Topps Scratch Cover, Ringaway
Furniture cleaner	For removing old wax and dirt.	Antiquax Furniture Cleaner
Furniture polish	Polishes are mainly wax pastes, creams or liquid sprays. Wax pastes need plenty of rubbing in and are best suited to antiques. Creams and sprays need only light rubbing and some can also be used for cleaning other surfaces such as glass and paintwork. For matt and oil finishes use oils and creams that do not shine. Many sprays clean as well as polish, and are intended mainly for hard modern finishes that do not absorb polish.	Antiquax, Mansion Wax, Goddard's Cabinet Maker's Wax, Johnson's Wax, Rentokil Wax (pastes); Stephenson's, Enriched Min, Pride (creams); Rentokil Teak Oil, Wood Care (for matt or oil finishes); Topps Original, Liquid Gold, Favor (sprays); Pledge, Mr Sheen, Mansion One-Two (multi-purpose sprays)
Glass cleaner	For cleaning windows, mirrors, tiles, flat glass. Aerosol foam, which clears without being wiped, can be used for chandeliers.	Ajax Window Cleaner, Miraglo, 1001, Winfield, Sparkle, Windolene; Sparkle-Plenty (foam)
Hand cleaner/protector	Barrier creams are rubbed into the hands while clean to protect them from grime. Other cleaners remove grime from dirty hands.	Savlon Barrier Cream, Swarfega, Duckhams, Dabs; Perox-Chlor (to scrub into grimy nails)

CLEANING AND PROTECTIVE AGENTS (CONTINUED)

AGENT	DESCRIPTION AND USE	SOME BRANDS
Hide food	For preserving, conditioning and cleaning hide upholstery, etc.	Connolly's Hide Food, Orkin Leather Food
Iron cleaner	For cleaning the base (soleplate) of irons (not a non-stick finish).	Vilene
Jewellery cleaner	For cleaning jewellery settings. Not all clean silver; always check.	Goddard's Jewellery Care Kit
Kettle de-scaler	For removing scale (furring) from elements of kettles, steam irons. Check before using in enamel ware. For some automatic kettles, use only citric acid.	Descalite, Kay-Dee, Ketlone, Cleanix, Borite JIDS, Albright Scale Away, Cadnit Kettle Fur Collector
Lavatory cleaner	Powders or blocks which contain bleach and disinfectant; blocks also contain detergent and are hung in cistern or pan. For stains, see Bath-stain remover.	Dot, Sanilav, Harpic (powders); Aquasan, Lu Blue, Flush Kleen, Racapan, Astral, Sani-Flush (blocks)
Leather polish	For cleaning and polishing leather shoes, luggage, etc. Polishes may include dyes for re-colouring, some have extra dye to hide scuff marks. A few are self-shine and need no rubbing in. Multi-purpose polishes clean, polish and give a water-resistant film; some can be used on all leathers. Use special polishes for white leather, aniline calf, soft leathers (kid and glove calf) and patent or wet-look leather.	Wren, Cherry Blossom, Kiwax (pastes); Meltonian, Tuxan All-purpose (creams); Kiwi Crown (self shine); Kids Stuff, Kiwi Guard (to hide scuff marks); Leather Groom (multi-purpose). Special types: Glo Calf (for soft and pearlised); Meltonian Antique or Aniline cream; Punch Patent or Wet Look
Leather protector	To rub or spray on leather after polishing to repel water.	Wren's Dubbin, Meltonian Waterstop
Leather soap	For occasional cleaning to keep leather soft and supple. Not suitable for aniline calf.	Propert's Saddle Soap, Meltonian Glycerine Soap
Leather softener	For rubbing into heavy leathers to prevent hardening, cracking.	Wren's Leather Oil, Propert's Neatsfoot Oil
Metal cleaner	Foam cleaner/polishers can be used for cutlery. Chemical dips are for cleaning tarnished silver.	Goddard's Town Talk (foam cleanser); Goddard's Silver Dip
Metal polish	All contain an abrasive – harsh for hard metals and milder for soft metals. Long-term or tarnish-inhibiting polishes also give a temporary protective finish.	Soft metals: Town Talk Silver/Chrome, Silvo. Hard metals: Bluebell, Brasso, Goddard's Glow, Hi Sheen, Polaris
Multi-purpose cleaner	For cleaning a range of household surfaces such as cookers, lino. Some can be used for laundry. Many are abrasive cleaners.	Flash, Jonquel, Handy Andy, Chemico GP, Jif, Scrubbs Cloudy Ammonia, Mr Sheen
Oven cleaner	For shifting burnt-on grease from oven interiors (see p. 325).	Force, Mansion Oven Pad, Kleenoff, Stovoid

CLEANING AND PROTECTIVE AGENTS (CONTINUED)

AGENT	DESCRIPTION AND USE	SOME BRANDS
Paintwork cleaner	Mild detergent or multi-purpose cleaners can be used; abrasive cleaners can be used diluted on stubborn marks. Sugar soap is for use before repainting.	Flash, Jonquel, Jif, Scrubbs Cloudy Ammonia, Mr Sheen, Sparkle, Manger's Sugar Soap
Polish stripper	For removing the build up of self-shine polish from floors.	Marley Floor Cleaner, Klear
Rust/scale inhibitor	For placing in the cold-water tank to prevent scaling in the hot-water system, or in the central-heating header tank to prevent corrosion.	Micromet (for hot-water system); Protec (for central-heating system)
Scouring pads	For cleaning badly soiled oven interiors, pans, etc. Plastic or fabric pads are gentler than soap-impregnated steel wool.	Brillo soap pads, Ajax pan shiners (steel wool); Brobat, Cadnit (plastic); Golden Fleece (fabric)
Shoe cleaners	See Fabric cleaner, Leather polish, Suede cleaner.	
Soap (household)	For general cleaning and rubbing fabrics before machine-washing.	Fairy, Lifeguard, Sunlight
Stain removers	See p. 326	
Starch	Sprays or powders for stiffening fabrics; applied before ironing.	Robin, Goddards, Easy-On, Scentinel
Sterilising agent	For sterilising bottles, jars and high-density plastic equipment.	Milton, Chempro SDP
Suede/leather stain removers	For removing water, dirt or grease stains from suede or leather shoes (not clothing). Stubborn stains may need grease-and-tar remover.	Lady Esquire Cleaner, Meltonian Stain Remover, Mel Grease and Tar Remover
Suede and leather protector	For spraying on clothing, shoes, etc., to protect against water and non-greasy stains.	Meltonian, Scotchgard, Miss Dylon, Swade Guard, Kiwi Wetpruf
Suede cleaner/ shampoo	Sprays or impregnated cloths or blocks for cleaning suede, sheepskin and brushed pigskin.	Meltonian, Lady Esquire, Miss Dylon, Swade Groom; Swade Aid
Suede dressing	For reviving colour of suede shoes. Do not use on clothing.	Meltonian
Upholstery cleaner	For cleaning upholstered furniture, cushions, etc.	Bissell Upholstery Shampoo, 1001
Washing powder	See p. 333	
Washing soda	Loosens dirt and grease; softens water. For cleaning and soaking.	ICI, Elco
Washing-up liquid	Mild detergent for hand-washing dishes, china, etc.	Fairy, Lux, Palmolive, Sqezy, Sunlight
Water softener	For adding to hard water to prevent soap scum (see p. 333).	Calgon, Aqua Softna, Boots

HOUSEHOLD STORE

A supply of cleaning materials and spares, such as light bulbs, is essential for a smoothly run home. A check list of some things to include is given below.

A central store place near the cleaning-equipment cupboard can be used for storing some articles, but things in use and some spares are best kept near to the place of use. Keep an emergency-repair kit securely fixed to and at hand, and check that it is stocked with spares such as fuse wire (see pp. 352-3).

A store cupboard should be dry, cool and well ventilated so that things keep in good condition as long as possible.

Keep the lids of fluids such as methylated spirit securely fixed to minimise evaporation. Do not store batteries near radiators or boilers – the storage temperature should be 10-25°C (50-77°F).

Things not stored in their original containers should be clearly labelled. Keep dangerous substances locked up out of a child's reach.

Abrasive cleaner
Adhesive tape
Air freshener
Bath cleaner
Batteries (torch, radio, etc.)
Bin bags/liners
Bleach
Candles/nightlights
Carpet cleaner
Cloths, disposable
Dishwashing-machine powder/rinse aid
Disinfectant
Dry-cleaning fluid
Dustbin powder
Floor cleaner/polish
Furniture polish
Hand cleaner
Lavatory cleaner
Light bulbs/tubes
Matches
Metal cleaner/polish
Methylated spirit
Multi-purpose cleaner
Oil (light machine)
Paper towel
Pesticides
Rubber gloves
Scouring pads
Shoe polish
Soap, household/toilet
String
Toilet paper
Vacuum-cleaner bags
Washing powder/liquid
Washing soda
Washing-up liquid
Window/glass cleaner
Wrapping paper

317

HOW TO CLEAN AND CARE FOR THINGS

Proper care and cleaning will add to the life and usefulness of materials and articles in your home. Products today are manufactured from a wide variety of materials, and a suitable way of cleaning one material may prove damaging for another. Old-fashioned scrubbing and scouring is likely to be bad for some products. The trend is for manufacturers to design articles using materials that make cleaning easier – self-cleaning ovens, for example, and furniture that needs only a wipe with a damp cloth rather than vigorous polishing. When you buy an article, always find out how it should be cleaned and looked after. If there are no directions, or if those given are not clear, check with the manufacturer.

• CARE AND CLEANING OF HARD FLOORS

Floors need more regular attention than any other part of the house. Without frequent sweeping or vacuum cleaning they quickly become dulled by ground-in dirt which then makes them more difficult to clean. When choosing new flooring, consider its practical qualities as well as its appearance.

Shiny floors are more resistant to dirt, but if polished too highly they can be dangerous to walk on. Never polish the floor under rugs.

Unsealed wooden floors need monthly waxing or oiling, although parts that take most wear may need more frequent attention. Wooden and cork floors (see pp. 33 and 35) can be sealed with a varnish or polyurethane sealer which need only be cleaned with a damp mop.

Sweep the floor carefully before polishing, and remove or hammer in any protruding nails which could damage mops or polishing equipment. After polishing, untangle fluff and hair from brushes and pads, and remove excess polish from cloths with spirit solvent or by washing them in hot, soapy water. Rinse and dry before storing.

• CARPET CARE AND CLEANING

Most new carpets shed fluff for the first few weeks. During this time they should be lightly cleaned with a hand brush or carpet sweeper. Cut off any tufts that stand up from the surface, do not pull them out.

After the first month, clean with a vacuum cleaner at least once a week, always making the last stroke in the direction of the pile, so that it lies flat.

To even out wear on the carpet, move furniture round occasionally so that indented pile can be brushed up. Parts that receive heavier wear, such as in front of a door or settee, can be protected by rugs. Avoid dragging heavy furniture over carpets as this damages the fibres.

Static electricity can be a problem in a centrally heated room that has carpets containing man-made fibres. It is caused by the combination of dry air and friction as people walk over the carpet. Carpet manufacturers are developing methods to counteract static. The householder can reduce it by installing humidifiers or keeping bowls of water and plants in the room.

HOME SHAMPOOING

It is possible to clean a carpet yourself with a carpet shampoo, but make sure the instructions are followed, and do not over-wet the carpet. There are several brands of wet shampoo on the market and some manufacturers produce their own hand applicators. Try to get the shampoo recommended by the carpet manufacturer.

The safest wet shampoo for home cleaning is dry foam, which is mixed with water and applied with a carpet shampooer. It absorbs dust and dries as crystals, which can then be removed with a vacuum cleaner. An aerosol type is also available; this dries faster, but is more expensive.

If a carpet shampooer is not available, or if the carpet is badly soiled, apply the shampoo with a cloth, sponge or brush, using a circular movement. Dilute the shampoo according to the maker's instructions. Electrically operated carpet shampooers can be hired from hardware shops, hire companies, dry cleaners and carpet shops.

When using a carpet shampoo, make sure the carpet is thoroughly dry before vacuuming. If heavy furniture has to be moved back before the carpet is completely dry, place foil under the feet to protect the carpet.

PROFESSIONAL CLEANING

Some professionals clean carpets in the home. Otherwise carpets must be sent away, a process which takes at least a week. It is better not to send fitted carpets away as there is a risk of slight shrinkage. Local carpet cleaners or agents of nationwide cleaners are usually listed in the telephone directory Yellow Pages. Many belong to the Carpet Cleaners' Association, which sets standards for work.

DYEING

A carpet that is faded or marked can be given new life by dyeing, but it is a job best left to the professional carpet dyer. Dyeing will not obliterate patterns or bad stains.

Most carpet-cleaning companies provide a dyeing service, but it is only worth the expense if there is still quite a lot of wear in the carpet.

Home dyeing can be successful if the carpet is dyed a darker shade of the original colour. Avoid using a colour which will combine with the original shade to form another colour (see Dyeing at home, p. 334).

If possible, test the colour on a spare piece of carpet or on a patch which will be covered by furniture. If the carpet is dirty, clean it before dyeing. Follow the dye manufacturer's instructions carefully. Home dyeing is not suitable for some carpets, particularly foam-backed types.

• CLEANING WALL COVERINGS

Before cleaning walls, remove any pictures, mirrors or ornaments. Push the furniture to the middle of the room and cover it. First wipe down the walls, with a cloth-covered brush or broom, or a vacuum cleaner attachment. Remove cobwebs and dust threads by dusting from the bottom up.

When washing painted walls or washable coverings, again work from the bottom up. If dirty water runs down a dry area of the painted wall or wallpaper, the streak may be difficult to remove. Wring out a sponge or cloth as dry as possible and clean a small area – about 60 cm. (2 ft) square; work in a circular movement. Wipe the washed area dry with a sponge wrung out in clear water, working from the top down. Move to the adjoining area, overlapping with the area just cleaned.

If you are uncertain whether the wallpaper is washable, rub a small area with a sponge wrung out in lukewarm water. Do not over-wet.

To remove stains and grease from wall coverings, see chart opposite.

FABRIC WALL COVERINGS

Clean fabrics according to the manufacturer's instructions. Do not use dry-cleaning fluids or upholstery cleaners, because these can cause discoloration and shrinkage.

CLEANING HARD FLOORING

TYPE	METHOD
Asphalt composition Bitumastic Mastic Pitchmastic Semastic Thermoplastic	Daily sweep and damp-mop. Occasionally apply self-shine polish. Never use wax polishes as the spirit in them will damage the surface. Remove marks by rubbing lightly with wire wool; then wipe over with sponge wrung out in warm water, and polish
Cement Concrete Clay tiles, quarry tiles Brick, stone	Sweep or dry-mop daily. Periodically wash or scrub with detergent suds. May be sealed to make the floor non-slip and resistant to dust, oil, water and grease. Polish quarry tiles with liquid tile polish, or self-shine tile polish
Glazed tiles, terrazzo	Sweep or dry-mop daily or wipe down with mild detergent solution. Avoid all abrasive cleaners
Cork	Daily sweep or damp-mop. Wax polish periodically. If sealed, use self-shine polish occasionally
Linoleum	Daily sweep or dry-mop, or wipe with cloth wrung out in warm water and detergent. Polish with wax or self-shine polish, or use combination cleaner/polisher
Marble	Sweep or dry-mop daily. Wash with soft cloth wrung out in warm water and detergent. Rinse well and dry. Remove light stains with mild abrasive, lemon juice, or vinegar; rinse off and dry. Get bad stains removed professionally
Rubber	Sweep and damp-mop daily. Apply self-shine polish weekly until pores are filled and non-absorbent. Wash only when very dirty, and do not over-wet. Avoid oil or spirit-based sealants or wax polishes
Vinyl, matt PVC, vinyl asbestos, felt-back vinyl	Sweep or damp-mop daily. Wash when needed with cloth wrung out in warm, soapy water. Polish with self-shine finish or combination cleaner/polisher. Avoid oil-based sealants, spirit cleaners and solvents. To remove marks, rub gently with wire wool
Wood, wood blocks, wood mosaic, hardwood strip, plywood, parquet	Daily sweep and occasionally mop or wash. If unsealed, apply wax polish periodically. If sealed, damp-mop and buff with dry mop; use self-shine polish periodically

CLEANING CARPETS AND RUGS

TYPE	METHOD
Carpets – wool, cotton, rayon, acrylic, nylon and mixtures Carpet tiles Cord	Carpet-sweep or vacuum daily. Shampoo periodically or arrange for professional cleaning. Mop up spills immediately with a cloth damped in cold water, except for grease-based stains. (See ABC of stain removal, p. 326, for specific treatments.) Mud stains should be left until they are dry. Then brush them off
Cotton and rag rugs	Daily clean as for carpets. Cotton and rag rugs are usually washable, but if not, treat as for carpets, above
Felt	Carpet-sweep or vacuum daily using slow, smooth strokes. Shampoo periodically but do not over-wet. Get professional advice on stains
Matting – coconut (coir), reed, rush, sisal	Carpet-sweep or vacuum daily. Lift matting occasionally to clean underneath as the open weave allows dirt to fall through. Periodically refresh matting with a brush dipped in detergent suds and wipe with cloth wrung out in cold water and salt solution (1 tablespoon salt to 1 pint). Dry in the open if possible. Avoid over-wetting the matting. This may cause shrinkage
Oriental and antique rugs	Daily light carpet-sweeping or vacuum-cleaning with slow, smooth strokes. Have them professionally cleaned when necessary and always get professional advice on removing any stains: inexpert treatment could easily do severe damage to a valuable rug
Shaggy and fur rugs	Shake outdoors daily. Avoid using carpet sweeper or vacuum cleaner except occasionally on the backs of rugs. Shaggy and fur rugs should be beaten occasionally – but do not hang them over a line. Lay them face down on an old sheet and beat gently with a rattan beater. Have them professionally cleaned when it becomes necessary
Sheepskin, goatskin	Daily clean as for carpets. Shampoo periodically without wetting the backs unless they are washable. Get professional advice on stains

CLEANING WALL COVERINGS

TYPE	METHOD
Cannolux (wall carpet) Felt Flock (paper-backed) Grass cloth Hessian Jute Linen Moiré Silk	Brush down with a soft, long-handled wall brush or use a vacuum-cleaner brush attachment. To remove stains, dab lightly with white baby powder on cottonwool. Leave for a few hours. Brush off. Do not use dry-cleaning or upholstery cleaners as they can cause discoloration and shrinkage, except on Hessian Con-tact, on which water will cause shrinkage
Cork	Brush or vacuum. Sponge marks gently with lukewarm water and mild detergent. Do not over-wet
Foils, flock (vinyl-backed)	Wipe over with sponge wrung out in warm water. Do not rub flock
Leather	See Leather chart (p. 321)
Paint – emulsion	Wipe down with sponge wrung out in mild detergent solution. Rinse with cold water
Paint – silk finish, vinyl, Vymura, gloss	Wash wall from bottom upwards using a sponge wrung out in mild detergent solution; rinse with cold water, working from the top down. If necessary, scrub gloss paint with a soft brush
Polyurethane varnish	Wipe with chamois wrung out in mild detergent solution. Occasionally spray lightly with aerosol furniture polish and rub up with soft cloth
Tiles – aluminium and ceramic	Wipe down with a sponge wrung out in mild detergent solution. Rinse well. Dry with chamois. Clean grouting with soft brush dipped in bleach solution. Rinse
Tiles – mirror	Wipe down with a chamois wrung out in vinegar water (1 tablespoon vinegar to 1 pint lukewarm water)
Wallpaper – including textured and embossed	Brush or lightly vacuum. Gently sponge marks with a mild detergent solution. For grease stains, dab lightly with white baby powder on cottonwool and brush off after a few hours; or rub area gently with stale white bread
Wallpaper – washable vinyls	Wipe down with sponge wrung out in mild detergent solution
Wood panelling	Brush or vacuum and rub with soft dusters. Treat as teak (see p. 320)

• CARE AND CLEANING OF FURNITURE

Because wood is porous, furniture is protected against dirt and moisture at manufacture with a finish such as wax or french polish, oil or plastic. French polish is now used for good quality reproduction furniture only; the whole surface may need replacing if damaged. Polish and oil finishes need regular polishing or oiling to keep them clean and in good condition.

Many modern finishes are hard-wearing lacquers that need little cleaning. For cleaning plastic laminate surfaces such as melamine and PVC, see Plastics chart opposite.

Antique wood surfaces will warp and crack in heat, strong sunlight or the dry atmosphere of central heating. Use blinds or sheer curtains to filter the sunlight, and use humidifiers to keep up humidity. House plants reduce dryness in the atmosphere.

Occasionally apply furniture cream to the underside and inside of wooden furniture to preserve the wood and discourage woodworm.

• CARE AND CLEANING OF UPHOLSTERY

Most modern upholstery fabrics have labels detailing cleaning methods. File these labels for reference.

Although many fabrics are stain-resistant, it is still necessary to mop or blot a spill immediately to prevent staining. For other fabrics, see p. 326, or comments in the chart opposite.

When wet-cleaning fitted upholstery fabrics, do not over-wet the fabric because this causes some foam fillings to break down. Dry-cleaning solvents can have the same effect if over-used. Mixed kapok fillings can cause staining if they become wet.

Use a hand hair-drier to speed the drying of the fabric – but do not scorch it by holding the drier too close. Clean upholstery surfaces and corners regularly with the vacuum-cleaner upholstery brush.

• CLEANING AND CARING FOR PLASTICS

Two main types of plastic are used in the home. Thermoplastic (soft plastic) softens when exposed to heat and hardens again when cool. Thermosetting (hard) plastics are moulded by heat and pressure and do not usually soften when they are reheated.

For normal cleaning, wipe or wash plastics with a soft cloth and soapy water or a mild detergent solution. Rinse and leave to dry. Never rub them with a dry cloth, as this increases their static electricity and makes them more likely to attract dust. Most thermoplastics can be damaged by nail varnish, dry-cleaning fluids and other solvents, especially if left in prolonged contact.

Many plastic surfaces will stain unless spills are wiped up quickly. Remove stains with a mild paste cleaner or a damp cloth dipped in bicarbonate of soda.

• HOW TO CLEAN AND CARE FOR LEATHER

The basic equipment for all leather cleaning is two soft brushes – one to remove surface dust and dirt, the other to apply polish – and a soft cloth or velvet pad to buff the polish.

Dust leather upholstery regularly, and periodically use a special hide cleaner. Clean soiled leather with saddle or leather soap. Rub a damp sponge across the soap and apply to the leather, working the lather well into the surface. Wipe off surplus lather with a clean, almost dry, sponge, and polish when dry with a hide polish.

Never try to clean or remove stains from leather with dry-cleaning fluid, petrol, ammonia or detergent.

CARE AND CLEANING OF FURNITURE

TYPE	METHOD	TYPE	METHOD
Antique wood	Dust and rub as needed. Remove greasy marks with a chamois wrung out in vinegar water (1 tablespoon vinegar to 1 pint water). Dry well and polish with wax paste. To remove water or heat marks, rub lightly with metal polish along the grain, then repolish the surface with wax polish	Marble	See Hard floors chart, p. 319
Bamboo	Clean with a brush or vacuum cleaner. Wash with detergent suds, rinse and dry. Polish with furniture cream. Occasionally rub in linseed oil to prevent dryness	Marquetry Inlay	Dust and rub as needed. Lightly polish with wax paste. Never wash, and avoid catching the edges of the strips when cleaning
Cane Rush Wickerwork	Dust or brush as needed. Wash or lightly scrub with warm salt water, which helps to stiffen, bleach and remove stains from cane. Do not over-wet. Dry in the open air if possible	Mother of pearl Imitation tortoiseshell	Dust. Wipe with chamois wrung out in tepid soapy water. Rinse and dry. Do not over-wet
Deal Painted furniture (modern)	Wipe (or scrub deal) with hot detergent suds. Rinse and wipe dry. Polish paint with silicone cream or spray	Oak – fumed, limed	Dust. Clean with chamois wrung out in vinegar water. Dry and polish with furniture cream
Ebony	Dust and rub. Periodically polish with furniture cream. Never wash	Oak – waxed Mahogany, Pine, Walnut, Beech, Elm	Dust and rub. Polish periodically with light-coloured wax polish
French polish	Dust and rub as needed. Clean if necessary with chamois wrung out in vinegar water. Dry well and polish with furniture cream or wax polish. Remove superficial heat marks by rubbing french-polish reviver along the grain. Mop up alcohol spills at once. (To restore surface, see p. 114)	Ormolu	Dust or brush gently. Wash sticky parts with vinegar water. Rinse, dry and buff. To remove tarnish, brush gently with soapy water containing a few drops of ammonia (cover woodwork). Rinse, dry and rub. Never use metal polish or lacquer
Garden furniture (cedar, hardwoods)	Remove marks with steel wool, rubbing along the grain. Treat with exterior-grade wood preservative	Papier mâché	Dust as needed. Wipe with cloth wrung out in warm, soapy water. Do not over-wet. Dry and polish with wax paste
Gilt	Dust as needed. Clean by wiping with a cloth lightly dipped in warm turpentine (stand it in a bowl of hot water) or white spirit. Remove stains by rubbing gently with a cut raw onion. Dry and buff	Parchment Vellum	Dust as needed. Wipe with clean cloth moistened with olive oil, or rub with proprietary paper cleaner (available from art shops)
		Teak Afrormosia	Dust as needed. Periodically apply teak oil or cream and rub in. Never use wax polishes
Ivory Bone Horn	Dust and rub. Remove marks with a soft cloth lightly dampened with methylated spirit. Never wash	Tortoiseshell (real)	Dust. Periodically rub in a few drops of olive oil on a soft cloth. Leave several minutes, rub off, buff
Lacquered finish Japanned	Dust as needed. Remove fingermarks with a damp chamois and rub with a soft duster. Polish a glossy surface with cream or spray polish occasionally	Veneer	Treat according to the type of wood. Mop up water spills at once. To reset bubbled veneer, press with a hot iron over several layers of blotting paper or ordinary brown paper
		Whitewood Plywood	Dust, then wipe with chamois wrung out in warm water. Rinse with cold water and dry. Remove stains by rubbing gently with fine wire wool along the grain. Avoid harsh scrubbing, hot water and strong abrasives. Remove small dents by pressing with a hot iron over several layers of damp blotting paper

CARE AND CLEANING OF UPHOLSTERY

TYPE	METHOD
Cotton Linen Wool Cotton, linen and wool mixtures	Fitted covers: remove surface dust and clean with dry foam upholstery shampoo. Loose covers: wash according to material (see p. 330) or maker's instructions. Treat stains before washing (see p. 326)
Dralon (acrylic fibre)	Fitted covers: remove surface dust with stiff brush or vacuum cleaner; apply dry foam shampoo with a sponge and remove with a vacuum cleaner. Loose covers: wash in soap or detergent solution at temperatures up to 30°C (86°F)
Dralon velvet	Clean fitted covers in the same way as Dralon, but be very careful not to over-wet. Loose covers must be dry-cleaned; washing may cause the cotton backing to shrink
Evlan Scandair	Remove surface dust; clean with dry foam upholstery shampoo
Hide-leather	See Leather chart
Horsehair	Brush with a stiff brush. Use dry-cleaning fluid on grease stains
Leather cloth, Vinyl-simulated hide Rexine Plastics	Wipe regularly with damp, soapy cloth. To remove stains, scrub gently with soft brush, rinse with cold water and dry. Do not use strong detergents, solvents, wax polish and cleaners
Modacrylic (flameproof)	This fabric can be dry-cleaned, but warn the dry-cleaner that it is heat sensitive. Loose covers: short machine wash at a temperature not over 40°C (104°F). Cold rinse. Do not wring. Drip-dry after a short spin. Press with a cool iron
Tapestry Gros point	Have these fabrics cleaned professionally. Remove small stains with dry-cleaning fluid (see p. 326)
Taffeta, Twill, Repp, Moiré, etc	Clean according to fabric; see Fabrics chart, pp. 292-5
Velvet, Velveteen	Remove surface dust with stiff brush or vacuum cleaner. Get cleaning done professionally
Water-repellent fabrics	Dry-clean or follow manufacturer's instructions. Blot wet spills immediately without rubbing

CARE AND CLEANING OF PLASTICS

THERMOPLASTICS

TYPE	METHOD
ABS (refrigerator parts, utensils, tool handles, radio cases)	Normal cleaning (see text, left); avoid abrasives
Acrylics (baths, basins, shower trays, light fittings, furniture, clear and opaque partitions)	Normal cleaning (see text, left). Use a mild abrasive cleaner (see p. 316) when necessary only on sinks, basins and baths. Rub scratches with liquid metal polish
Nylon (furniture, some utensils, curtain rails and fittings). Acetal (taps, door handles) Polycarbonate (bowls, kitchen appliances)	Normal cleaning (see text, left). Avoid abrasives. Will withstand boiling water
Polyethylene, Polythene (flexible ice-cube trays, buckets, tumblers, trays, dishes, washing-up bowls, bottles, colanders, food bags, cisterns, furniture)	Normal cleaning (see text, left). Do not use articles over a flame or in a hot oven
Polypropylene (packaging film and sheeting, sterilisable bottles, washing-machine tubs, hinges, furniture, tool handles)	Normal cleaning (see text, left). Avoid abrasives. Will withstand normal refrigeration and temperatures up to 100°C (212°F)
Polystyrene (high-impact polystyrene is used for kitchen items, doors, wall tiles, bathroom units, furniture, refrigerator containers. Expanded polystyrene is used for insulation, ceiling tiles, packaging)	Normal cleaning (see text, left). Avoid abrasives, grease solvents and boiling water. Will withstand normal refrigeration. High-impact polystyrene is tough, but will crack under severe impact or excessive flexing
Vinyl and PVC (raincoats, bags, shower curtains, upholstery, curtains, wall and floor coverings, kitchen and shower units, furniture, veneers, drawers, skirtings, cold-water pipes and fittings, venetian blinds)	Normal cleaning (see text, left). Avoid abrasives, concentrated detergents, grease solvents and wax polishes. Vinyls are resistant to common chemicals, oils, foods and water. Lightly buff PVC fittings – such as venetian blinds – with silicone cream to keep down dust

THERMOSETTING PLASTICS

TYPE	METHOD
Amino decorative laminates (table and work tops, furniture veneers)	Normal cleaning (see text, left). Avoid abrasives and do not polish. Never slice or chop food directly on a laminate surface. It can also be damaged by direct contact with hot dishes, irons, lighted cigarettes
Melamine formaldehyde, urea formaldehyde, phenol formaldehyde, glass-reinforced polyester, polyester mouldings (tableware, buttons, stove knobs and handles, electrical fittings, door furniture, toilet seats, etc.)	Normal cleaning (see text, left). Melamine tableware should not be used over a flame, in the oven, or put in a dishwasher

CARE AND CLEANING OF LEATHER

TYPE	METHOD
Alligator Crocodile Snake	Remove mud and dust with a soft brush, apply neutral shoe cream or tinted aniline calf cream
Buckskin Doeskin	Remove dust and mud with a soft brush. Apply white cleaner and allow to dry. Brush the surface lightly to roughen it if desired
Calf – aniline, antique or shadow	Remove dust and mud with soft brush. Use cream polish for lightweight calf and wax polish for heavier weight. For aniline and shadow calf use the special creams and cleaners available. Buff with a cloth or pad
Chamois	Wash in a solution of soap flakes and warm water. Squeeze gently but do not rinse out soap (which helps keep the leather soft) unless the chamois is to be used for window cleaning. Pull into shape and hang up to dry. When dry, rub between hands to soften
Goat skin	Wipe with a cloth wrung out in a warm glycerine and soap solution; apply hide cream while still damp
Hide upholstery/luggage	Dust as needed. Periodically, clean with leather soap (see text, left) before polishing with hide cleaner. Do not polish lacquered (shiny) hide; treat as simulated hide (see Upholstery chart)
Kid-glacé kid Glove calf	Remove dust and mud with a soft brush. Apply special kid cleaner and buff. Wash gloves on the hand with cream glove shampoo
Morocco	Rub with soft dusters. Occasionally apply silicone furniture cream and buff. To remove damp spots, lightly rub with methylated spirit; repolish
Patent Wet-look	Remove dust and dirt with a soft cloth (take care not to scratch surface). Apply patent-leather dressing or a wet-look spray; buff
Pearlised	Remove dust and dirt with a soft cloth. Take care not to rub in dirt. Apply pearlised leather polish or colourless aniline cream and buff
Suede, Pig skin, Sheepskin	See Looking after your wardrobe, p. 323; also (for sheepskin) Carpet chart, p. 319

STAFFORDSHIRE FIGURES

Staffordshire pottery figures – ranging from dull earthenware to fine porcelain – were very popular as chimney-piece ornaments in the second half of the 19th century. They were cast from moulds of original clay models made by local men, women and children.

Many figures were painted in bright colours and richly gilded. Early models were almost completely in the round, but after 1840 they became almost completely flat-backed. Subjects included royalty, heroes of the Crimean War, notorious villains, sportsmen, actors and writers.

Named figures of good quality are generally the most expensive. The value of untitled figures tends to increase once they have been identified. There are hundreds for whom the original model is unknown; trying to establish their identity is one of the attractions of collecting these figures.

The figure illustrated above is Queen Victoria on Horseback. The illustrations below include two Crimean War models – Marshal Arnaud (top left), and a naval gun crew usually referred to as The Rammers (bottom centre).

• CARE OF CHINA, EARTHEN-WARE AND GLASS

Hand-wash valuable or hand-painted china and earthenware separately in hot water and mild detergent in a plastic bowl. Do not pour very hot water over them, and do not use abrasives as they can damage and scar the surface. Use a soft brush to clean the crevices of ornaments and figurines. Rinse in clear, warm water.

Rinse crockery as soon as possible after use, especially if it has contained vinegar, salt, lemon juice or wine. Wipe away tea or coffee stains with a damp cloth dipped in bicarbonate of soda or borax and rinse. When machine-washing, avoid using too much detergent.

Hand-wash valuable pieces of glass separately, to avoid chipping. Rinse in warm water and drain upright (not on their delicate rims). Dry with a linen glass cloth. Clean engraved glass gently with a soft brush and drain on a soft towel.

• CARE AND CLEANING OF JEWELLERY

Store pieces of valuable jewellery separately, as hard stones such as diamonds can scratch other stones like pearls and opals. If a jewellery case does not have separate compartments, wrap gems individually in tissue or place them in small, chamois leather bags.

Take valuable antique jewellery for an occasional professional check on the clasps, settings and threading, and for insurance valuation. There is a percentage fee for valuation.

Clean jewellery regularly, as dirt on stones and mountings detracts from its appearance. Wash it in a bowl, never in the sink where small items can be lost down the wastepipe. Do not leave necklaces to soak, as the threading will be weakened.

CARE OF CHINA, EARTHENWARE, AND GLASS

TYPE	METHOD
Black basalt	Hand-wash in warm water and mild detergent
Bone china	Hand-wash antiques and all pieces not labelled as suitable for machine-washing
Borosilicate	See Ovenproof ware
Cut glass	Hand or machine-wash. Use a soft brush if necessary when hand-washing
Earthenware	Wash by hand or machine
English translucent china	Wash by hand or machine
Jasper	Hand-wash in water and mild detergent
Lead crystal glass	Hand-wash in warm water and mild detergent
Ovenproof ware (such as Pyrex) Flameproof ware (pottery or glass) Glass ceramics (ovenware, such as Pyroflame or Pyrosil)	Hand or machine-wash. Remove stubborn stains from pottery by soaking in warm water and mild detergent, and from glass with cleaning powder on a damp cloth or nylon scourer before washing
Porcelain Black porcelain	Hand-wash in warm water and mild detergent. Undecorated porcelain can be machine-washed
Soda glass or soda lime glass (includes most domestic glassware)	Machine-wash unless delicate or with painted decoration. Lift stemmed glasses by the stem, not the cup. To separate glasses stuck together, put cold water in the inner glass and hold the outer one in warm water. Remove stains from inside vases or decanters by filling them with a solution of warm water and biological detergent, or a solution of 150 ml. (¼ pint) vinegar and 1 tablespoon cooking salt. Leave to stand for 12 hours, shaking occasionally. To remove lime deposits, dissolve proprietary stain-removal tablets in water according to the manufacturer's instructions
Stoneware	Hand or machine-wash
Terracotta	Hand-wash only

CARE AND CLEANING OF JEWELLERY

TYPE	METHOD
Agate, Amethyst, Aquamarine, Bloodstone, Citrine, Coral, Cornelian, Emerald, Garnet, Moonstone (or feldspar), Mother of pearl, Onyx, Peridot, Rock crystal, Ruby, Sapphire, Topaz, Tourmaline, Zircon	Clean with a jewellery-care kit (see p. 317), or simply swish pieces about in warm soapy water. Loosen dirt with a mascara brush or soft toothbrush. Rinse in warm water and dry with a chamois leather or paper tissue
Amber, Tortoiseshell	Rub with chamois leather
Cameo	Clean with a soft, soapy toothbrush, rinse, and rub up with a chamois leather
Diamond	Swish in a solution of 1 tablespoon ammonia and a few soapflakes in 2 cups warm water, brushing gently with a mascara brush; rinse well and dip in surgical spirit
Filigree (delicate wire work)	Clean according to the metal (see p. 324)
Ivory, Jade, Jet, Lapis lazuli, Malachite	Wash in warm soapy water and loosen dirt with a fine toothbrush. Rinse in warm water and dry with a chamois leather or paper tissue
Marcasite, Pinchbeck	Rub up with a silver cloth
Metal	Clean according to the type of metal (see p. 324)
Obsidian	Wash in lukewarm soapy water; rinse well, dry, and rub up with a chamois leather
Opal	Clean gently with damp cloth; polish with chamois leather
Paste (coloured or clear glass made to imitate precious stones, e.g. rhinestone)	Best cleaned professionally, as stones are easily dislodged from their settings
Pearls	Wash in warm, soapy water, rinse, and dry with a chamois leather. Do not soak. Pearls can be damaged by make-up, perfume and hair lacquer. Do not store in cottonwool, as this dries them out
Turquoise	Polish gently with a chamois leather or soft cloth. Do not wet as the stone may discolour or crack
Wood	Wipe with a soft damp cloth, then rub up in palm of hand

• LOOKING AFTER YOUR WARDROBE

Clothes will look better and last longer if they are put on a hanger as soon as you have undressed. Button or zip them when you hang them, so they will keep their shape. Empty pockets or they will develop bulges.

Turn light-coloured clothes inside out or cover them with plastic bags to prevent them picking up dirt.

Always leave leather and suede clothes or shoes to air for a while before putting them away. Do not dry wet suede, leather or fur clothes near heat, as the skin may crack. Leave them on a hanger to dry naturally before putting them away.

After wearing a fur, give it a good shake to settle the pile. Avoid rubbing the pile against handbags or shopping baskets, as this can cause worn patches.

Stains on clothing should be treated while fresh (see p. 326).

CLEANING SUEDE AND LEATHER

Do not use spirit solvents on suede and smooth leathers, as they may remove the colour. Get badly soiled garments cleaned professionally.

Many leather and suede garments are washable. Each tannery has its own curing process, so follow the manufacturer's instructions carefully.

To refresh smooth leather, sponge gently with water containing a small amount of unscented white toilet soap. Try out a small area first, and if you have any doubts get the garment cleaned professionally.

Do not use a wire brush on suede, as it will destroy the nap (the fibre ends on the surface). Brush suede clothes regularly with a rubber brush or pad to raise the nap. Do not brush when wet as this flattens the nap.

Spots caused by rain can be removed when dry by vigorous rubbing with a rubber brush. Collars of suede coats soil very quickly; protect them by wearing a scarf.

If suede becomes grubby, it can be refreshed by using a suede cleaner (see p. 317), which also helps to keep the colour bright. Suede dressings or shampoos are not recommended for use on clothing or handbags.

LOOKING AFTER GLOVES

All gloves, leather gloves particularly, keep their shape longer if they are put on correctly.

Roll back the cuff to the bottom of the fingers, slip in the fingers only, and ease them well home by stroking them between the fingers and thumb of the other hand. Do not push down between the fingers, as this may break the stitches.

Then slip the thumb into position and fold the cuff back into place, pulling on the glove from the back of the hand. Take them off in a similar way – roll back the cuff and ease them gently off your fingers and thumb.

After wearing leather gloves, puff them up while they are still warm and gently pull the fingers into shape. Pull fabric gloves gently into shape after wearing.

Only a few dry-cleaners will clean leather gloves. Most leather gloves are guaranteed washable, but if you buy some that are not, it is best not to clean them at all, as the wrong cleaning fluid could damage the leather.

Washable leather gloves can be washed gently with soap flakes or glove soap dissolved in warm water. Wash gloves on the hand, except for doeskin, which tears easily when wet.

Rinse in clear, tepid water, but do not rinse doeskin gloves, which should be pressed lightly between towelling. Dry gloves flat on a towel, away from the sun or direct heat. Just before they are dry, ease them into shape by stretching gently or by putting them on your hands.

Wash gloves made from other fabrics in the same way as leather gloves, or according to the manufacturer's instructions.

SHOES AND BOOTS

Before wearing shoes or boots for the first time, give them a protective coating of polish or dressing. In winter spray with water-and-stain repellent before polishing.

If new shoes have leather soles, wear them for the first time on a dry day so that the soles can pick up a protective coating of dust and grit.

Do not wear the same shoes day after day – resting them increases their life and helps them to keep their shape. Use shoe or boot trees to help footwear keep its shape.

Remove mud or dust by brushing or wiping with a soft cloth when shoes (except suede) are dry. Before polishing, remove salt, snow or other stains with a proprietary stain remover. Very dirty leather shoes can be washed with saddle soap (see p. 317).

Apply the polish or dressing recommended for the fabric (see p. 316). Apply with a cloth unless the manufacturer instructs otherwise. Rub in with a cloth or soft brush, and give a final polish with a soft cloth.

Leave wet shoes to dry before cleaning; stuff them with paper so that they keep their shape while drying. Do not dry them near heat.

Rub up suede shoes frequently with a rubber brush, but do not brush when wet. Remove heavy mud from shoes by scraping gently with the back of a knife. Small kick and scuff marks can be sponged away gently with a mild soap and water solution. Use a suede shampoo to remove ingrained dirt; follow the maker's directions – shampoo applied incorrectly can make the nap lie flat. When shoes are clean and dry, use a suede dressing to retint and revive the nap.

HANDBAGS, BRIEFCASES, LUGGAGE

Cleaning handbags, briefcases and suitcases periodically helps to prolong their life, as well as keep them looking smart.

Remove dirt and dust from the interior by brushing or, for large trunks, with a vacuum-cleaner attachment. Treat any stains with the appropriate cleaner (see p. 326).

Freshen up a grubby or soiled lining by wiping it over with a cloth wrung out in warm water and mild detergent, but do not overwet it. Rinse with a chamois leather wrung out in clear water, and leave it to dry away from sun or heat.

Clean the outside of the bag according to the material from which it is made. On leather bags, do not use a shoe or furniture polish, as these may leave the surface sticky and stain clothing.

If a fabric exterior is very dirty, give it a preliminary clean with a chamois leather or cloth well wrung out in vinegar water. Over-wetting may damage the backing. Rinse with clear water and leave to dry before cleaning it according to its fabric type. See charts for Upholstery, Wall coverings.

Store handbags and luggage in a cool, dry place, not near heat, which can cause the surface to crack.

• SELF-SERVICE DRY-CLEANING

Most clothing, curtains and loose covers can be dry-cleaned in a coin-operated cleaner, but not articles containing metallic thread, plastic, leather, rubber, animal fur or adhesive patches.

Remove any stains before cleaning (see p. 326). Food stains are sometimes not visible until after cleaning, when the whitish residue can be removed with a brush or damp sponge.

Although dry-cleaning will not remove deep-set creases, clothes will come out almost wrinkle free if they are on hangers overnight before cleaning and are taken to the machine on hangers, not stuffed in a bag.

Before putting articles in the machine, turn pockets, cuffs and trouser turn-ups inside-out and brush off any loose dirt or mud. Close zips and fasten hooks to keep fabric from snagging. Remove curtain hooks and leather buttons or any clothes trimmings that might be damaged.

Turn sweaters, knitted dresses, trousers, and beaded garments inside-out to avoid loosening threads. Velvet, velveteen and corduroy garments also need to be turned inside-out because the pile attracts fluff.

Do not clean light and dark fabrics together, as the light material shows up fluff picked up from the dark. Put pale garments in a pillowcase and close it with tacking before cleaning. Put lightweight fabrics in by themselves, not with heavy, bulky articles.

Place garments on hangers as soon as possible after dry-cleaning. The fumes from the cleaning agent are dangerous. Open the window if you have newly cleaned clothing hung in a closed car. Do not use cleaned articles until they have been well aired.

Garments such as men's suits need professional pressing after cleaning. Some self-service establishments have a pressing service. If they do not, it is best to have suits professionally cleaned and pressed. Other clothes can be ironed with a steam iron after they have been on a hanger overnight.

• CARE AND CLEANING OF METALS

All metals can be worn away by corrosion. Iron and steel, the most commonly used metals, are particularly vulnerable to rust.

One way in which manufacturers combat rust is to give metal articles a protective coating of paint, enamel, zinc (galvanisation) or chromium. But if this protective coating is damaged, the metal will rust.

Cleaning with a harsh abrasive can damage a protective surface. So can prolonged contact with acids (such as those in rhubarb, lemons and tomatoes). Vitreous enamel (vitramel), although very hard, can be chipped by careless treatment – such as knocking the rim of a saucepan with a spoon. Stove enamel is only paint.

On metals other than iron and steel, mild corrosion usually shows as tarnish, a thin coating that dulls lustre, but it is much slower-acting than rust. Unless lacquered, or constantly and thoroughly cleaned, copper, brass and bronze eventually develop a green incrustation known as verdigris.

On some metals, particularly aluminium and chromium, tarnish inhibits further corrosion. On aluminium the natural coating can be thickened by a process known as anodising, which hardens the surface.

Oxidised metals have a protective coating induced in a similar way. Do not polish, as this may damage the coating; dust with a soft cloth.

On unprotected metals, tarnish can normally be removed with an abrasive polish. Use the right polish for the right metal; polishes for hard metals such as brass will scratch soft metals such as silver. Soft-metal polishes will not shine hard metals.

Wash unprotected iron and steel, using an abrasive powder, and keep it thoroughly clean and dry. Where practicable, a grease coating can be applied to prevent rust. (See also Pots and pans, p. 208.)

Once rust occurs, it can be cleaned off with emery paper, wire wool or proprietary rust remover, but it cannot be permanently stopped.

FACTS ABOUT SOME METALS

Most metals used today are alloys – blends of two or more basic metals. This gives them extra strength and increased resistance to corrosion.

Aluminium A soft, lightweight metal that forms high-strength alloys. It is a good heat conductor. Thick-bottomed pans are best for cooking; thin ones tend to distort. Aluminium is commonly used as the base for non-stick pans.

Brass An alloy of copper and zinc.

Copper Although a very good conductor of heat, copper can form poisonous salts with acids from foods. Copper cooking pots should be lined with tin.

Gold Pure gold is alloyed with copper or silver or both. A carat is a 24th part, so 9 carat gold is 9 parts gold and 15 parts other metal.

Pewter Old pewter is an alloy of tin and lead, and will darken with age. Modern pewter (Britannia metal) is normally an alloy of tin, antimony and copper, and does not discolour.

Silver That used in jewellery is normally about 80% silver. Sterling silver is just over 90% silver.

Steel An alloy of iron and carbon. Stainless steel, which also contains chromium and sometimes nickel, resists corrosion well. It is not a good heat conductor; cooking pans with an aluminium or copper base are best.

Tin A soft metal normally used only for plating or coatings; it has good resistance to corrosion. A tin can is usually steel coated with tin.

CARE AND CLEANING OF METALS AND ENAMEL

TYPE	METHOD	TYPE	METHOD
Aluminium (pots and pans, baking tins, kettles)	Hand-wash in hot water and mild detergent. Do not use soda. Scour with soap-impregnated steel wool pads or nylon pot scourer. Rinse and dry thoroughly. Remove dark discoloration with a strong solution of cream of tartar or vinegar in water; simmer for about 20 minutes	Gold, Platinum	Rub up with dusters or a chamois leather. Wash periodically in warm, mild detergent; rinse, dry and rub up with chamois. Clean tarnished low-carat gold with a long-term silver polish. When not in use, wrap gold in chamois leather or tissue paper
Anodised aluminium (trays, trolleys, light fittings, trim on household appliances, saucepan lids)	Wipe over with a damp cloth. Rub up with a dry cloth and a little liquid wax polish. Do not wash articles in a dishwasher	Iron and steel (not tinned, enamelled or stainless) (pots and pans, buckets, gates, etc.)	Wash painted or galvanised surfaces in hot detergent suds and dry well; rub up paint with a soft cloth. Clean crevices with a soft brush and dry thoroughly. Buff varnished iron with a soft cloth only. Clean rust off with a wire brush or proprietary fluid
Brass, Copper (saucepans, kettles, ornaments)	Wash pans and kettles with hot detergent suds. Soak to remove stubborn stains. Polish outside and remove light stains with lemon juice or vinegar and salt. Check that a tin lining is intact, and if not have it professionally re-lined. Polish ornaments with copper cleaner or with brass polish; apply polish to engraved surfaces with a soft brush and rub up with a soft brush inside a cloth. Rub up lacquered surfaces with a soft duster; avoid overhandling as the skin's natural acids will in time remove the lacquer	Lead (ornaments)	Scrub with turpentine. Remove white deposits by boiling in several changes of water. Then place in a solution of 1 part vinegar to 9 parts water. Rinse in water containing a little bicarbonate of soda, then rinse in several changes of distilled water
		Non-stick coatings (silicone, PTFE)	Wash immediately after use in hot soapy suds. Do not use abrasives. Rinse and dry. Use plastic or wooden implements when cooking
Bronze (ornaments)	Rub up with a soft duster. If very dirty, wash with a soft brush in very hot water and mild detergent. Rinse, dry and buff. Remove green verdigris by scraping lightly with a knife or rubbing with a brush; swab heavy incrustation with water containing 10% acetic acid. Rinse, dry and buff	Pewter, Britannia metal (ornaments, decorative plates, tankards)	Old pewter should be dusted and buffed with a soft cloth. Get professional advice if it is badly discoloured. Clean modern pewter (Britannia metal) with a proprietary polish
Chromium plating (on electrical appliances, plumbing fixtures, metal furniture)	Rub up with a soft duster. Occasionally polish with proprietary chrome cleaner, first washing, if very dirty, in hot detergent suds. Remove stains with a chrome cleaner	Silver, Silver plate, Sheffield plate, EPNS (ornaments, cutlery, jewellery)	Immediately after use, wash silverware in hot, mild detergent suds. Rinse and dry. Periodically use a proprietary silver cleaner. Avoid wire wool, abrasives or bleach
Enamel, vitreous enamel (a protective coating used for saucepans, cookers, oven interiors, sinks, baths)	Wash in hot detergent suds. For vitreous enamel use cleaners recommended by the Vitreous Enamel Development Council (stated with V symbol on packet). Remove stains by soaking in hot water and detergent or use a nylon brush and warm detergent suds. Stubborn stains can be moved by filling the pan with cold water and adding a teaspoon of household bleach. Soak for a few hours then clean normally	Stainless steel (pots and pans, cutlery, trim on household appliances)	Wash in, or wipe down with, hot detergent suds. Rinse well and dry with a soft cloth. Sticky food particles on pans can be removed gently with mild scouring powder or soap-impregnated steel wool. Rinse and dry well. Periodic cleaning with stainless-steel polish will remove most stains, but not burn marks on a pan exterior
		Tin (biscuit and cake tins, saucepan linings)	Wash after use in hot detergent suds; rinse and dry thoroughly (finish off tins in cool oven). Store in a dry place

• HARD CLEANING JOBS AROUND THE HOME

Hard or unpleasant jobs are less of a burden if they are not neglected. A lavatory pan thoroughly cleaned every week should not become stained. Drains regularly swilled are less likely to get blocked.

CLEANING A LAVATORY PAN

Dampen the inside of the pan, then sprinkle it with bleach or a proprietary cleaner. Do not use both, as the mixture can give off poisonous gas.

After about an hour, clean the base of the pan with a lavatory brush and the top part with a cloth. Rinse by flushing, and swill the water with the cloth to any parts of the bowl where it did not reach. If the bowl is stained, leave the bleach or cleaner to soak in the pan overnight. Next morning rub the stains with a brush, then rinse thoroughly. Wash the lavatory brush in hot suds after every use, then rinse it and hang it up to dry.

If the pan is badly marked due to hard water or rust in the cistern, it may be necessary to use a bath-stain remover (see p. 316). Use the stain remover according to the manufacturer's instructions.

Clean the seat and the outside of the lavatory pan with warm water and a mild detergent such as washing-up liquid. Rinse and then wipe dry with a paper towel so that the surface does not become streaky.

Flush-cleaners and toilet blocks include perfume to mask unpleasant smells, and also contain detergent which helps to keep the lavatory pan clean; they can be used in addition to regular cleaning.

Flush-cleaners are hung in the water in the cistern, and normally colour the flush water blue or green. They need renewing when the colour fades. Toilet blocks are hung by a wire from the rim of the lavatory pan, and are immersed and slightly dissolved when the pan is flushed.

CLEANING OPEN DRAINS

First remove the grid, using a strong piece of bent wire to lift it off if necessary. Clean off anything caught in the grid – such as hair or fluff – then soak and scrub the grid in a bucket of hot water and washing soda, rinsing in clear water.

Swill out the drain with clean, warm water, and scrub round the rim and walls with a brush kept specially for the purpose. If necessary, scrape out silt from the bottom of the drain gulley. Then swill the drain with a bucket of boiling water containing a handful of washing soda. Alternatively, use a proprietary disinfectant or liquid bleach according to the manufacturer's instructions.

Replace the grid and wash the scrubbing brush in warm water and disinfectant. For clearing a blocked drain, see p. 316 or p. 361.

CLEANING WINDOWS

Do not clean windows while the sun is shining directly on them, or streaks will appear when they dry.

Tepid water is the best cleaner. Use a chamois leather or soft cloth with no lint. Work with two leathers or cloths, one for washing and one for wiping.

Dip the washing leather into the water, wring it out well, then work round the edges of the pane and into the middle. Immediately afterwards wipe with the second leather, which should be just damp. Change the water frequently, so that it does not get too dirty.

For large areas of glass it saves time to use a rubber window mop – a rubber blade on a stick – instead of cloths or leathers. Work the mop smoothly downwards from the top of the pane. Wipe the blade on a cloth after each stroke.

If windows are very dirty, add a small amount of washing-up liquid to the tepid water. Alternatively, use a tablespoon of methylated spirit – especially if the weather is very cold, as it will stop the water from freezing on the glass.

After washing with anything other than clear water, rinse the windows with plain water and wipe them with a leather. Be sure to rinse thoroughly if using methylated spirit, as it could damage woodwork.

Using a proprietary window polish is a convenient but more costly way of cleaning. A very dirty window should be cleaned with water and a chamois leather before using polish.

Proprietary polishes are generally either aerosol sprays or liquid emulsions that have to be lightly applied with a cloth. They leave a white smear on the surface which is rubbed off with a soft cloth or paper towel.

CLEANING A COOKER

Stains from spilt food are easiest to remove while they are still fresh. Wipe round the edge of the burners with a dry cloth if the surface is hot, or with a damp cloth once it has cooled.

For general cleaning, make sure the cooker (gas or electric) is turned off and is cool. Dismantle all removable parts and wash them in the dishwasher or warm water containing detergent or washing soda.

Rub stubborn stains with a stiff brush. Do not scour. If stains persist, soak them in a solution of soda and warm water for an hour or two.

After washing each part, rinse it thoroughly and then dry. Use a tea towel or paper towel, or leave the part to drain and dry naturally. When reassembling, check that the pilot lights are working properly on a gas cooker. If necessary, turn off the gas at the main and clean the jets with a fine wire or pipe cleaner.

Clean an inner glass door of an oven by rubbing it with a spot of bicarbonate of soda on a damp cloth. Wash the inside of the oven while it is still warm with detergent or washing soda in warm water, or use a suitable proprietary cleaner. Most oven interiors are vitreous enamel, for which use a cleaner recommended by the Vitreous Enamel Development Council; these are marked on the packet with the council's V symbol.

Tackle persistent marks with a nylon brush or some more liberally soaped steel wool. Scouring with harsh abrasives will damage the oven surface; this makes it more likely to burn so that it becomes more stained. A badly stained oven can be cleaned with a strong proprietary cleaner specially manufactured for use on an oven interior (see p. 317).

Self-cleaning ovens are coated with a new type of enamel that cleans itself while cooking is taking place. Cleaning the sides is not necessary (see p. 195). Follow the cooker manufacturer's cleaning instructions.

CLEANING A BATH

Some modern baths have a plastic surface. Wipe it after use with warm water and soap or mild detergent solution. Persistent tide marks due to hard water can be moved with liquid metal polish on a soft cloth. Scratches can be rubbed with fine wire wool before polishing.

Clean a vitreous enamel bath with a cleaner recommended by the Vitreous Enamel Development Council (marked with a V on the packet). Dry with a soft cloth. Stains on old enamelled baths – usually caused by hard water from dripping taps – can sometimes be removed with lemon juice or citric acid, or a proprietary bath-stain remover (see p. 316).

LAYING AN OPEN FIRE

Brush soot from the back of the fireplace and round the damper. Remove the ashes, but keep large cinders for the new fire. When clearing out ashes, sprinkle them with water to keep the dust down. Wipe over the hearth with a damp cloth.

To lay a fire for lighting with matches, place plenty of dry, bunched-up newspaper on the bars of the grate. Some paper can be made into paper crackers, which burn longer and give the wood time to get well alight.

To make a paper cracker, take a sheet of newspaper and lay it flat. Then bend over one corner and roll it diagonally into a long, thin spill.

Press along the spill to flatten it, then fold it at the centre to make a V shape. Continue folding each arm of the V backwards over the other until the spill is formed into a short, concertina-like cracker.

Next take plenty of short, dry sticks of wood and place on the paper, building the wood up in criss-crossed layers, so that air can get through.

Finally, place a layer of coal, coke or other solid fuel, including large cinders from the previous fire. Build it round and on top of the wood. Use small and medium-sized pieces, not large pieces as these will smother the flames as the wood collapses when the paper burns up.

One or two firelighters can be used as an alternative to paper and wood.

It is far simpler to light a fire with an electric or gas poker, if a power point is at hand. Calor-gas pokers are available. The poker is placed in the base of a pyramid of cinders and solid fuel, ignited, and left in position until the fuel is well alight.

● ABC OF STAIN REMOVAL

Tackle freshly made stains at once, as most stains are difficult to remove when dried in. The best immediate action is to rinse (but not flood) with cold water, except for grease-based stains for which shake on an absorbent such as talcum powder.

After that the removal method depends on what has caused the stain, what will dissolve it, and the material stained. Take care when using chemicals; they may discolour or damage some fabrics.

If a stain persists after the appropriate treatment, get professional advice and tell the cleaner what made the stain and how you have treated it. Not all stains can be removed.

Very large stains or stains made by an unknown substance are best left to a professional cleaner, as are stains on rich, heavy, or waterproof fabrics and stains on suede or leather that cannot be removed by normal cleaning (see pp. 321–325).

The stain-removal methods given are mainly for fabrics, but where practicable can be used on floors and furniture; but see Care and cleaning, pp. 318-25. If in doubt about the effect on a surface, get professional advice. Many common household spills on solid surfaces do not stain if mopped up at once and then cleaned in the normal way. Stains on plastic fabrics can normally be removed with bicarbonate of soda (see p. 320).

STAIN REMOVERS

Many stain-removing agents are poisonous or inflammable or both. Keep them clearly labelled and out of the reach of children.

Absorbents Talcum powder, powdered starch, french chalk (fabrics); cat litter/sawdust (solid surfaces).

Acetone A cellulose solvent. Do not use on acetate, triacetate or viscose rayon (see Fabrics chart, p. 292). Inflammable.

Ammonia Use 1 tablespoon to 600 ml. (1 pint) of warm water. It is dangerous to use undiluted. Test fabric for colour-fastness (method 3), particularly rayon. Sponge, or soak for about three minutes. White silk and wool may be yellowed by too strong a solution – neutralise with white-vinegar solution. Fumes poisonous.

Amyl acetate Can be used in place of acetone on acetate, triacetate, or viscose rayon (see Acetone); test before using, as fabrics may discolour.

Borax Use 1 tablespoon of domestic borax in 600 ml. (1 pint) of warm water. Soak for about ten minutes.

Detergent Heavy-duty detergents (see p. 333) contain a mild bleach and will wash away some stains on washable fabrics; the bleach is most effective at high temperatures (60°-100°C). Use the lather only on non-washables. Liquid detergents are milder but can be used undiluted on some stains. Enzyme detergents will soak away protein stains (such as egg yolk, blood, gravy) from washable fabrics; their effectiveness depends on water temperature and soaking time (see p. 334).

Developer Use ½ teaspoon hypo to 300 ml. (½ pint) of warm water.

Dry-cleaner A grease solvent sold under various brand names; some will also remove stains other than grease. The cleaner may be liquid (such as Boot's Dry Cleaner or Beaucaire), an aerosol spray (such as Goddard's Dry Cleaner or Dabitoff Spray), or a paste (such as K2r). Spray or paste removers usually dry as powders.

Dry-cleaners cannot normally be used on leather, suede, rubber, plastics or waterproofed fabrics. Check the use when buying, and follow the instructions on the package carefully. Apply only to dry surfaces.

Do not smoke when using. Keep the container stoppered and use in a well-ventilated room.

Eucalyptus oil For heavy oil and tar stains. Use neat. It tends to leave a smell on garments for a while.

Glycerine This softens stains and is safe to use on most fabrics. Rinse the area thoroughly with lukewarm water after use; it cannot be removed by dry-cleaning but will dissolve in water.

Lemon juice A mild acid that can be used to counteract discoloration by alkalis such as ammonia.

Lighter fuel Can be used neat as a weak grease solvent. Inflammable.

Methylated spirit Use neat. Generally safe on all fabrics, but test before using. Poisonous, inflammable.

Nail-polish remover (non-oily) Contains acetone; use with the same precautions (see Acetone).

Paint remover A solvent for cleaning paint brushes, and so on, that can be used to remove some paint stains, and also grease and tar stains from carpets. Test the fabric first.

Peroxide (hydrogen peroxide) A mild bleach that can be used on white and some coloured fabrics (test first), but not on nylon. Use 1 part of 20-volume peroxide in 4 parts cold water, and add a few drops of ammonia. Soak whites overnight if necessary, coloureds for 5-15 minutes.

Turpentine (and white spirit) Safe for use on most fabrics, but test first. White spirit (turpentine substitute) is weaker. Inflammable.

Vinegar (white) A mild acid for counteracting discoloration from alkalis such as ammonia. Use 1 tablespoon in 600 ml. (1 pint) of warm water.

METHOD 1 DRY-CLEANING FABRICS

First test the cleaner on the fabric in an inconspicuous spot, such as an inside seam. Leave it for 15 minutes.

Do not use it if it dries hard or weakens or discolours the fabric. If no alternative remover can be used, get professional advice.

To remove a stain, place a clean, absorbent pad (such as cottonwool) underneath, where possible, with the inside of the fabric uppermost. Use another clean pad for the cleaner.

Do not apply too much cleaner at a time – flooding could spread the stain – and do not rub too hard. It is safer to use several weak applications rather than one strong one.

Work from the outer edge of the stain inwards to avoid it spreading or forming rings. Change the pads frequently. After each application of the cleaner, blot the stain dry.

Be careful about using a cleaner on a carpet with a rubber, latex, foam, or plastic backing. Soaking the carpet may damage the backing.

After stain removal, wash or dry-clean fabrics normally. If the stain reappears, get professional advice.

METHOD 2 USING AN ABSORBENT

Lay the fabric flat, where possible. Spread the absorbent over the stain and work it round gently with a spoon handle. Remove it by brushing, shaking or vacuuming after about an hour.

METHOD 3 WET-CLEANING FABRICS

Washables Rinse immediately with cold or lukewarm water. Soaking in a solution of the suggested cleaner will remove some stains, but do not soak wool, silk or non-colourfast or flameproof fabrics. Check under Stain removers (above) for the soaking time.

Test for colour-fastness by sponging the fabric with the cleaning solution in an inconspicuous spot such as an inside seam. Then put the wetted fabric between two pieces of white cloth and press with a warm iron. The fabric is colourfast if no colour is transferred to the white cloth.

Certain fresh stains on white or colourfast linens can sometimes be removed by drenching the stained area (not the whole area, which might shrink) with boiling water. Stretch the fabric over a basin and sprinkle a little dry borax or detergent on the stain; pour boiling water through, then rinse.

If the stain remains after rinsing, rub some cleaner gently into the stain, rinse, then wash. On suitable fabrics, any remaining stain may be removed by peroxide or bleach (see p. 333).

Non-washables Sponge gently with cold water or, if possible, stretch the fabric over a jug and pour cold water through the stain.

If the stain remains, place an absorbent pad under it (where possible) and work in the cleaning solution with a pad. With detergents, use the lather only. Sponge with clear water and blot dry. Repeat if necessary.

Carpets and upholstery First make sure that an upholstery fabric can be treated with shampoo (see p. 321). Dissolve liquid carpet or upholstery shampoo in lukewarm water until it foams (or use a foam shampoo).

Sponge the stain gently with the foam, blotting it frequently; be careful not to soak the fabric, as this may cause shrinkage or discoloration or both. Rinse in the same way, using cold water. Raise a carpet to dry it, if possible, so that air can circulate between the fibres to prevent mildew.

If the stain persists, try dry-cleaner (method 1) once the fabric is quite dry. If this is not successful, get professional advice.

Proprietary spotting kits or spot removers are available for removing small stains from upholstery and carpets. Follow the instructions on the container carefully.

A-Z OF STAINS

There is no guarantee that the suggested methods will be wholly effective. Check opposite that the cleaner is suitable for the material.

A

ADHESIVE
Clear and contact (e.g. Bostik, Evo-Stik Impact) Use acetone, amyl acetate, or non-oily nail-varnish remover (method 1).
Latex (e.g. Copydex) and model-maker's cement Take off with spatula then use dry-cleaner (method 1).
Epoxy resin (e.g. Araldite) Cannot be removed once hardened; try acetone, amyl acetate or lighter fuel before stain dries (method 1).

ALCOHOL See Spirits

AMMONIA
Try lemon juice, or white vinegar or developer solution (method 3).

ANIMAL DROPPINGS See Vomit

B

BALLPOINT See Ink

BEER
Use detergent or carpet shampoo (method 3). For dried-in stains add white vinegar – 1 egg cup to 600 ml. (1 pint) of water.

BEETROOT See Fruit juice

BLACKLEAD
Use white spirit (method 1).

BLEACH (Chlorine)
Use developer (method 3).

BLOOD
Soak fresh stains in cold water (method 3) – boiling water will set the stain. For dried-in stains, sponge with salt water (½ teaspoon salt to 600 ml./1 pint) or use enzyme detergent or carpet shampoo (method 3).

BUTTER See Grease

C

CANDLE WAX
Scrape off as much as possible with a blunt blade. Place slightly damp blotting paper or tissues over (and under if possible) fabric and press quickly with a warm iron; repeat until wax is absorbed. Otherwise try dry-cleaner (method 1). On furniture, chill with an ice cube then scrape off.

CARBON PAPER See Transfer pattern

CHEWING GUM
Chill with an ice cube to harden. Scrape off, then use dry-cleaner (method 1). Or use a spray such as Holloway Gum Remover.

CHOCOLATE/COCOA
Use enzyme detergent or borax solution (method 3). If stain persists use dry-cleaner (method 1).

COFFEE
Use borax or peroxide solution or carpet shampoo (method 3). Loosen dried-in stains with glycerine first.

COSMETICS
Use dry-cleaner (method 1).

CRAYON
Use dry-cleaner (method 1). On unwashable wallpaper try an aerosol spot remover (test first in an inconspicuous spot), but the clean part may show up more than the stain.

CREAM
Use dry-cleaner (method 1); for washables first try enzyme detergent or borax (method 3).

CREOSOTE
Scrape off as much as possible. Use eucalyptus oil, white spirit or dry-cleaner (method 1). Loosen old stains with glycerine first, then rinse with lukewarm water.

CURRY
Soften with glycerine (method 1), rinse, then use an enzyme detergent or carpet shampoo (method 3).

D

DEODORANT
Use white-vinegar solution (method 3). For persistent stains try methylated spirit (method 1).

DYE
Use enzyme detergent (for washables) or carpet shampoo (method 3). For white washables try Dygon Colour and Stain Remover. For non-washables try methylated spirit (method 1).

E/F

EGG See Blood

FAECES See Vomit

FELT PEN See Ink

FLOWER MARKS See Grass

FRUIT JUICE
On white table linen pour salt on a fresh stain to stop it spreading, then rinse with boiling water (method 3). Otherwise use peroxide, borax solution or carpet shampoo (method 3).

G

GRASS MARKS
Use eucalyptus oil, glycerine, or methylated spirit (method 1).

GRAVY
Use dry-cleaner (method 1). If stain is browning only (no grease), use enzyme detergent (method 3).

GREASE
Remove as much as possible with an absorbent (method 2), then use dry-cleaner (method 1). On wallpaper, dab lightly with baby powder

on cottonwool, or try holding blotting paper over the stain and pressing quickly with a warm iron. Or use an aerosol grease solvent (but this may bring up the cleaned patch brighter than the rest).

H/I

HAIR LACQUER
Some types can be removed with water, otherwise use methylated spirit (method 1) or acetone or amyl acetate.

HEAT MARKS
On polished wood furniture use brass polish sprinkled on a cloth and rubbed in the way of the grain. Then repolish.

ICE CREAM See Cream

INK
For ballpoint and felt-pen marks use methylated spirit (method 1). Most writing inks can be removed by rinsing at once in cold water; otherwise try soap flakes and water (method 3). Some proprietary dry-cleaners or rust removers may remove permanent inks.

IODINE (Tincture)
Use developer solution (method 1).

IRON MOULD See Rust marks

J/L

JAM See Fruit juice

LEAD PENCIL
Use a soft india-rubber on light marks on fabrics or wallpaper. Or try dry-cleaner (method 1) or a spray.

LEAF MARKS See Grass

LEMON JUICE
Use borax solution (method 3).

M

MAYONNAISE See Cream

MEDICINE
If you know the basic constituent – for example, syrup, iron, tar – use the method suggested for it. Or get professional advice.

METAL POLISH
Blot excess. Use white spirit or dry-cleaner (method 1).

MILDEW
Expose the article to sun and air to help kill the fungus; dry out books with an absorbent. On suitable washable fabrics use peroxide solution, on others rub with hard yellow soap then leave to dry in the sun before washing. On non-washables use a fungicide, Mystox, can be used.

MILK
Rinse fresh stains in lukewarm water. For dried-in stains use borax solution or carpet shampoo (method 3). For hot milk use dry-cleaner (method 1).

MUSTARD
For washables try detergent (method 3); for non-washables use methylated spirit or dry-cleaner (method 1). Soften old stains with glycerine, then rinse with lukewarm water and dry before using method 1.

N

NAIL VARNISH/LACQUER
Use acetone, amyl acetate, or non-oily nail-polish remover (method 1).

NICOTINE
Use eucalyptus oil or methylated spirit (method 1) or detergent or peroxide solution (method 3).

O/P

OIL
Soak up as much as possible with an absorbent (method 2), then use dry-cleaner (method 1). For bicycle or motor oil on fabrics, try

eucalyptus oil (method 1).

PAINT
For enamel and oil paints use paint remover or turpentine (method 1); for cellulose paint use acetone or amyl acetate (method 1). Fresh emulsion paint can be rinsed off with cold water; for dried-in stains try methylated spirit, but they cannot usually be removed.

PARAFFIN See Oil

PERFUME
Can normally be washed off washable fabrics. For dried-in stains or non-washables, use glycerine (method 1).

PERSPIRATION
Try enzyme detergent or ammonia, borax, or white-vinegar solution (method 3).

PLASTICINE
Scrape off as much as possible then use dry-cleaner (method 1).

R/S

RUST MARKS
Try lemon juice or, on whites, a proprietary remover such as Movol (method 1).

SALAD DRESSING See Cream

SCORCH MARKS
Try borax, peroxide or ammonia solution (method 3).

SHOE POLISH
Scrape off as much as possible then use dry-cleaner (method 1). On carpets first try shampoo (method 3).

SOOT
Vacuum up as much as possible; do not brush as it will rub in. On light-coloured fabrics use an absorbent (method 2) before vacuuming. Then use dry-cleaner (method 1), but try detergent or shampoo (method 3) first on washables and carpets. There are proprietary cleaners for

fireplaces (Bricktone, Stonekleen).

SPIRITS/SYRUP
Use detergent, peroxide or borax solution (method 3).

T

TAR See Grease and Oil

TEA See Coffee

TOMATO See Fruit juice

TRANSFER PATTERN
Use methylated spirit (method 1).

TURMERIC See Curry

U/V

URINE
Use enzyme detergent or carpet shampoo (method 3); add white vinegar – 1 egg cup per 600 ml. (1 pint) to shampoo solution.

VARNISH
For shellac use methylated spirit (method 1). For cellulose and polyurethane see Paint (cellulose).

VOMIT
If necessary, remove deposits with an absorbent, then use enzyme detergent, borax solution or carpet shampoo (method 3).

W

WATER
Remove rainspots on materials such as felt, velvet and taffeta by holding in steam from boiling kettle, not too near spout. Alkaline drinking water can discolour fabrics; sponge with white-vinegar solution (method 1).

WAX See Candle wax

WAX POLISH See Grease

WINE See Fruit juice

HOME LAUNDERING

Doing your washing at home in a washing machine is more convenient than taking it to a laundrette, but not always cheaper. For a family of four with an average of about 18 kg. (40 lb.) of washing a week, a machine at home is likely to be cheaper as long as the washing can be dried on the line – if it has to be dried by heat there is little difference in cost. In general, the laundrette proves cheaper for light loads, but as the load increases above about 18 kg., a home machine becomes more economic.

Using a laundrette generally means more hand washing; garments that can be given a cool wash in a home automatic, such as machine-knitted woollen jumpers, are best not included in a laundrette load as the machines are faster and have fewer programmes.

• WASHING MACHINES

Washing machines need servicing every year. Complex automatic machines are more likely to have troubles than twin tub or single-tub machines. Manufacturers usually have a home servicing scheme by which a yearly payment insures against repairs that may be needed.

Make sure that any machine you buy is approved by the British Electro-technical Approvals Board (see p. 370), which sets safety standards.

TWIN TUB

A twin-tub machine has one tub for washing and one for rinsing and spin drying. Water has to be fed in by hose from a tap, and is pumped out through a hose into the sink. The machine needs to be easy to move so that it can be pushed to the sink.

Machines can be filled with hot or cold water and set to heat the water to a selected temperature suitable for the wash. It is usually convenient to start with the hottest wash then move down the temperature range so that the same water can be used for white cottons (soaked while the water is heating) through to coloured man-made fibres, for example.

Heaters are usually 2 or 3 kW and may take about two hours to heat the water from cold to 85°C (for a cotton wash), or if filled with hot water (about 60°C), 30 or 40 minutes. They usually have a pilot light that goes out when the water has reached the selected temperature. In some models the wash will then start automatically; others have to be started by hand.

WASHING AND DRYING MACHINES

MACHINE	WHAT IT NORMALLY DOES	AVERAGE OPERATING TIME	AVERAGE LOAD – DRY WEIGHT	OTHER POINTS
Single-tub washer	Soak or boil. Wash. Each operation set by hand	Water heating ½-2 hrs. Wash 4 or 12 min. depending on action	1.8-2.7 kg. (4-6 lb.)	Fed by hose from taps. Used with wringer. Complete drying needed
Twin-tub washer	Soak or boil. Wash, rinse, spin dry. Each operation set by hand	Water heating ½-2 hrs. Wash 4 or 12 min. depending on action. Spin 30-60 sec. or 4 min.	2.7 kg. (6 lb.)	Fed by hose from taps. Load lifted to second tub for rinse and spin. More drying will be needed
Automatic washer	Pre-treatment. Wash (7 programmes), rinse, spin dry. All automatic from switch on	Pre-treatment ¼-1¼ hrs (bio-soak). Longest programme 1½ hrs from mixed fill, 2 hrs from cold	2.7-5.5 kg. (6-12 lb.)	Can be fed from taps but best plumbed in. Further drying will be needed
Automatic washer and tumble drier combined	Pre-treatment. Wash (7 programmes), rinse, spin, dry by warm air. Automatic from switch on; drying may have to be set separately	Pre-treatment ¼-1¼ hrs (bio-soak). Wash 2½-3 hrs, dry 1½-3 hrs	Wash 4 kg. (9 lb.) Dry 2.5 kg. (5½ lb.)	Best plumbed in. Wash and dry by warm air in same drum. May need a venting hose to remove steam. No more drying needed
Spin drier	Rinse (some types), spin dry. Each operation set by hand; sometimes automatic rinse	Spin dry 30-60 sec., or 4 min.	2.7 kg. (6 lb.)	Fed by hose from taps if used for rinsing. More drying will be needed
Tumble drier	Dries by warm air	35-40 min. (cottons)	2.7-4.5 kg. (6-10 lb.)	May need a venting hose to remove steam. No more drying needed

WASHING ACTION

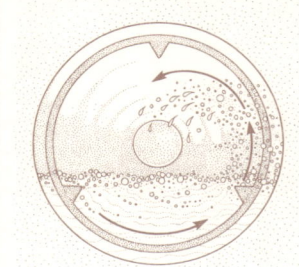

Revolving drum Clothes are lifted from the water and fall back in again as the drum slowly rotates. Some turn one way only, others alternate.

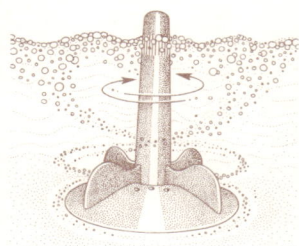

Agitator A flanged, upright paddle-like structure in the drum centre moves clothes clockwise then anticlockwise more than 60 times a minute.

Pulsator A flanged disc at the side or bottom of the drum revolves clockwise about 600 times a minute. This vigorous action can tangle clothes.

The washing action is by an agitator or pulsator. An agitator looks like a paddle and is in the centre of the tub, a pulsator is a disc at the side or bottom of the tub. The pulsator washing action is more vigorous and the maximum washing time is four minutes. The agitator action is gentler and there is less risk of tangling; maximum washing time is 12 minutes.

Most detergents can be used. A bad wash is usually due to insufficient detergent being used or the water not being hot enough.

To rinse, the spinner tub may have to be filled with water by hose and then spun, this being repeated until the water comes out clean. Some models have an automatic rinse, by which water can be pumped through while the tub is spinning.

The spinner usually operates only with the lid closed. Spinning speeds vary from about 1,800-3,000 revolutions per minute; the faster the speed, the drier the wash.

Some machines have an automatic spin timer, others have to be stopped by hand. Man-made fibres usually need to be spun for 30-60 seconds only, natural fibres for four minutes. Over-spinning will not get clothes drier, but may crease man-made fabrics, and tax the machine.

A twin tub may be slightly cheaper to run than an automatic, and the clothes come out drier. But you need to stand over a twin tub most of the time to operate it. Heavy, wet clothes have to be lifted from the washing tub to the spinning tub, and rinsing is not as efficient as in automatic machines. The spin tub is not large enough to take a bulky article such as a wet double blanket.

SINGLE TUB
A single-tub machine works in the same way as a twin-tub machine, but has no spinner – so heavy, wet clothes have to be lifted from the machine before and after rinsing.

A wringer is usually provided. It is possible to buy a machine without a wringer, but with a bridging piece to link the machine to a matching spin drier while they are in use.

AUTOMATIC
An automatic machine has one container for washing, rinsing and spin drying. It can be set to a different programme for each fabric group (see Garment labelling, p. 330), each programme including a wash at the required temperature, several rinses, and spin drying. Once set, the machine generally needs no attention until it switches off when finished.

Some automatic machines work from both the hot and cold-water supply at once, some from the cold supply only. Although a machine can be fed by hose from the taps, this means the taps will be blocked all the time the machine is operating. It is best to have it plumbed in (see p. 377).

A hot-and-cold-fill machine may be cheaper to run than a cold-fill one, depending on your hot-water heating system, but is more expensive to buy and plumb in. It uses less hot water than cold.

Machine manufacturers give recommended minimum hot and cold-water pressures for operation. Before buying a machine, check the water pressure you have available with a plumber. Cold-water pressures are usually higher than hot, and you may be able to use a cold-fill machine only.

Automatic machines are either top loaders or front loaders, and have either an agitator or revolving drum washing action. Front loaders are generally revolving drum types, top loaders can be either.

The drum machine is more economical since it uses less water and has shorter wash programmes, but it is limited to low-foaming detergent. An agitator machine can use any type of detergent. Both types may have a water-saver button for small loads – less than about 2.5 kg. (5½ lb.).

A top-loading machine can be interrupted in mid-programme (unless spinning) to put something in or take something out. A front-loading machine generally cannot.

In addition to the seven normal wash cycles, automatic machines have a programme for pre-treatment before a wash, and sometimes extra programmes such as a blanket wash, separate rinse and spin, or separate spin. The pre-treatment may be linked to some programmes so the machine can be set to go right through without attention, or you may have to set the wash programme afterwards.

Pre-treatment before a wash may take one of three forms: a pre-rinse to remove loose dirt from clothes; a pre-wash in detergent for heavily soiled clothes; or a pre-soak in biological detergent to remove stains.

A separate rinse and spin is useful for rinsing articles washed by hand and for treating fabrics with fabric softener or starch, although machines without this separate programme can usually be started at the rinse sequence on the programme dial. But it is not generally advisable to start a machine at the spin sequence, so a separate spin programme can be useful, especially for hand-washed clothes that need spinning but should not be rinsed.

Some machines have a spin delay – they can be set to stop at the final rinse with water still in the drum, and will not finish the programme until restarted. This is useful when washing man-made fibres if you will not be there to remove them as soon as the programme has finished; if left dry in the drum they are likely to crease.

Pre-wash detergent, wash detergent and fabric softener are automatically dispensed by some machines, others may only automatically dispense one or two of these stages, which means that you have to dispense the others manually.

Most automatics occupy less space than a twin tub, and rinse better, but they do not spin as much water from clothes. Spin speeds vary from about 400 to 1,000 rpm.

AUTOMATIC WITH INTEGRAL TUMBLE DRIER
In a machine with an integral tumble drier, washing and drying are done in the same drum. Some machines can be set to wash and dry automatically, others must be reset for drying at the end of the wash.

The washing action is the same as for an automatic machine. But as it is not possible to dry one load while another is being washed, the total programme time is longer. As most manufacturers recommend a smaller drying load than washing load, it may be necessary to remove some items from the machine before drying. Washing and drying a full load may take from six to nine hours.

A front-loading washing machine with a tumble drier on top is generally more useful. The only advantage of the combined machine is that it takes up less space and you do not have to lift damp clothes about.

SPIN DRIER
A separate spin drier is useful for those who have no washing machine, as it saves wringing by hand. There are two types – one drains from a spout into a bowl, the other pumps water into the sink.

The spout type is smaller and lighter and holds less water than the pump type. Pump-emptying driers are taller, heavier and more expensive, but more convenient to use. They can also be used for rinsing.

Always place the spinner mat on top of the load to prevent small articles being lost between the drum and outer casing. If no mat is supplied, tuck a folded tea cloth over the load.

If an article should fall between the drum and the casing, and you cannot retrieve it, call the service engineer, or the pump may get blocked.

TUMBLE DRIER
Clothes can be completely dried in a tumble drier or removed when damp enough for ironing. Garments dry while tumbling through warm air. Some driers are designed to fit on top of an automatic washing machine.

As the clothes dry, moist air is given off through a vent (usually at the back). The best position for the drier is near a window where the moist air can disperse. A venting kit is supplied as an optional extra, its hose passing through a window or a wall.

There is usually a choice of two or three heat settings for different fabrics. Some machines have a cold setting, in others the heat cuts off during the last few minutes so that the clothes tumble in cool air. Man-made fabrics need to be cooled after drying so that creases do not form. Remove them as soon as the tumbling stops.

Do not overload the machine, as the clothes will take longer to dry or will dry unevenly and get very creased. The load should be reduced for man-made fabrics to about 2 kg. (4½ lb.). Static electricity can be reduced by adding one or two dry towels as the clothes are drying. There is a removable filter (usually in the front of the machine) to collect fluff. Clear the filter after use.

• GARMENT LABELLING

Because of the wide range of man-made and natural fibres now available, there have been several attempts to create a labelling system that covers the washing techniques needed for different fabrics.

The result is that a garment may carry one of three types of label:
1. A washtub symbol, devised by the Home Laundering Consultative Council (HLCC). This numbers eight different washing processes – seven machine programmes and hand washing only.
2. A continental label showing four symbols – washtub, triangle, iron and circle – giving washing, bleaching, ironing and dry-cleaning instructions.
3. A combined label introduced in 1974, which uses the British wash-group number in conjunction with the continental symbols for bleaching, ironing and dry-cleaning.

When combining the UK and continental labelling schemes, some compromises had to be made. There is no confusion over the treatment of garments which carry the new labels, but if garments carrying the old labels are washed in a new machine – or garments with new labels are washed in an older machine – note the differences: the minimum wash temperature in group 1 has been increased from 85°C to 95°C, and the temperature in group 4 from 48°C to 50°C.

The new wash temperature is 95°C.

The new wash temperature is 50°C.

There are now nine machine processes instead of the seven of the HLCC system. The symbol for hand wash only has dropped the figure 8, and the two new machine symbols are as follows: group 8 is for silk and printed acetate fabrics with colours which are not fast at 40°C (so having to be washed at a very low temperature), and which need minimum agitation and spinning.

A new cool wash to avoid colour loss.

Group 9 is for cotton articles with special finishes which benefit from washing at a high temperature but need drip-drying.

A new wash for special-finish cottons.

The label on a garment is normally inside the collar or sleeves, or attached to a seam. Labels are also illustrated on the control panels of home automatic machines, irons, some tumble driers, and wash-powder packs.

Symbols that prohibit a certain treatment may be in red. A symbol printed in amber or orange means be especially careful with the treatment. If a symbol is in green, it is safe to use the treatment with normal care.

Sometimes labels have symbols introduced by a particular manufacturer. For example, drying instructions may be given by a square symbol containing three vertical lines for drip-dry, one horizontal line for dry flat, or a circle for tumble dry.

HLCC LABELS

The wash-tub symbol devised by the HLCC first appeared in 1966, giving recommended washing techniques for different groups of fabric. Automatic washing-machine programmes are numbered to correspond with the symbols on garment labels.

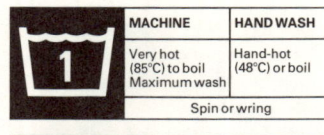

MACHINE	HAND WASH
1 Very hot (85°C) to boil Maximum wash	Hand-hot (48°C) or boil
Spin or wring	

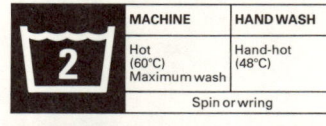

MACHINE	HAND WASH
2 Hot (60°C) Maximum wash	Hand-hot (48°C)
Spin or wring	

MACHINE	HAND WASH
3 Hot (60°C) Medium wash	Hand-hot (48°C)
Cold rinse. Short spin or drip-dry	

MACHINE	HAND WASH
4 Hand-hot (48°C) Medium wash	Hand-hot (48°C)
Cold rinse. Short spin or drip-dry	

MACHINE	HAND WASH
5 Warm (40°C) Medium wash	Warm (40°C)
Spin or wring	

MACHINE	HAND WASH
6 Warm (40°C) Minimum wash	Warm (40°C)
Cold rinse. Short spin. Do not wring	

MACHINE	HAND WASH
7 Warm (40°C) Minimum wash	Warm (40°C) Do not rub
Spin. Do not hand wring	

HAND WASH ONLY
8 Warm (40°C)
Warm rinse. Hand-hot final rinse. Drip-dry

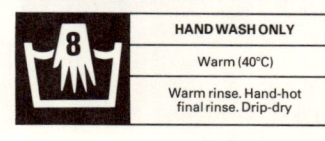

CONTINENTAL LABELS

Labels contain four basic symbols – a washtub, a triangle, an iron and a circle. Each symbol carries information, as shown below, giving instructions concerning washing, rinsing, bleaching, drying, ironing and dry-cleaning garments.

 Maximum wash temperature 95°C

 Maximum wash temperature 60°C

 Maximum wash temperature 30°C

 Do not wash

 The article can be treated with chlorine bleach

 Do not use chlorine bleach. (The symbol does not apply to other types of bleach)

 Use a hot iron (maximum temperature 210°C)

 Use a warm iron (maximum temperature 160°C)

 Use a cool iron (maximum temperature 120°C)

 Do not iron

 Can be dry-cleaned in all solvents

 Dry-cleaning restricted to certain solvents. Line under indicates special treatment

 Dry-cleaning restricted to certain solvent. Line under indicates special treatment

 Do not dry-clean

NEW INTERNATIONAL LABELS

HLCC and continental care labels – introduced in 1974 – are combined in the new International Textile Care Labelling Code, which is replacing the other two systems.

At present, there is no standard size or format for labels used on garments, although the sequence of symbols – washing, bleaching, ironing, dry-cleaning – is the same. Some follow the HLCC style and include written instructions. A few use the wash symbol only.

A summary of the new washing symbols and their related drying programmes is given opposite. An automatic machine will follow the programme dialled, but its spin period, which may be capable of variation in length, may have to be set by a separate control.

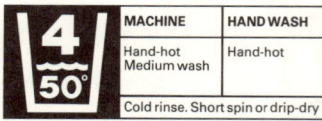

MACHINE	HAND WASH
4 Hand-hot Medium wash 50°	Hand-hot
Cold rinse. Short spin or drip-dry	

HLCC style with the new wash symbol.

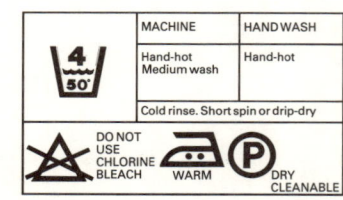

MACHINE	HAND WASH
4 Hand-hot Medium wash 50°	Hand-hot
Cold rinse. Short spin or drip-dry	

DO NOT USE CHLORINE BLEACH   WARM   DRY CLEANABLE

HLCC style with other symbols below.

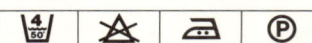

Continental style with new wash symbol.

MACHINE	HAND WASH
4 Hand-hot Medium wash 50°	Hand-hot
Cold rinse. Short spin or drip-dry	
DO NOT USE CHLORINE BLEACH	
WARM	
DRY CLEANABLE	

An arrangement used mostly on UK labels.

SUMMARY OF WASHING SYMBOLS ON NEW INTERNATIONAL LABELS

SYMBOL	MACHINE	HAND	AGITATION	RINSE	SPINNING	FABRIC	BENEFITS
1 / 95°	very hot 95°C to boil	hand hot 50°C or boil	maximum	normal	normal	White cotton and linen articles without special finishes	Ensures whiteness and stain removal
2 / 60°	hot 60°C	hand hot 50°C	maximum	normal	normal	Cotton, linen or rayon articles without special finishes where colours are fast at 60°C	Maintains colours
3 / 60°	hot 60°C	hand hot 50°C	medium	cold	short spin or drip-dry	White nylon; white polyester/cotton mixtures	Prolongs whiteness – minimises creasing
4 / 50°	hand hot 50°C	hand hot 50°C	medium	cold	short spin or drip-dry	Coloured nylon; polyester; cotton; rayon with special finishes; acrylic/cotton mixtures; coloured polyester/cotton mixtures	Safeguards colour and finish – minimises creasing
5 / 40°	warm 40°C	warm 40°C	medium	normal	normal	Cotton, linen or rayon articles where colours are fast at 40°C, but not at 60°C	Safeguards the colour fastness
6 / 40°	warm 40°C	warm 40°C	minimum	cold	short spin	Acrylics; acetate and triacetate, including mixtures with wool; polyester/wool blends	Preserves colour and shape – minimises creasing
7 / 40°	warm 40°C	warm 40°C	minimum do not rub	normal	normal spin do not hand wring	Wool, including blankets and wool mixtures with cotton or rayon; silk	Keeps colour, size and handling quality
8 / 30°	cool 30°C	cool 30°C	minimum	cold	short spin do not hand wring	Silk and printed acetate fabrics with colours not fast at 40°C	Prevents colour loss
9 / 95°	very hot 95°C to boil	hand hot 50°C or boil	maximum	cold	drip-dry	Cotton articles with special finishes capable of being boiled but requiring drip-drying	Prolongs whiteness, retains special crease-resistant finish
 ⊠	Do not wash						
 ⊠	Do not machine wash						

• SORTING THE CLOTHES

Before washing, sort clothes into groups needing different treatment, as indicated by the care label on each article. Correct sorting ensures that the washing method will get the clothes clean and will not cause the colours to run or creases to set into the fabric. If there is a blend of fibres – for instance, polyester (Terylene) and cotton – always use the method recommended for the most sensitive (it has a higher programme number).

Never take chances with garments that are irreplaceable or delicate. Wash them only by the correct method. If in doubt, use the gentlest machine programme or wash by hand in lukewarm water. This also applies to men's washable suits and raincoats and to furnishings washed only once or twice a year – net curtains made from man-made fibres can remain permanently creased if not washed separately and on the correct programme.

The weekly wash usually divides into two or three groups, with articles in the other groups needing to be washed only occasionally. Loads can be mixed to save time and money, but remember to use the programme for the most sensitive fabric in the load. The chart below gives examples of the groups commonly mixed, but if you mix loads in this way regularly, some articles are likely to deteriorate.

An alternative to mixing loads is to wash groups in which there are fewer items every other week.

WHEN THERE IS NO LABEL

If an article has no label, gently hand wash it, and after one or two hand washes try the gentlest machine programme. If you are not sure whether a fabric should be washed in the colourfast or the non-colourfast group, test to see if the colour runs.

Dip an inconspicuous part, such as inside a hem, in a bowl of warm suds. Squeeze out the water, then put the fabric between two layers of white material and press with a warm iron.

If any colour comes off on the white material, the colour is not fast at 40°C and the garment is best hand washed carefully on its own, or dry-cleaned. Never soak such garments. Wash cotton articles with dark red or blue dye separately when new, as there is always some colour-loss at first.

EXAMPLES OF COMMONLY MIXED GROUPS AND RESULTS

MIX AND PROGRAMME	RESULT
1 + 2 – white and coloured cotton. Wash on 2	The white cotton will gradually become grey from being washed at too low a temperature
2 + 5 – colourfast and non-colourfast cottons. Wash on 5	In time, colourfast cottons will look dull
3 + 4 – white nylon or white polyester/cotton with coloureds of the same fibre. Wash on 4	The white nylon or white polyester cotton will become grey from being washed at too low a temperature
Wash all man-made fabrics on 6	Some whites will become grey, and coloured nylon and polyester will look dull
Wash all man-made fabrics on 4	The acrylics (Orlon, Acrilan, Dacron) will become creased and lose shape

AVERAGE WEIGHTS OF CLOTHING

Use this list as a guide to calculating safe wash loads.

Apron 150 g. (5 oz.)
Baby's napkin 175 g. (6 oz.)
Bedspread (candlewick), single 1,300 g. (3 lb.)
Bedspread (candlewick), double 2.5 kg. (5½ lb.)
Blanket, cot 425 g. (15 oz.)
Blanket, single 1,300 g. (3 lb.)
Blanket, double 2.5 kg. (5½ lb.)
Blouse, woman's 150 g. (5 oz.)
Dress (cotton), child's 75 g. (3 oz.)
Dress (cotton), woman's 225 g. (8 oz.)
Jeans, boy's 375 g. (13 oz.)
Jeans, man's 525 g. (1 lb. 3 oz.)
Pants, man's 50 g. (2 oz.)
Pants, woman's/boy's 25 g. (1 oz.)
Pillowcase, cotton 150 g. (5 oz.)
Pillowcase, terylene/cotton 120 g. (4 oz.)
Pyjamas, cotton 450 g. (1 lb.)
Sheet, cot 300 g. (11 oz.)
Sheet (cotton), single 650 g. (1½ lb.)
Sheet (cotton), double 1,150 g. (2½ lb.)
Sheet (terylene/cotton), single 600 g. (1 lb. 5 oz.)
Sheet (terylene/cotton), double 1,000 g. (2½ lb.)
Shirt (cotton), man's 250 g. (9 oz.)
Sweater (Orlon), boy's 300 g. (11 oz.)
Sweater (Orlon), woman's 425 g. (15 oz.)
Tablecloth (linen) 575 g. (1¼ lb.)
Tea cloth 75 g. (3 oz.)
T-shirt, boy's 120 g. (4 oz.)
Towel, hand 225 g. (8 oz.)
Towel, bath 650 g. (1½ lb.)
Vest, boy's 50 g. (2 oz.)
Vest, man's 75 g. (3 oz.)

• MAKING UP A LOAD

Calculate the weight of the clothes either from the chart above or go by their volume, as described below. Do not exceed the manufacturer's recommended weight for the machine (usually 1.8 - 5.5 kg., see p. 328).

With a load of cottons, in an automatic machine, the drum is full when all garments are packed loosely but there is still room to put your hand in and turn it round. If the drum is packed too tightly, the clothes will be creased and badly washed.

It is best to mix large items, such as double sheets, with smaller items, such as shirts. This gives an even load and smoother operation of the machine.

Terry towelling is highly absorbent; as a wash load is usually calculated on a ratio of water to washing, reduce the load if it is all terry towelling (nappies or towels), or wash a mixture of towelling and other cottons.

With man-made or drip-dry non-iron fabrics, reduce the load so that the drum is only half or one-third full, according to the manufacturer's instructions. More than this can cause creasing.

In a twin tub or single-tub machine the clothes should be able to move freely in the water. If they are too tightly packed they are more liable to wear and will be washed less efficiently. Another drawback is that the water will tend to splash more as the bulk moves. If this happens, take out sufficient garments to ease the movement. As with automatics, reduce the load for man-made fibres and drip-dry non-iron materials according to the manufacturer's instructions.

POINTS TO WATCH

Always check the following points before washing, and you will save yourself time in the end.

Make sure all pockets are empty. Pins, coins, paper handkerchiefs and such items may block the pump of an automatic machine. Ball-point pens will run and stain garments. White handkerchiefs in the pockets of jeans will be stained blue.

Mend rips and tears. Even hand-washing will make a tear or hole bigger.

Tie belts and apron strings, and button shirt cuffs to the centre buttons. This prevents garments wrapping round each other. Wash fine fabrics such as tights in a pillowcase.

Close zips and hooks. They may snag other garments or hook into perforations on the sides of the wash drum or spinner drum. Wrap non-washable buttons tightly in foil.

Treat any stains (see p. 326). If untreated stains are washed at high temperatures they may set and become impossible to remove.

• GETTING THE BEST FROM YOUR MACHINE

To make the fullest use of your washing machine, check that a garment is machine-washable before buying, and that it has a care label so that you do not have to guess how to treat it. This also applies to material bought by the yard and to knitting yarns.

When buying coloured sheets, towels and underwear, make sure that dyes are colourfast so that you can use programme 2 on an automatic, because programme 5 – for non-colourfast fabrics – is not hot enough to get such articles really clean.

If you follow a policy of buying for the machine, it may be possible to divide the weekly wash between three automatic machine programmes – or even two. The programmes most used would be 2 for coloured cottons, 4 for coloured nylon and polyester and polyester/cotton mixtures, and 6 for acrylics and socks of a polyester/wool blend.

Hand-knitted garments should not be machine washed, but some manufacturers, particularly of woollens, are over-cautious. Some garments labelled hand wash can be washed in a machine if put into a low-temperature group; if your machine has a wool label, it has been designed for this purpose. 'Superwash' wool has been treated to withstand higher temperatures and can be washed on programme 5.

Do not dry woollens in a tumble drier unless the manufacturer states that it is safe to do so. The temperature is usually too high and the action too severe to dry wool successfully.

Soak large items such as curtains, bedspreads and loose covers in the bath before putting them in a single or twin-tub washing machine. Wash one at a time to get the best agitation and to allow the load to fit into the spin tub. In an automatic machine, use the cold prewash before the main wash to loosen the surface dirt. If uncertain about the material, use programme 5 or 6, no hotter, to avoid shrinkage and colour loss.

MACHINE WASHING BLANKETS

Blankets – except for single woollen blankets – are usually too bulky to wash in a single or twin-tub machine. They can generally be washed in an automatic – check to see whether they are listed in the programme printed on the machine or in the manufacturer's handbook.

Blankets can be soaked for a short while before machine washing if they are very dirty (see Hand washing p. 334). Use machine programme 6 for Acrilan and Courtelle blankets, and 7 for woollen blankets. Use a fabric conditioner in the final rinse (see opposite), and for Acrilan and Courtelle blankets use a spin delay if there is one. Take blankets from the machine when it stops, to avoid creasing.

If you dry in a tumble drier, use the cool setting and turn the blanket occasionally to ensure even drying. Do not use a drier if the blanket has to be forced in and bunched up, as it will crease as it dries.

• SOAPS AND OTHER WASHING PRODUCTS

Washing powders and products such as bleach and conditioner are most effective when properly used according to the washing method, the water quality, and the type of fabric.

WATER SOFTENING

Soft water washes better than hard. It stops soap deposits being left in clothes, which will make them feel stiff, and it stops scum forming on top of the water and making soap powder ineffective. Also, unlike hard water, it will not form scale on the heating elements of your washing machine.

When washing with soap or soap powder, it is best to add a softener to hard water. When washing with synthetic detergent, or a blend of soap powder and synthetic detergent, a water softener need not be used as these products are not affected by hard water in the same way as soap. But if the water is very hard, more detergent or blend has to be used, as it becomes less effective.

Your local water board should be able to tell you whether your water is hard. But you can test for yourself by rubbing soap in warm water – if scum forms and persists before lather appears, the water is hard or very hard.

Two softeners generally available are washing soda and Calgon. Washing soda is more alkaline, and can damage woollens or coloured fabrics. It may also set stains in other fabrics. It dissolves only in warm or hot water. Calgon does not increase the alkalinity of the water, so it can be used for all fabrics and will dissolve in hot or cold water.

When washing by hand or using a single or twin-tub machine, add the softener to the water and wait until it has dissolved – allow a couple of minutes for soda to take effect, then add soap powder.

Because most automatic washing machines take in cold water first (even if hot water is later mixed with it),

SOAPS, DETERGENTS, WHITENERS

Not all washing products are designed to do the same job. To get the best results, use the most suitable product for the purpose and the correct amount according to the instructions on the packet. Heavy-duty washing products normally contain a mild bleach (sodium perborate) that is most effective at a temperature of 85°C.

TYPE AND COMMON BRANDS	ACTION	USES
Soap powders: Persil, Fairy Snow	Heavy duty, high foaming. Best for soft-water areas; in hard-water areas add water softener (see opposite)	For normal washing of soiled articles in single tub, twin tub and top-loader agitator washing machines. Will also remove some stains (see p. 326)
Synthetic detergent powder: Omo, Surf, Daz, Tide	Heavy duty, high foaming. Best for hard-water areas; use extra amounts if the water is very hard (see opposite)	
Soap powder and synthetic detergent blend: Persil Automatic, Pat, (most brands with Automatic in name)	Heavy duty, low foaming	For normal washing of soiled articles in revolving-drum automatic machines, which take less water than other types, and work best with less lather. Will also remove some stains (see p. 326)
Soap flakes: Lux, Kudos	Light duty, high foaming. Best for soft-water areas (see opposite)	For hand washing lightly soiled articles and delicate woollens or man-made fabrics
Synthetic detergent flakes/liquid: Dreft flakes, Stergene, Lux Liquid, Fairy Liquid	Light duty, high foaming. Best for hard-water areas (see opposite)	
Biological detergents: Specifically designed for removing protein stains (such as egg yolk, blood, gravy, see p. 326) that cannot be removed by ordinary washing powders	Contains enzymes that break down proteins. These are most effective at a temperature of about 55°C. The lower the water temperature, the longer the soaking time (see Hand washing, p. 334)	For machines that have a biological soak or pre-wash treatment (this heats to 50°C) or for soaking away stains in hand-basins (see Hand washing, p. 334). Can be used for normal washing, but enzymes become ineffective at temperatures higher than 60°C
Ariel, Radiant, Biological Omo (most brands that include Biological in name)	Heavy duty, high foaming. Use extra in hard-water areas (see opposite)	
Bold Automatic	Heavy duty, low foaming	
Biotex	Light duty	For soaking in hand-basins only (see Hand washing, p. 334)
Woolite (liquid or powder)	Works in cold water	For hand washing colourfast woollens and other delicate fabrics without shrinking or stretching. Can also be used in top-loading automatic machines and spin driers
Fabric whiteners: Dylon Super-White (for nylon and wool) Dylon Nylon White Dylon Curtain White (for nets) Dylon-CC Curtain White (for use in cold water)	Each type is designed for a particular use	Added when washing or rinsing whites to restore the colour of those that have yellowed or greyed. Use the right product for the purpose

it is simpler to use Calgon. Dissolve it first in a jug, then either add it to the dispenser as the machine fills, or put it into the machine before adding the dry clothes. If you use too much softener or too much detergent, the machine will foam. Experiment until you have the right mix.

BLEACH

Modern detergents contain enough bleaching agents to keep clothes white. However, clothes can sometimes become grey or discoloured by other garments in the wash because of careless sorting. Chlorine bleach will restore their whiteness. For stains use a specific stain remover (see p. 326) rather than bleach, although it can be used finally to remove persistent marks remaining on whites and colour-fast articles.

If you use chlorine bleach, remember the following points:

Bleach will not damage the washing machine, provided it is diluted.

Never use chlorine bleach on wool, silk, rayon, drip dry or deep-coloured cottons, or articles with a flame-proof or crease-resistant finish.

For coloured articles, check the care label to see if bleach can be used. If there is no information, try a weak solution in an inconspicuous part first. If the fabric is damaged or discoloured, do not bleach it.

Never use neat bleach – always follow the instructions on the container.

It is better to give the material a few weak treatments than one strong one, which could damage or discolour it.

Rinse thoroughly afterwards to make sure all bleach is removed.

STARCH

Starch is normally used to stiffen cotton or linen fabrics only.

Hot-water starch is made by mixing starch powder to a paste with cold water, then adding boiling water to burst the starch grains and produce a thick whitish mixture. Use less water for a thick starch, and more for a thinner one. Dip the clothes into the mixture and make sure that the material has absorbed the starch evenly. Iron while still damp.

Cold-water starch is a powder in which the grains have been pre-treated, and will dissolve when mixed with cold water. Use in exactly the same way as hot-water starch.

It is easier to starch clothes in a basin or bath, rather than in the washing machine, because there are seldom enough clothes for starching to make a full load. If you have a machine, starch the clothes after the wash, and return them to the machine to spin off excess water. Rinse the spinner afterwards to get rid of starch deposits.

Aerosol starch, which is sprayed on before ironing, is expensive if used extensively. It lasts for one wash only, but is very convenient for small areas such as collars and cuffs, for freshening garments in between washes, or if only one or two items need starching.

FABRIC CONDITIONERS

Conditioners, or softeners, prevent fibres from becoming matted and so drying hard. They are useful for materials such as wool, acrylics (Orlon, Courtelle, Acrilan), terry towelling, chenille, corduroy, velvet and velveteen. They also cut down the static electricity produced in man-made fibres – the clinging effect is considerably reduced.

Fabric conditioners are used in the last rinse, and their effect lasts for one wash only. All detergent must be rinsed out of garments before they are used, otherwise a chemical reaction is produced that reduces the softening effect of the conditioner.

When hand washing, always dissolve the conditioner in the rinse water first and then add the garments. Neat softener can bleach coloured items or cause spots of colour change.

When using a single tub or twin-tub machine, treat articles needing fabric conditioner in a bowl after they have been rinsed, then spin or wring as usual.

If using an automatic machine, add the conditioner in the maker's recommended quantities directly into the special compartment in the dispenser. If dispensing is not automatic, wait until the programme has finished, then dilute the conditioner in a jug of water. Dial a separate rinse programme or the final rinse sequence, and add the diluted conditioner through the dispenser either before or as the machine fills.

• HAND WASHING

You may need to hand wash a garment for one of the following reasons (apart from a machine breakdown):

1. To protect the finish, such as pleats.

2. Because the colour runs in warm water, and it cannot safely be washed in a machine, even at 40° or 30°C.

3. Because some accessories, such as buttons, shoulder-pads, linings, cannot stand machine washing.

4. Because even medium agitation may shrink or spoil the shape of loose-knit sweaters and some blankets.

If you need to wash clothes by hand, sort the wash by the hand-wash part of the care label, which gives a temperature. Translate temperatures as follows: 30°C, cool, feels cool to the touch; 40°C warm, pleasantly warm to the hand; 50°C, hand hot, as hot as the hand can bear.

Soak clothes for about two hours before washing. Dissolve the soap powder or detergent in warm water before putting the clothes in. For articles such as loose covers or net curtains, soak overnight in cold water. Then let out the water, wash and rinse. Blankets can be soaked for about 15 minutes before washing.

Never soak wool, silk, fabrics with flame-resistant finishes, non-colourfast, drip-dry or crease-resistant fabrics or – when using biological detergent – clothing with metal zip fasteners. Do not soak white and coloured items together.

If you are soaking clothes in a biological detergent to remove stains (see Soap powders and detergents, p. 332), make up the solution recommended by the manufacturer – generally one-third of a cup for every gallon of water. Soaking times are normally as follows: cold water, 16 hours or overnight; 30°C, 6-8 hours; 40°C, 3-4 hours; 50°C, 1-2 hours. Agitate the load occasionally, and when the stain has gone, rinse and wash as usual.

To wash wool, dissolve the soap powder or detergent in warm water (up to 40°C) and move the garment gently under the surface. Try not to squeeze or rub. Rinse in warm water, using the same action as for the wash. Wash blankets in a bath or large sink so they will not get bunched up and creased. Squeeze out as much water as possible before drying, but do not twist or wring. Drip the blanket dry on a line, hung lengthways with the border vertical.

Garments with non-iron or drip-dry finishes should be washed separately in warm water. Rinse thoroughly in warm water, and then either put on a hanger to dry or, for flat items, fold evenly and drip-dry. Do not use hot water; do not leave wet garments in a heap; do not spin, wring or squeeze the fabric while it is warm.

Acrylics should be washed as for wool, but spin only when the fabric is cool. Spinning or pulling them while they are warm will permanently crease them or pull them out of shape.

IS DRY-CLEANING AVOIDABLE?

Manufacturers recommend dry-cleaning for one or more of the following reasons:

1. The colours will run in water.

2. Trimmings, pads or stiffening will not wash.

3. The fabric itself will not wash or will shrink alarmingly.

It is possible that the manufacturer is merely protecting the garment from any risk of bad handling, but unless the garment is old and you do not mind the trouble of washing it by hand and the risk of damaging it, it is safer and easier to dry-clean.

If you do try hand washing, be very careful indeed. Do not soak the garment; use cool water and dissolve the powder or detergent well before putting the article in. Wash separately and handle very gently, rinsing with warm water.

Remove as much moisture as possible as quickly as possible, by pressing with a towel. Do not spin, wring or tumble dry. Dry flat with an old towel between front and back to pick up any loose dyes, and keep the garment away from direct heat.

• LAUNDRETTES

Most laundrettes offer only two wash programmes – hot and warm. There may or may not be a pretreatment before the main wash, and some of the larger-capacity machines have what is described as a double wash – a short warm wash before the main one. Soak very soiled articles at home beforehand to loosen dust or dirt.

Wash groups 1, 2 and 3 can be washed on the hot programme; 4, 5 and 6 should be washed on the warm programme. Group 7 (wool) should not be washed at the laundrette, but washed at home by hand.

If there is enough laundry, separate white cotton items from coloured. White cottons need to be washed in very hot water in order to stay white. If the laundrette is very busy and a lot of water is being drawn off, the water temperature may fall, so try to take in the white load at a quiet time.

When washing man-made fibres – nylons, polyester mixtures and acrylics – try not to overload the machine. These fabrics need room to move freely, otherwise they will become creased.

Laundrette tumble driers operate at high temperatures, enabling the load to dry quickly. Dry groups 1, 2 and 5 on the hot setting, and groups 3, 4 and 6 on the cool setting. Do not pack man-made fabrics tightly into the drum, and fold them carefully as soon as they are dry. Overloading the drum or pushing warm garments into a bag will make creases which have to be ironed out later. The metal drum of the drier retains heat for some time after a hot dry, so if you need to dry on the cool setting, choose a drier which has already cooled down.

• DYEING CLOTHES AT HOME

Home dyeing is easy. It also saves money by giving new life to old clothes and fabrics. Most articles can be dyed in a basin, sink, bath, wash boiler or washing machine. There are four basic types of home dye:

Cold-water dye A powder that has to be mixed with water, it is completely colourfast, and so is suitable for articles frequently washed. It is best for natural fibres, but can also be used on polyester/cotton mixtures and viscose rayon. This is the dye to use for batik and tie-dye work.

Multi-purpose dye Sold in powder form, these dyes must be mixed exactly in accordance with the instructions on the packet. These are good for man-made materials – nylon, acetate and some rayons – as well as for natural fibres. They are more troublesome to use than cold-water dyes, as garments must be heated and stirred.

Hot-water liquid dye Ready-mixed dyes that can be used with most washable fabrics and man-made fibres, except for polyester. They are easy to use, and are economical because you need use only as much as you require, saving any left over for further use and matching.

Wash 'n dye A mixture of dye and detergent. The easiest way to dye articles in a washing machine, particularly large articles such as bedspreads, curtains and loose covers.

Dyes can be used on cottons, linens and nylons, but you can get only pale shades on polyesters; and mixtures containing nylon and polyester will dye with a two-tone effect.

Acrylics (Orlon, Courtelle, Acrilan, Dralon) cannot be dyed, and any fabric with a special finish – such as pleated Tricel, Fibreglass or drip-dry cottons – should not be dyed as the finish will be spoiled.

Wool can be dyed, but follow the dye manufacturer's recommendations closely. Never dye wool in an automatic machine, or the garment will probably shrink.

Remove stains before dyeing, or they will show through. Scorch marks cannot be covered by dye.

If the material is faded or streaked, strip the remaining colour with dye-remover to get an even colour before you start. If the material is patterned, dyeing will produce a two-tone effect.

It is not possible to obliterate a colour by dyeing – the dye will mix with it. For example, unless the fabric is stripped of dye first, a blue garment dyed yellow will turn green.

If you are using a washing machine, some dye will remain in the pump, so always run the machine through a hot wash with a tablespoon of detergent and a cup of bleach, or the next wash-load may pick up the dye.

When you have finished, you may notice that part of the machine is stained – usually the door seal or the gasket round the drum. This is not harmful and will fade in time. But if you prefer to remove it, dissolve dye stripper in the machine and run it through a hot-wash programme.

Always wear rubber gloves, to avoid staining your skin and nails, and use washing tongs to handle the wet clothes. Wipe up all spills before they stain, and wear old clothes or a large plastic apron.

POINTS TO REMEMBER

Always check the fibre before dyeing.

DYEING FABRIC AND CLOTHING

METHOD	QUANTITY	PREPARATION	DYEING
COLD-WATER DYE			
By hand	2 tins for each 450 g. (1 lb.) of fabric	Wash and rinse fabrics Add warm water to dye (600 ml., 1 pint, per tin). Stir Fill bowl with enough cold water to cover fabrics Add dye and 4 heaped tblspns salt per tin and either 1 sachet Cold Fix or 1 heaped tblspn soda dissolved in hot water. Stir **Wool** Fill bowl with hot water, but instead of salt and Cold Fix, use 1½ cups vinegar	Spread fabrics evenly in bowl Stir constantly for 10 minutes. Keep fabrics submerged Rinse Wash in very hot water and detergent Rinse until water clears
Washing machine	2 tins for each 450 g. (1 lb.) of fabric. Half a load at a time	Wash and rinse fabrics Mask inside of lid with foil. Dissolve dye (600 ml., 1 pint, of warm water per tin). Stir Run cold water into machine (4.5 litres, 1 gal., per tin) Add dye, and 4 heaped tblspns salt per tin and either 1 sachet Cold Fix or 1 heaped tblspn soda dissolved in hot water. Agitate **Wool** Fill machine with hot water, but instead of salt and Cold Fix, use 1½ cups vinegar	Add fabrics and agitate for 10 minutes, then occasionally for 20 minutes. If the machine is automatic, consult a dealer **Wool** Do not agitate, but stir gently Rinse Wash in very hot water and detergent Rinse until water clears
MULTI-PURPOSE DYE			
By hand	2 tins (4 if dyeing nylon or acetate black; 6 for Terylene or Tricel) for each 450 g. (1 lb.) of fabric	Wash fabrics. If clean, wet them Dissolve dye in boiling water (600 ml., 1 pint per tin) Fill fireproof bowl or boiler with very hot water to cover fabrics; add dye and 1 heaped tblspn salt per tin. Stir	Spread fabrics evenly in bowl or boiler. Keep submerged and moving. Simmer 20 minutes **Pastel shades** Do not simmer **Wool** Bring slowly to simmer; reduce immediately Stir gently for 10 minutes **Nylon, acetate, polyester, triacetate** Stir 15 minutes Rinse until water clears
Washing machine	2 tins (4 if dyeing nylon or acetate black, 6 for polyester or triacetate) for each 450 g. (1 lb.) of fabric. Half-load at a time	Wash and rinse fabrics Mask inside of lid with foil Dissolve dye in boiling water (600 ml., 1 pint, per tin) Run very hot water into machine (7 litres, 1½ gal., per tin) Add dye and 1 heaped tblspn salt per tin. Agitate	Add fabrics and agitate for 20 minutes. Keep heater on if possible. If automatic, use hottest cycle **Wool** Do not agitate: stir gently for 10 minutes **Blankets** Agitate for only 5 minutes Rinse until water clears
HOT-WATER LIQUID DYE			
By hand	½ bottle (dark colours, 1 bottle) for each 450 g. (1 lb.) of fabric	Wash and rinse fabrics Fill bowl with very hot water to cover fabrics Add dye and 2 tblspns salt per ½ bottle. Stir	Spread fabrics evenly in bowl. Keep submerged and stir for 20 minutes **Wool** Stir for only 10 minutes Rinse until water is clear
Washing machine	½ bottle (dark colours, 1 bottle) for each 450 g. (1 lb.) of fabric. Half-load at a time	Wash and rinse fabrics Mask inside of lid with foil Run very hot water into machine Add dye plus 2 tblspns salt per ½ bottle. Agitate	Add fabrics and agitate for 20 minutes. Keep heater on if possible. If automatic, use hottest cycle **Wool** Do not agitate: stir gently for 10 minutes **Blankets** Agitate for 5 minutes Rinse until water clears
WASH 'N DYE			
Washing machine	½ jar for each 450 g. (1 lb.) of fabric. Half-load at a time	Mask inside of lid with foil Run in very hot water (13.5 litres, 3 gal., per ½ jar) Add dye. Agitate	Add fabrics and agitate for 12 minutes. Keep heater on if possible. If the machine is automatic, use the hottest cycle **Wool** Wet before dyeing. Do not agitate: stir gently Rinse until water clears

FABRIC DYEING GUIDE

FIBRE	DYE
Acetate	Any except cold
Acrylic	Do not dye
Angora	Do not dye
Camel	Do not dye
Cashmere	Do not dye
Cotton	Any
Glass fibre	Do not dye
Leather	Brush-on dye for leather
Linen	Any
Mohair	Do not dye
Nylon	Any except cold
Polyester	Multi-purpose
Silk	Any
Suede	Brush-on dye for suede
Triacetate	Multi-purpose or liquid
Viscose Rayon	Any
Wool	Any

HOW COLOURS COMBINE

ORIGINAL COLOUR			RESULT
Red	+ Yellow	=	Orange/Red
Blue	+ Yellow	=	Green
Yellow	+ Pink	=	Coral
Green	+ Yellow	=	Lime
Light Brown	+ Medium Red	=	Rust
Red	+ Blue	=	Purple
Pale Blue	+ Pink	=	Lilac
Dark Brown	+ Light Red	=	Reddish Brown

IRONING A SHIRT

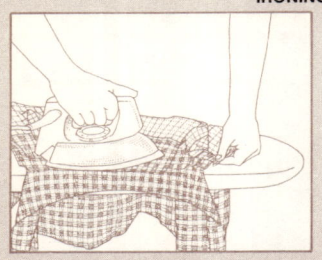

1. Iron seams and double thicknesses on the inside, including the collar.

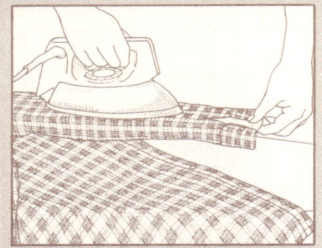

2. Next iron the sleeves. The easiest way to do them is on a sleeve board.

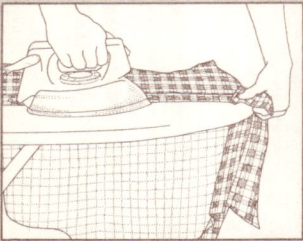

3. Place the right shoulder over the board edge and iron the right front.

4. With the collar at the round end of the board, iron the back of the shirt.

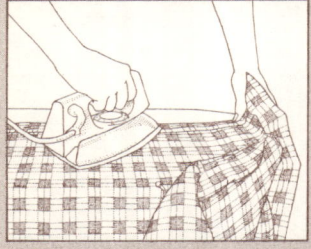

5. Place the left shoulder over the board edge and iron the left front.

6. Hang the shirt over the edge of the board and iron the back of the collar.

FOLDING A SHIRT

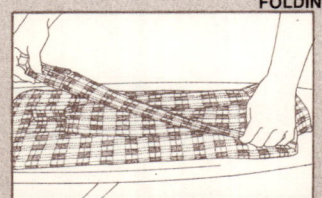

1. Place shirt face down, fold sides to middle, lay sleeves in line with edge.

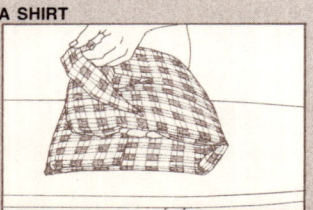

2. Fold tail end inwards, then carefully fold remainder back in half.

• IRONING

If you do not have much time to spare for ironing, or do not like doing it, buy clothes made from the various man-made fabrics that need no ironing. Do not iron articles for which a smooth appearance is not essential, such as tea cloths, or those for which ironing would flatten a desirable fluffiness, such as towels or blankets.

THE IRON

If you are buying a new hand-iron it will be one of three types: a dry iron, a steam iron or a steam-and-spray iron.

Steam irons have a chamber in which water is heated, and vents in the bottom (the sole plate) through which steam can be released to damp the material while ironing. Steam-and-spray irons have, in addition, a manual control for shooting a spray of water ahead of the iron for quick damping of a particular area – such as a bad crease or thick hem.

All three types of iron have a range of heat settings. The heat-setting control may be marked with the names of fabrics or with dots according to the care-labelling system (see p. 330). Settings correspond with the recommended ironing temperatures on garment labels. Older types of iron may have numbers – 1 indicates cool (110°C), 2 warm (150°C), 3 medium hot (180°C), 4 hot (200°C), and 5 very hot (250°C).

Steam irons normally have only one temperature setting at which steam can be produced; this is usually between the warm and hot settings, in the range 140-170°C (285-340°F). Fabrics that need a cool iron cannot therefore be steam-ironed.

A steam iron can also be used dry at the usual choice of temperatures. Modern irons can be switched directly from steam to dry. In earlier models the water chamber had to be emptied

before using the iron dry.

When you buy an iron, make sure it meets the safety standard of the British Electrotechnical Approvals Board (see p. 370). Design points to consider when buying are:

Handle An iron handle can be open at the front, or closed. The advantage of an open handle is that it is easier to move the iron into a fold – into pockets and cuffs for example. But, in general, a closed handle gives a better balance and a better grip.

Weight Irons vary in weight from just under 1 kg. (2 lb.) to more than 1.5 kg. (3 lb.). Steam irons are usually larger and heavier than dry irons, and can weigh 1.5-1.8 kg. (3-4 lb.) when filled

with water. Weight is a matter of preference.

Flex Irons may have the flex fixed to one side or to the top of the heel or handle. A top-fitting flex is better for left-handed people.

Pilot light Some irons have a pilot light that glows when the iron is switched on until it reaches the selected temperature.

Heel rest Irons are available with heel rests designed to prevent them from tipping over when upright.

Button grooves Slight grooves in the point of the iron are useful for ironing round buttons.

Sole-plate finish The bottom of some makes of iron are treated with a non-

IRONING GUIDE
For temperature see p. 330

FIBRE	IRONING SIDE	HEAT SETTING	DRY OR DAMP
Acetate	Wrong side	Cool	Iron slightly damp
Acrylic	Wrong side	Cool	Iron dry if ironing is needed. Do not iron mod-acrylics, which are easily damaged by a hot iron
Cotton	Right side unless dark coloured, cotton piqué or embroidered	Hot	Iron damp
Linen	Right side if you want it shiny, wrong for a dull finish	Hot	Iron damp
Nylon	Either side	Cool	Iron slightly damp
Polyester	Either side	Cool	Iron slightly damp
Polyester mixture	Either side	Warm	Iron slightly damp
Silk	Wrong side	Warm	Iron slightly damp. Do not sprinkle, it will water-mark. Can be steam-ironed
Triacetate	Wrong side	Cool	Iron slightly damp
Viscose rayon	Wrong side	Warm	Iron slightly damp. Do not sprinkle, it will water-mark. Can be steam-ironed
Wool	Wrong side	Warm	Iron slightly damp. Can be steam-ironed

AIDS FOR PRESSING

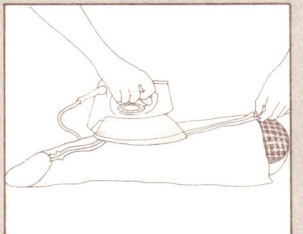

Seam roll Seams inside narrow areas can be pressed on this cylindrical pad.

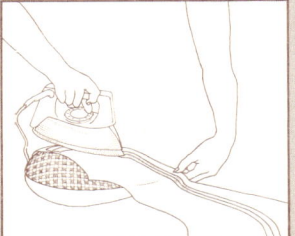

Tailor's ham A pear-shaped pad on which awkward shapes are pressed.

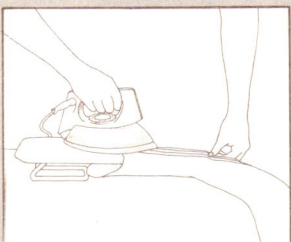

Sleeve board This provides a small, flat surface for ironing sleeves.

Pressing mitt Use it on the hand or sleeve board for pressing darts.

stick (PTFE) coating, to prevent stains or starch marking them.

When buying a steam iron, run your finger over the sole plate to check that the design of vent holes or screws and openings has not affected the smoothness of the iron. Make sure there are no metal burrs that could damage fabrics.

Water-level gauge On a steam iron, it is easier to top-up the water chamber without danger of overfilling if there is a water-level gauge.

ROTARY IRON

A rotary iron has a padded, rotating roller and a curved, heated metal ironing plate that is pressed against it. The roller is rotated by an electric motor, and the ironing plate raised or lowered by means of a foot pedal.

It is easy to use, and cuts down ironing time considerably for articles such as sheets, tablecloths and pillowcases. With practice, even shirts can be ironed quickly. But rotary irons are more expensive than hand irons and take up more room. Some are portable (although heavy) and can be used on a table or stand. They are difficult to dismantle and are best left up and ready to use.

THE IRONING BOARD

Most ironing boards are adjustable; make sure the board is at the right height for you to iron comfortably. Make sure also that it has a heat-proof place on which to stand the iron. Tie-on covers for boards are available in cotton, siliconised cotton, or a stain and scorch-resistant material.

A flex holder can be attached either to the ironing board or the iron. It helps to keep the flex out of the way and stops it catching on the side of the board and fraying.

A sleeve board, either loose or attachable, is useful for ironing shirts and blouses and for pressing pleats.

DAMPING

Unless you have a steam iron, damp most fabrics before ironing; give the moisture time to penetrate the fabric so that it is evenly damp.

If you have a lot of ironing, damp all the cottons and keep them in a polythene bag to stop them drying out. If you do not have time to finish the job, either hang the dampened fabrics out again or put them, still in the bag, in the freezer. This will stop mildew forming, and the clothes can be thawed before you iron again.

A pressure spray of the type used for house plants gives a good, even spray for damping It can also be used for damping on the board, or you can keep a bowl of warm water and a cloth (a piece of old sheet or towel) close by. When you come to a difficult crease, dampen the cloth, dab on the area, then iron.

USING THE IRON

When the iron is first turned on, allow five minutes before you use it. The thermostat takes time to settle, and the initial temperature may be a little hotter than that set on the dial.

It may be more convenient to iron from cool to hot, but it does not matter if you begin with the iron on the hot setting and allow it to cool for man-made fibres, as long as you give it enough time for the temperature to adjust. An iron takes longer to cool down than it does to heat up.

Always iron at the temperature given on the fabric label. The chart opposite gives a general guide. Test man-made fabrics on an inside piece first, particularly if the iron has just been used on a hotter setting.

Pull flat articles into shape before ironing, otherwise you may find that they are not absolutely square when

finished. Tack pleats into place.

Iron sheets folded; to keep the same side uppermost, fold lengthways twice with the right side inwards, then reverse the top flap.

Turn a garment inside-out and iron seams, hems and other double thicknesses first. Some fabrics are best ironed wholly on the wrong side (see the chart opposite).

There are parts of a sleeve or some gathers which are difficult to reach, even with a sleeve board. For seams in sleeves and trouser legs use a seam roll – a firmly packed cylindrical pad. This allows the fabric to drape so that only the seam is pressed. A tailor's ham is a similar, but pear-shaped, pad for pressing curves. Both are made with wool on one side, to hold steam, and cotton on the other, for high-temperature pressing. A pressing mitt – resembling an extra-thick oven-glove – copes with darts and gathers. It can be used on the hand or over the end of a sleeve board.

PRESSING

To give a good finish to tailored garments use a hot iron, a clean, damp tea cloth and a clothes brush. Place the material to be pressed on the ironing board under the tea cloth. Press the iron up-and-down over the tea cloth until the surface is dry.

Then take the cloth away, and with the back of the clothes brush – not the bristles – beat the crease to firm it up. Re-wet the tea cloth and treat the surface of the material wherever it needs to be pressed. Hang the garment up and allow it to air.

IRONING SAFELY

Do not use an electric iron connected to a lighting circuit. It should be wired to a 3-pin 13 amp plug with a 13 amp fuse (see p. 371).

Always unplug an iron if you have to leave it for any reason (but do not handle the plug with wet hands).

Do not attempt to lengthen the flex supplied with the iron – a join can be dangerous. Get a worn flex renewed.

Store the iron in an iron stand or by standing it on its heel. Do not wrap the flex round the iron while it is hot.

Starch marks can be cleaned from the sole plate by rubbing them with olive oil while the iron is warm. Clean stains by rubbing the hot iron over a piece of coarse, damp cloth held taut on the ironing board.

Rub persistent stains gently with a piece of fine wire wool when the iron is cold – hold a steam iron in the ironing position while doing so, otherwise something may get lodged in the steam vents.

Irons with non-stick sole plates should not need cleaning unless misused. They are best cleaned with a sponge dipped in warm water and detergent. Never use an abrasive.

Never fill a steam iron while it is connected to the electricity supply. Always follow the manufacturer's instructions for filling. Distilled water (bought from a chemist) should be used, as hard water from a tap causes the element to become furred and eventually clogs the iron.

If you run out of distilled water, do not use it from a garage as it may contain acid. Use either melted frost from the fridge or water that has been boiled in the kettle.

On some steam irons, the sole plate can be dismantled and the furred element cleaned with a special cleaning fluid according to the manufacturer's instructions. Do not try to dismantle an iron that does not have this provision – it could be extremely dangerous.

Empty the water chamber of the steam iron immediately after use, while it is still hot.

MANAGING YOUR MONEY

Whatever your income you can make the most of it by careful management of your money. It is in your interest to make sure you are getting all the tax allowances due to you. It is also worth having a bank account so that you can take advantage of the services offered by the bank. You can protect your home and provide security for yourself and your family with various forms of insurance, and ensure funds for your retirement with an annuity or pension. Any money left over can be put into a savings account or be invested. The following six pages give a guide to taxation, bank services, insurance and investment, and tell you how to make the best use of credit facilities.

• INCOME TAX

Taxable income includes wages and salaries, tips and bonuses, family allowances, some National Insurance benefits, retirement pensions, dividends from investments, rents from property or from letting a caravan, and so on.

You do not have to pay tax on National Insurance payments such as unemployment, sickness and maternity benefits, or war and disability pensions. Other forms of income which are tax-free are football pools and gambling winnings, Premium Bond prizes and the interest on some savings schemes (see p. 342).

Interest on money invested in a building society (see p. 342) is also paid tax-free, but you have to declare it in your annual tax return as it is taken into account in calculating your taxable income.

ALLOWANCES

Everyone is allowed a certain amount of tax-free earned income, called personal allowance. The amount of the allowance depends for example on whether you are single or married, or a wife whose earned income is taxed separately from her husband's. An age allowance is given to people over 65 whose total income is not more than a certain amount, which can be varied in each year's Budget. If the total income is higher, a reduced age allowance may be given. Personal allowances – and all other tax rules –

may also change from one year to another, according to the Budget.

In addition, tax relief can be claimed on life-assurance premiums and on the interest paid on mortgages or loans to buy or improve your home.

You can also claim tax relief for dependent relatives such as children, invalids and aged parents. Even if an aged parent is not living with you, you can still claim tax relief if you are helping to support him or her.

Claim your allowances on the yearly tax return, which is usually sent to you in April, with an explanatory leaflet. Read the leaflet: there may have been changes in the past year. Go through the form carefully and make sure you give all the information asked for. If you do not receive a tax return, or if your circumstances change after completing it, inform the tax office of anything which may affect your allowances. For example, you may have taken out a mortgage or life assurance, or had a baby.

Married couples are usually better off having their tax assessed jointly: that way they receive both the married man's personal allowance and the wife's earned income allowance. But if their combined earnings amount to more than £7,000 they may pay less if they are taxed separately.

CHECKING YOUR CODE NUMBER

If you are an employee, and therefore pay tax under the Pay As You Earn (PAYE) system, your tax is deducted

from your pay by your employer. The amount due is worked out from a code number based on the amount of your tax allowances.

To check that you have the right code number, delete the last figure of the total 'allowances against pay' shown on your Notice of Coding (form P2). The remaining figures should be the same as your code number. If your total allowances amount to £1,236, for example, your code number should be 123. The higher your code number, the greater your total allowances.

Self-employed people are taxed on their profits (after allowances and deduction of expenses) under a Schedule D assessment. Allowable expenses include a proportion of rates, lighting, heating and telephone bills if one's home is used as an office; but, in the event of selling, the owner might then be liable to some capital gains tax, since part of the home could be regarded as business premises. Travelling expenses on business trips and a proportion of the running expenses of a car may also be claimed, among other things, as allowances by a self-employed person.

If you have not claimed all your allowances in the past, it may not be too late to do so. You are allowed to claim within six years of the relevant assessment.

At present a person with up to £5,000 of taxable income pays income tax at the standard rate of 35%. For amounts above £5,000 the rates increase.

Investment income – including interest from bank deposit accounts above a certain amount, income from rents, and share dividends – is also taxable. If investment income exceeds £1,000 a year (£1,500 for people over 65) it is also liable

to an additional 'investment-income surcharge'.

PROFITS AND GIFTS

Capital gains tax is charged on the profits resulting from selling assets, such as antiques, shares, and property other than your main home, if the proceeds of the sale are £1,000 or more in any tax year. Losses can be set off against profits, and a net loss in any year can be taken into account against any future profits. The top rate of capital gains tax is 30%, but it can be less for low-rate taxpayers.

Capital transfer tax (which has replaced estate duty) is a tax on gifts made during one's lifetime and on property transferred at death. You can, however, give away up to £2,000 in every tax year without tax being levied. Gifts passing between husbands and wives are totally exempt from tax during their lifetime, and up to the death of the surviving partner. After that, anything in the estate exceeding £15,000 is taxable.

Gifts totalling up to £15,000 are tax-free – whether made during one's lifetime or as bequests at death. But capital transfer tax is cumulative – anything a person gives away while alive is added to the property bequeathed on death, and the rate of taxation then applied will be the rate for the total of all gifts made. So if a person dies leaving, say, £10,000, but has already given away £8,000, tax will be payable on £3,000.

There are special tax rates for gifts made during one's lifetime. Up to £100,000, the lifetime rate is only half the death rate. But if the donor does not live for three years after making a gift, the death rate of taxation is payable.

The rules applying to capital transfer tax, as to all other taxes, are liable to change from year to year, and anyone likely to leave a substantial amount of money should seek professional advice on how to minimise the tax burden on his heirs.

VALUE-ADDED TAX

Value-added tax is a tax on the price or value of goods or services, levied at each stage of manufacture and sale. It is payable by all firms involved in the making or preparation of any goods or services, and by all self-employed people with a business turnover of £5,000 a year or more.

Some items – for example most foods, books, magazines, newspapers, medicines and children's clothes – are not subject to VAT.

WHERE TO GET HELP ON TAX PROBLEMS

Your bank manager can give basic help with tax problems, or put you in touch with the bank's specialist tax division, which makes a small charge for its services. Do not hesitate to ask your tax office for guidance: its duty is to see that you pay your just dues – no more and no less.

Alternatively, you can get advice and help from an accountant. A list of accountants in your area is obtainable from the Institute of Chartered Accountants (see pp. 410 - 21).

• RATES, REBATES AND REDUCTIONS

The other major form of taxation in Britain is local rates – levied by every council on buildings in its area. Local authorities have two main sources of income to pay for their operations – grants from the central government and rates which are levied on buildings within each authority's area. Rates must be paid by the occupier – not necessarily the owner. It is advisable to check your rates to make sure you are not overpaying. You may be

able to get them reduced – either by being granted a rebate or by appealing against the valuation.

HOW THE RATES ARE FIXED

The amount you are asked to pay depends on three factors:

Gross Value This is calculated by Inland Revenue officers, not local council employees.

The value they fix is intended to be the yearly rent for which the property could be let in certain circumstances – not necessarily the actual rent.

All gross values are updated regularly. Premises built or altered between revaluations are assessed on the basis of the last revaluation.

Rateable value This is worked out by deducting from the gross value a theoretical amount to cover the cost of repairs and insurance.

Rate-in-the-£ Every council fixes each year the amount it will levy as a number of pence in the £. For example, if the rateable value of your house is £200 and your council fixes a rate of 70p in the £ you will be required to pay £140 in the year.

SEEKING A LOWER VALUATION

One way to pay less in rates is to challenge the assessment of your property.

If things have changed You may feel that circumstances have changed since the last valuation, causing the value of your property to drop. For example:

Difficulties over access.

Noise from an airport, road or long-term construction work.

The building of offensive structures – perhaps pylons or a sewage plant.

The removal of convenient shops and facilities.

Disturbance from neighbouring property.

Delay in providing street lighting and

made-up roads and footpaths. Garden affected by development.

Changes that are unlikely to influence the valuation officer to reduce his assessment include:

The state of repair of your property (unless you can prove that there is serious structural fault).

The fact that there is slightly more or less space in the home, compared with similar properties in the area.

If you have improved your home since the last valuation, you should inform the valuation officer. Changes that might increase his valuation include:

Extensions or alterations to create extra rooms or outbuildings.

The installation of (even partial) central heating.

Adoption of your road by the council. The building of new shops and schools.

If things have not changed Even if things have not changed since the last valuation, you may still be able to appeal successfully if you can persuade the valuation officer that he has over-valued your property compared with similar houses in your area. For this purpose, every ratepayer has the right to inspect the valuation list at the council office.

TAKING THE FIRST STEPS

To apply for a lower valuation, obtain a proposal form from the local valuation office, which is usually listed under Inland Revenue in the telephone directory. Complete the form, and return it to the valuation office. If you can persuade your neighbours to make a similar appeal at the same time, your case may be stronger. You do not have to say what you think the valuation should be, though it is advisable to suggest a figure.

The valuation officer has three months within which to challenge your

proposal. If he does not do so within that time, the valuation you have suggested will be accepted.

Normally, however, the officer will send you his objection in writing, and your case will come up for appeal before the local valuation court: this could take more than a year.

In the meantime, the valuation officer may offer you a compromise, but you have the right to reject it.

AT THE COURT HEARING

If your case does go to the local valuation court and you win, you can apply to the council rates office for a backdating of the reduction. If you lose, you can appeal (and so can the valuation officer if he is dissatisfied with the decision) to the Lands Tribunal.

Appeals to the tribunal are costly and usually require the help of professionals – a solicitor and perhaps even a surveyor.

FINDING OUT ABOUT REBATES

The other way to pay lower rates is to be granted a rebate by the council. Rebates are not only for the very poor; a couple earning £5,000, with two children and paying rates of £400 or more, could be entitled to some reduction in the form of a rebate.

To qualify, you must either own your home or be a tenant (furnished or unfurnished) who is responsible for paying the rates, either as part of the rent or separately. The rateable value of the property must be not more than £700 (£1,500 in Greater London, £300 in Scotland).

If your rates are so high that they are causing you financial hardship, the rates department of your local town hall will help you to calculate whether a rebate is due. There is a maximum rebate of £3 a week in Greater London and £2.50 in other parts of Britain.

APPLYING FOR THE REBATE

When you have established that you may be entitled to a rebate, ask the council rates office for the necessary application forms. Complete and return them.

Towards the end of the period for which the rebate is given you will have to re-apply if you think you are still entitled to a reduction. If the council does not send you the forms automatically, you should ask for them.

PAYING BY INSTALMENT

Demands for rates are normally issued yearly for payment in two instalments, but if you do not want to pay the full amount in two equal sums, you are entitled to pay monthly. It is usually worth arranging to pay by instalments even if you have enough money to pay the full sum due. If you were to invest the money, you could earn interest. If, on the other hand, the council gives a discount for cash, you will lose that amount by instalment payments. Ask at the council offices.

IF YOU FAIL TO PAY

If you cannot pay the rates in full, offer the council some money now and the rest later. Most authorities are willing to accept reasonable offers in such cases.

If, however, you simply fail or refuse to pay, you will be summoned to appear at the local magistrates' court. You do not have to attend the hearing, but if you cannot persuade the magistrates that you are entitled to withhold payment, they will issue a distress warrant, which gives the council the right to seize your goods and sell them to raise the amount due.

If you do not have enough property to raise the money, you can be sent to prison, or the council can put in a claim for unpaid rates if bankruptcy proceedings are started.

• BANKING

About six out of ten people in Britain do not have a bank account. But there are many advantages in having one – even for people with a small income. A bank account helps you to keep track of your money. It keeps your money safe, while allowing easy access to it, and enables you to pay bills and buy goods by cheque. Banks also pay interest on money not in current use and they offer loans, financial advice and help.

To open an account, ask to see the manager of the bank you select. He will explain the different types of account and will tell you what borrowing facilities there are. If you want to open a current account you may be asked for names of two referees. It is usual to give the names of a personal friend and your employer.

TYPES OF BANK ACCOUNT

Current accounts are for everyday expenditure. Customers can pay in and draw out their money when they wish. Regular bills, such as insurance premiums and mortgage payments, can be paid direct from a current account by means of standing orders to the bank. Cheque cards are also available. They guarantee that the bank will honour a cheque up to a limit of £30. A cheque card can also be used to cash a cheque from any bank in Britain, and many banks abroad.

If you have surplus funds in your current account, it is a good idea to transfer them to a deposit account on which interest will be paid. A budget account is convenient for coping with regular household bills such as those for gas, electricity, telephone and rates. Work out what these are likely to total in one year, basing your assessment on the previous year's accounts and allowing for increases. For a small charge, the bank will transfer an appropriate amount each month from your current account to a budget account. You can then pay your bills from the budget account and any adjustment is made at the year end.

WHEN SOMEONE HAS NO ACCOUNT

If you wish to send a cheque to someone who has no bank account, you can write an uncrossed cheque – which they can then cash at a bank. Generally, however, banks prefer customers – for safety – to use crossed cheques.

If an uncrossed cheque fell into the hands of someone who is dishonest, he could obtain cash for it. The only safe way to send a cheque is to cross it and write 'account payee only' on it. The recipient can then try to find someone who does have a bank account who would be willing to pay cash for the cheque after the recipient has signed it.

BANK SERVICES

Other services offered by banks include tax, investment and insurance advice, and the supplying of travellers' cheques. The bank will also act as executor and trustee of your will. Loans, overdrafts and credit cards are dealt with on p. 343.

Charges for these services vary. Some banks levy no charges on current accounts kept in credit. It may be worth comparing the charges of different banks to find the best one for your needs. Get to know your bank manager and let him know if you have, or foresee, any financial problems. It is in his interest to help you through financial difficulties.

The four largest banks are National Westminster, Barclays, Midland and Lloyds. Other banks offering comprehensive banking services include the Co-operative, the Yorkshire, the Bank of Scotland, Clydesdale, Coutts, and Williams & Glyn's. National Giro and the Trustee Savings Banks also have a wide, though not yet complete, range of banking services.

The Trustee Savings Banks, founded as safe depositories for the savings of working people, have been given government approval to become fully competitive with commercial banks. But customers cannot yet get personal loans or overdrafts at a Trustee Savings Bank.

Giro, the Post Office money transfer service, offers customers current accounts, cheque books, cheque guarantee cards and personal loans. Bills can be paid by sending a Giro transfer form to the National Giro Centre, but there is no bank manager to approach for advice.

• INSURANCE

It is possible to insure against almost any eventuality, but the main policies needed by a householder are life assurance, car and general household insurance.

Whatever form of insurance you want, choose a reputable company.

Advice about insurance can be obtained from an insurance broker, who is a specialist in selling insurance. But if you consult a broker, check that he belongs to a professional association (see pp. 410-21).

LIFE ASSURANCE

There are three basic types of protection: term, whole life and endowment. A term policy is taken out for an agreed period of time. If you die during this period your dependants receive benefits, but you get nothing back if you survive. A whole-life policy provides permanent protection for your family, who will receive benefits when you die.

An endowment policy provides death benefit if you die during the period of the policy, or a lump sum if you survive until the policy matures. The premiums are higher than for term and whole-life policies, but an endowment policy combines life-assurance cover with saving.

Endowment and whole-life schemes offer a choice between non-profit and with-profits policies. Non-profit policies are for a fixed amount. With-profits policies cost more but the lump sum payable on maturity is increased by bonuses which vary in proportion to any profits earned by the life-assurance company through their investments. For a higher premium, therefore, you get some protection against inflation.

Another alternative is an equity-linked assurance policy. This is linked to a unit trust, and the return will depend on the investment performance. Although there is a possibility of greater profit with this type of policy, there is also a greater element of risk.

Rates vary from company to company, so it is a good idea to get quotations from different companies to find the one that offers the best terms for the type of policy you need.

Husbands and wives should both have insurance cover on their lives if the family budget allows. The loss of a wife and mother could be a serious financial, as well as emotional, blow to a family. Legal and General Assurance came to the conclusion, in a recent survey, that the work in the home of a wife, with young children, could be worth more than £70 a week. As women have longer life expectancy than men, they have the advantage of cheaper life assurance.

Life assurance is a long-term contract. If you surrender your policy early, when most of the costs of setting up the policy are being paid out of the premiums, you will get back only a fraction of the amount you have paid, and you will have to repay tax relief. If you are in financial difficulties and cannot continue to pay the premiums, you can make the policy paid-up. This means that you arrange with the company to stop paying premiums, but you still get some benefit for the premiums already paid at the end of the term of the policy.

Life assurance policies can be linked to mortgages (see p. 8), and can be used as security against a loan.

LIFE ASSURANCE PREMIUMS

Life assurance costs vary from company to company. This table is compiled from annual premium rates quoted by a leading company for insuring the life of a man for £10,000. Comparable premiums for women are lower, because they tend to live longer. Premium age is age at next birthday.

TYPE OF POLICY	AGE 25	AGE 35	AGE 50
15 year term	£ 17.10	£ 27.10	£115.00
Whole life, non-profit	84.60	120.60	247.60
Whole life, with profits	182.60	250.60	431.60
20 year endowment, non-profit	309.60	315.60	368.60
20 year endowment, with profits	520.60	528.60	589.60
15 year endowment, non-profit	463.60	466.60	506.60
15 year endowment, with profits	700.60	704.60	749.60

THE LANGUAGE OF MONEY

Assets Anything which can be sold.
Assurance Type of insurance which guarantees some return in all circumstances.
Blue chips Shares in leading companies considered to be exceptionally sound.
Bond Document promising to repay a loan.
Compound interest Interest on capital plus accumulating interest. Some pensions and annuities increase in this way.
Comprehensive insurance Cover for most (but not necessarily all) risks.
Convertible loan Loan which may be converted into shares on stated terms.
Direct taxation Taxes paid on money received as wages, dividends, etc.
Equity Value of property after debts (e.g., mortgages) are paid off. Ordinary shares are sometimes called equities.
Estate The total value of everything a person owns, after all debts have been met.
Fiscal (tax) year April 6 to April 5.
Gilts Gilt-edged securities – loans to the government at a fixed interest, and usually for a fixed period.
Indirect taxation Taxes included in prices – e.g., beer, cigarettes, meals out.
Inflation Excess of money over production, resulting in rising prices and decline in purchasing power of currency.
Insurance Unlike assurance, pays out only if the risk (e.g., fire) happens.
Par Equality. Repayment of loan (e.g., gilt-edged security) at par means at face value regardless of purchase price.
R/D Refer to drawer – a bank's polite way of saying a cheque has 'bounced', because the person signing, or drawing, it has not enough money in his account to cover the amount.
Residue What is left of a dead person's estate after all bequests have been met.
Rights issue Method of raising capital whereby a company offers shareholders new shares on favourable terms.
Scrip issue Free or bonus shares issued by a company to its shareholders. They do not increase the shareholders' stake in the company, but merely split it up into smaller units.
Stock Loans to government, councils, and so on, usually in blocks of £100.
Zero-rated (VAT) Exempt. Zero-rated company pays VAT-included bills and reclaims tax from the government.

GENERAL INSURANCE

Having protected your family's future, and your own, you also need to insure your home and possessions. When buying a household policy, check that it covers all likely risks. Some comprehensive policies, for example, do not cover flooding.

To work out the amount of cover you need for your home, measure the ground area of the house, multiply the number of square feet by the number of floors, and multiply the result by at least £15-£18 to estimate the cost of rebuilding. Then list the value of all the contents. Anything particularly precious – such as jewellery or furs – should be covered by a separate 'all risks' policy which applies even when the items concerned are not in the home.

Premium rates for household insurance vary according to the area. Some areas of London, for example, are 'high risk'. Homes outside cities may be cheaper to insure. Rates range from £2 to £5 a year for every £1,000 of cover. Most companies charge a minimum yearly premium of £3 or more.

• ANNUITIES

The purpose of an annuity is to give you an income during retirement. You pay a lump sum and in return receive a fixed income until you die. The older you are when you take out the annuity, the higher the income a given sum will buy.

One drawback of an annuity is that, as the income is fixed, it gives no protection against inflation. And once you have bought an annuity, you cannot get your capital back.

A joint survivorship annuity enables the surviving spouse to continue to receive an income at a reduced rate.

If you are saving up for retirement, you can buy a deferred annuity which is paid for by instalments. House owners who have paid off their mortgage can take out a loan on their property and use the money to buy an annuity. The loan is paid off at death from the annuity holder's estate.

ANNUITY INCOMES

Income obtainable from buying an annuity depends very much on the general level of interest rates at the time of purchase: the higher this is, the greater the income a given sum of money will buy. The following annual incomes for a purchase price of £10,000 were quoted by a leading assurance company when the Minimum Lending Rate, the key to general interest rates, was 11½%. The figures quoted are gross and subject to tax. Payment may be half-yearly or monthly.

AGE	MAN	WOMAN
65	£1,725	£1,607
70	£1,935	£1,757
75	£2,235	£1,985

• PENSIONS

Beginning in 1978, the new state retirement pension scheme gives some protection against inflation, aiming to ensure that everyone will have a pension equal to at least half of his earnings on retirement. Full details are given in a book called *Pensions: Britain's Great Step Forward*, obtainable from Department of Health and Social Security offices.

Self-employed people will not benefit from this scheme and must continue to make their own arrangements. One way that makes the most of available tax relief is by contributing to a personal pension plan operated by an assurance company.

Arrangements should be made well in advance of retirement: the younger you are when you start contributing, the better the pension you get.

COLLECTING MONEY BOXES

Money boxes are probably as old as coinage itself. Some, made of clay, are believed to have been in use in Asia Minor as early as the 6th century BC, and in Britain a flint money box has been found containing coins of the 1st century BC.

In the Middle Ages, coins were saved in tall, open-necked jars, but by the 16th century, intricate money boxes, made of iron and designed as chests, were fitted with bolts or with locks and keys.

The manufacture of even more ingenious money boxes, like American mechanical boxes illustrated below, did not begin until the 19th century.

The 'organ bank' (left, below), patented in 1882, has a monkey on top of the organ which deposits the coin in the slot, at the same time raising its hat. Next to this is the 'kicking mule' (1879). A coin placed on the figure of the man depresses a spring, the donkey swings round, kicks the man over, and the coin drops into the slot.

In the foreground, right, is a figure of a notorious American politician of the late 19th century, Boss Tweed, whose party was linked with bribery and corruption. When the spring of the money box is operated, a coin placed in Boss Tweed's right hand is dropped into a slot in his coat pocket and the figure nods its head in acknowledgment of the 'bribe' (1875).

A coin given to Jonah (left, foreground) on the other hand, is deposited by him into the whale's open mouth (1890).

Such mechanical money boxes are extremely rare and expensive. It would be simpler to start a collection by concentrating on slotted money boxes such as those shown above. These were produced by the Victorians shaped as beehives, books, post boxes, human figures and animals.

Many of these 19th-century money boxes were made of brass or cast iron. In the same period several famous Staffordshire potteries produced specimens in their own style, often in the form of mantelpiece ornaments and decorative pieces to hang on the wall. Once 'banked', the only way to get the money out again was to break the box.

The pig has been, and still is, a universally popular shape for the money box, and this animal alone could well be the basis for starting a collection.

In certain cultures, the fish is equally popular and the 17th-century Sussex pottery money box (above left) combines the snout, ears and curly tail of the pig with the overall shape of the fish's body.

JONAH AND THE WHALE

• SAVINGS AND RISK-FREE INVESTMENT

Having provided basic protection for the future, you may wish to find safe ways of investing any money left over. The following schemes enable you to recover all the money invested and give you some return on your savings. The amount of interest you receive will depend on the current rate for any particular scheme, on whether it is tax free and on how long your money is invested.

NATIONAL SAVINGS

If you have an ordinary national savings account with the Post Office, the first £40 of annual interest is tax free, and you can withdraw up to £30 on demand at any Post Office. With a national savings investment account, one month's notice is required for withdrawals. The interest is taxable, but interest rates are considerably higher than for an ordinary savings account.

There are also longer-term national savings schemes. Savings certificates have a four-year life and pay tax-free interest at the end. Tax is payable on interest from British savings bonds, but there is a tax-free bonus after five years if you keep your bonds that long. Premium Bonds give no interest but provide the chance of winning tax-free prizes.

There are also two schemes which help to protect money against inflation: retirement certificates (for women over 60 and men over 65) and the index-linked save-as-you-earn monthly savings schemes. The return on your investment depends on the movement of the Retail Price Index (which monitors the cost of living) since the day of purchase. These are currently the only savings schemes which guarantee that the purchasing power of an investment is maintained. You cannot buy more than £500-worth of retirement certificates, and there is a £20 ceiling on the monthly SAYE contribution. SAYE contributions can be deducted from your salary by your employer, or you can pay them by banker's order or through the Post Office.

BUILDING SOCIETIES

These are non-profit-making organisations that lend people money to buy their homes, and finance these loans from money that investors lend them. Interest is paid with the standard rate of tax already deducted. People who do not pay tax cannot reclaim this deduction, so for them investing with a building society is not recommended.

For others, if you want ready access to your money, invest in a building society ordinary share account. Longer-term and regular savers can get higher interest rates.

LOCAL-AUTHORITY INVESTMENT

Local authorities borrow from the public in two main ways. Negotiable (or 'yearling') bonds are issued and quoted on the Stock Exchange. They can be bought and sold through bank managers, accountants and stockbrokers. Commission is charged. Interest (from which tax is deducted automatically at the basic rate before you get it) remains fixed.

Advertised or 'over-the-counter' bonds are obtained, at no cost, by applying to the council concerned. Interest is fixed for the life of the bond, with basic-rate tax deducted automatically, The term of the bond can vary between one and ten years and it is difficult to recover your money before the end of the set term. Usually, the larger the sum invested and the longer the life of the bond, the higher the interest.

• STOCKS AND SHARES

If you have money to spare and can afford to take a chance, you may wish to buy stocks and shares, which offer the possibility that your investment may increase in value, and the risk that it may go down.

Shares are just what the name suggests. You buy a share in the ownership of a company and receive part of its profits if there are any. Remember that profits – and dividends – can go down as well as up. And even if a company should be spectacularly successful, the amount of dividend it is allowed to pay to its shareholders is at present limited by law.

The Stock Exchange is the market place for all securities.

You can buy either ordinary or preference shares. A preference shareholder is paid a fixed percentage of the company's profits even if there is nothing left for the ordinary shareholders. An investor holding ordinary shares, however, although he bears the loss in a bad year, could do better than the preference shareholder in a good year.

You can also buy gilt-edged securities – safer, fixed-interest loan

---

FINANCIAL TIMES SHARE INFORMATION SERVICE

The Financial Times publishes a daily list of share prices, classified under headings such as Engineering, Shipping, Oils, together with certain relevant figures against which the prices can be compared. Company names in the examples below are fictitious. A blank in the + or − column indicates no change, or no recent deals. Blanks in other columns indicate that information on which to base the calculations is not available. It should be remembered that all the details in the last four columns are based on past, not future, dividends. Shrewd investors want to know much more about a company and its prospects than these figures can tell them.

1977 HIGH	LOW	STOCK	PRICE	+ OR −	DIV NET	C'VR	Y'LD GR'S	P/E
128	68	Biggs & Bloggs	85	+2	5.0	3.3	9.0	5.1
149	96	Ancient Mariners Co.	96xd	− 1	5.54	2.7	8.9	6.5
31	16	Smoothflow Oil Corp.	19	—	—	—	—	—

KEY TO TERMS

The highest and lowest prices (in pence) at which the shares have been dealt in during the year. Government, local government and certain other stocks are quoted in £100 units. Their prices are given in £s sterling and rises and falls are recorded in fractions of £1.	Name of the company or type of stock.	This is the 'middle' price: it normally varies slightly either way, depending on whether you are buying or selling. xd Ex-dividend. While this symbol appears against a share quotation, a buyer is not entitled to the current dividend payment.	Rise or fall in price during the day.	Total year's dividend, or payment to the shareholder, in pence per share after tax.	Cover – the number of times by which available profits exceed the dividend paid.	Gross yield – percentage income, subject to tax, on an investment at the quoted price.	Price/Earnings ratio – the number of times by which the share price exceeds the company's yearly earnings per share; in other words, the number of years of earnings (if maintained) required to cover the share price.

stock issued by the government to finance the running of the country. Gilt-edged securities offer opportunities both for income and for capital gain – which is exempt from capital gains tax if the securities are held for at least a year.

Another type of security dealt with on the Stock Exchange is debentures and loan stock – loans raised by companies to finance their operations. The companies pay regular interest on the money borrowed, and holders of debentures and loan stock have first claim on a company's assets before those holding shares.

There is no mystery about buying and selling on the Stock Exchange, and you can watch the performance of your investments in the financial pages of the newspapers – particularly the *Financial Times*.

Most people will, however, need advice before making investments, especially on choosing the type of investment best suited to the amount of tax they pay. Your bank manager will be able to assist. Alternatively, you can go direct to the experts – the stockbrokers. Write to the Public Relations Department of the Stock Exchange (see pp. 410-21), stating the amount you have to invest, and asking for names of brokers who would be willing to accept your business. Brokers charge commission based on the value of the transaction and the type of security bought or sold. Their advice is free.

UNIT TRUSTS

Small investors, however, may find it difficult to engage a broker willing to undertake their business. It is for this kind of investor that unit trusts were introduced, offering the small saver a way of sharing in Stock Exchange activity while minimising the risk.

Unit Trust investors pool their money into a single fund which is managed by professional experts, who use the money from the units the public buy to purchase all kinds of securities.

There are about 300 unit trusts, with many different investment aims. Most of them allow investment through monthly savings schemes for people who do not want to put down a large capital sum. The *Unit Trust Year Book* gives a description of the investment strategy and the past performance of all trusts available.

• CREDIT

The final step in money management is to find out how best to get credit to pay for things you want now but prefer to buy out of your future earnings. Hire purchase and other forms of credit sales are dealt with on p. 346.

Banks give overdrafts and personal loans. An overdraft is cheaper, as interest is charged only on the outstanding amount. Interest is linked to the bank's base rate – the amount charged above the base rate will depend largely on your past credit record. Overdrafts are usually granted only to tide people over temporary difficulties. Banks can withdraw the facility at any time, demanding payment of the outstanding amount, and may require the borrower to provide some tangible security.

A personal loan is granted according to the borrower's ability to repay. Interest is charged each month on the whole amount, not just the sum outstanding. Interest rates vary with different banks. Unlike an overdraft, which becomes a liability on your estate, a personal loan often includes life assurance, and is usually wiped out if you die leaving it unpaid. Tax relief is available on loans granted for house purchase and home improvements (not repairs).

Banks also issue credit cards, which can be used without a cheque to buy goods at any shop or petrol station which has an agreement with the bank. They can also be used to buy rail tickets and to pay restaurant and hotel bills. The credit is limited to a figure fixed by the bank. Every month, if he does not pay promptly, a bill is sent to the holder and monthly interest is charged on the unpaid balance. It is possible to obtain up to two months' free credit by taking full advantage of the time allowed to settle your account.

Money can be raised on the security of life-assurance policies from the company concerned, provided the policies have been running long enough to acquire a surrender value. Interest is payable, but the loan can usually run on and be deducted from the sum assured when the policy matures.

Second mortgages are further loans taken out on the security of one's home, taking advantage of any increase in value since purchase. Interest rates are much higher, however, than on a first mortgage.

Finally, there are moneylenders, who lend small amounts for short periods without security but charge customers a very high rate of interest for the money.

• MAKING A WILL

Anyone over the age of 18 can make a will provided he is of sound mind, memory and understanding. In Scotland a boy over 14 or a girl over 12 can make a will. If you have any property at all, it is certainly worthwhile considering doing so. Otherwise, you cannot be certain that your wishes will be respected.

A will is unique among legal documents for, when it becomes effective, the person who made it – called the testator or, if a woman, the testatrix – is not there to explain what it means. It is said to 'speak from the death' – which means that it is read as if it were the testator's last words, even although it may have been drawn up some time before his death.

This has led the courts to be very strict in interpreting wills. The testator must therefore ensure that there can be no doubt about names, addresses or property described. When a will says 'all my property', it means all the property at the time of death, not at the time of writing.

Similarly, when a will speaks of 'all my grandchildren' it is not restricted to those who were alive when the will was made. But if the testator writes 'my grandchildren' and then names those alive at the time, any children born later will be excluded. A will, once made, need not be final – the testator can change it at any time by adding an amendment, called a codicil, or by making a new will.

Every will should begin by stating that it is a will, and naming the testator or testatrix. The will must be dated, and it must make clear that it supersedes any previous will, or codicil.

The person who sees that the terms of the will are carried out and arranges payment of any taxes due is called an executor, or executrix in the case of a woman. At least one executor or executrix should be named in the will. Be sure to get the agreement of anyone who is to be named as an executor or trustee.

Most people choose a relative or close friend as executor. If he has business or professional experience, so much the better. Do not choose anyone who is unlikely to outlive you.

The testator should make sure that all his property is covered by the will. A will must be signed by the testator in the presence of at least two independent witnesses, who are not beneficiaries. If the testator is unable to sign, it can be signed for him by someone else, but it must be done in his presence. The will must have been read to him and he must have acknowledged in the presence of the two witnesses that it represents his wishes.

Most stationers sell will forms costing about 10p each. Although there is no need to use these forms – any piece of paper is satisfactory – a standard form helps the testator to remember the points to be included.

The drafting of a complex will is usually entrusted to a solicitor. An unqualified person who does it himself runs the risk that his intentions will not be carried out because of an ambiguity in the drafting of the clauses.

The testator has the right to state in the will his wishes about the disposal of his body, though what he says is not legally binding (except if he prohibits cremation). It is essential to tell relatives of such wishes, in case there is a delay in finding or reading the will.

A testator who wants any of his organs to be used after death for transplants or research (see under 'Death', pp. 410-21) should make separate arrangements. There is no point in mentioning this in the will, because by the time it is read it is usually too late to use them.

Once a will is made it governs what happens to the testator's estate – until he cancels it. In law, cancellation is called revoking the will.

A will is automatically revoked when a testator marries. The only exception to this rule is when the will is expressly stated to have been made in contemplation of marriage to a named person.

If a testator is married when he makes a will, the will is not revoked by a subsequent divorce.

SHOPPING AND CONSUMER PROBLEMS

To shop sensibly means to shop within a budget and to get value for money. When going shopping, always make out a list of items wanted and try to keep to it – one survey found that people without shopping lists can spend up to 25% more than they intended, much of it on items they already had at home. When goods are being weighed up, do not accept 'a little bit over' simply as a matter of course, and check that correct prices are rung up at the till. There are rules, too, that you should follow when complaining about goods. This section will help you to get the best value from your shopping, and explains the complex laws that protect today's consumer if goods are faulty or damaged.

• TYPES OF SHOPS

The biggest change in our shopping habits over the past few years has been the growth of self-service. This method of buying goods was unheard of in Britain as recently as 1953, but within the next three years 3,000 self-service food shops and supermarkets had sprung up around the country.

This growth continued steadily and by 1975 there were more than 28,000 self-service shops selling food and groceries alone. Today self-service shops sell not only food but also cosmetics, non-prescription medicines, clothes, china, glass, car accessories, wines, carpets, shoes, furniture, kitchen, garden and household equipment. These shops include the supermarkets, cash-and-carry stores, discount warehouses, vast superstores and the even more massive hypermarkets.

This retail revolution has brought a drastic decline in the numbers of neighbourhood grocery shops, greengrocers, butchers and bakers selling over the counter. Those that have survived have an important part to play in modern society, for although they may not always be able to compete with the price-cutting tactics of the supermarket giants, they provide the personal service that many shoppers prefer.

Your shopping habits will probably be dictated by your budget, by the amount of time you have to spare and by the sort of service you expect.

These are the various retail outlets that can meet the requirements of today's shopper:

MARKET STALLS

Prices of food, especially fruit and vegetables, are likely to be lower in street or covered markets where stallholders do not have costly overheads such as rents, heating and staff. Whether the quality of goods is equal may depend to some extent on competition from nearby shops and on the customers themselves. Always watch, for instance, that the apples or vegetables taken from the back of a display pile are as good as those shown at the front. Note, too, whether the hands of the stallholder handling fish and meat are clean. It is illegal to wrap fish or meat in newspaper and you should always wash food bought from open stalls where it has been exposed to dirt and fumes from the road.

THE CORNER SHOP

Prices will generally, though not always, be higher than those in the supermarket because small shop owners do not have the capital, the storage space, or the quick turnround of goods to enable them to buy in bulk and therefore to buy at a cheaper price.

You will, however, get a personal service and be able to buy more precise amounts of items such as bacon, cheese, ham and cold meats, which can be cut to your requirements instead of being pre-packed. Some small grocers will also order individual items for you, such as a special sauce or a cheese.

A few small shops give credit, allowing you to pay for your shopping at the end of each month; and some also deliver the groceries to your door for a small charge.

CONVENIENCE STORES

Some corner shops have taken a lead from the supermarkets, and have converted themselves into small self-service or 'convenience' grocery stores.

Others have joined small grocery groups – known as 'symbol groups' – to take advantage of bulk buying, so that they, too, can reduce their prices.

These 'mini supermarkets' retain much of the flavour of personal service and will save the shopper a lot of time if only two or three items are required.

SUPERMARKETS

More than 19% of the average family's income is spent on food, and most of this money goes into the tills of the 5,900 medium-to-large-size supermarkets. The great majority of these self-service stores are owned by big grocery chains and are to be found – sometimes half a dozen at a time – along almost every High Street.

The shopper's choice of supermarket is not always governed by price (and prices do vary considerably from store to store). Preference may be given to a supermarket that looks cleaner, or to one where the staff appear friendlier. Another may be more convenient because it is near a bus stop or car park. Or it has the range of goods a shopper wants to buy, at prices which are more or less what she wants to pay.

DISCOUNT STORES

Retailers who sell one particular range of goods – it can be carpets, electrical equipment, furniture or bedding – at cut prices, often operate from a large warehouse or showroom. The premises can be more austere than a department store and the staff are there principally to take money or to make hire-purchase arrangements. You are unlikely to get demonstrations of goods such as electrical equipment, or very much advice apart from the manufacturers' leaflets. You will save money by taking away the goods you purchase; a charge is normally made for delivery.

DEPARTMENT STORES

Stores in town and city centres selling a wide range of goods – which can include furniture, fabrics, bedding, light fittings, glass, china, clothes and cosmetics – are popular because of the wide selection on show and the amenities that go with it: the decor, the cloakrooms, the attractive displays, and the highly personalised service. There are many bargains to be picked up at department stores, especially in the sales.

SPECIALIST SHOPS

Shops that specialise in one range of products such as carpets, furniture, shoes, books, cameras and records can save a lot of shopping time because of the wide range of articles on show. And because their staffs sell within these narrow product ranges, assistants are generally more knowledgeable about the products.

BULK BUYING

If you have storage space to spare, considerable savings can be made by buying food, and household articles such as soap powders and toilet rolls, in bulk.

SUPERSTORES AND HYPERMARKETS

The giants of the retail business are the superstores (which take up floor areas of about 50,000 sq. ft – twice the size of the largest supermarket) and hypermarkets (which are anything over this size). They are sited on the outskirts of towns and cities and have their own car parks near the store.

These stores can pass on considerable savings through bulk-buying in vast quantities. They also reduce costs by having a relatively limited choice of goods and selling them cheaply so that they have a fast turnover and bigger sales.

It has been estimated, for instance, that food and groceries are, on average, 7% cheaper at superstores and hypermarkets. To a family spending £30 a week on these items, this would represent a saving of around £100 a year.

• BUYING FROM HOME

The smartly dressed young man or woman who knocks at your door, the friend who invites you to a party, the neighbour with a colourful catalogue to show you, the advertisement in the local newspaper . . . all these can be selling you something. There is nothing illegal or underhand about any of these sales methods, but there are important safeguards worth noting.

DIRECT SELLING

The most common form of direct selling is that done at the door. The most reputable firms will belong to the Direct Sales and Service Association (DSSA), who lay down standards on the quality of their members' products and have a code of conduct over the way in which customers' complaints are handled.

These companies do not expect cash with any order you are placing; this will be collected at the time the goods are delivered. If in the meantime the customer has had second thoughts, the order can be cancelled or alternative goods can be chosen.

PARTY SELLING

A housewife, normally chosen by a manufacturer or his agent through answers to newspaper advertising, invites her friends and neighbours round to a 'party' at which the guests are invited to buy from the manufacturer's display of goods. For organising the evening, the housewife-hostess usually gets a present, based on the value of the goods sold.

The problem with such parties is that many people feel obliged to buy something for the sake of the hostess, and prices are usually high. There can be difficulties, too, finding out who is responsible for complaints – the hostess, the agent, or the manufacturer.

MAIL ORDER

The large mail-order companies operate through agents who have their catalogue and who take orders from friends, neighbours, relatives or colleagues at work. Payment is usually by deposit, followed by regular weekly payments to the agent.

Most problems occur because the article you are buying cannot first be tried on or examined. But, apart from the inconvenience it can cause you, there is normally no difficulty in getting the agent to return faulty or wrongly sized goods – or even goods you do not like once you have seen them.

Direct Mail Goods, such as books and records, can be bought from brochures mailed directly to your home. The advantages of buying by direct mail are that goods can be inspected before being paid for and there is no obligation to pay anything if you return them to the advertiser within a given time – usually ten days. Most direct-mail offers can be paid for in one lump sum, or by monthly instalments over a fixed period. Interest will be charged on any long-term repayments for goods bought.

Mail-order advertisements All kinds of goods are offered for sale in newspapers and magazines, ranging from underwear and umbrellas to garages and garden swings. When sending money for such goods, make sure you keep a note of the publication in which the advertisement appeared, the date it appeared, the date of posting the order, and your cheque number (or postal-order counterfoil). You may need evidence to back up any claim you have if the order is lost or the goods are excessively delayed.

If the firm you are dealing with goes out of business, you may find that your money will be refunded. Contact the Newspaper Publishers Association (see pp. 410-21).

• VALUE FOR MONEY

The shopkeeper, whether a small village grocer or the managing director of a huge retail organisation, is in business to make a profit. Although he values your custom and will go to great lengths to keep it, he must always make money from you or he will be out of business. You, on the other hand, will probably have a budget to keep to and will want the best value you can get for your money.

SHOPPING AROUND

Supermarkets can stock as many as 5,000 different articles at any one time, and the prices of these can vary considerably between each supermarket. Going from one shop to another and buying the cheapest is an obvious way to save money, but if finding the cheaper-priced goods means a journey by bus or car, what you save on your purchases can disappear on fares or petrol costs.

OWN BRANDS

Savings of as much as £20 a year can be made on the shopping bill for a family of four simply by buying own-brand goods. These are the packaged goods that the big grocery chains sell under their own labels. They include washing-up liquid (which showed a saving of 30% in a survey carried out among more than 1,000 shops); scouring powder (20% saving); self-raising flour (15% saving); baked beans, cornflakes, coffee and tea (10% saving).

BARGAIN OFFERS

Supermarkets will often make a bargain offer on a particular product, the special price of which they have negotiated direct with the manufacturer. These prices will be available for a limited amount of time only.

Be wary, however, of those bargain offers where you have to buy in bulk to save money. Four cakes for the price normally charged for three may seem cheap; but ask yourself – will they all keep fresh until you need them?

SPECIAL PROMOTIONS

Offers made with packaged food – offers of camp beds, picnic equipment and toys, for example – where so many packet labels have to be sent to secure the goods at the reduced price, can be good value. But always make a note of the date you sent the money, the address of the company making the offer and the name and address of the company handling the offer, in case you have cause to complain later.

TRADING STAMPS

Trading stamps are incentives used by many shops and garages to bring in more trade. Stamps are issued in proportion to the value of your purchase and are stuck into a book, which can be exchanged, when the book is filled, for a gift or – under the Trading Stamps Act of 1964 – the cash value of the book.

To fill a book by one well-known trading stamp company will take 1,280 stamps.

Shops issue one stamp for every 2½p you spend, so when a book is complete you will have spent £32. A completed book is worth 70p in gifts, or 42½p in cash.

If when making your purchases there is a special offer of 'double stamps' or 'treble stamps', you will obviously not need to spend so much before the book is filled.

The method of issuing stamps at garages is slightly different. Because of the high tax levied on petrol, stamps are issued on the amount of petrol you buy rather than the cost.

The basic rate is five stamps for every gallon which, on petrol costing, say, 75p a gallon, would mean one stamp for every 15p you spend (as against one stamp for every 2½p spent in the supermarket).

The lowest number of stamps given by any garage, however, is 'treble stamps' which means you get 15 stamps to the gallon, or one stamp for every 5p you spend. This is still not as beneficial as stamps from the supermarket (you would have spent £64 on petrol filling your book), but considerable additional inducements are offered by many garages to encourage you on to their forecourts.

Some garages, for instance, give '20-fold stamps' – or 100 stamps for every gallon of petrol. If all your stamps had been collected from one of these garages and your petrol had cost you 78p a gallon, you would have spent £9.98 on filling your book, and would have made a saving equivalent to 7% (or 7p in every £).

Trading stamps give some people a satisfying feeling of 'something for nothing', but whether they actually gain anything is questionable. If by offering stamps a trader can increase his sales he will no doubt be happy to meet the cost out of his extra turnover, but competition from rivals can siphon off that additional business. Since he has to buy the stamps he 'gives away', this could mean either increasing his prices or reducing quality and service.

• PAYING FOR GOODS

The quickest and simplest way to pay for goods is by cash. But there are many occasions when it may be more convenient to buy on credit – by means of a credit card, by hire purchase, by bank loan or by operating an account at the shop or store.

Many of these methods increase the price of the goods because interest charges are added to the cost. So when you decide to buy on credit, always work out first what the interest charges are to be and compare the total with what it would cost you to pay cash. If the sum involved is one that you could invest, compare what you will lose in investment income with what you will pay in interest.

THE LAW AND CREDIT BUYING

There are special provisions and protections in law for consumers who buy goods on credit. First there are now restrictions on the kind of individual and organisation allowed to offer credit. Since the Consumer Credit Act 1974 became law, all the individuals and companies who offer credit for sums of less than £5,000 must be licensed by the Director-General of Fair Trading.

These include banks, building societies, moneylenders, pawnbrokers, finance houses, shops for selling goods on hire purchase, tally men and even secondhand-car dealers, if they supply credit.

Deals involving credit of more than £5,000 are not, at present, covered by the Consumer Credit Act, but the older laws – for example, the Moneylenders Act – still apply. These older laws will, however, be absorbed into the Consumer Credit Act in the next few years.

Under the Consumer Credit Act, any credit agreement that has been made with an unlicensed company or trader or with someone who has broken the provisions of the Act is not legally binding. This means that the consumer would be able to keep the goods he had obtained, and the credit company or trader would lose the money.

There is important protection, too, on interest rates. The true annual rate of interest – that is how much is actually payable in the course of a year – must now be stated clearly in any agreement and advertising. It is no longer enough to say 1½% interest per month. The true rate – in this instance, 19.6% per annum – must also be declared.

The Consumer Credit Act also gives the consumer protection against the operation of credit-reference agencies. Anyone who believes a reference agency may be holding inaccurate information about him has the right to see the agency records and is able, if necessary, to have incorrect information removed from the file and destroyed – provided that he applies in writing and pays a small fee.

Finally, the law allows a cooling-off period of five days in the case of an agreement that has been signed anywhere other than on the seller's trade premises. This means that if you sign a credit agreement in your own home, for example, you can withdraw from the deal without any financial commitment – provided only that you write to the seller and cancel the arrangement within five days of signing. But if you sign on the finance company's premises, this doesn't apply.

HIRE PURCHASE OR CREDIT SALE?

The two most common ways of buying consumer goods on credit are by hire purchase or by a credit-sale agreement. Technically, hire purchase is a hire contract, not a sale, for the shopper does not own the goods until he has paid the last instalment and a further nominal fee.

Under a hire-purchase contract, the shop or trader sells the goods to a finance company which becomes the legal owner and which then lends the goods to the customer, the hirer. The shopper signs the contract with the finance company. When the Consumer Credit Act is fully implemented, liability for putting right any matters concerning faulty goods will be shared between the finance company and the supplier of goods or services. A hirer will, however, put himself in the wrong if he stops making his payments just because the goods are defective.

All the legal protection and regulations covering the quality and condition of the goods (see pp. 348-9) apply equally to items bought under hire-purchase agreements.

Under any hire-purchase agreement, the owner (the finance company) has certain limited rights allowing it to recover the goods if the buyer (hirer) fails to keep up his payments.

If he defaults before he has paid one-third of the total hire-purchase price (that is, the selling price plus interest), the finance company can repossess the goods without a court order. But if the hirer defaults after he has paid one-third of the total price, the finance company must apply to the local county court for an order instructing the hirer to return the goods. If the hirer then refuses to hand over the property, the finance company can ask the court bailiff to execute the order – that is, take the goods by force if necessary.

The hirer, too, has certain rights. For example, he can decide to end the agreement, simply by returning the goods to the seller – provided that he has paid at least half the total hire-purchase price.

Credit sale is also an instalment system but, unlike hire purchase, the consumer legally owns the goods as soon as he has paid the first instalment. He therefore has no right to return the goods or cancel the contract at any stage, but neither the shop nor the finance company has any right to repossess them. The agreement is between the shopkeeper and the consumer. If the buyer defaults on his instalment payments the shopkeeper must sue for debt in the county court.

OTHER FORMS OF CREDIT

Credit cards allow the shopper to obtain goods up to a set limit, without paying until later. A monthly rate of interest of about 2% is charged – which means that the true annual rate is about 27%. On some credit cards – such as Access or Barclaycard – no interest is charged if payment is made in full within 25 days of receiving the monthly statement.

Some shops and stores operate their own credit schemes – for example, budget accounts. The shopper agrees to pay each month a given amount and can then buy goods worth up to several times the value of the monthly instalment. There is no charge for the credit.

Other shops operate option accounts – which allow the customers the choice of paying in full at the end of a month or allowing part of the account to remain outstanding and paying interest on it.

Cheque-trading companies issue cheques or vouchers entitling the holder to obtain goods from particular shops. The customers pay for the cheques by instalments (which include interest charges at especially high rates of 45%). Many traders charge a higher price for goods that are bought by trading cheque – which means that the customer is paying interest to the trading cheque company and is losing for a second time when he comes to buy the goods.

• COMPLAINING WHEN THINGS GO WRONG

When a product is faulty, the first point to remember is that the shopkeeper is legally responsible for putting matters right, not the manufacturer.

When goods are found to be faulty, the shopkeeper can either refund your money, repair the goods, or replace them. You have the right, however, to demand your money back, provided that you can prove to have bought the goods from him. The shopkeeper's receipt is good proof of purchase – so keep it.

Think carefully before you accept a credit note in place of a money refund. If you do so, you cannot later insist on having your money back if you find that there is nothing else in the shop you want to buy.

HOW TO COMPLAIN

If you need to complain to a shopkeeper do so immediately you realise that the goods or the services are in some way inadequate. Take the goods back to the shop if you can, though this is not necessary in the case of large items.

When you make a complaint in person, always take the bill and receipt and any guarantee. Ask to speak to someone in authority who deals with complaints. Most stores now have a procedure for dealing with complaints and this work is normally allocated to a senior person.

Make your complaint civilly and pleasantly, and do not make threatening statements which may create antagonism on both sides. If you wish, you can complain in writing – stating the case simply and quoting any receipt or invoice numbers. It is not necessary to send the receipts with the letter. Make sure, however, that you keep a copy of the letter.

If you are not satisfied with the answer you receive from the shop, write to the managing director of the company at its head office.

If you decide to make your complaint by telephone, make sure you speak to someone in authority, find out their name and keep a note for use later of the date, and what was said and agreed in the conversation.

WHEN NOTHING CAN BE DONE

There are cases in which you have no right to a cash refund or, indeed, to exchange goods with which you are dissatisfied. A shopkeeper, for example, does not have to refund the price of a product that has a design fault which is annoying, but does not make the item unusable or unsafe – for example, a hairdrier that develops an irritating noise. It would be possible to get a refund, legally, only if you had specified that the hairdrier must be silent when operating and had been assured that it would be.

Similarly, if you decide after you have taken the goods away from the shop that you simply do not like them, you have no right to a cash refund. The same rule applies to goods that are found to be the wrong size when you get them home.

In many cases, however, the shopkeeper will offer either to exchange the goods as a gesture of goodwill or will take back the goods in exchange for a credit note. In such cases, it is generally inadvisable to accept the offer of a credit note unless there is something in the shop that you want to buy at the time.

You have no cause for complaint

and no right to a refund or exchange if you damage the goods – for example, by dropping them, by failing to follow instructions given with them or by generally handling them badly.

IF YOU DO NOT GET SATISFACTION

When a shopkeeper refuses to put matters right, it may be because he does not understand your legal rights or that he has chosen to ignore them or that he doubts your complaint. Traders who have had to deal with many dishonest customers or habitual complainers can be suspicious of even genuine complaints.

If you do not get satisfaction from a shop, seek help from the local council's Consumer Advice Centre, which is staffed by people with experience of consumer law.

Another source of advice is the independent Citizens' Advice Bureau, which often also has consumer specialists. The address of a local Citizens' Advice Bureau is usually listed in telephone directories and post offices.

These people listen to the complaint and then contact the shopkeeper to ask for his side of the story. A complaint may be quickly settled simply because some influential local organisation takes an interest.

Every local authority also has a trading standards department, or consumer-protection department, which can be contacted at the council's main office and may be able to help if other bodies cannot do so. As a last resort you can take legal action in the county court under the small claims procedure.

COMPLAINING ABOUT FAULTY SERVICES

There is little written law about the standard of service that you are enti-

tled to expect, but in common law you have the right to expect any work done to be of a standard that could be reasonably expected from a person holding himself out as having a particular skill, and that the work should be done within a reasonable time.

The best protection against faulty workmanship is undoubtedly to choose a firm or individual carefully at the outset – asking friends for recommendations and seeking the advice if necessary of a trade or service organisation (see pp. 410-21).

Many of these trade groups have drawn up codes of practice under the guidance of the Office of Fair Trading and are prepared to help later if there are complaints about their members.

When you do have a complaint, first contact the firm or individual who did the job. Explain clearly what you expected and why the job was below the standard you expected. Ask that the faults should be put right as quickly as possible.

If you do not get satisfaction, or if you decide that you want in addition to claim compensation for inconvenience and possibly damage, consult a solicitor.

COMPLAINING ABOUT NATIONALISED INDUSTRIES

The gas, electricity and coal industries, the Post Office, British Rail and state airlines all have consumer councils, which investigate complaints. The addresses of the local organisations are usually published at the offices of the particular public bodies – for example, gas and electricity showrooms display the addresses of their local councils, and the address of the local committee of the Post Office Users' National Council, if there is one, is listed in all post offices in the area.

Try to resolve the problem in the normal way by complaining directly to

the local organisation concerned before taking the complaint to one of the consultative groups.

COMPLAINING ABOUT BAD FOOD

When food from a shop is bad or contains a 'foreign body', you can take it back and exchange it. If the shopkeeper refuses, take it to the local environmental, or public health, officer (who can be contacted at the council's main office). He or his staff will then inspect the product and the shop and find out whether there are grounds for prosecuting the shopkeeper or the manufacturer under the Food and Drugs Act.

● TAKING LEGAL ACTION

Legal action is the last resort in a dispute with a shop. It may very well be the only way to get satisfaction.

COUNTY COURT

The most common form of action in England and Wales is through the small claims procedure at the local county court – which can decide on claims up to a value of £1,000. The claimant brings the action himself under the Supply of Goods (Implied Terms) Act. He need not be represented by a lawyer; and if he wins a claim involving say, £80 or so, his costs will be limited to only about £5.

To bring an action, the claimant must go to the court office, obtain a claim form and complete it, giving details of the claim, the amount, and his name and address. Sample forms are available in the court office, and if the claimant has any difficulty in completing his form, the court officials should help.

Alternatively, the local Citizens' Advice Bureau or Consumer Advice Centre will give advice.

A court fee is payable at the start of any action and the amount depends

on the size of the claim. There is a minimum fee of 75p and a maximum of £8 for claims of more than £200. The claimant must also pay a charge of 50p to cover the cost of serving the summons on the trader or company being sued.

The advantage of county-court procedure is that in most cases the trader settles as soon as he receives the summons. If, however, he persists in not meeting the claim, the registrar will hear the action and will come to a decision which is binding on both parties.

The drawbacks are the legal atmosphere, which some people find disturbing, and the complexity of the documents and procedures.

Most important of all, judgment in the shopper's favour does not necessarily mean he is automatically reimbursed. If a trader is determined not to pay, it can often prove too costly and time-consuming to make the action worth while. The trader may also be unable to pay, so before embarking on any claim it is essential to find out if the person you are claiming against has the necessary money with which to pay.

A useful guide to the papers and procedures needed to pursue a legal action of this kind is *Small Claims in the County Court*, a booklet issued free by the Lord Chancellor's office. It is available from county court offices, Consumer Advice Centres and Citizens' Advice Bureaus.

Cases of this kind in Scotland are held in the local sheriff court.

For people living in the North-West, a simpler form of redress in disputes involving up to £250 is available through the Manchester Small Claims Arbitration Scheme (see pp. 410-21). The charge for bringing a case is only £1, but extra fees must be paid for any expert evidence that may be needed.

• SHOPPER AND THE LAW

Even the most apparently simple transaction in a shop, supermarket, market-place or on a garage forecourt is governed and protected by a formidable amount of legislation. There are more than a dozen British Acts of Parliament alone that deal with the shopper or buyer.

In addition, the Commission of the European Communities has a programme of harmonising consumer laws throughout the EEC. When the commission agrees a directive, this becomes incorporated in our national law.

It is in this increasingly complex world of laws and regulations that the present-day shopper has to pick her way as surely and safely as possible.

CONTRACT TERMS

Every sale is a contract between a buyer and seller, and both parties to the contract have rights and duties. Both sides have protection in law, but since the buyer parts with money (whose worth is known) in exchange for goods which must often be taken at face value, it is the buyer who is seen to be in the weaker position and so is given more legal protection.

The contract between buyer and seller is usually only spoken, although for expensive items – for example, a refrigerator, car or major piece of furniture – it may be written out in the form of an order or an invoice.

The terms of the contract – whether written or spoken – only come into effect after the seller has agreed to accept a certain sum of money for the goods that are being exchanged.

Two of the main laws protecting the shopper are the Sale of Goods Act 1893 and the Supply of Goods (Implied Terms) Act 1973.

Under the 1893 Act, the buyer has the right to demand back part or all of his money if the seller fails to fulfil his side of the contract. The seller, for example, must make sure that the goods he is selling have been correctly described; they must be of 'merchantable quality'; and they must be 'fit for the purpose for which they are intended'.

This means that the goods must work. If you buy a washing machine which consistently breaks down within a short period of your buying it, you are entitled to have your money refunded.

FITNESS

The law, however, goes further. When the 1893 Act established that the goods must be fit for the purpose for which they are normally used, it was intended to protect not only the buyer but also the seller. For, although it ensures for example that when you buy an electric toaster, it should be capable of toasting, it also lays down three conditions.

1. You must have bought the goods from a dealer who normally sells that kind of merchandise. You are not protected if you buy, say, a toaster from a hairdresser, or if you buy at a discount through the trade.

2. You must have told the shopkeeper or his staff the purpose for which you intend to use the goods. This means that if you, perhaps, try to save money by buying goods that are not intended to be used in the way you want (and that is something the shopkeeper would have pointed out to you), you are not entitled to have your money refunded if you later decide that you are dissatisfied. Using dress fabric to make curtains is an example.

3. You must not have asked for a *specific* article – say, by describing it by its brand name. When you do so, you relieve the shopkeeper or his assistants of any responsibility under the 'fitness' regulation. You are not relying on their skill and judgment in your choice of what you buy.

• GUARANTEES

Before the Supply of Goods (Implied Terms) Act was passed, guarantees by-passed the contractual relationship with the retailer, and established a relationship with the manufacturer. But this had no standing in law.

Since the Act was passed, confirming the consumer's right to redress from the retailer, the position over guarantee cards has been clarified.

Now, in the event of finding that you have bought faulty goods, you can go to the retailer, *or* use the guarantee card which may have additional advantages. For example, the guarantee may offer spare parts or service facilities. Make sure, however, that you keep any counterfoil to avoid possible dispute later.

WHEN NO REFUND NEED BE PAID

But although the 1973 Act reinforces the law's protection for the buyer in this way, it also limits his rights and further protects the shopkeeper.

No refund need be paid on unsatisfactory goods if the shopkeeper pointed out at the time of selling them that the goods were in some way faulty, or if the buyer examined the goods carefully before he paid for them and failed to notice a defect which he should have seen, or if the shopkeeper disclaimed any knowledge about whether the goods were fit for a particular purpose.

Above all, the 1973 Act confirms that the buyer's contract is with the seller – and not with the manufacturer of the goods he has bought. A shopkeeper cannot evade his responsibilities by later claiming that the manufacturer must put right any defects.

Both Acts are, however, civil legislation – that is, they deal with offences against the individual and the individual must take action on them in the civil courts. This means that the buyer who has a grievance because he has been refused a refund or replacement of the goods has got to take legal action (see p. 347) himself against the shopkeeper. He cannot simply report the shopkeeper to a local authority department and have his complaint handled for him.

WHEN THE SHOPKEEPER CAN BE REPORTED

There are, however, several other pieces of legislation that do give the buyer this right to report the shopkeeper. In general, laws that make the shopkeeper liable to inspection by officials and punishment in the criminal court only provide compensation where the consumer has suffered serious loss – perhaps over a second-hand car. Then compensation can be awarded under the Power of the Courts Act, 1973.

SAFETY LAW

The Consumer Protection Acts of 1961 and 1971 deal with safety. Regulations under the Acts cover the design, composition, construction and labelling of specified categories of products – for example, oil heaters, electric blankets, fire guards; the flammability of night clothes; the colour coding of wiring on electrical appliances; the cadmium and lead content in glazed cooking utensils; and the lead content of paint on toys and pencils.

• WEIGHT AND QUALITY

The Weights and Measures Act 1963 ensures that consumers know the exact quantity of pre-packed foods they are buying. Goods – mainly food – must not be sold under their declared weight, and the weight, volume or length of the articles must be marked on the packet, tin or bottle. Weight, volume and length must at present be declared in imperial units. Eventually only metric measures will be required.

Certain foodstuffs must be packed in 'prescribed quantities' or standard amounts.

Certain goods are not covered by the Weights and Measures Act. They include pre-packed cakes, and packets of sweets that weigh less than 3 oz.

Other items – for example, eggs and matches – must be sold by number, not by weight, volume or length.

FOOD QUALITY

The quality of food is also controlled by the Food and Drugs Act 1955, which makes it an offence for a shopkeeper or trader to sell food 'which is not of the nature, substance or quality ... demanded'. Regulations under the Act establish the composition of a wide range of canned and packaged foods. There are also regulations for the conditions in which food is made, prepared, sold and stored, and for the labelling of foods.

SLIMMING FOODS

Foods described as 'slimming' must declare their calories, and must state that they only work as 'part of a calorie-controlled diet'. Foods making claims about nutritional value or vitamin content can only do this where a significant percentage above the amount normally expected is present in the food.

BELIEVING WHAT YOU ARE TOLD

To ensure that the shopper can trust the information he is given, the Trade

Descriptions Act 1968 lays down that goods must be correctly described in all signs, publicity material and labelling that is used.

The 1968 Act also makes illegal the practice of advertising false price reductions. A shopkeeper, for example, could simply cross out £3 on a price ticket and add £2 as the new price. This mark-down is legal only if the shopkeeper had charged the higher price for at least 28 consecutive working days in the preceding six months.

If, however, the trader makes it clear on the sales card that the higher price was charged for a shorter time, he is not committing an offence.

Similarly, when a shopkeeper buys in special ranges of goods for sales, he must make clear which are special purchases and which are reduced prices of stock which he has been selling normally in the preceding months.

WHEN YOU BUY 'SECONDS'

The 1968 Act also ensures that if a shopkeeper decides to sell 'seconds' – goods that have small defects – they must be clearly marked as such, and if the faults are serious they should be described as 'imperfect' or 'substandard'.

The buyer, moreover, is still protected under the Sale of Goods Act, for the 'seconds' must be of merchantable quality and be fit for their purpose.

WHEN YOU BUY AT HOME

The buyer who does not go into a shop to make his purchase is protected quite separately.

If he decides to buy goods that are advertised in mail-order features in newspapers and magazines, he may be protected by guarantee schemes operated by the newspaper or magazine. Under these schemes, if the advertiser goes out of business and cannot fulfil orders, any money the buyer has sent the firm will be refunded. This does not apply, however, to goods advertised within the day-to-day private classified advertisements of a newspaper.

If he buys from a salesman on the doorstep, he is protected under the Consumer Credit Act if he buys on hire purchase (see p. 346), and he can also complain to the Direct Sales Service Association (see pp. 410-21) if the salesman was one of its members.

RECEIVING UNWANTED GOODS

Under the Unsolicited Goods and Services Act 1971 it is an offence for anyone to demand payment from people who have been sent goods which they did not order. Under the Act, a person who receives unsolicited goods need do nothing except wait for six months to see if the sender will collect them. If they have not been collected within that time they become the property of the person to whom they were sent. Alternatively, on receiving the goods he can write asking the firm to collect them. If after 30 days they have not done so, the goods become his property.

• FACTS ABOUT GOODS

Before buying any item – particularly an expensive piece of household equipment, for example – it is advisable to collect as much information as possible so that you compare and evaluate the number of possible choices.

LEAFLETS

The first source of information is leaflets and advertisements produced by the manufacturers. But although such information must, according to the Trade Descriptions Act, be accurate, much of it may confuse and cloud the choice rather than simplify it for you.

There are available throughout England and Wales more than 100 local government Consumer Advice Centres. To find out if there is one in your area, telephone the main office of the local council.

Trained staff, usually working in close co-operation with the local authority trading standards department, give advice and help on all kinds of consumer problems and some give pre-shopping advice.

There are too, many independent local consumer groups who may be able to help. Their addresses may be in the local telephone directory or they may be listed at main post offices.

The best sources of information can be the labels attached to the goods, or the handbook supplied with them. Under the Trade Descriptions Act, the information must be accurate. If a manufacturer does use labels, the following information may be given:
1. Facts about quantity, size, capacity, ingredients and types of fabric or fibre;
2. Information on how to use or care for the goods – covering washing, ironing and spin drying;
3. Information about safety – dealing with how to use potentially dangerous items, such as oil heaters.

FACT LABELLING

The labelling of pre-packed foods is the best example of informative fact labelling, for under the Labelling of Food Regulations, most pre-packed foods must have a description of all the ingredients in them, listed in order of quantity. There are some exceptions – mainly pre-packed, brand-named products that had been in existence for 30 years before the regulations came into force in 1970.

Bread is not covered by the labelling regulations. Nor are meals served in a restaurant. But in either case, if the food is 'not of the quality or substance demanded' proceedings might be taken under the Food and Drugs Act.

Although there is no legal requirement, many manufacturers add date marks to their food products telling either the retailer in code by which date he should sell the goods or the buyer by which date he should eat the food.

There is no legal requirement for the manufacturers of toothpaste, cleansers, polishes and washing powders to declare the ingredients on their labels or packaging. So in this field, the shopper has no special protection against their claims of 'bigger and best'.

The fibre content of fabrics must be declared on furnishings; clothes; and cloth sold by the metre. Because the information is given on removable labels or is stencilled on the material in such a way that it can eventually be obliterated, it is advisable always to make a separate note of the information given.

CARE LABELLING

Fabrics and furnishings usually also give details of how to care for the goods, according to the international system adopted by the Home Laundering Consultative Council (see p. 330).

OTHER LABELLING

Although manufacturers are not generally required by law to give details of how their products behave, any claims or descriptions that they do publish – whether in advertising material or labels attached to the goods – must be completely accurate and not misleading. Otherwise, an offence is committed.

TRADEMARKS AND SYMBOLS

Trademarks are names or emblems registered by companies for exclusive use on their own products, and to distinguish them from other companies' products.

They are, however, no more of a guide to quality than any other commercial symbol.

Long-established companies who want to stay in business will, of course, always be concerned about their company name and trademark. However, in many cases the trademark's chief use is as a form of identification, which can be an advantage to the shopper when choosing between similar goods on display.

SAFETY LABELLING

A more valuable mark is the British Standards Institution (BSI) safety mark, known as the Kitemark.

The British Standards Institution, financed by government and industry, specifies standards of manufacture or methods of testing.

There are BS numbers for 7,500 industrial and domestic goods, covering dimensions, quality, performance and other specifications including safety. A Kitemark or a BS number on a product is therefore a good guide for shoppers to follow.

The Kitemark symbol indicates that a consumer product meets the British Standard. It appears on a range of products from oil heaters to pressure cookers and from garden tools to safety belts. In addition, the British Electro-Technical Approvals Board awards its own mark of approval to electrical appliances which its tests have shown to conform to British Standards.

The British Gas Corporation awards a label 'Approved by British Gas' to appliances that have been satisfactorily tested for safety.

349

FAMILY MATTERS
SECTION 4

Coping in the home

There is only one thing certain about trouble: it always arrives when it is least expected. It is a good idea, therefore, to study this section now and become familiar with its main outline, so that in an emergency you will know where to turn. Basic household repairs tells you how to mend anything from a punctured air-bed to a broken window. The A–Z of useful information lists more than 400 organisations which offer help, from adoption societies to youth organisations. The chapter on home medical care covers first aid and family medical problems.

CONTENTS

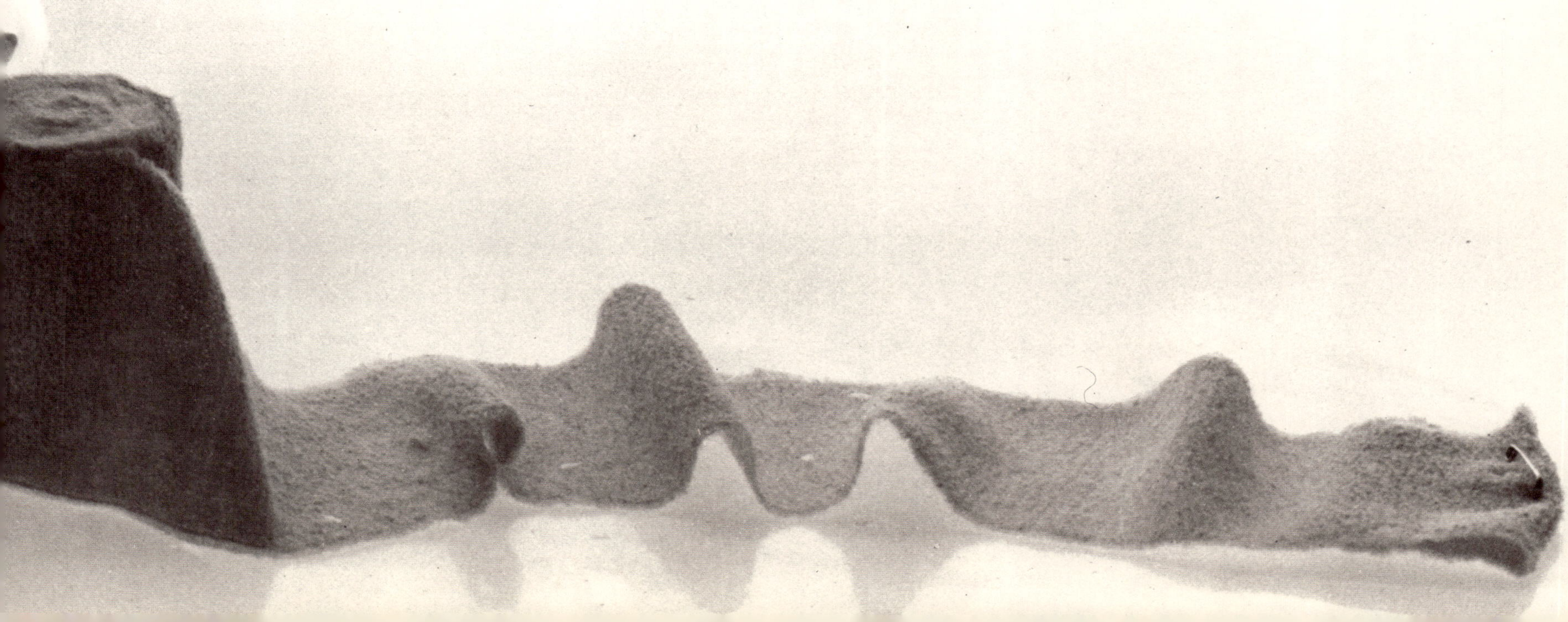

BASIC HOUSEHOLD REPAIRS

If you intend to do a lot of do-it-yourself work, it pays to buy the best tools you can afford. Buy those with an established manufacturer's reputation behind them; many cheap tools do not have this and may need to be replaced frequently. Learn how they work and how to use them. Handled with care and confidence, they will make it easier to do a job that gives satisfaction.

• ELECTRIC DRILLS

Although it is possible to do many jobs without an electric drill, this is such a versatile tool that it becomes essential for anyone who goes beyond the simplest of do-it-yourself tasks. Fitted with attachments, it makes light work of round-the-house jobs, such as drilling, sanding wood or metal, wire-brushing and polishing.

Start with the drill and bit, and buy other attachments as the need arises. Since drill leads are short, an extension cable will be invaluable.

Since different materials require different drilling speeds, drills are made with different capabilities. For the average handyman, a two-speed or variable-speed drill is the most useful, running at 900-3,000 rpm.

Drills are graded by their chuck capacity – the maximum diameter of bit or attachment that can be secured in the chuck. This is usually 6.5 or 8 mm. ($\frac{1}{4}$ or $\frac{5}{16}$ in.).

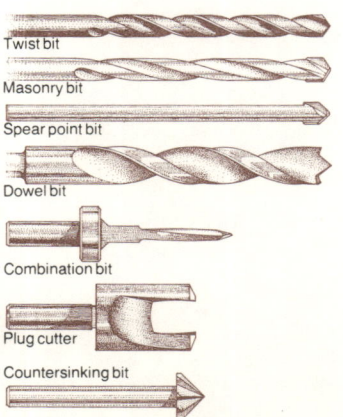

Chuck and fastening key on an electric drill.

TYPES OF BITS

The drilling tool – known as a bit – is fitted into the chuck and tightened with a key. Bits in general use are:

Twist bit Though designed for metalwork, twist bits are more often used for drilling wood. They are sold singly or in sets, in a range of sizes. For drilling metalwork, use drills marked HS (made of high-speed steel).

Masonry bit A twist bit with a hard alloy tungsten carbide tip, for drilling brick, concrete and tiles.

Spear point bit A bit for drilling holes in glass and mirrors.

Dowel bit Used for making flat-bottomed holes in wood to receive a dowel when hiding screwheads.

Combination bit A tool that will drill and countersink in one operation.

Plug cutter Cuts a plug of wood which can be glued back in the hole to conceal a screw head.

Countersinking bit Used so that the head of a countersunk screw will lie flush with the surface of the wood.

Flexible drive An attachment for drilling into awkward places.

Sanding attachments Paper or metal abrasive discs – used with a rubber backing pad which is fitted to the drill chuck – in grades from fine to extra coarse. A wire cup brush is useful for removing rust.

Twist bit

Masonry bit

Spear point bit

Dowel bit

Combination bit

Plug cutter

Countersinking bit

Seven bits suitable for most household jobs.

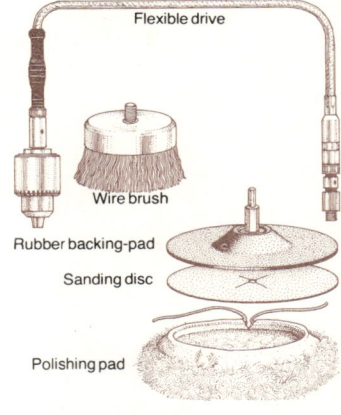

Flexible drive

Wire brush

Rubber backing-pad

Sanding disc

Polishing pad

Varied attachments for an electric drill.

Lambswool bonnet A polishing pad, tied over the rubber backing pad, simplifies polishing wood or metal.

USING AN ELECTRIC DRILL

Use a drill with firm steady pressure. Never use excessive force to make the drill work faster or it will overheat: withdraw it occasionally and let it free-wheel at full revs for a few seconds to allow it to cool. A drop in speed and lowering of motor pitch indicates overloading.

Small pieces of material can usually be held by hand to prevent them spinning; but for anything large or awkward, use a G-cramp to secure it to a bench or work top. Always keep the drill at right-angles to the surface being drilled.

Correct drilling speeds For drilling in wood up to 10 mm. ($\frac{3}{8}$ in.) dia., use 2,500-3,000 rpm.

For drilling in steel up to 6.5 mm. ($\frac{1}{4}$ in.) dia., use 2,500-3,000 rpm.

For wood from 10 to 25 mm. ($\frac{3}{8}$ to 1 in.) dia., use up to 1,000 rpm.

For steel from 6.5 to 10 mm. ($\frac{1}{4}$ to $\frac{3}{8}$ in.) dia., use up to 1,000 rpm.

For drilling in masonry or metals use up to 1,000 rpm.

For drilling glass, use up to 1,000 rpm.

Wheelbrace An alternative to a power-drill, the wheelbrace also uses twist bits, and will drill holes up to 8 mm. ($\frac{5}{16}$ in.) in diameter, in wood, metal and plastic. Keep a constant pressure when drilling, turn the handle at an even speed and prevent it from wobbling, or the hole will be enlarged.

Drilling wood Always rest the wood you are drilling on a piece of scrap wood. This prevents splintering as the drill breaks through.

Drilling metal To prevent the bit wandering over a smooth surface, make a starting indentation with a punch (see right). To drill a large hole, start with a small bit and then use a larger one. To help cutting and reduce friction and heat, use a lubricant round the edge of the hole: oil for steel; paraffin for brass and aluminium. A ragged edge, or burr, will form as the drill emerges on the other side of the metal. To remove the burr, use a larger bit and turn it slowly, by hand, anti-clockwise against the hole.

Drilling plastic Buy a specially designed twist bit, which has a steeper cutting angle. Select a high speed and use water to keep the plastic cool.

Drilling masonry Make a starting point with a nail or turn the chuck by hand to make an indentation.

Drilling ceramic tiles Mark the centre of the hole and cover it with a piece of transparent adhesive tape to prevent the tip of the bit wandering.

Drilling glass and mirrors Lay the glass – painted side up if it is a mirror – on a flat and firm surface, such as a blanket on a table. Place a ring of putty around the position of the hole and fill it with white spirit. Break through the glaze by alternately applying and releasing a gentle pressure. Continue drilling but stop before the bit breaks through the other side. Turn the glass over and drill from this side to complete the hole without splintering.

• OTHER TOOLS

Hammer Buy a 450 g. (16 oz.) claw hammer for simple jointing and general nailing work.

Saws Buy a ten-point – ten cutting points to the inch – panel saw, 560 mm. (22 in.) long, for general-purpose work; a 300 mm. (12 in.) tenon saw for cutting small woodworking joints; and a 250 or 300 mm. (10 or 12 in.) hacksaw for cutting metal and plastics. A junior hacksaw is a useful extra where a hacksaw is too large. A padsaw is for cutting holes in panels, such as keyholes; a coping saw for cutting curves.

Screwdrivers Different jobs require different-sized screwdrivers. The three most useful are 75, 150 and 200 mm. (3, 6 and 8 in.) long. You will also need a small screwdriver with an insulated handle for electrical work. Sizes refer to the length of blade. Buy a cross-head screwdriver for Phillip's and Pozidriv screws (see p. 355).

Pliers and pincers A pair of pliers, with insulated handles, are necessary for electrical work, and a pair of pincers, with a claw on one of the handles, for removing nails. Use pincers with a series of short and even pulls.

Planes Wood is smoothed and reduced to size with a plane. Buy a smoothing plane 200-250 mm. (8-10 in.) long.

Files and rasps Buy a 250 mm. (10 in.) long file, with fine teeth, and a half-round rasp – which has coarser teeth – for general wood-shaping jobs. Also useful is a Surform: a type of rasp with replaceable blades, available in a variety of shapes. In all cases, use the tool to smooth on the forward stroke.

Chisels and mallet Buy three chisels: 6, 12 and 25 mm. ($\frac{1}{4}$, $\frac{1}{2}$ and 1 in.); and a 110 mm. ($4\frac{1}{2}$ in.) mallet. There are two kinds of chisel: firmer and bevel-edge. Firmer chisels have a rectangular cross-section and are the stronger of the two; the bevel-edge is better for under-cutting work, such as when cutting holes or wood joints.

Adjustable spanner Useful for dealing with a wide range of nut sizes.

Cold chisel A 200 mm. (8 in.) long chisel can be used with a hammer for a number of jobs, such as cutting rusted nuts and bolts, raking brickwork joints, cutting bricks and stone.

Boring tools Buy a gimlet and bradawl for making pilot holes before screwing. The gimlet is best for small holes, such as cup hooks, screw-eyes and so on, but if used too near the edge of a piece of wood, it will split the grain. The bradawl has a small, flat, chisel-like point; insert it at right-angles to the grain and revolve it.

Punches A nail punch is essential for knocking nail heads below the surface of the wood; a centre-punch for making starter holes when drilling.

Bench hook If you do not have a vice this is a useful tool for steadying wood while sawing it. Hook one end over a bench, door-step or similar stable bench, door-step or similar stable

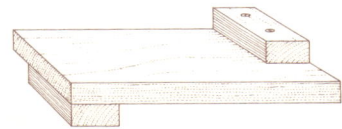

Bench hook – to steady wood while sawing.

surface, and hold the other – with the wood in place – while sawing.

Marking and measuring equipment Basic equipment includes: a 1 m. (3 ft) folding boxwood rule, or a 2 or 3 m. (6 or 10 ft) steel tape; try-square and a straight-edge or metal rule.

G-cramps Two cramps – 100 and 200 mm. (4 and 8 in.) – are useful for jobs where an extra pair of hands is an advantage, for example, to hold wood while drilling in.

Trimming knife Choose one with replaceable blades – including a special blade for cutting plastic laminates.

• MAKING FIXINGS IN WALLS

Solid walls To make a fixing use either a wall plug or a compound filler – both are sold in do-it-yourself shops and builders' merchants.

Plugs – plastic or fibre tubes – are made to match screw sizes; the screws should be long enough for the thread to be buried at least 20 mm. ($\frac{3}{4}$ in.) in the brickwork.

Insert the plug – so that it is flush with the surface of the wall – and position the item you are fixing. As the screw is tightened, the plug will

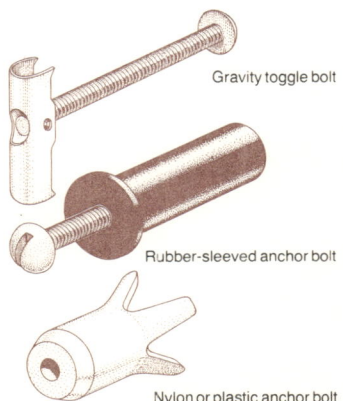

Gravity toggle bolt

Rubber-sleeved anchor bolt

Nylon or plastic anchor bolt

Patent fasteners for fixing to hollow walls.

expand to grip the side of the hole.

A compound filler consists of asbestos fibres and filler powder, and is useful for irregularly shaped holes. Moisten it with water to a putty-like consistency, and ram it tightly into the hole, to finish flush with the surface. Make a starter-hole in the filler – with the pointed tool supplied with the compound – and after a few minutes, when the filler has set, drive home the screw.

Hollow walls Normal screw fixings can be made into a timber-framed wall, faced with plasterboard. Locate the framing by tapping across the surface with a hammer handle. The high notes will indicate solid areas behind the plaster.

To make fixings against plasterboard where there is no framing, use either a gravity toggle, a rubber-sleeved anchor or a nylon or plastic anchor, available from builders' merchants and hardware shops.

A gravity toggle is a bolt with a swivel-fitting on the end. Drill a hole in the plasterboard and push the toggle through until it swivels down. Tighten the nut until the toggle bites into the back of the plasterboard. Once fixed, a gravity bolt cannot be removed intact.

A rubber-sleeved anchor is suitable for fixing plastic or sheet metal to a wall. Drill a hole the same diameter as the bolt, and insert the fitting. As the bolt is tightened, the rubber sleeve, attached to the tail of the bolt, is compressed against the back of the plasterboard. Its big advantage is that it can be taken out and used again.

A nylon or plastic anchor is used with a screw – as the screw is tightened the anchor is pulled against the back of the plasterboard. If the screw is removed, the anchor will drop into the cavity.

• USING LAMINATED PLASTIC

Always cut laminates about 1.5 mm. ($\frac{1}{16}$ in.) oversize to allow for final trimming when the sheet is fixed in place. Use a trimming knife – with a special laminate-cutting blade – and score a line through the decorative face into the brown layer underneath; use a metal straight-edge as a guide. Press on the straight-edge and lift the waste piece to snap the laminate cleanly.

A special laminate-cutter, sold in toolshops, is worth having for large sheets of plastic or those jobs involving curved work.

Spread contact adhesive (see p. 356) on both the laminate and the work surface to be covered and allow them to become touch-dry. Lay strips of wood – about 6 mm. ($\frac{1}{4}$ in.) square – across the work surface. Place laminate on the strips, aligning it carefully. Start at one end and withdraw each strip, one by one, pressing the laminate into position. When the adhesive is dry – about a day later – trim off the excess, using a fine smoothing file. Hold it at an angle and work downwards – do not file upwards or the edges will chip. Use fine glasspaper for final smoothing.

BASIC TOOL KIT

Start with a basic tool kit, adding to it with the tools shown on this and the pages overleaf, as the need arises. A handy-size tool-box can be bought from do-it-yourself shops.

The following items will be useful: hammer, pliers, pincers, adjustable spanner, tenon saw, hand-drill and bits, screwdrivers (large, electrician's and cross-head), cold chisel, knife, scissors, measuring rule, plug punch and plugs, insulating and masking tape, adhesives (see p. 356), assorted grades of glasspaper, cartridge fuses and fuse wire, wallpaper paste, external and internal fillers; machine and penetrating oils, assorted screws and nails, tap washers, ball of string and a length of 3-core flex.

• THE CHOICE AND USE OF WOOD

All wood contains moisture. When bought fresh from a timber merchant it may contain as much as 20%, by weight.

For outside use, wood with this moisture content is suitable; but for inside work the moisture content should not be more than 8-10% or, as it dries out, the wood will shrink and warp. Wherever possible, keep freshly bought timber inside the house for at least a month before using it – preferably in the room where it will ultimately be used. This method of maturing timber is essential in a house having central heating.

Estimate your requirements carefully in order to use wood as economically as possible. Timber is now sold in metric sizes, and a series of metric equivalents of the old imperial measures has been introduced. These sizes are usually on display at timber yards. Timber is sold in unit lengths, each unit 300 mm. long – about $\frac{3}{16}$ in. under 1 ft. If you are planning to use a 6 ft length of wood, for example, you would have to buy seven units, with a consequent wastage of 11 in. of timber. By adapting a design so that 5 ft 11 in. is adequate, only six units need be bought.

Wood is sold in either sawn or planed sizes. All planed wood is about 4 mm. ($\frac{5}{32}$ in.) smaller in width and thickness than the sawn (or nominal) size. If you want to buy timber that is planed to specific dimensions, ask for *finished* sizes, which will be more expensive.

Examine wood carefully when buying it, for warped shapes, knots and splits in the ends of boards. Knots, provided they are sound and tight, present no problem unless on the corners of boards used for shelving or built-in fittings.

Softwood Suitable for most household purposes – both inside and out – softwood is usually available from timber yards in a wide range of sizes as stock items. Other sizes have to be cut to size by the merchants and, consequently, cost a little more. Typical softwoods are pine, fir and cedar.

Hardwood This is stronger, denser and more expensive than softwood, used chiefly for decorative cladding, furniture and floors. The cheapest hardwood is about the same price as the dearest softwood.

Unlike softwood, the difference between actual and nominal sizes varies among timber merchants. Typical hardwoods are oak, teak and mahogany.

Chipboard Made from chips of wood bonded together under pressure, chipboard is the cheapest of manufactured boards. It is strong and will not warp, but unless supported at the edges it will sag under its own weight over a span of about a metre. Special grades are made for outside use, and plastic or hardwood-veneered chipboard is available for fitted furniture. Chipboard is suitable for utility shelving or, when veneered with plastic, for work tops and similar surfaces.

It is normally available in 2,440 mm. (8 ft) long sheets, 1,220 and 600 mm. (4 and 2 ft) wide, 12, 18, 22 and 25 mm. ($\frac{1}{2}$, $\frac{3}{4}$, $\frac{5}{8}$ and 1 in.) thick.

Blockboard Made of strips of softwood, sandwiched between sheets of wood veneer, blockboard is a strong and versatile material, ideal for cupboards, wardrobes and work tops. But it cannot be used for outside work, since the adhesives used in its manufacture are not waterproof.

For maximum strength when using blockboard to span between supports, cut it so that the inner strips run the length of the span.

Blockboard is available in 2,440 × 1,220 mm. (8 × 4 ft) sheets, and common thicknesses are 12, 18 and 25 mm. ($\frac{1}{2}$, $\frac{3}{4}$ and 1 in.).

In order to conceal the core construction of blockboard and to provide, where necessary, a fixing for screws, the exposed edges need to be lipped with hardwood or softwood. Glue and panel-pin 6 mm. ($\frac{1}{4}$ in.) thick lippings to the edges, with mitred corners.

Plywood Wood veneers are layered and bonded together under pressure to form plywood. The veneers are layered in odd numbers – three, five and so on – and alternate veneers are arranged at right-angles to each other to give maximum strength.

Only plywood marked EXTERIOR WBP – which is water and boil-proof – is suitable for outside use.

Chiefly used for decorative cladding and furniture, plywood is available in a range of sheet sizes from 1,220 × 1,220 mm. (4 × 4 ft) square up to 3,050 × 1,525 mm. (10 × 5 ft), and thicknesses from 3.2 to 12.5 mm. ($\frac{1}{8}$ to $\frac{1}{2}$ in.).

Hardboard Made from highly compressed softwood pulp, hardboard – if properly sealed – can be painted, papered or laminated. Manufactured in several different grades, one of which is suitable for outside use, it has one smooth and one textured face. Hardboard can also be bought with decorative, laminated, or perforated finishes.

It is suitable as a cladding material, and is often glued and panel-pinned to wooden frameworks – such as cupboard carcassing or flush doors.

Hardboard is available in 2,440 × 1,220 mm. (8 × 4 ft) sheets, up to 6.5 mm. ($\frac{1}{4}$ in.) thick. Hardboard can often be bought, cut to size, for facing a panelled door.

SIMPLE JOINTS AND FIXINGS

A few simple joints are adequate for many basic household carpentry jobs.

The halving joint is easy to make and suitable for framing work, particularly if a framework needs to be flush-faced for panelling or cladding.

Measure and cut the grooves carefully to size, so that the pieces can be pushed together by hand – a joint that needs to be hammered is too tight and may ultimately distort.

If the joint is used where it will be strained – in a chair, for instance – it should be screwed as well as glued.

Proprietary plastic corner units are easy to use and ideal for jointing man-made boards. The plastic joints have pre-formed holes in them and are simply screwed to the adjoining boards

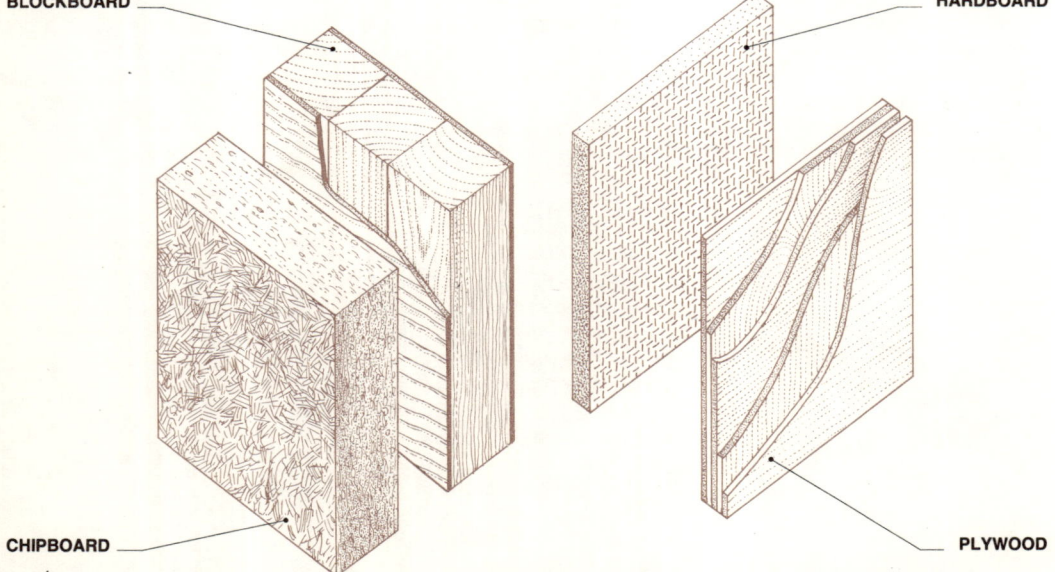

BLOCKBOARD

HARDBOARD

CHIPBOARD

PLYWOOD

MANUFACTURED BOARDS Some of the more useful man-made boards available that have a wide range of uses – both practical and decorative – for the handyman. Always ask for external quality if a board is needed for outside use.

and then bolted to each other to make a tight and accurate joint.

• SCREWS

These have two dimensions: their length, expressed in inches, and the thickness of the shank – that portion between the head and the thread – which has a gauge number. Gauge numbers do not vary with the length of the screw. For example, a 1 in. No. 8 gauge screw has the same size head and shank as a 3 in. No. 8 gauge screw. The thinner the screw the lower the gauge number.

Screws have differently shaped heads. The head of a countersunk screw allows it to be driven in flush with the surface, and is used for most woodworking joints. Metal fittings, such as coat hooks and toilet-paper holders, often have countersunk fixing holes.

Round-head screws, which have a flat surface underneath, are for gripping sheets of metal, hardboard or plywood.

Raised-head screws – rounded on top and countersunk underneath – are used for more decorative work, such as door handles.

Dome-head screws have two parts – a countersunk screw and a dome-shaped cap, with a stem on it which screws into a hole in the top of the screw. Dome-head screws are used as a decorative fixing for mirrors and bath panels.

Steel screws are suitable for most woodworking purposes; but use galvanised or zinc-coated steel for outside work to avoid rusting.

Brass screws – not as strong as steel – can be used for similar jobs inside the house, where appearance is important. Since a brass screw may snap when driven into hardwood, drill the pilot hole and drive a steel screw home first, then replace it with a brass screw of the same length and gauge. Other decorative screws available are chromium-plated, black japanned and aluminium.

Most screws have a slot in the head to receive the blade of a screwdriver. Two exceptions are Pozidriv and Phillip's screws, which have star-shaped and cross-shaped slots respectively; each needing its own type of screwdriver.

Always fix the thinner wood to the thicker in order to avoid splitting, and always drill a starting hole for the screw shank in the thinner of the two. Use a bit in a hand-drill for small holes; an electric drill for large holes.

Screw heads can be disguised beneath a painted surface by countersinking holes and using countersunk screws. Drive the head well in, and fill the surface indentation with plastic wood or a flexible wood filler. For woodwork that is to be sealed or polished, use a dowelling bit and drive the screw home about 6 mm. ($\frac{1}{4}$ in.) below the surface. Fill the hole with matching size dowelling rod – available from builders' merchants and do-it-yourself shops – glued into place and sanded smooth.

If you expect to use a lot of screws it is more economical to get them by the box of 100 or 200, rather than in smaller quantities.

• NAILS

Although much easier to use than screws, nails do not provide such a firm fixing and should therefore be used only where there is no frontal pull on the timber. A stronger fixing can often be made by dovetailing nails, that is, hammering them in at an angle to the surface of the wood, with adjacent nails in alternate directions.

For outside work use galvanised nails to avoid rusting.

Nails have either oval or round bodies: oval wire nails are neater and easier to drive below the surface and are less likely to split the wood; round wire nails have flat heads and are effective for gripping thin timber.

Panel pins are thin nails suitable for fixing such items as mouldings, hardboard and cork tiles. The heads can be driven below the surface with a hammer and nail punch.

Lost head nails have a smaller head and are more suitable for hidden fixings in good-quality work.

Clout nails have a large head in relation to their body and are suitable for fixing roofing felt, and the sash cords in windows.

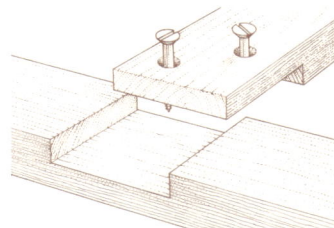

A T-halving joint is a simple substitute for the more difficult mortise and tenon. Cut the pieces to fit together – hand-tight.

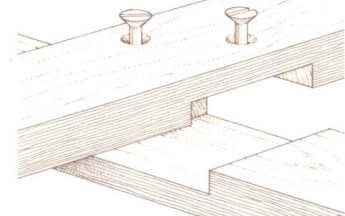

A cross-halving joint – suitable for framing jobs, where a flush face is needed in order to clad it with boarding or panelling.

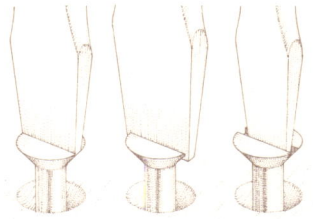

The blade of a screwdriver should always fit the slot exactly – too large or too small a blade will damage the head of the screw.

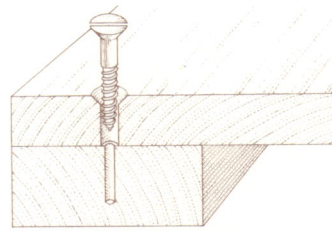

Drill a clearance hole for the screw through the wood being fixed, and a second, smaller hole, in the fixing timber.

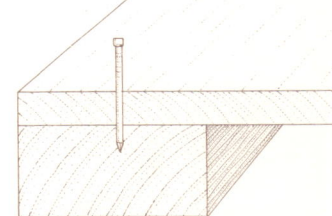

In order to avoid splitting, always nail the thinner of two pieces of wood to the thicker. Oval nails should line up with the grain.

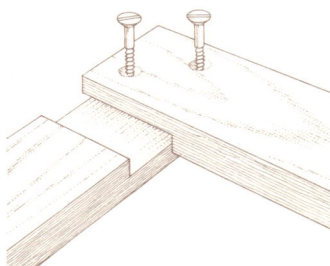

The corner-halving joint is an easy one to make since it needs only saw cuts.

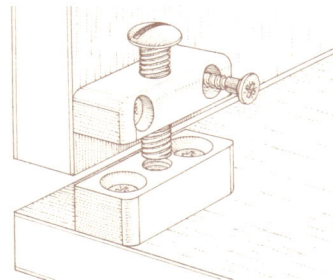

Proprietary plastic corner joints simplify jointing manufactured boards.

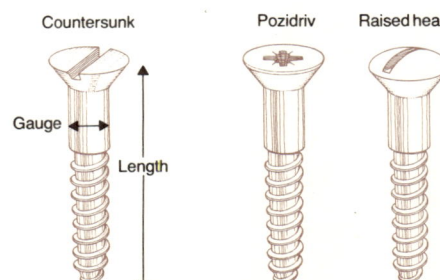

Countersunk   Pozidriv   Raised head   Round head   Dome head

Gauge   Length

A selection of different screws available for general woodworking purposes, as well as for fixing decorative hardware, such as door or cupboard handles.

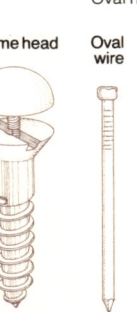

Oval wire   Round wire   Panel pin   Lost head   Clout

A range of nails that is suitable for most general repair jobs about the house.

ADHESIVES
The numbers, listing the adhesives (below), correspond with those numbers in the chart on the facing page.

ADHESIVE	SAMPLE BRAND NAMES	CHARACTERISTICS	ADVANTAGES	DISADVANTAGES	CLEANING UP
1. Animal glue	Britfix 33, Certofix, Chukka, Croid Aero, Certofix Multi-purpose, Gloy Liquid Glue	Traditional carpenters' glue made from animal and fish bones and skin. Used to be heated in old-fashioned kettles. Available in bar form or ready-mixed liquid	Forms a strong bond. Will stick wood veneers	Neither waterproof nor flexible. Difficult to use	With a damp cloth while still tacky; soak in warm water when set
2. Casein	Casco casein glue, Insol	In powder form for mixing	Can be used in low temperatures	Will stain hardwoods	With water before glue sets
3. Cellulose	Durofix, HMG Heat and waterproof adhesive, Joy Stixin	Useful for repairing awkward-shaped pieces that cannot be cramped	Dries quickly	Bond not strong. Adhesive not heatproof or waterproof	Acetone or nail-varnish remover
4. Clear	Bostik, Croid 1, Britfix 22, Gloy Household, Rawlplug Durafix, Uhu	General-purpose household glue. Will not stick expanded polystyrene or polythene	Versatile and hard	Although versatile, is not the ideal glue for every job. Useful in an emergency	In most cases a nail-varnish remover or cellulose thinners
5. Contact	Evostik Impact, Borden Superstick, Bostik 3, Clam 3, Dunlop Thixofix (T), Evostik Timebond (T), Gloy Contact	Bonds immediately when two surfaces are brought together, so is used where cramping would be difficult: for example, sticking laminates to a work top	Acts immediately and no cramping needed	Expensive, so use other types where cramping is possible. Because they bond straight away, you get no time to reposition objects correctly. But Thixofix types (marked T in brand list) do allow limited time in which to make small adjustments	Cellulose thinners or proprietary cleaners (e.g. Evostik cleaner)
6. Epoxy resin	Araldite, Devcon Clear Epoxy, Evostik Hard and Fast, Plastic Padding Super Epoxy	Strong, heat and water-resistant. Ideal for china, metal and glass repairs	Very strong. Can be used on a thin edge	Too expensive for large-scale work; most supplied in two parts (glue and hardener) that have to be mixed	With cellulose thinners while still tacky
7. Latex	Bostik Boscotex, Clam 5, Copydex, Gloy Lay-Tex, Devcon rubber	Mainly for sticking fabrics to themselves. Used extensively in carpet laying. White when wet, but dries to a translucent film	Dries rapidly. Withstands washing in hot water	Will not withstand dry-cleaning	With damp cloth while still wet; special solvent can be bought from manufacturers to remove dried adhesive
8. Polystyrene cements	HMG Polystyrene cement, Joy Polystyrene, Revell's 'S' Cement	Special-purpose adhesive for bonding rigid polystyrene	Dries quickly and clear	Will not stick expanded polystyrene, nylon or polythene	Acetone or nail-varnish remover. But may damage workpiece
9. PVA woodworking	Croid Polystik, Dunlop Woodworking, Evostik Woodworking, ICI Dufix	Ideal for all woodworking jobs	Strong and easily handled	Pieces being glued must be cramped or temporarily fastened with masking tape	With a damp cloth when still tacky. Difficult to remove when dry
10. PVA building	Unibond, Blue Circle Bonding Agent, Polybond	Ideal adhesive with good resistance to stress – for instance, joints in furniture. Useful for bonding timber, concrete, bricks and wood, and as a cement additive	An ideal primer for porous surfaces	Pieces being glued must be cramped or temporarily fastened with masking tape	With a damp cloth when still tacky. Difficult to remove when dry
11. Urea-formaldehyde (Synthetic resin)	Aerolite 306, Borden Cascamite	A powder mixed with water, or as fluids in separate containers that must be mixed	Makes a strong, heat-resistant and waterproof bond	Needs to be mixed and joints need to be cramped while setting	Virtually impossible to remove when set. Sponge with warm water when wet, wash hands thoroughly
12. Specialised wall adhesive	Bostik 10, Clam 2 or 143, Evostik Wall (for veneers)	Strong adhesives suitable for fixing ceramic wall tiles	Strong and easily handled	Difficult to remove when dry	With a damp cloth while still tacky

• GENERAL-PURPOSE ADHESIVES

Modern adhesives have a strength and versatility unknown until recent years. But with so many different types available, it can be confusing to know which sticks what.

Some adhesives are waterproof and suitable for outdoor use; others are only moisture-resistant and more appropriate for bathrooms and kitchens; while others differ according to the nature of the finished job.

Many adhesives have critical setting times – either before surfaces are stuck or after. Most manufacturers supply instructions with adhesives and it is important that you follow them closely in order to get satisfactory results.

CHOOSING AN ADHESIVE

Some materials have different textures on different surfaces – for example, a ceramic wall tile may be glazed on one side and absorbent on the other – so each surface may need a different adhesive.

Removing excess adhesive when making joints in woodwork may be a problem. If more than one adhesive is suitable, choose the one that can be wiped off, or removed with a solvent.

The chart, right, combines two lists of materials. If one of the materials to be joined is movable and the other fixed – as in the case of a tile to be stuck to a wall – look down the left-hand column for the movable material. Find the name of the second,

CHOOSING AN ADHESIVE

	Acoustic tiles	Bricks and concrete	Carpets	Ceramic tiles	Cork (except tiles)	Cork tiles and sheeting	Fabrics and cloth	Glass, china, pottery	Hardboard	Leather	Leathercloth	Metal	Paper and cardboard	Plaster	Plasterboard	Plastics – flexible	Plastics – rigid	Plastics – laminated	Plastic floor tiles	Polystyrene foam	Rubber	Rubber floor tiles/sheet	Stone	Wood
Acoustic tiles	5	5		5	7,5	5	7		5	5		5	9,5	5	5	4		4	4	8	5	5	5	5
Bricks and concrete			5									6											6	
Carpets		7,5	7	5	7	7	7		9,5	7	7,5	5	7	9,5	9,5	4	4,6	5		9	5		7,5	9,5
Ceramic tiles	12	12		5,6	5	5	12	5,6	12	5	5	5,6	12	12	12		5,6	5,6	4	12	5	5	12	12
Cork (except tiles)	5,7	4,5	7	5	4,5	4,5	7,5	4	9,5	5	4,5	5	9	9,5	9,5	4	4	5	10,4	8	5	5	4,5	9,5
Cork tiles and sheeting	5	10		5	4,5	5	7	4	10	4		5	4	10	10	4	5	5	10		5	5	10	10
Fabrics and cloth	7	7,5	7	12	7,5	7	7	4,1,2	9,1,2,5	7,1,2,5	7,5	4,5	7	9	9	4	5,6	4	7	5	5		7,5	9,1,2,5
Glass, china, pottery		4,6		5,6	4	4	4,1,2	4,6		4,1,2,6	4	4,6	4	4,6	4,6	4	4,6	5,6	4		5	4	4,6	
Hardboard	5	9,5		5,6	9,5	5	9,5		9,6	5	9,5	5,6	9,5	5	5	4	5,6	4		9	5	5	5,6	9
Leather	5	4	7	5	5	4	7,1,2,5	4,1,2,6	5	5,1,2	4	5	4	5	5	4	4,5	5		7	5	5	5	5,1,2
Leathercloth		4	7,5	5	4,5		7,5	4	9,5	5	4	4	4	4,5	4,5	4	4,5	5			5		4	9,5
Metal	5	5,6		5,6	5	5	4,5	4,6	5,6	5	4	5,6	4,5	5,6	5,6	4	5,6	5,6			5	5	5,6	5,1
Paper and cardboard	9,3,5	9,3,5	7	4,5	9,3	4	7	4	9,3,5	4	4	4,5	9,3	9,3	9,3	4	5	4	9,3	5	5		4	9,3,5
Plaster					9,5	5	9,5	4,6	5	5	4,5	5,6	9	9	9			5,6	4		5			9,6
Plasterboard		5			9,5	5	9,5	4,6	5	5	4,5	5,6	9	9	9			5,6	4		5		5	9
Plastics – flexible	4	4	4	4	4	4	4	4	4	4	4	4	4	4	4	4	4	4	4	4	5	4	4	4
Plastics – rigid		5,6	4,5	5,6	4	5	4,5	4,6	5,6	4,5	4,5	5,6	4	5,6	5,6	4	5,6	5,6	4		5	5	5,6	5,6
Plastics – laminated	5	5,6		5,6	5	5	5	5,6	5,6	5	5	5,6	5	5,6	5,6	4	5,6	5,6	4	9	5	5	5,6	5,6
Plastic floor tiles	4	10		4	10	10	4	4	10	4		4	4	10	10	4	4	4			4	5	10	10
Polystyrene foam	8	8			8		7		8	7			9	8	8					8			8	8
Rubber	5	5		5	5	5	5	5	5	5	5	5	5	5	5	5	5	5	4		5	5	5	5
Rubber floor tiles/sheet	5	10		5	5	5	5	4	10	5		5	5	10	10	4	5	5	4		5	5	10	10
Stone		6		5	5							6											6	
Wood	5	5,6,11		5,6,11	9,5	5	9,1,2,5		9,11	5,1,2	9,5	5,6,11	9,5	9,11	9,11	4	5,6	5,6,11	4	9	5	5	5,6,11	9,11

fixed, material in the top line of the chart. Where the two lists corresponding with these materials cross, is the number of the adhesive – listed on this page – suitable for use.

If both materials are movable – for example, a rubber sole on a leather shoe – use either list.

Where more than one adhesive is listed, the one in heavy type is the one recommended for work that will be subjected to extreme conditions.

PRECAUTIONS TO TAKE

Before using adhesive, surfaces to be stuck together should be clean and dry. Unless they are, you will, in effect, be sticking two layers of dirt together and the bond will not hold.

Adhesion can often be improved if you roughen the surfaces first – with glasspaper, emery cloth, a file or a wire brush.

Solvent-based adhesives and those having petroleum mixture in them give off inflammable vapours: use them in a well-ventilated room, do not smoke and avoid naked flames.

Certain adhesives contain chemicals that are an irritant to the skin. When using one of the instant-acting adhesives, use a barrier cream on the hands; alternatively, wash adhesive off immediately in fresh water.

Epoxy resin glues (see facing page) are supplied in two containers and need to be mixed before use. Do not allow either container to be contaminated by the other's glue or the adhesive will be ruined.

A-Z OF REPAIRS

A

AIR-BEDS: PUNCTURES
Repair kits are available from camping shops. Kits for rubberised canvas air-beds contain rubber solution; those for plastic beds contain PVC cement.

To mend a puncture, first inflate the bed and listen for escaping air, or hold the bed under water and look for bubbles. Mark the hole with a wax pencil and deflate the bed.

Clean the area around the hole. On a rubber air-bed use a rag soaked in lighter fuel or petrol. On a plastic bed use only water. Wipe dry. To mend a plastic bed spread a thin coat of PVC cement on both the patch and the bed, press the patch in place – smoothing it down from the centre outwards – and leave it under pressure for at least five hours. On a rubber air-bed smear rubber solution into the canvas around the hole and allow it to dry. Roughen the back of the patch with glasspaper, apply rubber solution and allow to dry. Apply a second coat to both surfaces and when dry press the patch in place. Leave to dry for about 12 hours.

Use the same techniques to repair other inflatable rubber and canvas items such as paddling pools, and so on.

B

BADMINTON RACKETS
See Tennis rackets.

BASKET HANDLES
Basket cane can be bought from craft shops. Take the damaged basket with you to match the new material to the original cane.

Handles are made from two different types of cane – a stout cane, called the bow, and a decorative binding, called lapping, which is wound around the bow, securing it to the basket. It is made by splitting ordinary cane down the middle and is available in various thicknesses. Plastic lapping is often used as an alternative.

To renew a handle, withdraw the ends of the old lapping from

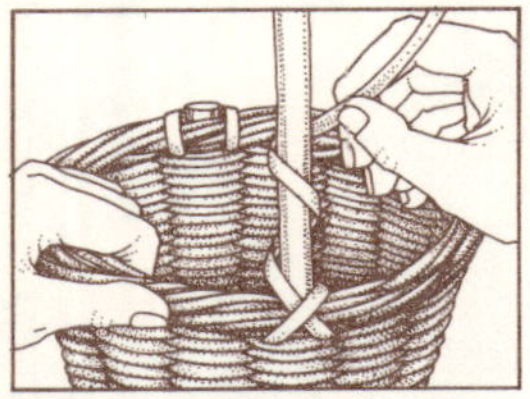

the basket and strip it off the bow. If the bow is cracked or broken, pull out broken stubs with pliers.

Soak the new bow in water until it is supple, sharpen one end and push it in through the border of the basket for about 50 mm. (2 in.), next to a vertical rib.

Bend the bow to the correct height, allow an extra 50 mm. (2 in.) and cut it to length. Sharpen the end and push it through the border, against a rib.

Soak the lapping to make it supple. Push one end, from the inside, into the border on the left side of one end of the bow. Bring the lapping across and outside the bow, then feed its end through the weave, under the border. Bring the lapping out, over the border again, then feed it through the weave, under the border and around the bow, so that the lapping forms a cross over both

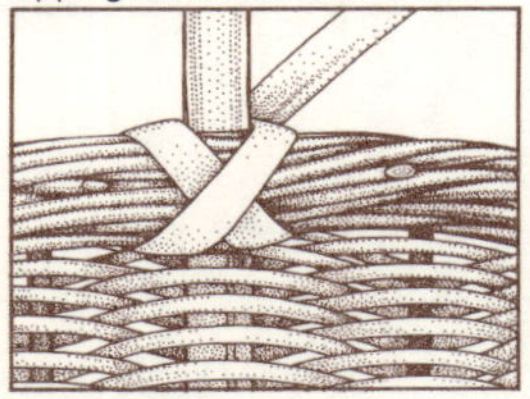

bow and border.

Pull the lapping tightly across the bow and, starting close to the border, wind it round the bow. Keep each turn tight up against the last. Repeat the cross-over pattern at the other end of the bow. Push the lapping out against the side of the first stave and cut it evenly at the stave with a knife.

BATHROOM CABINETS
Where there are small children, a bathroom medicine-cabinet should be locked and the key kept out of their reach.

A ratchet clip, available from ironmongers and suitable for sliding doors 4-8 mm. ($\frac{1}{6}$-$\frac{1}{3}$ in.) thick, requires no cutting or drilling to be fitted in place.

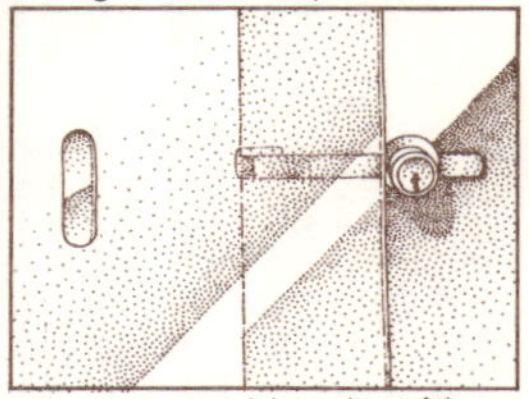

It wraps round the edge of the inner door and the lock slides on to the ratchet.

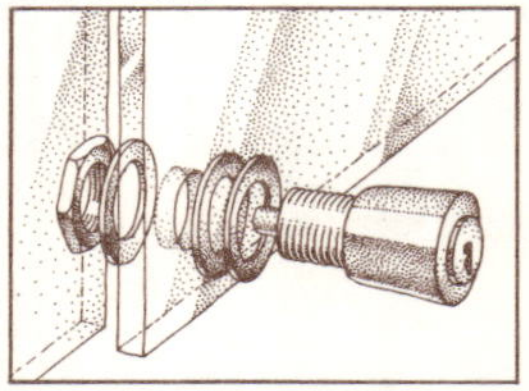

Another kind of lock can be fitted through a small hole in the front of a pair of sliding glass doors, with rubber washers protecting the glass. Get a glazier to drill the holes for you.

BATHS
A gap between bath and wall is unsightly and allows water to run down the wall, where it may rot floorboards and appear on the ceiling below as damp patches. Fill the gap with a sealer or a ceramic coving (see p. 52).

Since baths are prone to slight movement use a permanently flexible sealer.

A badly worn or chipped cast-iron bath can be repaired with an epoxy-resin based paint, sold specifically for this purpose.

A bath with a vitreous enamel finish cannot be painted – consult a firm that specialises in resurfacing a bath in the home.

BEACH BALLS
Use the same techniques as for air-bed punctures.

BEADS
Re-stringing Check a necklace regularly, and if the string holding the beads shows signs of stretching or weakness, renew it, using a strong matching thread.

Before removing the beads, note their order and replace them in the same way. To help keep them in the same order, fold a piece of paper in an M shape and place the beads in the V fold.

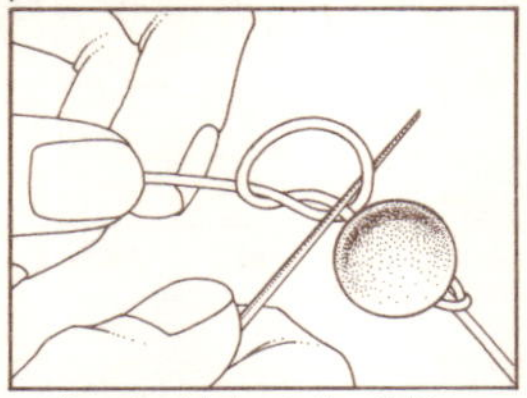

Tie a double knot about 40 mm. ($1\frac{1}{2}$ in.) in from one end of the thread and slide the first bead close up to the knot. Tie a second knot and, using a needle, push it close up to the other side of the bead before tightening it. Fix the rest of the beads in the same way. Rub a little balsa cement on the thread before tying the last knot behind the last bead.

Repairing a broken string When a necklace with a knotted thread breaks, it usually breaks between knots and at least one bead falls off. If the thread is in good condition, the necklace can be repaired without being re-strung.

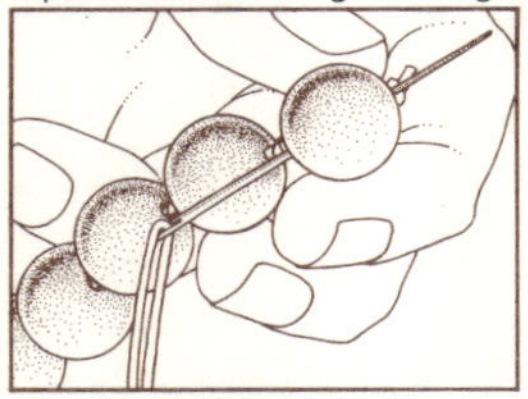

Push a needle with double thread out through one of the last soundly knotted beads. Wind the

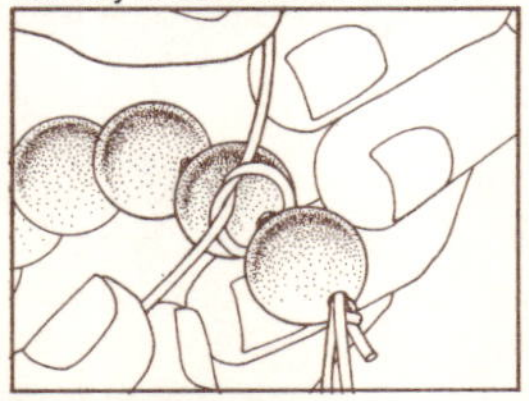

two ends of the new thread around the old thread, behind the second knot, and tie a reef knot.

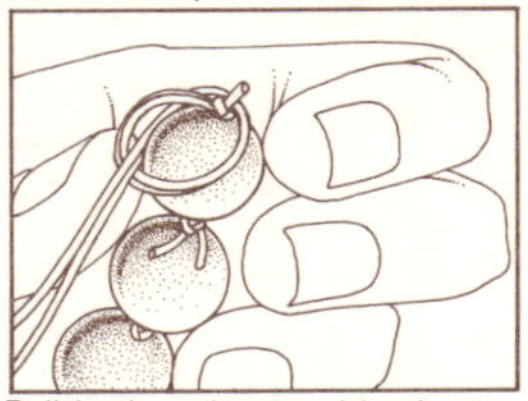

Pull the thread taut and tie a knot between the other side of the bead and the knot, at the broken end of the necklace.

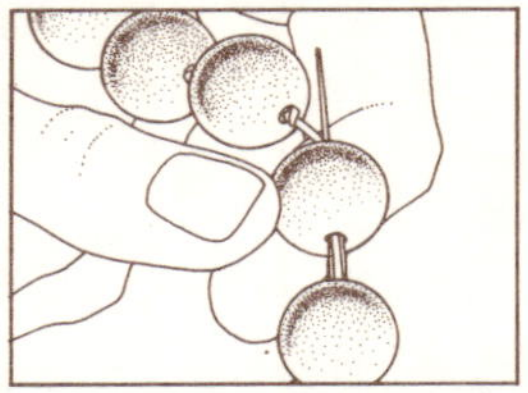

Thread the needle through the loose bead and through the secure bead on the other end of the necklace, draw the halves

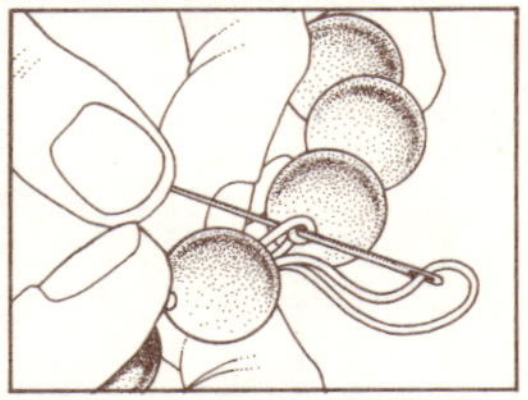

together and push the needle through the knot behind the secure bead. Pull the thread taut, cut it from the needle and tie the ends around the original thread.

Cut the new thread to leave 5 mm. ($\frac{1}{4}$ in.) ends, roll them together between the fingertips and a little balsa cement, and conceal the combined end by tucking it into the nearest bead hole. (See also Jewellery.)

BEDS
If the bed-head rattles and the framework is unsteady and squeaky, tighten up the bolts securing the bed-head and those holding the frame together.

The greatest strain put on the bolts is when the bed is moved with the legs in contact with the floor. This juddering effect can be eliminated by fitting castors.

Lever the castors out of their metal or plastic housings, turn the bed over and drill holes into the ends of the legs in which the housings can fit tightly.

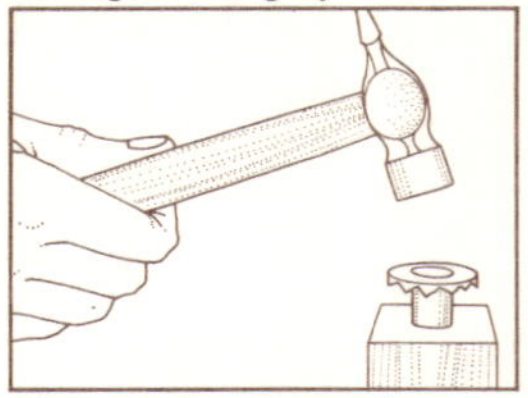

Insert the housings and hammer them home until the housings' spikes are firmly clenched in the wood. Fit the castors.

BICYCLE TYRES
Flat tyres are caused by either a faulty valve or a punctured inner-tube. Check the valve first, as this is the easier to repair or replace.

A puncture outfit should contain a wax pencil, an abrasive stick or glasspaper for cleaning the area around the puncture, some rubber solution, rubber patches and french chalk. You will also need three tyre levers.

To check a valve for leaks, wet your finger on your tongue, and moisten the top of the valve – covering it completely. If bubbles come from the valve, this indicates escaping air.

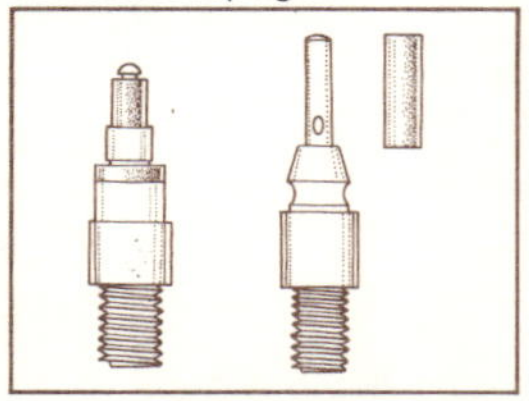

A faulty Schrader valve (left) must be replaced. With older-type valves (right), remove the rubber and blow through the valve to remove any grit. Wet the valve and fit a new rubber, pushing it over the valve shoulder.

Remove any nails or sharp objects in the tyre and note their position. This may help you to locate the puncture. To mend a

A-Z OF REPAIRS

puncture, first unscrew the valve-retaining nut, and withdraw the valve. Then remove the lock ring so that the valve stem can be pushed up inside the wheel rim when the tube is taken out.

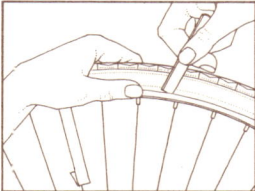

Insert tyre levers around the wheel, between rim and tyre, until one side of the tyre can be lifted off the wheel. Withdraw the tube carefully, replace the valve assembly and inflate the tube.

Pass the tube through water to find the puncture's exact position. Mark this with the pencil and deflate the tube. Clean the area with abrasive paper, spread adhesive thinly over the surface around the mark and, when almost dry, peel off the backing from a patch and press it, tacky side down, over the puncture. Dry any surplus adhesive with french chalk. If air is escaping from an old patch remove it with petrol and fit a new one.

While the tube is off, check that the rim-tape is in good condition and covering spoke ends.

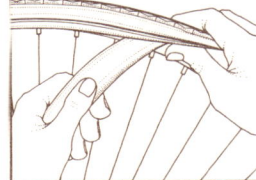

Replace the tube, inserting the section with the valve in it first and screw the lock ring finger-tight. Inflate the tube slightly and slip the tyre back into place with the balls of your thumbs. If the last section is difficult to snap into place, move your hands about 300 mm. (12 in.) to either side, and press the fitted part of the tyre well into the centre of the wheel rim. Carry on pressing, and move your hands towards the unfitted

section, which should now roll into place more easily. If you need to use tyre levers take care not to nip the inner-tube. Check that no part of the tube is trapped between rim and tyre, tighten the lock ring, and inflate the inner-tube.

BOOK REPAIRS
If a valuable book is damaged take it to an expert. However, an amateur can tackle basic repairs to less-valuable books.
To repair a broken hinge
Support the cover on another book, tear away the loose end-paper and then scrape the pasted down end-paper from the inside of the cover – the serrated blade of a bread-knife is ideal.

With the cover of the book open, measure from the front edge of the pages to the far edge of the cover and add on 5 mm. (¼ in.). Cut a new end-paper to this size, from good-quality typing or similar paper.

Lay the new end-paper in position on the hinges, fold it at the hinges and press along the crease with a curved bone knife handle or a wooden spatula.

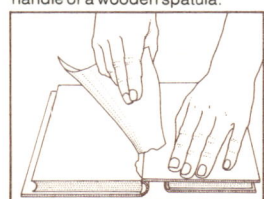

Remove the folded end-paper from the book and, using a piece of scrap paper, cover it – except for a 3 mm. (⅛ in.) wide strip from the folded edge. Apply PVA adhesive (see p. 356) to this strip.

Align the end-paper with the edges of the pages and press down the glued fold. Close the book, put a weight on it and allow the glue to dry.

Open the book again and insert a sheet of waxed paper and a sheet of waste paper between the free end and the pasted down end-paper. Apply adhesive to the surface to be pasted to the cover. Smooth it down over the cover, remove the waste paper and close the book, leaving the waxed paper in position. Weight the

book and leave it for 24 hours.

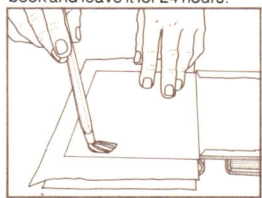

To repair a torn page Position a piece of waxed paper under the page, thinly coat the edges of the tear with a white PVA adhesive, then press the torn edges firmly together on the waxed paper.

Place a second piece of waxed paper over the repaired page, close and weight the book and allow the adhesive to dry.
To secure a loose page Place a piece of waxed paper over the page, to within 3 mm. (⅛ in.) of the inside edge and brush adhesive on to the 3 mm. strip. Position the page in the book and press down along the entire length of the glued edge. Place a second piece of waxed paper over the repaired page, close the book and leave the adhesive to dry.

Trim the outer edges of frayed pages before gluing them back in the book.

BRASS AND COPPER
Brass and copper objects dent easily if dropped, and handles or other riveted attachments can be knocked loose. To remove dents, shape one end of a piece of hardwood to match the curve of the damaged article. Use a chisel and rasp (see p. 352) to pare off the wood. Secure the wood in a vice and push out the dent by pressing and rubbing the damaged area of the article on the shaped wood. Keep the article on the wood and lightly hammer out any remaining irregularities,

constantly moving the article over the shaped surface to obtain an even finish. Clean with a soft cloth and metal polish.

Remove broken or badly worn rivets by nipping off the heads with pincers, or punching the centre of the heads with a nail-punch and hammering or drilling them out. Cut off loose rivets with a hacksaw. Buy matching rivets from an ironmongers.

Insert a tight-fitting rivet from the inside of the article and, holding the head of the rivet against a metal surface, hammer the rivet flat. Use a concave punch if the head is to be left proud. If it is to be countersunk, use a flat punch and file the rivet down.

BRICKWORK: STAINING
White powder appearing on new brickwork is efflorescence – salts in the bricks brought to the surface as rainwater evaporates. It can be removed temporarily by brushing with a stiff broom, but will reappear after some months. A permanent cure is to brush on two coats of neutralising liquid – available from builders' merchants. Allow 15 minutes between coats.

To remove vegetation stains, first trace and cure any dampness (see p. 378) that may be causing it. Then brush on a coat of colourless fungicide, available from do-it-yourself shops.

Grimy and paint-stained brickwork can be cleaned with Disclean – an acid-based fluid available from builders' merchants. Wear rubber gloves and goggles and apply the fluid with a bristle brush. Leave it for five to ten minutes and hose it off with fresh water.

BRIEFCASES
Replacement handles These can be bought from leatherware shops in various sizes, but the rivets which retain the handle on a case are difficult to replace. Blind-head nails – available from do-it-yourself shops – are a good substitute.

Remove the flattened ends of the existing rivets with a fine-toothed file and pull out the rivets with a pair of pliers.

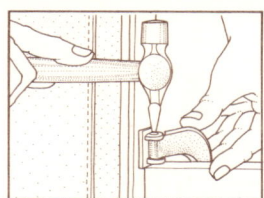

Hold the new handle in position and slide in the two nails. Hold the heads of the nails against a hard surface and flatten the other ends with a hammer.

If the lock spring breaks it is not usually possible to repair it, so fit a new part – available from craft shops. If the broken lock has only one locking position it is worth fitting a three-position replacement to make the bag more convenient to use. But this

entails cutting extra holes for the tongues of the lock. If the bag is lined, cut a flap in the lining before starting the repair, to expose the back of the lock. Use a new razorblade to avoid applying excessive pressure and scarring the leather.

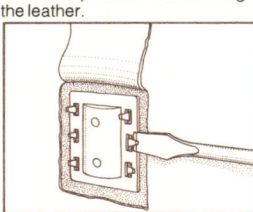

Use a small-bladed screwdriver to prise up the tongues of the damaged lock.

Prise up the body of the lock and carefully remove it from the holes. Position the new lock and slip the back plate over the tongues inside the case. Check that the lock engages and make any necessary adjustments. This

can be done by slightly enlarging the slots in the leather with the tip of a sharp knife.

Push the tongues over to grip the leather tightly with a pair of pliers, then coat the flap of the lining and the back plate of the lock with neoprene cement. Leave them to dry and then stick them together.
Fitting a new hasp The hasp is the metal end of the briefcase flap with a D-shaped pin in it, which fits into the lock. If the pin snaps a new hasp can be fitted.

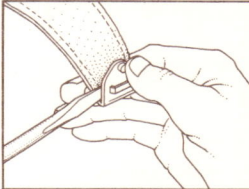

Prise the damaged hasp off the flap with a small-bladed screwdriver. Work from both sides of the hasp, taking care not to damage the leather.

If the pins necessary to fix the hasp to the flap are difficult to obtain use 13 mm. (½ in.) fine brass nails. Take the case to a dealer to determine the correct gauge nails. Slide on the new hasp and push the brass nails through the holes – from the outside in. Cut off the ends of the nails with pliers.

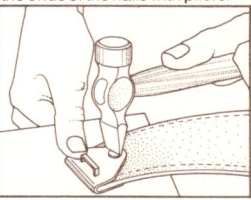

Hold the outside of the hasp against a flat surface, protect the hasp with a cloth, if necessary, and flatten the cut ends of the nails. Turn the hasp over and hammer gently on the heads of the nails.

If necessary, use a sharp knife to trim the leather flush with the edge of the hasp.

BROOMHEADS
See Mops.

A-Z OF REPAIRS

CANDLESTICKS

During use, candlesticks become caked by wax. Break off as much of the wax by hand as possible, then wash the candlestick in hot, soapy water before polishing it.

When the wax has soaked into an absorbent surface such as wood, the soapy-water method still holds good. It will not always remove every trace of ingrained wax, but it will leave the surface with an even finish.

CARPETS

A small area – up to 23 cm. (9 in.) square – of a torn or worn carpet can easily be repaired. Use a latex adhesive (see p. 356).

To patch an Axminster or Wilton carpet, turn it back and mark a square around the damaged area. Coat the area plus about 25 mm. (1 in.) extra on all sides with latex adhesive and rub it in with a rag.

Place a piece of wood under the damaged area and, using a sharp knife, cut out the square.

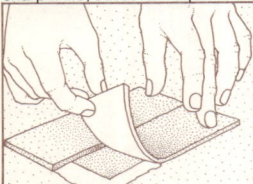

Cut two strips of hessian tape, about 50 mm. (2 in.) longer than the square and, covering the hole, stick them to the back of the carpet.

Lay the square over a remnant, or part of the carpet that is permanently covered by furniture, taking care that the pile runs the same way in square and remnant,

and matching the patterns, if the carpet is patterned. Use the square as a template or pattern to cut out a patch.

Apply adhesive to the back and edges of the new patch, taking care not to get it on the tufts, and press it into place. Lightly hammer down the edges.

When repairing foam-backed carpets cut out the damaged area from the tufted side.

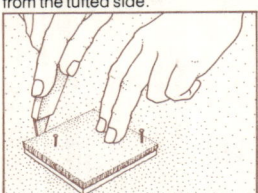

First, cut a patch slightly larger than the damaged area, lay and temporarily pin it in place. Cut around its edges through the carpet, then remove the patch so that the damaged area below can be withdrawn.

Turn back the carpet and stick strips of adhesive tape along the edges of the hole to overlap the hole by half their width.

Turn down the carpet and press the patch in place on to the adhesive-tape strips, then lightly hammer along the joins to get a firm bond.

Burns Trim off singed or damaged tufts then wind enough 4-ply wool for the repair round the fingers of one hand, and cut through both ends. The colour of the wool should match the carpet as near as possible.

Cut bunches of 15 mm. (½ in.) lengths from the pieces, then dab latex adhesive into the hole and stand a bunch of strands in the adhesive. Use a toothpick or sharpened matchstick to work the strands into position, and add

more as required. Trim and leave to dry, then work the strands into position again and add more as required. Trim and leave to dry, then use a pin to blend the tufts with the surrounding wool.

CARPET SWEEPERS

If a carpet sweeper becomes clogged with hair or cotton, remove the brushes and, if necessary, the wheels.

On some sweepers the brush is held in place by a hinged clip which, when rotated or pressed inwards, will release the brush.

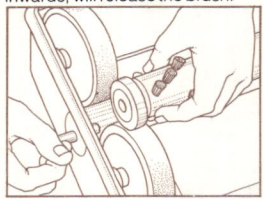

On other sweepers the brush is held by the sides of the frame.

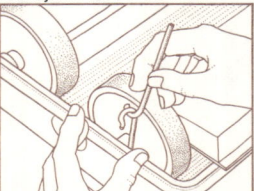

The wheels are held in place by a spring at each end and can easily be unhooked once the brush has been removed. When the brush has been taken out, it is easy to tease out any hair or cotton. An old comb is ideal.

Use a little light oil on a pipe cleaner to lubricate the brush roller and wheels.

A badly worn tyre – the kind cemented to the wheels – can be replaced: pre-cemented tyres are

available from manufacturers. Immerse the wheel in boiling water for five minutes and then prise off the old tyre. Clean the rim with glasspaper and fit the new tyre. Immerse the wheel in boiling water for a minute. Remove it from the water and leave the cement to harden.

CASTORS
See Beds.

CHINA AND ORNAMENTS

Repairs to handles of china are unlikely to be strong enough for normal use.

Wipe broken pieces clean with a piece of silk dipped in methylated spirit – silk will not leave lint on jagged edges. Apply a thin coat of epoxy resin on the surfaces to be joined and press them together. Use a frayed matchstick and methylated spirit to remove the surplus adhesive before it dries. Remove any dried adhesive with a razor blade and smooth the surface with dampened 600–700 grade wet-and-dry paper. To achieve a really good join with such items as cups, saucers and plates, apply pressure on the glued joint by putting on a weight, where possible, or binding the object with 40 mm. (1½ in.) wide gummed brown paper, which shrinks as it dries and exerts tension to cramp the join. Self-adhesive tape is unsuitable.

Place dampened strips at right-angles across the glued join. Leave the join to set, then soak off the strips and remove any surplus adhesive with glasspaper and a razor blade.

Fill chips in china with a mixture of epoxy resin and whiting – finely powdered chalk available from craft shops. Allow the resin to set for five minutes, then cut off the surplus with a sharp knife and smooth the filled surface with dampened wet-and-dry paper.

Leave the china to dry before using it – some slow-drying resins take up to 12 hours to dry. Consult the manufacturer's instructions.

The same procedure can be used for repairing ornaments. With an awkward-shaped figure, support it in a bowl of sand, with the broken portion only

protruding. Position it so that the broken piece can balance on the matching surface, before gluing the pieces together.

COPPER
See Brass and copper.

CRACKS
See Floorboards; Sinks; Skirting boards; Walls; Washbasins.

CUPBOARDS

If treated roughly, wall cupboards can pull away from the wall on their fixings.

If the screws will not retighten securely the cupboard will have to be taken down, and the holes in the wall re-plugged to give the screws extra grip (see p. 353).

To repair a badly fitting catch, first loosen the catch-striker's plate screws and adjust its position until the doors close efficiently. Fixing-holes in catches are usually elongated for this purpose. Make sure that the doors are fixed properly at their hinges before tightening the screws.

If the lock jams, lubricate it and operate it vigorously. If the lock becomes increasingly difficult to operate and jams regularly a new one may have to be fitted.

If handles and door knobs are loose, tighten their fixing screws or securing nuts. If the holes of fixing screws have become oversize, plug them with matchsticks. When fitting knobs with a shaft make sure that the hole is slightly larger than the diameter of the shaft. (See also Doors.)

D

DECKCHAIRS

Canvas deckchair covers wear through in time and need to be replaced. You will need a hammer, an old screwdriver and some 10 mm. (⅜ in.) tacks.

Prise out the old tacks with the screwdriver, and remove the canvas from the frame of the chair. Measure the old cover and buy a new one from a hardware shop to match.

Fold under one end of the new canvas cover by 25 mm. (1 in.) to make a double thickness, and tuck it round the top rail of the

chair. Tack the cover to the underside of the rail at its mid-point. Keeping the doubled seam tight, hammer in tacks at each end of the rail and two more, midway between the end tacks and the middle tack.

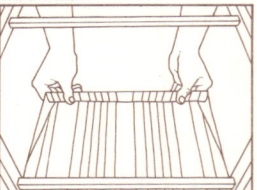

The bottom rail is shorter than the top rail, so taper each side of the canvas to fit by folding the edges over. Fold the end of the canvas 25 mm. (1 in.) under, and tack it to the underside of the rail. Tack the canvas in position using the same sequence as that used for the top rail.

DOORS

Doors can stick, refuse to shut, rattle or jam. Knobs and hinges can work loose and locks jam.

Fitting a new lock is an expert's job. If the lock jams, try adding light lubricating oil and operating the lock vigorously, or inserting some powdered graphite.

When a door hinge works loose,

tighten its fixing screws. If the screws cannot be tightened the holes have become oversize. Plug them with matchsticks or

A-Z OF REPAIRS

dowels. Do the same for loose-fitting door knob screws.

If the door is tight on the hinge side unscrew one hinge at a time, supporting the bottom of the door with wedges, and pack the recess with cardboard or thin timber. If

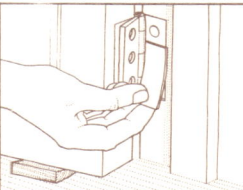

the door is tight on the jamb side, pare off some wood from the hinge recesses, using a chisel. Keep hinges well oiled.

The likeliest cause of a rattling door is that the timber has shrunk and the door no longer butts tightly against its stop.

Close the door and measure the gap between the jamb and the edge of the door. Remove the latch keep, and mark and chisel out a new recess for it so that the door will close against the stop. Plug the original fixing holes with matchsticks or dowels, then refit the latch keep.

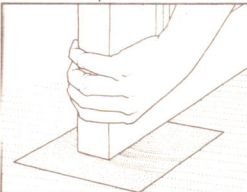

A door that scrapes the floor when opened, can be eased slightly by placing a sheet of abrasive paper on the floor and pulling the door backwards and forwards over it.

If the door is oversize to the

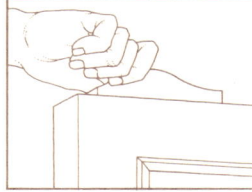

extent that it jams on the floor or at the top – due to distortion or settlement – remove it and plane off the excess.

To ensure smooth-running sliding doors in timber grooves, apply a little grated candle grease to the grooves. Sliding doors that are higher than they are wide rarely operate smoothly.

DOWNPIPES AND GUTTERS
Downpipes and gutters overflow if they are not kept clean and free of debris. They leak if joints are loose, or if the pipe or guttering is holed or cracked. You will need to use a ladder to reach gutters. Make sure that the bottom of the ladder is firmly supported and do not overreach when you are working on the ladder. Tie it at the top if possible; better still, get someone to hold it at the bottom.

Scrape out silt from gutters with a trowel, or a hardboard scraper cut roughly to the shape of the gutter, then flush water along the gutter. If water stays around the downpipe outlet the downpipe is blocked. Check that the blockage is not at the bottom of the pipe. Tie a rag securely to the end of a length of cane and push it down the pipe.

If the obstruction does not clear, lift out the upper section of downpipe. If there is insufficient play to manipulate the pipe from the one below it, undo the clips securing the pipes to the wall. Start from the bottom and clean each section of the pipe separately. Flush with clean water before refitting. Reconnect the pipe sections and refix the clips by hammering masonry nails into the plugs, holding the clips, or by fitting new plugs.

Plastic gutters are fitted in sections connected by pieces called union clips, lined with replaceable rubber seals. To replace a leaking seal, unclip the gutters and peel off the old seal. Use petrol to remove any perished rubber. Fit the new seal and reclip the gutters in place.

Cast-iron gutters overlap each other and bolt together. If the joint is loose, tighten the bolt. Apply penetrating oil if the bolt is stiff. Replace badly damaged sections of guttering with new sections to

match the old. Seal the joints with putty.

If joints are loose, tighten up the downpipe clips. Apply penetrating oil if necessary. Loose joints can also be packed with a proprietary mastic and sealed with a coat of bitumen paint. (See also Rust.)

DRAINS
An overflowing gully beneath an outside downpipe, or a sink, bath, basin or lavatory pan that empties slowly, may be a sign that an underground drainpipe is blocked.

A rubber-headed plunger might shift an obstruction in an external gully, but if this fails send for a firm specialising in clearing drain blockages. Such firms are listed in Yellow Pages. Remember, if you call out a firm to clear your drain – which is shared with other properties – it will be your responsibility to pay the bill, even though the blockage may not ultimately be found in your part of the drain.

In an emergency, local authorities will clear blockages free.

Provided gullies and fittings, such as baths and lavatories, are cleaned regularly, blockages in the drains are rare.

F

FILTERS
Many items of household equipment have filters which are designed to stop dust, fluff or grit from damaging mechanisms. Most filters (for example, the filter trays on washing machines) are cleaned automatically when the equipment is in use. But other filters are tucked away and need to be cleaned manually from time to time.

If an automatic washing machine takes a long time to fill, prise out the filter and rinse it under running water. Filter positions vary according to the machine – consult the handbook.

If it fills too slowly, remove the cold and hot-water inlet hoses where they enter the back of the machine. The solenoid valves which control water intake are

situated here. Remove, clean and replace the small metal filters which protect the valves.

Fluff filters are found behind the doors of tumble driers or at the back of the drum. If they are not cleaned regularly the thermal overload switch will cut out the heater and fan motor. When these have cooled the machine can be re-started, but constant operation of the overload cut-out indicates dirty filters or more serious trouble.

Empty the waste trap in a dishwasher after each wash. Every two or three months thoroughly clean the inside of the large rectangular filter which is situated at the bottom of the tank. Lift out the waste trap, remove the central screw which holds the filter in place, remove the filter and clean it under a tap.

FIREPLACES
Cracked firebacks These allow heat and smoke to penetrate behind the fireplace and eventually weaken the chimney structure.

If the fireback is badly cracked it will need to be replaced. Small cracks can be filled with plastic fire clay, obtainable from builders' merchants.

Use a stiff bristle brush to remove soot and dirt from the fireback, then rake out the cracks with a sharp-pointed tool. Remove any loose particles with a wire brush, then soak the cracks thoroughly with water, using an old paint brush.

Use a putty knife and apply the plastic fire clay to the cracks before the water dries. Press it firmly in a place, wet a finger and scrape off any excess, smoothing over the filled surfaces.

Loose tiles Refix any loose tiles in the hearth or surround with a 1 : 4 cement-and-sand mix. Replace those which are broken or badly damaged. Take a sample with you to a builders' merchants in order to get a good match.

Sealing the opening Before blocking off a disused fireplace have the chimney swept.

The opening can be temporarily or permanently sealed: in either case, have the chimney swept beforehand.

For a permanent job, get a builder to brick up the opening and plaster the surface to match the existing wall. To avoid condensation forming in the flue and possibly causing staining on

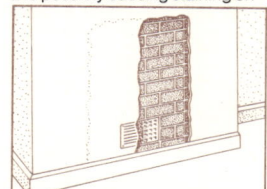

the walls, have a 225 × 150 mm. (9 × 6 in.) air-brick built into the centre of the wall, near the bottom. Fix a metal, plastic or fibrous plaster louvre over the air-brick.

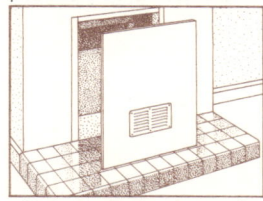

To seal an opening temporarily, plug and screw 50 × 25 mm. (2 × 1 in.) softwood battens around the edge of the opening. Set them back from the front of the wall by about 5 mm. (¼ in.).

Cut a piece of hardboard to fit the opening and drill and screw the board to the battens. Use either raised-head screws (see p. 355) or cups and screws – which are easy to remove – available from builders' merchants or DIY shops.

Use a padsaw to cut a hole in the centre, near the bottom, of the hardboard and fit a louvred grille.

FLOORBOARDS
To cure squeaky floorboards try shaking french chalk or talcum powder into the gaps between them. This acts as a lubricant when the boards are walked on and rubbed together.

Check that the nails holding down the boards have a firm grip. If they have not, replace them with 38 mm. (1½ in.) screws, countersinking the holes. Joist positions can be established from

the positions of the nails, but there is still a danger of drilling through a pipe or cable. To be safe, remove a floorboard first and check that there is nothing in the way of the screws.

Filling gaps Fill cracks and small holes with a proprietary wood filler, then sand them smooth after the filler has set. Add a small amount of stain to the filler to match the floor finish.

Fill wide gaps between floorboards by inserting slightly tapered wood strips. Cut a piece of the same thickness timber as the floorboards, a little wider than the gap to be filled and plane it to a taper. Coat the edges of the area to be filled with glue and tap the tapered strip in place with a mallet or piece of wood and a hammer; if the strips are wide enough, nail them to the joists. Plane the strip flush with the floorboards if it protrudes.

For an old house, where there may be a lot of gap-filling to be done, it is worthwhile visiting a timber yard – often a variety of suitable off-cuts of timber, of the correct thickness, can be bought cheaply.

FURNITURE LEGS
To prevent heavy furniture from leaving its impression on a floor covering, use one of three types of fitting: castor cups, rubber thimbles or rubber studs.

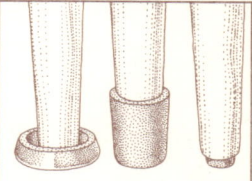

Castor cups are made of Bakelite and are simply placed under the legs to spread the weight. Rubber thimbles are fitted over the bottom of the legs. And rubber studs, which have half-round heads on a three-pronged metal base, are hammered into the ends of the legs to provide permanent protection.

FUSES
See p. 370.

A-Z OF REPAIRS

G

GLASS

When mending broken glass, all parts must be scrupulously clean. Wash glass in warm, soapy water and scrub broken edges with scouring powder. Thoroughly rinse, then allow all parts to dry. Use a hair-drier to speed drying.

Before gluing an item, arrange the fragments in order of rebuilding. Without using adhesive, see how the parts fit together. In some cases it may be necessary to make a jig from scrap timber to hold parts while the adhesive sets. With a quick-setting epoxy adhesive (see p. 356) it is often convenient to hold pieces by hand while the adhesive hardens.

Roughen the surfaces of the edges to be joined, using fine emery cloth. This gives a key for the adhesive to make a strong bond.

Put the thinnest possible coat of adhesive on each broken surface and press them together. Remove surplus adhesive with a watercolour brush dipped in methylated spirit. Avoid touching the actual crack. Maintain pressure while the glue sets by clamping or weighting. If this is not possible due to an awkward shape, hold the pieces together with a 40 mm. wide (1½ in.) brown paper, gummed strip, placed at right-angles across the crack. As it dries the paper shrinks and exerts pressure on the crack. Self-adhesive tape will not do this.

When the adhesive has dried, the gummed strip can be removed by soaking in warm water. Remove excess adhesive by rubbing with fine (00 or 000 grade) steel wool.

If the glass is broken into fragments, rebuild it piece-by-piece, allowing each joint to harden before another is added.

Sharp edges can be smoothed by rubbing them with a fine carborundum stone which should occasionally be dipped in water. The edge will assume a matt finish. (See also Mirrors; Windows.)

GUTTERS
See Downpipes and gutters.

H

HANDBAGS

If a handle frays or breaks, a ready-made matching replacement may be obtainable from a leather shop. If not, buy a strip of calf leather, double the width of the damaged handle and about 75 mm. (3 in.) longer, and two capping rivets.

Fold the outside edges of the leather in to meet at the back and glue them with neoprene cement.

Cut off the old handle. Trim the fabricated handle by cutting the corners off each end of the strip. If necessary, stain the leather, including the cut edges, to match the bag. Turn each end under about 30 mm. (1½ in.) to make a loop large enough to fit over a D-ring, and punch a hole through both thicknesses. Use a leather or a nail punch or a skewer.

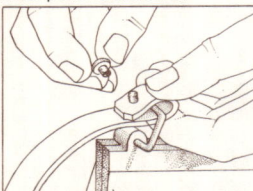

Loop one end of the handle through a D-ring on the bag – the short end on the inside. Push a rivet pin through the hole, rest the head of the rivet on a hard surface, fit a rivet cap and hammer the rivet cap home.

Fit and rivet the other end of the handle.

To replace a faulty turn fastener cut a flap in the top of the bag's lining to expose the fabric patch on the back of the fastener.

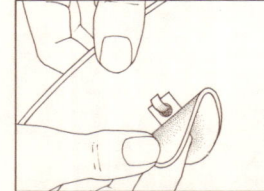

Remove the patch and lever up the metal tongues to remove the fastener. Buy a new fastener that fits the slot in the top plate.

Push the tongues of the new fastener through the slots in the bag. Slip the backing plate over

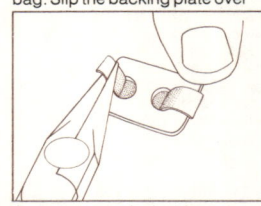

the tongues on the inside and bend the tongues down to the plate with pliers. Replace the fabric patch over the back of the fastener using a latex adhesive and refix the lining.

A bag with a hidden fastener has a pin fastener fitted to the underside of the flap, and a spring fastener fitted to the body of the bag. The pin fastener can, in time, pull away from the flap and a new piece of soft leather must be fitted to the back of the flap – the fastener may be re-used. Cut the leather slightly smaller than the existing flap. Lay the leather on the flap and mark the position of the fastener by closing the bag.

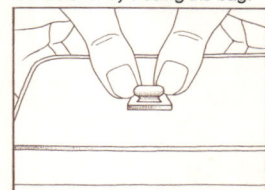

Cut two slots for the tongues of the fastener and fit it to the piece of leather. Glue the leather to the back of the flap with a contact adhesive.

HINGES
See Doors.

HOSES

A split in a garden hose can be repaired by cutting out the split section and joining the hose with a short piece of copper pipe which has roughly the same outside diameter as the internal bore of the hose. Copper pipe can be bought from a builders' merchants. Use two adjustable screw clips to hold the hose firmly to the tube. If it is difficult to push the hose over the tube, lubricate the tube with soap and soften the ends of the hose by immersing them in boiling water for a few minutes.

A repair can also be made with a hose union. Plastic types with a compression ring to grip the hose are simple to fit and reliable. Cut out the split section, push each end of the hose over the centre tube of the fitting and tighten the threaded nuts against the compression rings.

Some connectors have a simple snap-together action and because they are quickly disconnected this type is ideal for joining two long lengths of hose.

Hose care After use, drain water from the hose and coil it neatly for storage. Prevent the hose from forming kinks which encourage splits. A hose reel makes coiling easier and prolongs the life of the hose. In cold weather run warm water through the hose to make it pliable.

I

IRONS

Never carry out repairs while the iron is plugged in. Melted nylon and other burn marks can be cleaned from the iron by using special cleaning fluid, sold for the purpose, or by rubbing with a wet cloth and a mild scouring powder. Stubborn burns can be removed by scouring with very fine 00 or 000 grade steel wool.

To renew a worn flex, undo the screw holding the insulating plate at the back of the iron and remove the plate. The flex terminals will be seen. They are marked neutral (N), earth (E), and live (L) (see p. 370). Make a note of the positioning of the old flex so that the new flex can be connected in the same way. Loosen the terminals and the flex-securing screws and remove the old flex. Slide off the rubber sleeve that holds the flex clear of the body of the iron and fit it over the new flex. Use the old flex as a pattern and cut through the sheathing of the flex to expose the three wires. Remove about 15 mm. (½ in.) of insulation from each wire. Connect the wires to the correct terminals – brown to the terminal marked L; blue to N and green and yellow to E. Slide the rubber sleeve into place, secure the clamp and refit the plate.

Some irons have a plug-in flex coupler. Undo the screw in the end of the coupler and slide back the collar to expose the flex terminals. Connect the wires, as described above, and replace the coupler.

If any other repairs are necessary, do not attempt them yourself. Take the iron to a dealer or manufacturer.

IRONING BOARDS

A worn ironing-board cover can usually be replaced with a ready-made one. But if the board is not standard in size, buy some sheeting material or use an old linen sheet and make a cover to fit.

To remove the old cover it may be necessary to prise off a metal or wooden strip that retains the edge against the asbestos pad. Use a screwdriver to ease the strip off sufficiently for the nails to be withdrawn with pincers.

Fold the new sheeting material in half and lay the old cover on it. Mark and cut the sheet with a 25 mm. (1 in.) margin at the sides and a 15 mm. (½ in.) margin at the end.

Open the sheet out, and fold a 15 mm. wide hem over the straight end and machine across. Tack-stitch and machine a seam 15 mm. from the edge all round the cover. Turn the cover inside out, then iron it. Form a slot by sewing all round the sides of the cover, 15 mm. from the edge.

Use a safety pin and thread elastic through the seam.

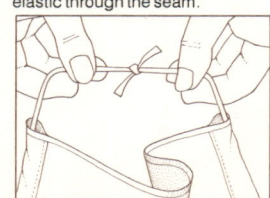

Remove safety pin and tie the ends of the elastic together. Take the knotted elastic over the straight end of the board. When this end is positioned, pull the other end of the cover over the tip of the board. Smooth the edges of the cover to remove wrinkles and adjust the tension of the elastic as necessary. Finally, refit the retaining strip.

To replace a worn asbestos pad, first prise off the nailed flange – or hardwood beading – with a screwdriver and pull out the nails with pincers. Undo the wing-nuts holding a metal retaining strip in place and remove the asbestos pad. On some metal boards the asbestos is riveted to the board. Turn the board upside-down and hammer an old screwdriver round the edge of the rivet to cut off the tongue.

New asbestos pads are obtainable from hardware shops and can be fitted merely by replacing the retaining strip, wing-nuts and flange or beading. If the old pad was riveted, the new one must be drilled. Position the mat, and mark the rivet holes from underneath with a pencil. Remove the asbestos pad, and drill through it with a bit the same size as the rivets (see p. 352). Refit the pad with rivets, tapping them flat with a hammer.

As a safety precaution when using asbestos, work in a well-ventilated space, dampen the pad and use a hand-drill to make the holes.

J

JEWELLERY

If a claw-mounted stone works loose, the claws can be tightened by gently squeezing them together, using long-nosed pliers. If a claw is broken, get it replaced by a jeweller.

In fashion jewellery, stones are often held by adhesive. If this fails the stone can be re-stuck using epoxy resin. Scrape old adhesive from the mounting and roughen the surfaces with emery cloth wrapped round a file. Apply a thin coating of adhesive to both surfaces.

If the mount has a spike or shaped part to fit the stone, use a little glass-fibre filler-paste – obtainable from DIY shops – to refix the stone.

A-Z OF REPAIRS

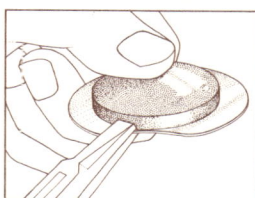

Fashion jewellery is made of soft metal which dents easily. Dented edges can be partly flattened with pliers, as illustrated, and the edges finished with light hammering, from the back, against a metal block.

If a safety chain is strained the link between the chain and the bracelet will open up. The link can be closed with long-nosed pliers.

Use long-nosed pliers to straighten a brooch pin. If the

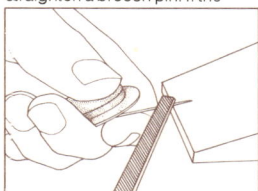

point of a pin is hooked, lay it in a groove cut in a scrap of wood and smooth the pin with a fine file. If necessary, adjust the hook so that it still engages the pin.

K

KETTLES
A hard layer of chalk, called furring, develops inside kettles in hard-water areas. This can be removed using descaling liquids based on formic acid – available from hardware shops. Because these solutions contain acid, do not allow them to come into contact with the eyes, skin or fabrics. Follow the directions on the bottle. Buy about 113 ml. (4 fl. oz.) of the descaling solution for a 1.5 litre (3 pint) kettle. Fill the kettle two-thirds full with clean, tepid water and add half the solution. The water will effervesce as it dissolves the chalk deposit. If furring remains, refill the kettle with fresh water and use the

remainder of the solution. Before using the kettle, fill it with fresh water, boil it and rinse the inside with running water.

If you need to fit a new electric-kettle element, take the kettle to a dealer to be sure of getting a replacement element of the correct shape and wattage.

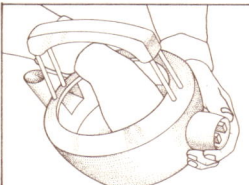

Unscrew the outer plastic or metal shroud on the coupler housing while holding the old element. Twist the old element

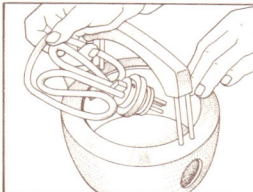

and lift it out of the kettle. Clean around the plug port and scrape stubborn scale away from the inside.

Put the rubber sealing ring over the threaded part of the new element and fit the element in place. Slip the outer fibre sealing washer over the threads and screw on the shroud. Fill the kettle with water and check for leaks.

Some kettles have a spring-loaded pin that ejects the lead plug if the kettle overheats, preventing it from boiling dry. Switch off and unplug the lead, and push the pin back with a stick until it clicks into position.

KITCHEN UTENSILS
If the prongs of a fork are bent towards each other, straighten them by using a wooden rule as a lever. If the prongs are out of line, wrap a thick cloth around the fork, lay it in a vice and gently tighten to clamp and realign the prongs.

If the bowl of a spoon is dented inwards, lay the bowl on a flat

surface and gently beat out the dent with the ball end of a hammer.

If the bowl bulges outwards, use the spoon to make a glass-fibre filler-paste – obtainable from DIY shops – cast of the bowl. Follow the manufacturer's instructions when mixing the paste and apply a thin film of Vaseline to the surface of the spoon to prevent sticking. When the cast is dry, stick it to a piece of wood and hold it in a vice. File the bump off to leave a smooth contour. When satisfied with the

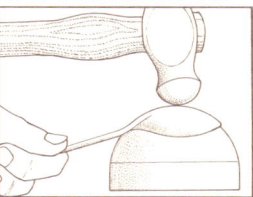

shape, hold the bowl of the spoon over the cast and with a fibre mallet or ball hammer tap the distortion out of the bowl. (See also, Knives; Saucepans.)

KNIVES
The tang of a blade is the spiked end that is glued into a bone or wooden handle. If the tang is intact a loose handle can be repaired using epoxy adhesive. Use a pointed tool to scrape as much old adhesive out of the handle as possible. Pack the handle two-thirds full of adhesive and press the blade in place. Wipe surplus adhesive from the handle and clean up with a rag soaked in methylated spirit. Bind with sticky tape until the adhesive has hardened. (See also Sharpening blades.)

L

LADDERS
From time to time check metal tie rods for tightness. These rods, which strengthen the structure of the ladder, are fixed just below the rungs. But if the ladder has aluminium rungs, the tie rods may be the rungs themselves. Tie rods usually can be tightened with a screwdriver or spanner, but if they

are held with rivets rest the ladder on its side and tap them firmly with a hammer.

Sliders and brackets on an extending ladder may work loose. Tighten their nuts or screws as necessary.

Do not attempt to replace broken or loose rungs. These can indicate general deterioration, so have the ladder checked and repaired by a builder.

Ladders should be stored under cover, and from time to time treated with clear wood preservative. Before treatment rub ladder stiles (the sides of the ladder) with glasspaper to remove any splinters. When the wood preservative has dried, apply one or two coats of clear varnish. Never paint a ladder, for this may hide splits and other defects which could lead to an accident.

Check ropes on step-ladders and, if necessary, replace them. Make sure that the hinges are sound and properly secured.

LAMPSHADES
To remove scorch marks, dab the area with a solution of equal parts of peroxide and water. First test the effect of the peroxide solution on an inconspicuous part of the shade. After tackling the scorch rub the area with a damp cloth to remove the peroxide. If the mark is still there, the shade must be re-covered.

A shade may fail to hang straight because the joints of the hinged metal framework supports are loose. Hold a metal block beneath each joint and gently tap the rivet head with a small hammer. If the frame is distorted because a stave – a vertical framing-wire – has come adrift from the ring, remove the cover, lining and tape to expose the joint. Repair the frame by resoldering. Alternatively, it may be possible to remake the joint using epoxy adhesive. Whichever method is used, the metal must be thoroughly cleaned.

LAVATORIES
See Water closets.

LETTER BOX: FITTING A NEW SPRING
If a letter-box return-spring

breaks, or loses its tension, a new one can be fitted. First remove the nuts holding the letter-plate assembly to the back of the door. At the back of the assembly is a metal rod on which the letter-box flap is mounted. The return-spring is also mounted on this rod. Tap the rod to one side to remove it from its mounting, then slide off the flap and the old spring. Buy a new spring from a hardware shop or locksmiths, and reassemble in reverse order to dismantling.

If a new spring is unobtainable, the old spring can often be re-used by carefully unwinding two turns to increase the tension. Initially, this may make the flap stiff to operate.

LIDS AND STOPPERS
To remove a sticking jar-top, try improving the grip by doubling a wide elastic band round the jar-top, or try holding the lid with a strip of glasspaper. A stubborn lid can sometimes be freed by gently tapping the jar upside-down on a hard surface or using the hinged side of a door as a vice. Another method is to hold the lid under hot running water. Wrap the jar in a cloth to prevent water running on to the glass. Special tools with handles for clamping round sticking jar-tops are available from hardware shops.

To remove a ground-glass stopper that is jammed in a decanter, run hot water over the neck of the decanter until the glass expands and releases the stopper. If this fails, or the stopper has broken off inside the neck, apply a mixture of 2 parts white spirit, 1 part glycerine, and 1 part salt to the join between bottle and stopper. Leave it for a day, then gently tap the stopper with your hand or a piece of wood wrapped in cloth, to loosen it.

LINOLEUM AND VINYL: PATCHING
Patch holes with a piece taken from beneath furniture or under a carpet. Cut a patch larger all round than the hole, and place it over the hole, matching any pattern as carefully as possible. Remember, an irregularly shaped patch will show up less than a square one. Using a sharp

trimming-knife, cut through the patch into the linoleum beneath. Remove the waste pieces and glue the patch to the floor, using a flooring adhesive (see p. 356). Weight down the patch until the adhesive dries.

Repair the area from which the patch was cut with glass-fibre filler-paste, of the type used for car-body repairs – available from car-accessory shops. Use glass-fibre paste to make the main repair if a patch cannot be used. First make sure that the lino around the hole is stuck down. Fill the hole with the paste and rub down level with the floor surface when hardened. Paint the repair with polyurethane gloss paint to match the linoleum.

M

MIRRORS
A mirror should have a space of about 3 mm. (⅛ in.) behind it to allow air to circulate between the mirror and the wall.

Small, lightweight mirrors or mirror-tiles can be fixed to a clean, non-powdery wall surface using double-sided sticky pads which are available from hardware shops and stationers.

Heavier unframed mirrors must be fixed with screws. If a mirror has fixing holes fix it with dome-head mirror screws. Tighten the screws to hold the mirror firmly, but not too tightly or the mirror may distort or crack. Use rubber packing washers to hold the mirror away from the wall.

To fix a mirror that is not drilled, use clips or corner plates. Fixed clips are screwed to the wall to hold the bottom of the mirror; the top and sides are retained with sliding clips fitted 20 mm. (¾ in.) from the top corners. Tighten the screws holding the sliding clips so that the clips can just be moved. Use washers to hold the clips away from the wall. Place the mirror on the bottom clips and push the sliding clips into position so that the mirror is held firmly, but without undue stress.

Resilvering is a complicated process, and results are unsatisfactory unless the work is carried out by a glass merchant.

A-Z OF REPAIRS

MOPS

To fit a new mop-head, remove the screw securing the old head to the handle. Tap off the head. Try the new head on the old handle and if it is a good fit, replace the securing screw. If it is too tight, use a Surform to shave the end of the handle slightly.

Mop-heads usually have parallel-sided sockets. In this case, use a chisel or Surform to shape the handle until a snug fit is obtained. Fit the securing screw.

In the unlikely event of the mop-socket being too large for the handle, obtain a good fit by binding close turns of string round the handle end.

MOULDINGS

See Picture framing, p. 164: Plaster.

PICTURES AND PRINTS

Work on valuable pictures should be left to an expert.

To re-mount a print, remove it from its old mount by lifting it carefully if it is fixed with paper hinges, or – if it is glued to a backing card – moistening the back of the card. Separate print and card carefully to avoid tearing. Hold the print flat between sheets of clean blotting paper and boards until it is dry.

Brown stains on a print can usually be removed by soaking it in a solution of 5 ml. of Chloromine T in 600 ml. (1 pint) of water. This bleach is obtainable through chemists. Test it on an obscure corner before treating the entire print. After treatment, rinse the print in clean water and dry as above.

To mend a tear, paste a good-quality artists' paper over the back of the damaged area. Any white paper showing through the print must be touched-in using matching tints on a fine brush. See also Picture framing, pp. 164-5; Stains, p. 326.

PLASTER

To fill a hole in plasterboard, use a cellulose plaster filler, available from do-it-yourself shops. This will fill a hole up to about 12 mm. (½ in.)

across. With a larger hole than this the repair must be reinforced with scrim cloth, which can be bought from builders' merchants.

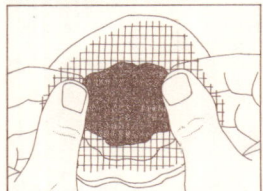

Cut a border about 12 mm. (½ in.) wide and 5 mm. (¼ in.) deep round the hole. Cut a piece of scrim cloth to fit into the hole and border. Dampen the edge of the plasterboard with water and apply dabs of plaster. Press the scrim into place, leave it to set and then plaster over the repair. To get a smooth finish, when the plaster is nearly set, dampen it and polish with a metal float or a trowel.

Lath and plaster is found in older houses – the plaster is keyed on to wooden laths nailed to the partition or ceiling. If the laths are undamaged there should be no difficulty in repairing the plaster after damping with water. If the laths have broken away, reinforce the hole by inserting a plug of stiff paper, soaked first in water and then in plaster of a creamy consistency. Fill the hole with plaster to just below the surface. When this has hardened, apply a surface coat.

Ceilings in old houses are often spoiled by an accumulation of paint and distemper in the decorative cornices. Soften it with water – an old scent spray filled with water is ideal – and leave it to soak for half an hour. Then, using

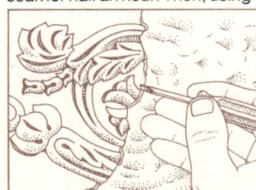

a small screwdriver, carefully scrape the paint from the moulding. Use a small stiff brush to clean away loose and flaking

material. Replace missing sections of mouldings by using the technique described under Picture framing, p.164.

POTS AND PANS

See Saucepans.

PRESSURE COOKERS

If the safety plug on a pressure cooker opens, take the cooker off the heat and wait for steam to stop escaping. Reset the plug by pressing the pin back into the rubber plug. After resetting, check that the steam vent is not blocked. If the plug holes blow frequently and holes in the steam vent are clear, buy a new safety plug from a dealer.

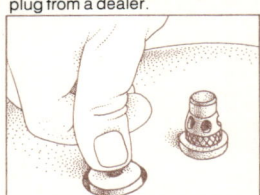

Remove the old plug by pressing back the pin and pulling it out from the underside. Then push out the rubber plug, using a screwdriver as a lever if necessary. Press the new plug into place from below. Take care to ensure that the side marked TOP is uppermost.

A faulty gasket is indicated by steam escaping around the cooker lid. Turn the lid upside-down and carefully lever out the

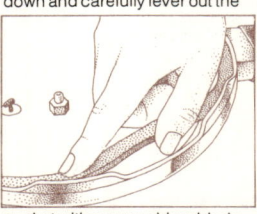

gasket with a screwdriver blade. Wash the inside of the rim with luke-warm soapy water and dry it thoroughly before fitting the new gasket. Press the gasket into place round the rim.

PUNCTURES

See Air-beds.

RECORD PLAYERS

A faulty record player should be repaired only by a technician.

RUSH SEATS

If one or two pieces of rush break away at the edges, temporary repairs can be made with PVA or contact adhesive. Such damage indicates, however, that rush seats will shortly need to be remade. Foam seat cushions will protect the rush from further damage and improve comfort until the seats are permanently repaired.

To renew a rush seat, buy rushes from a good craft shop. A bolt is sufficient for four chairs. Soak the rushes in cold water for 15 minutes, then lay them flat under a heavy cloth for 24 hours.

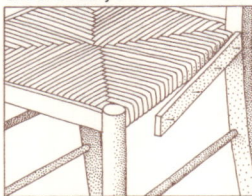

Remove protective wood edging strips from the old seats and cut away the old rushes to expose the frame.

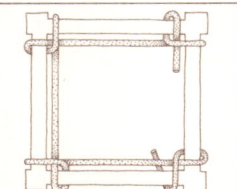

Form the new seat by wrapping the rushes round and round the frame. Start in the front left-hand corner and lay the first rush over the front rail, twisting it firmly in a clockwise direction. Still twisting the rush, wrap it round the front rail then turn it sharply up and over the left-hand rail. Without twisting, pull the rush straight over to the front right-hand corner. Work this corner in a similar manner to the first corner, then take the rush on

to the back right-hand corner. Complete this corner, then take the rush on to the back left-hand corner and then to the front left-hand corner to complete one round. At each corner the rush is twisted clockwise as it lies on the top surface, but it is untwisted on the straight lays.

The rushes must be tightly packed against one another and the process continued until the seat is filled. New rushes are joined on with knots arranged so that they fall on the underside. The rushes should be of even thickness. If some are too thin, two can be twisted together.

As the work progresses, stuff the gap between the upper and under layers of rushes with bundles made from broken rushes and spare ends. Firm packing will prevent sagging and loosening in the seat.

A square seat will fill symmetrically on all sides; a rectangular seat will fill at the sides before the front and back, leaving an oblong space at the centre to be filled. Weave the rush from front to back only.

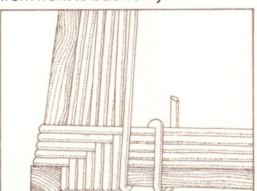

With a chair that is slightly wider at the front, wrap an extra turn around the bar at the front corners, complete a full round as before, then wrap two extra turns around the front corners. Alternate this procedure until the space at the centre is square or rectangular, then fill from front to back only.

RUST

A rust-remover tool-kit consists of a wire brush, scraper, emery paper, wire wool, rust-removing liquid, such as Jenolite, and metal primer. Alternatively, a combined rust-inhibiting liquid and metal primer – such as Kurust – can be used.

Remove thick rust by scraping. In serious cases rust scales can be chipped off with a hammer and cold chisel. Thoroughly wire-brush, then rub with emery paper to get back to bright metal, if possible. Apply the rust-remover liquid, rub with wire wool and leave for 15 - 20 minutes. Wipe the surface dry, then leave it for a further 20 minutes before applying metal primer. Zinc-base, cold galvanising paint is ideal. Apply the finishing coats in the normal way.

If a combined rust inhibitor and primer is used, brush it liberally over the prepared metal surface and leave it to dry. It dries quickly on rusty surfaces; slowly on bright metal. It will not dry on painted surfaces. Wait until the primer has dried over the metal, then wipe the excess away using a cloth soaked in methylated spirit. Finish by applying two coats of paint.

To loosen rusted nuts and bolts, apply penetrating oil, or paraffin, and leave it to soak in. Wire-brush to remove loose rust from the threaded portion. Tap the nut to break the rust seal. If the nut still does not turn, try heating it with a blow-torch or blow-lamp flame.

To loosen a rusted screw, use penetrating oil and a long screwdriver – the longer the tool the more force you can exert.

SAUCEPANS

Handles are usually screwed or riveted. Pans bearing the British Standard kitemark usually have their handles screwed to a metal bracket, and can be tightened easily with a screwdriver if the handle works loose.

To tighten riveted handles, fix a hammer firmly in a metal vice. The hammer head will act as an anvil. Support the pan, with the handle upwards, on the hammer head.

A-Z OF REPAIRS

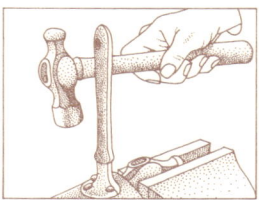

Use another hammer to tap the rivets in the handle fixing, and flatten them out. Rub smooth with emery paper afterwards.

There are several products on the market designed to resurface non-stick pans, but usually these are rarely successful for long. Pans whose surfaces are badly damaged should be discarded or the manufacturer informed. If you feel that a non-stick surface has worn out prematurely, inform the manufacturer of the pan. To minimise wear, use only wood or plastic spatulas, not metal slicers. Avoid using steel wool.

SCALES
Bathroom or kitchen scales should be accurate to within 1 oz. per lb. If they are not, they cannot be repaired by the amateur and should be sent to the makers.

Each time kitchen scales are used, set the pointer to zero. Check the scales regularly for accuracy by using a package of a known weight.

SCISSORS
When scissors fail to cut properly, the joint between the blades may be loose. The joint is usually made with a rivet with a screw head.

If turning the screw fails to tighten the joint, place the screw head on a metal surface – a metal vice, for example – and give the rivet end a few sharp taps with a hammer. If this does not improve the cutting action, the blades need sharpening.

SHARPENING BLADES
Knives Sharpen on a whetstone – available from hardware stores – on a steel, a hand-sharpener or with an electric sharpener. Most kitchen knives are ground at an angle of 30 degrees and should be held at this angle when sharpening on a stone or steel.

Sharpen blades gradually, first on one side, then the other, then again on the first side and so on.

To use a whetstone draw one side of the blade along the stone, then turn and pull it back across the surface several times.

To use a hand-sharpener pull the blade firmly through the discs, in the same direction, several times. Do not saw the blade backwards and forwards.

Scalloped and saw-edged blades Sharpen with special tools, available from hardware stores.

Scissors Blunt edges can be sharpened with a fine slipstone – available from hardware stores. Keep it at right-angles to the face of the blade.

If the blade edges are damaged, smear light oil on the slipstone and run it over the inner face of the blade.

Garden shears Put the shears in a metal vice and use a fine single-cut file to sharpen the blade. Hold the file at a slight angle.

Blades cannot be sharpened properly by an amateur if they are chipped or distorted. Take them to a specialist.

Lawn mowers Cylinder blades can be sharpened by turning them backwards to grind them against the fixed bottom blade, using valve-grinding paste, available from garages.

Remove the drive casing. Stand the machine on wood blocks to keep the blades off the ground.

Remove the chain from chain-driven machines. Use a screwdriver and prise off the clip connecting the ends of the chain and remove the link between them. Unwrap the chain from the

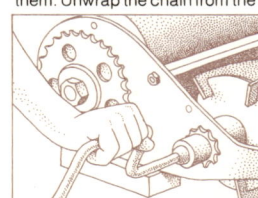

sprocket wheels. Use a brace and socket to turn the sprocket-nut on the cylinder shaft.

There is a special hole on some gear-driven mowers in the roller gear with a screwed thread.

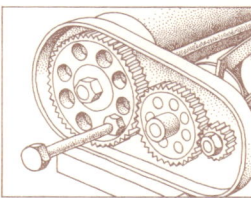

Screw in a bolt to make a handle and secure it with a nut.

On gear-driven mowers, slide the central idle gear off the shaft. This prevents the roller assembly turning. Fit a brace and socket to

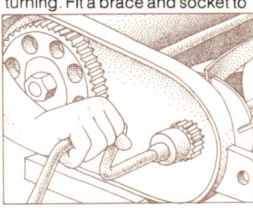

the nut on the end of the shaft.

Adjust the rotating blades so

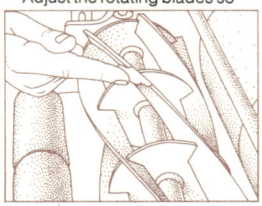

that they meet the fixed blade with only a minute, even gap between them.

Use coarse grinding paste, applying it with the fingertips to the edge of each blade, and then turn the blades anti-clockwise.

Adjust the height of the blades so that they will cut thin paper cleanly throughout the length of the cylinder when rotated.

Wipe off paste from blades and bottom blade with a rag. Remove the handle and refit the chain.

If the bottom, fixed blade becomes rounded, it is no longer worth sharpening. Unscrew it, and fit a matching replacement – available from ironmongers.

Chisels Apply a few spots of oil to an oil-stone. If there are high spots along the cutting edge of the back, hone the back of the blade

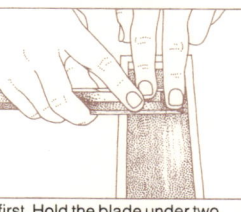

first. Hold the blade under two fingers, across the width and the end 50 mm. (2 in.) of the blade.

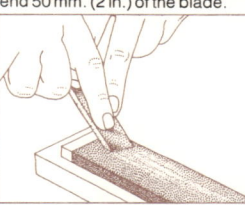

With the bevelled edge of the chisel facing down, rub the chisel up and down the stone, in the oil, several times. Work diagonally in both directions to use the stone evenly.

To remove burr, hone the back edge of the blade, then the front edge alternately.

SHOE REPAIRS
Repairs to modern shoes are limited to fixing stick-on soles, renewing leather or rubber heels and renovating toe-caps which have become scuffed.

Soles and heels made of PVC cannot be repaired by an amateur. To find out if a shoe is made of PVC, touch the sole with a hot copper wire and then put the wire back in the flame. If the wire turns green, the sole is PVC.

Heels To replace a leather heel with a rubber one, remove at least two thicknesses of leather, as a rubber heel is thicker than a layer

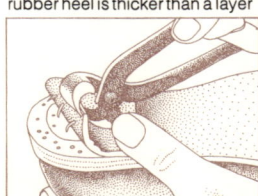

of leather. Use a screwdriver to

prise up the first and second layers on the worn heel and peel them off with pincers.

Clean the heel on the shoe with medium-grade glasspaper and roughen the new heel to provide a key for the adhesive.

Coat the shoe heel with neoprene cement – available in tubes from DIY shops – working it well into the leather. Wait ten minutes or so for the cement to dry. Position the new rubber heel on the shoe heel and hammer in nails just below the ridges of the holes – rubber heels have prepared nail holes in which metal washers are fitted.

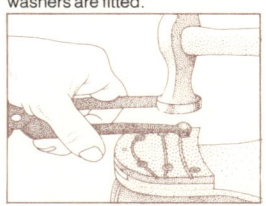

Drive the nails below the heel's surface using a nail punch and hammer. Stop when the nail heads contact these washers.

Support shoes when nailing with a block of wood held firmly in a vice.

With a wet knife blade, trim around the new heel and along the instep until it is flush with the rest of the heel. Smooth off with a rasp and glasspaper.

To colour the heel, use a wood stain or water-based ink. When dry, apply several coats of shoe polish.

Scuffed toe-cap Use methylated spirit to remove all the old polish, and smooth the scuffed area with glasspaper. Brush off the dust and use a matching proprietary shoe colouring to resurface the damaged area. Apply further coats until the area blends with the rest of the shoe.

Stick-on soles The method of fixing these soles is the same for both rubber and leather-soled shoes, but the preparation methods are different.

Use a rasp to remove dirt and grease from leather soles. Use a solvent, such as lighter fuel, to clean rubber soles. Finish with coarse glasspaper.

Buy a tube of neoprene cement and a tin rasp. Stick-on soles are sold in the same sizes as shoes.

The stick-on soles will be fixed about 2 mm. ($\frac{1}{16}$ in.) inside the edge of the shoe sole. First, position the sole and draw a pencil line around it on the shoe. If the sole is too large it can be trimmed: pencil the outline of the

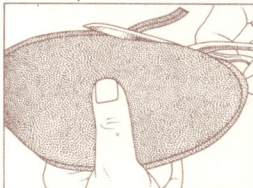

shoe on the stick-on sole, and cut 2 mm. inside the pencilled line, using scissors or a sharp knife.

Chamfer the edge of the new sole with glasspaper or a rasp.

Coat both soles with cement, rubbing it well into the new sole. When both soles are tacky, fit the new sole.

Starting from the toe, work downwards towards the centre of the sole, then outwards, pressing

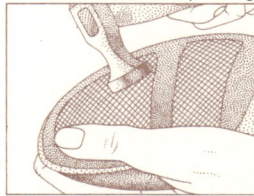

hard all the time. Place a hand inside the shoe, and hammer over the whole surface of the new sole.

SILVER AND GOLD
Repairs or replating of either silver or gold should be done by a craftsman. Silver is usually hard-soldered at the joints and the soldering temperature is crucial. A mistake could damage the article.

Dents, too, should also be hammered out by an expert, or the thin metal may stretch or fracture.

To remove slight scratches on silver use jeweller's rouge or fine crocus powder – do not use any other abrasives on valuable silver or the surface may be scored.

A-Z OF REPAIRS

SINKS

Chipped enamel can be repaired with Porcelainit, a proprietary paint. Clean the area and apply the paint in accordance with the manufacturer's instructions.

Cracked sinks can be repaired temporarily with an epoxy resin filler. But a cracked sink is dangerous and should be replaced as soon as possible. (See also Washbasins.)

SKIRTING BOARDS

Fill cracks with a wood filler such as Brummer and leave the filling proud of the surface. Rub down with glasspaper when dry.

To conceal gaps below skirtings, fix strips of timber mouldings to the floor – not the skirting.

Choose mouldings which have two sides forming a right-angle to fit between the floor and the skirting.

Pin the moulding to the floor with 25 mm. (1 in.) panel pins spaced 150 mm. (6 in.) apart. Punch nail heads below the surface and fill the holes with plastic wood or a similar filler.

SPECTACLES

A broken frame can be temporarily repaired, but should be attended to by an expert as soon as possible. Other repairs should be limited to tightening loose hinge screws and replacing partly rimless lenses, which are held in place by a nylon thread. All other repairs should be left to an optician.

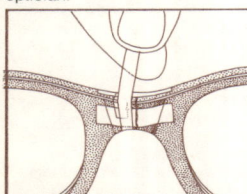

A break in a side arm or across the bridge – the main stress point in a pair of spectacles – can be repaired with clear adhesive tape. Clean the frame thoroughly with a dry cloth, and cut six 5 mm. (¼ in.) wide strips of tape to size, 25 mm. (1 in.) long.

Get someone to hold the broken pieces together. Then use the tip of a needle to place the strips in place. Put one on each side of the break, one on the top and the bottom of the break. Bind the last two round the other four on either side of the break.

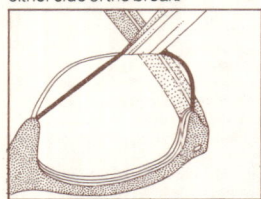

To refit a lens that has slipped from its nylon thread, place the lens in the groove of the frame. Hook a piece of narrow fabric through the nylon thread and pull the tape to draw the thread into the lens groove. Hold the lens firmly in place and carefully withdraw the tape.

SQUASH RACKETS

See Tennis rackets.

STAIRS

A common cause of creaking is that the bottom edge of a riser rubs against the top of the tread below it. First try brushing french chalk into any cracks between tread and riser. If this fails, a more complicated repair is necessary.

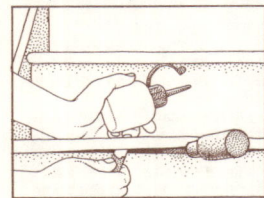

On most staircases it is possible to prise the squeaking tread and riser apart slightly, using an old chisel or screwdriver, and push in PVA adhesive on a piece of thin cardboard.

Drive nails at an angle through the top of the tread into the riser beneath. Drive the nail heads below the surface and fill the holes with plastic wood.

Staircases that are open underneath are easier to deal with. Triangular blocks of wood or metal brackets can be fixed behind the tread and riser joints, to give them rigidity.

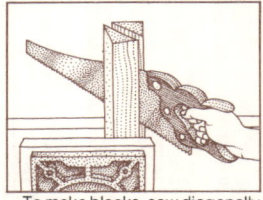

To make blocks, saw diagonally through a length of 45 × 45 mm. (1¾ × 1¾ in.) softwood held in a vice.

Cut two blocks 75 mm. (3 in.) long for each tread and riser. Partly hammer two panel pins into each block.

Apply PVA woodworking adhesive to each block and press in place from below, one at each end of the joint between tread and riser. Then hammer in the panel pins.

Metal brackets – the kind sold for shelving – can also be effective in extreme cases to stop stairs creaking. Brackets should be a little shorter than the steps and be fixed with screws shorter than the thickness of tread or riser. Position one bracket 150 mm. (6 in.) in from each side, tight up underneath the treads and risers.

STEPS

Concrete steps that are cracked or crumbling at the edges can be repaired by patching with new concrete.

Use 3 parts aggregate – small quantities can be bought from builders' merchants – 2 parts sand and 1 part cement. Add a PVA liquid adhesive such as Unibond or Polybond to assist bonding. The makers' instructions will tell how much to add.

Using a hammer and cold chisel, chip off 50 - 75 mm. (2 - 3 in.) of concrete around the damaged area. Brush out well.

Fix a board in place, the same height as the step and wider than the damaged area, and support it with bricks.

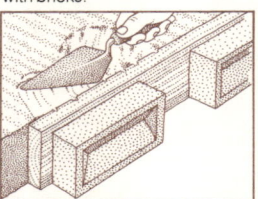

Brush PVA liquid adhesive on the damaged surface and then fill the hole with concrete. Do this gradually, firming it down well with a piece of wood to exclude air pockets.

Smooth the mortar with a trowel and leave the board in place for at least 24 hours. Do not use the step for at least seven days.

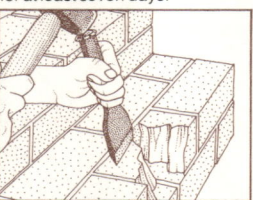

Broken brick steps can be dangerous. Remove broken bricks with a hammer and cold chisel. Take care not to damage or disturb sound bricks. Clean

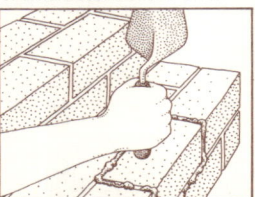

holes with a wire brush and apply a mix of 4 parts sand and 1 part cement. Set a new brick in place, tapping it gently with the trowel handle. Remove surplus mortar.

In hot weather, soak the brick to prevent too much moisture being absorbed from the mortar.

Use a board to check that the surface is level. After 24 hours, finish the joints with a mix of 3 parts sand and 1 part cement.

STEREOS

A faulty stereo should be repaired only by a technician.

SUITCASES

To remove a broken handle, use pliers to open the D-rings at each end of the old one, and remove it. Put the D-rings through the loops at each end of the new handle and tighten with pincers.

To fit a new lock, cut the lining in the case to expose the back of the lock and use a screwdriver to prise open the tongues.

Take out the old lock and insert the new one. Bend down the tongues and stick the lining back.

If the corners of a case are worn but not rounded, they can be reinforced with fibre corner pieces fixed with bifurcated rivets: both are available from shoe-repair or leatherware shops.

Cut away part of the case to make room for the curved surface inside the corner piece.

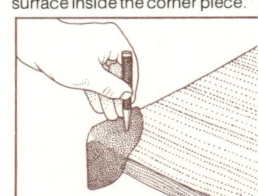

Hold the corner piece on a firm edge and punch holes in the centre 15 mm. (½ in.) from each edge. Push a rivet into the hole in the top face and position the corner piece.

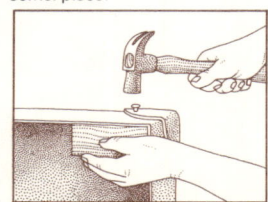

Using a metal block as a support, hammer the top of the rivet firmly. Drive home the other two rivets. Flatten the tails of the rivets on the inside.

T

TELEVISION

A faulty television should be repaired only by a technician. It can be dangerous to attempt repairs yourself – even when the set is unplugged.

TENNIS RACKETS

A worn or broken grip on a tennis racket can be replaced with a special adhesive tape obtainable from a sports' equipment shop.

Strip off the old grip. If any tacks have been used, remove them with pincers. Clean the handle with fine glasspaper. Stick the end of the new tape to the side of the handle, at the top. Use a trimming knife to cut a triangular piece from the end of the tape. Start the cut just down from the top corner and angle it downwards, making the cut as long as the circumference of the handle. Peel off the triangle of cut tape. Wind the rest of the tape round the shaft, following the

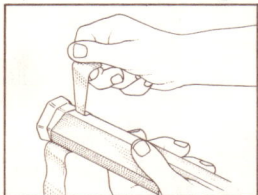

angle of the cut and overlapping it slightly. Continue winding down the shaft at this angle. When the area of the original grip is covered, cut the tape straight across the shaft, at this angle. Insert a small tack at the end of the tape if one was used on the original grip. Seal the end of the grip with a narrow strip of adhesive tape.

The same method of repair can be used to fit new grips to the handles of badminton or squash rackets.

TOILET-ROLL HOLDERS

Ceramic stick-on toilet-roll holders are made to match wall tiles, and are fixed in the same way (see pp. 66-67). If the wall is already tiled, one of the tiles will have to be removed to make way for the holder. First check that the

A-Z OF REPAIRS

size of the tile matches the size of the holder. If it does, break the tile occupying the position where the holder will go, and lever out the pieces from the centre, using a screwdriver. If you try to lever it out in one piece, you may damage surrounding tiles. If the wall surface is damaged it must first be made good with a cellulose filler. When the filler has dried, rub it down flat with a glasspaper block.

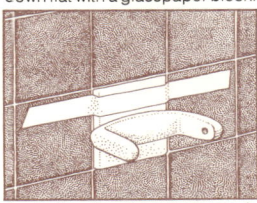

Apply tile adhesive to the back of the holder, using a notched spreader, press the holder in place and tape it to the surrounding tiles. Leave it taped until the adhesive sets. Finally, press tile grout into the gap around the holder and, when dry, polish with a soft cloth. To refix screw-on types, see p. 353.

TOWEL RAILS
See p. 353.

TOYS
Dolls The limbs of plastic dolls are usually fixed with push-on flanges. Limbs fall off if a flange splits or tears.

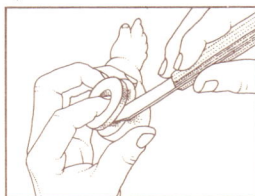

To refix a limb, heat the blade of an old knife. Hold it on the flange until the plastic starts to melt.
Take the blade off and squeeze the split edges together. Repair 15 mm. (½ in.) lengths at a time. Reinforce the inside of the flange with adhesive tape. Fit the limb back into the doll by pressing and turning the flange at the same time.

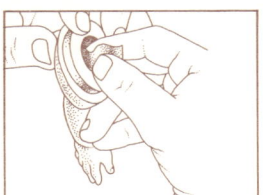

If the elastic breaks inside a strung vinyl doll, cut a length of 5 mm. (¼ in.) thick elastic twice the length of the doll's body and tie the ends together.
Secure the tied ends with zinc-oxide tape, available from hardware stores. Push the elastic loop into the head, past the bar.

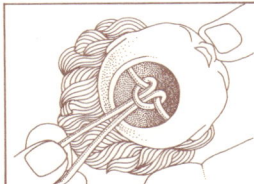

Hook the end of the elastic over the bar, out of the head and through the other side of the loop.

Push the free side of the loop into the neck hole and push head and body together. Push a hooked wire into the body through a leg hole. Pull the elastic out through the hole.

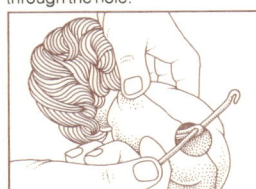

Hook the leg on to the loop, and pull out the wire. Catch the elastic

through the other leg hole and fix. Fit arms in the same way, except on large dolls, which need a separate small loop to fix arms.

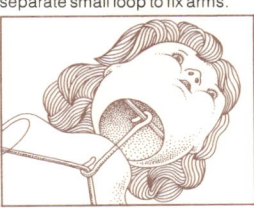

If the doll has a metal hook from the head bar, the elastic should be fitted over the hook, not around the bar.
Teddy bears To repair a loose limb, unstitch the main body seam and remove stuffing until the loose joint can be seen.
Push the limb against the body. Grip the joint plate with one hand and use long-nosed pliers to tighten the pin.

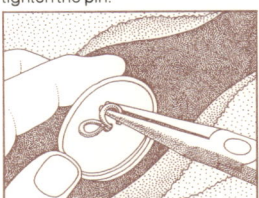

Tighten the curl on wire joints with pliers. On a split-pin joint, curl both ends of the pin to tighten it and flatten the loop with pliers.
To replace stuffing, add new kapok, or foam-rubber chips, if necessary. Sew up the seam, pulling it tight every four stitches.
New eyes, to replace those that

are broken or lost, can be obtained from toy or handicraft shops.
Electric trains Power is supplied through pick-ups in contact with the wheels and transmitted to a collector screwed to the engine base.
If the pick-ups are damaged, fit a new collector.

Release the two screws holding the collector, unsolder the pick-up lead from the others and release the connector.
Push the new collector lead up through the chassis between the first two wheels.

Resolder the new lead to the others with core solder. Fit and tighten the collector screws.
Smoke-unit element: A burnt-out electric element can cause the smoke unit to fail. When buying a new element, quote the make and type of engine.

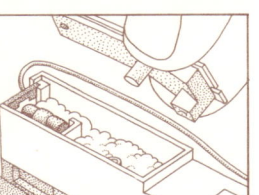

Release the securing smoke-unit screw and lift off the lid. Prise out the old element, fit the new one and replace the lid and screw. Renewing carbon brushes: Carbon brushes in the electric motor can wear down. To renew

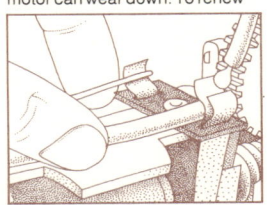
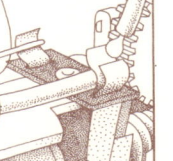

them, compress the spring clip and remove old brushes. Fit new brushes with the tag on the same side as the insulating sleeve. Replacing points springs: Take off the crank lever and fit the new spring with tweezers.

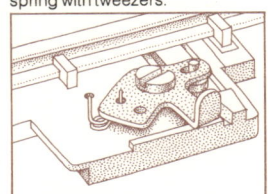

Replace the crank lever and trap the new spring in position. Renewing fishplates: Fit new fishplates if the rails slide off the sleepers. Press down on the sleeper at the damaged fishplate

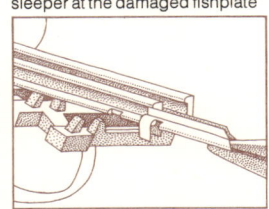

end. Gently ease out the rail with the fishplate.
Widen the tags carefully with pliers and remove the fishplate.
Insert a new fishplate; press in the tags. Slide the rail back in place, slotting the tags into the hole in the second sleeper from the end.
Balls To repair a puncture in a vinyl ball with a valve, put the ball in a bowl of water to find the hole. Mark the area with chalk.
Heat a screwdriver blade on a gas ring and rub it gently over the hole. This moulds the vinyl.
Let the vinyl harden for five minutes before inflating it with an adaptor and bicycle pump.
A vinyl ball without a valve cannot be repaired since it cannot be inflated. (See also Air-beds.)

U

UMBRELLAS
Few repairs can be made to umbrellas because of their complicated construction.
Mending holes To patch small holes, up to the size of a 10p piece, buy matching nylon from a haberdashers. Use clear adhesive and coat one side of the patch. With the umbrella up and taut, fix the patch on the inside, pressing down any loose threads from the outside.
Plastic handle Carefully break off a damaged handle with a hammer and clean out the recessed piece of metal into which it fits. Fix the replacement handle in place, using an epoxy-resin adhesive (see p. 356).
Loose cover The stitching securing the edge of the cover to a rib tip sometimes works loose.

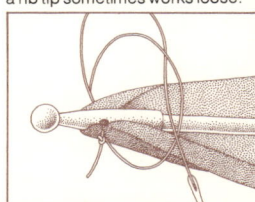

Cut away the loose nylon cotton and re-sew the cover, with a stitch through the hem and the eye of the rib tip, ending with a slip knot.

367

A-Z OF REPAIRS

UPHOLSTERY

To replace one or more broken straps of rubber webbing on a chair or sofa, buy matching material from a furniture dealer or craft shop.

There are two kinds of rubber webbing – all-rubber and reinforced rubber. Reinforced webbing has a core of rubber sandwiched between two layers of rayon cord, and has different stretching characteristics from all-rubber webbing.

Webbing is tacked to wooden frames or fixed to wooden or metal frames with metal clips. Various types of clips are sold for the purpose and provide simple fixing methods.

The neatest type fits into a groove cut in the perimeter rails of the frame, ensuring that all straps are under equal tension.

Allow 10% tension when measuring and cutting rubber webbing to length, for example, for a 750 mm. (30 in.) span, cut webbing in 675 mm. (27 in.) lengths.

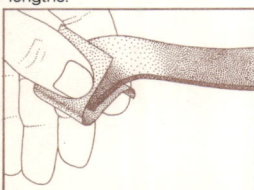

If you are using clip-fixings, cut the webbing to length first and fit clips to each end of the straps – pinching them tight with pliers. Fit

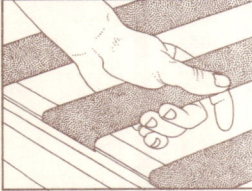

the clips into the grooves on the frame.

If you are using tacks, measure and mark on the webbing the unstretched length. Fix one end of the webbing to the frame with three tacks, and stretch the webbing until the mark lines up

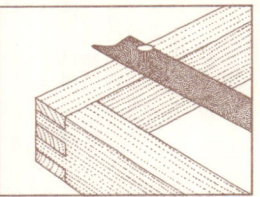

with the edge of the opposite frame. Tack the webbing in place and then cut off the surplus. (See also pp. 122-33.)

V

VACUUM CLEANERS

Before making any repairs, switch off the cleaner and remove the plug from the socket.

Splits or frays in a broken hose can be repaired temporarily by binding it with plastic fabric tape or masking tape.

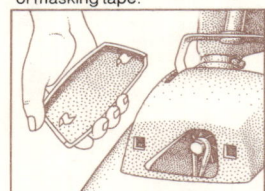

To fit a new drive belt or roller brush to an upright cleaner, take off the cover plate at the front of the cleaner and remove the belt from the pulley.

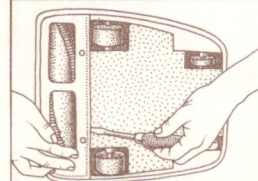

Turn the cleaner on its side and loosen the screws securing the metal shield behind the brush roller.

Beside the roller there may be a catch. If so, free it, lift out the brush and belt and discard the worn belt.

Fit the new belt round the slot in the middle of the roller and re-fit

the roller and shield.

Turn the cleaner upright. Twist the belt clockwise and stretch it

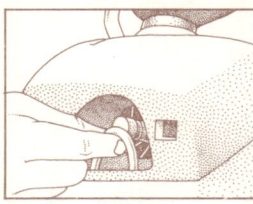

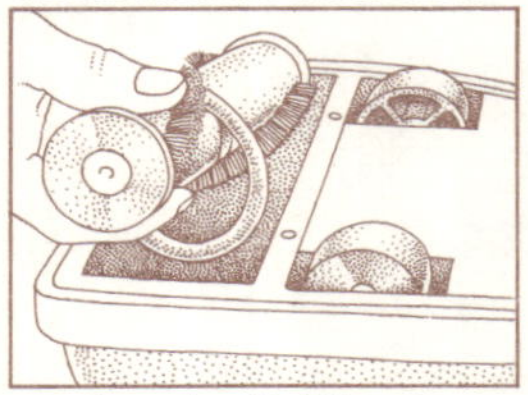

over the pulley. Re-fit the cover plate.

A vacuum cleaner's efficiency can be impaired if the filters become blocked. They should be cleaned regularly and renewed when worn.

On some models, the filters are behind the dust bag. They collect those particles of dust which pass through the bag. On other models, the filters are at the motor end or blow end. They prevent particles of dust being dispersed into the room. On other cleaners, the filters will be found in front of the motor.

VACUUM FLASKS

Metal vacuum flasks tend to rust, making it difficult to unscrew the top of the flask when fitting a replacement liner. Modern flasks are usually made of plastic and are easier to repair.

If a silvered-glass liner breaks, a replacement can be bought from a hardware shop. Handle liners with great care – they are extremely brittle and can easily be broken when being fitted.

Unscrew the top of the flask, empty out the fragments and unscrew the inner lining cap to remove the remainder of the broken liner. Fit the new one so that it rests on the concave mount, inside the flask, and screw the inner lining cap back on.

W

WALLS

Remove loose plaster around cracks and minor holes and enlarge the crevices slightly to give a key for the filler. Brush off dust.

Dampen the area and apply plaster filler proud of the surface.

When dry, rub down with wet-and-dry abrasive paper and leave it for 24 hours before painting.

Large cracks which appear persistently at the corners between walls and ceiling can be disguised with plaster coving fixed in place with coving adhesive – both available from builders' merchants.

The coving sticks only to plaster, so any wall covering or ceiling paper on the area to be covered must be removed first.

Hold the coving against the corner of the ceiling and mark the area which will be covered on walls and ceiling.

If the walls are papered, cut the paper 3 mm. (⅛ in.) inside the coving lines and strip off the paper.

Score the surface of the wall and ceiling to be covered, with a sharp knife to improve adhesion for the coving.

Measure the lengths of wall and mark the lengths of coving needed.

Use a sharp fine-toothed saw to cut the coving. Saw from the face of it to keep the edges clean.

To mitre the corners, cut out the paper templates supplied with the coving, checking whether each mitre is internal or external, and trace the appropriate template on the coving.

Cut mitres with the saw from the face of the coving. Use a 45 degree mitre block for 90 degree corners. Carefully smooth cut edges with fine glasspaper.

Use an old paint brush to wet the areas to be covered.

Mix enough adhesive to be used in 20 minutes and spread it thickly on the back of the coving.

With the aid of a helper, press the coving firmly in place and hold it until stuck – a minute or so. On uneven surfaces, fix it with a nail every 600 mm. (24 in.). Punch nail

heads below the surface. Remove surplus adhesive and use it to fill any gaps or nail-head holes.

Leave 3 mm. (⅛ in.) gaps between adjoining lengths of coving and fill them with adhesive.

Butt mitred edges tightly at the corners and fill the joints with adhesive, applied upwards with a flexible knife.

Clean any remaining adhesive with water and a clean brush.

WASHBASINS

Minor cracks and small holes can be repaired with an epoxy-resin filler (Isopon or Plastic Padding).

Enlarge the crack or hole very slightly to give the filler a good key. Make sure the surface is dry and clean.

Fill the crevice with the filler, mixing it as directed so that it is slightly raised above the surface of the washbasin.

When the filler has set, rub it down with fine glasspaper until smooth.

If a washbasin is coming away from the wall, provide new plugs and refix it (see p. 352).

WASTE DISPOSERS

Before attempting any repairs, turn off the power at the mains.

If the waste disposer jams, reach into the unit and try to clear the obstruction. Tangled hairs are a major cause of jamming.

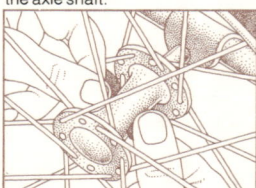

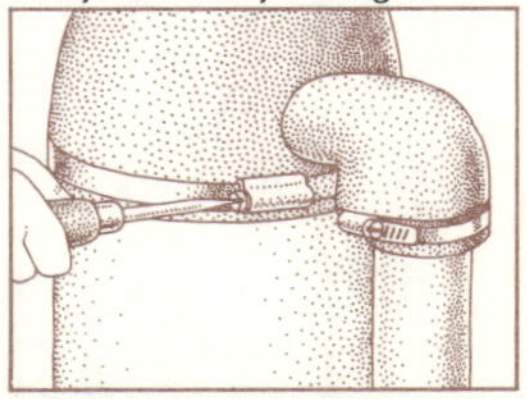

If this fails, fit the release tool – supplied with the unit – through the sink outlet on to the hexagon

nut and turn it backwards and forwards. If this does not free the motor, undo the screw which holds the clip at the base of the rubber shroud.

Raise the motor and grinder unit from the shroud, remove the obstruction and reassemble the parts.

Switch on at the mains, press the reset button and switch on. If the machine is fitted with a reversing control, minor jams may be cleared by switching to reverse.

WATER CLOSETS

Although minor cracks can be repaired with an epoxy-resin adhesive (see Washbasins), this is a temporary measure only.

It is not possible to make a repair which will restore the pan to a hygienic, self-cleansing piece of equipment, and a damaged pan should be replaced as soon as possible.

WHEELS

If a new wheel or tyre is needed, take the old one to a dealer so that it can be matched.

Pram wheels are secured by spring clips, sliders or plungers. All three types fit into a groove in the axle shaft.

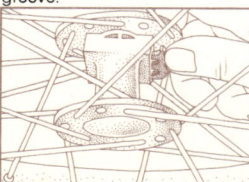

To remove a wheel, push the ends of the spring clips apart with the thumbs and push it to the side, to unhook its lug from the shaft groove.

Pull a spring-loaded slider from

A-Z OF REPAIRS

its housing at the side of the wheel axle.

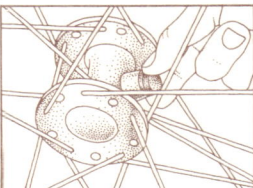

A plunger is usually in the middle of the axle. Pull it up and slide the wheel off the shaft. Reverse the procedure in all cases to fit a new wheel.

Replacement wheels for wheelbarrows can be obtained from the manufacturer. Make sure you have the address when buying a new wheelbarrow.

To remove a wheel from a metal wheelbarrow, take off the nuts and washers from each side of the spindle.

Spring the frame forks and body stays apart and slide the wheel from the frame.

Draw the spindle out of the hub. Grease and insert the new one and reassemble.

WINDOWS
Double-hung sashes If one sashcord breaks, it is best to renew the other three at the same time. You will need sashcord – waxed and plaited rope obtainable from builders' merchants and hardware stores – 25 mm. (1 in.) galvanised clout nails, a ball of string and 1 in. panel pins.

Prise off the interior beading on each side of the window with a chisel.

Lift out the lower, inner sash. Cut the cord if it is intact and lower the weight to the box bottom. Prise out the centre beading between the sashes. Cut the

cords and lift out the upper sash.

Remove the wooden caps from the pockets and lift the weights out of each box section.

Pull out the clout nails holding the cords to the sash and use the old cords as a guide when cutting the new ones to length.

Tie string to a bent nail. Run the nail and string over a pulley wheel and lower the nail, pulling it out through the bottom of the pocket. Oil the pivot of the pulley if it does not run smoothly.

Remove the nail and tie the string to the end of a new cord. Pull it over the pulley and cut through the pocket.

Remove the string and tie the bottom of the cord to a weight, using a figure-of-eight knot. Push the weight in through the pocket and into the box section.

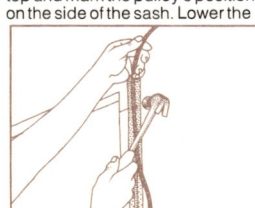

Hold the lower sash against the top and mark the pulley's position on the side of the sash. Lower the

sash and pull the cord tight. Nail the cord in a groove, 355 mm. (14 in.) down from the mark. Repeat on the other side.

Lower the upper sash cords

over the outside pulleys and hold the sash at the bottom.

Cut the cords to length and nail to the sash at both sides. Re-fit the beading and the pockets.

Use clout nails when fixing cords to the framework and fix beadings with panel pins.
Casements Loose hinges are a common cause of jammed casements. Tighten the screws in the hinges to pull the frame into place.

If this fails, slide a piece of carbon paper in the spot where the window is binding and open and shut the window. The paper will leave a mark only on the jamming points.

Shave off enough wood from these points to enable the window to close with a clearance of the thickness of a coin. Prime and repaint.

If handles and stays work loose, it is usually only necessary to tighten the fixing screws. Handles on metal windows may become hard to move owing to a heavy build-up of paint. Strip off the paint, treat with a rust inhibitor and re-paint (see pp. 58-59). Oil the handles when dry.
Sills If the drip grooves, under the projecting edges of sills, get clogged up with paint, rain can run back into the frame at the joint where wall and frame meet. Use an old screwdriver, or similar tool, to clean out all drip grooves.
Sealing gaps Leaks can be

caused by gaps between the frame and the wall, or if there is cracked putty around the glass.

To seal gaps, rake out the jointing material between window frame and wall and fill them with a non-setting mastic, obtainable from do-it-yourself shops and builders' merchants.

Make sure the mastic adheres to both surfaces.

If rain seeps in around the glass, remove the pane and re-bed it in new putty.
Broken window Use polythene sheeting or hardboard as a temporary cover for a broken window.

To mend a broken window in a

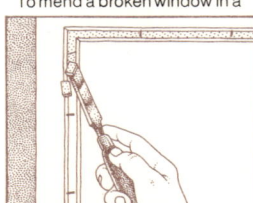

wooden frame, scrape out the putty with an old chisel or screwdriver and tap out any remaining fragments of glass with the handle of a hammer. Pull out sprigs – glazier's nails – with a pair of pincers, and clean the rebate – or recess in which the glass fits – with glasspaper. Paint the rebate with primer and leave it for two hours to dry.

Measure the size of the opening and get a glazier to cut glass to size for you, 1.5 mm. ($\frac{1}{16}$ in.) smaller than the opening.

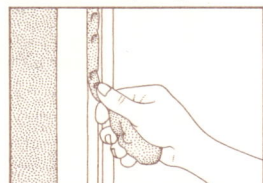

Make a thin sausage of putty between the palms, and squeeze a bed of putty into the rebate with thumb and forefinger. Press the glass firmly into place but avoid applying pressure at the centre of the pane.

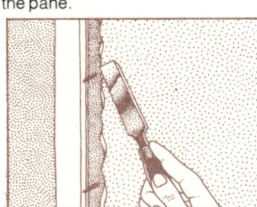

Tap glazing sprigs or headless panel pins into the rebate, flush with the glass, using the edge of a wide chisel as a hammer. Apply

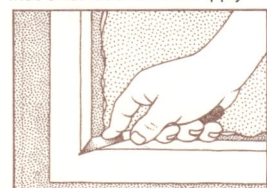

putty to the face edges of the window with a putty knife to form a neat bevel, and mitre the corners.

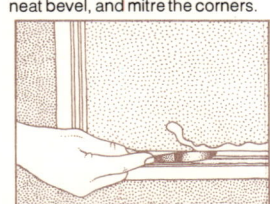

Scrape off excess putty from inside the window and clean off

fingerprints with methylated spirit. Paint the putty after 7-14 days.

To mend a window in a metal frame follow the same procedure, with the exception of special glazing clips that are used instead of glazier's sprigs.

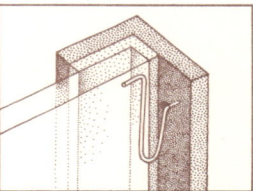

After removing the putty, prise out the glazing clips – one end is clamped over the glass; the other fitting into a hole in the frame. Note the positions of each clip and re-use them in the same holes. Scrape off any rust and apply a rust inhibitor – such as Kurust – where necessary.

A leaded light has cames – H-shaped lead strips – holding small panes of square or diamond-shaped panes of glass. To replace a broken pane, work from the outside and snick the four corners of the enclosing cames with a sharp knife. Bend back the cames to expose the edges of the pane and remove it. Scrape the recess clean.

Buy glass from a glazier to fit the opening. Press gold-size putty – available from builders' merchants – into the recess with a putty knife. Fit the glass, bend back the cames, and trim off surplus putty from both sides of the window. Use gentle pressure when replacing the cames.

Burnish the cut corners with a fine-grade glasspaper. Apply a blob of solder to them, with a moderately hot iron and flux.

If the glass is unbroken but the cames leak during wet weather, mark the leaks with a wax crayon on the glass. In dry weather, prise open the cames slightly, and prick out the old putty, which will probably have dried and crumbled. Use the point of a sharp penknife or similar tool.

Press gold-size putty into place so that it squeezes up behind the inside of the glass, and replace the cames. Clean off surplus.

ELECTRICITY, GAS AND WATER

Although the supply of electricity, gas and water is the responsibility of the appropriate authorities, the householder is responsible for the way they are used. When moving into a new house, therefore, familiarise yourself with the controls, and find out where supplies can be turned off in an emergency. Keep a list near the telephone of the names and telephone numbers of local people and organisations who provide emergency services.

• UNDERSTANDING AND USING ELECTRICITY

Electricity flows along wires rather as water flows in a pipe – except that electricity cannot flow until a circuit is completed. The amount of electricity flowing along the wire is measured in amps (A). The pressure, pushing electricity along the wires, is measured in volts (V). When an appliance is switched on, the amount of power consumed, or watts (W), is calculated by multiplying the volts by the amps.

Every appliance has at least two wires: one live (brown), carrying the electricity in, and one neutral (blue), returning it to the circuit. In addition, there is usually a third wire – the earth wire (green and yellow). This is a safety device which carries electricity harmlessly to earth if there is any failure in an appliance.

The previous colour-coding used before Britain switched to the continental standard was: live (red), neutral (black) and earth (green). Old appliances still in use may be wired in these colours.

EXTERNAL ELECTRICAL WORK
Weatherproof socket outlets are made for outdoor use, but there are strict regulations about electricity outside the house. Wiring for lights or power or garden tools should be installed by a qualified electrician.

REPAIRS AND INSTALLATIONS
Minor electrical repairs can be done by the householder, but anything involving complicated work, or the wiring of new circuit installations,

should be done by a competent electrician and expertly tested.

The electricity board or a registered contractor will test any wiring installation for safety and quote for repairs or rewiring. The board will also check – often without charge – the wiring when you move into a new house. Only the local board can connect up their supply to a house, and they may refuse to do so if the wiring is considered unsafe.

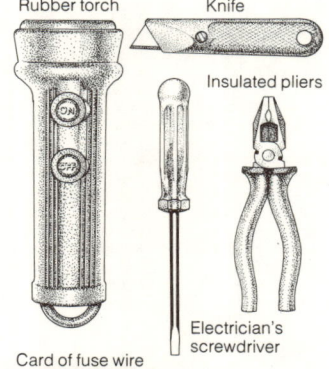

Rubber torch / Knife / Insulated pliers / Electrician's screwdriver / Card of fuse wire / Cartridge fuses

TOOL KIT FOR MINOR REPAIRS
A torch, rubber or plastic covered; an electrician's screwdriver with insulated handle; pliers with insulated handles; a card of fuse wire; spare cartridge fuses; a small, sharp knife; insulating tape; wire stripper.

READING APPLIANCE LABELS
Every appliance has fixed to it a rating plate which shows the maker's name,

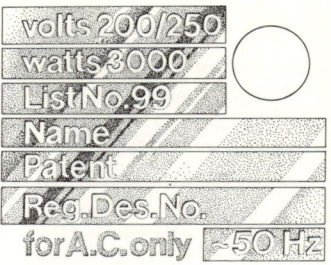

volts 200/250
watts 3000
List No. 99
Name
Patent
Reg. Des. No.
for A.C. only ~50 Hz

Appliance label

the model number (which is quoted for servicing), the wattage, the voltage, and sometimes the amperage.

The standard voltage for the domestic supply of electricity in Britain is 240 volts. The rating plate also shows the type of current it is designed to use – AC (alternating current) or DC (direct current). AC is in general use throughout the country; DC is rare.

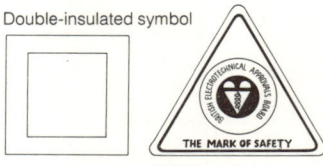

Double-insulated symbol / BEAB symbol / THE MARK OF SAFETY

THE MARKS OF SAFETY
Some modern appliances carry a label to show they are double-insulated – an indication that they have two-core wire and do not need earthing. They may also carry the BEAB (British Electrotechnical Approvals Board) symbol (above), proving that a sample of the appliance has been tested and satisfied the requirements set by the British Standard's Institution for electrical safety.

ESTIMATING THE COST
The wattage used by an appliance gives a guide to the running costs – 1,000 watts used for one hour is 1

kilowatt-hour (kWh) – the unit by which electricity is measured on the meter. Therefore, a fire supplied with 240 volt current at 12.5 amps consumes 3,000 watts or 3 kW per hour.

The price of electricity varies from region to region – consult your local electricity board for the relevant tariff in your area, which is also stated on your bills. Ask, too, about the different kinds of off-peak tariff rates.

UNITS USED PER HOUR
As a guide to the amount of electricity used, the following table shows the average consumption of units per hour of various appliances.

APPLIANCE	UNITS/HOUR
Heating	
3 kW radiant fire	3
2 kW immersion heater	2
2 kW fan heater	2
2 kW convector heater	2
1 kW infra-red heater	1
Towel rail	$\frac{1}{4}$
Electric overblanket	$\frac{1}{7}$
Electric underblanket	$\frac{1}{10}$
Lighting	
100 watt bulb	$\frac{1}{10}$
80 watt fluorescent tube	$\frac{1}{12}$
Kitchen equipment	
Kettle	1
Food mixer	$\frac{1}{5}$
Refrigerator	$\frac{1}{10}$
Food freezer (8 cu. ft)	$\frac{1}{12}$
Cooker hood	$\frac{1}{10}$
Extractor fan	$\frac{1}{15}$
Spin drier	$\frac{1}{4}$
Tumble drier	2
Iron	$\frac{1}{2}$
Vacuum cleaner	$\frac{1}{4}$
Floor polisher	$\frac{1}{10}$
Living-room	
Television (colour)	$\frac{1}{8}$
Television (black and white)	$\frac{1}{16}$
Stereo system	$\frac{1}{10}$
Record player/tape recorder	$\frac{1}{24}$
Workshop and garage	
Power tool	$\frac{1}{4}$
Battery charger	$\frac{1}{30}$

READING THE METER

There are two kinds of meter: the digital meter and the dial meter. Both record the total number of units used since the meter was installed. To check consumption, subtract the previous reading – which is recorded on the account – from the new reading.

The digital meter shows the units used by a simple row of figures. The special White Meter uses two digital indicators: one for the lower-priced night-rate electricity and the other for the day rate.

The dial meter has six dials and each pointer goes round in the opposite direction to its neighbour. From left to right, the dials record units in ten thousands, thousands, hundreds, tens and singles. Ignore the dials registering tenths or hundredths of a unit – usually coloured red.

Note the figures down in order, starting at the dial showing 10,000 units. Always write down the number the pointer has passed. For example, if the pointer is anywhere between 3 and 4, write down 3.

PAYING THE BILL

Most people get their bills quarterly, but paying a monthly estimated sum

by banker's order or Giro can help with household budgeting. It is also possible to pay weekly, if you wish to ease the burden of sudden large bills; or to have a coin-in-the-slot meter. Write to the electricity board for details.

All bills contain a standing charge which covers the cost of making a supply available, and is payable whether or not any power is used. Some boards spread the amount over the first 100 or so units in each quarter while the remainder are charged at a lower price. Other boards impose a separate standing charge, then charge for the units at a stated price.

Electricity can be cheaper if used during off-peak periods, normally the night hours. Thermal storage heaters and electric water-heaters benefit from the off-peak White Meter tariff, as also do all appliances and lighting used between about 11 p.m. and 7 a.m. on this cheap-rate tariff. Thus, if it is practicable to use a cooker, dishwasher or automatic washing machine during these hours – appliances which use a lot of power – you gain the maximum benefits.

The bill may also include a fuel adjustment clause or surcharge which

covers fluctuations in basic fuel prices.

MAINS SUPPLY AND FUSE BOX

A thick, two-core service cable brings power into the home to a sealed fuse unit which must not be touched by the householder, and is the property of the electricity board. From the sealed fuse box the service cable goes through the meter to the main switch. In old houses the main switch is in a separate box, but in recently built homes it is part of a consumer's unit, or fuse box, where the main circuit is split into a number of sub-circuits, each having its own fuse.

FUSES

Fuses are safety devices designed to protect wiring and appliances. If more current flows through a wiring circuit than it is designed to carry, the flex or cable could get dangerously hot. The fuse wire is made of weaker material, so that it melts or 'blows' when overloading occurs. This stops the flow of current and prevents further trouble.

The most common form of installation has one fuse that can be rewired for each circuit. All fuse wire is sold with its amperage marked on the package and it is essential that it should match the amperage of the cable. Some fuse boxes now have cartridge fuses which can be replaced as easily as those in 13 amp plugs.

In either case, label each fuse-holder so that it is easy to tell which belongs to which circuit and what rooms or appliances it serves.

The fuse carriers on modern fuse units are colour coded: 5A is white (for lighting), 15A is blue (for immersion heaters and other 3 kW circuits), 20A is yellow (for some types of water heaters), 30A is red (ring circuits), 45A is green (cookers).

REPLACING A FUSE

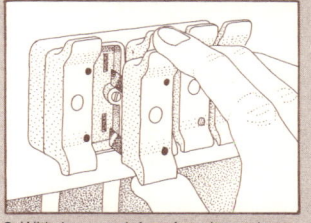

1. Turn off the supply at the mains switch before handling any fuses. Unscrew and remove the fuse-box cover.

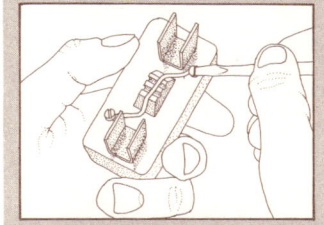

2. Withdraw each fuse from its socket to find the blown fuse. Ratings are marked by a coloured spot or a number.

3. If the wire bridging a fuse has parted, unscrew it and fit new wire. Replace a cartridge fuse with a new one.

CIRCUIT BREAKERS

Some of the newer systems have miniature circuit breakers in place of these removable fuses. Looking like ordinary switches or push buttons, they flick themselves off if any circuit is overloaded or if a fault in the wiring system fails to blow the plug or socket fuse. The circuit can be brought back into use simply by pressing the switch down or pushing the button in.

If after finding and repairing a fault a fuse blows repeatedly, this indicates a serious fault which must be rectified. Call in an electrician. Do not use a fuse wire of a higher rating – this may cause a fire.

SEALED FUSE BOX

If this blows, call the Board's emergency service – write the number on the wall close to the meter. To check if this fuse has blown, first check to see if all fuses in the consumer unit are intact, second, turn on all switches (do not leave them switched on), and third, check with neighbours to see if there is a power cut. As a final check put your ear against the meter. If you can hear a faint hum, the Board's fuse is intact and there is a fault between their fuse and your consumer unit. Call an electrician.

Board fuses are unlikely to fail, but may do so if you make additions to the system without informing the Board.

• EMERGENCIES AND POWER CUTS

Keep matches and candles, a torch and possibly camping lighting equipment in the house. Power cuts stop the electric pump motors used in central heating, so a paraffin stove is a useful standby.

Voltage reductions cause lights to dim, the TV picture to reduce, a cooker to burn more slowly and electric fires to burn dull. If the power is cut, turn off all electrical appliances, such as refrigerator, fires, blankets, irons and kettles, or when power is restored an accident may occur.

Keep a refrigerator door closed as much as possible. Keep the lid or door of a freezer closed and food will remain in perfect condition for at least ten hours – longer than a power cut is likely to last.

DIAL METER
Start reading the dials from left to right, ignoring the one marked 1/10. If the pointer is between two figures, write down the lowest one. If the pointer is on a figure, say 7, look at the next dial to the right and, if the number is between 9 and 0, write down 6; if it is between 0 and 1, write down 7. The meter reads 18558.

DIGITAL METER
Read the figures from left to right. The total number of units consumed is 1,381.

ELECTRICITY METER Read meters carefully when checking your consumption.

• WIRING, SOCKETS AND PLUGS

Separate circuits of cable distribute power from the consumer's unit to the various appliances, via power points or socket outlets, each cable protected with plastic and containing three wires: a red, live wire; a black, neutral wire; and a bare, earth wire.

Circuits are wired in one of two ways: by the ring-main system or by the radial-wired system.

RING-MAIN SYSTEM

Many houses built since 1947 have ring-main wiring, with separate circuits providing the power to socket outlets on each floor. An electric cooker has its own circuit. Each circuit has its own fuse, so that should one circuit fail, the others remain unaffected. The sockets – designed to take flat-pin plugs – have shutters

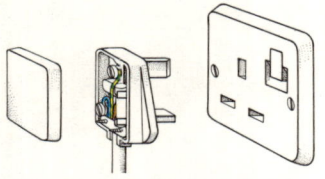

13 amp fused plug and socket outlet

which close when a plug is withdrawn, so that children cannot poke anything in to touch the live terminal. Plugs are fitted with 13, 3, 2 or 1 amp fuses to suit the appliances to which they are wired.

RADIAL-WIRING SYSTEM

This is no longer installed, but still exists in many houses. Radial wiring has a separate circuit supplying each 15 amp socket with additional circuits supplying 2 amp or 5 amp sockets. Each separate circuit has its own fuse.

Sockets take round-pin plugs only.

Never use a plug and socket which are too low-rated for an appliance. The power demanded by a heater will overheat a 5 amp plug and socket and might start a fire. It is safer to rewire a house with 13 amp sockets.

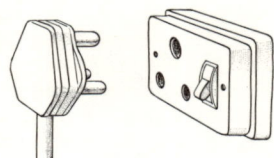

15 amp plug and socket outlet

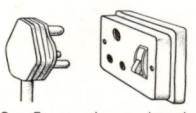

Typical 2 or 5 amp plug and socket outlet

FLEX

Power is carried from plug to appliance through flexible cable – called flex. All three-core flexes are colour-coded to the European standard: brown insulation for live wires, blue for neutral, and green-and-yellow stripes for earth. Two-core flexes are neutral colours without an earth. Before these colours were introduced, three-core flexes were red for live, black for neutral and green for earth; two-core flexes were red and black.

Flex of both old and new colour-coding may be found in a house. They

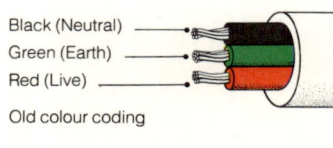

Black (Neutral)
Green (Earth)
Red (Live)

Old colour coding

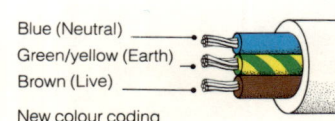

Blue (Neutral)
Green/yellow (Earth)
Brown (Live)

New colour coding

3 amp

6 amp

13 amp

Typical two and three-core flexes

must be connected correctly or an appliance or circuit may be damaged. Old-colour flex is quite safe to use in this way. The flex must also be the correct type and amperage to match the appliance. The commonly used flexes are: 0.5 mm.^{2} (3 amp) for up to 720 watts – lamps, radios and blankets; 0.75 mm.^{2} (6 amp) for up to 1,400 watts – irons, refrigerators and small fires; and 1.5 mm.^{2} (13 amp) for up to 3,000 watts – two or three-bar electric fires and kettles.

Never extend flex by taping on an extra length. It is unsafe. Get an electrician to fit a new length of flex to the appliance.

CARTRIDGE FUSES

A 13 amp plug can be used for appliances with a lower fuse rating, provided the correct cartridge fuse is fitted. Each fuse is colour-coded: the 3 amp (red) fuse is suitable for appliances rated up to 720 watts; the 13 amp (brown) fuse for those with a rating of 720-3,000 watts. Other colours and fuse ratings exist but are gradually being phased out; only the 3 and 13 amp fuses are necessary except in the case of electric clocks which may be 1 or 2 amp.

Some appliances which incorporate an electric motor may need a 13 amp fuse – even though rated below 720 watts – due to the higher starting current required. The same applies to colour television receivers; but black-and-white sets need only 3 amp fuses.

WIRING A 13 AMP PLUG

Unscrew the back of the plug (1). Loosen the screws holding the fibre clamp and remove one screw. Remove the fuse (2).

Strip the flex sheathing to expose 50 mm. (2 in.) of the insulated wires. Lay flex in the plug, position the wires against their respective terminals and cut them to length (3). Strip off the last 12 mm. ($\frac{1}{2}$ in.) of insulation.

The green-and-yellow striped lead (green in older flexes) is the earth lead and goes to the largest of the three pins, marked E or ⊥.

The brown lead (formerly red) is fitted to the pin marked 'L' – for live – or 'R' – for red. The blue lead (formerly black) goes to the pin marked 'N' for neutral. A two-core flex from a table lamp or a double-insulated appliance can be wired to a three-pin plug, with the earth pin left unconnected.

Make sure that the outer sheath of flex is gripped under the clamp where the lead enters the plug (4). Replace the fuse and the back of the plug.

RATINGS FOR PLUG FUSES

Always check the rating marked on an appliance before selecting and fitting a fuse.

APPLIANCE	FUSE RATING
Colour television	13 amp
Dishwasher	13 amp
Electric kettle	13 amp
3 kW fire	13 amp
Tumble drier	13 amp
Vacuum cleaner	13 amp
Washing machine	13 amp
Black-and-white television	3 amp
Electric blanket	3 amp
Extractor fan	3 amp
Food mixer	3 amp
Power tools	3 amp
Radio	3 amp
Record player	3 amp
Standard or table lamp	3 amp
Electric clock	1 or 2 amp

HOW TO WIRE A PLUG

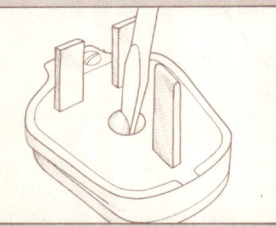

1. With pins facing upwards, loosen the central screw and remove the plug cover. Loosen the fibre-clamp screws.

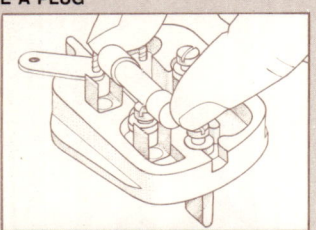

2. Swing the clamp to one side, remove the fuse and unscrew the three terminal screws. Strip 50 mm. sheathing from flex.

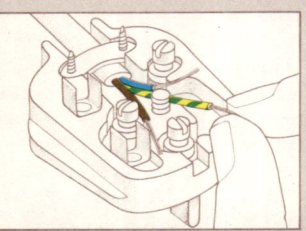

3. Cut wires to reach appropriate terminal screws: brown lead to pin marked L or R; blue to N, and green/yellow to E.

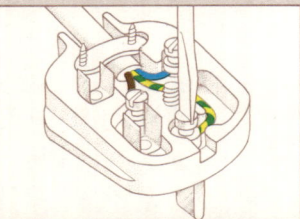

4. Tighten terminal screws around wires and tighten clamp screws. Replace fuse and screw the plug cover back in place.

• THE SUPPLY OF GAS

Most households are now supplied with natural gas – those still receiving town gas can expect to have their supply converted in 1978. Although natural gas is non-poisonous it can still cause explosions or fires if used carelessly, and it is important therefore that the installation of appliances, and repairs, are carried out either by your local gas service centre or by a suitably qualified specialist. Consult your local gas showroom or a CORGI installer, i.e., someone listed by the Confederation for the Registration of Gas Installers.

Gas appliances and all pipework beyond the meter are the householder's responsibility; the meter and service pipes from the street mains are the gas industry's.

READING THE METER

There are two kinds of meter: one having dials and one a row of digits.

To read a meter with dials, read only the four dials which have black hands. Reading from left to right, copy down the figures in the order

they appear. If the hands are between two figures, record the lower figure. However, if the hands are between 9 and 0, write down 9.

With a digital meter, read the first four figures only.

To find the amount of gas consumed since the last reading, subtract the figures shown on your last bill, from those on the meter. The figures refer to hundreds of cubic feet.

PAYING FOR GAS

British Gas offers two alternative tariffs, but all consist basically of two parts: the standing charge and rate per therm. If you have gas-fired central heating or add more gas appliances to your home, you probably qualify for the cheap rate – a tariff having a higher standing charge, but with a lower rate per therm. These vary slightly from region to region.

Gas bills are normally sent every three months, but if you prefer to pay a regular amount monthly this can be arranged, provided the bill is likely to exceed £4 a month. An estimate of the year's consumption is made and

agreed between the householder and British Gas. A twelfth of this sum is then paid each month. Periodic adjustments are made if necessary.

With a slot meter you insert coins for gas as you use it. The meter is emptied quarterly, or more frequently if requested.

CALCULATING THE GAS BILL

Although gas is measured in hundreds of cubic feet it is charged for in therms, a therm being 100,000 British thermal units (Btu's). A Btu is the amount of heat required to raise the temperature of one pound of water one degree Fahrenheit.

To convert cubic feet into therms, you need to know the calorific value of the gas. This is shown on a gas bill as CV. Multiply this figure by the number of hundreds of cubic feet used and divide by 1000 to get the number of therms. The formula is:

$$\frac{\text{Calorific Value (CV)} \times \text{hundreds of cubic feet}}{1000} = \text{Therms}$$

For example, if you have consumed 2,800 cubic feet of natural gas, with a calorific value of 1035, the number of therms used is:

$$\frac{1035 \times 28}{1000} = \text{approximately 29 therms}$$

HELP FOR THE ELDERLY AND DISABLED

Information about adaptors that make gas taps and slot meters easier for elderly or disabled people to use is available at showrooms. Home Service Advisers will call on the disabled at home to discuss their needs, free of charge.

A meter that is inconveniently positioned for an aged or disabled person will usually be repositioned by British Gas at little or no charge.

• USING GAS SAFELY

Make sure you know where your mains gas tap is and how to operate it. The tap is usually near the meter and has two positions: ON and OFF. If it is stiff to turn, ring the local gas service centre.

The top of the valve has a groove cut in it which must be in line with the centre-line of the pipe when the supply is ON; across it when OFF.

If you are leaving your house unoccupied for more than a day or two, turn off all taps to gas-using equipment, including pilot lights, and then turn off the main gas supply. Before turning the supply on again, check that all taps and pilot lights are turned off. Turn on the main gas tap and then light all pilot lights.

If you have a slot meter and the supply runs out, turn off all taps and appliances served by the meter before inserting fresh coins.

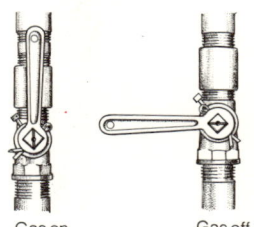

Gas on   Gas off

All fuel-burning appliances must have plenty of fresh air in order to operate safely as well as efficiently. Without adequate ventilation, poisonous fumes – the products of combustion – may enter a room. Never block or cover ventilators installed for gas appliances.

SAFETY PRECAUTIONS

If you smell gas, the cause is often the pilot light or burner of a cooker or other appliance that has gone out, or been left on unlit. This could happen,

for instance, when normal supply is resumed after a temporary failure, or drop in pressure. Put out any cigarettes or naked flames. Do not use matches. Check all pilot lights and burners. If one is turned on, but not burning, turn it off, and if there is an electric fire in the same room, switch it off and remove it, if possible.

Open all doors and windows and wait for the smell to disappear. If the smell persists, or you are in any doubt, turn off the supply at the mains gas tap and call the local gas service centre immediately.

Do not try to deal with the leak yourself or hunt for it with a naked flame.

A brown discoloration around the edge of a gas fire or water heater, or an unusual smell from either of these fittings, are signs of potential danger. The flue extracting the burned gases could be blocked, cracked or inadequate, causing fumes to flow back in a room. Turn off the appliance and call the gas board immediately.

MAINTENANCE

It is dangerous to service your own gas fittings. British Gas operate various schemes that provide a maintenance service on a regular basis for central-heating systems. Emergency repair service is always available.

THE SYMBOL OF SAFETY

The BSI Safety Mark indicates that an appliance has been certified by the British Standards Institution as conforming to the required levels of the Quality Assurance Council.

BSI safety mark

DIAL METER
Start reading from left to right the bottom four dials only. If the pointer is between two figures write down the lowest one. If the pointer is on a figure, say 7, look at the next dial to the right and, if the number is between 9 and 0, write down 6; if it is between 0 and 1, write down 7. The dial here shows 7519.

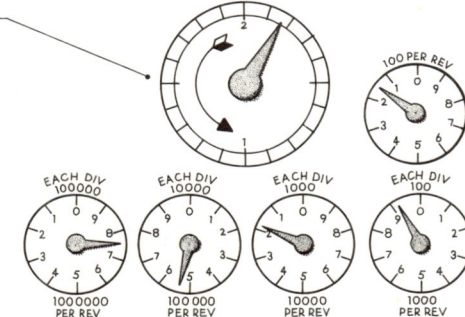

EACH DIV 100000 · EACH DIV 10000 · EACH DIV 1000 · EACH DIV 100

1000000 PER REV · 100000 PER REV · 10000 PER REV · 1000 PER REV

100 PER REV

DIGITAL METER
Read the first four digits from left to right. Here the meter reads 7519.

7 5 1 9 1 0

GAS METERS The two kinds now in use: one with dials and one with digits.

• HOW WATER IS SUPPLIED AND DISTRIBUTED

Before you have any new water fittings installed – a shower, a bath or an extra lavatory, for instance – the local water authority demands at least seven days' notice in writing.

This applies to new fittings only, not to the repair or renewal of existing fittings. If you are having the job done by a plumber, he should give the required notice on your behalf. Check that he does so – for the water authority can demand that the fitting be removed at the householder's expense if its by-laws are broken. A good plumber is knowledgeable about all the by-laws relating to installation or repair work. The Institute of Plumbing recommends plumbers whose work conforms to its standards, and complies with by-laws.

THE MAINS SUPPLY

A mains stop-valve (often called the stop-cock) isolates the water supply to a house from the water-authority's main in the road. It is usually situated close to the house – at least 750 mm. (2 ft 6 in.) below ground to protect it from frost – with a hinged cast-iron cover on the pavement or garden path. To simplify access in an emergency, keep a piece of wood near by – about 1 m. (39 in.) long, and 50 × 25 mm. (2 × 1 in.), with a V cut in one end – to turn the valve clockwise.

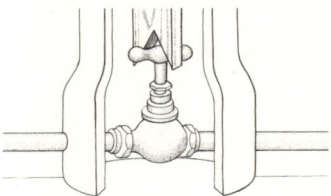

Reaching down to the mains stop-valve

THE RISING MAIN

The service pipe – usually referred to as the rising main – enters a house through the kitchen floor close to the sink. Ideally, a rising main will have a stop-valve, combined with a drain-cock, so that in an emergency – such

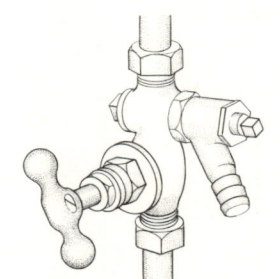

Stop-valve (left) and drain-cock

as a burst pipe – the valve can be closed from inside the house, enabling the pipe to be drained.

INTERNAL SUPPLIES

Water is distributed either by direct or indirect supply. With a direct supply, the mains pipe feeds all taps, cisterns and some types of water heaters. With an indirect supply, the mains pipe feeds a cistern with a minimum capacity of 50 gallons, and one tap at the kitchen sink. Two pipes run from the cistern: one supplying water to a hot-water cylinder and the other pipe feeding the lavatories, basins and bath. Both pipes should have a stop-valve.

A preliminary precaution when moving into a house is to identify and label all stop-valves so that the right one can be closed in an emergency.

• FROST PRECAUTIONS

Lag all pipework in the roof space to protect it from frost (see p. 382).

When a severe frost is expected, check that the main stop-valve is accessible and working properly, so that it can be closed in an emergency. Sprinkle common salt over the hinged cover to prevent it from icing up.

Make sure there are no taps left dripping and put the plugs in the sink, bath and basin waste outlets.

Check that ball-valves are working correctly. Water dripping from an overflow pipe can freeze, block the pipe and cause flooding.

If it is not intended to use an outside lavatory in freezing weather, empty the cistern and tie up the ball-valve.

Keep the temperature in the house above freezing point. If you do not have central heating, a small portable heater or oil lamp (see p. 388), strategically placed – usually in the hallway – will be sufficient to prevent freezing.

If a house is to be left unoccupied during the winter, drain both the hot and cold-water systems. This can be a tricky operation in some houses, due to the complexity of some designs. If in doubt, consult a plumber.

Leave a note in a prominent place as a reminder that the heating should not be turned on again until the system has been refilled.

• IN CASE OF EMERGENCY

If a pipe bursts, close the main stop-valve at once and open all the taps. If

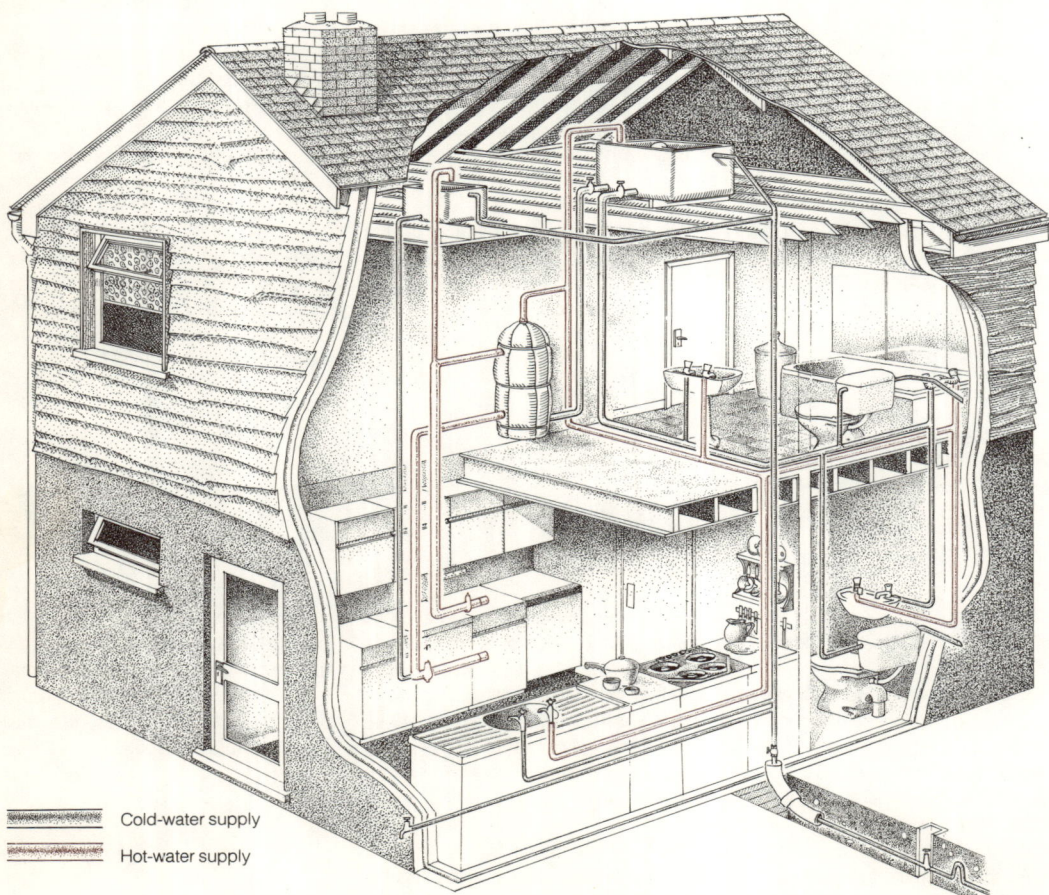

─────── Cold-water supply

─────── Hot-water supply

TYPICAL PLUMBING LAYOUT Cold water enters the house from the water-authority's main in the road, and rises to feed a storage cistern, or tank, in the roof. Pipework distributes water to taps, lavatory cisterns and the hot-water cylinder.

the burst is in a distribution pipe fed from a cistern, close the control-valve for that pipe, if there is one.

Send for a plumber, and in the meantime tie up the arm of the ball-valve in the cistern.

Water emerging from an overflow pipe means that a ball-valve has jammed or failed, or a ball float is faulty. Cut off the water supply by lifting the arm of the ball-valve and tying it to a stick placed across the cistern (see right). Then replace ball-valve or float.

VALVES AND BALL FLOATS

The supply of water to a cold-water storage cistern and to a lavatory's flushing cistern is controlled by ball-valves, operated by a ball float on the end of a lever arm. As water enters the cistern, the float rises, until the supply is cut off by the valve.

REPLACING A VALVE WASHER

Most cisterns have one of two types of valve: the Portsmouth – which has a horizontal piston – or the Croydon, with a vertical piston.

The procedure of replacing a washer is the same, in principle, for both types of ball-valve.

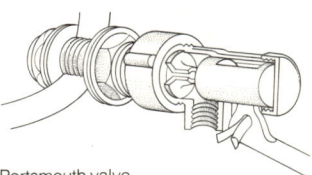

Portsmouth valve

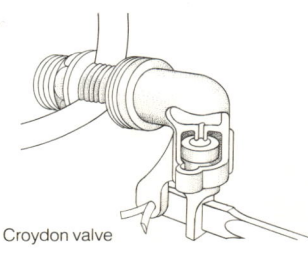

Croydon valve

MATERIALS AND EQUIPMENT

Replacement washer; wire wool; Vaseline; pliers; screwdriver.

Turn off the water. Using pliers, close the split ends of the split-pin (A1), taking care not to pinch them; if the shape of the pin is distorted it will be difficult to remove.

Remove the split-pin and withdraw the arm from its slot. Unscrew the cap of the valve – if it has one – and slide out the piston (A2). If there is nothing embedded in the washer, fit a new one. Take the piston apart by inserting the blade of a screwdriver in the half with the slot, unscrewing the other half with a pair of pliers (A3). Prise out the old washer and clean off any rubber adhering to the metal (A4). Insert a new washer, and screw the two parts of the piston together again. Clean the piston with wire wool and

REPLACING A WORN VALVE WASHER

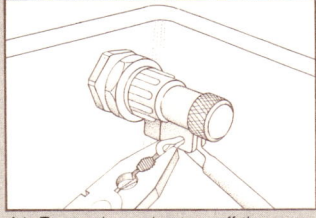

A1. To repair a valve turn off the water, remove split-pin and withdraw ball-float arm from slot.

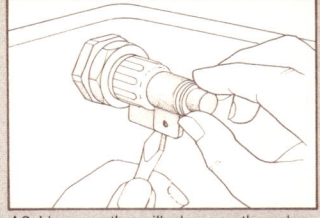

A2. Unscrew the milled cap on the valve – if one is fitted – and, using the tip of a screwdriver, ease out the piston.

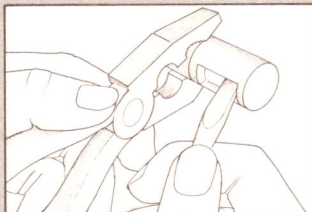

A3. Grip the piston with a pair of pliers, and, using the blade of a screwdriver, unscrew the end with a groove in it.

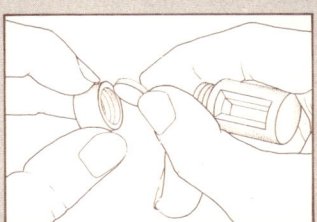

A4. Prise out the washer from the smallest half of the piston. Make sure there is no grit inside and fit a new washer.

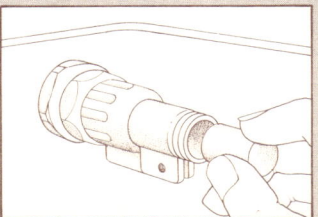

A5. Screw halves together, clean with wire wool and smear with Vaseline. Replace the piston – grooved end last.

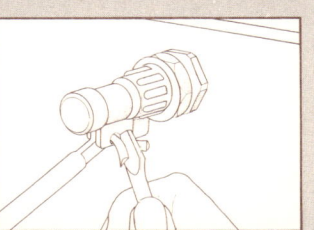

A6. Fit lever arm in place, and replace split-pin – opening ends slightly with screwdriver. Switch on supply to refill.

Tying up the ball

smear the surface with Vaseline or grease. Reassemble the valve (A5). Insert the split-pin and open the ends slightly with a screwdriver (A6).

If the seating of the valve is damaged or other parts are badly worn, install a new ball-valve.

REPLACING A BALL FLOAT

Each cistern has an overflow pipe leading to an outside wall. In a full

REPLACING A BALL FLOAT

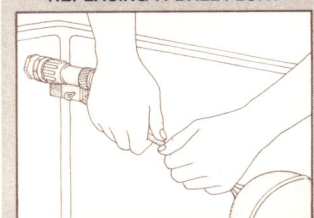

B1. If water level rises above overflow outlet, turn off supply and flush cistern. Bend lever arm down slightly and refill.

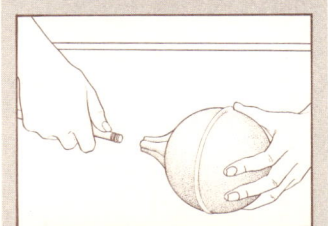

B2. If a ball does not float it may be punctured. Tie up the lever arm, unscrew and replace the existing ball.

storage cistern the level of the water should be an inch or two below the level of the overflow pipe. In a flushing cistern the level is marked 'water line'. If water drips from this pipe, bend the lever arm slightly (B1), to make the necessary adjustment to lower the water level. If water pours from the overflow pipe, either the ball float has become detached or is waterlogged, or the ball-valve is defective.

If you need to change a ball float, first tie up the lever arm to a piece of wood or a broom handle to close the valve. Flush the lavatory, or empty the storage tank, then unscrew the ball float. Take it to a plumbers' merchant and buy a plastic replacement of the same size, and screw it back on to the lever arm (B2).

CLEARING AIR-LOCKS

Knocking noises when a tap is used, or an erratic flow of water from a hot-water tap may mean there is an air-lock in the pipework – possibly as a result of alteration work.

This can sometimes be cured by using the mains water pressure. Fit a length of hose between the hot and cold-water taps in the kitchen, open hot-water taps in the bathroom, and then open both taps in the kitchen. The mains water should force the air to escape through the bathroom taps, until water flows freely.

If this fails to clear air-locks, or they occur frequently, there may be a fault in the system. Consult a plumber.

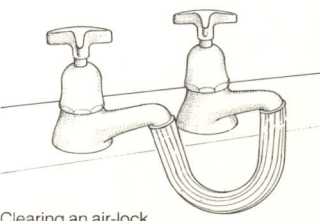

Clearing an air-lock

● BLOCKAGES

Beneath each basin, sink and bath outlet, there is a trap – usually a U-shape in the pipework – which retains water at all times, preventing odours entering the house from the sewers. Modern fittings have 'bottle' traps, which are fitted to the waste pipe to perform the same function.

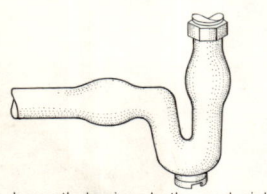

U-trap beneath basins, baths and sinks

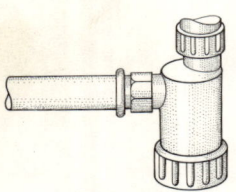

Bottle trap

Blockages in a basin, sink or bath are often caused by an accumulation of soap, grease and hair clinging to the trap or the pipe walls. A blockage caused by grease may be cleared by pouring boiling water and soda crystals down the outlet, or using wire to dislodge an obstruction.

If not, try using a rubber plunger – available from hardware shops and builders' merchants. Block the overflow with a wet rag, and pump the

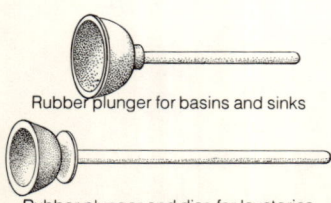

Rubber plunger for basins and sinks

Rubber plunger and disc for lavatories

plunger up and down with a vigorous action [A1]. If this fails to clear the blockage it is necessary to dismantle the trap.

With a sink or basin trap, place a bucket underneath and unscrew the small clearing-eye in the elbow of the pipe [A2]. Once the accumulation causing the blockage has been removed, push a piece of wire or cane into the pipe and wriggle it about to clear any remaining debris [A3]. If the fitting is a bottle trap, unscrew the bottom half [A4].

Clearing a bath-trap blockage is more awkward. First, empty all water from the bath, then remove the bath panel. Place a large shallow tray beneath the trap. If there is insufficient space, use a sheet of plastic – about 400 mm. (16 in.) square – and with damp rags around the edge and under the plastic, make a tray-shaped

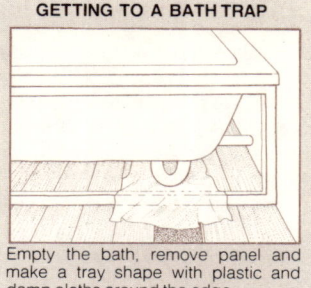

GETTING TO A BATH TRAP

Empty the bath, remove panel and make a tray shape with plastic and damp cloths around the edge.

depression. Undo the nut on a pipe trap, or the bottom portion of a bottle trap, and use flexible curtain wire to clear the blockage. On some traps it may also be necessary to remove a floorboard to gain additional access space.

To clear a blockage in the trap of a WC pan, use a cup-shaped rubber

CLEARING A BLOCKAGE IN A BASIN OR SINK

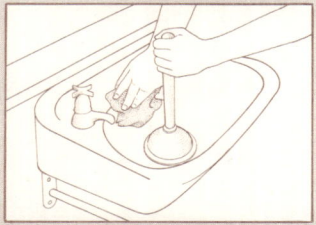

A1. Seal the overflow with a damp cloth. Place a rubber plunger over the outlet and pump it up and down vigorously.

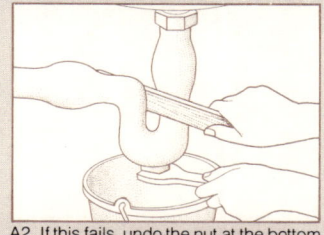

A2. If this fails, undo the nut at the bottom of the trap, using a piece of wood to counteract pressure and strain on pipe.

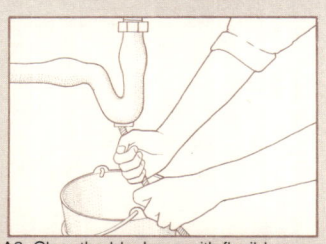

A3. Clear the blockage with flexible curtain wire – first from the outlet down to the trap, then up through the clearing hole.

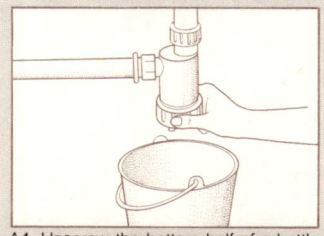

A4. Unscrew the bottom half of a bottle trap to release blockage. Flush outlet and pipe with hot water and refit nut or bottle.

plunger, with a metal plate above it – available from builders' merchants. The plate prevents the cup from turning inside out. Work the plunger up and down in a series of short and sharp movements. Take care not to damage the pan. Flush the cistern when the blockage has been cleared. If this fails send for a plumber.

DRIPPING AND LEAKING TAPS

With most kinds of tap, the water must be turned off at the rising main before a new washer is fitted. There is one exception – the Supatap. This kind of tap is easily identified by its revolving nozzle.

A dripping tap means that the washer is worn and needs replacing. A tap that seeps water around the base of the spindle needs the gland nut either tightening or repacking with string rubbed with Vaseline. Both repairs are simple and some do-it-yourself shops sell tap-repair kits containing all the necessary parts.

REPLACING A WORN TAP WASHER

Use replacement washers that are the same size as the existing washers, but if the worn ones are of fibre or

leather, use rubber or nylon replacements. They last longer and are more efficient.

MATERIALS AND EQUIPMENT

Washers: 13 mm. ($\frac{1}{2}$ in.) for sink and basin taps, 20 mm. ($\frac{3}{4}$ in.) for bath taps; washer plate for Supataps; adjustable spanner; screwdriver; pliers.

Turn off the water supply at the rising main, except with Supataps. Open the tap to empty the water in the system. Unscrew the protective shield or head and lift it to expose the hexagonal head nut, forming part of the tap head. Using a spanner, unscrew the tap head from the body, turning the nut anti-clockwise. Remove the jumper (or washer plate) and holding its stem with pliers, unscrew the retaining nut beneath the washer. Discard the old washer and fit a new one of the same diameter on the jumper and tighten the nut again. Fit the new washer so that the maker's name faces the washer plate. Before putting the jumper back into the tap, check to see that the seating of the washer plate is not damaged in any way and is clean. Before screwing back the head, see that the fibre washer which seals the joint with the

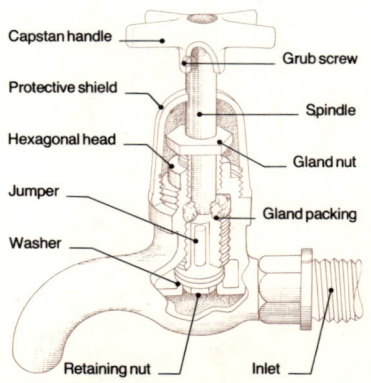

Capstan handle — Grub screw
Protective shield — Spindle
Hexagonal head — Gland nut
Jumper — Gland packing
Washer
Retaining nut — Inlet

How a bib tap is constructed

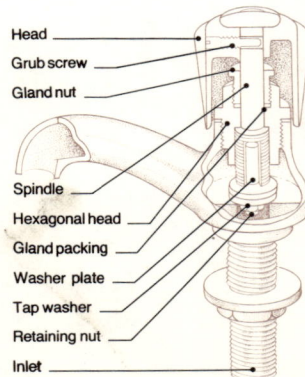

Head
Grub screw
Gland nut
Spindle
Hexagonal head
Gland packing
Washer plate
Tap washer
Retaining nut
Inlet

How a pillar tap is constructed

body has not fallen off the threaded part of the head. Close the tap and turn on the water.

SUPATAPS

Hold the nozzle with one hand and unscrew the locking gland nut with a spanner. Unscrew the capstan head. When the water has ceased to run, push out the anti-splash device, to which the washer is attached, with a pencil. Change the washer and reassemble the anti-splash device, screwing the capstan head back on the pipe stem. Water will begin to flow again. Tighten the locking gland-nut in a clockwise direction.

CURING A LEAKING TAP

It may not be necessary to shut off the water supply at the mains to mend a tap leaking between the spindle and the protective shield. But the tap must be left closed. Undo the shield to expose the gland nut and tighten it. If it still leaks, then turn off the supply and remove the capstan handle by unscrewing the grub screw which secures it to the spindle. If handle sticks, hold a piece of wood underneath it, and tap the wood gently with a hammer. Remove the gland nut and pick

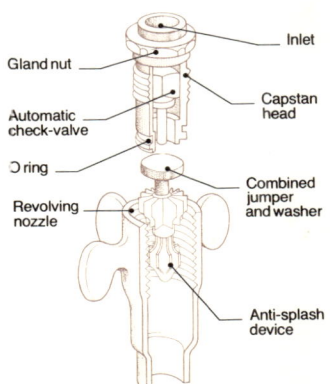

How a Supatap is constructed

Labels: Inlet / Gland nut / Automatic check-valve / O ring / Revolving nozzle / Capstan head / Combined jumper and washer / Anti-splash device

out the old packing from the thread. Repack the gland nut with lamp cotton (available from builders' merchants) or soft white string, soaked in Vaseline. Make two or three clockwise turns and push string down around the spindle with a small screwdriver. Replace the gland nut and screw it down firmly. Too little string will leave the gland leaking; too much will make the tap difficult to turn.

REPACKING A GLAND NUT

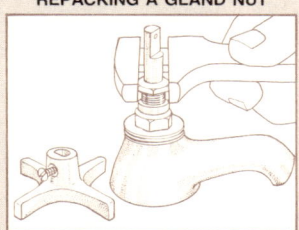

B1. Undo the grub screw, remove the capstan handle and tighten gland nut with a spanner. Refit handle and test.

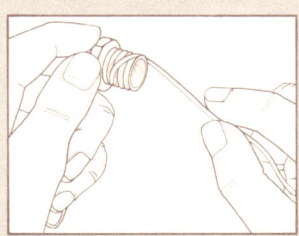

B2. If tap still leaks turn off supply, undo gland nut and wrap new string, rubbed in Vaseline, around stem.

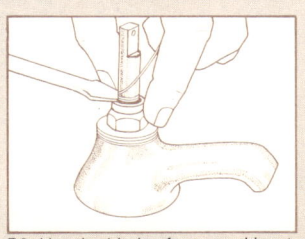

B3. Use the blade of a screwdriver to pack similar string around spindle. Reassemble tap and turn on supply.

REWASHERING A BIB/PILLAR TAP

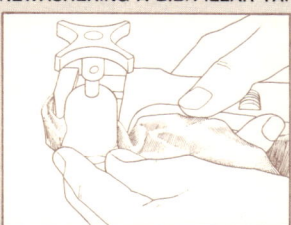

C1. Turn off the water supply and open the tap. Undo the protective shield and the hexagonal head nut.

C2. Lift off the top half of the tap, withdraw combined jumper and washer. Check that washer-seating is clean.

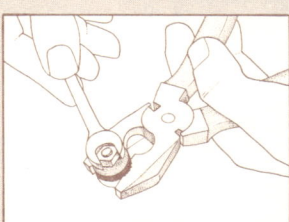

C3. Grip the jumper with a pair of pliers and, using a spanner, undo the small retaining nut holding the washer.

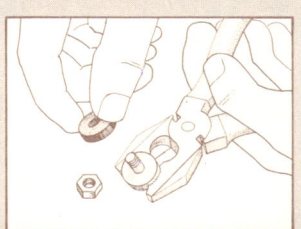

C4. Remove the old washer and fit a new washer with the maker's name against the face of the jumper plate.

REWASHERING A SUPATAP

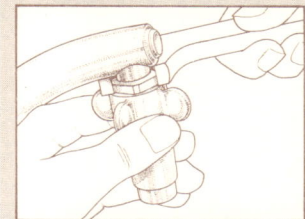

D1. Hold the nozzle steady with one hand and, using a spanner, undo the locking gland nut fixing it to the stem.

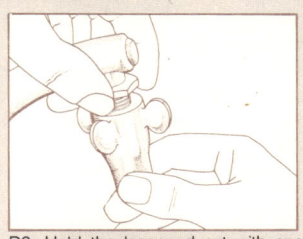

D2. Hold the loosened nut with one hand and unscrew the revolving nozzle with the other, turning it anti-clockwise.

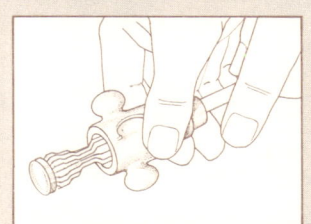

D3. Insert the unsharpened end of a pencil in the outlet end of the tap and push out the anti-splash device.

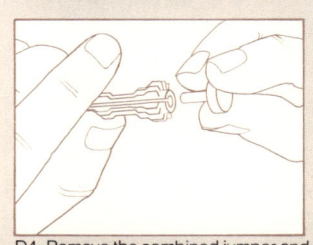

D4. Remove the combined jumper and washer. Scrub the anti-splash device with a nail brush, and fit a new washer.

HOW WASHING MACHINES AND DISHWASHERS ARE PLUMBED IN

A washing machine that is permanently plumbed in position is more convenient to use than one that has to be moved to a sink with hose connections made to the taps.

Check with the local water authority before buying a machine. Some authorities impose conditions regarding the use of mains water for washing machines.

The water supply cannot be taken to a machine from a mixer tap – in case mains water is accidentally contaminated – or from an instantaneous gas or electric water heater, having only a single outlet.

Water pressure is also important, whether you live in a bungalow or a high block of flats. Manufacturers' recommendations vary, but most suggest a minimum pressure of 4-5 lb. per square inch, and a maximum of 150 lb. per square inch for hot-water supplies; for cold water the pressure required is that exerted by a minimum head of at least 8 ft – measured from the bottom of the cold-water storage cistern and the top of the appliance.

The local water board will tell you your mains water pressure.

Pressure can sometimes be adjusted by a valve attached to an appliance; but this must be checked beforehand with the manufacturers.

Most machines have a built-in water heater and need only to be connected to a cold-water supply.

A permanently plumbed-in machine can also have a permanent waste connection or be emptied by a drain hose. Manufacturers supply hoses with each machine – the average length being 130-150 cm. (51-59 in.).

The same principles for plumbing-in washing machines apply to dishwashers. In either case the job should be done by a plumber.

377

PROTECTING THE HOME

A house and its contents are open to attack both from the weather and three main groups of living enemies: fungi, insects and rodents. The main danger from weather is damp, which can find its way into the house through the roof, walls and even up through the ground. Dampness provides the conditions in which timber is exposed to attack by fungi, such as wet rot and dry rot. The main insect assault comes from wood-boring beetles such as the furniture beetle and the death-watch beetle. Rodents – mice and rats – cause no structural damage, but are carriers of disease and leave unsightly evidence of their occupation.

• DAMPNESS

Once dampness is allowed to take hold on a house it creates an unhealthy atmosphere, damages decorations and provides conditions in which wet and dry rot can flourish.

Dampness can be due to a number of causes; some need expert attention – others can be dealt with by the householder.

Rising damp, which can be a major problem, is often the result of a missing or defective damp-proof course (dpc). It shows on inside walls as tide-marks or staining above the skirting board. A dpc is a layer of impervious material built into walls, at least 150 mm. (6 in.) above ground level. If it has deteriorated, or is missing – houses built before 1875 did not have them – call in a specialist.

In some cases local authorities may make a grant towards the cost of a dpc (see p. 14).

Never allow earth, plants or paths to cover a dpc, or the wall above will become damp. Similarly, an obstruction across an air-brick will prevent proper ventilation.

Water may penetrate the structure of a house if there are missing or defective flashings – the strips of metal or felt used to weatherproof the junctions of a roof and the surrounds of doors and windows. Missing or broken tiles or slates will also cause leaks. These are defects that should be dealt with by a builder.

If the mortar between bricks on the outside walls is loose or crumbling, driving rain will soak the walls. They need re-pointing.

The things you can do yourself: keep gutters and downpipes clean; fill the gaps around door and window frames with a non-hardening mastic; and keep the drips – the grooves on the undersides of sills – clean. If they become clogged, moisture will creep back and soak into the wall.

Dampness is also caused by condensation. This occurs when moisture-laden air comes into contact with a cold surface.

• ROT

Two fungi, wet rot and dry rot, can cause serious structural damage. A third, mould, can ruin decorations. But it also gives warning that the conditions in which the other two thrive may be present. To prevent attack by fungus, remove all sources of damp and keep the house dry and well ventilated.

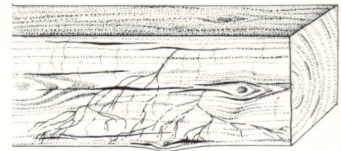

WET ROT
This is a general term for a group of related fungi which attack timber with a moisture content of more than 30%.

Wet rot

Dry rot

Woodworm

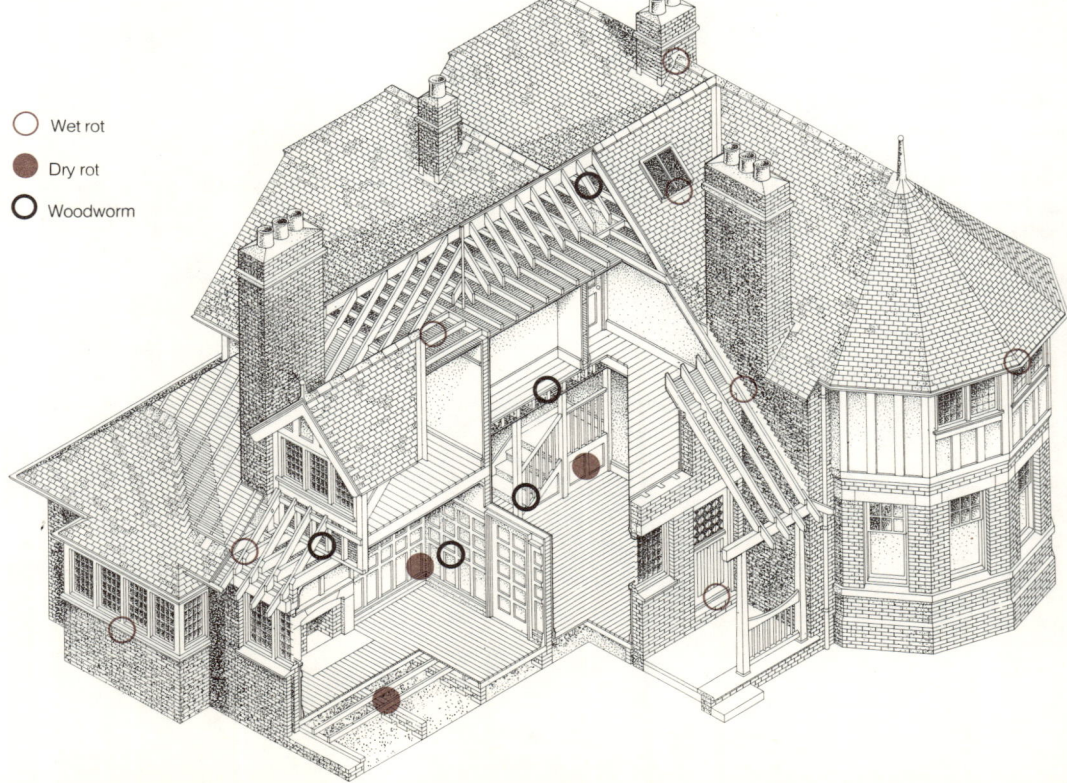

POINTS OF ATTACK All timber in the house is liable to attack by wet rot, dry rot and wood-boring insects. The main danger points shown here should be inspected regularly for signs of dampness or insect infestation.

It is more common than dry rot, though it is usually less serious.

Inside the house it is most likely to be found in kitchens, bathrooms, roofs and cellars. Outside, it attacks window frames and sills, doors and door frames where water has penetrated paintwork.

Affected timber becomes dark brown to black, is spongy when wet and brittle when dry. Yellow or brown streaks or patches are often found in decayed timber. Sometimes, decay can be present beneath a seemingly sound surface.

It is not always easy to detect on painted wood, though the surface may bubble or peel.

Cure It is best to call in a specialist firm. If you wish to do the job yourself, cut out all affected timber. If necessary, replace with an entirely new section which has been treated with fungicidal preservatives (these include anti-rot fluids). Treat all adjacent timber with preservative also. Apply water-repellent preservative, such as Cuprinol WR or Rentokil water repellent, to external timber.

DRY ROT

Despite its name, dry rot is a fungus which thrives in damp, still, warm conditions. If structural defects or plumbing faults lead to damp, it can take hold. The fungus spreads by means of strands, some of which transport water to create ideal conditions for it to start up on a new site. The strands look like a mass of white or grey cotton wool. They can climb from cellar to attic, even through the adjoining brick wall of two houses.

Eventually, fruiting bodies form, looking like giant pancakes. These liberate microscopic spores, like red dust, which can be blown to new areas – again spreading the rot.

Areas most likely to be affected are under floorboards, behind skirtings, embedded joist ends and timber in cellars. Suspended timber ground floors in houses with faulty or non-existent damp-proof courses are vulnerable. The first signs may be a musty, mushroom-like smell. The timber may appear to be warped, paint could flake, unpainted timber will split both with and across the grain. When touched, decayed timber will crumble into dry powder.

Cure Eradication of dry rot must be thorough. For this reason it is best to leave the job to experts. The British Wood Preserving Association will supply a list of specialist companies, many of whom offer a 20-year guarantee that treated timbers will not be re-infected.

MOULDS

Apart from ruining decorations, moulds are harmless – some can be brushed away. However, an outbreak is caused usually by condensation or damp which, if not eradicated, can lead to greater trouble.

Particularly vulnerable are modern houses with solid concrete floors and well-fitting doors and windows. When the house is left cold during the day and heated during the evening, ideal conditions are created for condensation.

Cure Ventilation, adequate insulation and heating are essential to combat condensation. Thorough painting protects a surface. You can go a stage further and treat a surface with anti-condensation paint, to poison any mould that may settle. Proprietary fungicides specially made for the purpose are effective and dry quickly. Cavity-wall insulation often alleviates condensation problems (see p. 382).

If condensation is severe, get a builder to dry-line the affected walls. This involves fixing softwood battens to the wall and fitting plasterboard to them, backed with glass-fibre or similar insulation.

• WOODWORM

The furniture beetle is responsible for most woodworm damage. It feeds off structural timbers as well as furniture. Sapwood, rough, or unpainted timber, plywood and wickerwork are specially vulnerable. Old furniture stored in a loft is also a prime target.

Timber becomes infested when an adult beetle lays eggs in cracks in timber. Beetles may fly into the house or they can be brought in with second-hand furniture or packing cases. Grubs hatch from the eggs and tunnel through the wood for about three years, before emerging as adults in the summer. They live for four weeks, in which time the female can lay up to 80 eggs in cracks or the holes made by the emerging grubs. So the cycle continues.

Signs to look for are neat, circular holes, about 2 mm. ($\frac{1}{16}$ in.) in diameter, on the surface of the timber. If a hole is old, it will appear dark. In this case it is likely that remedial treatment has been carried out or that the beetles have moved on. A fresh hole will have clean, white wood inside and be surrounded by a small pile of wood dust. This indicates that the woodworm is active.

Cure Paint *all* surfaces of infested furniture, inside and out, with a proprietary woodworm killer. Then use the nozzle of the applicator to force fluid into some of the holes. An insecticidal polish can be used as an added precaution for all polished furniture. Valuable furniture should be given fumigation treatment by a specialist.

Outbreaks in structural timbers should be treated by a specialist. Treatment must be painstaking. In roofs, all surfaces must be painted and pressure-sprayed with appropriate woodworm-killer fluid (wear protective clothing, goggles and a mouth mask). Infested floorboards must be lifted to give access to joists below. The fluid can affect the insulation around electric wires, so this must be masked during treatment. Roof insulation must be removed before treatment.

• MICE

The house mouse lives indoors all year round. The field mouse intrudes mainly in autumn and winter.

Mice gnaw anything, so look for teeth marks and droppings.

They enter houses through heating and ventilation ducts, from under floorboards and along plumbing or through broken air-bricks. They often breed in outhouses.

Cure Proprietary ready-to-use poison baits or traps can be set in places where there are signs of mice. Chocolate is a better trap-bait than the traditional cheese.

Many mice are now immune to conventional warfarin-type bait. A quick-acting, humane killer is Alpha-kil. Fill holes with cement reinforced with wire wool. A cat may be a deterrent.

• RATS

Rats carry serious disease, so the local authority should be notified of any persistent problem. Fortunately, domestic infestation is fairly rare.

Rats have poor eyesight and prefer to skirt walls and fences rather than cross open spaces. They spoil more food than they eat.

Cure Bait with poison such as Rodine. Fill holes with cement reinforced with wire wool.

INSECT PESTS IN THE HOME AND HOW TO ERADICATE THEM

INSECT		WHERE FOUND	ACTION
	Furniture beetle 5 mm. ($\frac{3}{16}$ in.)	Structural timber, furniture	Paint and inject wood with woodworm killer
	Death-watch beetle 6 mm. ($\frac{1}{4}$ in.)	Timber in older properties	Paint affected timber with woodworm-killing fluid and inject fluid into holes
	Carpet beetle 3 mm. ($\frac{1}{8}$ in.)	Birds' nests in roof, under carpets	Remove birds' nests. Spray carpets, skirtings and furnishings with insecticides
	House moth, clothes moth, 10 mm. ($\frac{3}{8}$ in.)	Clothing, upholstery, carpets	Spray moth repellent on fabrics. Store clothes in plastic bags with repellent, such as moth balls
	Cockroach 2.5 cm. (1 in.)	Crevices in kitchens. They emerge at night	Cover food. Wrap waste before disposal. Spread insecticide on their runs
	Flea 2 mm. ($\frac{1}{12}$ in.)	Domestic animals, carpets, upholstery	Use proprietary flea powder on animals. Aerosol insecticide

• LOCKS AND ALARMS

Every year about 200,000 homes in Britain suffer from break-ins.

An average household is unlikely to be troubled by a professional house-breaker. The enemy is the sneak thief taking advantage of unlocked windows and doors.

A typical break-in takes no more than five minutes – a snatch-and-run affair where the thief is looking for money or small, portable items such as a transistor radio.

The peak period is between 3 p.m. and 8 p.m. Two-thirds of all break-ins are committed by children and young people under the age of 17.

Though you probably have household insurance to cover losses or breakages, a burglary can leave a disturbing mental effect, especially on the elderly and the nervous.

It may not be possible to make your house completely thief-proof, but simple precautions such as locking doors and windows, and not leaving the key dangling behind the letter-box, will reduce the risk of burglary.

Elementary precautions such as these will prevent the casual thief from gaining immediate entry, which is his object. He is not likely to hang around outside a house when there is easier game elsewhere.

DOORS

Front doors are used as the entry point in about one-third of burglaries. Suspicion is rarely aroused by someone walking boldly through the front door as though entitled to do so.

Most doors are fitted with a cylinder lock which can be opened easily with a strip of celluloid or an adapted Yale key, unless it is double-locked from inside. The best security is provided by a mortise deadlock, which is set in the woodwork of the door. When its key is turned a thick, square-edged

bolt slots deeply into the door frame.

Not all mortise locks give adequate protection – a two-lever type is easy to pick. For the maximum practicable security, fit a precision-built, bored, cylindrical lock with a deadlocking latch and at least six levers. Make sure it meets the British Standard; it will have saw-proof steel roller inserts in the bolt, and be drill-proof.

The enormous number of permutations offered by a six-lever cylinder mechanism makes it unlikely that anyone will have a matching key. Manufacturers operate a key-registration system through which only registered holders can obtain duplicate keys.

On glass-panelled doors fit a double-cylinder deadlock, which needs a key to unlock it from either side. This type is needed also where there is a window that could be broken to reach the lock, or if a hand pushed through the letter-box could reach the lock.

Do not lock doors inside the house. This is likely to invite unnecessary damage. Having got inside, the housebreaker is going to be tempted by anything locked, so he is likely to break down locked doors.

Most french windows open outwards, which means that the hinges are exposed. This makes it a simple job to knock out the hinge pins. Hinge bolts, fitted close to the existing hinges, will prevent this. In addition to the lock, fit bolts at the top and bottom of the outer one of the pair of french windows.

Do not forget to fit locks to the garage door, the connecting door between garage and house, the shed door, and the doors to other outbuildings. An insecure garden shed may even provide a thief with tools to break into your house. Lock-fitting is best left to a locksmith.

Guard chains For anyone with a front

door which cannot be seen from a window, so that visitors cannot be identified, a guard chain or door viewer is useful.

A guard chain allows the door to be opened a few inches so that visitors can be identified and turned away if they seem undesirable.

Peep holes A door viewer can be fitted to standard doors quickly and

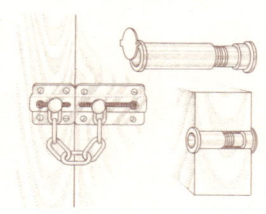

Chain guard   Peephole

simply. The one-way optical lens gives an angle of vision of about 170 degrees.

Padlocks A security padlock with a door fitting of equal strength should be used on the main garage door. Two padlock types are in general use. One opens when the combination is 'dialled'. The other needs a key.

Some key-operated padlocks have raised 'shoulders' on the sides of the main body of the lock to protect the shackle from attack from all directions. The key cylinder is armoured on the outside. Padlocks must be used with padlock bars suited to the door.

WINDOWS

Hinged windows with standard latches are reasonably secure. Single-pane windows are less vulnerable than those made of many small panes. It is far safer for a housebreaker to break a small pane to reach through and open the window or an adjacent door.

All ground-floor windows, including all top-hung ventilation windows,

Security bolt   Lockable handle

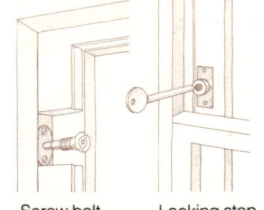

Screw bolt   Locking stop

however small, should be lockable. Some housebreakers – particularly children – can squeeze through very small openings. Unused windows can be screwed closed.

There are locks to suit all types of window. These include lockable handles and devices for locking stays, which enable the window to be locked in a slightly open position for ventilation. Wooden sash windows can be fitted with a barrel lock which is screwed into the frame.

ALARMS

A simple burglar alarm frightens off would-be intruders by triggering a bell or buzzer. The operation of most do-it-yourself systems is known to the professional housebreaker, so they are unlikely to stop him, but they will usually deter sneak thieves.

A do-it-yourself burglar-alarm kit consists of simple switches fitted to windows, doors, under doormats, etc., that are wired up to a central control unit hidden in the house. The central unit is the only place where the alarm can be switched off.

An electric system must have stand-by batteries in case of power cuts, and you must always switch on before going to bed or going out.

An efficient system should allow people who have legitimate reasons to be in the house to enter without the alarm operating – by using a special key, for example.

Before buying a kit, make sure it has easy-to-follow fitting instructions.

Insurance companies will recommend approved installers if you do not want to install an alarm yourself.

A dog will also act as a burglar alarm. A barking dog will scare off a burglar as effectively as an alarm bell.

ANTI-CLIMB PAINT

Applied to the upper part of a house, anti-climb paint is a useful deterrent. It is non-setting and can be applied to most types of surfaces – metal, concrete, brick, wood, asbestos, etc. It remains greasy and is strictly for use on surfaces not normally touched by family or visitors. On drainpipes, for example, the coating should commence just over 2 m. (7 ft) from ground level. It is available in black, dark grey, red and green.

SAFES

There is no point in locking money, jewellery, passports and other valuables or documents in desks and cupboards. This often results in damage as well as loss.

Floor safes A floor safe fitted in a cupboard can be installed simply. A portable container locks on to a baseplate screwed to the floor. If fitted in a corner, it is even more difficult for a thief to tamper with.

The container is immovable when locked to the baseplate and there are no weak points such as a hinge, lid or seam exposed. The only entry to the container is through the baseplate, which is anchored with shielded bolts.

Another type of floor safe (see illustration below) can be embedded in concrete under the floor. A trapdoor is made by cutting out a square of floorboards and this can be concealed by a carpet or rug.

Wall safes A wall safe can be concealed by a picture, curtains or furniture. Safes for use in the home are made in several sizes for fitting into a 9 in. wall.

SAFETY-DEPOSIT BOX IN A BANK

Systems for obtaining a safety-deposit box vary from bank to bank. Basically, two systems are operated. One is a simple safe-custody system under which the bank will store valuables in their strongroom.

In London and other large cities the main banks also rent out private steel boxes in their strong rooms. Rent depends on the size of the box, and starts from about £1.50 per year.

• PREVENTION

Let the police know if your house is to be empty for any length of time. The police also recommend telling your neighbours, the milkman and the postman so they can report anything suspicious that they see.

SUSPICIOUS CHARACTERS

Anyone seen 'hanging about' or taking more than a casual interest in a house should be reported to the police immediately. Often a criminal examines a house during daytime to find the best way in.

If anyone unknown calls at the house to 'inspect the electricity system', or claims he has some other official reason for his visit, ask for identification. If you are not satisfied, check with the authority concerned.

LIGHTS ON A TIME SWITCH

Time switches that operate one or more lights in the right room at the right time make the house seem occupied when empty.

SIMPLE PRECAUTIONS

Do not put identification tags on keys in case they are lost. If this happens tell the police at once and get all exterior locks changed immediately.

Do not leave the house in response to a telephone call purporting to be from the police. It might be a thief who has found your keys who will get in when you go to the police station.

Do not tell everyone you meet that you will be away for a while.

Do not leave the key of the door 'under a mat' or in some other favourite hiding place. Leave the door key with neighbours, and ask them to draw the curtains and leave the light on each evening.

Do not leave notes on the doorstep cancelling milk or papers.

Do not leave an empty dustbin at the front of the house.

Do not leave ladders lying around. Padlock them together, or to a fence-post or drainpipe.

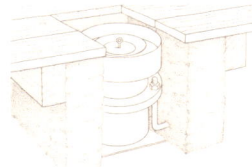

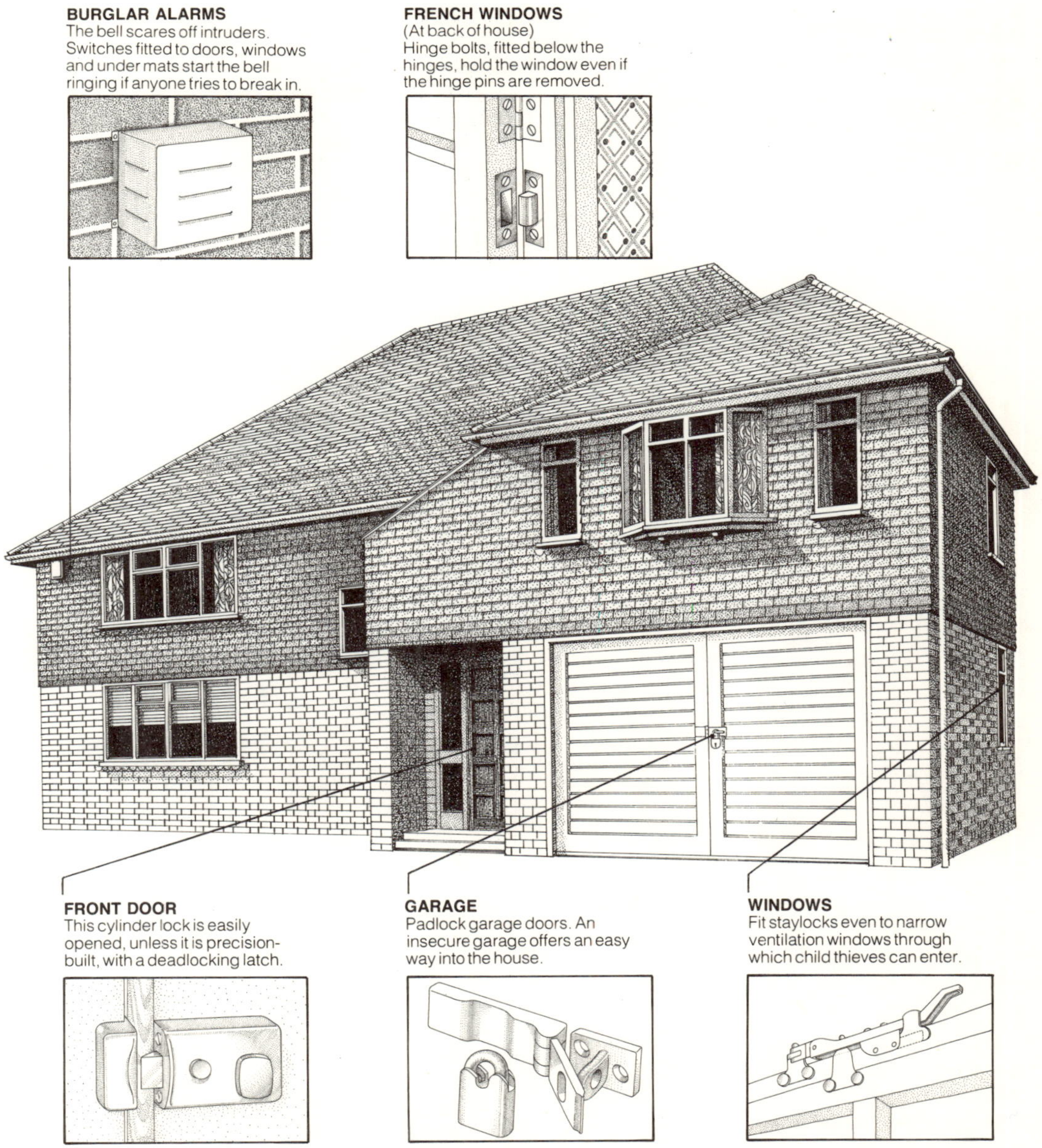

Floor safe

Wall safe

BURGLAR ALARMS
The bell scares off intruders. Switches fitted to doors, windows and under mats start the bell ringing if anyone tries to break in.

FRENCH WINDOWS
(At back of house)
Hinge bolts, fitted below the hinges, hold the window even if the hinge pins are removed.

FRONT DOOR
This cylinder lock is easily opened, unless it is precision-built, with a deadlocking latch.

GARAGE
Padlock garage doors. An insecure garage offers an easy way into the house.

WINDOWS
Fit staylocks even to narrow ventilation windows through which child thieves can enter.

GUARDING THE WEAK POINTS Special locks are available for every type of door and window. Overall protection is secured by fitting a burglar alarm with switches connected to every point of entry.

KEEPING THE HOUSE WARM AND QUIET

The British climate, with its dampness, winds and rapid changes of temperature, finds the weak points in the structure of a house. In a poorly insulated house you may enjoy only a quarter of the heat you pay for. As much as 20% can be lost through the roof; 20% through doors, windows and flues; 10% through floors and 25% through the outer walls. There are several ways in which these weak points can be strengthened to make a house warm, draught-proof and quiet. Some are interlinked. For example, insulating the loft and double-glazing the windows will not only make the house warmer but also help to insulate it from outside noise. It will also, like any insulation work, add to the value of the house.

However much insulation is used, it will never be possible to prevent some heat being lost. There is a limit beyond which the cost of extra insulation is greater than the value of the energy saved.

There are various steps which can be taken to improve a traditional, uninsulated house: insulating the roof; draught-proofing windows and doors; foam-injection or other filling to cavity walls; and double-glazing windows. Various firms specialise in filling cavity brickwork with insulating material and provide a guarantee of workmanship. Materials used are either mineral wool, blown into the cavity, or plastic foam that is pumped in under pressure and solidifies.

With the exception of cavity infilling, these jobs can be undertaken by the average householder with little experience in handicrafts or do-it-yourself.

• LOFT INSULATION
Laying a glass-fibre quilt between the joists in the roof space will reduce the amount of heat lost through a roof by 60-80%, depending on the thickness of the quilt – a fuel saving for the whole house of about 8%.

Building Regulations require a 50 mm. (2 in.) thick glass-fibre quilt, or its equivalent in other loft-insulation materials. The Department of the Environment recommends a thickness of at least 75 mm. (3 in.).

GLASS-FIBRE INSULATION
Materials and equipment: Glass-fibre quilting; planks; walking-stick or similar length of wood; dustpan and brush.

Wear gloves when handling glass-

fibre – it can be an unpleasant skin irritant – and a face mask to prevent particles being inhaled into the lungs. Inexpensive masks can be bought from builders' merchants and chemists' shops.

Before starting, sweep up dust from between the joists and check the wood for signs of woodworm infestation (see p. 377). Kneel on planks across the joists to avoid putting your knee through the ceiling.

Start at the eaves and unroll the material towards the centre of the loft. If possible, buy rolls 50 mm. wider than the space between the joists, to allow for turning up at the sides. Push the material well into the eaves, and fill any odd gaps with pieces torn from a roll. Cover the top of the ceiling hatch

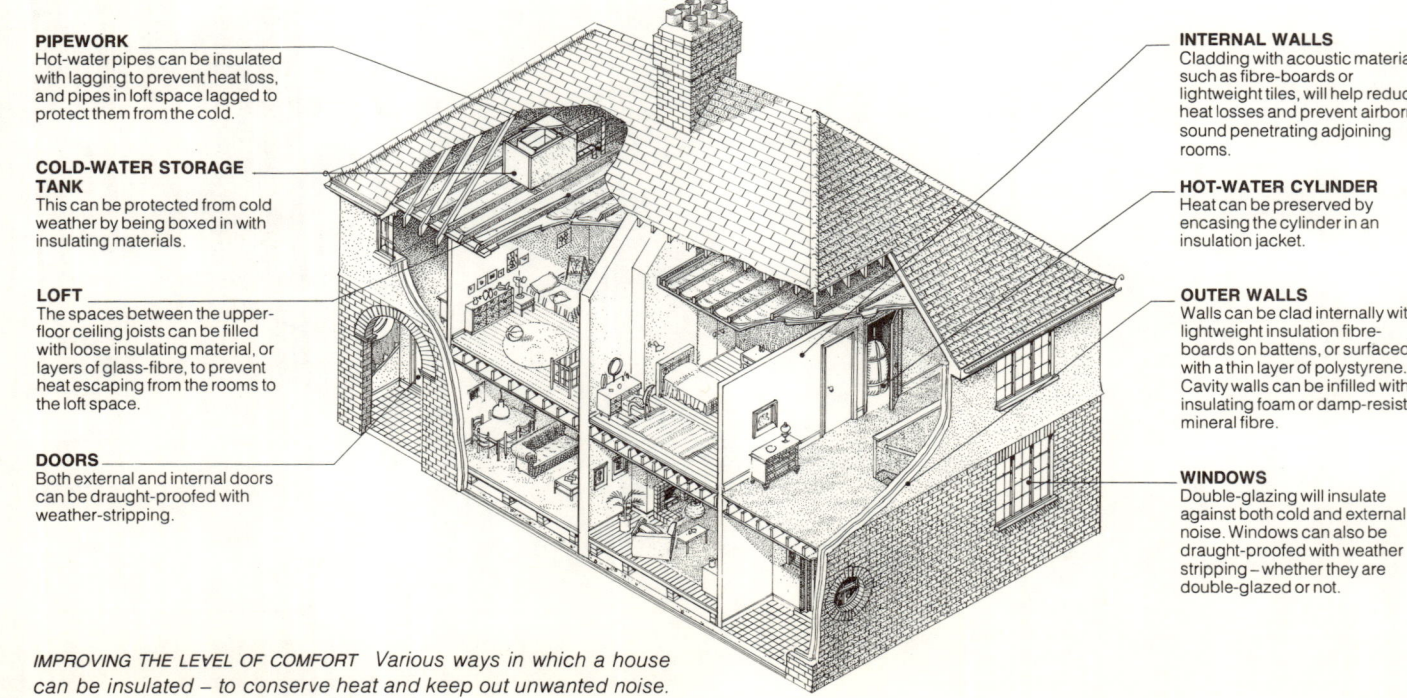

PIPEWORK
Hot-water pipes can be insulated with lagging to prevent heat loss, and pipes in loft space lagged to protect them from the cold.

COLD-WATER STORAGE TANK
This can be protected from cold weather by being boxed in with insulating materials.

LOFT
The spaces between the upper-floor ceiling joists can be filled with loose insulating material, or layers of glass-fibre, to prevent heat escaping from the rooms to the loft space.

DOORS
Both external and internal doors can be draught-proofed with weather-stripping.

INTERNAL WALLS
Cladding with acoustic materials, such as fibre-boards or lightweight tiles, will help reduce heat losses and prevent airborne sound penetrating adjoining rooms.

HOT-WATER CYLINDER
Heat can be preserved by encasing the cylinder in an insulation jacket.

OUTER WALLS
Walls can be clad internally with lightweight insulation fibre-boards on battens, or surfaced with a thin layer of polystyrene. Cavity walls can be infilled with insulating foam or damp-resistant mineral fibre.

WINDOWS
Double-glazing will insulate against both cold and external noise. Windows can also be draught-proofed with weather stripping – whether they are double-glazed or not.

IMPROVING THE LEVEL OF COMFORT Various ways in which a house can be insulated – to conserve heat and keep out unwanted noise.

with a piece of insulation board fixed with PVA adhesive.

GRANULATED INSULATION

Materials and equipment: Insulating material; planks; hardboard; dustpan and brush; tenon saw.

Instead of quilt, loose granulated material such as cork, expanded polystyrene, vermiculite or mineral wool can be tipped between joists.

LINING THE CEILING

A possible hazard in houses where a pitched roof is lined with waterproof material – bitumen felt, aluminium foil or plastic sheets – is condensation in the roof space. The insulation keeps the roof space cold, and vapour passing through the plaster-board ceiling below condenses – a condition which could lead to moisture collecting on top of the ceiling and causing staining. Line the ceiling with vinyl paper or use several coats of oil paint to stop heat rising from the room below and penetrating the roof space.

• LAGGING TANKS AND PIPES

An insulated loft exposes the cold-water tank to the risk of freezing, so the tank will also need insulating. There are three ways of doing this: with polystyrene slabs; with a glass-fibre blanket; or, if the floor is boarded, by surrounding the tank with a hardboard box filled with granulated material.

All pipework in the roof should be lagged – including the small overflow pipes from tanks and cisterns. Wrap felt strip round them like a bandage, or slip on lengths of flexible foam-plastic lagging secured with tape.

LAGGING WITH FOAM

Materials and equipment: Foam plastic; waterproof plastic adhesive tape; scissors or trimming knife.

Foam plastic can be bought from builders' merchants or do-it-yourself shops to fit pipes between 6 mm. (¼ in.) and 75 mm. (3 in.) in diameter. It is in the form of a split tube which is opened and taped round the pipes. It is normally available in 915 mm. (3 ft) or 1.8 m. (6 ft) lengths.

LAGGING WITH FELT

Materials and equipment: Rolls of felt strip; ball of string; scissors or knife.

Felt strip is sold in rolls 75 mm. (3 in.) wide and 3.6 m. (12 ft) long. If the strip is backed with a waterproof material, make sure that the felt surface is against the pipework.

LOOSE MATERIAL

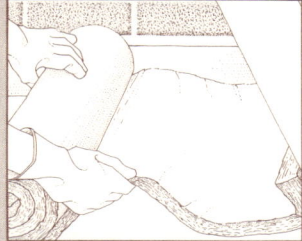

1. Cut hardboard T-shaped spreader, 50 mm. shallower than ceiling joists. Spread material evenly between joists.

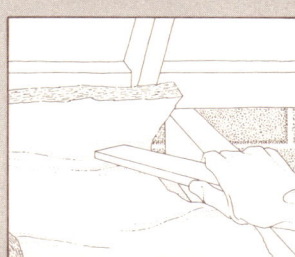

2. Spread material under obstructions, such as parts of a roof truss, by hand to the same depth as the remainder.

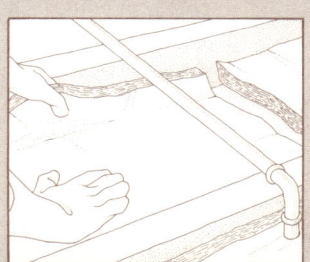

3. Where there are pipes more than 50 mm. above the ceiling finish, spread material level with tops of joists.

LAYING GLASS FIBRE

1. Start at the eaves and unroll the fibre, working towards the centre of the roof space. Kneel on planks for safety.

2. Use a stick to push the fibre quilting into the far corners of the eaves. Use odd pieces of fibre to patch gaps.

3. Push fibre beneath obstructions, such as pipework or structural timbers. Tear the fibre to fit if necessary.

LAGGING A CYLINDER

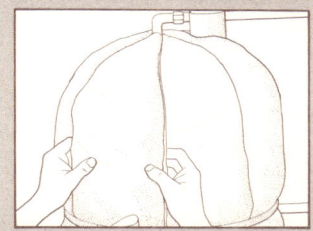

More fuel will be used, so that heating costs will be higher, if heat is allowed to escape from an unlagged hot-water cylinder. Plastic jackets, containing polystyrene or glass-fibre, can be bought to fit most sizes of cylinder.

LAGGING WITH FOAM

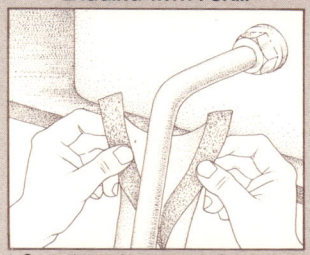

1. Start where pipes emerge from a tank or cistern. Slip the foam round a pipe and push into position. Seal with tape.

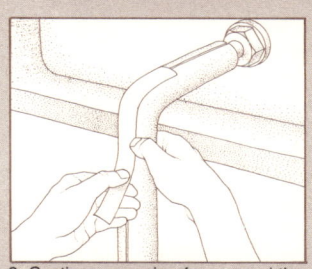

2. Continue wrapping foam round the pipework. Tape all joins, including those enclosing elbows or bends.

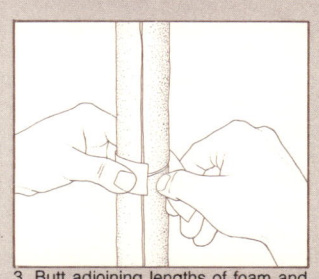

3. Butt adjoining lengths of foam and seal the edges with adhesive tape. Cut foam if odd lengths are needed.

LAGGING WITH FELT

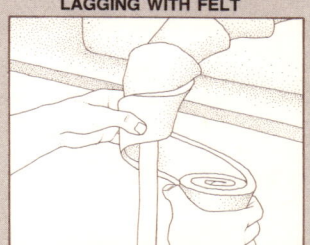

1. Start by tying felt to pipes and wrapping it bandage fashion, so that the felt overlaps throughout by half its width.

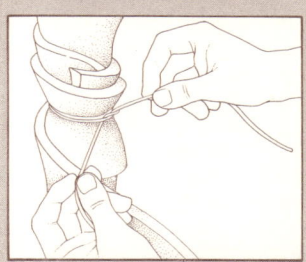

2. Join lengths of felt by overlapping the end of one length with the start of another, by one full turn. Tie the join.

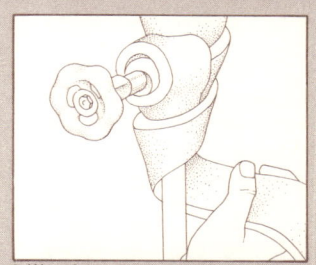

3. Wrap felt round the necks of valves or taps to form a collar of insulation. Double insulate pipes against walls.

• INSULATING WALLS, FLOORS AND WINDOWS

Insulation may save from one-half to two-thirds of the heat loss through cavity or solid walls.

CAVITY WALLS

The best way of dealing with cavity brick walls is for urea-formaldehyde (UF) foam to be injected from the outside, through holes drilled in the mortar joints.

Liquid UF is pumped into the gap between the two leaves of the wall and expands to become a high-insulating foam infill. Another specialised technique – particularly suitable for walls in exposed positions – is to fill the cavity with damp-resistant mineral fibres blown into the gap under pressure. In neither case is the efficiency of the wall impaired.

The infill keeps the wall warm on the inside, and prevents the house from cooling down too quickly after heating is switched off.

The local authority should be contacted before cavities are filled. This is not a job you can do yourself – engage a firm that belongs to the National Cavity Insulation Association, who lay down standards of workmanship.

SOLID WALLS

Solid brick or stone walls can be surfaced internally with insulation board, before being plastered. If the inside cannot be disturbed, the insulation can be put on the outside of the wall and surfaced with cement and sand rendering.

An alternative method of internal insulation is to fix 45 × 19 mm. (1¾ × ¾ in.) wooden battens to the wall, vertically, with their centres 405 mm. (16 in.) apart. Fill the spaces between them with glass-fibre or slabs of polystyrene before fixing plaster-board sheets to the wall battens.

A thickness of 25 mm. (1 in.) of rigid board such as polystyrene, or plaster-board and infill, will reduce heat loss through the wall by more than half, and keep the inner surface warm. As with an insulated roof, vapour can diffuse through the board and condense in the air space or wall structure. Use a vapour barrier – a surface finish of vinyl paper or paint, or a polythene film behind the plaster-board – which prevents the wall 'breathing'.

FLOORS

Only 10% of the total heat loss from a house leaves through the ground floor, and solid floors transmit less heat than suspended floors (see pp. 30-31).

Solid floors feel cold to the touch because of their high surface conductivity: cork tiles make them feel warmer but, in fact, add little extra insulation. Carpets and underfelts reduce the heat lost into suspended floors.

DOUBLE-GLAZING

The advantages of double-glazing cannot always be measured in terms of money. The cost of an expensive installation will rarely be recouped by the saving in fuel costs, although it will add to the resale value of a house. Heat lost through single-glazed windows forms only 20% of the total needed to keep a house warm. Even though double-glazing will cut this loss in half, this means a mere 5-10% cut in fuel consumption.

However, double-glazing can greatly reduce noise from outside, eliminate the chilling effect felt near single-glazed windows, and permit more humidity without condensation.

Radiators can also be placed more freely as they do not need to go beneath windows, where – with single-glazing – warm air escapes. Down draughts are reduced with double-glazing and windows better sealed.

There are three DIY methods of double-glazing existing windows:
1. Replacing the existing glass with an hermetically sealed double-pane unit. This usually means that the rebate, or recess, on a window frame must be deepened with a chisel or plane. A simpler alternative is to use a 'stepped unit' – a fitting specially designed to fit the narrow rebate on standard-size windows.
2. Secondary sashes – hinged or sliding frames in metal or plastic – which are secured to the inside of existing windows.
3. Double-glazing kits that provide plastic edging strips and fixing clips, and for which you supply the glass.

For ideal heat insulation the air space should be no more than 20 mm. (¾ in.) wide; in factory-sealed units it is 6 mm. (¼ in.) wide. Narrower air spaces are unsuitable for double-glazing – increasing conductivity and causing greater heat loss. For sound insulation, an air gap must be at least 100 mm. (4 in.) wide, and heavy-grade glass used. Ask a glazier for advice, or engage a double-glazing specialist to install it for you.

CONDENSATION

When warm moist air comes into contact with cold, non-porous surfaces it turns into droplets which run down walls and collect on window-sills.

Plaster becomes soaked and the surface is marred by salt deposits. Wallpaper peels, and mould appears. Condensation is likely to affect a house that has been left empty and unheated for any length of time. It is most common in kitchens and bathrooms, where steam is present.

The best means of prevention are insulation and improved heating. An extractor fan fitted in an outside wall will also improve ventilation. Painting walls with anti-condensation paint, or lining them with polystyrene under wallpaper, helps.

• DRAUGHT-PROOFING

Many of the draughts in a house are caused by badly fitting doors and windows. These may swell in wet

FITTING A SPRUNG FELT SEAL

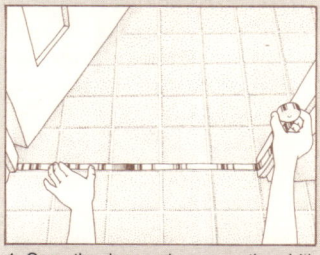

1. Open the door and measure the width from one side of the door frame to the other – that is, the narrowest width of the door opening.

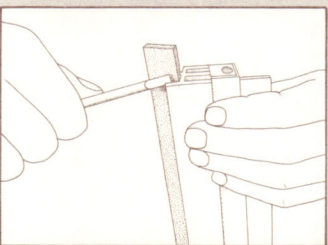

2. Transfer this measurement, less 6 mm., to the metal felt holder. Measure from the push-rod end. Prise the opposite end of the felt holder open with a screwdriver.

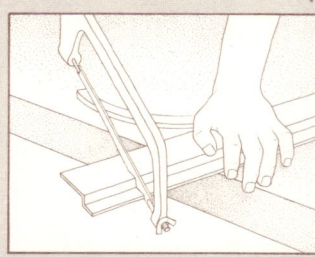

3. Pull back carefully about 150 mm. of felt, and cut the metal to size with a fine-toothed hacksaw. Smooth the cut metal with glasspaper.

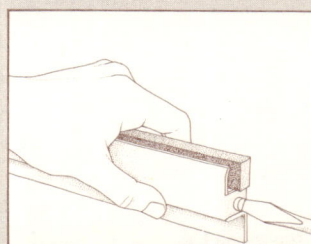

4. Push felt into holder to project 12 mm. Tap corners to grip felt. Cut felt to leave 6 mm. projecting. Loosen screw until rod moves freely.

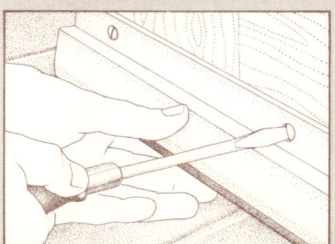

5. Hold the seal across the opening to check if the length is correct. Trim the felt, if necessary, and screw the seal to the door so that the felt is touching the floor.

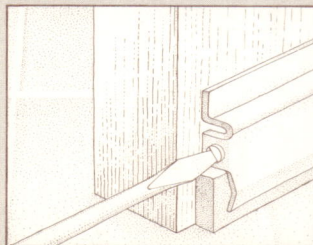

6. Open and close the door to test how well the felt rises and falls. If the felt is too loose or too tight, adjust the screw on the end of the push rod accordingly.

weather and need planing to allow them to close properly. Draught-proofing will, on average, bring about a saving of 6% on fuel costs.

If it is overdone, however, it can reduce the amount of fresh air and cause condensation on windows and walls. Furthermore, fresh air is needed for boilers and direct-burning stoves and many open fires.

Some manufacturers of draught-proofing materials provide an installation service.

MATERIALS AND EQUIPMENT

Four methods of draught-proofing are shown here. For a sprung felt seal you need: spring seal, glasspaper; hacksaw; scissors; screwdriver; hammer; tape measure and pencil; for V-

shaped seal: a copper V-strip with recommended nails or adhesive; tape measure; scissors; bradawl; hammer and nail punch; for plastic strip with felt: felt strip; felt pen; scissors; for self-adhesive plastic strip: plastic strip; scissors; clean rag.

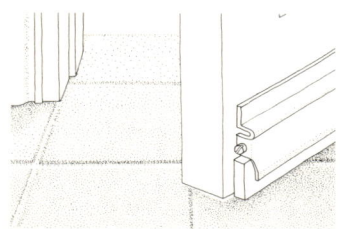

SPRUNG FELT SEAL

For gaps up to 20 mm. ($\frac{3}{4}$ in.) wide below an internal door, use a felt seal

fitted with a spring mechanism.

The seal has a spring-loaded holder, containing a strip of felt, with a push-rod projecting at one side. As the door is closed the rod presses against the jamb on the hinge side and the felt drops flush with the floor.

V-SHAPED SEAL

Seal doors with a V-shaped sprung metal strip – usually copper – which can be nailed or stuck to door frames.

Check before starting that there is at least 2 mm. ($\frac{1}{16}$ in.) clearance between the frames and the doors. If not, adjust the hinges (see p. 361).

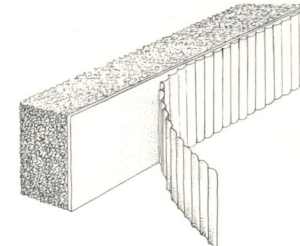

SELF-ADHESIVE PLASTIC STRIP

Plastic strip draught-proofing is easier and cheaper to fasten than more sophisticated draught excluders, but needs replacing each year,

as it discolours and perishes, losing its flexibility.

Use self-adhesive foam-backed plastic strip to weatherproof the edges of doors and window frames; the strip is 6 mm. ($\frac{1}{4}$ in.) deep and available in two widths: 9 and 12 mm. ($\frac{3}{8}$ and $\frac{1}{2}$ in.) wide, sold in rolls of varying lengths. It can be bought from do-it-yourself shops and hardware stores.

First clean the surface of the door or window frame with a clean and damp rag, making sure all grease and dust is removed.

When the surface is dry, peel back about 300 mm. (12 in.) of backing paper on the foam strip and press the sticky side down on to the surface. Start at the top of a door or window frame, and work downwards. Stop just short of the bottom, and cut the strip to length with a pair of sharp scissors. Leave the backing paper on unused lengths of foam.

FITTING A V-SHAPED SEAL

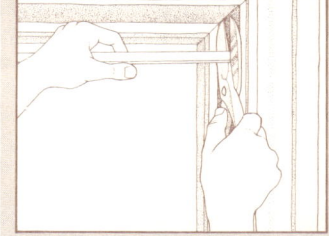

1. Measure the inside width and length of the door frame and cut one width and two lengths of V-strip, allowing 12 mm. extra on each piece.

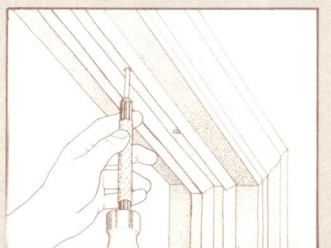

4. Nail the strip to the framework, using the non-ferrous nails sold with the seal. Punch heads flush with the surface; loose nails impair the seal's efficiency.

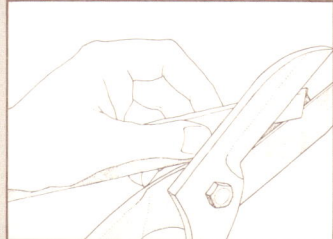

2. Hold the strips in position and cut them so that they touch the frame on both sides. Snip the ends of the narrow edge to a 45 degree angle to make mitred corners.

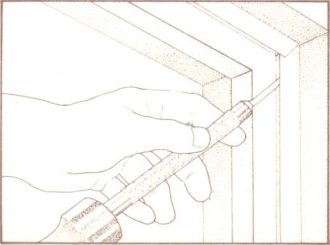

5. Fit top length of seal first, then the sides, with the ends tucked into the corners to complete the mitres. Fix nails as close to the corners as possible.

3. Hold the strip in place, narrow edge downwards, and using the bradawl make holes in the broad edge, positioned approximately 100 mm. apart.

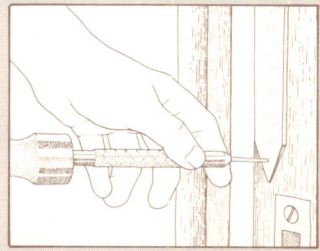

6. Cut the strip to fit just above and below the hinges and the striker plate on the lock. Cut ends straight against hinges and pointed against the striker plate.

FITTING SELF-ADHESIVE STRIPS

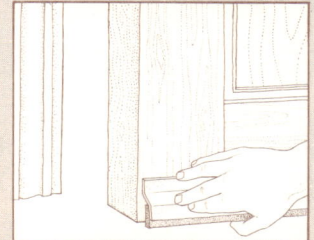

Plastic and felt Cut strip to length, remove backing paper and press the strip to the bottom of the door, so that the felt touches the floor covering.

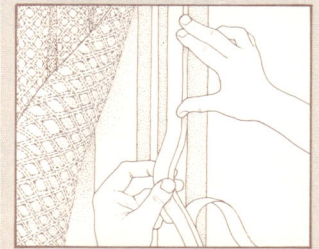

Foam-backed plastic Peel back part of the backing paper and press the strip in place along edges of the door and window frames. Cut with scissors.

PLASTIC STRIP WITH FELT

Close gaps at the bottom of inside doors with self-adhesive plastic strips, incorporating a ribbon of felt.

Clean the surface of the door with a damp rag. Hold the strip against the bottom of the door, and mark the width of the door with a felt pen. Cut the strip to length and peel off the brown paper backing.

Press the adhesive side of the strip against the door so that the bottom edge of the felt fits snugly against the floor covering.

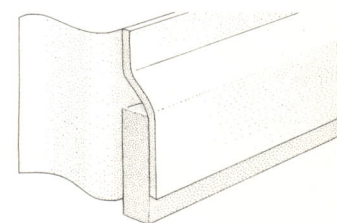

• CHOOSING A CENTRAL-HEATING SYSTEM

There are three kinds of central-heating systems: full central heating, providing pre-set temperatures in all living areas; background central heating, supplying heat to all living areas – but with lower temperatures; and partial central heating, providing some but not all living areas with full heat.

Additional heat is generated by equipment used in the home – cooker, television, refrigerator, washing machine, lighting, and even by occupants themselves.

This incidental heat can, collectively, contribute between 1-2 kW (see p. 370) – about a quarter of the total heat needed for a house in winter; in well-insulated houses, incidental heat can be as much as one-third.

A good heating system provides comfort, with sufficient movement of air to avoid a stuffy atmosphere.

BOILERS

The most common form of central heating has water heated by a boiler at a central source and circulated through pipework to various heat distributors, such as radiators, skirting tubes or fan convectors. The water may circulate by gravity – that is, the water rises from the boiler as it is heated and returns to the boiler again, by gravity, as it cools. Alternatively, the water may be circulated by a pump.

Boilers are supplied with thermostats, to regulate temperature, and safety controls. A few also incorporate a means of storing water in the same casing, making it unnecessary to add a hot-water cylinder elsewhere in the house.

Boilers range from floor-standing models, intended to fit alongside kitchen units, to those that hang on the wall – similar to an instantaneous water heater. Other types include a master radiator/boiler which heats the living-room directly as well as supplying other radiators; and various kinds of back boiler – boilers integrated with the backs of stoves or open fires.

SOLID-FUEL BOILERS

Most solid-fuel boilers must be fuelled by hand, but one type is the gravity-fed boiler which is designed to simplify refuelling and ash disposal. This has a storage compartment for anthracite, which needs topping up about once a day. It also has thermostatic controls and an electric fan. This produces sufficient air flow for high temperatures during burning, capable of turning the fine ash into an easily removed clinker. Solid-fuel heaters have been greatly improved. Open fires have flue restrictors, which prevent the chimney sucking up too much air from the room, and back-boilers to supply radiators and hot-water cylinders. There are stoves with window fronts and built-in boilers whose burning rate can be closely controlled.

GAS-FIRED BOILERS

There are two basic types of gas-fired boiler. The first must be connected to a conventional flue, and the second type can have a balanced flue outlet – a smaller and simpler device than a conventional flue – provided the boiler is on or near an outside wall.

Where a gas boiler is connected to a conventional chimney, the flue must be lined with a material capable of preventing burnt gases and moisture affecting the brickwork and staining the walls.

OIL-FIRED BOILERS

There are different types, identified by the kind of burner they use: the vaporising burner, and the pressure-jet – or atomising – burner.

The first is used on small boilers up to about 60,000 Btu's per hour (see p. 373). The second is used for larger boilers which, because they are a little noisier to run, require a separate boiler compartment. Like gas-fired heating, oil-fired boilers also need suitably lined flues.

ELECTRIC HEATING UNIT

Although not strictly a boiler, this is a heating unit that performs a similar function, using off-peak electricity. The unit consists of a concrete block in the centre of an insulated metal casing. This is heated like a night-storage radiator. Water is pumped through a series of pipes, arranged like a car radiator and positioned near the concrete. An electric fan directs the hot air over the pipes and a pump circulates the heated water to a radiator system.

The unit does not need a flue. Some makes are, however, fairly bulky.

PIPING SYSTEMS

Two widely used piping systems are small-bore and microbore. Both have small diameter pipework – microbore is the smaller of the two – with water circulating under pressure from a small electric pump. The advantages of these systems are that they are relatively easy to install, the pipework is unobtrusive and heating is more rapid than in larger-piped systems, because of the small amount of water in them.

RADIATORS

Radiators are controlled by valves: either simple ON/OFF, or thermostats, which can be pre-set to maintain a selected room temperature.

Long, low radiators distribute heat more evenly than tall narrow ones. Radiators are best placed under windows because, as well as activating air movement, they help to offset the cool air stream created by the glass, and they heat draughts entering through cracks. Positioning is less critical if you have double-glazed windows because of the higher level of insulation that double glazing provides.

STORAGE RADIATORS

Storage radiators are heated by off-peak electricity. They are usually used for background heating with supplementary heat from conventional heaters – gas, electric or open fires. Thermostatic storage radiators are better for full heating as they incorporate a fan which can deliver warm air when needed, for example, towards the end of the day when an ordinary storage radiator starts to cool off.

CONVECTORS

Convectors comprise a heating element of finned tubes mounted in a metal cabinet with louvres at the top and the bottom. Cold air is drawn in through grilles at the bottom, and the heated air is discharged through a grille at the top. Like radiators they can be used with any heating system (see chart opposite).

Some convectors contain a fan which forces air over the elements. This type takes up less space, and the output can be controlled by varying the speed of the fan.

SKIRTING HEATING

This is fixed in place of the traditional wooden skirting in a room and is in effect a low-level convector.

The warmth is spread along the walls and creates an even room temperature without occupying extra space, as with radiators.

UNDERFLOOR HEATING

The most common form of underfloor heating has electrically heated elements, embedded in the ground floor concrete slab. Since this is best done during construction it is most suited to new houses. Unobtrusive and providing the ideal conditions of comfort – with the lower part of the room having a slightly higher temperature than the upper – underfloor heating also uses off-peak current.

Less common is the underfloor-heating system that has water circulating through pipework. Although it can be sufficient to heat a well-insulated house it may need supplementary radiators or convectors.

WARM-AIR HEATING

Ducts from a gas-fired or oil-fired boiler, or electric storage heater, discharge the warm air through grilles in the floors or walls of the rooms. Thermostatic control is rapidly effected by switching the fan motor on or off. Some makes incorporate a second heater for hot water.

Ducts are generally built into a house during construction – occasionally added in old houses – and so occupy no extra wall space. Good design will, however, overcome the system's possible drawbacks. These could be noisy operation, the risk of conversation being heard between rooms and the possible spread of smoke and smells.

• CONTROLLING THE TEMPERATURE

The temperature of a central-heating system may be controlled by a single thermostat on the boiler, or separate thermostats positioned strategically throughout the house, linked to a time switch or programmer.

A thermostat on the boiler automatically switches off the burner once

THE CHOICE OF CENTRAL-HEATING SYSTEMS
* Cannot be installed in an existing house easily

FUEL	TYPES OF SYSTEMS AVAILABLE	
GAS No fuel-storage problems and always on tap. It can be controlled automatically by time clock and thermostat. Boilers have to be linked to conventional flues or balanced flues	Radiant or convector heaters Skirting convectors Fan convectors * Underfloor heating	Supplied by separate boiler or a back boiler with a gas fire
	* Warm-air heating Individual heaters	
SOLID FUEL Fuel-storage space necessary and supply is dependent upon deliveries. Refuelling and removing ashes or clinker is necessary, although some types are cleaner and easier to maintain than others. Some boilers have semi-automatic controls	Radiant or convector heaters Skirting convectors Fan convectors * Underfloor heating	Supplied by separate boiler or open fire/stove with back boiler
	Open fire or room heater	
ELECTRICITY Clean, safe and requires minimum maintenance. No fuel-storage problems and supply is always available. Individual heaters are easy to install and easy to take if you move house	* Warm air heating Radiant or convector heaters Skirting convectors Fan convectors	Supplied by central unit (generally off-peak current)
	* Underfloor heating (storage) Individual heaters (on-peak panel or off-peak storage)	
OIL Storage tank needed outside the house and consequently some screening may be considered desirable. Supply is dependent upon deliveries. Fully automatic controls	Radiant or convector heaters Skirting convectors Fan convectors * Underfloor heating	Supplied by separate boiler or room heater with back boiler
	* Warm-air heating Individual heaters	

water has been heated to the required temperature. It can also be adjusted manually to control the maximum temperature throughout the house. Separate thermostats, however, give more sensitive temperature control and better fuel economy.

Each room, hall and landing space, can have its own thermostat that controls the temperature in that area by switching the circulation pump on or off once the temperature drops below, or rises above, a certain setting. Fixed to the wall at least 1.5 m. (5 ft) above the floor, away from draughts or separate heaters, the room thermostat operates independently of the boiler's thermostat.

Recommended minimum temperatures for central heating in different parts of the home are:

Living-room	21°C	(70°F)
Dining-room	21°C	(70°F)
Bedsitting-room	21°C	(70°F)
Bathroom	21°C	(70°F)
Hall/Landing	16°C	(61°F)
Kitchen	18°C	(64°F)
Lavatory	16°C	(61°F)
Bedrooms	16°C	(61°F)

Higher temperatures are often desirable for children's rooms, studies and elderly people's bedrooms.

A radiator thermostat, fitted in place of a manual on/off control, can be pre-set to ensure water flows through a radiator at the correct temperature.

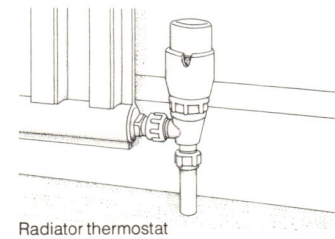

Radiator thermostat

A radiator thermostat is ideal for a room with a single radiator, permitting temperature changes to be made to suit individual needs.

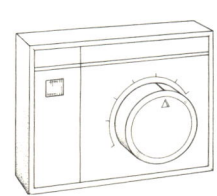

Room thermostat

• REMOVING AIR FROM RADIATORS

An air lock in a radiator will stop it heating correctly. Turn off the radiator and when the water is warm – not hot – open the vent valve at the top of the radiator. Use a hollow, square-ended key, obtainable from ironmongers.

Hold a container beneath the valve to collect water, insert the key and turn it anti-clockwise to 'bleed' the radiator. Air will start to escape. Stop turning. If you turn too far, the valve may come out, and water will jet out of the radiator. As soon as the air stops escaping and water starts to flow, turn the key to tighten the valve.

If air locks are a frequent trouble, get a plumber to replace the vent-valve with an air eliminator available from builders' merchants. This is a valve having a porous gland that allows air to escape automatically.

• ADJUSTING A THERMOSTAT ON AN IMMERSION HEATER

Immersion-heater thermostats can be adjusted to heat water to 60°C (140°F) or 70°C (158°F). For economical use, 60°C is usually sufficient. It is the lowest temperature at which water is hot enough for most domestic purposes.

Turn off the electricity supply first. It is dangerous to adjust a thermostat while it is still switched on.

Unscrew the cover disc and remove it. Use a screwdriver to prise off a metal cap covering the regulator and, with the blade, turn the regulator screw to the required temperature. Replace the cap and the disc.

Despite the thermostat, an immersion heater is more economical to run for average use, if the heater is switched on for an hour in the morning and again in the evening, rather than being on all day.

REMOVING AIR FROM RADIATORS

1. Turn the valve anti-clockwise with the key. Collect the water in a container.

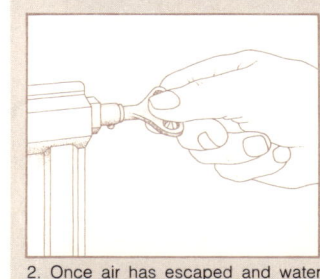

2. Once air has escaped and water starts to appear, tighten the valve.

ADJUSTING A THERMOSTAT

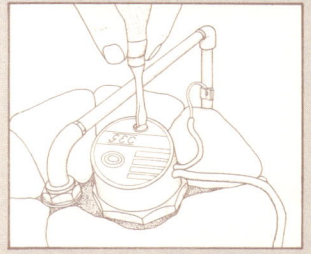

1. Turn off supply. Unscrew cover disc and prise off cap covering regulator.

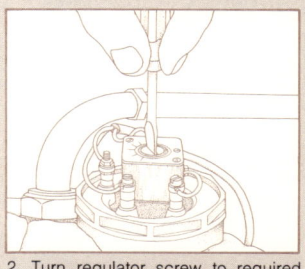

2. Turn regulator screw to required temperature. Replace cap and disc.

OTHER FORMS OF HEATING/ELECTRICITY

APPLIANCE	HOW IT WORKS	EFFICIENCY	MAINTENANCE	TYPES AND CONTROLS	SAFETY ASPECTS
Radiant Heater	Emits heat directly. Simplest types consist of one or more ceramic or fireclay rods – with wire elements coiled around them – mounted in front of a polished reflector plate.	Instant heat in the vicinity of the heater. If used for full heating can produce stuffy conditions by overheating the upper portion of the room.	None.	Portable, wall hung and large floor-standing models – some of which are designed to be set in a fireplace opening. Ratings range from 750 watt to 3 kW, with two or three switch settings so that only part of a fire need be turned on at a time.	Choose heaters that have a guard on them to stop clothing touching the elements. Never use a portable electric heater in a bathroom – it could kill if splashed with water or touched with wet hands. The only kind of radiant heater that is both safe and suitable for use in a bathroom, has a single element, 800-1,000 watt, sheathed in silica. The heater should be wired by a qualified electrician only, and fixed either to the ceiling or high on a wall, with a pull cord switch. A conventional switch can be used only if it is positioned outside the bathroom door. If the heater has an angled reflector, the fire should be positioned so that it is not possible for anyone standing in a bath or shower to adjust it.
Convector Heater	Cold air enters the bottom of the heater. As it is warmed, it rises rapidly, escaping through grilles in the top of the casing to create a current of moving air that raises the room temperature.	Ordinary convectors tend to overheat the upper part of a room; fan convectors provide a better distribution of heat.	Regular dusting to keep inlet and outlet grilles clean and dust-free.	Portable, floor-standing and some wall-hung types, with ratings ranging from 1 to 3 kW. Some types have thermostats, time switches or manual controls for several different heat settings; most have a pilot light to show when the heater is switched on.	Wall-hung types are particularly appropriate where there are small children. Convectors must not be covered with clothing or the air flow will be blocked and the elements will overheat. This usually causes a safety cut-out to operate but may, in some cases, also damage the heater.
Radiant Convector Heater	A combination of radiant and convector heater in the same casing.	Has the combined advantages of both radiant and convector heaters.	Regular dusting to keep inlet and outlet grilles clear of dust and fluff.	Floor-standing and wall-mounted types available, ranging from 2 to 3 kW. Different switch settings for one or more elements and controls that enable radiant or convected heat to be used jointly or separately.	Must not be covered with clothing or the air supply may be blocked.
Fan Heater	Cold air is drawn in at the back and sides of the casing, passes over hot elements and is blown out at the front as hot air.	Will heat a room quickly but tends to be noisy in operation. Portable model provides convected heat that can be directed where required.	Occasional cleaning to remove dust and fluff that may clog the mechanism. With the heater unplugged, use a vacuum cleaner and blow through it, holding the nozzle about 10 cm. (4 in.) away from the fan.	Portable, floor-standing and wall-mounted types, with ratings ranging from ½ to 3 kW, and one or two switches to provide different heat levels. Some types have a thermostat and will keep a room at a constant temperature. Most fan heaters can be run without heat, to act as a circulating fan in hot weather.	Must not be covered with clothing or the air flow will be blocked. In some cases the elements may also be damaged. Since fan heaters must be kept on a level surface to operate properly, they should not be used as hand-held hair-dryers.
Oil-Filled Radiator	Column or panel-shaped radiators, filled with oil. The oil, which distributes the heat evenly through the panel, is sealed inside – heated by an insulated element – and does not need to be replaced. Oil-filled radiators heat a room in the same way as a water-filled radiator in a conventional central-heating system.	Provides part radiant and part convected heat. Equally suitable for full heating or background heating.	None.	Portable and floor-standing heaters and some makes that can be bracketed to the wall. Available in ratings from ½ to 3 kW; all with thermostatic controls.	Some types can become too hot to touch – a disadvantage where there are small children.
Tubular Heater	Consists of low-power heating elements inside a perforated metal tube.	Produces convected heat at a low output. Can be linked, in lines, to provide heat similar to skirting heaters.	Keep perforations clean by regular dusting.	Portable and wall-hung models, varying in length from 50 cm. - 5 m. (20 in. - 16 ft). Utilitarian in appearance, tubular heaters are particularly suitable for garages or workshops, or for providing a low level of background heat in a clothes cupboard or similar situation. Ratings from 60 to 80 watts for approximately every 30 cm. (12 in.) length.	Must not be covered with material or the air flow will be blocked.

OTHER FORMS OF HEATING/GAS

APPLIANCE	HOW IT WORKS	EFFICIENCY	MAINTENANCE	TYPES AND CONTROLS	SAFETY ASPECTS
Radiant Convector Heater	Gas heats elements which provide radiant heat, while grilles in the top of the casing release convected heat. Fresh air enters through inlets underneath the heater.	Radiant heat providing immediate warmth near the heater. Convected heat provides good distribution of warmth throughout a room.	Keep inlet and outlet grilles free of fluff. Occasional replacement of ignition battery, and service on jets.	Floor-standing and wall-mounted models available – most with automatic ignition and thermostatic controls. Switches may have different settings to allow all or part of a heater to be used. Ratings from 5 kW to 7.5 kW. Radiant convector heaters must be fixed permanently in position, with the rear outlet sealed with an air-tight joint to a flue. With some makes of gas convector, several heaters can be wired to a central time-switch.	Inlet grilles must not be covered or the air flow for convected heat will be blocked and the elements will overheat. Some models have thermal cut-out devices. Radiant elements should be protected by wire guards.
Balanced Flue Convector	Convector heater	Emits and circulates warm air – ideal as a background heater.	Regular dusting to keep inlet and outlet grilles clean and dust-free. Occasional replacement of ignition battery, and service on jets.	Similar to conventional convector heaters but larger and more suitable therefore for large houses or open-planned interiors. Needs a balanced flue – a small unit containing two ducts: a fresh-air inlet, and an outlet duct to exhaust the products of combustion. The flue fits into an outer wall, terminated by a grille. The heater must therefore be fitted on or near an outside wall with a flexible duct connected to it. Floor-standing types with ratings up to 4 kW.	Inlet and outlet grilles must not be blocked. Balanced flue grille must also be kept free of obstructions.

OTHER FORMS OF HEATING/SOLID AND BOTTLED FUELS

APPLIANCE	HOW IT WORKS	EFFICIENCY	MAINTENANCE	TYPES AND CONTROLS	SAFETY ASPECTS
Open Fire – Inset Grate	Traditional inset open fire that burns coal, coke or smokeless fuels, such as anthracite. Transmits most heat by radiation.	Slow to heat a room, providing localised warmth.	None, apart from emptying ash cans.	An adjustable damper, fitted in the chimney just above the fire will help reduce room draughts. An ash-pit air controller is essential, and combined with an electric fan, will improve the rate of burning and give a rapid boost when starting. Some types draw air from under the floor or through an outer wall. The fire can be fitted with different kinds of ash box – some that need to be emptied only once a week.	Provide a guard in a room where there are children or old people.
Open Fire – Free-Standing Heater	A heater that can be positioned anywhere in a room, provided it has a chimney.	More efficient than an open fire since the casing also disperses heat into a room.	None, save emptying the ash and occasional renewal of fire bars and fire bricks.	Free-standing heaters with a rating output up to 5 kW, varying from types styled to look like an ordinary open fire to those resembling old-fashioned stoves. Some need to be fuelled only once a day.	The casing gets hot enough to burn if touched. Not ideal, therefore, where there are children.
Room Heater	An enclosed fire with a glass front, sealed so that the heater takes only the minimum air needed. Provides radiated and convected heat.	One of the most efficient means of burning solid fuel. The chimney also gets warmed and more heat is left in the house.	None beyond emptying the ash and occasional renewal of fire bars and fire bricks.	A hearth boiler has a hopper within the heater's casing, filled with anthracite that is automatically fed to the fire. At full output the supply will last about six hours; for normal use, eight to ten hours. Some room heaters can be had with time switches, air controllers, programmers and thermostats.	None.
Bottled Fuel – Paraffin	Fuels both radiant and convector heaters.	Highly efficient since all heat goes into the room. Can cause condensation if it is the only heater in a poorly ventilated room.	Wicks must be trimmed regularly to avoid smoking. Use only clean fuel to prevent smells.	In addition to the more commonplace and traditional designs, there are heaters similar in appearance to gas heaters. Most are available as floor-standing models, but some are made to fix on a wall to provide permanent background heat. Ratings up to 3 kW.	Modern heaters have built-in safety devices and conform with BS 3300 and carry the BS Kitemark (see p. 349). Never leave a heater where it can be knocked over by children or animals. Use it only in a ventilated room, positioned away from draughts, which can cause smoking and flaring. Never move or fill a heater while it is alight and never fill it to capacity – paraffin expands when hot. Never store paraffin in the house and mark the can clearly – a heater filled with petrol will explode.
Bottled Fuel – Gas	Bottled (butane) gas is a convenient substitute for natural gas where there are no main supplies available. The gas is in liquid form, contained, under pressure, in steel bottles.	Comparable with natural gas (above).	None.	In addition to a range of portable heaters made specifically for bottled gas, manufacturers offer specially adapted radiant fires and convectors. Consult the manufacturers of the heaters or the distributors of bottled gas. The gas bottles are hired: start with two so that while one is in use the other can be returned for filling. Controls on portable heaters can be bought with three heat settings and battery or manual ignition.	The same care is necessary with portable gas heaters as with paraffin fires. Adequate ventilation in a room heated by bottled gas is essential.

HOME MEDICAL CARE

There is little point in asking your doctor for advice about minor illnesses and injuries which cause symptoms for only a few days. The common cold, the occasional stomach upset or headache, a small cut or bruise can be treated at home. However, if the symptoms persist, or the injury does not heal, it is advisable to go to the doctor.

• HOME NURSING

When caring for a seriously ill patient at home, try to make the surroundings clean, pleasant and comfortable. A person, particularly a child, can quickly become bored and despondent if the room in which he is lying is drab. Hanging colourful pictures or posters can brighten a sick room.

Give the patient books, newspapers and writing materials to keep him entertained. Put a radio or television near the bed. When looking after a bed-ridden child, set aside a time for reading aloud and playing.

Most children, when they are ill, constantly demand attention. Try not to feel harassed by this; it is natural. Even if the patient is undemanding, do not leave him on his own too long.

Throughout the day, adjust the pillows and the position of the patient. When the patient regains his strength, encourage him to sit on the edge of the bed and then in a chair for a short time each day.

A seriously ill patient may need special nursing treatment at home. NHS and voluntary help is available, and information about this can be obtained from local health centres, local authority offices and post offices.

THE NURSING ROUTINE

Always carry out the doctor's instructions exactly. Give the right amount of medicine at the right times. The patient should take the full course, and only medicine prescribed by the doctor should be given to him.

Before giving the medicine, read the label on the bottle to check the contents. Shake a bottle of liquid medicine before removing the cork or cap. After use, put it away out of reach of the children.

Meal times can help to break up a dull day. Serve food at the same times each day, and try to make the meal on the tray look attractive. A small bowl of flowers, for instance, can add brightness. If possible, get the patient to sit up, or give support by holding his head. Serve one course at a time and do not hurry the patient. Cut up any food that he cannot cut himself. In some cases it may be necessary to spoon-feed the patient. If he is lying flat in bed and cannot drink normally, use a beaker with a lid and a spout.

THE PATIENT'S PROGRESS

When you are caring for a patient at home, the doctor may ask you to watch his progress. He may want to know how much sleep the patient has had, how much he has eaten and drunk, whether he has been in pain, or whether the prescribed medicine has been effective. These observations will help the doctor to make a diagnosis or to change a treatment. The doctor may also need a daily record of the rise and fall of the patient's temperature, pulse and respiration.

TAKING A TEMPERATURE

A patient's temperature may be taken at regular intervals in the mouth or under the arm by using a clinical thermometer. The normal temperature under the tongue is 37°C (98.6°F), but the skin temperature, under the arm, is about 0.5°C (1°F) lower. A rectal thermometer should be used only by someone trained in this method.

The patient should be lying or sitting quietly before his temperature is taken. Never take a reading less than 20 minutes after the patient has had a meal or drink, or has taken a bath, as these distort the temperature.

Keep the thermometer in a weak solution of antiseptic. Rinse it in cold water and wipe with dry cotton wool. Shake the thermometer until the mercury has gone down into the bulb.

Place the bulb under the patient's tongue and ask him to close his mouth. Leave the thermometer in place for two minutes, then remove it and read the level of mercury. After taking the reading, shake the thermometer down, rinse it in cold water and return it to the antiseptic solution.

If the patient has a mouth injury or cannot breathe through his nose, the skin temperature can be taken. Put the thermometer under the armpit for two minutes.

PULSE AND RESPIRATION

The pulse is caused by the contraction of the heart as it pumps blood round the body. The average adult pulse rate is between 72 and 80 beats per minute; for a baby the rate is 120 to 140 times per minute. The rate, regularity and strength of the pulse is an indication of the patient's health. An increase in this rate may be due to fever or an emotional state, such as anxiety.

The pulse can be felt wherever an artery crosses the bone near the surface of the skin. The most convenient place for taking the pulse is at the wrist. Put three fingers on the artery just above the thumb. Do not take a pulse with your thumb, because the thumb has a pulse of its own. Count the number of beats per minute, using a watch with a second hand. A patient's pulse can be taken at the same time as his temperature.

A patient's respiration rate can be counted after taking the pulse rate. A new-born baby breathes 30 to 50 times a minute, but in an adult the rate is 16 to 20 times a minute. Try not to make the patient aware that you are counting his breathing rate, as this may alter his respiration. If necessary, the respiration rate can be counted while the patient is sleeping.

• THE FAMILY MEDICINE CHEST

You can economise on home doctoring by buying bandages and other medical products which carry the letters 'BP' or 'BPC'. This indicates that they conform to the British Pharmacopoeia or the British Pharmaceutical Code. These products are much cheaper than their branded equivalents. For example, aspirin tablets BP are about one fifth the price of proprietary aspirin tablets.

People react in different ways to pills and other forms of medicine. If a medical product has no effect, or seems to be making things worse, stop taking it. When taking drugs on a doctor's prescription, check with the chemist or doctor that they do not clash with any other medicines you may be taking.

Do not clutter up the medicine chest with bottles containing a few left-over tablets from a prescription. Drugs should not be kept too long because they may deteriorate and become ineffective or dangerous. At the end of a course of treatment, throw them away or empty them down the toilet, unless they are being kept as an emergency supply. Get rid of other medical products which have lost their labels or whose use you have forgotten.

Keep medicine out of the reach of children. Place it on a high shelf, or in a cupboard with a child-proof lock.

PARACETAMOL
This drug is an alternative to aspirin and alleviates the same problems. It does not irritate the stomach. Codeine is another pain-relieving pill, but it can cause drowsiness and constipation.

OIL OF CLOVES
Painting an aching tooth with oil of cloves provides temporary relief.

METHYL SALICYLATE OINTMENT
Rub this ointment into a strained or bruised muscle. It will also ease spasm and pain.

ASPIRIN
This pill is for relieving pain and lowering a raised temperature. It may irritate the stomach lining, causing internal bleeding. Therefore, never take an aspirin for a pain in the stomach. Anyone who suffers stomach discomfort by taking aspirin can prevent this by taking it with milk. Soluble aspirin is less likely to cause stomach upset.

MAGNESIUM TRISILICATE
Available in tablets or as a liquid, magnesium trisilicate gives relief from heartburn. This burning sensation is caused by stomach acid irritating the gullet or oesophagus. Other simple antacid tablets, liquids and fizzy powders, including sodium bicarbonate, can be taken to relieve mild indigestion.

CALAMINE LOTION
This is the familiar name for a medicated liquid containing zinc carbonate. It has a soothing effect when applied with cottonwool to a painful sunburn. Calamine lotion also helps to relieve any itching, such as nettle rash, insect bites and stings.

KAOLIN AND MORPHINE MIXTURE
This mixture is used to relieve diarrhoea by slowing down bowel movements. Lomotil tablets have the same effect. If the diarrhoea is caused by bacterial food poisoning, anti-bacterial drugs may be prescribed by the doctor.

ANTISEPTIC CREAM
This is useful for cuts and grazes. Do not put creams on burns, which are best left uncovered.

ANTIHISTAMINE CREAM
This lotion can be rubbed on bites, stings and sunburns.

TRAVEL-SICKNESS TABLETS
These can be taken before a journey, or as directed by a doctor.

FINGER BANDAGE AND APPLICATOR
A seamless tubular gauze bandage covers finger injuries. Use the applicator to fit the bandage.

DRESSING SCISSORS
When cutting away dressings or bandages, keep the blunt-ended blade next to the skin.

SPADE-ENDED TWEEZERS
These will remove splinters from the skin. Use in good light.

CLINICAL THERMOMETER
The clinical thermometer is used either in the mouth or under the arm. Clean with antiseptic.

SAFETY PINS
These are used for fixing bandages or slings.

UNBLEACHED TRIANGULAR BANDAGE
This type of bandage makes a sling to support a sprained wrist or an elbow injury.

STERILISED WHITE ABSORBENT GAUZE
This dressing can be used dry, with no cream or ointment, to dress a minor wound.

COTTONWOOL
This can be used to pad a dressing or, with soap and hot water, to clean an injury.

CRÊPE BANDAGE
This may be needed to bandage a joint, such as wrist or knee.

ADHESIVE-PLASTER DRESSINGS
Plasters can be used on minor wounds or to secure a dressing.

OPEN-WEAVE BANDAGES
These protect wounds from dirt and from contact with clothing.

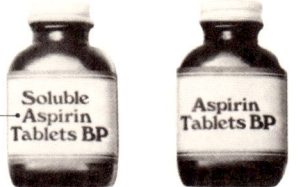

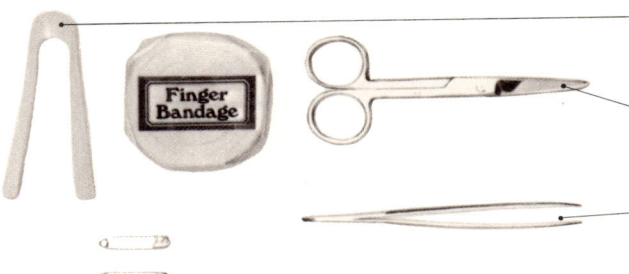
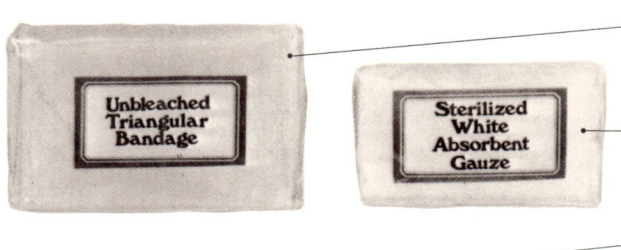
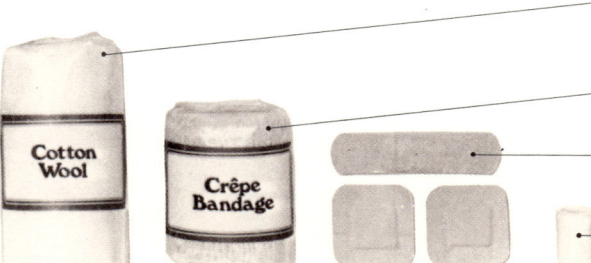

HOME MEDICAL SUPPLIES *The medicines, bandages and other equipment shown above are sufficient for treating minor illnesses and injuries. They should be kept in a locked cupboard.*

MINOR COMPLAINTS AND INJURIES

A

ATHLETE'S FOOT
This disorder of the feet is caused by infection with various fungi, such as ringworm, that thrive in warm wet places, such as showers and swimming pools. The symptoms are cracks in the skin, and blisters and scaling between the toes. Athlete's foot can be treated by gently rubbing away the scaly and damp patches with cottonwool and drying the foot. Apply water mixed with a little rubbing alcohol. Dry the foot again and apply dusting powder. A fungicidal ointment should be applied before going to bed and in the morning. Bathing the feet in a solution of potassium permanganate, in a dilution suggested by the doctor, is useful if the blisters are oozing. After soaking the feet for 10-15 minutes, dry and apply calamine.

B

BLEEDING
Minor bleeding stops on its own or under slight pressure. Wash away any dirt from the wound, and dry. See Emergency treatment, p. 398.

BLISTERS
These are due to damage to the skin, as the result of a burn, an insect bite, or friction – from an ill-fitting shoe, for example. Do not burst blisters, because infection is likely to follow. Protect the blister with an adhesive plaster, padded if needed, and treat its cause.

BOILS
A boil is a gland in the skin which has become blocked or infected. Pressure inside the blocked gland rises, and the swelling becomes hot and inflamed. In a teenager a boil may be due to acne, caused by excessive secretion of the oil that lubricates the skin.

Squeezing a boil is likely to spread the infection to other parts of the skin. Most boils need no special treatment. The pain will be eased and the infection brought to a head if a kaolin poultice is applied as hot as can be borne and renewed as necessary.

Medical treatment should be sought for recurrent boils.

BRUISES AND BLACK EYES
A bruise is a surface discoloration or swelling resulting from a blow or pressure. The small blood vessels under the skin rupture, but the skin does not break and the blood cannot drain away quickly. The internal bleeding produces the black or blue mark. Once the blood has leaked out, it has to be removed by the body's internal cleansing system. The cleansing is partly a chemical process in which the dark-red blood pigment is converted into yellowish-green breakdown products. This explains the discoloration around a bruise.

Immediately after an injury, the application of a cold compress may prevent bruising. But once the bruise has formed, there is nothing that can be done to speed its breakdown. If the blood causes a soft swelling beneath the skin, known as a haematoma, a doctor may remove the clotted blood through a small incision.

A black eye, like other bruises, is due to bleeding beneath the skin. Because of the many blood vessels, and the looseness and transparency of the skin near the eye, the bruise may be darker than elsewhere. To reduce pain and swelling, apply ice packs or cloth soaked in cold water.

BUNION
An overgrowth of bone, usually just below the base of the big toe. This painful swelling turns the big toe inwards against the other toes. The cause is ill-fitting shoes, probably worn in childhood. A corn or callus on the bunion adds to the pressure and the pain. Bunions can be avoided by wearing broad shoes. Resting the foot on a jacketed hot-water bottle may relieve the pain. However, surgery is the only effective cure.

BURNS, MINOR
Put the burnt part immediately under a running cold-water tap and keep it there for a few minutes, or until the pain subsides. Then apply a dry dressing to protect from dirt and damage and fix it with a plaster.

BURNS AND SCALDS
See First aid, p. 399.

C

CALLUSES AND CORNS
This is a pad of hard skin formed where the skin is under pressure. A corn, for example, is a callus caused by ill-fitting shoes pressing against a prominent bone. For immediate relief, soak the foot in hot water and then rub away the thickened skin with an emery board, or apply corn plasters. Over a long period, a right-fitting shoe is the cure.

CHILBLAINS
This is an inflammation of the skin accompanying poor circulation, often caused by exposure to cold, dry weather. The parts affected are the fingers, toes, ears and nose. To prevent chilblains, wear gloves, thick socks and protective clothing. Chilblains should not be warmed in front of the fire. Allow the skin to reheat slowly and then apply a soothing dressing, such as compound benzoin tincture (Friar's Balsam) or Iodex ointment.

CHOKING
See First aid, p. 399.

COLD SORE
A slightly swollen, painful, red patch usually on the lip or the border of the nostrils. Small blisters arise on this patch, turn yellow, crust and come off as scabs. Cold sores last about ten days and are not contagious. They are caused by a virus, known as herpes simplex, which breaks out repeatedly in people who carry the virus in their skin. Calamine lotion may soothe and dry the blisters. In serious cases, idoxuridine may be prescribed.

COLDS AND COUGHS
The common cold is an infectious disease of the upper respiratory system – the nose, throat and the bronchial tubes particularly – which is caused by viruses. It is highly contagious, and its symptoms – a running or stuffy nose, headache and cough – appear 18-48 hours after infection. The patient may feel chilly and develop a high temperature. A cold may last from a few days to a few weeks.

There is no need to call a doctor for a cold, unless there are complications, such as an infection of the middle ear, the sinuses or the lungs. Treatment is with aspirin or paracetamol.

A patient with a feverish cold and cough should be kept warm, but need not be confined to bed. Give him plenty to drink to make up for the fluid which is lost from sweating. A soothing cough linctus may help the person to sleep at night. But frequent doses of a powerful cough medicine are not recommended, because coughing is caused by the need to remove fluid or sputum from the lungs. Get a doctor's advice if the sputum becomes discoloured or sticky, which suggests bronchitis may have developed.

CONJUNCTIVITIS
An inflammation of the conjunctiva, the membranes which cover the eyeball and the lining of the eyelids. The infection, also known as pink eye, may be caused by bacteria, a virus or an allergy. It is contagious and can be transmitted by fingers or towels. The eye is inflamed and there may be a sticky discharge inside the lids. Bathe the eyes in boiled warm water several times a day. Dip cottonwool in the water and hold it against the eye. If the infection persists, the doctor will prescribe eyedrops or ointment.

CRAMP
A painful spasmodic contraction of a muscle or a group of muscles. It may come on after violent exercise or any other activity resulting in the accumulation of lactic acid, a waste product of muscular activity, in body tissue. It may also occur without warning in bed at night. Abdominal cramp is common at the onset of a menstrual period (see p. 402). Pregnant women get cramp in the muscles of the calf and feet, as do many elderly people.

For immediate relief, massage the cramped muscles. If you suffer regularly from cramp at night, try sleeping with the foot of the bed raised about 6 in. A medical prescription of quinine tablets may also help.

CUTS, GRAZES, SCRATCHES
Minor injuries need only be washed clean in warm water and then covered with a plaster. If the cut, graze or scratch is dirty, add a tablespoon of antiseptic, such as Dettol, to the basin of water. If an injury is embedded with dirt, consult the doctor or take the patient to the hospital in case an antibiotic or anti-tetanus injection is needed. Extensive, superficial scratches – of the kind caused by falling into a blackberry bush, for example – need no dressing.

D

DOG BITE
Although the risk of rabies is slight in Britain, the mere possibility means that any dog bite must be considered dangerous. Get immediate medical advice.

E

ELECTRIC SHOCK
See First aid, p. 399.

EYE INJURY
See Object in the eye, and First aid, p. 399.

F

FAINTING
See First aid, p. 399.

FEVER
This is a high temperature accompanied by restlessness, sweating and chills. The average normal body temperature is 37°C (98.6°F), but many people – particularly children – have a temperature that is half a degree above or below this value. If the temperature rises to 37.8°C (100°F), the patient is said to be running a fever. If the fever reaches 38.3°C (101°F), consult the doctor. A fever is almost always a sign of infection.

FITS
See First aid, p. 399.

FOREIGN BODY
See Object in the eye (opposite), or see First aid, p. 399, (Ear Blockages or Nose).

FRACTURES
See First aid, p. 399.

H

HANGOVER
Alcohol is a poisonous substance that affects the entire body, and it takes time to recover from the unpleasant after-effects of excessive drinking. The severity of a hangover depends on a person's tolerance for drink and the amount of alcohol he has drunk. The best treatment is to drink plenty of water to relieve thirst and to take paracetamol for the headache. Do not take aspirin together with alcohol.

HAY FEVER
An allergic disorder affecting the tissues lining the nose and eyes. The symptoms are a watery discharge and sneezing, often combined with a burning or itching sensation. The hay-fever sufferer is sensitive to the pollen of plants in their flowering stage. Animal hairs and household dust may also cause hay fever.

In some cases a skin test may pinpoint the substance that is causing the allergy. A doctor can try to make the hay-fever sufferer immune to it by giving a course of injections of this substance.

The doctor prescribes drugs to control hay fever. For example, decongestant nosedrops give relief, but their action is only temporary and treatment has to be repeated. Antihistamines may help, but these drugs can cause unpleasant side-effects, such as extreme drowsiness, and so could be dangerous if taken, for instance, before driving a car.

HEAD LICE
These tiny parasites lay their eggs, the nits, on the hairs close to the scalp. The nits – greyish-white, shiny oval structures – are visible on the hairs. Head lice are passed by contact from one person to another, and are more

MINOR COMPLAINTS AND INJURIES

common among children than among adults. The bites of the lice cause head-scratching and itching of the scalp. Wash the hair in malathion shampoo and then comb out the dead nits with a fine comb.

HEADACHE
This may be the result of mistreatment of the body – too many alcoholic drinks (see Hangover), excessive exposure to the hot sun (see Sunburn), or long hours spent in a smoky, noisy atmosphere. In all cases, the headache will pass as the body recovers. All that is needed is a simple pain-relieving drug, such as paracetamol.

Migraine is a distinct illness, in which the headache is accompanied by a sensation of lights or patterns before the eyes and nausea or vomiting. Medical advice should be taken for this or other recurrent headaches.

HEAT EXHAUSTION
This follows extremely strenuous exercise carried out in a very hot environment. Extra salt taken with drinks prevents heat exhaustion.

HICCUPS
A spasmodic contraction of the diaphragm, the muscular sheet between the chest and the abdomen. The sound of a hiccup is caused by the sudden closure of the lid that shuts off the airways during swallowing. Hiccups are caused by eating too quickly or drinking too much alcohol, by disorders of the digestive and respiratory system and by nervous tension. Most hiccups go away within an hour. There are many cures for hiccups: sipping water, sucking sugar, holding the breath, or deep breathing. In the case of a prolonged and severe attack, consult your doctor.

INDIGESTION
Stomach discomfort or pain, heartburn or waterbrash (the backflow of an acid into the back of the throat) are signs of indigestion. A glass of milk or an antacid preparation, such as Milk

of Magnesia or Gelusil, may be all that is needed for relief. Some people find that they are upset by only one or two foods, which they learn to avoid.

Recurrent indigestion may be due to a stomach ulcer or other disease – consult your doctor.

INFLUENZA
An acute, infectious disease caused by a virus. The symptoms are pains in the throat and in the joints, fever, headache and sometimes a cough. In an uncomplicated case, the symptoms pass in two or three days, although the patient may feel weak for a week or more.

Anyone with influenza should stay at home and go to bed. This is the best way to recover and it reduces the danger of passing the disease to other people. Plenty of fluids should be taken, and the temperature can be lowered by taking two aspirin or paracetamol tablets every four hours. A sore throat may be relieved by gargling with two soluble aspirin dissolved in water.

There is no need to call the doctor for an attack of influenza in a healthy individual. However, anyone with chronic bronchitis, or an elderly person, should see a doctor early in the illness to forestall complications. A doctor should also be consulted if the illness causes difficulty in breathing, or the patient becomes drowsy or confused.

An injection of vaccine gives temporary immunity against a particular kind of influenza virus. A person who has received an injection takes about two weeks to develop immunity. Once influenza has begun, it is useless to have an injection.

INGROWING TOE-NAILS
The edge of the nail sometimes grows into the side of the toe, causing a painful swelling of the tissues which may become infected. Generally, ingrowing toe-nails are caused by poorly fitting shoes. The condition is less likely to occur if the toe-nail is cut square across and kept short. If the ingrowing toe-nail becomes infected, medical treatment may be the only effective cure.

INSECT BITES AND STINGS
These usually cause little more than pain and temporary discomfort in most people. The barbed bee sting can be removed using tweezers, and the injury dressed with an antihistamine cream, such as Caladryl, and a plaster. Occasionally, an allergic reaction to the sting may cause puffing of the skin of the whole body and difficulty with breathing. Urgent medical attention is needed to counteract this.

Mosquito, midge and gnat bites cause skin irritation and itching. Scratching can damage the skin further and lead to the bites becoming infected. Frequent applications of calamine lotion soothe the irritation.

MOUTH ULCERS
Isolated mouth ulcers are due to a virus infection and clear up within seven to ten days. The soreness and discomfort can be relieved by a mouth-wash or mouth pastilles. Broken or jagged teeth, or ill-fitting dentures, can cause mouth ulcers. Anyone with a recurrent condition should see the dentist.

NETTLE STINGS
Treat these with calamine lotion or antihistamine cream.

NOSE BLEEDS
Make the victim sit down with his head over a sink or bowl. Pinch the sides of the nose together, apply a cold pad to the bridge of the nose, and wait. Instruct the patient to breathe through his mouth and not to sniff. If the bleeding has not stopped within 15 minutes, take him to the hospital emergency department or to a doctor.

OBJECT IN THE EYE
Remove any tiny object, such as a speck of dirt or dust, with a wisp of cottonwool. However, do not attempt to remove anything from

the cornea, which is the transparent, domed front of the eyeball. If necessary, the eyelid can be folded back over a toothpick to get at the object. Get medical attention if a metal particle enters the eye while using a high-speed tool.

SHOCK
See First aid, p. 399.

SNAKE BITE
See First aid, p. 399.

SORE THROAT
An inflammation of the throat tissues, due to infection or to inhaling smoke or dust. The discomfort can be relieved by gargling with soluble aspirin (two tablets to a glass of water) every four hours. Swallow the gargle; do not spit it out. Glycerine, thymol, blackcurrant and other throat pastilles also give relief.

SPLINTERS
Remove splinters with a pair of eyebrow tweezers after the surrounding skin has been softened by washing in warm soapy water. A splinter can also be eased out of the skin with a needle which has been sterilised by boiling in water or by passing through a gas flame. Do not attempt to remove the splinter by squeezing the surrounding skin.

SPRAINS AND STRAINS
Any joint can be strained if it is bent further than its normal range of movement. If the strain tears the ligament around the joint, it is called a sprain. There will be bleeding beneath the skin, causing swelling and bruising. A painful swollen joint should be examined by a doctor who will know whether or not bones or ligaments have been damaged.

Remove the boots, shoes and anything else that causes tightness around the swelling. If footwear is left in place on a sprained ankle, swelling may make it difficult to remove later. Apply a cold compress – a cloth soaked in ice-cold water – to the swelling. If the sprain occurs in

open country, try to improvise a crutch. Walking on a damaged joint may damage it further.

STYE
An inflammation of the gland at the base of an eyelash. Styes frequently come in crops – one stye following another. The painful, red swelling lasts for several days, but usually disappears without special treatment. A stye clears up more quickly with hot compresses. Dip balls of cottonwool in a basin of hot water, and apply to the inflammation.

SUNBURN
This can be more easily prevented than cured. Avoid intense sunlight early in a holiday or heatwave, particularly if you have a pale skin. As little as 15 minutes' exposure to the noon sun at a Mediterranean resort at the start of a holiday can cause severe burning. Some protection is given by tablets, such as Sylvasun, containing vitamin A, and by sun-screening creams.

Sunburn has to be treated like any other burn. Some relief can be given by calamine lotion or a cold cream. Drink plenty of fluid, together with two or three aspirin or paracetamol tablets.

SUNSTROKE
See Heat exhaustion.

TOOTHACHE
Temporary relief may be given by a mild pain-killer, such as aspirin, or by placing a covered hot-water bottle on the cheek. Painting the tooth with oil of cloves may also bring relief. For permanent relief, see a dentist.

TRAVEL SICKNESS
A feeling of nausea, sometimes followed by vomiting, which is experienced by some people when travelling by car, bus, train, aircraft or boat. It is caused by an overstimulation of the organs of balance in the ear.

Anyone who suffers from travel sickness should avoid looking at things in motion – for example, the

shifting landscape seen through a car or train window. Do not read while travelling because this can bring on sickness. The lack of fresh air or unpleasant fumes in a car or train can start an attack. If possible, adjust the ventilation so that there is enough fresh air.

The effects of travel sickness disappear at the end of the journey. An attack of travel sickness can be prevented by taking tablets containing cyclizine and Ancolan.

VOMITING AND DIARRHOEA
Most cases of vomiting and diarrhoea are caused by food poisoning – the result of eating food infected with microbes or their toxins. Although the symptoms may be alarming and unpleasant, they rarely last more than 24 hours. No harm results if the fluid lost is replaced. Therefore, as soon as the vomiting ceases, a little water or fruit squash should be drunk every 30 minutes or so.

Diarrhoea rarely lasts for more than a day or two. Treatment with kaolin and morphine mixtures or Lomotil tablets relieves the symptoms. An antibiotic may be prescribed by a doctor. When going abroad, precautionary treatment with antibiotic Streptotriad tablets can prevent attacks of travellers' diarrhoea.

WARTS AND VERRUCAS
A small growth, hard but harmless, formed on and rooted in the skin, caused by a virus. They appear on the fingers, face or feet, but they may develop anywhere. A verruca is a wart which grows on the soles of the feet. Because of the pressure on the foot, the verruca grows into the deeper layers of the skin, causing pain.

Most warts disappear without treatment, but this may take years. Get a doctor's advice about getting rid of warts or verrucas. Warts on the genitals are associated with venereal disease and need specialist treatment.

DANGER SIGNALS OF DISEASE

Persistent and recurrent coughing and hoarseness, dizziness, excessive indigestion, loss of appetite, sleeplessness, and bowel-habit changes, may be symptoms of serious illness. Do not neglect these symptoms or mask them with home remedies - see a doctor.

DO NOT TRY TO TREAT YOURSELF FOR:

1. Any persistent or recurrent pain anywhere in the body.

2. Any fatigue without an obvious cause, such as failure to get enough sleep or poor diet.

3. Any persistent loss of appetite or weight.

4. Any unusual bleeding from the skin or any body opening, such as the rectum.

5. Any mild but persistent indigestion or abdominal distress after meals, particularly if it interferes with sleep or causes loss of appetite.

6. Any changes in the skin, such as a rash, an unhealed sore or unexplained change in the colour of the skin or the complexion.

7. Any unexplained swelling, especially in the abdomen, joints or legs.

8. Any lumps or growths, usually painless, on or under the skin, especially if they keep increasing in size.

9. Any unaccustomed breathlessness after exertion.

10. Any hoarseness, loss of voice, or cough that lasts more than a week or so.

11. Any loss of appetite, or difficulty in swallowing.

12. Any excessive thirst.

13. Any painful urination, or any blood in the urine.

14. Any dizziness or giddiness.

15. Any problems with vision, such as seeing double.

• FINDING A DOCTOR

When moving to a new district, you can find a doctor by consulting the list of doctors at the local National Health Service executive office. The address of this office can be found under 'National Health' in the telephone book or it may be obtained from the town hall. Lists of doctors are also available in the main post office, public library or Citizens' Advice Bureau.

The choice of doctor is limited by the number within easy access of your home. Few doctors are willing to treat patients living a long way from their surgeries because it may be difficult for them to make home visits and answer emergency calls.

In some areas, where there are few doctors, the general practitioner of your choice may have a full list of patients and so be unable to take you. Anyone who has difficulty in finding a doctor can ask the clerk of the local NHS executive office for help. The clerk will help you to find another doctor whose list is not full; he also has powers to insist that a local doctor accepts a patient.

When you go to a doctor's surgery to register, take your medical card, particularly if you wish to consult him at the same time. Different members of the family may wish to register with different doctors. This is possible but not advisable. The family is a unit. An illness in one member may affect the others, particularly in the case of infectious illness. The more the doctor knows about your family background, the better he will be able to deal with your problems.

APPOINTMENTS AND VISITS

Many practices have two or more partners. In some cases, there will be a nurse, a midwife and even a health visitor, who between them can give the patient the full range of community health care. There is a trend towards group practice in which several doctors work together from health centres.

Some practitioners operate on an appointment system, which involves telephoning for an appointment first, and others still have the traditional 'open surgery' which allows the patient to attend any day within surgery hours.

If you are telephoning to make an appointment, it is best to do so after 10 a.m., because doctors prefer to have their telephone lines clear before that time for patients asking for a home visit.

The doctor decides whether to visit a patient on the basis of the information given to him, or on his knowledge of the previous condition of the patient. But a doctor is not legally bound to make a visit, simply because it is requested.

However, if a doctor fails to visit a patient who later becomes seriously ill or dies, his conduct can be investigated by the NHS or by the General Medical Council. He can also be sued for negligence by members of the patient's family.

TALKING TO YOUR DOCTOR

Discuss health problems frankly with your doctor. To reach his diagnosis, he will want to know what your symptoms are, when they started and in what order they appeared. Make your description as brief as possible. And, when going to the surgery, wear clothing that can be removed and replaced quickly, in case the doctor needs to examine you.

Before making a diagnosis, a doctor may arrange for you to have blood tests and X-rays at the local hospital or health centre. If there is still doubt about the diagnosis, the doctor may refer you to a hospital consultant.

Take the doctor's letter to the hospital to arrange an appointment. Waiting time for an appointment with a consultant varies according to the nature and urgency of your complaint. If there is any difficulty or delay in making an appointment, go back to the doctor. If necessary, he can telephone the hospital to arrange a consultation.

If you are worried or dissatisfied about the progress of your case, you can get another opinion. Your doctor will agree to refer you to a specialist, but this second examination may be on a private basis.

SPECIAL CLINICS

If you wish to bypass your doctor because of some embarrassing complaint, such as a venereal disease, there are clinics attached to many large hospitals for which no doctor's referral is required. To find out about these special clinics, ask in the outpatients' department or the casualty department, or telephone the hospital. At the special clinic the patient's problem is treated confidentially.

Family-planning clinics and pregnancy advisory services can also be attended without a note from the doctor. However, the clinic doctor may want details of your previous health from your doctor and will want to inform him of any treatment prescribed. The consultation may be kept confidential if you wish, but in most cases it is more convenient for medical details to be exchanged.

CHANGING DOCTORS

You can change your doctor without giving any explanation, although it is normal and courteous to do so. Similarly, a doctor can remove a patient from his list without offering any reason. The procedure is simple. The patient's medical card is signed by the doctor whose list he is leaving and the card is then taken by the patient to be signed by the new doctor.

If you are too embarrassed to tell your doctor that you wish to change, send your card to the local NHS family-practitioner committee with a letter stating that you wish to change to another doctor. Make certain that you have been accepted by the new doctor before making a change.

Anybody wishing to make a complaint about a doctor, because he failed to give all the proper and necessary treatment, can go to the local NHS family-practitioner committee. If the patient decides to bring an action against a doctor, he must first show that whatever was done caused some damage. He must also establish that the doctor did not follow customary practice. Proving that a doctor or surgeon mishandled a patient's case can be extremely complicated.

GOING INTO HOSPITAL

If a patient is to go into hospital for an operation or treatment, he may first be put on a waiting list. Notification that a bed is ready may come by letter, telephone or even telegram.

The waiting time to get into hospital depends on the condition of the patient and the length of the waiting list. If a case is urgent, admission may be within a few days or a week. If the case is 'routine', the waiting time may be months. The hospital should be notified as soon as possible if for any reason the patient cannot go in.

Before going into hospital, the patient will be told what to take, whether it is possible to smoke, use an electric razor, make a telephone call, what the visiting hours are and whether children are allowed in the ward.

It is best to leave unnecessary personal property at home because there is not sufficient space to store things in the hospital. The hospital is liable for the loss or damage to property due to the negligence of the staff. But hospitals do not accept liability for items kept by the patient in the ward.

Money and valuable jewellery should be handed over to the ward sister for safe keeping. Personal possessions, such as dentures, are removed before an operation, but a wedding ring can be left on.

Any drugs that the patient brings into the hospital should be handed to the ward staff. While the patient is in hospital, his medication is controlled by the nurses. The interaction of some drugs can have serious consequences. However, regular 'maintenance' drugs, such as anti-coagulants, steroids or insulin, will be continued.

CHILDREN IN HOSPITAL

In many hospitals there is unrestricted visiting to the children's ward. A mother who is not working may be encouraged to stay with a very small child if overnight accommodation is available. A few hospitals have 'play ladies' who explain to children what goes on in hospital to help allay any fears that they may have.

HOSPITAL PROCEDURES

On admission to the hospital the patient will be examined by a house doctor. Some tests – for example, blood tests – may be done in the ward. In some cases, nothing may be done for a day or so, because some factor, such as a swelling, delays treatment.

Any major surgery or treatment for a serious illness will be explained to the patient by the consultant, or his deputy, who may also perform the operation. The patient can also ask any questions about medical procedures that are worrying him.

It is unreasonable for friends and distant relatives to expect to be given confidential details about a patient's condition. However, a parent, wife or husband, son or daughter can ask the doctor for information.

In teaching hospitals, the patient may be examined by students. If the patient has strong objections to this, he or she can refuse.

Before an operation or test requiring a general anaesthetic the patient must fill in a form. In the case of a child, parents must give their written consent to an operation or test. In the case of an emergency, where parents cannot be reached, the age of consent is 16. However, if someone is under that age and there is a delay in contacting the parents, or the patient is an unconscious, unaccompanied adult, the surgeon may proceed without waiting for an authorisation.

Before an operation, a nurse will prepare the patient, who will be issued with some form of identification – for example, a bracelet – giving his name and the type and site of the operation. The patient will not be given anything to eat for some hours before an operation. This is to avoid the possibility of being sick while under the anaesthetic. The patient will be given a sedative before going to the operation, and a general anaesthetic before surgery.

After an operation, a patient is encouraged to get up and move around to stimulate the circulation and prevent thrombosis, or blood clot. As soon as possible, the patient will be discharged from the hospital if there is someone to look after him at home. For example, after an uncomplicated operation, such as removal of the appendix, the patient may leave hospital within four or five days.

When entering or leaving hospital, it is advisable to be accompanied by a

relative or friend. Relatives may be asked to take clothes home when you are admitted and to bring them back when you leave.

MAKING A COMPLAINT

Any complaint about hospital treatment should first be talked over with the ward sister or the consultant. If no satisfaction is obtained, write to the hospital secretary or the administrative officer of the district health board. The local Member of Parliament can arrange for a complaint to be investigated by the Health Service Commissioner. Advice on problems of this kind can also be obtained from the Patients Association.

Dissatisfied patients can discharge themselves from hospital, even against medical advice. Before leaving, the patient is asked to sign a form which protects the hospital against the charge of negligence, which might arise at a later date, if the patient becomes seriously ill. The hospital cannot refuse to re-admit a patient who has discharged himself, but he would have to wait for a bed.

TREATING MENTAL ILLNESS

Going into hospital for the treatment of mental illness is on an informal voluntary basis, unless the patient is a danger to himself and others. Once the acute stage of the illness is over, the patient may spend his time in group activities or occupational therapy.

The use of drugs has meant that the mentally ill person does not have to be treated as an in-patient. In some areas there are special day hospitals where the mentally ill can go during the day, returning home in the evening or at weekends.

• FINDING A DENTIST

Dentists do not have lists of patients in

the same way as doctors. They take on patients for a course of treatment but neither the dentist nor the patient is under any legal obligation concerning future treatment. In practice, though, most dentists operate exactly as if they had lists of patients.

A dentist is allowed to choose whether or not he will carry out work under the NHS terms or as a private practitioner, but he must tell the patient what he proposes at the first visit. If a patient wishes to be treated under the National Health Service, he should sign a NHS treatment form provided by the dentist.

The choice of dentists is not limited to the patient's residential area, as it is with doctors. Some people find that it may be more convenient to attend a dentist near their place of work. To find a NHS dentist, make inquiries at the local post office.

There is usually an interval of at least six months between the end of one course of NHS treatment and the start of the next. NHS patients are required to pay half the cost of dental treatment and appliances – for example, false teeth – up to a maximum of £10 for each course. However, there are exemptions on the grounds of age, pregnancy or low income.

Some dentists may not be prepared to give cosmetic treatment, such as capping teeth, under the NHS. If a patient wants more expensive treatment than is provided for under the NHS, such as gold fillings, or more expensive false teeth, he may be allowed to have it by paying the excess above the NHS allowance.

Complaints about dental treatment should be made to the local executive council, as in the case of medical treatment. Complaints about the conduct of a dentist may also be taken to the General Dental Council, the dentists' professional organisation.

COLLECTING DRUG JARS

Drug jars have been used for centuries by apothecaries and chemists to store their stock-in-trade, from leeches to ointments and liquid medicines. The jars, made in many shapes and sizes and often colourfully decorated, have become collectors' items.

There are many varieties – tall albarellos from Italy, used to hold liquids, fat elixir containers and daintily waisted syrup jars. Two basic types evolved in the 16th century – straight-sided earthenware jars for ointments, and narrow-necked phials for liquids. Leech jars have perforated lids to admit air into them.

The first English jars, which date from the early 17th century, were made of white tin-glazed earthenware. They were often decorated with birds. By the middle of the 18th century, jars were being made of cream-coloured earthenware and decorated with angels' heads and wings. Towards the end of the century decoration became more ornate – cherubs, birds, shells and sprays of leaves or flowers spread over the jars.

Labels on jars often name fantastic concoctions that were held to have equally fantastic curative properties. Well into the 19th century apothecaries still stocked preparations such as *O. Vulpin*, or oil of foxes, made by boiling a fox's carcase in herbs and wine.

The 19th century saw glass take over as the principal material for drug jars. By 1830 most pharmacies stocked blue syrup bottles, ribbed green poison bottles, and round bottles in varying colours. Carboys – the pear-shaped glass vessels used to store coloured medicines – became the very symbol of pharmacy itself.

Drug jars are sold in antique shops, and a few can still be seen in old-fashioned pharmacies. There is a comprehensive collection at the Wellcome Institute of the History of Medicine in London.

• FURNISHING THE SICK ROOM

If possible, position a comfortable bed where the patient has a view out of the window. There should be enough room on both sides for the nurse to move round the bed easily.

Place a table or locker by the bed for personal possessions, medicines, a jug of drinking water or fruit juice and a glass. Leave a handbell on the top that the patient can ring for attention. Nursing equipment can be arranged on the top of a dressing-table or chest of drawers, or kept in the drawers. There should also be comfortable chairs for visitors and for the patient when he is allowed to get up.

Keep the sick-room temperature at 16-19°C (61-66°F). Central heating, gas and electric fires take moisture from the air, and this may be harmful for a patient with a chest infection. If the room is too dry, boil water in an electric kettle to give off steam.

Depending on the weather, a window can be left open to provide fresh air. A screen placed across the window will divert draughts.

MAKING THE BED COMFORTABLE

Equipment to make the bedridden patient more comfortable may be obtained through the social services department of the local authority.

Backrests can be used to keep the patient upright. Alternatively, additional pillows arranged like an armchair can be effective.

A bedcradle can be used to lift the weight of the top sheet and the blankets from injured legs or feet. A bedcradle can be improvised from a stool.

A patient who is immobile for a long time may suffer from bedsores. These occur at the toes, heels, knees, elbows and shoulders, which rub against the bedclothing and the pyjamas. If neglected, these areas break into open sores.

The best method of avoiding bedsores is to change the patient's position every two hours. Moisture, such as excessive sweat, causes soreness. Therefore, the skin should be kept clean and dry. Apply talcum powder or dab the tender spots with surgical spirit.

Foam pads can be used to relieve pressure on heels, elbows and the back of the head. Place an inflated air ring, enclosed in a pillowcase, under the buttocks to provide comfort.

WASHING THE PATIENT

Give a bedridden patient a blanket bath every day, if possible. You need warm water, soap, flannel, towels and talcum powder. After removing the patient's pyjamas, place a bath towel or thin blanket underneath him. Cover him with a bath towel.

Begin by washing round the face. When washing the rest of the body, uncover each part of the patient in turn, and cover it when washed, rinsed, dried and powdered (see illustrations). Let the patient wash himself where he can.

After washing, let the patient brush his teeth and gargle. Clean his nails and cut when necessary. Then help him put on his pyjamas and remake the bed.

CHANGING THE BOTTOM SHEET

If the patient is too ill to get up, the bottom bedsheet can be changed while he is still in bed by making the bed a half at a time length-ways.

Remove the blankets first and then the top sheet. Cross the patient's arms and legs before turning him on his side to start changing the bottom sheet (see illustrations).

LIFTING THE PATIENT

A bedridden patient may develop complications other than sores due to inactivity. As soon as possible, get the patient sitting up in bed or in a chair. If he is weak he may have to be lifted.

Never try to lift a patient on your own. Get someone to help you. You and your helper should stand on either side of him, with your backs straight, your knees slightly bent and your feet apart. Your thighs, rather than your back, should take the weight of the patient. Grasp wrists under his thighs and join hands round his back. The patient sits in the well formed by the two pairs of arms. Let him rest his arms round you.

If the patient is being moved higher up the bed, he should put his hands on his knees, and bow his head. Lift him in one movement.

DEALING WITH INCONTINENCE

A rubber drawsheet can be used for an incontinent patient. Some local authorities collect, launder and return linen. Special incontinence pads are also available on prescription.

A bedpan or urinal must be made available for a bedridden patient. A commode – a movable toilet – can be obtained through the local authority social services department.

WASHING A PATIENT

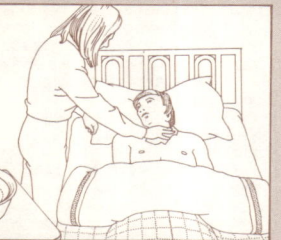

1. Fold back the blanket and towel to wash and dry the chest and abdomen.

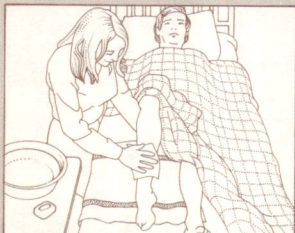

2. Cover the patient to the chin, before washing and drying each leg and foot.

3. Turn the patient on to his side to wash and dry his back.

CHANGING A BOTTOM SHEET

1. Turn the patient on his side and roll the old bedding up against his back.

2. Tuck in the clean sheet and roll the patient on to it. Remove old bedding.

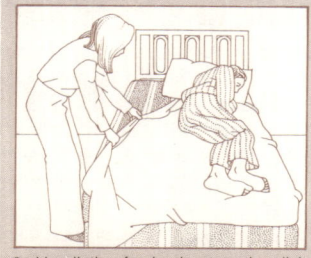

3. Unroll the fresh sheet and pull it tightly so that there are no creases.

LIFTING A PATIENT

1. Help the patient to swing his legs over the side of the bed.

2. To lift the patient, support his back and clasp wrists under his knees.

3. Lift and carry the patient to a chair and place him gently on to it.

ACCIDENTS IN THE HOME: SAFETY CHECK-LIST

WHERE ACCIDENTS CAN HAPPEN

Every day about 20 people die in Britain as a result of home accidents. In a year there are more fatal accidents in British homes than on the country's roads. More than 1½ million people have to be treated in hospital for serious domestic injuries.

The largest group involved in home accidents are women between the ages of 15 and 64. However, children, particularly those under the age of five, and elderly people are more likely to suffer fatal accidents.

The most frequent types of home accidents are falls, cuts, bruises, poisonings, and burns and scalds. Such accidents are less likely to occur if the following precautions are taken.

GENERAL

1 Awkwardly placed fittings, such as cupboards, can cause cuts and bruises. If possible move them; if not, pad or guard dangerous edges and corners.

2 Throw out plastic bags after use or keep them out of reach of children. A child may pull a plastic bag over his head and suffocate.

3 Sloppy slippers, run-down shoes and trailing dressing-gown hems can cause falls. Repair faulty footwear and clothing.

4 Make sure clothing, particularly children's, is non-flammable. Untreated fabrics can flare and envelop a child in flames.

ENTRANCE

1 Keep the entrance well lit. Keep the entrance stairs in good repair.

2 Recess the doormat into the floor: it cannot slide or be tripped over.

3 Make sure that a faulty front-door latch will not allow a toddler to run out into the road.

KITCHEN

1 Have a non-slip surface on the floor.

2 Keep shelving low, where possible.

3 Keep a strong step-ladder to reach high shelves.

4 Wipe up grease spills on the floor immediately.

5 Fit a gate to keep toddlers from wandering into the working area.

6 Keep knives out of the reach of children.

7 Do not try to prise off open can lids with the fingers.

8 Store cleaning materials, disinfectants, bleaches, paraffin and the like out of the reach of children.

9 Use electrical kitchen equipment with care. Electric slicers, grinders, mincers, stewpans and toasters can cause burns and electric shocks.

10 If possible, cook on the back burners. Turn kettle spouts and steam vents away from the front of the cooker.

11 Do not let the handles of saucepans and frying pans project over the edge of a cooker or a kitchen table.

12 If possible, buy a cooker fitted with a safety guard for saucepans.

13 Keep all vessels containing hot liquids – for example, teapots – off tablecloths that a child might be able to reach and pull.

14 Never use a thin or wet oven-cloth.

15 Never leave chip pans unattended.

LIVING-ROOM

1 Fit a fire-guard over a fireplace or a wall-mounted heater.

2 When cleaning a fireplace, use gloves and keep children clear.

3 Use self-closing or deep ashtrays.

4 Repair worn carpets and rugs.

5 Fix rugs to the floor.

6 Use non-slip polish on wooden floors.

7 Keep flexes from lamps and other appliances as short as possible. Long, trailing flexes can cause people to trip and fall.

8 Never run flexes under the carpet.

9 At night, always switch off and unplug the television set and other appliances.

HALL, STAIRS AND LANDINGS

1 Have good lighting to dispel gloom, glare and shadows.

2 Make sure that the stair carpet is in good repair, and firmly fixed.

3 Make sure the banisters are secure.

4 Fit gates at the top and bottom of the stairs to stop toddlers falling.

5 Check from time to time that there are no toys or other objects lying on the stairs.

6 Remove loose mats by the stairs or on landings.

BEDROOM AND NURSERY

1 Before going to bed, disconnect an electric under-blanket.

2 Never take medicine in the dark.

3 Do not smoke in bed.

4 Guard bedroom heaters properly.

5 Never put a heater close to airing clothes or beneath curtains.

6 Never share a bed with a baby.

7 Never put a soft pillow on a baby's cot.

8 In a child's room, guard the windows with vertical bars.

9 Never let a cat or dog sleep in a baby's cot or pram.

10 Never give a child toys which have sharp edges or are inflammable.

11 Make sure the paint used on cots and toys is lead-free.

BATHROOM

1 Do not have a power point in the bathroom.

2 Never bring portable electrical appliances into the bathroom.

3 Have a properly insulated shaver point for electric shavers.

4 When filling a bath, always put in the cold water first, to prevent scalding. Test the water in a bath or a shower before stepping into it.

5 Help an infant or elderly person into the bath.

6 Never leave children alone in the bath.

7 Put a mat with a non-slip backing on the bathroom floor.

8 Keep all medicines labelled and out of reach of children.

GARAGES AND WORKSHOPS

1 Do not smoke where inflammable liquids are stored.

2 Keep pesticides or weedkillers and any other poisonous substances locked up. Pour any left-over poison solutions down the drain. Store nothing poisonous or corrosive in old drink bottles.

3 Do not leave a car engine running in garage. Exhaust fumes can be fatal.

GARDEN

1 Keep the garden path in good condition, with no loose or uneven stones on which people may trip.

2 Do not leave tools, such as rakes, lying about the garden.

3 Enclose or cover a pond. A child could drown in an unguarded pool.

4 Do not let a child use a lawn mower, or play near a mower in use.

5 Check that there are no plants with poisonous berries or seeds that children might be tempted to eat. Poisonous berries include those of yew, woody and black nightshade, mistletoe, holly and privet. Laburnum and lupin seeds are dangerous.

6 Control the size of a bonfire and never light it with petrol or paraffin. When lighting fireworks, follow the instructions exactly. Never leave children to light bonfires or fireworks on their own.

FIRE

Keep a fire extinguisher in a handy place such as the hall or kitchen.

Always keep a fire-smothering cloth, woven from non-flammable glass-fibre, near the cooker, ready for any emergency.

SMALL FIRES

1 Use water at once on all fires – including paraffin heaters – except those fires which involve fats, cooking oils and electricity.

2 If fat catches fire in a cooking pan, smother with a cloth – preferably damp – a plate, earth or sand.

3 If electricity is involved, first switch off at the mains or unplug the appliance, then use water or a fire extinguisher. *Exception* Do not use water or an extinguisher on a television set. After switching off the electricity at the mains, smother the fire with a rug or blanket.

CHIMNEYS

1 Call the fire brigade immediately. Do not attempt to tackle the fire yourself.

2 Remove furniture, rugs and carpets from around the fireplace.

3 Close doors and windows to starve the fire of air.

MAJOR FIRES

1 Get everyone out of the house. Close all doors and windows to isolate the fire.

2 Outside, check to make sure that everyone is out. Telephone 999 for the fire brigade.

3 Do not go back in the house for pets or valuables.

4 If trapped, try to reach a room facing the street if possible. Stay near the floor. Block gaps round the door. Open the window at the top to let out smoke, at the bottom to breathe and call for help.

5 Do not jump except as a last resort.

6 Do not try to get through smoke-filled halls or stairways.

• EMERGENCY CARE

Call a doctor, or telephone for an ambulance by dialling 999, as quickly as possible after an accident or a sudden illness. Give your name, and say what has happened. Give the address or location clearly and precisely.

While waiting for help, confine first aid to what is needed to preserve the patient's life, prevent his condition from becoming worse and lessen his pain. If you are alone, confused, and upset yourself, simply call for help.

If you are able to help, stop the cause of injury, such as escaping gas. A seriously injured person should not be moved unless the cause cannot be stopped.

If the victim is conscious and able to move about without causing further injury to himself, take him to the doctor or the hospital casualty department or accident unit. If the victim is unconscious with no obvious cause, search for identification which may give instructions for emergency care. Check that he is breathing. If you put your ear close to his nose or mouth, you should be able to hear the air passing in and out of his throat.

If the victim is not breathing, lay him on his back and check that the tongue is not blocking the throat. Once the patient starts breathing, place him in the recovery position (see lower drawing, right).

• GIVING THE KISS OF LIFE

If the patient is still not breathing, try artificial respiration. The mouth-to-mouth method of forcing air into the victim's lungs – known as the 'kiss of life' – is the easiest.

• STARTING THE HEART

If the victim's condition still does not improve quickly with artificial respiration, his heart may have ceased beating. In such a case, try to start the heart beating by giving the breast bone, in the centre of the chest, a single firm blow with a clenched fist.

If the victim of a heart attack is still breathing, he should be made to rest with head and shoulders propped up. Loosen any tight clothing.

• CONTROLLING BLEEDING

Any severe bleeding must be stopped immediately. However, if the patient is not breathing, artificial respiration is the priority. Give the kiss of life. Then attend to the bleeding.

Lay the victim flat. Find out where the bleeding is coming from. Remove or cut away clothing only if necessary. Bleeding can be stopped by pushing the sides of a large wound together or by pressing on it a pad of the cleanest material available.

Do not apply pressure if there is a suspected fracture or foreign bodies are embedded in the wound. If the pad becomes saturated with blood, put another on top. A firm bandage can be used to secure the pad, but never use a tourniquet unless you have first-aid training.

If the injury is to an arm or leg, and provided it is not fractured, raise it to reduce the flow of blood.

If pressure cannot be applied to the area around the wound or is ineffective, indirect pressure can be applied at one of the major 'pressure points' – just below the armpit for the arm, and below the groin for the leg.

Scalp wounds may bleed profusely. If a skull fracture is suspected, do not apply any pressure. Put on a large dressing and bandage it in position.

Once the bleeding has been brought under control, treat for shock (see panel on p. 399). If you suspect internal bleeding, keep the patient lying down and loosen tight clothing. Do not give the victim food or drink.

HOW TO GIVE THE KISS OF LIFE

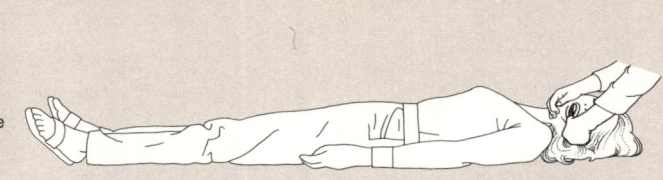

If the victim is unconscious and is not breathing, make sure that the tongue has not fallen back in the throat. Tilt the head to one side to prevent a blockage. Remove any obstruction, such as false teeth, blood, or vomit, from the mouth, using a handkerchief if necessary. Place the victim in the recovery position (see bottom drawing).

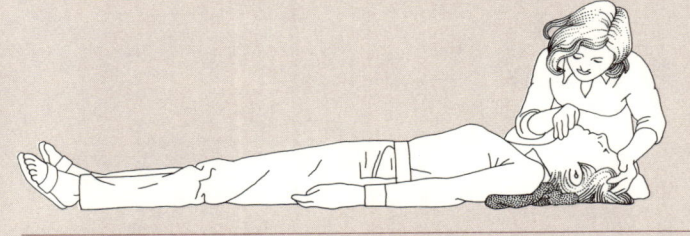

If the victim does not breathe immediately after tilting the head or removing an obstruction, then give the kiss of life. Place a folded coat under the victim's shoulders, if possible. Press the forehead down with one hand and lift the chin up with the other.

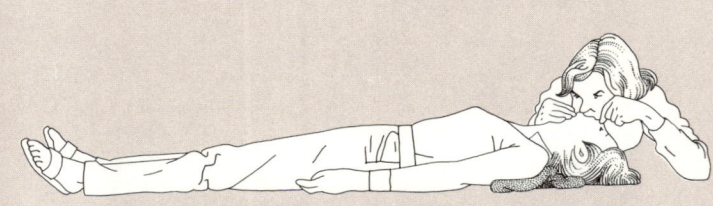

Support the victim's neck and pinch the nostrils together. Open your mouth wide and seal your lips around the victim's mouth. Blow gently into the lungs until the chest rises. Remove your mouth and watch the chest fall. With a small child, cover the nose and mouth with your mouth. If the victim's lips are stained with poison, blow through the victim's nose.

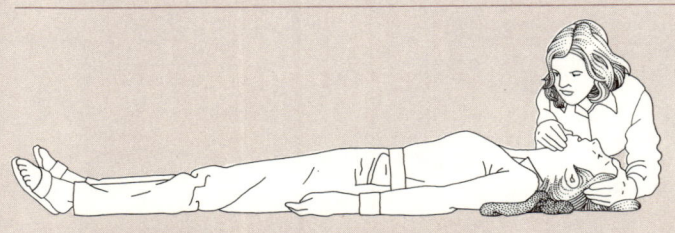

Repeat this procedure six times as quickly as possible. Then continue at the rate of between 10 and 15 blows per minute. In the case of a child, give 20 blows per minute.

RECOVERY POSITION
If the victim is unconscious and breathing, use the recovery position – one arm and leg drawn up as shown, and the head tilted to the side to keep the mouth and nose clear.

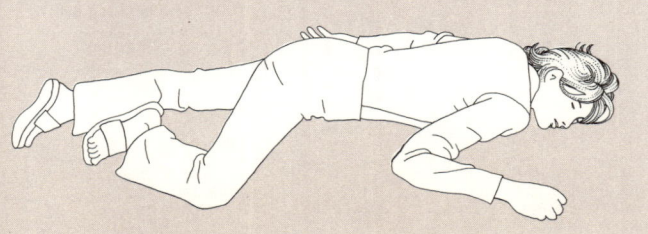

FIRST AID

ASPHYXIA
see Suffocation.

BURNS AND SCALDS
For minor burns on the limbs, hold the injury under cold running water for five minutes. Pain is quickly relieved and damage to the skin is kept to a minimum. A small burn needs no further treatment. It should be exposed to the air, but if this is inconvenient, then a dry gauze dressing may be applied. Do not apply any oil, grease, butter or ointment to the burn, and do not prick or remove blisters.

Large burns, covering more than about 3 in. square, or deep burns, need medical attention. If possible, relieve pain by immersing the area in cold water or applying cold wet cloths. Wrap or cover the injury with a clean cloth and lightly bandage. Treat the victim for shock while waiting for medical help. If the victim can be moved, it may be best to take him to the hospital.

Chemical burns These are usually caused by a strong acid, such as nitric or sulphuric, or by an alkali, such as caustic soda, and can cause serious damage, particularly to the eye. See Eye injuries.

If large areas of the body have been burned by a chemical, put the victim under cold running water – a shower, if possible – or pour cold water over him.

Fire burns If the victim's clothing is on fire, smother the flames in a rug, blanket or other heavy material. Afterwards, lay him flat. Remove any smouldering clothing if it is not adhering to the skin. Otherwise, dampen the smouldering cloth with cold water but do not press the wet cloth against the patient's skin. If possible, remove any jewellery, watch, socks or shoes near the burned area before the tissues have time to swell.

Cover the burns with a clean cloth which can be held in position with a light bandage.

While waiting for medical help to arrive, treat for shock by keeping the patient quiet and covering him lightly with a blanket.
Powder burns These are caused by careless handling of fireworks, cap pistols or firearms. The skin may be broken and exposed to infection. Therefore, remove any splinters and dirt from the wound. Wash it with soap and water, and apply a dry sterile dressing. Treat for shock until medical help arrives.
Scalds Remove any very hot clothing from the skin immediately, and pour plenty of cold water over the burned area. If the scald is caused by hot tar, do not remove clothing because in trying to do this you may also remove surface skin and aggravate the injuries.

CHOKING
The victim will probably cough violently, because food or some foreign body is caught in the windpipe. If the coughing does not clear the blockage, get the victim to bend over and give a hard slap between the shoulder blades. If this does not dislodge the object, put the victim face down on a table or chair, with his head and chest hanging downwards, and give him another hard slap. In the case of a child, hold him upside-down and slap him on the back. If this is not successful, get medical help at once.

CONVULSIONS OR FITS
Anyone who falls to the ground with violent movements of the arms and legs may be having an epileptic fit. Move furniture out of the way to reduce the risk of further injury. If you get the opportunity, slip a knotted handkerchief between his teeth to stop him biting his tongue. Otherwise, do not attempt to force anything between the victim's teeth. On regaining consciousness, the epileptic may be dazed and should be prevented from wandering off in this state. If the attack recurs, · call a doctor immediately.

DISLOCATION
When a joint is dislocated, the victim is unable to move it in the usual way. There may be a swelling and a numbness beyond the point where the dislocation is. Do not attempt to replace the bone in its proper place. Keep the part as still as possible. Get medical help.

DROWNING
Make sure the airway is clear, by removing any obstruction. Give artificial respiration, with the kiss of life, immediately the victim has been rescued, and continue until breathing is restored or medical help arrives.

DRUG ABUSE
see Poisoning.

EAR BLOCKAGES
If a foreign body is lodged in the ear, and cannot be very easily removed, leave it alone and get medical aid.

ELECTRIC SHOCK
If the victim is still in contact with electrical equipment, he should not be touched until the electric current has been switched off. It may be necessary to try to drag the appliance away from the victim by pulling the insulating wire leading to it. If this is not possible, separate the victim from the electrical source, using a non-conductor, such as a dry wooden stick.

If his heart does not seem to be beating, give the breast bone in the centre of the chest a sharp thump. If the victim is not breathing, start artificial respiration at once, with the kiss of life, and continue until medical help arrives.

If the victim is breathing but unconscious, place him in the recovery position. Treat for burns and shock.

EXPOSURE
A healthy person who is out in the open for a long period during extremely cold weather may suffer from exposure. If the victim is conscious, remove any wet clothing and dry him. Give him fresh clothing, and wrap him in blankets. Give him a hot drink. Call a doctor or an ambulance.

EYE INJURIES
If rapid blinking fails to dislodge an object in the eye, lift the lid of the affected eye by the lashes and try to remove the object with the corner of a clean handkerchief. If the object is embedded in the eyeball or cannot be seen, cover the eye with a gauze pad, held lightly in place with a plaster, and arrange immediate transport to the hospital.
Acid or other corrosive fluid in the eye This should be washed out immediately. Bathe the eye copiously with cold water keeping it under running water, if possible, for 10-15 minutes to ensure that all the acid is washed out. Get medical help as soon as possible.

FAINTING
This is caused by a sudden reduction in the blood-flow to the head, which may be the result of a slowing down in the heartbeat from a shock, anxiety or hormonal changes in early pregnancy. If someone feels faint, get him to lie down with his feet raised above head level. Alternatively, sit the victim in a chair with his head between his knees. If someone has already fainted, loosen any tight clothing around the neck, chest and waist. If indoors, open the windows.

FRACTURES
The signs of a bone fracture are pain, tenderness at even a gentle touch, swelling and bruising, or loss of control or deformity of the affected limb. A broken bone needs treatment by a doctor. While waiting for medical help, keep the victim still, stop bleeding and treat for shock. Do not attempt to move the victim, unless absolutely necessary, and do not try to straighten the bone. Do not loosen any of the victim's clothing, except around the neck.

NOSE
Do not try to dislodge any object in the nose, if it cannot be easily removed. Any attempt to remove it may make it go backwards down the windpipe and cause more trouble. Tell the victim to breath through his mouth. Take him to the doctor.
Nose bleeds see Minor complaints, p. 392.

OBJECTS IN THE EYE
see Minor complaints, p. 392.

POISONING
If someone has taken an overdose of a drug, swallowed some harmful substance or absorbed chemicals – pesticides, for example – through the skin, telephone the doctor even if no ill-effects have appeared.

If the victim is not breathing, give him the kiss of life. Use the mouth-to-nose method if you think there is still poison in his mouth.

The lips and mouth will be burned or stained if the victim has swallowed an acid or alkaline substance. Do not give him an emetic – a medicine to make the victim vomit.

If the victim is unconscious but breathing, place him on his side, with the uppermost arm and leg drawn up and his head tilted back to keep the airway open. Note any bottles, tablets, berries, or the smell of petrol, paraffin or cleaning fluid. If the victim is slipping into unconsciousness, try to find out what poison has been swallowed. Tell the doctor because this information makes diagnosis quicker.

POISONOUS PLANTS
Children sometimes eat the poisonous berries of deadly or woody nightshade, or laburnum seeds. In such a case, take the child to the hospital immediately. Do not waste time giving an emetic or any other treatment.

SHOCK
After even a minor accident, the victim may experience shock – a condition in which the blood pressure is low and the heartbeat weak. The effect of shock can be lessened by stopping bleeding, by trying to ease any discomfort and by talking reassuringly to the victim. Keep the victim quiet and warm by covering him lightly with a blanket. Where possible, have the victim lying down with the head low and the legs raised a little. In the case of a heart, chest or abdominal injury, the victim's shoulders should be raised slightly and supported. Turn his head to one side.

SNAKE-BITE
In Britain the adder, or viper, is the only poisonous snake. Adder bites are serious only for the very young, the very old or sick people. In most cases fright causes more symptoms than the bite. Wash the wound with soap and water, and apply a dry dressing to it. Do not give the victim anything to eat or drink. Reassure him, while arranging medical help.

SUFFOCATION
This may be due to poisonous gas, or something may be smothering the victim.

Find the cause of suffocation and remove it. Turn off escaping gas. Or, if the victim has been overcome by car-exhaust fumes, turn off the engine. Open the windows or take the victim out into the open.

In the case of smothering, remove the obstruction from the victim's nose and mouth. In all cases, give artificial respiration if the breathing has stopped, using the kiss of life (see opposite).

SWALLOWED OBJECTS
For pills, drug overdoses and poisons, see Poisoning.

Children sometimes swallow buttons, coins and other small objects, which pass through the body easily. If you think that a sharp object has been swallowed, take the child to hospital without delay.

• BETTER ADULT HEALTH

Doctors are aware that the major killing diseases, such as lung cancer and heart disease, are more likely to occur among those who smoke and eat and drink too much, and who take too little exercise.

SMOKING

There is growing evidence that smokers run a high risk of developing cancer of the lung, chronic bronchitis, heart disease, as well as cancer of the mouth, throat, gullet and bladder. For cigarette smokers the risks are particularly grave. In Britain, it is estimated that more than 20,000 deaths a year in men between 35 and 64 are due to cigarette smoking.

If a woman smokes during pregnancy, the health of her unborn child may suffer. And the risk of a miscarriage or stillbirth is greater among women who smoke.

Drugs, psychotherapy and hypnotism may be useful methods of giving up smoking. But the best way is to make a complete break. Stop smoking when you are relaxed and not under stress. If this is not possible, give up cigarettes gradually during weekends or on holidays, and then cut down during the working week. Some smokers find that joining an anti-smoking group helps them. Those who cannot give up cigarettes should buy lower tar brands or switch to cigars or a pipe.

Among those who give up smoking, there is a drop in the death rates. After ten years of abstinence, the risk of developing a disease, such as lung cancer, is the same for the ex-smoker as for the non-smoker.

ALCOHOLISM

Used in moderation, alcohol can serve as a relaxant and an appetite stimulant.

But excessive indulgence in alcohol can produce chronic alcoholism. Doctors make a distinction between this condition and intoxication, or ordinary drunkenness.

Chronic alcoholism is a disease which is related to an underlying personality disorder. The alcoholic has a compulsive need for drink, which he uses either as a sedative or as a prop against personal, social or financial worries. The condition can lead to serious physical disorders, such as stomach ulcers and liver disease, and possibly death. The behaviour of the alcoholic has a shattering effect on his relationships with his family, friends and associates.

In Britain there are about 400,000 chronic alcoholics. The percentage of female and teenage alcoholics is also growing. Alcoholism can be treated under the NHS or by one of the voluntary agencies, such as Alcoholics Anonymous.

TRANQUILLISERS

Many people who suffer from serious depression or anxiety may be prescribed tranquillisers or sleeping pills to get over their unhappy mental state. These drugs can be dangerous when mixed with alcohol or when taken to excess. And many people tend to become dependent on them. It may be better if the patient and his or her doctor try to find the cause of the worry and attempt to remove it, rather than continue taking these kinds of drugs.

WEIGHT PROBLEMS

Obesity or being overweight is the second most common physical disorder after tooth decay in the Western world. It occurs when the body takes in more energy calories – in food and drink units – than it uses. Only 100 calories above the normal requirement every day – for example, the amount in a medium-sized boiled potato or a very large apple – can increase weight by 4 kg. (10 lb.) a year.

Obesity puts a strain on all parts of the body and can cause disorders such as diabetes and arthritis. It reduces the capacity for physical effort. As a result, anyone who has become overweight tends to take less exercise. Unless the intake of calories is cut down to match the lower physical activity, more weight will be gained.

Anyone who is 10% over his ideal weight (see chart, opposite page) should consider slimming. A dietician or a general practitioner can help an obese person to find a suitable diet.

THE EFFECTS OF EXERCISE

Apart from controlling weight, taking exercise is health-giving. It improves the appearance by toning up flabby muscles, and gives a sense of fitness. It also provides protection against heart disease and stroke.

The best form of exercise is the kind that you enjoy and can go on taking regularly for years. This may be solitary swimming. But most people enjoy company and a sense of competition, in which case games like badminton, golf, tennis and squash may be preferred to solitary pursuits.

Effective exercise will make you slightly breathless and sweaty. It will also raise the pulse rate from its normal rate of 80 beats a minute to 120 beats a minute. For a person under 30, this is not risky. But for those over this age, it is unwise to plunge suddenly into strenuous exercise. If there is any doubt about exercising, see your doctor. The chart (right) gives a daily exercise routine that will not tax your strength, but will tone up your muscles and prepare you for more demanding exercises.

EXERCISING FOR FITNESS

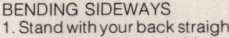

The following exercises, to be carried out daily, will strengthen muscles and keep the body toned up. At first, do each exercise only a few times, increasing gradually.

ARM CIRCLING
1. Stand with your back straight, your feet slightly apart, and your hands at your sides.

2. Make large circles by swinging your left arm forward and up. Swing your arm forward 5 to 10 times. Repeat the exercise with the right arm.

3. Repeat the exercise, but swing your arms backwards. Do 5 to 10 circles with each arm.

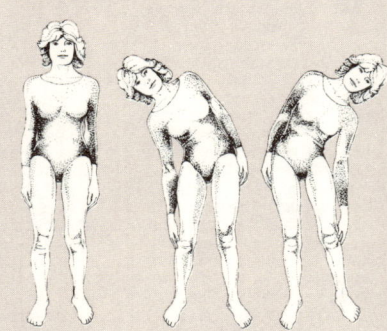

BENDING SIDEWAYS
1. Stand with your back straight and your hands at your sides.

2. Keeping your back straight, bend sideways from the waist, sliding your hand on one side down as far as you can go.

3. Repeat the sideways movement on the other side. Bend 5 to 10 times on each side.

KNEE RAISING
1. Stand with your back straight, your feet together and hands at your sides.

2. Raise your right knee as high as possible. Repeat with the left leg. Raise each leg 5 to 10 times.

3. Try the same exercise with your hands on your hips.

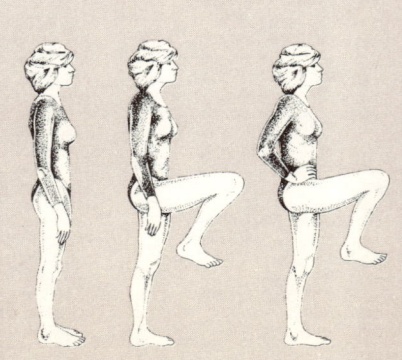

EXERCISING FOR FITNESS

LEG RAISING SIDEWAYS

1. Lie on your side with your legs straight. Stretch your lower arm under your head along the floor.

2. Raise your leg about 18 in. and lower it slowly. Repeat the exercise about 5 to 10 times. Then roll to the other side and repeat the exercise with the other leg.

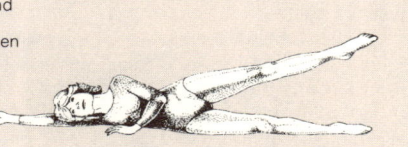

HEAD AND SHOULDER RAISING

1. Lie on your back, with your arms at your sides, your legs straight and your toes pointed.

2. Raise your head and shoulders off the floor and lower them again. Repeat the exercise 6 to 12 times.

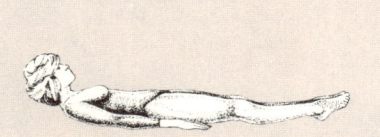

LEG LIFT

1. Lie on your back, with your legs straight and together, arms at your sides. Press the palms of your hands against the floor.

2. Raise your left leg until it is upright and lower it slowly. Do this 4 to 8 times. Repeat this exercise with the right leg.

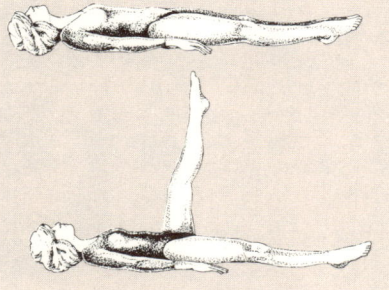

PARTIAL PUSH-UPS

1. Lie face down with your legs straight and your toes pointed. Put your hands under your shoulders.

2. Push your body off the floor but not your knees or shins. Lower the body to the floor. Repeat this exercise 5 to 10 times.

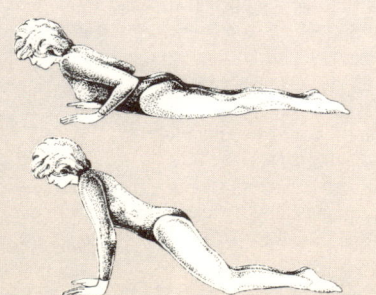

IDEAL WEIGHT

The ideal weight of a person – the weight that medical records show is associated with good health – depends as much on build as on height. Ideal weights can vary by well over 6.2 kg. (14 lb.) between a man of light build and a man of large bone structure whose heights are identical. The weight will also vary according to age. A 25-year-old person should be within 1.4-1.8 kg.(3-4 lb.) of the figure shown in this chart, but the weight then rises by about 1 lb. each year up to the age of 45. Weights and heights given exclude clothing and shoes.

	HEIGHT		SMALL BUILD		MEDIUM BUILD		LARGE BUILD	
WOMEN Add 2 kg. (4½ lb.) to weight for clothes	1.42 m.	(4 ft 8 in.)	43.1 kg.	(6 st. 11 lb.)	46.3 kg.	(7 st. 4 lb.)	50.8 kg.	(8 st. 0 lb.)
	1.44 m.	(4 ft 9 in.)	44.5 kg.	(7 st. 0 lb.)	47.2 kg.	(7 st. 6 lb.)	51.7 kg.	(8 st. 2 lb.)
	1.47 m.	(4 ft 10 in.)	45.4 kg.	(7 st. 2 lb.)	48.5 kg.	(7 st. 9 lb.)	53.1 kg.	(8 st. 5 lb.)
	1.49 m.	(4 ft 11 in.)	46.7 kg.	(7 st. 5 lb.)	49.9 kg.	(7 st. 12 lb.)	54.4 kg.	(8 st. 8 lb.)
	1.51 m.	(5 ft 0 in.)	48.1 kg.	(7 st. 8 lb.)	51.3 kg.	(8 st. 1 lb.)	55.8 kg.	(8 st. 11 lb.)
	1.54 m.	(5 ft 1 in.)	49.4 kg.	(7 st. 11 lb.)	52.6 kg.	(8 st. 4 lb.)	57.2 kg.	(9 st. 0 lb.)
	1.57 m.	(5 ft 2 in.)	50.8 kg.	(8 st. 0 lb.)	54.4 kg.	(8 st. 8 lb.)	59.0 kg.	(9 st. 4 lb.)
	1.60 m.	(5 ft 3 in.)	52.2 kg.	(8 st. 3 lb.)	55.8 kg.	(8 st. 11 lb.)	60.8 kg.	(9 st. 8 lb.)
	1.62 m.	(5 ft 4 in.)	54.0 kg.	(8 st. 7 lb.)	58.1 kg.	(9 st. 2 lb.)	62.6 kg.	(9 st. 12 lb.)
	1.65 m.	(5 ft 5 in.)	55.8 kg.	(8 st. 11 lb.)	59.9 kg.	(9 st. 6 lb.)	64.4 kg.	(10 st. 2 lb.)
	1.67 m.	(5 ft 6 in.)	57.6 kg.	(9 st. 1 lb.)	61.7 kg.	(9 st. 10 lb.)	66.2 kg.	(10 st. 6 lb.)
	1.70 m.	(5 ft 7 in.)	59.4 kg.	(9 st. 5 lb.)	63.5 kg.	(10 st. 0 lb.)	68.0 kg.	(10 st. 10 lb.)
	1.72 m.	(5 ft 8 in.)	61.2 kg.	(9 st. 9 lb.)	65.3 kg.	(10 st. 4 lb.)	69.9 kg.	(11 st. 0 lb.)
	1.75 m.	(5 ft 9 in.)	63.0 kg.	(9 st. 13 lb.)	67.1 kg.	(10 st. 8 lb.)	72.1 kg.	(11 st. 5 lb.)
	1.77 m.	(5 ft 10 in.)	64.9 kg.	(10 st. 3 lb.)	68.9 kg.	(10 st. 12 lb.)	74.4 kg.	(11 st. 10 lb.)
MEN Add 3.2 kg. (7 lb.) to weight for clothes	1.57 m.	(5 ft 2 in.)	54.0 kg.	(8 st. 7 lb.)	57.6 kg.	(9 st. 1 lb.)	62.1 kg.	(9 st. 11 lb.)
	1.60 m.	(5 ft 3 in.)	55.3 kg.	(8 st. 10 lb.)	59.0 kg.	(9 st. 4 lb.)	63.5 kg.	(10 st. 0 lb.)
	1.62 m.	(5 ft 4 in.)	56.7 kg.	(8 st. 13 lb.)	60.3 kg.	(9 st. 7 lb.)	65.3 kg.	(10 st. 4 lb.)
	1.65 m.	(5 ft 5 in.)	58.5 kg.	(9 st. 3 lb.)	62.1 kg.	(9 st. 11 lb.)	66.7 kg.	(10 st. 7 lb.)
	1.67 m.	(5 ft 6 in.)	60.3 kg.	(9 st. 7 lb.)	64.0 kg.	(10 st. 1 lb.)	68.9 kg.	(10 st. 12 lb.)
	1.70 m.	(5 ft 7 in.)	62.1 kg.	(9 st. 11 lb.)	65.8 kg.	(10 st. 5 lb.)	71.2 kg.	(11 st. 3 lb.)
	1.72 m.	(5 ft 8 in.)	64.0 kg.	(10 st. 1 lb.)	67.6 kg.	(10 st. 9 lb.)	73.0 kg.	(11 st. 7 lb.)
	1.75 m.	(5 ft 9 in.)	65.8 kg.	(10 st. 5 lb.)	69.4 kg.	(10 st. 13 lb.)	74.8 kg.	(11 st. 11 lb.)
	1.77 m.	(5 ft 10 in.)	67.6 kg.	(10 st. 9 lb.)	71.7 kg.	(11 st. 4 lb.)	76.7 kg.	(12 st. 1 lb.)
	1.80 m.	(5 ft 11 in.)	69.4 kg.	(10 st. 13 lb.)	73.5 kg.	(11 st. 8 lb.)	78.9 kg.	(12 st. 6 lb.)
	1.82 m.	(6 ft 0 in.)	71.2 kg.	(11 st. 3 lb.)	75.7 kg.	(11 st. 13 lb.)	81.2 kg.	(12 st. 11 lb.)
	1.85 m.	(6 ft 1 in.)	73.5 kg.	(11 st. 8 lb.)	77.6 kg.	(12 st. 3 lb.)	83.5 kg.	(13 st. 2 lb.)
	1.88 m.	(6 ft 2 in.)	75.3 kg.	(11 st. 12 lb.)	79.8 kg.	(12 st. 8 lb.)	85.7 kg.	(13 st. 7 lb.)
	1.90 m.	(6 ft 3 in.)	77.1 kg.	(12 st. 2 lb.)	82.1 kg.	(12 st. 13 lb.)	87.5 kg.	(13 st. 11 lb.)

• THE HEALTH PROBLEMS OF WOMEN

The child-bearing years of a woman's life last from the teens, when menstruation and ovulation begin, to the late forties, when the 'change of life' occurs. The physical and emotional changes of these years bring with them problems which may call for special help.

THE MENSTRUAL CYCLE

Menstruation is the monthly loss of blood and mucus from the womb. During the first half of the menstrual cycle, an egg develops in the ovary and is released towards the Fallopian tubes which lead to the womb. This process is called ovulation.

During the second half of the cycle, the egg travels slowly down a Fallopian tube into the womb, where the lining has been thickened under the influence of hormones produced in the ovaries. If the egg is not fertilised by the male sperm, the process ceases abruptly. The lining of the womb collapses and the debris forms the menstrual flow, which lasts about five days.

Menstruation normally begins between the ages of 10 and 14. Between 15 and 45, the most common cause of a missed period is pregnancy. But anxiety about exams, emotional problems, or physical ill-health may also upset the normal menstrual cycle.

MENSTRUAL PROBLEMS

Some women have physical symptoms before a period begins. The breasts become larger, heavier and are often slightly sore. There may be a gain of a few pounds in weight and ankle swelling. There may be backache. Many women experience a sense of bloating in the lower abdomen. This sensation is due to the accumulation of fluid in the body as a consequence of hormonal changes.

The retention of fluid has a common side-effect known as premenstrual tension. A woman suffers from headache and feels nervous, irritable and depressed. All these symptoms may be treated by the use of a diuretic – a substance which enables people to pass extra urine. This removes the excess fluid from the body and relieves the side-effects.

Sometimes a cramping pain, called dysmenorrhoea, occurs for the first day or two of the period. It rarely occurs in the early years of adolescence and among women who have had children. But it may be distressing for girls in their late teens and early twenties. The pain seems to be triggered by ovulation. If ovulation is suppressed by an oral contraceptive – the pill – the symptoms of dysmenorrhoea disappear.

Heavy periods – menorrhagia – occur in women approaching the menopause, but may also be caused by disorders of the womb or poor health. A doctor should be consulted.

The absence of menstruation, known as amenorrhoea, may be primary or secondary. Primary amenorrhoea is the term used if menstruation has not occurred, although the age of 15 has been reached. If it begins and then ceases, the term used is secondary amenorrhoea. It may be due to pregnancy or an early menopause, or to hormonal disorders. In both cases, a doctor should be consulted.

OTHER HEALTH PROBLEMS

Painful intercourse may be due to an inflammation of the vagina wall as a result of oestrogen deficiency at or after the menopause. Occasionally, it may be due to scarring after a gynaecological operation. However, the most common cause is a muscular spasm provoked by anxiety or by a psychological or emotional problem.

Cervical erosion is an area of thinning and redness in the covering of the cervix – the lower end of the uterus. Sometimes an erosion causes no symptoms. However, it may cause a vaginal discharge or some bleeding or discomfort after sexual intercourse. If the erosion becomes infected, these symptoms are increased. Erosions are caused by hormonal changes in the body, and they appear to be more common in women on the pill. They are treated by local cauterisation.

Cystitis is an inflammation of the bladder. It may be caused by an infection of the bladder or by a bruising of the outlet of the bladder during sexual intercourse. The symptoms are discomfort and frequency in passing urine. Antibiotics can control any infection quickly. Symptoms may also be eased by drinking plenty of fluids. Cystitis is less likely if the genital region is washed before intercourse and if urine is passed within 20 minutes afterwards.

HYSTERECTOMY

Heavy periods and other menstrual irregularities may sometimes be caused by a disease of the womb. This condition is best treated by removing the womb – an operation called a hysterectomy. It has no effect on health or sexual activity.

In a young woman a hysterectomy does not cause an early menopause, although the menstrual periods cease after the operation. Most women who have the operation find that relief from the symptoms leads to a general improvement in their health.

CANCER OF THE CERVIX AND THE BREAST

Every woman over 25 should have regular tests for cervical cancer, one of the more common serious diseases of middle life. During an examination by a doctor or nurse, a few cells are taken from the lower end of the womb. This examination is called taking a cervical smear.

It takes only a few seconds and is completely painless. Tests on these cells will show whether there are any grounds for anxiety. The test should be repeated every two to three years. It is always done six weeks after a woman has given birth.

Like cervical cancer, breast cancer can be cured if detected early. Every woman should learn to examine her breasts every month throughout her adult life. This is best done just after a menstrual period. Some swelling often appears in the breasts for a few days before a period, only to disappear after it.

Look at your breasts while sitting in front of a mirror to see if there are any changes in appearance in the shape of the nipple or in the skin. Then lie on your back with your head on a pillow or cushion, and examine each breast in turn – see panel, opposite page. If there is anything unusual, such as a lump, consult a doctor as soon as possible.

THE CHANGE OF LIFE

Most women cease to be fertile between the ages of 45 and 50. This change of life, known as the menopause, is as natural as the start of menstruation. About the age of 35 to 40 the output of oestrogen begins to decline. As a result, the menstrual periods first become irregular and eventually stop.

In many women, the menopause causes no other symptoms at all. In others, however, a rapid fall in oestrogen level causes troublesome symptoms, such as irregular menstruation, heavy periods, hot flushes in the face, neck and arms, and excessive perspiration.

Any women troubled by these symptoms should go to her doctor.

• PLANNING A FAMILY

The wide range of contraceptive methods and devices allows a couple to plan the size of their family and the timing of pregnancies. Sexual harmony is more likely if both partners are satisfied with their method of birth control which may change as a relationship develops.

For example, the pill may be best at the start of a woman's active sex life, because it is certain and does not affect spontaneity. However, after the birth of the first child, there may be a case for switching to the loop or coil. The small risk of unplanned pregnancy may be acceptable at that time.

Before choosing a particular method, a woman may wish to discuss the subject with her doctor.

Advice may also be obtained from birth-control clinics.

THE PILL

Contraception by taking the pill is nearly 100% reliable. The standard pill contains synthetic forms of progesterone and oestrogen, the female sex hormones normally produced by the ovaries during each menstrual period. The pill is taken regularly, usually every day for 21 days, beginning on the fifth day after the start of menstruation. During this time, the synthetic hormones suppress the release of the egg, or ovum. The pill also causes changes in the linings of the cervix and the womb, or uterus, and these changes make pregnancy, or conception, unlikely even if an egg does form. Menstruation takes place during the seven days when the woman takes no pill. Some women

EXAMINING THE BREASTS

1. Place towel under left shoulder and left hand under head. Examine the upper, inner quarter of the left breast with the right hand using flats of the fingers.

2. Examine the lower, inner quarter of the breast. When examining the breasts, start feeling well out from the breast and move inwards towards the nipple.

3. Bring the left arm down to your side when examining the lower, outer quarter. Start the examination well out from the ribs below and at the side.

4. Move the fingers to the upper, outer quarter of the breast. Give special attention to the breast tissue between the upper, outer quarter and the armpit.

5. Examine the armpit itself, feeling for any lumps. When you have finished the left breast use your left hand to examine the right breast in the same way.

find that the pill has unpleasant side-effects, such as depression, an increase in weight, swelling of the ankles, or skin discoloration. These problems can be kept to a minimum if the doctor chooses a pill to suit the natural hormonal make-up of the woman.

THE COIL AND THE LOOP

The methods which are second only to the pill in effectiveness (about 97% reliable) are the intra-uterine devices (IUDs) – small plastic coils or loops, and mixed plastic and copper devices. IUDs prevent conception by making the lining of the womb unsuitable for the growth of a fertilised egg. They can be easily inserted by a doctor and provide reliable contraception for many women.

Pain, heavy periods, backache and other unpleasant symptoms may sometimes occur after insertion, but these discomforts usually soon disappear.

SHEATH AND DIAPHRAGM

There are two types of rubber devices – the condom, or french letter, which is fitted over the penis, and the dia-phragm, or dutch cap, which is fitted inside the vagina. Both are designed to prevent the male sperm from reaching the womb. They are not as effective as the loop and the coil – for example, the diaphragm is about 88% reliable.

NATURAL METHODS

The rhythm method of contraception and coitus interruptus are used mainly by couples with religious or ethical objections to all contraceptive drugs and devices.

The rhythm method is based on abstinence from sexual intercourse close to the time when the egg is released. Because sperm cells can survive in the female reproductive tract for 48 hours, the period of abstinence must start about two days before ovulation.

Although ovulation occurs at the mid-point of the menstrual cycle, it is not likely to take place at exactly the same time each month. As a result, if ovulation occurs earlier than expected in the menstrual cycle, and sexual intercourse takes place within the previous two days, conception might occur.

However, a woman who keeps a calendar record of her menstrual cycles for a year, can roughly forecast when ovulation occurs. The time of ovulation can be predicted with greater accuracy if a woman keeps a record of her daily temperature for several months (taken first thing in the morning). There is a slight rise in temperature when ovulation occurs. If this is consistent from month to month, the time of ovulation can be forecast with confidence. It is unlikely that conception will occur if intercourse is delayed for 72 hours after the rise in temperature.

Coitus interruptus, also called the withdrawal method, is the simplest but least-reliable method of birth control. The unreliability is due mainly to the fact that sperm may emerge before ejaculation. The method may also impose a nervous strain on both partners.

STERILISATION

This may be the most satisfactory method of birth control for couples with growing children.

Male sterilisation by vasectomy is a simple, safe procedure that takes only a few minutes. The sperms are carried from the testicles to the penis by two tubes, the vas deferens. If these tubes are cut or blocked, the man is no longer fertile. The operation is done under local anaesthetic, and two small surgical incisions are made in the scrotum to reach the vas deferens. Vasectomy does not affect sexual desire, and has no effect on orgasm or ejaculation. The operation is considered to be reversible, but in practice this has not always proved to be the case.

Female sterilisation is a similar procedure. It involves cutting or blocking the two Fallopian tubes that carry the eggs from the ovaries to the womb. Because these tubes are inside the abdomen, the operation is slightly more difficult than a vasectomy, but it can be done under local anaesthetic through a single tiny incision just beneath the navel. The operation is usually irreversible.

CHILDLESS MARRIAGES

Infertility – the failure to have children – may be due to physical or psychological defects of either the man or the woman. A couple who fail to conceive in two years with regular intercourse, and without the use of contraceptives, probably need help. They can get advice from their doctor, the Marriage Guidance Council, or the Family Planning Association. The couple may then be referred to an infertility clinic in a local hospital. A medical examination may reveal disorders affecting fertility – for example, mumps in the teenage years has been known to make a male infertile.

However, if the couple are in good health, the problem may be due to the frequency and timing of sexual intercourse, or to some sexual defect.

Once the cause of infertility has been identified, it is possible to estimate if treatment will be successful. Two-thirds of couples seen by infertility clinics have a child within four years of attendance.

Intending parents should ask for advice if there has been a family history of inherited disorders. This advice can be obtained from genetic counselling clinics, which are located in most large teaching hospitals. Parents will be told if they might have an abnormal child and what can be done to prevent this happening.

• PREGNANCY AND CHILDBIRTH

The first noticeable sign of pregnancy is usually a missed menstrual period. Confirmation comes within a few weeks from other symptoms. The breasts increase in size and tenderness, there is a need to pass urine more frequently, and there can be vomiting or a feeling of nausea in the early morning.

A laboratory test of a sample of urine can give a reliable answer as to whether or not a woman is pregnant. It detects a hormone – chorionic gonadotrophin – produced by the membranes which surround the developing embryo.

Information about pregnancy tests can be obtained from the Family Planning Association (see pp. 410-21).

CARE DURING PREGNANCY

Although a pregnant woman is entitled to medical care at the local NHS antenatal clinic, there is no fixed schedule of clinic visits. Most women usually attend the clinic at the eighth or tenth week of pregnancy for an initial health check.

During this first visit the 'expected day of delivery', or EDD, is calculated. This is done by adding 280 days to the date of the last period – or by subtracting three calendar months from that date and adding seven days.

Further visits are made to the clinic every four weeks until the 28th week of pregnancy. After this the visits are fortnightly until the 36th week. From then on, the woman attends every week until the baby is born. At these visits a check is kept on the growth of the baby and the health of the mother.

Antenatal clinics provide mothercraft classes for women having their first baby. At these classes the expectant mother learns about baby care and can ask about the problems of pregnancy.

DIET DURING PREGNANCY

During pregnancy, the expectant mother should eat a balanced diet to maintain her strength and ensure the health of her child. It is essential that she guards against over-eating and putting on too much weight. Protein-rich foods, such as meat and fish, are preferable to starchy foods.

The most common cause for medical concern in pregnancy is excessive weight. This can lead to possible complications during pregnancy, and may cause obesity after birth. At the end of a normal pregnancy, a woman should have gained no more than 9-12½ kg. (20-28 lb.).

Milk is an excellent food during pregnancy since it contains the calcium needed for the baby's bones. But it is also high in calories, and too much milk may lead to weight problems. Plenty of fluid should be taken – 2.5 litres (4 pints) or more a day.

Even with a balanced diet there is always a risk of anaemia during pregnancy. Tablets of iron and the vitamin folic acid may be given to prevent this.

HEALTH DURING PREGNANCY

One of the early signs of pregnancy is tiredness. In the first few weeks, a two-hour rest in the afternoon may be needed in addition to eight hours' sleep at night. In the later stages of pregnancy, sleeping may be difficult because of the increased bulk of the baby. Warm milk at bedtime may help, but sleeping pills may be needed. No medicines should be taken without medical approval.

Morning sickness is a troublesome symptom of pregnancy. But it rarely lasts beyond the fourth month.

Indigestion may become the main complaint later in pregnancy. Symptoms are relieved by sitting propped up in bed. Antacid tablets give relief, but should be used only with medical approval.

Some women suffer from constipation during pregnancy. This difficulty can be overcome by making sure that the diet includes enough roughage, such as green vegetables, fruit and whole-grain cereals.

Backache during pregnancy is caused by carrying the weight of the baby, combined with the slackness of the ligaments in the back. Lying on a firm, flat surface may give relief.

The rise in blood pressure during pregnancy may cause varicose veins. Symptoms such as aching legs can be relieved by wearing an elastic stocking and by resting with the legs up. Piles – varicose veins in the rectum – can be treated with cream and suppositories. Varicose veins often disappear after the birth of the child.

Women who are prone to recurrent miscarriage may be advised against sex in the early months of pregnancy. But in the absence of any illness, sexual relations can be continued throughout pregnancy. Exercise is not harmful, unless the pregnant woman has experienced recurrent miscarriage. Doctors discourage horse-riding and any form of sport where there is a risk of a fall.

Any serious condition leading to illness, premature delivery or stillbirth will be quickly detected at the antenatal clinic. One of the most serious problems is toxaemia, a condition caused by the presence of poisonous substances in the blood. It affects one in every 20 expectant women. Swollen hands, feet and ankles in the 20th to 30th week are warning signs.

Another troublesome complaint is vaginal discharge, which is caused by a fungus infection. Report any such discharge to the doctor. Treatment is simple and effective.

Pregnant women are not free from disease, but few of these disorders can harm a growing baby. The major exceptions are virus infections, particularly German measles, which can cause mental deficiency in the child.

MISCARRIAGE AND ABORTION

A miscarriage, or spontaneous abortion, usually results from some defect in the development of the foetus or some accident or illness affecting the mother. Abortion – the artificial termination of pregnancy – is induced either by drugs or by an operation.

Any bleeding in pregnancy can be a sign of possible miscarriage, and the woman should call her doctor.

If a miscarriage is only threatened, rest in bed may be all that is needed. A miscarriage is usually no bar to a normal pregnancy later.

The Abortion Act 1967 permits termination of pregnancy if there are adequate grounds certified by two doctors. Abortion is permissible if the pregnancy is a danger to the woman's life, or her physical or mental health; if it endangers the physical or mental health of other children in the family; or if there is risk of grave physical or mental deformity in the baby.

Any woman, married or unmarried, who believes she has grounds for termination can get advice from her doctor or a pregnancy advisory service.

STAGES OF CHILDBIRTH

When labour begins, the muscles of the womb go into contractions, each lasting for about 45 seconds. At first these pains occur every 20 minutes, then more frequently.

Labour may start with a 'show' – a loss of blood or a gushing of clear amniotic fluid in the womb. This fluid cushions the baby against shocks. As the labour contractions raise the pressure inside the womb, the sac containing the fluid breaks and the fluid escapes. The loss of fluid brings the baby's head further down into the pelvis and speeds up labour.

During the first and longest stage of labour, the contractions become stronger and more frequent. The cervix, or neck of the womb, stretches to its fullest extent and the woman is told by the doctor or midwife to help the baby out of the womb by holding her breath and pushing down with her abdominal muscles during each contraction. This stage may last only a few minutes if the woman has had several children. But it usually takes about an hour with a first baby. The third and final stage is the expulsion of the placenta, or afterbirth.

Although the risks of home delivery are small, obstetricians encourage admission to hospital, where a woman may be given gas, supplemented with drugs, to relieve pain.

If the birth is difficult, an incision may be made in the skin and muscles at the side of the vagina. This prevents any permanent damage to the vagina or its surroundings.

If the baby's condition or position during childbirth gives rise to anxiety, it may have to be delivered by caesarean section. The obstetrician makes an incision through the abdominal muscles and the womb, extracting the baby and placenta.

A mother may begin breast-feeding the baby six to eight hours after birth. She will be allowed to get up for short periods during the first days after birth, and may leave the hospital as early as the third day if she is in good health. Sexual relations may normally be resumed after two weeks or so. The mother and baby have a check-up about six weeks after birth.

CHANGES DURING PREGNANCY

6th WEEK	8th WEEK	12th WEEK	16th WEEK	20th WEEK	24th WEEK	28th WEEK	32nd WEEK	36th WEEK	40th WEEK

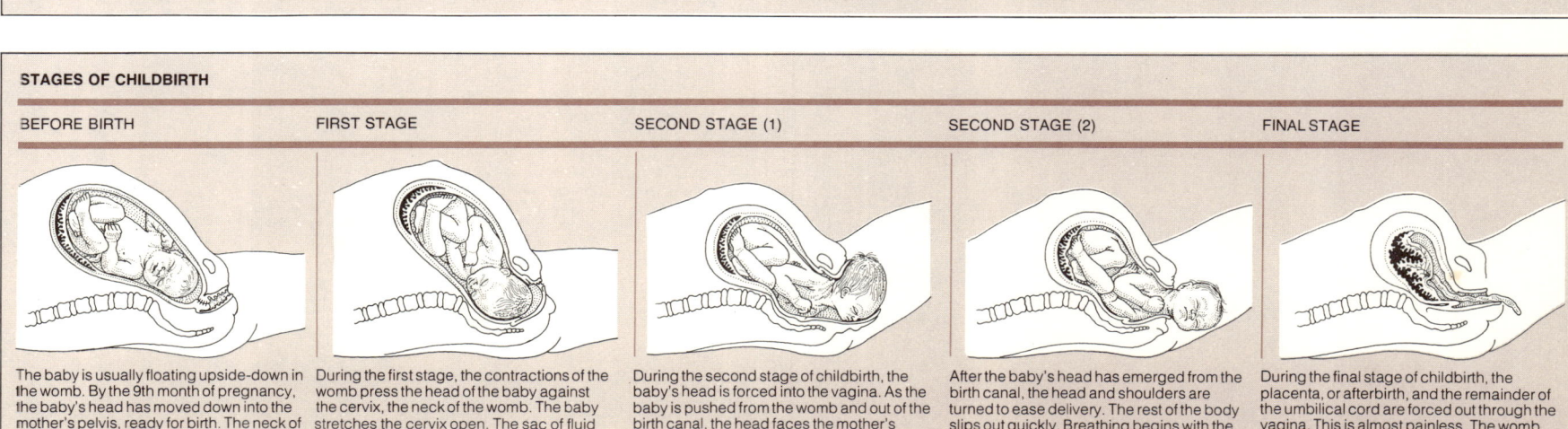

The first signs of pregnancy occur: periods missed; morning sickness; breasts feeling uncomfortable. At 6 weeks the baby is 25 mm. long, weighs only 1 g. but already has a human look.

Toward the end of the 2nd month, the baby's skeleton begins to develop. It is made of soft cartilage which soon turns to bone.

For the first 3 months of pregnancy there is little change in a woman's shape, but the baby's brain, heart, lungs, stomach, intestines, nerves and bladder are fully formed.

The baby grows from 50 to 125 mm. By the 4th month the enlargement of the abdomen is noticeable to the mother, but other people will not notice for another month.

The baby is about 160 mm. long, weighs 225 g. or more. At the 5th month the baby has a thin layer of wrinkled skin. As the baby gains fat, the skin will smooth out.

The mother feels the baby kicking and churning inside her. As the baby moves about, the umbilical cord, which provides the baby's circulation, slips over the body but does not become knotted.

By the 7th month the baby has developed enough so that he can live if born prematurely. The baby is now about 350 mm. long and weighs 1.1 kg.

The baby gains the fat and the strength needed to live outside the womb. His muscles are developed, his blood is circulating, and his digestive system is ready for food.

The mother's womb has grown nearly to the rib cage. The mother experiences 'lightening' as the baby's head sinks into the pelvis. The baby's weight is about 2.5 kg.

In the 9th month the womb is about 300 mm. long. The baby is about 3 kg., 500 mm. long, and is curled up awaiting birth. The baby takes up most of the womb and moves little.

STAGES OF CHILDBIRTH

BEFORE BIRTH	FIRST STAGE	SECOND STAGE (1)	SECOND STAGE (2)	FINAL STAGE

The baby is usually floating upside-down in the womb. By the 9th month of pregnancy, the baby's head has moved down into the mother's pelvis, ready for birth. The neck of the womb has not dilated or opened.

During the first stage, the contractions of the womb press the head of the baby against the cervix, the neck of the womb. The baby stretches the cervix open. The sac of fluid surrounding the baby breaks.

During the second stage of childbirth, the baby's head is forced into the vagina. As the baby is pushed from the womb and out of the birth canal, the head faces the mother's back.

After the baby's head has emerged from the birth canal, the head and shoulders are turned to ease delivery. The rest of the body slips out quickly. Breathing begins with the baby's first cry. The umbilical cord is cut.

During the final stage of childbirth, the placenta, or afterbirth, and the remainder of the umbilical cord are forced out through the vagina. This is almost painless. The womb returns to normal size about ten days later.

HOW A BABY DEVELOPS IN THE FIRST YEAR

MONTH 1	MONTH 2	MONTH 3	MONTH 4	MONTH 5	MONTH 6	MONTH 7	MONTH 8	MONTH 9	MONTH 10	MONTH 11	MONTH 12

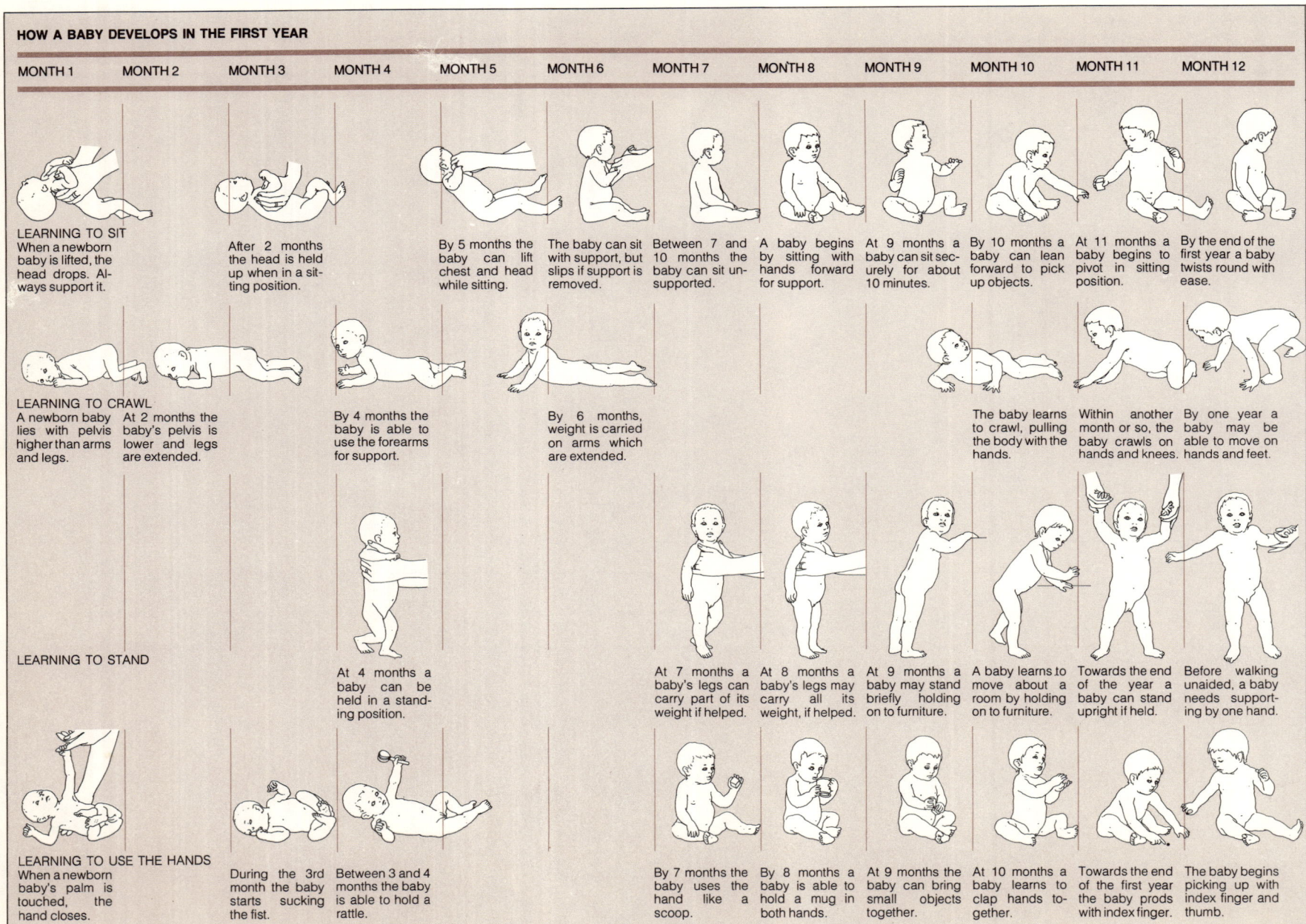

LEARNING TO SIT
When a newborn baby is lifted, the head drops. Always support it.

After 2 months the head is held up when in a sitting position.

By 5 months the baby can lift chest and head while sitting.

The baby can sit with support, but slips if support is removed.

Between 7 and 10 months the baby can sit unsupported.

A baby begins by sitting with hands forward for support.

At 9 months a baby can sit securely for about 10 minutes.

By 10 months a baby can lean forward to pick up objects.

At 11 months a baby begins to pivot in sitting position.

By the end of the first year a baby twists round with ease.

LEARNING TO CRAWL
A newborn baby lies with pelvis higher than arms and legs.

At 2 months the baby's pelvis is lower and legs are extended.

By 4 months the baby is able to use the forearms for support.

By 6 months, weight is carried on arms which are extended.

The baby learns to crawl, pulling the body with the hands.

Within another month or so, the baby crawls on hands and knees.

By one year a baby may be able to move on hands and feet.

LEARNING TO STAND

At 4 months a baby can be held in a standing position.

At 7 months a baby's legs can carry part of its weight if helped.

At 8 months a baby's legs may carry all its weight, if helped.

At 9 months a baby may stand briefly holding on to furniture.

A baby learns to move about a room by holding on to furniture.

Towards the end of the year a baby can stand upright if held.

Before walking unaided, a baby needs supporting by one hand.

LEARNING TO USE THE HANDS
When a newborn baby's palm is touched, the hand closes.

During the 3rd month the baby starts sucking the fist.

Between 3 and 4 months the baby is able to hold a rattle.

By 7 months the baby uses the hand like a scoop.

By 8 months a baby is able to hold a mug in both hands.

At 9 months the baby can bring small objects together.

At 10 months a baby learns to clap hands together.

Towards the end of the first year the baby prods with index finger.

The baby begins picking up with index finger and thumb.

• CHILD CARE

First-year parents watch the development of their baby (see chart, opposite page) and will learn to deal with the everyday problems of feeding, crying and sleeping. Few parents escape worry when a baby or toddler is ill. For them, it is important to know how to cope with first-year illnesses and upsets (see chart, p. 408).

FEEDING

Breast milk is the ideal food for a baby. It contains the correct mixture of fat, protein and sugar and provides all the food a baby needs for the first six months of life. It is always at the right temperature; it cannot become infected; and it is available when needed, day and night. Breast feeding is psychologically satisfying for the mother and baby because it helps to 'bond' the infant to his mother. It need only be stopped if the mother has to return to work or if she develops a breast abscess or a cracked nipple.

Breast feeding also plays a part in protecting the baby against disease. In the early months of life the breast-fed baby is immune against many of the common diseases, such as measles, because antibodies are passed to him from his mother in breast milk. Even if a mother breast feeds for only a week or two, she will help to provide this immunity.

The problem with breast feeding is that it is not easy to see how much milk the baby is getting. One way to be certain that the baby is getting enough milk is to weigh him every week on a baby scale. A healthy baby weighing 3.2 kg. (7 lb.) at birth gains about 200 g. (7 oz.) a week in the first three months of life, and then about 140 g. (5 oz.) a week in the second three months. If the baby gains more than this, reduce the food intake. A baby who is overweight is prone to chesty illnesses. It is also likely to become a fat child and grow up as an obese adult.

BOTTLE FEEDING

Although breast feeding brings psychological benefits to both mother and child, babies still thrive on bottle feeding. Any suitable dried or evaporated milk, used according to instructions, is satisfactory for a bottle-feed.

Take care in making up the feeds to get the proportions of milk, sugar and water right. Milk made up too strong, or with too much sugar, can upset the baby.

Undiluted cow's milk is not suitable for a baby immediately after birth because its composition is different from human milk. But a baby of two or three months may be given boiled, diluted cow's milk and may digest it happily.

A baby needs about 70 g. (2½ oz.) of fresh milk each day for every pound of body weight. For example, a 4.4 kg. (10 lb.) baby can be given about 650 g. (25 oz.) of fluid in a day. This quantity is usually split into five feeds of 130 g. (5 oz.) each, timed to suit the mother's convenience.

Cleanliness is vital in the preparation of babies' bottle-feeds. The work of sterilising the bottle after use can be eased by using a solution of hypochlorite, sold under various brand names, often with a tank in which to immerse the bottle. After filling the bottle with a fresh feed, cool under a cold tap and test the temperature of the milk by shaking a few drops on to the back of the hand.

No single feeding routine is right for all babies. Some mothers prefer feeding on demand when the baby cries. However, many babies are content with a regular schedule of feeds (every four hours during the first weeks of life).

A baby who feeds too fast and greedily may swallow a lot of wind, while one who sucks too slowly may become exhausted before he has taken enough milk. Twenty minutes or so is a reasonable time for a baby to drink a bottle of milk. If he regularly takes longer, it may be best to switch to a teat with a larger hole.

A baby will swallow some air as he feeds and will not be comfortable until this has been burped up. An effective form of relief is to hold the baby upright against the shoulder and gently rub or pat his back. A little milk may be brought up with the wind. Only if the baby vomits a large quantity after every feed is there reason to consult a doctor. There is no need to start solids until the baby is four to six months old, when he has doubled his birth weight.

At eight to nine months the baby should be weaned on to three meals a day with an additional drink first thing in the morning and last thing at night. Cut down the amount of milk as the intake of solid food, such as sieved vegetables and meats, increases. The infant will still need fluid and can be given diluted orange or black-currant juice instead of milk.

SLEEPING

There are no hard-and-fast rules about the number of hours that a baby should sleep. The best guide is the baby himself. If a baby is contented and cheerful on 12 hours' sleep a day, that is clearly all he needs.

An average newborn baby spends only an hour or two a day awake, in addition to the time he spends feeding. By the end of the first year, time spent sleeping drops to about 15 hours. However, some two-year-olds need 16 hours of sleep a day, while others are satisfied with eight. Ideally, the baby should be encouraged to have a long uninterrupted sleep at night and take the rest in naps after each feed. An infant who wakes at night may cry, but will often go back to sleep quickly. However, a baby who is picked up and soothed by its parents every time he stirs is less likely to develop into a sound sleeper.

CRYING

From birth onwards babies cry because they are hungry or uncomfortable from wind or a wet nappy. But it is only too easy for a mother to assume that these are the only possible causes. A newborn baby that has been changed, fed and burped may cry the moment he is returned to the cot.

A baby who has been a model of contentment may often start to scream after his feeds at the age of three months. This 'three-month colic', which is most troublesome in the evenings, seems to be due to uncomfortable spasms of the bowel after a meal. This condition rarely lasts more than a week or two, and the baby is no worse for it.

Teething may be a cause of crying. But it is only the first half-a-dozen teeth that cause discomfort. An infant may find cutting some of his teeth a little uncomfortable, but too much blame should not be placed on teething for infant discomforts. There could be other causes.

Boredom may be the underlying explanation for crying. As babies grow, they begin to feel bored or lonely when left to themselves.

Babies like the reassuring presence of their mothers. If a baby is to be content in his cot or pram, then he should be propped up so that he can watch his mother. If left lying flat on his back looking at a ceiling he will become frustrated. But by giving him a few simple toys to investigate, chew and manipulate, misery can be converted to contentment.

COLLECTING DOLLS

The hand-made dolls of the 19th century are today prized for their beauty. In the above selection, most of the dolls are from Germany, the largest doll-producing country in Victorian times.

If starting a collection, go to antique shops and auctions. You could well come across the doll known as 'dream baby' (third from left), manufactured by Germany's Armand Marseille, and often marked with his initials.

Two families famous for their doll-making in England at this time were the Montanaris, who gave their dolls individual strands of hair and individual eyelashes; and the Pierottis, who marked out finger-nails and dimples and gave faces realistic flesh creases.

Most of these dolls, made of wax, china, or a highly coloured unglazed clay-mix known as bisque, are expensive, but a collection of wooden dolls or modern folk-art dolls would not cost a lot. The Japanese doll c. 1890 (below) is a rare example of a folk-art doll.

Antique dolls can be seen in London at the Bethnal Green, Victoria and Albert, and London museums, and at Edinburgh's Museum of Childhood.

MINOR FIRST-YEAR HEALTH PROBLEMS

A baby is a delicate creature, yet tougher and more robust than many parents imagine. During the first year of its life, a baby develops symptoms that are normal and can be easily dealt with by parents.

BOWEL MOVEMENTS
Bowel movement may at first cause the mother some concern. For the first two or three days the movement will be sticky and tar coloured. If the baby is bottle-fed this will change to green, then yellow. At first, movements will correspond with feeding – one for each feed – but they will become less frequent, maybe as few as once a day in a bottle-fed baby. The pattern is similar for breast-fed babies except that the movement is likely to be more orange in colour.

A sudden change from passing soft movements to hard movements indicates that the baby may be constipated.

If the baby is constipated, try giving him sugared water during the day. About 4 oz. of boiled water with half a teaspoon of sugar twice a day should be enough, but if this fails try orange or prune juice. If the child does not respond to these measures, consult the doctor.

A bottle-fed baby who is troubled by frequent, semi-liquid stools may well be getting too much sugar. A frequent and excessively watery bowel movement is a symptom of diarrhoea. This condition should be reported to the doctor.

BODY TEMPERATURE
The body temperature of a newborn baby tends to fluctuate. The child can overheat or get very cold quite easily. Avoid exposing the baby to any temperature much warmer than 24°C (75°F) or below 13°C (55°F).

BONE DEFORMITIES
Talipes, or club foot, is a minor deformity and if properly treated by special splints, can usually be cured by the first birthday. More serious abnormalities affecting the joints, bones and muscles may require longer periods of specialist treatment, but in every case early medical advice is vital.

A baby's head is often compressed during birth so that immediately afterwards its shape may appear a little odd. The fontanelles – membranous areas at the junction of the main skull bones – are designed to allow for these changes in shape. Within a few days the skull will be normal.

BREAST ENLARGEMENT
During the first two months there is an enlargement of the baby's breasts, whether male or female. This is normal and disappears in time. Inform the doctor only if the nipples become red and hot.

CIRCUMCISION
In many baby boys, the foreskin – the covering of skin at the end of the penis – cannot be retracted, and it was formerly thought that circumcision (removal of the foreskin) was necessary so that the glans could be washed. This is not necessary. If the foreskin is tight and will not retract, then it should not be stretched. It will loosen by the time the boy starts school.

COLDS AND RUNNY NOSE
Many babies get a stuffy nose, which is no cause for concern. If the child has a cold he will show the usual symptoms – watery eyes, runny nose. Call the doctor.

CRADLECAP
This is excessive scaliness of the baby's scalp. It clears up with regular washing. Use an infant-medicated shampoo.

CROUP
This is a difficulty in breathing associated with a chest or throat infection. It may be relieved by keeping the air warm and moist.

JAUNDICE
It is common and normal for a baby to become slightly yellow on the third or fourth day after birth. This is caused by a yellow pigment in the blood which is normally cleared by the liver. But in the newborn baby the liver is not sufficiently developed to clear the pigment quickly. Nothing needs to be done, but if the baby is excessively yellow or the yellowness lasts beyond the sixth day after birth, call the doctor.

LOSS OF APPETITE
If a baby will not feed, it may be due to a cold or some other minor ailment. Tell the doctor if the loss of appetite persists.

RASHES
The most common is nappy rash, caused by leaving a wet nappy on too long, or insufficient rinsing of the nappy after washing.

If nappy rash occurs, change the nappies frequently, and if they smell of ammonia soak them in a bucket of water to which have been added two tablespoons of vinegar.

A barrier cream, such as a zinc-based ointment or yellow soft paraffin BP, helps to prevent nappy rash. It helps to leave the nappy off for as long as possible between changes. Do not use boracic powder.

If the rash persists, or if a rash appears on any other part of the body, take the baby to the doctor.

THRUSH
This is a whitish appearance of the mouth and throat due to a fungus infection. It should be treated by a doctor.

VAGINAL DISCHARGE
Occasionally, baby girls bleed slightly from the vagina in the first few days after birth. This is quite normal, but if the discharge is excessive or persists after the first two weeks tell the doctor.

MAJOR FIRST-YEAR HEALTH PROBLEMS

The chances of a baby being born with some abnormality are slight. Some disorders can be treated within a few hours of the baby's birth. For the more chronic diseases there are organisations which help and advise parents. See pp. 410-21.

AUTISM
The autistic child lives in a world of his own, and does not respond normally to parental love or to the world around him. Treatment is by psychological and occupational therapy. The organisation that deals with autistic children is The National Society for Autistic Children.

BLUE BABY
This is the name given to a baby whose lips and skin have a blue tinge as a result of a heart defect at birth. This defect prevents some of the baby's blood getting the oxygen that gives blood its normal bright red colour. The blueness is not always present immediately after birth, but the baby will grow more slowly and tire more easily than a normal child. Because it is easily detectable, the condition can normally be corrected by surgery before any permanent damage is done.

CEREBRAL PALSY
Damage to the brain, either during or after birth, can cause cerebral palsy or spastic paralysis. It is a disorder of movement and posture. Although the child may show some symptoms in the early days, it is not usually detected until the fifth or sixth month.

Facilities for treatment and care of spastics are provided by The Spastics Society.

CLEFT PALATE
A small cleft at the back of the palate, or roof of the mouth, is not serious and requires no treatment. Where the cleft extends from the back of the palate to the front, it may include a cleft of the upper lip, sometimes known as a hare lip. Both can be treated surgically and in both cases, results are extremely good.

COT DEATH
About 2,000 babies are found unexpectedly dead in their cots each year, usually during the winter. Medical experts do not fully understand the causes. Tests have shown that many of these babies are killed by unsuspected virus pneumonia.

Cot deaths are most common in babies under a year old. Bottle-fed babies are more likely to die than those that are breast-fed. Usually, it is found that the babies who die have been ill for a day or two with a respiratory infection. Parents of small babies should not hesitate to call their doctor if they are worried.

MENINGITIS
Although not a birth disorder, meningitis is a serious illness which must be treated at once. It is caused by inflammation of the membranes covering the brain and spinal cord, and can lead to brain damage. Early symptoms are vomiting and high fever. The child may also whimper and go stiff when picked up.

PHENYLKETONURIA
This rare disease arises from a defect in the way the body uses phenylalanine, a constituent of protein in food. This abnormal process produces poisonous substances that harm the baby's nervous system and brain. These substances can be prevented from forming by putting the infant on a diet containing proteins from which most of the phenylalanine has been removed.

PREMATURITY
A baby is considered to be premature if it weighs less than 2.5 kg. (5½ lb.) when it is born. All maternity hospitals are equipped with a premature-baby unit where the baby's progress can be watched carefully. If the baby is very small, it will be placed in an incubator, a transparent box which keeps the baby warm while it is being observed.

The baby is not allowed home until it has reached the weight of 2.5 kg. and even then special care is still needed. The baby's room must be kept warm and the baby must be protected from contact with people infected with a cold, sore throat or cough.

RHESUS DISEASE
Most people have a substance in their blood called the Rhesus factor, and are said to be Rhesus positive. Those without this factor are Rhesus negative. If a Rhesus-negative mother has Rhesus-positive babies in her second and subsequent pregnancies, the babies' blood cells may be destroyed by antibodies in the mother's blood.

The condition can now be prevented by treating the mother with antibodies, given shortly after the birth of the first child and each subsequent child.

SPINA BIFIDA
The cause of spina bifida is not known, although it can be inherited. The condition is a malformation of the spine which leaves the spinal cord unprotected. The type and severity of the condition varies, and mild cases can benefit from surgery if carried out in the first few days of birth.

Severe cases may lead to hydrocephalus, excessive fluid in and around the brain. This can sometimes be treated by an operation.

The Association for Spina Bifida and Hydrocephalus arranges talks for parents to help them to cope with the problems and needs of a child suffering from these conditions.

• CHILDHOOD INFECTIONS

During the first year or two at school a child may suffer from coughs, colds, sore throats and other recurrent illnesses. With each bout of illness, the child adds to his store of immunity, and by the time he is eight or nine he can go through the winter with little trouble or time off from school.

A child who has had his full course of immunisations, including his booster shots at the age of five, is protected against diphtheria, measles, whooping cough and poliomyelitis (see chart on right). Despite recent doubts about its value, it is advisable that children should be given whooping-cough vaccine.

Girls should be given German measles (rubella) vaccine at the age of 13, to protect them against this disorder, which can harm a baby during pregnancy. Smallpox vaccination is no longer recommended because the vaccine can cause complications.

Another recurrent problem for many children is tonsilitis – the swelling of the tonsils at the back of the throat. This problem disappears as the child grows and most doctors now believe that removal of the tonsils is necessary only in a few cases.

EAR INFECTIONS

Earache is common in small children. Because the Eustachian tubes connecting the internal ear to the back of the throat are short and straight in infants, infections travel easily to the ear from a sore throat. This problem is made worse because small children tend to sniff instead of blow their noses. As the child grows, the tube lengthens, the child learns to blow his nose, and earache becomes less frequent.

Ear infection can be serious at this age if neglected. Get medical advice if symptoms persist.

TABLE OF INFECTIOUS DISEASES

DISEASE	CAUSE	SPREAD BY	SITE OF INFECTION	SYMPTOMS	TREATMENT	OUTLOOK	VACCINATION AVAILABLE
Bronchitis	Bacteria	Discharge from the nose	Lungs	Cough, chills, fever, pain in back and muscles	Antibiotics, aspirin, absolute bed rest, fluids	Recovery in 4-5 days, unless there are complications	None
Chicken pox	Virus	Discharge from the nose, contact with infected articles, direct contact	Blood-stream and skin	Mild fever, weakness, pustules or pimples	Relief of itching and prevention of infection and scarring of pustules	Usually not serious	None
Diphtheria	Bacteria	Discharge from the nose, infected articles, carriers	Throat, lungs	Sore throat, fever, hoarseness, nasal discharge	Antitoxin serum and antibiotics	Good, with serum and antibiotics	Yes
Hepatitis	Virus	Contaminated food, water, direct contact or blood of infected persons	Liver and blood-stream	Jaundice, fever, nausea, headache, pain over liver, reddening and itching of hands and feet	Bed rest, fat-free diet, high in carbohydrates and protein	Rarely fatal, often lasts several months	None
Influenza	Virus	Discharge from the nose, contact with contaminated articles	Throat, lungs	Sudden fever, weakness, ache in back and limbs, sore throat	Bed rest, fluids	Good, unless complications develop	Vaccine effective few months
Jaundice	Virus	Contamination of food or drink	Liver	Loss of appetite, nausea, skin turns yellow	Rest and diet	Serious cases may require specialist care	None, but reinfection unlikely
Measles, red	Virus	Discharge from the nose, contact with contaminated articles	Throat, lungs, skin	Fever, cough, red swollen eyes, rash spreading from face to body, spots in mouth	Bed rest in a darkened room, antibiotics to prevent complications	Rarely fatal unless complications develop	Yes
Measles, German (rubella)	Virus	Discharge from the nose, contact with contaminated articles	Throat, lungs	Slight fever, neck glands swollen, rash resembling scarlet fever	Bed rest until rash has faded	Not serious, unless complications develop	Yes
Mumps	Virus	Direct contact and contaminated articles	Salivary glands	Fever, pain and swelling in salivary glands	Local applications, gamma globulin, and serum	Usually not serious, but complications may develop	Vaccine gives immunity at least 2 years
Poliomyelitis (polio)	Virus	Discharge from nose and throat, and faeces of carriers	Spinal cord and motor-nerve roots, spinal bulb	Headache, stiff neck and spine, fever about 37°C (100°F), paralysis of limbs in some cases	No specific treatment, therapy to regain use of limbs	Rarely fatal	Yes
Tonsilitis	Bacteria and virus	Nasal discharge	Throat and tonsils	Sore throat, difficulty in swallowing	Antibiotics, gargles	Good with antibiotics	None. Less common after the age of 5-6
Whooping cough	Bacteria	Nasal infection, contact with contaminated articles	Lungs	Cough, followed by a 'whoop', and lasting 1-2 months, fever, vomiting	Immune serum, antibiotics	Dangerous in infants, less serious in older children	Yes

A-Z OF USEFUL INFORM- ATION

Throughout *Household Manual*, reference has been made to various organisations that can be of use to you when seeking advice or when dealing with a specific problem.

In compiling this list of their names, and a brief resumé of the work they do, we have taken the opportunity to include many other organisations – clubs, consumer associations, trusts, societies, public departments, federations and so on – whose services can be helpful in many different ways.

To find a particular activity or organisation, first look under the main section heading where it is likely to be listed. For example, you may want to give some of your time to helping elderly people. Turn to the section headed 'Voluntary Work' and you will find a list, in alphabetical order, of those organisations dealing with all types of welfare work.

Telephone numbers have been given where possible. The addresses of most organisations can be traced through the local library reference section.

A

ACCIDENTS
Keep emergency telephone numbers handy. Dial 999 for the police, ambulance, or in case of fire. For shelter after a fire or flood go to the Social Services Department of the local council.

British Safety Council (01 - 741 1231)
The council operates a round-the-clock telephone line (01 - 741 3117) for emergencies, but is not open for general complaints. It is mainly an organisation for industry, but will direct inquiries from the public to the right authorities.

Fire Protection Association (01 - 248 5222)
Provides general and technical information on all aspects of fire and its prevention. There is a telephone inquiry service.

Royal Society for the Prevention of Accidents (01 - 668 4272)
The society supplies information

on all aspects of safety in the home, especially in the fields of education, training and advice on consumer product safety.

ADOPTION
More than 24,000 children are adopted in Britain each year through some 70 voluntary charitable adoption agencies and societies, which include various church organisations. When making preliminary inquiries to adopt a child, also contact the children's department of the local authority, your doctor, hospital matrons or almoners, and the district nurse. The major adoption organisations are listed here:-

Adoption Resource Exchange (01 - 837 0496/7)
A clearing house for bringing together those interested in adopting coloured children, and those children with special needs.

Association of British Adoption and Fostering Agencies (01 - 242 8951)
Publishes books on adoption and fostering, and booklets giving advice and the names of adoption agencies.

Independent Adoption Society (01 - 693 9611)
Provides a counselling and advice service for natural parents; a placement service for children; a service for adoptive parents and services needed after adoption.

National Foster Care Association (01 - 852 6821)
Provides information on fostering services and assists in providing facilities for education, training and recreation for those working in foster care.

ANIMALS AND PETS
Dogs must be licensed from the age of six months. Licences can be bought at any Post Office. Working dogs such as guide dogs, sheep dogs and hunting dogs do not need licences, nor do any other animals.

Animal owners can insure themselves against injury or damage caused by their animal by taking out a public liability policy. This covers the owner if,

say, his dog bites the postman.

To bring an animal into the country an import licence is required. Apply to:
The Ministry of Agriculture, Fisheries and Food (01 - 337 6611)
The Department of Agriculture, and Fisheries, for Scotland (Edinburgh 443 4020)

All imported animals susceptible to rabies will be kept in quarantine on arrival for six months. These include pets such as dogs, cats and rabbits, mice and monkeys. Dogs and cats must be vaccinated twice while in quarantine.

There is no national register of kennels so it is best to inspect a kennel before putting your dog in its care.

There must be a valid reason for destroying a pet, and animal societies such as the Blue Cross and the RSPCA will be able to advise and help.

Animal Defence Society Limited Animal Defence Trust (01 - 734 5922/1566)
Provides an educational and advisory service on domestic animals or birds. Can help needy dog and cat owners with money for spaying or neutering. Members of the Society pay £1 a year. The Trust is a charity.

Animal Welfare Trust (01 - 930 7698)
Finds homes for lost or unwanted dogs and cats, and helps elderly owners with vet's fees.

Blue Cross (01 - 834 4224/5556)
Maintains three animal hospitals – two in London and one at Grimsby – and clinics. They provide treatment for animals when their owners cannot afford to pay for it.

Cats Protection League (Slough 20173)
Caters for stray, unwanted, sick and injured cats or kittens. Prospective owners can get cats free through the league which has cat homes throughout Britain.

Dogs' Home, Battersea (01 - 622 4454)
Aims to restore lost dogs to their owners and gives temporary

shelter to homeless, starving dogs in London. Also cares for cats. Offers cats and dogs for sale. Will destroy an animal when either illness or age makes it absolutely necessary. Operates a free clinic for animals whose owners are unable to pay.

National Canine Defence League (01 - 935 5511)
Runs a mobile clinic for dogs whose owners cannot afford to pay vet's fees. Maintains homes for stray, lost or abandoned dogs, and will collect a dog from owners unable to look after it.

Pedigree Petfoods Education Centre (01 - 409 0291)
Provides information on the social responsibilities of pet owners, and on caring for and feeding dogs, cats and budgerigars.

People's Dispensary for Sick Animals (Dorking 81691)
A charitable trust which offers free treatment for animals owned by people who cannot afford to pay.

Royal Society for the Prevention of Cruelty to Animals (Horsham 64181)
Aims to prevent and eliminate cruelty to all animals. Maintains two hospitals in London, 71 clinics, 60 homes, one hostel at Heathrow Airport, London. It has more than 200 branches throughout the country.

Royal Society for the Protection of Birds (Sandy 80551)
Advises on making gardens suitable for birds and on how to discourage birds while observing the law. (See also Conservation.)

B

BUILDING TRADES AND MATERIALS
Brick Advisory Centre (01 - 637 0047)
Provides information and advisory service on types of bricks and the uses of bricks and their cleaning and preservation.

British Ceramic Tile Council (Stoke-on-Trent 45147)
A trade association which gives

information on all aspects of the manufacture, supply and fixing of ceramic glazed tiles and ceramic unglazed floor tiles. Provides addresses of tilers.

British Wood Preserving Association (01 - 580 3185)
Offers a free advisory service on the preservation of timber, and issues leaflets on how to deal with problems such as woodworm, dry rot and wet rot. List of qualified members available.

Cement and Concrete Association (01 - 235 6661)
Publishes do-it-yourself information on concrete.

Draughtproofing Advisory Service (01 - 950 5310)
Gives information and advice on draughtproofing homes to conserve heat.

Federation of Master Builders (01 - 242 7583)
Admits only experienced builders, and will supply a list of local qualified members.

Glass Advisory Council (01 - 629 8334)
Provides information on all kinds of flat glass, including mirrors.

Institute of Building (Ascot 23355)
The professional institute for the building industry. Advises on sources of information.

Insulation Glazing Association (01 - 629 8334)
Offers an advisory service on double-glazing and provides a list of qualified members who work to established standards.

National Association of Building Centres (01 - 637 1022)
An information service on building, building materials and products. It has centres at Bristol, Cambridge, Glasgow, Manchester and Southampton. Also advises on heating.

National Cavity Insulating Association (01 - 402 5411)
Will investigate complaints against contractors approved by the association, and runs a general advisory service.

A-Z OF USEFUL INFORMATION

**National Council of Building Material Producers
(01 - 730 9233)**
Provides information on building materials and components.

**National Federation of Builders' and Plumbers' Merchants
(01 - 439 1753)**
Provides addresses of home improvement centres in Britain.

National Federation of Building Trade Employers (01 - 637 4771; 01 - 580 4041)
Provides, through its local branches, names and addresses of members who undertake building and repair work. Investigates complaints.

National Federation of Roofing Contractors (01 - 439 1753)
Provides names of members and information on roofing, and will investigate complaints.

National Home Improvement Council (01 - 637 9709)
Shows a comprehensive range of household units and appliances at 500 centres throughout Britain. Also provides help in choosing from them. Publishes information on improving homes, getting grants, etc.

Scottish National Federation of Building Trades Employers (Glasgow 332 7144)
The federation operates in Scotland in the same way as the English organisation does.

**Tile Advisory Service
(01 - 950 5310)**
Gives information and advice on the use and availability of floor and wall tiles.

**Timber Research and Development Association
(01 - 636 8761)**
Maintains advisory services throughout the country on the uses of timber.

CHARITIES
There are literally thousands of charities in Britain and anyone who wants to leave a gift to charity

should take care to get the name of the charity right. The name of the charity can be checked in the *Annual Charities Register and Digest* available in most public libraries. A list of most charities is also kept by the Charity Commission
(01 - 214 6000).

CHILD WELFARE
(See also Adoption)
Some local councils register baby-sitters and child minders. It is best to get in touch with them through the councils.

**British Toymakers' Guild
(01 - 947 5662)**
Is concerned with maintaining quality and standards in the production and design of toys. The guild also assists individuals interested in toy-making at home.

**National Childbirth Trust
(01 - 229 9319)**
Offers help and advice on childbirth and on caring for the new baby.

CLUBS AND SOCIETIES
There are many specialised clubs and societies, and the local library or telephone directory should be able to provide a detailed list of those in your area. Further information about specialised clubs can be obtained from the organisations listed below.

**National Association of Decorative and Fine Arts Societies
(Princes Risborough 4587)**
Dedicated to the enjoyment and care of the visual arts. Members are trained to assist at houses of historic or artistic interest, museums and exhibitions.

National Association of Flower Arrangement Societies of Great Britain (01 - 828 5145)
Aims to promote interest in gardening, artistic flower arrangement, and the understanding of plants.

National Association of Women's Clubs (01 - 636 4066)
The national organisation for 1,100 women's clubs in England and Wales, which provide

informal education and social activities.

National Federation of Eighteen Plus Groups (Dartford 23591)
An independent organisation providing social and cultural recreation for 18 - 30 age group.

National Federation of Solo Clubs (Birmingham 236 2879)
Organises activities for those under 60 years of age who are either living alone, divorced, separated or widowed.

National Federation of Women's Institutes (01 - 730 7212)
Aims to improve and develop rural life in Britain through social and cultural activities.

National Housewives' Register
Aims to form groups to encourage discussion and friendship among women.

National Union of Townswomen's Guilds (01 - 589 8817/8/9)
Assists women in leisure-time activities to make life fuller and improve citizenship.

Scottish Women's Rural Institutes (Edinburgh 225 6490)
Provides social, educational and recreational opportunities for women who live and work in villages or in small towns.

**Women's Corona Society
(01 - 222 2251/2)**
A voluntary and non-political association of women of all races. Since 1950 it has aimed to provide a link between women of different countries; to promote friendship and understanding by increasing knowledge of other countries and their customs and cultures.

Women's Institutes of Northern Ireland (Belfast 26335)
Aims to improve and develop rural life through social, educational and cultural activities.

CONSERVATION
There are many specialist organisations concerned with the conservation of particular groups of plants or animals as well as other parts of the national heritage, including the landscape

and architecture. These specialist groups can usually be located through one or other of the major organisations listed below.

Council for Environmental Education (Reading 85234)
The central co-ordinating agency for organisations and individuals with an interest in environmental education. Operates an information service for teachers.

Council for Nature (01 - 722 7111)
Represents voluntary wildlife organisations at a national level. Operates an information service and publishes literature.

**Council for the Protection of Rural England (01 - 235 9481)
Scotland (Glasgow 639 2069)
Wales (Welshpool 7525)**
These bodies organise concerted action to improve, protect and preserve the scenery and amenities of the countryside and its towns and villages. They act as centres to give or obtain advice and information.

**Countryside Commission (Cheltenham 21381, Ext. 296)
Countryside Commission for Scotland**
Give advice and undertake research on conservation, recreation and public access to the countryside. They provide for parks, picnic sites, farm trails, etc.

**Royal Forestry Society of England, Wales and Northern Ireland (Tring 2028)
Royal Scottish Forestry Society (Edinburgh 577 1017)**
Membership is open to owners of small woodlands; land agents, foresters, woodmen, forest officers and consultants, and others interested in forestry.

Royal Society for the Protection of Birds (Sandy 80551)
Safeguards wild birds in their natural habitat in Britain, and manages about 60 nature reserves. Its activities include education, research and conservation planning.

Society for the Protection of Ancient Buildings (01 - 405 2646)
Provides an information service

on the treatment and repair of old buildings. Lists of old buildings for sale available.

Soil Association
Gives information on organic farming, gardening, nutrition and health. Conducts short courses.

CONSUMER PROBLEMS
The Department of Prices and Consumer Protection is responsible for administering a wide range of laws that protect the consumer. It has encouraged the setting up of consumer advice centres and provides a grant to the central services of the Citizens' Advice Bureaus. Consumers' committees have been appointed under the Agricultural Marketing Act to consider complaints about products regulated by marketing boards, particularly milk and potatoes. The Trading Standards Department of the local town hall should be contacted for complaints.

British Housewives' League Limited (Sudbury, Suff. 76374)
Established to provide housewives with an effective voice in matters concerning their welfare, and gives them information and advice. Publishes *Housewives Today* monthly.

**British Standards Institution
(01 - 629 9000)**
Participates in establishing standards for consumer goods. The Kitemark, its symbol, indicates that goods conform to those standards.

**Consumers' Association
(01 - 839 1222)**
Campaigns for improvements in consumer products, and is the largest independent consumer organisation in Britain. It publishes comparative test reports on consumer goods and services and the monthly magazine *Which?*

Housewife's Trust
An independent watchdog organisation to help the housewife in shopping for food and cleaning materials. Deals with members' complaints.

**Jewellery Advisory Centre
(01 - 353 7886/7)**
Answers general inquiries and will recommend specialised organisations for others.

Mail Order Traders' Association of Great Britain (Liverpool 236 7581)
Member firms must subscribe to the rules of the association, which provides for the protection of customers. It will take up complaints by customers.

Metrication Board (01 - 242 6828)
Provides information on the metric system, and supplies free leaflets, films and displays to familiarise people with the metric system.

National Association of Retail Furnishers (01 - 636 1778/9)
Publishes pamphlets for members to give to customers and will deal with written complaints about member firms.

National Consumer Protection Council (01 - 202 5787/6303)
Gives advice on complaints about goods or services. It is a private organisation with no membership fee and expects a contribution in return for advice.

National Inspection Council for Electrical Installation Contracting
(See Electricity.)

CRAFTS AND CRAFTSMEN
Crafts are mainly associated with traditional skills. The following organisations can advise you on individuals and firms in your area who specialise in various crafts.

**Council for Small Industries in Rural Areas (Salisbury 24411)
Scotland (Edinburgh 225 2846)**
Advisory and credit service organisation sponsored by the government to assist small firms in rural areas, and provide work. A firm is eligible for credit if it is situated in a rural area or in a country town with a population of less than 10,000, and employs not more than 20 skilled people.

**Crafts Advisory Committee
(01 - 839 8000)**
Maintains an index of crafts in each county and can supply the addresses of specialist societies.

A-Z OF USEFUL INFORMATION

CRAFTS (continued)
Craftsmen Potters Association of Great Britain (01-437 7605)
Encourages artistic ceramics. Members sell their work through The Craftsmen Potters Shop, which also provides information.

Federation of British Craft Societies (01-278 2214)
Represents craft societies, guilds and groups, and through them runs an information pool for craftsmen.

DEATH
When a death occurs in the family, there are a number of problems that have to be dealt with. If death is by natural causes, the first thing to do is to register the death. A medical certificate giving the cause of death will be made out by the doctor attending the person, or by the hospital where the person died. This will be either handed to you to take to the local registrar of births and deaths (you will find the appropriate office in the local telephone book under 'Registration of Births, Deaths and Marriages'), or posted to the registrar by the doctor, leaving you with a detachable portion to take to the registrar. He in turn will issue a 'disposal certificate', made out either for burial or cremation, which will be needed by the undertaker. The registrar will also issue a 'certificate of registration' which entitles you to a death grant (normally £30) which can be collected from your local social security office.

If a coroner has had to be called in – and this will be necessary if the death occurred while the person was not under the care of a doctor or hospital, or if the cause of death was by violence, poisoning, a road accident and so on – the registration of death will be held up until the coroner's investigations have been completed. If the coroner is involved, do not move the body until the coroner gives his permission.

Always check the deceased's papers to see whether he has expressed certain wishes for the funeral, or whether he has made any special requests for disposal of his body or parts of his body.

Body bequests are dealt with by **HM Inspector of Anatomy (01-636 6811, Ext. 3752/3576)**, who will bear funeral costs. Kidneys can be donated to a hospital but need removing immediately after death and the bequest normally applies only if death occurs in hospital. Would-be donors should apply to the **Department of Health and Social Security**. Eye donors should contact the **Royal National Institute for the Blind (01-388 1266)**. Again, these need to be extracted quickly, and are useful only up to 12 hours after death.

Cruse Organisation (01-940 4818/9047)
A national organisation providing advice and information for widows and their children.

Department of Health and Social Security (HQ: 01-407 5522)
Publishes leaflets on widows' and welfare benefits. Application cards for donation of kidneys for re-use sent on request.

Foundation for the Study of Infant Deaths (01-245 9421)
Provides support and information to bereaved parents and is a research centre for infant deaths.

National Association of Funeral Directors (01-242 9388)
Provides a list of local funeral directors who are its members. Will investigate complaints.

National Association of Master Masons (01-437 0328)
Can provide names of local master masons for headstones, and will investigate complaints against members.

Probate Personal Application Department (01-836 7366)
Grants permission to distribute among claimants the estate left by a deceased person. Grants of probate or administration made in England and Wales since 1858 are indexed, and copies of any grant or will that has been proved can be obtained for a search fee.

Record Keeper's Department (01-405 7641, Ext. 3652)
Keeps a record of all wills.

EDUCATION
Every child from the age of 5 to 16 must receive a full-time education, geared to the child's age, ability and aptitude. Parents and guardians are responsible for a child's attendance at school, but if they can give the child an education as good as, or better than, he or she would receive at school – for instance, by providing private tutors – they do not have to send the child to school.

In theory, most parents have the right to choose the school where their children will be educated but, in practice, other factors often override the choice. Local education authorities have the right to ignore parents' wishes if the choice of school would mean that the child did not receive efficient instruction, that it would involve the local authority in 'unreasonable expense'; or if the school can be shown to be unsuitable for the age, ability and aptitude of the child.

The type of course the child follows will depend on the school, the head teacher and the child's abilities. In many instances, of course, the head teacher will take the parents' wishes into account as far as possible.

Parents who are dissatisfied with any decision by a head teacher may appeal to the local education authority.

For information on grants towards school uniforms, education maintenance and travel expenses, apply to the local education authority.

Further education Many institutes and colleges offer specialist courses – for example in home economics, child nursing, newspaper work and so on. The journal of the Advisory Centre for Education, *Where?*, should be consulted for these. Local education authorities run day and evening classes in a wide variety of subjects, and the local library will usually have details of classes in the area.

Advisory Centre for Education (Cambridge 51456)
Provides an advisory service, but does not answer telephone inquiries. Runs courses for teachers and parents, and *Watch,* an environmental club for children. Publishes booklets, and the monthly magazine, *Where?*

British Association for Early Childhood Education (01-582 8744)
Will answer inquiries on the education of children up to the age of eight and will give advice on related topics.

British Council (01-930 8466)
Promotes a wider knowledge of Britain and the English language abroad; develops closer cultural relations between Britain and other countries; and administers, on behalf of the British government, educational and book aid in many developing countries. The council's overseas services department meets overseas students on arrival in London and helps certain categories of them to find long-term accommodation in London. It arranges hospitality for them in private homes and maintains contact with official and volunteer bodies.

City and Guilds of London Institute (01-580 3050)
Offers examinations and awards certificates on a wide range of technical subjects. Regulations and syllabus available.

Council for the Accreditation of Correspondence Colleges (01-935 5391)
Will provide addresses of accredited correspondence colleges.

Duke of Edinburgh's Award (01-937 5205)
The scheme offers people between the ages of 14 and 25, and those who are handicapped, a chance to win awards for activities ranging from community service to athletics.

Educational Grants Advisory Service (01-636 4066)
Provides advice to parents and students on possible sources of financial help towards educational fees, in cases of unforeseen misfortune.

Further Education
Regional advisory councils in London, Norwich, Nottingham, Newcastle upon Tyne, Manchester, Reading, Taunton, Birmingham, Leeds and Cardiff.

Independent Schools Information Service (01-222 7274/7353)
Aims to uphold the cause of independent education, and provides information about independent schools recognised as efficient.

National Adult School Union (01-387 5920)
Organises discussion groups in various parts of England, and weekend and summer schools.

National Association for Gifted Children (01-499 1188)
This association caters entirely for the needs of gifted children, helps to bring their parents together, and organises activities.

National Book League (01-493 9001)
Provides an information service on books, for adults and children.

National Extension College (Cambridge 63465)
A non-profit college which offers correspondence courses towards elementary and GCE 'O' and 'A' Level examinations, for admission to the Open University, and London University external degrees.

National Institute of Adult Education (01-637 4241)
Advises on education for mature people and publishes calendars of short residential courses.

National Union of Students (01-387 1277)
Central organisation for student activities.

Open University (Milton Keynes 74066)
Details of how the Open University works and courses leading to its degrees are available on request.

Pre-school Playgroups Association (01-582 8871)
Scottish (Glasgow 331 1340)
A national network of independent playgroups for children under five based on community involvement.

Scottish Institute of Adult Education (Edinburgh 226 7200)
Provides information and advice on adult education opportunities in Scotland for part-time and full-time study, and study at home.

Universities Central Council on Admissions (Cheltenham 5909)
This is the central office dealing with applications for admission to full-time first degree and first diploma courses at British universities (except the Open University and the University College at Buckingham). Handbook available.

White Lion Street Free School (01-837 6379)
Publishes a pamphlet on the law on alternative education and on educating children at home.

Workers' Educational Association (01-402 5608/9)
Organises evening or daytime and day-release courses, and one-day, weekend and residential summer schools at home and abroad. Has branches in most towns in Britain.

ELDERLY PEOPLE
Although there are numerous organisations which help the elderly, the social services department of the local council should be contacted first for advice on problems, such as meals on wheels, home help, etc. For advice on welfare rights of the elderly, Age Concern is the central clearing house.

Abbeyfield Society (Potters Bar 43371)
Helps elderly people living on their own through its local branches, and a list of these is available. Provides some accommodation.

Age Concern (01-640 5431)
This is the national information and advice centre on the welfare

A-Z OF USEFUL INFORMATION

of the elderly. It acts as the headquarters for 1,100 local volunteer groups which provide regular visits, clubs, day centres, transport and advice on welfare rights and benefits.

Anchor Housing Association (Oxford 22261)
Provides purpose-built self-contained flats for the elderly, with common facilities and wardens.

British Association of Retired Persons (Edinburgh 225 7334)
Aims to help elderly and retired people who live on fairly fixed incomes and find it difficult to meet the rapid increases in the cost of essentials. Members receive The Bulletin.

Department of Health and Social Security (HQ: 01 - 407 5522)
Publishes leaflets on pensions and benefits for the elderly.

Elderly Invalids Fund (01 - 353 1892)
Subsidises the cost of private homes for the elderly in Britain. This registered charity also provides an advisory service on accommodation and services.

Family Welfare Association Ltd. (See Social Problems.)

Hanover Housing Association (Egham 5451)
Provides specially designed unfurnished flats all over the country, with wardens. Can help to organise rent allowances.

National Benevolent Fund for the Aged (01 - 283 3287; 01 - 626 9509)
Aims to make the lives of lonely and needy old people happier, through activities such as outings and holidays, and television sets for those who are housebound.

National Listening Library (See Handicapped and Disabled.)

Outset (01 - 930 4255)
Conducts surveys, through volunteers, to discover disabled and chronically sick people in need of help. Volunteers also offer to do odd jobs for them.

Pre-retirement Association (01 - 767 3225/6 or 3854)
Helps people to prepare for retirement through courses and specialist publications, and its magazine, Choice.

Royal United Kingdom Beneficent Association (01 - 602 6274)
Makes annuities, grants and accommodation available for old and needy people of the professional and kindred classes.

ELECTRICITY
Lists of contractors approved by the National Inspection Council for Electrical Installation and of local consultative councils dealing with consumer problems are displayed in local shops of the Electricity Board. The board also offers advice on appliances to suit the particular needs of householders.

British Electrotechnical Approvals Board for Household Equipment (01 - 549 2202/7)
Aims to safeguard and protect the public by testing and approving household electrical equipment for safety and durability in accordance with British standards, and publishes a list of approved equipment. The board's Mark of Safety is given to approved equipment.

Dishwasher Development Council (01 - 499 0414)
Provides information on a wide range of dishwashers and detergent products.

Electrical Association for Women (01 - 437 5212)
A forum for women to express their views on the design and performance of electrical equipment. Promotes the safe and efficient use of electricity.

Electrical Contractors' Association (01 - 229 1266) Scotland (Edinburgh 225 7221/3)
Guarantees installation work of its members and its completion at the price quoted if a member goes out of business before the job is finished. Will provide a list of members or put a customer in touch with a member firm.

Electricity Council (01 - 834 2333, Ext. 387)
Promotes and protects the interests of all consumers and will investigate their complaints through consultative councils. It is advisable to make the first approach through the local electricity board.

Food Freezer and Refrigerator Council (01 - 499 0414)
Provides information on the choice of food freezers and refrigerators, packaging materials and frozen foods.

National Inspection Council for Electrical Installation Contracting (01 - 582 7746)
Guarantees consumers against faulty and unsafe wiring installations, and provides a list of approved contractors.

Radio and Television Retailers' Association Ltd (01 - 836 1463/4/5/6)
A customer advisory panel deals with complaints from the public. Will arbitrate in disputes.

EMPLOYMENT AND CAREERS
The addresses of employment exchanges and job centres, which provide an advisory service on government training schemes, may be obtained through any post office or local telephone directory. (See also Education.)

Careers Research and Advisory Centre (Cambridge 69811)
Recognised as an educational charity, this is an independent non-profit organisation, which has many publications.

Central Council for Education and Training in Social Work (Edinburgh 556 2953)
Gives information about careers and training in social work.

Claimants Union
Deals with problems members face when claiming social security. The main branches are in South-East London, East London and Birmingham.

Department of Employment (HQ: 01 - 214 6000)
Advises on terms and conditions

of employment, safety and health at places of employment, and on redundancy. Unemployment benefit forms, leaflets, available at local centres.

Department of Health and Social Security (HQ: 01 - 407 5522)
Publishes leaflets on unemployment and industrial injuries benefits, national insurance, earnings-related supplement and other welfare benefits.

Equal Opportunities Commission (Manchester 833 9244)
Provides information and advice on the Sex Discrimination Act and will help those with complaints.

National Advisory Centre on Careers for Women (01 - 589 9237)
An appointment can be made for personal advice, and other information can be obtained by post or through publications.

Over Forty Association for Women Workers (01 - 828 2867)
Helps women over the age of 40 to obtain employment, particularly those who have given up work to look after elderly parents or to bring up families, and now want to take up training courses.

Vocational Guidance Association (01 - 935 8017/2600)
Makes a scientific assessment of a person's interests, aptitudes and personality, and collects information to help a person choose the right career. This voluntary non-profit association will do a vocational test for a fee.

FABRICS AND CLOTHING
General information on fabrics can be obtained from the British Fabric Federation.

British Fabric Federation (01 - 580 4535)
A trade organisation, but will provide answers to such questions as who manufactures a particular kind of fabric, and where to buy it.

Leather Institute (01 - 407 1582)
Will advise the public on problems such as cleaning leather.

FINANCE
All the major banks have specialist departments dealing with most aspects of family finance, from arranging budgets to executing wills. They can also advise on the services provided by other financial organisations.

Building Societies Association (01 - 629 0515)
Will help with queries about obtaining a mortgage, and will investigate complaints against member societies. It will not recommend individual societies. Publications available on saving with building societies and buying a house.

Corporation of Mortgage and Finance Brokers Ltd (Wokingham 785672)
Will provide a list of members who will help with loans and mortgages, and will deal with complaints against them.

Finance Houses Association (01 - 930 3391)
Gives free advice on raising loans, and provides a list of members who lend money.

Registry of Friendly Societies (01 - 629 7001, Ext. 1)
Will duly safeguard the investments of a small investor, but does not itself give any financial aid. It is a government organisation which makes sure that friendly societies are properly run and will investigate complaints about societies.

Save-As-You-Earn Office (SAYE) (Durham 64900)
Sells National Savings Certificates and Retirement Certificates. Should be informed if any savings certificates are lost.

Savings Certificates (Durham 64900)
Men over the age of 65 and women over 60 may buy Retirement Certificates through Post Offices. Leaflets are available. The office should be notified if certificates are lost.

Stock Exchange (01 - 588 2355)
Will provide prospective investors with the addresses of reputable stockbrokers. Publications about the Stock Exchange and business also available.

Wider Share Ownership Council (01 - 236 3011)
Offers guidance to prospective investors, though not detailed advice on such matters as the selection of a portfolio of shares. Will give information on different methods of investing money.

FOOD
Complaints about food should normally be referred to the Environmental Health Department of the local council.

British Bacon Curers Federation (Tring 4124)
Supplies information and recipes on request for bacon, ham and other cured pork products.

British Egg Information Service (01 - 839 7258)
Provides cookery demonstrations, talks and films on loan, and has a demonstration theatre for up to 40 people at a time. Publishes information and books; and runs a telephone information service.

British Farm Produce Council (01 - 235 5077)
Provides up-to-date basic information about British foodstuffs, and advice on how to choose and use them, for those who write about cookery or give talks to women about food. Has a range of illustrated leaflets giving recipes and hints on quality. A telephone recipe service is available through 51 centres.

British Sugar Bureau (01 - 493 4546)
Gives information on sugar and will supply leaflets and a recipe book for a small charge.

Butter Information Council (Tonbridge 65243)
Provides information on how butter is made, different types of butter, its nutritional value and recipes for a wide variety of dishes.

A-Z OF USEFUL INFORMATION

FOOD (continued)
Dairy Produce Advisory Service
(01 - 398 4101)
Provides leaflets and recipes on how to make the best use of milk and dairy products.

Flour Advisory Bureau (01 - 493 2521)
Operates a nutrition and cookery advisory service on flour, bread and other flour products. Provides lecturers, recipe leaflets and books and films for teachers.

Health Food Manufacturers' Association (01 - 242 2746)
Provides information about health foods and allied products.

Meat Promotion Executive
(01 - 251 1264)
Gives information and advice on choosing, buying, cooking and freezing meat.

National Association of Wine and Beer Makers (York 58238)
Members meet in local groups to exchange information on techniques to improve the quality of wines and beers made by home-brew enthusiasts.

National Farmers' Union
(01 - 235 5077)
Provides discussion material for groups and organisations concerned with British foodstuffs from both the producer's and consumer's point of view. Will not deal with individual complaints. Has regional information centres in County Durham, Worcestershire, Huntingdon, Wiltshire, Hampshire, and Powys.

Potato Marketing Board
(01 - 589 4874)
Publishes low-cost cookery books and free information leaflets on potatoes. Will look into complaints from the public on potato quality.

Tea Council Ltd (01 - 248 1024)
Provides comprehensive information on types of tea and tea-making.

Vegan Society (Leatherhead 72389)
Aims to provide information on an alternative life-style for vegans, who eat only plant products.

Vegetarian Society of the United Kingdom Ltd (Manchester 928 0793)
Runs an information service on vegetarianism, organises talks, discussions and cookery demonstrations.

GARDENING
For those interested in particular plants, such as chrysanthemums, there are special societies, and the Royal Horticultural Society will advise on individual clubs.

Arboricultural Association (incorporating the Association of British Tree Surgeons and Arborists) (Guildford 2424)
Encourages proper and adequate tree planting and tree care in Britain. Maintains a directory of consultants and contractors for tree work.

Royal Horticultural Society's Garden (Ripley, Surrey 2163)
Provides an information service and advice on all aspects of gardening.

GAS
At the slightest suspicion of any gas leak at home or in the neighbourhood, call the local gas board, which has a 24 hour emergency telephone number.

British Gas Corporation
(01 - 723 7030)
There are 12 British gas regions. Their showrooms throughout the country provide leaflets and sell a wide range of appliances. They also offer a kitchen planning service. Approved appliances carry a label. A list of registered installers of gas heating is also available.

HANDICAPPED AND DISABLED
Contact the local health authority and ask for a health visitor to call to deal with any problem arising from disability, or telephone the local Social Services department. Aids needed in education or employment may be supplied by local education authorities or the Department of Employment.

Special controls can be fitted to gas cookers, fires, etc., for a standard charge, and braille controls for the blind are usually available free through the local gas or electricity board.

To find out about benefits, allowances or grants, telephone or visit the local office of the Department of Health and Social Security for leaflets. To attend one of the special training colleges for the disabled a person must be registered as disabled, and the Disablement Resettlement Officer at the local job centre can help with this.

Association for All Speech Impaired Children
This registered charity maintains regional offices which provide information to parents whose children suffer from speech or language difficulties, and helps professionals concerned with these problems.

Association for Spina Bifida and Hydrocephalus
(01 - 486 6100; 01 - 935 9060)
Provides help and care for all those with these conditions, and holidays, publications, information, equipment, grants, advice on education, training and employment, and other assistance as needed. There are local associations in most areas.

Break (Sheringham 3170)
A registered charity which provides holidays and residential care throughout the year for handicapped and deprived children.

Breakthrough Trust
(01 - 857 4170; 01 - 318 1564)
Provides information for integrating the deaf with adults and children who can hear. It organises courses on communication.

British Association of the Hard of Hearing
Gives advice on hearing aids, lip reading, and employment problems; organises home visits, educational weekend courses, and holidays at home and abroad;
runs social clubs, and will help with any problem due to partial or total deafness.

British Council for the Rehabilitation of the Disabled
(01 - 387 4037/8)
Publishes hundreds of leaflets for the disabled, particularly on holidays and travel. Publications, including motel guides, are available on request. The council gives advice and information but not aids or treatment.

British Deaf Association
Publishes books on sign-language for the deaf, provides interpreters and organises educational courses for them.

British Dyslexia Association (Bath 20554)
The association researches into the problems of dyslexia – also known as 'word blindness'. Parents of children with dyslexia can seek advice about education from the association.

British Polio Fellowship and Polio Fellowship of Ireland (Ruislip 75515)
This national voluntary organisation for those disabled by polio provides a personal welfare service, holiday and residential centres, and promotes recreational and social activities.

British Wireless for the Blind Fund (01 - 388 1266)
Provides radio sets free on permanent loan to registered blind people over the age of 16 in Britain. Applications for a set should not be made direct to the fund, but to the organisation with which the blind person is registered.

Camphill Village Trust (Watford 6006)
Assists mentally handicapped people to be independent and to adjust socially within the communities set up by the trust, and gives them guidance towards open employment and integration within society.

Central Council for the Disabled (01 - 821 1871)
Gives advice and information for
disabled people, but not aids or treatment. Publishes hundreds of useful leaflets for the disabled, including subjects such as travel and hotel accommodation.

Children and Youth Action Group Ltd (See Holidays for Children.)

Committee on Sexual Problems of the Disabled (01 - 727 4426)
Deals with sexual problems of disabled people. Prefers to answer inquiries by post.

Cripples' Help Society (Manchester 832 3678/9)
Provides a welfare and casework service for families who have disabled or deprived children; and an advisory and information service for disabled persons.

Disabled Drivers' Association (Fundenhall 449)
Does not teach disabled persons to drive but has local group activities at local and national level, such as motor rallies, driving tests and competitions. The association also arranges holidays abroad.

Disabled Drivers' Insurance Bureau (01 - 950 4455/6/7)
Arranges policies for disabled drivers at fair rates with insurance underwriters. Offers a nationwide list of assessors to deal quickly and efficiently with claims.

Disabled Living Foundation (01 - 602 2491)
Provides a comprehensive advisory service for the disabled. Maintains a showroom with aids for the handicapped, and gives postal advice on aids available to those concerned with disabled or elderly people.

Disablement Income Group Charitable Trust (01 - 247 2128)
Maintains an advisory service, and publishes an information booklet of services available for disabled persons. Provides economic and social assistance to those whose income is affected through their disablement.

Elizabeth Fitzroy Homes (Liss 3577)
Provide residential family care for
the mentally handicapped in small Christian homes, and special holidays for physically disabled youngsters.

Guide Dogs for the Blind Association (01 - 567 7001/3)
Arranges training of guide dogs at training centres. The dogs are trained mainly from puppies bred by the association, and the ownership of a dog can be transferred to a blind person on payment of a small fee. A feeding allowance and assistance with veterinary expenses are also provided.

Handicapped Adventure Playground Association (01 - 352 2321)
Provides specially designed and staffed playgrounds for handicapped children in London. There are other playground groups in the country run by hospitals and local councils and the association can provide information about them.

Hearing Aid Council
Appointed by the Board of Trade, it maintains a register of people qualified to sell hearing aids, and sets examinations for them. Will deal with complaints.

In touch
Runs a correspondence scheme for parents of mentally handicapped children or adults. A directory of addresses helpful to parents is available at a small fee.

Invalid Children's Aid Association (01 - 730 9891)
Provides an advisory service on the care of handicapped children. Does supportive work with families in parts of London and Surrey in co-operation with statutory services. Runs special schools for chronic asthmatics and children with speech problems.

Invalids at Home (01 - 452 2074)
Offers advice, help, grants, equipment and loans to invalids permanently confined at home.

Multiple Sclerosis Society (01 - 834 8231/2/3)
Promotes research into the

A-Z OF USEFUL INFORMATION

disease. Its branches throughout Britain will help disabled members.

Muscular Dystrophy Group of Great Britain (01-720 8055)
Raises funds for research into muscular dystrophy and allied neuromuscular diseases and to give help to sufferers and those who care for them. Provides a friendly link for those who suffer from the disease, both from headquarters and through its voluntary branches.

National Association for Deaf/Blind and Rubella Handicapped
Gives assistance to members and their children. Organises holidays and tries to help with the special problems of young adults who have to live permanently in hospitals.

National Deaf Children's Society (01-486 3251/2)
Parents, teachers of the deaf, otologists, welfare workers and active well-wishers of deaf children can become members. Provides a nationwide advisory and welfare service.

National Library for the Blind (01-222 2725)
Provides a free book service for all blind people, although it prefers to help those registered as blind.

National Listening Library (01-723 5008)
Supplies a postal 'talking book' library service for those who are unable to read or handle a book in the ordinary way because of physical disability or old age. A similar service for blind persons is provided by the British Talking Book Service for the Blind.

National Society for Autistic Children (01-458 4375)
An advisory service for parents, to help them with educational or hospital placement for autistic children. Aims to provide and promote centres for the care of such children.

National Society for Mentally Handicapped Children (01-229 8941; 01-727 0536)

Scottish Society for Mentally Handicapped Children (Glasgow 332 4590)
Support and help parents of mentally handicapped children through a network of local societies and regional offices. Provide an advisory and information service on mental handicaps.

Partially Sighted Society
Advises partially sighted people about careers and employment opportunities and provides information about them. This is not a registered charity but a self-help society, with regional branches.

Possum Users Association (Bristol 683596)
Originally this association was formed from the initials POSM, which stands for Patient Operated Selector Mechanism, covering a wide range of electronic aids for the severely physically disabled. The association assists people with the purchase of equipment.

Royal Association in Aid of the Deaf and Dumb (01-743 6187)
Provides a service to deaf people and helps with their day-to-day problems through trained staff. Has churches, social clubs and recreational facilities for them.

Royal National Institute for the Blind (01-388 1266)
Produces music, books and periodicals in braille, and in the raised type known as 'Moon books', and has a 'talking books' library. Runs nursery schools for blind babies and young children; special schools for blind children; holiday and residential homes; training courses, and an employment service.

Royal National Institute for the Deaf (01-387 8033)
Voluntary organisations which aim to protect the interests of all deaf people. They have a scientific and technical department which gives advice and help, a library open to the public and rehabilitation centres.

Shaftesbury Society (01-834 2656)
Maintains residential schools for

children and special homes for young men physically disabled. Also has holiday centres for the elderly and disabled, and clubs for social activities.

Spastics Society (01-636 5020) Scottish Council for Spastics (Edinburgh 337 2804)
Voluntary bodies which are concerned with the care, treatment, welfare and training of spastics – sufferers from cerebral palsy. Will provide addresses of affiliated local groups, and special schools and centres.

Toy Libraries Association (01-247 1386)
Runs lending centres for toys for handicapped children. Provides the address of the nearest one.

Voluntary Council for Handicapped Children (01-278 9441)
Refers children with special handicaps to specialised organisations. Publishes a leaflet advising parents on the services available from local councils.

Wider Horizons
Promotes wider interests among handicapped and housebound people. Those with similar interests are brought together through correspondence groups. Provides information on welfare and aids.

Winged Fellowship Trust (01-222 2589/3761)
An organisation which takes severely handicapped people for holidays in special centres.

HARDWARE
The societies listed here are only those likely to be of use to consumers. (See also Building Trades and Materials.)

Council of British Ceramic Sanitary Ware Manufacturers (Stoke-on-Trent 48675/47074)
This trade association will handle inquiries about ceramic sanitary ware. Publishes two brief consumer leaflets on bathroom fittings and care of bathrooms, which are available on request, and also a children's 'Time to Wash' leaflet.

Paintmakers Association of Great Britain (01-686 3111)
Gives information on the best sources of paint for particular uses, and lists of members.

Shower Bath Advisory and Information Service (01-353 3541/2/3)
Answers inquiries about the care and maintenance of shower baths, and will send manufacturers' catalogues on request.

Vitreous Enamel Development Council Ltd (Ticehurst 200152)
A trade association of the vitreous enamel industry, which can provide information about cleaners suitable for such surfaces and hints on looking after vitreous enamel articles.

HEALTH AND MEDICINE
Many organisations offering help to people suffering from particular diseases are charities, and it would help to send a stamped addressed envelope with a written inquiry. Contact the local authority for public health or environmental matters.

Action on Smoking and Health (01-637 9843)
Aims to discourage smoking. Runs an information service on smoking, its health hazards and methods of giving up. Maintains a list and details of smoking withdrawal clinics and aids.

Acupuncture Association and Register Ltd (01-834 1012/3353)
Provides a list of qualified practitioners of acupuncture and will deal with complaints against those on its register.

Asthma Research Council (01-229 1149)
Publishes books to help people understand about asthma and its causes, but does not provide medical advice to sufferers.

Blood Transfusion Service
There are 15 regional centres throughout the country where information can be obtained on giving blood. Would-be donors should contact their nearest centre, listed in the local telephone directory or library.

British Cancer Council (01-274 4002)
Advises the public on facilities available to cancer sufferers.

British Chiropractors' Association (Guildford 62830)
Provides a register of members recognised by the association; publishes explanatory leaflets.

British Dental Association (01-935 0875)
Will not recommend individual dentists, but will give advice on such dental topics as the value of fluoridation, recommended toothpastes, brushes and so on.

British Dental Health Foundation (01-580 0778)
A charity to educate people on oral hygiene. Will give advice and help on dental care and dentistry.

British Diabetic Association (01-636 7355)
Gives help and advice to diabetics of all ages, runs holiday camps for children and supports research.

British Epilepsy Association (01-580 2704) Scottish Epilepsy Association (Glasgow 4911)
Give help and advice on epilepsy and how to cope with it. Free literature on request.

British Homeopathic Association (01-935 2163)
Deals with inquiries about where homeopathic treatment is available. Issues publications.

British Hypnotherapy Association (01-723 4443)
The organisation for qualified psychotherapists trained in hypnotherapy. Lays down standards for the profession, maintains registers for different areas, arranges talks, broadcasts and written material about the association, and refers inquirers to qualified practitioners.

British Library of Tape Recordings for Hospital Patients (01-253 1790/3851)
Provides recorded readings of popular books for patients unable to handle books.

British Migraine Association (Ottershaw 3242)
A registered charity run by migraine sufferers, which offers help and understanding.

British Pregnancy Advisory Service (Henley-in-Arden 3225)
Owns and runs its own clinics (for abortions). Gives advice on contraceptives, sterilisation and pregnancy, including unwanted pregnancies. List of branches and nursing homes available. Charges around £65 for abortions and £3 a year for fertility control.

British Red Cross Society
(See Voluntary Work.)

British Rheumatism and Arthritis Association (01-935 9905)
Provides information, advice and aid. This welfare association has more than 100 branches in the country and a special group for sufferers aged 15-40.

British Spas Federation (Bath 66573)
Supplies information about spas in Britain.

British United Provident Association (BUPA) (01-353 9451)
Offers protection against the cost of private treatment for illness through branches in major centres in Britain.

Cancer Aftercare and Rehabilitation Society (Timsbury 70731)
An association of cancer patients, and their friends or relatives, which helps patients to return to normal life through visits and discussions. Runs social events.

Cancer Information Association (Oxford 46654)
Publishes booklets and leaflets about cancer, and provides visual aids, including films. Organises educational programmes, and lectures suitable for Women's Institutes and community centres.

Chest, Heart and Stroke Association (01-387 3012) Northern Ireland (Belfast 20184) Scottish (Edinburgh 225 6527)
Will answer inquiries, and give

A-Z OF USEFUL INFORMATION

HEALTH (continued)
advice and information. Will also give nominal sums of money, subject to the approval of the welfare officer. Does not provide medical advice, but will assist in coping with disabilities.

Colostomy Welfare Group
(01 - 828 5175)
Provides a welfare service for patients who have had or are to have a colostomy operation.

Crediton Project (Honiton 3165)
Promotes vasectomy and gives information about it.

Department of Health and Social Security (HQ: 01 - 407 5522)
Publishes leaflets on national insurance benefits.

Family Planning Association
(01 - 636 7866)
Provides birth-control services at clinics throughout the country, and gives some information on vasectomy and sub-fertility treatment, and some psycho-sexual counselling.

General Council and Register of Osteopaths Ltd (01 - 828 0601)
Members are required to meet the standards of the council. Publishes an annual directory of members which may be found in many public libraries and Citizens' Advice Bureaus.

Guideposts Trust (Witney 3981/2)
Provides a home and cares for mental patients who have recovered but remain in psychiatric hospitals only because they have no homes.

HM Inspector of Anatomy (See Death.)

Hospital Saving Association
(01 - 723 7601)
A non-profit contributory association which helps families with consultation and hospitalisation, provides spectacles and dentures, and home help.

Institute of Chiropodists
(01 - 935 6874/5)
A professional body whose main aim is to look after the interests of

its members, but will provide information about training in chiropody and addresses of qualified chiropodists. Send a stamped addressed envelope.

Keep Fit Association
This association (and the Scottish, Northern Ireland and Wales associations) works with local education authorities and evening institute classes. Will provide the name of a local secretary to help those who wish to attend classes.

Leukaemia Society
A charitable society which operates in various areas. Provides information and help for leukaemia sufferers.

Marie Curie Memorial Foundation
(01 - 730 9157/9)
Is concerned with the welfare of cancer patients. Will send educational leaflets and arrange for grants through local authorities for patients who have to be nursed at home, and for special diets, appliances, etc.

Mastectomy Association
(01 - 654 8643)
An association of women who have had a mastectomy – an operation for the removal of a breast. Will provide help, advice and information on the operation, clothing and other personal matters.

Medic-Alert Foundation
(01 - 499 2261)
A registry for those with special medical complaints and allergies. Members registered wear a bracelet or necklet inscribed with details of the condition or allergy. Operates a 24 hour telephone service for doctors or authorised persons to get further information from the member's doctor.

Mental After Care Association
(01 - 839 5953)
Provides homes and hostels for long and short-term care of adults recovering from mental illness.

National Association for Mental Health (MIND) (01 - 637 0741)
A charity which helps patients and families and promotes mental

health. Provides an advisory service for those needing help, and runs homes, schools and hostels.

National Association for the Welfare of Children in Hospital
(01 - 261 1738)
Provides an information service for parents who wish to visit their children more frequently in hospital, and a variety of welfare services. Details of children's wards, for visiting or living-in with children, are made available.

National Association of Leagues of Hospital Friends (01 - 584 7713)
A central organisation to which are affiliated over 1,000 Leagues of Hospital Friends, whose members give their time and money to provide services and amenities in local hospitals.

National Eczema Society
Helps sufferers and their families with information and through local self-help groups.

National Schizophrenia Fellowship (01 - 390 3651/2)
A voluntary association of relatives or friends of those who have this illness, or professional workers dealing with them. Aims to help families to cope with a schizophrenic person.

National Society for Cancer Relief
(01 - 402 8125)
Provides financial help to cancer sufferers in need. It maintains homes where special care is provided for those who can no longer be kept in hospitals and whose families are unable to nurse them at home.

Parkinson's Disease Society of the UK (01 - 946 2500)
A registered charity which sponsors research into the disease. Provides welfare services, which include a free information and advisory branch, and help through local groups.

Patients Association
(Oxford 50306)
Will investigate complaints about the National Health Service or private treatment, and will take up individual cases.

Phobics Society
(Manchester 881 1937)
Gives advice and help to those suffering from phobias. Branches throughout the country.

Pregnancy Advisory Service
(01 - 409 0281/4)
Gives information and advice on pregnancy and unwanted pregnancy. The service includes diagnosis, counselling, referral for either abortion or ante-natal care, and contraceptive advice.

Psychiatric Rehabilitation Association (01 - 254 9753)
Promotes research into mental illness and organises activities for the mentally ill. Provides organised hospital visiting, and day centres for discharged hospital patients.

Psychotherapy Centre
(01 - 262 8852)
Provides training in psychotherapy treatment for nervous problems, and will refer patients to psychotherapists.

Renal Society
Gives encouragement to kidney patients, especially those who have to cope with a stringent diet or a kidney machine.

Richmond Fellowship for Mental Welfare and Rehabilitation
(01 - 603 6373/4/5)
Runs an educational programme in mental health, and 'halfway houses' where those who have been emotionally disturbed or mentally ill stay temporarily.

Society of Chiropodists
(01 - 580 3228)
Provides names and addresses of its members in private practice. Literature on foot health is available on request.

Ulster Pregnancy Advisory Association Ltd
(Belfast 667345)
Has counsellors for advice on pregnancy, including unwanted pregnancy.

Women's League of Health and Beauty (01 - 769 3577)
Arranges exercises classes throughout the country.

Women's National Cancer Control Campaign (01 - 499 7532)
An educational charity concerned with cervical and breast cancers. Leaflets on these are available on request if a stamped addressed envelope is enclosed. Its mobile clinics provide screening facilities for women, in association with health authorities and industry.

HEATING
It is advisable to consult a qualified heating engineer.

Coal Merchants Federation of Great Britain (01 - 405 8218/0034)
Will provide the name of an approved merchant in a particular area. Also gives information about coal and has a training officer to advise the public on the correct fuel for a particular type of boiler.

Heating and Ventilating Contractors' Association
(01 - 229 5543)
Gives advice on heating and ventilation and will put a householder in touch with a member in a local area.

National Federation of Builders and Plumbers Merchants
(01 - 439 1753)
Provides advice about heating at home improvement centres throughout the country. A list of central-heating installers in local areas is also available.

Solid Fuel Advisory Service
(01 - 235 2020)
Supplies information on solid fuel heating and appliances, particularly central heating. Will provide the address of a local heating engineer, and will investigate a complaint if the customer has failed to get satisfaction from the engineer. Will provide a list of addresses of showrooms in the country.

HOLIDAYS AND LEISURE
Under the Trade Descriptions Act it is an offence to give false or misleading information about holiday facilities. The customer has, in law, the same protection as anyone who pays for goods or services. However, unlike the general shopper, he cannot 'examine' what he is paying for

before handing over the money. It is important, therefore, in studying holiday brochures and comparing prices, to read the 'small print' and understand exactly what is offered.

Different tour operators often offer what may appear to be identical holidays, but at different prices. But it could be a mistake to assume that the cheaper holiday is necessarily the better value. For example, it may entail travelling by night or on inconvenient days. The cost of day excursions may be extra, whereas they may be included in a higher-priced holiday. Single rooms, and rooms with special amenities, such as a balcony and sea view, may incur an expensive supplementary charge. Meals may be only 'half board' – which means that if you want a midday meal you have to pay for it out of your own pocket. Also, the bigger and more expensive hotels often provide entertainments that are not available at the more modest establishments.

Holidaymakers should insure themselves against sickness, loss or theft, and cancellation through illness or accident. Such insurance can be arranged by tour operators and travel agencies.

Many organisations run 'holidays with a difference', such as farm holidays or holidays for a special craft group. Check with the British Tourist Authority or regional tourist boards for these. Consult the telephone directory or the Sports Council for particular sports.

For sport and leisure facilities, such as swimming pools or squash in the area, inquire at the local council or library.

Association of British Travel Agents (01 - 580 8281)
Establishes and maintains a code of conduct between member firms and the public, and has conciliation machinery to deal with complaints. Travel agents who are members contribute to a fund which helps to safeguard the public if a member-firm fails or defaults. Tour operators who are members must take out a bond with the association, which is

A-Z OF USEFUL INFORMATION

used to safeguard a customer's payment if a tour company fails.

British Federation of Film Societies (01-437 4355)
Local film societies can get practical help, advice and information from the federation.

British Railways Board
Special fares offered by British Rail often last only a few months, so it is advisable to get in touch with the nearest mainline station or BR office for up-to-date information. Offers also vary from area to area, but in general there are cheap day-return tickets available. Other facilities include all-inclusive fares for visits to stately homes or zoos; excursion fares for school parties and other groups; railcards for senior citizens; and cheap tickets for children.

British Tourist Authority (01-629 9191)
This is the national tourist organisation which issues a vast range of literature about holidays and travel within Britain.

British Waterways Board (01-262 6711, Ext. 6361, 6364)
Gives information about waterways in the country and canal walks in London.

Camping Club of Great Britain and Ireland (01-828 1012)
A membership fee is required from campers or caravanners who wish to join, and an advisory service is available only to its members. This national organisation maintains a large network of sites in Britain, and provides a list of these sites.

Caravan Club (East Grinstead 26944)
An organisation for people who tour with caravans. Provides information on sites.

Forestry Commission (Edinburgh 334 0303)
Gives information about camping sites and holiday homes in forest areas throughout Britain. Maintains forest walks and woodland exhibition centres. See also Conservation.

Motor Caravanners' Club (01-874 5105/1929)
Subscribing members receive: a monthly magazine; information on insurance and suppliers of motor caravans and accessories; and lists of caravan sites at home and abroad.

National Caravan Council Ltd (Weybridge 51376/9)
A trade organisation representing most manufacturers catering for caravanners or equipment for them. Has about 4,000 caravan park operators as members. Will advise on where to buy, hire or stay, and will help with problems or complaints.

National Playing Fields Association (01-584 6445)
Gives advice and help on children's play and play leadership. This covers adventure playgrounds, holiday play schemes, conventional playgrounds, and play for the handicapped.

National Trust for Places of Historic Interest or Natural Beauty (01-930 0211)
National Trust for Scotland (Edinburgh 225 5922)
The trust owns hundreds of square miles of countryside and hundreds of properties, from stately homes to cottages. Much of the land and most of the buildings are open to the public. See also Conservation.

Passport Office
Gives information on passports and visas. There are passport offices in London, Belfast, Glasgow, Liverpool, Newport and Peterborough. (See Passports.)

Ramblers' Association (01-262 1477)
Subscribing members are entitled to its journal and annual accommodation list. Publishes guide books, maps and literature relevant to ramblers.

Scottish Tourist Board (Edinburgh 332 2433)
Assists in improving tourist amenities in Scotland; and provides information about holidays and travel in Scotland.

Sports Council (01-589 3411)
Sports Council for Wales (Cardiff 397571)
Scottish Sports Council (Edinburgh 225 5544)
The councils give information on national sports centres and run courses in sports at them. They offer grant aid and, in some cases, grants for training.

Wales Tourist Board (Cardiff 27281)
Provides a comprehensive range of literature on tourism and holiday activities in Wales.

HOLIDAYS FOR CHILDREN
Amitié Internationale des Jeunes (01-786 6857)
Arranges for British and French children and young people between the ages of 10 and 20 to exchange visits and stay at each other's homes.

Central Bureau for Educational Visits and Exchanges (01-487 5961)
Is the national information office for all educational travel and exchange, for groups as well as individuals.

Children and Youth Action Group Ltd (01-222 0261)
A non-profit organisation which provides information on children's play. Helps handicapped children. Publications sent for a fee, and a list of them is sent if a stamped addressed envelope is enclosed.

Council for Colony Holidays for Schoolchildren (Colwall 40501)
Offers, through 40 holiday centres, constructive holidays for children between the ages of 9 and 14. It is a non-profit trust supported by the Department of Education and Science.

Educational Interchange Council (Incorporated) (01-580 9137)
Arranges for young people from abroad to stay as paying guests with families in Britain.

HOUSEHOLD GOODS
The following organisations can assist you with advice on choosing and purchasing household items.

China and Glass Retailers' Association (01-839 6171)
Will give advice on where to get a particular pattern of china or glass, or the name of the manufacturer or importer.

Continental Quilt Association (Hungerford 2532)
Gives advice about problems with continental quilts.

Cutlery and Allied Trades Research Association (Sheffield 663084)
Offers advice on the care of cutlery but does not deal with complaints.

Design Centre (01-839 8000)
Scottish Design Centre (Glasgow 221 6121)
Products which bear the Design Centre label are chosen for safety, suitability of materials used, value for money and beauty of design. The centre maintains a display of well-designed products of all kinds, a design index and a photographic record of thousands of British products.

Glass Advisory Council (See Building Trades and Materials.)

National Association of Retail Furnishers (See Consumer Problems.)

National Bedding Federation (01-589 4888)
Supplies free leaflets on choosing a bed and its care afterwards.

Scottish House Furnishers' Association (Glasgow 332 6381)
This association of retail furnishers dealing in Scotland offers members a comprehensive service dealing with consumer complaints, and other matters.

UK Cutlery and Silverware Manufacturers' Association (Sheffield 663084)
Will advise on buying cutlery and silverware made in Britain and on tracing patterns or trade marks.

Wallcovering Manufacturers' Association (01-686 3111)
Gives information on the best

wallcovering for particular purposes, and a list of its members.

HOUSEHOLD SERVICES
Some household services may be provided by the local council. Local public health inspectors will look at septic and drainage tanks and advise on their installation and use and, in some cases, will eliminate pests. Commercial companies which provide the same services can be found in the telephone directory or in the classified Yellow Pages under the respective heading.
The local police station will have a list of locksmiths in the area, and the security officer will be able to advise on protecting a home against burglars. Local water boards will often renew washers for taps free of charge, and will recommend a qualified plumber in an emergency.

Association of British Picture Restorers (Littlewick Green 3288)
Advises on restoration, and puts inquirers in touch with members of the association.

Association of Master Upholsterers (01-965 3565)
Will supply a list of members and will investigate a complaint against a member.

British Antique Dealers' Association Limited (01-589 4128)
Irish Antique Dealers' Association (Dublin 722142)
Members of both associations will assist and advise on buying, selling and valuing antiques. A list of members is published.

British Association of Removers (01-837 3088/9)
Will recommend a local removal firm which is accepted as reliable by the association. Has no established code of practice but will investigate a complaint against a member. Also offers overseas services. Publishes a leaflet on helpful hints and a list of members.

British Decorators' Association (Harrogate 67292)
Members (including master

painters) conform to a code of practice, and the association will take up a complaint against a member company. Will put an inquirer in touch with the relevant regional office.

British Institute of Design (Nottingham 397250)
Will put the public in touch with members and operates a code of practice for members. Has branches serving Scotland and Ireland. Gives information on educational courses in design.

British Pest Control Association (01-582 8268)
Has a code of practice and, for a fee, will provide a directory of its members explaining the services they offer. Will investigate a complaint against a member.

British Society of Dowsers (Daventry 60525)
Gives information about water divining and maintains a list of registered qualified dowsers.

British Waste Paper Association (01-353 8420)
Collects, processes and bales waste paper to be recycled. Gives advice on the kind of paper to save and a list of local merchants who will collect waste paper in large quantities.

Carpet Cleaners Association (01-445 2899)
Will send a list of its members and will deal with complaints.

Dylon International Ltd (01-650 4801)
Runs a consumer advice bureau dealing with inquiries about the use of its products. It will advise on how to dye particular fabrics.

Good Housekeeping Institute (01-834 2331)
Gives advice on household, cookery and consumer problems.

Hard Water Information Bureau (01-636 2461)
Provides a free information service to the public, home economists, schools and colleges. A technical unit, backed by experienced chemists, deals with problems caused by hard

A-Z OF USEFUL INFORMATION

HOUSEHOLD SERVICES (cont.)
water in the home – such as scale in hot-water systems and damage to washing machines.

Home Laundering Consultative Council (01 - 493 7446)
Provides information and guidance on the International Textile Care Labelling code. Its labels tell how to wash garments.

Institute of Plumbing (Hornchurch 51236)
Members are qualified plumbers. The institute will investigate complaints of incompetence of members, providing the matter has not been referred to a solicitor.

Master Locksmiths Association (01 - 427 1123)
Will recommend a qualified locksmith in your area and will investigate a complaint against a member.

National Federation of Master Window Cleaners (Manchester 432 8754)
Will recommend window cleaners who are members; investigates complaints against members.

National Federation of Painting and Decorating Contractors (01 - 580 4041)
Is affiliated to the National Federation of Building Trades Employers. Will recommend a member to do a particular job, but does not operate a code of practice. Publications available.

Pianoforte Tuners' Association (Ashford, Kent, 27254)
Aims to maintain high professional standards. Will put the public in touch with recognised tuners; investigates complaints against members.

Sotheby and Co. (01 - 493 8080)
Will value antiques or objects of art free of charge.

HOUSING
There is a Rent Officers' Service for those who think they are being charged too high a rent. It can be located through the local town hall, where information about the Rent Tribunal is also available.

House Owners' Co-operative Ltd (01 - 427 6218)
Arranges for members the legal work of transferring property at less than the usual rates. A non-profit organisation.

Housing Centre Trust (01 - 240 3424)
Offers an information service on property (but not on individual accommodation problems), conversions, housing policy and so on. Administers a bookshop, and a library which has almost every current publication on housing available.

Incorporated Society of Valuers and Auctioneers (01 - 235 2282)
Its services for the public include recommending estate agents and auctioneers; advising on fees and scales of charges; publishing leaflets such as *Buying a House, Buying and selling at Auction*; and investigating complaints against members, who are designated by the initials FSVA and ASVA.

Mobile Homes Residents' Association Ltd (01 - 598 6017)
Gives information on how to select a mobile home and site, and get a licence.

National Council of Co-ownership Housing Societies
Provides advice and information about co-ownership of houses and represents the interests of co-owners to the government and other authorities.

National Federation of Owner-occupiers' and Owner-residents' Associations (Manchester 445 6567)
Advises members on owner-occupation, and represents them on the National House Building Council. Provides information on housing legislation and will assist with names of local solicitors and councillors if legal help is needed over difficult problems.

National Union of Ratepayers' Associations (01 - 222 6220; 01 - 886 8114)
Protects the interests of ratepayers, and provides an advisory service to members and affiliated organisations.

Rating and Valuation Association (01 - 730 7250/8/9)
A professional society whose members are involved in the operation of the present rating system, and will answer general inquiries on rating and valuation.

J

JURY SERVICE
Most people over the age of 18 and under 65 who are on the electoral register are liable for service as jurors in a criminal trial. The exceptions are those whose job is concerned with the law, clergymen, people who are mentally ill or have a prison record, and those who have not lived in Britain for at least five years since the age of 13.

Others may be excused from jury service because they cannot be away from their work (as can happen, for example, with a doctor), because of language difficulties, illness or disablement, or because they have already served on a jury within the last two years. The Jury Summoning Officer of the local Crown Court may also, at his own discretion, excuse you for a reason.

Your name is selected at random. A jury summons usually comes by post, from the local Crown Court on behalf of the Lord Chancellor's department, about a month before a trial begins. With it is an explanatory leaflet, information about your local court, and a form for you to return.

If you are selected you may have to try more than one case during the session. However, not many jurors are involved in long, complex trials, and most trials do not last more than two weeks. Attendance normally is from 9.30 a.m. to 4.30 p.m., and you are given a daily travelling and subsistence allowance, and compensation for any loss of earnings if your employer will not pay you during jury service.

L

LEGAL ADVICE
Citizens' Advice Bureaus will advise on many problems. The address of the nearest bureau can be obtained at the council offices or any Post Office or library. In some areas there are legal advice centres, either funded by the local council or run independently. Fact sheets on the rights of citizens are also available from the National Council for Civil Liberties.

For specific legal problems look under relevant headings. You can contact the Member of Parliament for your constituency by writing to him at the House of Commons. If you do not know his name, ask at the council offices.

Legal aid There are three kinds of legal aid – for giving advice, for providing a solicitor in civil court proceedings, and a solicitor in criminal court cases. The legal aid is free if a person is adjudged poor, but people with limited means have to make a contribution towards the cost. A booklet, *Guide to Legal Aid*, explains in full the circumstances in which assistance can be given and shows how individual contribution rates are worked out. It is available from law societies (see below), to whom applications for aid should be made.

Under the Legal Advice and Assistance Scheme, aid can be given with legal documents, including wills, and in disputes over redundancy payments.

Citizens' Rights Office (01 - 405 5942/4517)
Provides assistance and advice to people with problems about supplementary benefit, national insurance and housing benefits (afternoon service only).

Criminal Injuries Compensation Board (01 - 636 2812)
Anybody who has not been able to get compensation following injury due to a criminal act should write to the board.

Institute of Patentees and Inventors (01 - 222 1616)
Offers advice and guidance to inventors and research workers at all stages through to commercial adoption of ideas. Provides information on the procedure for applying for patents.

Law Society (01 - 242 1222)
Law Society of Scotland (Edinburgh 226 7411)
Law Society of Northern Ireland, Incorporated (Belfast 31614)
Will provide a list of local law societies which, in turn, will recommend a local solicitor. Deal with complaints. All three have a committee which deals with applications for legal aid.

Married Women's Association (01 - 435 2281)
Promotes the recognition of a wife as a financially and legally equal partner in marriage.

National Association for the Care and Resettlement of Offenders (01 - 735 1151/2/3)
Scottish Association for the Care and Resettlement of Offenders (Edinburgh 225 5232)
These organisations co-ordinate and help voluntary groups concerned with assisting offenders.

National Association of Citizens' Advice Bureaus (01 - 636 4066)
Northern Ireland Citizens' Advice Bureaus (Belfast 43986)
Offer free guidance and information on any subject including consumer complaints, hire purchase and buying on credit, personal and family problems, landlord and tenant obligations, welfare benefits, national insurance, employment and legal aid. The address of the nearest bureau can be obtained from the local telephone directory, or from the council offices, library or Post Office.

National Council for Civil Liberties (01 - 278 4575)
Scottish Council for Civil Liberties (Glasgow 221 4921)
Northern Ireland Civil Rights Association (Belfast 2335)
These councils are active on a wide range of issues. They publish a number of fact sheets and pamphlets about legal rights, and details of publications and membership are available on request. A rights-for-women unit advises women and takes up cases under the Equal Pay and Sex Discrimination Acts.

The councils do not take legal action but can give legal advice on arrest, bail, police questioning, police complaints, solicitors and so on.

Preservation of the Rights of Prisoners (01 - 435 1215)
Helps prisoners to rehabilitate themselves in society, with accommodation and friends.

M

MARRIAGE AND DIVORCE
People who are too closely related are not allowed to marry according to the laws in Britain. For example, a man may not marry his brother's or sister's daughter, or daughter-in-law, and a woman may not marry her brother's or sister's son, or a stepson. In England and Wales, marriage is not permitted when one party is below the age of 16.

Anybody in England and Wales over the age of 16, but under 18, must obtain the consent to marry of both parents, or the parent who has custody (in the case of a divorced couple), or the local authority which has assumed parental rights over a child.

The marriage must be properly conducted, either in a church or in the marriage room of a Registrar of Marriages. All marriages must be registered. Both the church authorities and the Registrar of Marriages require a minimum residential qualification in the district, or parish.

Even though parental consent is still not required in Scotland, for a person over 16 to marry, a minimum residence in Scotland of 15 days must now be established, followed by seven clear days of public notice of marriage.

The Registrar of Marriages normally requires that notice of intended marriage is displayed for 21 days before he issues a Certificate of Marriage – valid for three months, during which time the marriage must take place or the whole process is repeated again. He will, in some cases, issue a certificate, and a licence to allow a marriage to take place after the elapse of one clear weekday, but an extra fee is charged.

A-Z OF USEFUL INFORMATION

The Church of England will also help a couple who wish to marry at short notice, or even issue a special licence in exceptional circumstances – for example, if a couple need to avoid publicity, or one partner is dying – to take place according to church rites but outside church premises.

A polygamous marriage is one in which a man or woman takes more than one wife or husband. Such a marriage is illegal in Britain and would be void if it took place. If, however, a polygamous marriage is valid by the law of the domicile of both the partners, the marriage is generally recognised as valid in Britain. But the parties of a polygamous or potentially polygamous marriage cannot take action under English law to seek a divorce, a separation, annulment, or a maintenance order, even if they permanently live in this country.

Most churches offer marriage guidance and help services.

Changes in the divorce laws were made in 1963 to make it easier for estranged husbands and wives to become reconciled. However, the Divorce Reform Act of 1969 made it possible for divorce to be obtained by consent. The only ground for divorce is irretrievable breakdown of the marriage and it is no longer necessary to prove a matrimonial offence. Five years' separation is recognised as proof that the breakdown is irretrievable, even though one partner might be unwilling to end the marriage. A two-year separation is sufficient if both partners consent.

Divorce Registry
(01 - 405 7641, Ext. 3392)
Deals with divorce, judicial separation and nullity of marriage (in common with county courts throughout England and Wales). A leaflet briefly explaining how to go about getting a divorce is available from the local divorce county court (for address see local telephone directory).

Divorce Registry and Probate Office, Belfast (Belfast 35111)
Registers divorces in Northern Ireland and deals with probate.

Family Welfare Association Ltd
(See Social Problems.)

Institute of Marital Studies
(01 - 435 7111)
Undertakes casework with marital problems, and offers training and consultation to professional groups who are working with marriage and related problems. Conducts research into these, and has specialised caseworkers and psychiatric consultants.

National Marriage Guidance Council (Rugby 73241)
Northern Ireland (Belfast 23454)
Scottish (Edinburgh 225 5006)
There are about 140 marriage guidance councils in Britain affiliated to the national councils; addresses may be got from local telephone directories. These provide a personal counselling service for marriage and family problems. Many of them also provide family life education for schools and adult groups, and run courses in preparation for marriage. Many books and pamphlets available.

MOTORING
Your local Citizens' Advice Bureau can help you to find out if a secondhand car is still carrying any hire purchase or credit sale liability. There is no fee.

Automobile Association (AA)
(HQ: Basingstoke 20123)
The largest of the country's motoring organisations. It issues a handbook to members that grades hotels and garages according to standards of service and facilities, and operates a vehicle breakdown and recovery service. Also gives touring and travel information, technical and legal assistance, and insurance benefits. It campaigns vigorously for motorists' rights and motoring reforms, and it publishes guide books and books on motoring.

Motor Agents' Association Ltd
(01 - 580 9122)
Scottish Motor Trade Association Ltd (Edinburgh 225 3643/4)
These two associations maintain a code of practice for the retail motor trade, and deal with complaints against member firms.

Motor Insurers Bureau
(01 - 248 4477)
Deals only with compensation to victims of uninsured or untraced motorists, and will not give advice on other insurance questions.

Motor Schools Association of Great Britain Ltd
(01 - 385 3589/3128)
This is a trade association and professional body. It is concerned with standards of behaviour, staff training, road safety, and educating the public in traffic matters. It will take up a complaint against a member.

Pedestrians' Association for Road Safety (01 - 836 7220)
Campaigns for speed limits, alcohol checks, controlled pedestrian crossings, pedestrian precincts, walkways and for traffic-free areas. A registered charity, it has local affiliates.

Royal Automobile Club (RAC)
(HQ: 01 - 930 4343)
Offers members a car rescue and recovery service; telephone boxes; service centres; road signs; touring; a travel information bureau; legal aid; technical aid; insurance benefits; and the RAC finance plan.
Approves rallies and has offices throughout Britain.

Society of Motor Manufacturers and Traders (01 - 235 7000)
Operates a code of practice under the Fair Trading Office. Anybody who buys a new car and gets no satisfaction from the dealer on complaints about a defect can complain to the society which will investigate the matter.

PASSPORTS
It is not necessary to write to any of the regional Passport Offices for an application form: these can be obtained from most travel agencies or any local employment exchange. The form must be countersigned by a doctor, lawyer, minister of religion, police officer, or someone of similar standing who knows the applicant.

A standard passport is valid for ten years, after which it can be renewed. It allows the holder to travel anywhere in the world, but most countries outside western Europe also require the traveller to obtain a visa – a separate permit to visit their territory. Visas are obtainable from the embassies or consulates of the countries concerned in London. A simpler and cheaper form of passport, valid for one year only, can be used for visits to a restricted list of countries, which includes most of western Europe and Scandinavia.

Husbands and wives can have a joint passport, with their children included. This is cheaper than the cost of separate passports.

A bride-to-be, planning a honeymoon abroad, may apply for a passport in her future married name, but she must agree to surrender it if for any reason the marriage does not take place.

PENSIONS
An application for pension should be made through the Department of Health and Social Security, and the address of the local office may be obtained from the telephone directory, under 'Health and Social Security, Department of'. (See also Elderly People.)

National Federation of Old Age Pensions Associations
Offers advice and assistance on retirement, pensions, etc.

Royal British Legion
(01 - 930 8131)
Members of this organisation are concerned with caring for and helping ex-service men and women and their dependants, particularly in matters affecting their health, employment, housing for the elderly, and entitlement to war disability or war widows' pensions.

PETS (see Animals and Pets.)

PROFESSIONAL SERVICES
Before employing anyone in your home, make sure that your household insurance policy includes cover for them. A small extra premium may be needed.

Association of Insurance Brokers
(Colchester 44343)
Will provide a list of members who can advise on insurance, will recommend a local broker, and will investigate complaints against a member.

British Insurance Association
(01 - 248 4477)
Irish Insurance Association (Dublin 681162/681962)
Publish information leaflets, statistics and lists of members, who include about 300 insurance companies. Aim to promote and protect members' interests but also to provide an information service, on household, car insurance, etc., and to deal with complaints about members.

Chartered Insurance Institute
(01 - 606 3835)
Will give the address of insurance companies, and advice in the event of a company going bankrupt.

Corporation of Insurance Brokers
(01 - 588 4387)
Represents 630 member companies and members who have passed its test, and who must be able to give sound advice. Will recommend a member and will take up a complaint against broker companies.

Faculty of Architects and Surveyors Ltd (01 - 935 9966/7)
Incorporates the Institute of Registered Architects. Will supply the name and address of a suitable architect or surveyor.

Federation of Insurance Brokers
(Coventry 21999)
Represents the interests of both members and consumers, and will investigate a complaint against a member. List of members available.

Incorporated Society of Valuers and Auctioneers
(See Housing.)

Institute of Chartered Accountants in England and Wales
(01 - 628 7060)
A professional body for chartered accountants, with over 60,000 members who are either practising public accountants, or provide specialised services in auditing, accountancy, company work, taxation, etc. Will investigate a complaint against a member. The list of members can be seen in most public libraries.

Irish Auctioneers and Valuers Institute (Dublin 762011/763451)
Will send a list of its members, and will investigate a complaint against a member.

Life Offices' Association
(01 - 248 4477; 01 - 236 5117)
Associated Scottish Life Offices (Edinburgh 556 7171)
A list of member companies offering life insurance is available on request and the association will investigate a complaint against a member. They also provide an information service on life insurance.

Royal Institute of British Architects
(01 - 580 5533; 01 - 323 0687)
Royal Incorporation of Architects in Scotland (Edinburgh 229 7205)
The clients' advisory service of the Institute will provide the address of a local architect for home improvement or construction. It will investigate a complaint against a member and publishes a booklet giving advice on employing an architect. The Scottish organisation is affiliated to RIBA and offers the same kind of services.

Royal Institution of Chartered Surveyors (01 - 839 5600)
Will provide names of surveyors who can undertake particular types of work, and will investigate a complaint against a member.

PUBLIC SERVICES
Council offices provide many services, such as putting a person in touch with the district surveyor or health inspector, or with a Chamber of Commerce which may be able to supply the address of a local firm for a particular job. The Post Office also offers a wide range of services.

Post Office
Most people are not aware of the range of services offered by the

A-Z OF USEFUL INFORMATION

PUBLIC SERVICES (continued)
Post Office. Comprehensive information about these services and how to use them is given in *The Post Office Guide* which is available for inspection at any Post Office and on sale at main Post Offices.

The guide gives detailed information on matters ranging from how to pack parcels, to what can and cannot be sent by post, inland and external services, and savings and banking facilities. Not all the services are available at all the Post Offices in the country. In general, the local electoral register and a list of useful addresses, such as local Citizens' Advice Bureaus or the local Department of Health and Social Security, can be found at main Post Offices.

Over the counter Apart from stamps, stamped envelopes and air-letters, there are many application forms which can be obtained over the counter at any Post Office. These include licence forms for a dog, game, game dealer, or gamekeeper; renewal of vehicle licence or of change of ownership; driving tests and vehicle tests; British Passport or British Visitor's Pass.

A licence for a television set can be obtained from a Post Office; it costs less for those who are blind, and a composite licence is available for those who live in an old people's home.

You can buy: National Insurance stamps, and stamps for contracts and legal forms (for example, for leases); money orders, National Savings Certificates, and Premium Savings Bonds. The Post Office operates a Save As You Earn (SAYE) service, and a National Savings Bank, and provides a low-cost current banking account and money-transfer service.

You can apply for refunds on National Health prescriptions and collect pensions, including Sickness and Invalidity Benefit, Supplementary Pension, Maternity or Family and other allowances, Widow's Retirement, Old Persons and War Pensions. You can also buy Thomas Cook Traveller's Cheques.

Postal service extras Letters can be registered and insured up to a value of £600. A certificate of posting can be obtained. Letters can be addressed to a person to be collected at any Post Office (except a town sub-office).

Letters can also be handed in at a railway station, sent by the first available train and collected at another station; or from one airport to another served by British Airways.

Many postal areas operate a special service by which first-class mail can be delivered by a messenger. If you send an international reply-paid coupon with a letter posted abroad the person receiving it can exchange the coupon for stamps to send a reply.

Telegrams can also be sent reply paid. You can ask for a telegram to be delivered, transmitted by phone to the receiver, or by telex, or sent to a temporary address, such as a caravan, a ship or an aircraft.

In rural areas a postman on his delivery rounds will accept letters, or postal parcels, for posting.

In special circumstances the Post Office will collect money specified by a sender (Cash on Delivery).

Exemption from postage Books and papers for blind people (and letters to or from them) can be sent free by first-class post. Packets should be clearly marked *Article for the Blind*. Overseas mail, guide dog harnesses and braille books and maps for the blind can be sent free by post. Petitions to the Queen, or to Parliament through a Member of Parliament, may be posted free of charge.

Telephone services The Post Office also provides a range of special telephone services, which differ from one part of the country to another. For example, you can dial a bedtime story in Welsh, or current rates of foreign exchange. The numbers for most of these services are given in the local directory or the local STD code book. You may dial for the time, a record, reports on road conditions, a recipe for the day, cricket scores, or business news. You can ask for an alarm call to wake you up at a specified time.

Credit cards are issued for telephone calls or telegrams by telephone to be made without prepayment. The cost of a call made through an operator can be ascertained after the call has been made, if the operator is told beforehand. When a call is made to a particular person by name (as against to a number) it is charged for only if the person is available to answer. The Post Office will install, if you wish, a flameproof, lockable, or showerproof telephone, or a coin-box. It will also replace the normal ringing tone with neon signalling, buzzer, or hooter.

National Giro This is a low-cost current account banking and money transfer service, and conditions of the service are set out in the Giro Handbook, available for reference at any Post Office.

Envelopes with free first-class postage are provided for all account transactions sent to the Giro centre. Standing orders can be issued to pay regular bills. Statements of accounts, receipts and payments, are issued frequently. Giro cheques can be used to draw cash at a Post Office.

Complaints In case of difficulties, or for complaints against the Post Office, contact the *Post Office Users' National Council (01-928 9458)*. This is a government-sponsored organisation for consumers, with councils also in Scotland, Wales and Northern Ireland.

For telephone services there is an independent consumer organisation for members, the *Telephone Users' Association (01-883 7229)*.

Public Record Office
(01-405 0741, Ext. 205)
Scottish Record Office
(Edinburgh 556 6585, Ext. 43)
Public Record Office in Northern Ireland (Belfast 661621)
These offices keep records of government departments and courts of law which go back to the time of William the Conqueror. Search rooms are open to the public. The Scottish and Northern Ireland offices also have exhibitions of documents, and keep their own records.

Registry of Business Names
All firms (including individual proprietors trading under the name of a firm) are required to register under the Registration of Business Names Act of 1916. The particulars (such as the name of the company under which a person is operating, address of principal place of business, nature of business, etc.) may be inspected on payment of a standard search fee.

Society of Genealogists
(01-373 7054)
Undertakes research into family history. Non-members may use library (for fee).

SOCIAL PROBLEMS
There are numerous organisations tackling social problems in different fields. If the name of a particular society is not given below, contact the National Council of Social Services. Many churches also have welfare and assistance units.

Al-Anon Family Groups UK and Eire (01-403 0888)
A fellowship of relatives and friends of alcoholics who try to help each other to live with an alcoholic.

Albany Trust (01-582 0972)
Gives help and free advice on psycho-sexual matters, by appointment. Will refer an inquirer to a specialist.

Alcoholics Anonymous
(01-352 9779)
Aims to help people with a drink problem to stop drinking alcohol. Serves Great Britain and Ireland through many branches, addresses of which may be got from the telephone directory.

Alive and Well (01-567 5339)
An answering service for young people who have left home and who wish to inform their parents that they are all right without directly contacting them.

Association for the Childless
Provides information and advice to childless persons concerning fertility, loneliness, other interests, etc., and arranges social outings.

Brook Advisory Centre
(01-580 2991)
Advises young people on contraception methods. Has centres in Birmingham, Bristol, Cambridge, Coventry, Edinburgh, Liverpool, London.

Child Poverty Action Group
(01-242 3225/9149)
Campaigns for better understanding and help for poor families. Gives such families information on their rights and advice on how to get the maximum in welfare benefits and from the law. Operates a citizens' legal rights advice office.

Department of Health and Social Security (HQ: 01-407 5522)
Publishes pamphlets on benefits available through sickness, unemployment, retirement, and on general welfare benefits.

Family Welfare Association Ltd
(01-254 6251)
Offers professional counselling services on all problems of family relationships. Teaches and trains people in social work. Publishes a *Charities Digest* and a *Guide to the Social Services*.

Gamblers Anonymous
(01-352 3060)
This is a self-help fellowship for those with a gambling problem. Also runs a sister fellowship for families of compulsive gamblers.

Gingerbread (01-734 9014)
A self-help organisation for one-parent families which has groups throughout the country offering mutual help and advice, social activities, babysitting rotas, clothing and toy pools.

Helping Hand Organisation
(01-222 6862/3)
Has hostels, and offers help for people disabled by mental or emotional illness associated with alcoholism or other dependencies. Offers rehabilitation and training.

Institute for the Study of Drug Dependence (01-328 5541/2)
Maintains details of sources of help and advice for drug users, their parents and others involved with them, throughout Britain. No treatment is given at the institute.

National Advisory Centre on the Battered Child (01-361 1181)
Will give help and advice to members of the public who have a battered-child problem, and will refer people to local centres.

National Association for Maternal and Child Welfare (01-387 1874)
Aims to further understanding of maternity and child welfare, and offers an advisory service.

National Council for One-parent Families (01-267 1361)
Offers information, advice and free help to lone parents and pregnant single women.

National Council for the Single Woman and Her Dependants
(01-828 5511)
Provides advice and help for single women with dependants.

National Council of Social Service (01-636 4066)
Offers families and individuals under stress a social welfare service. Has many publications on such subjects as handicaps, health and women's rights. A list of women's organisations in Great Britain is available for a small fee.

National Federation of Community Associations
(01-636 4066)
Provides an information service on community work through visits and by correspondence. It is part of the National Council of Social Service, and aims to promote a spirit of community, fill gaps in community services and bring individuals together. Gives advice and assistance to those seeking to form a community association.

National Society for the Prevention of Cruelty to Children (01-580 8812)
Royal Scottish Society for the Prevention of Cruelty to Children (Edinburgh 225 5377/2912)
Help parents who have financial

A-Z OF USEFUL INFORMATION

or other problems because of their children and marriage. Investigate reports of neglect or ill-treatment of children.

National Women's Aid Federation (01 - 586 0104)
Provides refuge for battered women and their children.

New Life Foundation Trust (Newark 2807)
Offers residential counselling for long-term after-care for young persons with a serious drug problem.

Parents Inquiry (01 - 698 1815)
Deals with families with homosexual children, providing counselling and social facilities.

Phoenix House (01 - 699 5748/1515)
Financed by the government, it aims to rehabilitate people who have been dependent on drugs. People with a problem of drug abuse may apply directly to Phoenix House, but it does not offer a general information service.

Release (01 - 289 1123)
A legal and welfare aid organisation primarily to help young people in trouble with the law over drugs. It is also concerned with women's rights, and gives general advice about arrest, housing, tenants' rights, and pregnancy and abortion.

Salvation Army Family Services Department (01 - 985 1181)
Answers inquiries from fathers and husbands on reconciliation and maintenance.

Salvation Army Investigation Department (01 - 247 6831)
Helps to find relatives (but not husbands or reputed fathers) over the age of 17 for reconciliation.

Samaritans (Slough 32713/4)
A confidential, free 24-hour service which will listen to and befriend those in despair and with suicidal urges. Can be contacted by telephone, letter or visit, and the number and address of the nearest branch can be obtained from the telephone directory.

Scottish Council for Single Parents (Edinburgh 556 3899)
Ensures that single parents get the help they need, and will direct inquiries to an appropriate source of help. It is affiliated with similar organisations and brings these together for consultation on the welfare of single parents and their children in Scotland.

SOS Society (01 - 584 3717/8)
A registered charity, it runs homes and hostels for elderly men and women of limited means, those without relatives and friends, those recuperating from mental illness, or young men starting work away from home.

Women's Aid Ltd (01 - 995 4430)
A refuge, open as a centre and a community for the long and short-term difficulties faced by women, such as wife battering, isolation, problems of growing children, work and so on.

VOLUNTARY WORK
There are many voluntary bureaus attached to particular groups, such as those concerned with disabled people, children, and conservation. Many are charities, and if you cannot find a group you would like to work with look under the heading Social Problems. Most churches have some kind of voluntary organisation and many boroughs or local councils now have volunteer bureaus.

Board for Information on Youth and Community Service (Edinburgh 566 8671)
Answers inquiries on voluntary youth services in Scotland.

British Red Cross Society (01 - 235 5454)
Is concerned with first aid, nursing and welfare in peace time. Needs and welcomes volunteers, even with only a few hours to spare, for a wide range of activities in hospitals and communities to help the frail, sick, elderly or handicapped, as well as with administration. Ring the local branch for information.

Community Service Volunteers (01 - 278 6601)
An advisory service which gives materials, ideas and kits to teachers and others who wish to establish local programmes of part-time community service. It gives young people the opportunity to give full time service to the community, for periods from four to 12 months, throughout the British Isles. They are located at adventure playgrounds, in Borstal institutions, with children in care, hospitals for the handicapped, or community projects.

Concordia (01 - 629 3367/8)
A programme of international agricultural work camps for volunteer workers.

Contact (01 - 240 0630)
Brings lonely old people companionship through younger people.

Council for British Archaeology (01 - 486 1527)
Publishes a list of sites where volunteers are needed for archaeological digging.

International Voluntary Service (Leicester 541862)
Selects volunteers with professional or technical qualifications for long-term service in developing countries. Also places volunteers in international work camps in the UK. These camps in the UK are concerned with community development and mental health, and carry out such work as building a community playground or teaching English to immigrants.

National Association of Leagues of Hospital Friends
(See Health and Medicine.)

National Conservation Corps (01 - 722 7112/3)
Volunteers join work parties to make a practical contribution to conservation.

Oxfam (Oxford 56777)
Raises funds to help the poorer peoples of the world. It has local branches in many parts of Britain.

St John Ambulance Association (01 - 235 5231)
Gives training and crash courses for householders, and its volunteer members attend public functions to provide first aid.

Scottish Council for Social Service
Publishes a directory of voluntary organisations in Scotland.

Task Force (01 - 602 1469)
Needs volunteers, but only in London, to visit lonely old people and to do decorating, gardening or household jobs for them.

Voluntary Service Overseas (01 - 262 2611/2485)
Provides information and help to volunteers working abroad.

Volunteers Advisory Service (01 - 388 0241)
Puts inquirers in touch with volunteer bureaus in various parts of London.

Women's Royal Voluntary Service (01 - 499 6040)
Undertakes welfare work for government departments, local authorities and local community services, and trains its members to give help in emergencies.

YOUTH ORGANISATIONS
Air Cadets (East Bridgford 771, Ext. 403)
Promotes and encourages a practical interest in aviation and in the RAF. Can be joined by boys aged between 13 years and 17 years 9 months, who can be members up to the age of 22, depending on rank attained. Fosters a spirit of adventure and develops qualities of leadership, through lectures, adventure, training, sport, gliding and flying. The associated **Combined Cadet Force** is open to both boys and girls, but membership for girls depends on the number waiting to join (a minimum of ten) and the availability of a woman instructor.

Army Cadet Force Association (01 - 834 1727)
Open to boys of 13 to 18 years, with detachments in all parts of Britain where training is given in camping, drill, shooting, games and citizenship.

Boys' Brigade (01 - 736 8481)
A church-based organisation, operating in Britain and in 64 other countries, for boys from the age of eight who are taught to lead a fuller life based on Christian principles.

Girl Guides Association (01 - 834 6242)
A voluntary uniformed organisation open to girls from the age of 7 and to women, regardless of race, religion or other differences, but on condition they take the Guide Promise (that is, swear duty to God and the Queen, and to help others). Wide range of activities.

Girls' Brigade (01 - 736 8481)
Open to girls from five years old upwards. The organisation is church-based and has aims similar to those of the Boys' Brigade.

National Association of Boys' Clubs (01 - 636 5357)
Co-ordinates the activities of 1,912 affiliated clubs in Britain which aim to help their members grow into good citizens. It is also a clearing house for ideas and information. Organises national and regional sports and artistic competitions, promotes training courses for its members.

National Association of Youth Clubs (Nuneaton 61921/2)
Aims to provide information, advice and publications on youth club work, and to organise training courses and conferences for young people and club members and run national sports competitions.

National Federation of Young Farmers' Clubs (Coventry 56131) Scottish Association of Young Farmers' Clubs (Edinburgh 333 2445/6) The Young Farmers' Clubs of Ulster (Belfast 744292/3)
Open to anyone under the age of 26 who has an interest in farming and the countryside. There are clubs in all parts of Britain, not confined to rural areas.

National Youth Bureau (Leicester 538811/6)
This organisation offers information on youth and field work, and research and training services. It has publications and visual teaching aids.

Scout Association (01 - 584 7030)
Uniformed organisation open to boys and youths from the ages of 8 to 20, to prepare them for manhood through progressive training. Members are encouraged to use their abilities to develop self-confidence and self-reliance. The Scout Fellowship is open to men and women over the age of 18 who are prepared to support the Scout movement in any way, even if they have not previously been active in the movement. Adults up to the age of 65 can become Leaders – previously known as Scoutmasters.

Sea Cadet Corps (01 - 540 8222)
A voluntary youth organisation formed to develop leadership, devotion to duty and self-respect in boys between the ages of 12 and 18. Helps boys who are considering a seafaring career.

Young Men's Christian Association (01 - 520 5599) Young Women's Christian Association of Great Britain (01 - 636 9722/6)
Provide hostels and residential clubs for young people and are involved with national camps, colleges, educational research programmes, holiday centres and refugees. An accommodation advisory service is available for women and girls.

Youth Hostels Association (England and Wales) (St Albans 55215) Scottish Youth Hostels Association Youth Hostel Association of Northern Ireland Ltd
The associations aim to encourage knowledge and use of the countryside. They run hostels, mainly in areas of natural beauty, which provide inexpensive overnight accommodation for their members.

INDEX

INDEX

INDEX

INDEX

INDEX

INDEX

ACKNOWLEDGMENTS

Many people and organisations assisted in the preparation of this book. The publishers wish to thank all of them for their help or for allowing their houses to be photographed.

Adeptus Designs Ltd (London)
Afia Carpets
R. Allen & Co. Ltd (Butchers)
Aluminium Federation Ltd
American Folk Art Ltd
Antiference Ltd
Aram Designs Ltd
Armstrong Cork Co. Ltd
Sally M. Ashworth
B. P. Chemicals International Ltd
John Baily & Sons Ltd
Bamboo Prosperity
Corinna Bateman
Bayliss & Sons Ltd
Kenneth A. Beckett
Beckfoot Mill
Bedlam
Bissell Appliances Ltd
David Black Oriental Carpets
The Boots Company Limited
Peter Boswell (Restorations) Ltd
British Carpet Industry Technical Ass.
British Gas Corporation
British Safety Council
The British Standards Institution
Browns
The Building Centre (London)
Alastair and Sarah Campbell
Fiona Campbell Ltd
Casa Pupo Ltd
Chubb and Sons Ltd (Leonard W. Dunham, Deputy Chairman)
Michele G. Clarke, BA (Hons)
Martaine Clason
Clevedon Court and the National Trust
Click Shelving Ltd
Margot Coatts
Concord Lighting International Ltd
Condotti
The Conran Shop
The Consumers' Association
Continental Quilt Association
Courtaulds Ltd
John Crossley & Sons Ltd
Crown Decorative Products Ltd (Tom Pearson)
CubeStore Ltd
Margaret Currie
Danish Food Centre (London)
Delomosne and Sons
The Design Council
Designers Guild
Divertimenti
June Dixon
Dixons Technical Ltd
Terence Donovan
Peta and Michael Drew
Roger DuBern
Dunlop Semtex Ltd
Dunlopillo Industrial Division
The Dutch Dairy Bureau
Dyno-Rod Ltd
E. Eaton Wholesale Ltd
Faith Eaton
The Electricity Council
Fish Trader (Graham Large)
Floor Treatments Ltd
Food Freezer and Refrigerator Council
Formica Ltd
Fortnum and Mason

Felicia France
Anna French
French Dairy Farmers Ltd
Fruit Trades Journal (Barbara Coyle)
Furnishing Textile Association Ltd
Furniture Industry Research Association
Robin Gage (Antiques)
Frederic Gaiger
Galt Toys
General Trading Company
Gilt Edge Carpets Ltd
J. Goddard & Sons Ltd
E. Gomme Ltd
Habitat Shops
I. G. E. Harrison-Hansley
Harrods (Knightsbridge)
Robin Hartley
Harvey Nichols
John Harvey Wine Museum, Bristol
Heals
Leslie Hersham
Heuga Carpet Tiles
Nicholas Hills, M.Des. (RCA), ARIBA
Home Heating Advisory Centre
Hygena Ltd
IBM United Kingdom Ltd
Ibstock Building Products Ltd
ICI Paints Division
ICI Plastics Division (D. N. Buttrey)
In Pine Ltd
Institute of Plumbing (W. A. Watts)
Jackson Day Designs
Robert Jacksons and Co. Ltd
Bernard Jacobsen
Jewellery Advisory Centre
Derek G. John, Dip. Arch., MRTPI
Johnson Wax Ltd
Kosset Carpets Ltd
Dr Walter Lachmann
The Leather Institute
Lever Brothers Information Service
John Lewis Partnership
Liberty & Co. Ltd
Lighting Industries Federation
Lillywhites Ltd
Lina Stores Ltd
Mark Livingston
Albert Locke
London Bedding Centre
London College of Furniture
London Lighting Co. Ltd
Loot Antiques
Carol Macartney
John and Moira McConnell
Hugh Mackay & Co. Ltd
Henry S. McNeil
Victor Mann & Co. Ltd
Marianne Interior Designs
Marley Retail Supplies Ltd
Mattessons Meats Ltd
David Mellor
Mercury Antiques
Metal Weatherstrips Ltd
The Metrication Board
Molton Brown
Dinah Morrison
Mr Stone's Flooring and Tiling Shop Ltd
Nairn Floors Ltd
National Association of Flower Arrangement Societies (Jean Taylor)
National Bedding Federation

Heinz Norden
Michael O'Connor (Cellarmaster of the Dorchester Hotel)
Oliver-Sutton Antiques
O. M. K. Design Ltd
Robert Opie
William and Clare Packer
Ron Page
Paperchase
Parker Knoll Textiles Ltd
Parrots
Paxton & Whitfield Ltd
Primrose Peacock
Penguin Books Ltd
William Perring Ltd
Philips Electrical Ltd
Peter Phillips, Member of the Master Locksmiths' Association
Pirelli Ltd
Pulbrook and Gould Ltd
Quintiques Too (Barrie Quinn)
C. Rassell Ltd
The Rating and Valuation Association
Reckitt and Colman Ltd
Reed Harris Ltd
Rentokil Ltd (Peter Bateman)
Retail Trading Standards Association
Royal Doulton Tableware Ltd
Royal Institute of British Architects
Royal Institution of Chartered Surveyors (David Blake)
Rufflette Ltd
Ryman Ltd
Sandersons
Christine Schell
The Singer Company (U.K.) Ltd
Sleepeezee Ltd
Slumberland Ltd
Spillers Ltd
Sterling Roncraft
Sunway Blinds
Swish Products Ltd
Swiss Cheese Union
Guy Talbot
Tamesa
Joanna Tanlaw
David A. Taylor, BA (Edin.), ARIBA
Kate Taylor
Tebrax Ltd
John and Sally Thompson
Maureen Thompson
Thorn Lighting Ltd
Tomorrow Antiques
Treasure Island
Jane Tresidder
Tretford Carpets Ltd
Betty and Vera Vandekar Antiques
Verity Mirrors
Victoria and Albert Museum
Vigers, Stevens and Adams Ltd
The Waddington Galleries
Josiah Wedgwood & Sons Ltd
Westminster College
Robert Whiting Designs Ltd
Mrs Victor Whitworth
Wicanders (Great Britain) Ltd
Hugh W. Wilson
Zoë Woolrych
F. W. Woolworth & Co. Ltd
Christopher Wray's Lighting Emporium
Zella Nine

REFERENCE

The publishers also acknowledge their indebtedness to the following books which were consulted for reference.

Antique Finder; The Antiques of the Pharmacy L. G. Matthews (G. BELL & SONS); *Antique Toys and their Background* G. White (B. T. BATSFORD LTD); *Baby and Child Care* Dr Benjamin Spock (BODLEY HEAD); *The Book of Carpets* R. G. Hubel (BARRIE & JENKINS); *Book of Child Care* Hugh Jolly (GEORGE ALLEN & UNWIN); *The Book of Fish Cookery* Elspeth Robertson (SPECTATOR PUBLICATIONS); *Building Construction* J. K. McKay (LONGMANS); *Buttons for the Collector* P. Peacock (DAVID & CHARLES); *The Complete Book of Woodwork* Charles Hayward (EVANS BROTHERS LTD); *Complete Indoor Gardener* ed. Michael Wright (PAN); *The Consumer Jungle* Marian Giordan (FONTANA); *Cookery and Household Management* Mrs Beeton (WARD LOCK); *Cooking Explained* Barbara Hammond (LONGMANS); *The Dairy Book of Home Management* (WOLFE PUBLISHING LTD); *Design to Fit the Family* Phoebe De Syllas and Dorothy Meade (PENGUIN); *Discovering Oil Lamps* C. A. Meadows (SHIRE PUBLICATIONS LTD); *DIY Magazine; Dolls* A. Fraser (OCTOPUS BOOKS LTD); *Early English Drug Jars* G. Howard (THE MEDICI SOCIETY); *The Economist Measurement Guide and Reckoner* (THE ECONOMIST NEWSPAPER LTD); *Eggs, Milk and Cheese* Ninette Lyon and Peggie Benton (FABER & FABER); *Electricity* (CONSUMERS' ASSOCIATION); *Fabric Furnishings* Margaret G. Butler and Beryl S. Greves (B. T. BATSFORD LTD); *Flower Arranging and House-Plants* Violet Stevenson (GOOD HOUSEKEEPING/EBURY PRESS); *Foliage Plants* Christopher Wright (COLLINS); *Glass and British Pharmacy 1600-1900* J. K. Crellin and J. R. Scott (WELLCOME INSTITUTE OF THE HISTORY OF MEDICINE); *Glass Through the Ages* E. B. Haynes (PENGUIN); *Good Housekeeping Cookery Book* Good Housekeeping Institute (EBURY PRESS); *Good Housekeeping Magazine; Heating* Nigel Chapman (DESIGN CENTRE PUBLICATION); *Help Yourself* Mavis Nicholson (CORONET); *Home Lighting* Anthony Byers (PELHAM BOOKS); *Household Insect Pests* Norman E. Hickin (HUTCHINSON); *How to Clean Everything* Alma Chestnut-Moore (TOM STACEY LTD); *Interior Decorating Made Simple* Barty Phillips (ALDUS BOOKS LTD); *Interior Design* Diana Rowntree (PENGUIN); *Investing in Georgian Glass* W. Lloyd (BARRIE & ROCKLIFFE, THE CRESSET PRESS); *Keys: Their History and Collection* E. Monk (SHIRE PUBLICATIONS LTD); *Kitchens* John Prizeman (DESIGN CENTRE PUBLICATION); *Kitchens and Laundering Spaces* Department of the Environment (HMSO); *Know Your Rights* Ronald Irving and Charles Anthony (DAVID & CHARLES); *Locks and Keys Throughout the Ages* V. J. M. Eras (LIPS' SAFE AND LOCK MANUFACTURING CO.); *The Book of Meat Cookery* Mrs Bee Nilson (SPECTATOR PUBLICATIONS); *Medical Ceramics Volume I* J. K. Crellin (WELLCOME INSTITUTE OF THE HISTORY OF MEDICINE); Mitchells Building Construction (B. T. BATSFORD LTD); *Nailsea Glass* K. Vincent (DAVID & CHARLES); *The New Childbirth* Erna Wright (TANDEM); *Package and Print* A. Davis (FABER & FABER); *Planning Your Lighting* Derek Phillips (DESIGN CENTRE PUBLICATION); *The Practical Plumbing Guide* James Haig (STANLEY PAUL); *Practical Upholstery* Geoffrey Howes (EVANS BROTHERS LTD); *Space in the Home* Department of the Environment (HMSO); *Specification* ed. Dex Harrison (THE ARCHITECTURAL PRESS); *Standard Processes in Dressmaking* E. Lucy Towers (UNIVERSITY OF LONDON PRESS); *Storage* Geoffrey Salmon (DESIGN CENTRE PUBLICATIONS); *Superwoman* Shirley Conran (SIDGWICK & JACKSON); *Taste of Wine* Pamela Vandyke Price (MACDONALD); *Textiles, Properties and Behaviour* Edward Miller (B. T. BATSFORD LTD); *Tiles: A General History* A. Berendsen et al (FABER & FABER); *Upholstery* Malcolm Flitman (B. T. BATSFORD LTD); *Victorian Ceramic Tiles* J. Barnard (STUDIO VISTA); *The Victorian Staffordshire Figure* A. Oliver (WILLIAM HEINEMANN); *The Vogue Sewing Book* ed. Patricia Perry (VOGUE PATTERNS NEW YORK); *Which?; Womancraft; Women's Rights: A Practical Guide* Anna Coote and Tess Gill (PENGUIN).

ADDITIONAL PHOTOGRAPHY

Photographs supplied by

La Maison de Marie Claire
Femina
Zuhause – Stegeman
Schöner Wohnen – Atelier
Deimling
Morenberg
Rogers
Rosenfeld
Schmutz
Seekamp
Stradtmann
Tecklenborg
Willig

PROPS AND STYLING

Penny Croucher
Lizi Freeman
Sarah Harrington
Minnette Shepard
Designers Guild

Paper, printing and binding by
Bemrose Spondon Ltd, Derby
Bowater Paper Sales, Sittingbourne
Sir Joseph Causton & Sons Ltd, Eastleigh
Culver Graphics Ltd, Lane End
Gilchrist Brothers Ltd, Leeds
Hazell Watson and Viney Ltd, Aylesbury
Koninklijke Nederlandse Papierfabrieken NV, Maastricht
Reprocolor Llovet, Barcelona
Vantage Photosetting Ltd, Rownhams, Southampton

METRIC SHOPPING

Metrication is fraught with snags and apparent inconsistencies. Different trades have worked out their own standards of weights and measures, and not all follow a uniform basis of conversion. Some products are still manufactured in the old sizes, which are expressed in metric terms. Others are made or packed in metric units, so that exact imperial equivalents can seldom be given in round figures. Some materials, such as fabrics, are measured in centimetres and metres, whereas timber is sold by the millimetre and metre.

The conversion tables on the inside front cover of this book are based on the strict mathematical formulae. The principle followed on this and the next page is to adapt these to the working metric/imperial equivalents according to the standard practice adopted by the trades concerned.

CLOTHING

The basic metric unit of measurement for all ready-made clothing is the centimetre. No fractions are used, and sizes increase generally in steps of 4, 5 or 6 cm. Hats are marked with the actual number of centimetres to fit round the head. Metric shoe sizes give the length and breadth of the foot in millimetres, but these are not likely to replace the traditional British system for some time.

WOMEN'S CLOTHES
British and US sizes and average cm./in. equivalents:

British	US	BUST		HIPS		WAIST	
8	6	76 cm.	30 in.	81 cm.	32 in.	58 cm.	23 in.
10	8	81	32	86	34	58	23
12	10	86	34	91	36	61	24
14	12	91	36	97	38	66	26
16	14	97	38	102	40	71	28
18	16	102	40	107	42	76	30
20	18	107	42	112	44	81	32

MEN'S CLOTHES
Metric chest measurements for jackets, cardigans and pullovers, and waist/inside-leg measurements for trousers are given in centimetres. The same applies to shirt-collar sizes, which go up in stages of 1 cm.

CHILDREN'S CLOTHES
Most children's clothes are marked in centimetres and inches. Up to the age of 12 months, the size is related mainly to the child's weight; after 12 months to the child's height, increasing in 6 cm. steps. Ages are often marked, too, as an approximate guide.

AGE	HEIGHT		WEIGHT		CHEST	
3 months	$24\frac{1}{2}$ in.	62 cm.	12 lb.	5·5 kg.	$17\frac{3}{8}$ in.	45 cm.
6	27	68	18	8	$18\frac{1}{8}$	46
9	29	74	21	9·5	$18\frac{7}{8}$	48
12	$31\frac{1}{2}$	80	24	11	$19\frac{5}{8}$	50
18	34	86			$20\frac{1}{4}$	52
2 years	36	92			$20\frac{7}{8}$	53
3	38	98			$21\frac{1}{2}$	55
4	40	104			$22\frac{1}{8}$	57

DO-IT-YOURSELF

TIMBER
Standard widths and thicknesses, with the nearest imperial equivalents, are:

mm.	in.	mm.	in.
12	$\frac{1}{2}$	50	2
16	$\frac{5}{8}$	63	$2\frac{1}{2}$
19	$\frac{3}{4}$	75	3
22	$\frac{7}{8}$	100	4
25	1	125	5
32	$1\frac{1}{4}$	150	6
38	$1\frac{1}{2}$	then in 25 mm. stages to 300 (12 in.)	

Standard lengths begin at 1·8 m. and increase in stages of 0·3 m. (300 mm. or approximately 1 ft):

m.	ft in.	m.	ft in.
1·8	5 $10\frac{7}{8}$	4·2	13 $9\frac{3}{8}$
2·1	6 $10\frac{5}{8}$	4·5	14 $9\frac{1}{4}$
2·4	7 $10\frac{1}{2}$	4·8	15 9
2·7	8 $10\frac{1}{4}$	5·1	16 $8\frac{3}{4}$
3·0	9 $10\frac{1}{8}$	5·4	17 $8\frac{5}{8}$
3·3	10 $9\frac{7}{8}$	5·7	18 $8\frac{3}{8}$
3·6	11 $9\frac{3}{4}$	6·0	19 $8\frac{1}{8}$
3·9	12 $9\frac{1}{2}$	6·3	20 8

BOARD
Boards and manufactured sheets are still made in the old imperial sizes, but these are described in millimetres: e.g., a 2,440 x 1,220 mm. sheet of hardboard is the same size as the old 8 x 4 ft sheet.

PAINT, HARDWARE, etc.
Metric sizes of tins of paint are 250 and 500 ml.; 1, 2·5 and 5 litres.

Wood screws and self-tapping screws have not been metricated.

Glass is graded by the thickness, ranging from 2 mm. for picture-framing to 12 mm. for heavy plate.

Precast concrete paving slabs, 50 or 63 mm. thick, and 600 mm. wide, are available in lengths of 450, 600, 750 and 900 mm.

Sand, cement, ready-mixed concrete and plaster are sold in metric packs ranging from 5 to 50 kg.

CARPETS
A square metre is approximately 20% more than a square yard. Equivalent widths:

imperial	metric	imperial	metric
27 in.	0·69 m.	9 ft	2·74 m.
3 ft	0·91 m.	12 ft	3·66 m.
6 ft	1·83 m.	15 ft	4·57 m.

SEWING
Household and dress fabrics are now sold by the metre, the width being expressed in centimetres. The standard cutting unit of $\frac{1}{8}$ yd. – the smallest unit cut in the shops – is replaced by 10 cm. (4 in.).

Examples of the new metric widths and the imperial widths they are replacing are:

90 cm. instead of 35–36 in.	
115 cm. instead of 44–45 in.	
120 cm. instead of 48 in.	
140 cm. instead of 54–56 in.	
150 cm. instead of 60 in.	